THE FIREFLY FRENCH/ENGLISH VISUAL DICTIONARY

SECOND EDITION

Jean-Claude **Corbeil**
Ariane **Archambault**

FIREFLY BOOKS

Published by Firefly Books Ltd. 2010

First printing

Publisher Cataloging-in-Publication Data (U.S.)

Corbeil, Jean Claude.
The Firefly French/English visual dictionary / Jean-Claude Corbeil ; Ariane Archambault.
Rev. ed.
[vi, 586]p. : col. ill., col. maps ; cm.
Includes index.
Summary: A comprehensive general reference visual dictionary featuring terms in English and French, including sections on astronomy, geography, the animal and vegetable kingdoms, human biology, the home, clothing and accessories, art and architecture, communication, transportation, energy, science, society and sports.
ISBN-13: 978-1-55407-715-1
ISBN-10: 1-55407-715-X
1. Picture dictionaries, French. 2. Picture dictionaries, English. 3. French language – Dictionaries – English. 4. English language – Dictionaries – French. I. Archambault, Ariane. II. Title.
443/.21 dc 22 PC2629.C6732 2010

Library and Archives Canada Cataloguing in Publication

Corbeil, Jean-Claude, 1932–
The Firefly French/English visual dictionary / Jean-Claude Corbeil, Ariane Archambault. – Rev. ed.
Text in English and French.
Includes indexes.
ISBN-13: 978-1-55407-715-1
ISBN-10: 1-55407-715-X
1. Picture dictionaries, English. 2. Picture dictionaries, French. 3. French language–Dictionaries–English. 4. English language–Dictionaries–French. I. Archambault, Ariane, 1936-2006 II. Title.
AG250.C66373 2010 443'.17 C2010-901649-1

Published in the United States by
Firefly Books (U.S.) Inc.
P.O. Box 1338, Ellicott Station
Buffalo, New York 14205

Published in Canada by
Firefly Books Ltd.
66 Leek Crescent
Richmond Hill, Ontario L4B 1H1

Cover design: Gareth Lind

Printed in China
11 10 9 8 7 6 5 4 3 2 13 12 11 10
429, Version 3.5.4

The publisher gratefully acknowledges the financial support for our publishing program by the Government of Canada through the Canada Book Fund as administered by the Department of Canadian Heritage

ACKNOWLEDGMENTS

Our deepest gratitude to the individuals, institutions, companies and businesses that have provided us with the latest technical documentation for use in preparing *The Firefly French/English Visual Dictionary*.

Arcand, Denys (réalisateur); Association Internationale de Signalisation Maritime; Association canadienne des paiements (Charlie Clarke); Association des banquiers canadiens (Lise Provost); Automobiles Citroën; Automobiles Peugeot; Banque du Canada (Lyse Brousseau); Banque Royale du Canada (Raymond Chouinard, Francine Morel, Carole Trottier); Barrett Xplore inc.; Bazarin, Christine;Bibliothèque du Parlement canadien (Service de renseignements); Bibliothèque nationale du Québec (Jean-François Palomino); Bluechip Kennels (Olga Gagne); Bombardier Aéronautique; Bridgestone-Firestone; Brother (Canada); Canadien National; Casavant Frères ltée; C.O.J.O. ATHENES 2004 (Bureau des Médias Internationaux); Centre Eaton de Montréal; Centre national du Costume (Recherche et de Diffusion); Cetacean Society International (William R. Rossiter); Chagnon, Daniel (architecte D.E.S. – M.E.Q.); Cohen et Rubin Architectes (Maggy Cohen); Commission Scolaire de Montréal (École St-Henri); Compagnie de la Baie d'Hudson (Nunzia Iavarone, Ron Oyama); Corporation d'hébergement du Québec (Céline Drolet); École nationale de théâtre du Canada (Bibliothèque); Élevage Le Grand Saphir (Stéphane Ayotte); Énergie atomique du Canada ltée; Eurocopter; Famous Players; Fédération bancaire française (Védi Hékiman); Fontaine, PierreHenry (biologiste); Future Shop; Garaga; Groupe Jean Coutu; Hôpital du Sacré-Cœur de Montréal; Hôtel Inter-Continental; Hydro-Québec; I.P.I.Q. (Serge Bouchard); IGA Barcelo; International Entomological Society (Dr. Michael Geisthardt); Irisbus; Jérôme, Danielle (O.D.); La Poste (Colette Gouts); Le Groupe Canam Manac inc.; Lévesque, Georges (urgentologue); Lévesque, Robert (chef machiniste); Manutan; Marriot Spring Hill suites; MATRA S.A.; Métro inc.; ministère canadien de la Défense nationale (Affaires publiques); ministère de la Défense, République Française; ministère de la Justice du Québec (Service de la gestion immobilière – Carol Sirois); ministère de l'Éducation du Québec (Direction de l'équipement scolaire- Daniel Chagnon); Muse Productions (Annick Barbery); National Aeronautics and Space Administration; National Oceanic and Atmospheric Administration; Nikon Canada inc.; Normand, Denis (consultant en télécommunications); Office de la langue française du Québec (Chantal Robinson); Paul Demers & Fils inc.; Phillips (France); Pratt & Whitney Canada inc.; Prévost Car inc.; Radio Shack Canada ltée; Réno-Dépôt inc.; Robitaille, Jean-François (Département de biologie, Université Laurentienne); Rocking T Ranch and Poultry Farm (Pete and Justine Theer); RONA inc.; Sears Canada inc.; Secrétariat d'État du Canada : Bureau de la traduction ; Service correctionnel du Canada; Société d'Entomologie Africaine (Alain Drumont); Société des musées québécois (Michel Perron); Société Radio-Canada; Sony du Canada ltée; Sûreté du Québec; Théâtre du Nouveau Monde; Transports Canada (Julie Poirier); Urgences-Santé (Éric Berry); Ville de Longueuil (Direction de la Police); Ville de Montréal (Service de la prévention des incendies); Vimont Lexus Toyota; Volvo Bus Corporation; Yamaha Motor Canada Ltd.

QA International wishes to extend a special thank you to the following people for their contribution to *The Firefly French/English Visual Dictionary*:

Jean-Louis Martin, Marc Lalumière, Jacques Perrault, Stéphane Roy, Alice Comtois, Michel Blais, Christiane Beauregard, Mamadou Togola, Annie Maurice, Charles Campeau, Mivil Deschênes, Jonathan Jacques, Martin Lortie, Frédérick Simard, Yan Tremblay, Mathieu Blouin, Sébastien Dallaire, Hoang Khanh Le, Martin Desrosiers, Nicolas Oroc, François Escalmel, Danièle Lemay, Pierre Savoie, Benoît Bourdeau, Marie-Andrée Lemieux, Caroline Soucy, Yves Chabot, Anne-Marie Ouellette, Anne-Marie Villeneuve, Anne-Marie Brault, Nancy Lepage, Daniel Provost, François Vézina, Brad Wilson, Michael Worek, Lionel Koffler, Maraya Raduha, Dave Harvey, Mike Parkes, George Walker, Anna Simmons, Guylaine Houle, Sophie Pellerin, Tony O'Riley.

The Firefly French/English Visual Dictionary was created and produced by
QA International
329, rue de la Commune Ouest, 3e étage
Montréal (Québec) H2Y 2E1 Canada
T 514.499.3000 F 514.499.3010
www.qa-international.com

EDITORIAL STAFF

Publisher: Jacques Fortin
Authors: Jean-Claude Corbeil and Ariane Archambault
Editorial Director: François Fortin
Editor-in-Chief: Serge D'Amico
Graphic Design: Anne Tremblay

PRODUCTION

Guy Bonin
Salvatore Parisi

TERMINOLOGICAL RESEARCH

Sophie Ballarin
Jean Beaumont
Catherine Briand
Nathalie Guillo
Anne Rouleau

ILLUSTRATIONS

Art Directors: Jocelyn Gardner, Anouk Noël
Jean-Yves Ahern
Rielle Lévesque
Alain Lemire
Mélanie Boivin
Yan Bohler
Claude Thivierge
Pascal Bilodeau
Michel Rouleau
Carl Pelletier
Raymond Martin

LAYOUT

Pascal Goyette
Janou-Ève LeGuerrier
Véronique Boisvert
Josée Gagnon
Karine Raymond
Geneviève Théroux Béliveau

DOCUMENTATION

Gilles Vézina
Kathleen Wynd
Stéphane Batigne
Sylvain Robichaud
Jessie Daigle

DATA MANAGEMENT

Programmer: Daniel Beaulieu
Éric Gagnon
Gabriel Trudeau St-Hilaire

REVISION

Marie-Nicole Cimon
Liliane Michaud
Veronica Schami

PREPRESS

Julien Brisebois
François Hénault
Karine Lévesque
Patrick Mercure

Jean-Claude Corbeil is an expert in linguistic planning, with a world-wide reputation in the fields of comparative terminology and socio-linguistics. He serves as a consultant to various international organizations and governments.

Ariane Archambault, a specialist in applied linguistics, has taught foreign languages and is now a terminologist and editor of dictionaries and reference books.

Introduction to *The Firefly French/English Visual Dictionary*

A DICTIONARY FOR ONE AND ALL

The Firefly French/English Visual Dictionary uses pictures to define words. With thousands of illustrations and thousands of specialist and general terms, it provides a rich source of knowledge about the world around you.

Designed for the general reader and students of language, *The Firefly French/English Visual Dictionary* responds to the needs of anyone seeking precise, correct terms for a wide range of objects. Using illustrations enables you to "see" immediately the meaning of each term.

You can use *The Firefly French/English Visual Dictionary* in several ways:

By going from an idea to a word. If you are familiar with an object but do not know the correct name for it, you can look up the object in the dictionary and you will find the various parts correctly named.

By going from a word to an idea. If you want to check the meaning of a term, refer to the index where you will find the term and be directed to the appropriate illustration that defines the term.

For sheer pleasure. You can flip from one illustration to another or from one word to another, for the sole purpose of enjoying the illustrations and enriching your knowledge of the world around us.

STRUCTURE

The Firefly French/English Visual Dictionary is divided into CHAPTERS, outlining subjects from astronomy to sports.

More complex subjects are divided into THEMES; for example, the Animal Kingdom chapter is divided into themes including insects and arachnids, mollusks, and crustaceans.

The TITLES name the object and, at times, the chief members of a class of objects are brought together under the same SUBTITLE.

The ILLUSTRATIONS show an object, a process or a phenomenon, and the most significant details from which they are constructed. It serves as a visual definition for each of the terms presented.

TERMINOLOGY

Each word in *The Firefly French/English Visual Dictionary* has been carefully chosen and verified. Sometimes different words are used to name the same object, and in these cases the word most commonly used was chosen.

COLOR REFERENCE

On the spine and back of the book this identifies and accompanies each theme to facilitate quick access to the corresponding section in the book.

TITLE

It is highlighted in English, and the French equivalent is placed underneath in smaller characters. If the title runs over a number of pages, it is printed in gray on the pages subsequent to the first page on which it appears.

SUB-THEME

Most themes are subdivided into sub-themes. The sub-theme is given both in English and in French.

NARROW LINES

These link the word to the item indicated. Where too many lines would make reading difficult, they have been replaced by color codes with captions or, in rare cases, by numbers.

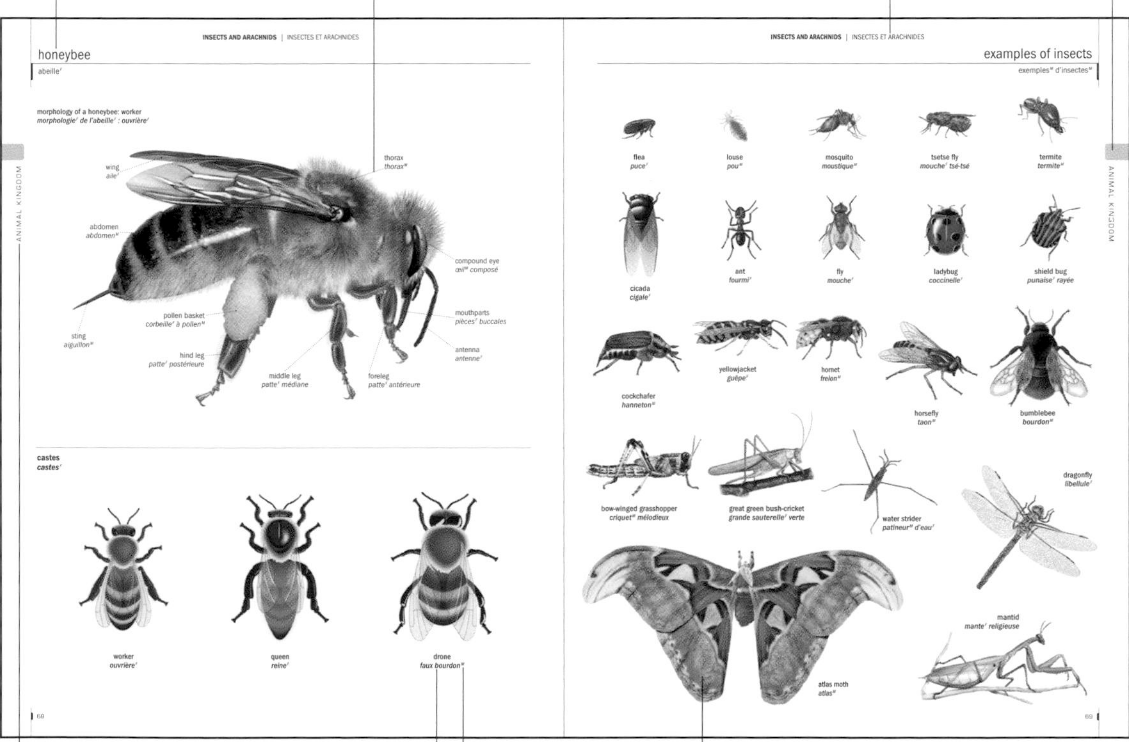

INSECTS AND ARACHNIDS | INSECTES ET ARACHNIDES
honeybee
abeille[F]
morphology of a honeybee: worker
morphologie[F] de l'abeille[F] : ouvrière[F]
wing
aile[F]
thorax
thorax[M]
abdomen
abdomen[M]
compound eye
œil[M] composé
pollen basket
corbeille[F] à pollen[M]
mouthparts
pièces[F] buccales
sting
aiguillon[M]
hind leg
patte[F] postérieure
antenna
antenne[F]
middle leg
patte[F] médiane
foreleg
patte[F] antérieure
castes
castes[F]
worker
ouvrière[F]
queen
reine[F]
drone
faux bourdon[M]
ANIMAL KINGDOM
68
INSECTS AND ARACHNIDS | INSECTES ET ARACHNIDES
examples of insects
exemples[M] d'insectes[M]
flea
puce[F]
louse
pou[M]
mosquito
moustique[M]
tsetse fly
mouche[F] tsé-tsé
termite
termite[M]
cicada
cigale[F]
ant
fourmi[F]
fly
mouche[F]
ladybug
coccinelle[F]
shield bug
punaise[F] rayée
cockchafer
hanneton[M]
yellowjacket
guêpe[F]
hornet
frelon[M]
horsefly
taon[M]
bumblebee
bourdon[M]
bow-winged grasshopper
criquet[M] mélodieux
great green bush-cricket
grande sauterelle[F] verte
water strider
patineur[M] d'eau[F]
dragonfly
libellule[F]
mantid
mante[F] religieuse
atlas moth
atlas[M]
ANIMAL KINGDOM
69

THEME

It is always unilingual, in English.

ILLUSTRATION

It serves as the visual definition for the terms associated with it.

GENDER INDICATION

F: feminine M: masculine N: neuter

The gender of each word in a term is indicated.

The characters shown in the dictionary are men or women when the function illustrated can be fulfilled by either. In these cases, the gender assigned to the word depends on the illustration; in fact, the word is either masculine or feminine depending on the sex of the person.

TERM

Each term appears in the index with a reference to the pages on which it appears. It is given in both languages, with English as the main index entry.

Contents

List of chapters

solar system

système[M] solaire

outer planets
planètes[F] externes

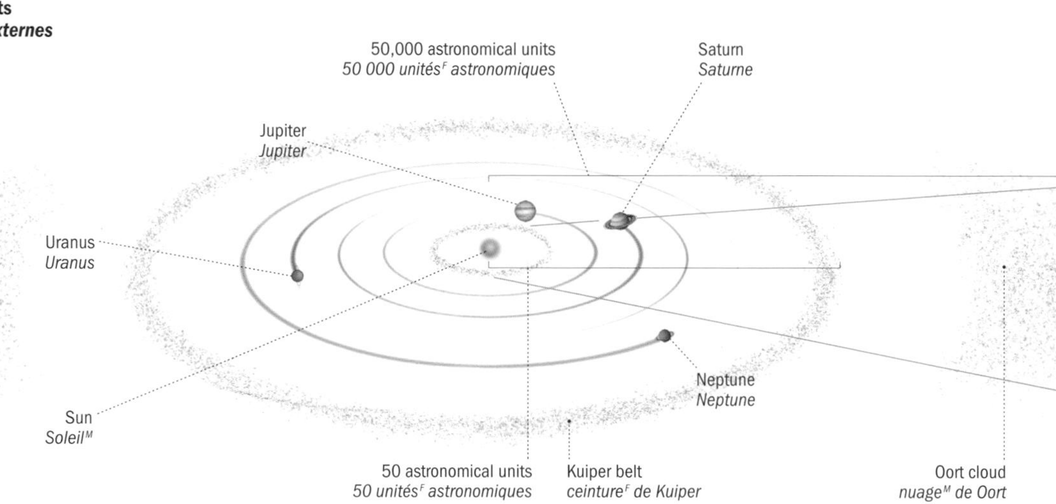
50,000 astronomical units
50 000 unités[F] astronomiques
Saturn
Saturne
Jupiter
Jupiter
Uranus
Uranus
Neptune
Neptune
Sun
Soleil[M]
50 astronomical units
50 unités[F] astronomiques
Kuiper belt
ceinture[F] de Kuiper
Oort cloud
nuage[M] de Oort

planets and satellites

planètes[F] et satellites[M]

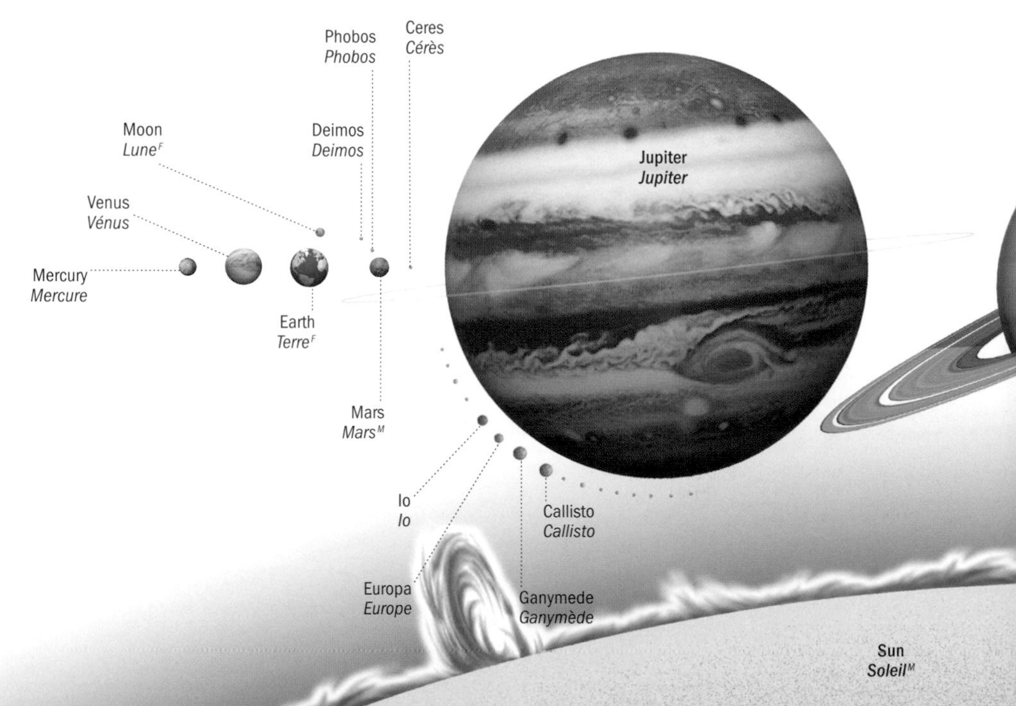
Phobos
Phobos
Ceres
Cérès
Moon
Lune[F]
Deimos
Deimos
Jupiter
Jupiter
Venus
Vénus
Mercury
Mercure
Earth
Terre[F]
Mars
Mars[M]
Io
Io
Callisto
Callisto
Europa
Europe
Ganymede
Ganymède
Sun
Soleil[M]

solar system

inner planets
planètes[F] internes

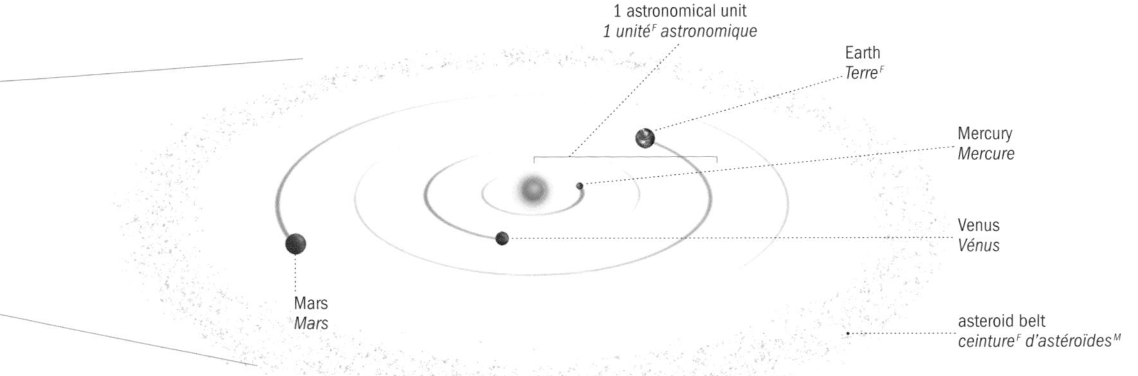
1 astronomical unit
1 unité[F] astronomique
Earth
Terre[F]
Mercury
Mercure
Venus
Vénus
Mars
Mars
asteroid belt
ceinture[F] d'astéroïdes[M]

planets and satellites

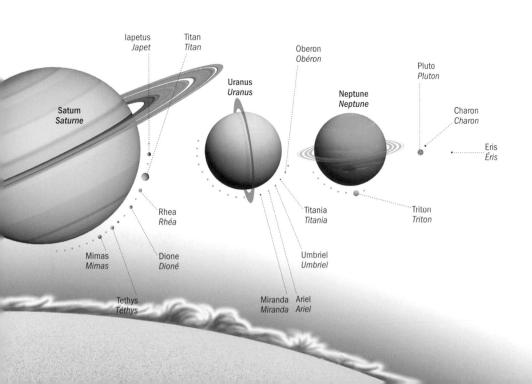

Iapetus
Japet
Titan
Titan
Oberon
Obéron
Pluto
Pluton
Uranus
Uranus
Neptune
Neptune
Saturn
Saturne
Charon
Charon
Eris
Éris
Rhea
Rhéa
Titania
Titania
Triton
Triton
Umbriel
Umbriel
Mimas
Mimas
Dione
Dioné
Tethys
Téthys
Miranda
Miranda
Ariel
Ariel

Sun

Soleil[M]

structure of the Sun
structure[F] du Soleil[M]

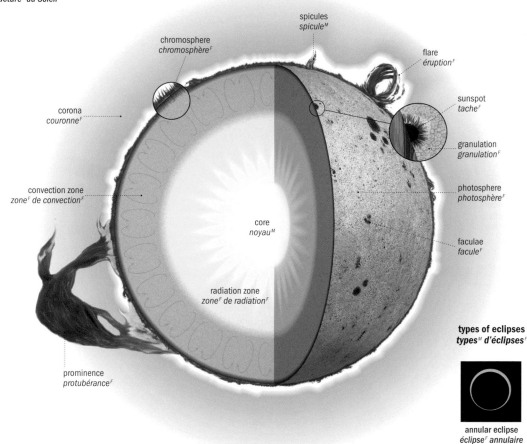

spicules
spicule[M]

chromosphere
chromosphère[F]

flare
éruption[F]

sunspot
tache[F]

corona
couronne[F]

granulation
granulation[F]

convection zone
zone[F] de convection[F]

photosphere
photosphère[F]

core
noyau[M]

faculae
facule[F]

radiation zone
zone[F] de radiation[F]

prominence
protubérance[F]

types of eclipses
types[M] d'éclipses[F]

annular eclipse
éclipse[F] annulaire

solar eclipse
éclipse[F] de Soleil[M]

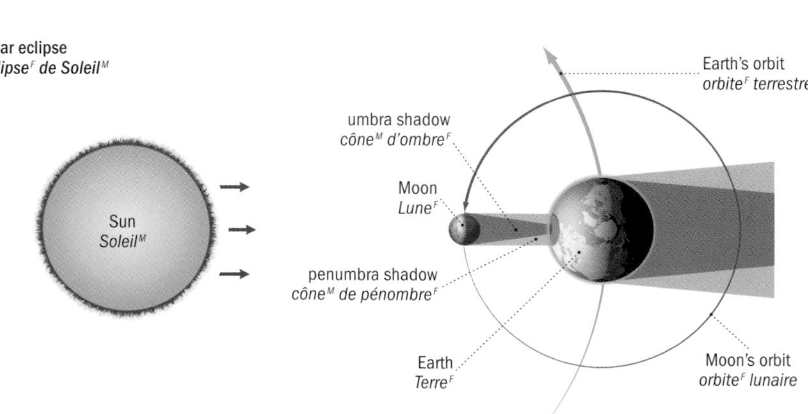
Earth's orbit
orbite[F] terrestre
umbra shadow
cône[M] d'ombre[F]
Moon
Lune[F]
Sun
Soleil[M]
penumbra shadow
cône[M] de pénombre[F]
Earth
Terre[F]
Moon's orbit
orbite[F] lunaire

partial eclipse
éclipse[F] partielle

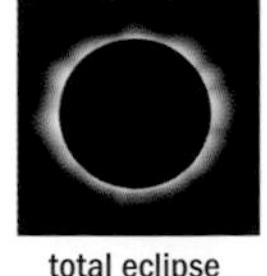

total eclipse
éclipse[F] totale

Moon

Lune[F]

types of eclipses
types[M] d'éclipses[F]

partial eclipse
éclipse[F] partielle

total eclipse
éclipse[F] totale

lunar features
relief[M] lunaire

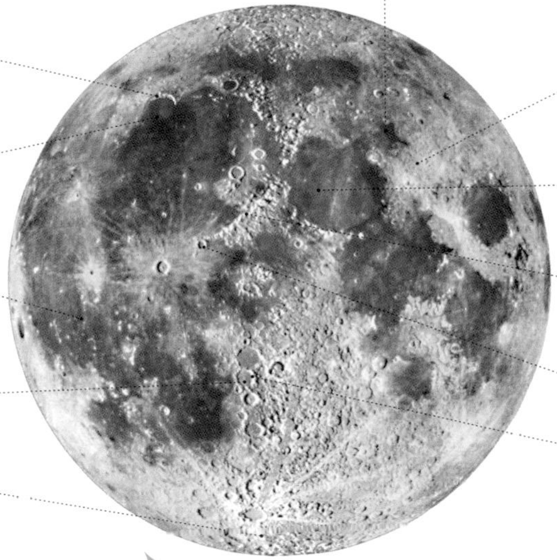

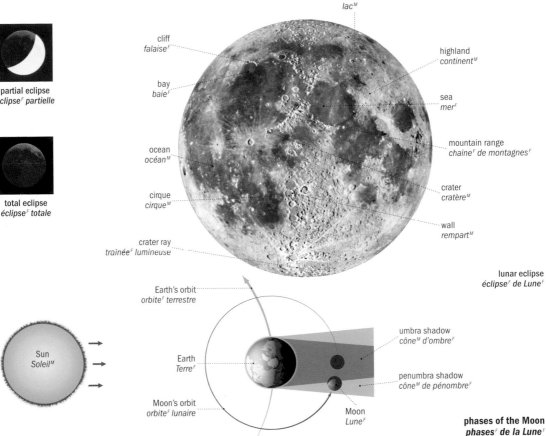

lake
lac[M]

cliff
falaise[F]

highland
continent[M]

bay
baie[F]

sea
mer[F]

mountain range
chaine[F] de montagnes[F]

ocean
océan[M]

crater
cratère[M]

cirque
cirque[M]

wall
rempart[M]

crater ray
trainée[F] lumineuse

lunar eclipse
éclipse[F] de Lune[F]

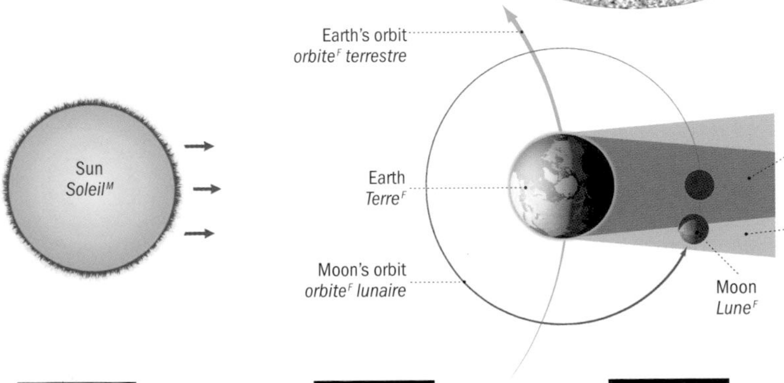

Earth's orbit
orbite[F] terrestre

Sun
Soleil[M]

Earth
Terre[F]

umbra shadow
cône[M] d'ombre[F]

penumbra shadow
cône[M] de pénombre[F]

Moon's orbit
orbite[F] lunaire

Moon
Lune[F]

phases of the Moon
phases[F] de la Lune[F]

new moon
nouvelle Lune[F]

new crescent
premier croissant[M]

first quarter
premier quartier[M]

waxing gibbous
gibbeuse[F] croissante

full moon
pleine Lune[F]

waning gibbous
gibbeuse[F] décroissante

last quarter
dernier quartier[M]

old crescent
dernier croissant[M]

galaxy

galaxie^F

Milky Way
Voie^F Lactée

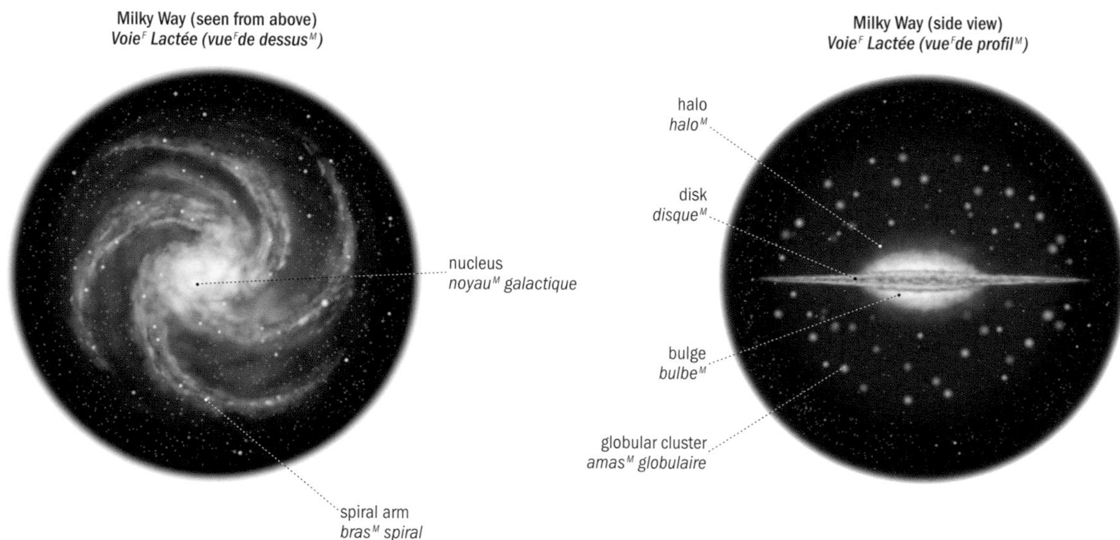
Milky Way (seen from above)
Voie^F Lactée (vue^F de dessus^M)
nucleus
noyau^M galactique
spiral arm
bras^M spiral
Milky Way (side view)
Voie^F Lactée (vue^F de profil^M)
halo
halo^M
disk
disque^M
bulge
bulbe^M
globular cluster
amas^M globulaire

comet

comète^F

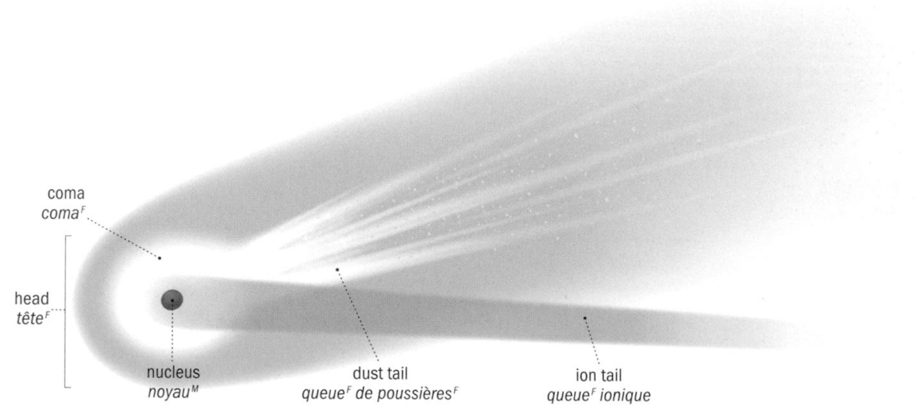
coma
coma^F
head
tête^F
nucleus
noyau^M
dust tail
queue^F de poussières^F
ion tail
queue^F ionique

Hubble space telescope

télescope[M] spatial Hubble

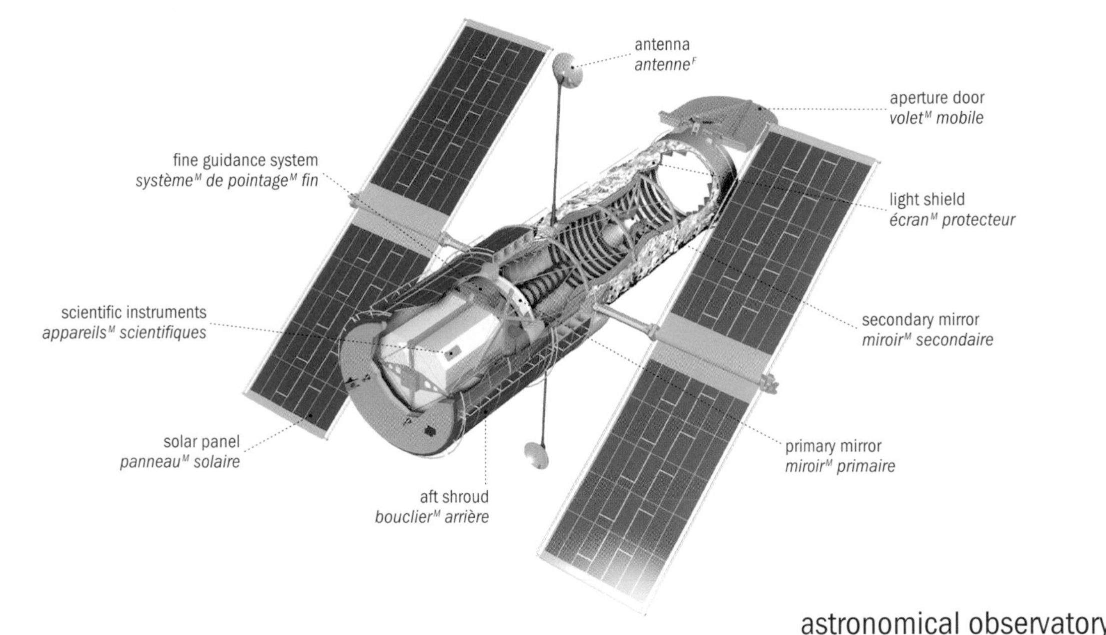
antenna
antenne[F]
aperture door
volet[M] mobile
fine guidance system
système[M] de pointage[M] fin
light shield
écran[M] protecteur
scientific instruments
appareils[M] scientifiques
secondary mirror
miroir[M] secondaire
solar panel
panneau[M] solaire
primary mirror
miroir[M] primaire
aft shroud
bouclier[M] arrière

astronomical observatory

observatoire[M] astronomique

cross section of an astronomical observatory
coupe[F] d'un observatoire[M] astronomique

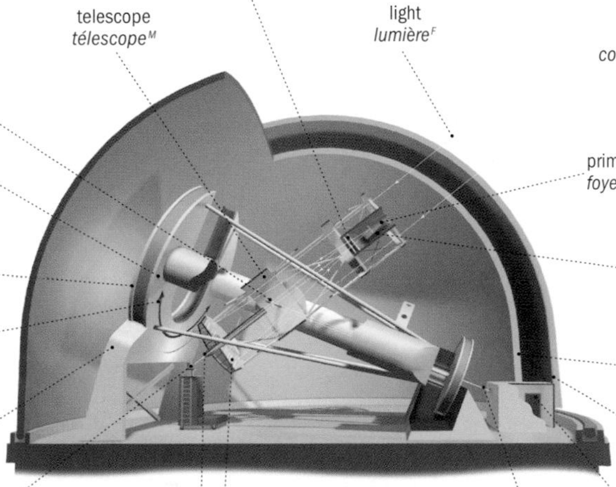

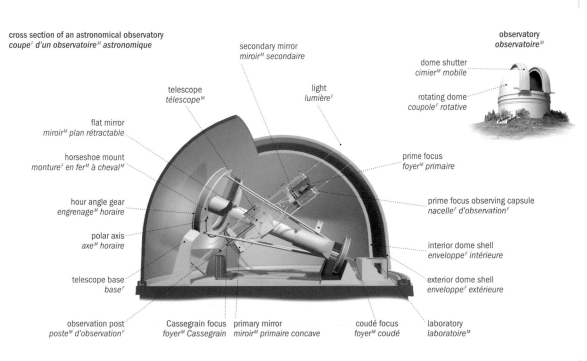

secondary mirror
miroir[M] secondaire

telescope
télescope[M]

light
lumière[F]

flat mirror
miroir[M] plan rétractable

horseshoe mount
monture[F] en fer[M] à cheval[M]

prime focus
foyer[M] primaire

hour angle gear
engrenage[M] horaire

prime focus observing capsule
nacelle[F] d'observation[F]

polar axis
axe[M] horaire

interior dome shell
enveloppe[F] intérieure

telescope base
base[F]

exterior dome shell
enveloppe[F] extérieure

observation post
poste[M] d'observation[F]

Cassegrain focus
foyer[M] Cassegrain

primary mirror
miroir[M] primaire concave

coudé focus
foyer[M] coudé

laboratory
laboratoire[M]

observatory
observatoire[M]

dome shutter
cimier[M] mobile

rotating dome
coupole[F] rotative

refracting telescope

lunette[F] astronomique

finderscope
chercheur[M]

cradle
bride[F] de fixation[F]

main tube
tube[M]

dew shield
pare-soleil[M]

eyepiece
oculaire[M]

eyepiece holder
tube[M] porte-oculaire[M]

star diagonal
oculaire[M] coudé

declination setting scale
cercle[M] de déclinaison[F]

azimuth clamp
vis[F] de blocage[M] (azimut[M])

focusing knob
bouton[M] de mise[F] au point[M]

altitude clamp
vis[F] de blocage[M] (latitude[F])

azimuth fine adjustment
réglage[M] micrométrique (azimut[M])

right ascension setting scale
cercle[M] d'ascension[F] droite

altitude fine adjustment
réglage[M] micrométrique (latitude[F])

counterweight
contrepoids[M]

fork
fourche[F]

tripod accessories shelf
plateau[M] pour accessoires[M]

tripod
trépied[M]

cross section of a refracting telescope
coupe[F] d'une lunette[F] astronomique

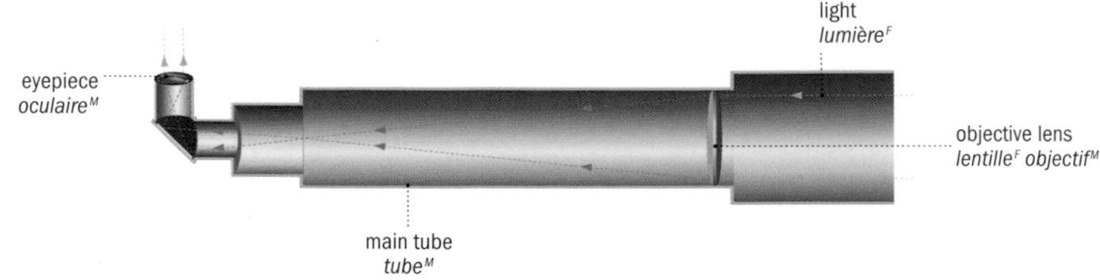

light
lumière[F]
eyepiece
oculaire[M]
objective lens
lentille[F] objectif[M]
main tube
tube[M]

reflecting telescope

télescope[M]

finderscope
chercheur[M]

eyepiece
oculaire[M]

cradle
bride[F] de fixation[F]

support
support[M] de fixation[F]

main tube
tube[M]

focusing knob
bouton[M] de mise[F] au point[M]

declination setting scale
cercle[M] de déclinaison[F]

right ascension setting scale
cercle[M] d'ascension[F] droite

azimuth fine adjustment
réglage[M] micrométrique (azimut[M])

azimuth clamp
vis[F] de blocage[M] (azimut[M])

altitude fine adjustment
réglage[M] micrométrique (latitude[F])

altitude clamp
vis[F] de blocage[M] (latitude[F])

cross section of a reflecting telescope
coupe[F] d'un télescope[M]

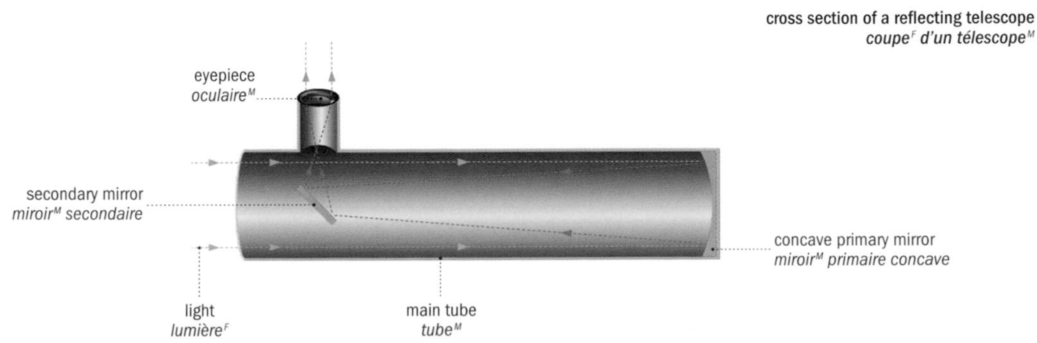
eyepiece
oculaire[M]
secondary mirror
miroir[M] secondaire
concave primary mirror
miroir[M] primaire concave
light
lumière[F]
main tube
tube[M]

spacesuit

scaphandre^M spatial

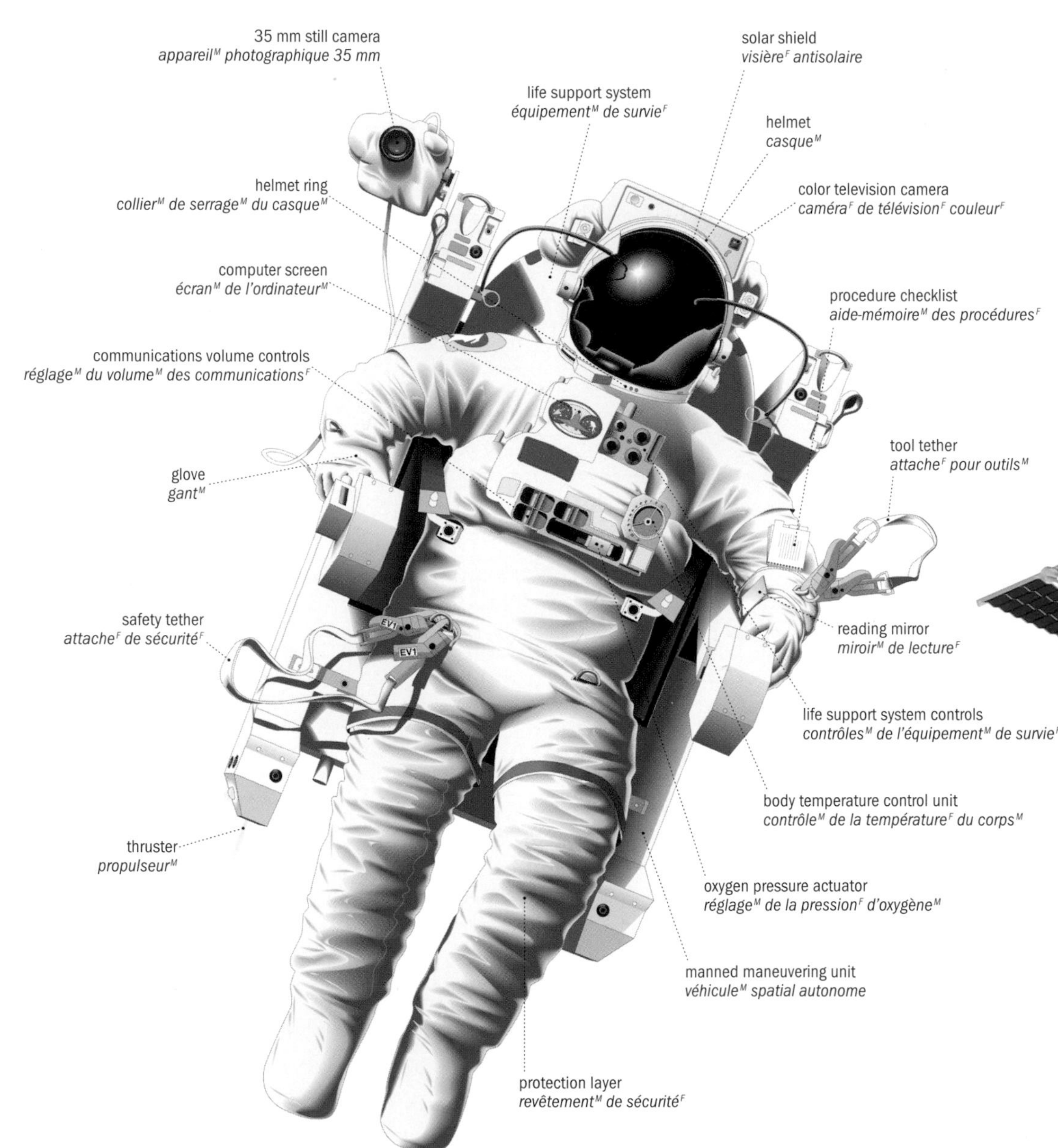
35 mm still camera
appareil^M photographique 35 mm
solar shield
visière^F antisolaire
life support system
équipement^M de survie^F
helmet
casque^M
helmet ring
collier^M de serrage^M du casque^M
color television camera
caméra^F de télévision^F couleur^F
computer screen
écran^M de l'ordinateur^M
procedure checklist
aide-mémoire^M des procédures^F
communications volume controls
réglage^M du volume^M des communications^F
tool tether
attache^F pour outils^M
glove
gant^M
EV1
EV1
safety tether
attache^F de sécurité^F
reading mirror
miroir^M de lecture^F
life support system controls
contrôles^M de l'équipement^M de survie^F
body temperature control unit
contrôle^M de la température^F du corps^M
thruster
propulseur^M
oxygen pressure actuator
réglage^M de la pression^F d'oxygène^M
manned maneuvering unit
véhicule^M spatial autonome
protection layer
revêtement^M de sécurité^F

international space station

station^F spatiale internationale

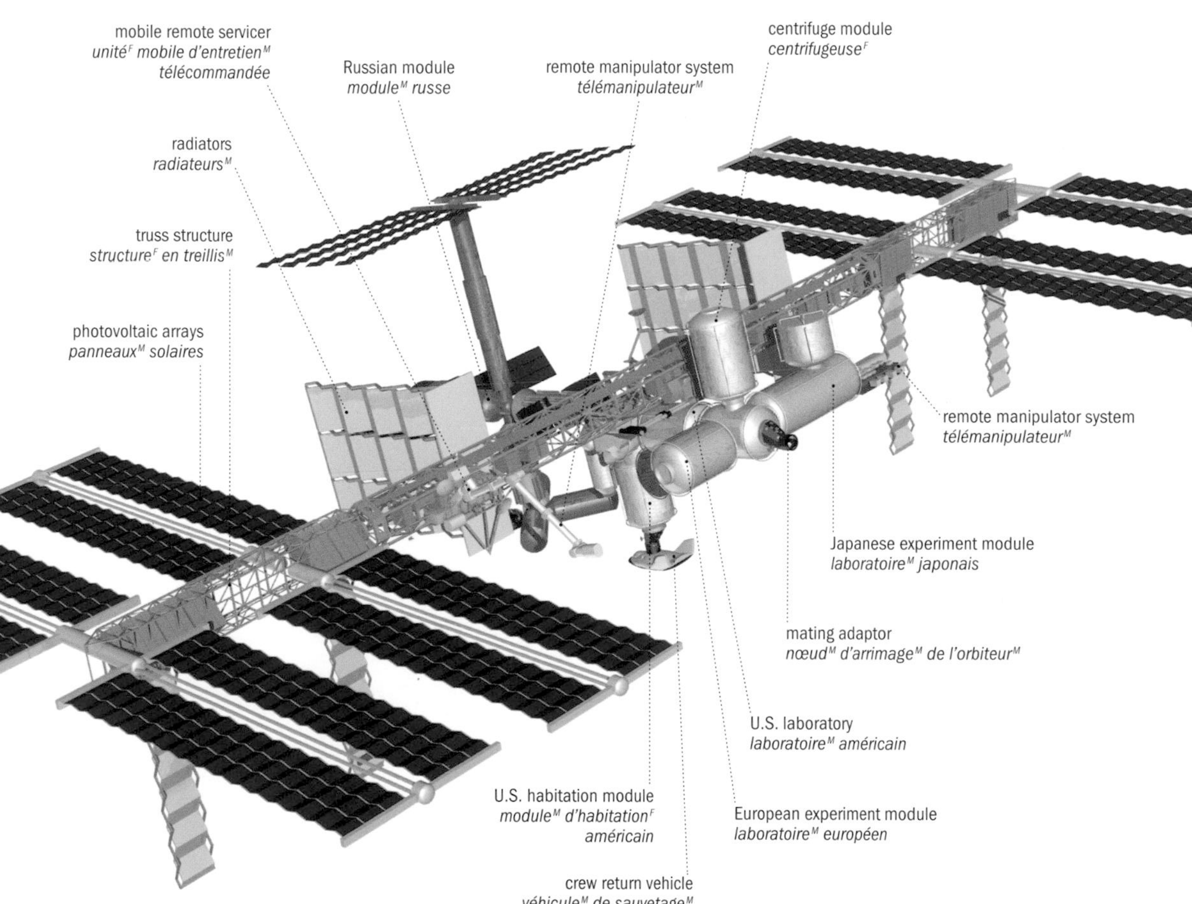
mobile remote servicer
unité^F mobile d'entretien^M télécommandée
Russian module
module^M russe
remote manipulator system
télémanipulateur^M
centrifuge module
centrifugeuse^F
radiators
radiateurs^M
truss structure
structure^F en treillis^M
photovoltaic arrays
panneaux^M solaires
remote manipulator system
télémanipulateur^M
Japanese experiment module
laboratoire^M japonais
mating adaptor
nœud^M d'arrimage^M de l'orbiteur^M
U.S. laboratory
laboratoire^M américain
U.S. habitation module
module^M d'habitation^F américain
European experiment module
laboratoire^M européen
crew return vehicle
véhicule^M de sauvetage^M

space shuttle

navette^F spatiale

space shuttle at takeoff
navette^F spatiale au décollage^M

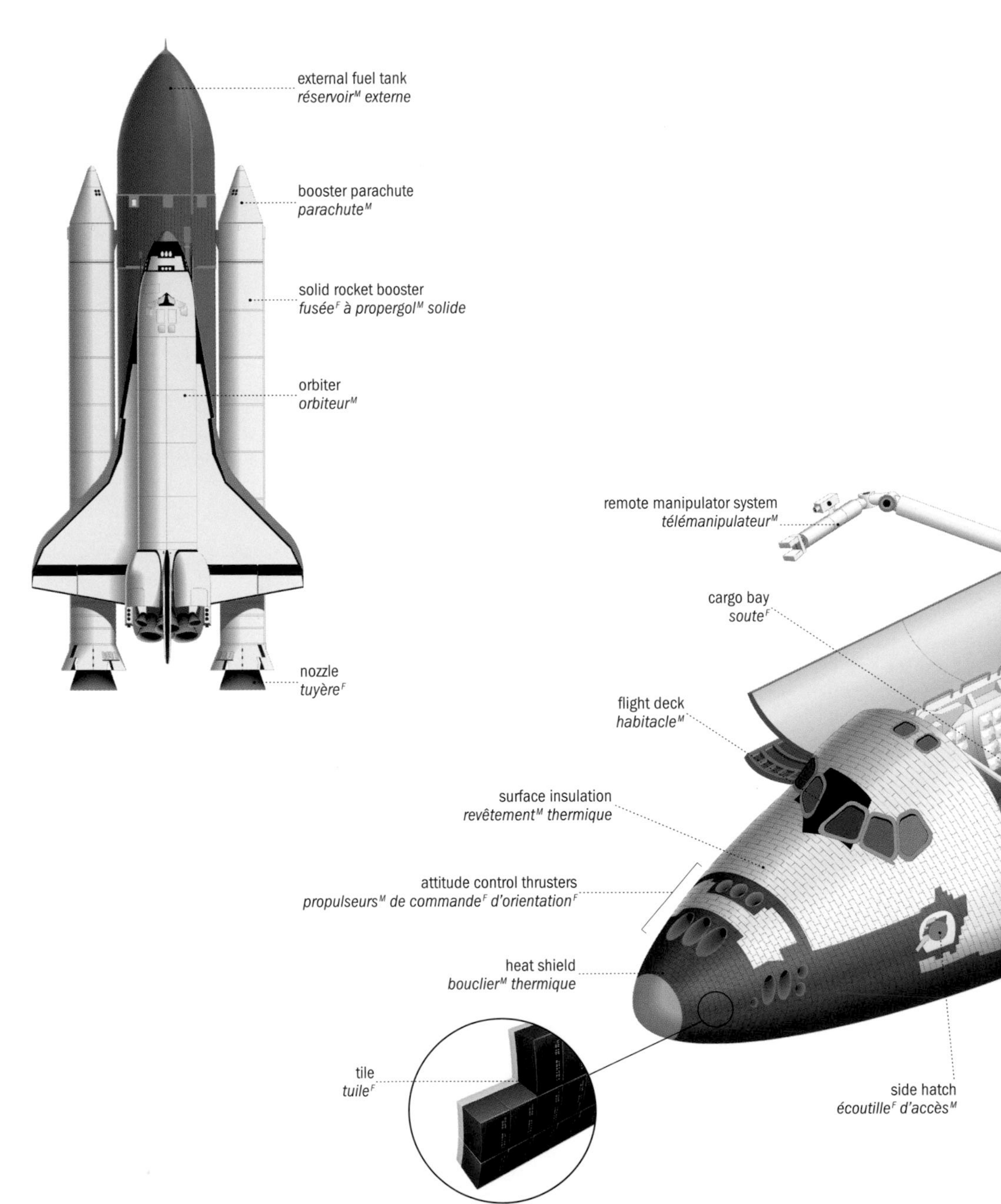
external fuel tank
réservoir^M externe
booster parachute
parachute^M
solid rocket booster
fusée^F à propergol^M solide
orbiter
orbiteur^M
nozzle
tuyère^F
remote manipulator system
télémanipulateur^M
cargo bay
soute^F
flight deck
habitacle^M
surface insulation
revêtement^M thermique
attitude control thrusters
propulseurs^M de commande^F d'orientation^F
heat shield
bouclier^M thermique
tile
tuile^F
side hatch
écoutille^F d'accès^M

orbiter
orbiteur[M]

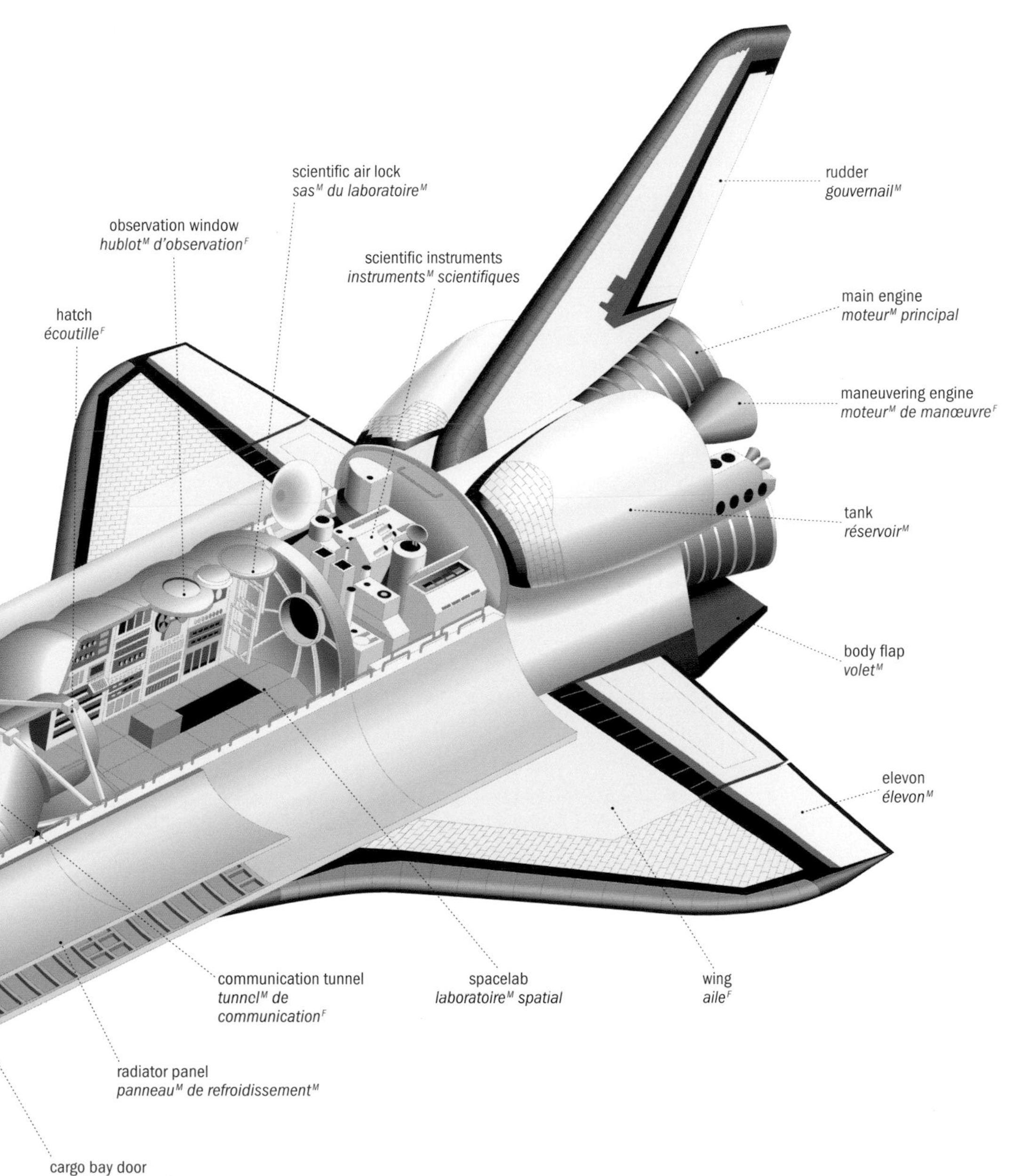
scientific air lock
sas[M] *du laboratoire*[M]
observation window
hublot[M] *d'observation*[F]
scientific instruments
instruments[M] *scientifiques*
hatch
écoutille[F]
rudder
gouvernail[M]
main engine
moteur[M] *principal*
maneuvering engine
moteur[M] *de manœuvre*[F]
tank
réservoir[M]
body flap
volet[M]
elevon
élevon[M]
communication tunnel
tunnel[M] *de communication*[F]
spacelab
laboratoire[M] *spatial*
wing
aile[F]
radiator panel
panneau[M] *de refroidissement*[M]
cargo bay door
porte[F] *de la soute*[F]

configuration of the continents

configuration[F] des continents[M]

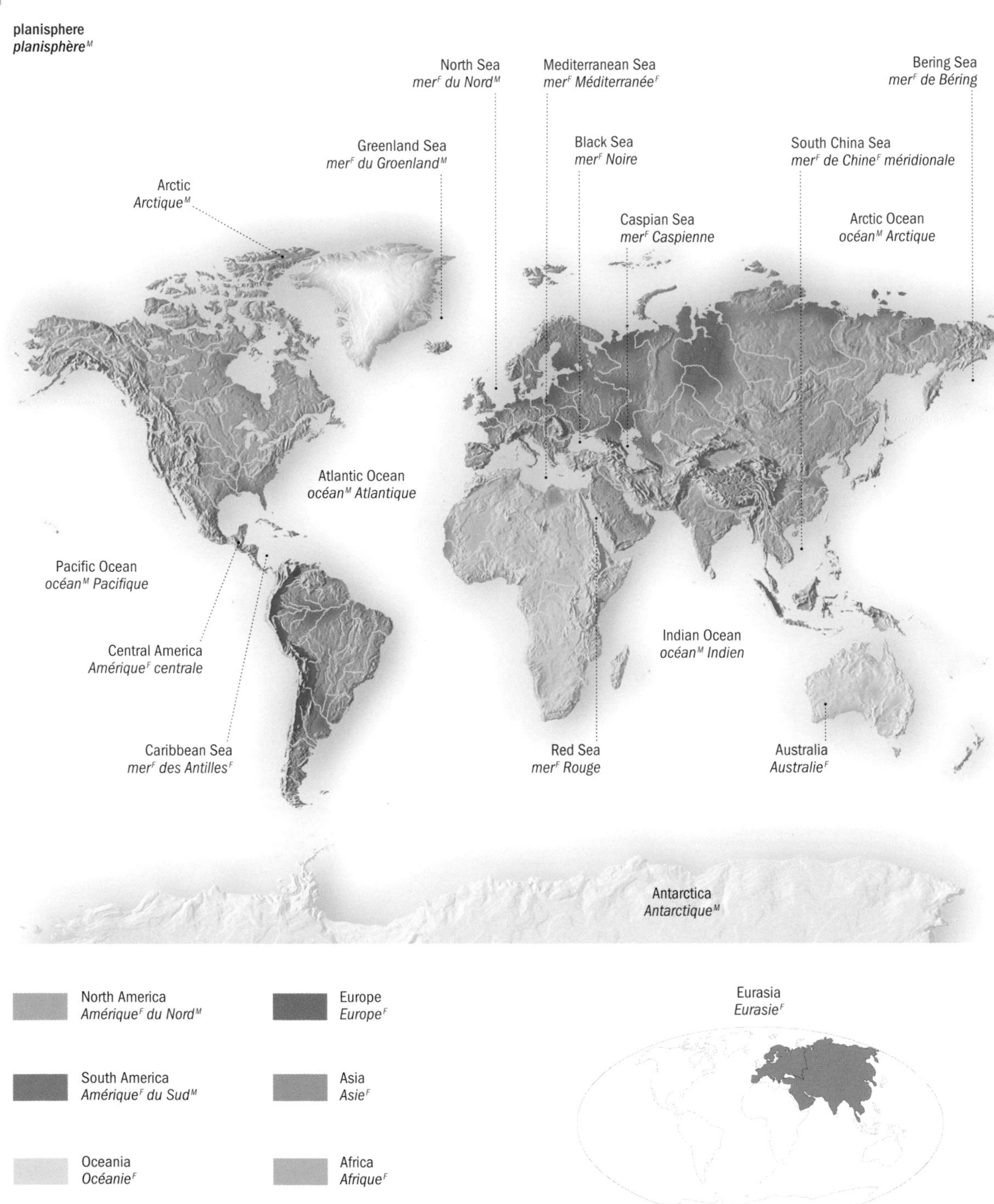
planisphere
planisphère[M]
North Sea
mer[F] du Nord[M]
Mediterranean Sea
mer[F] Méditerranée[F]
Bering Sea
mer[F] de Béring
Greenland Sea
mer[F] du Groenland[M]
Black Sea
mer[F] Noire
South China Sea
mer[F] de Chine[F] méridionale
Arctic
Arctique[M]
Caspian Sea
mer[F] Caspienne
Arctic Ocean
océan[M] Arctique
Atlantic Ocean
océan[M] Atlantique
Pacific Ocean
océan[M] Pacifique
Indian Ocean
océan[M] Indien
Central America
Amérique[F] centrale
Caribbean Sea
mer[F] des Antilles[F]
Red Sea
mer[F] Rouge
Australia
Australie[F]
Antarctica
Antarctique[M]
North America
Amérique[F] du Nord[M]
Europe
Europe[F]
South America
Amérique[F] du Sud[M]
Asia
Asie[F]
Oceania
Océanie[F]
Africa
Afrique[F]
Eurasia
Eurasie[F]

Antarctica
Antarctique[M]

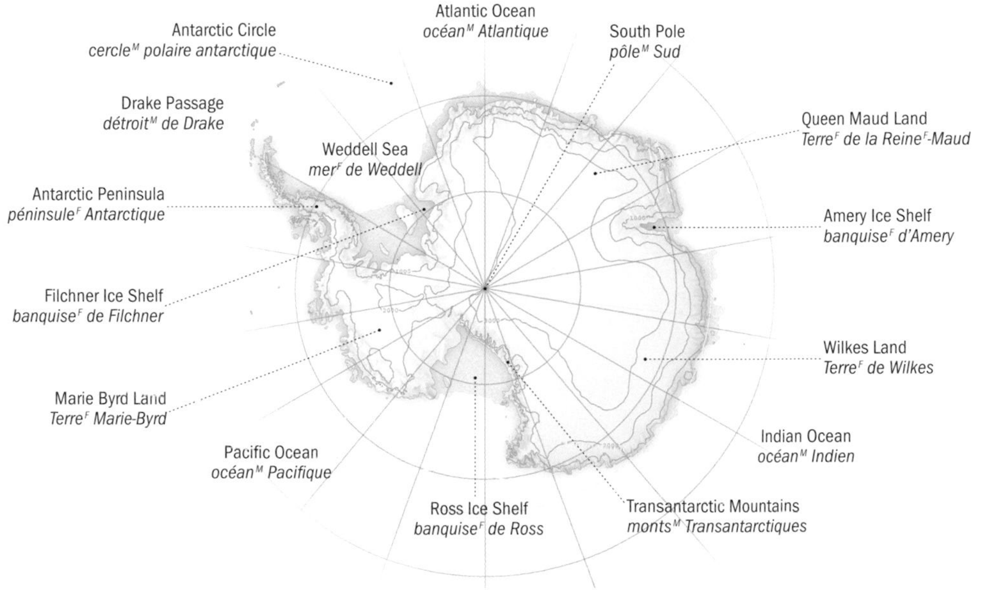

Atlantic Ocean
océan[M] *Atlantique*
Antarctic Circle
cercle[M] *polaire antarctique*
South Pole
pôle[M] *Sud*
Drake Passage
détroit[M] *de Drake*
Queen Maud Land
Terre[F] *de la Reine*[F]*-Maud*
Weddell Sea
mer[F] *de Weddell*
Antarctic Peninsula
péninsule[F] *Antarctique*
Amery Ice Shelf
banquise[F] *d'Amery*
Filchner Ice Shelf
banquise[F] *de Filchner*
Wilkes Land
Terre[F] *de Wilkes*
Marie Byrd Land
Terre[F] *Marie-Byrd*
Indian Ocean
océan[M] *Indien*
Pacific Ocean
océan[M] *Pacifique*
Ross Ice Shelf
banquise[F] *de Ross*
Transantarctic Mountains
monts[M] *Transantarctiques*

Oceania
Océanie[F]

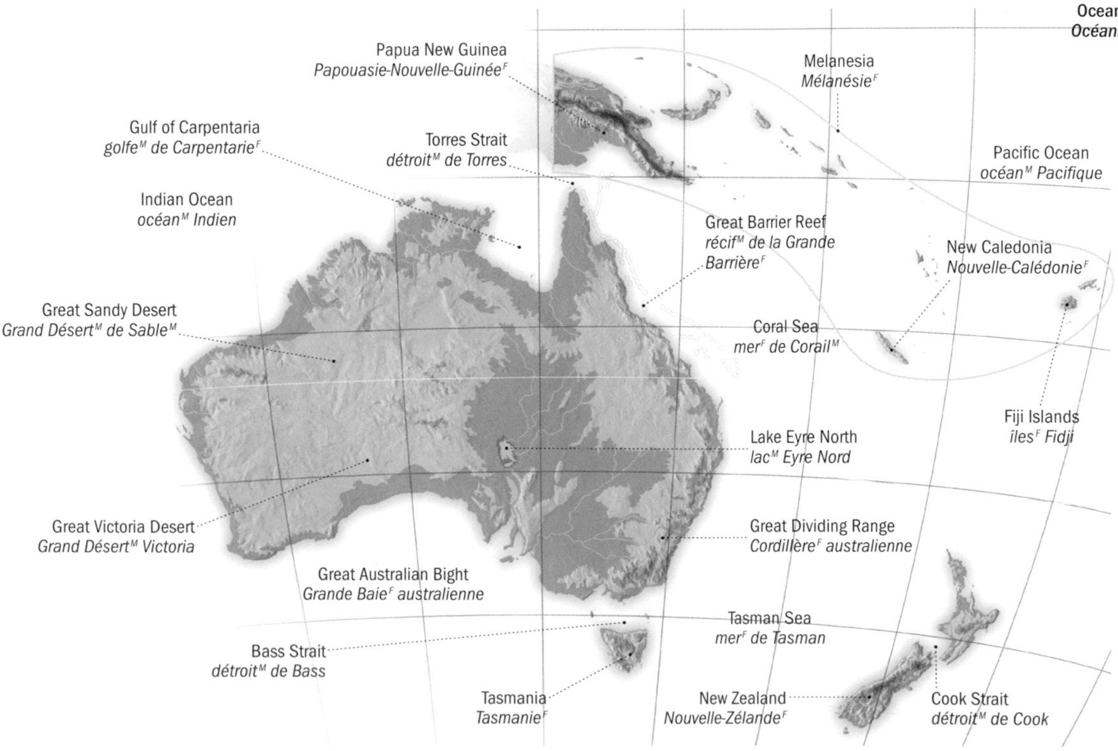

Papua New Guinea
Papouasie-Nouvelle-Guinée[F]
Melanesia
Mélanésie[F]
Gulf of Carpentaria
golfe[M] *de Carpentarie*[F]
Torres Strait
détroit[M] *de Torres*
Pacific Ocean
océan[M] *Pacifique*
Indian Ocean
océan[M] *Indien*
Great Barrier Reef
récif[M] *de la Grande Barrière*[F]
New Caledonia
Nouvelle-Calédonie[F]
Great Sandy Desert
Grand Désert[M] *de Sable*[M]
Coral Sea
mer[F] *de Corail*[M]
Fiji Islands
îles[F] *Fidji*
Lake Eyre North
lac[M] *Eyre Nord*
Great Victoria Desert
Grand Désert[M] *Victoria*
Great Dividing Range
Cordillère[F] *australienne*
Great Australian Bight
Grande Baie[F] *australienne*
Tasman Sea
mer[F] *de Tasman*
Bass Strait
détroit[M] *de Bass*
Tasmania
Tasmanie[F]
New Zealand
Nouvelle-Zélande[F]
Cook Strait
détroit[M] *de Cook*

North America
Amérique^F du Nord^M

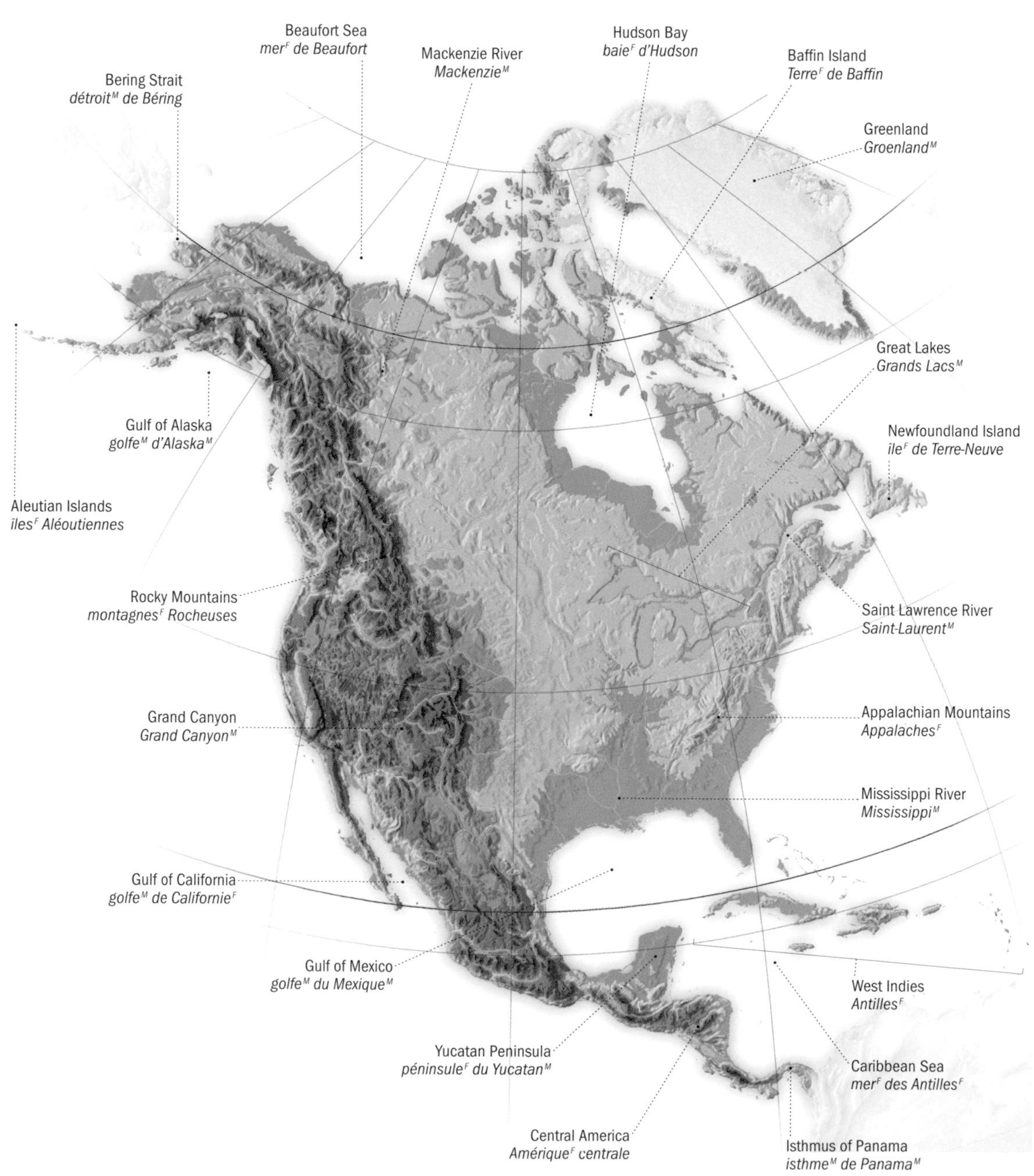
Beaufort Sea
mer^F de Beaufort
Hudson Bay
baie^F d'Hudson
Mackenzie River
Mackenzie^M
Baffin Island
Terre^F de Baffin
Bering Strait
détroit^M de Béring
Greenland
Groenland^M
Great Lakes
Grands Lacs^M
Newfoundland Island
île^F de Terre-Neuve
Gulf of Alaska
golfe^M d'Alaska^M
Aleutian Islands
îles^F Aléoutiennes
Rocky Mountains
montagnes^F Rocheuses
Saint Lawrence River
Saint-Laurent^M
Grand Canyon
Grand Canyon^M
Appalachian Mountains
Appalaches^F
Mississippi River
Mississippi^M
Gulf of California
golfe^M de Californie^F
Gulf of Mexico
golfe^M du Mexique^M
West Indies
Antilles^F
Yucatan Peninsula
péninsule^F du Yucatan^M
Caribbean Sea
mer^F des Antilles^F
Central America
Amérique^F centrale
Isthmus of Panama
isthme^M de Panama^M

South America
Amérique[F] du Sud[M]

Orinoco River
Orénoque[M]
Amazon River
Amazone[F]
Gulf of Panama
golfe[M] de Panama[M]
Equator
équateur[M]
Andes Cordillera
cordillère[F] des Andes
Lake Titicaca
lac[M] Titicaca
Atacama Desert
désert[M] d'Atacama
Paraná River
Paraná[M]
Patagonia
Patagonie[F]
Falkland Islands
îles[F] Falkland
Tierra del Fuego
Terre[F] de Feu[M]
Cape Horn
cap[M] Horn
Drake Passage
détroit[M] de Drake

Europe
Europe[F]

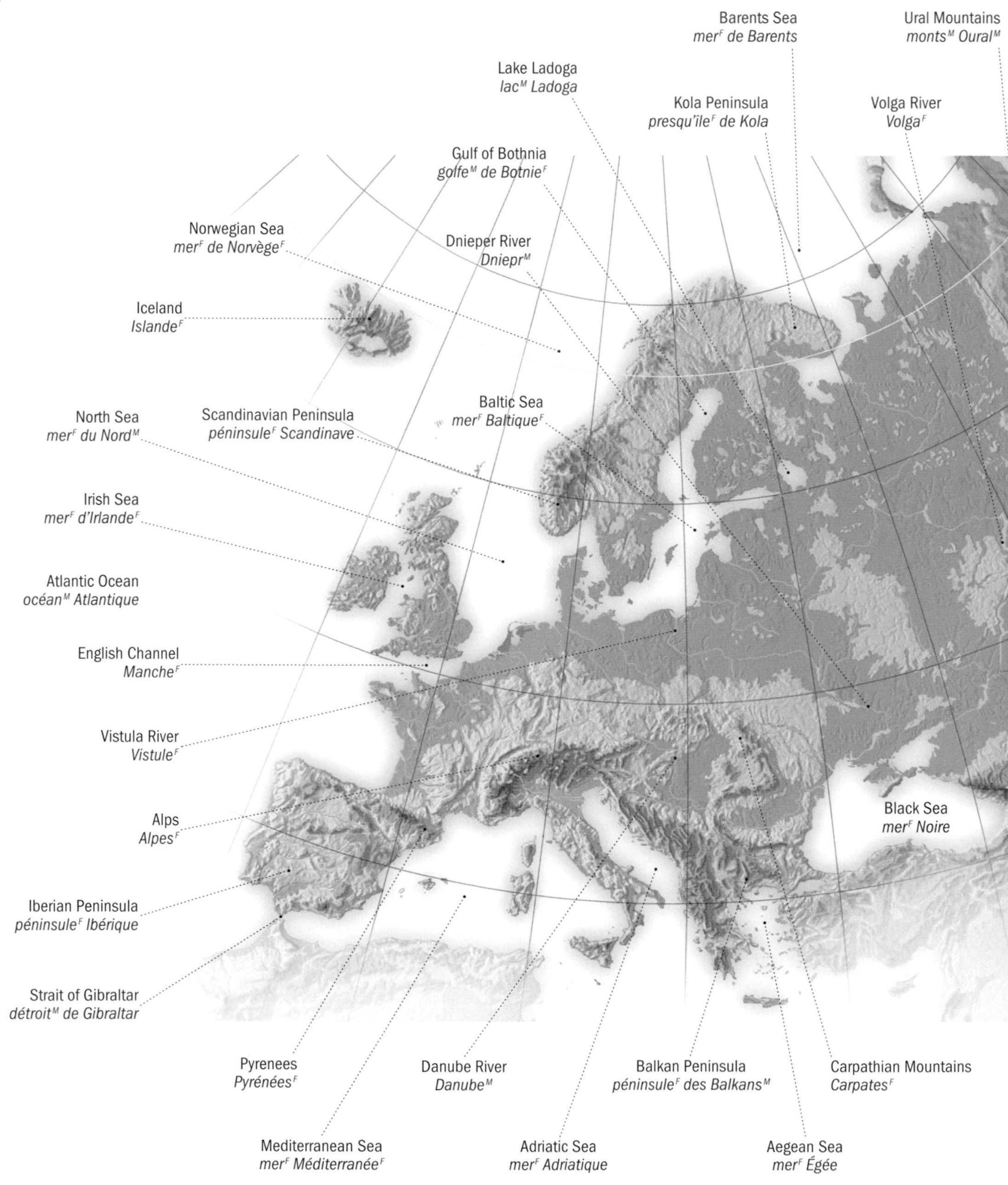
Barents Sea
merF de Barents
Ural Mountains
montsM OuralM
Lake Ladoga
lacM Ladoga
Kola Peninsula
presqu'îleF de Kola
Volga River
VolgaF
Gulf of Bothnia
golfeM de BotnieF
Norwegian Sea
merF de NorvègeF
Dnieper River
DnieprM
Iceland
IslandeF
North Sea
merF du NordM
Scandinavian Peninsula
péninsuleF Scandinave
Baltic Sea
merF BaltiqueF
Irish Sea
merF d'IrlandeF
Atlantic Ocean
océanM Atlantique
English Channel
MancheF
Vistula River
VistuleF
Alps
AlpesF
Black Sea
merF Noire
Iberian Peninsula
péninsuleF Ibérique
Strait of Gibraltar
détroitM de Gibraltar
Pyrenees
PyrénéesF
Danube River
DanubeM
Balkan Peninsula
péninsuleF des BalkansM
Carpathian Mountains
CarpatesF
Mediterranean Sea
merF MéditerranéeF
Adriatic Sea
merF Adriatique
Aegean Sea
merF Égée

Asia
*Asie*F

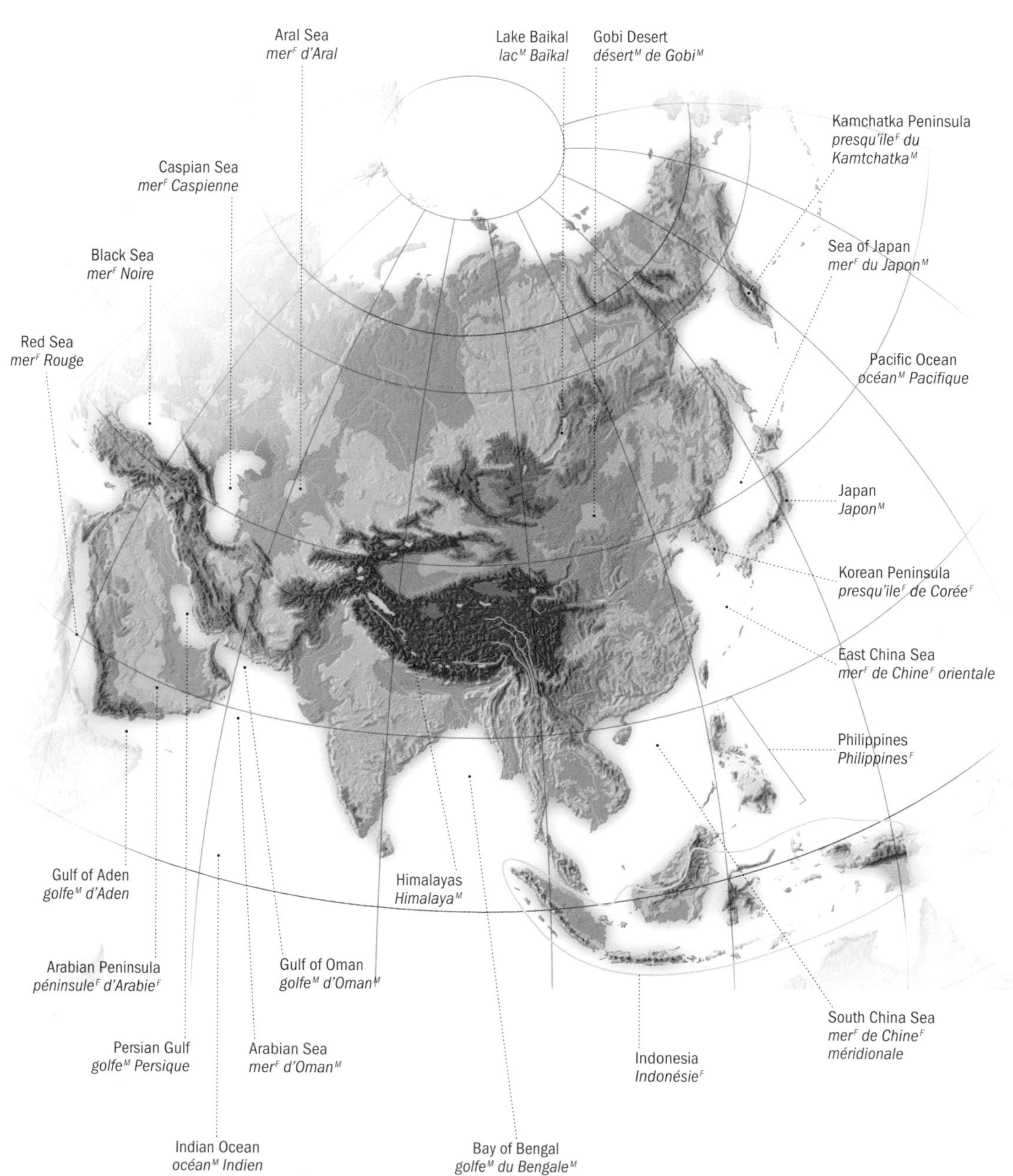
Aral Sea
merF d'Aral
Lake Baikal
lacM Baïkal
Gobi Desert
désertM de GobiM
Kamchatka Peninsula
presqu'îleF du KamtchatkaM
Caspian Sea
merF Caspienne
Black Sea
merF Noire
Sea of Japan
merF du JaponM
Red Sea
merF Rouge
Pacific Ocean
océanM Pacifique
Japan
JaponM
Korean Peninsula
presqu'îleF de CoréeF
East China Sea
merF de ChineF orientale
Philippines
PhilippinesF
Gulf of Aden
golfeM d'Aden
Himalayas
HimalayaM
Arabian Peninsula
péninsuleF d'ArabieF
Gulf of Oman
golfeM d'OmanM
South China Sea
merF de ChineF méridionale
Persian Gulf
golfeM Persique
Arabian Sea
merF d'OmanM
Indonesia
IndonésieF
Indian Ocean
océanM Indien
Bay of Bengal
golfeM du BengaleM

configuration of the continents

Africa
***Afrique*^F**

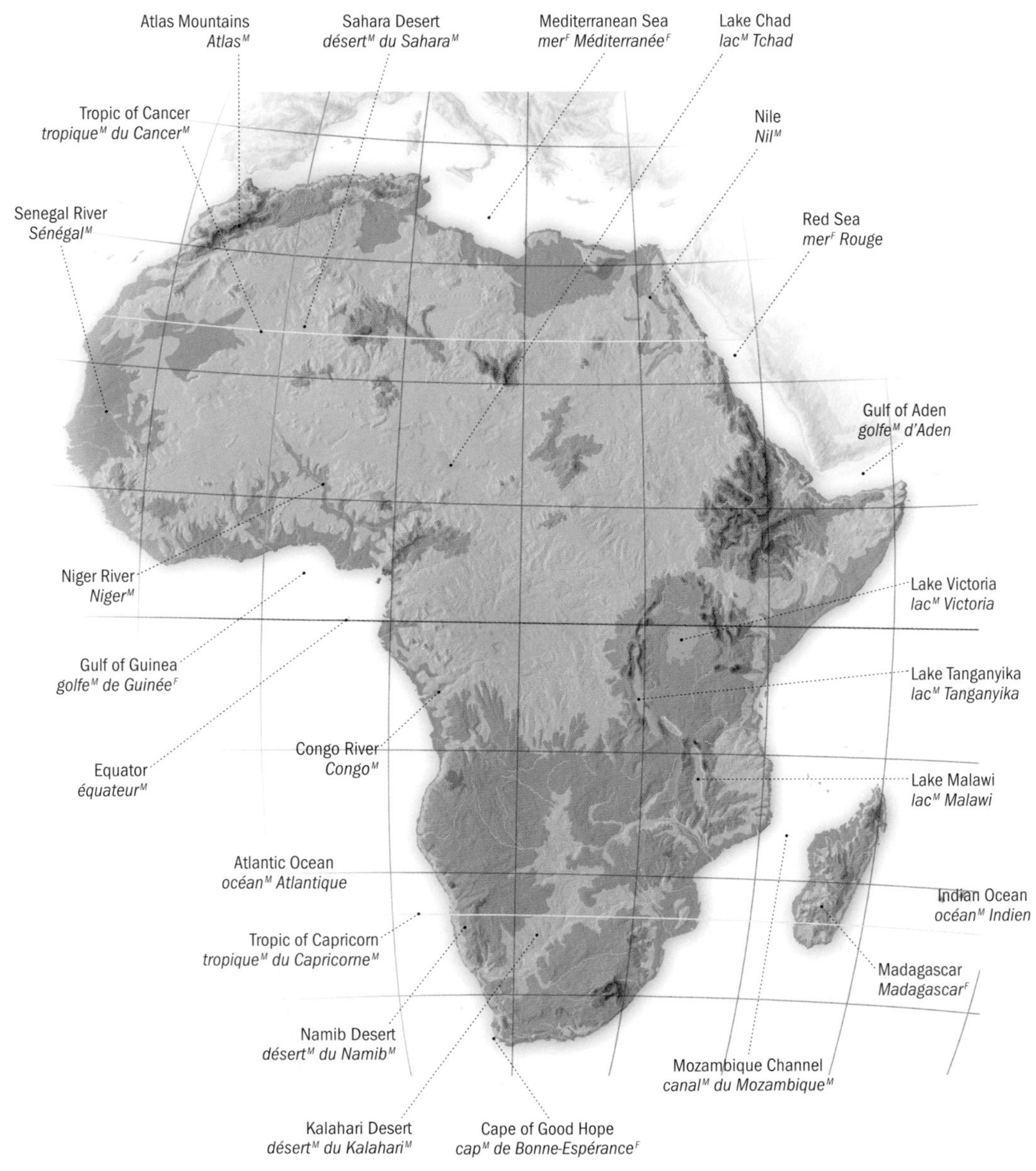
Atlas Mountains
Atlas^M
Sahara Desert
désert^M du Sahara^M
Mediterranean Sea
mer^F Méditerranée^F
Lake Chad
lac^M Tchad
Tropic of Cancer
tropique^M du Cancer^M
Nile
Nil^M
Senegal River
Sénégal^M
Red Sea
mer^F Rouge
Gulf of Aden
golfe^M d'Aden
Niger River
Niger^M
Lake Victoria
lac^M Victoria
Gulf of Guinea
golfe^M de Guinée^F
Lake Tanganyika
lac^M Tanganyika
Congo River
Congo^M
Equator
équateur^M
Lake Malawi
lac^M Malawi
Atlantic Ocean
océan^M Atlantique
Indian Ocean
océan^M Indien
Tropic of Capricorn
tropique^M du Capricorne^M
Madagascar
Madagascar^F
Namib Desert
désert^M du Namib^M
Mozambique Channel
canal^M du Mozambique^M
Kalahari Desert
désert^M du Kalahari^M
Cape of Good Hope
cap^M de Bonne-Espérance^F

cartography

cartographie[F]

Earth coordinate system
coordonnées[F] terrestres

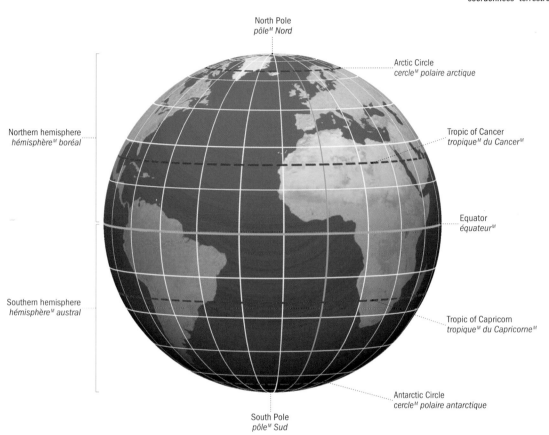

North Pole
pôle[M] Nord

Arctic Circle
cercle[M] polaire arctique

Northern hemisphere
hémisphère[M] boréal

Tropic of Cancer
tropique[M] du Cancer[M]

Equator
équateur[M]

Southern hemisphere
hémisphère[M] austral

Tropic of Capricorn
tropique[M] du Capricorne[M]

Antarctic Circle
cercle[M] polaire antarctique

South Pole
pôle[M] Sud

hemispheres
hémisphères[M]

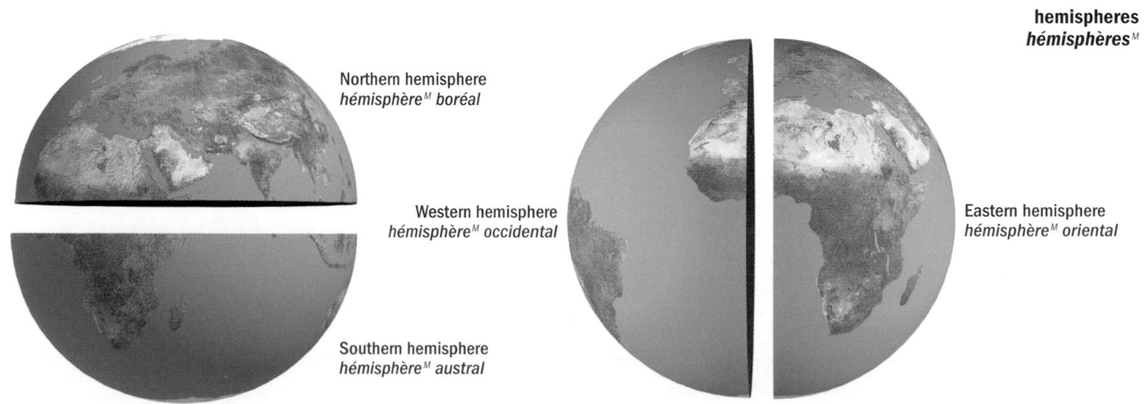
Northern hemisphere
hémisphère[M] boréal
Western hemisphere
hémisphère[M] occidental
Eastern hemisphere
hémisphère[M] oriental
Southern hemisphere
hémisphère[M] austral

cartography

grid system
divisions^F cartographiques

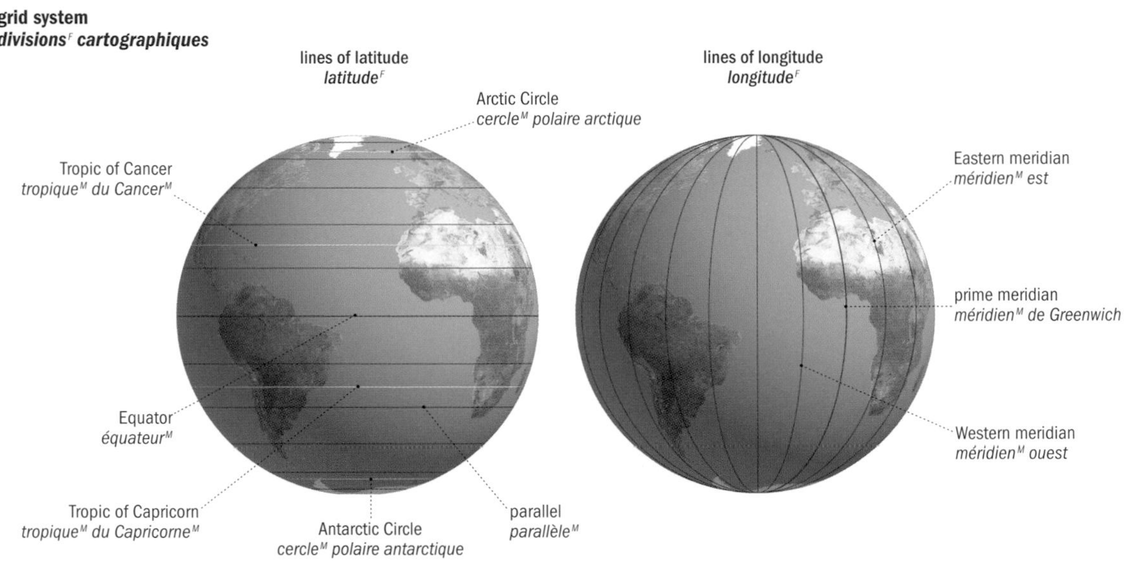
lines of latitude
latitude^F
Arctic Circle
cercle^M polaire arctique
Tropic of Cancer
tropique^M du Cancer^M
Equator
équateur^M
Tropic of Capricorn
tropique^M du Capricorne^M
Antarctic Circle
cercle^M polaire antarctique
parallel
parallèle^M
lines of longitude
longitude^F
Eastern meridian
méridien^M est
prime meridian
méridien^M de Greenwich
Western meridian
méridien^M ouest

map projections
projections^F cartographiques

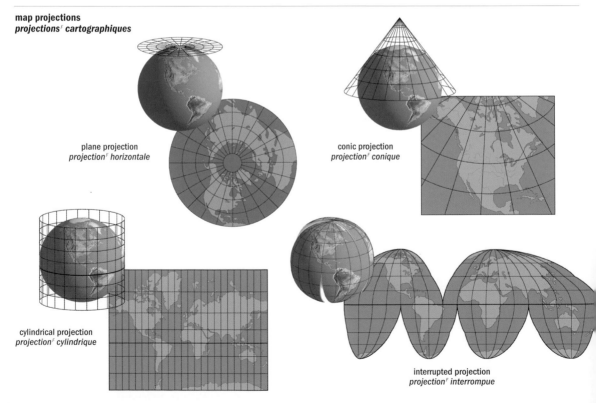

plane projection
projection^F horizontale

conic projection
projection^F conique

cylindrical projection
projection^F cylindrique

interrupted projection
projection^F interrompue

compass rose
rose[F] des vents[M]

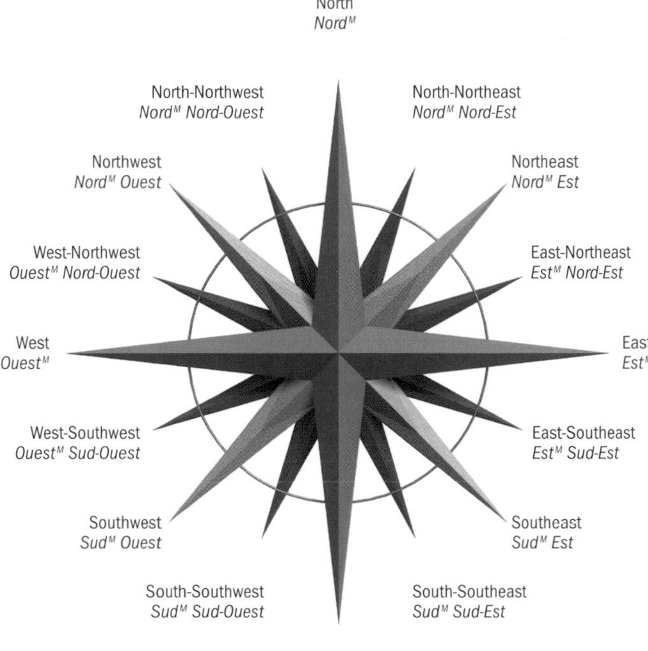
North
Nord[M]
North-Northwest
Nord[M] Nord-Ouest
North-Northeast
Nord[M] Nord-Est
Northwest
Nord[M] Ouest
Northeast
Nord[M] Est
West-Northwest
Ouest[M] Nord-Ouest
East-Northeast
Est[M] Nord-Est
West
Ouest[M]
East
Est[M]
West-Southwest
Ouest[M] Sud-Ouest
East-Southeast
Est[M] Sud-Est
Southwest
Sud[M] Ouest
Southeast
Sud[M] Est
South-Southwest
Sud[M] Sud-Ouest
South-Southeast
Sud[M] Sud-Est
South
Sud[M]

political map
carte[F] politique

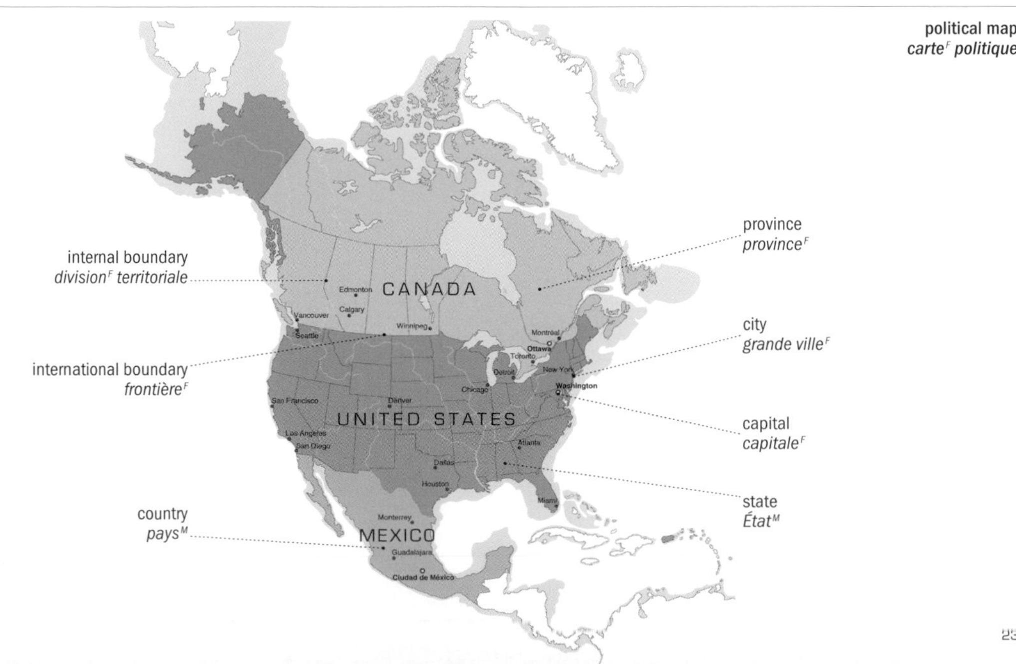
province
province[F]
internal boundary
division[F] territoriale
CANADA
Edmonton
Calgary
Vancouver
Seattle
Winnipeg
Montréal
Ottawa
Toronto
city
grande ville[F]
international boundary
frontière[F]
Detroit
New York
Washington
Chicago
Denver
San Francisco
UNITED STATES
capital
capitale[F]
Los Angeles
San Diego
Atlanta
Dallas
Houston
state
État[M]
Miami
country
pays[M]
Monterrey
MEXICO
Guadalajara
Ciudad de México

physical map
carte*[F] *physique

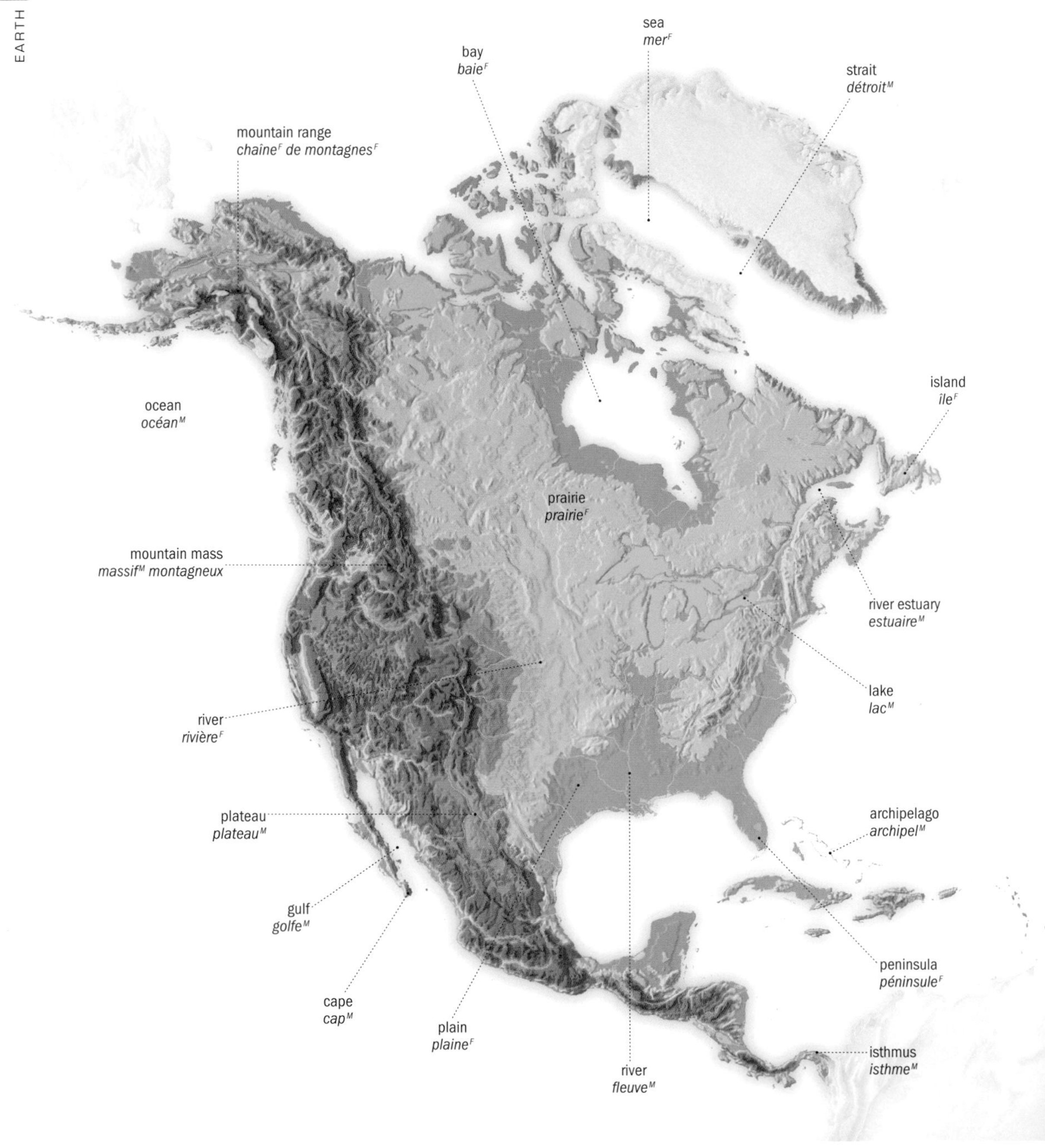
sea
merF
bay
baieF
strait
détroitM
mountain range
chaîneF de montagnesF
island
îleF
ocean
océanM
prairie
prairieF
mountain mass
massifM montagneux
river estuary
estuaireM
lake
lacM
river
rivièreF
archipelago
archipelM
plateau
plateauM
gulf
golfeM
peninsula
péninsuleF
cape
capM
plain
plaineF
isthmus
isthmeM
river
fleuveM

urban map
plan[M] urbain

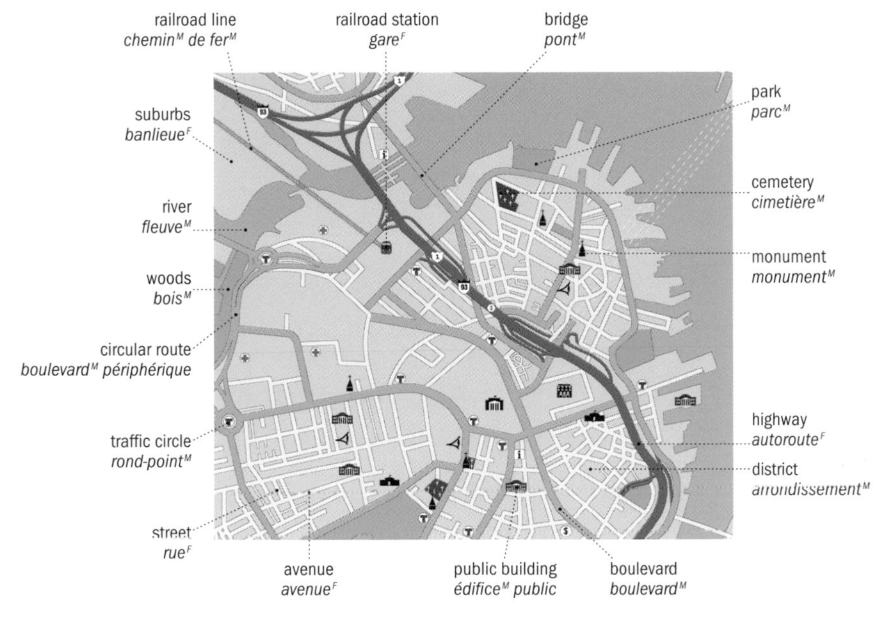
railroad line
chemin[M] de fer[M]
railroad station
gare[F]
bridge
pont[M]
suburbs
banlieue[F]
river
fleuve[M]
woods
bois[M]
circular route
boulevard[M] périphérique
traffic circle
rond-point[M]
street
rue[F]
avenue
avenue[F]
public building
édifice[M] public
boulevard
boulevard[M]
park
parc[M]
cemetery
cimetière[M]
monument
monument[M]
highway
autoroute[F]
district
arrondissement[M]

road map
carte[F] routière

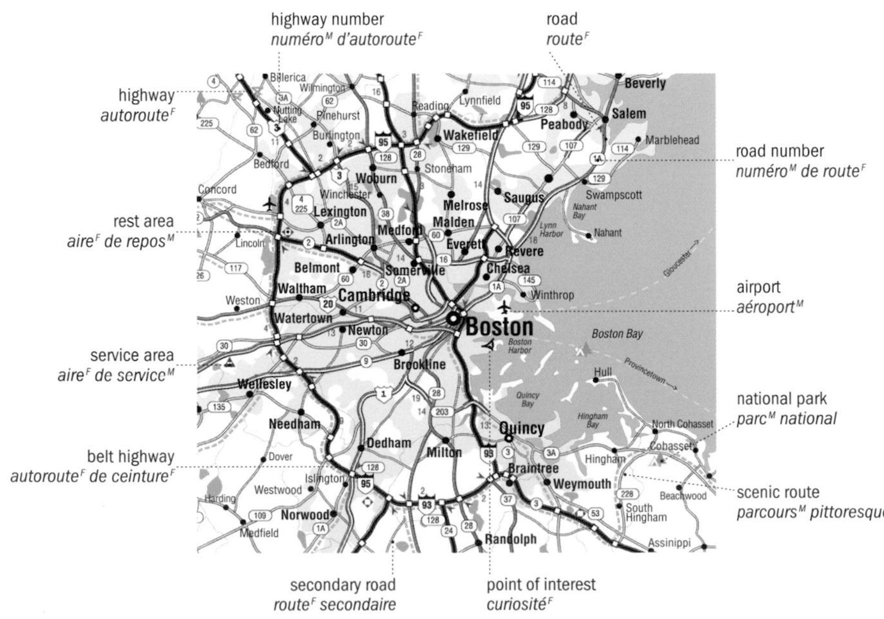
highway number
numéro[M] d'autoroute[F]
road
route[F]
highway
autoroute[F]
rest area
aire[F] de repos[M]
service area
aire[F] de service[M]
belt highway
autoroute[F] de ceinture[F]
secondary road
route[F] secondaire
point of interest
curiosité[F]
road number
numéro[M] de route[F]
airport
aéroport[M]
national park
parc[M] national
scenic route
parcours[M] pittoresque
Boston
Cambridge
Quincy

section of the Earth's crust

coupe^F de la croûte^F terrestre

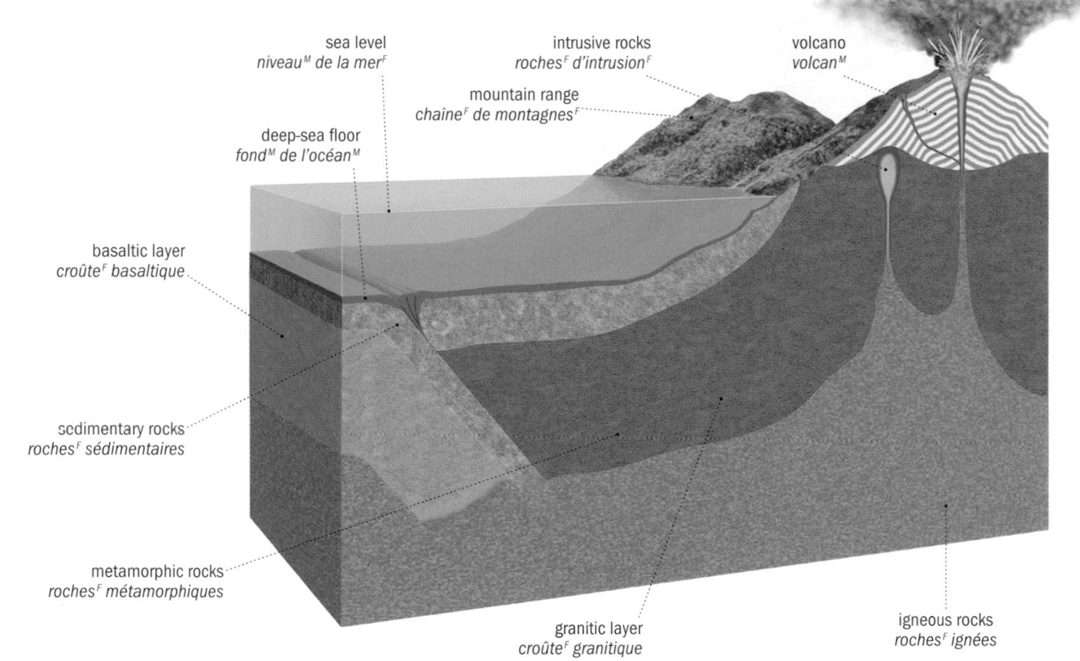
sea level
niveau^M de la mer^F
intrusive rocks
roches^F d'intrusion^F
volcano
volcan^M
mountain range
chaîne^F de montagnes^F
deep-sea floor
fond^M de l'océan^M
basaltic layer
croûte^F basaltique
sedimentary rocks
roches^F sédimentaires
metamorphic rocks
roches^F métamorphiques
granitic layer
croûte^F granitique
igneous rocks
roches^F ignées

structure of the Earth

structure^F de la Terre^F

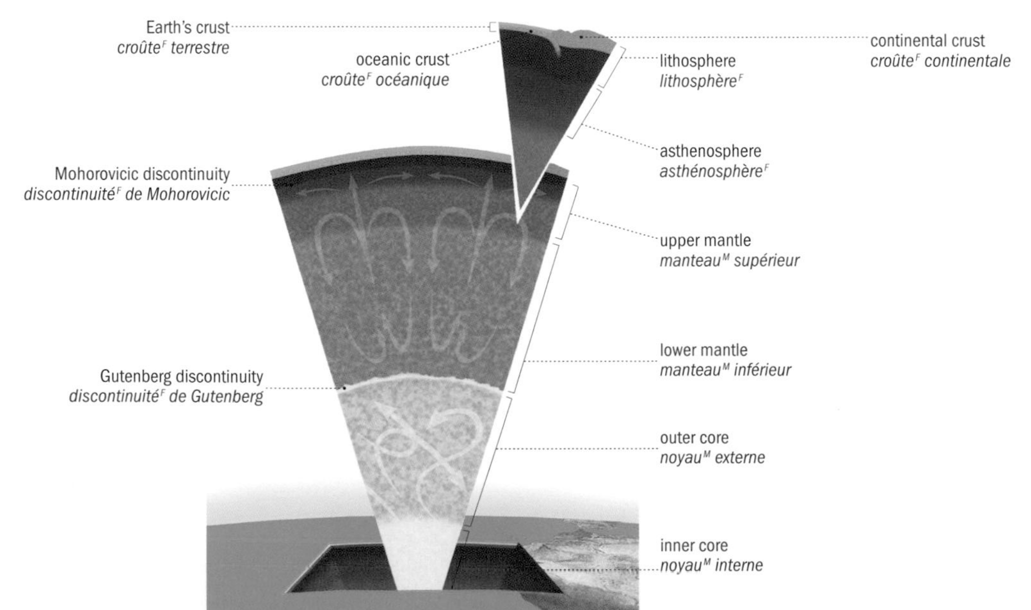
Earth's crust
croûte^F terrestre
oceanic crust
croûte^F océanique
continental crust
croûte^F continentale
lithosphere
lithosphère^F
asthenosphere
asthénosphère^F
Mohorovicic discontinuity
discontinuité^F de Mohorovicic
upper mantle
manteau^M supérieur
lower mantle
manteau^M inférieur
Gutenberg discontinuity
discontinuité^F de Gutenberg
outer core
noyau^M externe
inner core
noyau^M interne

tectonic plates

plaques^{F} tectoniques

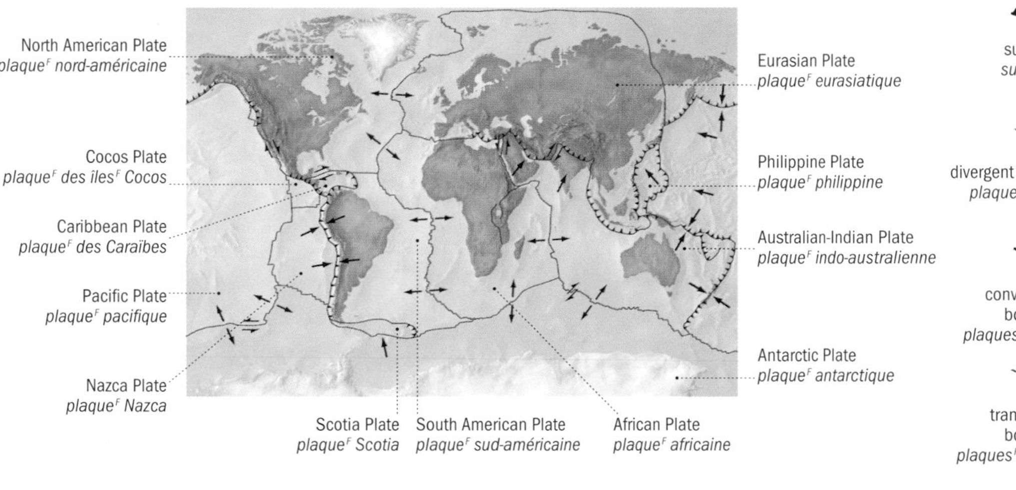
North American Plate
plaque^{F} nord-américaine
Cocos Plate
plaque^{F} des îles^{F} Cocos
Caribbean Plate
plaque^{F} des Caraïbes
Pacific Plate
plaque^{F} pacifique
Nazca Plate
plaque^{F} Nazca
Scotia Plate
plaque^{F} Scotia
South American Plate
plaque^{F} sud-américaine
African Plate
plaque^{F} africaine
Eurasian Plate
plaque^{F} eurasiatique
Philippine Plate
plaque^{F} philippine
Australian-Indian Plate
plaque^{F} indo-australienne
Antarctic Plate
plaque^{F} antarctique
subduction
subduction^{F}
divergent plate boundaries
plaques^{F} divergentes
convergent plate boundaries
plaques^{F} convergentes
transform plate boundaries
plaques^{F} transformantes

earthquake

séisme^{M}

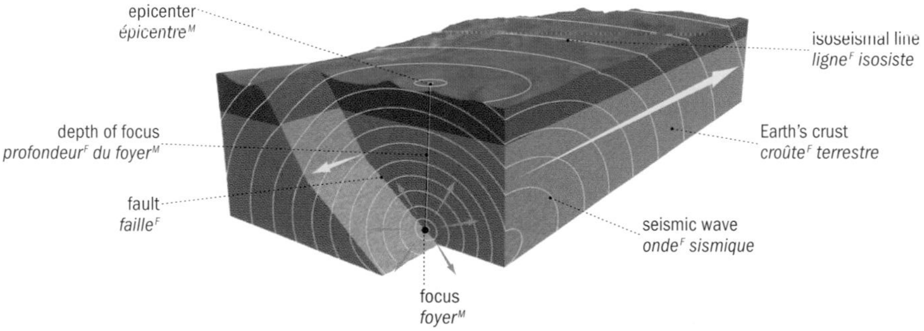

epicenter
épicentre^{M}
isoseismal line
ligne^{F} isosiste
depth of focus
profondeur^{F} du foyer^{M}
Earth's crust
croûte^{F} terrestre
fault
faille^{F}
seismic wave
onde^{F} sismique
focus
foyer^{M}

seismographs
sismographes^{M}

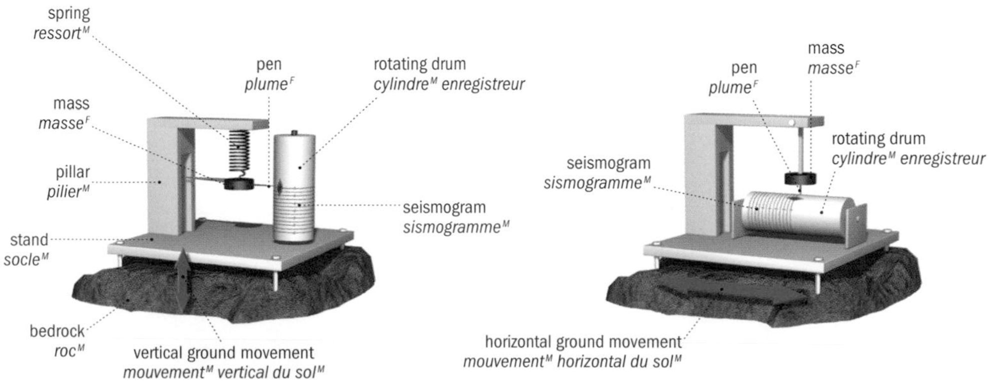

vertical seismograph
sismographe^{M} vertical

spring
ressort^{M}
pen
plume^{F}
rotating drum
cylindre^{M} enregistreur
mass
masse^{F}
pillar
pilier^{M}
seismogram
sismogramme^{M}
stand
socle^{M}
bedrock
roc^{M}
vertical ground movement
mouvement^{M} vertical du sol^{M}

horizontal seismograph
sismographe^{M} horizontal

mass
masse^{F}
pen
plume^{F}
rotating drum
cylindre^{M} enregistreur
seismogram
sismogramme^{M}
horizontal ground movement
mouvement^{M} horizontal du sol^{M}

volcano

volcan^M

volcano during eruption
volcan^M en éruption^F

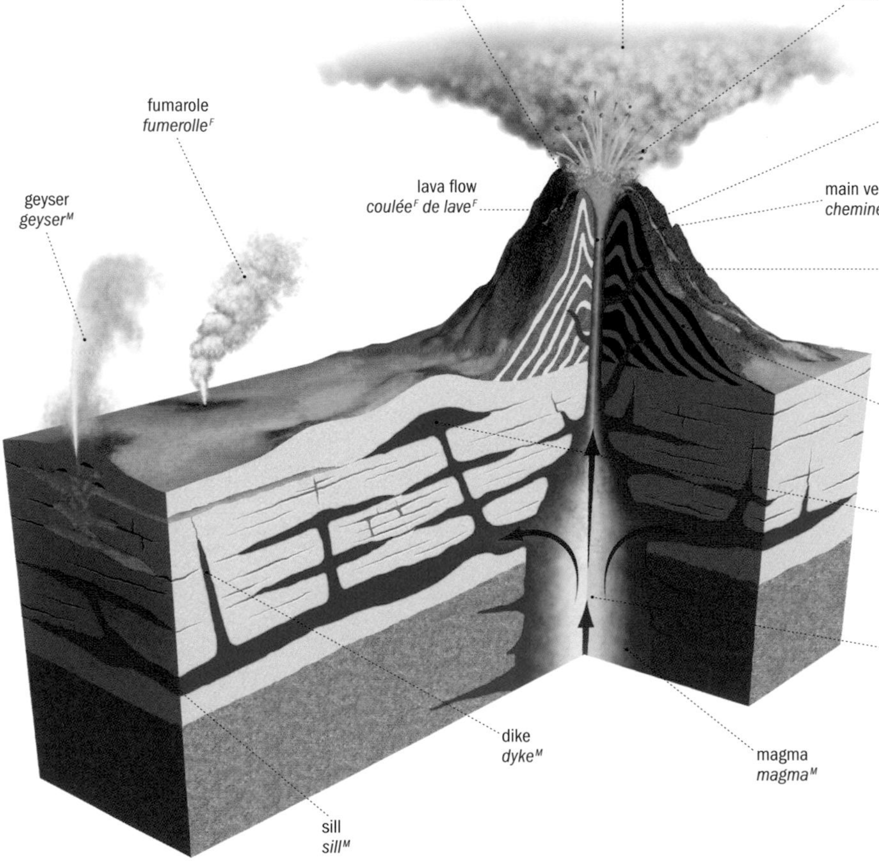

crater
cratère^M

cloud of volcanic ash
nuage^M de cendres^F

volcanic bomb
bombe^F volcanique

fumarole
fumerolle^F

lava layer
couche^F de laves^F

geyser
geyser^M

lava flow
coulée^F de lave^F

main vent
cheminée^F

side vent
cône^M adventif

ash layer
couche^F de cendres^F

laccolith
laccolite^F

magma chamber
réservoir^M magmatique

dike
dyke^M

magma
magma^M

sill
sill^M

examples of volcanoes
exemples^M de volcans^M

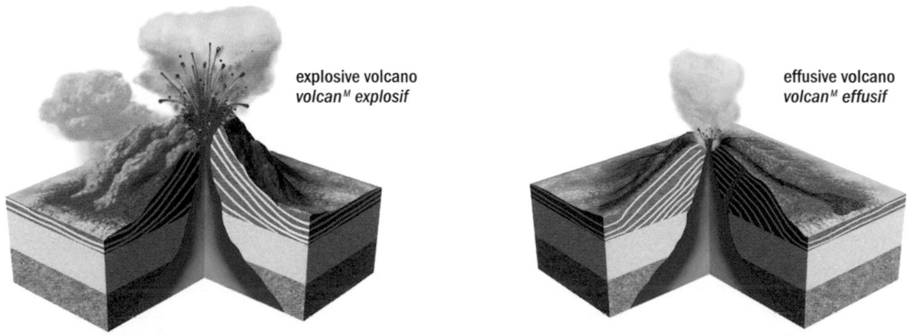
explosive volcano
volcan^M explosif
effusive volcano
volcan^M effusif

mountain

montagne[F]

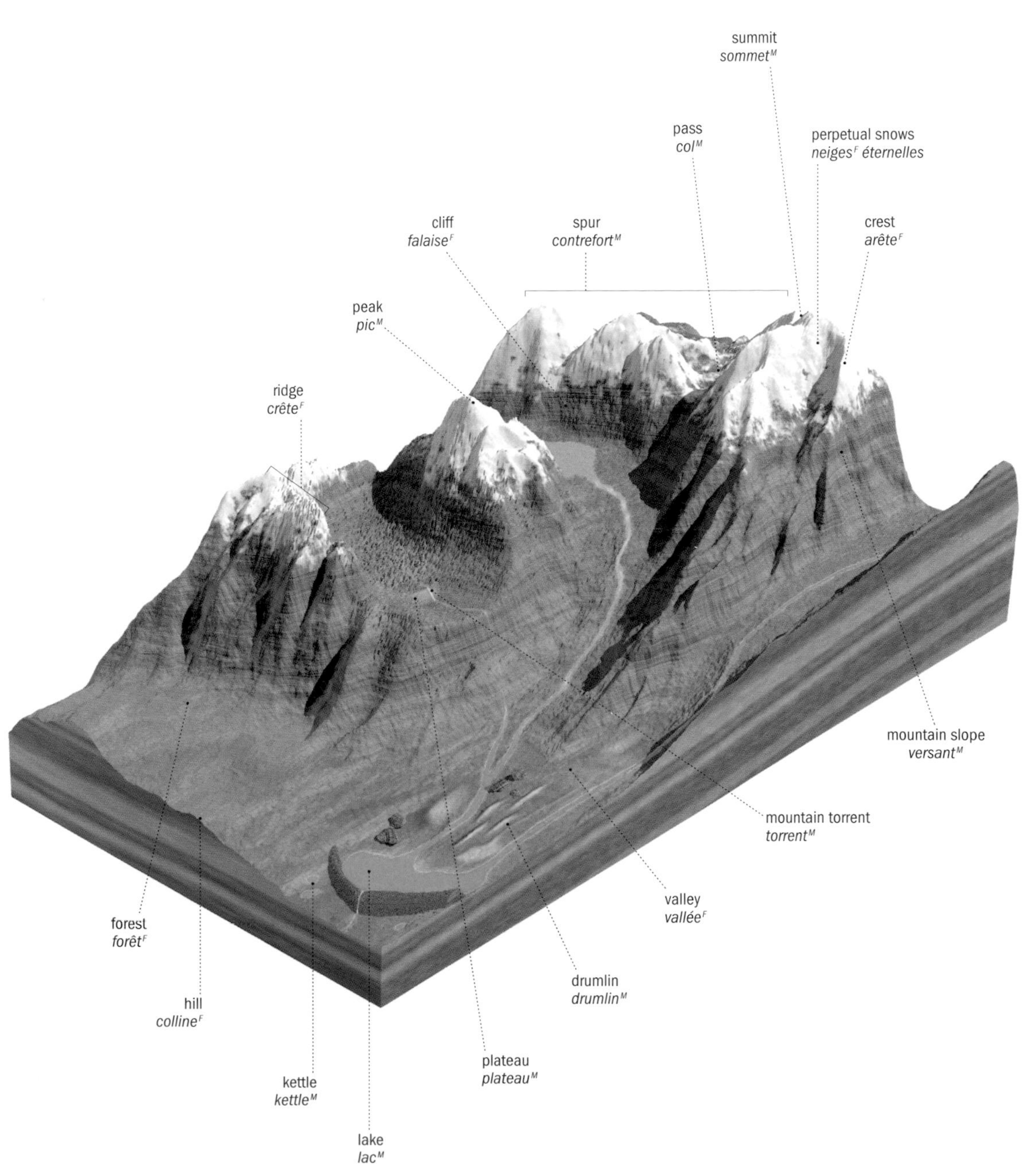
summit
sommet[M]
pass
col[M]
perpetual snows
neiges[F] éternelles
cliff
falaise[F]
spur
contrefort[M]
crest
arête[F]
peak
pic[M]
ridge
crête[F]
mountain slope
versant[M]
mountain torrent
torrent[M]
valley
vallée[F]
forest
forêt[F]
drumlin
drumlin[M]
hill
colline[F]
plateau
plateau[M]
kettle
kettle[M]
lake
lac[M]

glacier

glacier[M]

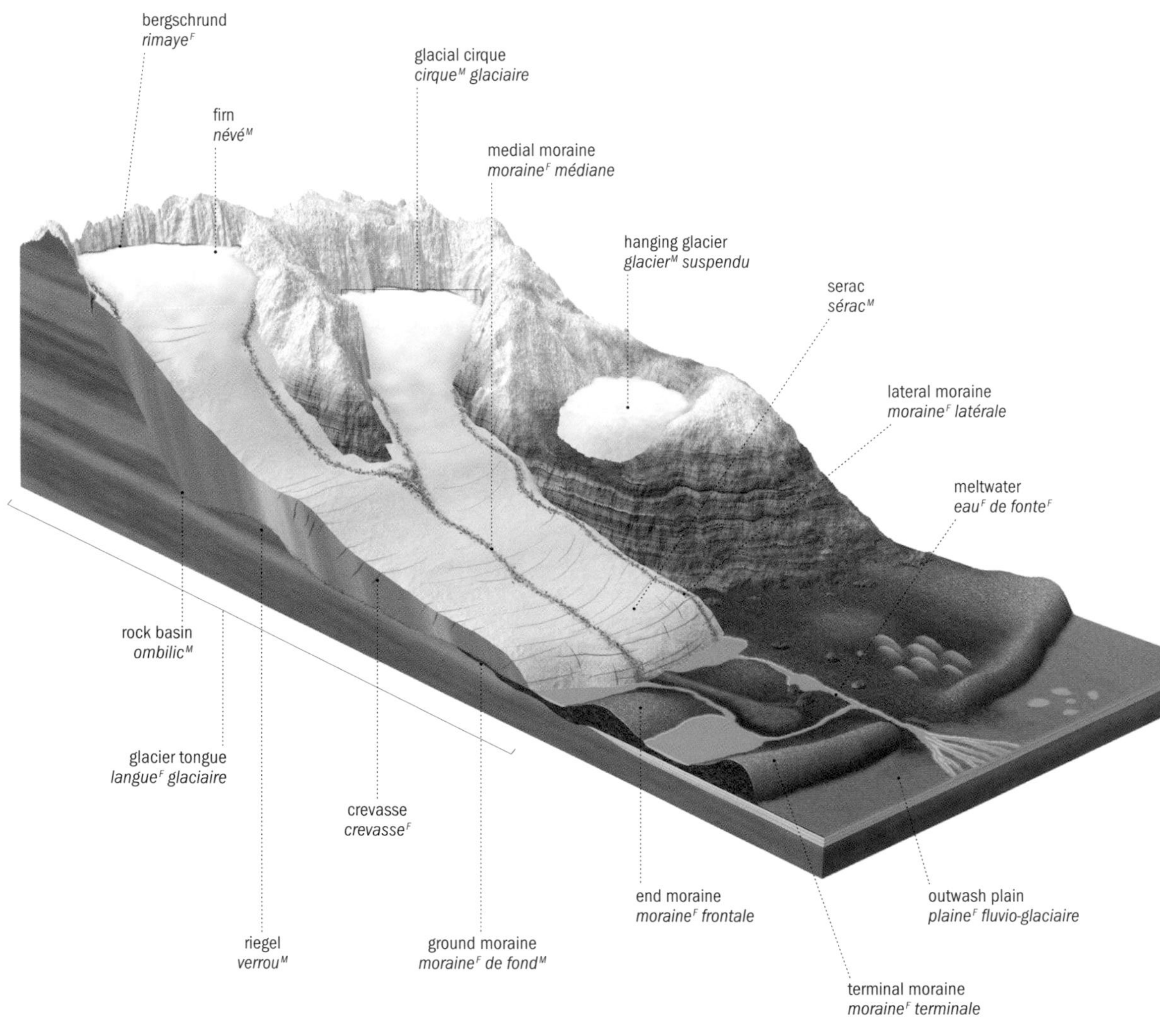
bergschrund
rimaye[F]
firn
névé[M]
glacial cirque
cirque[M] glaciaire
medial moraine
moraine[F] médiane
hanging glacier
glacier[M] suspendu
serac
sérac[M]
lateral moraine
moraine[F] latérale
meltwater
eau[F] de fonte[F]
rock basin
ombilic[M]
glacier tongue
langue[F] glaciaire
crevasse
crevasse[F]
riegel
verrou[M]
ground moraine
moraine[F] de fond[M]
end moraine
moraine[F] frontale
outwash plain
plaine[F] fluvio-glaciaire
terminal moraine
moraine[F] terminale

cave

grotte[F]

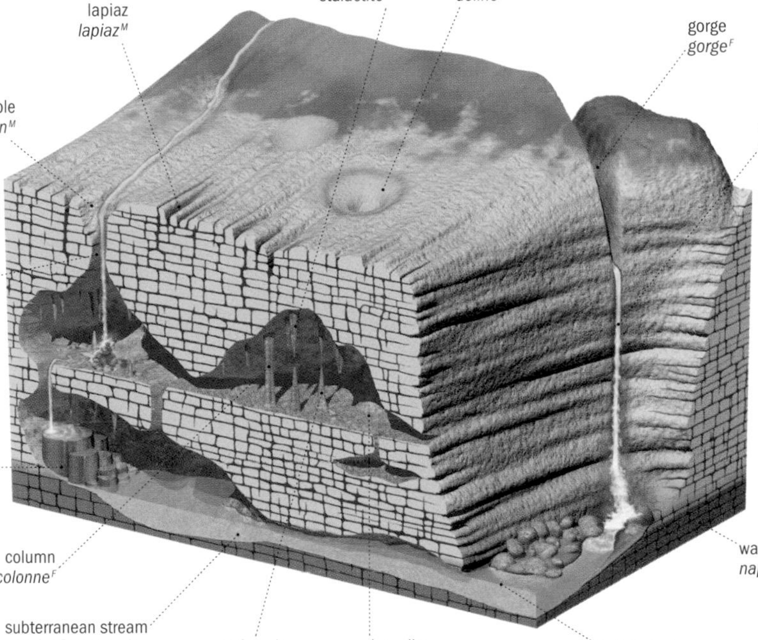

lapiaz
lapiaz[M]

stalactite
stalactite[F]

sinkhole
doline[F]

gorge
gorge[F]

pothole
aven[M]

waterfall
chute[F]

swallow hole
gouffre[M]

gour
gour[M]

water table
nappe[F] phréatique

column
colonne[F]

subterranean stream
rivière[F] souterraine

stalagmite
stalagmite[F]

dry gallery
galerie[F] sèche

resurgence
résurgence[F]

landslides

mouvements[M] de terrain[M]

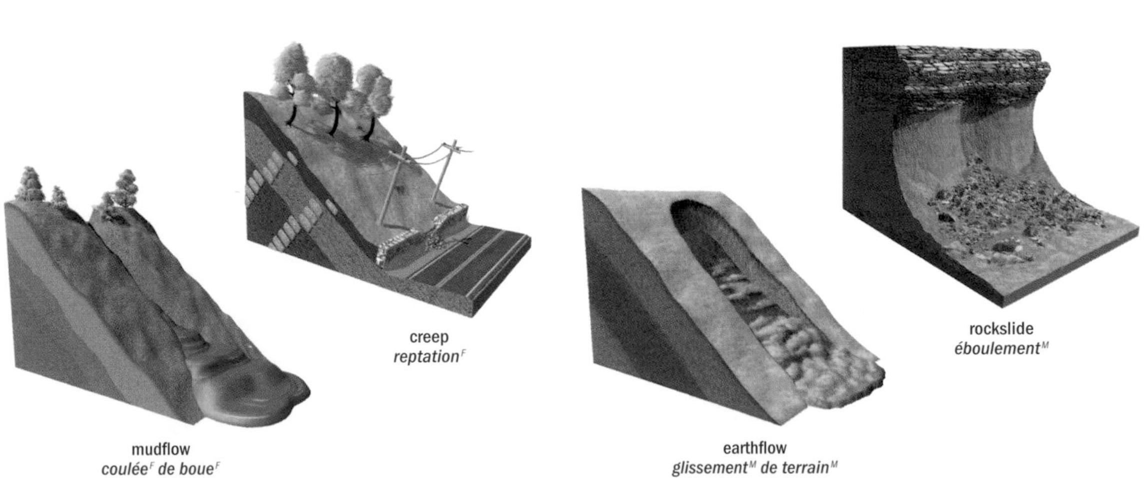

creep
reptation[F]

rockslide
éboulement[M]

mudflow
coulée[F] de boue[F]

earthflow
glissement[M] de terrain[M]

watercourse

cours^{M} d'eau^{F}

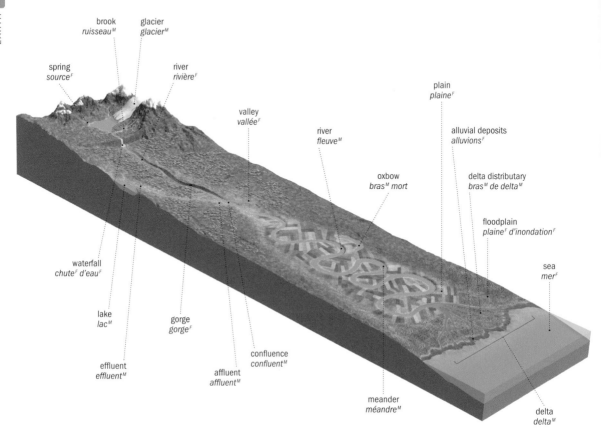

brook
ruisseau^{M}

glacier
glacier^{M}

spring
source^{F}

river
rivière^{F}

plain
plaine^{F}

valley
vallée^{F}

river
fleuve^{M}

alluvial deposits
alluvions^{F}

oxbow
bras^{M} mort

delta distributary
bras^{M} de delta^{M}

floodplain
plaine^{F} d'inondation^{F}

waterfall
chute^{F} d'eau^{F}

sea
mer^{F}

lake
lac^{M}

gorge
gorge^{F}

confluence
confluent^{M}

effluent
effluent^{M}

affluent
affluent^{M}

meander
méandre^{M}

delta
delta^{M}

lakes

lacs^{M}

glacial lake
lac^{M} d'origine^{F} glaciaire

volcanic lake
lac^{M} d'origine^{F} volcanique

tectonic lake
lac^{M} d'origine^{F} tectonique

oxbow lake
lac^{M} en croissant^{M}

oasis
oasis^{F}

artificial lake
lac^{M} artificiel

wave

vague[F]

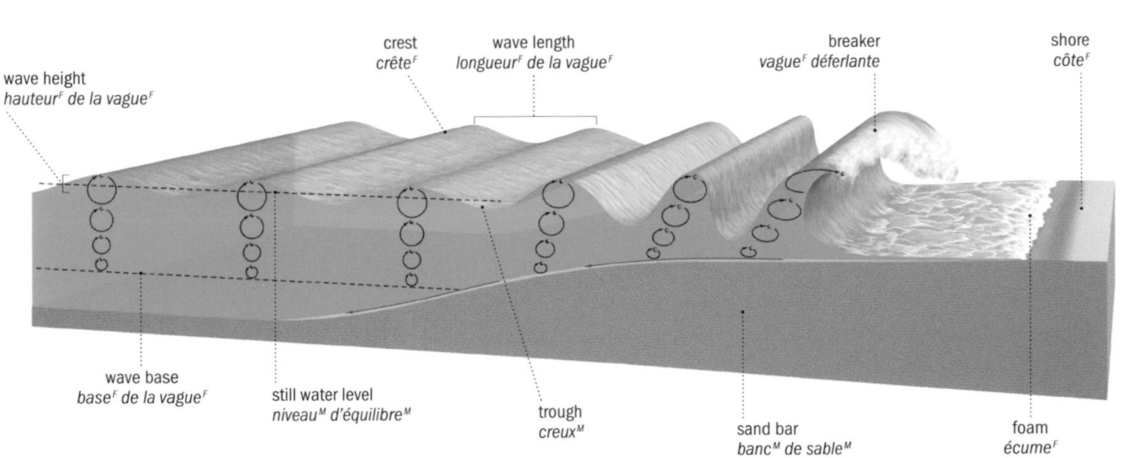
wave height
hauteur[F] de la vague[F]
crest
crête[F]
wave length
longueur[F] de la vague[F]
breaker
vague[F] déferlante
shore
côte[F]
wave base
base[F] de la vague[F]
still water level
niveau[M] d'équilibre[M]
trough
creux[M]
sand bar
banc[M] de sable[M]
foam
écume[F]

ocean floor

fond[M] de l'océan[M]

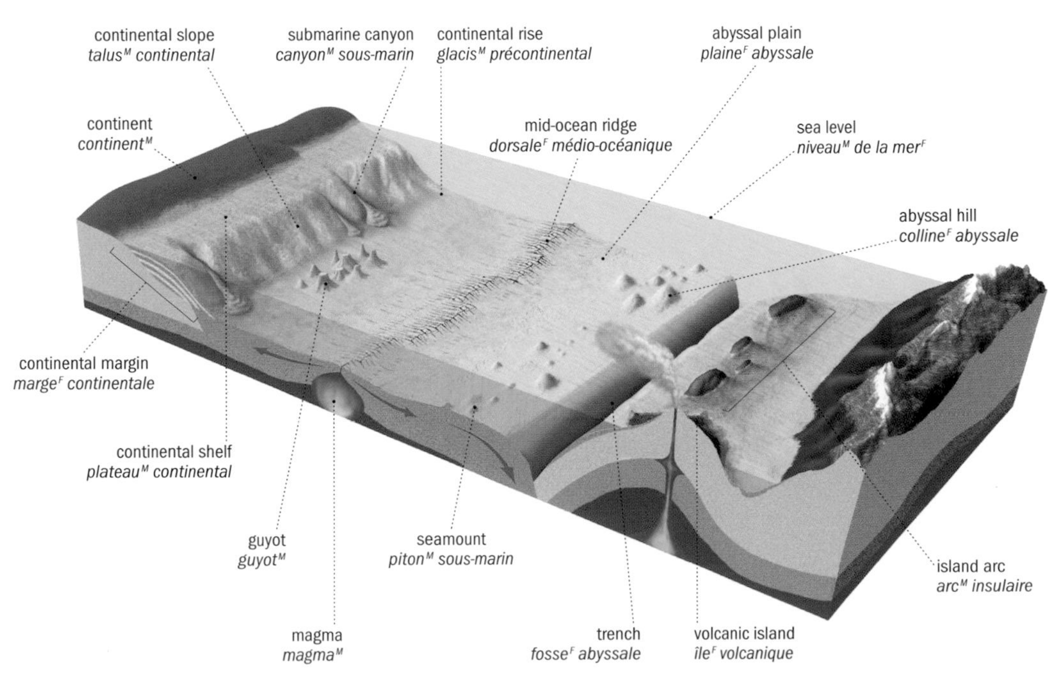
continental slope
talus[M] continental
submarine canyon
canyon[M] sous-marin
continental rise
glacis[M] précontinental
abyssal plain
plaine[F] abyssale
continent
continent[M]
mid-ocean ridge
dorsale[F] médio-océanique
sea level
niveau[M] de la mer[F]
abyssal hill
colline[F] abyssale
continental margin
marge[F] continentale
continental shelf
plateau[M] continental
guyot
guyot[M]
seamount
piton[M] sous-marin
island arc
arc[M] insulaire
magma
magma[M]
trench
fosse[F] abyssale
volcanic island
île[F] volcanique

ocean trenches and ridges

fosses[F] et dorsales[F] océaniques

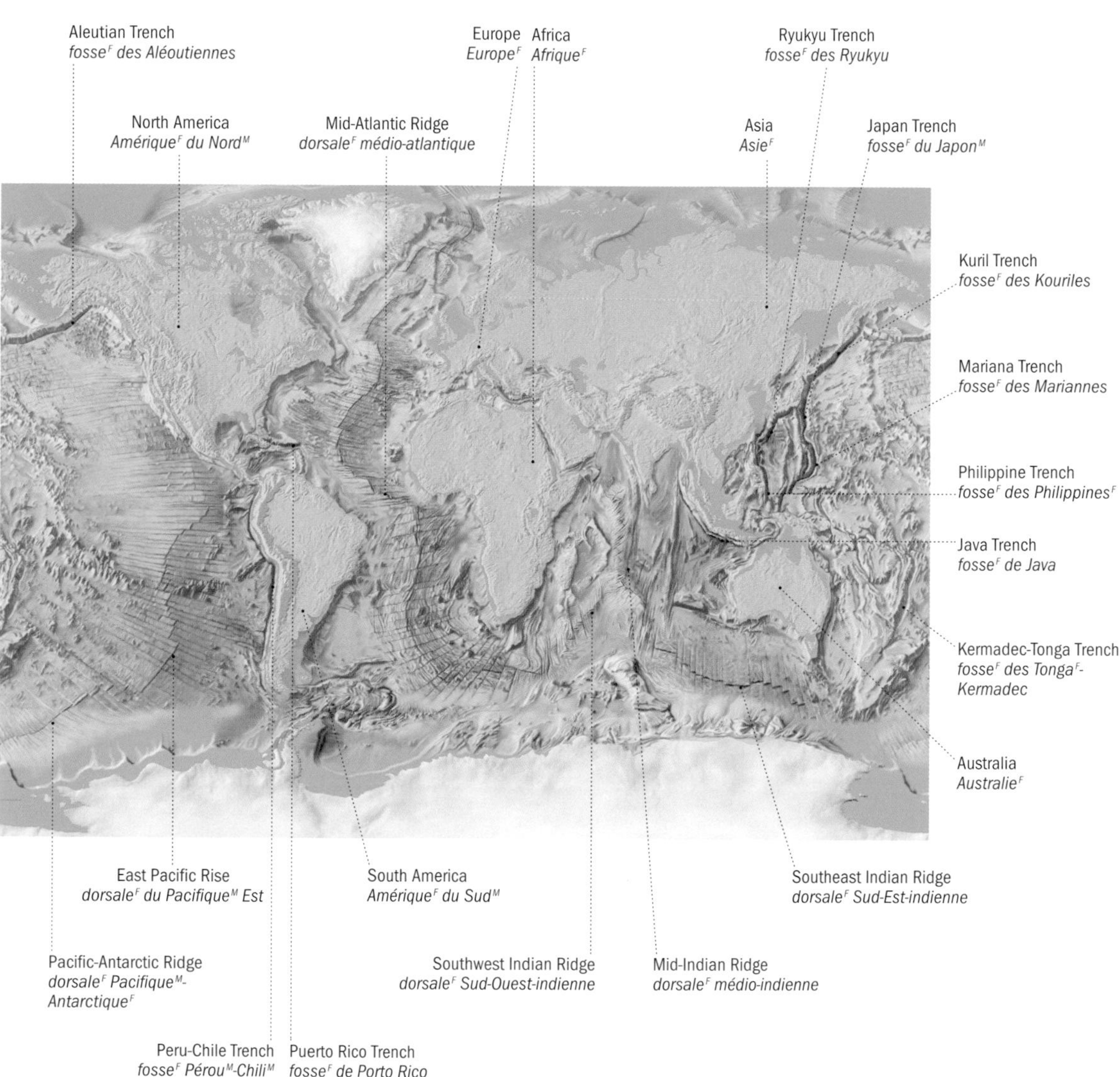
Aleutian Trench
fosse[F] des Aléoutiennes
Europe
Europe[F]
Africa
Afrique[F]
Ryukyu Trench
fosse[F] des Ryukyu
North America
Amérique[F] du Nord[M]
Mid-Atlantic Ridge
dorsale[F] médio-atlantique
Asia
Asie[F]
Japan Trench
fosse[F] du Japon[M]
Kuril Trench
fosse[F] des Kouriles
Mariana Trench
fosse[F] des Mariannes
Philippine Trench
fosse[F] des Philippines[F]
Java Trench
fosse[F] de Java
Kermadec-Tonga Trench
fosse[F] des Tonga[F]-Kermadec
Australia
Australie[F]
East Pacific Rise
dorsale[F] du Pacifique[M] Est
South America
Amérique[F] du Sud[M]
Southeast Indian Ridge
dorsale[F] Sud-Est-indienne
Pacific-Antarctic Ridge
dorsale[F] Pacifique[M]-Antarctique[F]
Southwest Indian Ridge
dorsale[F] Sud-Ouest-indienne
Mid-Indian Ridge
dorsale[F] médio-indienne
Peru-Chile Trench
fosse[F] Pérou[M]-Chili[M]
Puerto Rico Trench
fosse[F] de Porto Rico

common coastal features

configuration^F du littoral^M

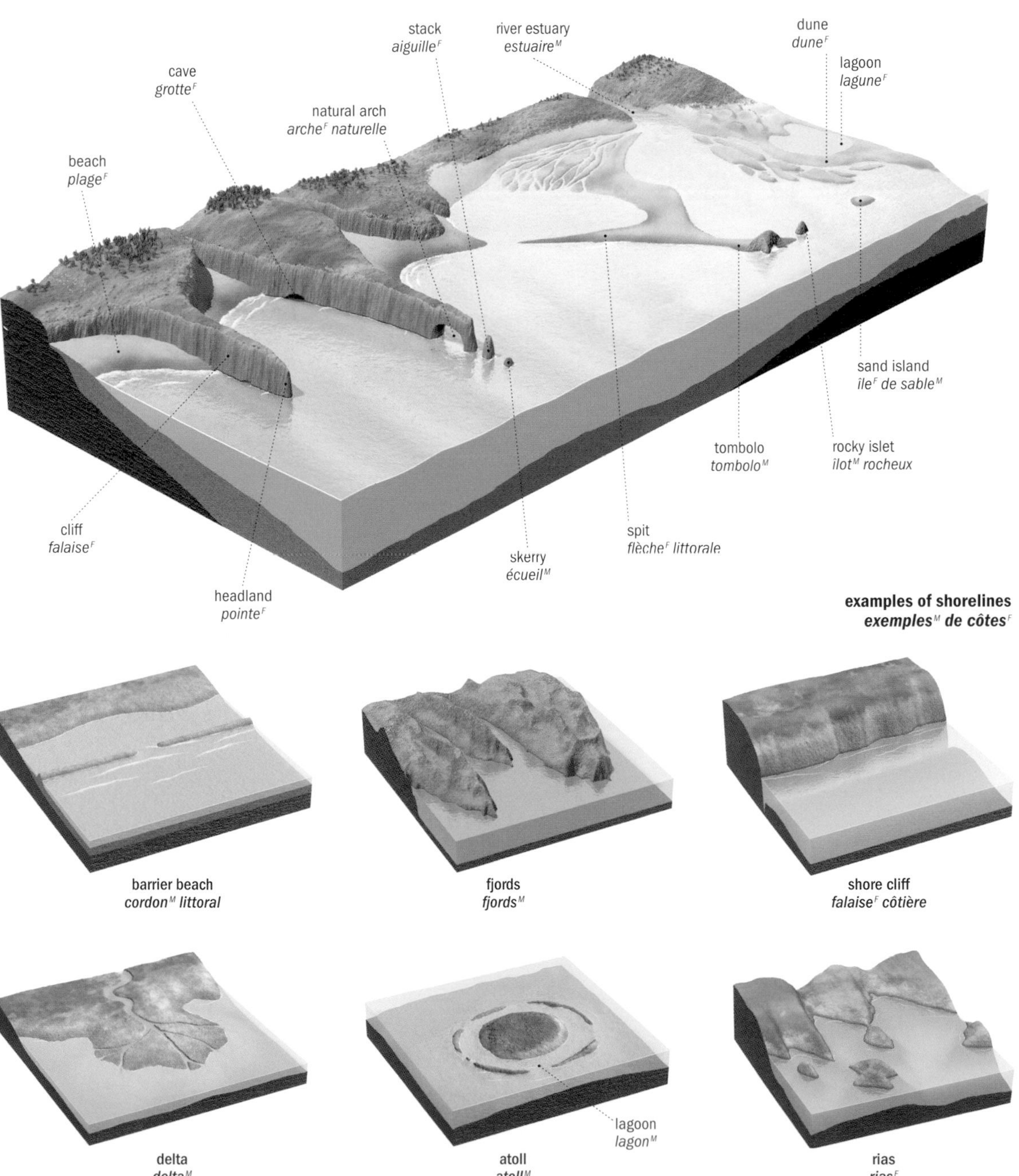
stack
aiguille^F
river estuary
estuaire^M
dune
dune^F
lagoon
lagune^F
cave
grotte^F
natural arch
arche^F naturelle
beach
plage^F
sand island
île^F de sable^M
tombolo
tombolo^M
rocky islet
ilot^M rocheux
cliff
falaise^F
spit
flèche^F littorale
skerry
écueil^M
headland
pointe^F
examples of shorelines
exemples^M de côtes^F
barrier beach
cordon^M littoral
fjords
fjords^M
shore cliff
falaise^F côtière
lagoon
lagon^M
delta
delta^M
atoll
atoll^M
rias
rias^F

desert

désert[M]

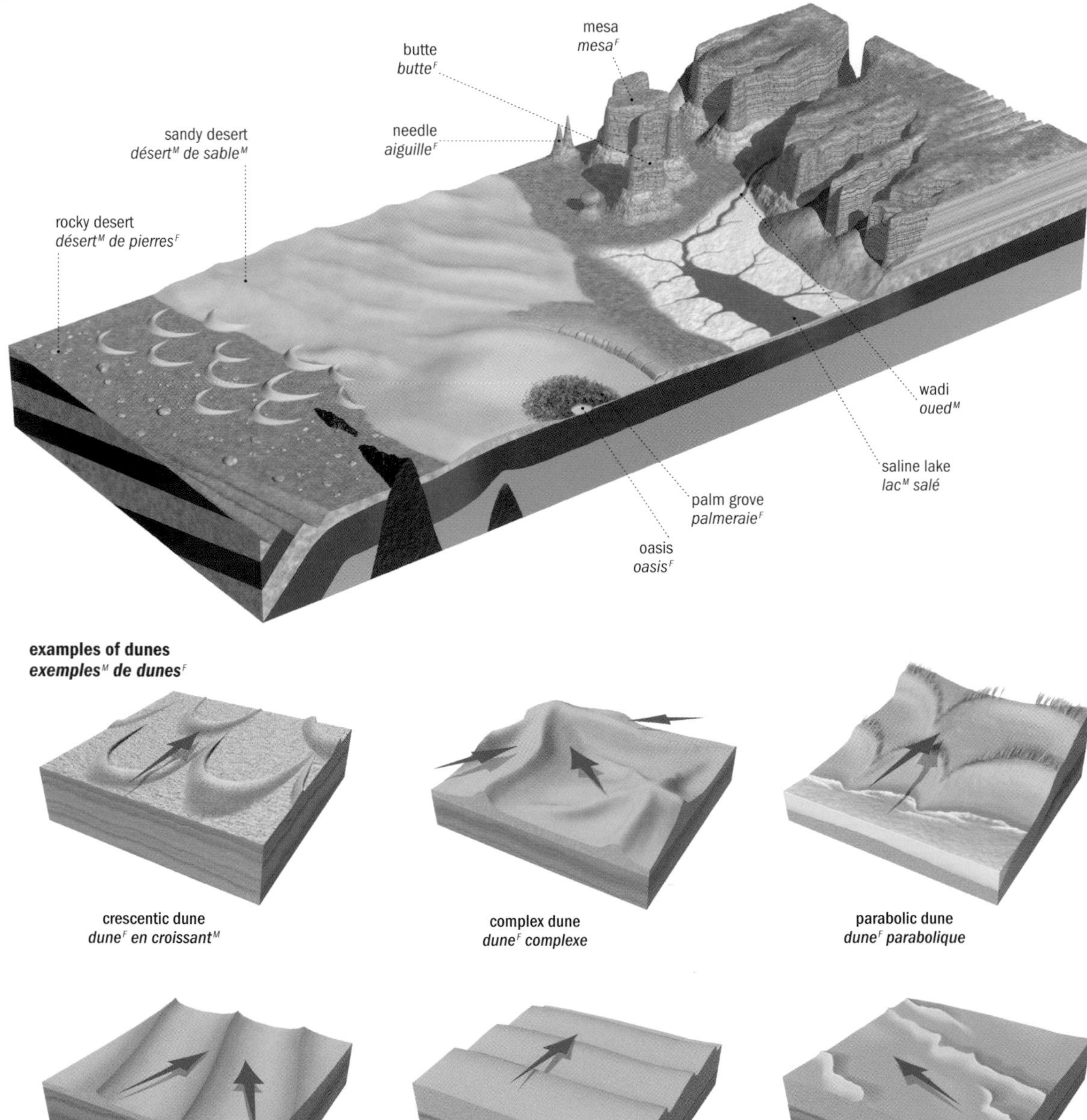

mesa
mesa[F]
butte
butte[F]
needle
aiguille[F]
sandy desert
désert[M] de sable[M]
rocky desert
désert[M] de pierres[F]
wadi
oued[M]
saline lake
lac[M] salé
palm grove
palmeraie[F]
oasis
oasis[F]
examples of dunes
exemples[M] de dunes[F]
crescentic dune
dune[F] en croissant[M]
complex dune
dune[F] complexe
parabolic dune
dune[F] parabolique
longitudinal dunes
dunes[F] longitudinales
transverse dunes
dunes[F] transversales
chain of dunes
cordon[M] de dunes[F]

profile of the Earth's atmosphere

coupe[F] de l'atmosphère[F] terrestre

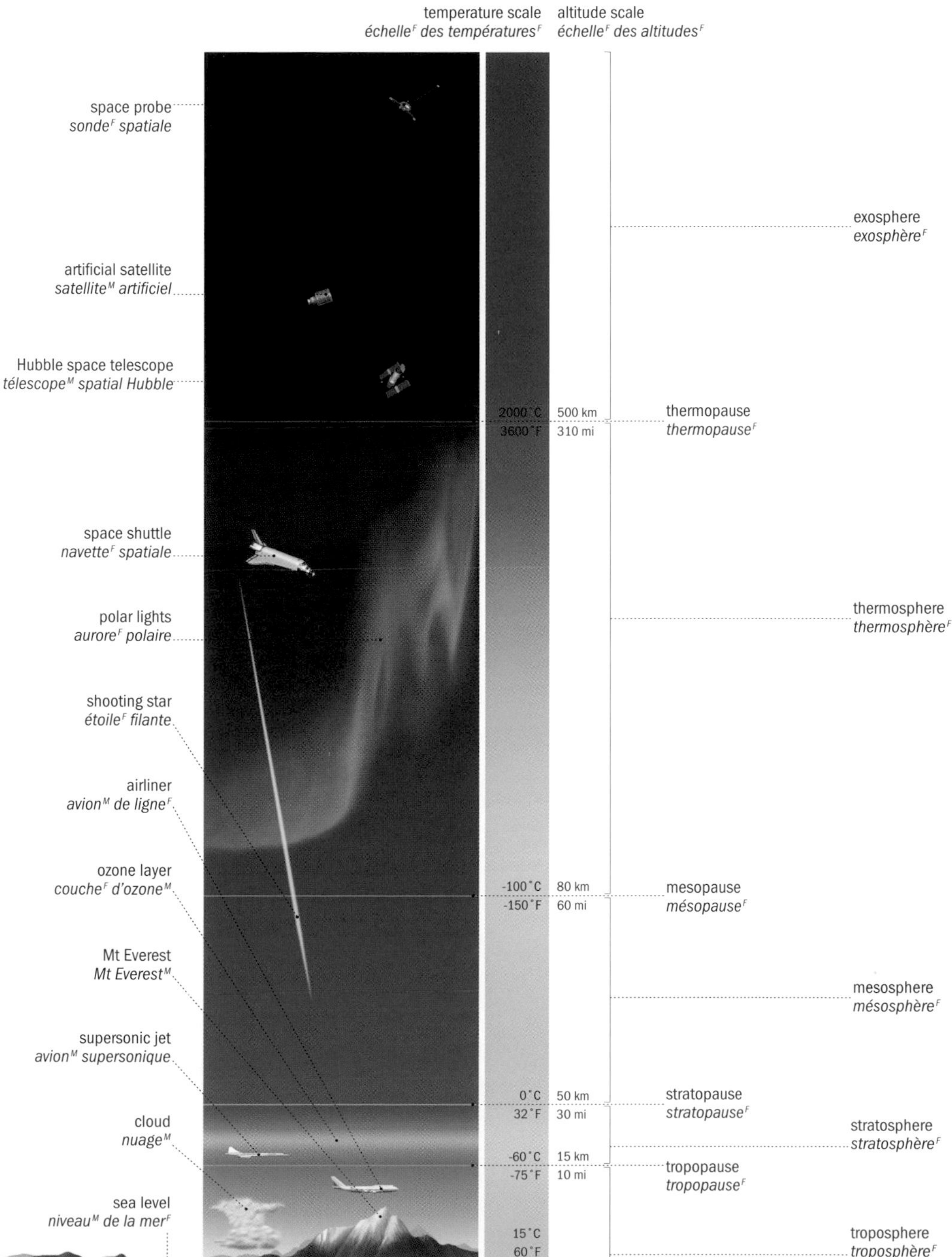

temperature scale
échelle[F] des températures[F]
altitude scale
échelle[F] des altitudes[F]
space probe
sonde[F] spatiale
exosphere
exosphère[F]
artificial satellite
satellite[M] artificiel
Hubble space telescope
télescope[M] spatial Hubble
2000 °C
3600 °F
500 km
310 mi
thermopause
thermopause[F]
space shuttle
navette[F] spatiale
polar lights
aurore[F] polaire
thermosphere
thermosphère[F]
shooting star
étoile[F] filante
airliner
avion[M] de ligne[F]
ozone layer
couche[F] d'ozone[M]
-100 °C
-150 °F
80 km
60 mi
mesopause
mésopause[F]
Mt Everest
Mt Everest[M]
mesosphere
mésosphère[F]
supersonic jet
avion[M] supersonique
0 °C
32 °F
50 km
30 mi
stratopause
stratopause[F]
cloud
nuage[M]
stratosphere
stratosphère[F]
-60 °C
-75 °F
15 km
10 mi
tropopause
tropopause[F]
sea level
niveau[M] de la mer[F]
15 °C
60 °F
troposphere
troposphère[F]

seasons of the year

cycle[M] des saisons[F]

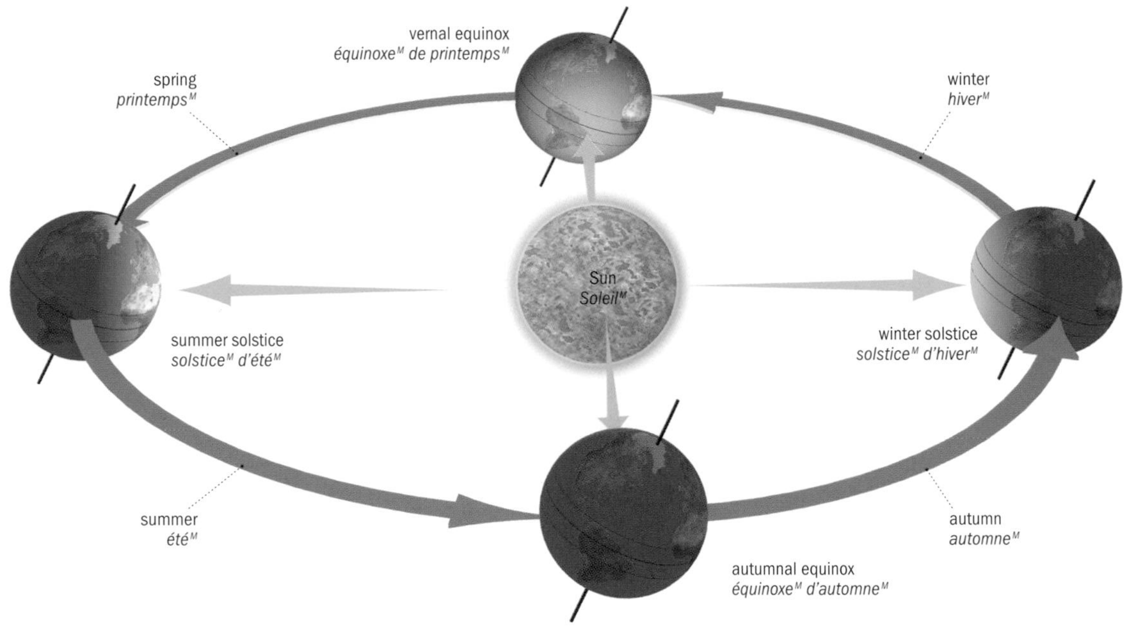
vernal equinox
équinoxe[M] de printemps[M]
spring
printemps[M]
winter
hiver[M]
Sun
Soleil[M]
summer solstice
solstice[M] d'été[M]
winter solstice
solstice[M] d'hiver[M]
summer
été[M]
autumn
automne[M]
autumnal equinox
équinoxe[M] d'automne[M]

meteorological forecast

prévision[F] météorologique

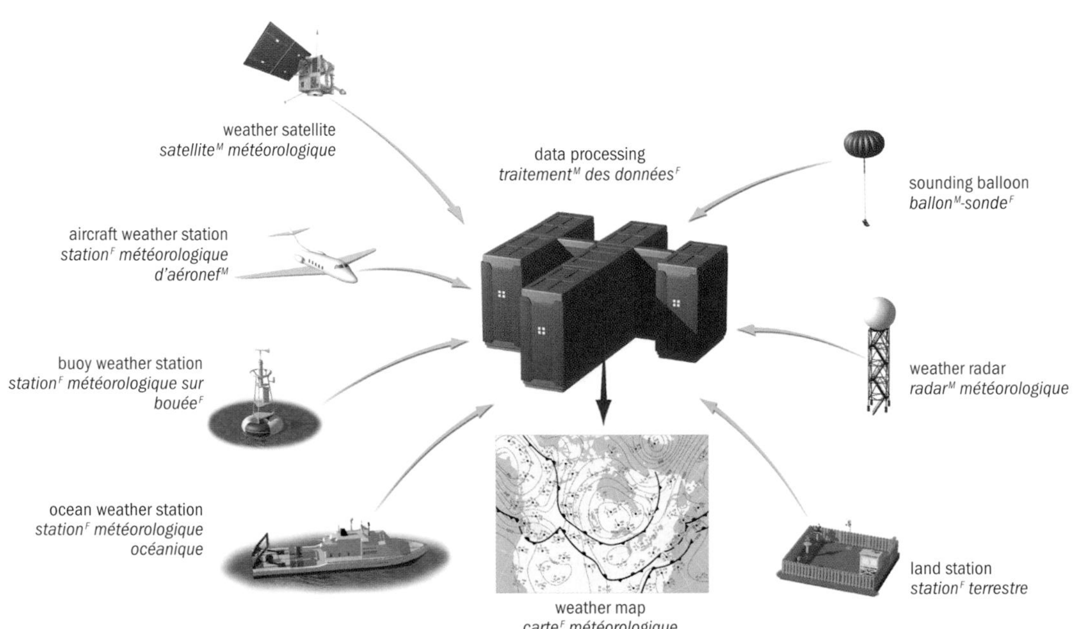
weather satellite
satellite[M] météorologique
data processing
traitement[M] des données[F]
sounding balloon
ballon[M]-sonde[F]
aircraft weather station
station[F] météorologique d'aéronef[M]
buoy weather station
station[F] météorologique sur bouée[F]
weather radar
radar[M] météorologique
ocean weather station
station[F] météorologique océanique
land station
station[F] terrestre
weather map
carte[F] météorologique

weather map

carte[F] météorologique

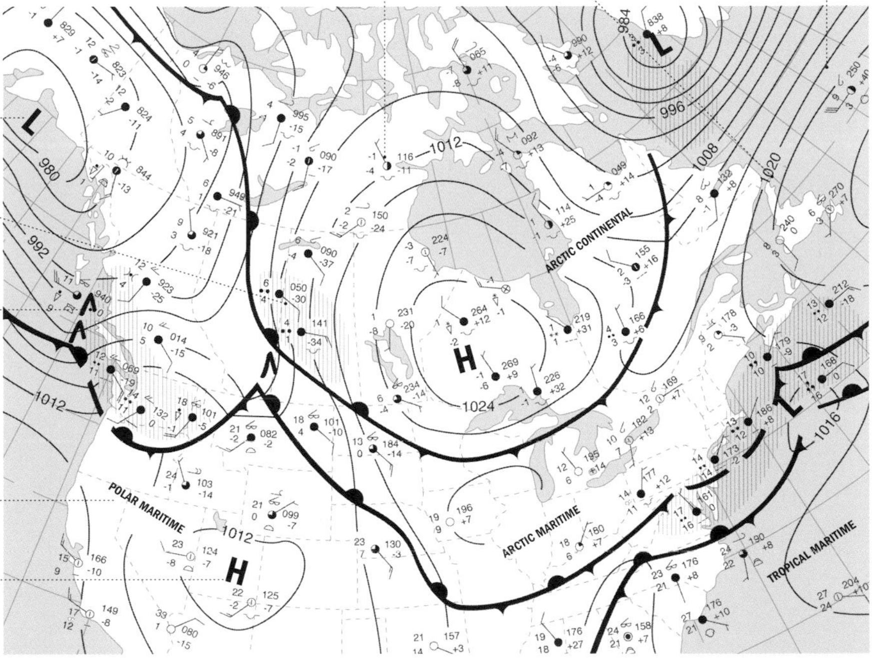

wind direction and speed
direction[F] et force[F] du vent[M]

barometric pressure
pression[F] barométrique

isobar
isobare[F]

low-pressure center
dépression[F]

precipitation area
zone[F] de précipitation[F]

trough
creux[M] barométrique

type of the air mass
type[M] de la masse[F] d'air[M]

high-pressure center
anticyclone[M]

station model

disposition[F] des informations[F] d'une station[F]

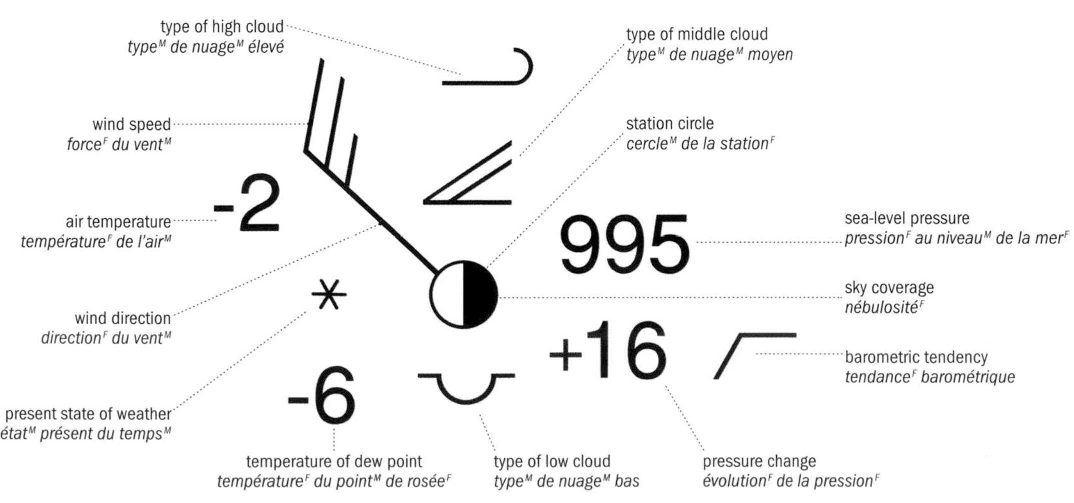
type of high cloud
type[M] de nuage[M] élevé
wind speed
force[F] du vent[M]
air temperature
température[F] de l'air[M]
wind direction
direction[F] du vent[M]
present state of weather
état[M] présent du temps[M]
temperature of dew point
température[F] du point[M] de rosée[F]
type of low cloud
type[M] de nuage[M] bas
pressure change
évolution[F] de la pression[F]
barometric tendency
tendance[F] barométrique
sky coverage
nébulosité[F]
sea-level pressure
pression[F] au niveau[M] de la mer[F]
station circle
cercle[M] de la station[F]
type of middle cloud
type[M] de nuage[M] moyen
-2
995
+16
-6

climates of the world

climats[M] du monde[M]

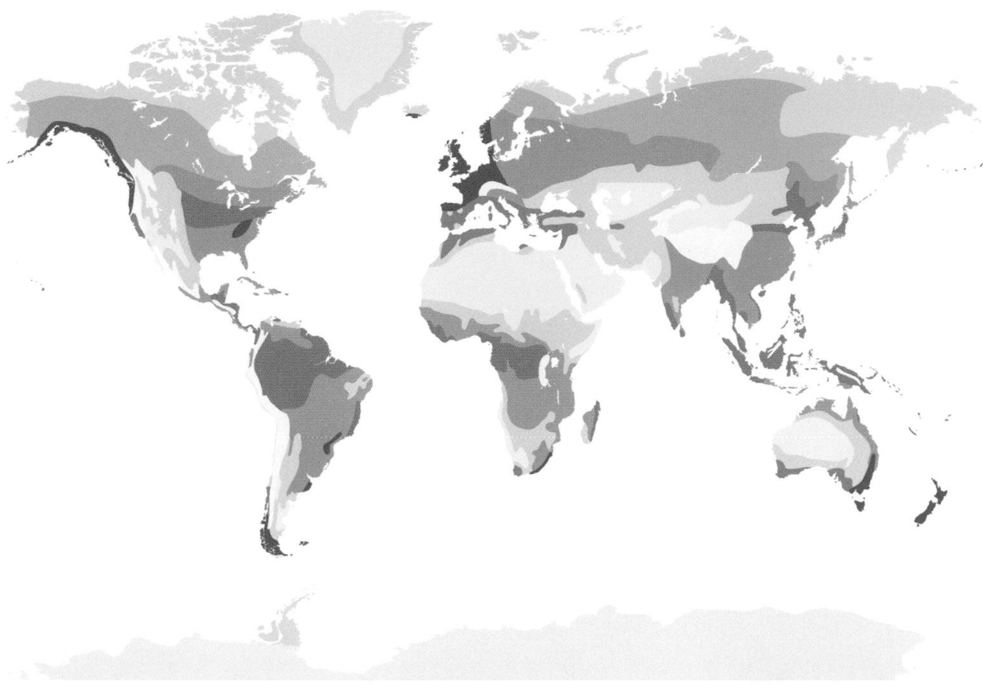

tropical climates
climats[M] tropicaux

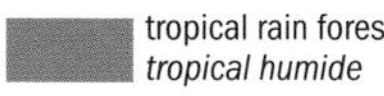
tropical rain forest
tropical humide

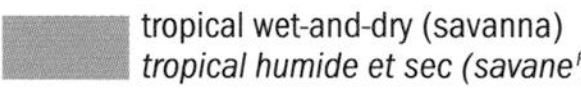
tropical wet-and-dry (savanna)
tropical humide et sec (savane[F])

dry climates
climats[M] arides

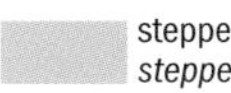
steppe
steppe[F]

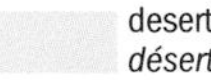
desert
désert[M]

cold temperate climates
climats[M] tempérés froids

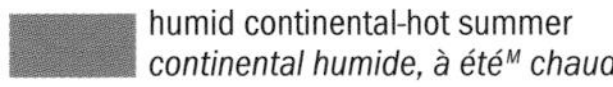
humid continental-hot summer
continental humide, à été[M] chaud

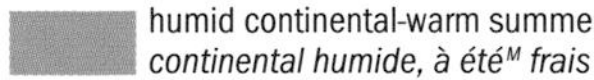
humid continental-warm summer
continental humide, à été[M] frais

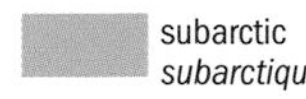
subarctic
subarctique

warm temperate climates
climats[M] tempérés chauds

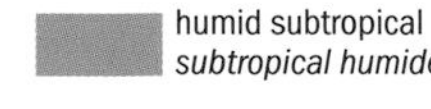
humid subtropical
subtropical humide

Mediterranean subtropical
méditerranéen

marine
océanique

polar climates
climats[M] polaires

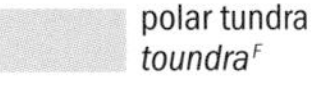
polar tundra
toundra[F]

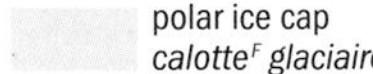
polar ice cap
calotte[F] glaciaire

highland climates
climats[M] de montagne[F]

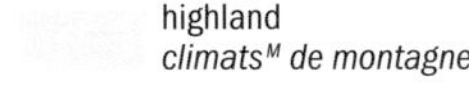
highland
climats[M] de montagne[F]

precipitation

précipitations[F]

winter precipitation
précipitations[F] hivernales

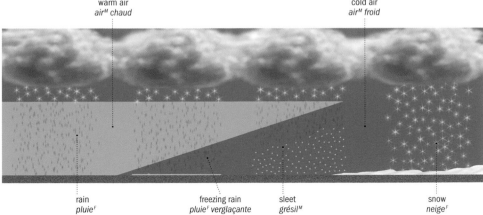

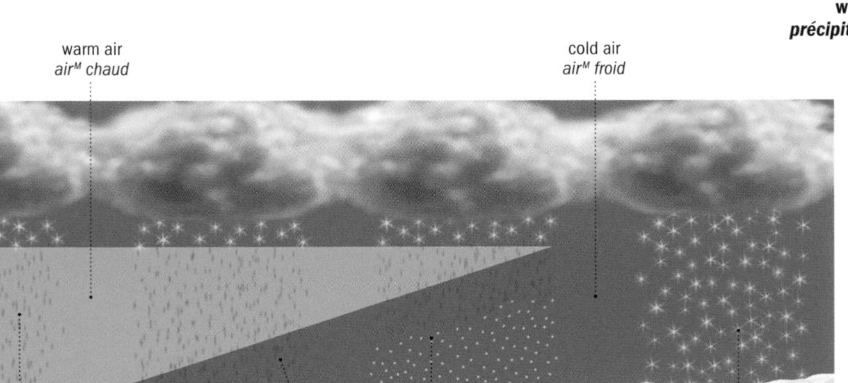
warm air
air[M] chaud
cold air
air[M] froid
rain
pluie[F]
freezing rain
pluie[F] verglaçante
sleet
grésil[M]
snow
neige[F]

stormy sky
ciel[M] d'orage[M]

cloud
nuage[M]
lightning
éclair[M]
rainbow
arc-en-ciel[M]
rain
pluie[F]

dew
rosée[F]

mist
brume[F]

fog
brouillard[M]

rime
givre[M]

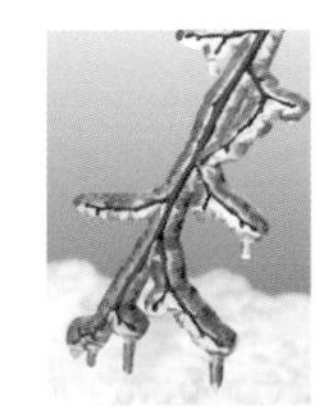

frost
verglas[M]

clouds

nuages[M]

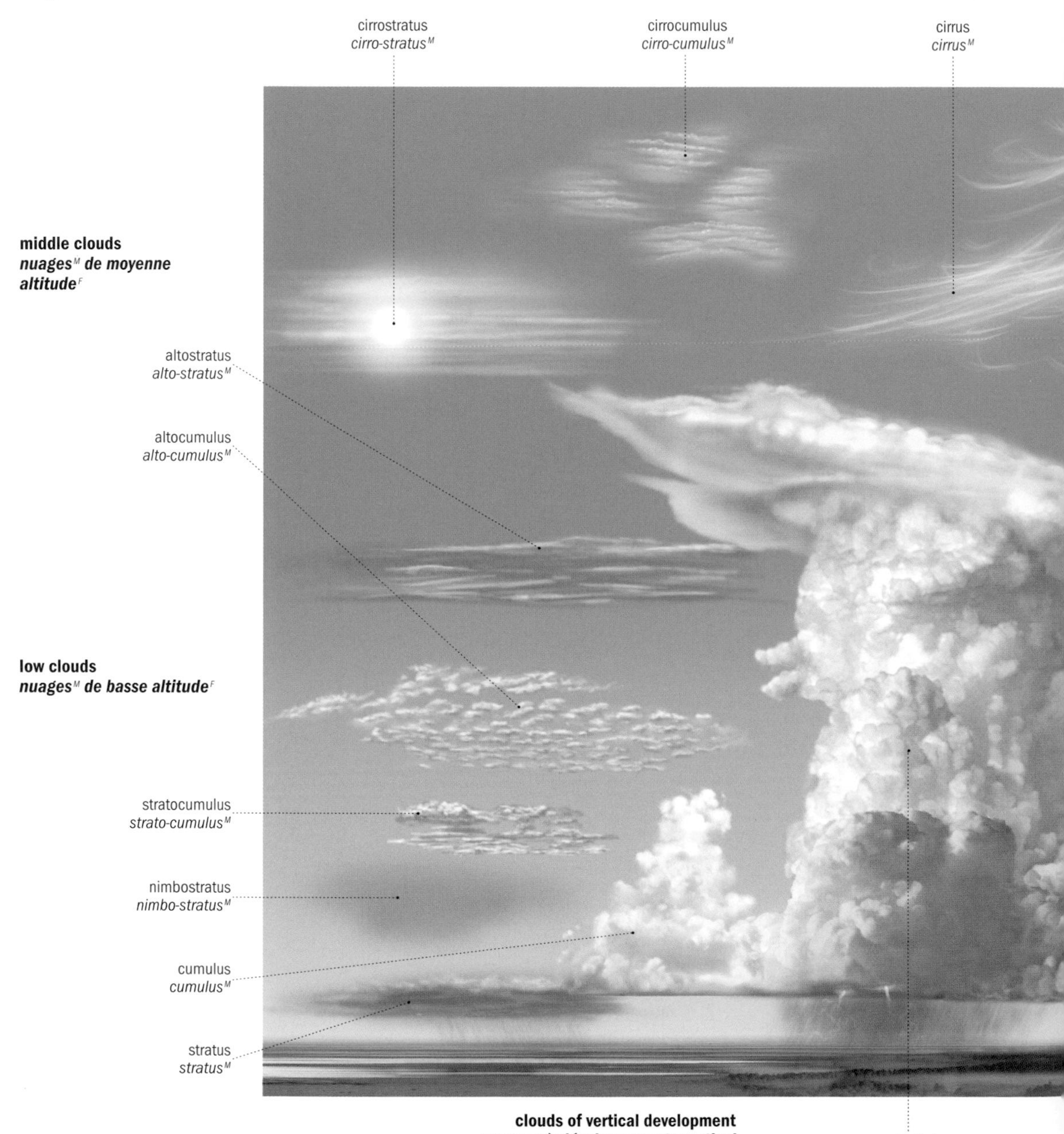
high clouds
nuages[M] de haute altitude[F]
cirrostratus
cirro-stratus[M]
cirrocumulus
cirro-cumulus[M]
cirrus
cirrus[M]
middle clouds
nuages[M] de moyenne altitude[F]
altostratus
alto-stratus[M]
altocumulus
alto-cumulus[M]
low clouds
nuages[M] de basse altitude[F]
stratocumulus
strato-cumulus[M]
nimbostratus
nimbo-stratus[M]
cumulus
cumulus[M]
stratus
stratus[M]
clouds of vertical development
nuages[M] à développement[M] vertical
cumulonimbus
cumulo-nimbus[M]

tornado and waterspout

tornade[F] et trombe[F] marine

waterspout
trombe[F] marine

wall cloud
mur[M] de nuages[M]
funnel cloud
nuage[M] en entonnoir[M]
debris
buisson[M]

tornado
tornade[F]

tropical cyclone

cyclone[M] tropical

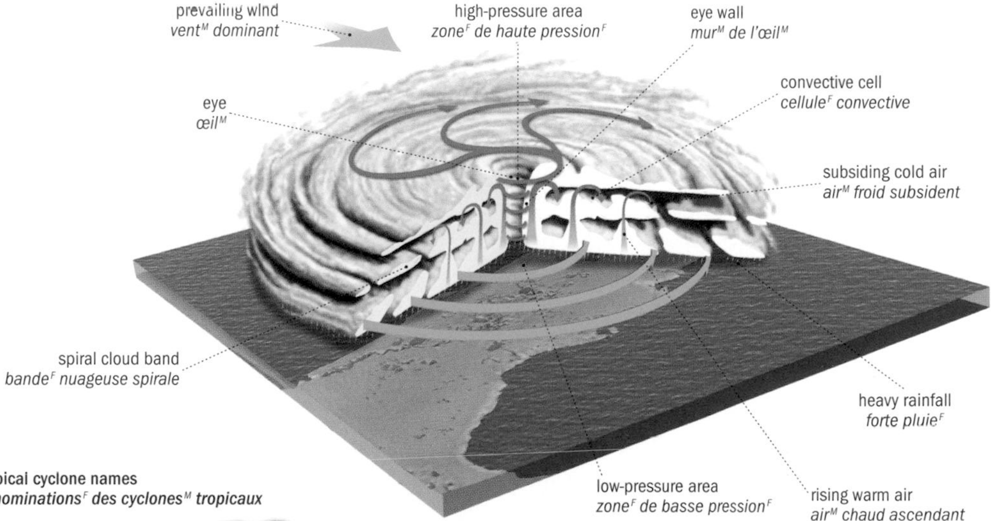

prevailing wind
vent[M] dominant

high-pressure area
zone[F] de haute pression[F]

eye wall
mur[M] de l'œil[M]

convective cell
cellule[F] convective

eye
œil[M]

subsiding cold air
air[M] froid subsident

spiral cloud band
bande[F] nuageuse spirale

heavy rainfall
forte pluie[F]

low-pressure area
zone[F] de basse pression[F]

rising warm air
air[M] chaud ascendant

tropical cyclone names
dénominations[F] des cyclones[M] tropicaux

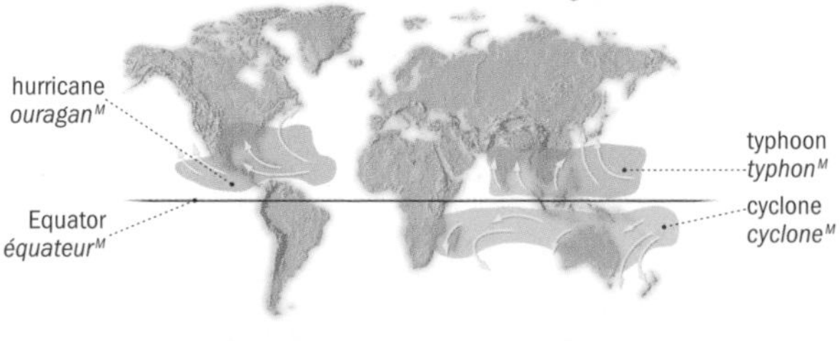

hurricane
ouragan[M]

typhoon
typhon[M]

Equator
équateur[M]

cyclone
cyclone[M]

vegetation and biosphere

végétation[F] et biosphère[F]

vegetation regions
distribution[F] de la végétation[F]

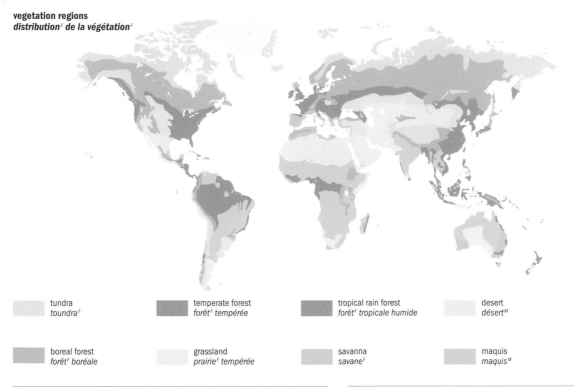

tundra
toundra[F]

temperate forest
forêt[F] tempérée

tropical rain forest
forêt[F] tropicale humide

desert
désert[M]

boreal forest
forêt[F] boréale

grassland
prairie[F] tempérée

savanna
savane[F]

maquis
maquis[M]

elevation zones and vegetation
paysage[M] végétal selon l'altitude[F]

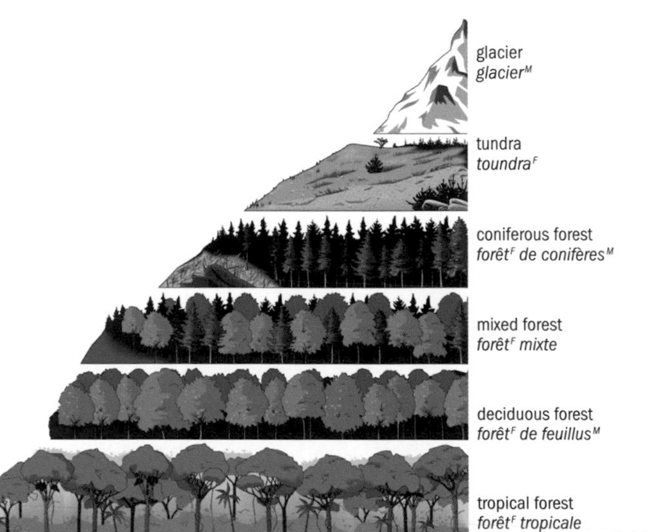
glacier
glacier[M]
tundra
toundra[F]
coniferous forest
forêt[F] de conifères[M]
mixed forest
forêt[F] mixte
deciduous forest
forêt[F] de feuillus[M]
tropical forest
forêt[F] tropicale

structure of the biosphere
structure[F] de la biosphère[F]

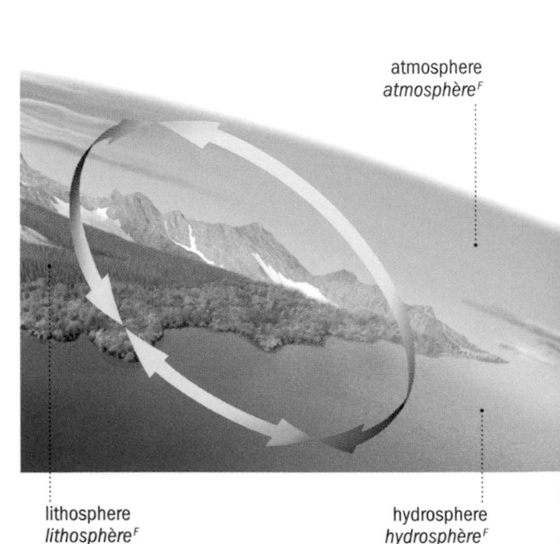
atmosphere
atmosphère[F]
lithosphere
lithosphère[F]
hydrosphere
hydrosphère[F]

food chain

chaîne alimentaire

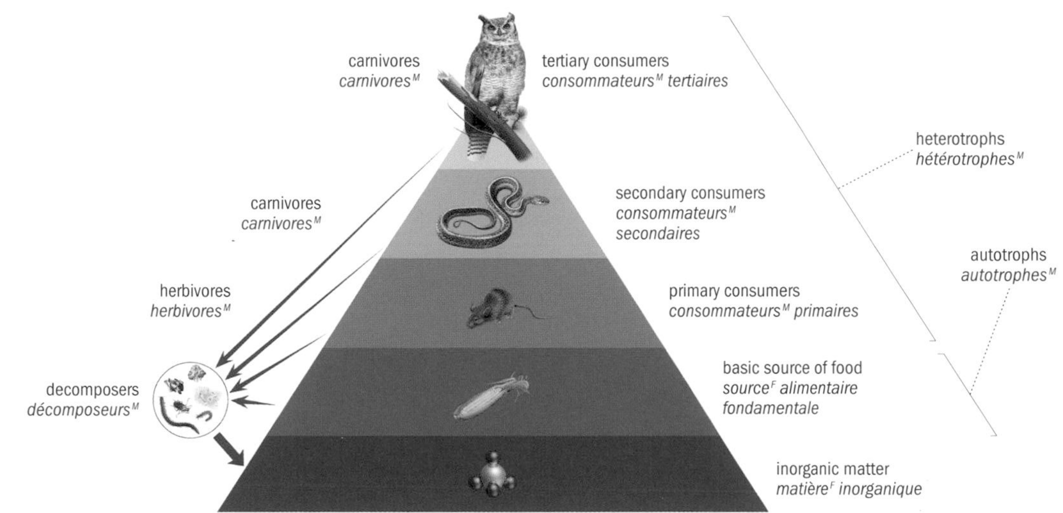
carnivores
carnivores
tertiary consumers
consommateurs tertiaires
heterotrophs
hétérotrophes
carnivores
carnivores
secondary consumers
consommateurs
secondaires
autotrophs
autotrophes
herbivores
herbivores
primary consumers
consommateurs primaires
decomposers
décomposeurs
basic source of food
source alimentaire
fondamentale
inorganic matter
matière inorganique

hydrologic cycle

cycle de l'eau

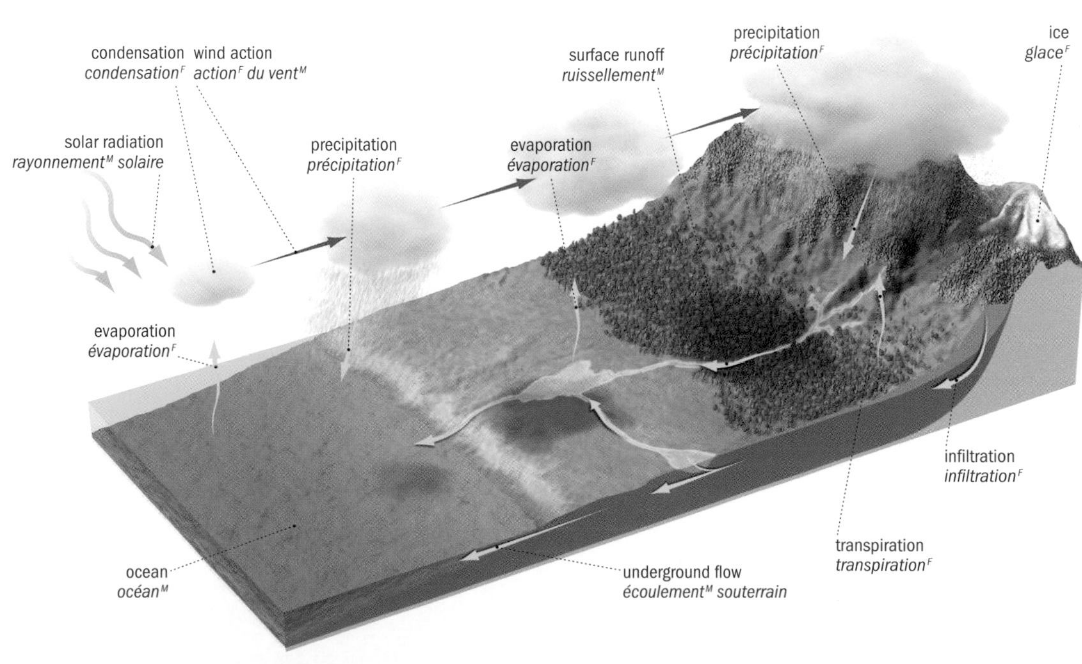
condensation
condensation
wind action
action du vent
surface runoff
ruissellement
precipitation
précipitation
ice
glace
solar radiation
rayonnement solaire
precipitation
précipitation
evaporation
évaporation
evaporation
évaporation
infiltration
infiltration
transpiration
transpiration
ocean
océan
underground flow
écoulement souterrain

greenhouse effect

effet^M de serre^F

natural greenhouse effect
effet^M de serre^F naturel

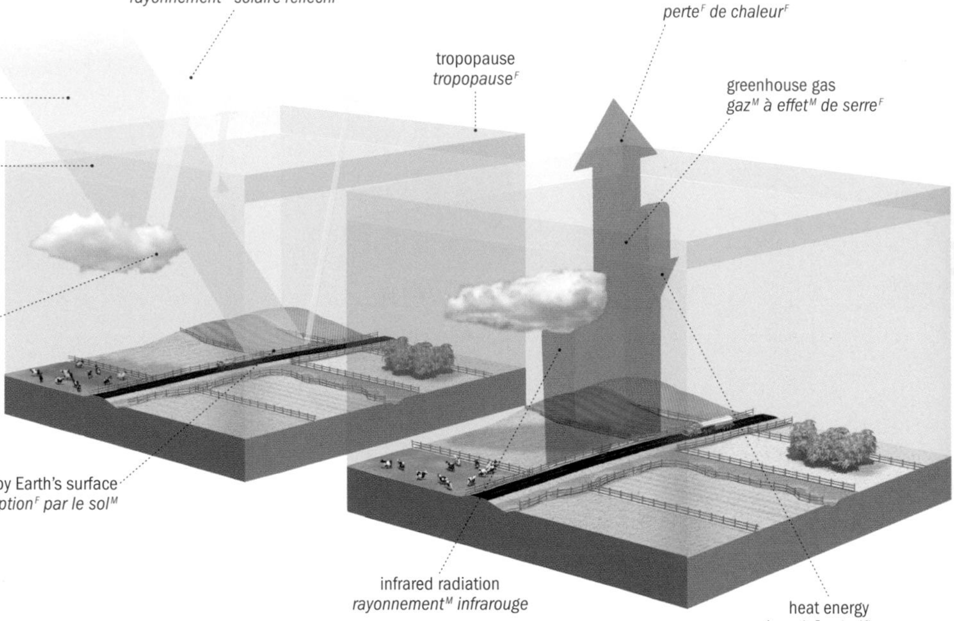

reflected solar radiation
rayonnement^M solaire réfléchi
heat loss
perte^F de chaleur^F
tropopause
tropopause^F
solar radiation
rayonnement^M solaire
greenhouse gas
gaz^M à effet^M de serre^F
absorbed solar radiation
rayonnement^M solaire absorbé
absorption by clouds
absorption^F par les nuages^M
absorption by Earth's surface
absorption^F par le sol^M
infrared radiation
rayonnement^M infrarouge
heat energy
énergie^F calorifique

enhanced greenhouse effect
augmentation^F de l'effet^M de serre^F

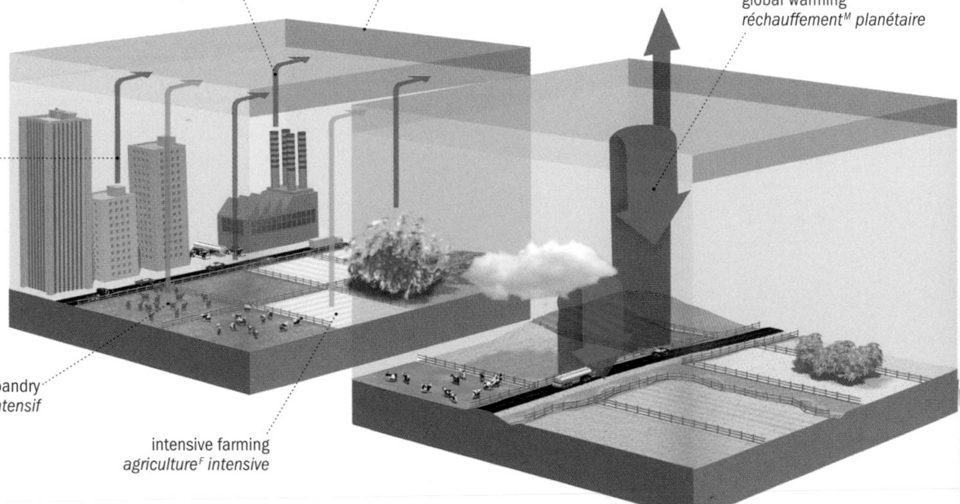

fossil fuel
combustible^M fossile
greenhouse gas concentration
concentration^F des gaz^M à effet^M de serre^F
global warming
réchauffement^M planétaire
air conditioning system
système^M de climatisation^F
intensive husbandry
élevage^M intensif
intensive farming
agriculture^F intensive

air pollution

pollution[F] de l'air[M]

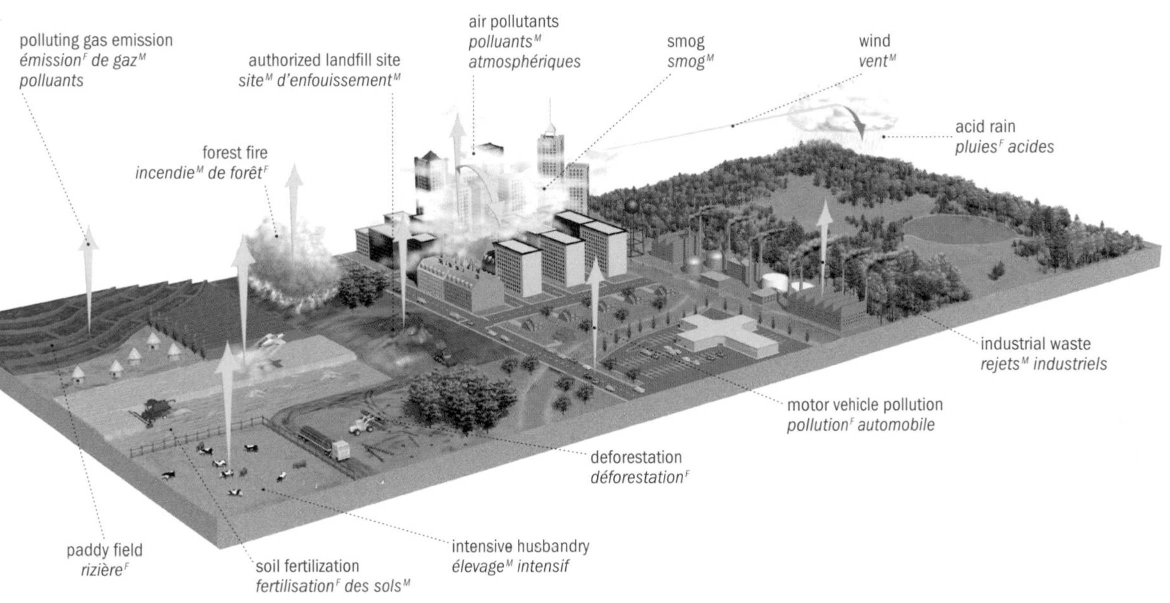

polluting gas emission
émission[F] de gaz[M] polluants
authorized landfill site
site[M] d'enfouissement[M]
air pollutants
polluants[M] atmosphériques
smog
smog[M]
wind
vent[M]
acid rain
pluies[F] acides
forest fire
incendie[M] de forêt[F]
industrial waste
rejets[M] industriels
motor vehicle pollution
pollution[F] automobile
deforestation
déforestation[F]
paddy field
rizière[F]
soil fertilization
fertilisation[F] des sols[M]
intensive husbandry
élevage[M] intensif

land pollution

pollution[F] du sol[M]

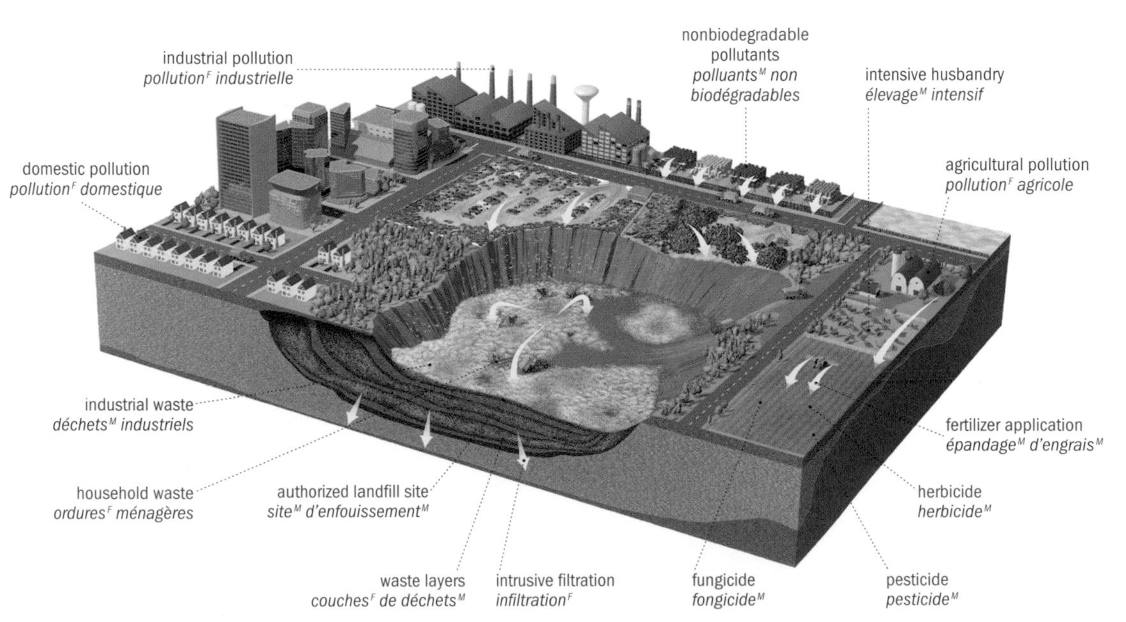

industrial pollution
pollution[F] industrielle
nonbiodegradable pollutants
polluants[M] non biodégradables
intensive husbandry
élevage[M] intensif
domestic pollution
pollution[F] domestique
agricultural pollution
pollution[F] agricole
industrial waste
déchets[M] industriels
fertilizer application
épandage[M] d'engrais[M]
household waste
ordures[F] ménagères
authorized landfill site
site[M] d'enfouissement[M]
herbicide
herbicide[M]
waste layers
couches[F] de déchets[M]
intrusive filtration
infiltration[F]
fungicide
fongicide[M]
pesticide
pesticide[M]

water pollution

pollution^F de l'eau^F

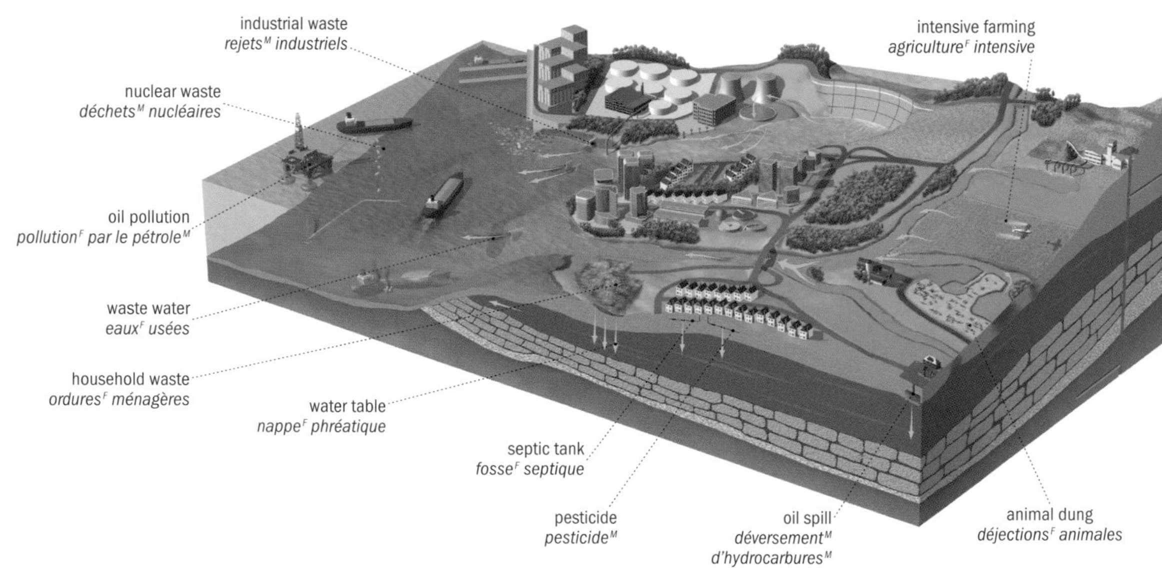
industrial waste
rejets^M industriels
nuclear waste
déchets^M nucléaires
oil pollution
pollution^F par le pétrole^M
waste water
eaux^F usées
household waste
ordures^F ménagères
water table
nappe^F phréatique
septic tank
fosse^F septique
pesticide
pesticide^M
oil spill
déversement^M d'hydrocarbures^M
animal dung
déjections^F animales
intensive farming
agriculture^F intensive

acid rain

pluies^F acides

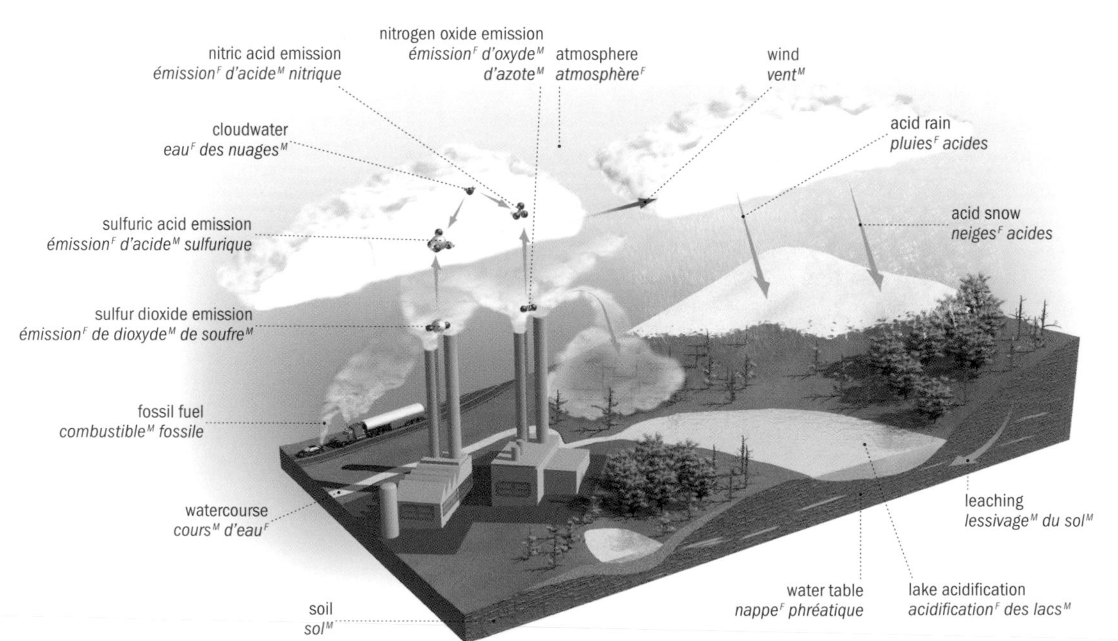
nitric acid emission
émission^F d'acide^M nitrique
nitrogen oxide emission
émission^F d'oxyde^M d'azote^M
atmosphere
atmosphère^F
wind
vent^M
cloudwater
eau^F des nuages^M
acid rain
pluies^F acides
sulfuric acid emission
émission^F d'acide^M sulfurique
acid snow
neiges^F acides
sulfur dioxide emission
émission^F de dioxyde^M de soufre^M
fossil fuel
combustible^M fossile
watercourse
cours^M d'eau^F
leaching
lessivage^M du sol^M
soil
sol^M
water table
nappe^F phréatique
lake acidification
acidification^F des lacs^M

selective sorting of waste

tri[M] sélectif des déchets[M]

sorting plant
centre[M] de tri[M]

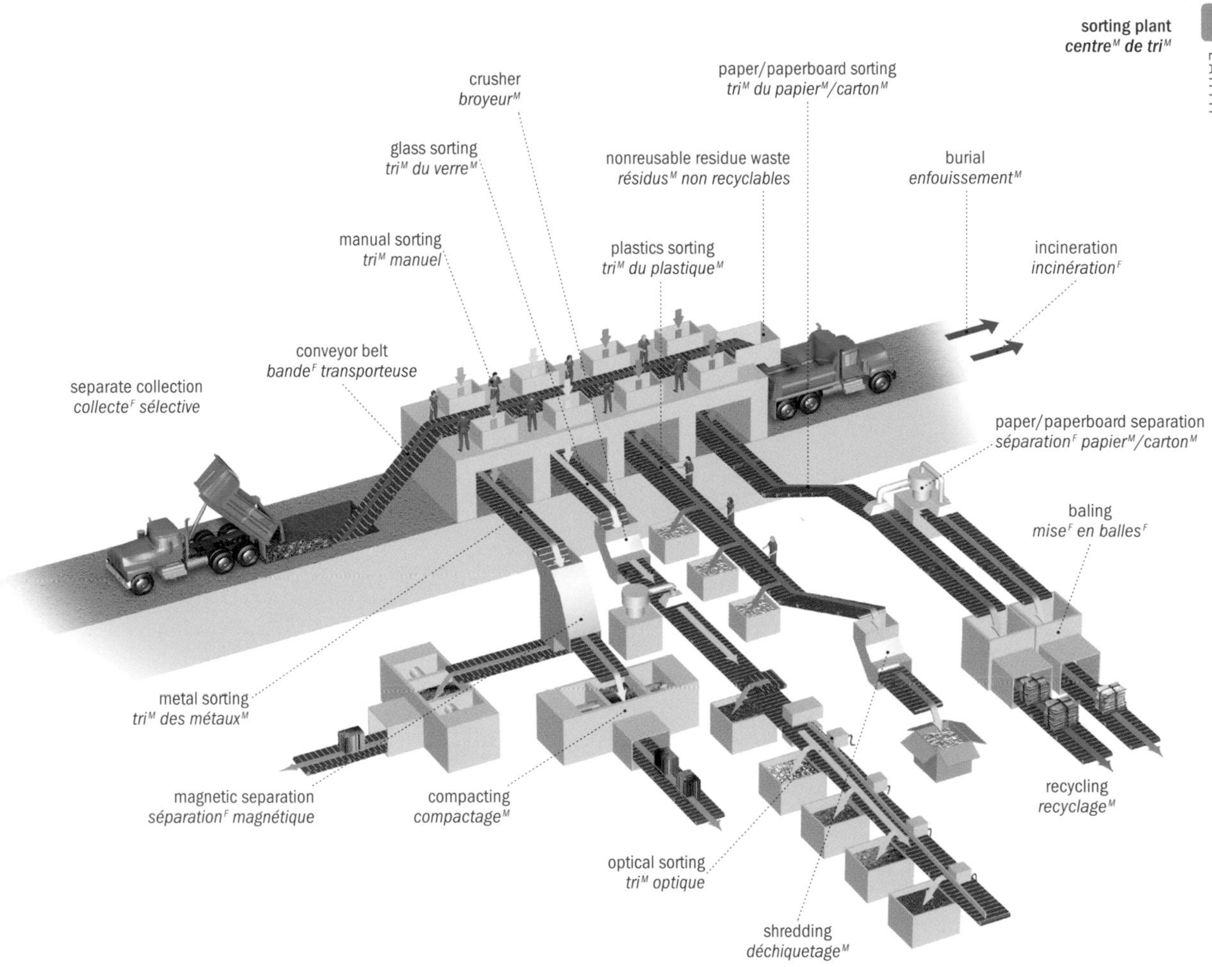

crusher
broyeur[M]

paper/paperboard sorting
tri[M] du papier[M]/carton[M]

glass sorting
tri[M] du verre[M]

nonreusable residue waste
résidus[M] non recyclables

burial
enfouissement[M]

manual sorting
tri[M] manuel

plastics sorting
tri[M] du plastique[M]

incineration
incinération[F]

conveyor belt
bande[F] transporteuse

separate collection
collecte[F] sélective

paper/paperboard separation
séparation[F] papier[M]/carton[M]

baling
mise[F] en balles[F]

metal sorting
tri[M] des métaux[M]

magnetic separation
séparation[F] magnétique

compacting
compactage[M]

recycling
recyclage[M]

optical sorting
tri[M] optique

shredding
déchiquetage[M]

recycling containers
conteneurs[M] de collecte[F] sélective

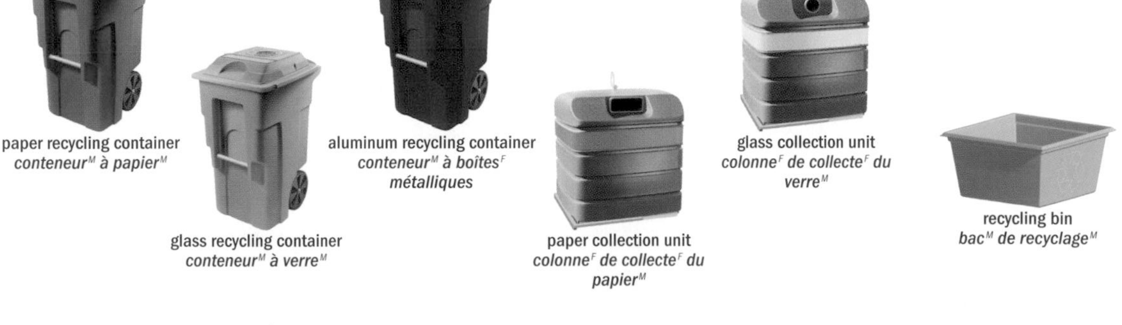

paper recycling container
conteneur[M] à papier[M]

aluminum recycling container
conteneur[M] à boîtes[F] métalliques

glass collection unit
colonne[F] de collecte[F] du verre[M]

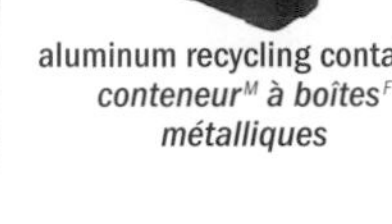

recycling bin
bac[M] de recyclage[M]

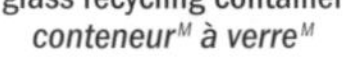

glass recycling container
conteneur[M] à verre[M]

paper collection unit
colonne[F] de collecte[F] du papier[M]

plant cell

cellule^F végétale

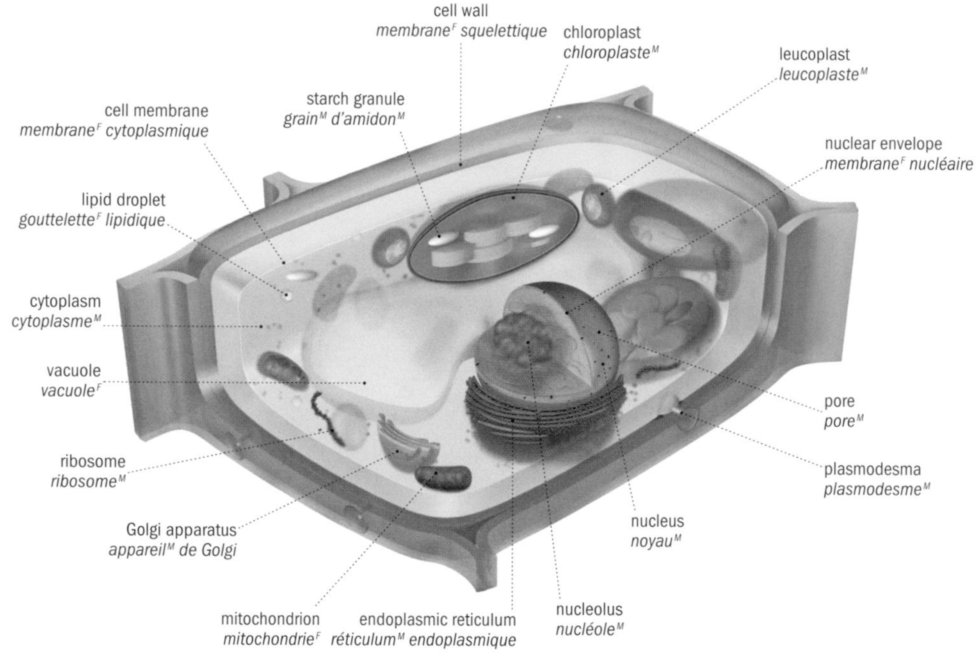
cell wall
membrane^F squelettique
chloroplast
chloroplaste^M
leucoplast
leucoplaste^M
starch granule
grain^M d'amidon^M
cell membrane
membrane^F cytoplasmique
nuclear envelope
membrane^F nucléaire
lipid droplet
gouttelette^F lipidique
cytoplasm
cytoplasme^M
vacuole
vacuole^F
pore
pore^M
ribosome
ribosome^M
plasmodesma
plasmodesme^M
Golgi apparatus
appareil^M de Golgi
nucleus
noyau^M
mitochondrion
mitochondrie^F
endoplasmic reticulum
réticulum^M endoplasmique
nucleolus
nucléole^M

lichen

lichen^M

structure of a lichen
structure^F d'un lichen^M

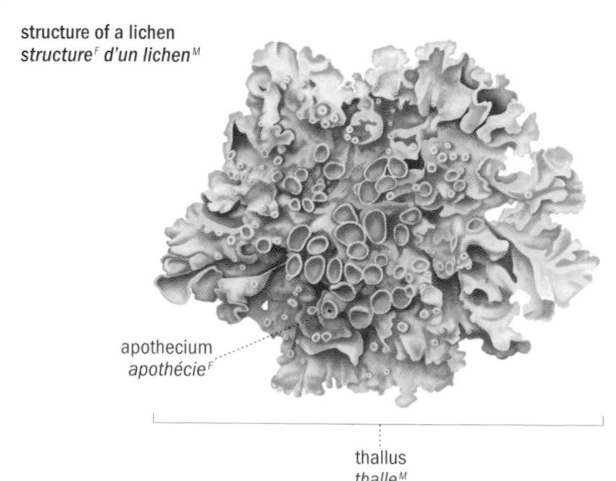
apothecium
apothécie^F
thallus
thalle^M

examples of lichens
exemples^M de lichens^M

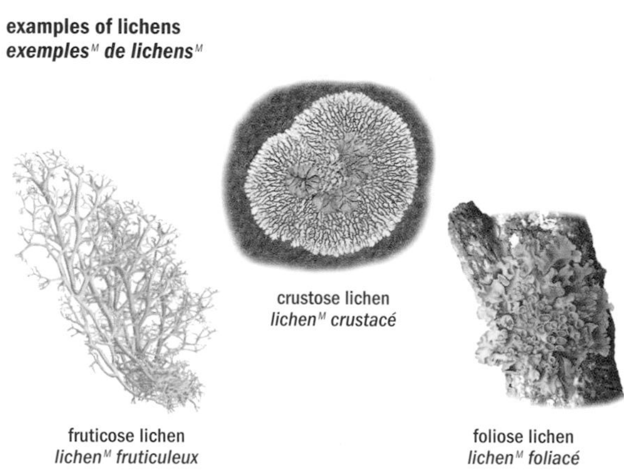
crustose lichen
lichen^M crustacé
fruticose lichen
lichen^M fruticuleux
foliose lichen
lichen^M foliacé

moss

mousse[F]

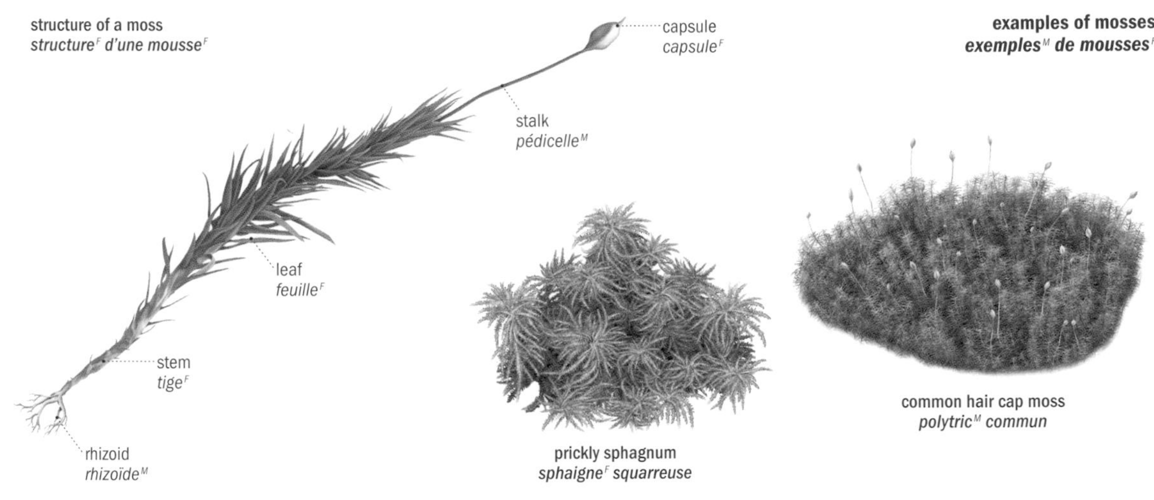
structure of a moss
structure[F] d'une mousse[F]
capsule
capsule[F]
stalk
pédicelle[M]
leaf
feuille[F]
stem
tige[F]
rhizoid
rhizoïde[M]
examples of mosses
exemples[M] de mousses[F]

prickly sphagnum
sphaigne[F] squarreuse

common hair cap moss
polytric[M] commun

algae

algues[F]

structure of an alga
structure[F] d'une algue[F]

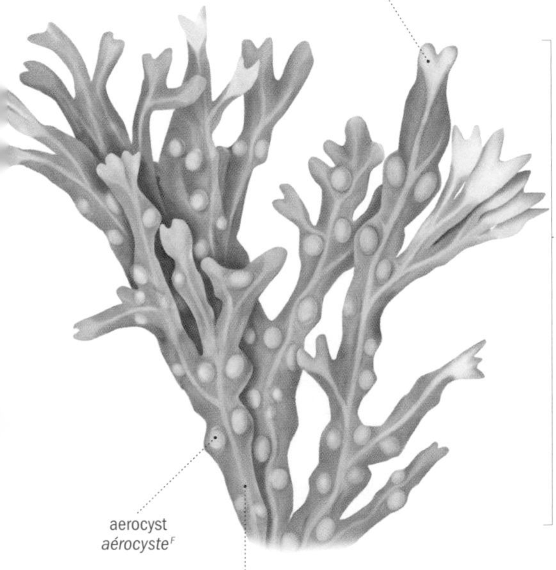

receptacle
réceptacle[M]

thallus
thalle[M]

aerocyst
aérocyste[F]

midrib
nervure[F] médiane

examples of algae
exemples[M] d'algues[F]

lamina
fronde[F]

hapteron
haptère[F]

red alga
algue[F] rouge

green alga
algue[F] verte

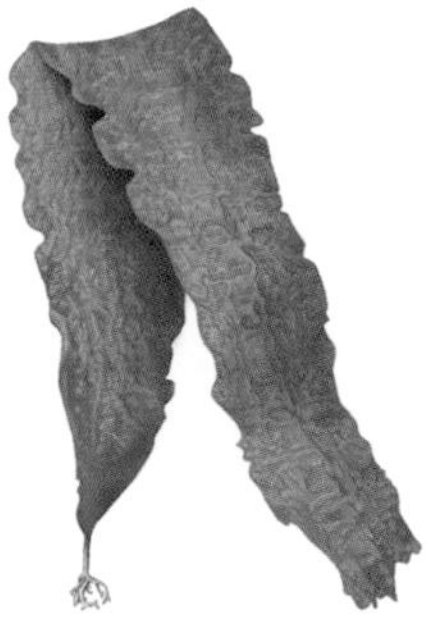

brown alga
algue[F] brune

mushroom

champignon[M]

structure of a mushroom
structure[F] d'un champignon[M]

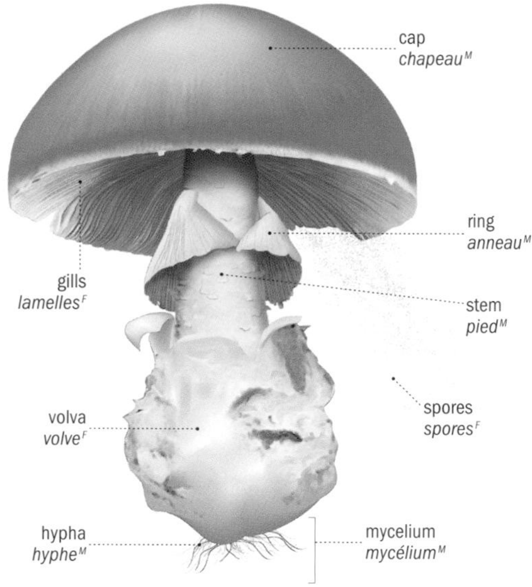
cap
chapeau[M]
ring
anneau[M]
gills
lamelles[F]
stem
pied[M]
spores
spores[F]
volva
volve[F]
hypha
hyphe[M]
mycelium
mycélium[M]

deadly poisonous mushroom
champignon[M] mortel

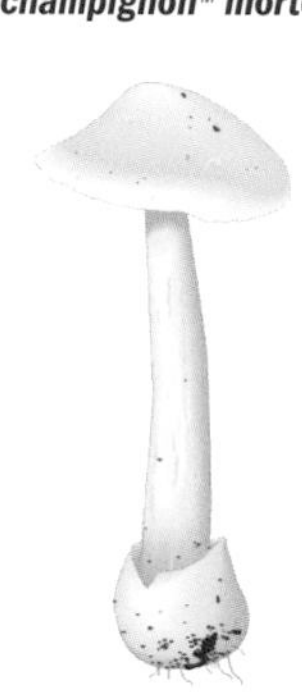

destroying angel
amanite[F] vireuse

poisonous mushroom
champignon[M] vénéneux

fly agaric
fausse oronge[F]

fern

fougère[F]

structure of a fern
structure[F] d'une fougère[F]

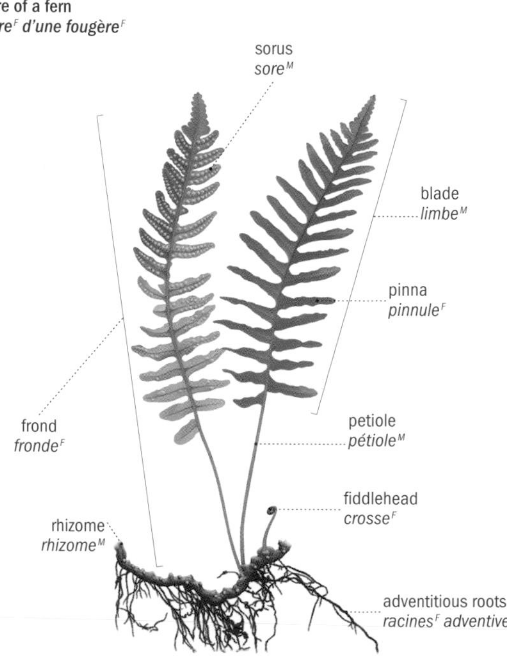
sorus
sore[M]
blade
limbe[M]
pinna
pinnule[F]
frond
fronde[F]
petiole
pétiole[M]
fiddlehead
crosse[F]
rhizome
rhizome[M]
adventitious roots
racines[F] adventives

examples of ferns
exemples[M] de fougères[F]

tree fern
fougère[F] arborescente
trunk
tronc[M]
common polypody
polypode[M] commun
bird's nest fern
fougère[F] nid[M] d'oiseau[M]

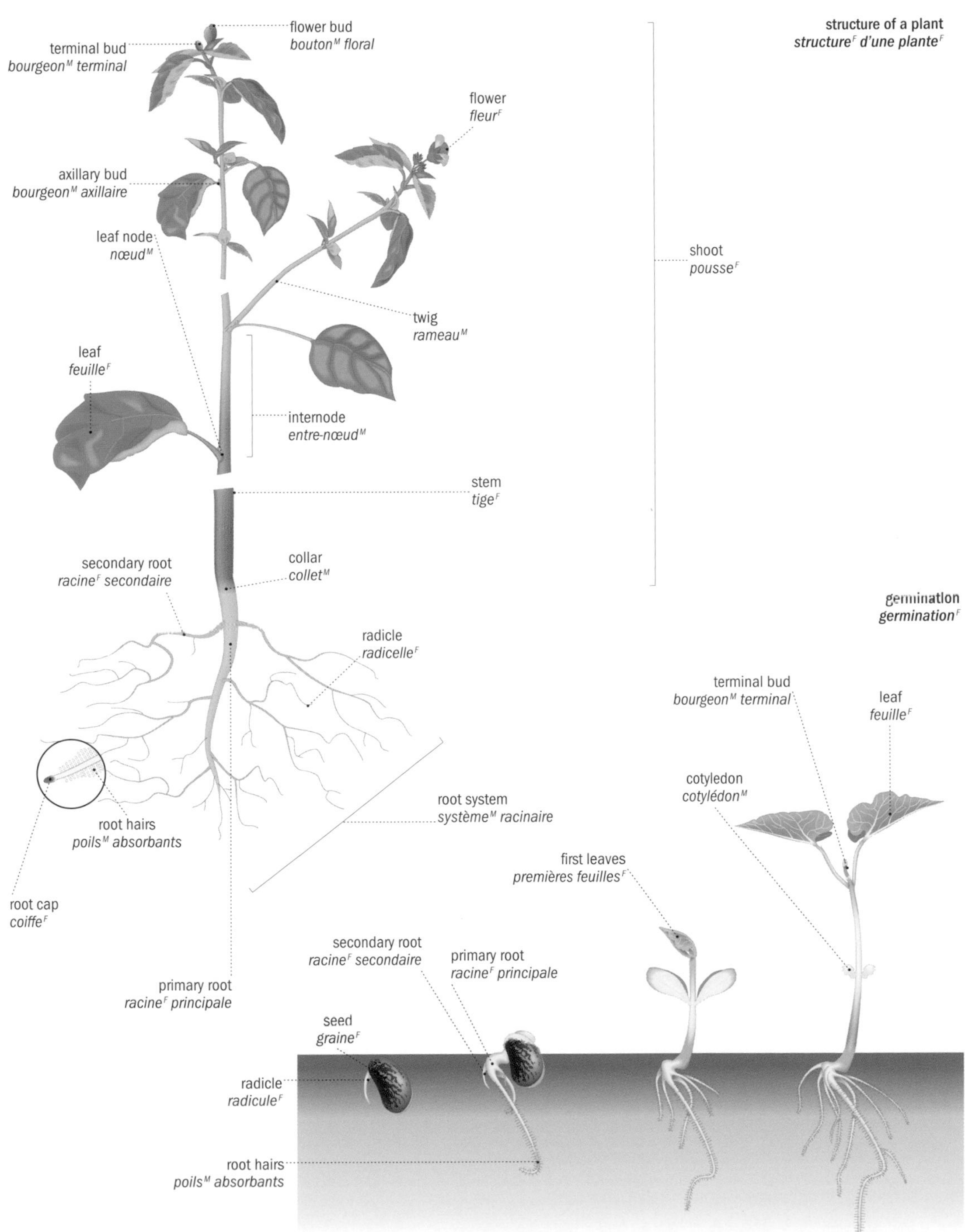

structure of a plant
structure[F] d'une plante[F]
flower bud
bouton[M] floral
terminal bud
bourgeon[M] terminal
flower
fleur[F]
axillary bud
bourgeon[M] axillaire
leaf node
nœud[M]
shoot
pousse[F]
twig
rameau[M]
leaf
feuille[F]
internode
entre-nœud[M]
stem
tige[F]
secondary root
racine[F] secondaire
collar
collet[M]
radicle
radicelle[F]
root system
système[M] racinaire
root hairs
poils[M] absorbants
root cap
coiffe[F]
primary root
racine[F] principale
germination
germination[F]
terminal bud
bourgeon[M] terminal
leaf
feuille[F]
cotyledon
cotylédon[M]
first leaves
premières feuilles[F]
secondary root
racine[F] secondaire
primary root
racine[F] principale
seed
graine[F]
radicle
radicule[F]
root hairs
poils[M] absorbants

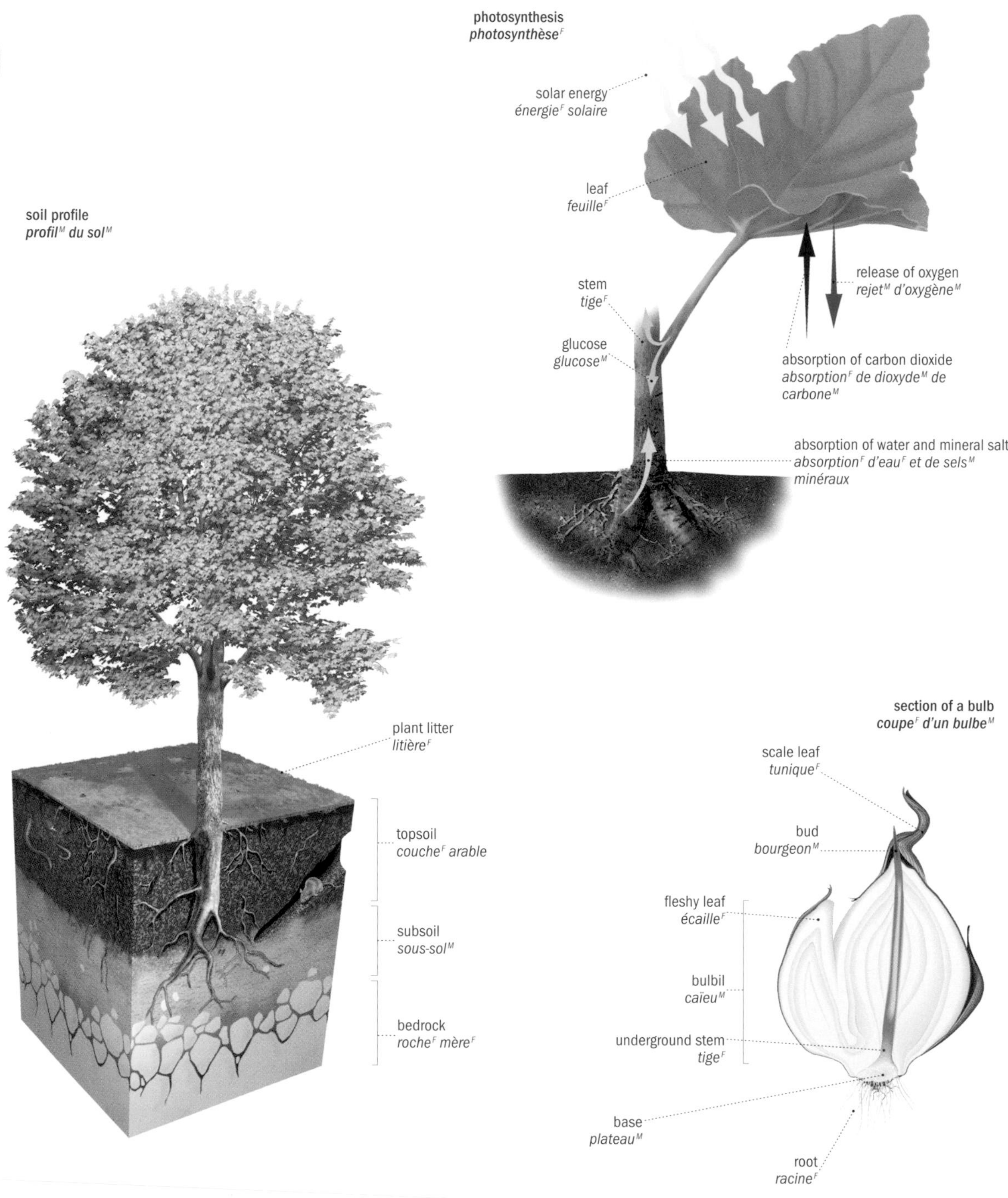
photosynthesis
photosynthèse^F
solar energy
énergie^F solaire
leaf
feuille^F
stem
tige^F
glucose
glucose^M
release of oxygen
rejet^M d'oxygène^M
absorption of carbon dioxide
absorption^F de dioxyde^M de carbone^M
absorption of water and mineral salts
absorption^F d'eau^F et de sels^M minéraux
soil profile
profil^M du sol^M
plant litter
litière^F
topsoil
couche^F arable
subsoil
sous-sol^M
bedrock
roche^F mère^F
section of a bulb
coupe^F d'un bulbe^M
scale leaf
tunique^F
bud
bourgeon^M
fleshy leaf
écaille^F
bulbil
caïeu^M
underground stem
tige^F
base
plateau^M
root
racine^F

leaf
feuille[F]

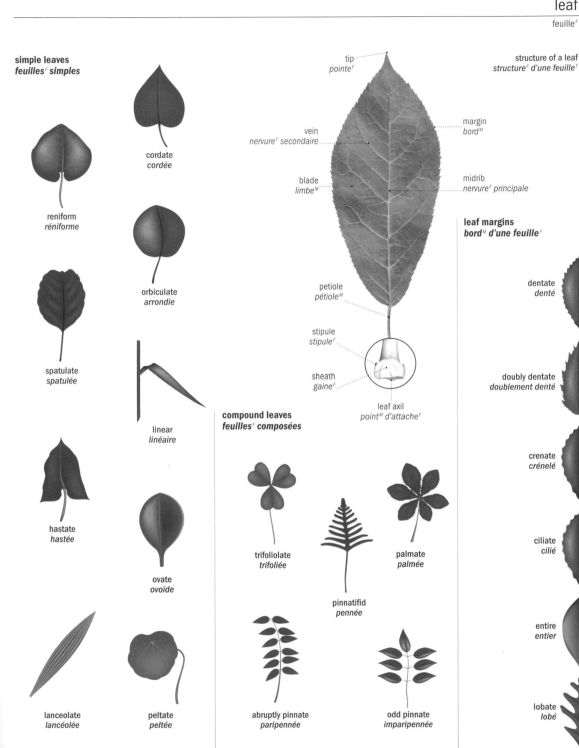

simple leaves
feuilles[F] simples

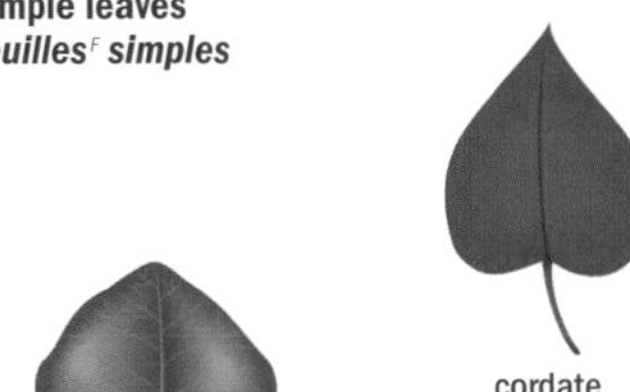

cordate
cordée

reniform
réniforme

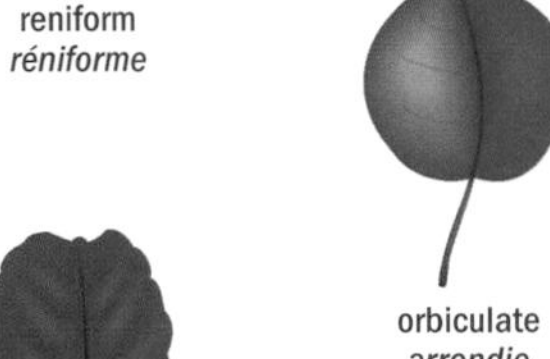

orbiculate
arrondie

spatulate
spatulée

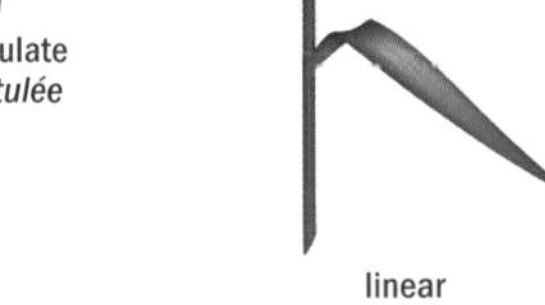

linear
linéaire

hastate
hastée

ovate
ovoïde

lanceolate
lancéolée

peltate
peltée

structure of a leaf
structure[F] d'une feuille[F]

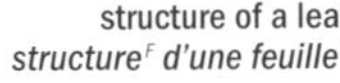

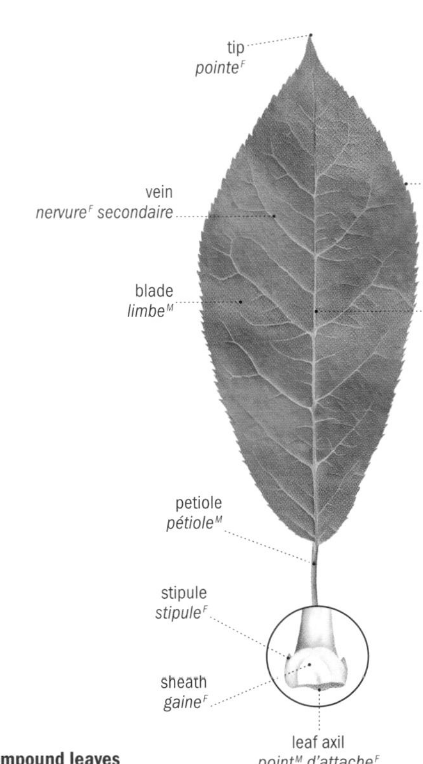
tip
pointe[F]
vein
nervure[F] secondaire
margin
bord[M]
blade
limbe[M]
midrib
nervure[F] principale
petiole
pétiole[M]
stipule
stipule[F]
sheath
gaine[F]
leaf axil
point[M] d'attache[F]

leaf margins
bord[M] d'une feuille[F]

dentate
denté

doubly dentate
doublement denté

crenate
crénelé

ciliate
cilié

entire
entier

lobate
lobé

compound leaves
feuilles[F] composées

trifoliolate
trifoliée

pinnatifid
pennée

palmate
palmée

abruptly pinnate
paripennée

odd pinnate
imparipennée

flower

fleur[F]

structure of a flower
structure[F] d'une fleur[F]

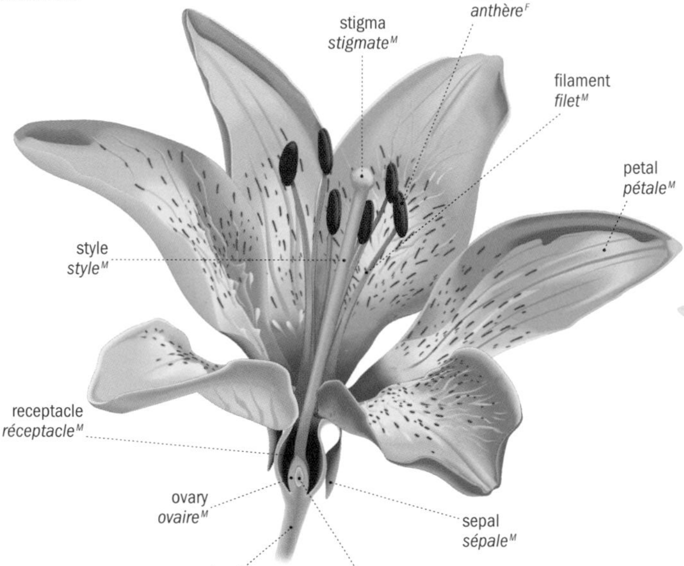

stigma
stigmate[M]

anther
anthère[F]

filament
filet[M]

petal
pétale[M]

style
style[M]

receptacle
réceptacle[M]

ovary
ovaire[M]

sepal
sépale[M]

peduncle
pédoncule[M]

ovule
ovule[M]

pistil
pistil[M]

corolla
corolle[F]

stamen
étamine[F]

calyx
calice[M]

examples of flowers
exemples[M] de fleurs[F]

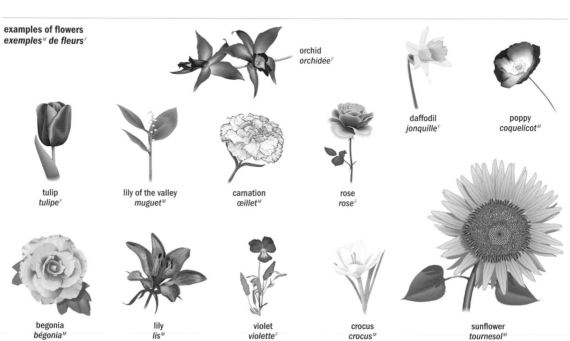

orchid
orchidée[F]

daffodil
jonquille[F]

poppy
coquelicot[M]

tulip
tulipe[F]

lily of the valley
muguet[M]

carnation
œillet[M]

rose
rose[F]

begonia
bégonia[M]

lily
lis[M]

violet
violette[F]

crocus
crocus[M]

sunflower
tournesol[M]

types of inflorescences
modes[M] d'inflorescence[F]

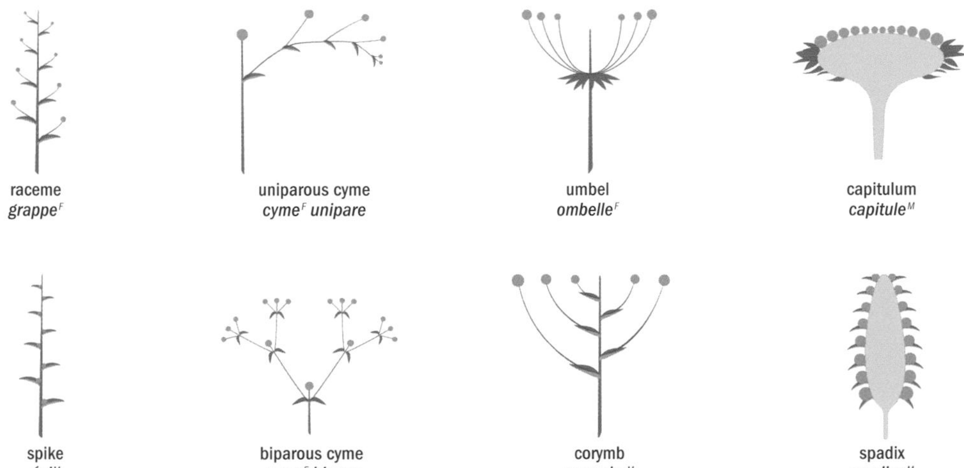
raceme
grappe[F]
uniparous cyme
cyme[F] unipare
umbel
ombelle[F]
capitulum
capitule[M]
spike
épi[M]
biparous cyme
cyme[F] bipare
corymb
corymbe[M]
spadix
spadice[M]

fruit
fruits[M]

fleshy fruit: stone fruit
fruit[M] charnu à noyau[M]

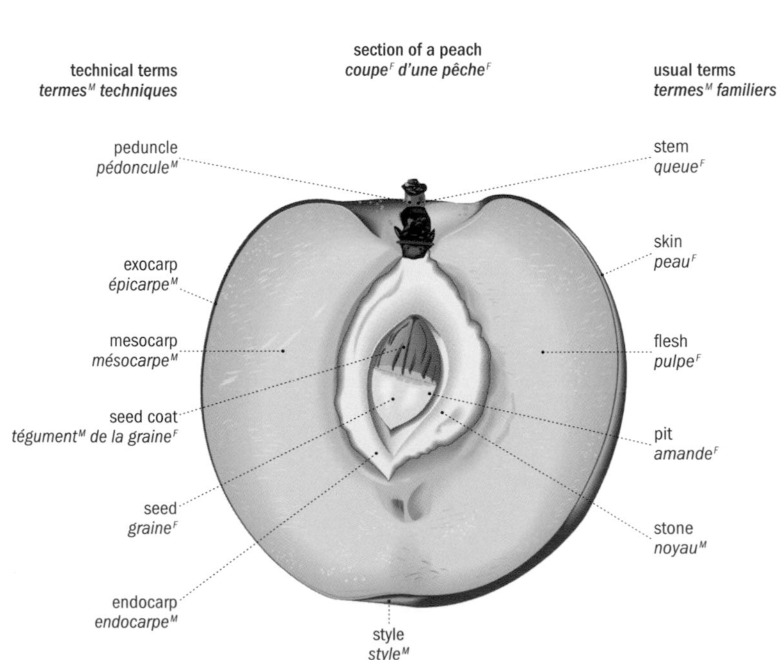
section of a peach
coupe[F] d'une pêche[F]
technical terms
termes[M] techniques
usual terms
termes[M] familiers
peduncle
pédoncule[M]
stem
queue[F]
exocarp
épicarpe[M]
skin
peau[F]
mesocarp
mésocarpe[M]
flesh
pulpe[F]
seed coat
tégument[M] de la graine[F]
pit
amande[F]
seed
graine[F]
stone
noyau[M]
endocarp
endocarpe[M]
style
style[M]

fleshy fruit: pome fruit
fruit[M] charnu à pépins[M]

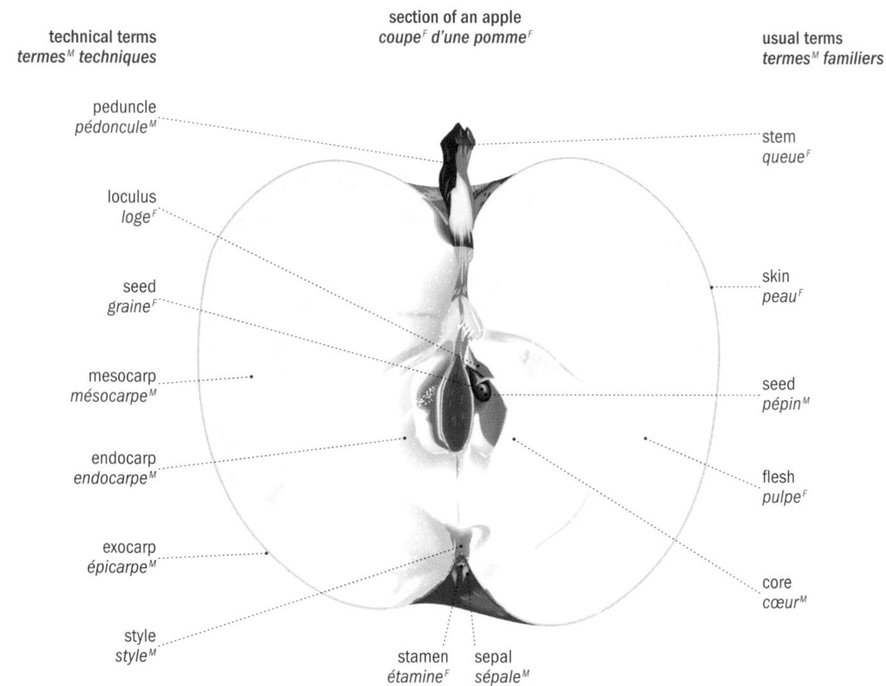
section of an apple
coupe[F] d'une pomme[F]
technical terms
termes[M] techniques
usual terms
termes[M] familiers
peduncle
pédoncule[M]
stem
queue[F]
loculus
loge[F]
skin
peau[F]
seed
graine[F]
mesocarp
mésocarpe[M]
seed
pépin[M]
endocarp
endocarpe[M]
flesh
pulpe[F]
exocarp
épicarpe[M]
core
cœur[M]
style
style[M]
stamen
étamine[F]
sepal
sépale[M]

fleshy fruit: citrus fruit
fruit[M] charnu : agrume[M]

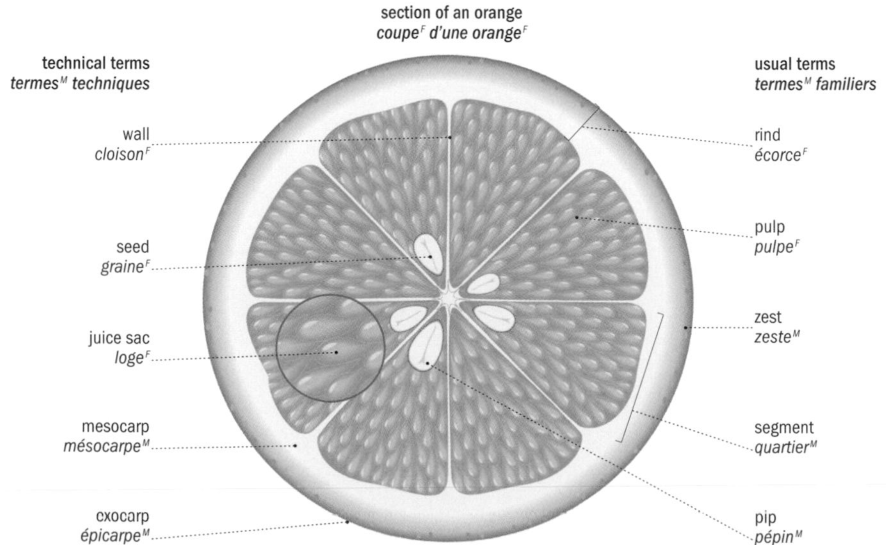
section of an orange
coupe[F] d'une orange[F]
technical terms
termes[M] techniques
usual terms
termes[M] familiers
wall
cloison[F]
rind
écorce[F]
pulp
pulpe[F]
seed
graine[F]
zest
zeste[M]
juice sac
loge[F]
mesocarp
mésocarpe[M]
segment
quartier[M]
exocarp
épicarpe[M]
pip
pépin[M]

fleshy fruit: berry fruit
fruit^M charnu : baie^F

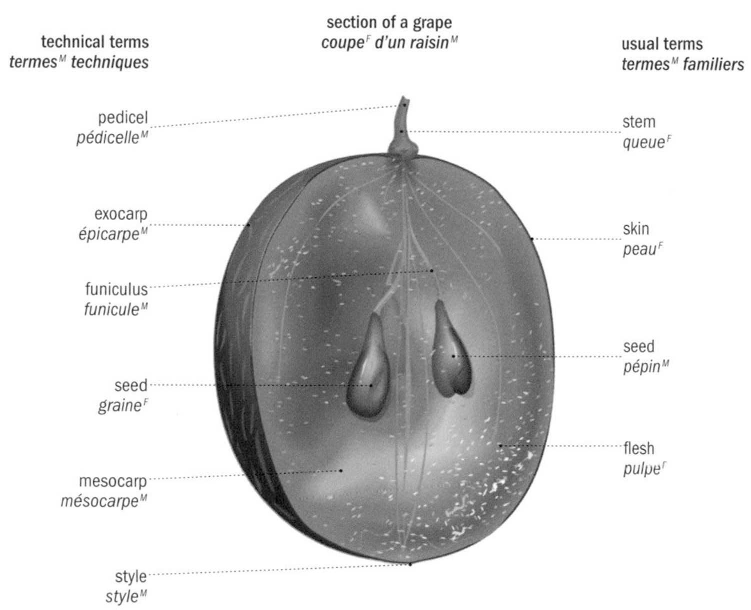
section of a grape
coupe^F d'un raisin^M
technical terms
termes^M techniques
usual terms
termes^M familiers
pedicel
pédicelle^M
stem
queue^F
exocarp
épicarpe^M
skin
peau^F
funiculus
funicule^M
seed
pépin^M
seed
graine^F
flesh
pulpe^F
mesocarp
mésocarpe^M
style
style^M

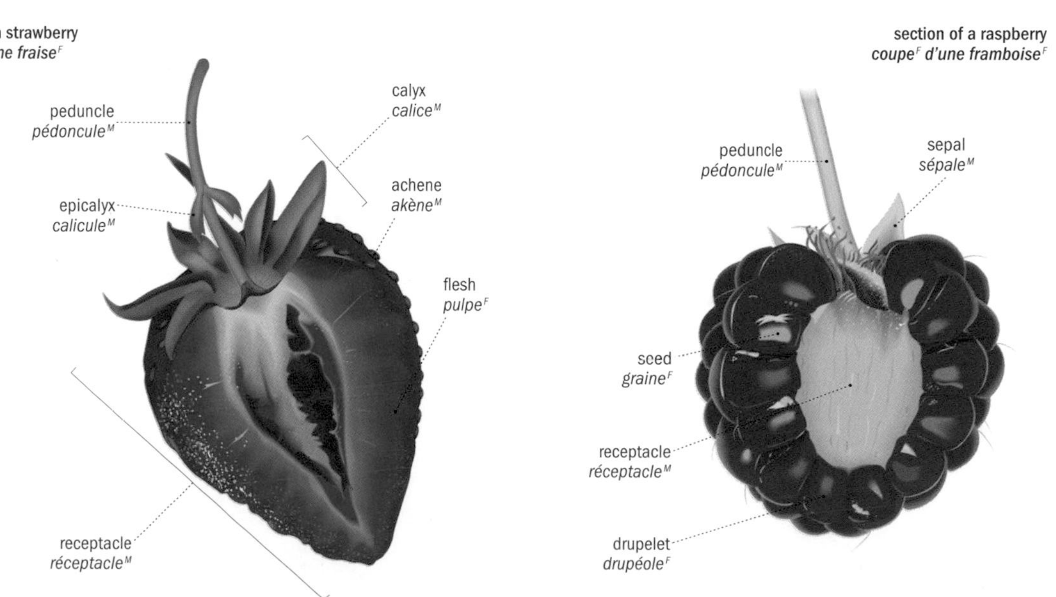
section of a strawberry
coupe^F d'une fraise^F
peduncle
pédoncule^M
calyx
calice^M
achene
akène^M
epicalyx
calicule^M
flesh
pulpe^F
receptacle
réceptacle^M
section of a raspberry
coupe^F d'une framboise^F
peduncle
pédoncule^M
sepal
sépale^M
seed
graine^F
receptacle
réceptacle^M
drupelet
drupéole^F

dry fruits
fruits*[M] *secs

husk
***brou*[M]**

section of a follicle: star anise
coupe*[F] *d'un follicule*[M] *: anis*[M] *étoilé

section of a silique: mustard
***coupe*[F] *d'une silique*[F] *: moutarde*[F]**

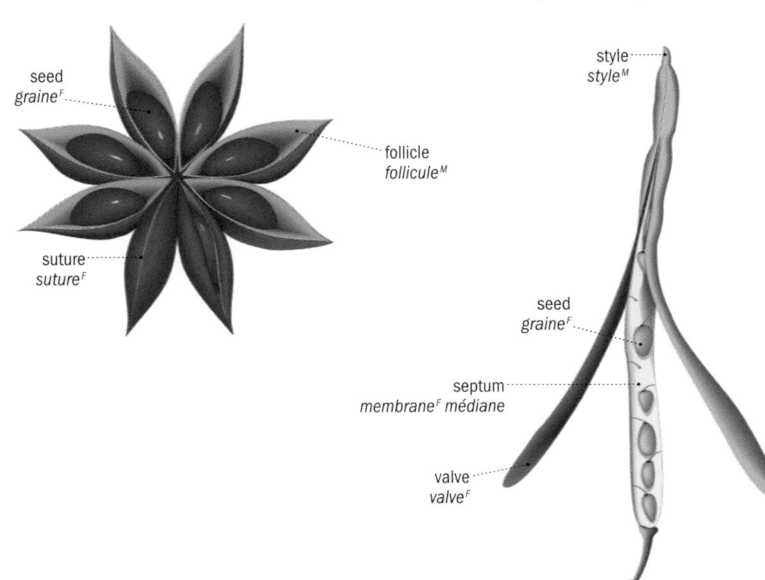
seed
graine[F]
follicle
follicule[M]
suture
suture[F]
style
style[M]
seed
graine[F]
septum
membrane[F] médiane
valve
valve[F]

section of a hazelnut
***coupe*[F] *d'une noisette*[F]**

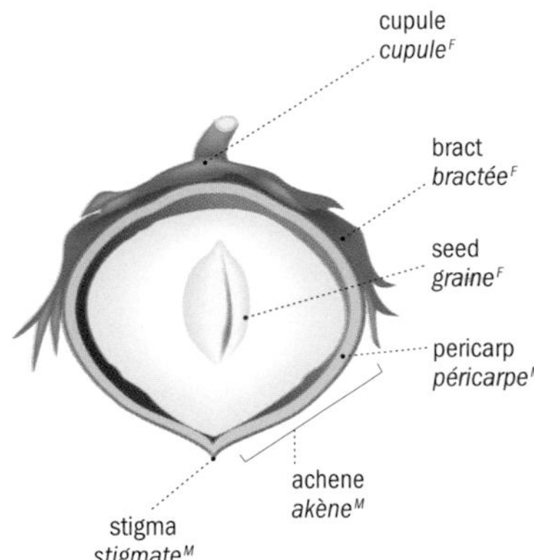
cupule
cupule[F]
bract
bractée[F]
seed
graine[F]
pericarp
péricarpe[M]
achene
akène[M]
stigma
stigmate[M]

section of a walnut
***coupe*[F] *d'une noix*[F]**

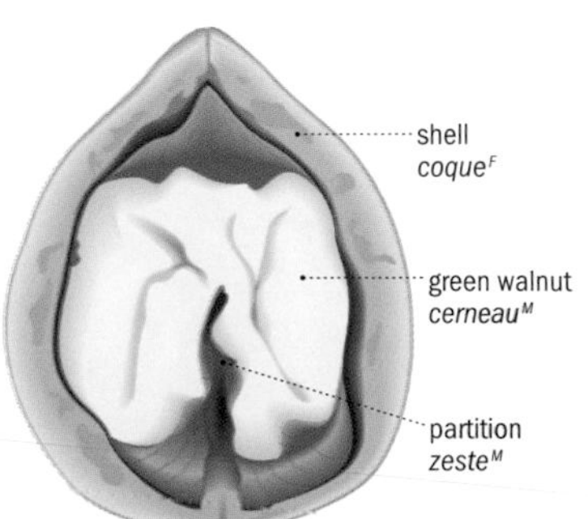
shell
coque[F]
green walnut
cerneau[M]
partition
zeste[M]

section of a legume: pea
***coupe*[F] *d'une gousse*[F] *: pois*[M]**

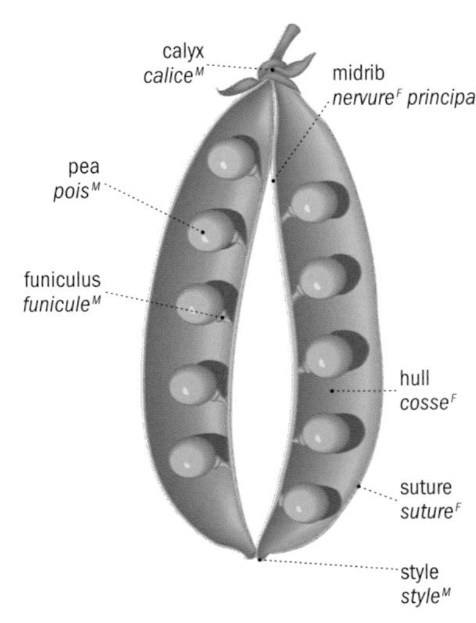
calyx
calice[M]
midrib
nervure[F] principale
pea
pois[M]
funiculus
funicule[M]
hull
cosse[F]
suture
suture[F]
style
style[M]

section of a capsule: poppy
***coupe*[F] *d'une capsule*[F] *: pavot*[M]**

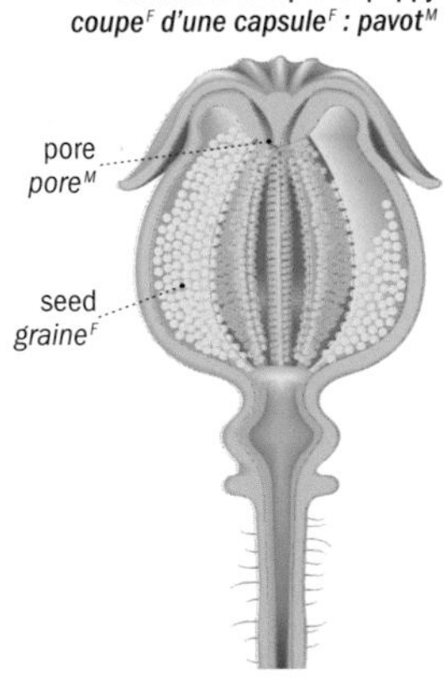
pore
pore[M]
seed
graine[F]

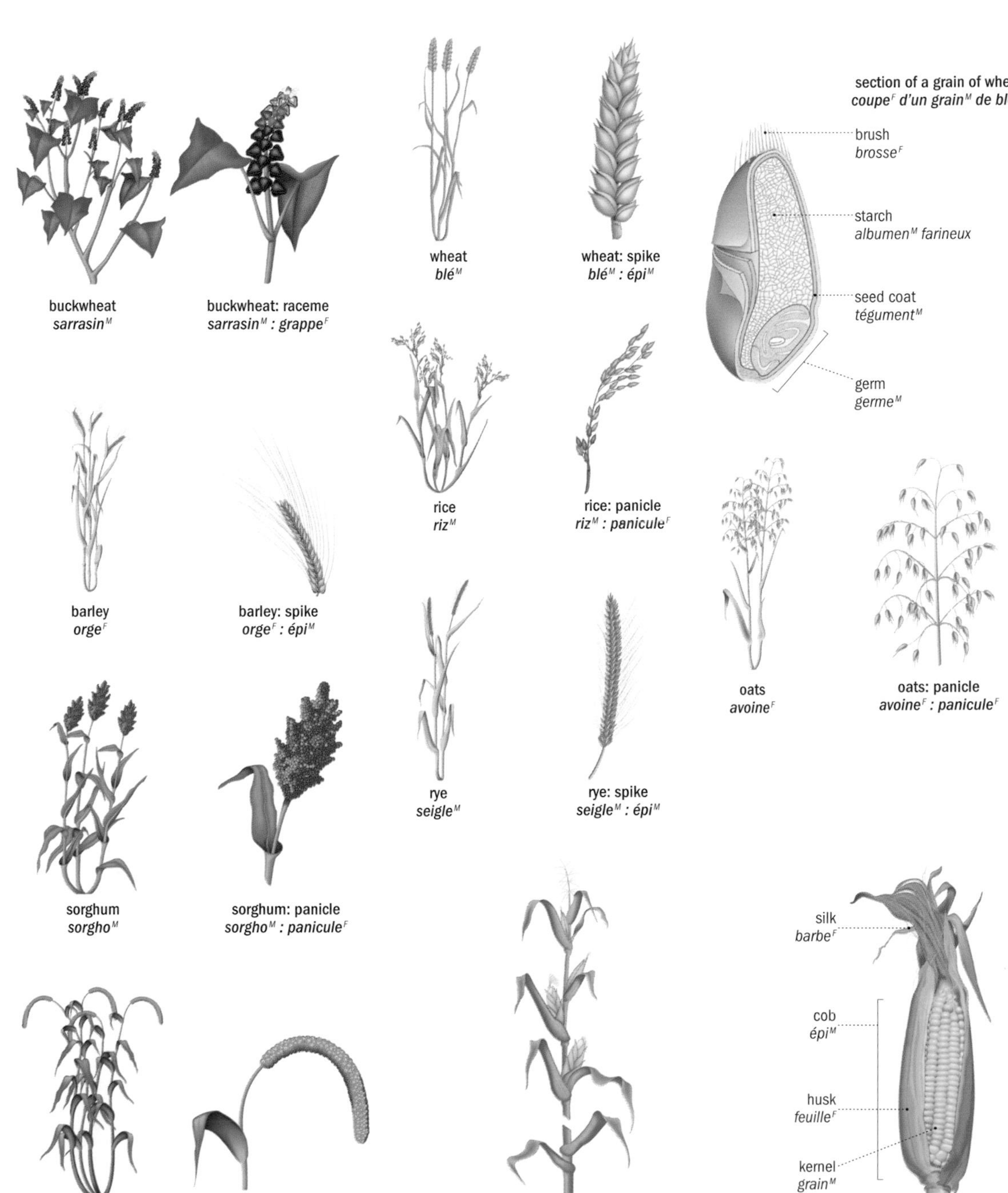
buckwheat
sarrasin[M]
buckwheat: raceme
sarrasin[M] : grappe[F]
wheat
blé[M]
wheat: spike
blé[M] : épi[M]
section of a grain of wheat
coupe[F] d'un grain[M] de blé[M]
brush
brosse[F]
starch
albumen[M] farineux
seed coat
tégument[M]
germ
germe[M]
barley
orge[F]
barley: spike
orge[F] : épi[M]
rice
riz[M]
rice: panicle
riz[M] : panicule[F]
oats
avoine[F]
oats: panicle
avoine[F] : panicule[F]
sorghum
sorgho[M]
sorghum: panicle
sorgho[M] : panicule[F]
rye
seigle[M]
rye: spike
seigle[M] : épi[M]
silk
barbe[F]
cob
épi[M]
husk
feuille[F]
kernel
grain[M]
millet
millet[M]
millet: spike
millet[M] : épi[M]
corn
maïs[M]
corn: cob
maïs[M] : épi[M]

grape

vigne[F]

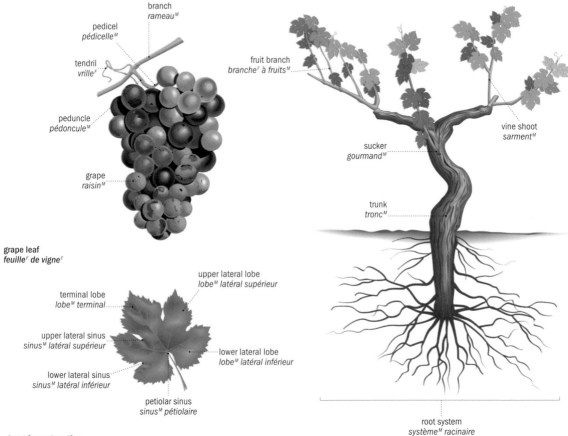

bunch of grapes
grappe[F] de raisin[M]

branch
rameau[M]

pedicel
pédicelle[M]

tendril
vrille[F]

peduncle
pédoncule[M]

grape
raisin[M]

vine stock
cep[M] de vigne[F]

fruit branch
branche[F] à fruits[M]

vine shoot
sarment[M]

sucker
gourmand[M]

trunk
tronc[M]

root system
système[M] racinaire

grape leaf
feuille[F] de vigne[F]

upper lateral lobe
lobe[M] latéral supérieur

terminal lobe
lobe[M] terminal

upper lateral sinus
sinus[M] latéral supérieur

lower lateral lobe
lobe[M] latéral inférieur

lower lateral sinus
sinus[M] latéral inférieur

petiolar sinus
sinus[M] pétiolaire

steps in maturation
étapes[F] de maturation[F]

flowering
floraison[F]

fruition
nouaison[F]

ripening
véraison[F]

ripeness
maturité[F]

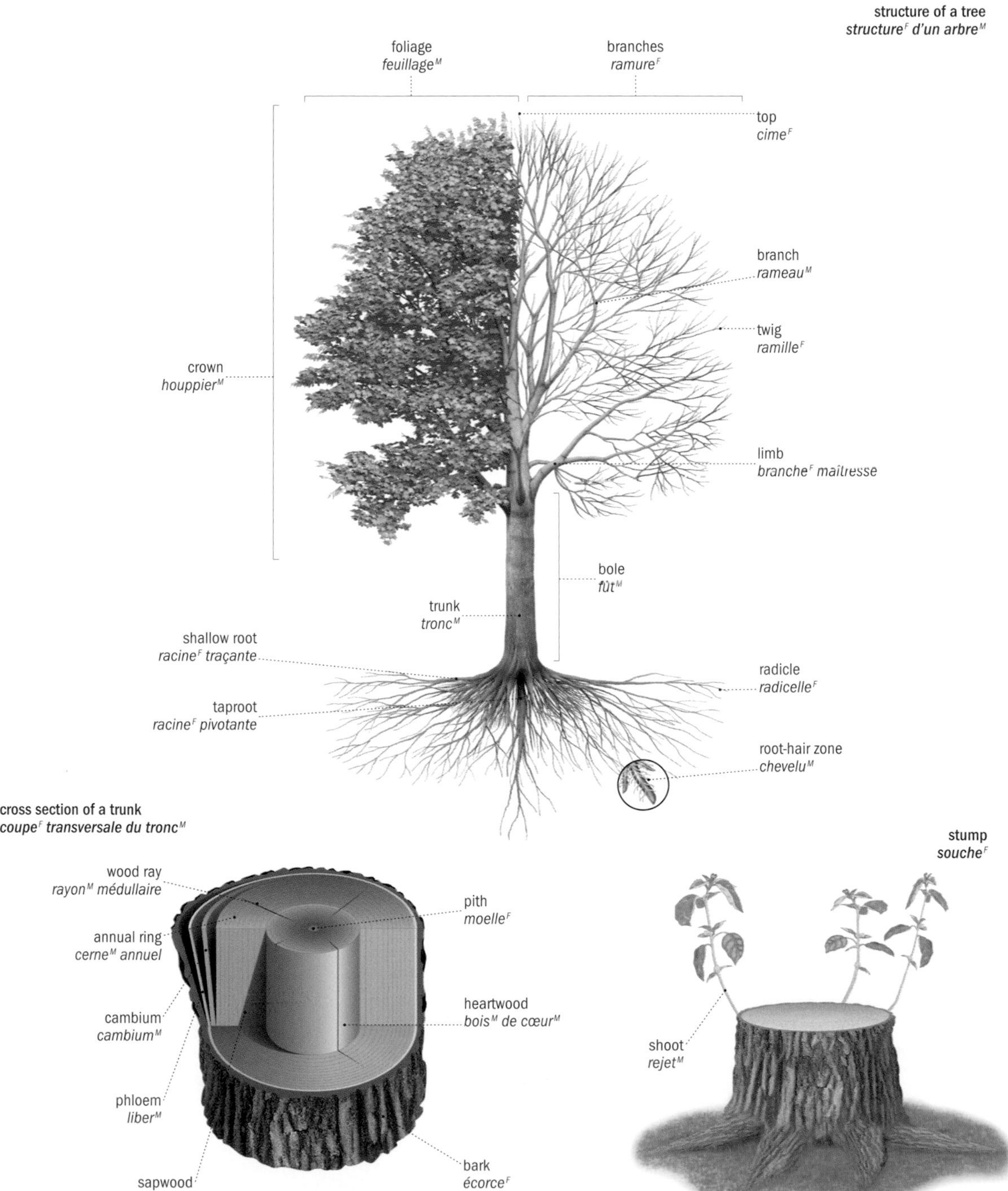

structure of a tree
structure[F] d'un arbre[M]
foliage
feuillage[M]
branches
ramure[F]
top
cime[F]
branch
rameau[M]
twig
ramille[F]
crown
houppier[M]
limb
branche[F] maîtresse
bole
fût[M]
trunk
tronc[M]
shallow root
racine[F] traçante
radicle
radicelle[F]
taproot
racine[F] pivotante
root-hair zone
chevelu[M]
cross section of a trunk
coupe[F] transversale du tronc[M]
wood ray
rayon[M] médullaire
pith
moelle[F]
annual ring
cerne[M] annuel
heartwood
bois[M] de cœur[M]
cambium
cambium[M]
phloem
liber[M]
sapwood
aubier[M]
bark
écorce[F]
stump
souche[F]
shoot
rejet[M]

examples of broadleaved trees
exemples*[M] *d'arbres*[M] *feuillus

oak
chêne[M]
birch
bouleau[M]
weeping willow
saule[M] *pleureur*
poplar
peuplier[M]
palm tree
palmier[M]
maple
érable[M]
beech
hêtre[M]
walnut
noyer[M]

pinecone
cône[M]

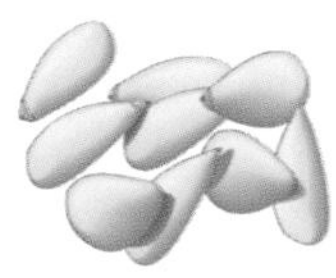

pine seed
pignon[M]

branch
rameau[M]

female cone
cône[M] femelle
male cone
cône[M] mâle

examples of leaves
exemples[M] de feuilles[F]

fir needles
aiguilles[F] de sapin[M]

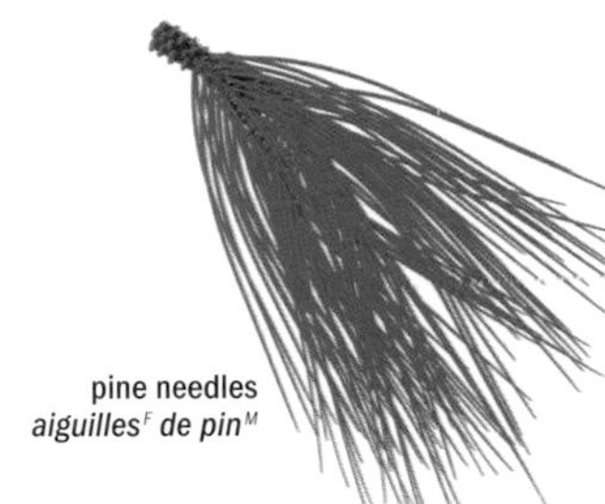

pine needles
aiguilles[F] de pin[M]

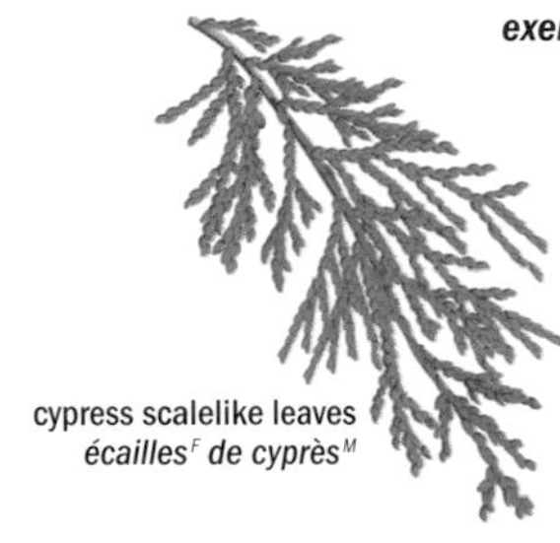

cypress scalelike leaves
écailles[F] de cyprès[M]

examples of conifers
exemples[M] de conifères[M]

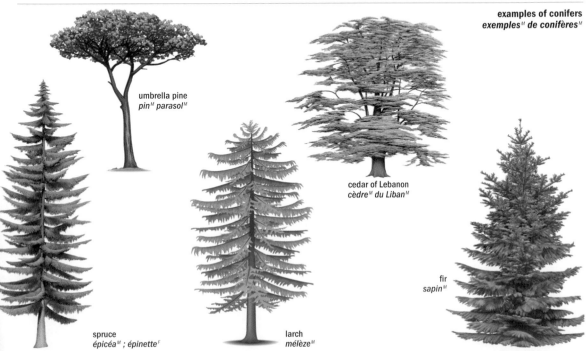

umbrella pine
pin[M] parasol[M]

cedar of Lebanon
cèdre[M] du Liban[M]

spruce
épicéa[M] ; épinette[F]

larch
mélèze[M]

fir
sapin[M]

animal cell

cellule^F animale

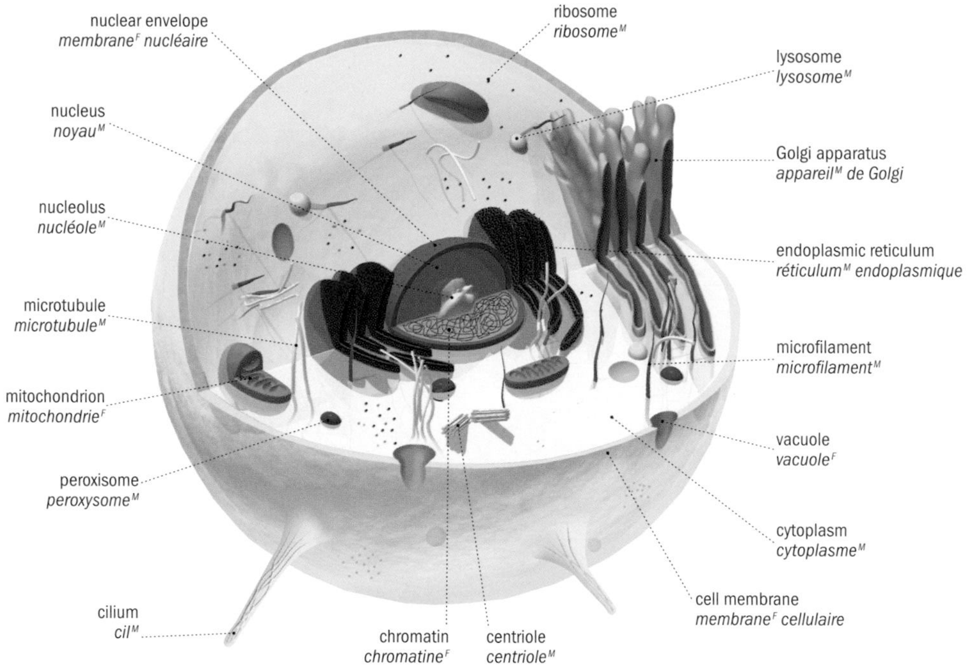
nuclear envelope
membrane^F nucléaire
ribosome
ribosome^M
lysosome
lysosome^M
nucleus
noyau^M
Golgi apparatus
appareil^M de Golgi
nucleolus
nucléole^M
endoplasmic reticulum
réticulum^M endoplasmique
microtubule
microtubule^M
microfilament
microfilament^M
mitochondrion
mitochondrie^F
vacuole
vacuole^F
peroxisome
peroxysome^M
cytoplasm
cytoplasme^M
cell membrane
membrane^F cellulaire
cilium
cil^M
chromatin
chromatine^F
centriole
centriole^M

unicellulars

unicellulaires^M

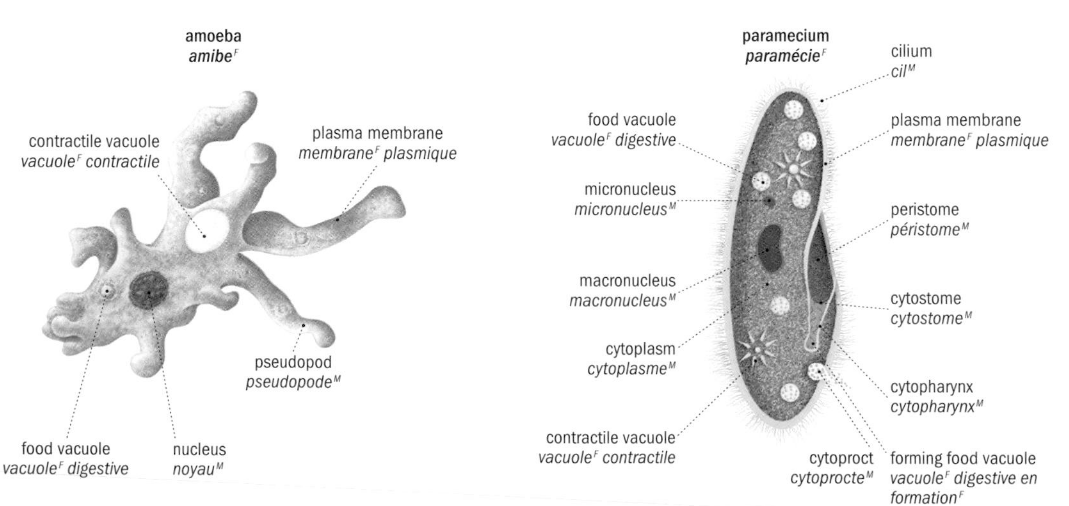
amoeba
amibe^F
contractile vacuole
vacuole^F contractile
plasma membrane
membrane^F plasmique
pseudopod
pseudopode^M
food vacuole
vacuole^F digestive
nucleus
noyau^M
paramecium
paramécie^F
cilium
cil^M
food vacuole
vacuole^F digestive
plasma membrane
membrane^F plasmique
micronucleus
micronucleus^M
peristome
péristome^M
macronucleus
macronucleus^M
cytostome
cytostome^M
cytoplasm
cytoplasme^M
cytopharynx
cytopharynx^M
contractile vacuole
vacuole^F contractile
cytoproct
cytoprocte^M
forming food vacuole
vacuole^F digestive en formation^F

butterfly

papillon[M]

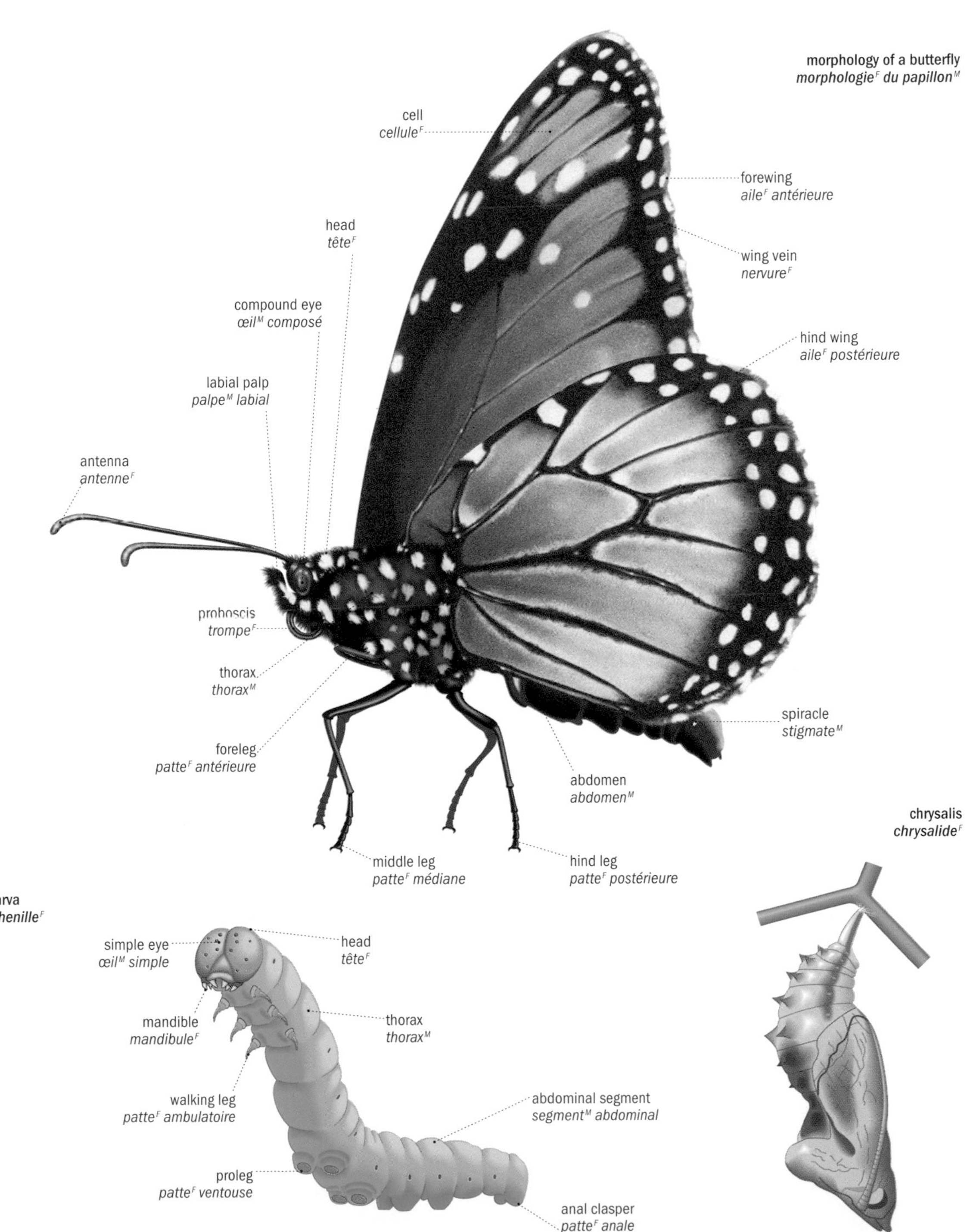
morphology of a butterfly
morphologie[F] du papillon[M]
cell
cellule[F]
forewing
aile[F] antérieure
head
tête[F]
wing vein
nervure[F]
compound eye
œil[M] composé
hind wing
aile[F] postérieure
labial palp
palpe[M] labial
antenna
antenne[F]
proboscis
trompe[F]
thorax
thorax[M]
spiracle
stigmate[M]
foreleg
patte[F] antérieure
abdomen
abdomen[M]
chrysalis
chrysalide[F]
middle leg
patte[F] médiane
hind leg
patte[F] postérieure
larva
chenille[F]
simple eye
œil[M] simple
head
tête[F]
mandible
mandibule[F]
thorax
thorax[M]
walking leg
patte[F] ambulatoire
abdominal segment
segment[M] abdominal
proleg
patte[F] ventouse
anal clasper
patte[F] anale

honeybee

abeille^F

morphology of a honeybee: worker
morphologie^F de l'abeille^F : ouvrière^F

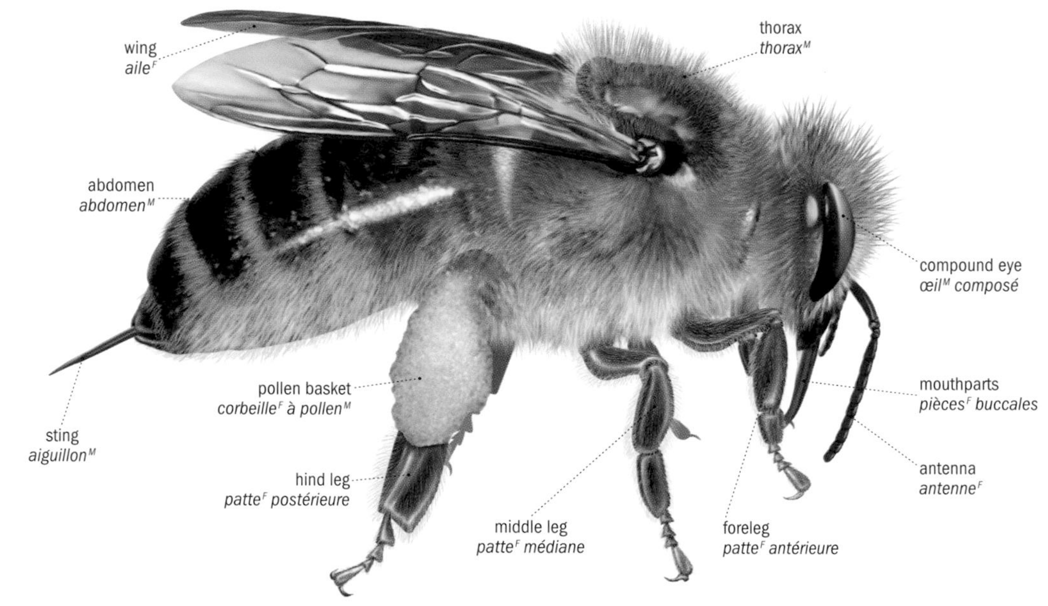

wing
aile^F
thorax
thorax^M
abdomen
abdomen^M
compound eye
œil^M composé
pollen basket
corbeille^F à pollen^M
mouthparts
pièces^F buccales
sting
aiguillon^M
hind leg
patte^F postérieure
antenna
antenne^F
middle leg
patte^F médiane
foreleg
patte^F antérieure

castes
castes^F

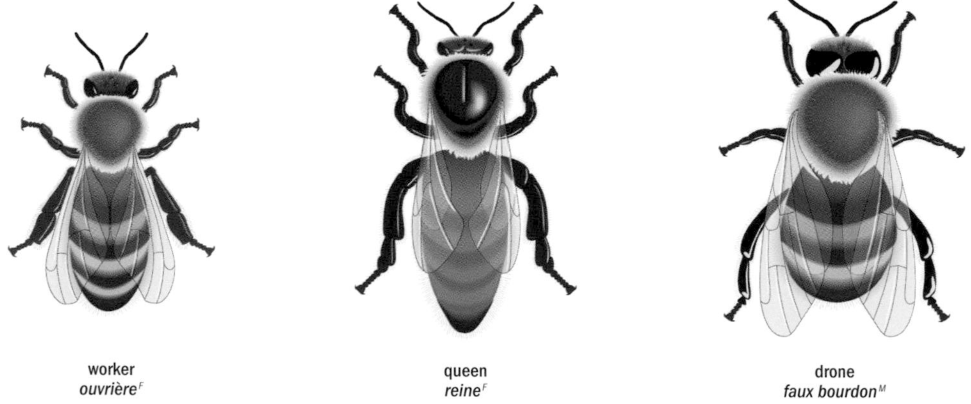

worker
ouvrière^F
queen
reine^F
drone
faux bourdon^M

examples of insects

exemples[M] d'insectes[M]

flea
puce[F]

louse
pou[M]

mosquito
moustique[M]

tsetse fly
mouche[F] tsé-tsé

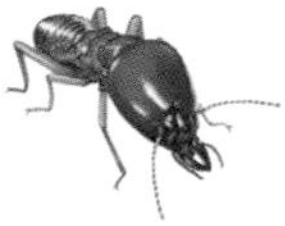

termite
termite[M]

cicada
cigale[F]

ant
fourmi[F]

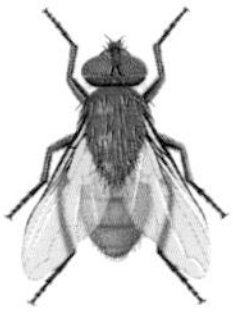

fly
mouche[F]

ladybug
coccinelle[F]

shield bug
punaise[F] rayée

cockchafer
hanneton[M]

yellowjacket
guêpe[F]

hornet
frelon[M]

horsefly
taon[M]

bumblebee
bourdon[M]

bow-winged grasshopper
criquet[M] mélodieux

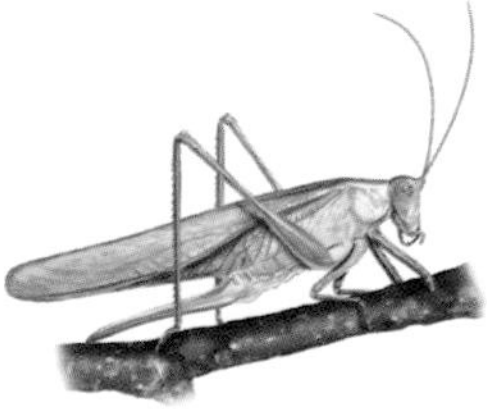

great green bush-cricket
grande sauterelle[F] verte

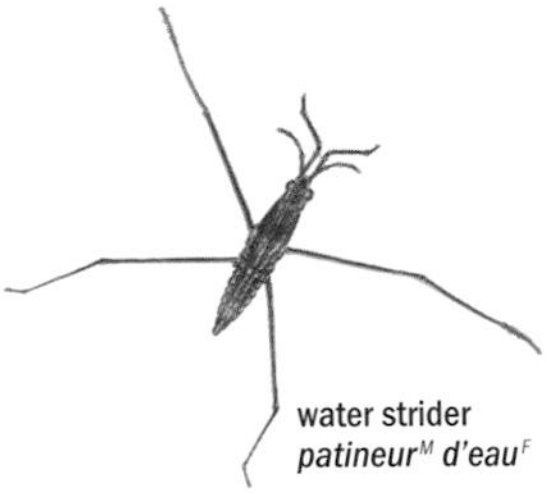

water strider
patineur[M] d'eau[F]

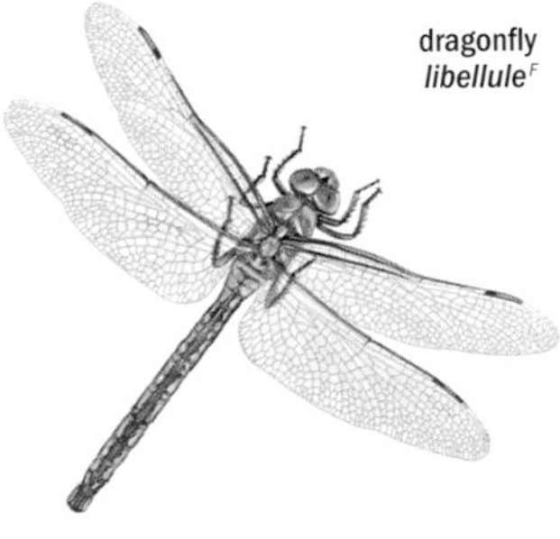

dragonfly
libellule[F]

atlas moth
atlas[M]

mantid
mante[F] religieuse

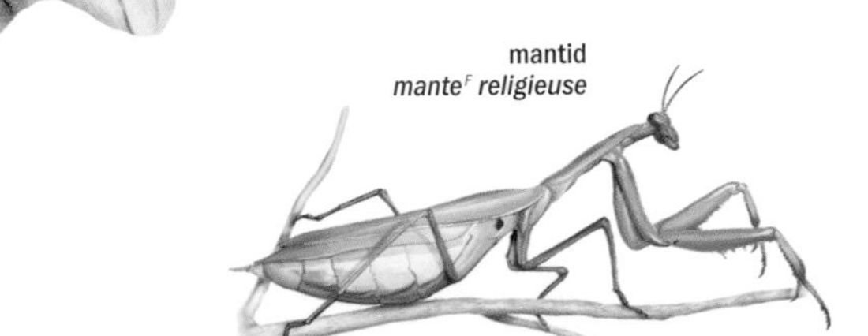

spider

araignée[F]

spider web
toile[F] d'araignée[F]

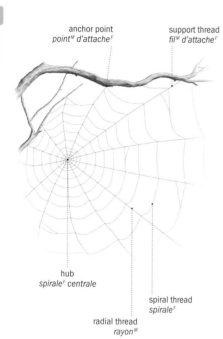

anchor point
point[M] d'attache[F]

support thread
fil[M] d'attache[F]

hub
spirale[F] centrale

spiral thread
spirale[F]

radial thread
rayon[M]

morphology of a spider
morphologie[F] de l'araignée[F]

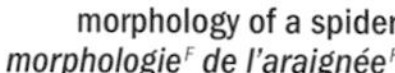

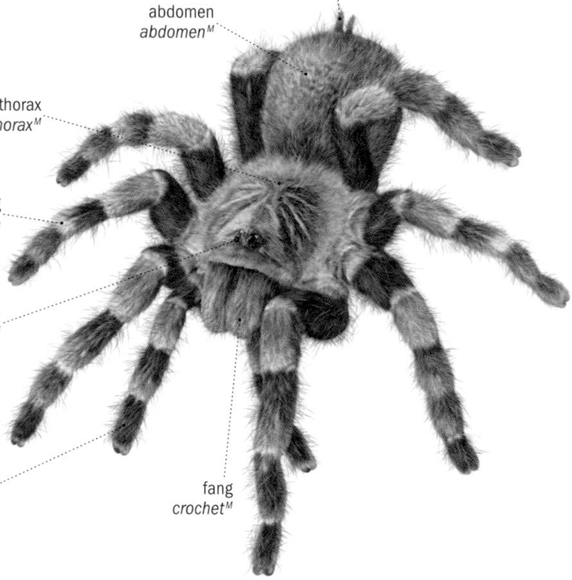

spinneret
filière[F]

abdomen
abdomen[M]

cephalothorax
céphalothorax[M]

leg
patte[F] locomotrice

eye
œil[M]

pedipalp
pédipalpe[M]

fang
crochet[M]

examples of arachnids

exemples[M] d'arachnides[M]

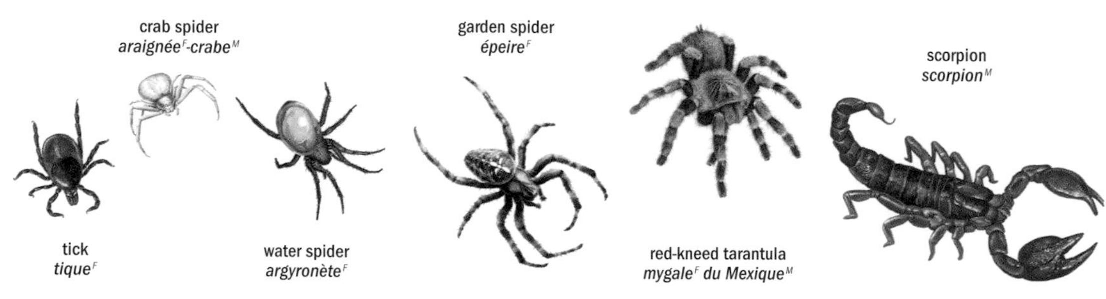

crab spider
araignée[F]-crabe[M]
garden spider
épeire[F]
scorpion
scorpion[M]
tick
tique[F]
water spider
argyronète[F]
red-kneed tarantula
mygale[F] du Mexique[M]

lobster

homard[M]

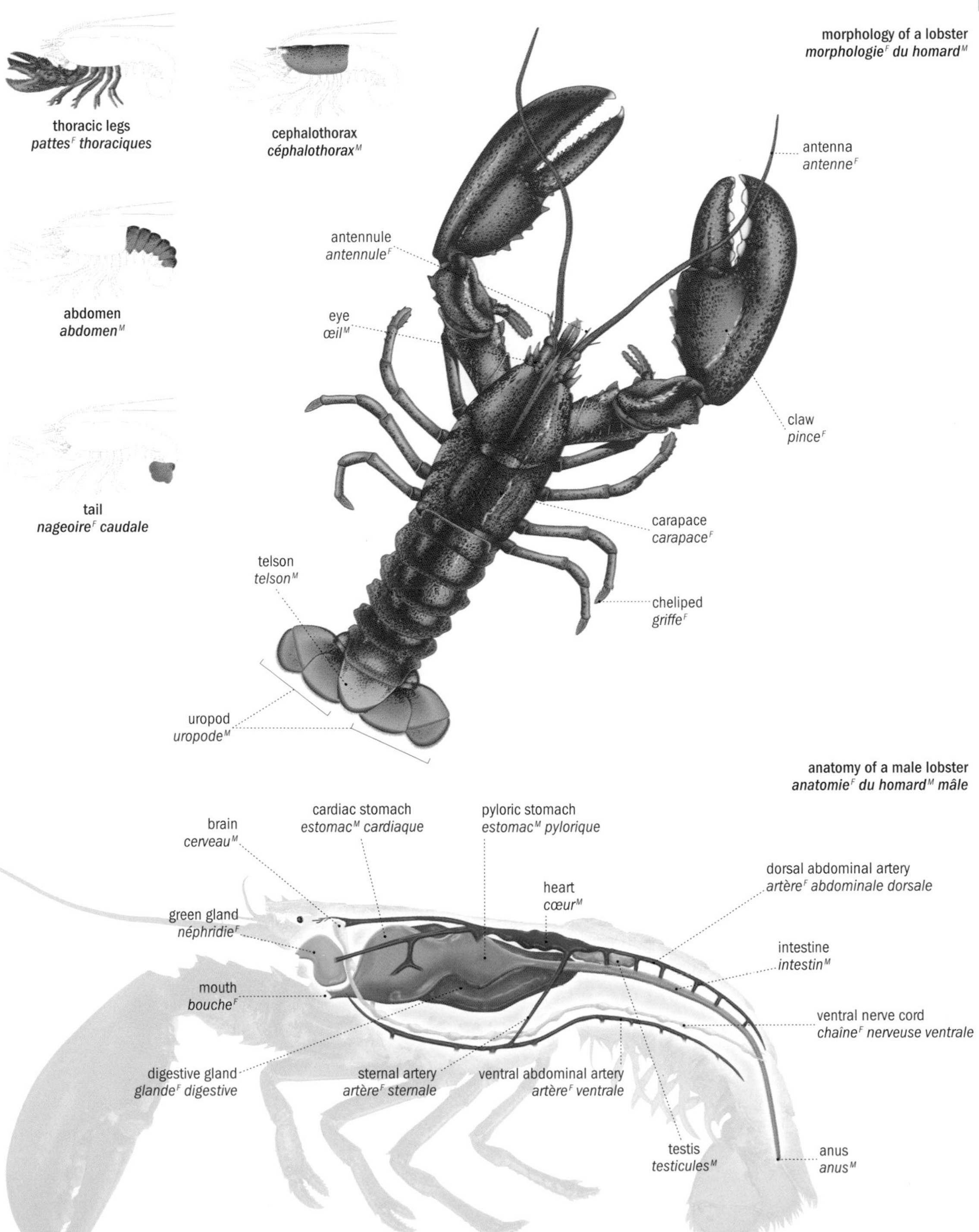
morphology of a lobster
morphologie[F] du homard[M]
thoracic legs
pattes[F] thoraciques
cephalothorax
céphalothorax[M]
abdomen
abdomen[M]
tail
nageoire[F] caudale
antenna
antenne[F]
antennule
antennule[F]
eye
œil[M]
claw
pince[F]
carapace
carapace[F]
telson
telson[M]
cheliped
griffe[F]
uropod
uropode[M]
anatomy of a male lobster
anatomie[F] du homard[M] mâle
brain
cerveau[M]
cardiac stomach
estomac[M] cardiaque
pyloric stomach
estomac[M] pylorique
dorsal abdominal artery
artère[F] abdominale dorsale
heart
cœur[M]
green gland
néphridie[F]
intestine
intestin[M]
mouth
bouche[F]
ventral nerve cord
chaîne[F] nerveuse ventrale
digestive gland
glande[F] digestive
sternal artery
artère[F] sternale
ventral abdominal artery
artère[F] ventrale
testis
testicules[M]
anus
anus[M]

snail

escargot[M]

morphology of a snail
morphologie[F] de l'escargot[M]

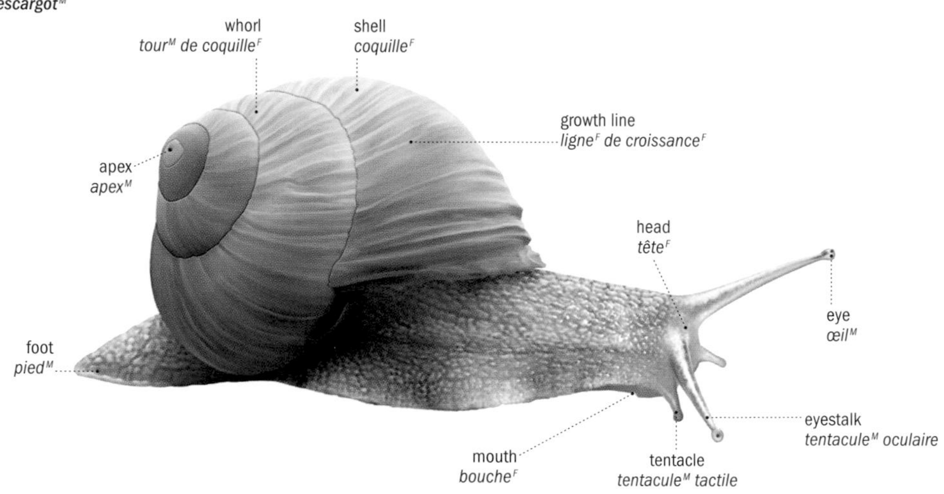
whorl
tour[M] de coquille[F]
shell
coquille[F]
growth line
ligne[F] de croissance[F]
apex
apex[M]
head
tête[F]
eye
œil[M]
foot
pied[M]
eyestalk
tentacule[M] oculaire
mouth
bouche[F]
tentacle
tentacule[M] tactile

octopus

pieuvre[F]

morphology of an octopus
morphologie[F] de la pieuvre[F]

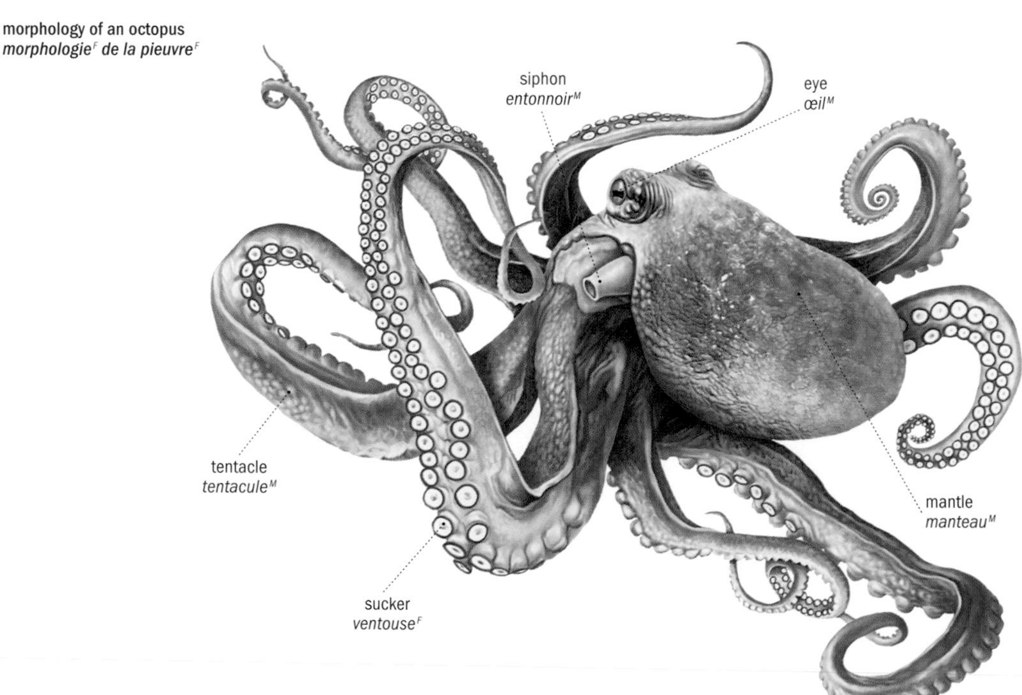
siphon
entonnoir[M]
eye
œil[M]
tentacle
tentacule[M]
mantle
manteau[M]
sucker
ventouse[F]

univalve shell

coquillage[M] univalve

morphology of a univalve shell
morphologie[F] du coquillage[M] univalve

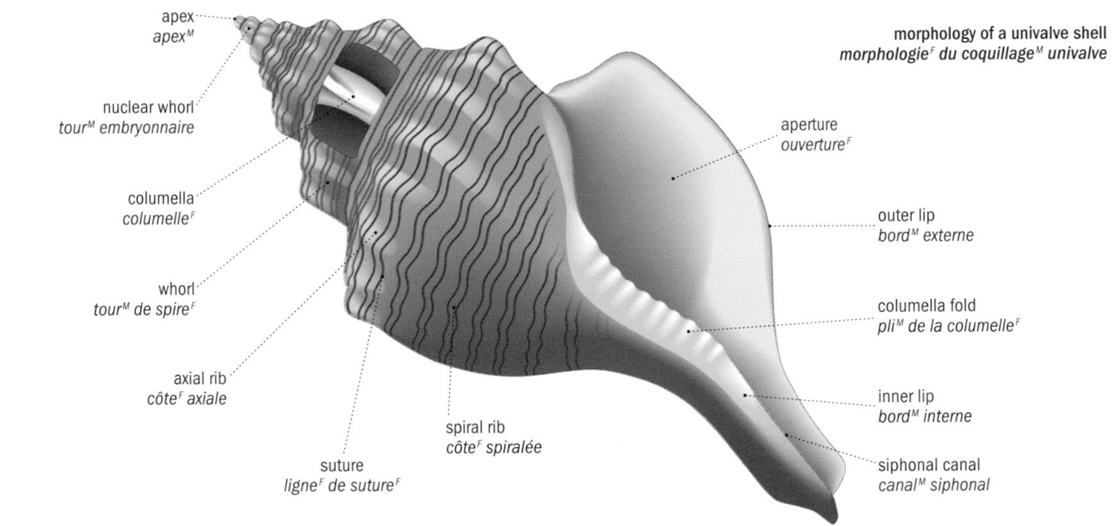
apex
apex[M]
nuclear whorl
tour[M] embryonnaire
columella
columelle[F]
whorl
tour[M] de spire[F]
axial rib
côte[F] axiale
suture
ligne[F] de suture[F]
spiral rib
côte[F] spiralée
aperture
ouverture[F]
outer lip
bord[M] externe
columella fold
pli[M] de la columelle[F]
inner lip
bord[M] interne
siphonal canal
canal[M] siphonal

bivalve shell

coquillage[M] bivalve

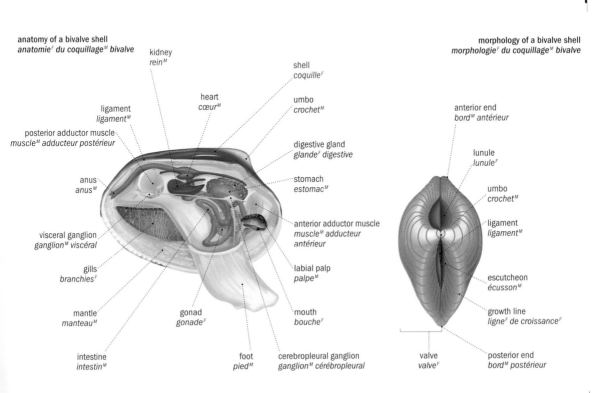

anatomy of a bivalve shell
anatomie[F] du coquillage[M] bivalve

kidney
rein[M]

shell
coquille[F]

heart
cœur[M]

ligament
ligament[M]

umbo
crochet[M]

posterior adductor muscle
muscle[M] adducteur postérieur

digestive gland
glande[F] digestive

anus
anus[M]

stomach
estomac[M]

anterior adductor muscle
muscle[M] adducteur antérieur

visceral ganglion
ganglion[M] viscéral

labial palp
palpe[M]

gills
branchies[F]

mantle
manteau[M]

gonad
gonade[F]

mouth
bouche[F]

intestine
intestin[M]

foot
pied[M]

cerebropleural ganglion
ganglion[M] cérébropleural

morphology of a bivalve shell
morphologie[F] du coquillage[M] bivalve

anterior end
bord[M] antérieur

lunule
lunule[F]

umbo
crochet[M]

ligament
ligament[M]

escutcheon
écusson[M]

growth line
ligne[F] de croissance[F]

valve
valve[F]

posterior end
bord[M] postérieur

cartilaginous fish

poisson[M] cartilagineux

morphology of a female shark
morphologie[F] du requin[M] femelle

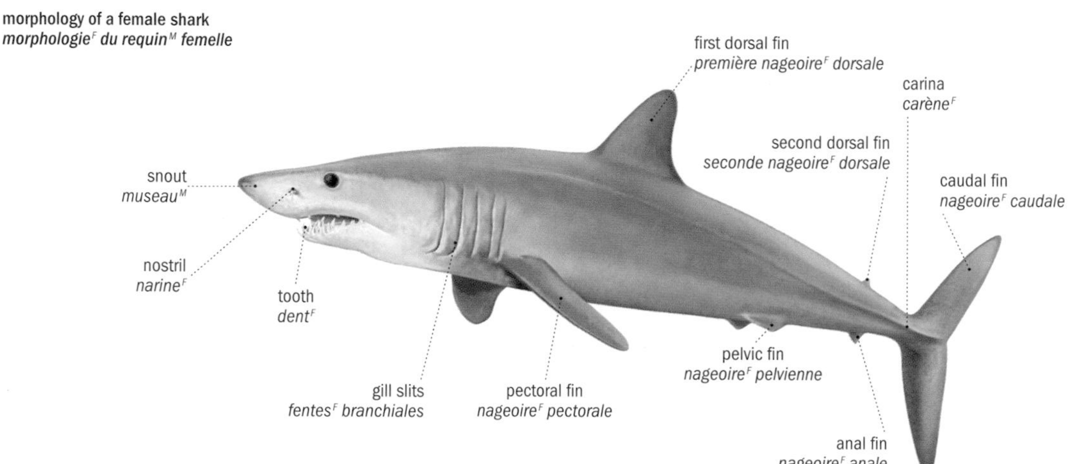
first dorsal fin
première nageoire[F] dorsale
carina
carène[F]
second dorsal fin
seconde nageoire[F] dorsale
caudal fin
nageoire[F] caudale
snout
museau[M]
nostril
narine[F]
tooth
dent[F]
gill slits
fentes[F] branchiales
pectoral fin
nageoire[F] pectorale
pelvic fin
nageoire[F] pelvienne
anal fin
nageoire[F] anale

bony fish

poisson[M] osseux

morphology of a perch
morphologie[F] de la perche[F] ; morphologie[F] de la perchaude[F]

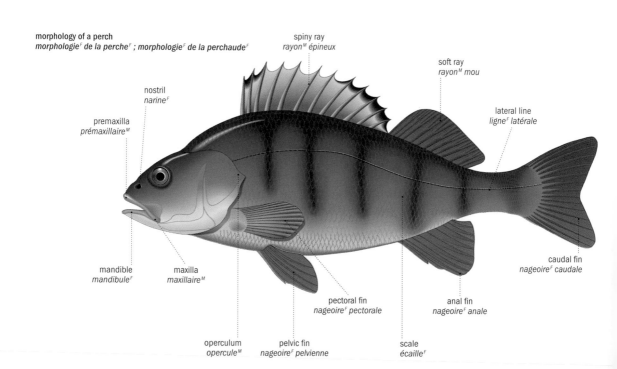

spiny ray
rayon[M] épineux
soft ray
rayon[M] mou
nostril
narine[F]
premaxilla
prémaxillaire[M]
lateral line
ligne[F] latérale
caudal fin
nageoire[F] caudale
mandible
mandibule[F]
maxilla
maxillaire[M]
pectoral fin
nageoire[F] pectorale
anal fin
nageoire[F] anale
operculum
opercule[M]
pelvic fin
nageoire[F] pelvienne
scale
écaille[F]

frog

grenouille^F

morphology of a frog
morphologie^F de la grenouille^F

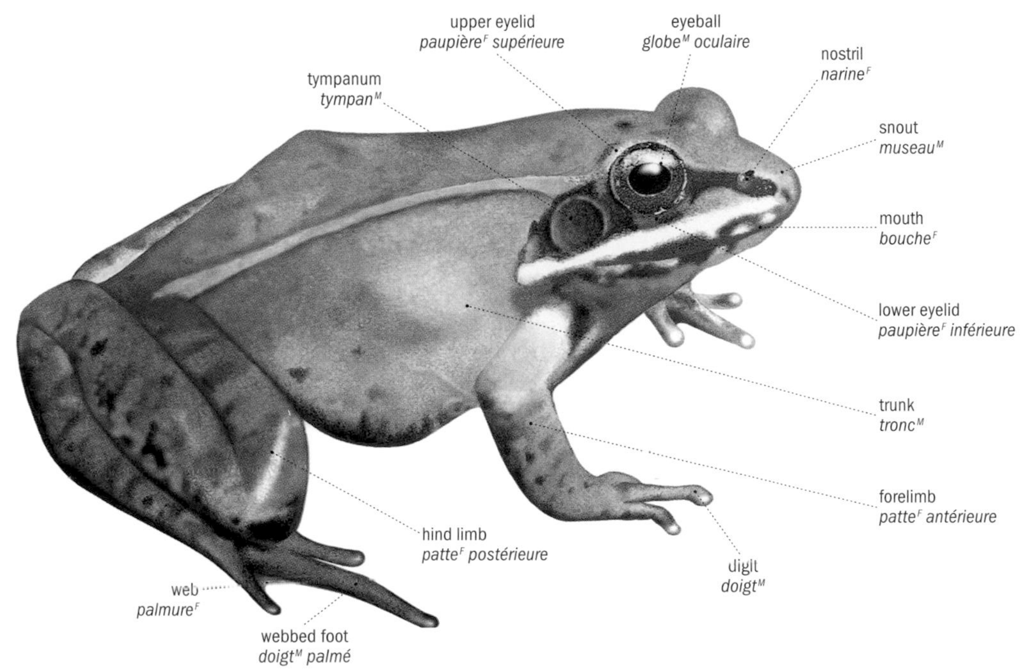
upper eyelid
paupière^F supérieure
eyeball
globe^M oculaire
nostril
narine^F
tympanum
tympan^M
snout
museau^M
mouth
bouche^F
lower eyelid
paupière^F inférieure
trunk
tronc^M
forelimb
patte^F antérieure
hind limb
patte^F postérieure
digit
doigt^M
web
palmure^F
webbed foot
doigt^M palmé

examples of amphibians

exemples^M d'amphibiens^M

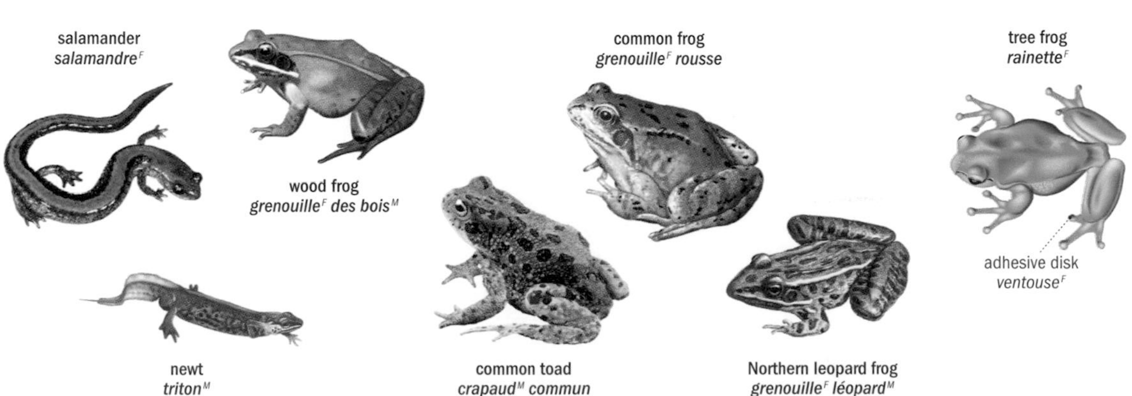
salamander
salamandre^F
common frog
grenouille^F rousse
tree frog
rainette^F
wood frog
grenouille^F des bois^M
adhesive disk
ventouse^F
newt
triton^M
common toad
crapaud^M commun
Northern leopard frog
grenouille^F léopard^M

snake

serpent^M

morphology of a venomous snake: head
morphologie^F du serpent^M venimeux : tête^F

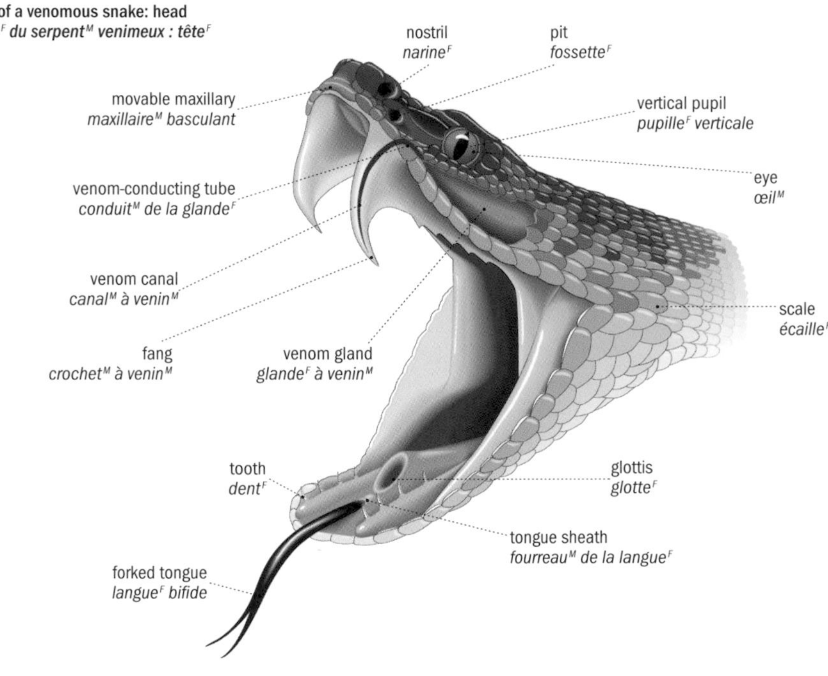
nostril
narine^F
pit
fossette^F
movable maxillary
maxillaire^M basculant
vertical pupil
pupille^F verticale
venom-conducting tube
conduit^M de la glande^F
eye
œil^M
venom canal
canal^M à venin^M
scale
écaille^F
fang
crochet^M à venin^M
venom gland
glande^F à venin^M
tooth
dent^F
glottis
glotte^F
tongue sheath
fourreau^M de la langue^F
forked tongue
langue^F bifide

turtle

tortue^F

morphology of a turtle
morphologie^F de la tortue^F

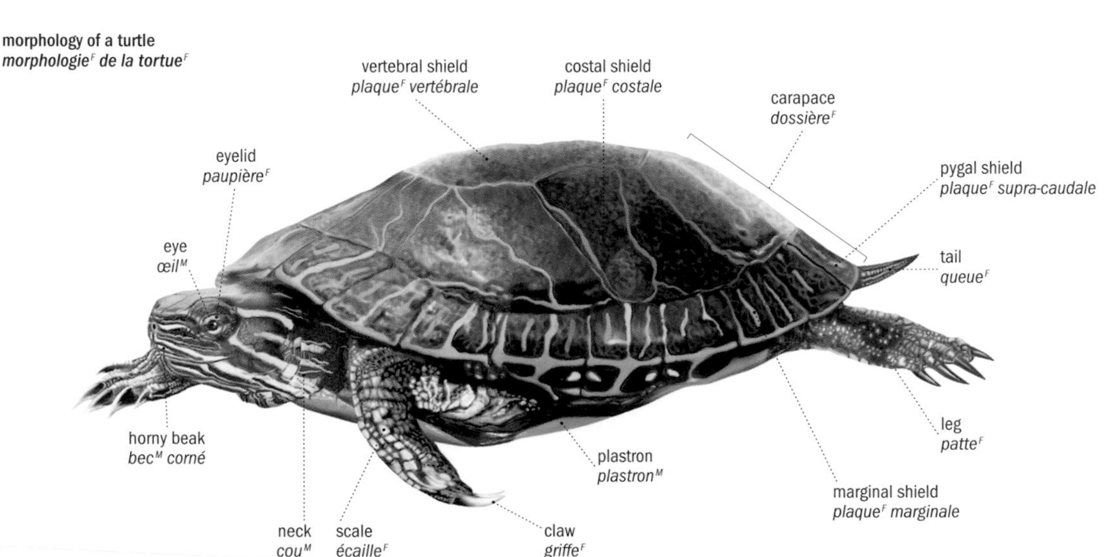
vertebral shield
plaque^F vertébrale
costal shield
plaque^F costale
carapace
dossière^F
eyelid
paupière^F
pygal shield
plaque^F supra-caudale
eye
œil^M
tail
queue^F
horny beak
bec^M corné
leg
patte^F
plastron
plastron^M
marginal shield
plaque^F marginale
neck
cou^M
scale
écaille^F
claw
griffe^F

examples of reptiles

exemples[M] de reptiles[M]

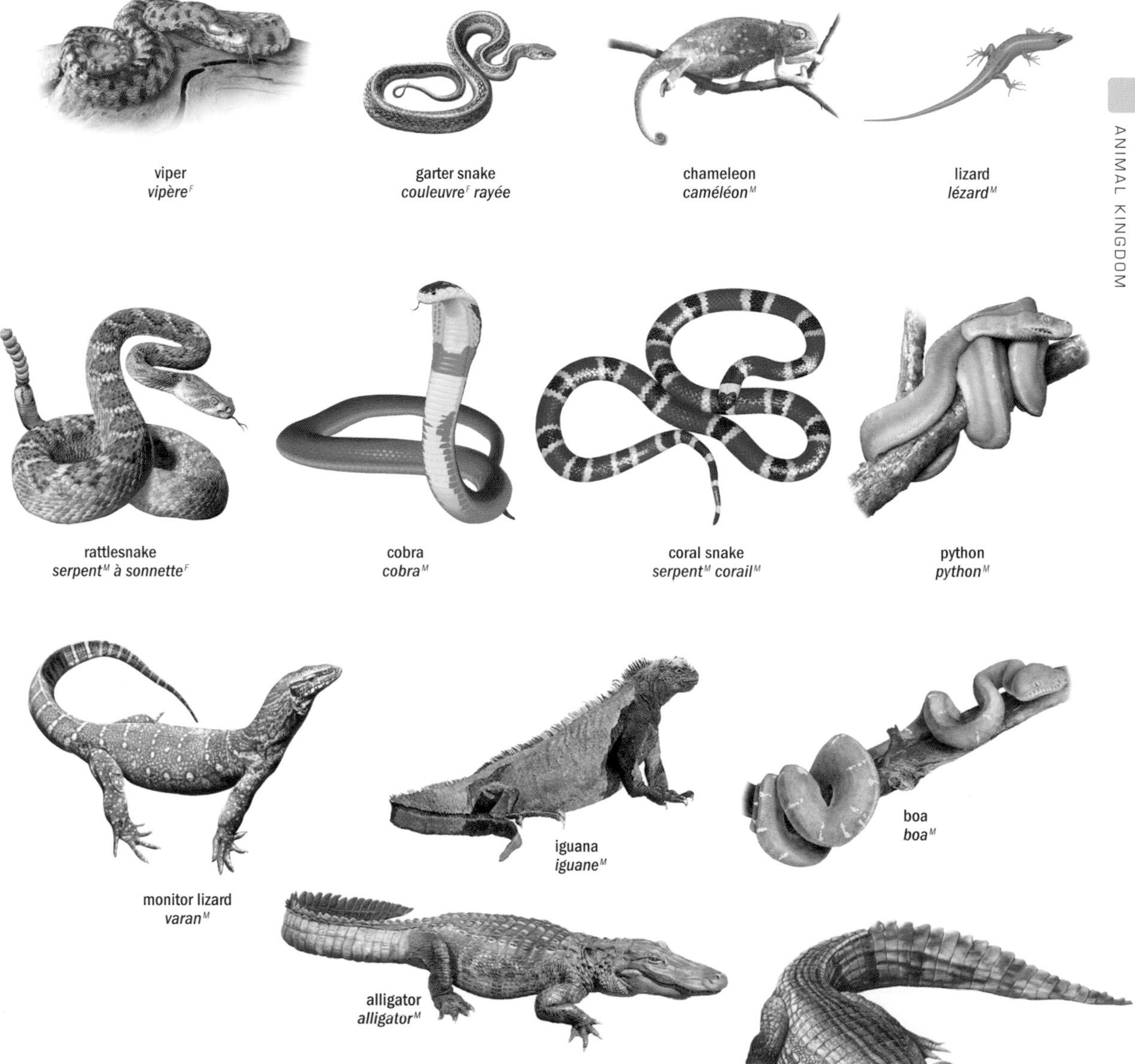
viper
vipère[F]
garter snake
couleuvre[F] rayée
chameleon
caméléon[M]
lizard
lézard[M]
rattlesnake
serpent[M] à sonnette[F]
cobra
cobra[M]
coral snake
serpent[M] corail[M]
python
python[M]
monitor lizard
varan[M]
iguana
iguane[M]
boa
boa[M]
alligator
alligator[M]
crocodile
crocodile[M]
caiman
caïman[M]

bird

oiseau[M]

morphology of a bird
morphologie[F] de l'oiseau[M]

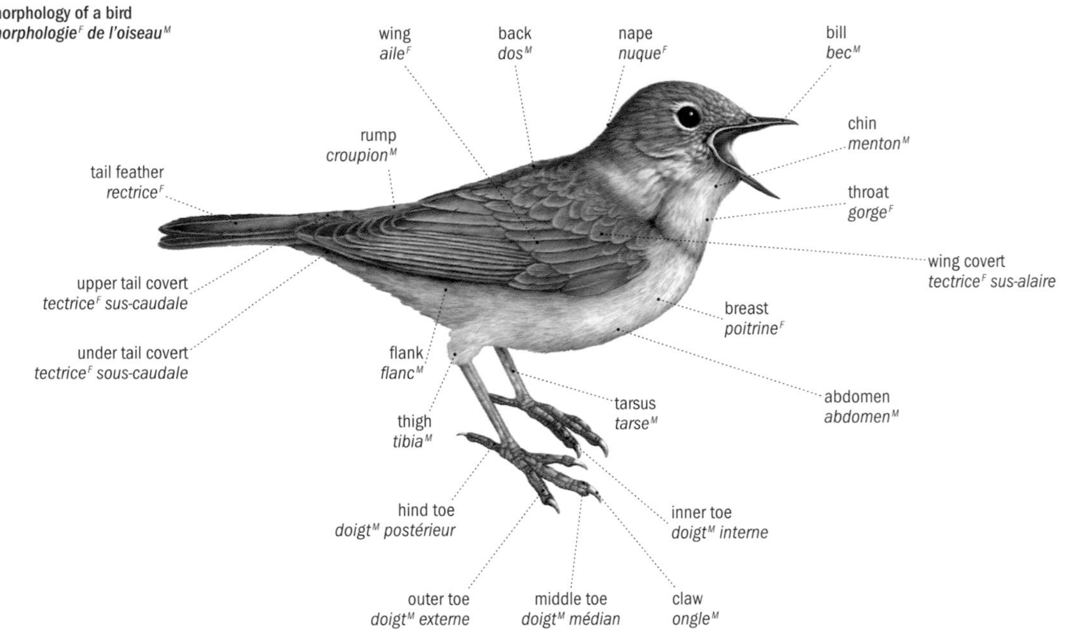
wing
aile[F]
back
dos[M]
nape
nuque[F]
bill
bec[M]
rump
croupion[M]
chin
menton[M]
tail feather
rectrice[F]
throat
gorge[F]
wing covert
tectrice[F] sus-alaire
upper tail covert
tectrice[F] sus-caudale
breast
poitrine[F]
under tail covert
tectrice[F] sous-caudale
flank
flanc[M]
tarsus
tarse[M]
abdomen
abdomen[M]
thigh
tibia[M]
hind toe
doigt[M] postérieur
inner toe
doigt[M] interne
outer toe
doigt[M] externe
middle toe
doigt[M] médian
claw
ongle[M]

head
tête[F]

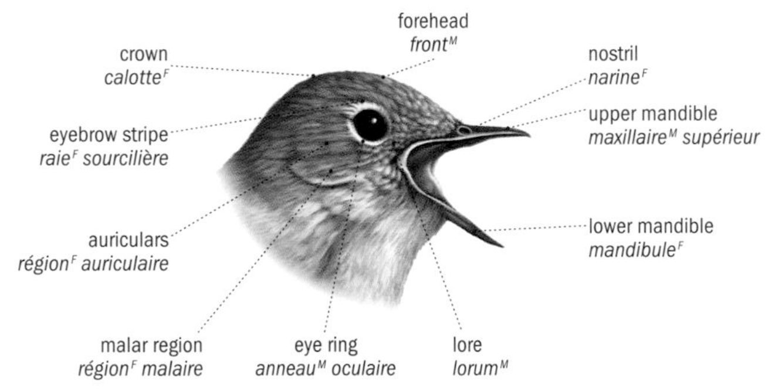
forehead
front[M]
crown
calotte[F]
nostril
narine[F]
upper mandible
maxillaire[M] supérieur
eyebrow stripe
raie[F] sourcilière
lower mandible
mandibule[F]
auriculars
région[F] auriculaire
malar region
région[F] malaire
eye ring
anneau[M] oculaire
lore
lorum[M]

wing
aile[F]

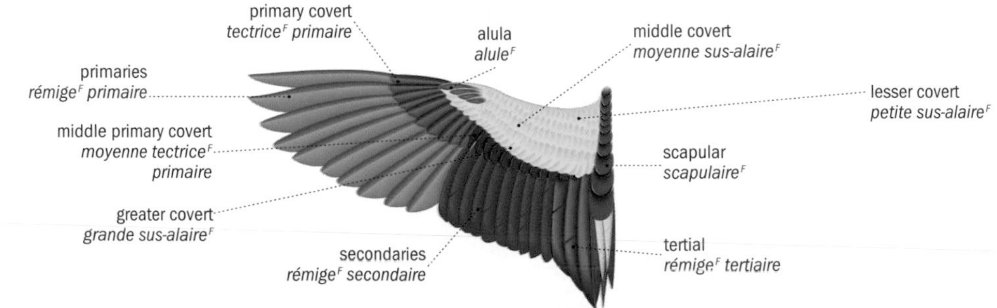
primary covert
tectrice[F] primaire
alula
alule[F]
middle covert
moyenne sus-alaire[F]
primaries
rémige[F] primaire
lesser covert
petite sus-alaire[F]
middle primary covert
moyenne tectrice[F] primaire
scapular
scapulaire[F]
greater covert
grande sus-alaire[F]
tertial
rémige[F] tertiaire
secondaries
rémige[F] secondaire

egg
œuf[M]

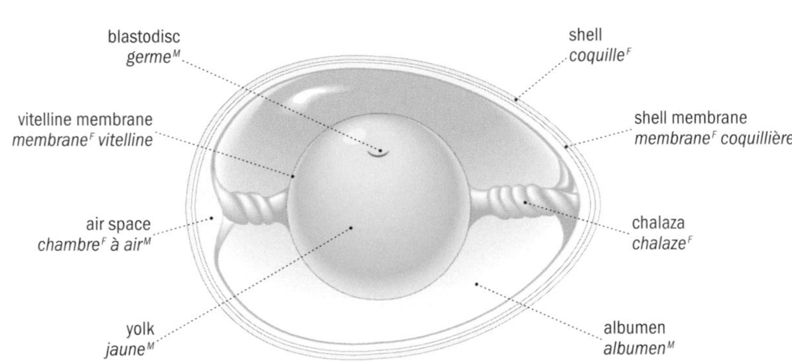

blastodisc
germe[M]
shell
coquille[F]
vitelline membrane
membrane[F] vitelline
shell membrane
membrane[F] coquillière
air space
chambre[F] à air[M]
chalaza
chalaze[F]
yolk
jaune[M]
albumen
albumen[M]

examples of bills
exemples[M] de becs[M]

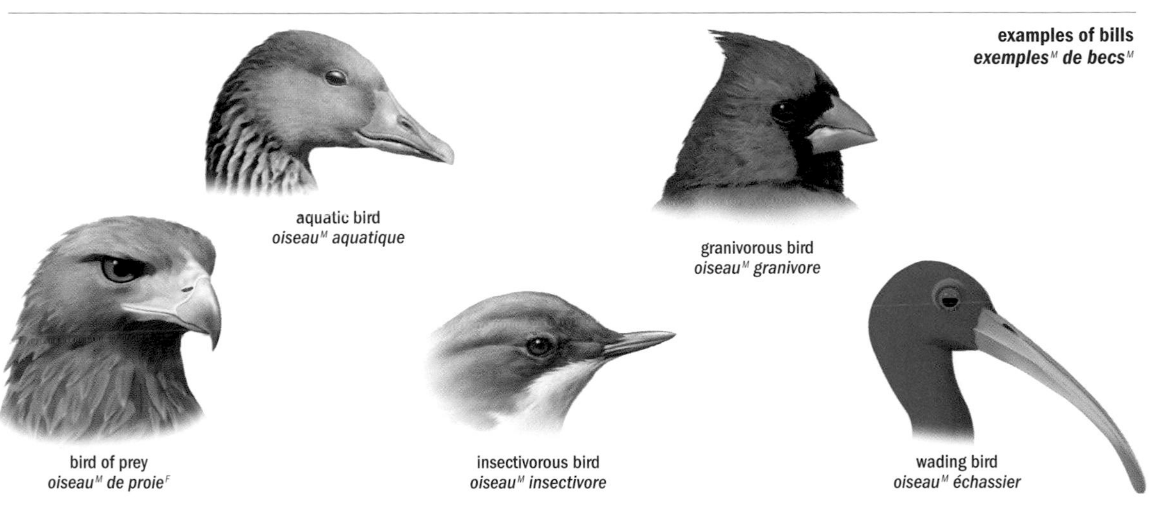

aquatic bird
oiseau[M] aquatique
granivorous bird
oiseau[M] granivore
bird of prey
oiseau[M] de proie[F]
insectivorous bird
oiseau[M] insectivore
wading bird
oiseau[M] échassier

examples of feet
exemples[M] de pattes[F]

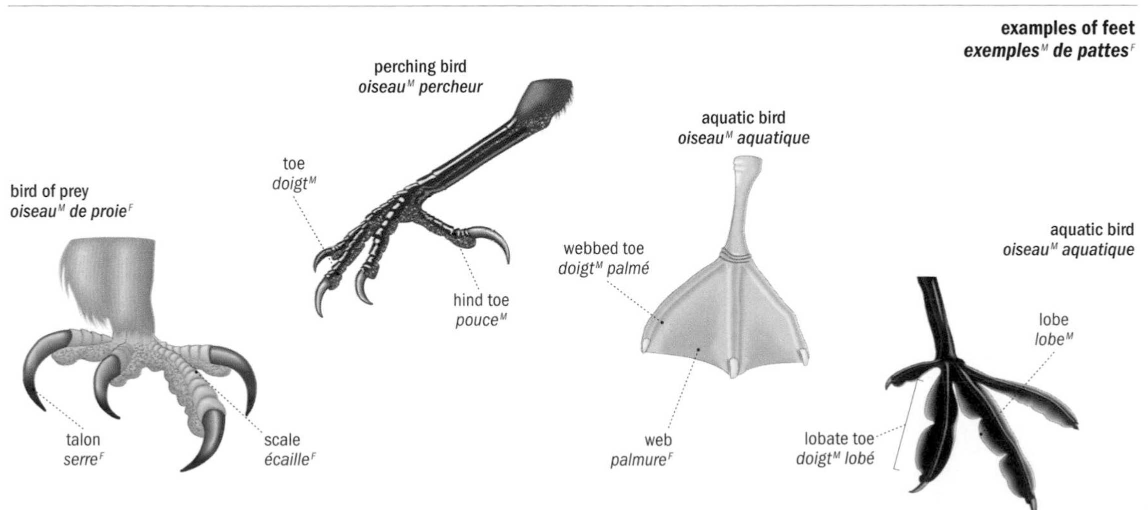

perching bird
oiseau[M] percheur
aquatic bird
oiseau[M] aquatique
toe
doigt[M]
bird of prey
oiseau[M] de proie[F]
aquatic bird
oiseau[M] aquatique
webbed toe
doigt[M] palmé
hind toe
pouce[M]
lobe
lobe[M]
talon
serre[F]
scale
écaille[F]
web
palmure[F]
lobate toe
doigt[M] lobé

examples of birds

exemples[M] d'oiseaux[M]

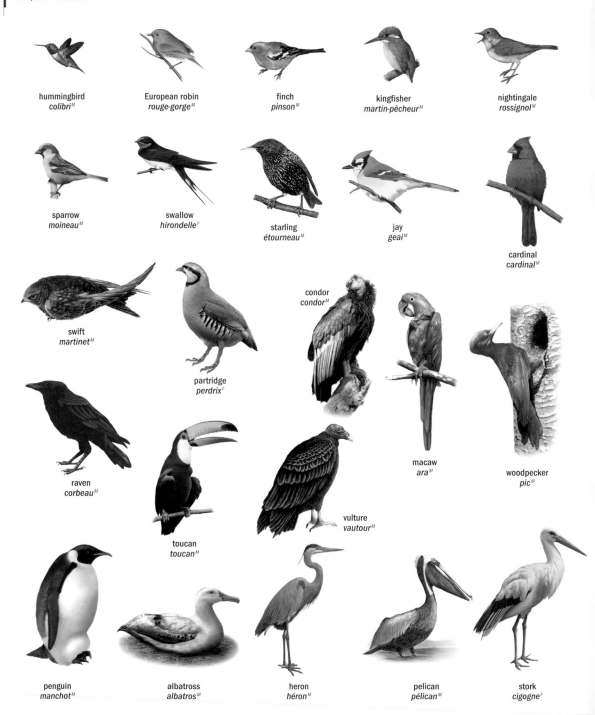

hummingbird
colibri[M]

European robin
rouge-gorge[M]

finch
pinson[M]

kingfisher
martin-pêcheur[M]

nightingale
rossignol[M]

sparrow
moineau[M]

swallow
hirondelle[F]

starling
étourneau[M]

jay
geai[M]

cardinal
cardinal[M]

swift
martinet[M]

partridge
perdrix[F]

condor
condor[M]

macaw
ara[M]

woodpecker
pic[M]

raven
corbeau[M]

toucan
toucan[M]

vulture
vautour[M]

penguin
manchot[M]

albatross
albatros[M]

heron
héron[M]

pelican
pélican[M]

stork
cigogne[F]

pheasant
*faisan*M
great horned owl
*grand duc*M *d'Amérique*F
falcon
*faucon*M
quail
*caille*F
eagle
*aigle*M
duck
*canard*M
pigeon
*pigeon*M
hen
*poule*F
turkey
*dindon*M
guinea fowl
*pintade*F
goose
*oie*F
rooster
*coq*M
ostrich
*autruche*F
peacock
*paon*M
flamingo
*flamant*M

rodent

rongeur[M]

morphology of a rat
morphologie[F] du rat[M]

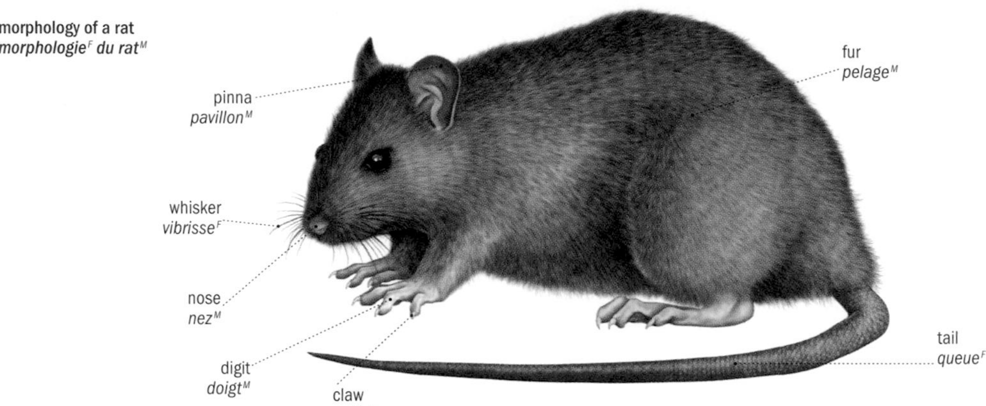
pinna
pavillon[M]
fur
pelage[M]
whisker
vibrisse[F]
nose
nez[M]
digit
doigt[M]
claw
griffe[F]
tail
queue[F]

examples of rodents

exemples[M] de mammifères[M] rongeurs[M]

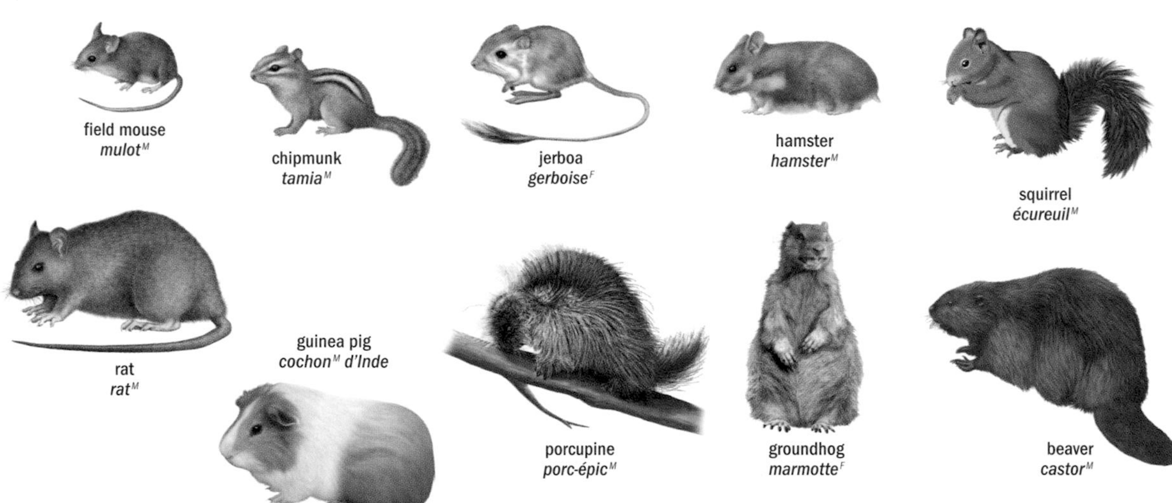
field mouse
mulot[M]
chipmunk
tamia[M]
jerboa
gerboise[F]
hamster
hamster[M]
squirrel
écureuil[M]
rat
rat[M]
guinea pig
cochon[M] d'Inde
porcupine
porc-épic[M]
groundhog
marmotte[F]
beaver
castor[M]

examples of lagomorphs

exemples[M] de mammifères[M] lagomorphes[M]

pika
pika[M]

rabbit
lapin[M]

hare
lièvre[M]

horse

cheval[M]

morphology of a horse
morphologie[F] du cheval[M]

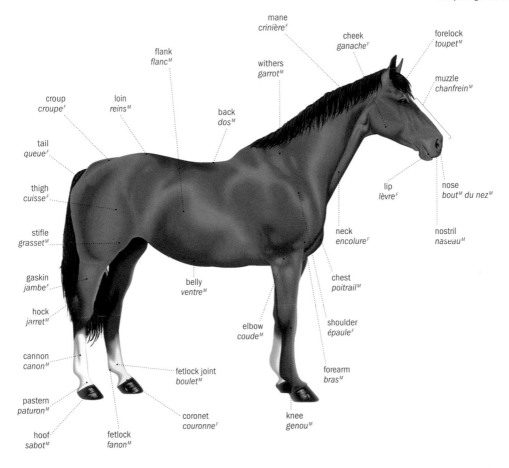

mane
crinière[F]

cheek
ganache[F]

forelock
toupet[M]

flank
flanc[M]

withers
garrot[M]

muzzle
chanfrein[M]

croup
croupe[F]

loin
reins[M]

back
dos[M]

tail
queue[F]

thigh
cuisse[F]

lip
lèvre[F]

nose
bout[M] du nez[M]

stifle
grasset[M]

neck
encolure[F]

nostril
naseau[M]

gaskin
jambe[F]

belly
ventre[M]

chest
poitrail[M]

hock
jarret[M]

elbow
coude[M]

shoulder
épaule[F]

cannon
canon[M]

fetlock joint
boulet[M]

forearm
bras[M]

pastern
paturon[M]

coronet
couronne[F]

knee
genou[M]

hoof
sabot[M]

fetlock
fanon[M]

gaits
allures[F]

walk
pas[M]

pace
amble[M]

trot
trot[M]

canter
galop[M]

examples of ungulate mammals

exemples[M] de mammifères[M] ongulés

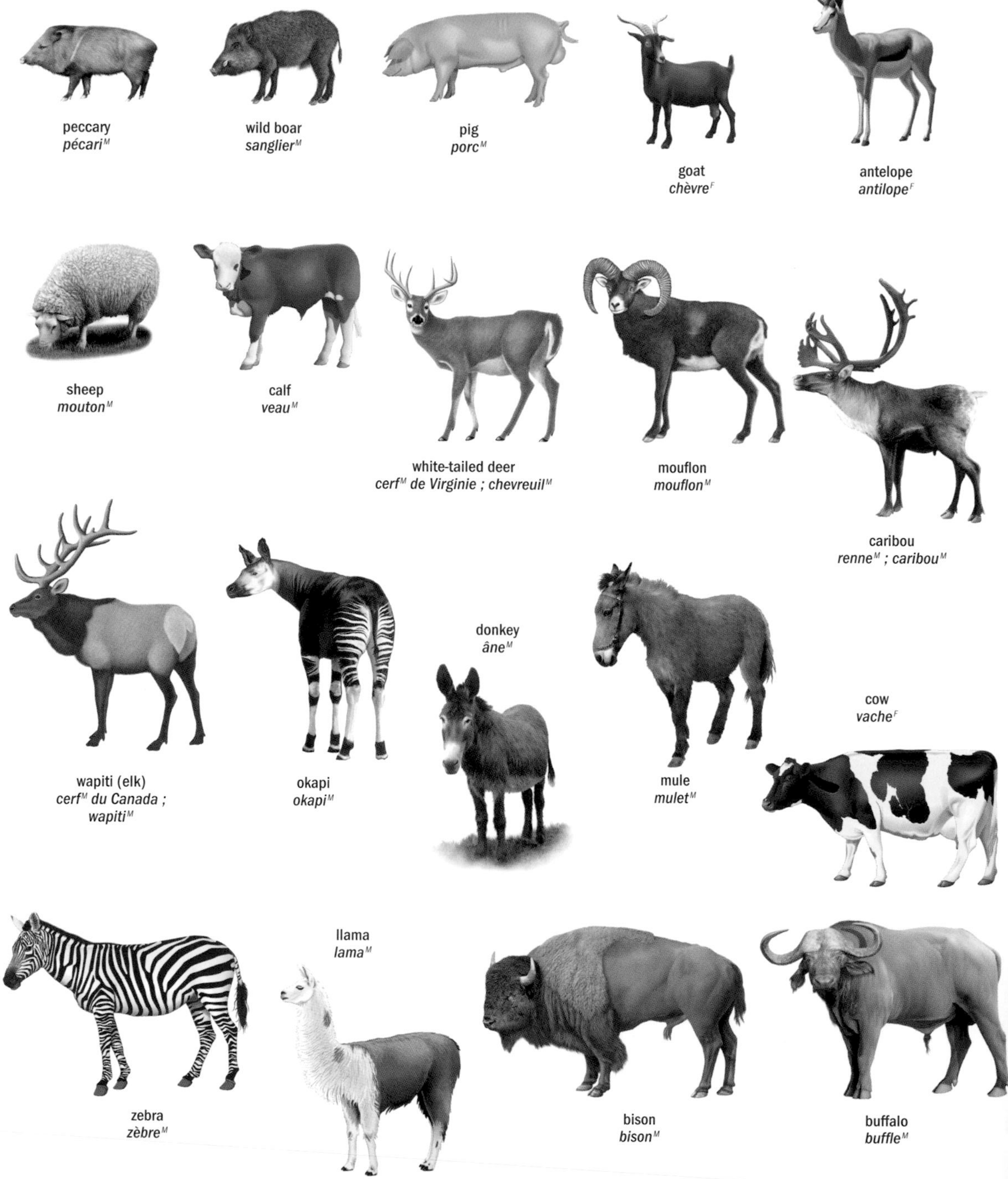
peccary
pécari[M]
wild boar
sanglier[M]
pig
porc[M]
goat
chèvre[F]
antelope
antilope[F]
sheep
mouton[M]
calf
veau[M]
white-tailed deer
cerf[M] de Virginie ; chevreuil[M]
mouflon
mouflon[M]
caribou
renne[M] ; caribou[M]
wapiti (elk)
cerf[M] du Canada ;
wapiti[M]
okapi
okapi[M]
donkey
âne[M]
mule
mulet[M]
cow
vache[F]
zebra
zèbre[M]
llama
lama[M]
bison
bison[M]
buffalo
buffle[M]

examples of ungulate mammals

ox
bœuf[M]

yak
yack[M]

horse
cheval[M]

moose
élan[M] *; orignal*[M]

bactrian camel
chameau[M]

dromedary camel
dromadaire[M]

rhinoceros
rhinocéros[M]

hippopotamus
hippopotame[M]

giraffe
girafe[F]

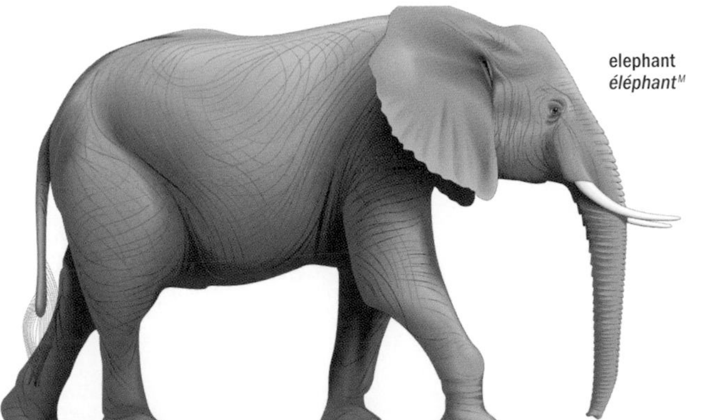
elephant
éléphant[M]

dog

chien[M]

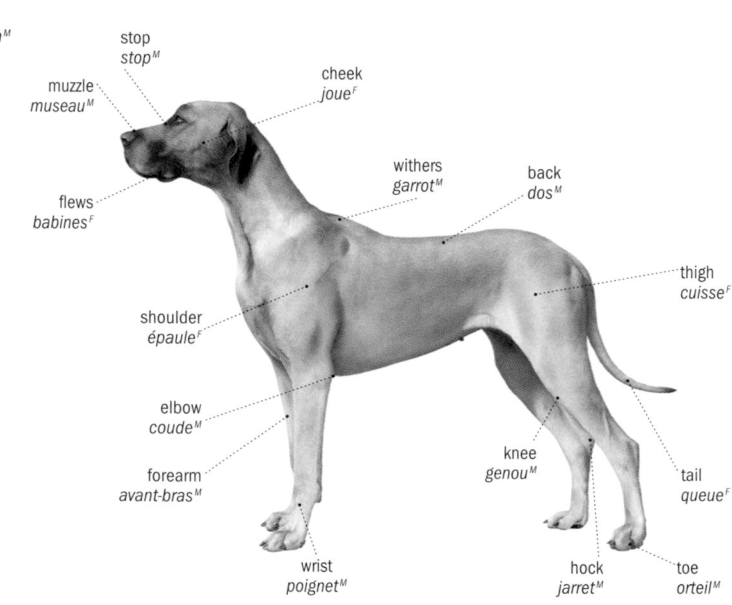

stop
stop[M]
muzzle
museau[M]
cheek
joue[F]
flews
babines[F]
withers
garrot[M]
back
dos[M]
thigh
cuisse[F]
shoulder
épaule[F]
elbow
coude[M]
forearm
avant-bras[M]
knee
genou[M]
tail
queue[F]
wrist
poignet[M]
hock
jarret[M]
toe
orteil[M]

morphology of a dog
***morphologie*[F] *du chien*[M]**

examples of dog breeds

races[F] de chiens[M]

bulldog
***bouledogue*[M]**

collie
***colley*[M]**

Dalmatian
***dalmatien*[M]**

poodle
***caniche*[M]**

schnauzer
***schnauzer*[M]**

Great Dane
***danois*[M]**

German shepherd
berger*[M] *allemand

Saint Bernard
***saint-bernard*[M]**

cat
chat^M

cat's head
tête^F

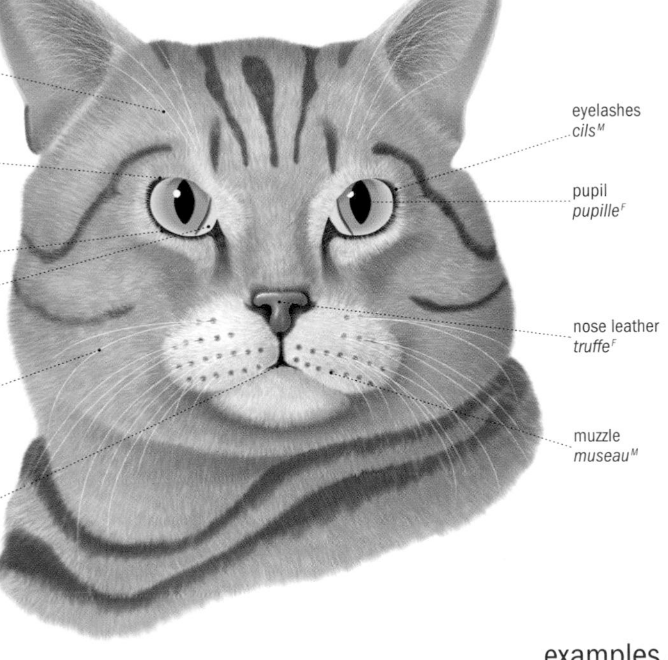

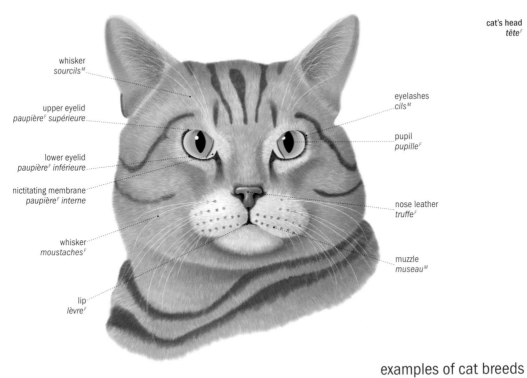

whisker
sourcils^M
upper eyelid
paupière^F supérieure
lower eyelid
paupière^F inférieure
nictitating membrane
paupière^F interne
whisker
moustaches^F
lip
lèvre^F
eyelashes
cils^M
pupil
pupille^F
nose leather
truffe^F
muzzle
museau^M

examples of cat breeds
races^F de chats^M

Siamese
siamois^M
Abyssinian
abyssin^M
Persian
persan^M
Maine coon
Maine coon^M
Manx
chat^M de l'île^F de Man

examples of carnivorous mammals

exemples[M] de mammifères[M] carnivores

weasel
belette[F]
mink
vison[M]
stone marten
fouine[F]
marten
martre[F]
fox
renard[M]
raccoon
raton[M] *laveur*
mongoose
mangouste[F]
fennec
fennec[M]
river otter
loutre[F] *de rivière*[F]
skunk
moufette[F]
badger
blaireau[M]
hyena
hyène[F]
lynx
lynx[M]
wolf
loup[M]
cougar
puma[M]

examples of carnivorous mammals

cheetah
guépard[M]
leopard
léopard[M]
lion
lion[M]
jaguar
jaguar[M]
tiger
tigre[M]
black bear
ours[M] *noir*
polar bear
ours[M] *polaire*

dolphin

dauphin[M]

morphology of a dolphin
morphologie[F] du dauphin[M]

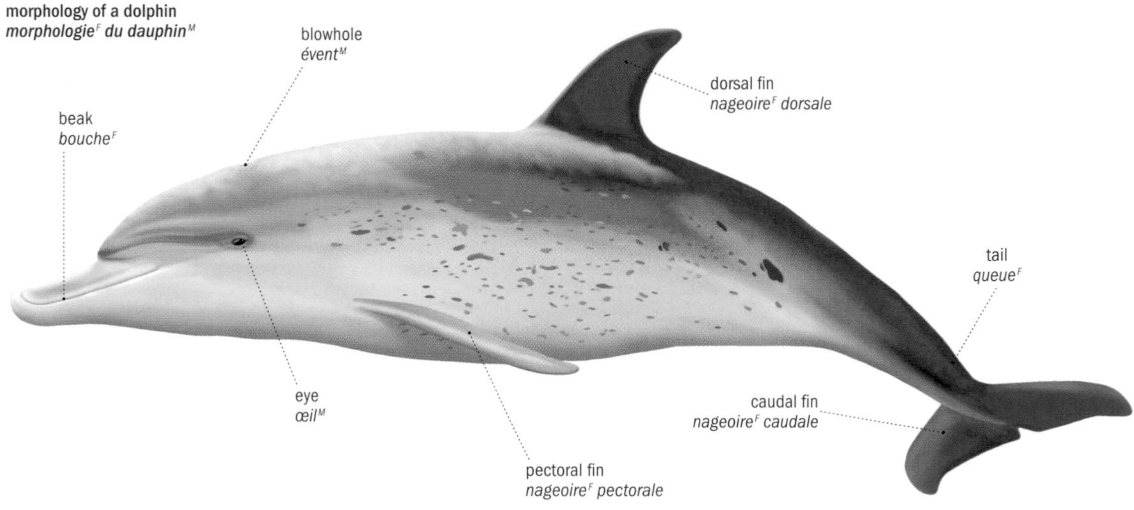
blowhole
évent[M]
dorsal fin
nageoire[F] dorsale
beak
bouche[F]
tail
queue[F]
eye
œil[M]
caudal fin
nageoire[F] caudale
pectoral fin
nageoire[F] pectorale

examples of marine mammals

exemples[M] de mammifères[M] marins

killer whale
orque[F]

seal
phoque[M]

humpback whale
rorqual[M]

northern right whale
baleine[F] franche

sperm whale
cachalot[M]

sea lion
otarie[F]

gorilla

gorille[M]

morphology of a gorilla
morphologie[F] du gorille[M]

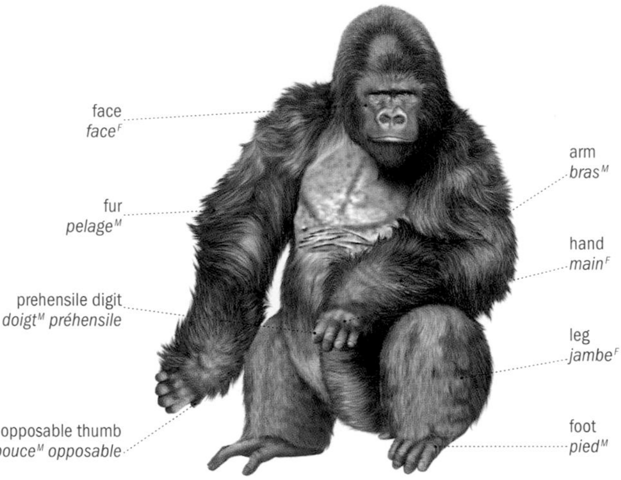
face
face[F]
fur
pelage[M]
prehensile digit
doigt[M] préhensile
opposable thumb
pouce[M] opposable
arm
bras[M]
hand
main[F]
leg
jambe[F]
foot
pied[M]

examples of primates

exemples[M] de mammifères[M] primates[M]

tamarin
tamarin[M]

baboon
babouin[M]

macaque
macaque[M]

marmoset
ouistiti[M]

orangutan
orang-outan[M]

chimpanzee
chimpanzé[M]

lemur
lémurien[M]

gibbon
gibbon[M]

man

homme[M]

anterior view
face[F] antérieure

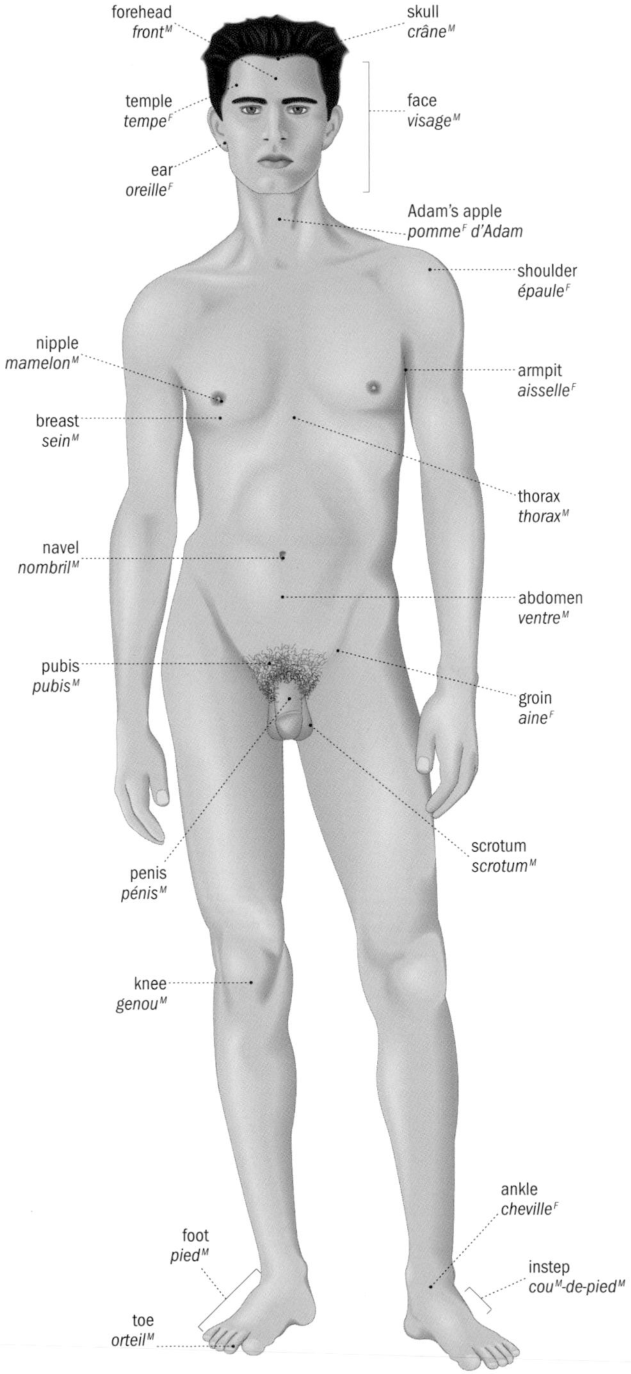

forehead
front[M]

skull
crâne[M]

temple
tempe[F]

face
visage[M]

ear
oreille[F]

Adam's apple
pomme[F] d'Adam

shoulder
épaule[F]

nipple
mamelon[M]

armpit
aisselle[F]

breast
sein[M]

thorax
thorax[M]

navel
nombril[M]

abdomen
ventre[M]

pubis
pubis[M]

groin
aine[F]

scrotum
scrotum[M]

penis
pénis[M]

knee
genou[M]

ankle
cheville[F]

foot
pied[M]

instep
cou[M]-de-pied[M]

toe
orteil[M]

posterior view
face[F] postérieure

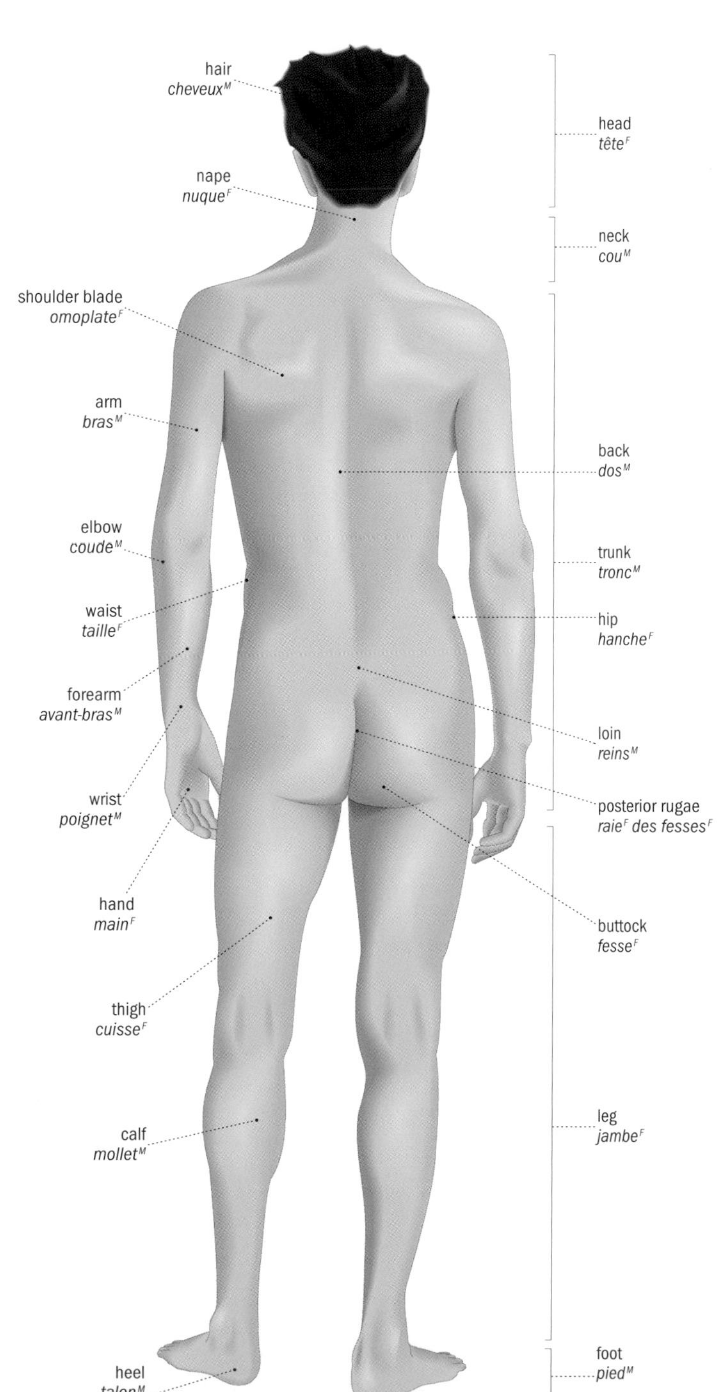
hair
cheveux[M]
nape
nuque[F]
shoulder blade
omoplate[F]
arm
bras[M]
elbow
coude[M]
waist
taille[F]
forearm
avant-bras[M]
wrist
poignet[M]
hand
main[F]
thigh
cuisse[F]
calf
mollet[M]
heel
talon[M]
head
tête[F]
neck
cou[M]
back
dos[M]
trunk
tronc[M]
hip
hanche[F]
loin
reins[M]
posterior rugae
raie[F] des fesses[F]
buttock
fesse[F]
leg
jambe[F]
foot
pied[M]

woman

femme[F]

anterior view
face[F] antérieure

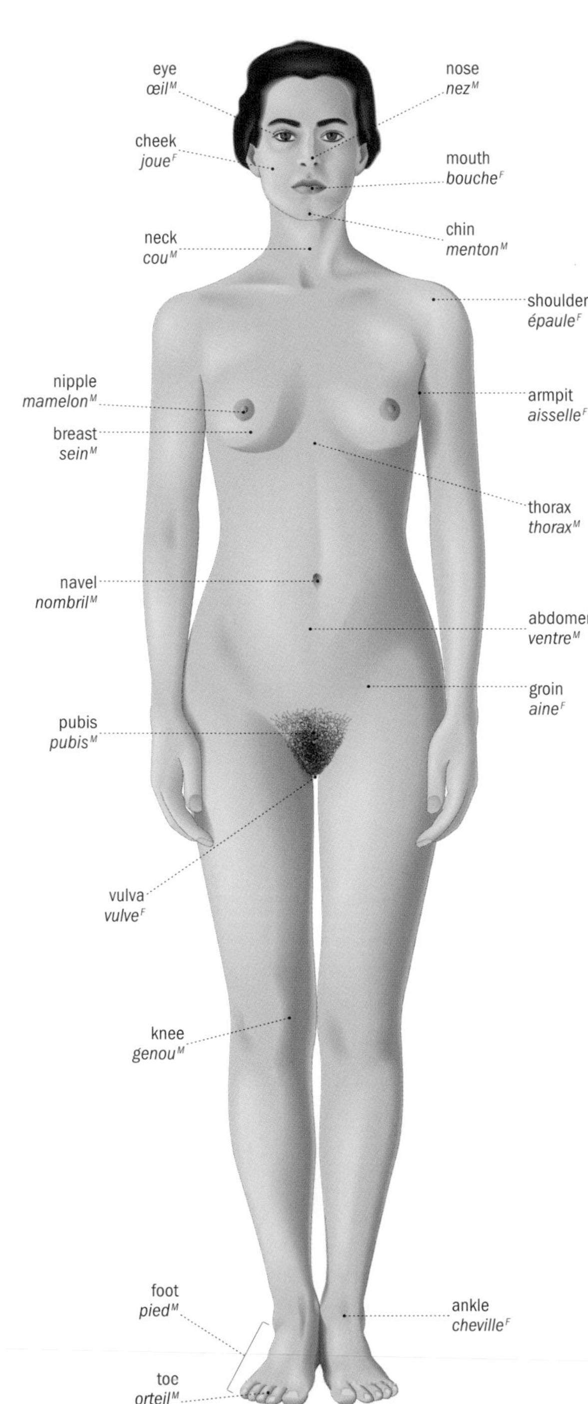
eye
œil[M]
nose
nez[M]
cheek
joue[F]
mouth
bouche[F]
chin
menton[M]
neck
cou[M]
shoulder
épaule[F]
nipple
mamelon[M]
armpit
aisselle[F]
breast
sein[M]
thorax
thorax[M]
navel
nombril[M]
abdomen
ventre[M]
groin
aine[F]
pubis
pubis[M]
vulva
vulve[F]
knee
genou[M]
foot
pied[M]
ankle
cheville[F]
toe
orteil[M]

posterior view
face^F postérieure

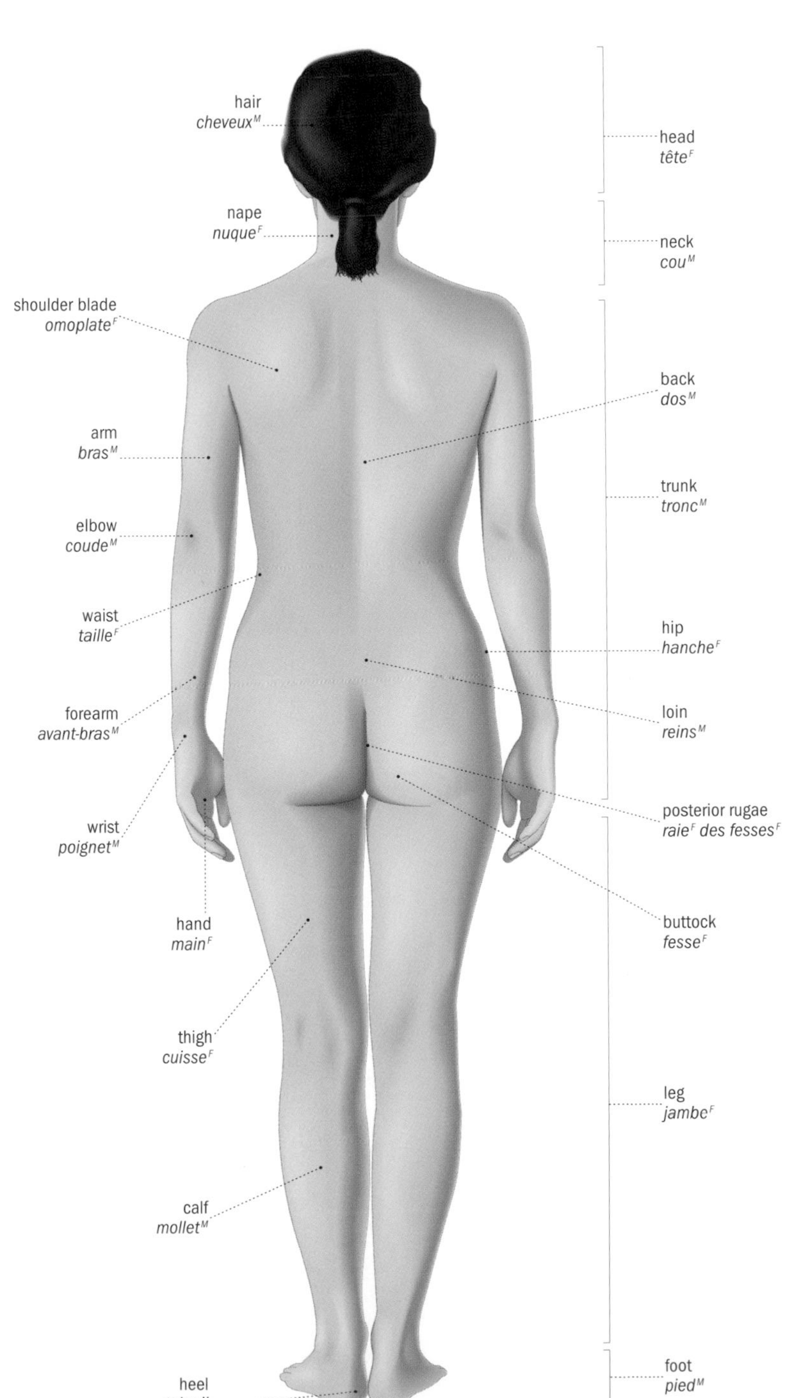
hair
cheveux^M
nape
nuque^F
shoulder blade
omoplate^F
arm
bras^M
elbow
coude^M
waist
taille^F
forearm
avant-bras^M
wrist
poignet^M
hand
main^F
thigh
cuisse^F
calf
mollet^M
heel
talon^M
head
tête^F
neck
cou^M
back
dos^M
trunk
tronc^M
hip
hanche^F
loin
reins^M
posterior rugae
raie^F des fesses^F
buttock
fesse^F
leg
jambe^F
foot
pied^M

muscles

muscles^M

anterior view
face^F antérieure

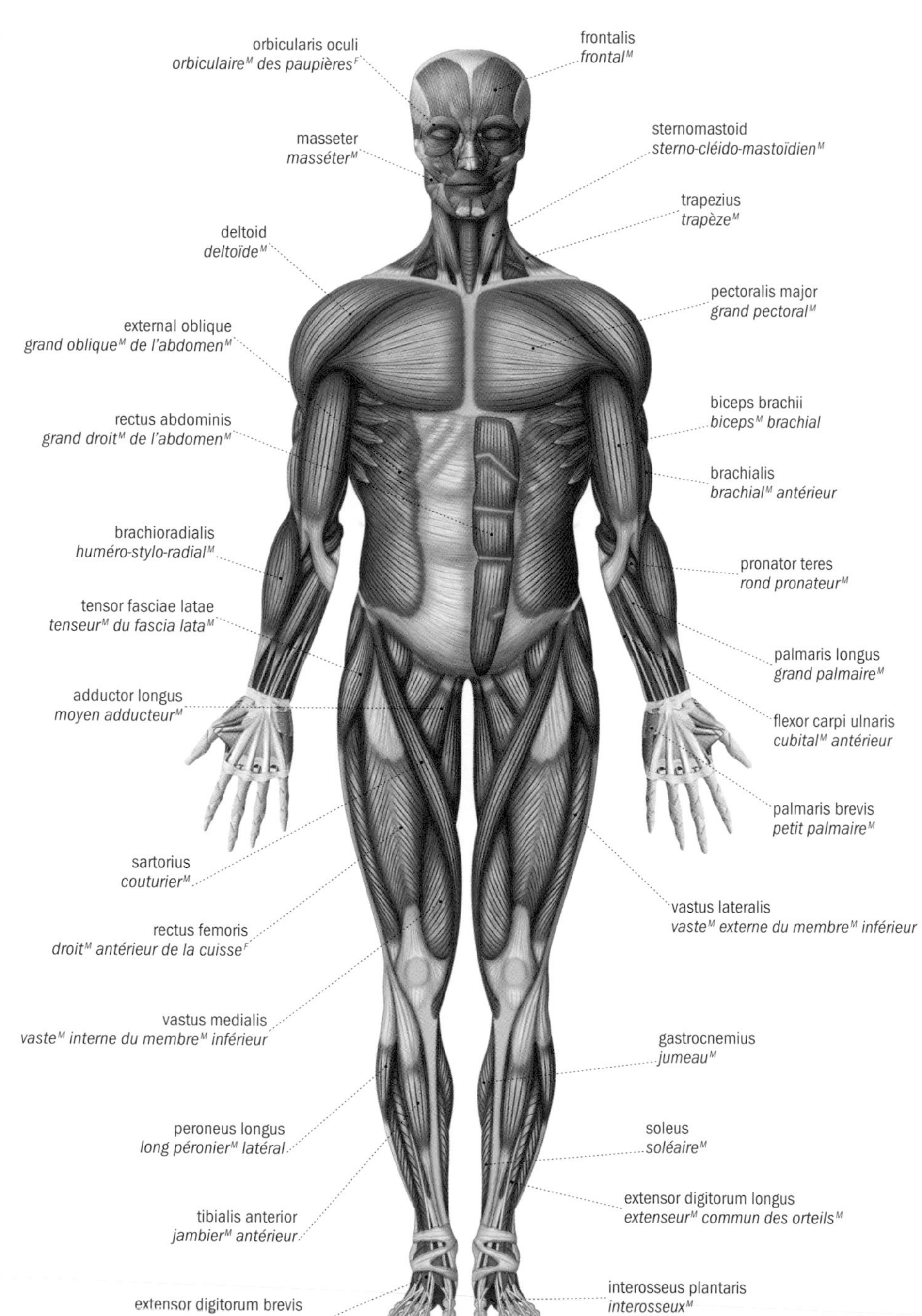
orbicularis oculi
orbiculaire^M des paupières^F
frontalis
frontal^M
masseter
masséter^M
sternomastoid
sterno-cléido-mastoïdien^M
trapezius
trapèze^M
deltoid
deltoïde^M
pectoralis major
grand pectoral^M
external oblique
grand oblique^M de l'abdomen^M
biceps brachii
biceps^M brachial
rectus abdominis
grand droit^M de l'abdomen^M
brachialis
brachial^M antérieur
brachioradialis
huméro-stylo-radial^M
pronator teres
rond pronateur^M
tensor fasciae latae
tenseur^M du fascia lata^M
palmaris longus
grand palmaire^M
adductor longus
moyen adducteur^M
flexor carpi ulnaris
cubital^M antérieur
palmaris brevis
petit palmaire^M
sartorius
couturier^M
vastus lateralis
vaste^M externe du membre^M inférieur
rectus femoris
droit^M antérieur de la cuisse^F
vastus medialis
vaste^M interne du membre^M inférieur
gastrocnemius
jumeau^M
peroneus longus
long péronier^M latéral
soleus
soléaire^M
extensor digitorum longus
extenseur^M commun des orteils^M
tibialis anterior
jambier^M antérieur
interosseus plantaris
interosseux^M
extensor digitorum brevis
pédieux^M

posterior view
face^F postérieure

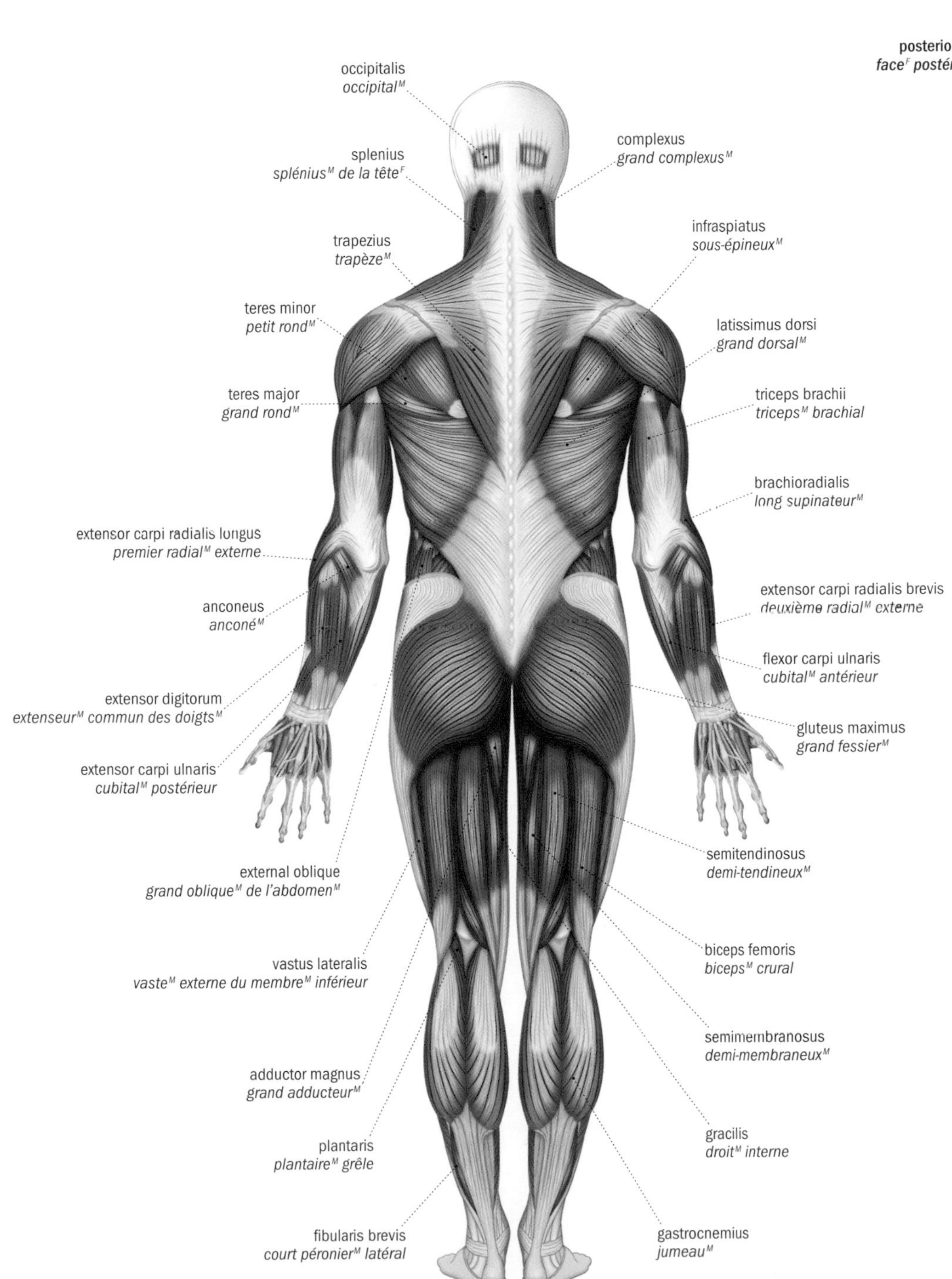
occipitalis
occipital^M
complexus
grand complexus^M
splenius
splénius^M de la tête^F
infraspiatus
sous-épineux^M
trapezius
trapèze^M
teres minor
petit rond^M
latissimus dorsi
grand dorsal^M
teres major
grand rond^M
triceps brachii
triceps^M brachial
brachioradialis
long supinateur^M
extensor carpi radialis longus
premier radial^M externe
extensor carpi radialis brevis
deuxième radial^M externe
anconeus
anconé^M
flexor carpi ulnaris
cubital^M antérieur
extensor digitorum
extenseur^M commun des doigts^M
gluteus maximus
grand fessier^M
extensor carpi ulnaris
cubital^M postérieur
semitendinosus
demi-tendineux^M
external oblique
grand oblique^M de l'abdomen^M
biceps femoris
biceps^M crural
vastus lateralis
vaste^M externe du membre^M inférieur
semimembranosus
demi-membraneux^M
adductor magnus
grand adducteur^M
gracilis
droit^M interne
plantaris
plantaire^M grêle
fibularis brevis
court péronier^M latéral
gastrocnemius
jumeau^M

skeleton

squelette[M]

anterior view
vue[F] antérieure

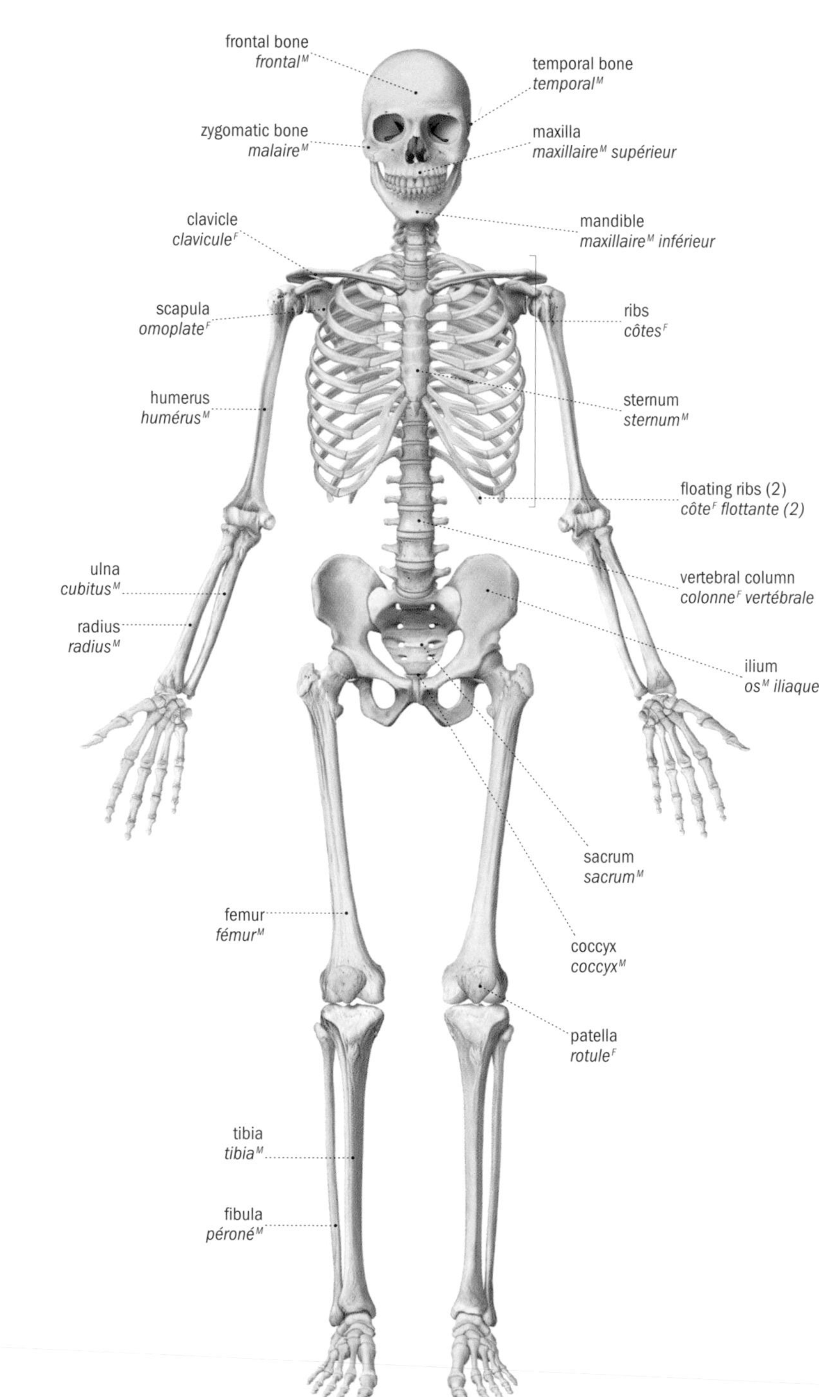

frontal bone
frontal[M]
temporal bone
temporal[M]
zygomatic bone
malaire[M]
maxilla
maxillaire[M] supérieur
clavicle
clavicule[F]
mandible
maxillaire[M] inférieur
scapula
omoplate[F]
ribs
côtes[F]
humerus
humérus[M]
sternum
sternum[M]
floating ribs (2)
côte[F] flottante (2)
vertebral column
colonne[F] vertébrale
ulna
cubitus[M]
radius
radius[M]
ilium
os[M] iliaque
sacrum
sacrum[M]
femur
fémur[M]
coccyx
coccyx[M]
patella
rotule[F]
tibia
tibia[M]
fibula
péroné[M]

posterior view
vue^F postérieure

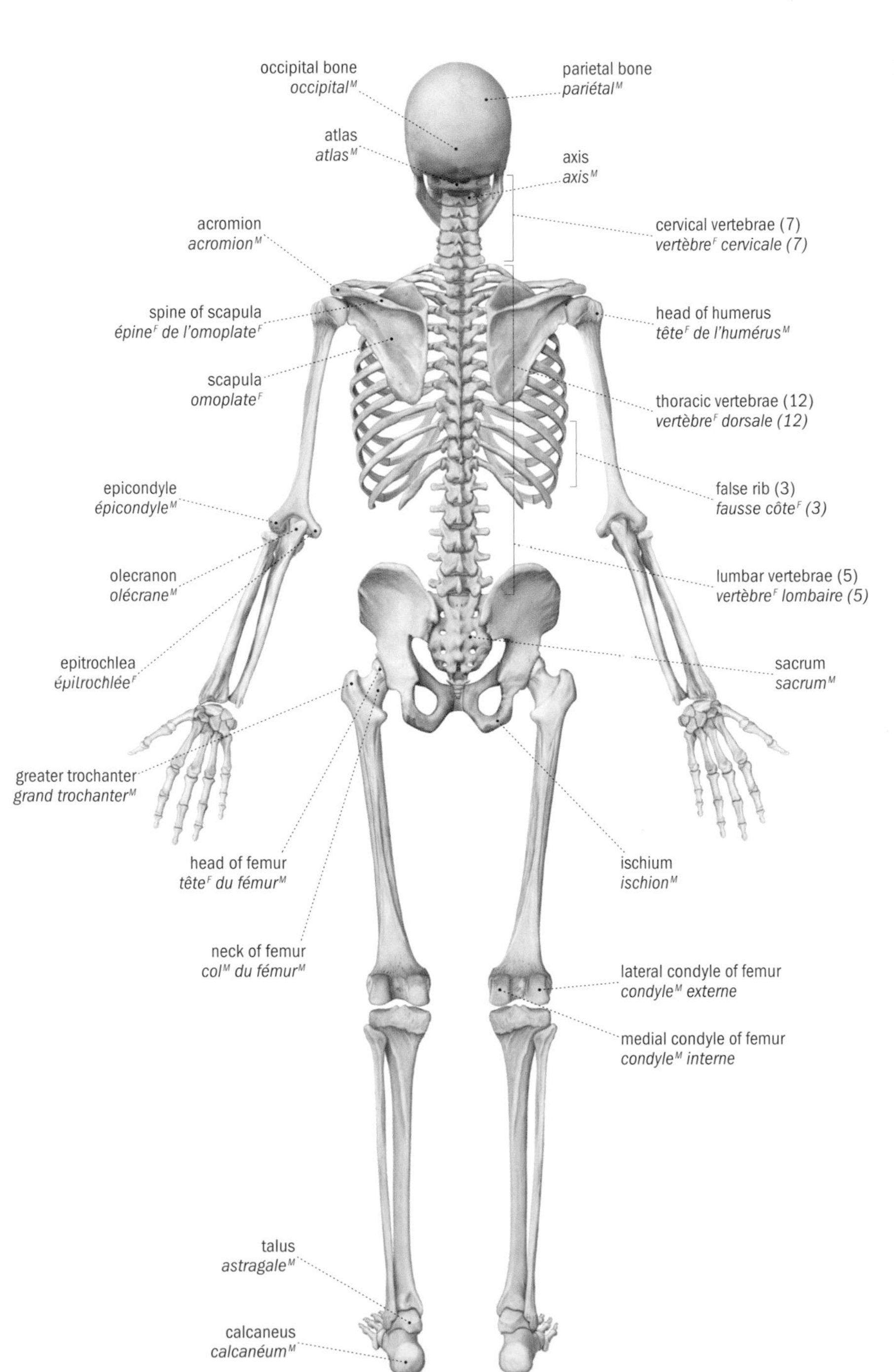
occipital bone
occipital^M
parietal bone
pariétal^M
atlas
atlas^M
axis
axis^M
acromion
acromion^M
cervical vertebrae (7)
vertèbre^F cervicale (7)
spine of scapula
épine^F de l'omoplate^F
head of humerus
tête^F de l'humérus^M
scapula
omoplate^F
thoracic vertebrae (12)
vertèbre^F dorsale (12)
epicondyle
épicondyle^M
false rib (3)
fausse côte^F (3)
olecranon
olécrane^M
lumbar vertebrae (5)
vertèbre^F lombaire (5)
epitrochlea
épitrochlée^F
sacrum
sacrum^M
greater trochanter
grand trochanter^M
head of femur
tête^F du fémur^M
ischium
ischion^M
neck of femur
col^M du fémur^M
lateral condyle of femur
condyle^M externe
medial condyle of femur
condyle^M interne
talus
astragale^M
calcaneus
calcanéum^M

skeleton

HUMAN BEING

lateral view of adult skull
vue[F] latérale du crâne[M] adulte

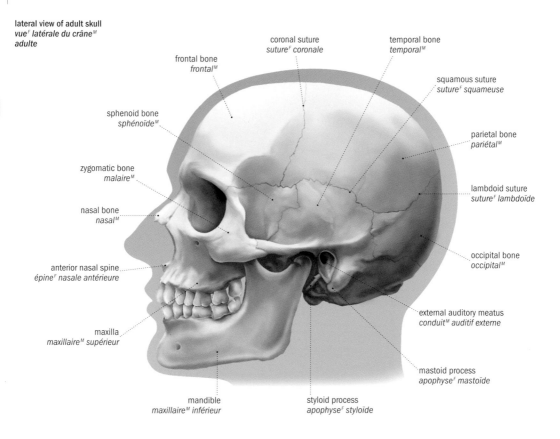

coronal suture
suture[F] coronale

temporal bone
temporal[M]

frontal bone
frontal[M]

squamous suture
suture[F] squameuse

sphenoid bone
sphénoïde[M]

parietal bone
pariétal[M]

zygomatic bone
malaire[M]

lambdoid suture
suture[F] lambdoïde

nasal bone
nasal[M]

occipital bone
occipital[M]

anterior nasal spine
épine[F] nasale antérieure

external auditory meatus
conduit[M] auditif externe

maxilla
maxillaire[M] supérieur

mastoid process
apophyse[F] mastoïde

mandible
maxillaire[M] inférieur

styloid process
apophyse[F] styloïde

lateral view of child's skull
vue[F] latérale du crâne[M] d'enfant[M]

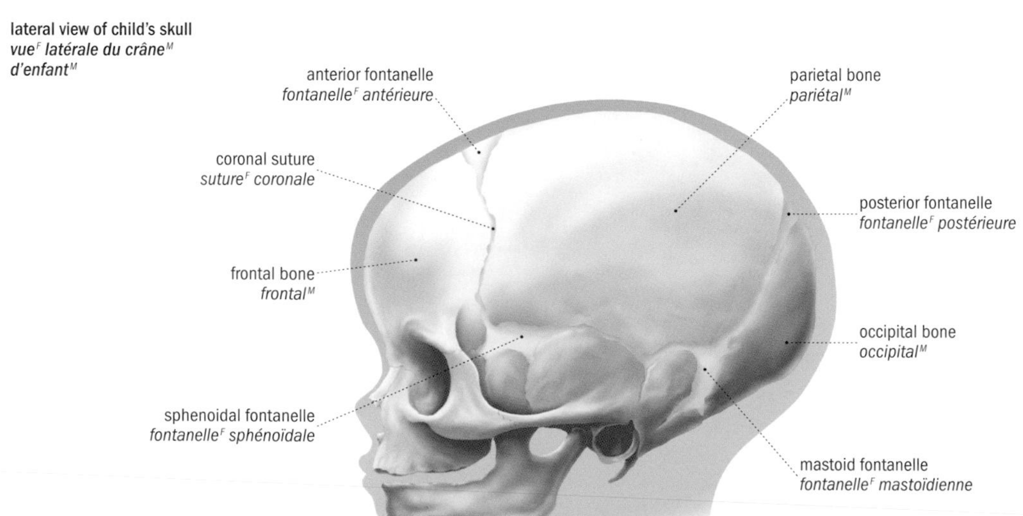
anterior fontanelle
fontanelle[F] antérieure
parietal bone
pariétal[M]
coronal suture
suture[F] coronale
posterior fontanelle
fontanelle[F] postérieure
frontal bone
frontal[M]
occipital bone
occipital[M]
sphenoidal fontanelle
fontanelle[F] sphénoïdale
mastoid fontanelle
fontanelle[F] mastoïdienne

teeth

dents[F]

human denture
denture[F] humaine

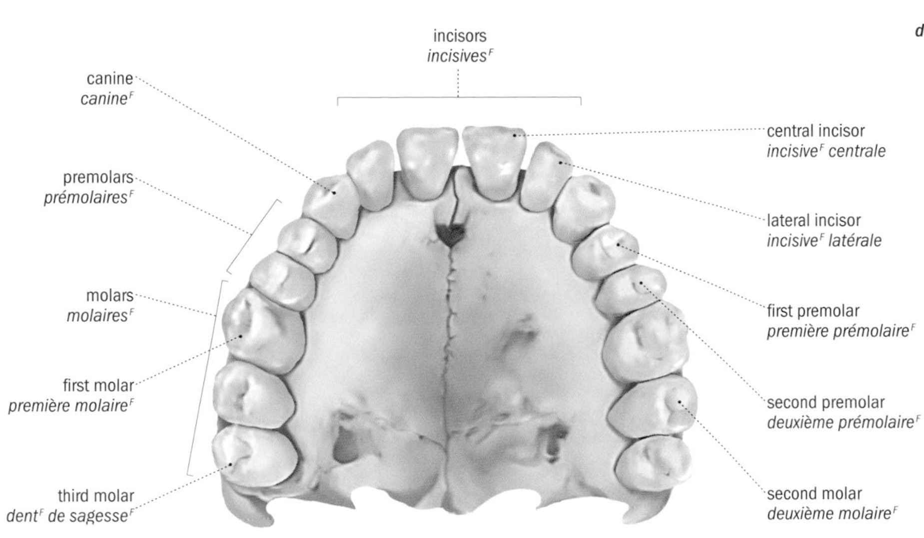
incisors
incisives[F]
canine
canine[F]
central incisor
incisive[F] centrale
premolars
prémolaires[F]
lateral incisor
incisive[F] latérale
molars
molaires[F]
first premolar
première prémolaire[F]
first molar
première molaire[F]
second premolar
deuxième prémolaire[F]
third molar
dent[F] de sagesse[F]
second molar
deuxième molaire[F]

cross section of a molar
coupe[F] d'une molaire[F]

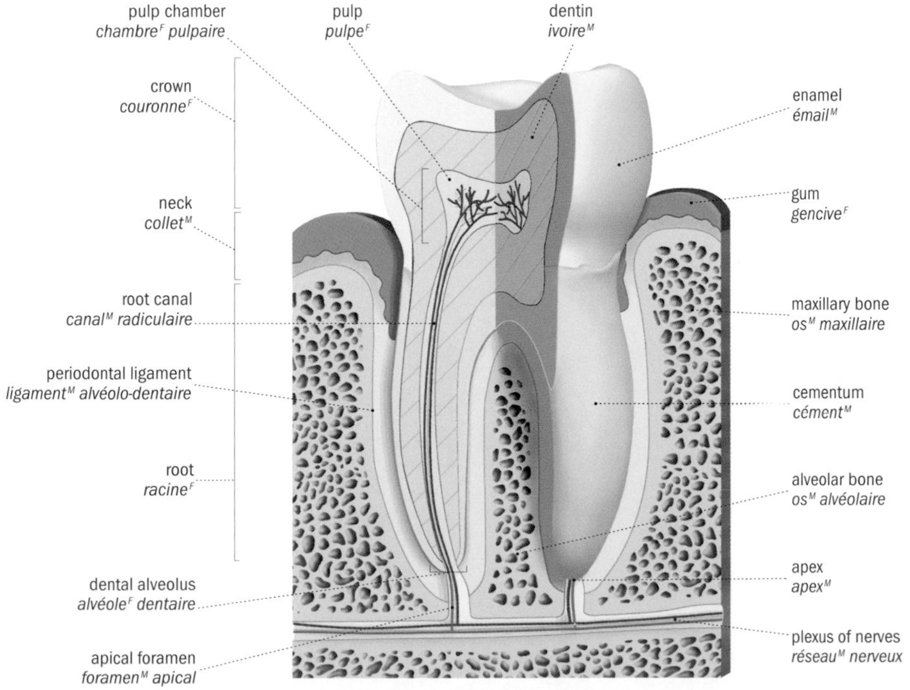

pulp chamber
chambre[F] pulpaire

pulp
pulpe[F]

dentin
ivoire[M]

crown
couronne[F]

enamel
émail[M]

neck
collet[M]

gum
gencive[F]

root canal
canal[M] radiculaire

maxillary bone
os[M] maxillaire

periodontal ligament
ligament[M] alvéolo-dentaire

cementum
cément[M]

root
racine[F]

alveolar bone
os[M] alvéolaire

apex
apex[M]

dental alveolus
alvéole[F] dentaire

plexus of nerves
réseau[M] nerveux

apical foramen
foramen[M] apical

blood circulation

circulation^F sanguine

principal veins and arteries
principales veines^F et artères^F

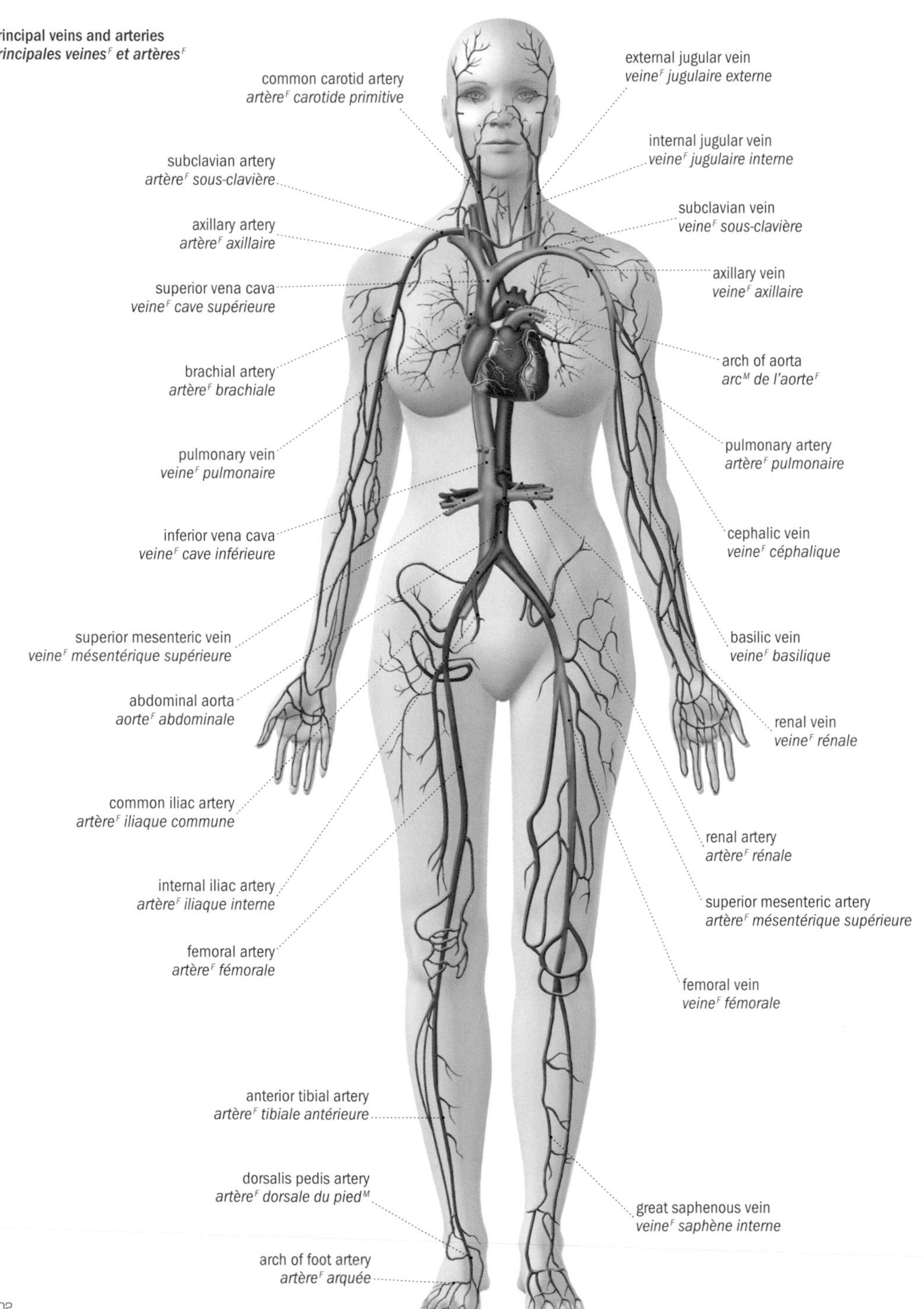

common carotid artery
artère^F carotide primitive
subclavian artery
artère^F sous-clavière
axillary artery
artère^F axillaire
superior vena cava
veine^F cave supérieure
brachial artery
artère^F brachiale
pulmonary vein
veine^F pulmonaire
inferior vena cava
veine^F cave inférieure
superior mesenteric vein
veine^F mésentérique supérieure
abdominal aorta
aorte^F abdominale
common iliac artery
artère^F iliaque commune
internal iliac artery
artère^F iliaque interne
femoral artery
artère^F fémorale
anterior tibial artery
artère^F tibiale antérieure
dorsalis pedis artery
artère^F dorsale du pied^M
arch of foot artery
artère^F arquée
external jugular vein
veine^F jugulaire externe
internal jugular vein
veine^F jugulaire interne
subclavian vein
veine^F sous-clavière
axillary vein
veine^F axillaire
arch of aorta
arc^M de l'aorte^F
pulmonary artery
artère^F pulmonaire
cephalic vein
veine^F céphalique
basilic vein
veine^F basilique
renal vein
veine^F rénale
renal artery
artère^F rénale
superior mesenteric artery
artère^F mésentérique supérieure
femoral vein
veine^F fémorale
great saphenous vein
veine^F saphène interne

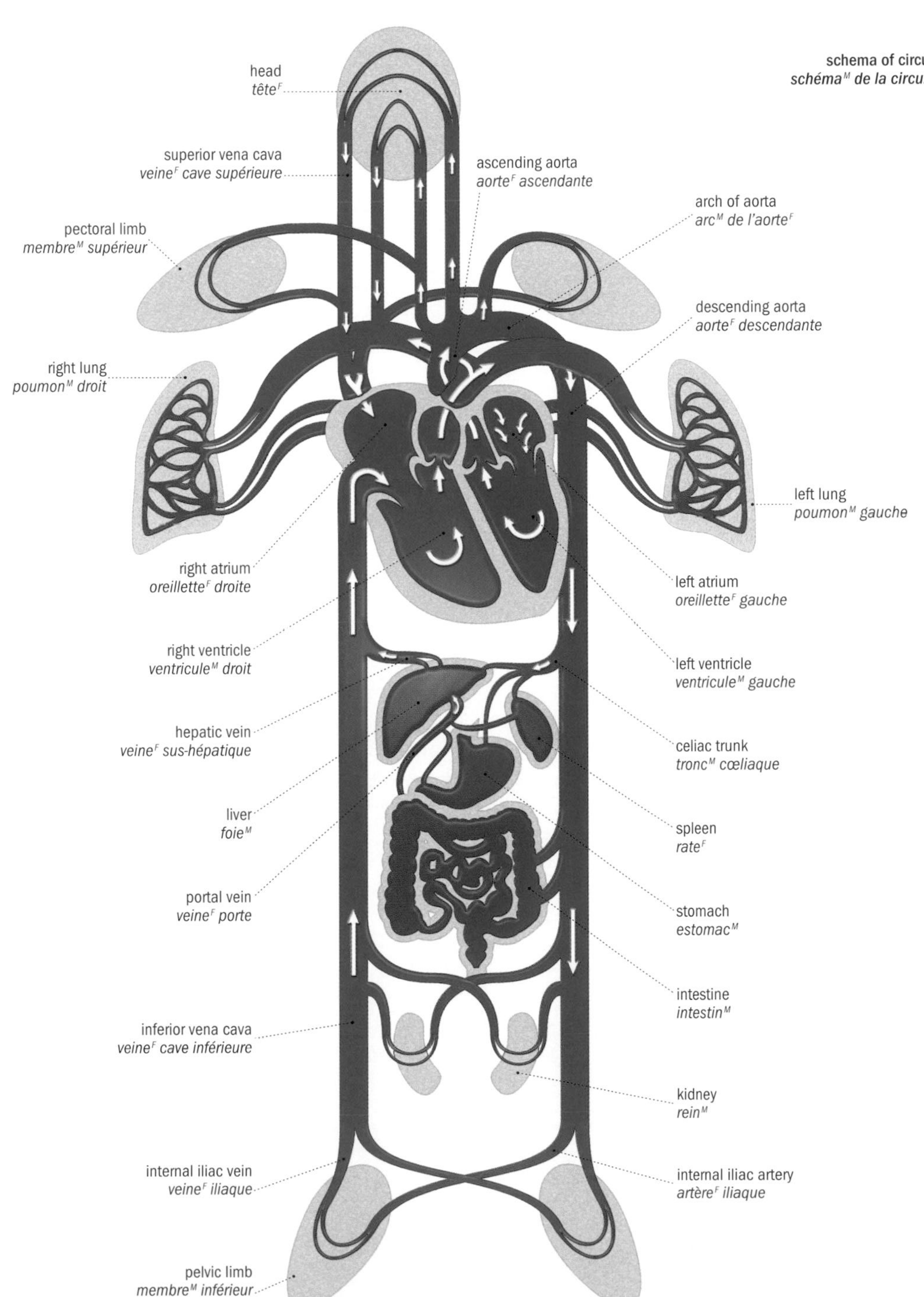
schema of circulation
schéma de la circulation
head
tête
superior vena cava
veine cave supérieure
ascending aorta
aorte ascendante
arch of aorta
arc de l'aorte
pectoral limb
membre supérieur
descending aorta
aorte descendante
right lung
poumon droit
left lung
poumon gauche
right atrium
oreillette droite
left atrium
oreillette gauche
right ventricle
ventricule droit
left ventricle
ventricule gauche
hepatic vein
veine sus-hépatique
celiac trunk
tronc cœliaque
liver
foie
spleen
rate
portal vein
veine porte
stomach
estomac
intestine
intestin
inferior vena cava
veine cave inférieure
kidney
rein
internal iliac vein
veine iliaque
internal iliac artery
artère iliaque
pelvic limb
membre inférieur

blood circulation

composition of the blood
composition[F] du sang[M]

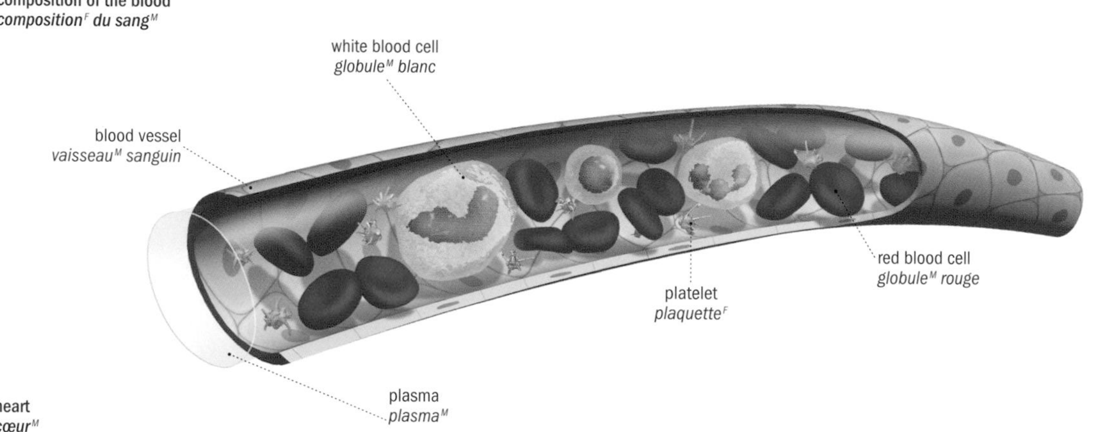
white blood cell
globule[M] blanc
blood vessel
vaisseau[M] sanguin
red blood cell
globule[M] rouge
platelet
plaquette[F]

plasma
plasma[M]

heart
cœur[M]

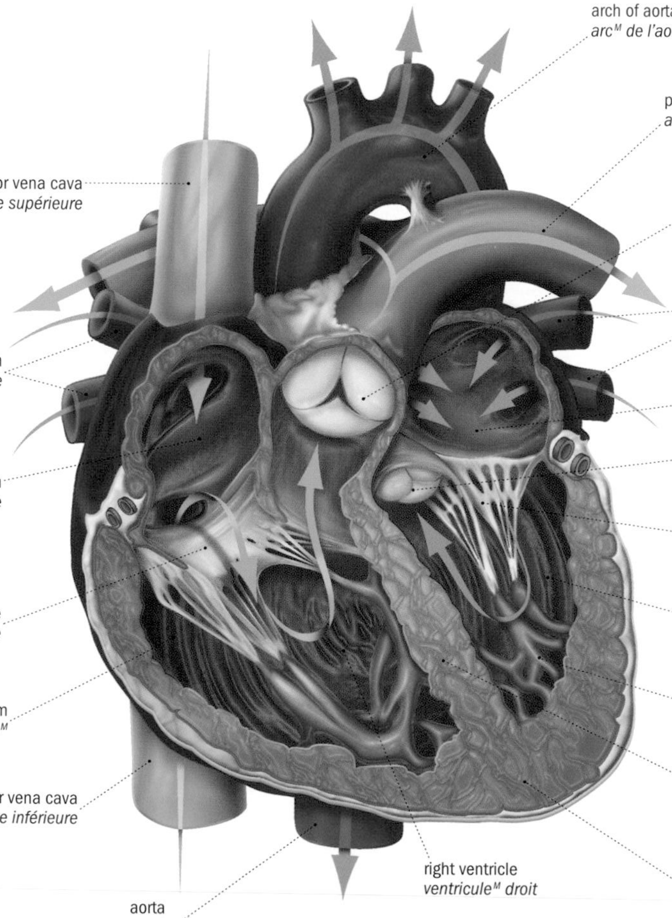

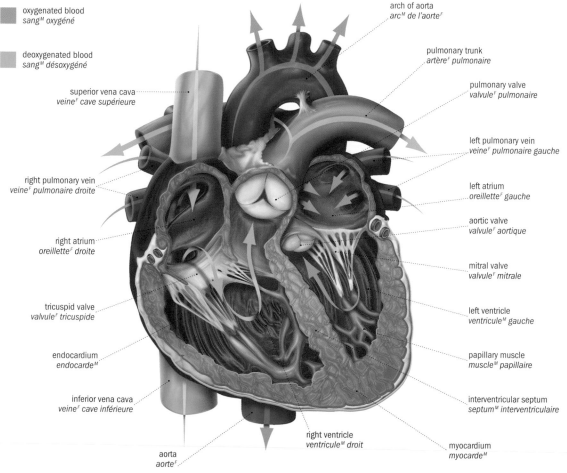

oxygenated blood
sang[M] oxygéné

deoxygenated blood
sang[M] désoxygéné

superior vena cava
veine[F] cave supérieure

right pulmonary vein
veine[F] pulmonaire droite

right atrium
oreillette[F] droite

tricuspid valve
valvule[F] tricuspide

endocardium
endocarde[M]

inferior vena cava
veine[F] cave inférieure

aorta
aorte[F]

right ventricle
ventricule[M] droit

arch of aorta
arc[M] de l'aorte[F]

pulmonary trunk
artère[F] pulmonaire

pulmonary valve
valvule[F] pulmonaire

left pulmonary vein
veine[F] pulmonaire gauche

left atrium
oreillette[F] gauche

aortic valve
valvule[F] aortique

mitral valve
valvule[F] mitrale

left ventricle
ventricule[M] gauche

papillary muscle
muscle[M] papillaire

interventricular septum
septum[M] interventriculaire

myocardium
myocarde[M]

respiratory system

appareil[M] respiratoire

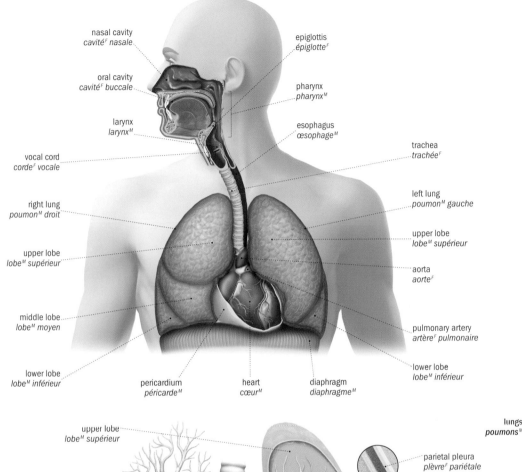

nasal cavity
cavité[F] nasale

oral cavity
cavité[F] buccale

larynx
larynx[M]

vocal cord
corde[F] vocale

right lung
poumon[M] droit

upper lobe
lobe[M] supérieur

middle lobe
lobe[M] moyen

lower lobe
lobe[M] inférieur

pericardium
péricarde[M]

heart
cœur[M]

diaphragm
diaphragme[M]

epiglottis
épiglotte[F]

pharynx
pharynx[M]

esophagus
œsophage[M]

trachea
trachée[F]

left lung
poumon[M] gauche

upper lobe
lobe[M] supérieur

aorta
aorte[F]

pulmonary artery
artère[F] pulmonaire

lower lobe
lobe[M] inférieur

lungs
poumons[M]

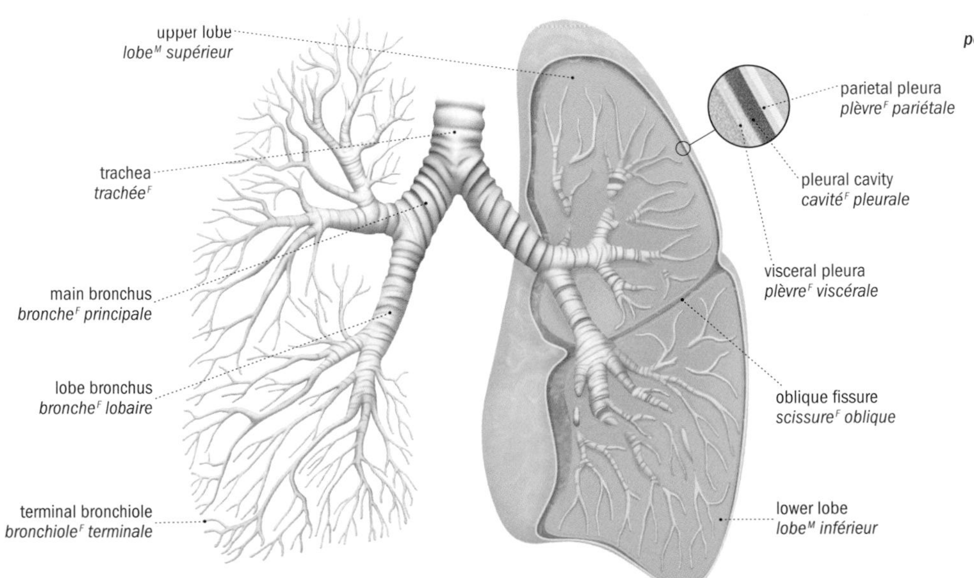
upper lobe
lobe[M] supérieur
trachea
trachée[F]
main bronchus
bronche[F] principale
lobe bronchus
bronche[F] lobaire
terminal bronchiole
bronchiole[F] terminale
parietal pleura
plèvre[F] pariétale
pleural cavity
cavité[F] pleurale
visceral pleura
plèvre[F] viscérale
oblique fissure
scissure[F] oblique
lower lobe
lobe[M] inférieur

digestive system

appareil[M] digestif

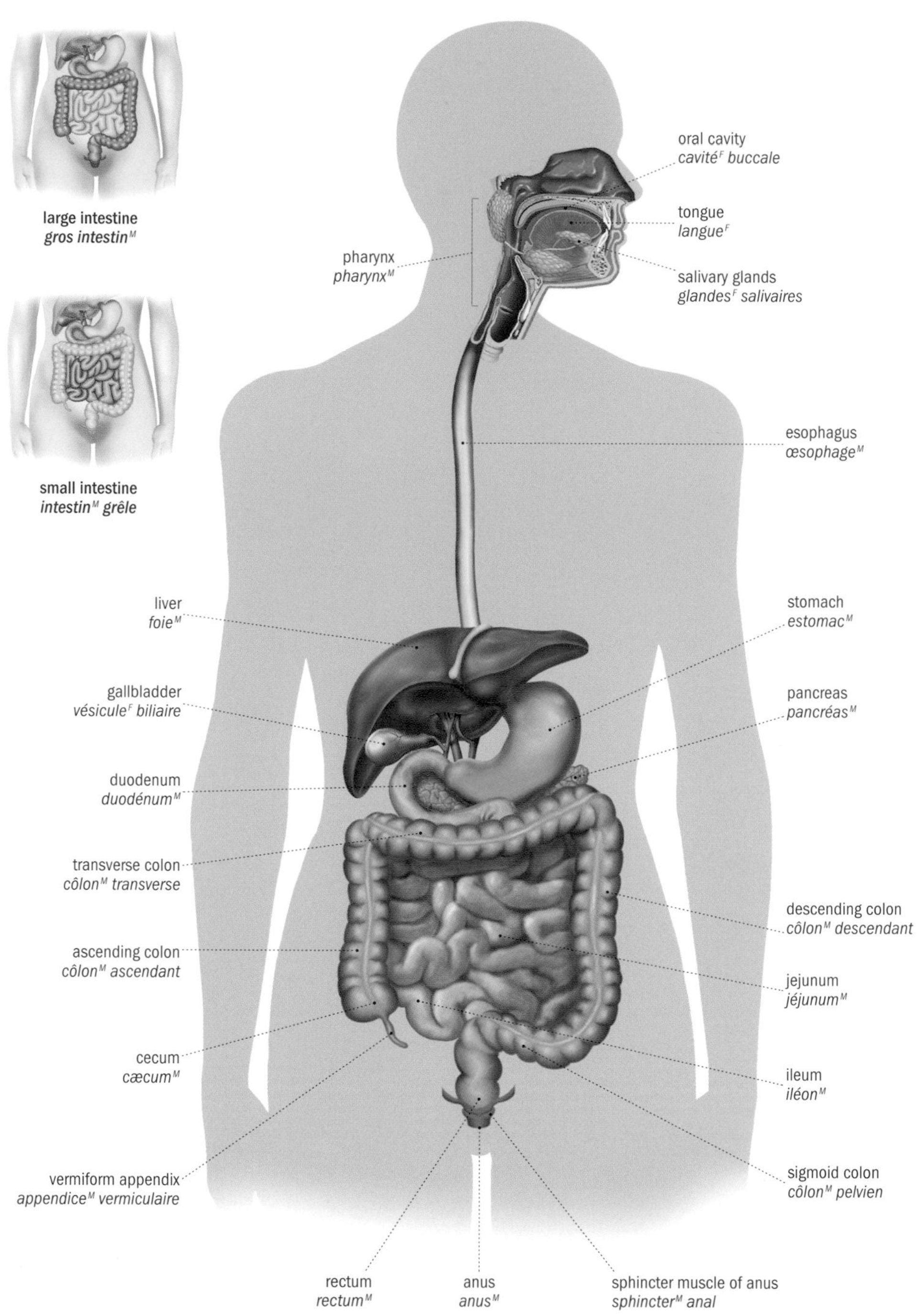
large intestine
gros intestin[M]
small intestine
intestin[M] grêle
oral cavity
cavité[F] buccale
tongue
langue[F]
pharynx
pharynx[M]
salivary glands
glandes[F] salivaires
esophagus
œsophage[M]
liver
foie[M]
stomach
estomac[M]
gallbladder
vésicule[F] biliaire
pancreas
pancréas[M]
duodenum
duodénum[M]
transverse colon
côlon[M] transverse
descending colon
côlon[M] descendant
ascending colon
côlon[M] ascendant
jejunum
jéjunum[M]
cecum
cæcum[M]
ileum
iléon[M]
vermiform appendix
appendice[M] vermiculaire
sigmoid colon
côlon[M] pelvien
rectum
rectum[M]
anus
anus[M]
sphincter muscle of anus
sphincter[M] anal

urinary system

appareil^M urinaire

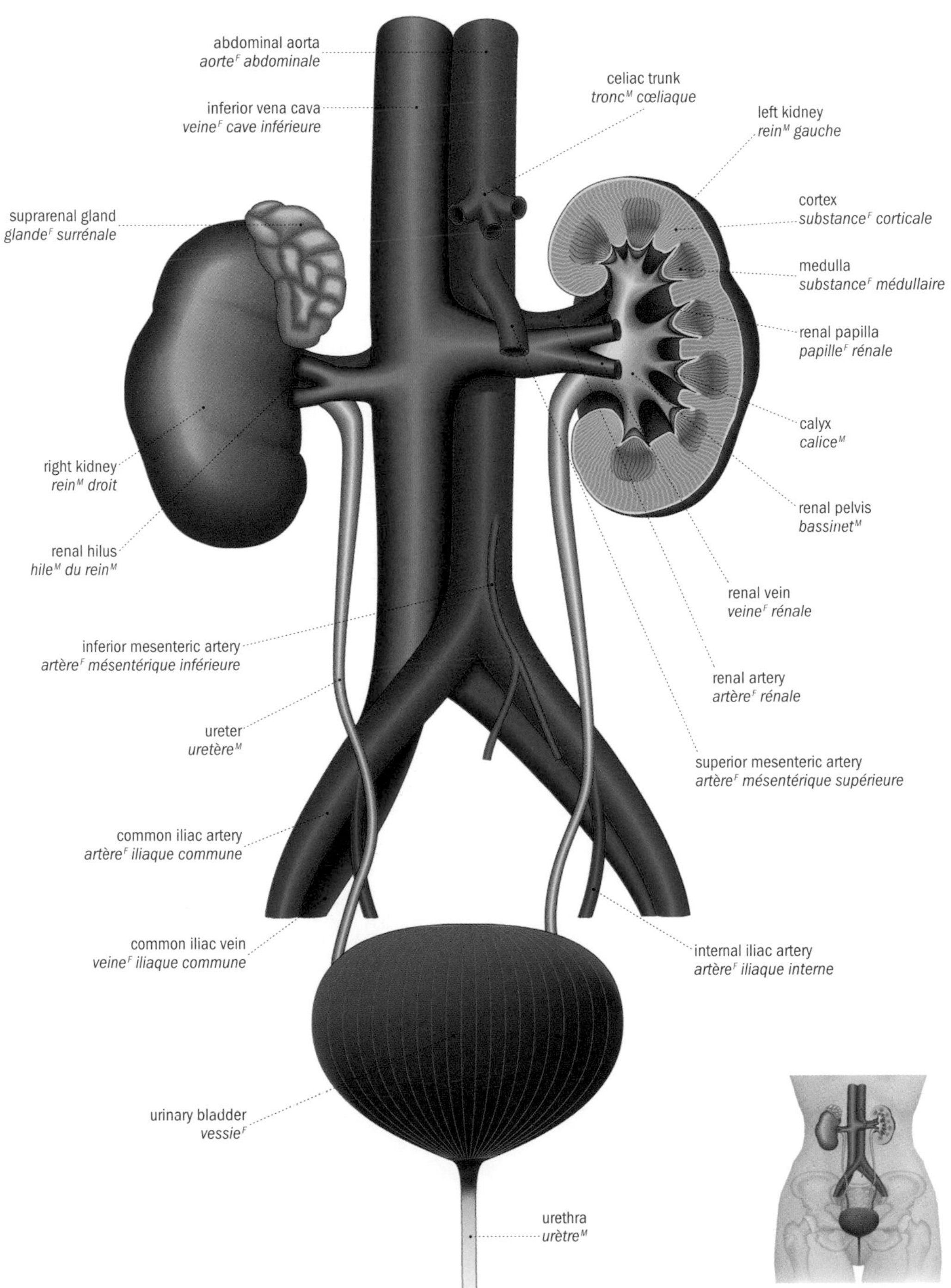

abdominal aorta
aorte^F abdominale
inferior vena cava
veine^F cave inférieure
celiac trunk
tronc^M cœliaque
left kidney
rein^M gauche
suprarenal gland
glande^F surrénale
cortex
substance^F corticale
medulla
substance^F médullaire
renal papilla
papille^F rénale
calyx
calice^M
right kidney
rein^M droit
renal pelvis
bassinet^M
renal hilus
hile^M du rein^M
renal vein
veine^F rénale
inferior mesenteric artery
artère^F mésentérique inférieure
renal artery
artère^F rénale
ureter
uretère^M
superior mesenteric artery
artère^F mésentérique supérieure
common iliac artery
artère^F iliaque commune
common iliac vein
veine^F iliaque commune
internal iliac artery
artère^F iliaque interne
urinary bladder
vessie^F
urethra
urètre^M

nervous system

système^M nerveux

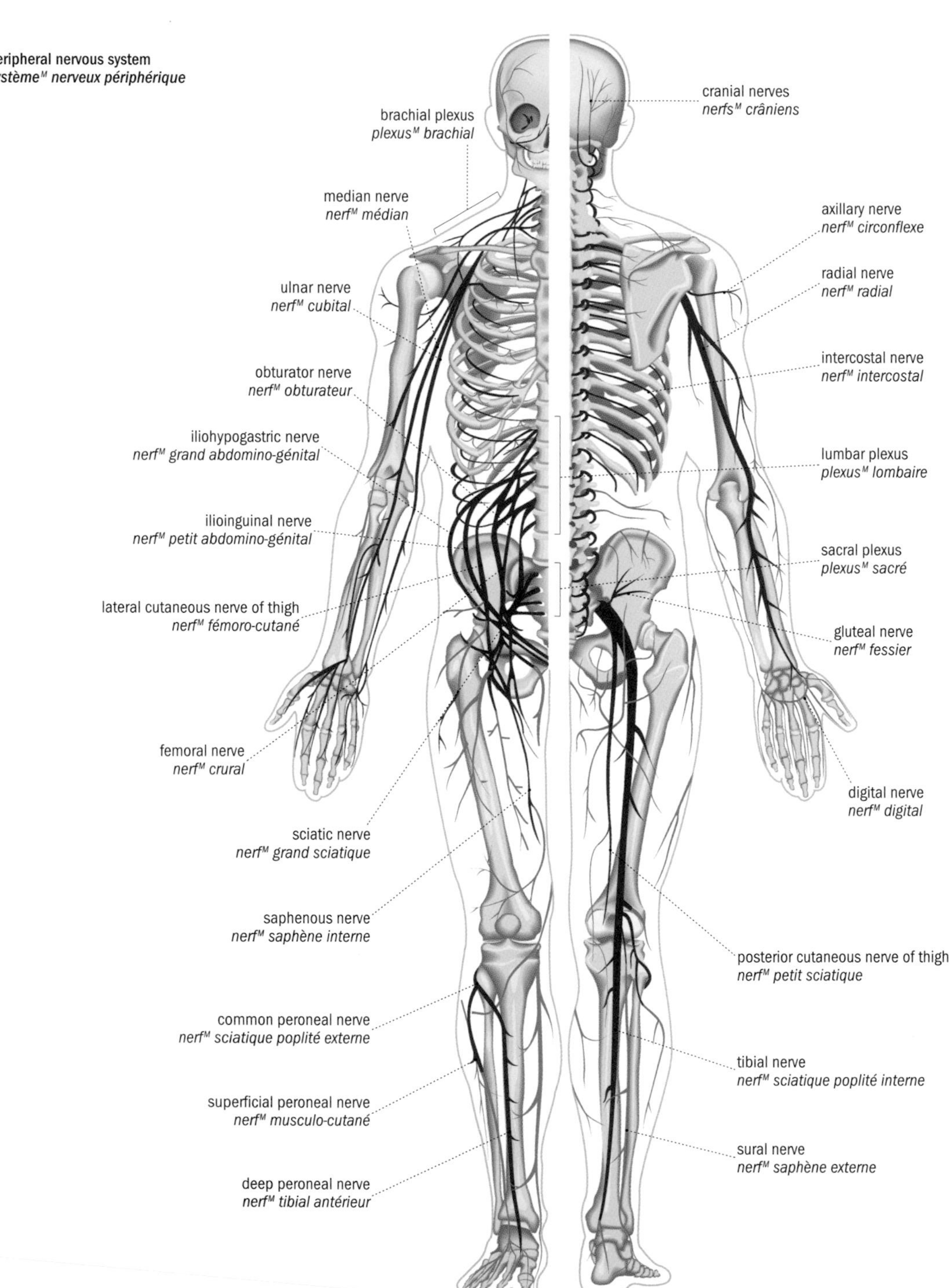
peripheral nervous system
systèmeᴹ nerveux périphérique
cranial nerves
nerfsᴹ crâniens
brachial plexus
plexusᴹ brachial
median nerve
nerfᴹ médian
axillary nerve
nerfᴹ circonflexe
radial nerve
nerfᴹ radial
ulnar nerve
nerfᴹ cubital
obturator nerve
nerfᴹ obturateur
intercostal nerve
nerfᴹ intercostal
iliohypogastric nerve
nerfᴹ grand abdomino-génital
lumbar plexus
plexusᴹ lombaire
ilioinguinal nerve
nerfᴹ petit abdomino-génital
sacral plexus
plexusᴹ sacré
lateral cutaneous nerve of thigh
nerfᴹ fémoro-cutané
gluteal nerve
nerfᴹ fessier
femoral nerve
nerfᴹ crural
digital nerve
nerfᴹ digital
sciatic nerve
nerfᴹ grand sciatique
saphenous nerve
nerfᴹ saphène interne
posterior cutaneous nerve of thigh
nerfᴹ petit sciatique
common peroneal nerve
nerfᴹ sciatique poplité externe
tibial nerve
nerfᴹ sciatique poplité interne
superficial peroneal nerve
nerfᴹ musculo-cutané
sural nerve
nerfᴹ saphène externe
deep peroneal nerve
nerfᴹ tibial antérieur

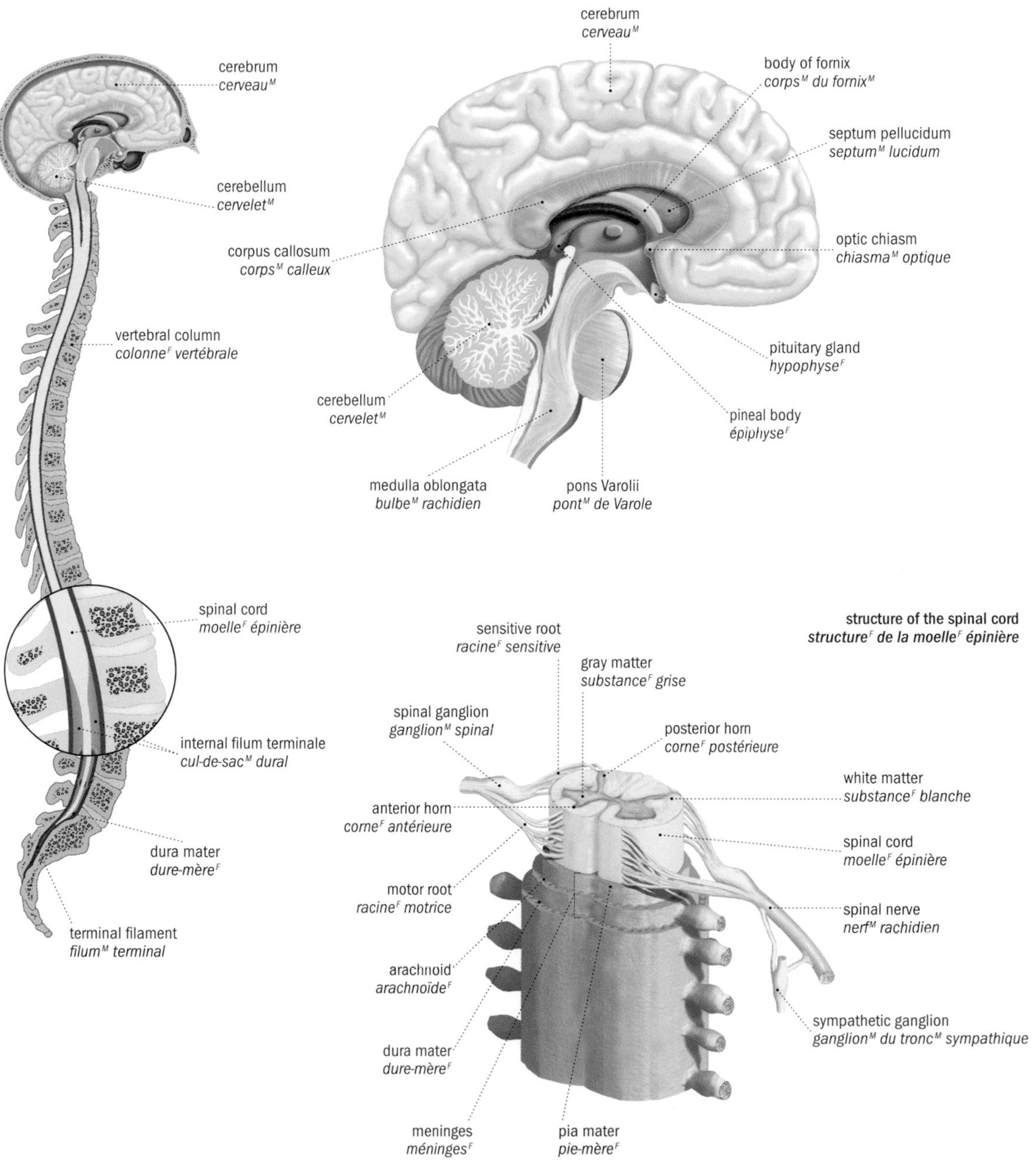
central nervous system
système^M nerveux central
cerebrum
cerveau^M
cerebellum
cervelet^M
vertebral column
colonne^F vertébrale
spinal cord
moelle^F épinière
internal filum terminale
cul-de-sac^M dural
dura mater
dure-mère^F
terminal filament
filum^M terminal
cerebrum
cerveau^M
body of fornix
corps^M du fornix^M
septum pellucidum
septum^M lucidum
optic chiasm
chiasma^M optique
corpus callosum
corps^M calleux
pituitary gland
hypophyse^F
cerebellum
cervelet^M
pineal body
épiphyse^F
medulla oblongata
bulbe^M rachidien
pons Varolii
pont^M de Varole
structure of the spinal cord
structure^F de la moelle^F épinière
sensitive root
racine^F sensitive
gray matter
substance^F grise
spinal ganglion
ganglion^M spinal
posterior horn
corne^F postérieure
white matter
substance^F blanche
anterior horn
corne^F antérieure
spinal cord
moelle^F épinière
motor root
racine^F motrice
spinal nerve
nerf^M rachidien
arachnoid
arachnoïde^F
sympathetic ganglion
ganglion^M du tronc^M sympathique
dura mater
dure-mère^F
meninges
méninges^F
pia mater
pie-mère^F

nervous system

chain of neurons
chaîne[F] de neurones[M]

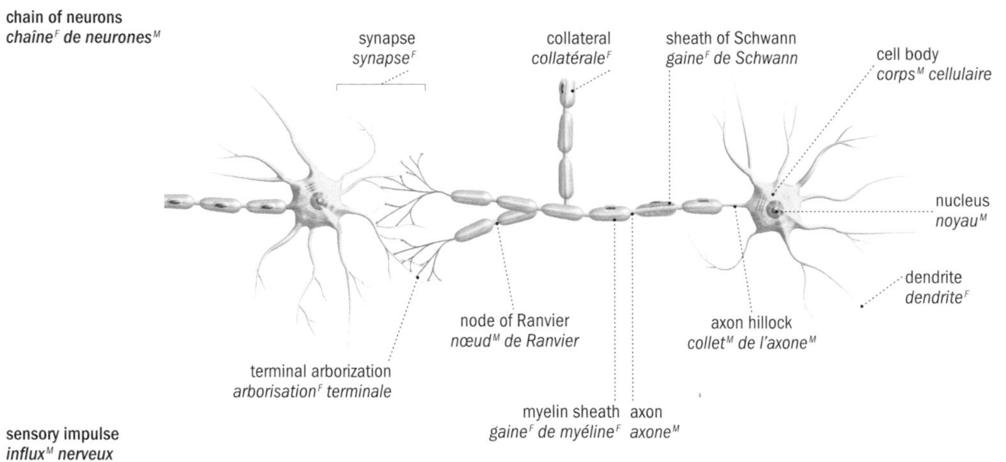
synapse
synapse[F]
collateral
collatérale[F]
sheath of Schwann
gaine[F] de Schwann
cell body
corps[M] cellulaire
nucleus
noyau[M]
dendrite
dendrite[F]
node of Ranvier
nœud[M] de Ranvier
axon hillock
collet[M] de l'axone[M]
terminal arborization
arborisation[F] terminale
myelin sheath
gaine[F] de myéline[F]
axon
axone[M]

sensory impulse
influx[M] nerveux

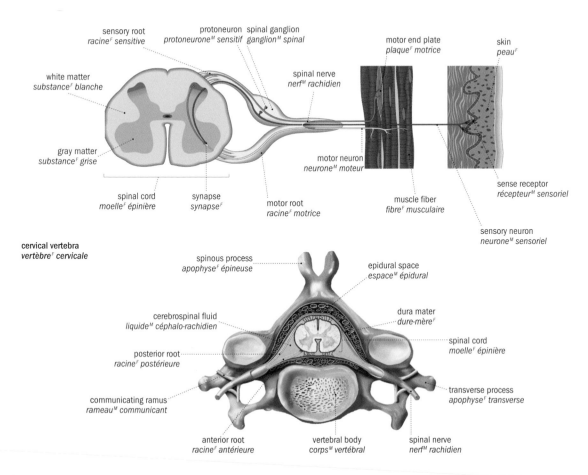

sensory root
racine[F] sensitive

protoneuron
protoneurone[M] sensitif

spinal ganglion
ganglion[M] spinal

motor end plate
plaque[F] motrice

skin
peau[F]

white matter
substance[F] blanche

spinal nerve
nerf[M] rachidien

gray matter
substance[F] grise

motor neuron
neurone[M] moteur

sense receptor
récepteur[M] sensoriel

spinal cord
moelle[F] épinière

synapse
synapse[F]

motor root
racine[F] motrice

muscle fiber
fibre[F] musculaire

sensory neuron
neurone[M] sensoriel

cervical vertebra
vertèbre[F] cervicale

spinous process
apophyse[F] épineuse

epidural space
espace[M] épidural

dura mater
dure-mère[F]

cerebrospinal fluid
liquide[M] céphalo-rachidien

spinal cord
moelle[F] épinière

posterior root
racine[F] postérieure

transverse process
apophyse[F] transverse

communicating ramus
rameau[M] communicant

anterior root
racine[F] antérieure

vertebral body
corps[M] vertébral

spinal nerve
nerf[M] rachidien

male reproductive organs

organes[M] génitaux masculins

sagittal section
coupe[F] sagittale

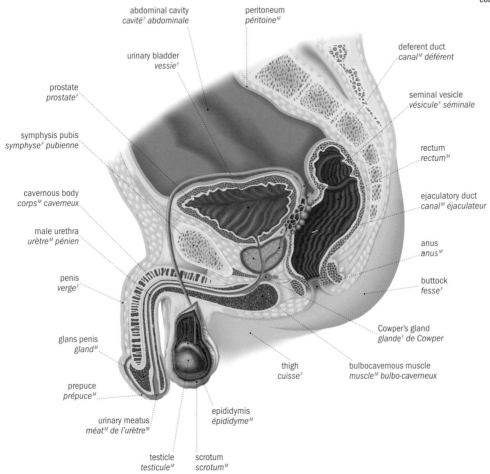

abdominal cavity
cavité[F] abdominale

peritoneum
péritoine[M]

urinary bladder
vessie[F]

deferent duct
canal[M] déférent

prostate
prostate[F]

seminal vesicle
vésicule[F] séminale

symphysis pubis
symphyse[F] pubienne

rectum
rectum[M]

cavernous body
corps[M] caverneux

ejaculatory duct
canal[M] éjaculateur

male urethra
urètre[M] pénien

anus
anus[M]

penis
verge[F]

buttock
fesse[F]

Cowper's gland
glande[F] de Cowper

glans penis
gland[M]

thigh
cuisse[F]

bulbocavernous muscle
muscle[M] bulbo-caverneux

prepuce
prépuce[M]

urinary meatus
méat[M] de l'urètre[M]

epididymis
épididyme[M]

testicle
testicule[M]

scrotum
scrotum[M]

spermatozoon
spermatozoïde[M]

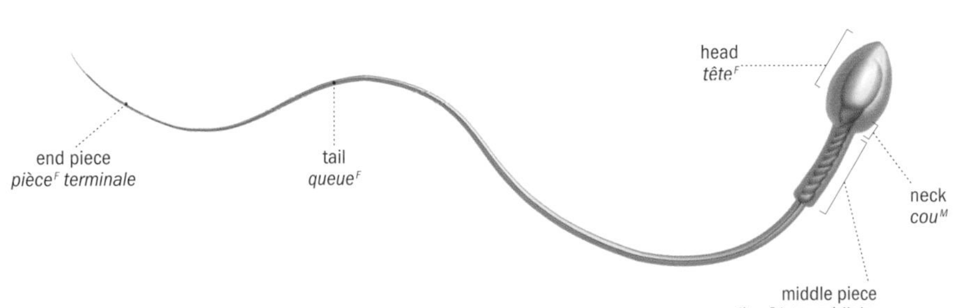
head
tête[F]
end piece
pièce[F] terminale
tail
queue[F]
neck
cou[M]
middle piece
pièce[F] intermédiaire

female reproductive organs

organes[M] génitaux féminins

sagittal section
coupe[F] sagittale

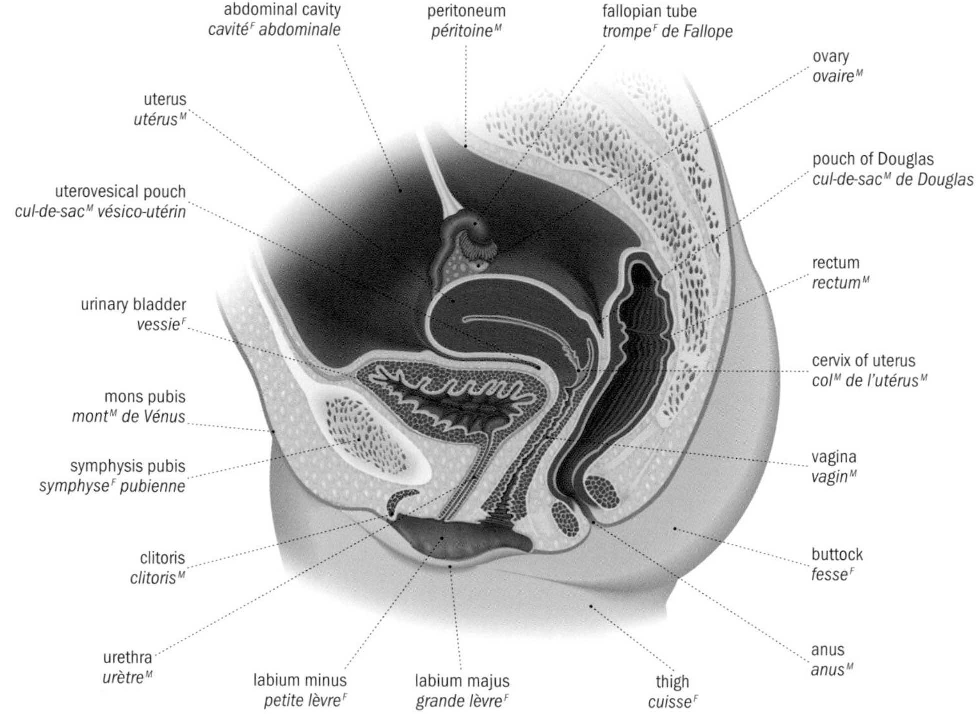

abdominal cavity
cavité[F] abdominale
peritoneum
péritoine[M]
fallopian tube
trompe[F] de Fallope
ovary
ovaire[M]
uterus
utérus[M]
pouch of Douglas
cul-de-sac[M] de Douglas
uterovesical pouch
cul-de-sac[M] vésico-utérin
rectum
rectum[M]
urinary bladder
vessie[F]
cervix of uterus
col[M] de l'utérus[M]
mons pubis
mont[M] de Vénus
vagina
vagin[M]
symphysis pubis
symphyse[F] pubienne
clitoris
clitoris[M]
buttock
fesse[F]
urethra
urètre[M]
labium minus
petite lèvre[F]
labium majus
grande lèvre[F]
thigh
cuisse[F]
anus
anus[M]

egg
ovule[M]

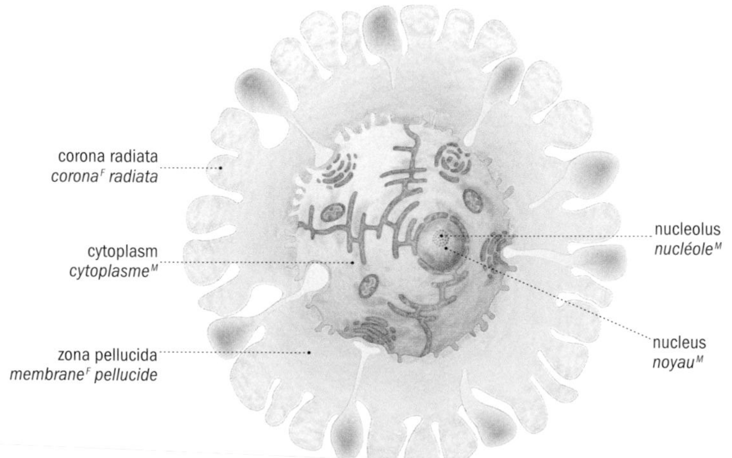

corona radiata
corona[F] radiata
nucleolus
nucléole[M]
cytoplasm
cytoplasme[M]
zona pellucida
membrane[F] pellucide
nucleus
noyau[M]

female reproductive organs

posterior view
vue[F] postérieure

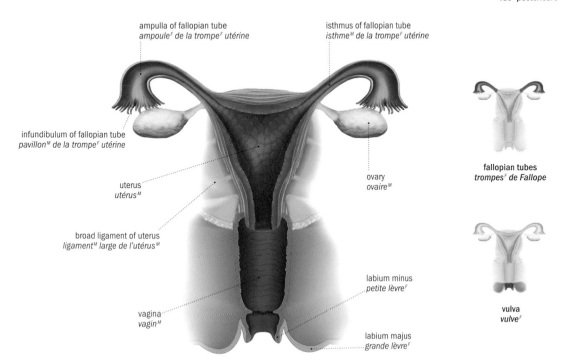

ampulla of fallopian tube
ampoule[F] de la trompe[F] utérine

isthmus of fallopian tube
isthme[M] de la trompe[F] utérine

infundibulum of fallopian tube
pavillon[M] de la trompe[F] utérine

uterus
utérus[M]

ovary
ovaire[M]

broad ligament of uterus
ligament[M] large de l'utérus[M]

labium minus
petite lèvre[F]

vagina
vagin[M]

labium majus
grande lèvre[F]

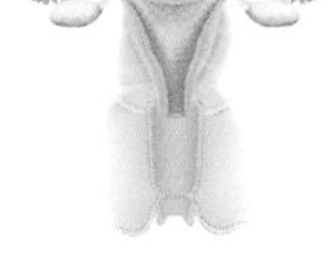

fallopian tubes
trompes[F] de Fallope

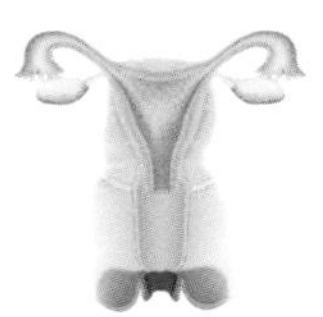

vulva
vulve[F]

breast

sein[M]

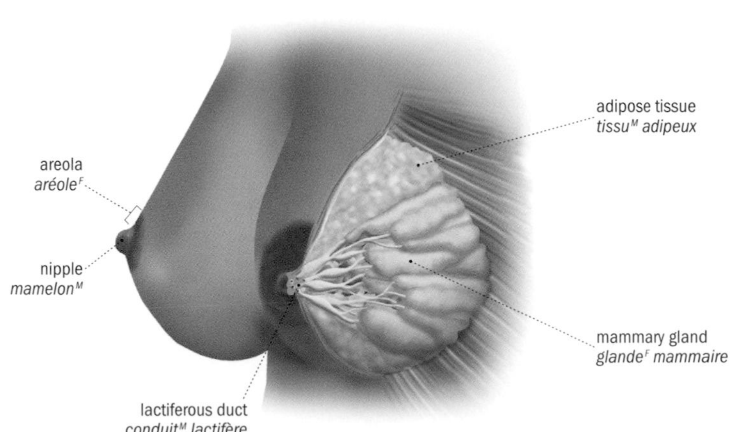
adipose tissue
tissu[M] adipeux
areola
aréole[F]
nipple
mamelon[M]
mammary gland
glande[F] mammaire
lactiferous duct
conduit[M] lactifère

touch

toucher[M]

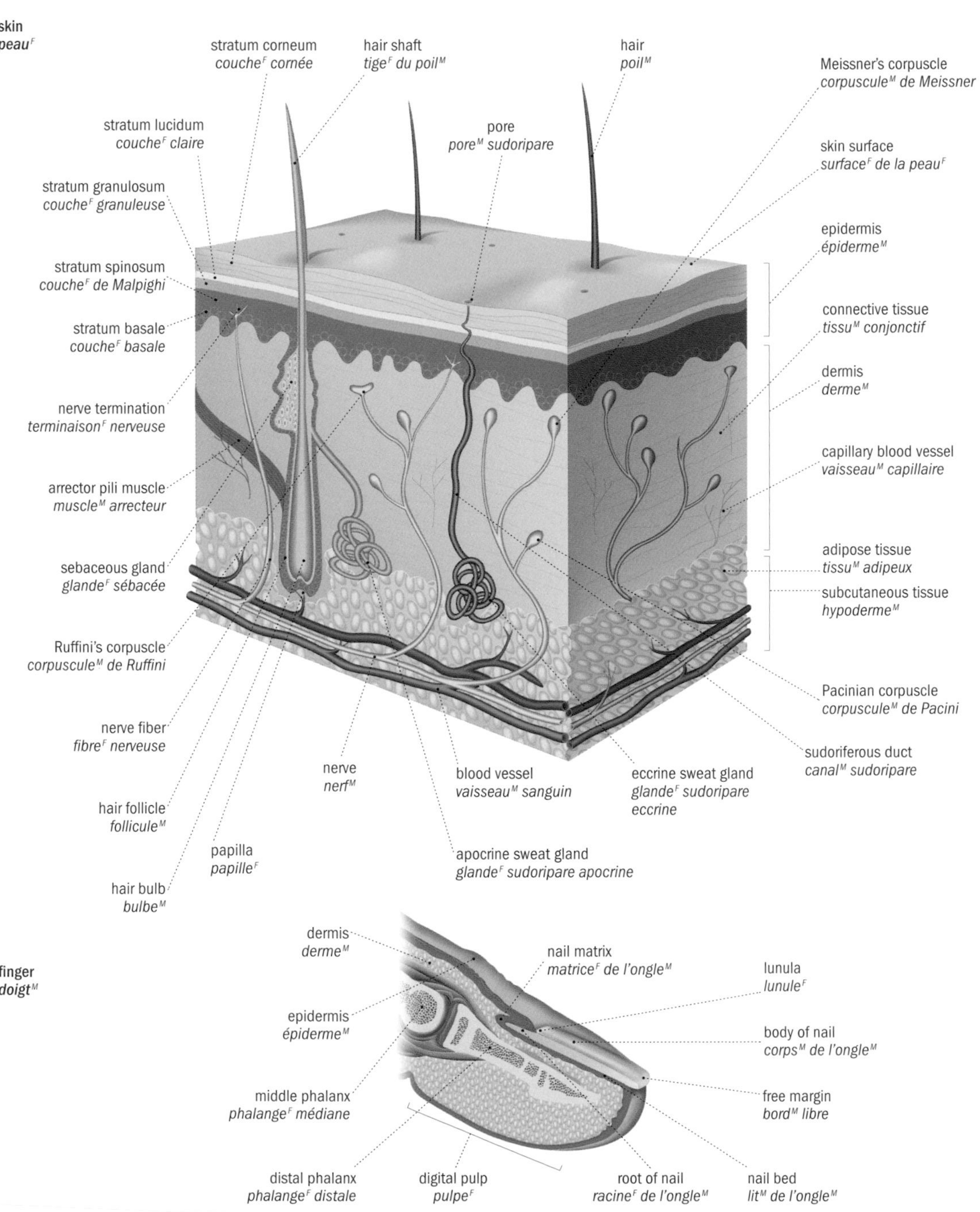
skin
peau[F]
stratum corneum
couche[F] cornée
hair shaft
tige[F] du poil[M]
hair
poil[M]
Meissner's corpuscle
corpuscule[M] de Meissner
stratum lucidum
couche[F] claire
pore
pore[M] sudoripare
skin surface
surface[F] de la peau[F]
stratum granulosum
couche[F] granuleuse
epidermis
épiderme[M]
stratum spinosum
couche[F] de Malpighi
connective tissue
tissu[M] conjonctif
stratum basale
couche[F] basale
dermis
derme[M]
nerve termination
terminaison[F] nerveuse
capillary blood vessel
vaisseau[M] capillaire
arrector pili muscle
muscle[M] arrecteur
adipose tissue
tissu[M] adipeux
sebaceous gland
glande[F] sébacée
subcutaneous tissue
hypoderme[M]
Ruffini's corpuscle
corpuscule[M] de Ruffini
Pacinian corpuscle
corpuscule[M] de Pacini
nerve fiber
fibre[F] nerveuse
sudoriferous duct
canal[M] sudoripare
nerve
nerf[M]
blood vessel
vaisseau[M] sanguin
eccrine sweat gland
glande[F] sudoripare eccrine
hair follicle
follicule[M]
papilla
papille[F]
apocrine sweat gland
glande[F] sudoripare apocrine
hair bulb
bulbe[M]
finger
doigt[M]
dermis
derme[M]
nail matrix
matrice[F] de l'ongle[M]
lunula
lunule[F]
epidermis
épiderme[M]
body of nail
corps[M] de l'ongle[M]
middle phalanx
phalange[F] médiane
free margin
bord[M] libre
distal phalanx
phalange[F] distale
digital pulp
pulpe[F]
root of nail
racine[F] de l'ongle[M]
nail bed
lit[M] de l'ongle[M]

touch

hand
main[F]

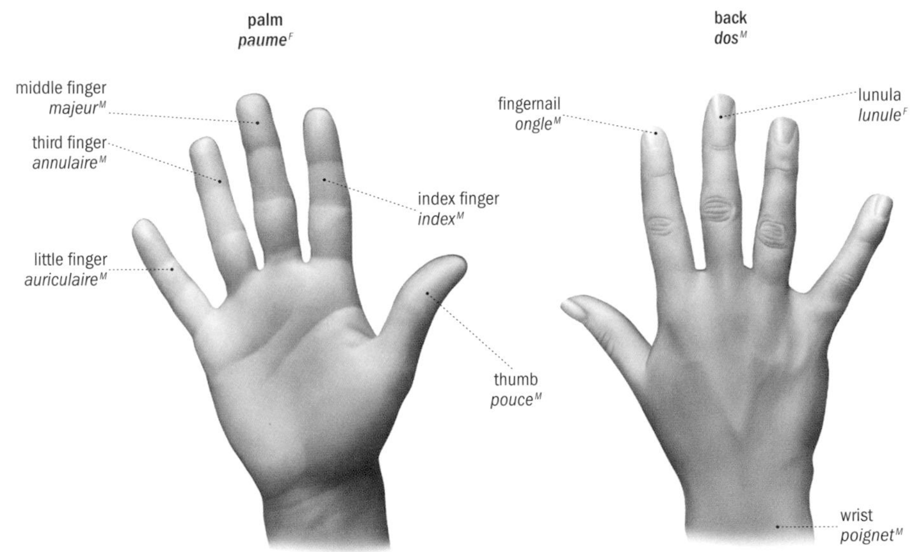
palm
paume[F]
back
dos[M]
middle finger
majeur[M]
third finger
annulaire[M]
little finger
auriculaire[M]
index finger
index[M]
thumb
pouce[M]
fingernail
ongle[M]
lunula
lunule[F]
wrist
poignet[M]

hearing
ouïe[F]

auricle
pavillon[M]

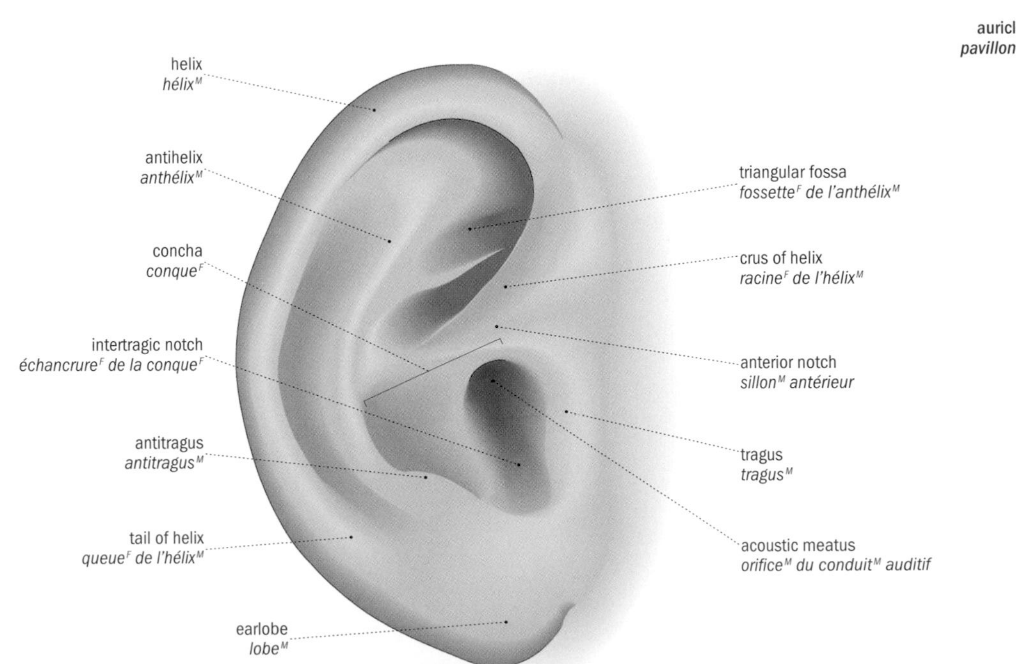
helix
hélix[M]
antihelix
anthélix[M]
concha
conque[F]
intertragic notch
échancrure[F] *de la conque*[F]
antitragus
antitragus[M]
tail of helix
queue[F] *de l'hélix*[M]
earlobe
lobe[M]
triangular fossa
fossette[F] *de l'anthélix*[M]
crus of helix
racine[F] *de l'hélix*[M]
anterior notch
sillon[M] *antérieur*
tragus
tragus[M]
acoustic meatus
orifice[M] *du conduit*[M] *auditif*

structure of the ear
structure[F] de l'oreille[F]

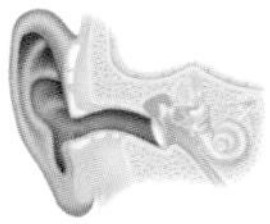

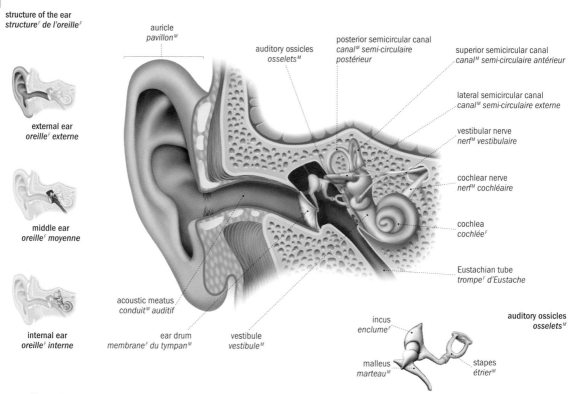

external ear
oreille[F] externe

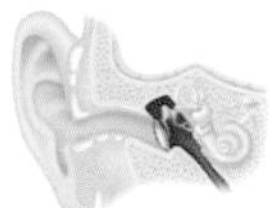

middle ear
oreille[F] moyenne

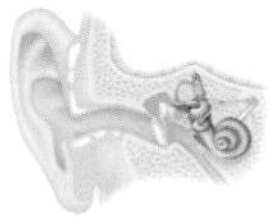

internal ear
oreille[F] interne

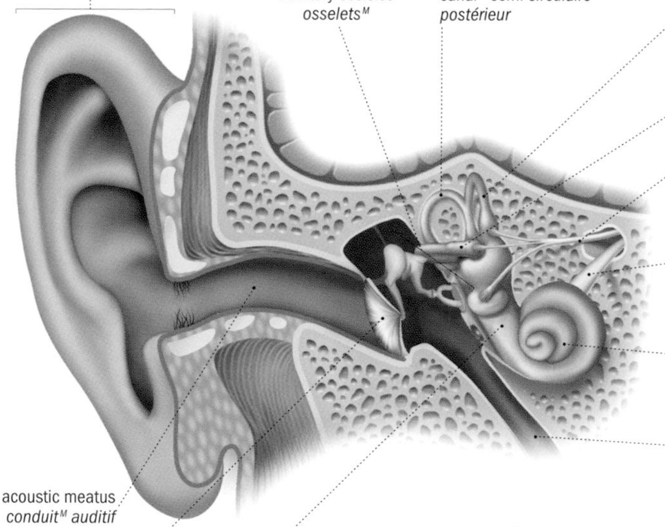

auricle
pavillon[M]

auditory ossicles
osselets[M]

posterior semicircular canal
canal[M] semi-circulaire postérieur

superior semicircular canal
canal[M] semi-circulaire antérieur

lateral semicircular canal
canal[M] semi-circulaire externe

vestibular nerve
nerf[M] vestibulaire

cochlear nerve
nerf[M] cochléaire

cochlea
cochlée[F]

Eustachian tube
trompe[F] d'Eustache

acoustic meatus
conduit[M] auditif

ear drum
membrane[F] du tympan[M]

vestibule
vestibule[M]

auditory ossicles
osselets[M]

incus
enclume[F]

malleus
marteau[M]

stapes
étrier[M]

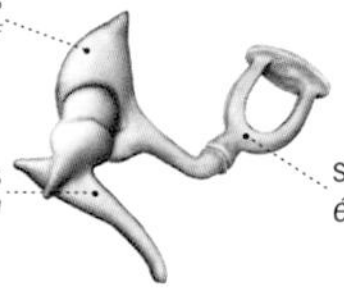

smell and taste

odorat[M] et goût[M]

mouth
bouche[F]

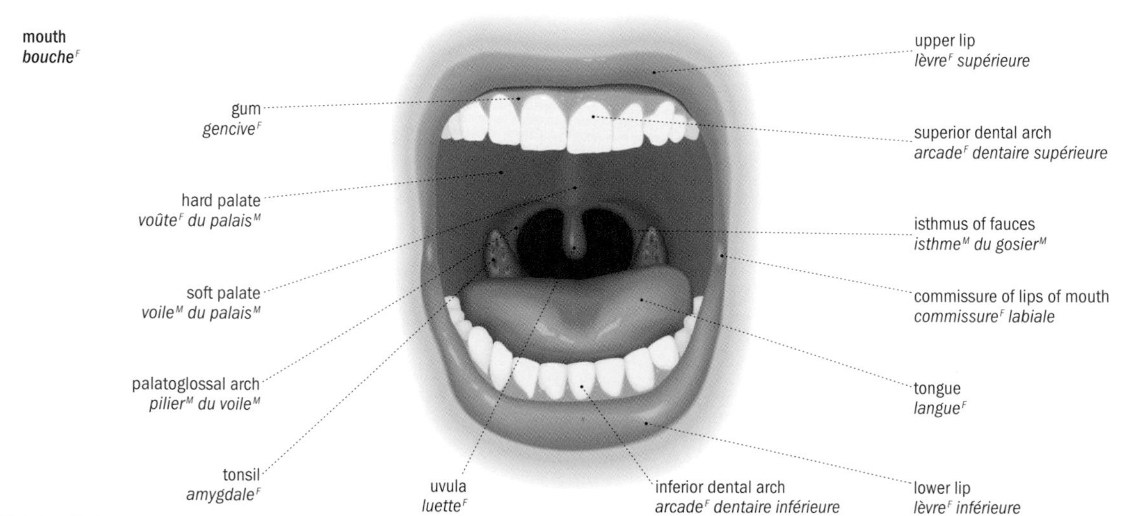
gum
gencive[F]
hard palate
voûte[F] du palais[M]
soft palate
voile[M] du palais[M]
palatoglossal arch
pilier[M] du voile[M]
tonsil
amygdale[F]
uvula
luette[F]
inferior dental arch
arcade[F] dentaire inférieure
upper lip
lèvre[F] supérieure
superior dental arch
arcade[F] dentaire supérieure
isthmus of fauces
isthme[M] du gosier[M]
commissure of lips of mouth
commissure[F] labiale
tongue
langue[F]
lower lip
lèvre[F] inférieure

external nose
parties[F] externes du nez[M]

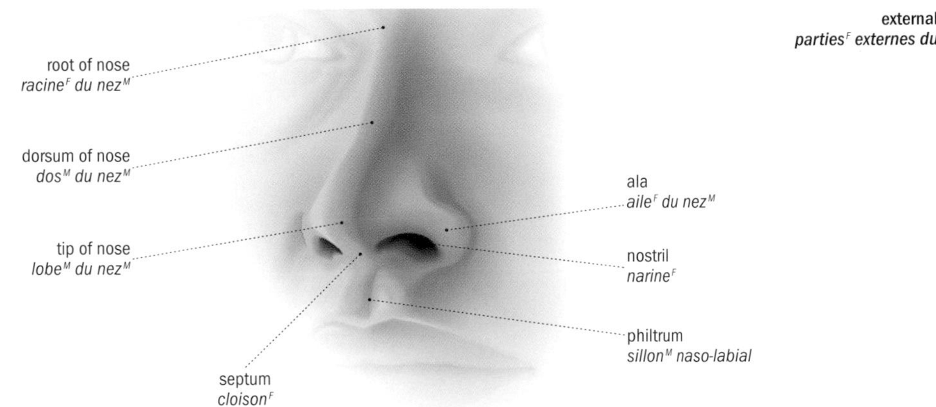
root of nose
racine[F] du nez[M]
dorsum of nose
dos[M] du nez[M]
tip of nose
lobe[M] du nez[M]
septum
cloison[F]
ala
aile[F] du nez[M]
nostril
narine[F]
philtrum
sillon[M] naso-labial

nasal fossae
fosses[F] nasales

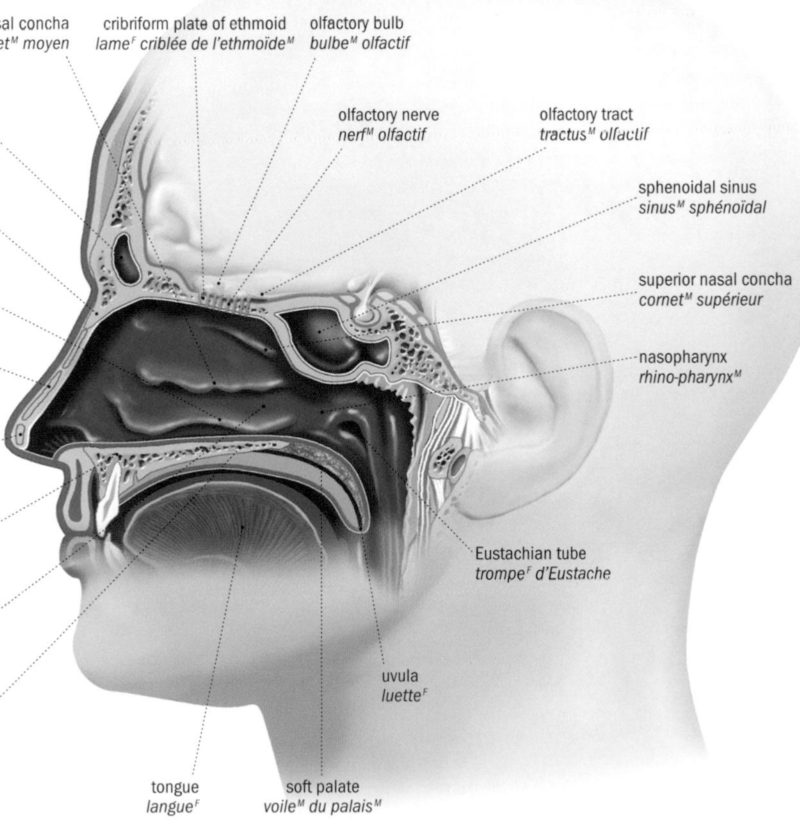

middle nasal concha
cornet[M] moyen
cribriform plate of ethmoid
lame[F] criblée de l'ethmoïde[M]
olfactory bulb
bulbe[M] olfactif
frontal sinus
sinus[M] frontal
olfactory nerve
nerf[M] olfactif
olfactory tract
tractus[M] olfactif
nasal bone
os[M] propre du nez[M]
sphenoidal sinus
sinus[M] sphénoïdal
inferior nasal concha
cornet[M] inférieur
superior nasal concha
cornet[M] supérieur
septal cartilage of nose
cartilage[M] de la cloison[F]
nasopharynx
rhino-pharynx[M]
greater alar cartilage
cartilage[M] de l'aile[F] du nez[M]
maxilla
maxillaire[M]
Eustachian tube
trompe[F] d'Eustache
olfactory mucosa
muqueuse[F] olfactive
uvula
luette[F]
hard palate
voûte[F] du palais[M]
tongue
langue[F]
soft palate
voile[M] du palais[M]

HUMAN BEING

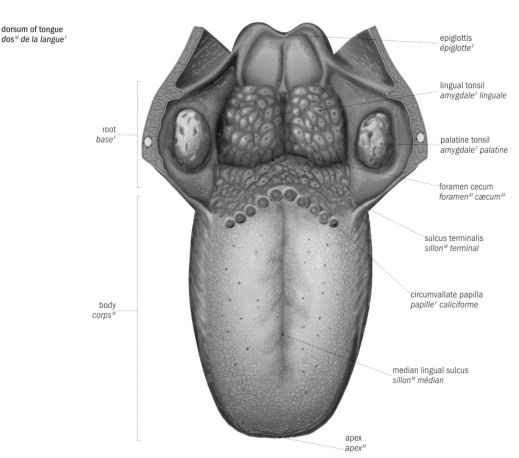

dorsum of tongue
dos[M] de la langue[F]

epiglottis
épiglotte[F]

lingual tonsil
amygdale[F] linguale

root
base[F]

palatine tonsil
amygdale[F] palatine

foramen cecum
foramen[M] cæcum[M]

sulcus terminalis
sillon[M] terminal

circumvallate papilla
papille[F] caliciforme

body
corps[M]

median lingual sulcus
sillon[M] médian

apex
apex[M]

taste receptors
récepteurs[M] du goût[M]

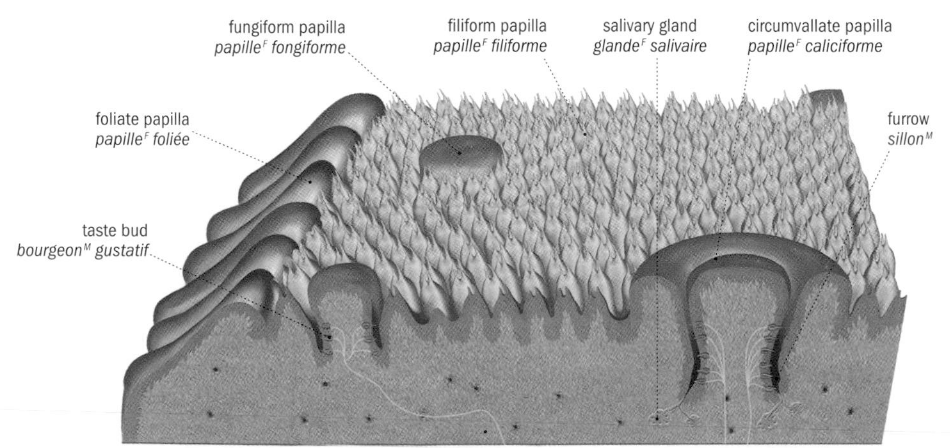
fungiform papilla
papille[F] fongiforme
filiform papilla
papille[F] filiforme
salivary gland
glande[F] salivaire
circumvallate papilla
papille[F] caliciforme
foliate papilla
papille[F] foliée
furrow
sillon[M]
taste bud
bourgeon[M] gustatif

sight

vue[F]

eye
œil[M]

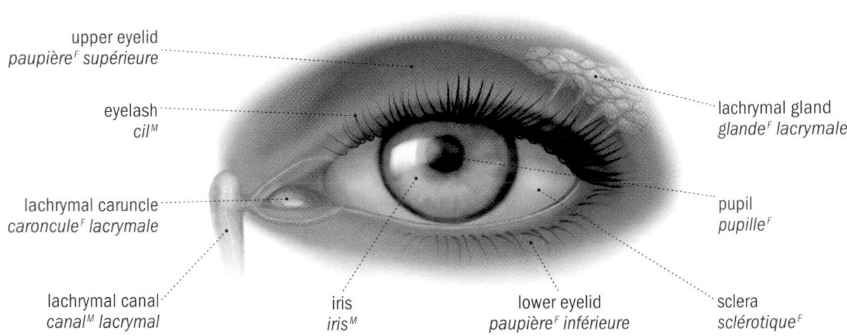
upper eyelid
paupière[F] supérieure
eyelash
cil[M]
lachrymal caruncle
caroncule[F] lacrymale
lachrymal canal
canal[M] lacrymal
iris
iris[M]
lower eyelid
paupière[F] inférieure
lachrymal gland
glande[F] lacrymale
pupil
pupille[F]
sclera
sclérotique[F]

eyeball
globe[M] oculaire

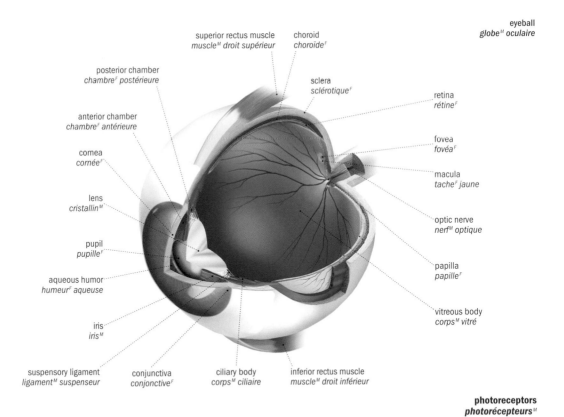

superior rectus muscle
muscle[M] droit supérieur

choroid
choroïde[F]

posterior chamber
chambre[F] postérieure

sclera
sclérotique[F]

retina
rétine[F]

anterior chamber
chambre[F] antérieure

fovea
fovéa[F]

cornea
cornée[F]

macula
tache[F] jaune

lens
cristallin[M]

optic nerve
nerf[M] optique

pupil
pupille[F]

papilla
papille[F]

aqueous humor
humeur[F] aqueuse

vitreous body
corps[M] vitré

iris
iris[M]

suspensory ligament
ligament[M] suspenseur

conjunctiva
conjonctive[F]

ciliary body
corps[M] ciliaire

inferior rectus muscle
muscle[M] droit inférieur

photoreceptors
photorécepteurs[M]

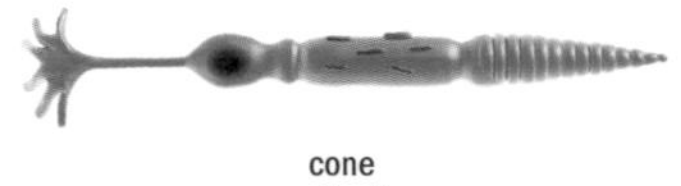

cone
cône[M]

rod
bâtonnet[M]

supermarket

supermarché[M]

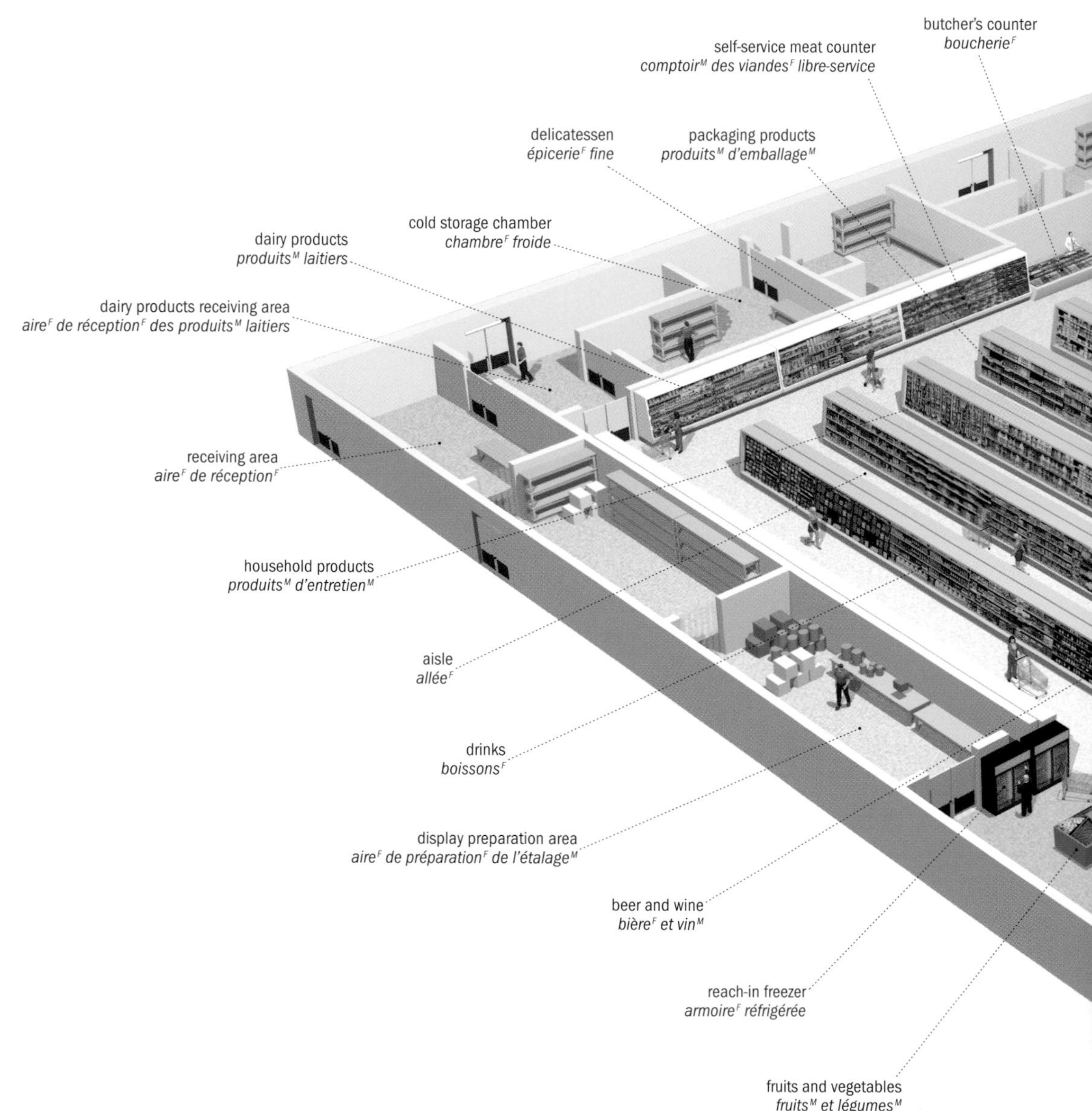
butcher's counter
boucherie[F]
self-service meat counter
comptoir[M] des viandes[F] libre-service
delicatessen
épicerie[F] fine
packaging products
produits[M] d'emballage[M]
cold storage chamber
chambre[F] froide
dairy products
produits[M] laitiers
dairy products receiving area
aire[F] de réception[F] des produits[M] laitiers
receiving area
aire[F] de réception[F]
household products
produits[M] d'entretien[M]
aisle
allée[F]
drinks
boissons[F]
display preparation area
aire[F] de préparation[F] de l'étalage[M]
beer and wine
bière[F] et vin[M]
reach-in freezer
armoire[F] réfrigérée
fruits and vegetables
fruits[M] et légumes[M]

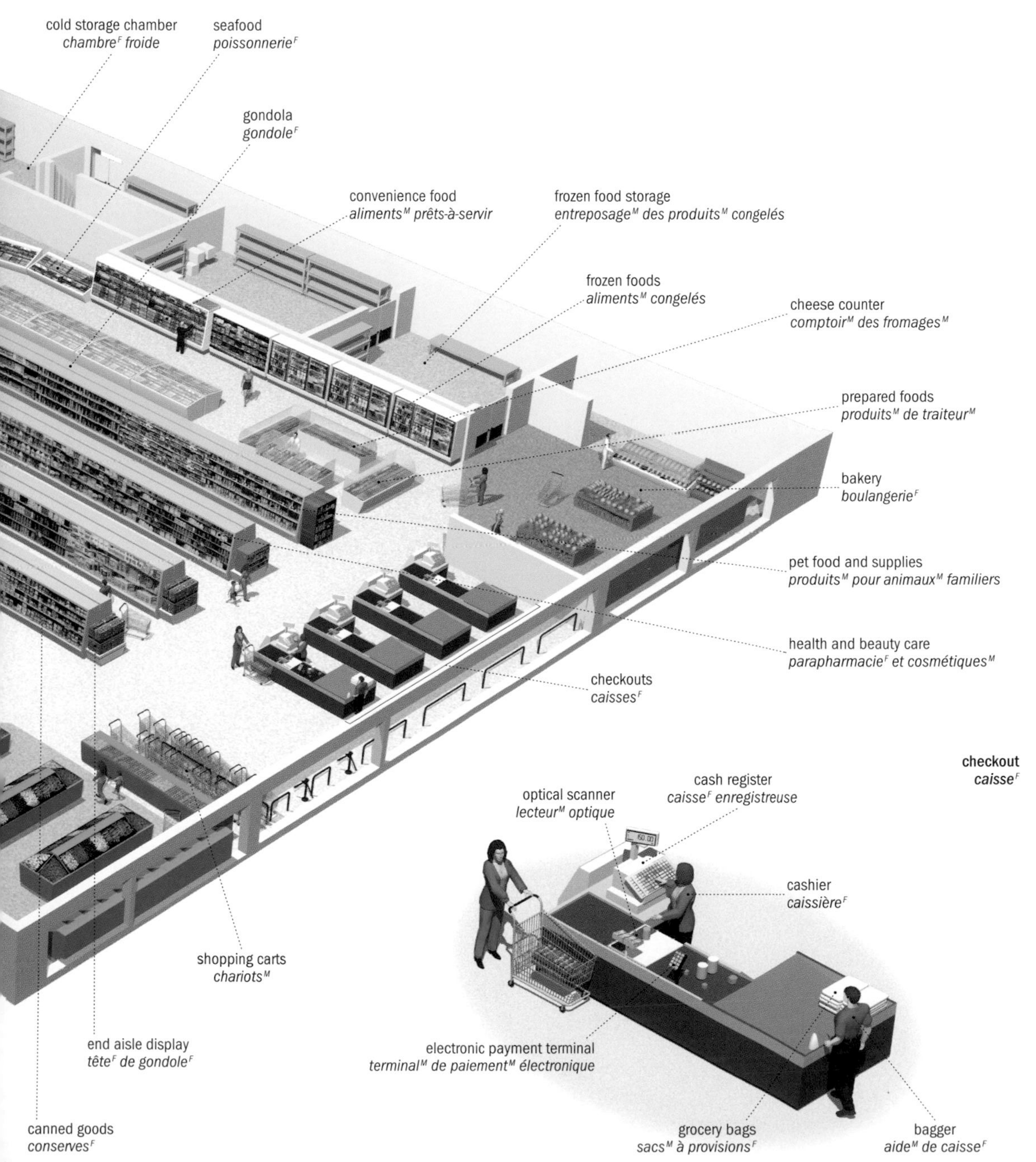
cold storage chamber
chambre^F froide
seafood
poissonnerie^F
gondola
gondole^F
convenience food
aliments^M prêts-à-servir
frozen food storage
entreposage^M des produits^M congelés
frozen foods
aliments^M congelés
cheese counter
comptoir^M des fromages^M
prepared foods
produits^M de traiteur^M
bakery
boulangerie^F
pet food and supplies
produits^M pour animaux^M familiers
health and beauty care
parapharmacie^F et cosmétiques^M
checkouts
caisses^F
shopping carts
chariots^M
end aisle display
tête^F de gondole^F
canned goods
conserves^F
checkout
caisse^F
optical scanner
lecteur^M optique
cash register
caisse^F enregistreuse
cashier
caissière^F
electronic payment terminal
terminal^M de paiement^M électronique
grocery bags
sacs^M à provisions^F
bagger
aide^M de caisse^F

farmstead

ferme[F]

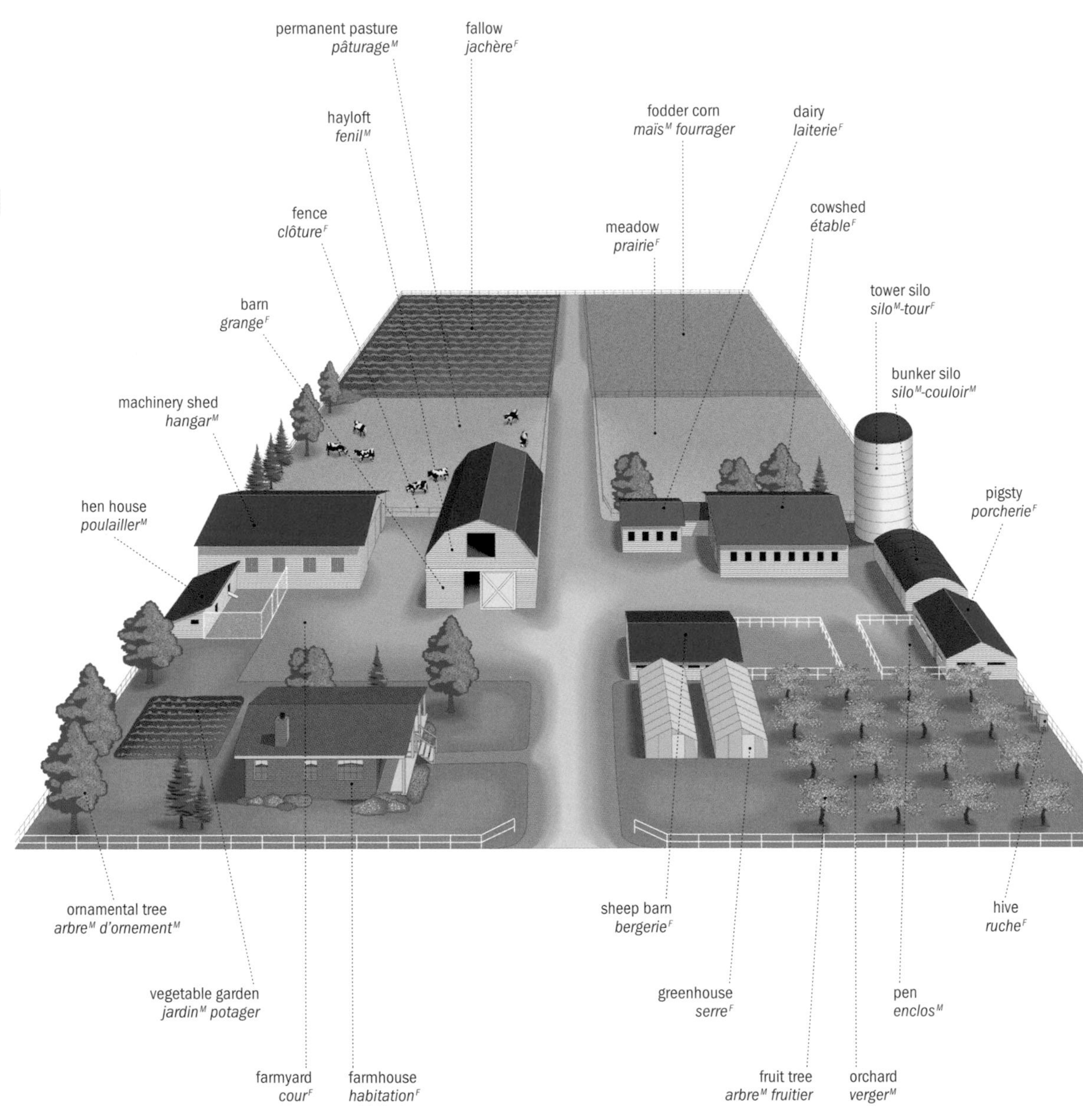

permanent pasture
pâturage[M]
fallow
jachère[F]
hayloft
fenil[M]
fodder corn
maïs[M] fourrager
dairy
laiterie[F]
fence
clôture[F]
meadow
prairie[F]
cowshed
étable[F]
barn
grange[F]
tower silo
silo[M]-tour[F]
machinery shed
hangar[M]
bunker silo
silo[M]-couloir[M]
hen house
poulailler[M]
pigsty
porcherie[F]
ornamental tree
arbre[M] d'ornement[M]
sheep barn
bergerie[F]
hive
ruche[F]
vegetable garden
jardin[M] potager
greenhouse
serre[F]
pen
enclos[M]
farmyard
cour[F]
farmhouse
habitation[F]
fruit tree
arbre[M] fruitier
orchard
verger[M]

mushrooms

champignons[M]

truffle
truffe[F]

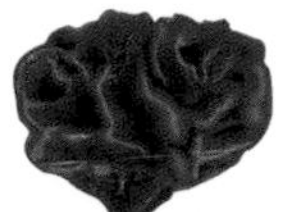
wood ear
oreille-de-Judas[F]

royal agaric
oronge[F] *vraie*

delicious lactarius
lactaire[M] *délicieux*

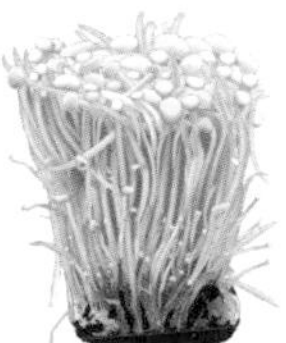
enoki
collybie[F] *à pied*[M] *velouté*

oyster
pleurote[M] *en forme*[F] *d'huître*[F]

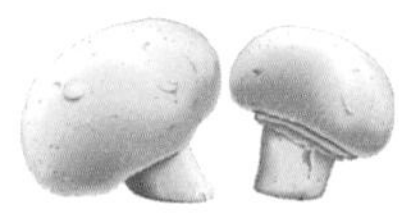
cultivated mushrooms
champignon[M] *de couche*[F]

green russula
russule[F] *verdoyante*

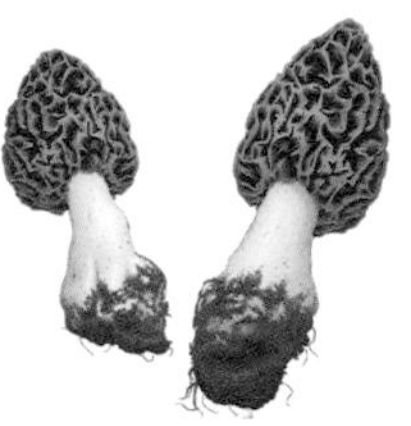
morels
morille[F]

edible boletus
cèpe[M]

shitake
shiitake[M]

chanterelles
chanterelle[F] *commune*

seaweed

algues[F]

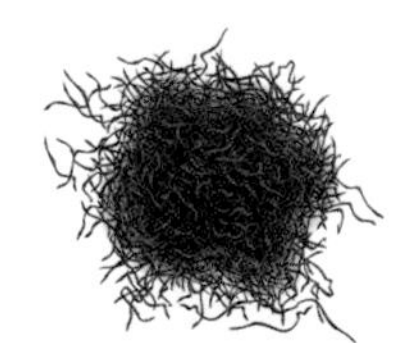
arame
aramé[M]

wakame
wakamé[M]

kombu
kombu[M]

spirulina
spiruline[F]

Irish moss
mousse[F] *d'Irlande*[F]

hijiki
hijiki[M]

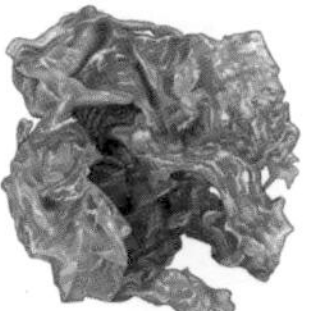
sea lettuce
laitue[F] *de mer*[F]

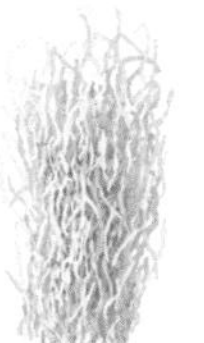
agar-agar
agar-agar[M]

nori
nori[M]

dulse
rhodyménie[M] *palmé*

vegetables

légumes^{M}

bulb vegetables
légumes^{M} bulbes^{M}

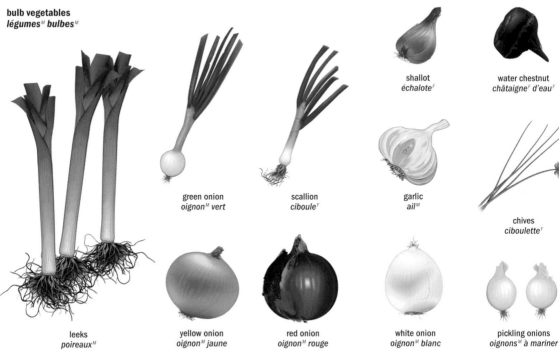

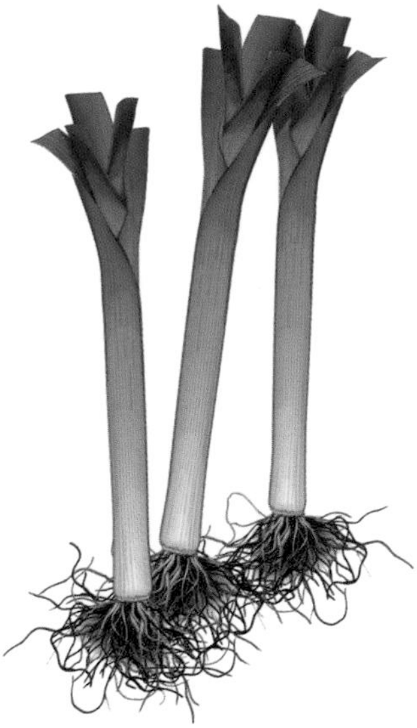

shallot
échalote^{F}

water chestnut
châtaigne^{F} d'eau^{F}

green onion
oignon^{M} vert

scallion
ciboule^{F}

garlic
ail^{M}

chives
ciboulette^{F}

leeks
poireaux^{M}

yellow onion
oignon^{M} jaune

red onion
oignon^{M} rouge

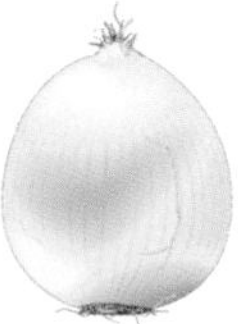

white onion
oignon^{M} blanc

pickling onions
oignons^{M} à mariner

tuber vegetables
légumes^{M} tubercules^{M}

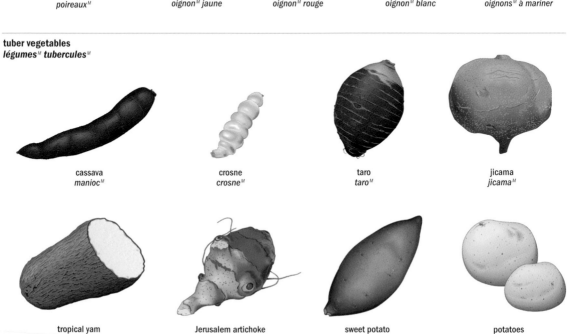

cassava
manioc^{M}

crosne
crosne^{M}

taro
taro^{M}

jicama
jicama^{M}

tropical yam
igname^{F}

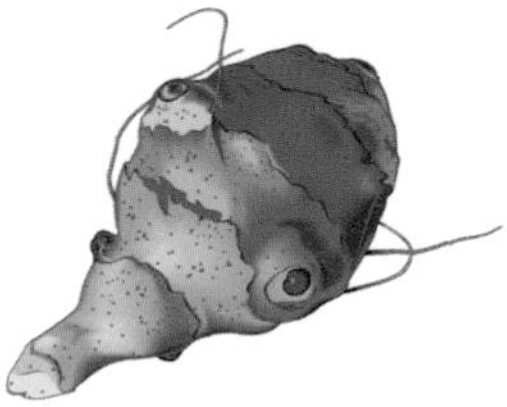

Jerusalem artichoke
topinambour^{M}

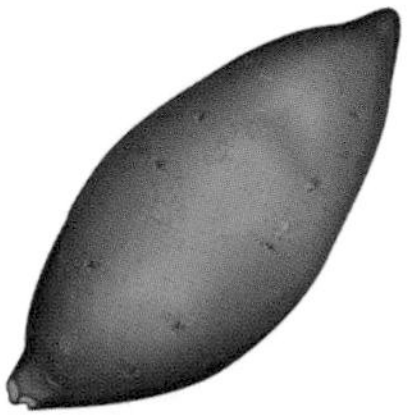

sweet potato
patate^{F}

potatoes
pommes^{F} de terre^{F}

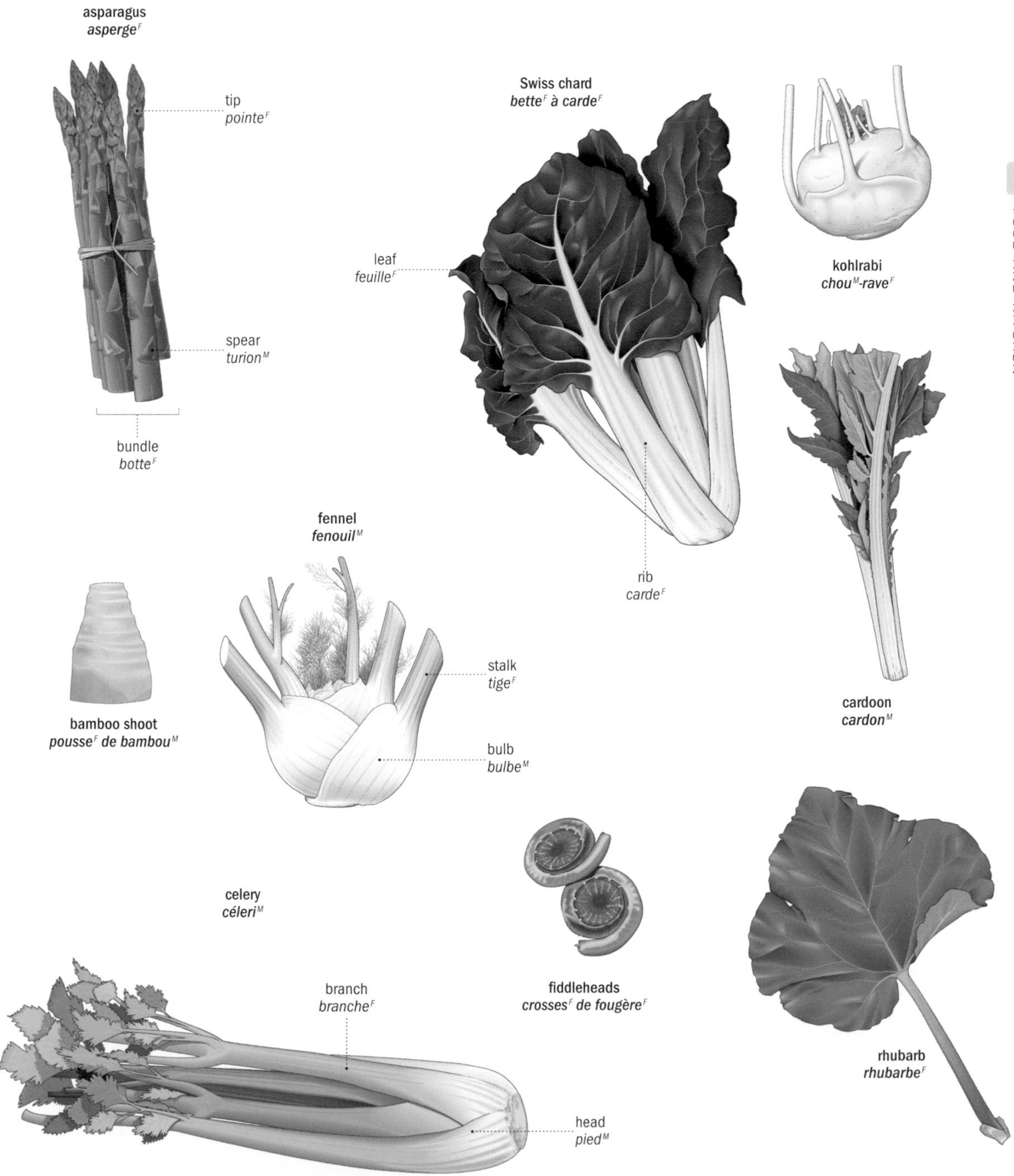
stalk vegetables
légumes^M tiges^F
asparagus
asperge^F
tip
pointe^F
spear
turion^M
bundle
botte^F
Swiss chard
bette^F à carde^F
leaf
feuille^F
rib
carde^F
kohlrabi
chou^M-rave^F
cardoon
cardon^M
fennel
fenouil^M
stalk
tige^F
bulb
bulbe^M
bamboo shoot
pousse^F de bambou^M
celery
céleri^M
branch
branche^F
head
pied^M
fiddleheads
crosses^F de fougère^F
rhubarb
rhubarbe^F

vegetables

leaf vegetables
***légumes*ᴹ *feuilles*ᶠ**

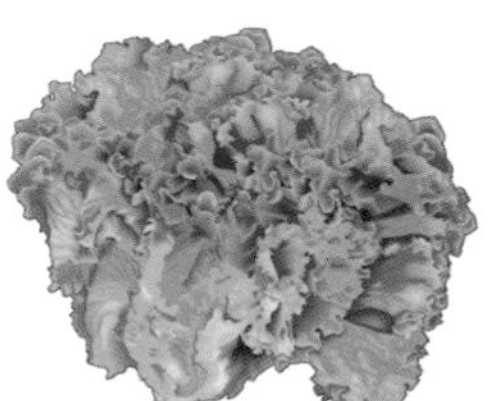

leaf lettuce
*laitue*ᶠ *frisée*

romaine lettuce
*romaine*ᶠ

celtuce
*laitue*ᶠ *asperge*ᶠ

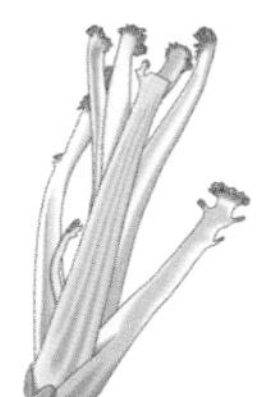

sea kale
*chou*ᴹ *marin*

collards
*chou*ᴹ *cavalier*ᴹ

escarole
*scarole*ᶠ

butter lettuce
*laitue*ᶠ *pommée*

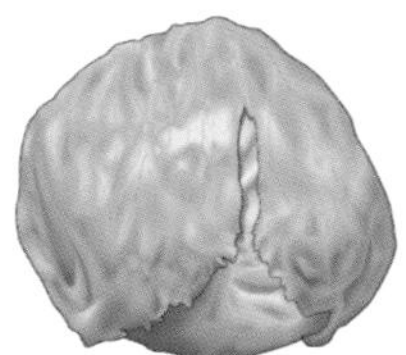

iceberg lettuce
*laitue*ᶠ *iceberg*ᴹ

radicchio
*chicorée*ᶠ *de Trévise*

ornamental kale
*chou*ᴹ *laitue*ᶠ

curly kale
*chou*ᴹ *frisé*

grape leaves
*feuille*ᶠ *de vigne*ᶠ

brussels sprouts
*choux*ᴹ *de Bruxelles*

red cabbage
*chou*ᴹ *pommé rouge*

white cabbage
*chou*ᴹ *pommé blanc*

savoy cabbage
*chou*ᴹ *de Milan*

green cabbage
*chou*ᴹ *pommé vert*

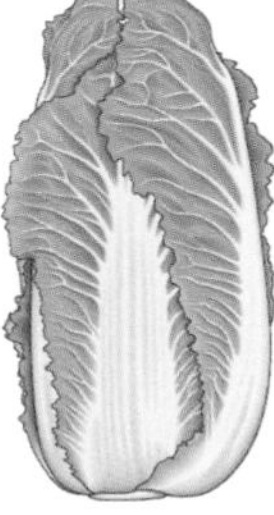

pe-tsai
*pe-tsaï*ᴹ

bok choy
*pak-choï*ᴹ

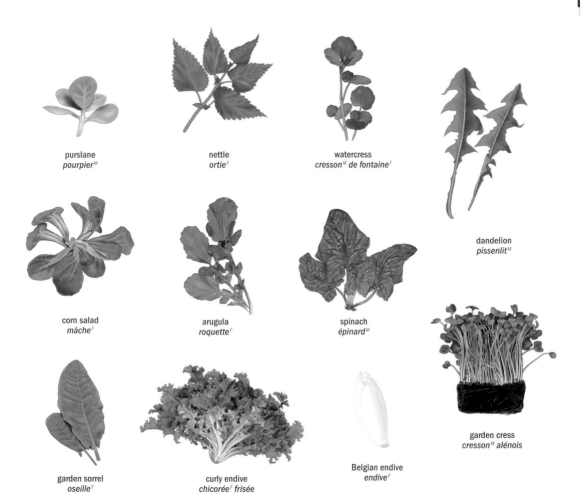

purslane
pourpier[M]

nettle
ortie[F]

watercress
cresson[M] de fontaine[F]

dandelion
pissenlit[M]

corn salad
mâche[F]

arugula
roquette[F]

spinach
épinard[M]

garden cress
cresson[M] alénois

garden sorrel
oseille[F]

curly endive
chicorée[F] frisée

Belgian endive
endive[F]

inflorescent vegetables
légumes[M] fleurs[F]

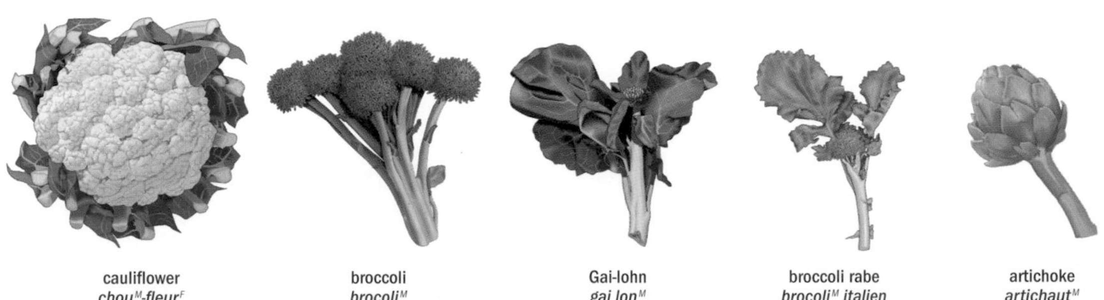

cauliflower
chou[M]-fleur[F]

broccoli
brocoli[M]

Gai-lohn
gai lon[M]

broccoli rabe
brocoli[M] italien

artichoke
artichaut[M]

vegetables

FOOD AND KITCHEN

fruit vegetables
légumes^M fruits^M

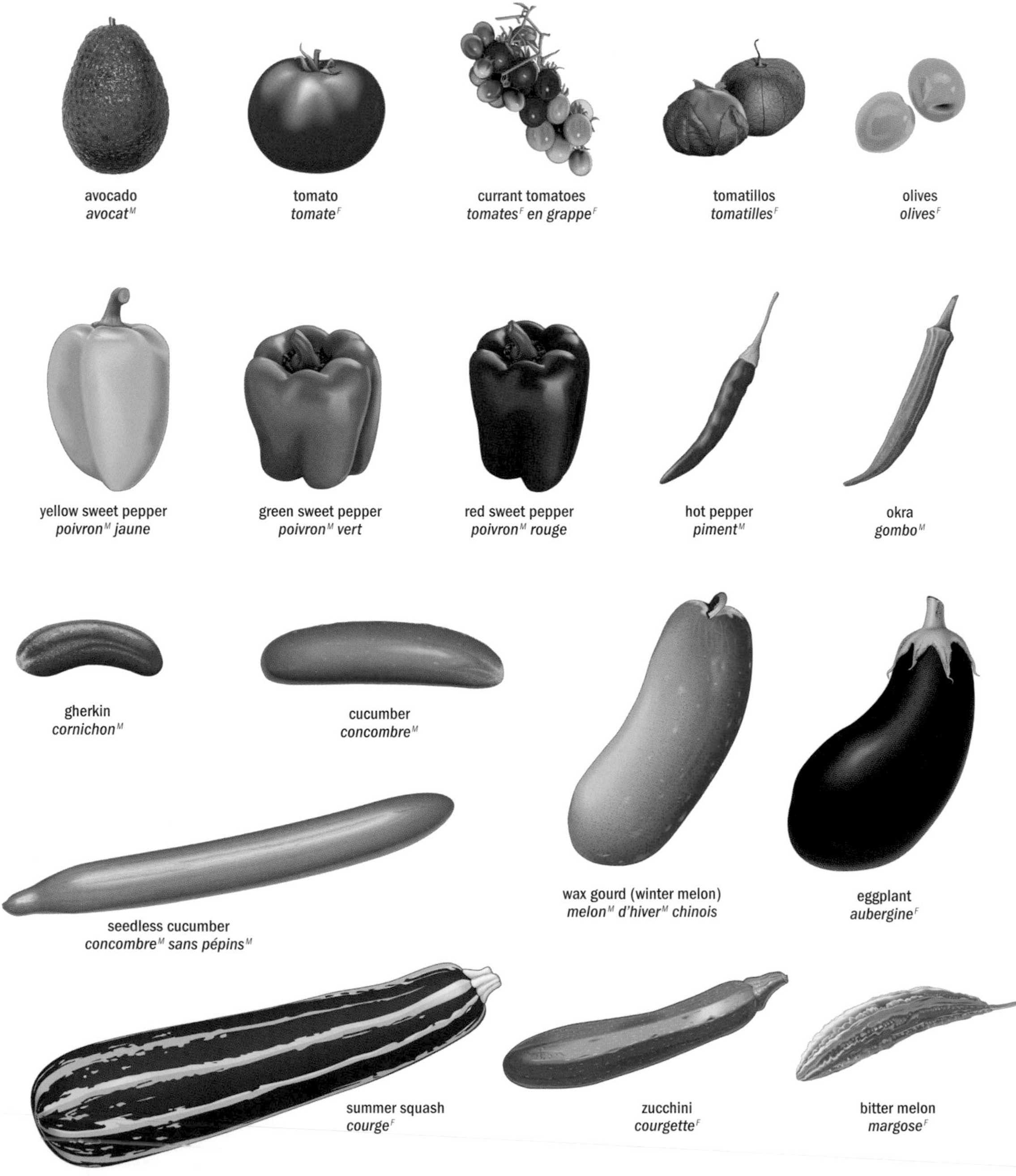
avocado
avocat^M
tomato
tomate^F
currant tomatoes
tomates^F en grappe^F
tomatillos
tomatilles^F
olives
olives^F
yellow sweet pepper
poivron^M jaune
green sweet pepper
poivron^M vert
red sweet pepper
poivron^M rouge
hot pepper
piment^M
okra
gombo^M
gherkin
cornichon^M
cucumber
concombre^M
wax gourd (winter melon)
melon^M d'hiver^M chinois
eggplant
aubergine^F
seedless cucumber
concombre^M sans pépins^M
summer squash
courge^F
zucchini
courgette^F
bitter melon
margose^F

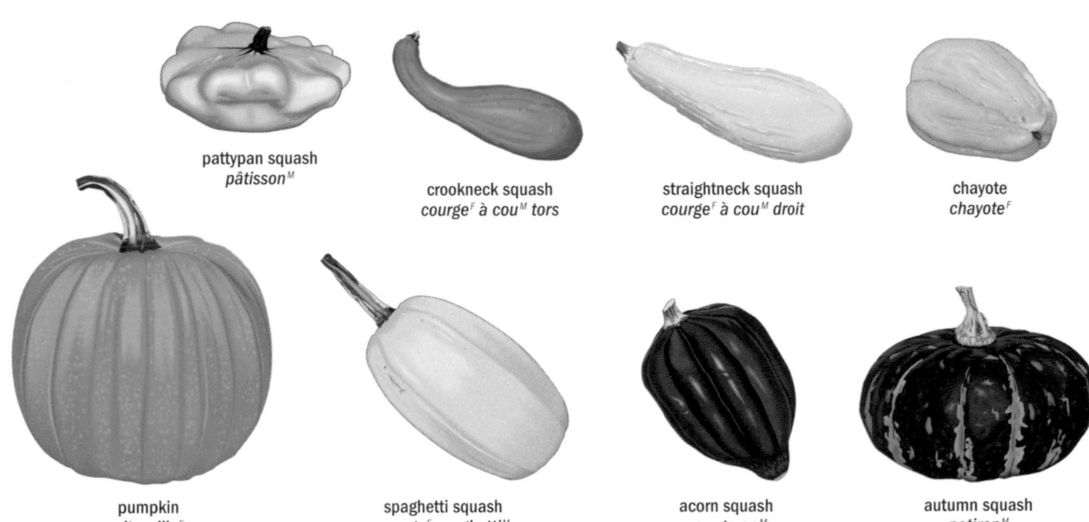

pattypan squash
pâtisson[M]

crookneck squash
courge[F] *à cou*[M] *tors*

straightneck squash
courge[F] *à cou*[M] *droit*

chayote
chayote[F]

pumpkin
citrouille[F]

spaghetti squash
courge[F] *spaghetti*[M]

acorn squash
courgeron[M]

autumn squash
potiron[M]

root vegetables
légumes[M] *racines*[F]

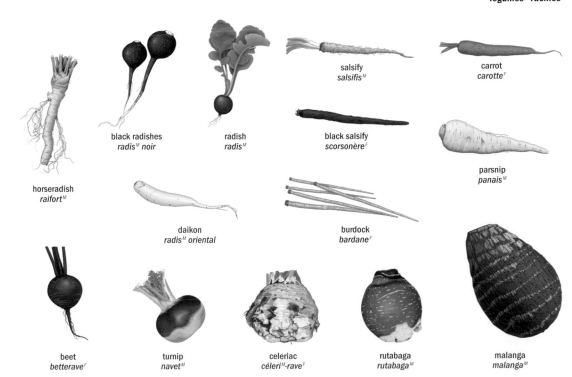

salsify
salsifis[M]

carrot
carotte[F]

black radishes
radis[M] *noir*

radish
radis[M]

black salsify
scorsonère[F]

horseradish
raifort[M]

parsnip
panais[M]

daikon
radis[M] *oriental*

burdock
bardane[F]

beet
betterave[F]

turnip
navet[M]

celeriac
céleri[M]*-rave*[F]

rutabaga
rutabaga[M]

malanga
malanga[M]

legumes

légumineuses[F]

alfalfa sprouts
luzerne[F]

lupines
lupin[M]

lentils
lentilles[F]

peanut
arachide[F]

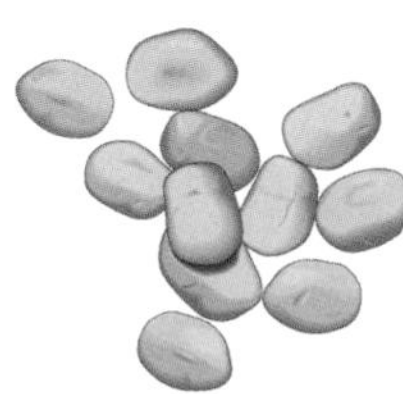

broad beans
fèves[F]

peas
pois[M]

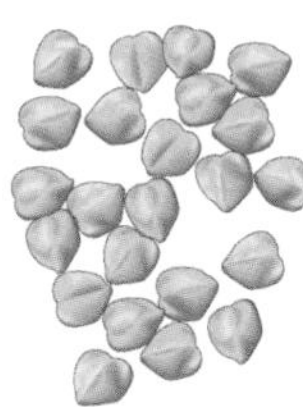

chick peas
pois[M] chiches

split peas
pois[M] cassés

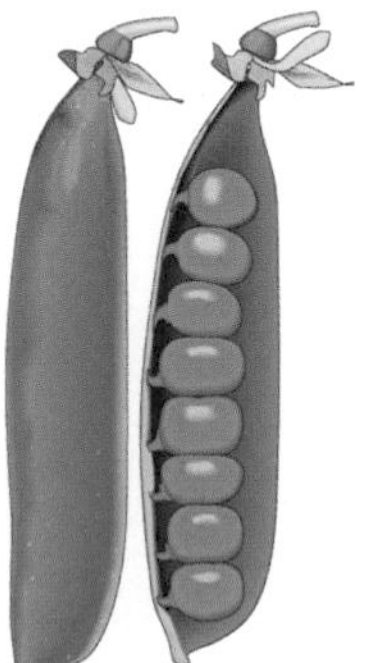

green peas
petits pois[M]

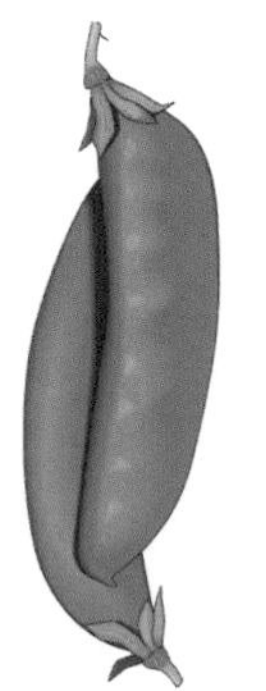

snow peas
pois[M] mange-tout[M]

dolichos beans
doliques[M]

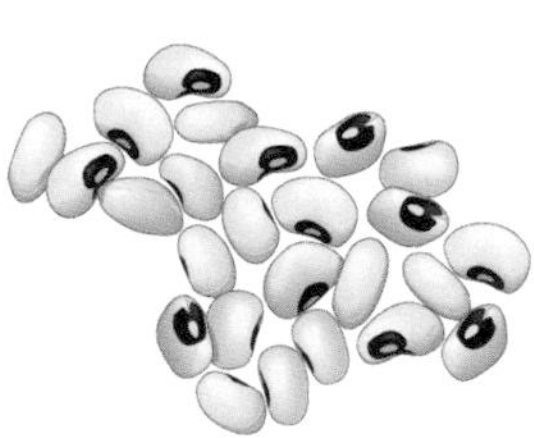

black-eyed peas
dolique[M] à œil[M] noir

lablab beans
dolique[M] d'Égypte[F]

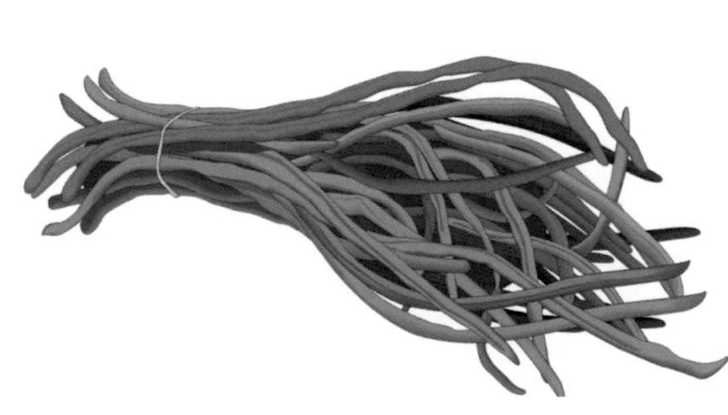

yard-long beans
dolique[M] asperge[F]

beans
haricots[M]

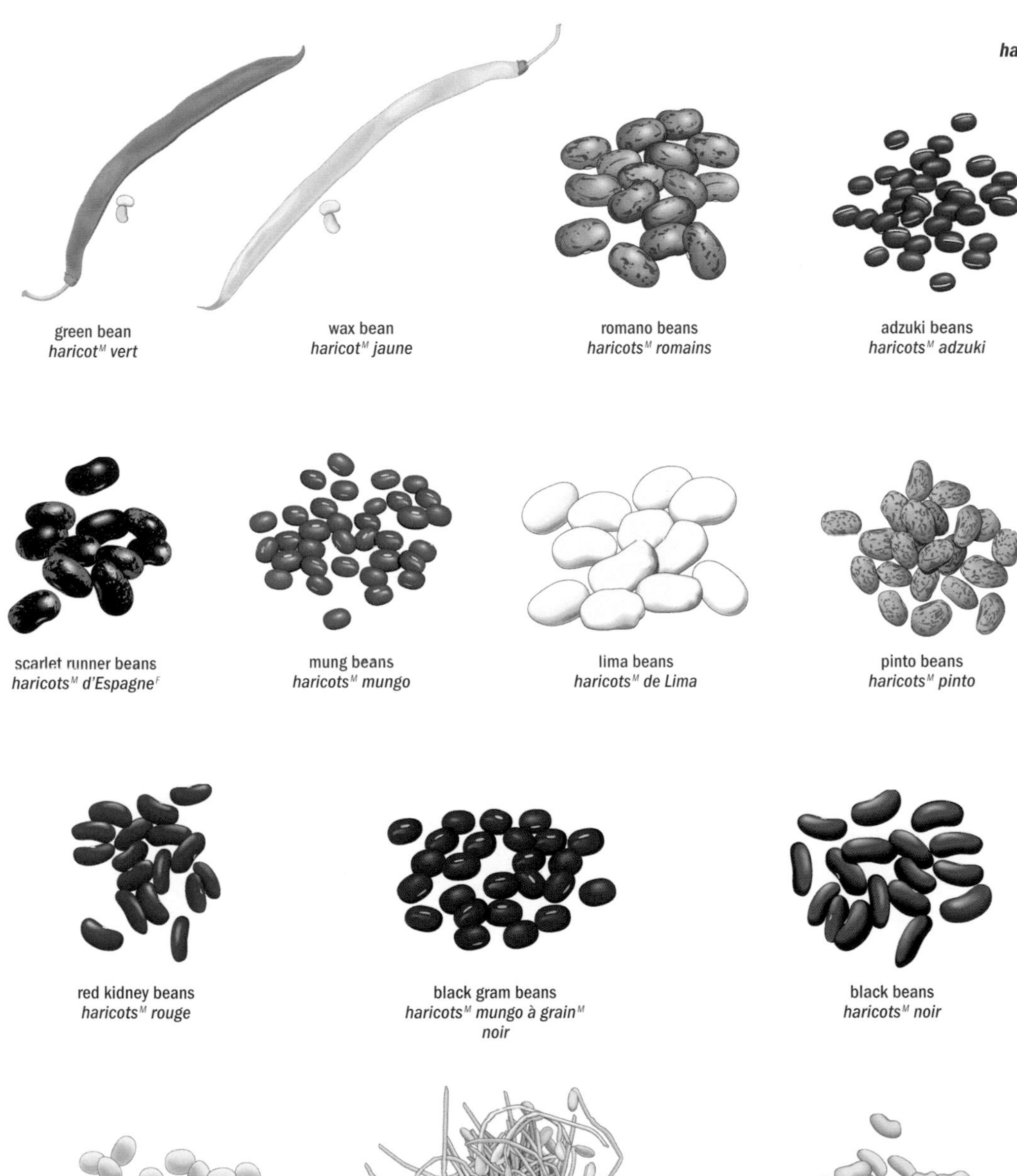

green bean
haricot[M] vert

wax bean
haricot[M] jaune

romano beans
haricots[M] romains

adzuki beans
haricots[M] adzuki

scarlet runner beans
haricots[M] d'Espagne[F]

mung beans
haricots[M] mungo

lima beans
haricots[M] de Lima

pinto beans
haricots[M] pinto

red kidney beans
haricots[M] rouge

black gram beans
haricots[M] mungo à grain[M] noir

black beans
haricots[M] noir

soybeans
graine[F] de soja[M] ; graine[F] de soya[M]

soybean sprouts
germes[M] de soja[M] ; germes[M] de soya[M]

flageolets
flageolets[M]

fruits

fruits[M]

berries
***baies*[F]**

currants
groseilles[F] *à grappes*[F] *; gadelle*[F]

black currants
cassis[M]

gooseberries
groseilles[F] *à maquereau*[M]

grapes
raisins[M]

blueberries
bleuets[M]

bilberries
myrtilles[F]

red whortleberries
airelles[F]

alkekengi
alkékenge[M]

cranberries
canneberges[F] *; atoca*[M]

raspberries
framboises[F]

blackberries
mûres[F]

strawberries
fraises[F]

stone fruits
***fruits*[M] *à noyau*[M]**

plums
prunes[F]

peach
pêche[F]

nectarine
nectarine[F]

apricot
abricot[M]

cherries
cerises[F]

dates
dattes[F]

dry fruits
fruits[M] secs

macadamia nuts
noix[F] de macadamia[M]

ginkgo nuts
noix[F] de ginkgo[M]

pistachio nuts
pistaches[F]

pine nuts
pignons[M]

cola nuts
noix[F] de cola[M]

pecan nuts
noix[F] de pacane[F]

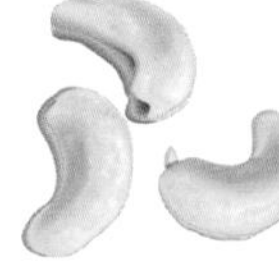
cashews
noix[F] de cajou[M]

almonds
amandes[F]

hazelnuts
noisettes[F]

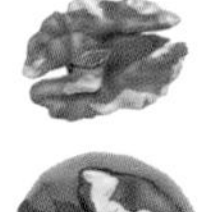
walnut
noix[F]

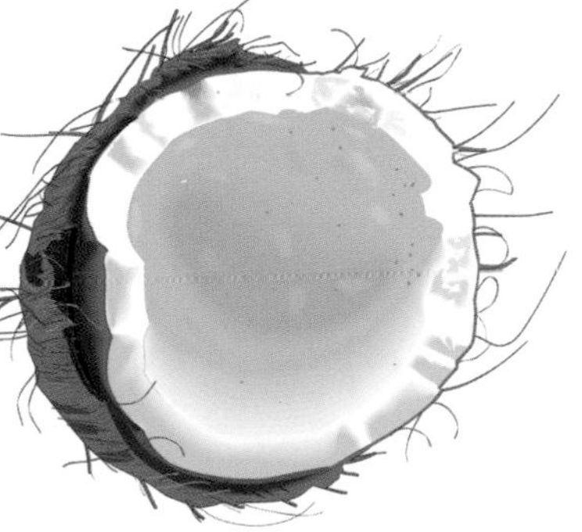
coconut
noix[F] de coco[M]

chestnuts
marrons[M]

beechnut
faîne[F]

Brazil nuts
noix[F] du Brésil[M]

pome fruits
fruits[M] à pépins[M]

pear
poire[F]

quince
coing[M]

apple
pomme[F]

Japanese plums
nèfles[F] du Japon[M]

citrus fruits
agrumes[M]

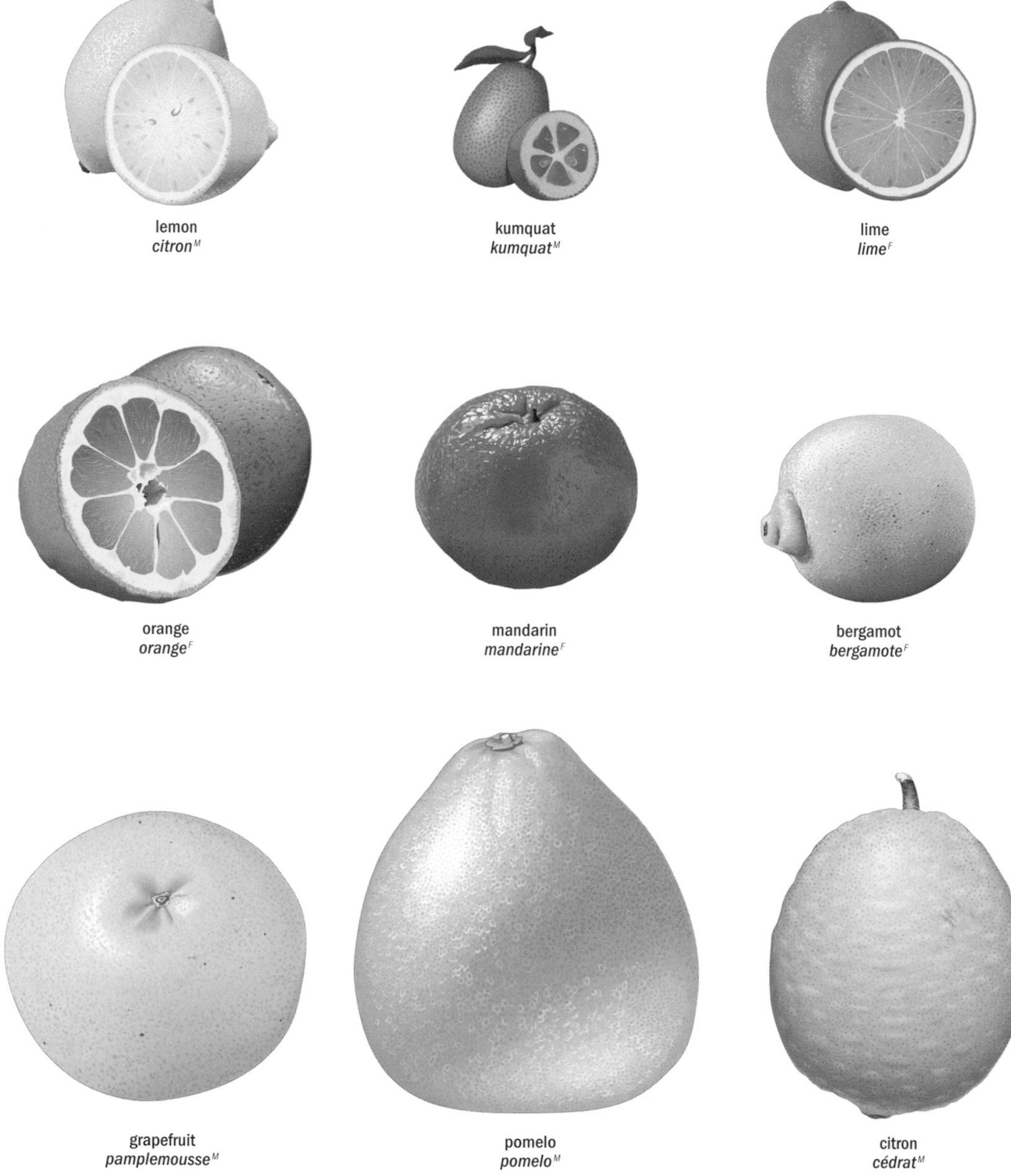
lemon
citron[M]
kumquat
kumquat[M]
lime
lime[F]
orange
orange[F]
mandarin
mandarine[F]
bergamot
bergamote[F]
grapefruit
pamplemousse[M]
pomelo
pomelo[M]
citron
cédrat[M]

melons
*melons*ᴹ

cantaloupe
*cantaloup*ᴹ

casaba melon
*melon*ᴹ *Casaba*

honeydew melon
*melon*ᴹ *miel*ᴹ

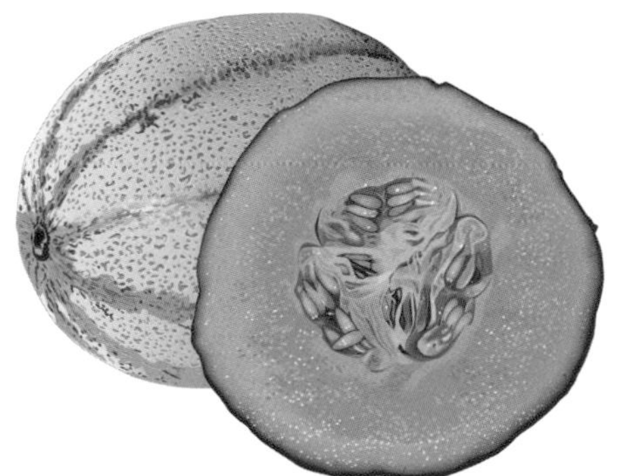
muskmelon
*melon*ᴹ *brodé*

canary melon
*melon*ᴹ *d'Espagne*ᶠ

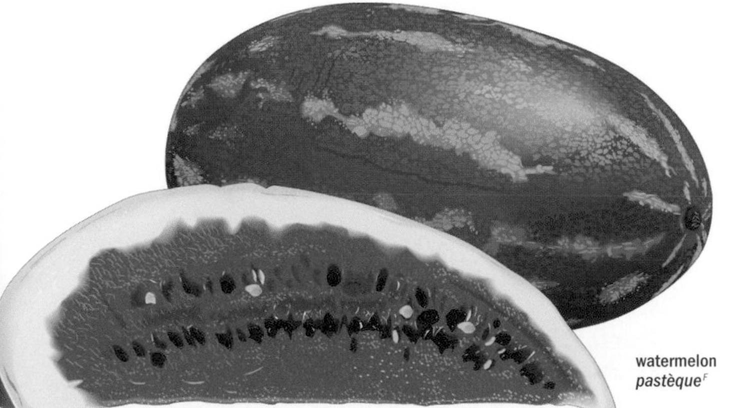
watermelon
*pastèque*ᶠ

Ogen melon
*melon*ᴹ *d'Ogen*

tropical fruits
fruits[M] tropicaux

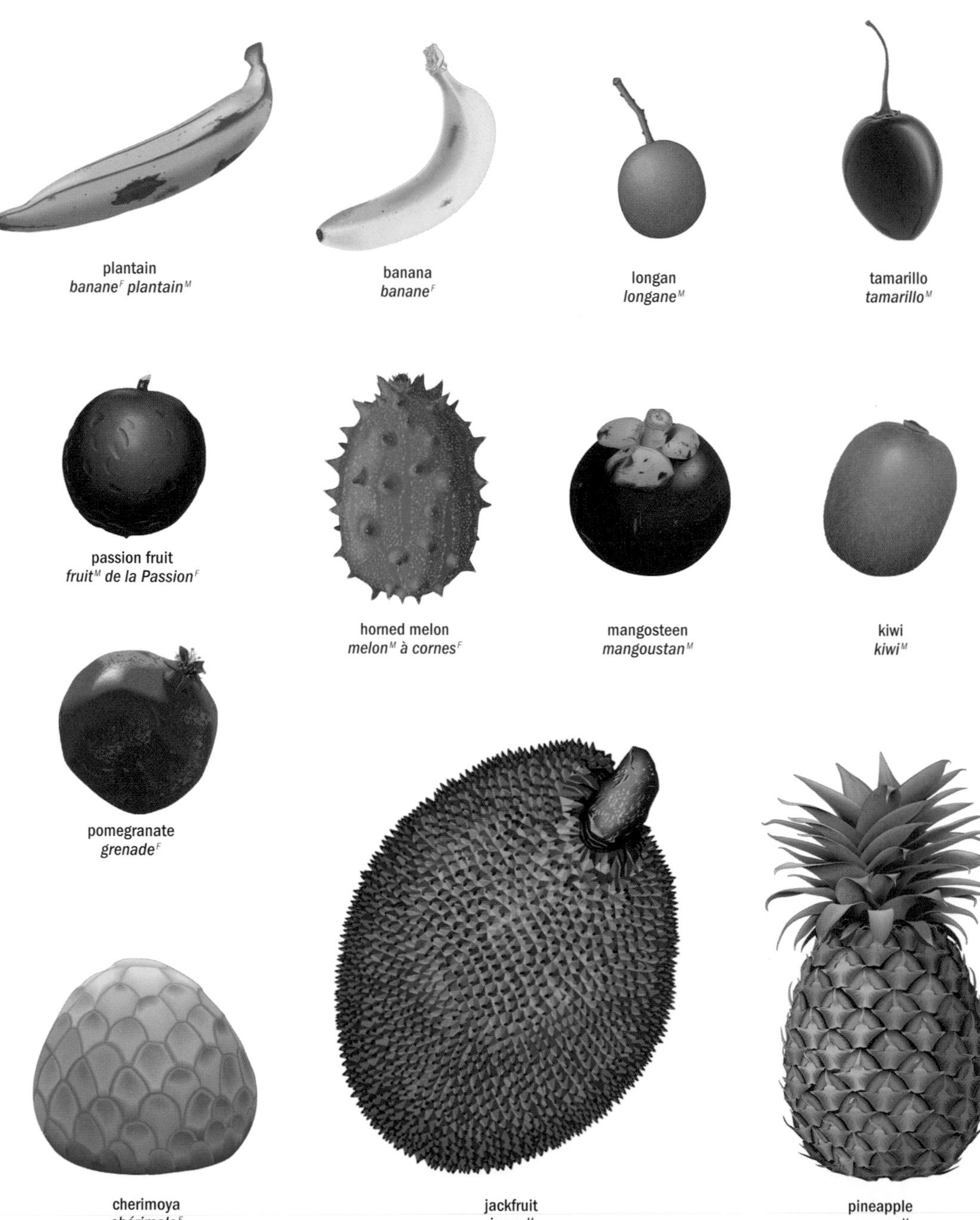

plantain
banane[F] plantain[M]

banana
banane[F]

longan
longane[M]

tamarillo
tamarillo[M]

passion fruit
fruit[M] de la Passion[F]

horned melon
melon[M] à cornes[F]

mangosteen
mangoustan[M]

kiwi
kiwi[M]

pomegranate
grenade[F]

cherimoya
chérimole[F]

jackfruit
jaque[M]

pineapple
ananas[M]

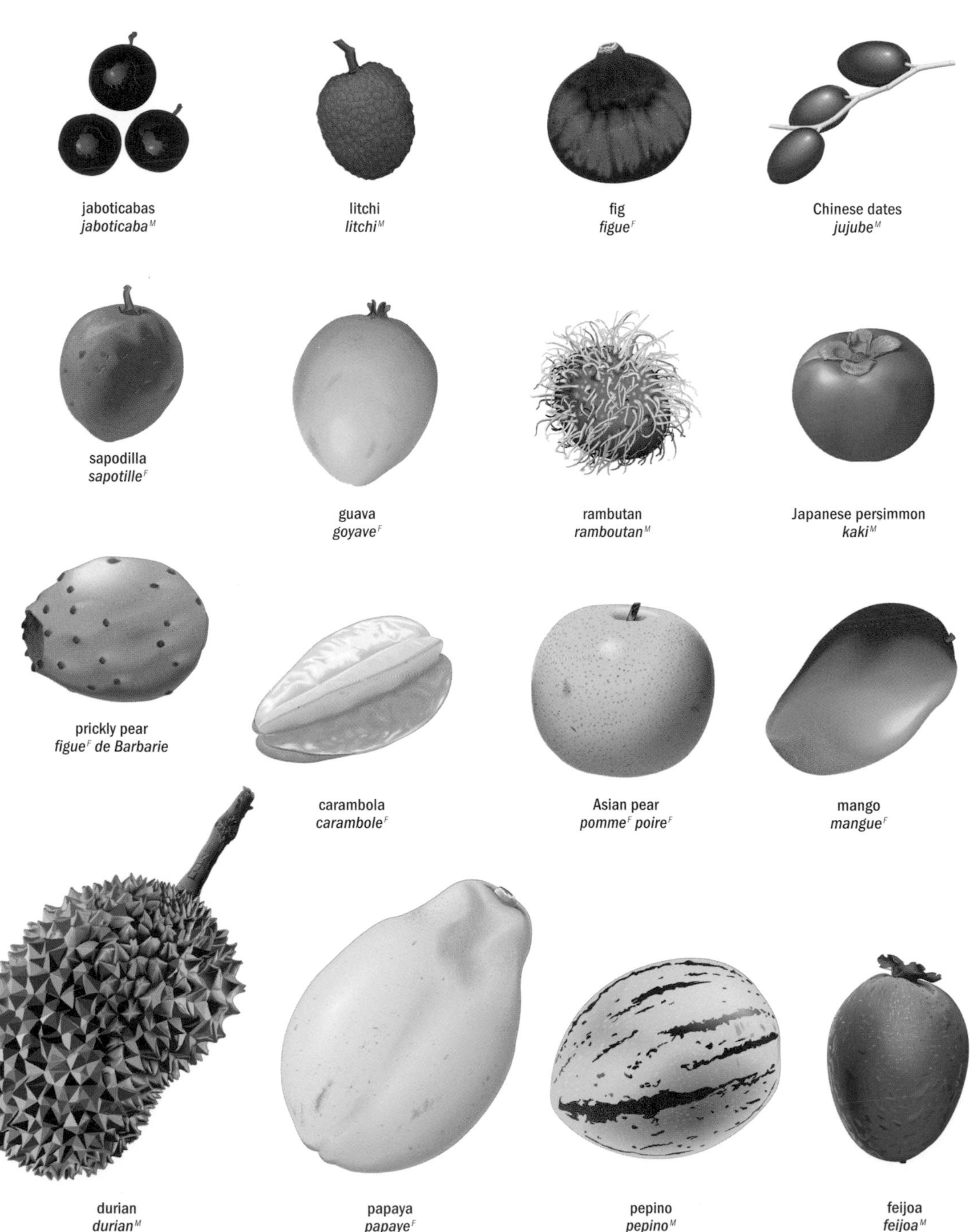

jaboticabas
jaboticaba^M

litchi
litchi^M

fig
figue^F

Chinese dates
jujube^M

sapodilla
sapotille^F

guava
goyave^F

rambutan
ramboutan^M

Japanese persimmon
kaki^M

prickly pear
figue^F *de Barbarie*

carambola
carambole^F

Asian pear
pomme^F *poire*^F

mango
mangue^F

durian
durian^M

papaya
papaye^F

pepino
pepino^M

feijoa
feijoa^M

spices

épices[F]

juniper berries
baies[F] de genièvre[M]

cloves
clou[M] de girofle[M]

allspice
piment[M] de la Jamaïque[F]

white mustard
moutarde[F] blanche

black mustard
moutarde[F] noire

black pepper
poivre[M] noir

white pepper
poivre[M] blanc

pink pepper
poivre[M] rose

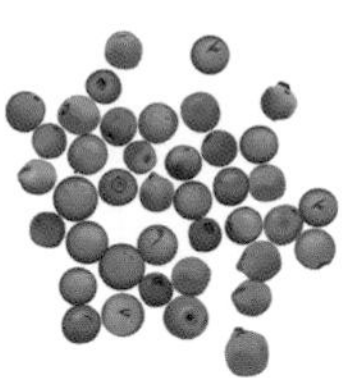

green pepper
poivre[M] vert

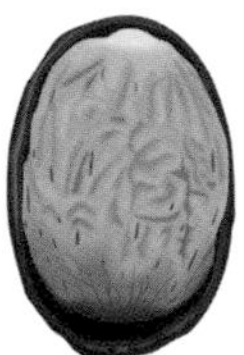

nutmeg
noix[F] de muscade[F]

caraway
carvi[M]

cardamom
cardamome[F]

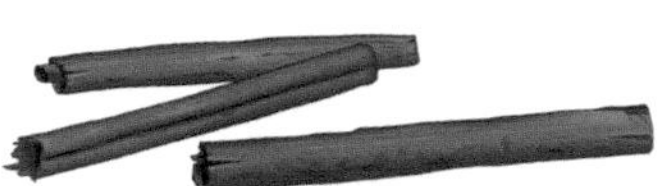

cinnamon
cannelle[F]

saffron
safran[M]

cumin
cumin[M]

curry
curry[M]

turmeric
curcuma[M]

fenugreek
fenugrec[M]

jalapeño chile
piment[M] *Jalapeño*

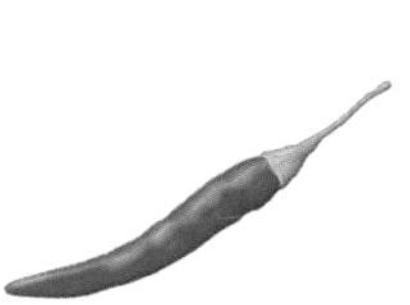

bird's eye chile
piment[M] *oiseau*[M]

crushed chiles
piments[M] *broyés*

dried chiles
piments[M] *séchés*

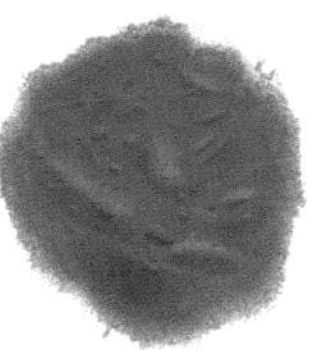

cayenne pepper
piment[M] *de Cayenne*

paprika
paprika[M]

ajowan
ajowan[M]

asafetida
asa-fœtida[F]

garam masala
garam masala[M]

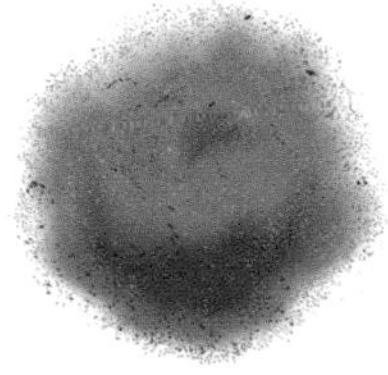

cajun spice seasoning
mélange[M] *d'épices*[F] *cajun*

marinade spices
épices[F] *à marinade*[F]

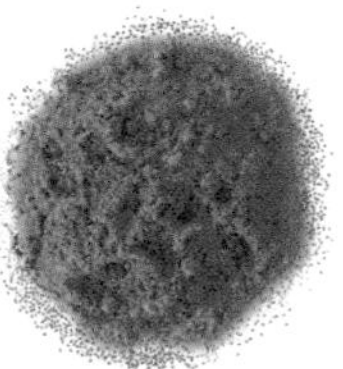

five spice powder
cinq-épices[M] *chinois*

chili powder
assaisonnement[M] *au chili*[M]

ground pepper
poivre[M] *moulu*

ras el hanout
ras-el-hanout[M]

sumac
sumac[M]

poppy seeds
graines[F] *de pavot*[M]

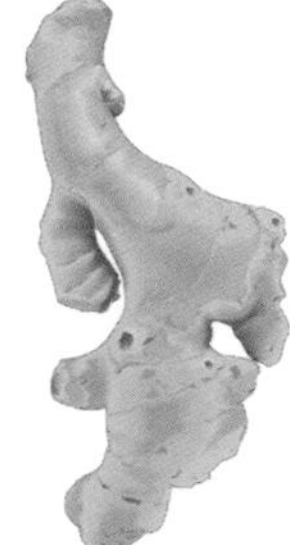

ginger
gingembre[M]

condiments

condiments[M]

Tabasco® sauce
sauce[F] Tabasco®[M]

Worcestershire sauce
sauce[F] Worcestershire

tamarind paste
pâte[F] de tamarin[M]

vanilla extract
extrait[M] de vanille[F]

tomato paste
concentré[M] de tomate[F]

tomato sauce
coulis[M] de tomate[F]

hummus
hoummos[M]

tahini
tahini[M]

hoisin sauce
sauce[F] hoisin

soy sauce
sauce[F] soja[M] ; sauce[F] soya[M]

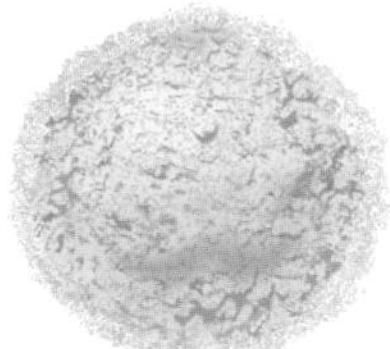

powdered mustard
moutarde[F] en poudre[F]

wholegrain mustard
moutarde[F] à l'ancienne[F]

Dijon mustard
moutarde[F] de Dijon

German mustard
moutarde[F] allemande

English mustard
moutarde[F] anglaise

American mustard
moutarde[F] américaine

plum sauce
sauce^F aux prunes^F

mango chutney
chutney^M à la mangue^F

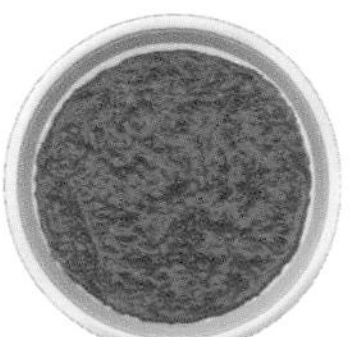
harissa
harissa^F

sambal oelek
sambal oelek^M

ketchup
ketchup^M

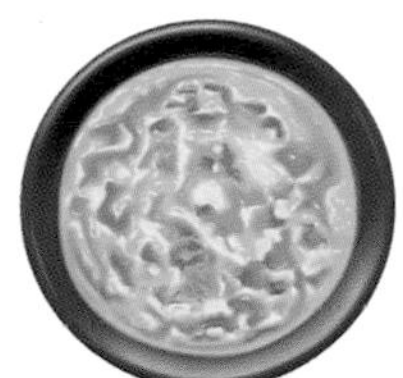
wasabi
wasabi^M

table salt
sel^M fin

coarse salt
gros sel^M

sea salt
sel^M marin

balsamic vinegar
vinaigre^M balsamique

rice vinegar
vinaigre^M de riz^M

apple cider vinegar
vinaigre^M de cidre^M

malt vinegar
vinaigre^M de malt^M

wine vinegar
vinaigre^M de vin^M

herbs

fines herbes[F]

dill
aneth[M]

anise
anis[M]

sweet bay
laurier[M]

oregano
origan[M]

tarragon
estragon[M]

basil
basilic[M]

sage
sauge[F]

thyme
thym[M]

mint
menthe[F]

parsley
persil[M]

chervil
cerfeuil[M]

coriander
coriandre[F]

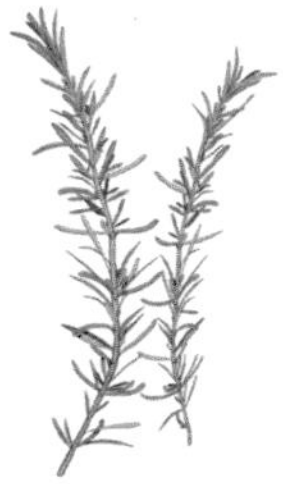

rosemary
romarin[M]

hyssop
hysope[F]

borage
bourrache[F]

lovage
livèche[F]

savory
sarriette[F]

lemon balm
mélisse[F]

cereal

céréales[F]

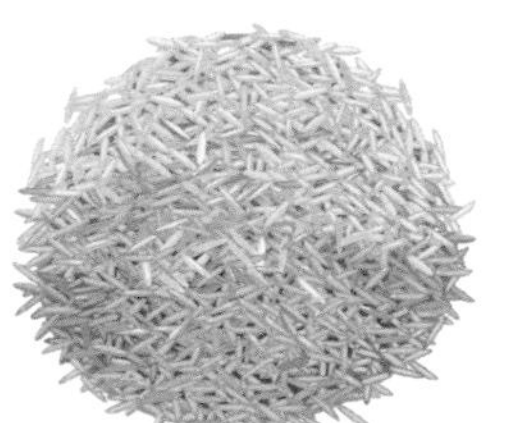

rice
riz[M]

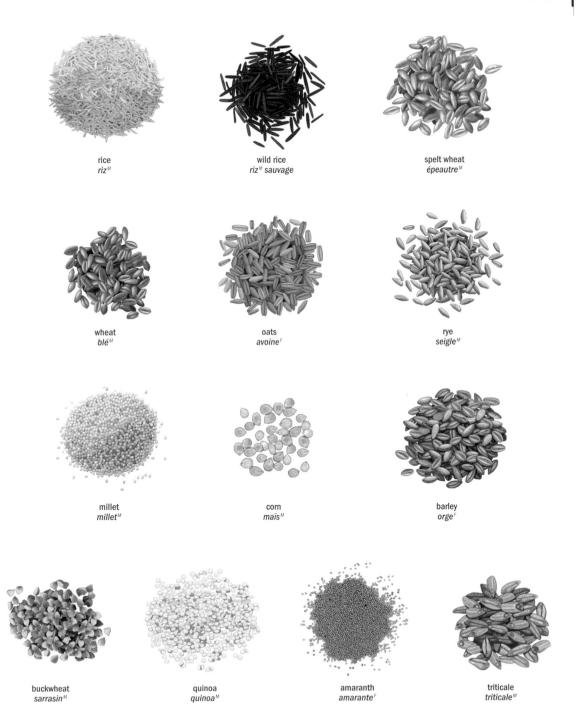

wild rice
riz[M] *sauvage*

spelt wheat
épeautre[M]

wheat
blé[M]

oats
avoine[F]

rye
seigle[M]

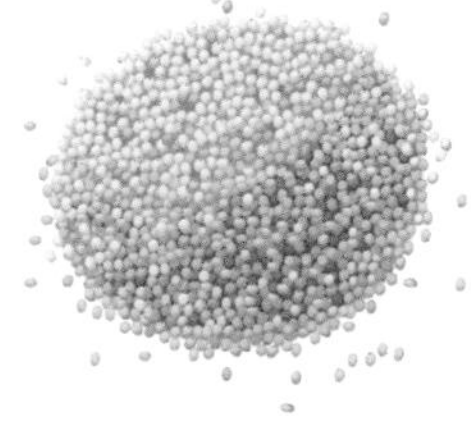

millet
millet[M]

corn
maïs[M]

barley
orge[F]

buckwheat
sarrasin[M]

quinoa
quinoa[M]

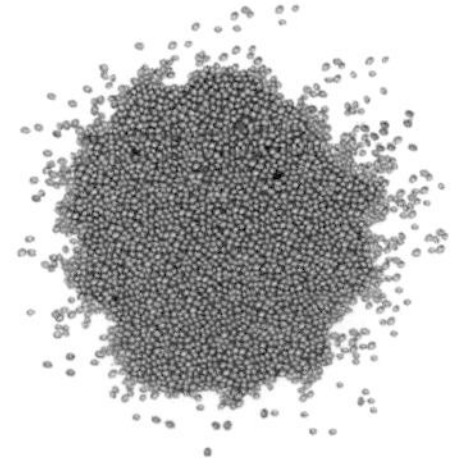

amaranth
amarante[F]

triticale
triticale[M]

cereal products

produits[M] céréaliers

flour and semolina
farine[F] et semoule[F]

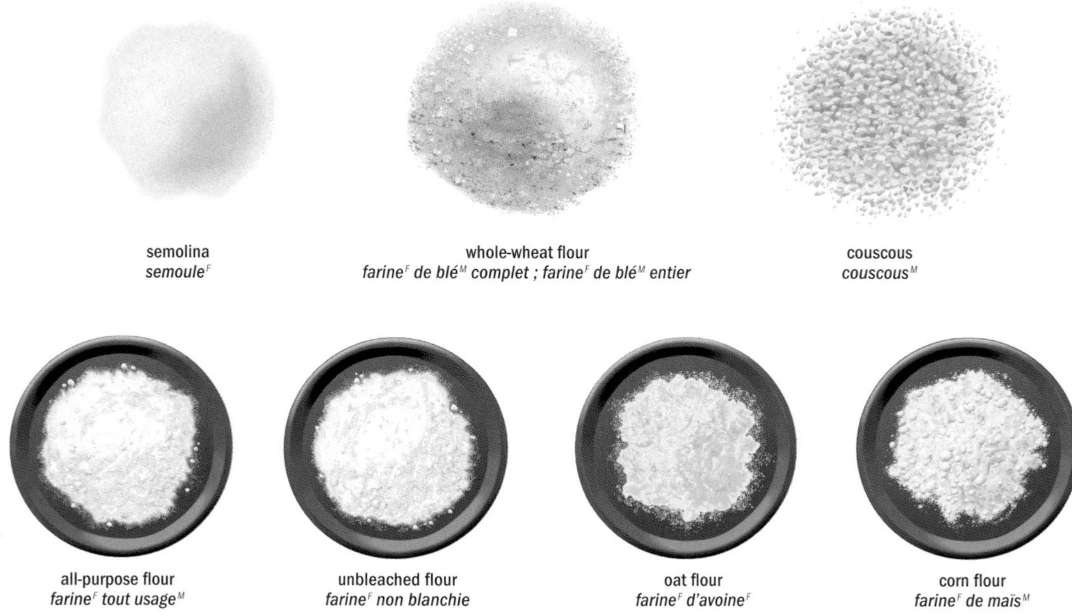

semolina
semoule[F]

whole-wheat flour
farine[F] de blé[M] complet ; farine[F] de blé[M] entier

couscous
couscous[M]

all-purpose flour
farine[F] tout usage[M]

unbleached flour
farine[F] non blanchie

oat flour
farine[F] d'avoine[F]

corn flour
farine[F] de maïs[M]

bread
pain[M]

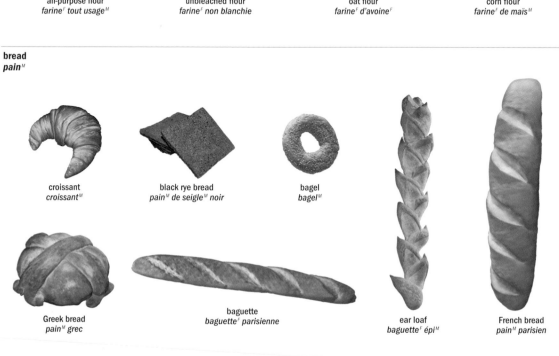

croissant
croissant[M]

black rye bread
pain[M] de seigle[M] noir

bagel
bagel[M]

Greek bread
pain[M] grec

baguette
baguette[F] parisienne

ear loaf
baguette[F] épi[M]

French bread
pain[M] parisien

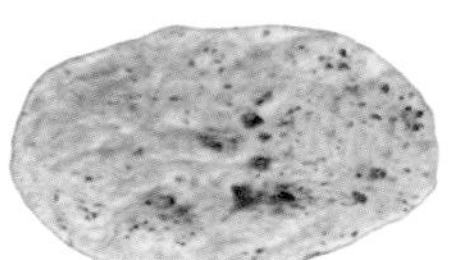
chapati
pain^M chapati indien

tortillas
tortillas^F

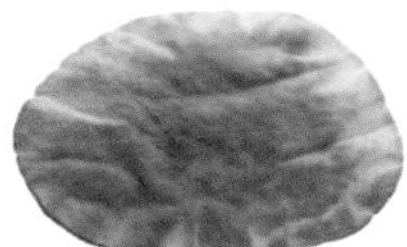
pita bread
pain^M pita

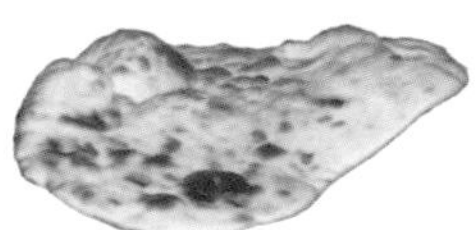
naan
pain^M naan indien

unleavened bread
pain^M azyme

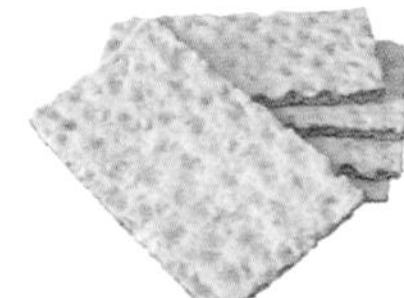
cracked rye bread
cracker^M de seigle^M

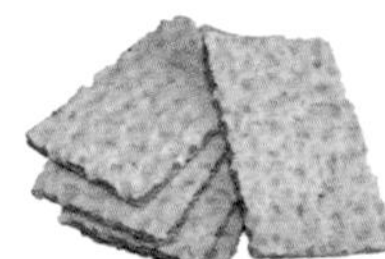
Scandinavian cracked bread
cracker^M scandinave

phyllo dough
pâte^F phyllo^F

Danish rye bread
pain^M de seigle^M danois

American corn bread
pain^M de maïs^M américain

multigrain bread
pain^M multicéréales

Russian pumpernickel
pain^M noir russe

German rye bread
pain^M de seigle^M allemand

challah
pain^M tchallah juif

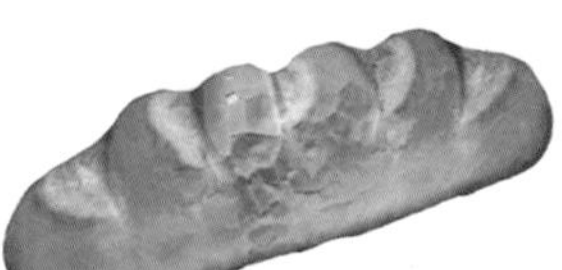
white bread
pain^M blanc

wholemeal bread
pain^M complet

farmhouse bread
pain^M de campagne^F

Irish soda bread
pain^M irlandais

English loaf
pain^M de mie^F

pasta
pâtes*[F] *alimentaires

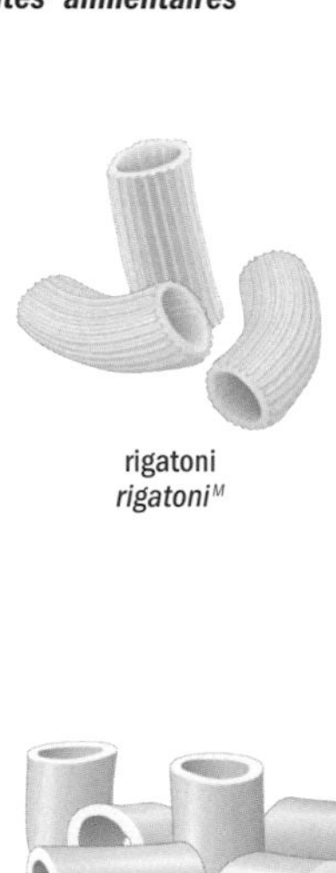

rigatoni
rigatoni[M]

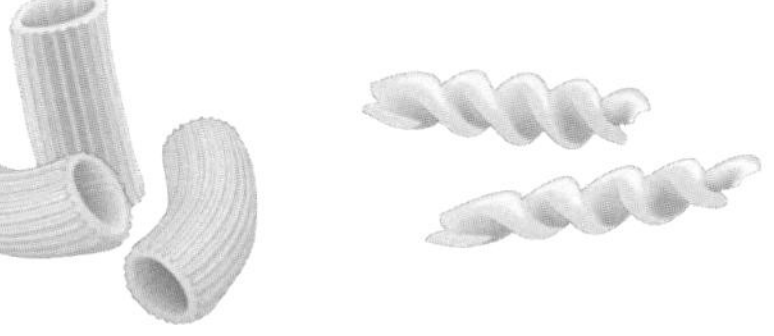

rotini
rotini[M]

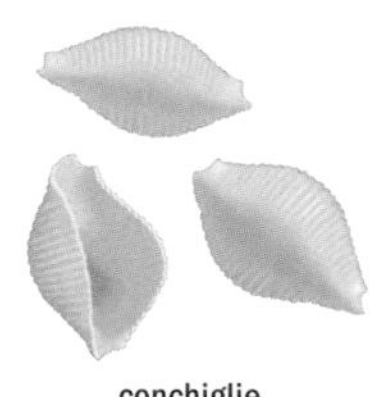

conchiglie
conchiglie[F]

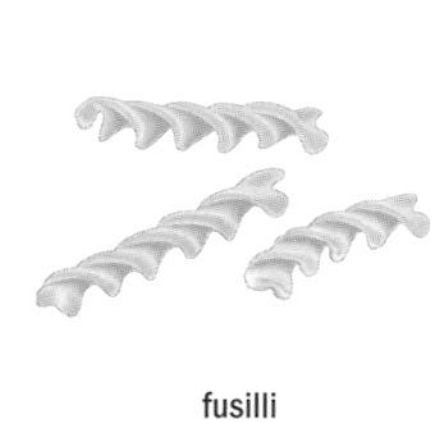

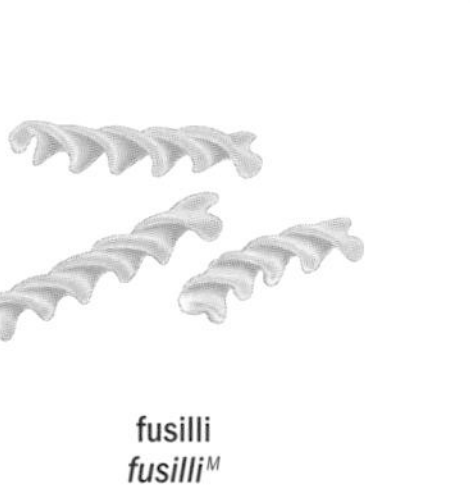

fusilli
fusilli[M]

spaghetti
spaghetti[M]

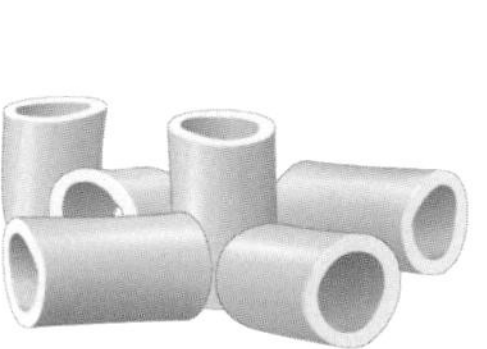

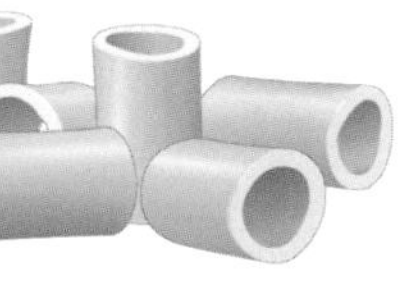

ditali
ditali[M]

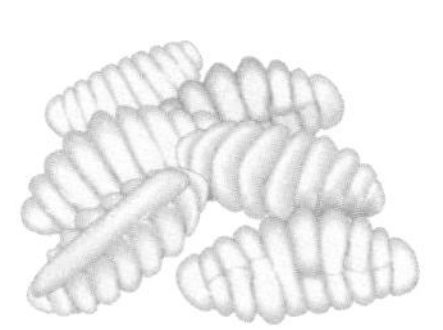

gnocchi
gnocchi[M]

tortellini
tortellini[M]

spaghettini
spaghettini[M]

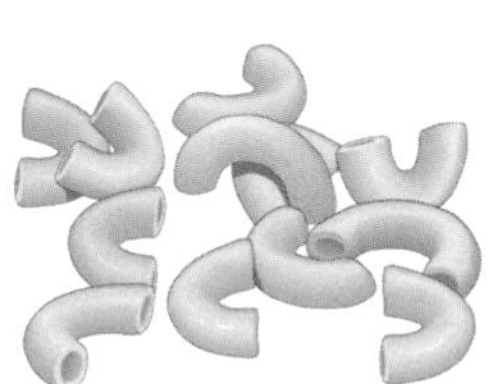

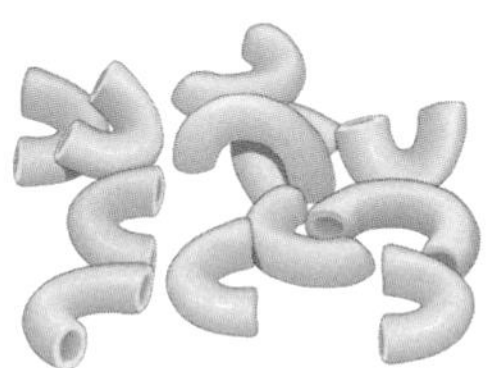

elbows
coudes[M]

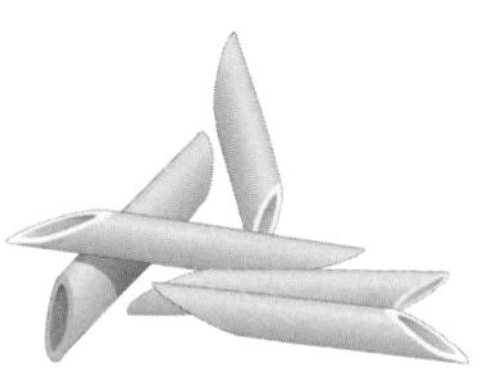

penne
penne[M]

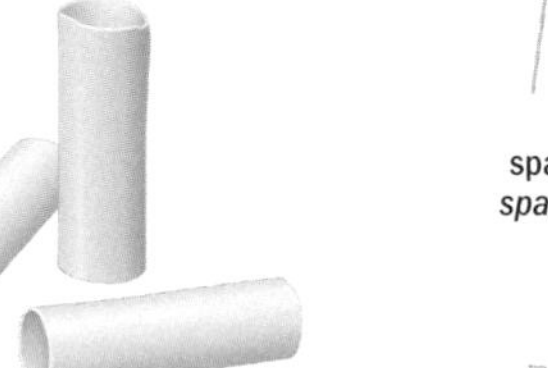

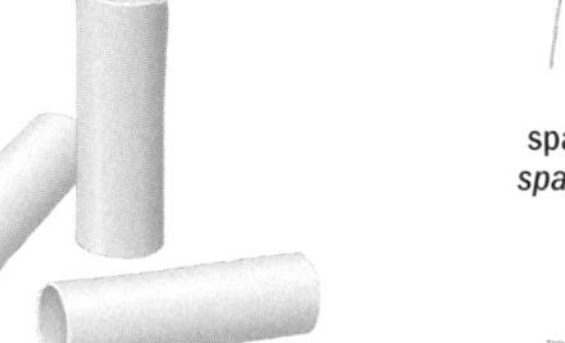

cannelloni
cannelloni[M]

lasagna
lasagne[F]

ravioli
ravioli[M]

spinach tagliatelle
tagliatelle[M] *aux épinards*[M]

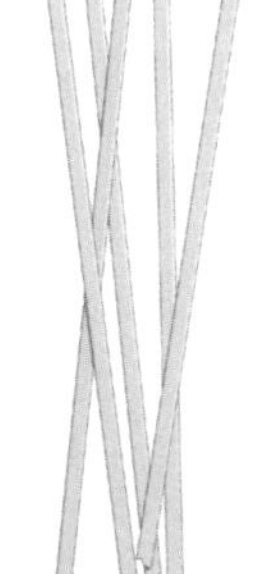

fettucine
fettucine[M]

Asian noodles
nouilles[F] *asiatiques*

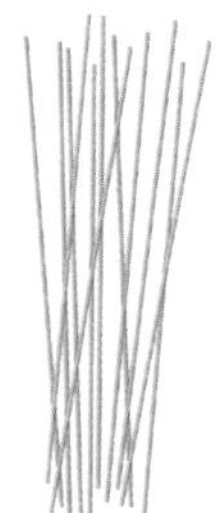
soba noodles
nouilles[F] *soba*

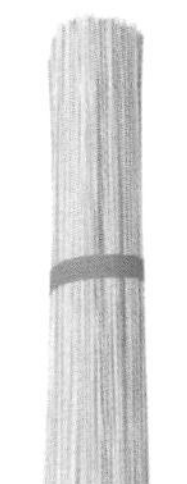
somen noodles
nouilles[F] *somen*

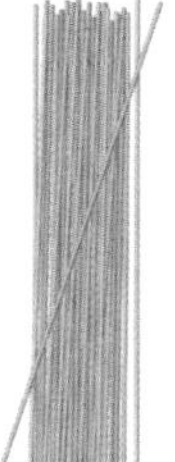
udon noodles
nouilles[F] *udon*

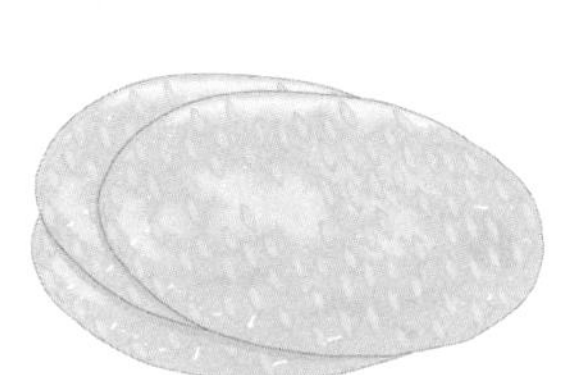
rice paper
galettes[F] *de riz*[M]

rice noodles
nouilles[F] *de riz*[M]

bean thread cellophane noodles
nouilles[F] *de haricots*[M] *mungo*

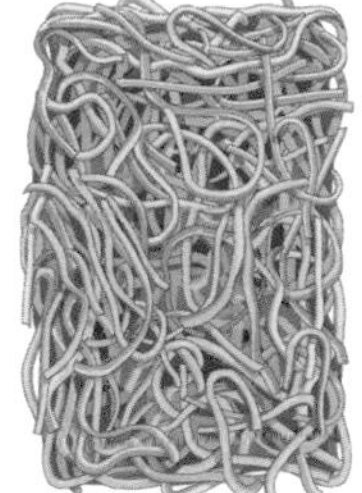
egg noodles
nouilles[F] *aux œufs*[M]

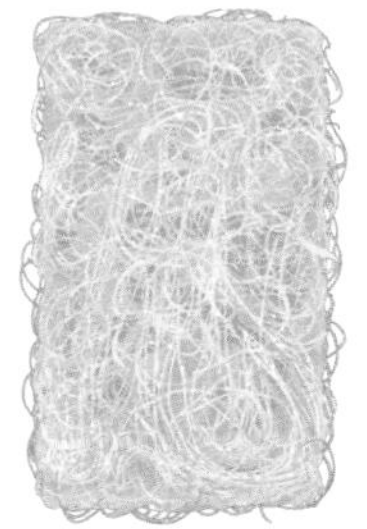
rice vermicelli
vermicelles[M] *de riz*[M]

won ton skins
pâtes[F] *won-ton*

rice
riz[M]

white rice
riz[M] *blanc*

brown rice
riz[M] *complet*

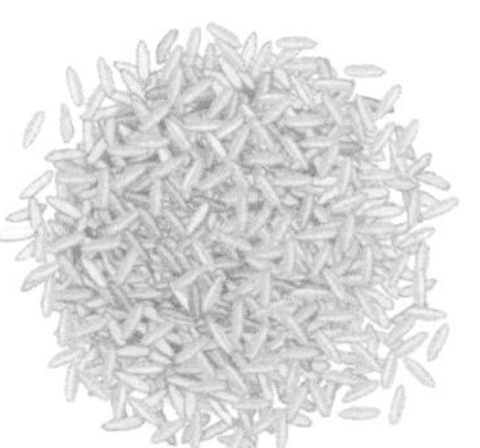
parboiled rice
riz[M] *étuvé*

basmati rice
riz[M] *basmati*

coffee and infusions

café[M] et infusions[F]

coffee
café[M]

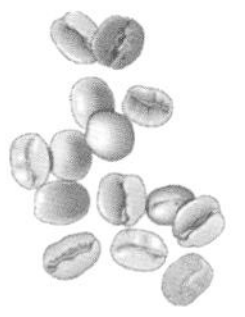

green coffee beans
grains[M] de café[M] verts

roasted coffee beans
grains[M] de café[M] torréfiés

herbal teas
tisanes[F]

linden
tilleul[M]

chamomile
camomille[F]

verbena
verveine[F]

tea
thé[M]

green tea
thé[M] vert

black tea
thé[M] noir

oolong tea
thé[M] oolong

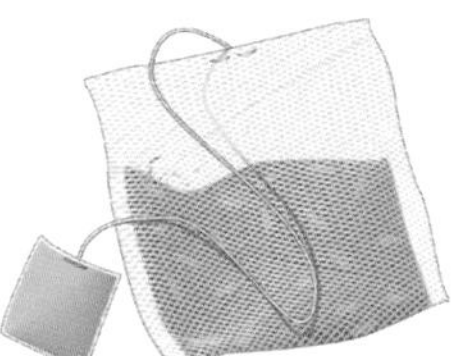

tea bag
thé[M] en sachet[M]

chocolate

chocolat[M]

dark chocolate
chocolat[M] noir

milk chocolate
chocolat[M] au lait[M]

cocoa
cacao[M]

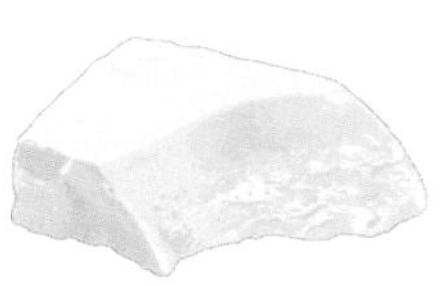

white chocolate
chocolat[M] blanc

sugar

sucre[M]

granulated sugar
sucre[M] granulé

powdered sugar
sucre[M] glace[F]

brown sugar
cassonade[F]

rock candy
sucre[M] candi

molasses
mélasse[F]

corn syrup
sirop[M] de maïs[M]

maple syrup
sirop[M] d'érable[M]

honey
miel[M]

fats and oils

huiles[F] et matières[F] grasses

corn oil
huile[F] de maïs[M]

olive oil
huile[F] d'olive[F]

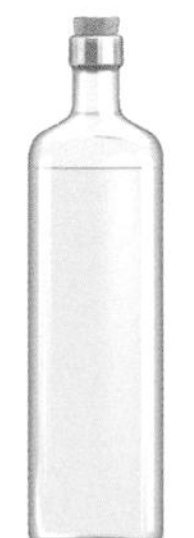
sunflower-seed oil
huile[F] de tournesol[M]

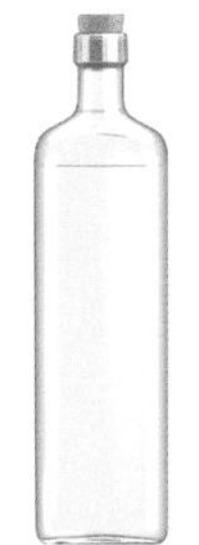
peanut oil
huile[F] d'arachide[F]

sesame oil
huile[F] de sésame[M]

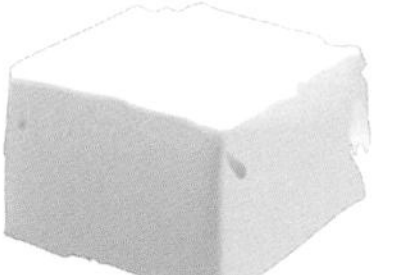
shortening
saindoux[M]

lard
lard[M]

margarine
margarine[F]

dairy products

produits^M laitiers

yogurt
yaourt^M ; yogourt^M

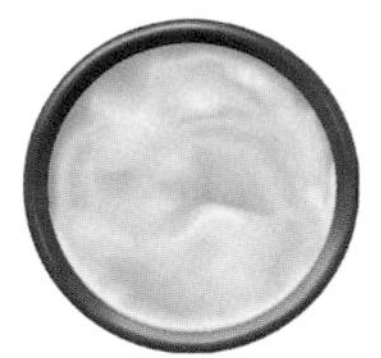

ghee
ghee^M

butter
beurre^M

cream
crème^F

whipping cream
crème^F épaisse ; crème^F à fouetter

sour cream
crème^F aigre ; crème^F sure

milk
lait^M

homogenized milk
lait^M homogénéisé

goat's milk
lait^M de chèvre^F

evaporated milk
lait^M concentré

buttermilk
babeurre^M

powdered milk
lait^M en poudre^F

fresh cheeses
fromages^M frais

cottage cheese
cottage^M

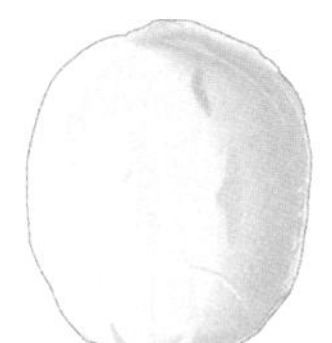

mozzarella
mozzarella^F

ricotta
ricotta^F

cream cheese
fromage^M à la crème^F

goat's-milk cheeses
fromages^M de chèvre^F

chèvre cheese
chèvre^M frais

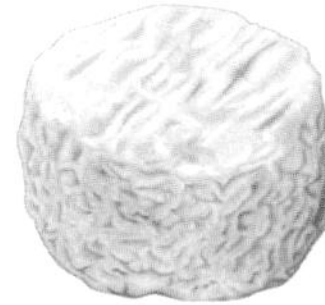

Crottin de Chavignol
crottin^M de Chavignol

pressed cheeses
fromages[M] à pâte[F] pressée

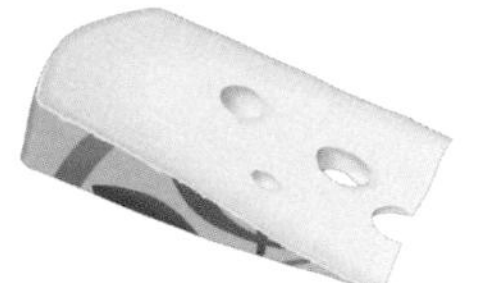

Jarlsberg
jarlsberg[M]

Emmenthal
emmenthal[M]

raclette
raclette[F]

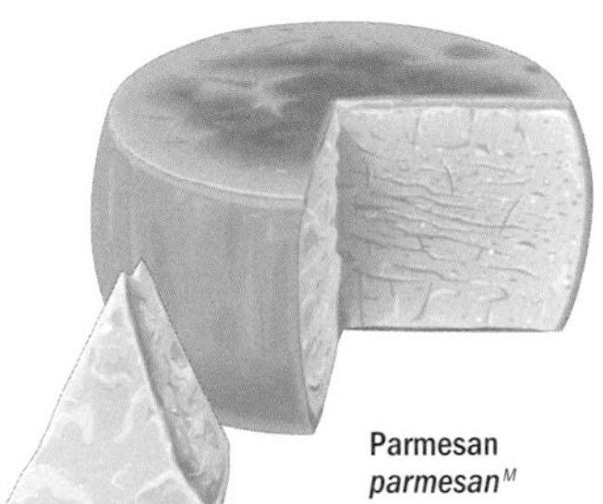

Parmesan
parmesan[M]

Gruyère
gruyère[M]

Romano
romano[M]

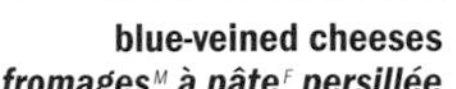

blue-veined cheeses
fromages[M] à pâte[F] persillée

Roquefort
roquefort[M]

Stilton
stilton[M]

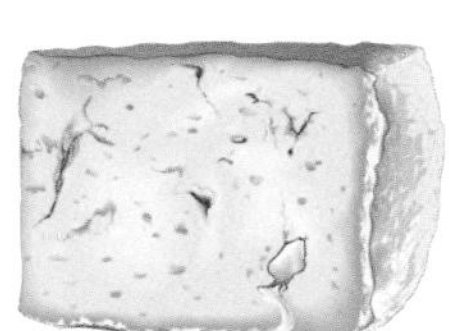

Gorgonzola
gorgonzola[M]

Danish Blue
bleu[M] danois

soft cheeses
fromages[M] à pâte[F] molle

Pont-l'Évêque
pont-l'évêque[M]

Coulommiers
coulommiers[M]

Camembert
camembert[M]

Brie
brie[M]

Munster
munster[M]

meat

viande[F]

cuts of beef
découpes[F] de bœuf[M]

steak
bifteck[M]

beef cubes
cubes[M] de bœuf[M]

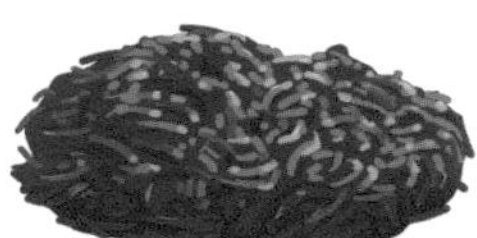

ground beef
bœuf[M] haché

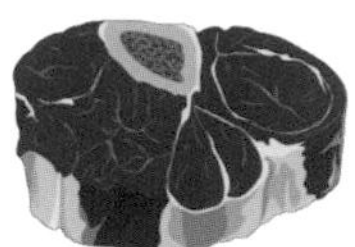

shank
jarret[M]

tenderloin roast
filet[M] de bœuf[M]

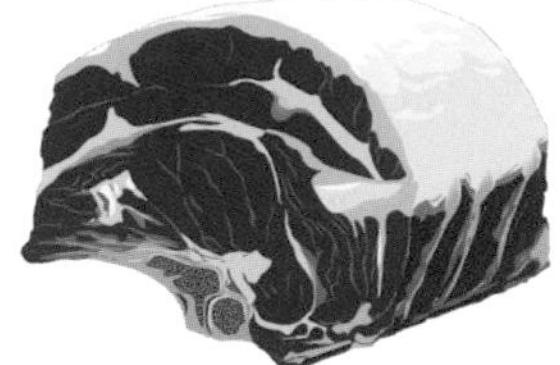

rib roast
rôti[M] de côtes[F]

back ribs
côtes[F] levées de dos[M]

cuts of veal
découpes[F] de veau[M]

veal cubes
cubes[M] de veau[M]

ground veal
veau[M] haché

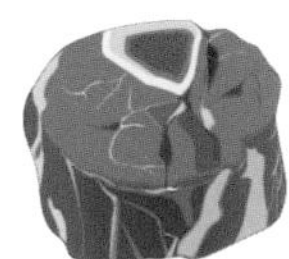

shank
jarret[M]

roast
rôti[M]

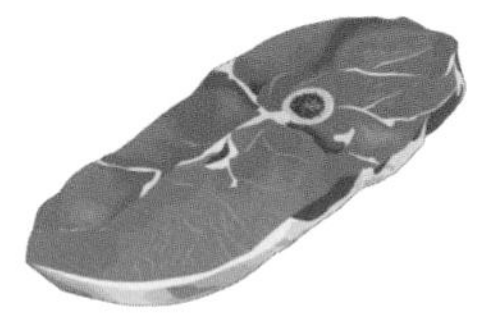

steak
bifteck[M]

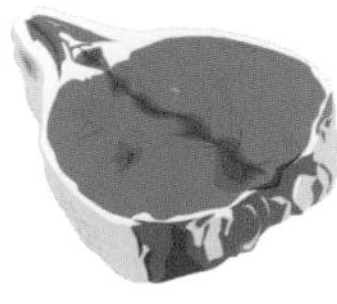

chop
côte[F]

cuts of lamb
découpes[F] d'agneau[M]

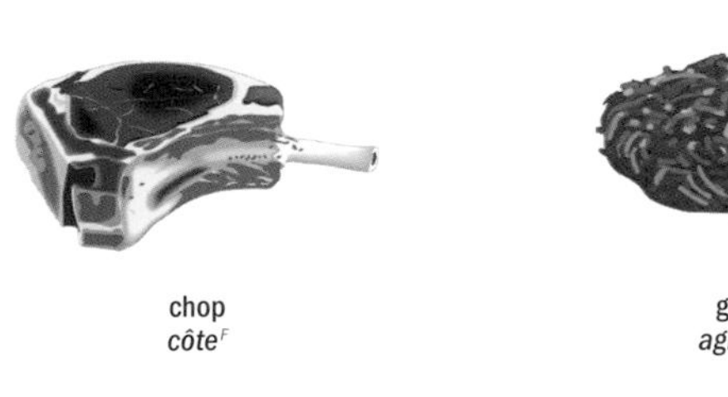

chop
côte[F]

ground lamb
agneau[M] haché

lamb cubes
cubes[M] d'agneau[M]

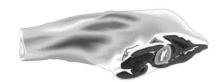

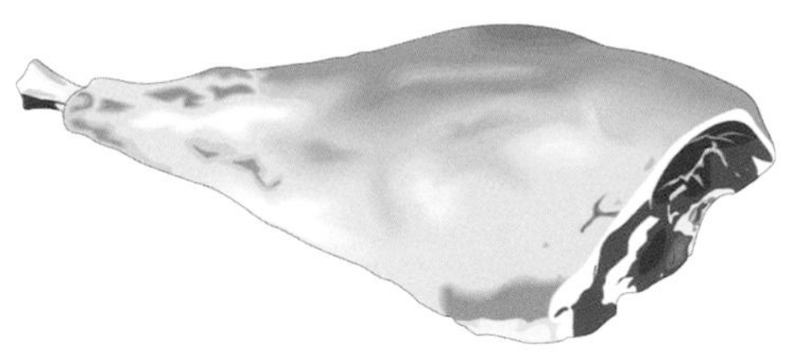

roast
rôti[M]

shank
jarret[M]

cuts of pork
découpes[F] de porc[M]

spareribs
travers[M] ; côtes[F] levées

ground pork
porc[M] haché

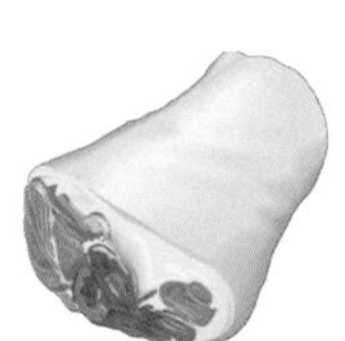

hock
jarret[M]

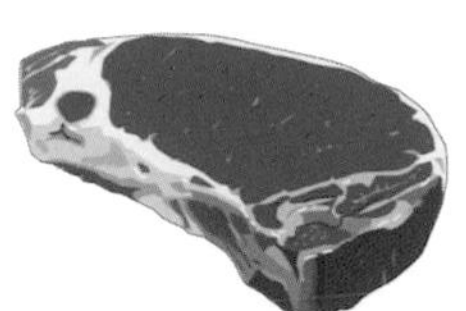

loin chop
côtelette[F]

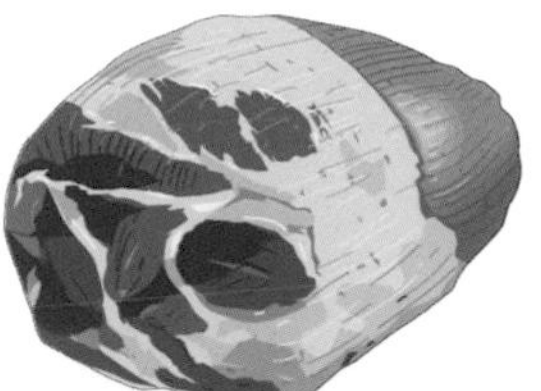

smoked ham
jambon[M] fumé

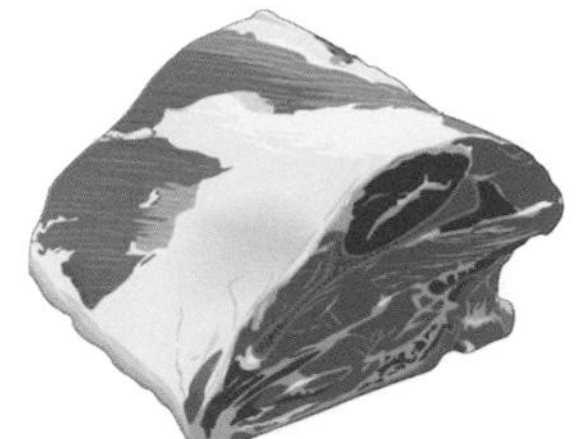

roast
rôti[M]

organ meat

abats[M]

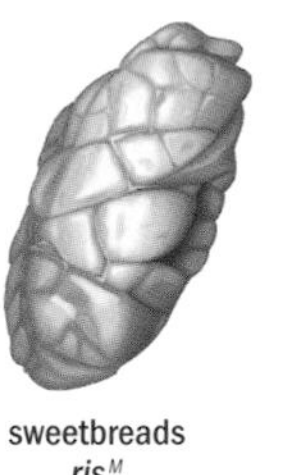

sweetbreads
ris[M]

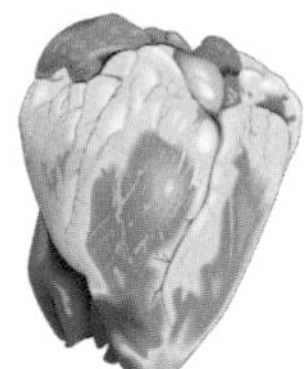

heart
cœur[M]

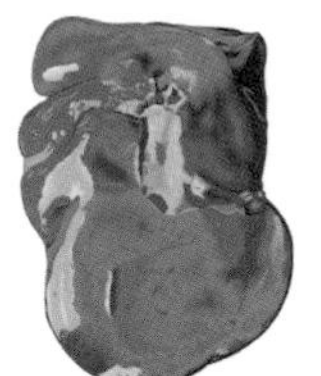

liver
foie[M]

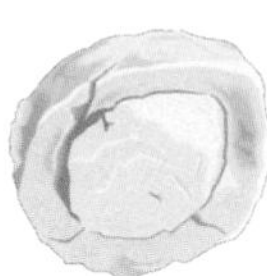

marrow
moelle[F]

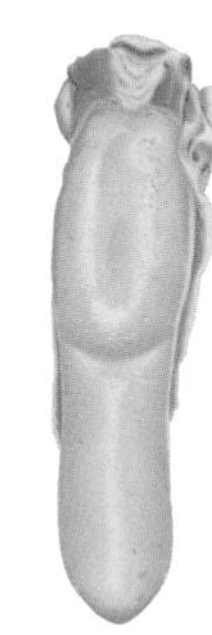

tongue
langue[F]

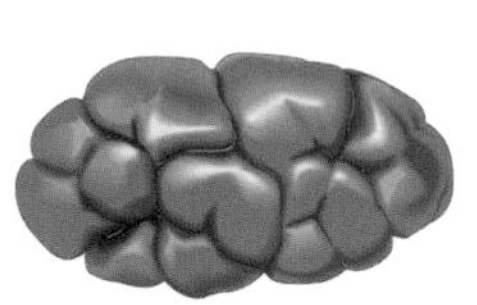

kidney
rognons[M]

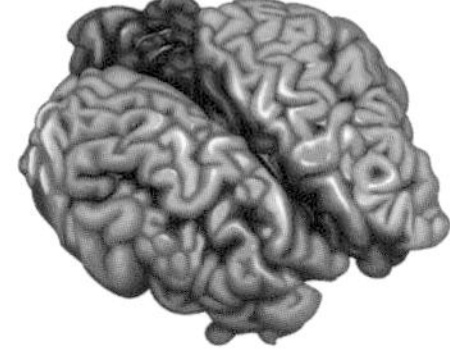

brains
cervelle[F]

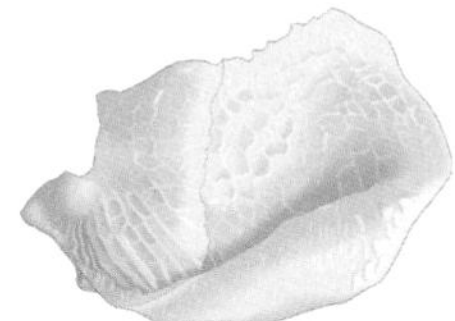

tripe
tripes[F]

game

gibier[M]

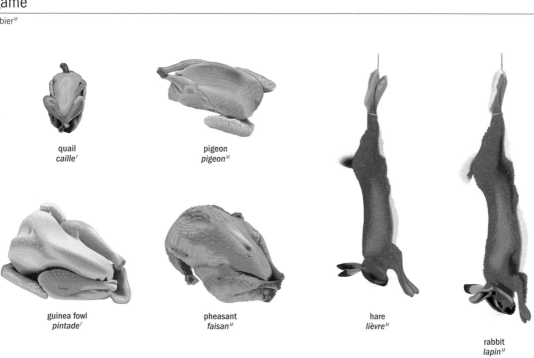

quail
caille[F]

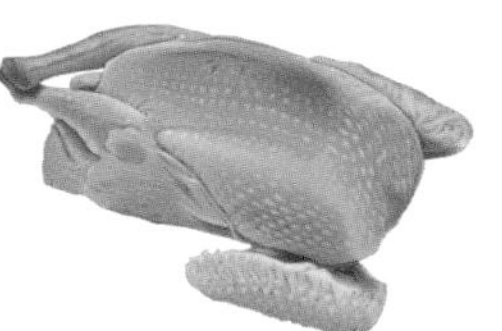

pigeon
pigeon[M]

guinea fowl
pintade[F]

pheasant
faisan[M]

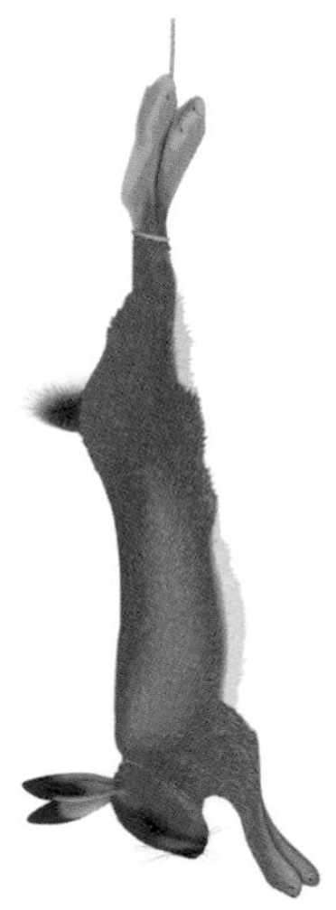

hare
lièvre[M]

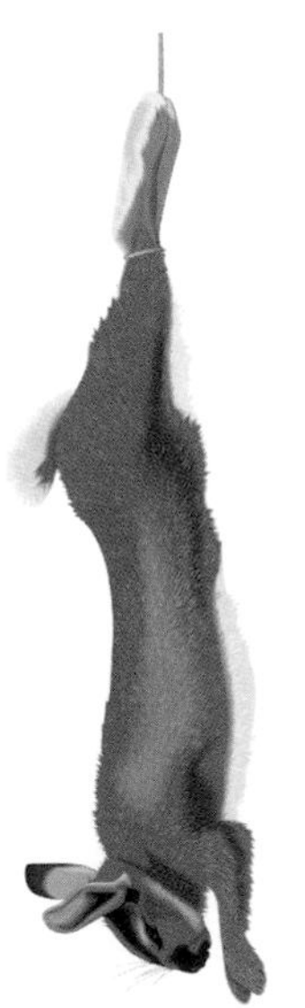

rabbit
lapin[M]

poultry
volaille[F]

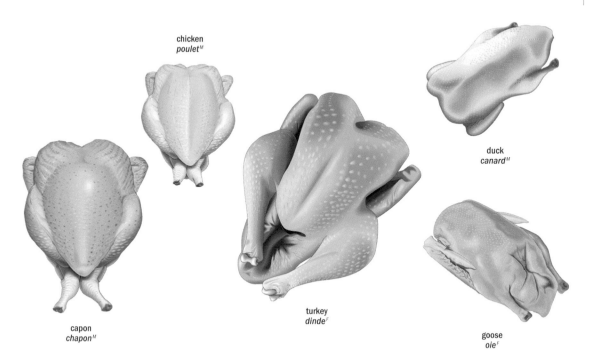

chicken
poulet[M]

duck
canard[M]

capon
chapon[M]

turkey
dinde[F]

goose
oie[F]

eggs
œufs[M]

quail egg
œuf[M] *de caille*[F]
pheasant egg
œuf[M] *de faisane*[F]
goose egg
œuf[M] *d'oie*[F]
ostrich egg
œuf[M] *d'autruche*[F]
duck egg
œuf[M] *de cane*[F]
hen egg
œuf[M] *de poule*[F]

delicatessen

charcuterie[F]

rillettes
rillettes[F]

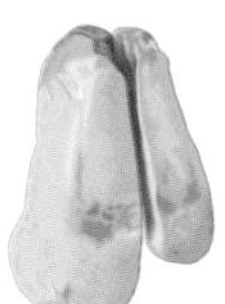

foie gras
foie[M] gras

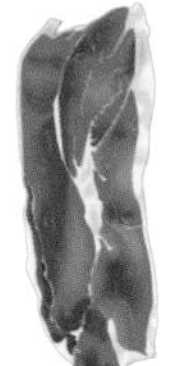

prosciutto
prosciutto[M]

kielbasa sausage
saucisson[M] kielbasa

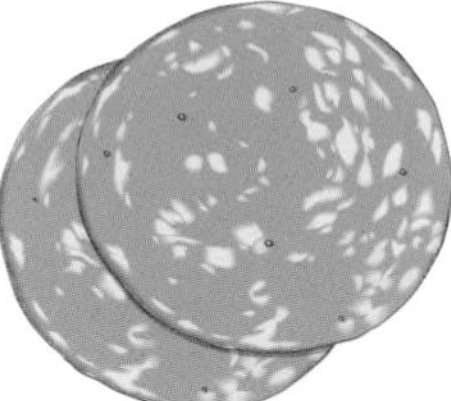

mortadella
mortadelle[F]

blood sausage
boudin[M]

chorizo
chorizo[M]

pepperoni
pepperoni[M]

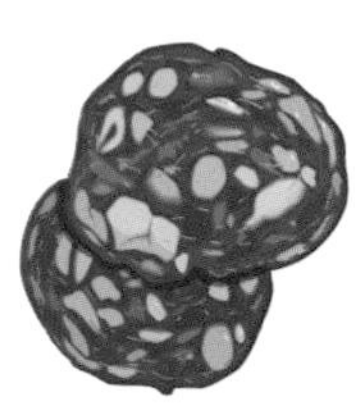

Genoa salami
salami[M] de Gênes

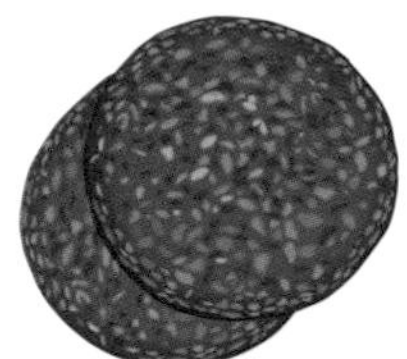

German salami
salami[M] allemand

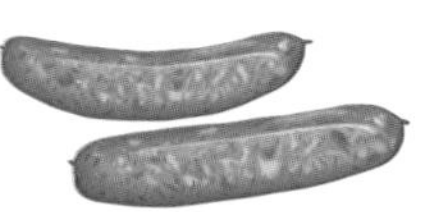

Toulouse sausages
saucisse[F] de Toulouse

merguez sausages
merguez[F]

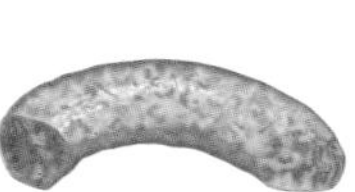

andouillette
andouillette[F]

chipolata sausage
chipolata[F]

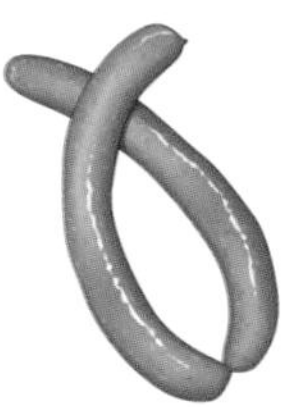

frankfurters
saucisse[F] de Francfort

pancetta
pancetta[F]

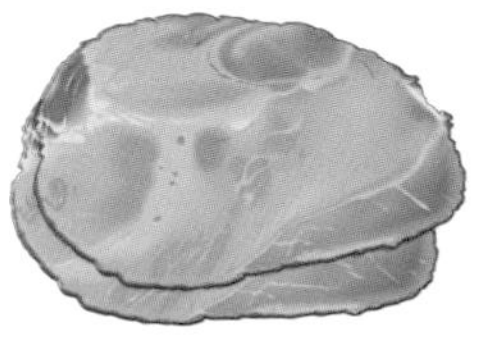

cooked ham
jambon[M] cuit

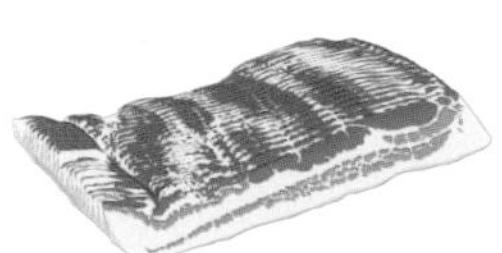

American bacon
bacon[M] américain

Canadian bacon
bacon[M] canadien

mollusks

mollusques^M

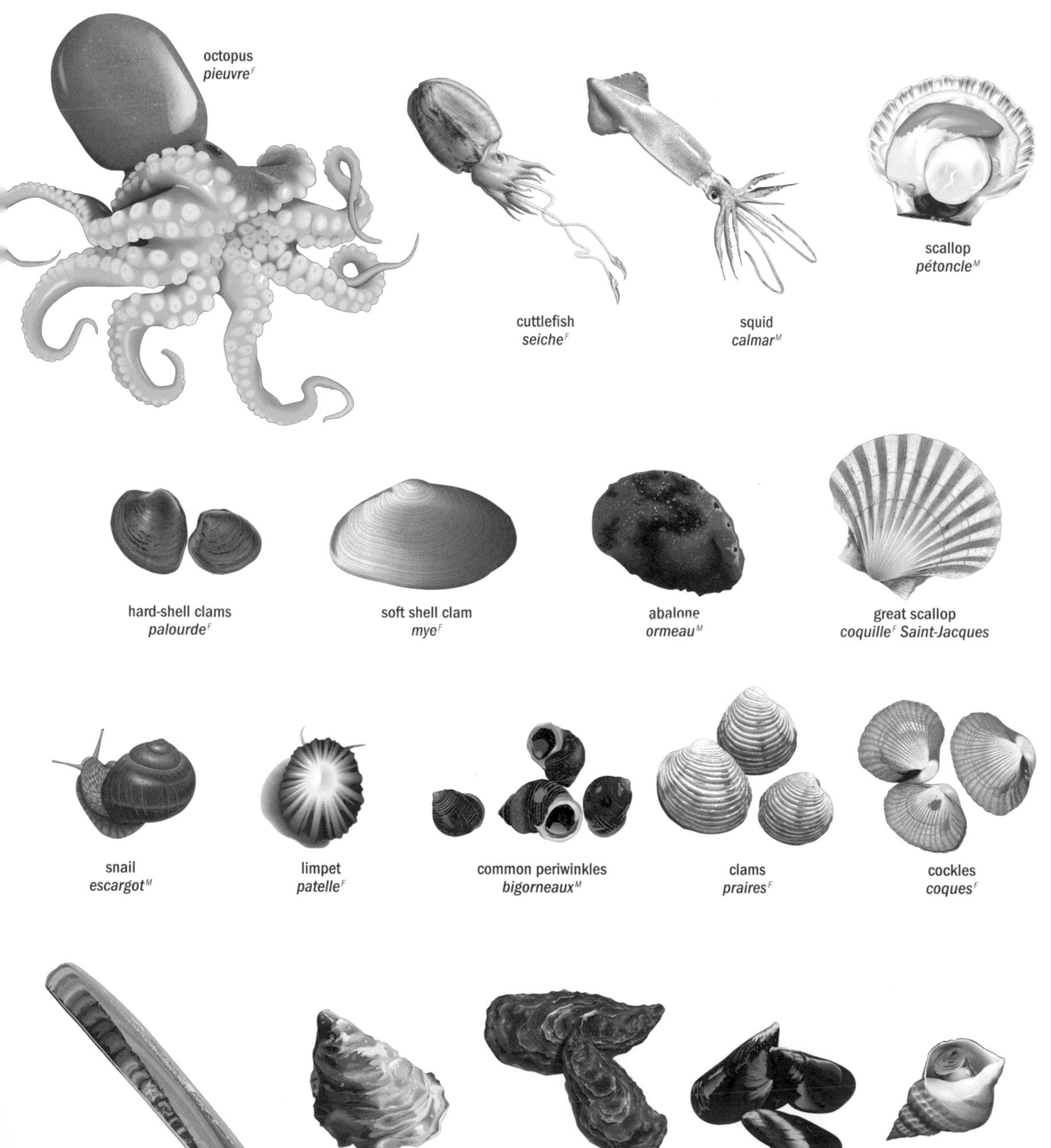
octopus
pieuvre^F
cuttlefish
seiche^F
squid
calmar^M
scallop
pétoncle^M
hard-shell clams
palourde^F
soft shell clam
mye^F
abalone
ormeau^M
great scallop
coquille^F Saint-Jacques
snail
escargot^M
limpet
patelle^F
common periwinkles
bigorneaux^M
clams
praires^F
cockles
coques^F
razor clam
couteau^M
flat oyster
huître^F plate
cupped Pacific oysters
huîtres^F creuses du Pacifique^M
blue mussels
moules^F
whelk
buccin^M

crustaceans

crustacés[M]

spiny lobster
langouste[F]

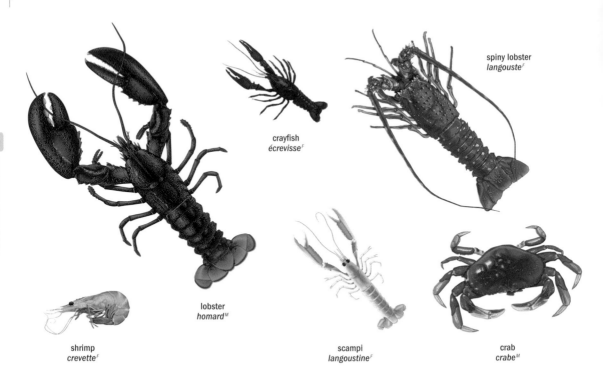

crayfish
écrevisse[F]

lobster
homard[M]

shrimp
crevette[F]

scampi
langoustine[F]

crab
crabe[M]

cartilaginous fishes

poissons[M] cartilagineux

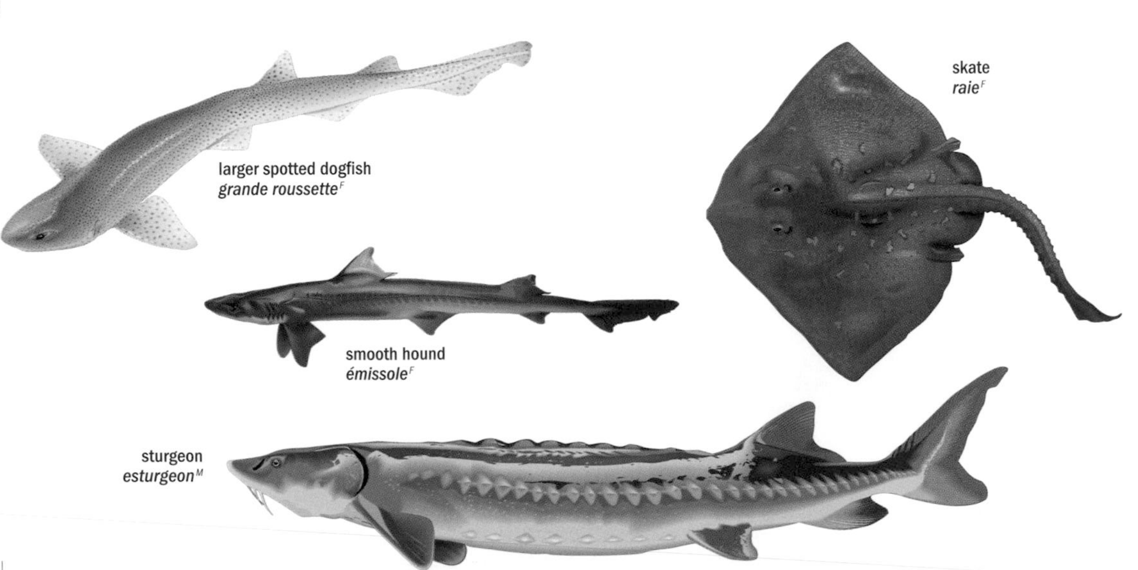
skate
raie[F]
larger spotted dogfish
grande roussette[F]
smooth hound
émissole[F]
sturgeon
esturgeon[M]

bony fishes

poissons^M osseux

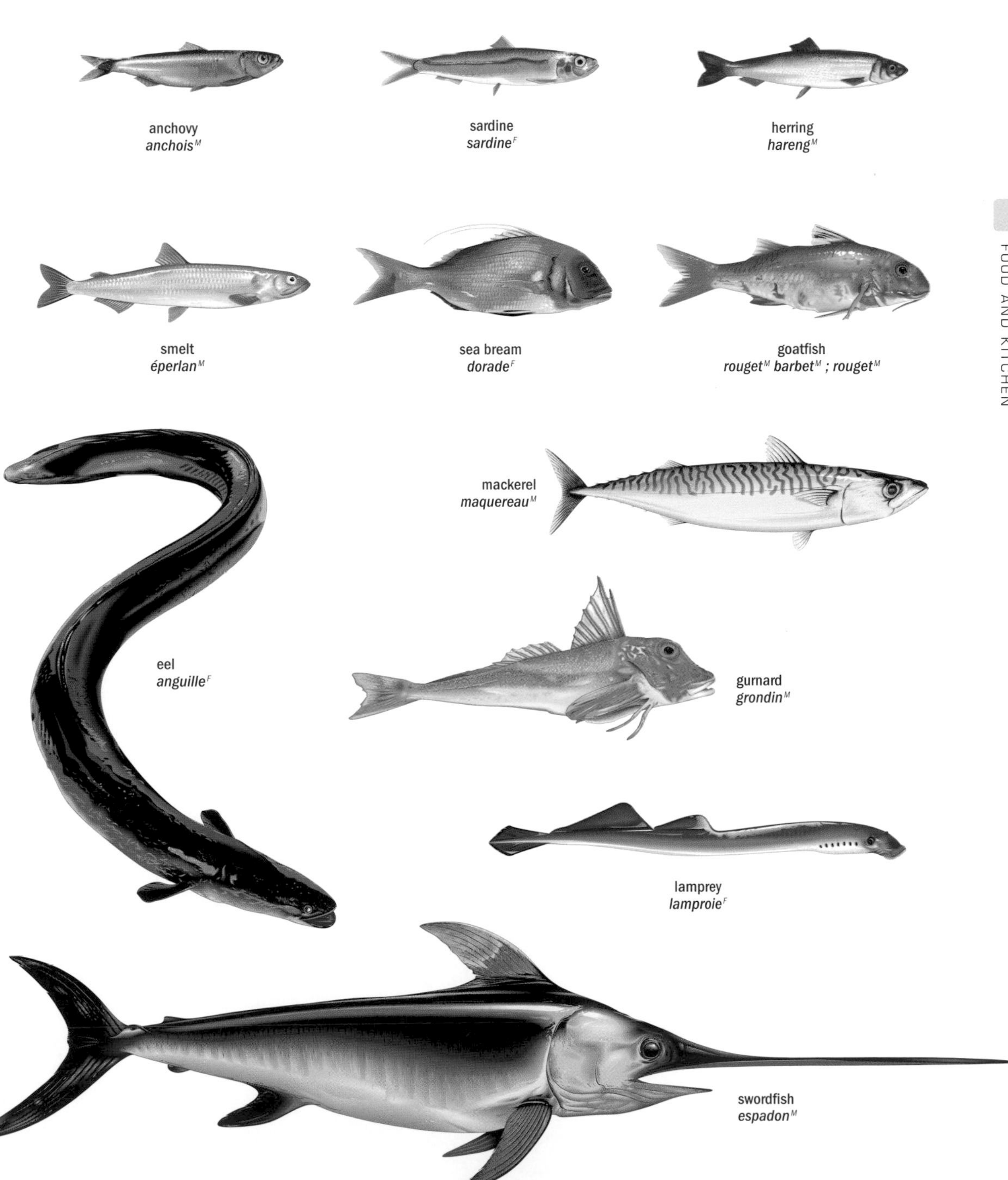
anchovy
anchois^M
sardine
sardine^F
herring
hareng^M
smelt
éperlan^M
sea bream
dorade^F
goatfish
rouget^M barbet^M ; rouget^M
mackerel
maquereau^M
eel
anguille^F
gurnard
grondin^M
lamprey
lamproie^F
swordfish
espadon^M

bony fishes

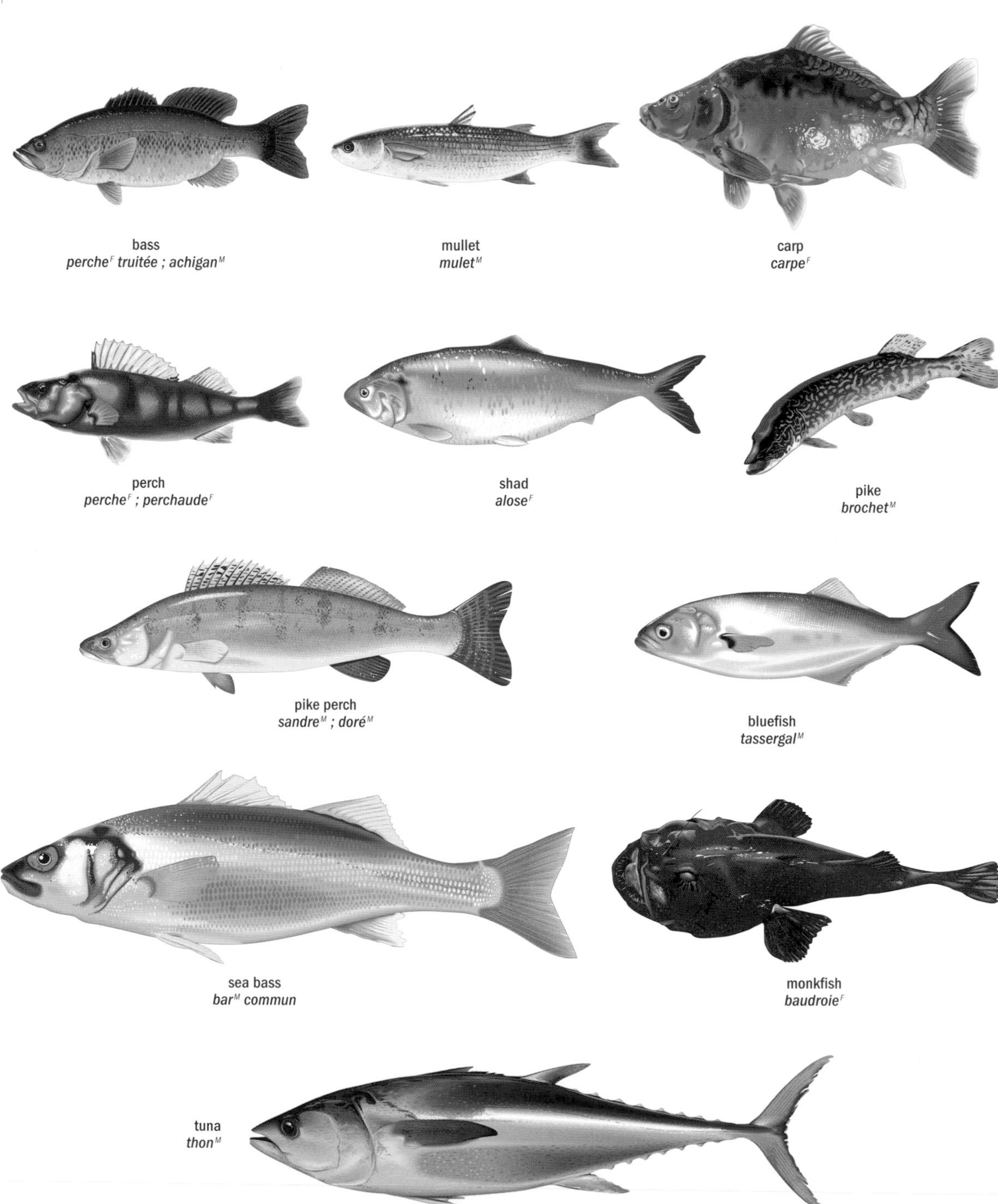
bass
perche[F] truitée ; achigan[M]
mullet
mulet[M]
carp
carpe[F]
perch
perche[F] ; perchaude[F]
shad
alose[F]
pike
brochet[M]
pike perch
sandre[M] ; doré[M]
bluefish
tassergal[M]
sea bass
bar[M] commun
monkfish
baudroie[F]
tuna
thon[M]

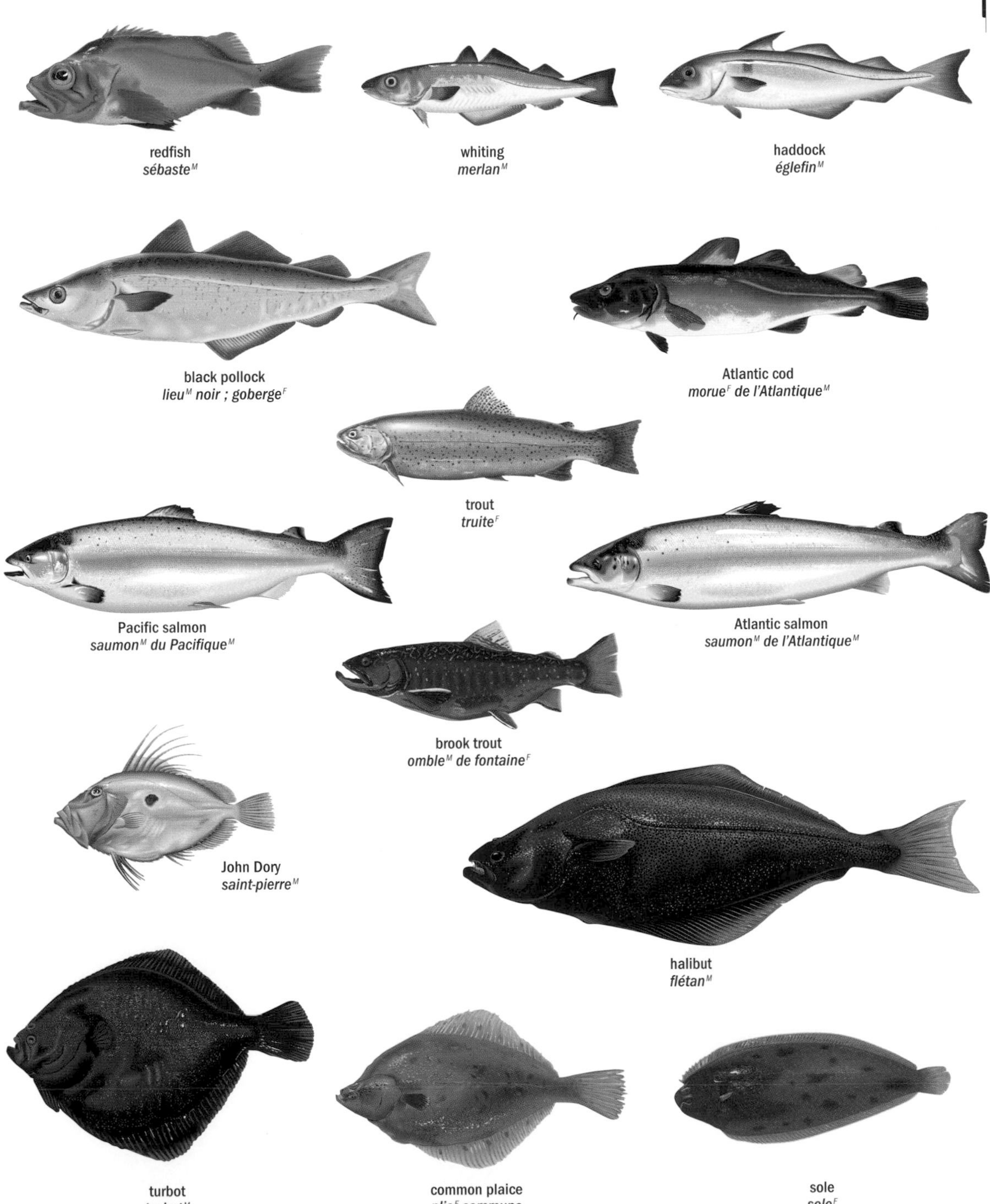
redfish
sébaste[M]
whiting
merlan[M]
haddock
églefin[M]
black pollock
lieu[M] noir ; goberge[F]
Atlantic cod
morue[F] de l'Atlantique[M]
trout
truite[F]
Pacific salmon
saumon[M] du Pacifique[M]
Atlantic salmon
saumon[M] de l'Atlantique[M]
brook trout
omble[M] de fontaine[F]
John Dory
saint-pierre[M]
halibut
flétan[M]
turbot
turbot[M]
common plaice
plie[F] commune
sole
sole[F]

packaging

emballage[M]

pouch
sachet[M]

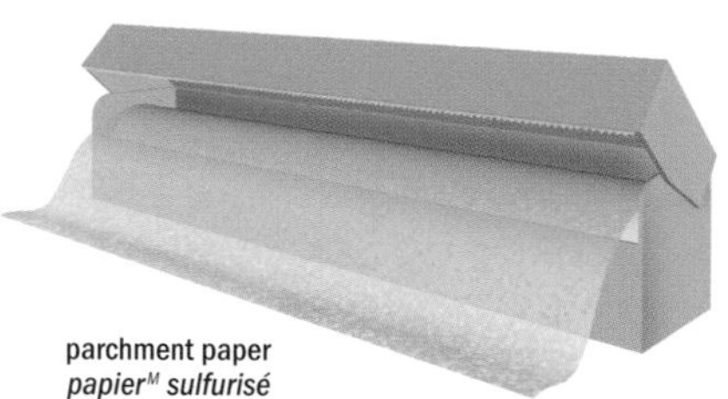
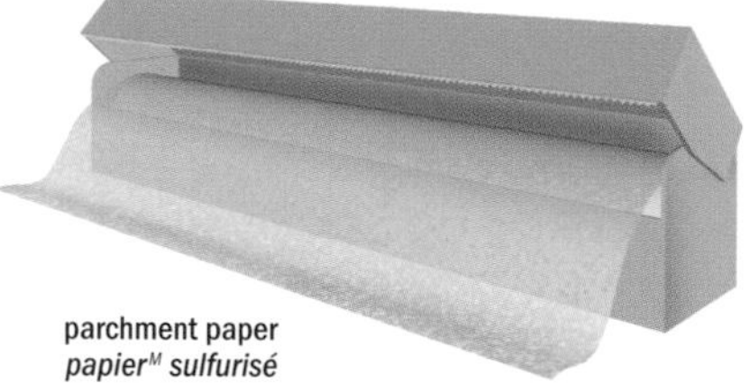

parchment paper
papier[M] *sulfurisé*

aluminum foil
papier[M] *aluminium*[M]

freezer bag
sac[M] *de congélation*[F]

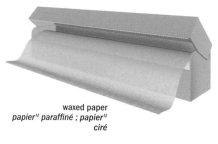

waxed paper
papier[M] *paraffiné ; papier*[M] *ciré*

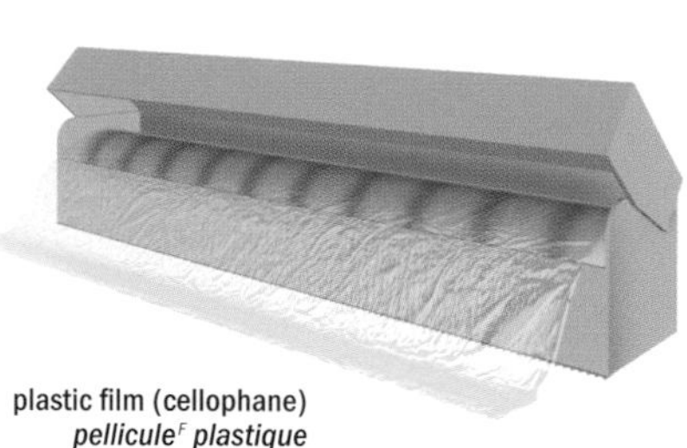

plastic film (cellophane)
pellicule[F] *plastique*

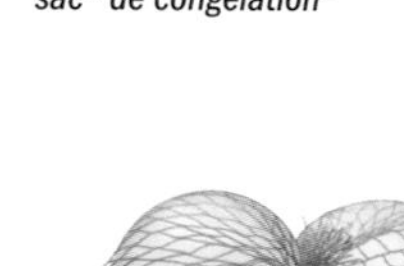
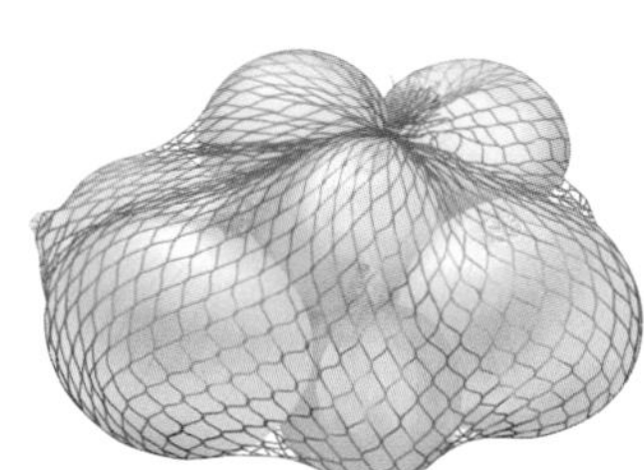

mesh bag
sac[M]*-filet*[M]

canisters
boîtes[F] *alimentaires*

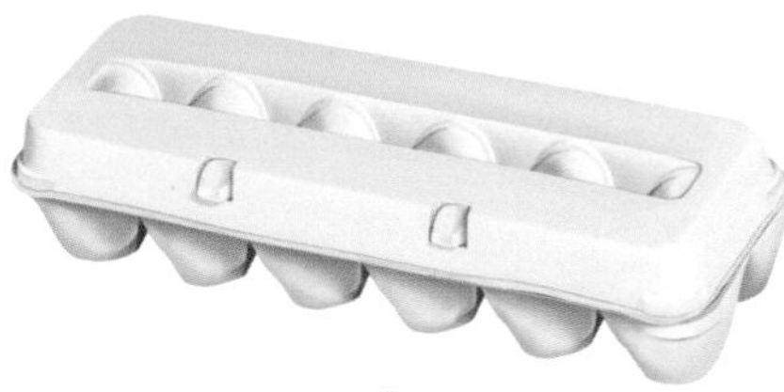

egg carton
boîte[F] *à œufs*[M]

food tray
barquette[F]

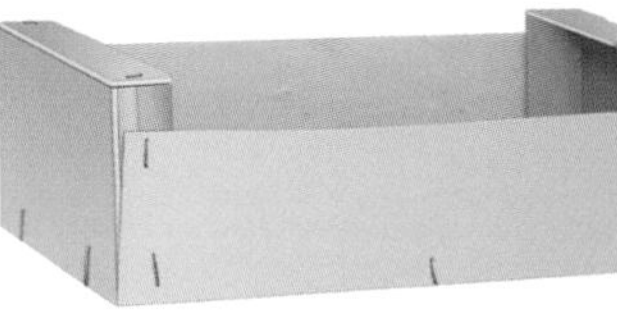
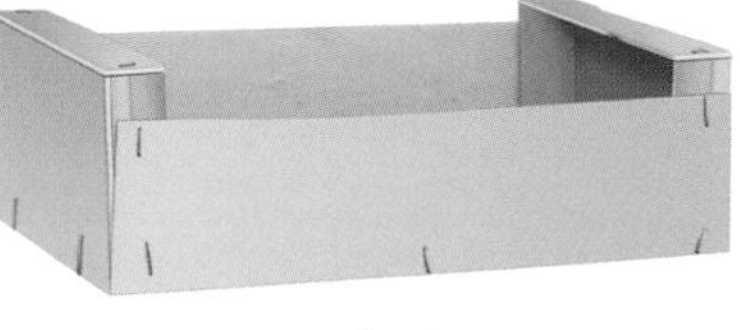

small crate
caissette[F]

small open crate
cageot[M]

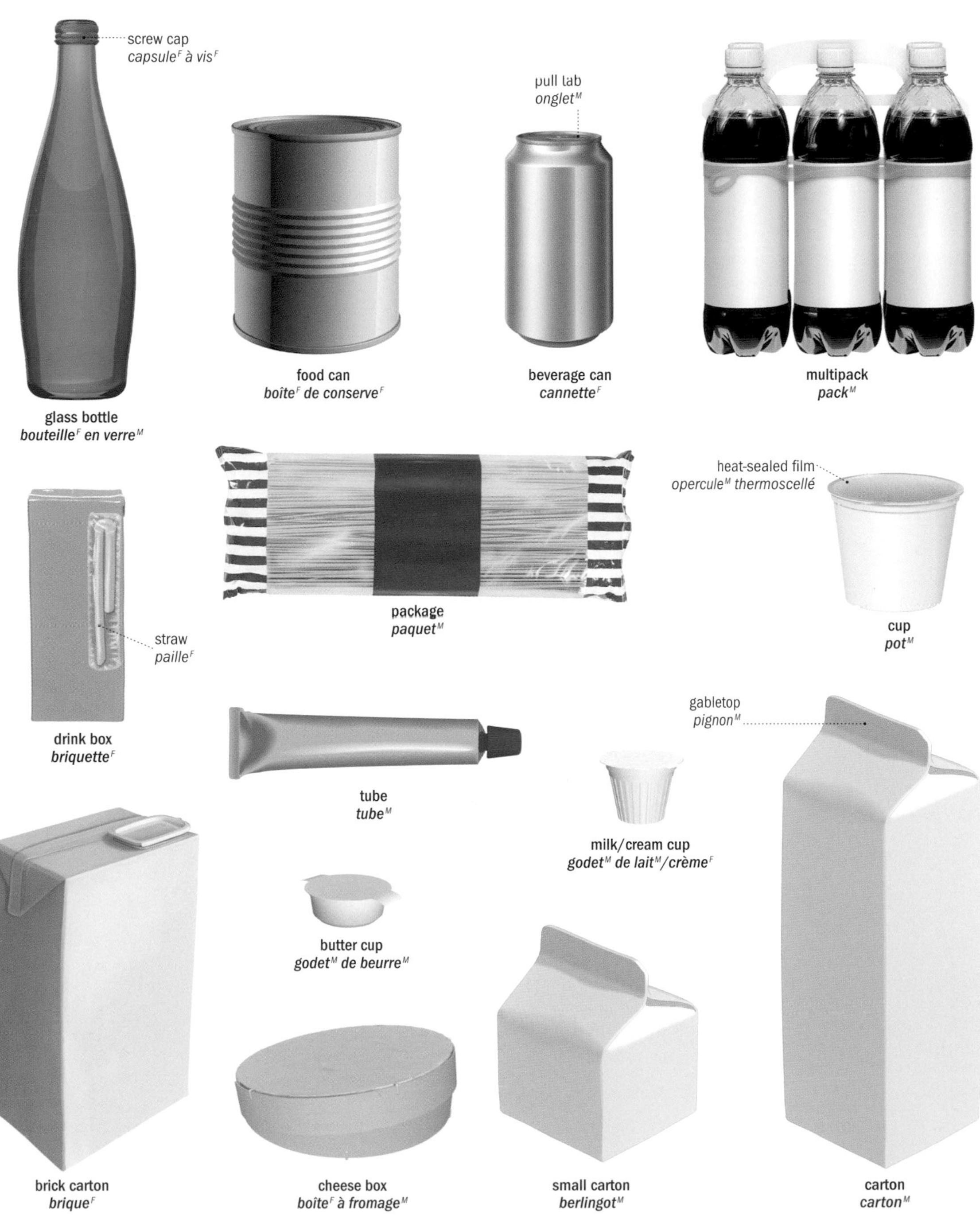
screw cap
capsule F à vis F
pull tab
onglet M
food can
boîte F de conserve F
beverage can
cannette F
multipack
pack M
glass bottle
bouteille F en verre M
heat-sealed film
opercule M thermoscellé
package
paquet M
cup
pot M
straw
paille F
gabletop
pignon M
drink box
briquette F
tube
tube M
milk/cream cup
godet M de lait M/crème F
butter cup
godet M de beurre M
brick carton
brique F
cheese box
boîte F à fromage M
small carton
berlingot M
carton
carton M

kitchen

cuisine[F]

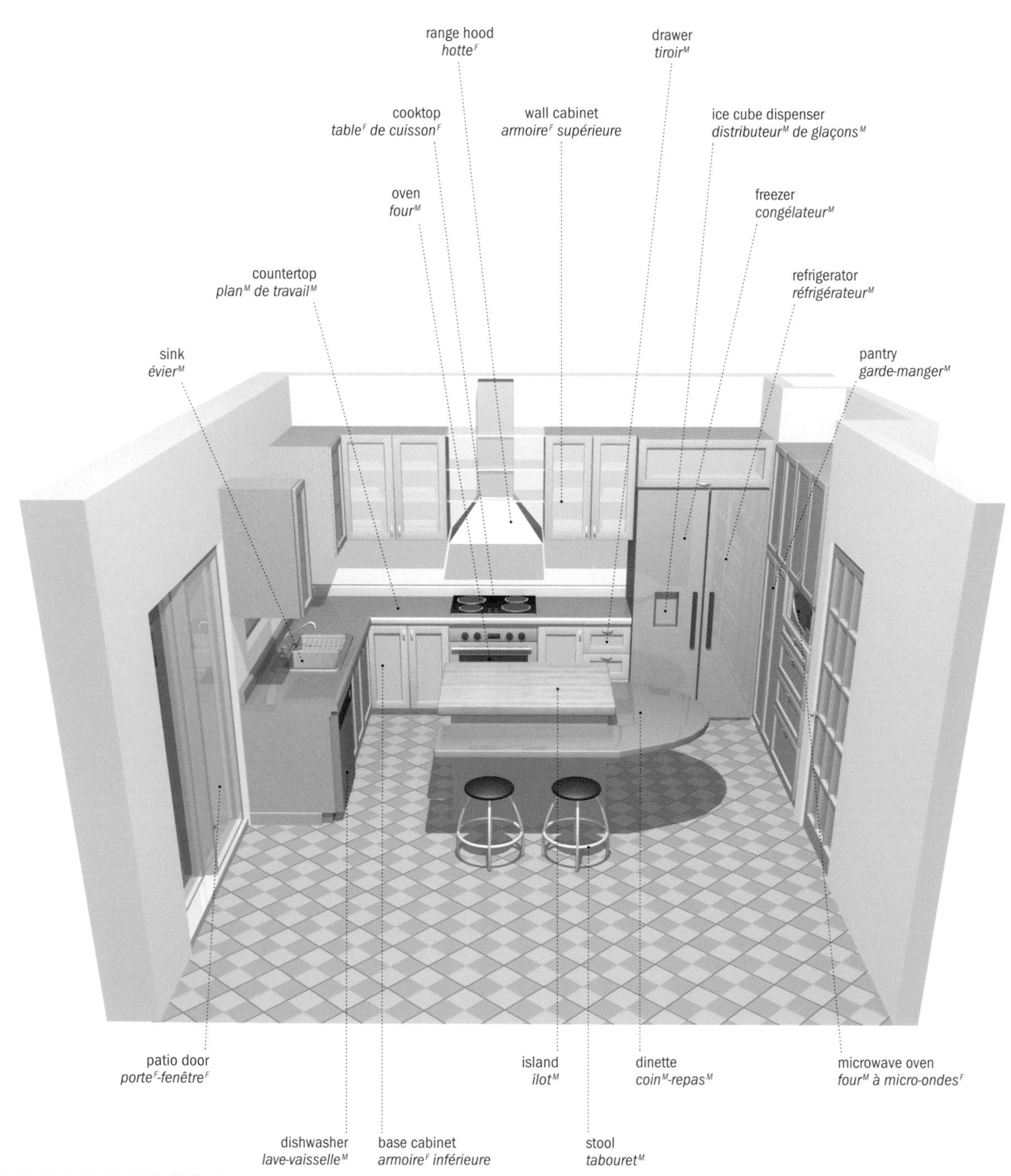
range hood
hotte[F]
drawer
tiroir[M]
cooktop
table[F] de cuisson[F]
wall cabinet
armoire[F] supérieure
ice cube dispenser
distributeur[M] de glaçons[M]
oven
four[M]
freezer
congélateur[M]
countertop
plan[M] de travail[M]
refrigerator
réfrigérateur[M]
sink
évier[M]
pantry
garde-manger[M]
patio door
porte[F]-fenêtre[F]
island
îlot[M]
dinette
coin[M]-repas[M]
microwave oven
four[M] à micro-ondes[F]
dishwasher
lave-vaisselle[M]
base cabinet
armoire[F] inférieure
stool
tabouret[M]

glassware

verres[M]

liqueur glass
verre[M] à liqueur[F]

port glass
verre[M] à porto[M]

sparkling wine glass
coupe[F] à mousseux[M]

brandy snifter
verre[M] à cognac[M]

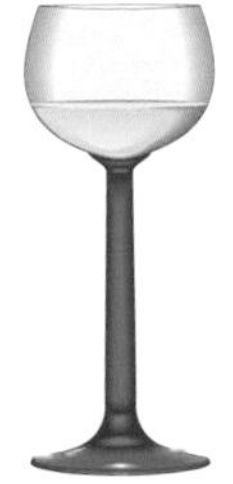

Alsace glass
verre[M] à vin[M] d'Alsace[F]

burgundy glass
verre[M] à bourgogne[M]

bordeaux glass
verre[M] à bordeaux[M]

white wine glass
verre[M] à vin[M] blanc

water goblet
verre[M] à eau[F]

cocktail glass
verre[M] à cocktail[M]

highball glass
verre[M] à gin[M]

old-fashioned glass
verre[M] à whisky[M]

beer mug
chope[F] à bière[F]

champagne flute
flûte[F] à champagne[M]

small decanter
carafon[M]

decanter
carafe[F]

dinnerware

vaisselle[F]

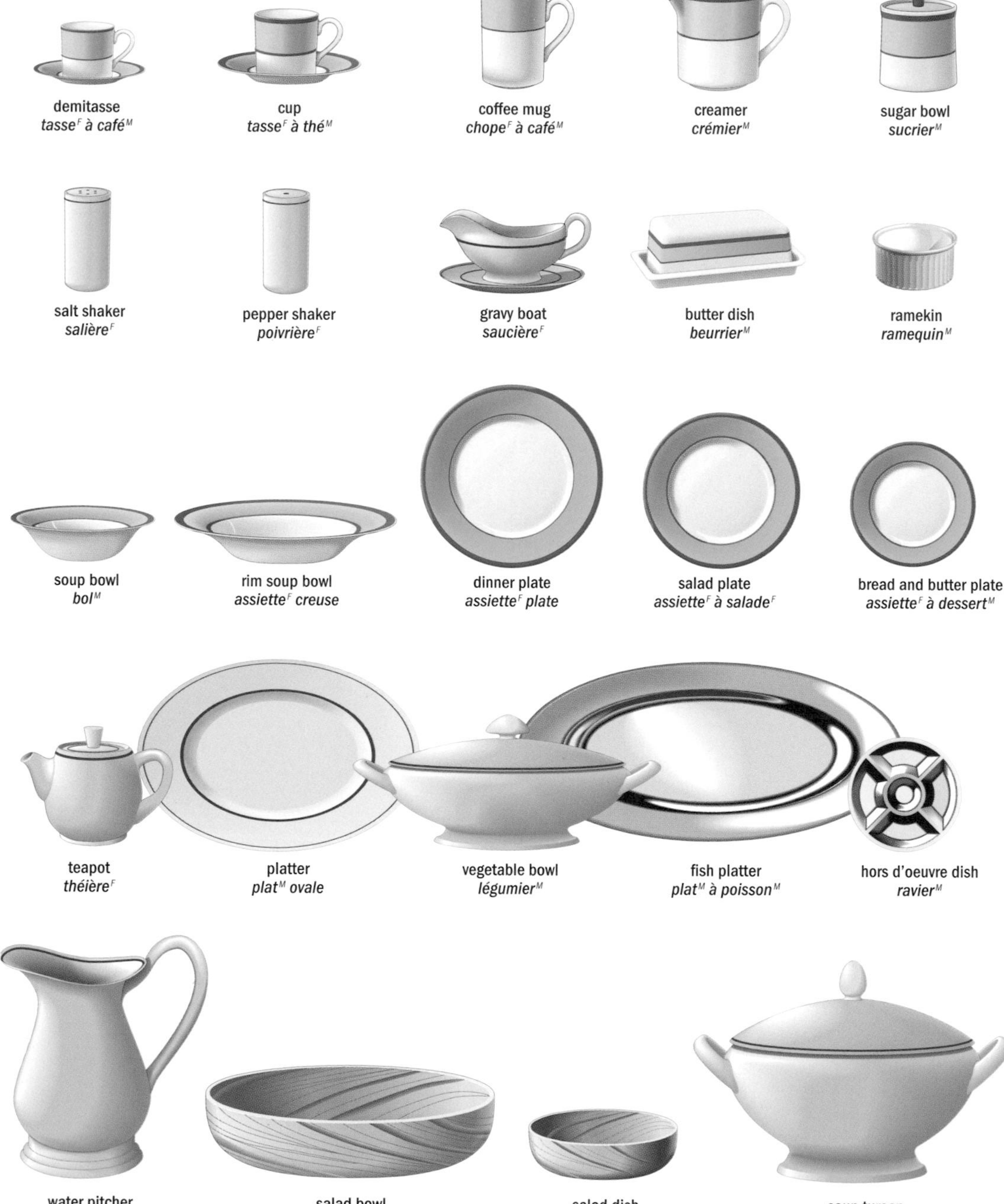
demitasse
tasse[F] à café[M]
cup
tasse[F] à thé[M]
coffee mug
chope[F] à café[M]
creamer
crémier[M]
sugar bowl
sucrier[M]
salt shaker
salière[F]
pepper shaker
poivrière[F]
gravy boat
saucière[F]
butter dish
beurrier[M]
ramekin
ramequin[M]
soup bowl
bol[M]
rim soup bowl
assiette[F] creuse
dinner plate
assiette[F] plate
salad plate
assiette[F] à salade[F]
bread and butter plate
assiette[F] à dessert[M]
teapot
théière[F]
platter
plat[M] ovale
vegetable bowl
légumier[M]
fish platter
plat[M] à poisson[M]
hors d'oeuvre dish
ravier[M]
water pitcher
pichet[M]
salad bowl
saladier[M]
salad dish
bol[M] à salade[F]
soup tureen
soupière[F]

silverware
couvert[M]

knife
couteau[M]

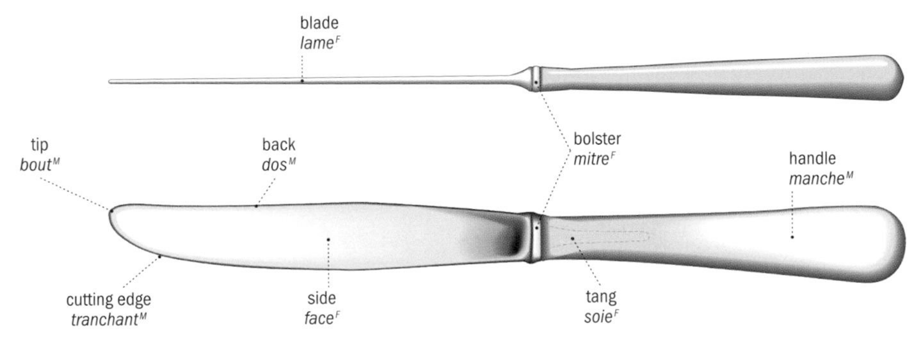
blade
lame[F]
tip
bout[M]
back
dos[M]
bolster
mitre[F]
handle
manche[M]
cutting edge
tranchant[M]
side
face[F]
tang
soie[F]

fork
fourchette[F]

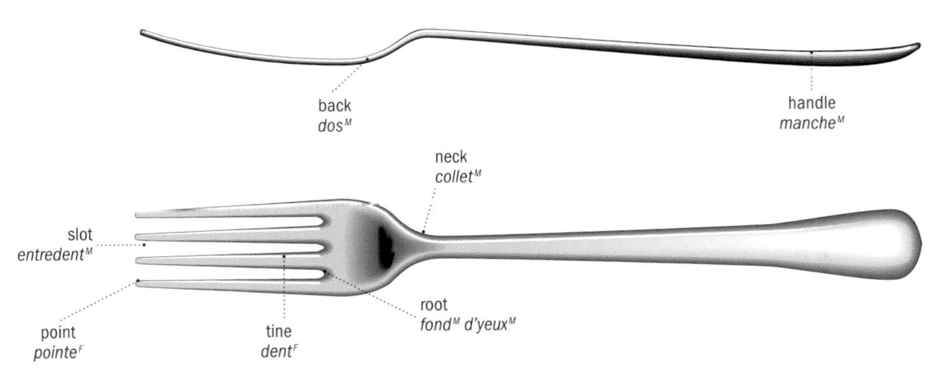
back
dos[M]
handle
manche[M]
neck
collet[M]
slot
entredent[M]
point
pointe[F]
tine
dent[F]
root
fond[M] *d'yeux*[M]

spoon
cuiller[F]

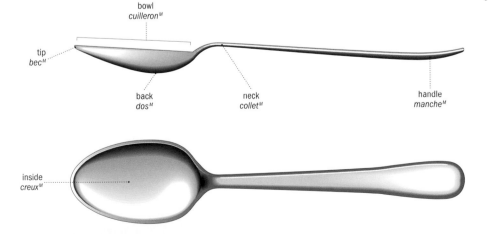

bowl
cuilleron[M]
tip
bec[M]
back
dos[M]
neck
collet[M]
handle
manche[M]
inside
creux[M]

silverware

examples of forks
exemples^M de fourchettes^F

examples of knives
exemples^M de couteaux^M

examples of spoons
exemples^M de cuillers^F

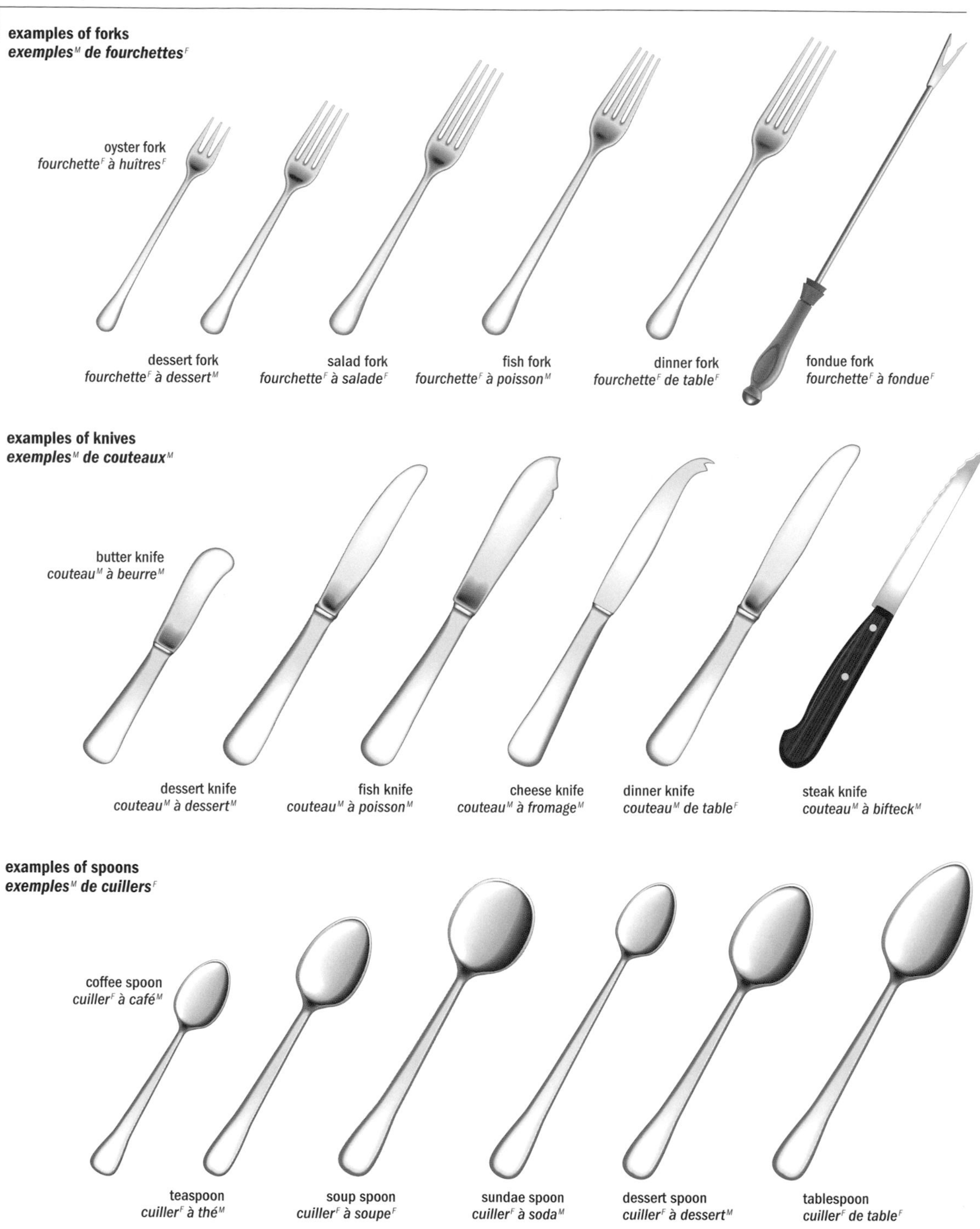
oyster fork
fourchette^F à huîtres^F
dessert fork
fourchette^F à dessert^M
salad fork
fourchette^F à salade^F
fish fork
fourchette^F à poisson^M
dinner fork
fourchette^F de table^F
fondue fork
fourchette^F à fondue^F
butter knife
couteau^M à beurre^M
dessert knife
couteau^M à dessert^M
fish knife
couteau^M à poisson^M
cheese knife
couteau^M à fromage^M
dinner knife
couteau^M de table^F
steak knife
couteau^M à bifteck^M
coffee spoon
cuiller^F à café^M
teaspoon
cuiller^F à thé^M
soup spoon
cuiller^F à soupe^F
sundae spoon
cuiller^F à soda^M
dessert spoon
cuiller^F à dessert^M
tablespoon
cuiller^F de table^F

kitchen utensils

ustensiles[M] de cuisine[F]

kitchen knife
couteau[M] de cuisine[F]

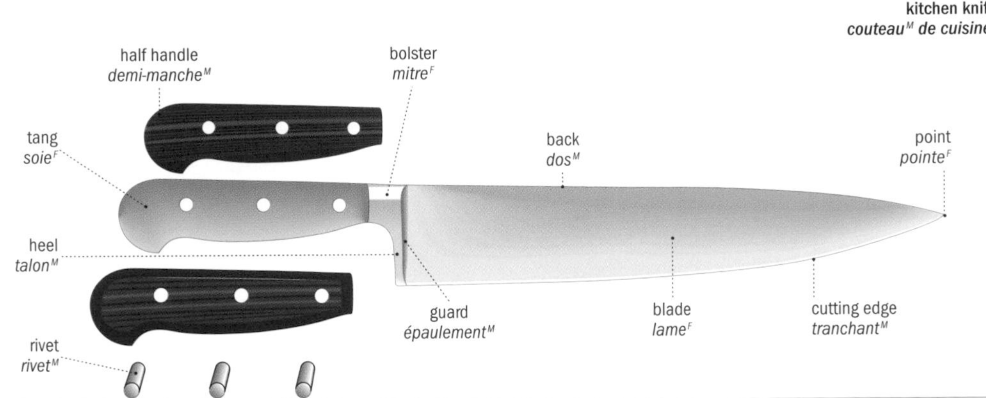
half handle
demi-manche[M]
bolster
mitre[F]
tang
soie[F]
back
dos[M]
point
pointe[F]
heel
talon[M]
guard
épaulement[M]
blade
lame[F]
cutting edge
tranchant[M]
rivet
rivet[M]

examples of utensils for cutting
exemples[M] de couteaux[M] de cuisine[F]

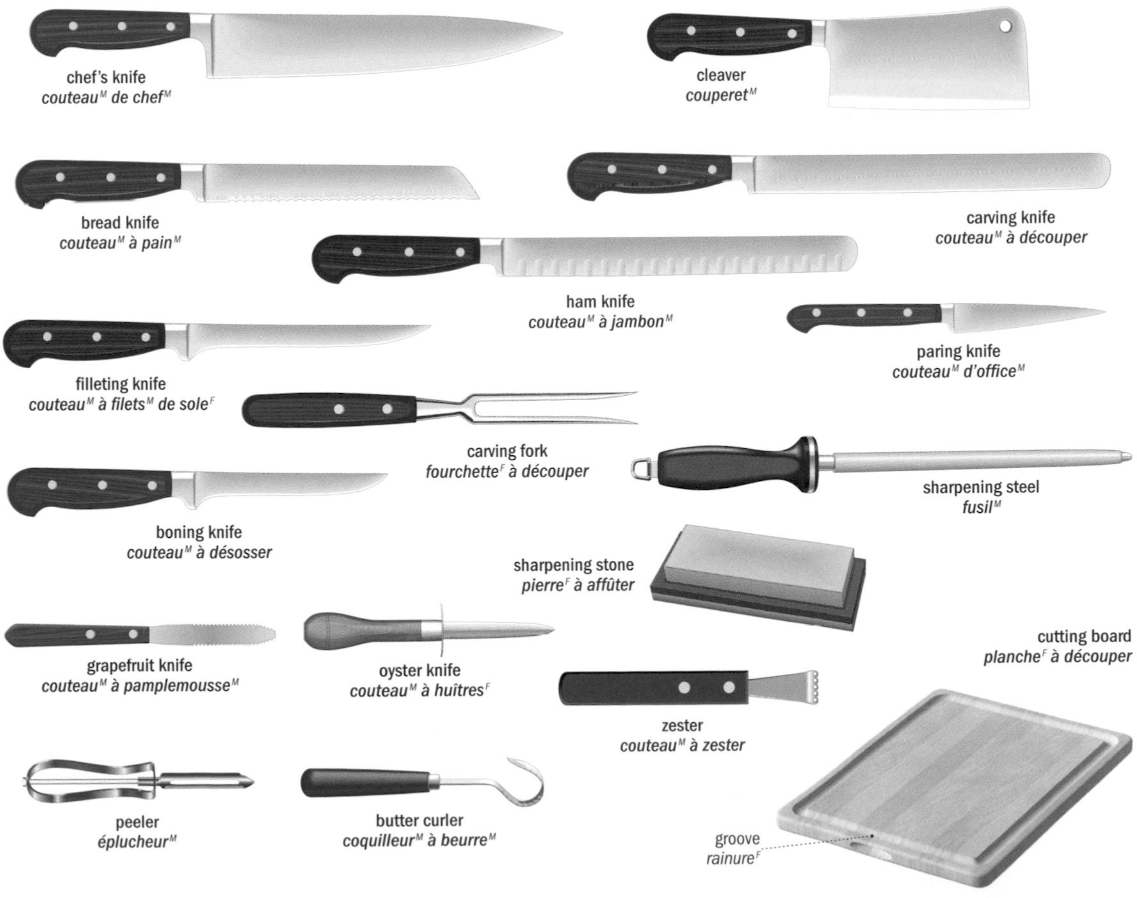

chef's knife
couteau[M] de chef[M]

cleaver
couperet[M]

bread knife
couteau[M] à pain[M]

carving knife
couteau[M] à découper

ham knife
couteau[M] à jambon[M]

paring knife
couteau[M] d'office[M]

filleting knife
couteau[M] à filets[M] de sole[F]

carving fork
fourchette[F] à découper

sharpening steel
fusil[M]

boning knife
couteau[M] à désosser

sharpening stone
pierre[F] à affûter

cutting board
planche[F] à découper

grapefruit knife
couteau[M] à pamplemousse[M]

oyster knife
couteau[M] à huîtres[F]

zester
couteau[M] à zester

peeler
éplucheur[M]

butter curler
coquilleur[M] à beurre[M]

groove
rainure[F]

for opening
pour ouvrir

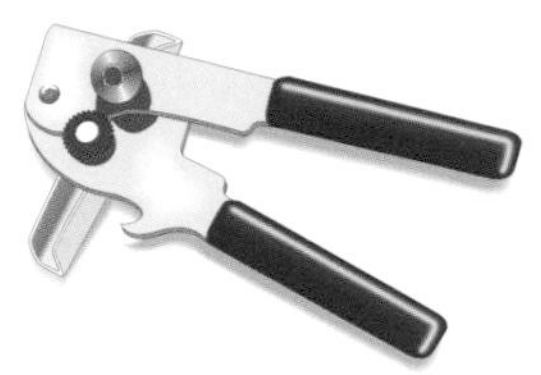

can opener
ouvre-boîtes[M]

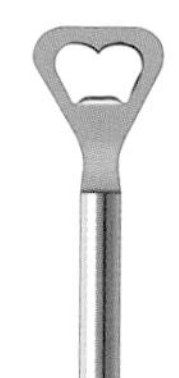

bottle opener
décapsuleur[M]

waiter's corkscrew
tire-bouchon[M] *de sommelier*[M]

lever corkscrew
tire-bouchon[M] *à levier*[M]

for grinding and grating
pour broyer et râper

nutcracker
casse-noix[M]

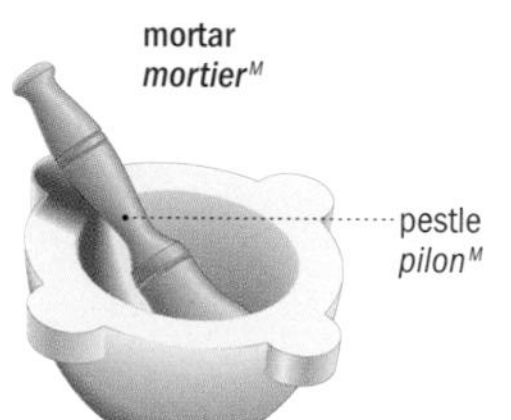
pestle
pilon[M]

mortar
mortier[M]

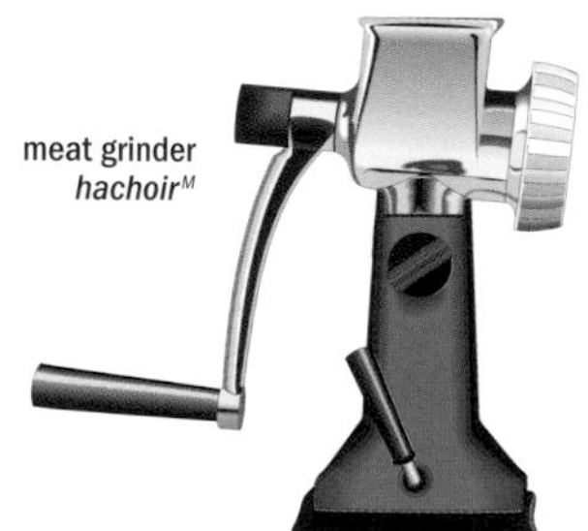

meat grinder
hachoir[M]

garlic press
presse-ail[M]

citrus juicer
presse-agrumes[M]

nutmeg grater
râpe[F] *à muscade*[F]

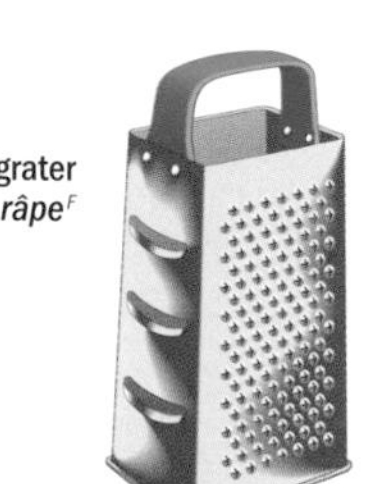

grater
râpe[F]

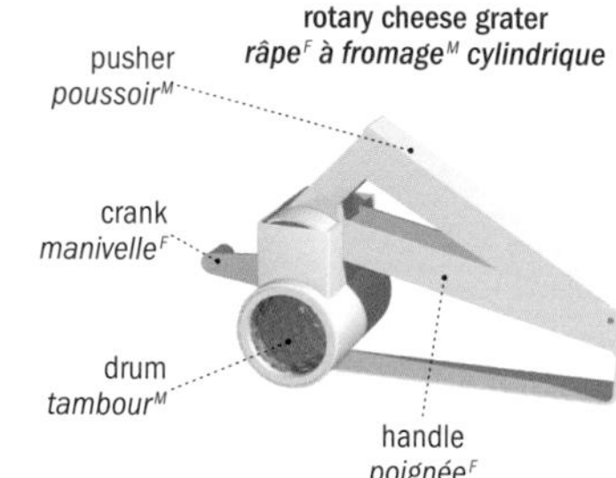
pusher
poussoir[M]
crank
manivelle[F]
drum
tambour[M]
handle
poignée[F]

rotary cheese grater
râpe[F] *à fromage*[M] *cylindrique*

pasta maker
machine[F] *à faire les pâtes*[F]

food mill
moulin[M] *à légumes*[M]

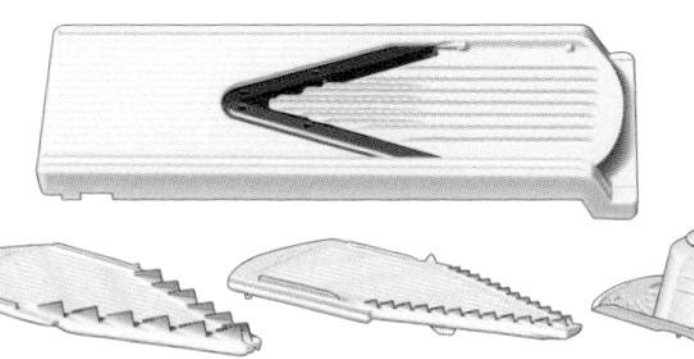

mandoline
mandoline[F]

for measuring
pour mesurer

measuring spoons
cuillers^F doseuses

measuring cups
mesures^F

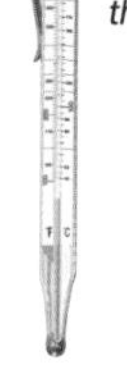

candy thermometer
thermomètre^M à sucre^M

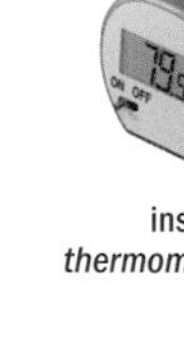

instant-read thermometer
thermomètre^M à mesure^F instantanée

measuring cup
tasse^F à mesurer

meat thermometer
thermomètre^M à viande^F

oven thermometer
thermomètre^M de four^M

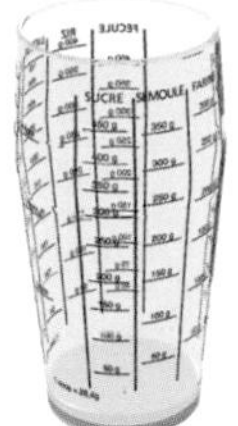

measuring beaker
verre^M à mesurer

kitchen timer
minuteur^M

egg timer
sablier^M

kitchen scale
balance^F de cuisine^F

for straining and draining
pour passer et égoutter

mesh strainer
passoire^F fine

muslin
mousseline^F

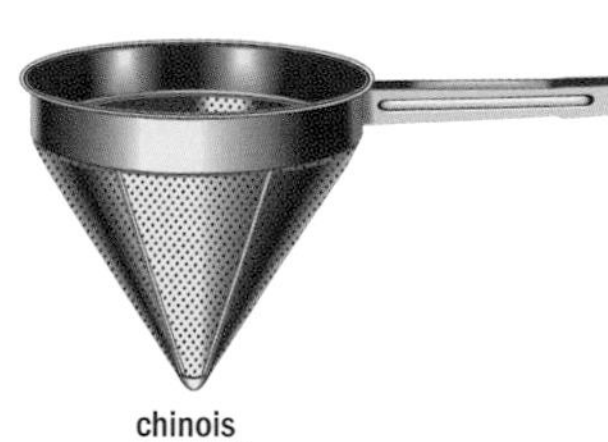

chinois
chinois^M

funnel
entonnoir^M

colander
passoire^F

fry basket
panier^M à friture^F

sieve
tamis^M

salad spinner
essoreuse^F à salade^F

FOOD AND KITCHEN

baking utensils
pour la pâtisserie[F]

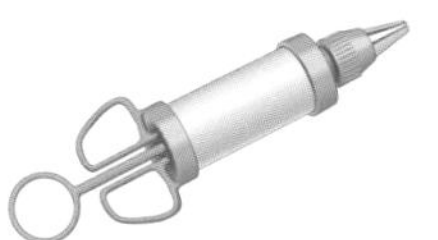

icing syringe
piston[M] à décorer

pastry cutting wheel
roulette[F] de pâtissier[M]

pastry brush
pinceau[M] à pâtisserie[F]

egg beater
batteur[M] à œufs[M]

whisk
fouet[M]

pastry bag and nozzles
poche[F] à douilles[F]

sifter
tamis[M] à farine[F]

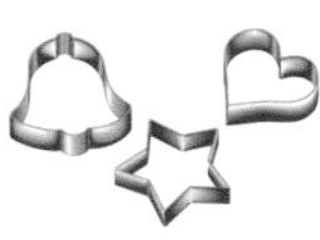

cookie cutters
emporte-pièces[M]

dredger
saupoudreuse[F]

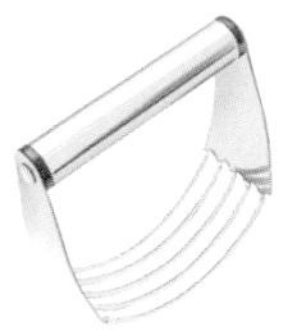

pastry blender
mélangeur[M] à pâtisserie[F]

mixing bowls
bols[M] à mélanger

rolling pin
rouleau[M] à pâtisserie[F]

baking sheet
plaque[F] à pâtisserie[F]

muffin pan
moule[M] à muffins[M]

soufflé dish
moule[M] à soufflé[M]

charlotte mold
moule[M] à charlotte[F]

spring-form pan
moule[M] à fond[M] amovible

pie pan
moule[M] à tarte[F]

quiche plate
moule[M] à quiche[F]

cake pan
moule[M] à gâteau[M]

set of utensils
jeu[M] d'ustensiles[M]

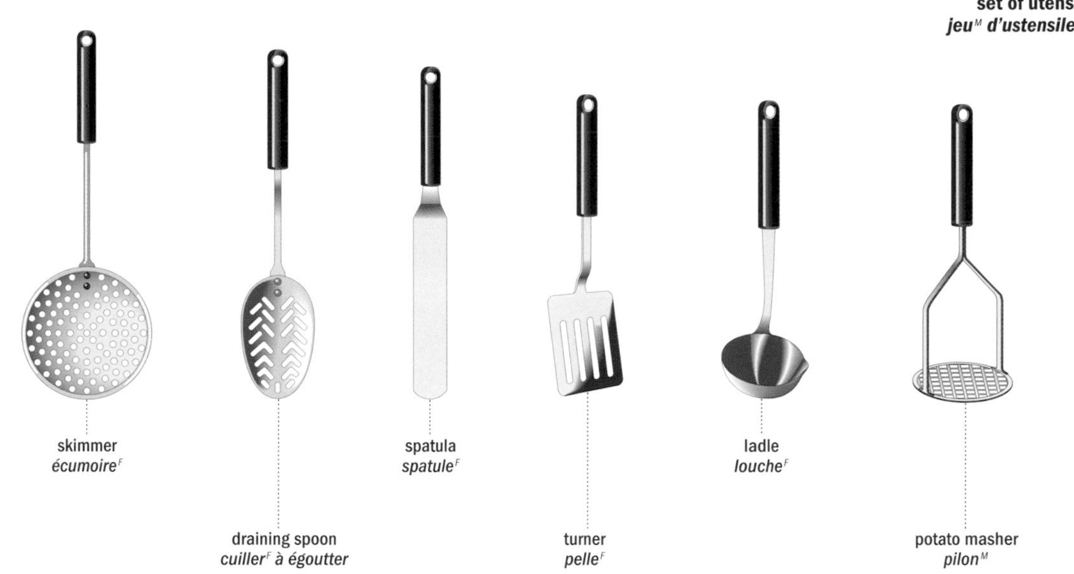
skimmer
écumoire[F]
draining spoon
cuiller[F] à égoutter
spatula
spatule[F]
turner
pelle[F]
ladle
louche[F]
potato masher
pilon[M]

miscellaneous utensils
ustensiles[M] divers

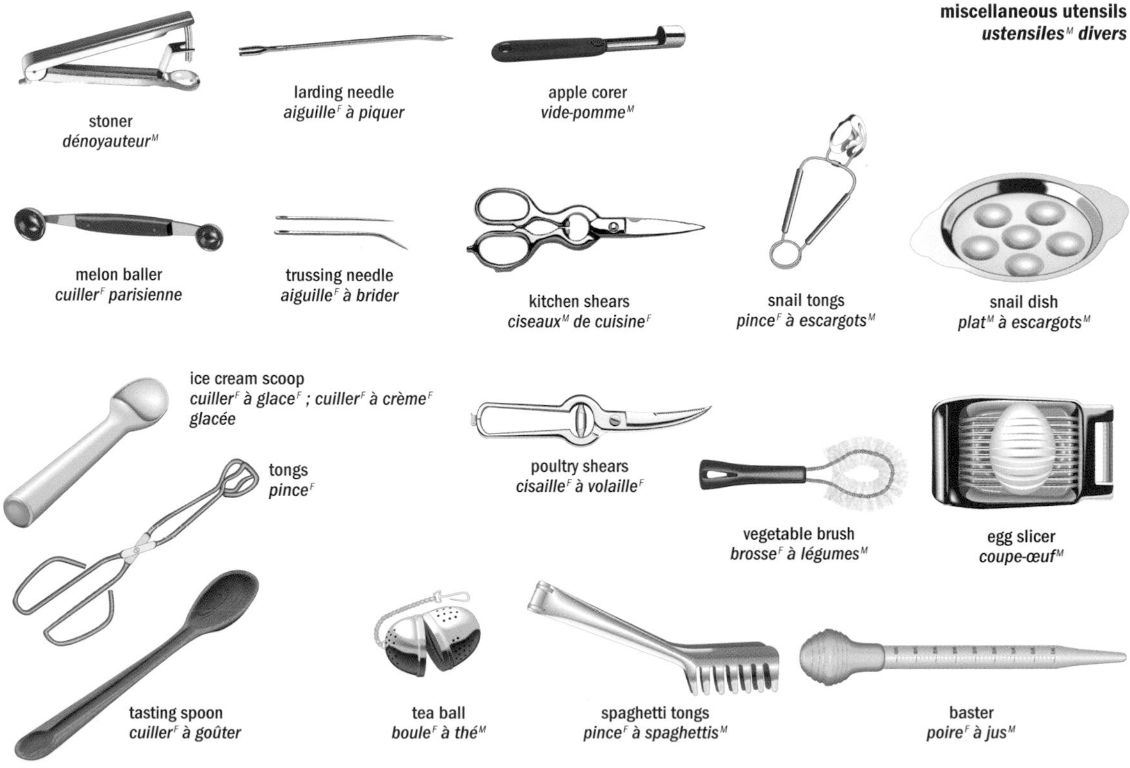

stoner
dénoyauteur[M]

larding needle
aiguille[F] à piquer

apple corer
vide-pomme[M]

melon baller
cuiller[F] parisienne

trussing needle
aiguille[F] à brider

kitchen shears
ciseaux[M] de cuisine[F]

snail tongs
pince[F] à escargots[M]

snail dish
plat[M] à escargots[M]

ice cream scoop
cuiller[F] à glace[F] ; cuiller[F] à crème[F] glacée

tongs
pince[F]

poultry shears
cisaille[F] à volaille[F]

vegetable brush
brosse[F] à légumes[M]

egg slicer
coupe-œuf[M]

tasting spoon
cuiller[F] à goûter

tea ball
boule[F] à thé[M]

spaghetti tongs
pince[F] à spaghettis[M]

baster
poire[F] à jus[M]

cooking utensils

batterie^F de cuisine^F

wok set
wok^M
lid
couvercle^M
rack
grille^F
wok
wok^M
burner ring
collier^M
tagine
tajine^M
fondue set
service^M à fondue^F
fondue pot
caquelon^M
stand
support^M
burner
réchaud^M
fish poacher
poissonnière^F
rack
grille^F
lid
couvercle^M
dripping pan
lèchefrite^F
terrine
terrine^F
roasting pans
plats^M à rôtir
pressure cooker
autocuiseur^M
pressure regulator
régulateur^M de pression^F
safety valve
soupape^F

Dutch oven
faitout[M]

stock pot
marmite[F]

couscous kettle
couscoussier[M]

frying pan
poêle[F] *à frire*

steamer
cuit-vapeur[M]

egg poacher
pocheuse[F]

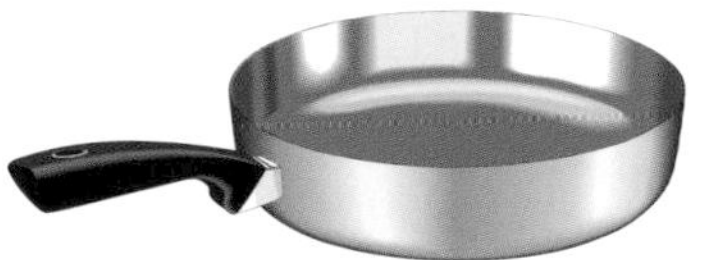
sauté pan
sauteuse[F]

small saucepan
poêlon[M]

diable
diable[M]

crêpe pan
poêle[F] *à crêpes*[F]

steamer basket
panier[M] *cuit-vapeur*[M]

double boiler
bain-marie[M]

saucepan
casserole[F]

domestic appliances

appareils^M électroménagers

for mixing and blending
pour mélanger et battre

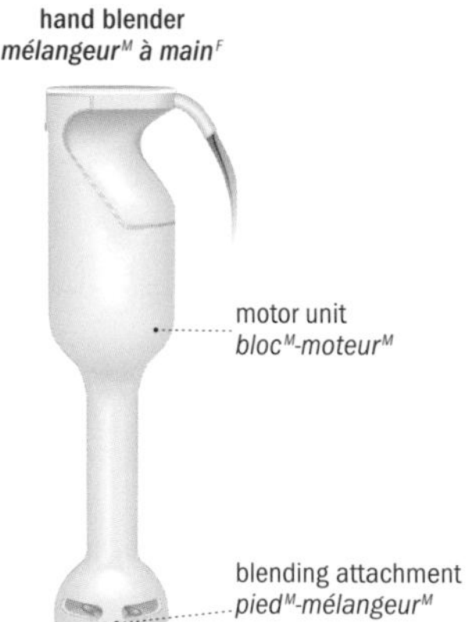
hand blender
mélangeur^M à main^F
motor unit
bloc^M-moteur^M
blending attachment
pied^M-mélangeur^M

blender
mélangeur^M
cap
bouchon^M
container
récipient^M
cutting blade
couteau^M
motor unit
bloc^M-moteur^M
control button
touche^F de commande^F

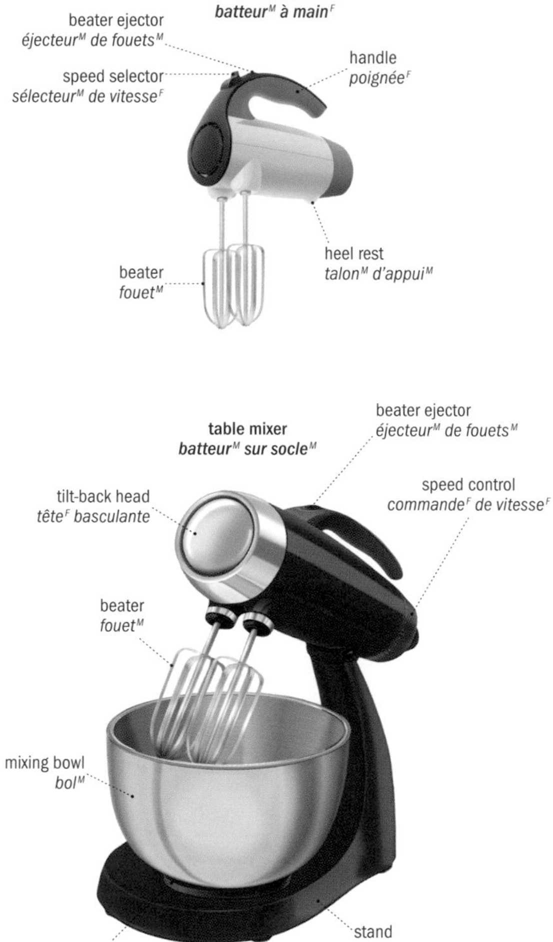
hand mixer
batteur^M à main^F
beater ejector
éjecteur^M de fouets^M
speed selector
sélecteur^M de vitesse^F
handle
poignée^F
heel rest
talon^M d'appui^M
beater
fouet^M
table mixer
batteur^M sur socle^M
beater ejector
éjecteur^M de fouets^M
speed control
commande^F de vitesse^F
tilt-back head
tête^F basculante
beater
fouet^M
mixing bowl
bol^M
turntable
plateau^M tournant
stand
socle^M

beaters
fouets^M

four blade beater
fouet^M quatre pales^F

spiral beater
fouet^M en spirale^F

wire beater
fouet^M à fil^M

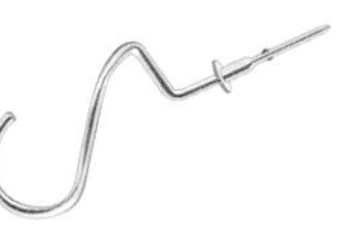

dough hook
crochet^M pétrisseur

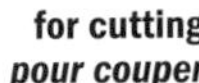

for cutting
pour couper

food processor
robot^M de cuisine^F

feed tube
entonnoir^M
lid
couvercle^M
bowl
bol^M
spindle
arbre^M
blade
couteau^M
handle
poignée^F
motor unit
bloc^M-moteur^M

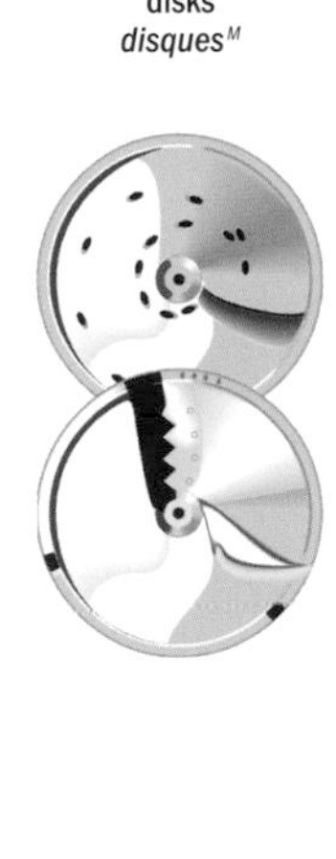
disks
disques^M

electric knife
couteau^M électrique

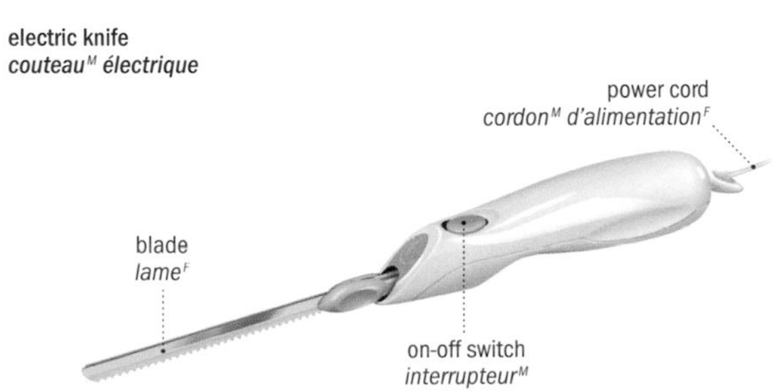
power cord
cordon^M d'alimentation^F
blade
lame^F
on-off switch
interrupteur^M

for juicing
pour presser

citrus juicer
presse-agrumes^M

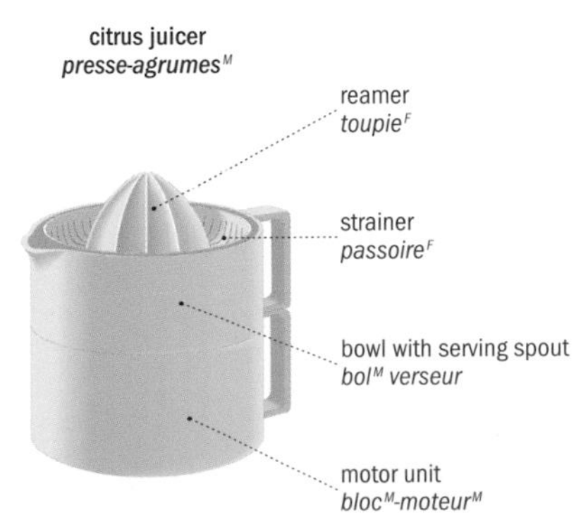
reamer
toupie^F
strainer
passoire^F
bowl with serving spout
bol^M verseur
motor unit
bloc^M-moteur^M

for cooking
pour cuire

microwave oven
four[M] à micro-ondes[F]

door
porte[F]
window
hublot[M]
clock timer
horloge[F] programmatrice
control panel
tableau[M] de commande[F]
latch
loquet[M]

waffle iron
gaufrier[M]-gril[M]

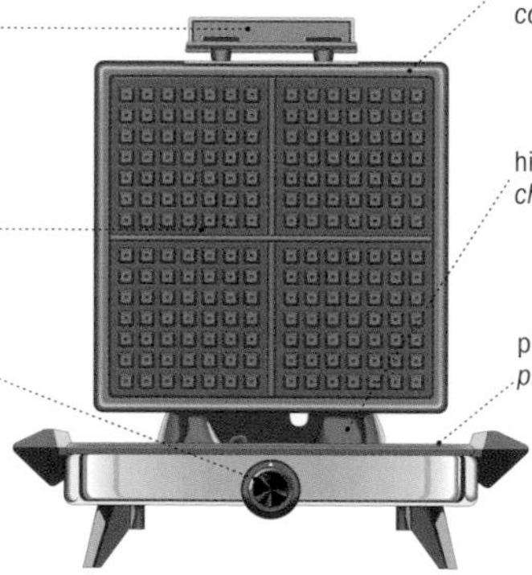

handle
poignée[F]
lid
couvercle[M]
hinge
charnière[F]
plate
plaque[F]
temperature selector
sélecteur[M] de température[F]
plate
plaque[F]

toaster
grille-pain[M]

slot
fente[F]
bread guide
guide[M]
lever
manette[F]
temperature control
thermostat[M]

deep fryer
friteuse[F]

basket
panier[M]
lid
couvercle[M]
handle
poignée[F]
thermostat
thermostat[M]
signal lamp
voyant[M] lumineux
timer
minuterie[F]

raclette with grill
raclette^F-gril^M
dish
poêlon^M
cooking plate
surface^F de cuisson^F
base
socle^M
electric steamer
cuit-vapeur^M électrique
cooking dishes
bols^M de cuisson^F
water level indicator
indicateur^M de niveau^M d'eau^F
signal lamp
voyant^M lumineux
timer
minuterie^F
indoor electric grill
gril^M barbecue^M
insulated handle
poignée^F isolante
drip pan
bac^M ramasse-jus^M
cooking surface
surface^F de cuisson^F
adjustable thermostat
thermostat^M réglable
bread machine
robot^M boulanger^M
lid
couvercle^M
control panel
tableau^M de commande^F
window
hublot^M
loaf pan
moule^M à pain^M
electric griddle
gril^M électrique
cooking surface
surface^F de cuisson^F
handle
poignée^F
detachable control
commande^F amovible
grease well
collecteur^M de graisse^F

miscellaneous domestic appliances

appareils^M électroménagers divers

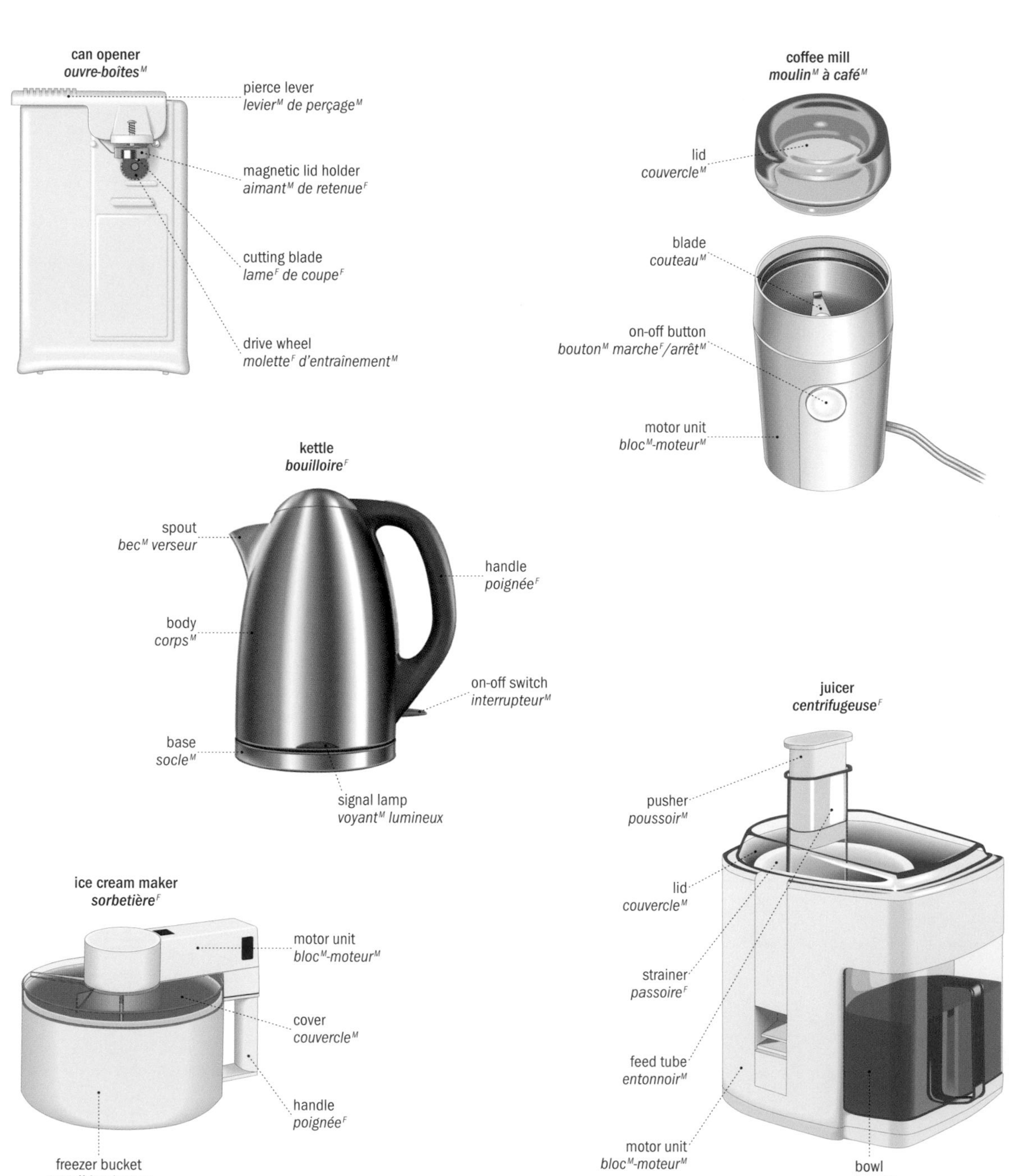
can opener
ouvre-boîtes^M
pierce lever
levier^M de perçage^M
magnetic lid holder
aimant^M de retenue^F
cutting blade
lame^F de coupe^F
drive wheel
molette^F d'entraînement^M
coffee mill
moulin^M à café^M
lid
couvercle^M
blade
couteau^M
on-off button
bouton^M marche^F/arrêt^M
motor unit
bloc^M-moteur^M
kettle
bouilloire^F
spout
bec^M verseur
handle
poignée^F
body
corps^M
on-off switch
interrupteur^M
base
socle^M
signal lamp
voyant^M lumineux
juicer
centrifugeuse^F
pusher
poussoir^M
lid
couvercle^M
strainer
passoire^F
feed tube
entonnoir^M
motor unit
bloc^M-moteur^M
bowl
pichet^M
ice cream maker
sorbetière^F
motor unit
bloc^M-moteur^M
cover
couvercle^M
handle
poignée^F
freezer bucket
seau^M isotherme

coffee makers

cafetières[F]

automatic drip coffee maker
cafetière[F] filtre[M]

lid
couvercle[M]
reservoir
réservoir[M]
basket
panier[M]
water level
niveau[M] d'eau[F]
carafe
verseuse[F]
signal lamp
voyant[M] lumineux
on-off switch
interrupteur[M]
warming plate
plaque[F] chauffante

Neapolitan coffee maker
cafetière[F] napolitaine

espresso machine
machine[F] à espresso[M]

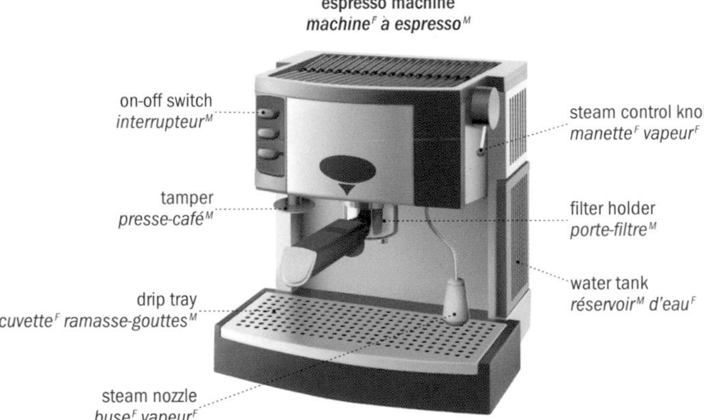
on-off switch
interrupteur[M]
steam control knob
manette[F] vapeur[F]
tamper
presse-café[M]
filter holder
porte-filtre[M]
water tank
réservoir[M] d'eau[F]
drip tray
cuvette[F] ramasse-gouttes[M]
steam nozzle
buse[F] vapeur[F]

vacuum coffee maker
cafetière[F] à infusion[F]

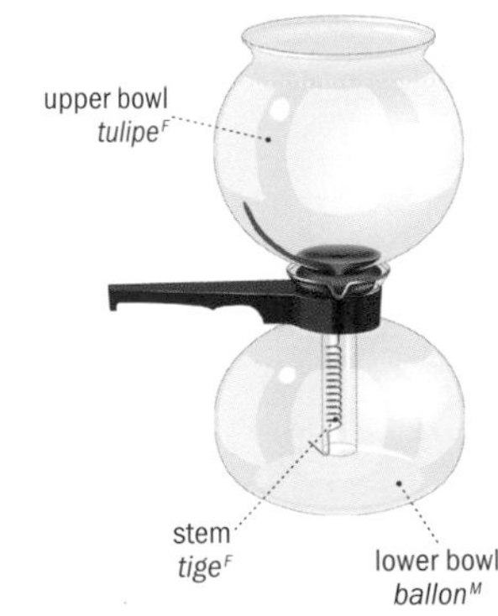
upper bowl
tulipe[F]
stem
tige[F]
lower bowl
ballon[M]

French press
cafetière[F] à piston[M]

espresso maker
cafetière[F] espresso[M]

percolator
percolateur[M]

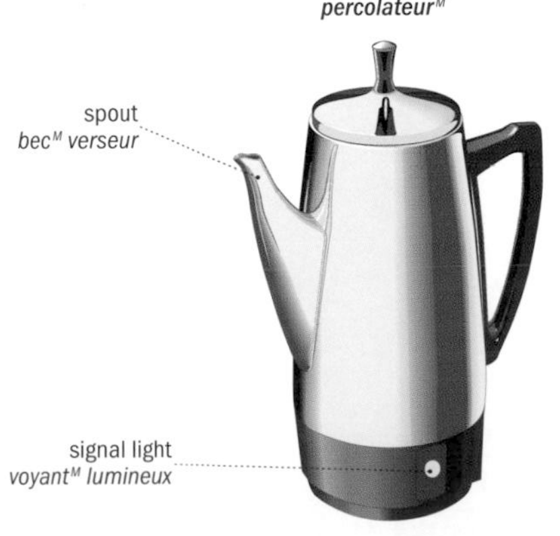
spout
bec[M] verseur
signal light
voyant[M] lumineux

exterior of a house

extérieurᴹ d'une maisonᶠ

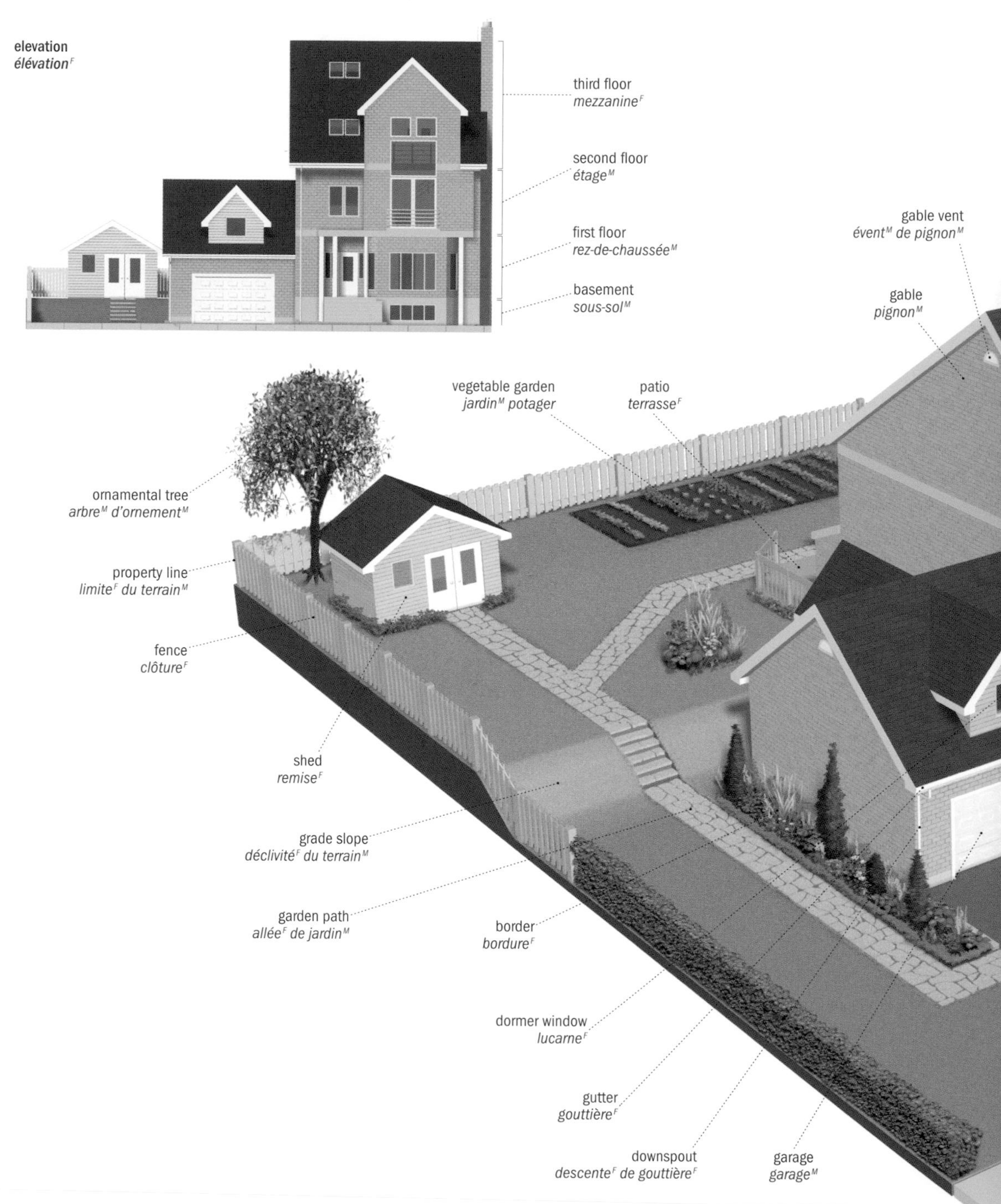
elevation
élévationF
third floor
mezzanineF
second floor
étageM
first floor
rez-de-chausséeM
basement
sous-solM
gable vent
éventM de pignonM
gable
pignonM
vegetable garden
jardinM potager
patio
terrasseF
ornamental tree
arbreM d'ornementM
property line
limiteF du terrainM
fence
clôtureF
shed
remiseF
grade slope
déclivitéF du terrainM
garden path
alléeF de jardinM
border
bordureF
dormer window
lucarneF
gutter
gouttièreF
downspout
descenteF de gouttièreF
garage
garageM

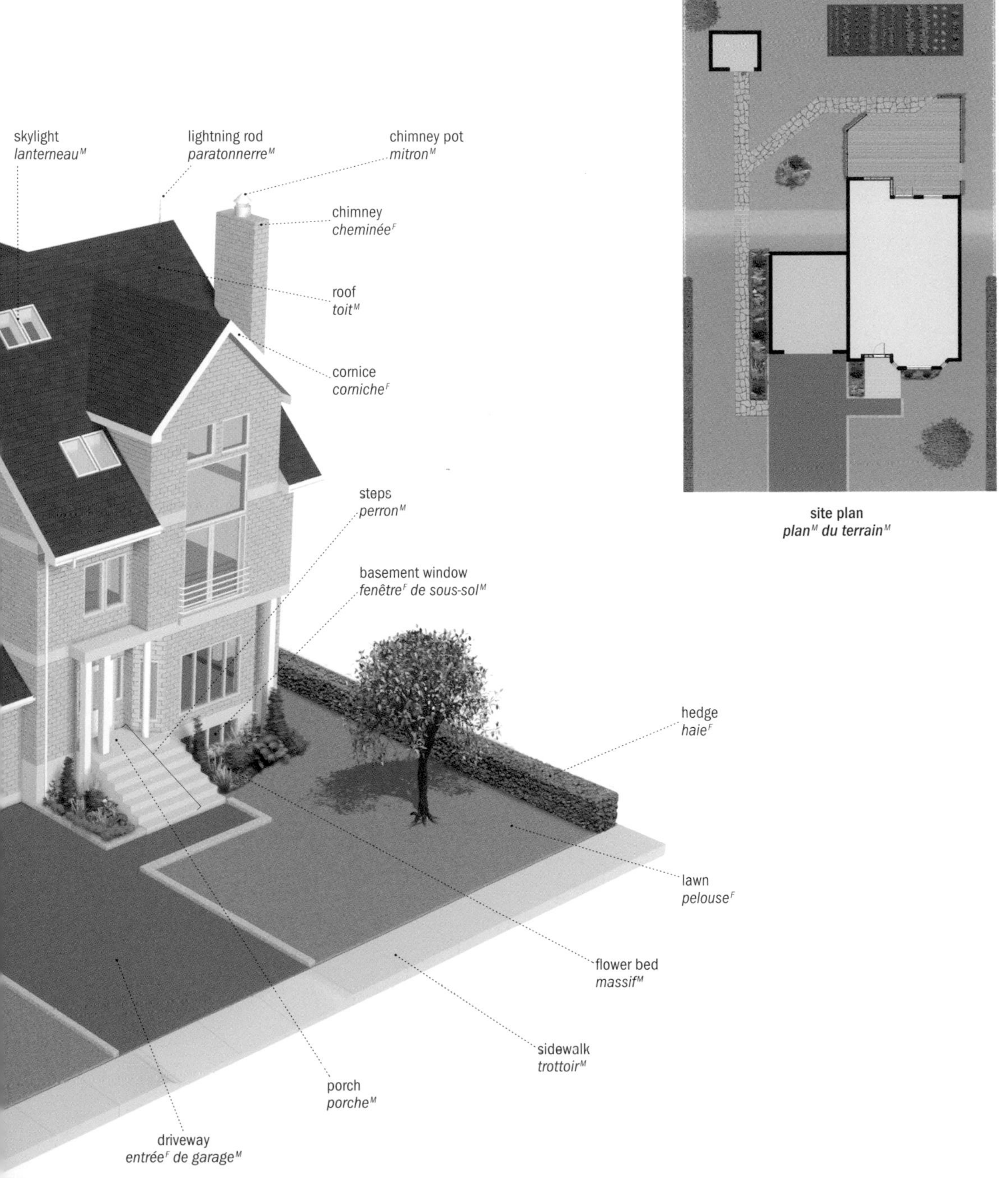
skylight
lanterneau^M
lightning rod
paratonnerre^M
chimney pot
mitron^M
chimney
cheminée^F
roof
toit^M
cornice
corniche^F
steps
perron^M
basement window
fenêtre^F de sous-sol^M
hedge
haie^F
lawn
pelouse^F
flower bed
massif^M
sidewalk
trottoir^M
porch
porche^M
driveway
entrée^F de garage^M

site plan
plan^M du terrain^M

pool

piscine[F]

hot tub
spa[M]

above-ground swimming pool
piscine[F] hors sol[M]

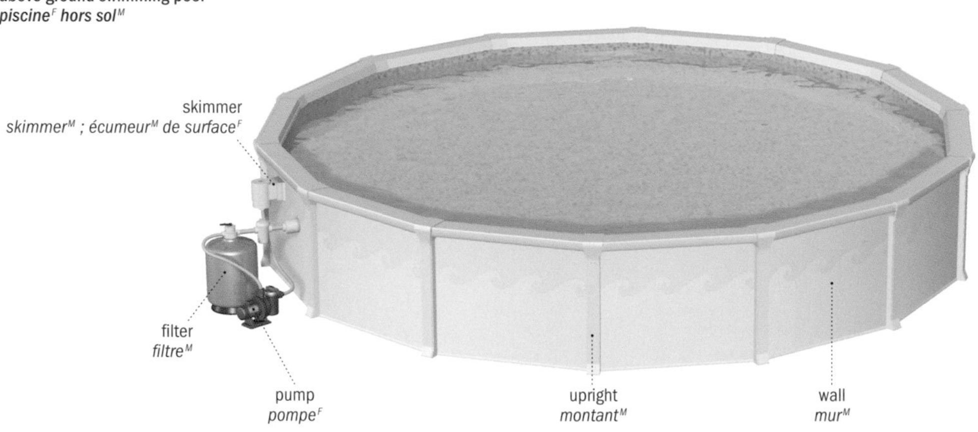
skimmer
skimmer[M] ; écumeur[M] de surface[F]
filter
filtre[M]
pump
pompe[F]
upright
montant[M]
wall
mur[M]

in-ground swimming pool
piscine[F] enterrée ; piscine[F] creusée

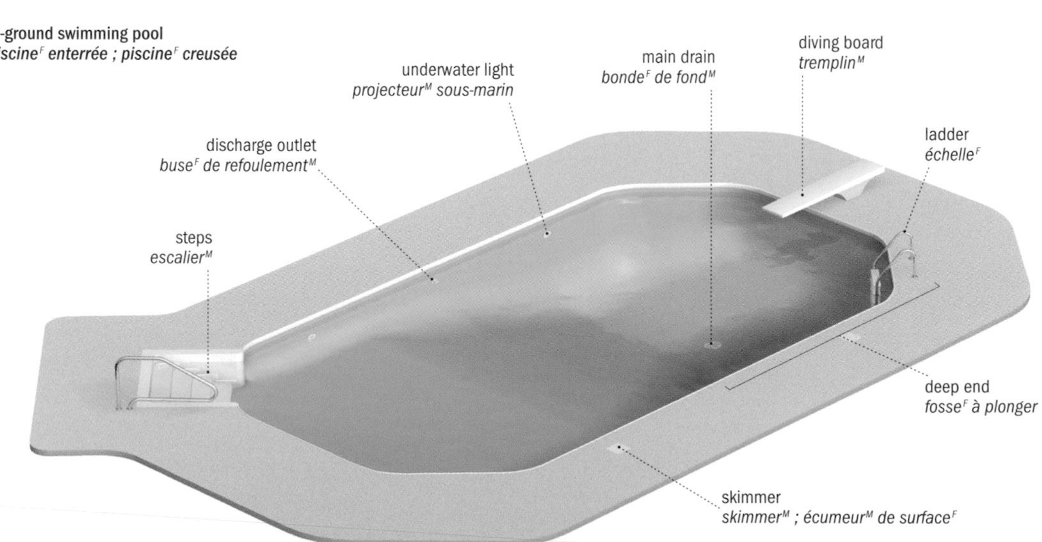
underwater light
projecteur[M] sous-marin
main drain
bonde[F] de fond[M]
diving board
tremplin[M]
discharge outlet
buse[F] de refoulement[M]
ladder
échelle[F]
steps
escalier[M]
deep end
fosse[F] à plonger
skimmer
skimmer[M] ; écumeur[M] de surface[F]

exterior door

porte^F extérieure

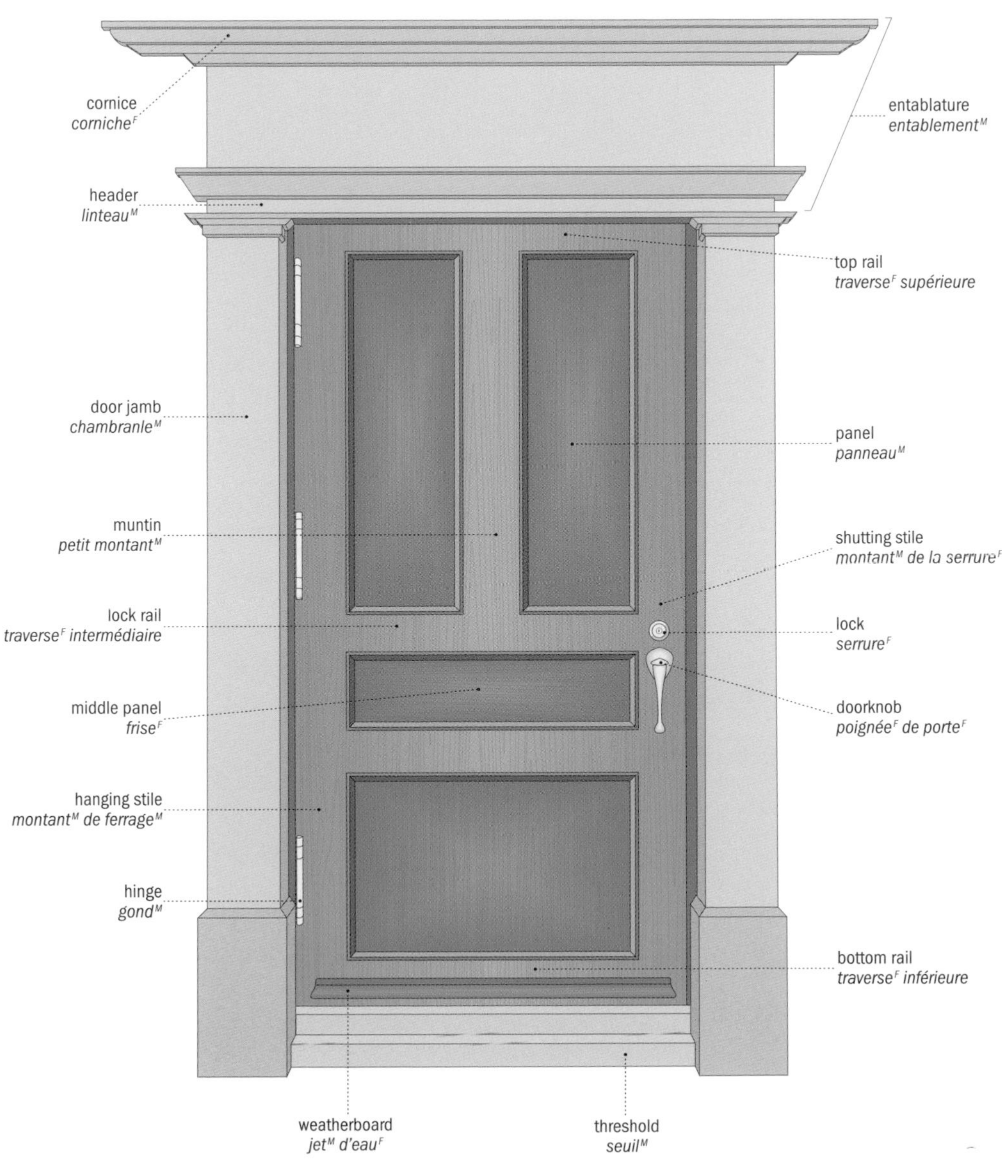
cornice
corniche^F
entablature
entablement^M
header
linteau^M
top rail
traverse^F supérieure
door jamb
chambranle^M
panel
panneau^M
muntin
petit montant^M
shutting stile
montant^M de la serrure^F
lock rail
traverse^F intermédiaire
lock
serrure^F
middle panel
frise^F
doorknob
poignée^F de porte^F
hanging stile
montant^M de ferrage^M
hinge
gond^M
bottom rail
traverse^F inférieure
weatherboard
jet^M d'eau^F
threshold
seuil^M

lock

serrure^F

general view
vue^F d'ensemble^M

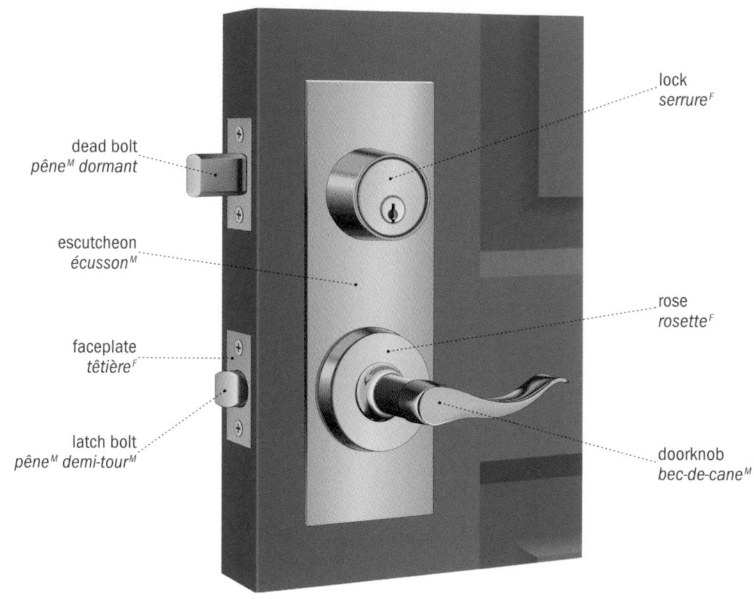
lock
serrure^F
dead bolt
pêne^M dormant
escutcheon
écusson^M
rose
rosette^F
faceplate
têtière^F
latch bolt
pêne^M demi-tour^M
doorknob
bec-de-cane^M

window

fenêtre^F

structure
structure^F

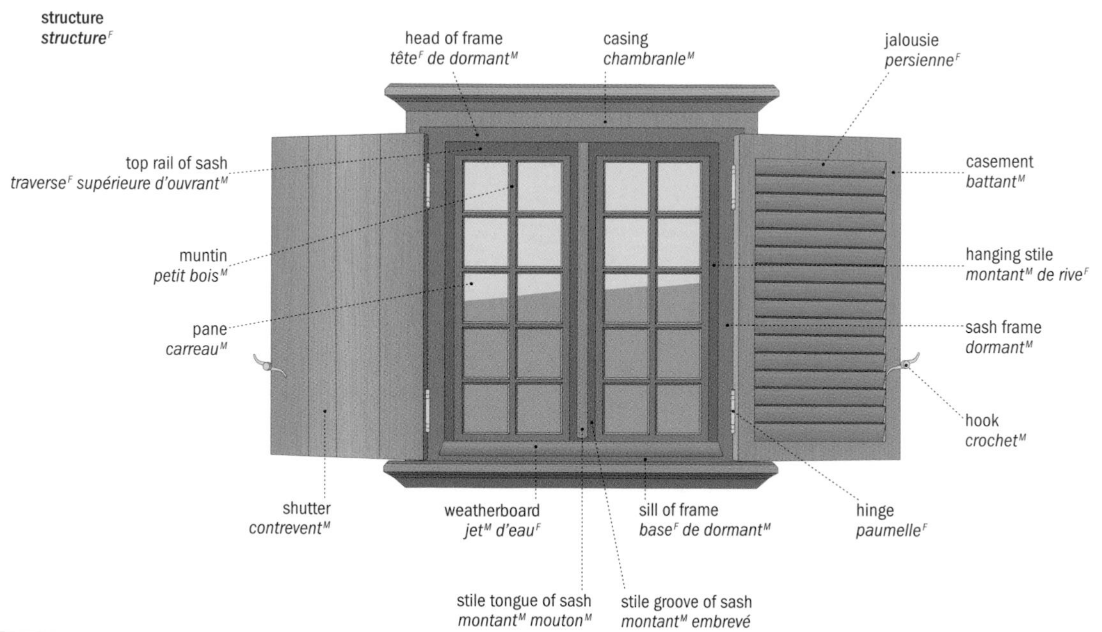
head of frame
tête^F de dormant^M
casing
chambranle^M
jalousie
persienne^F
top rail of sash
traverse^F supérieure d'ouvrant^M
casement
battant^M
muntin
petit bois^M
hanging stile
montant^M de rive^F
pane
carreau^M
sash frame
dormant^M
hook
crochet^M
shutter
contrevent^M
weatherboard
jet^M d'eau^F
sill of frame
base^F de dormant^M
hinge
paumelle^F
stile tongue of sash
montant^M mouton^M
stile groove of sash
montant^M embrevé

HOUSE

frame

charpente[F]

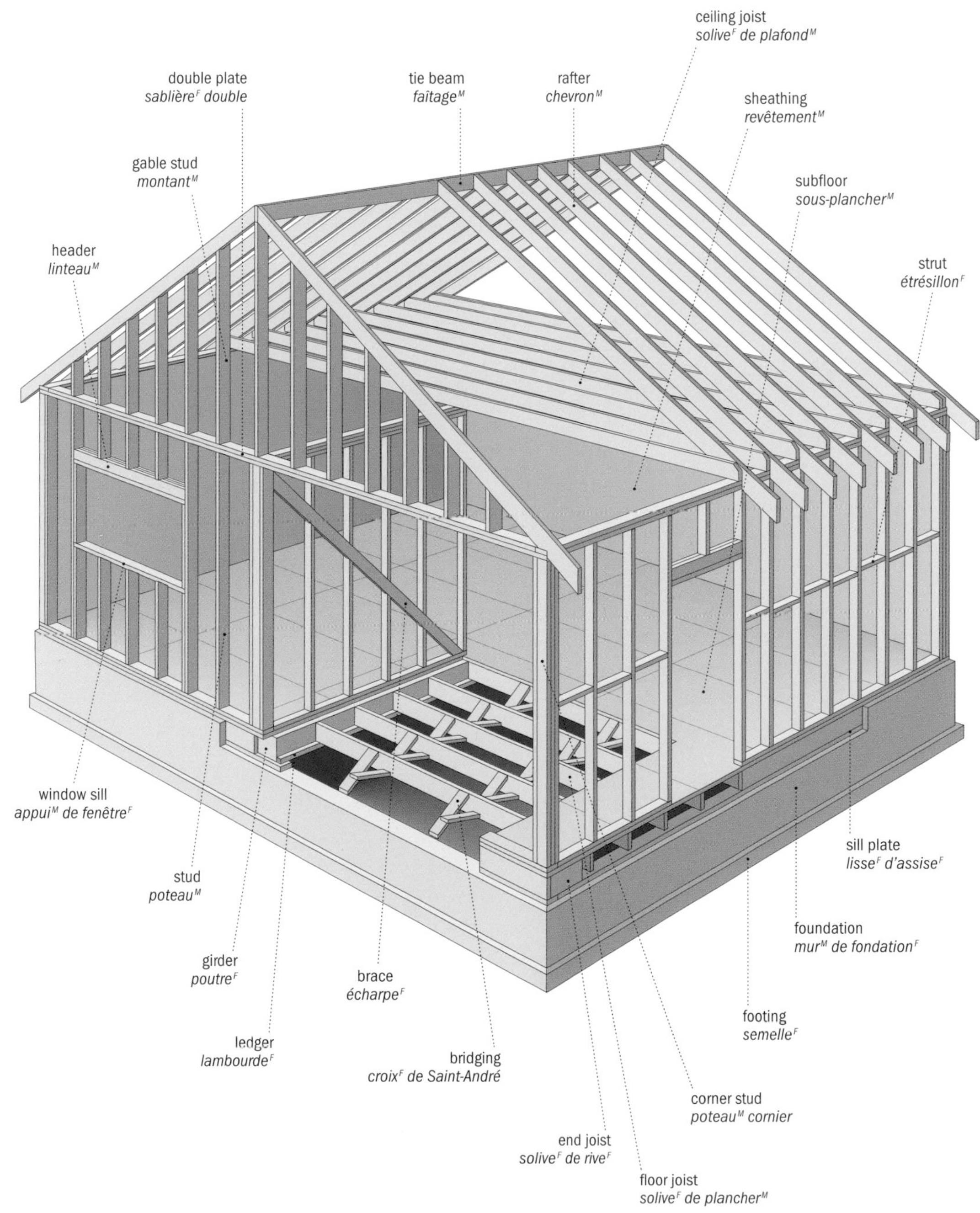
ceiling joist
solive[F] de plafond[M]
double plate
sablière[F] double
tie beam
faîtage[M]
rafter
chevron[M]
sheathing
revêtement[M]
gable stud
montant[M]
subfloor
sous-plancher[M]
header
linteau[M]
strut
étrésillon[F]
window sill
appui[M] de fenêtre[F]
sill plate
lisse[F] d'assise[F]
stud
poteau[M]
foundation
mur[M] de fondation[F]
girder
poutre[F]
brace
écharpe[F]
footing
semelle[F]
ledger
lambourde[F]
bridging
croix[F] de Saint-André
corner stud
poteau[M] cornier
end joist
solive[F] de rive[F]
floor joist
solive[F] de plancher[M]

main rooms

principales pièces^F d'une maison^F

first floor
rez-de-chaussée^M

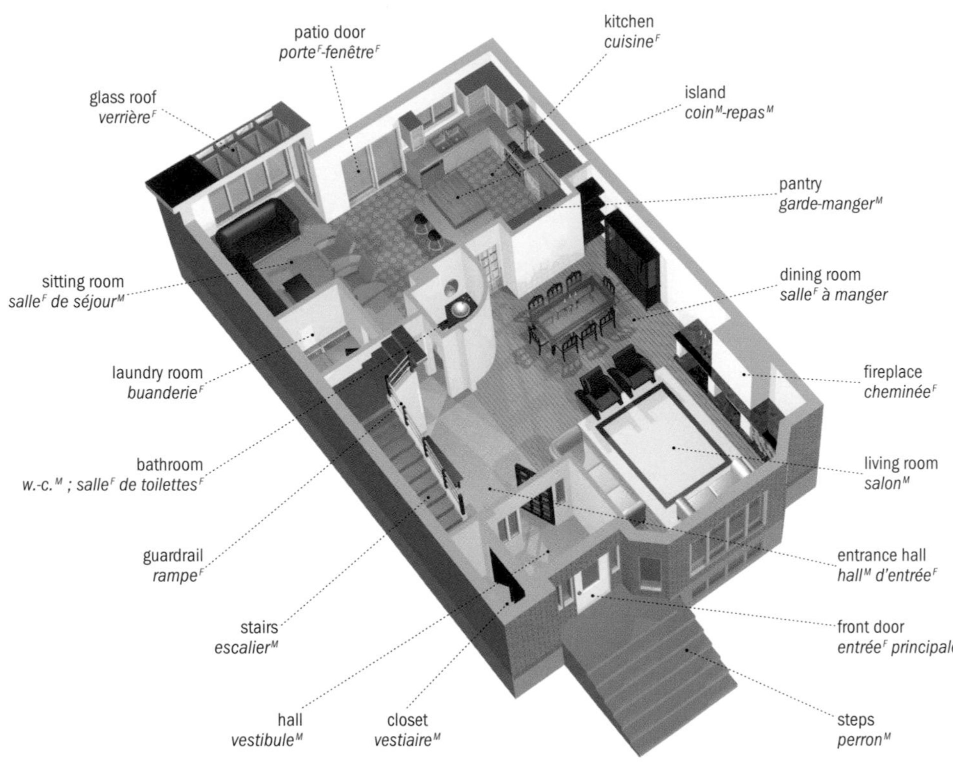
patio door
porte^F-fenêtre^F
kitchen
cuisine^F
glass roof
verrière^F
island
coin^M-repas^M
pantry
garde-manger^M
sitting room
salle^F de séjour^M
dining room
salle^F à manger
laundry room
buanderie^F
fireplace
cheminée^F
bathroom
w.-c.^M ; salle^F de toilettes^F
living room
salon^M
guardrail
rampe^F
entrance hall
hall^M d'entrée^F
stairs
escalier^M
front door
entrée^F principale
hall
vestibule^M
closet
vestiaire^M
steps
perron^M

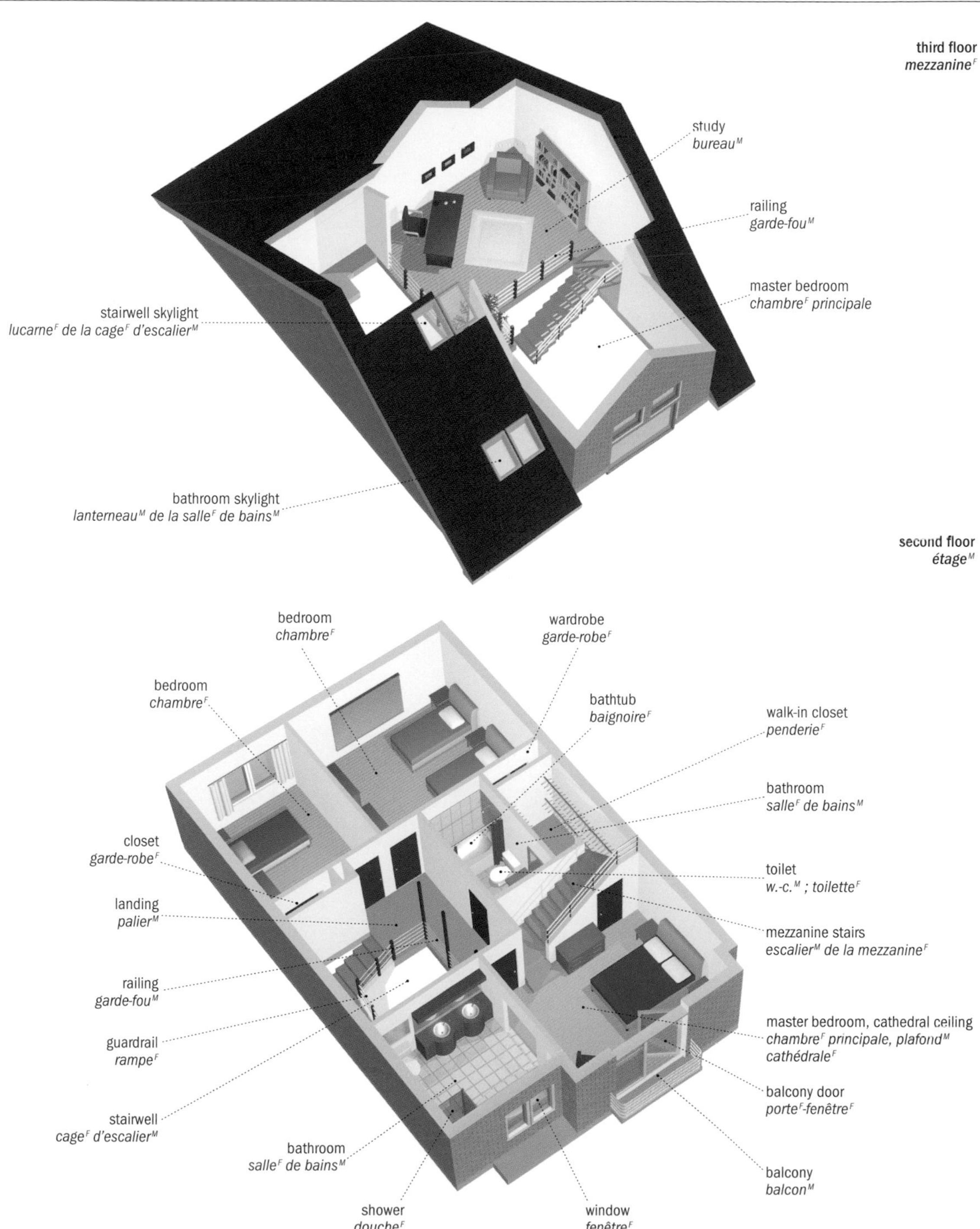
third floor
mezzanine
study
bureau
railing
garde-fou
master bedroom
chambre principale
stairwell skylight
lucarne de la cage d'escalier
bathroom skylight
lanterneau de la salle de bains
second floor
étage
bedroom
chambre
wardrobe
garde-robe
bedroom
chambre
bathtub
baignoire
walk-in closet
penderie
bathroom
salle de bains
closet
garde-robe
toilet
w.-c. ; toilette
landing
palier
mezzanine stairs
escalier de la mezzanine
railing
garde-fou
guardrail
rampe
master bedroom, cathedral ceiling
chambre principale, plafond cathédrale
balcony door
porte-fenêtre
stairwell
cage d'escalier
bathroom
salle de bains
balcony
balcon
shower
douche
window
fenêtre

wood flooring

parquet[M]

wood flooring on cement screed
parquet[M] sur chape[F] de ciment[M]

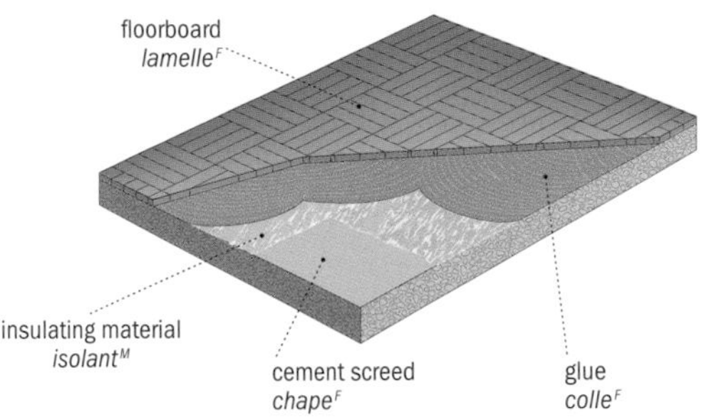
floorboard
lamelle[F]
insulating material
isolant[M]
cement screed
chape[F]
glue
colle[F]

wood flooring on wooden structure
parquet[M] sur ossature[F] de bois[M]

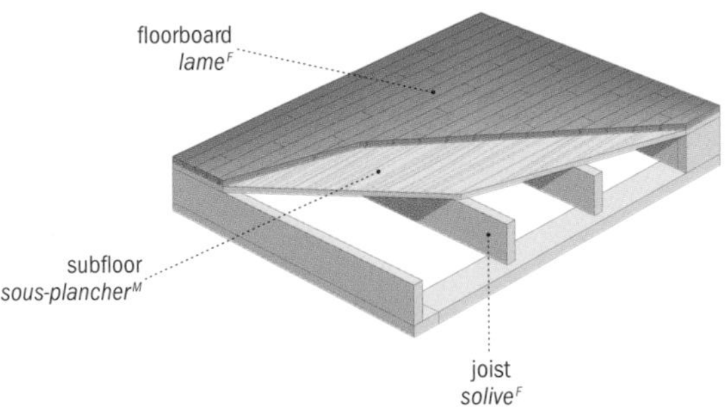
floorboard
lame[F]
subfloor
sous-plancher[M]
joist
solive[F]

wood flooring arrangements
arrangements[M] des parquets[M]

overlay flooring
parquet[M] à coupe[F] perdue

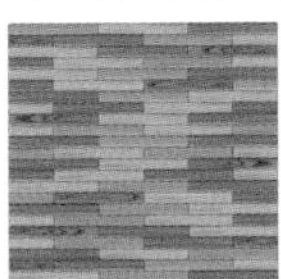

strip flooring with alternate joints
parquet[M] à coupe[F] de pierre[F]

herringbone parquet
parquet[M] à bâtons[M] rompus

herringbone pattern
parquet[M] en chevrons[M]

inlaid parquet
parquet[M] mosaïque[F]

basket weave pattern
parquet[M] en vannerie[F]

Arenberg parquet
parquet[M] d'Arenberg

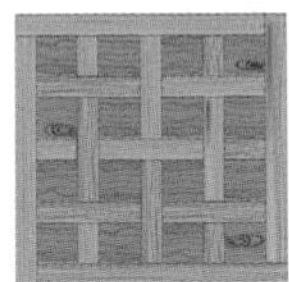

Chantilly parquet
parquet[M] Chantilly

Versailles parquet
parquet[M] Versailles

textile floor coverings

revêtements[M] de sol[M] textiles

rug
tapis[M]

pile carpet
moquette[F]

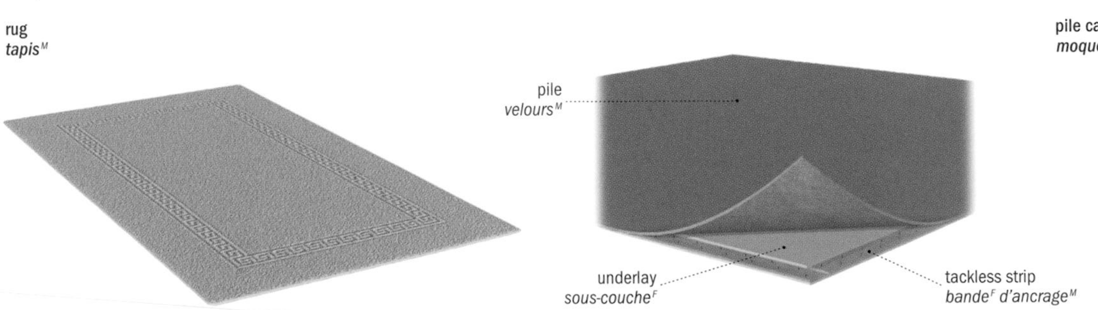
pile
velours[M]
underlay
sous-couche[F]
tackless strip
bande[F] d'ancrage[M]

stairs

escalier[M]

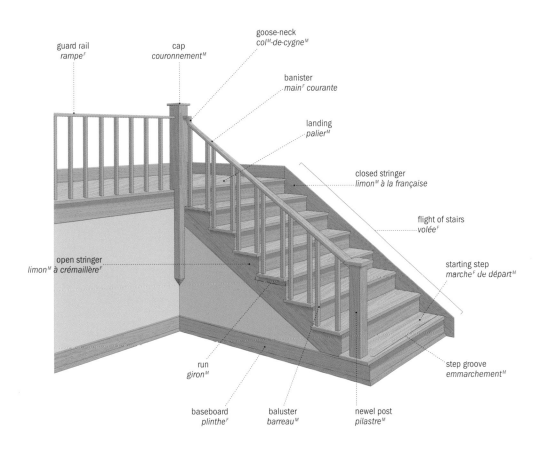

guard rail
rampe[F]

cap
couronnement[M]

goose-neck
col[M]-de-cygne[M]

banister
main[F] courante

landing
palier[M]

closed stringer
limon[M] à la française

flight of stairs
volée[F]

open stringer
limon[M] à crémaillère[F]

starting step
marche[F] de départ[M]

run
giron[M]

step groove
emmarchement[M]

baseboard
plinthe[F]

baluster
barreau[M]

newel post
pilastre[M]

step

marche[F]

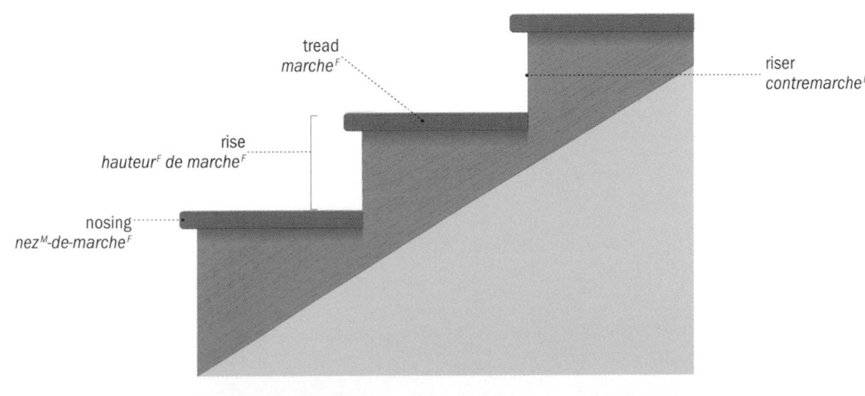
tread
marche[F]
riser
contremarche[F]
rise
hauteur[F] de marche[F]
nosing
nez[M]-de-marche[F]

wood burning

chauffage^M au bois^M

fireplace
cheminée^F à foyer^M ouvert

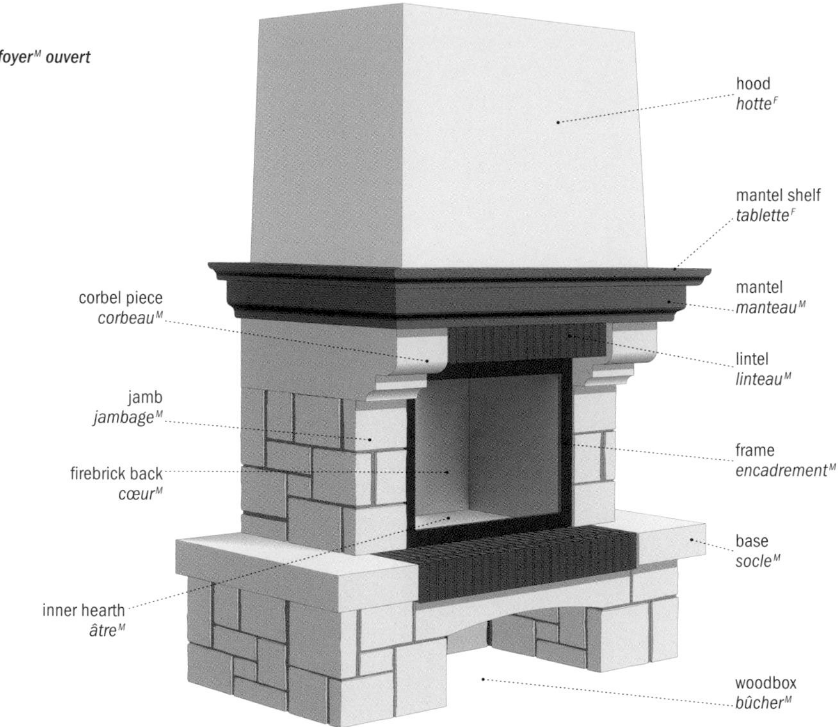
hood
hotte^F
mantel shelf
tablette^F
mantel
manteau^M
corbel piece
corbeau^M
lintel
linteau^M
jamb
jambage^M
frame
encadrement^M
firebrick back
cœur^M
base
socle^M
inner hearth
âtre^M
woodbox
bûcher^M

slow-burning wood stove
poêle^M à combustion^F lente

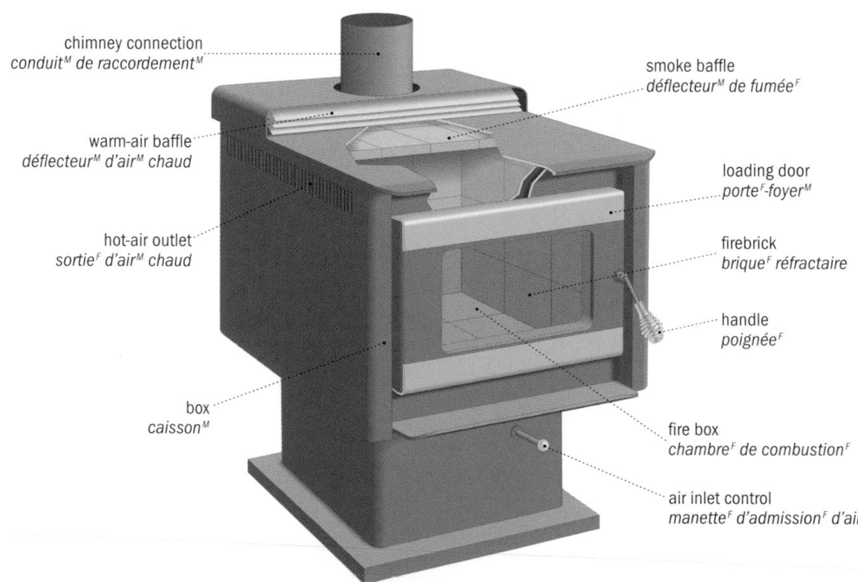
chimney connection
conduit^M de raccordement^M
smoke baffle
déflecteur^M de fumée^F
warm-air baffle
déflecteur^M d'air^M chaud
loading door
porte^F-foyer^M
hot-air outlet
sortie^F d'air^M chaud
firebrick
brique^F réfractaire
handle
poignée^F
box
caisson^M
fire box
chambre^F de combustion^F
air inlet control
manette^F d'admission^F d'air^M

chimney
cheminée[F]

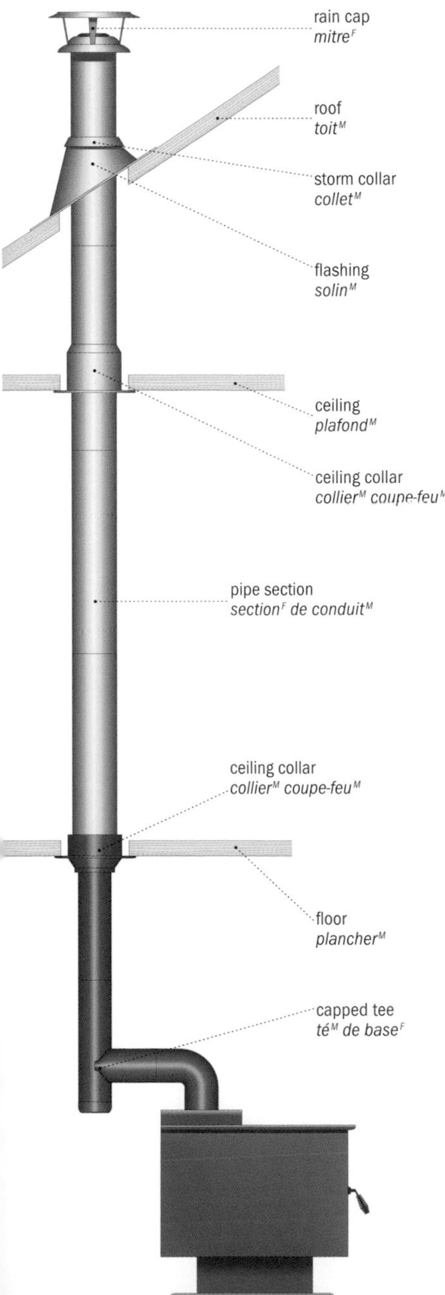
rain cap
mitre[F]
roof
toit[M]
storm collar
collet[M]
flashing
solin[M]
ceiling
plafond[M]
ceiling collar
collier[M] *coupe-feu*[M]
pipe section
section[F] *de conduit*[M]
ceiling collar
collier[M] *coupe-feu*[M]
floor
plancher[M]
capped tee
té[M] *de base*[F]

fire irons
***accessoires*[M] *de foyer*[M]**

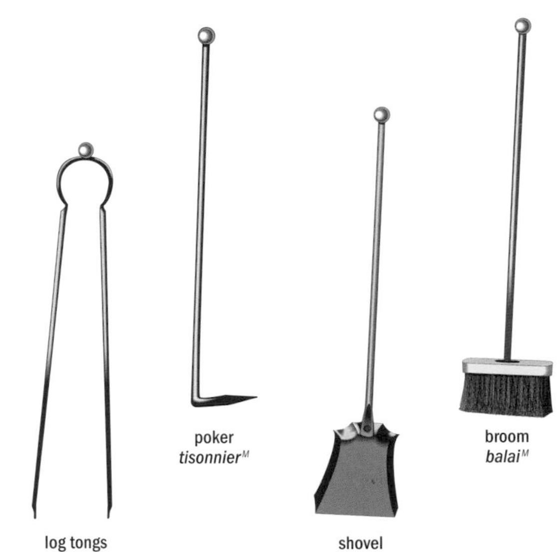
poker
tisonnier[M]
broom
balai[M]
log tongs
pince[F]
shovel
pelle[F]

andirons
chenets[M]
log carrier
porte-bûches[M]

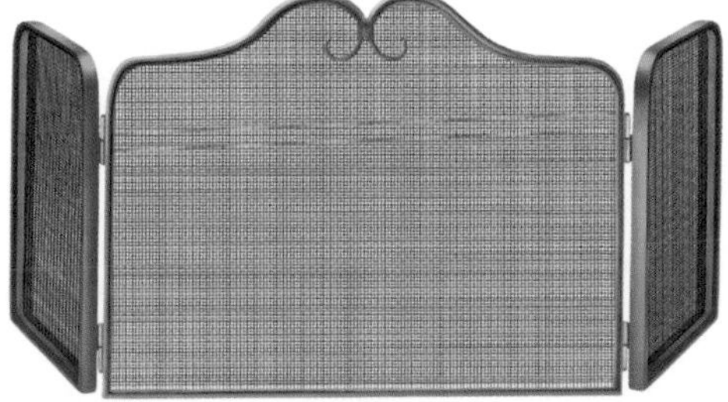
fireplace screen
pare-feu[M]

HOUSE

plumbing system

circuit[M] de plomberie[F]

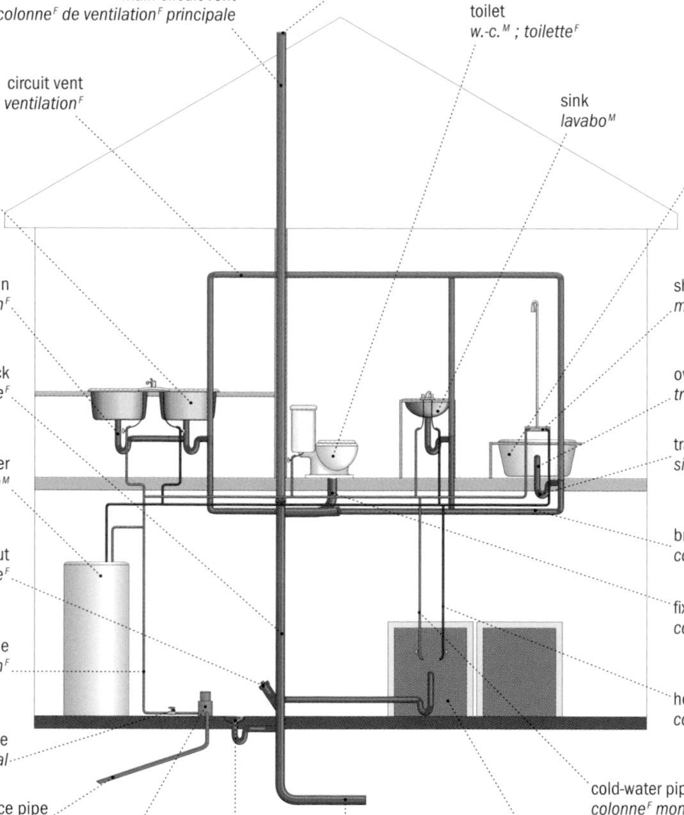

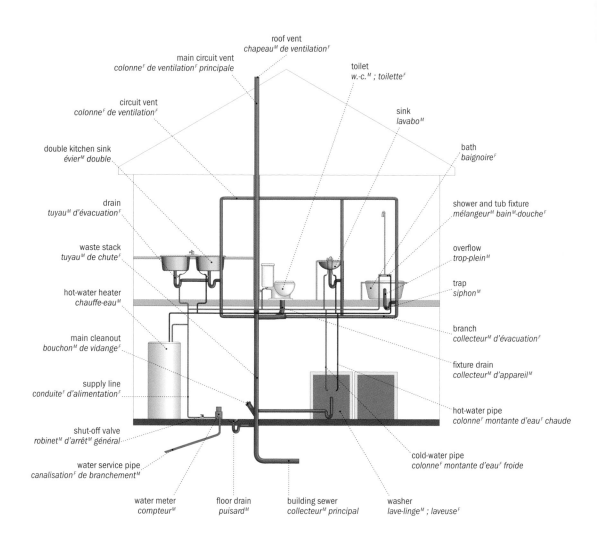

roof vent
chapeau[M] de ventilation[F]

main circuit vent
colonne[F] de ventilation[F] principale

toilet
w.-c.[M] ; toilette[F]

circuit vent
colonne[F] de ventilation[F]

sink
lavabo[M]

double kitchen sink
évier[M] double

bath
baignoire[F]

drain
tuyau[M] d'évacuation[F]

shower and tub fixture
mélangeur[M] bain[M]-douche[F]

waste stack
tuyau[M] de chute[F]

overflow
trop-plein[M]

hot-water heater
chauffe-eau[M]

trap
siphon[M]

branch
collecteur[M] d'évacuation[F]

main cleanout
bouchon[M] de vidange[F]

fixture drain
collecteur[M] d'appareil[M]

supply line
conduite[F] d'alimentation[F]

hot-water pipe
colonne[F] montante d'eau[F] chaude

shut-off valve
robinet[M] d'arrêt[M] général

cold-water pipe
colonne[F] montante d'eau[F] froide

water service pipe
canalisation[F] de branchement[M]

water meter
compteur[M]

floor drain
puisard[M]

building sewer
collecteur[M] principal

washer
lave-linge[M] ; laveuse[F]

ventilating circuit
circuit[M] de ventilation[F]

draining circuit
circuit[M] d'évacuation[F]

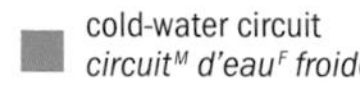

cold-water circuit
circuit[M] d'eau[F] froide

hot-water circuit
circuit[M] d'eau[F] chaude

bathroom

salle^F de bains^M

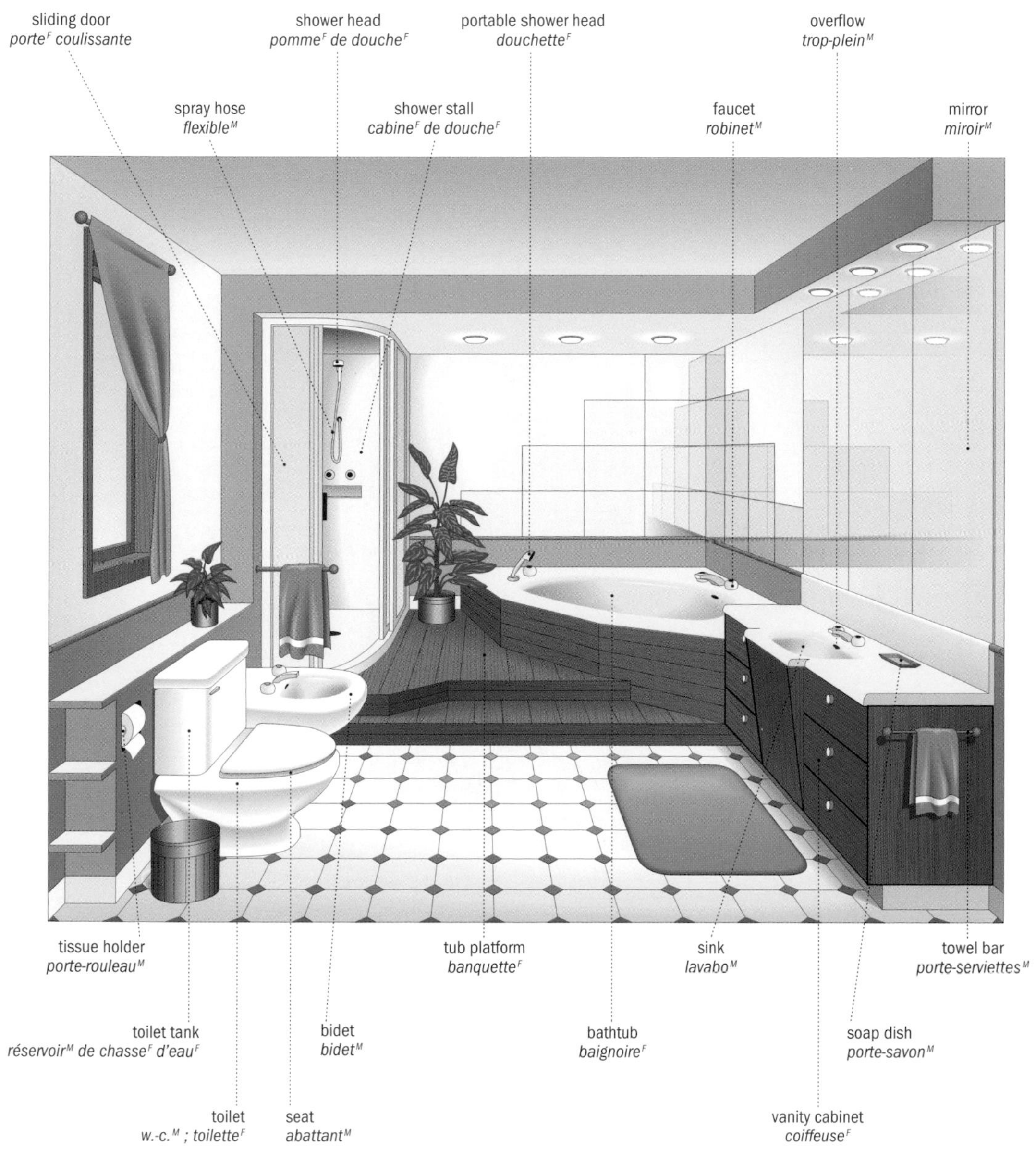
sliding door
porte^F coulissante
shower head
pomme^F de douche^F
portable shower head
douchette^F
overflow
trop-plein^M
spray hose
flexible^M
shower stall
cabine^F de douche^F
faucet
robinet^M
mirror
miroir^M
tissue holder
porte-rouleau^M
tub platform
banquette^F
sink
lavabo^M
towel bar
porte-serviettes^M
toilet tank
réservoir^M de chasse^F d'eau^F
bidet
bidet^M
bathtub
baignoire^F
soap dish
porte-savon^M
toilet
w.-c.^M ; toilette^F
seat
abattant^M
vanity cabinet
coiffeuse^F

toilet

w.-c.M ; *toiletteF*

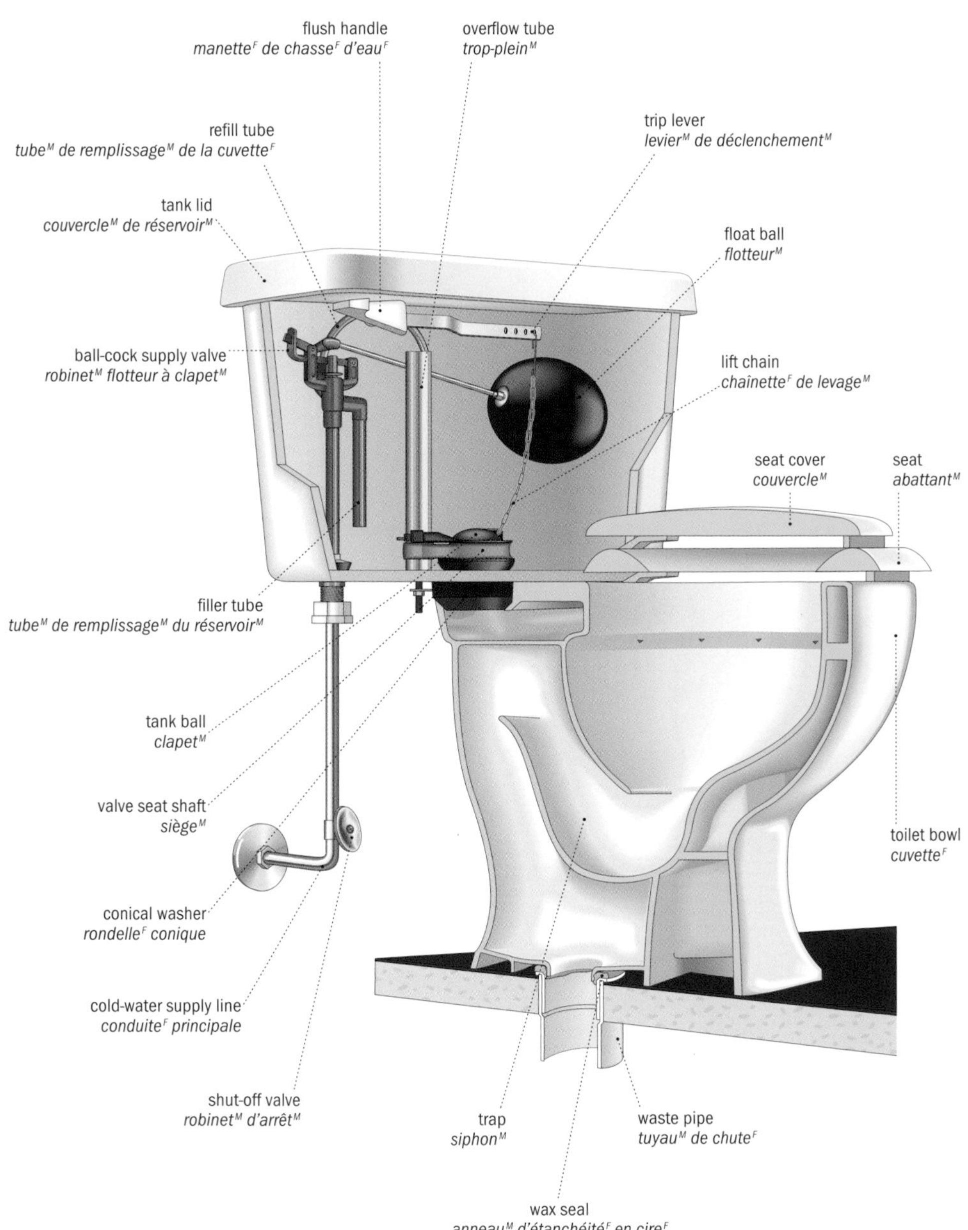
flush handle
manetteF de chasseF d'eauF
overflow tube
trop-pleinM
refill tube
tubeM de remplissageM de la cuvetteF
trip lever
levierM de déclenchementM
tank lid
couvercleM de réservoirM
float ball
flotteurM
ball-cock supply valve
robinetM flotteur à clapetM
lift chain
chaînetteF de levageM
seat cover
couvercleM
seat
abattantM
filler tube
tubeM de remplissageM du réservoirM
tank ball
clapetM
valve seat shaft
siègeM
toilet bowl
cuvetteF
conical washer
rondelleF conique
cold-water supply line
conduiteF principale
shut-off valve
robinetM d'arrêtM
trap
siphonM
waste pipe
tuyauM de chuteF
wax seal
anneauM d'étanchéitéF en cireF

examples of branching

exemples[M] de branchement[M]

garbage disposal sink
évier[M]-broyeur[M]

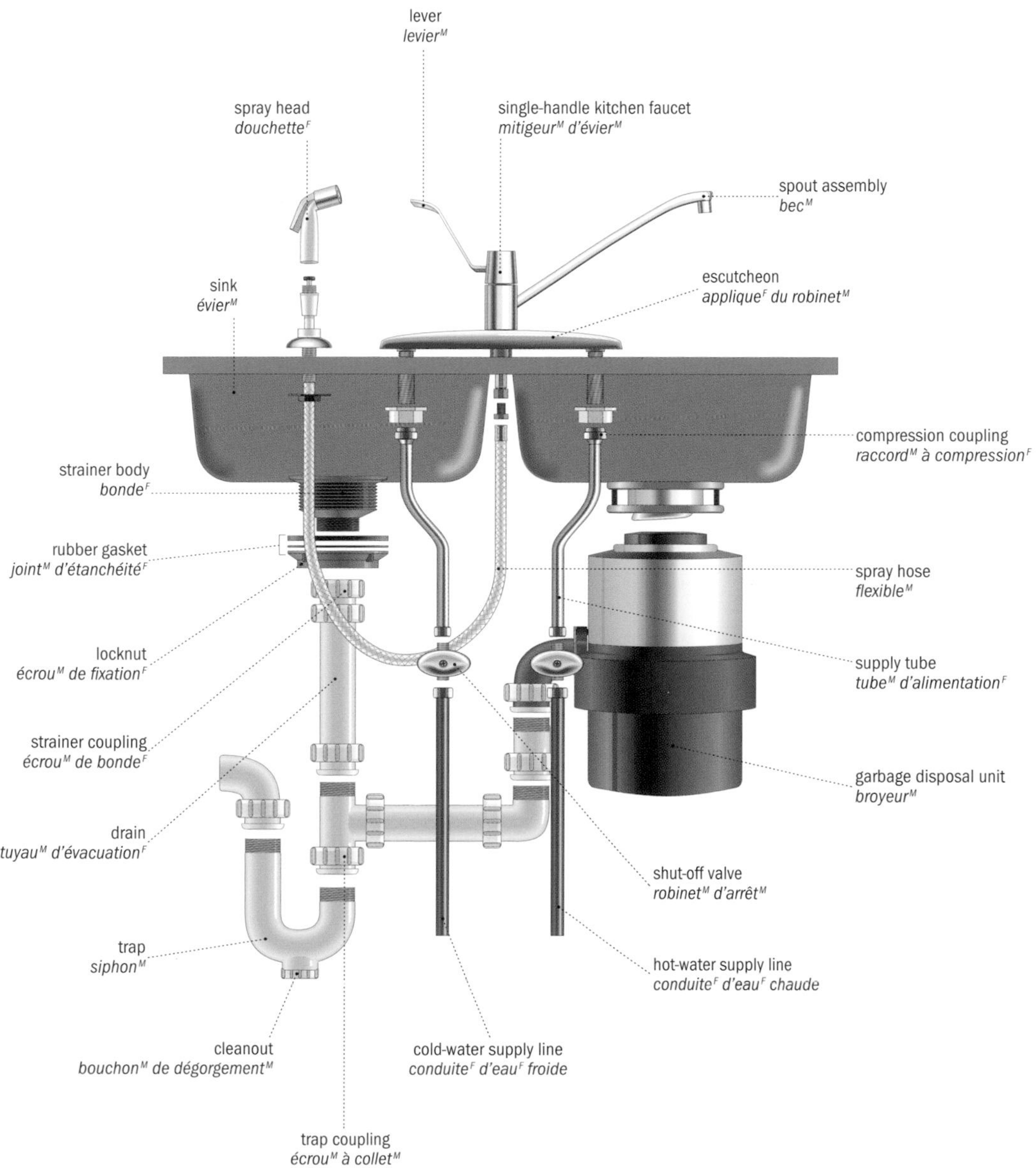
lever
levier[M]
spray head
douchette[F]
single-handle kitchen faucet
mitigeur[M] d'évier[M]
spout assembly
bec[M]
sink
évier[M]
escutcheon
applique[F] du robinet[M]
compression coupling
raccord[M] à compression[F]
strainer body
bonde[F]
rubber gasket
joint[M] d'étanchéité[F]
spray hose
flexible[M]
locknut
écrou[M] de fixation[F]
supply tube
tube[M] d'alimentation[F]
strainer coupling
écrou[M] de bonde[F]
garbage disposal unit
broyeur[M]
drain
tuyau[M] d'évacuation[F]
shut-off valve
robinet[M] d'arrêt[M]
trap
siphon[M]
hot-water supply line
conduite[F] d'eau[F] chaude
cleanout
bouchon[M] de dégorgement[M]
cold-water supply line
conduite[F] d'eau[F] froide
trap coupling
écrou[M] à collet[M]

network connection

branchement[M] au réseau[M]

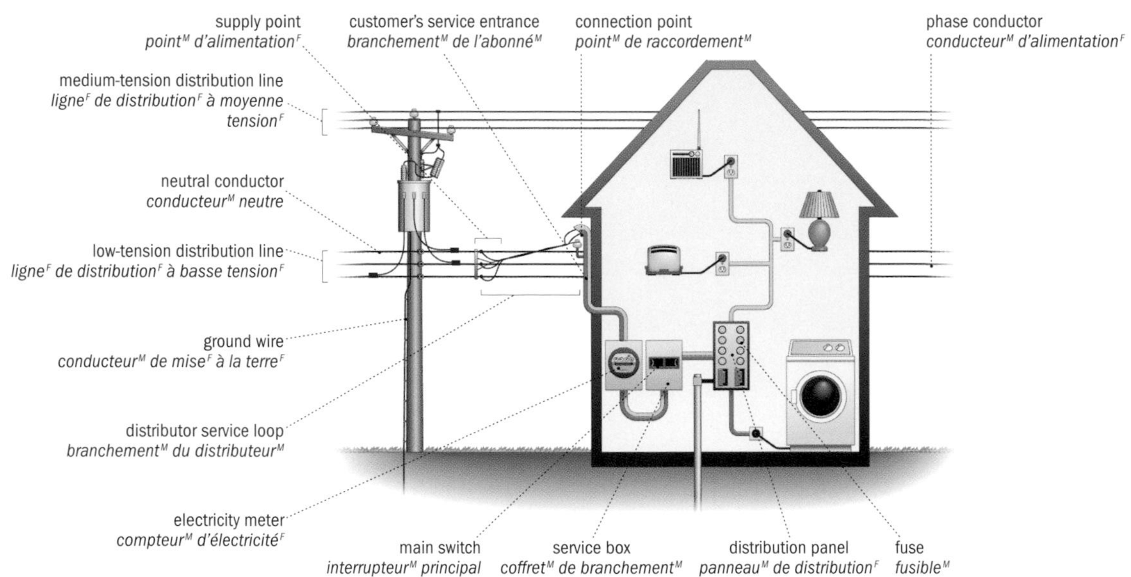
supply point
point[M] d'alimentation[F]
customer's service entrance
branchement[M] de l'abonné[M]
connection point
point[M] de raccordement[M]
phase conductor
conducteur[M] d'alimentation[F]
medium-tension distribution line
ligne[F] de distribution[F] à moyenne tension[F]
neutral conductor
conducteur[M] neutre
low-tension distribution line
ligne[F] de distribution[F] à basse tension[F]
ground wire
conducteur[M] de mise[F] à la terre[F]
distributor service loop
branchement[M] du distributeur[M]
electricity meter
compteur[M] d'électricité[F]
main switch
interrupteur[M] principal
service box
coffret[M] de branchement[M]
distribution panel
panneau[M] de distribution[F]
fuse
fusible[M]

contact devices

dispositifs[M] de contact[M]

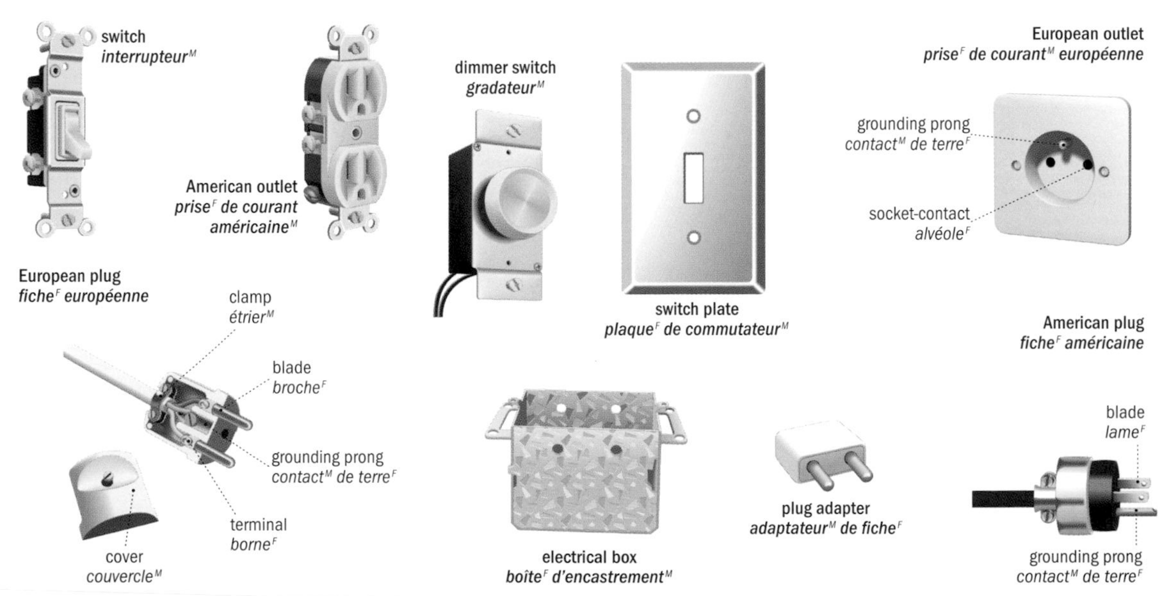
switch
interrupteur[M]
American outlet
prise[F] de courant américaine[M]
dimmer switch
gradateur[M]
switch plate
plaque[F] de commutateur[M]
European outlet
prise[F] de courant[M] européenne
grounding prong
contact[M] de terre[F]
socket-contact
alvéole[F]
European plug
fiche[F] européenne
clamp
étrier[M]
blade
broche[F]
grounding prong
contact[M] de terre[F]
terminal
borne[F]
cover
couvercle[M]
electrical box
boîte[F] d'encastrement[M]
plug adapter
adaptateur[M] de fiche[F]
American plug
fiche[F] américaine
blade
lame[F]
grounding prong
contact[M] de terre[F]

HOUSE

lighting
éclairage[M]

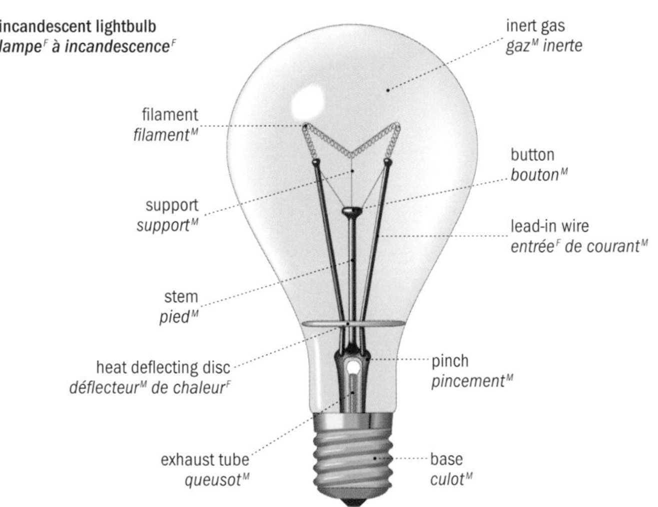
incandescent lightbulb
lampe[F] à incandescence[F]
inert gas
gaz[M] inerte
filament
filament[M]
button
bouton[M]
support
support[M]
lead-in wire
entrée[F] de courant[M]
stem
pied[M]
heat deflecting disc
déflecteur[M] de chaleur[F]
pinch
pincement[M]
exhaust tube
queusot[M]
base
culot[M]

lamp socket
douille[F] de lampe[F]

bulb
ampoule[F]

screw base
culot[M] à vis[F]

energy-saving bulb
lampe[F] à économie[F] d'énergie[F]

fluorescent tube
tube[M] fluorescent
bulb
ampoule[F]
tube retention clip
attache[F] du tube[M]
mounting plate
plaque[F] de montage[M]
electronic ballast
ballast[M] électronique
housing
boîtier[M]
base
culot[M]

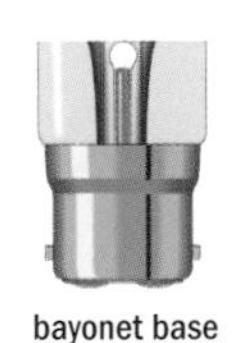
bayonet base
culot[M] à baïonnette[F]

tungsten-halogen lamp
lampe[F] à halogène[M]

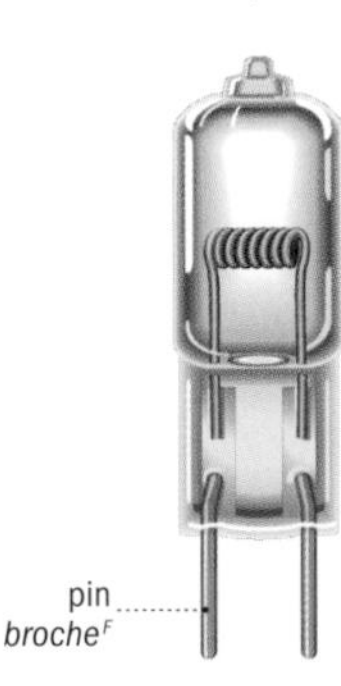
pin
broche[F]

fluorescent tube
tube[M] fluorescent

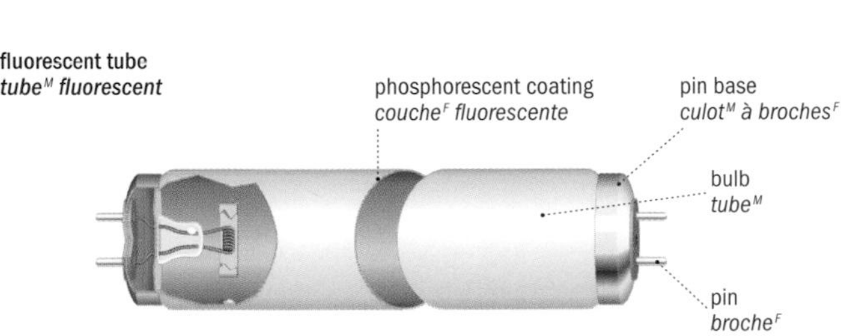
phosphorescent coating
couche[F] fluorescente
pin base
culot[M] à broches[F]
bulb
tube[M]
pin
broche[F]

armchair

fauteuil[M]

parts
parties[F]

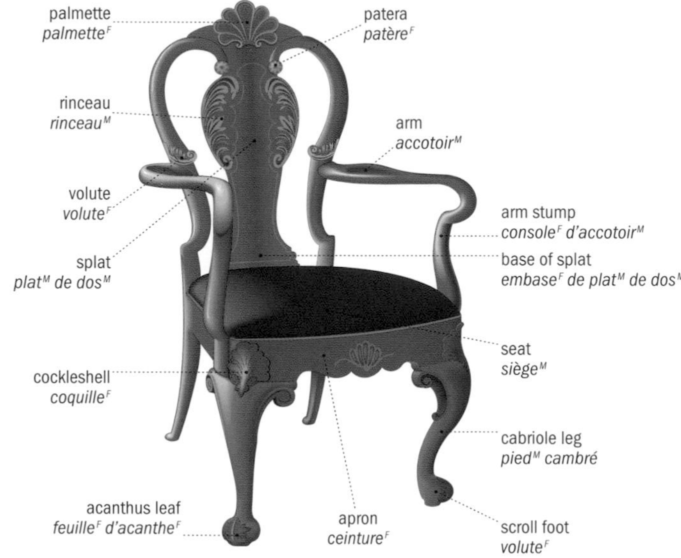
palmette
palmette[F]
patera
patère[F]
rinceau
rinceau[M]
arm
accotoir[M]
volute
volute[F]
arm stump
console[F] d'accotoir[M]
splat
plat[M] de dos[M]
base of splat
embase[F] de plat[M] de dos[M]
seat
siège[M]
cockleshell
coquille[F]
cabriole leg
pied[M] cambré
acanthus leaf
feuille[F] d'acanthe[F]
apron
ceinture[F]
scroll foot
volute[F]

examples of armchairs
exemples[M] de fauteuils[M]

Wassily chair
fauteuil[M] Wassily

director's chair
fauteuil[M] metteur[M] en scène[F]

rocking chair
berceuse[F]

cabriolet
cabriolet[M]

méridienne
méridienne[F]

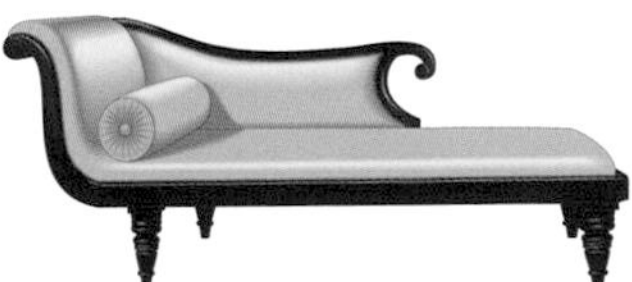

récamier
récamier[M]

club chair
fauteuil[M] club[M]

bergère
bergère[F]

sofa
canapé[M]

love seat
causeuse[F]

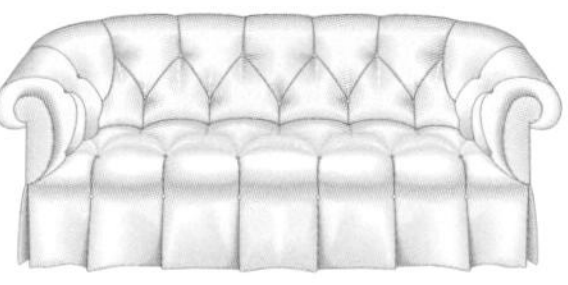

chesterfield
canapé[M] capitonné

side chair

chaise^F

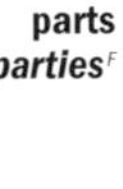

parts
parties^F

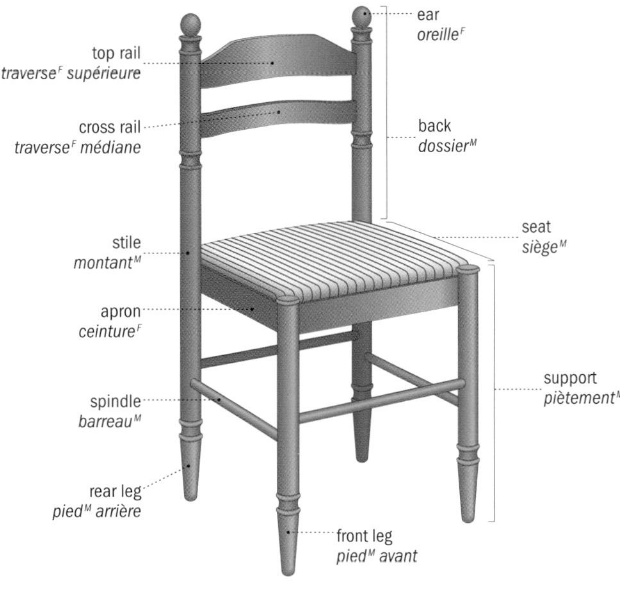
ear
oreille^F
top rail
traverse^F supérieure
cross rail
traverse^F médiane
back
dossier^M
seat
siège^M
stile
montant^M
apron
ceinture^F
support
piètement^M
spindle
barreau^M
rear leg
pied^M arrière
front leg
pied^M avant

examples of chairs
exemples^M de chaises^F

rocking chair
chaise^F berçante

stacking chairs
chaises^F empilables

folding chairs
chaises^F pliantes

chaise longue
chaise^F longue

seats

sièges^M

ottoman
pouf^M

bench
banc^M

banquette
banquette^F

bean bag chair
fauteuil^M-sac^M

step chair
chaise^F-escabeau^M

footstool
tabouret^M

bar stool
tabouret^M-bar^M

table

table^F

gate-leg table
table^F à abattants^M

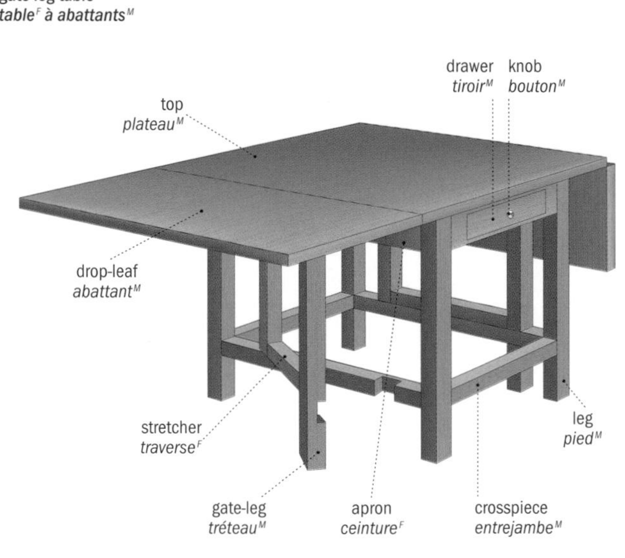

drawer
tiroir^M
knob
bouton^M
top
plateau^M
drop-leaf
abattant^M
stretcher
traverse^F
leg
pied^M
gate-leg
tréteau^M
apron
ceinture^F
crosspiece
entrejambe^M

examples of tables
exemples^M de tables^F

extension table
table^F à rallonges^F

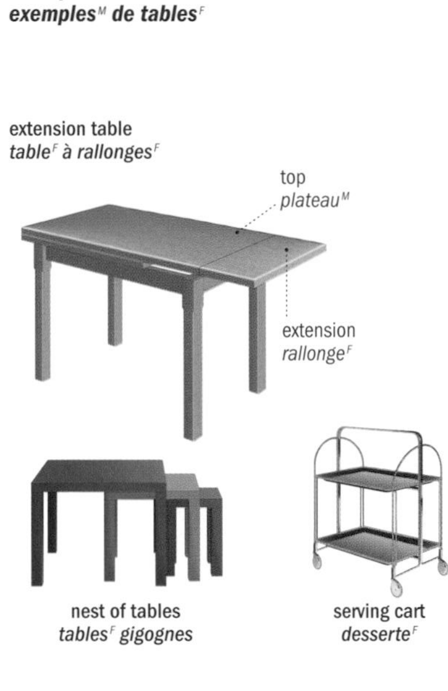

top
plateau^M
extension
rallonge^F

nest of tables
tables^F gigognes

serving cart
desserte^F

storage furniture

meubles^M de rangement^M

armoire
armoire^F

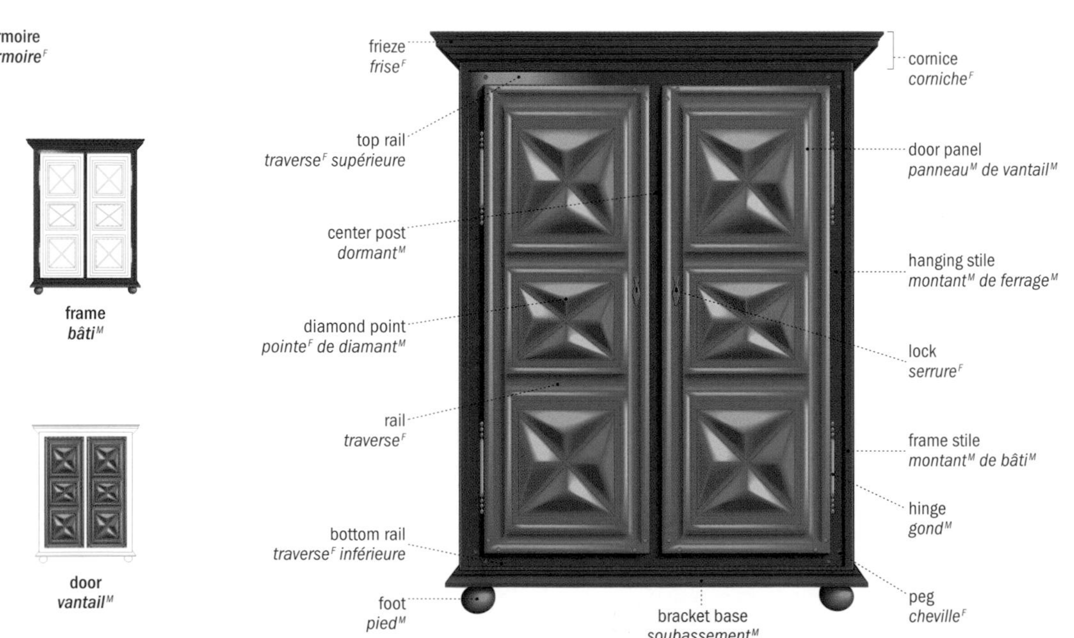

frieze
frise^F
cornice
corniche^F
top rail
traverse^F supérieure
door panel
panneau^M de vantail^M
center post
dormant^M
hanging stile
montant^M de ferrage^M
diamond point
pointe^F de diamant^M
lock
serrure^F
rail
traverse^F
frame stile
montant^M de bâti^M
hinge
gond^M
bottom rail
traverse^F inférieure
peg
cheville^F
foot
pied^M
bracket base
soubassement^M

frame
bâti^M

door
vantail^M

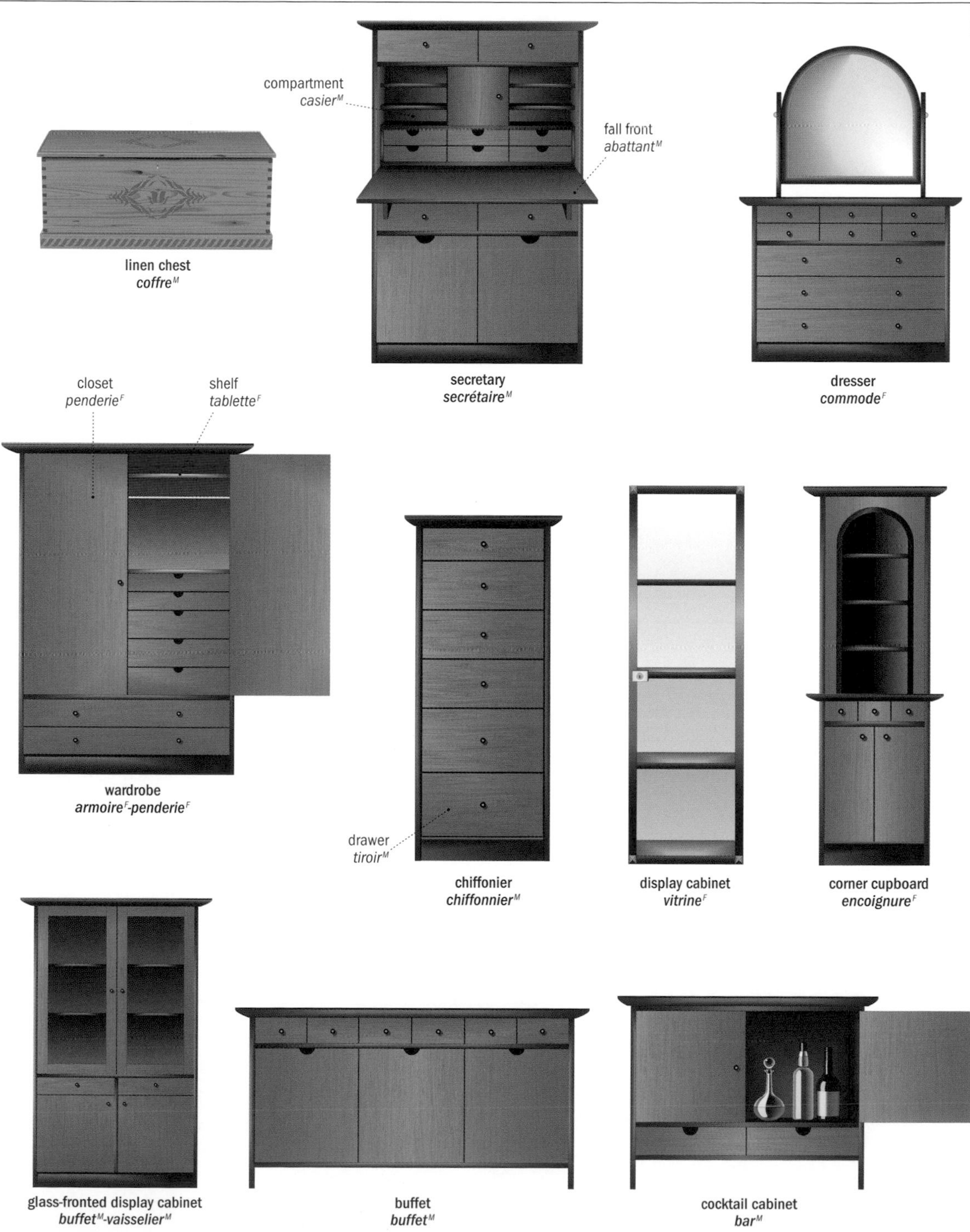
compartment
casier[M]
fall front
abattant[M]
closet
penderie[F]
shelf
tablette[F]
drawer
tiroir[M]

linen chest
coffre[M]

secretary
secrétaire[M]

dresser
commode[F]

wardrobe
armoire[F]*-penderie*[F]

chiffonier
chiffonnier[M]

display cabinet
vitrine[F]

corner cupboard
encoignure[F]

glass-fronted display cabinet
buffet[M]*-vaisselier*[M]

buffet
buffet[M]

cocktail cabinet
bar[M]

bed
lit[M]

sofa bed
canapé[M] convertible

futon
futon[M]
frame
cadre[M]

parts
parties[F]

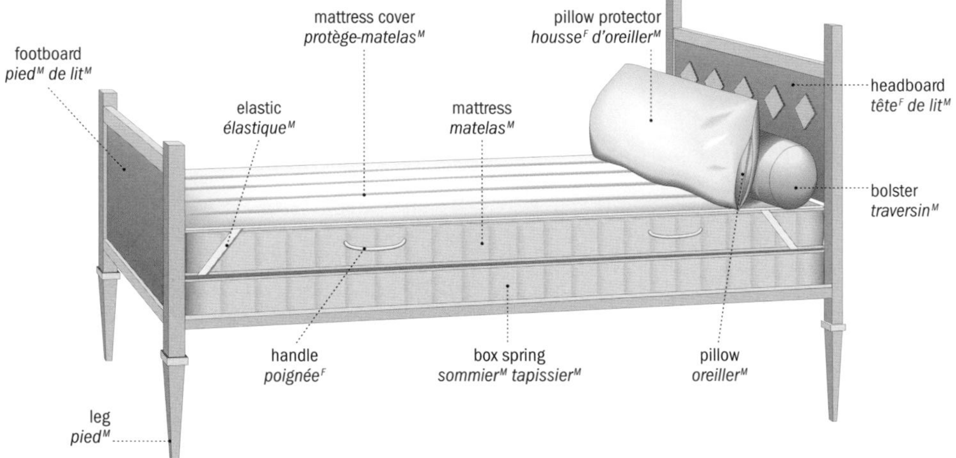
mattress cover
protège-matelas[M]
pillow protector
housse[F] d'oreiller[M]
footboard
pied[M] de lit[M]
elastic
élastique[M]
mattress
matelas[M]
headboard
tête[F] de lit[M]
bolster
traversin[M]
handle
poignée[F]
box spring
sommier[M] tapissier[M]
pillow
oreiller[M]
leg
pied[M]

linen
literie[F]

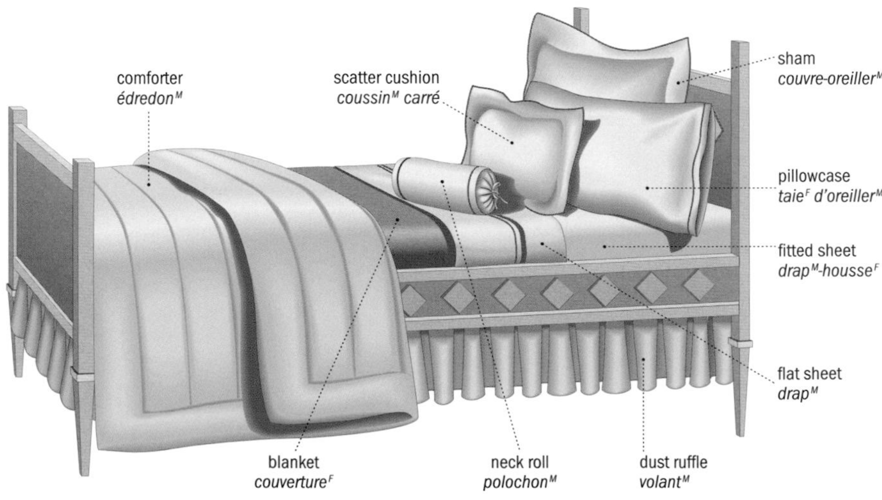
comforter
édredon[M]
scatter cushion
coussin[M] carré
sham
couvre-oreiller[M]
pillowcase
taie[F] d'oreiller[M]
fitted sheet
drap[M]-housse[F]
flat sheet
drap[M]
blanket
couverture[F]
neck roll
polochon[M]
dust ruffle
volant[M]

children's furniture

meubles[M] d'enfants[M]

playpen
lit[M] pliant

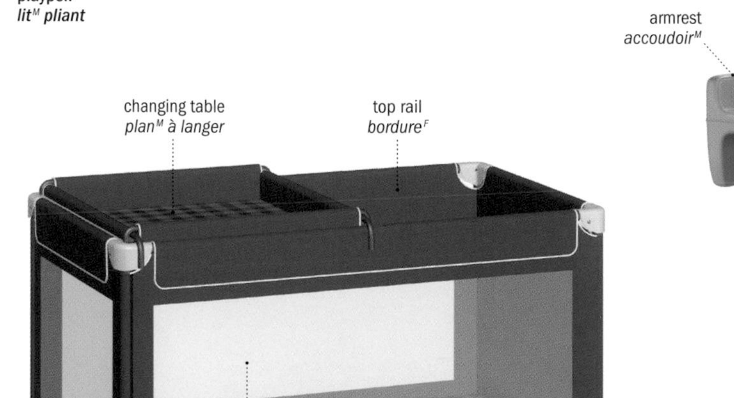
changing table
plan[M] à langer
top rail
bordure[F]
mesh
filet[M]
mattress
matelas[M]

booster seat
rehausseur[M]

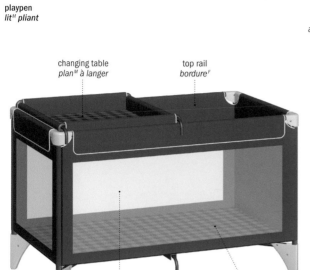

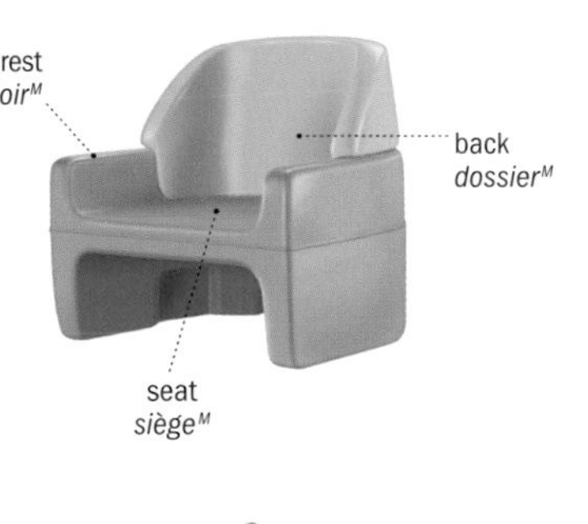
armrest
accoudoir[M]
back
dossier[M]
seat
siège[M]

changing table
table[F] à langer

high chair
chaise[F] haute

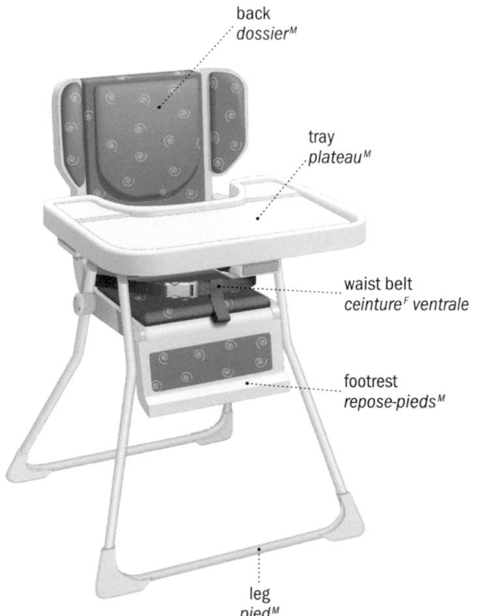
back
dossier[M]
tray
plateau[M]
waist belt
ceinture[F] ventrale
footrest
repose-pieds[M]
leg
pied[M]

crib
lit[M] à barreaux[M]

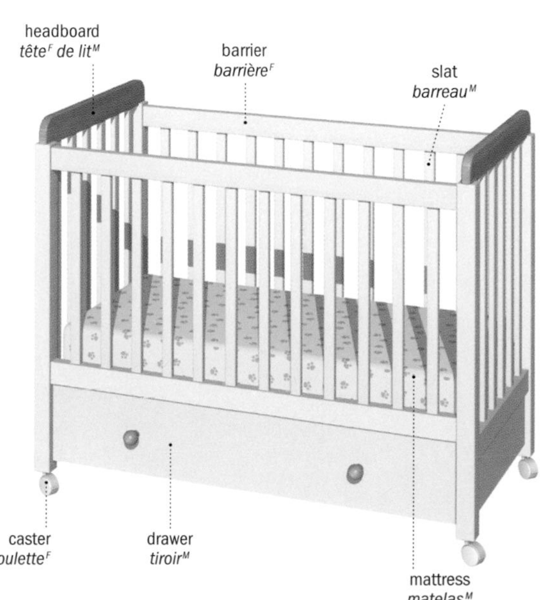
headboard
tête[F] de lit[M]
barrier
barrière[F]
slat
barreau[M]
caster
roulette[F]
drawer
tiroir[M]
mattress
matelas[M]

HOUSE

lights

luminaires^{M}

clamp spotlight
spot^{M} à pince^{F}

ceiling fixture
plafonnier^{M}

hanging pendant
suspension^{F}

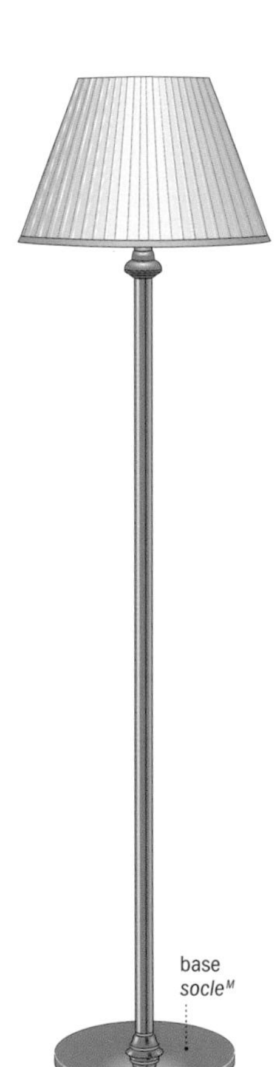
base
socle^{M}

floor lamp
lampadaire^{M}

arm
bras^{M}
base
socle^{M}
shade
abat-jour^{M}
stand
pied^{M}

halogen desk lamp
lampe^{F} de bureau^{M} halogène

reading lamp
lampe^{F} liseuse

table lamp
lampe^{F} de table^{F}

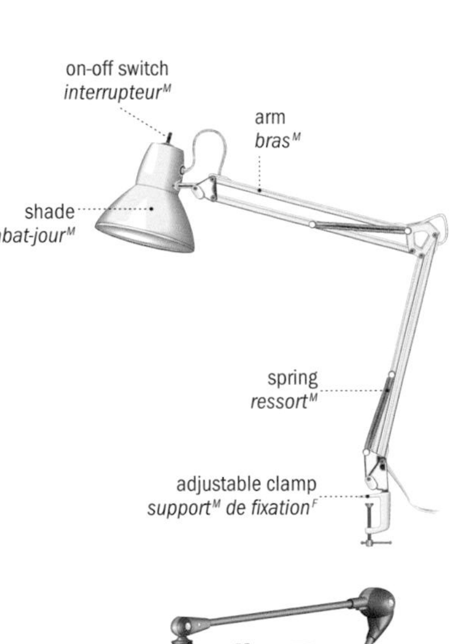
on-off switch
interrupteur^{M}
arm
bras^{M}
shade
abat-jour^{M}
spring
ressort^{M}
adjustable clamp
support^{M} de fixation^{F}

adjustable lamp
lampe^{F} d'architecte^{M}

desk lamp
lampe^{F} de bureau^{M}

chandelier
lustre^M
bobeche
coupelle^F
crystal drop
pendeloque^F
crystal button
pampille^F
column
fût^M
track lighting
rail^M d'éclairage^M
bar frame
gouttière^F
transformer
transformateur^M
contact lever
manette^F de contact^M
spot
spot^M
wall lantern
lanterne^F murale
wall sconce
applique^F
swivel wall lamp
applique^F orientable
strip lights
rampe^F d'éclairage^M
post lantern
lanterne^F de pied^M

domestic appliances

appareils[M] électroménagers

steam iron
fer[M] à vapeur[F]

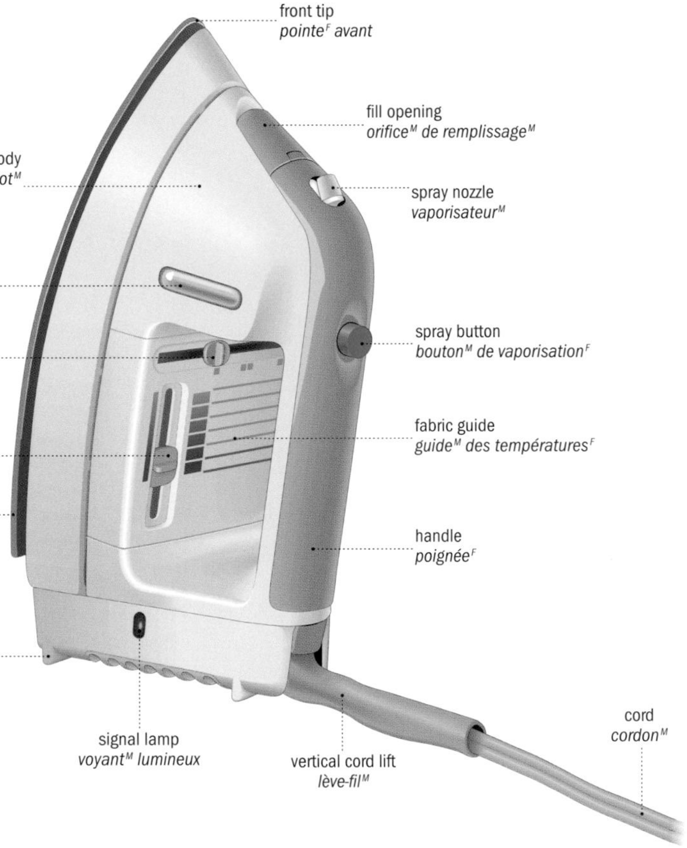

front tip
pointe[F] avant

fill opening
orifice[M] de remplissage[M]

body
capot[M]

spray nozzle
vaporisateur[M]

water-level tube
repère[M] de niveau[M] d'eau[F]

spray button
bouton[M] de vaporisation[F]

spray control
contrôle[M] de la vapeur[F]

fabric guide
guide[M] des températures[F]

temperature control
réglage[M] des températures[F]

soleplate
semelle[F]

handle
poignée[F]

heel rest
talon[M] d'appui[M]

cord
cordon[M]

signal lamp
voyant[M] lumineux

vertical cord lift
lève-fil[M]

hand held vacuum cleaner
aspirateur[M] à main[F]

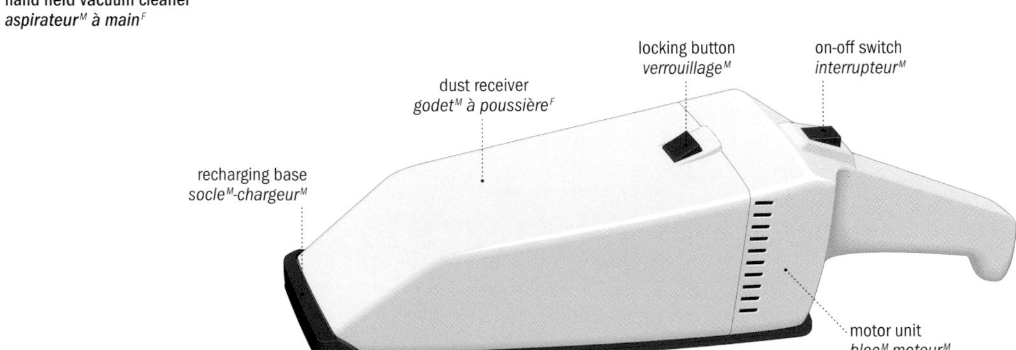
locking button
verrouillage[M]
on-off switch
interrupteur[M]
dust receiver
godet[M] à poussière[F]
recharging base
socle[M]-chargeur[M]
motor unit
bloc[M]-moteur[M]

upright vacuum cleaner
aspirateur[M]-balai[M]

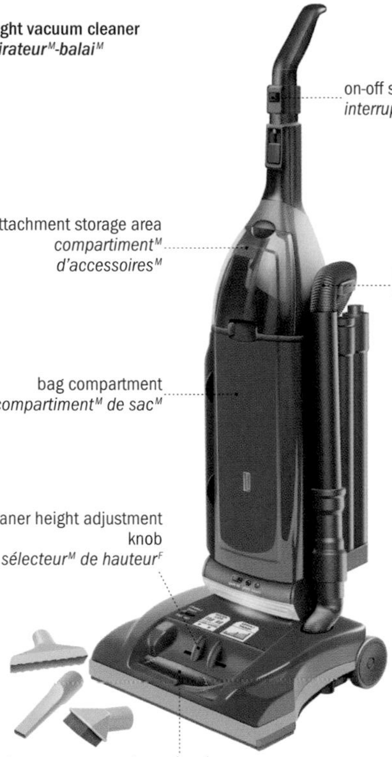

on-off switch
interrupteur[M]

attachment storage area
compartiment[M] d'accessoires[M]

hose
tuyau[M] flexible

bag compartment
compartiment[M] de sac[M]

cleaner height adjustment knob
sélecteur[M] de hauteur[F]

attachments
accessoires[M]

brush
brosse[F]

cylinder vacuum cleaner
aspirateur[M]-traîneau[M]

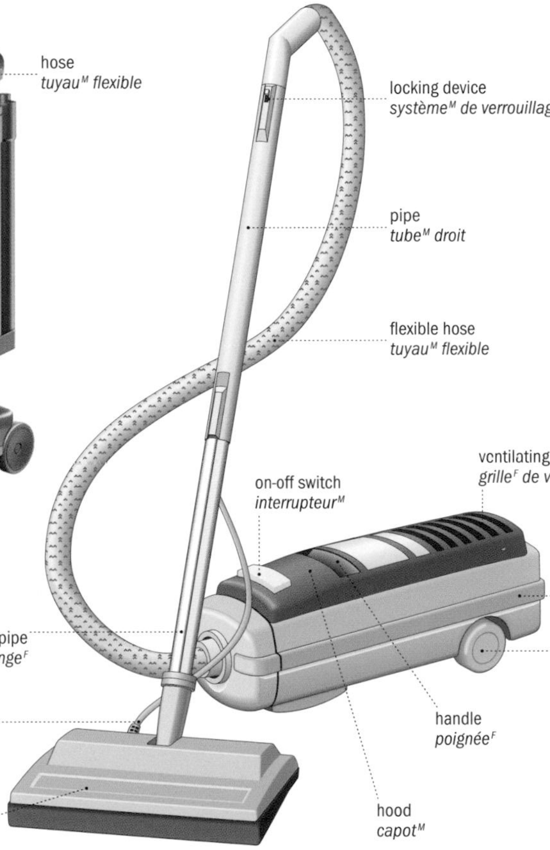

locking device
système[M] de verrouillage[M]

pipe
tube[M] droit

flexible hose
tuyau[M] flexible

ventilating grille
grille[F] de ventilation[F]

on-off switch
interrupteur[M]

bumper
pare-chocs[M]

caster
roulette[F]

extension pipe
rallonge[F]

cord
cordon[M]

handle
poignée[F]

rug and floor brush
suceur[M] à tapis[M] et planchers[M]

hood
capot[M]

vacuum cleaner attachments
accessoires[M]

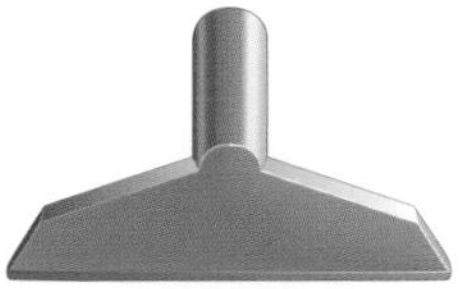

upholstery nozzle
suceur[M] triangulaire à tissus[M]

dusting brush
brosse[F] à épousseter

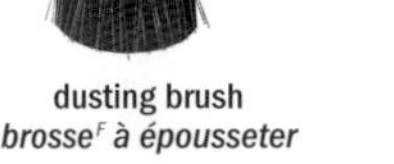

crevice tool
suceur[M] plat

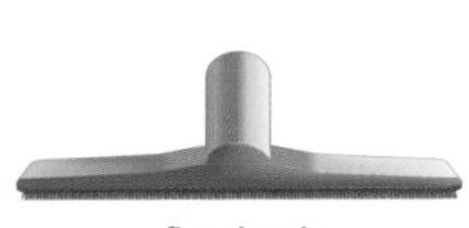

floor brush
brosse[F] à planchers[M]

domestic appliances

range hood
hotte[F]

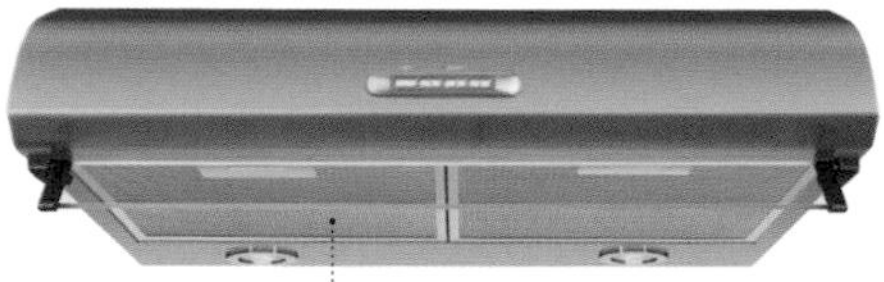

filter
filtre[M]

electric range
cuisinière[F] électrique

cooking element
élément[M] de cuisson[F]

clock timer
horloge[F] programmatrice

cooktop
surface[F] de cuisson[F]

control panel
tableau[M] de commande[F]

cooktop edge
rebord[M]

control knob
bouton[M] de commande[F]

oven
four[M]

handle
poignée[F]

window
hublot[M]

rack
grille[F]

drawer
tiroir[M]

surface element
serpentin[M]

tubular element
élément[M] tubulaire

terminal
borne[F]

drip bowl
cuvette[F]

trim ring
anneau[M]

gas range
cuisinière[F] à gaz[M]

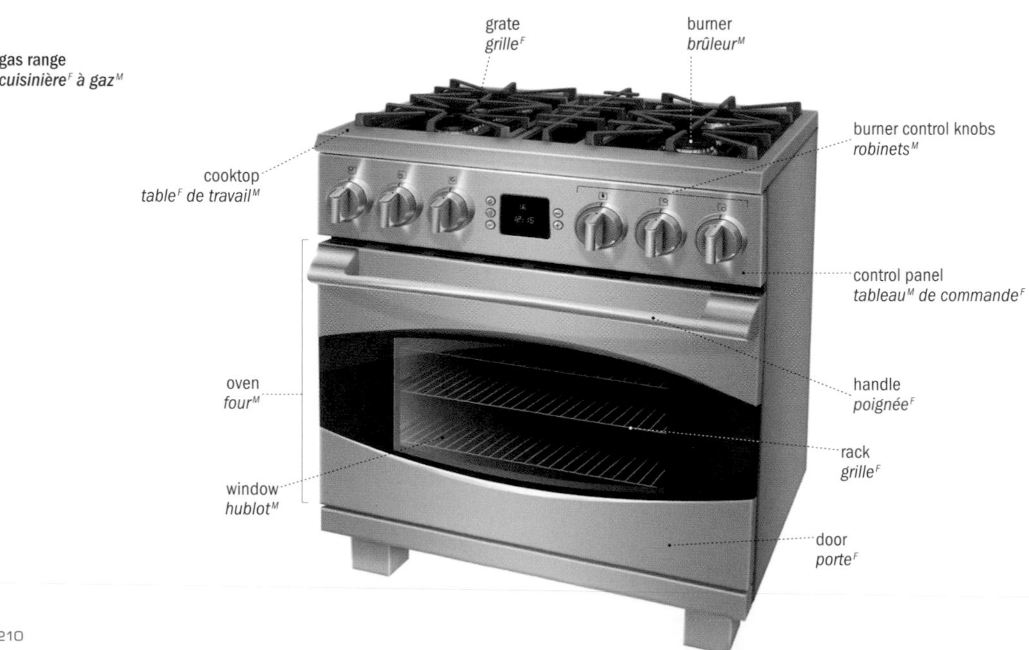
grate
grille[F]
burner
brûleur[M]
burner control knobs
robinets[M]
cooktop
table[F] de travail[M]
control panel
tableau[M] de commande[F]
handle
poignée[F]
oven
four[M]
rack
grille[F]
window
hublot[M]
door
porte[F]

chest freezer
congélateur[M] coffre[M]

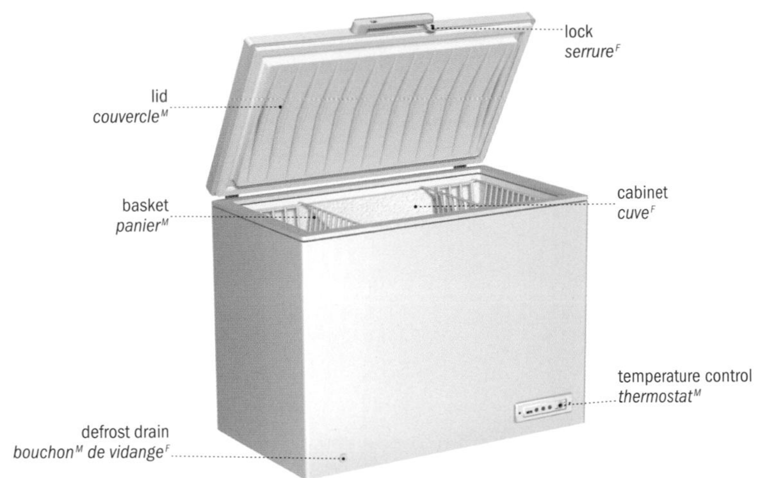
lock
serrure[F]
lid
couvercle[M]
basket
panier[M]
cabinet
cuve[F]
temperature control
thermostat[M]
defrost drain
bouchon[M] de vidange[F]

refrigerator
réfrigérateur[M]

switch
interrupteur[M]

door stop
butée[F] de porte[F]

magnetic gasket
joint[M] magnétique

butter compartment
casier[M] à beurre[M]

shelf
clayette[F]

handle
poignée[F]

meat keeper
bac[M] à viande[F]

water dispenser
distributeur[M] d'eau[F]

shelf channel
crémaillère[F]

refrigerator compartment
réfrigérateur[M]

freezer compartment
congélateur[M]

storage door
porte[F] étagère[F]

guard rail
barre[F] de retenue[F]

dairy compartment
casier[M] laitier

crisper
bac[M] à légumes[M]

domestic appliances

front-loading washer
lave-linge[M] à chargement[M] frontal ; laveuse[F] à chargement[M] frontal

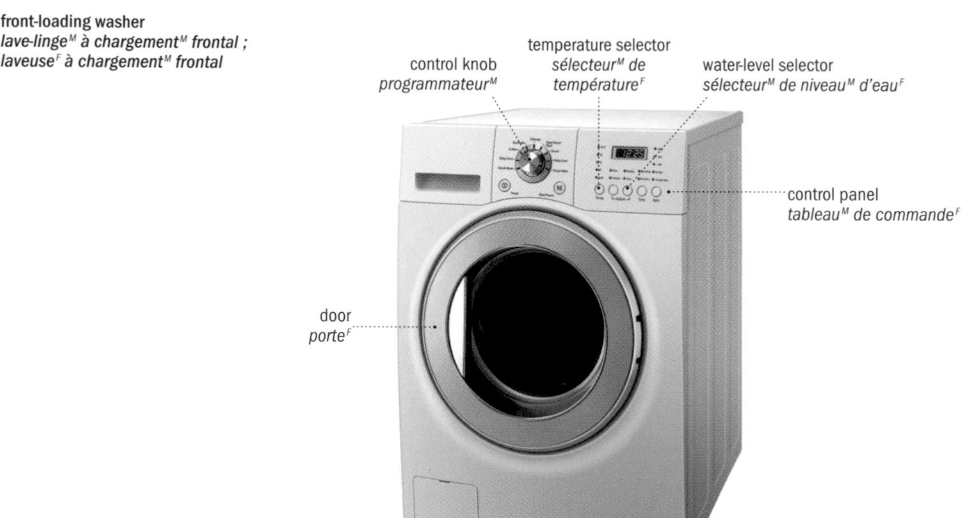
control knob
programmateur[M]
temperature selector
sélecteur[M] de température[F]
water-level selector
sélecteur[M] de niveau[M] d'eau[F]
control panel
tableau[M] de commande[F]
door
porte[F]

top-loading washer
lave-linge[M] à chargement[M] vertical ; laveuse[F] à chargement[M] vertical

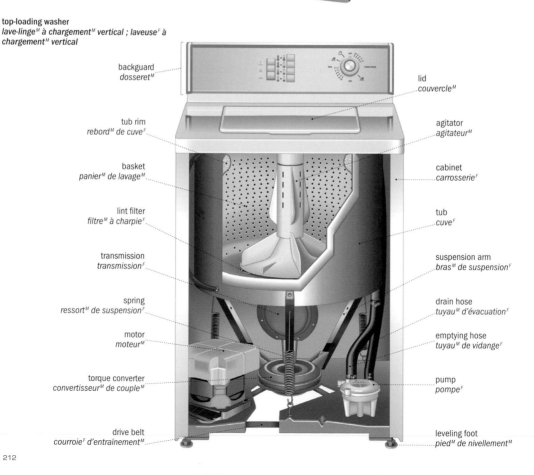

backguard
dosseret[M]

lid
couvercle[M]

tub rim
rebord[M] de cuve[F]

agitator
agitateur[M]

basket
panier[M] de lavage[M]

cabinet
carrosserie[F]

lint filter
filtre[M] à charpie[F]

tub
cuve[F]

transmission
transmission[F]

suspension arm
bras[M] de suspension[F]

spring
ressort[M] de suspension[F]

drain hose
tuyau[M] d'évacuation[F]

motor
moteur[M]

emptying hose
tuyau[M] de vidange[F]

torque converter
convertisseur[M] de couple[M]

pump
pompe[F]

drive belt
courroie[F] d'entraînement[M]

leveling foot
pied[M] de nivellement[M]

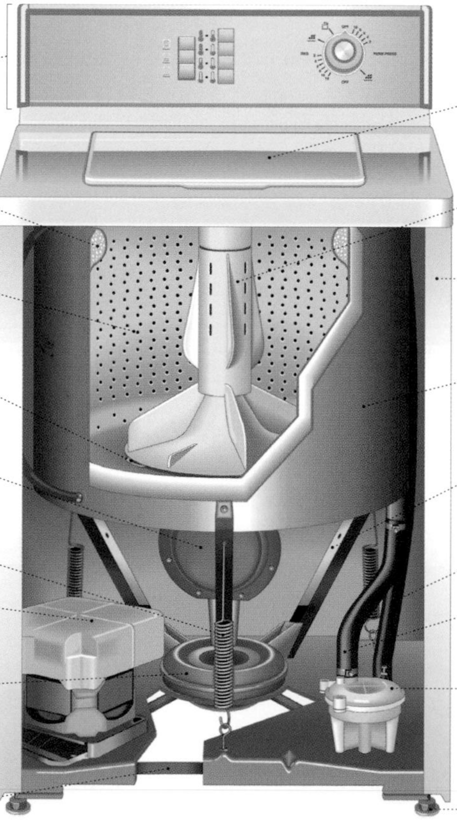

dryer
***sèche-linge*[M] *électrique ; sécheuse*[F]**

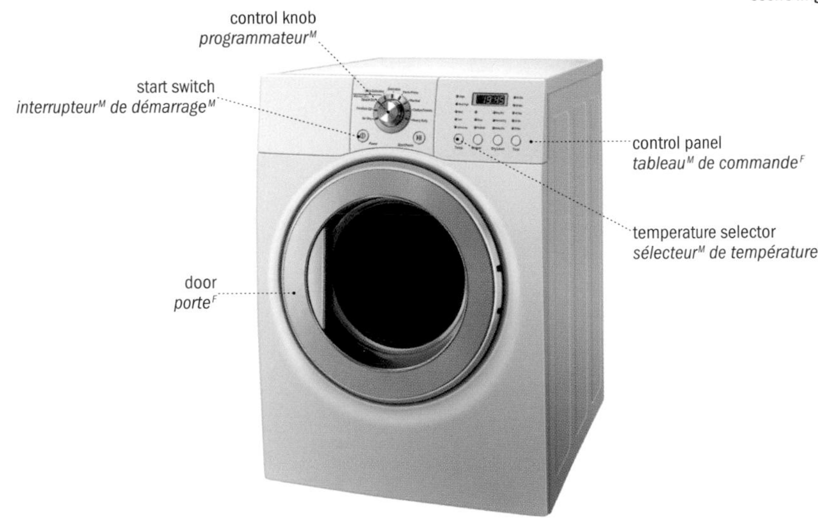
control knob
programmateur[M]
start switch
interrupteur[M] *de démarrage*[M]
control panel
tableau[M] *de commande*[F]
temperature selector
sélecteur[M] *de température*[F]
door
porte[F]

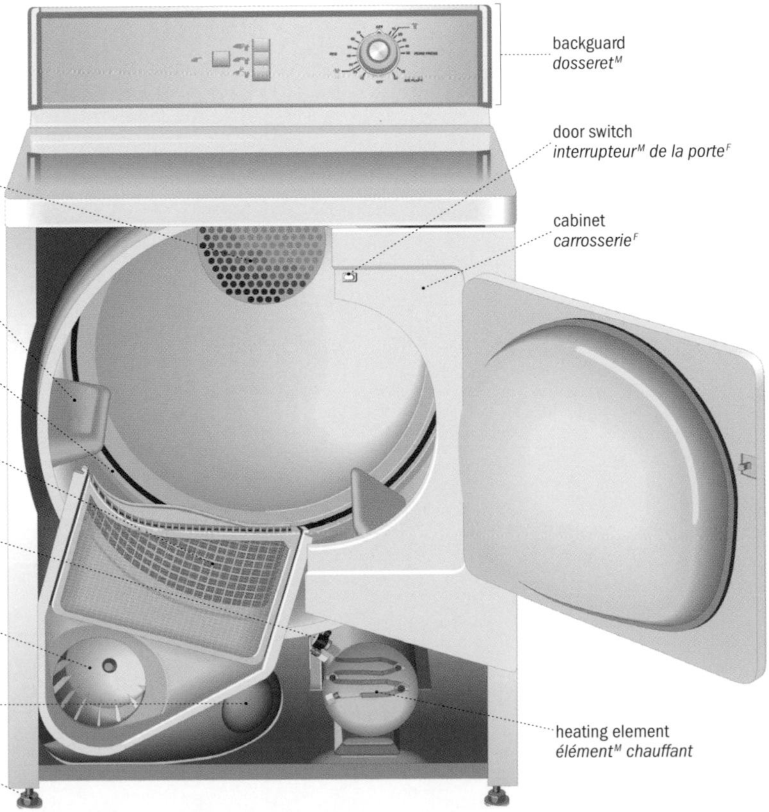

backguard
dosseret[M]

door switch
interrupteur[M] *de la porte*[F]

cabinet
carrosserie[F]

heating duct
conduit[M] *de chauffage*[M]

vane
ailette[F]

drum
tambour[M]

lint trap
filtre[M] *à charpie*[F]

safety thermostat
limiteur[M] *de surchauffe*[F]

fan
ventilateur[M]

motor
moteur[M]

leveling foot
pied[M] *de nivellement*[M]

heating element
élément[M] *chauffant*

control panel: dishwasher
tableau[M] de commande[F]

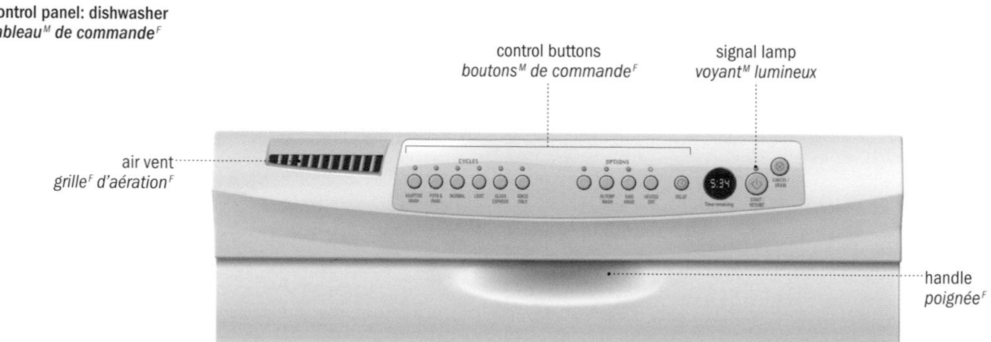
control buttons
boutons[M] de commande[F]
signal lamp
voyant[M] lumineux
air vent
grille[F] d'aération[F]
handle
poignée[F]

dishwasher
lave-vaisselle[M]

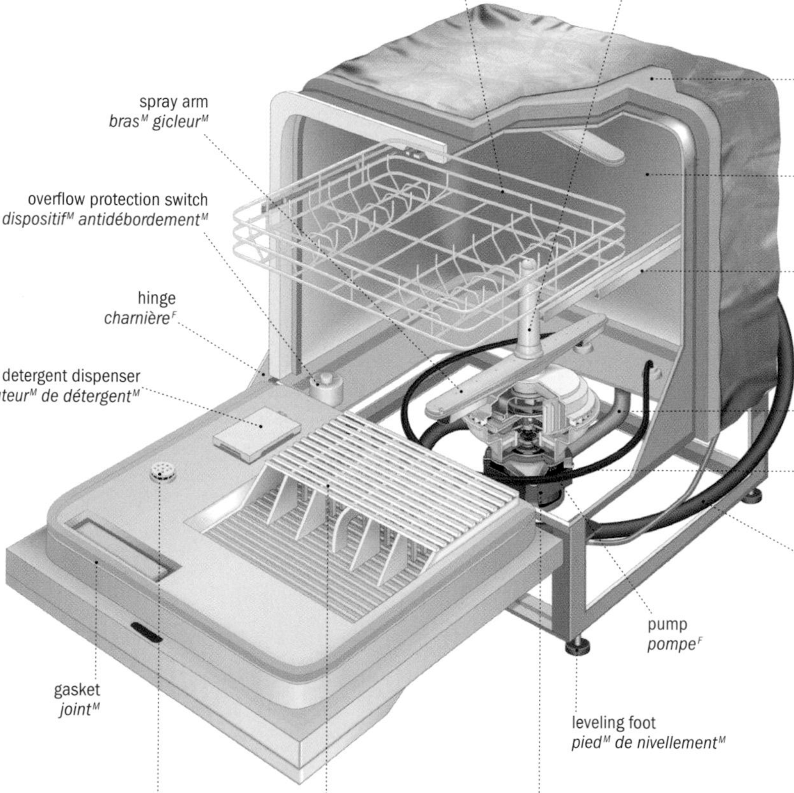

rack
panier[M]

wash tower
tourelle[F]

insulating material
isolant[M]

spray arm
bras[M] gicleur[M]

tub
cuve[F]

overflow protection switch
dispositif[M] antidébordement[M]

slide
glissière[F]

hinge
charnière[F]

detergent dispenser
distributeur[M] de détergent[M]

water hose
conduite[F] d'eau[F]

heating element
élément[M] chauffant

drain hose
tuyau[M] de vidange[F]

pump
pompe[F]

gasket
joint[M]

leveling foot
pied[M] de nivellement[M]

rinse-aid dispenser
distributeur[M] de produit[M] de rinçage[M]

cutlery basket
panier[M] à couverts[M]

motor
moteur[M]

household equipment

articles^M ménagers

tea towel
torchon^M
dustpan
pelle^F à poussière^F ; porte-poussière^M
broom
balai^M
mop
balai^M à franges^F ; vadrouille^F
scouring pad
éponge^F à récurer
handle
manche^M
brush
brosse^F
block
monture^F
fibers
fibres^F
garbage can
poubelle^F
lid
couvercle^M
handle
poignée^F
fibers
fibres^F
pail
seau^M
pouring spout
bec^M verseur
handle
anse^F

plumbing tools

plomberie^F : outils^M

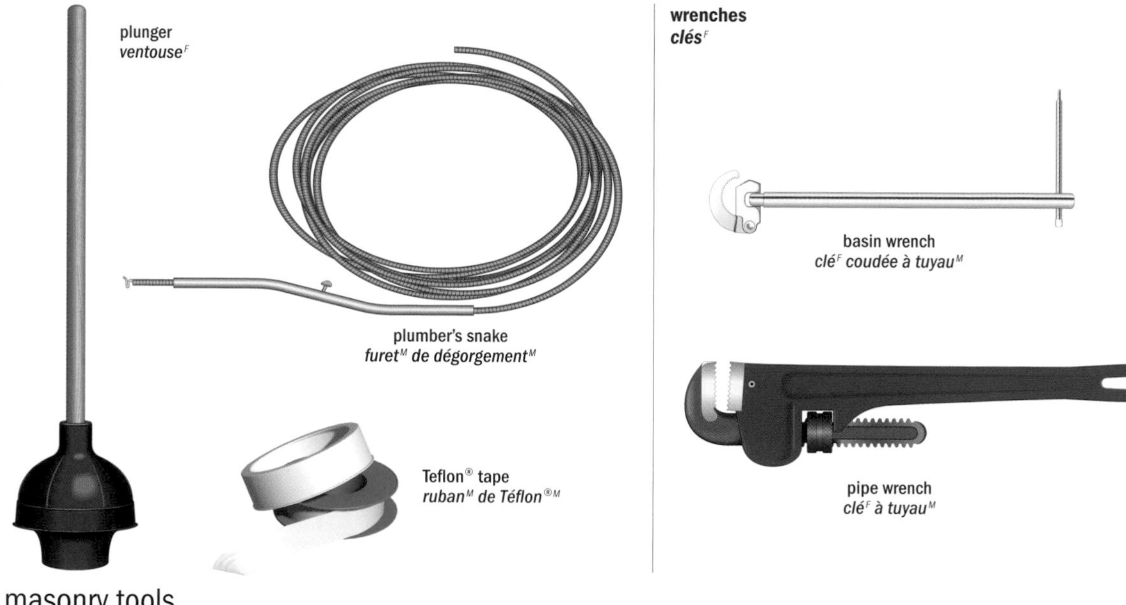
plunger
ventouse^F
plumber's snake
furet^M de dégorgement^M
Teflon® tape
ruban^M de Téflon®^M
wrenches
clés^F
basin wrench
clé^F coudée à tuyau^M
pipe wrench
clé^F à tuyau^M

masonry tools

maçonnerie^F : outils^M

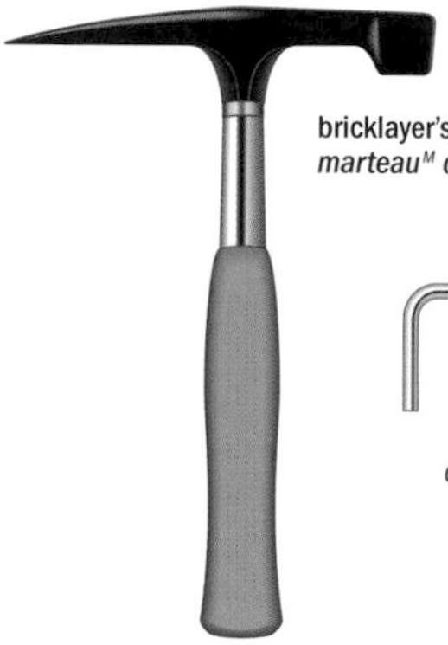

bricklayer's hammer
marteau^M de maçon^M

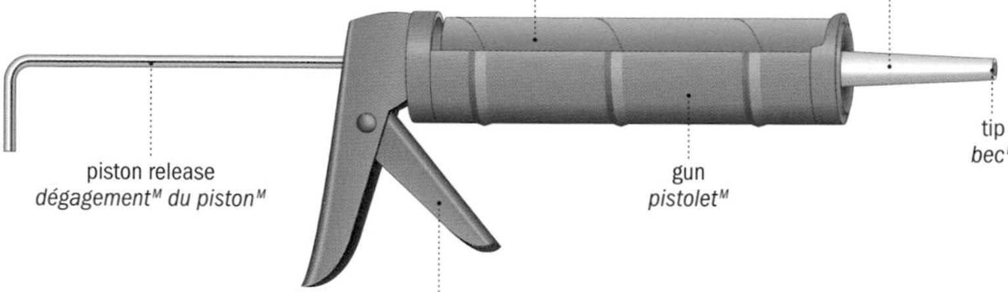

caulking gun
pistolet^M à calfeutrer

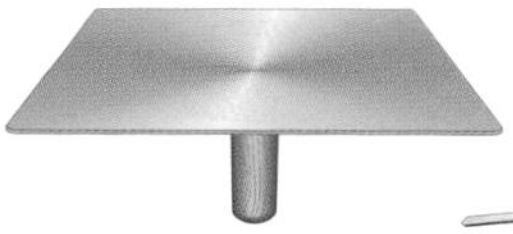

cartridge
cartouche^F

nozzle
buse^F

piston release
dégagement^M du piston^M

gun
pistolet^M

tip
bec^M

piston lever
levier^M du piston^M

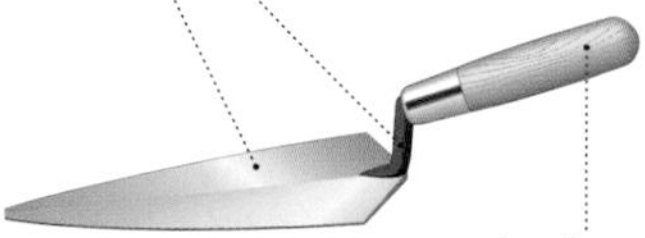

mason's trowel
truelle^F de maçon^M

blade
lame^F

tang
soie^F

handle
manche^M

hawk
taloche^F

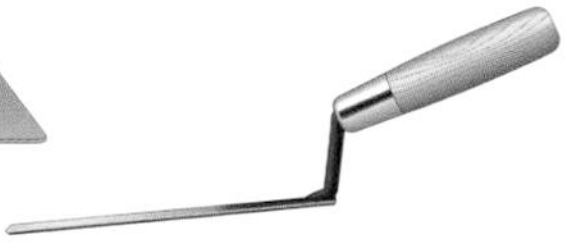

joint filler
tire-joint^M

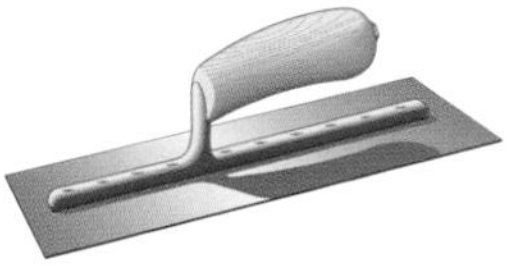

square trowel
truelle^F de plâtrier^M

electricity tools

électricité^F : outils^M

drop light
baladeuse^F

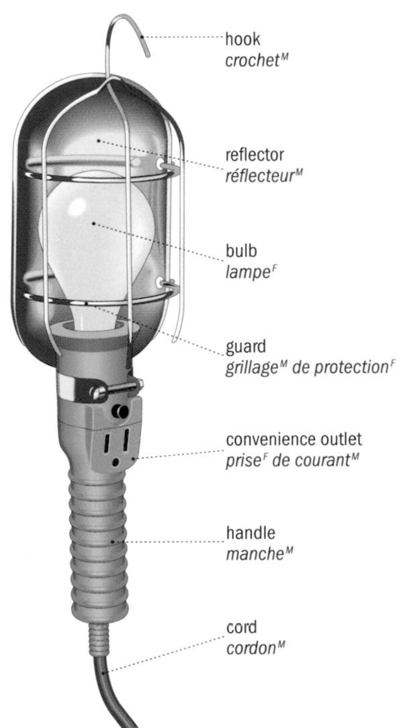
hook
crochet^M
reflector
réflecteur^M
bulb
lampe^F
guard
grillage^M de protection^F
convenience outlet
prise^F de courant^M
handle
manche^M
cord
cordon^M

neon tester
vérificateur^M de circuit^M

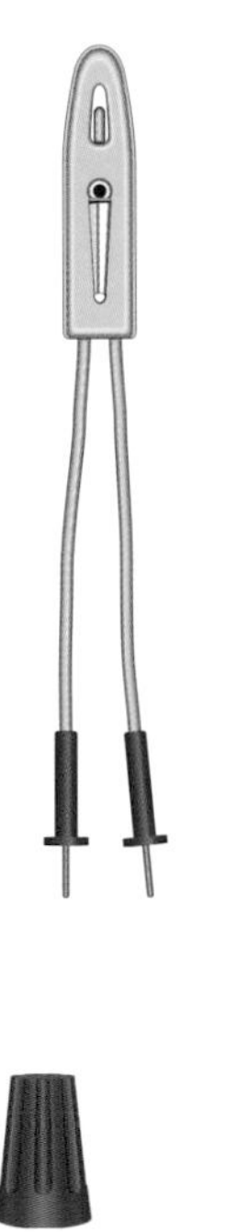

voltage tester
vérificateur^M de tension^F

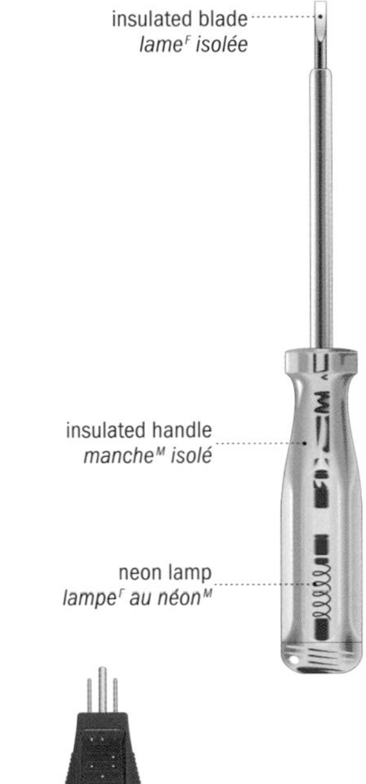
insulated blade
lame^F isolée
insulated handle
manche^M isolé
neon lamp
lampe^F au néon^M

wire nut
capuchon^M de connexion^F

receptacle analyzer
vérificateur^M de prise^F de courant^M

multipurpose tool
pince^F universelle

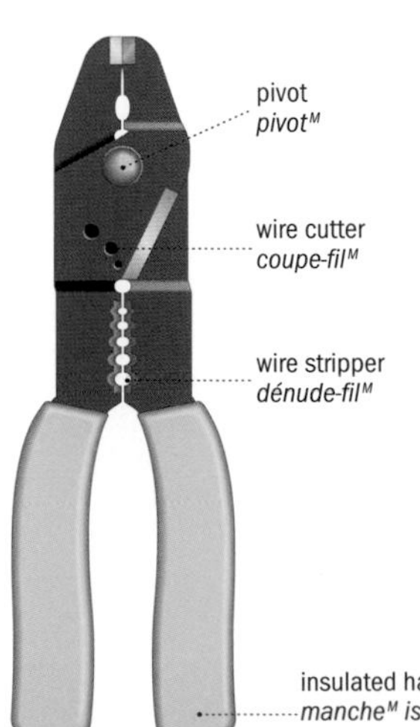
pivot
pivot^M
wire cutter
coupe-fil^M
wire stripper
dénude-fil^M
insulated handle
manche^M isolant

needle-nose pliers
pince^F à long bec^M

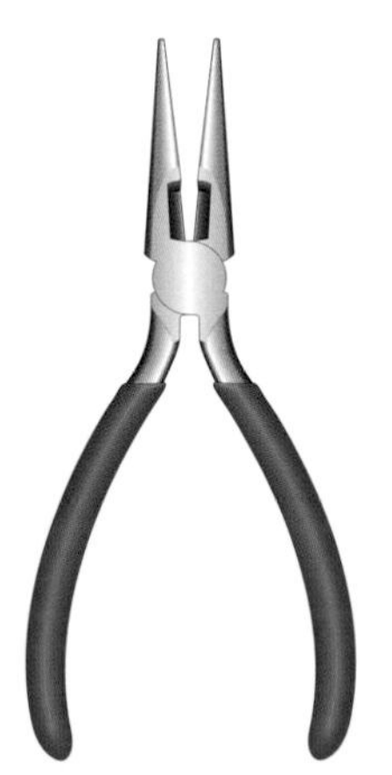

lineman's pliers
pince^F d'électricien^M

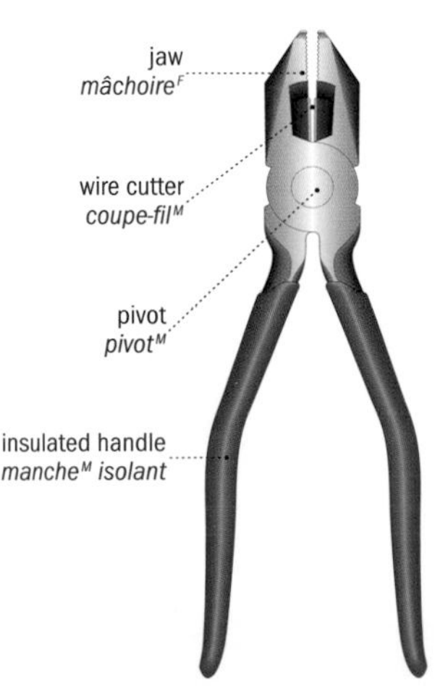
jaw
mâchoire^F
wire cutter
coupe-fil^M
pivot
pivot^M
insulated handle
manche^M isolant

soldering and welding tools

soudage[M] : outils[M]

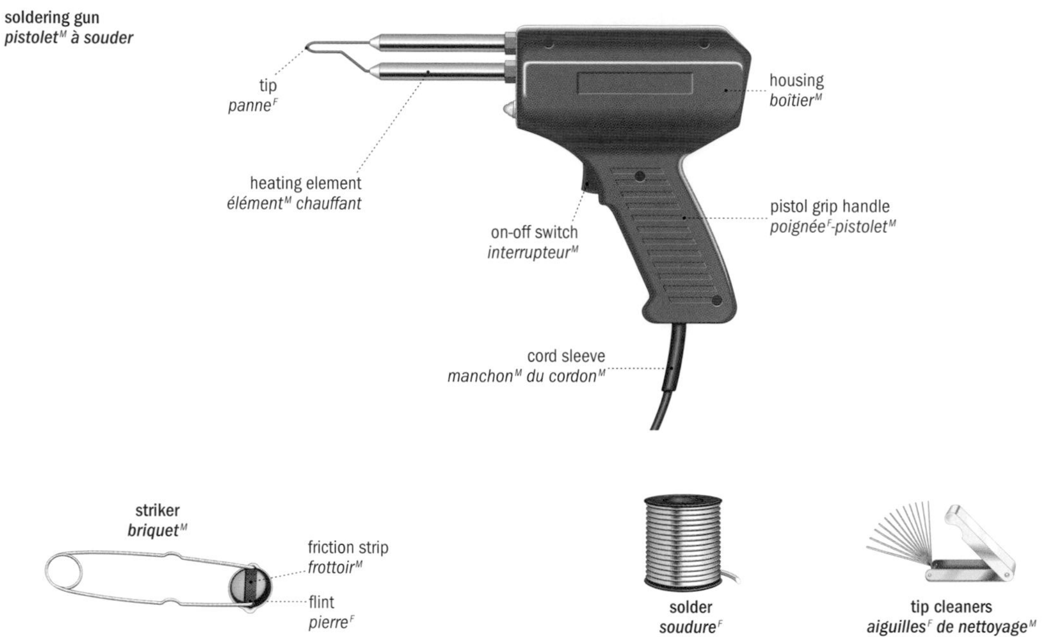
soldering gun
pistolet[M] à souder
tip
panne[F]
heating element
élément[M] chauffant
housing
boîtier[M]
on-off switch
interrupteur[M]
pistol grip handle
poignée[F]-pistolet[M]
cord sleeve
manchon[M] du cordon[M]
striker
briquet[M]
friction strip
frottoir[M]
flint
pierre[F]
solder
soudure[F]
tip cleaners
aiguilles[F] de nettoyage[M]

soldering torch
lampe[F] à souder

pencil-point tip
brûleur[M] flamme[F] crayon[M]

disposable fuel cylinder
cartouche[F] jetable

flame spreader tip
brûleur[M] bec[M] plat

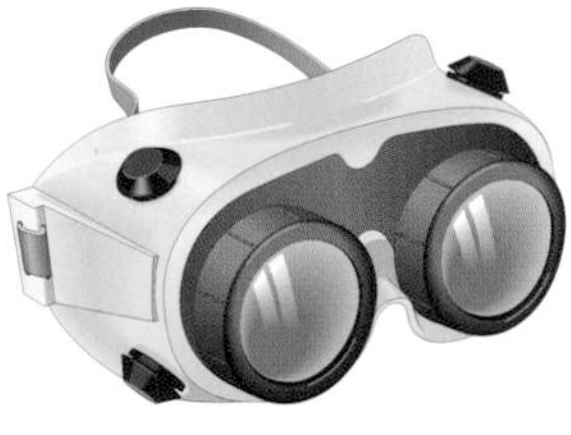

goggles
lunettes[F]

soldering iron
fer[M] à souder

painting

peinture[F] d'entretien[M]

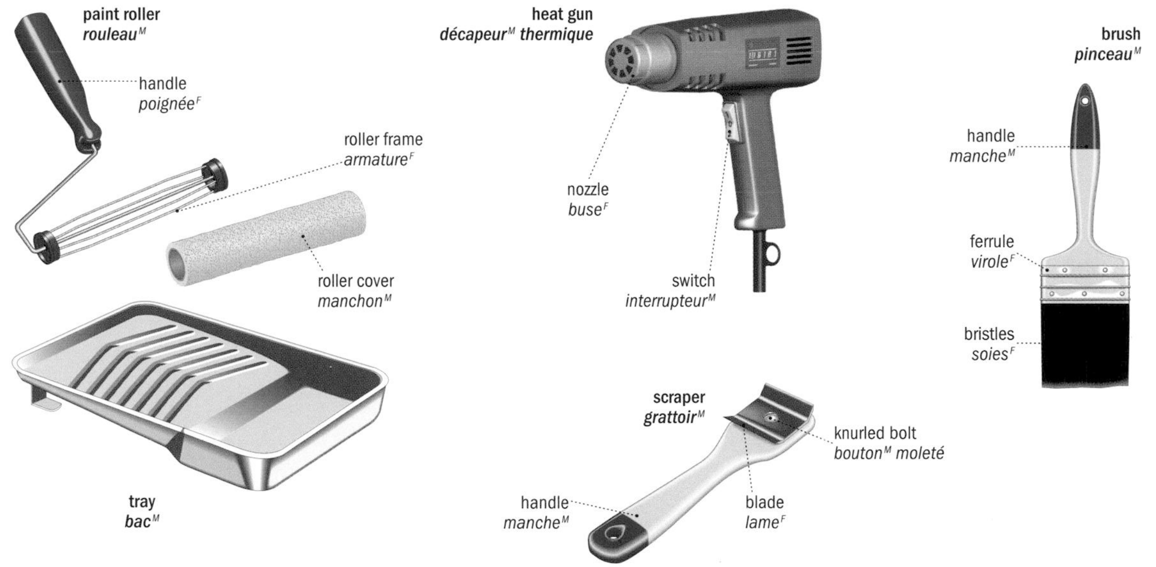
paint roller
rouleau[M]
handle
poignée[F]
roller frame
armature[F]
roller cover
manchon[M]
tray
bac[M]
heat gun
décapeur[M] thermique
nozzle
buse[F]
switch
interrupteur[M]
scraper
grattoir[M]
knurled bolt
bouton[M] moleté
handle
manche[M]
blade
lame[F]
brush
pinceau[M]
handle
manche[M]
ferrule
virole[F]
bristles
soies[F]

ladders and stepladders

échelles[F] et escabeaux[M]

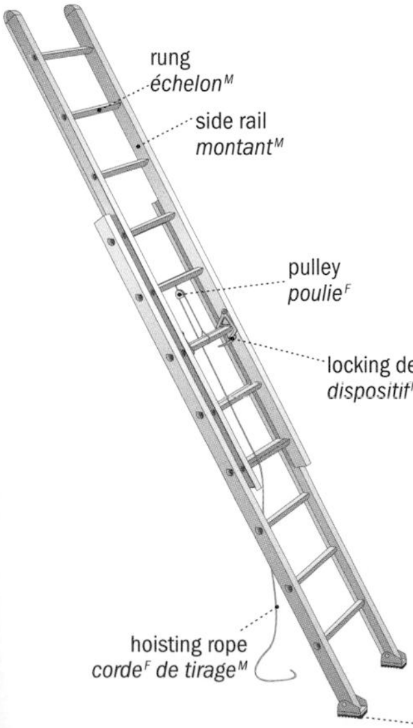

extension ladder
échelle[F] coulissante

rung
échelon[M]

side rail
montant[M]

pulley
poulie[F]

locking device
dispositif[M] de blocage[M]

hoisting rope
corde[F] de tirage[M]

antislip shoe
patin[M] antidérapant

platform ladder
marchepied[M]

safety rail
garde-corps[M]

shelf
tablette[F]

frame
piètement[M]

platform
plate-forme[F]

rubber tip
embout[M]

step
marche[F]

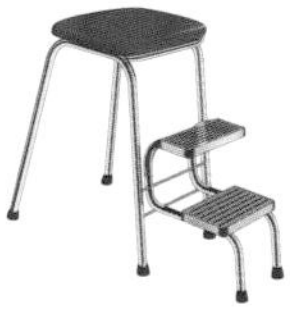

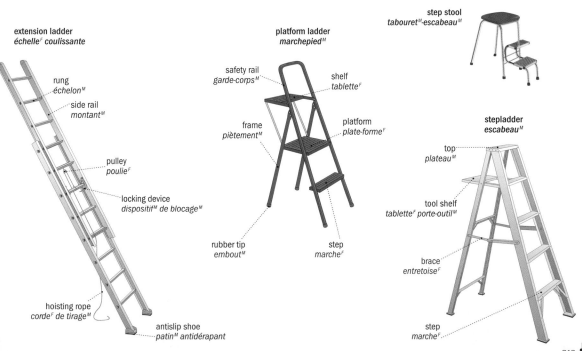

step stool
tabouret[M]-escabeau[M]

stepladder
escabeau[M]

top
plateau[M]

tool shelf
tablette[F] porte-outil[M]

brace
entretoise[F]

step
marche[F]

carpentry: nailing tools

menuiserie[F] : outils[M] pour clouer

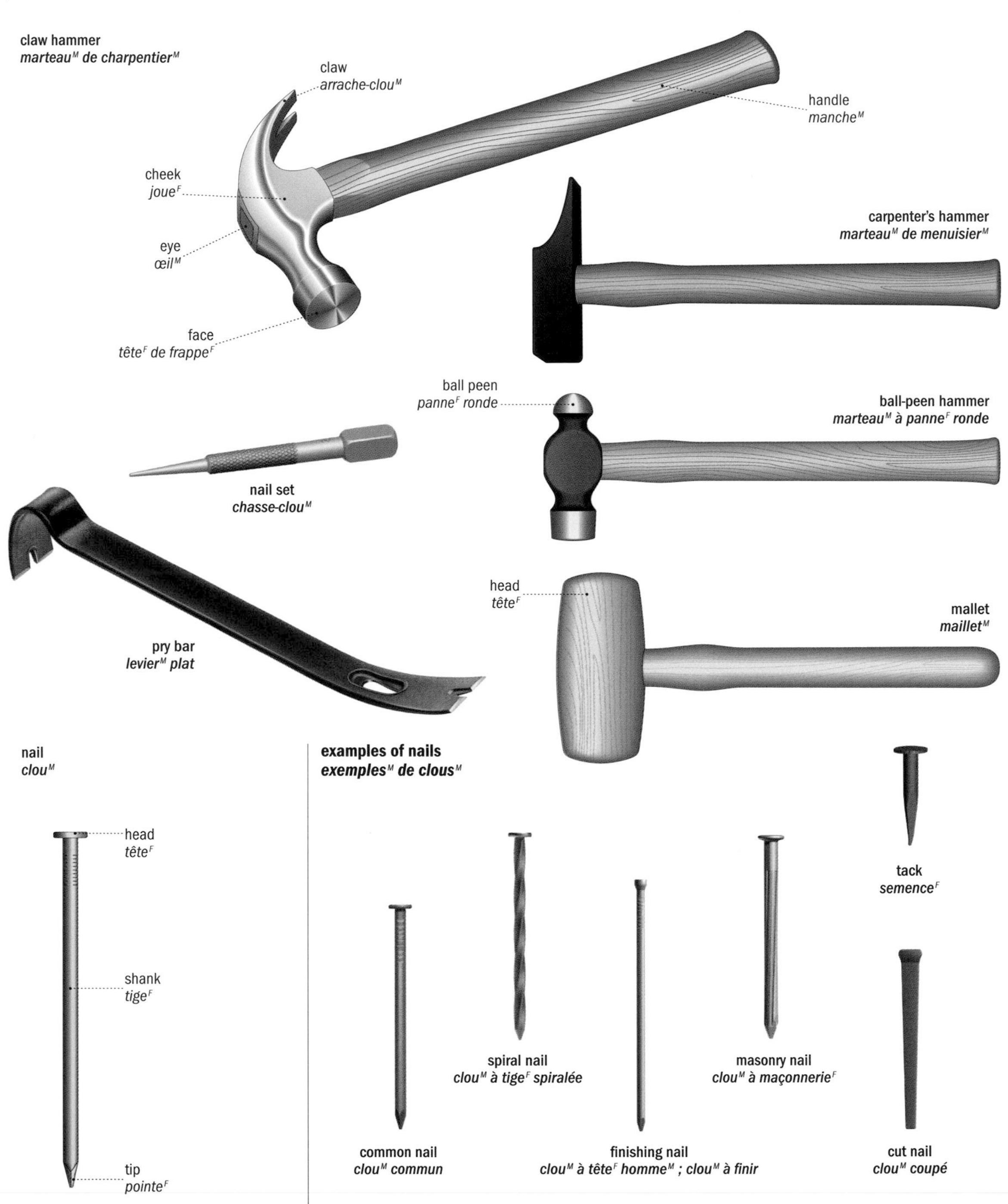
claw hammer
marteau[M] de charpentier[M]
claw
arrache-clou[M]
handle
manche[M]
cheek
joue[F]
eye
œil[M]
face
tête[F] de frappe[F]
carpenter's hammer
marteau[M] de menuisier[M]
ball peen
panne[F] ronde
ball-peen hammer
marteau[M] à panne[F] ronde
nail set
chasse-clou[M]
head
tête[F]
mallet
maillet[M]
pry bar
levier[M] plat
nail
clou[M]
head
tête[F]
shank
tige[F]
tip
pointe[F]
examples of nails
exemples[M] de clous[M]
tack
semence[F]
spiral nail
clou[M] à tige[F] spiralée
masonry nail
clou[M] à maçonnerie[F]
common nail
clou[M] commun
finishing nail
clou[M] à tête[F] homme[M] ; clou[M] à finir
cut nail
clou[M] coupé

carpentry: screw-driving tools

menuiserie[F] : outils[M] pour visser

screwdriver
tournevis[M]

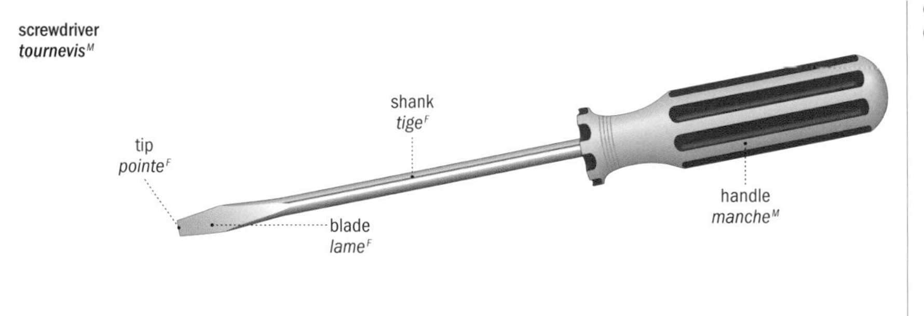
shank
tige[F]
tip
pointe[F]
blade
lame[F]
handle
manche[M]

spiral screwdriver
tournevis[M] à spirale[F]

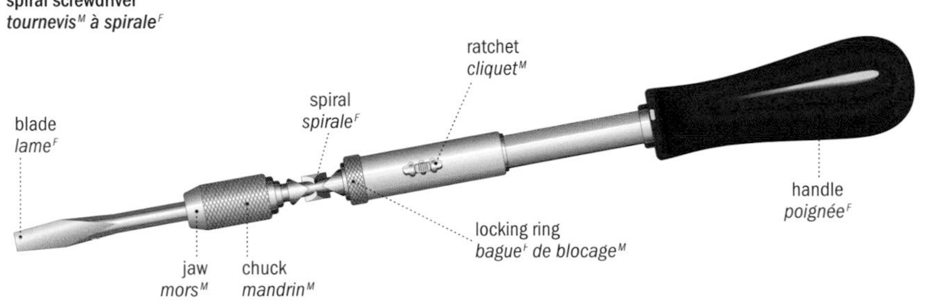
ratchet
cliquet[M]
spiral
spirale[F]
blade
lame[F]
handle
poignée[F]
locking ring
bague[F] de blocage[M]
jaw
mors[M]
chuck
mandrin[M]

cordless screwdriver
tournevis[M] sans fil[M]

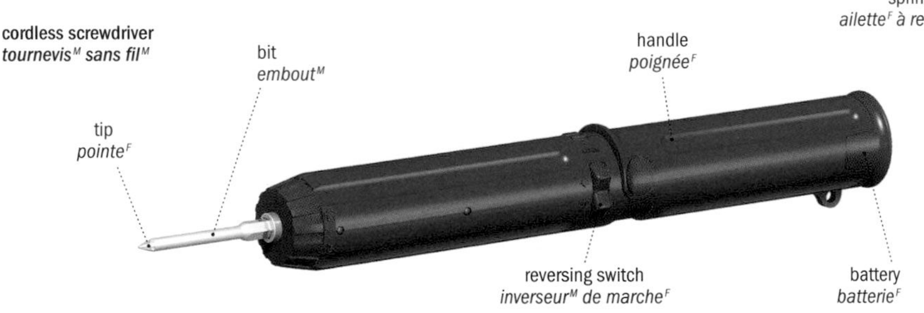
bit
embout[M]
handle
poignée[F]
tip
pointe[F]
reversing switch
inverseur[M] de marche[F]
battery
batterie[F]

screw
vis[F]

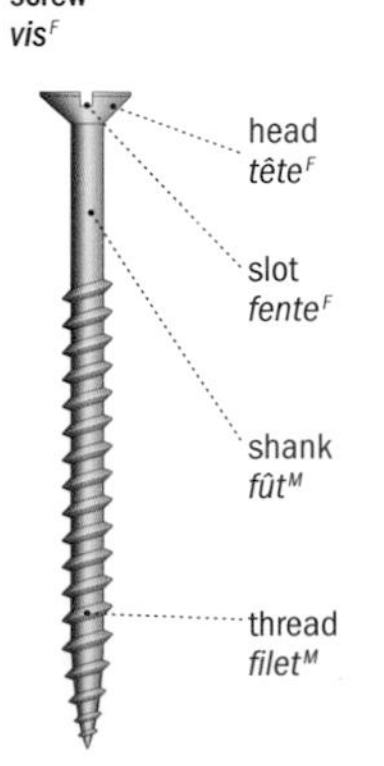
head
tête[F]
slot
fente[F]
shank
fût[M]
thread
filet[M]

examples of tips
exemples[M] de pointes[F]

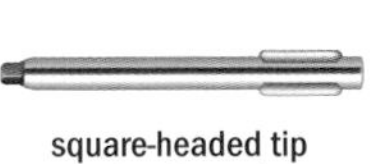

square-headed tip
pointe[F] carrée

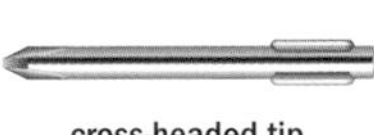

cross-headed tip
pointe[F] cruciforme

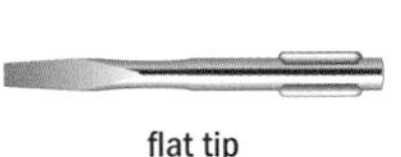

flat tip
pointe[F] plate

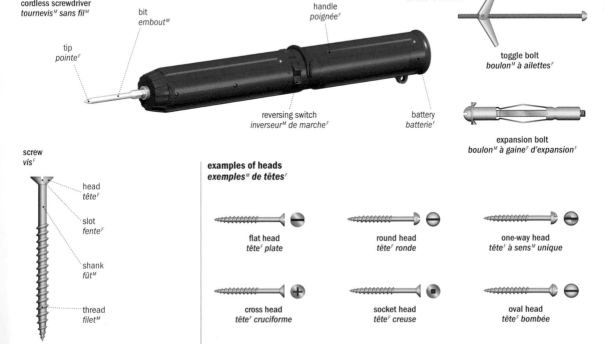

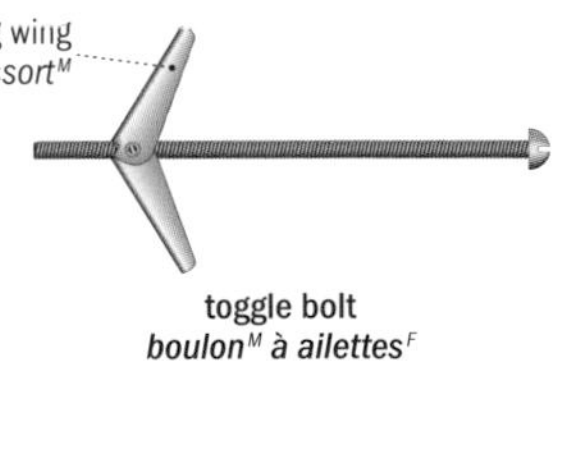
spring wing
ailette[F] à ressort[M]

toggle bolt
boulon[M] à ailettes[F]

expansion bolt
boulon[M] à gaine[F] d'expansion[F]

examples of heads
exemples[M] de têtes[F]

flat head
tête[F] plate

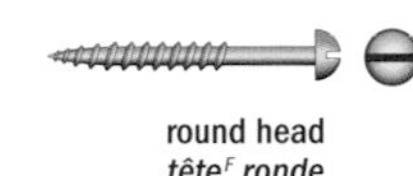

round head
tête[F] ronde

one-way head
tête[F] à sens[M] unique

cross head
tête[F] cruciforme

socket head
tête[F] creuse

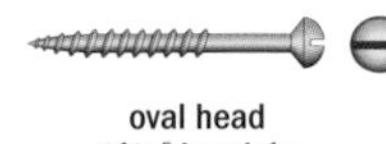

oval head
tête[F] bombée

DO-IT-YOURSELF AND GARDENING

carpentry: gripping and tightening tools

menuiserie[F] : outils[M] pour serrer

pliers
pinces[F]

slip joint pliers
pince[F] à joint[M] coulissant

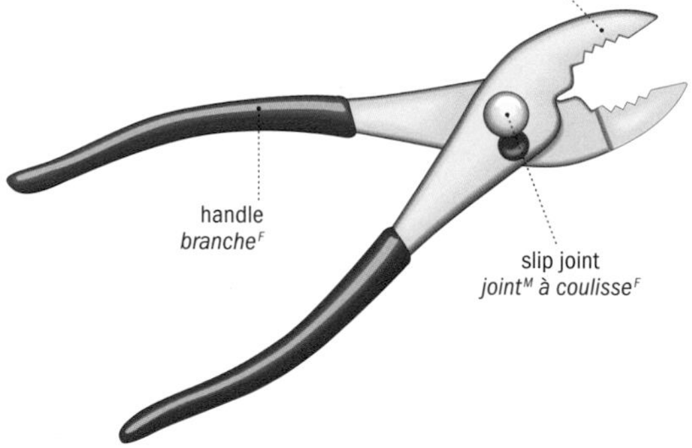

curved jaw
mâchoire[F] incurvée

handle
branche[F]

slip joint
joint[M] à coulisse[F]

rib joint pliers
pince[F] multiprise

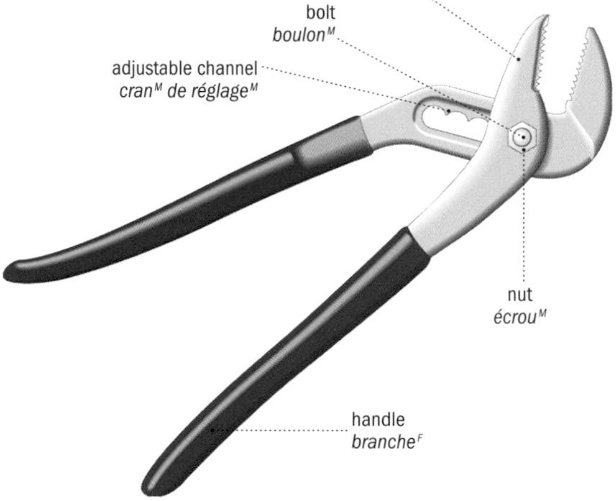

straight jaw
mâchoire[F] droite

bolt
boulon[M]

adjustable channel
cran[M] de réglage[M]

nut
écrou[M]

handle
branche[F]

locking pliers
pince[F]-étau[M]

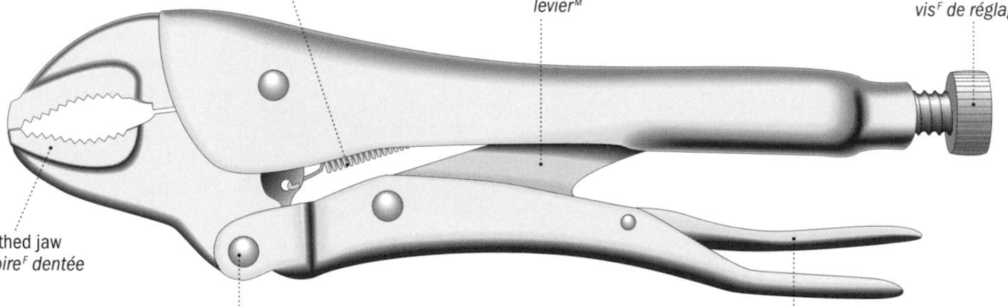

spring
ressort[M]

lever
levier[M]

adjusting screw
vis[F] de réglage[M]

toothed jaw
mâchoire[F] dentée

rivet
rivet[M]

release lever
levier[M] de dégagement[M]

washers
rondelles[F]

flat washer
rondelle[F] plate

lock washer
rondelle[F] à ressort[M]

external tooth lock washer
rondelle[F] à denture[F] extérieure

internal tooth lock washer
rondelle[F] à denture[F] intérieure

wrenches
clés[F]

crescent wrench
clé[F] à molette[F]

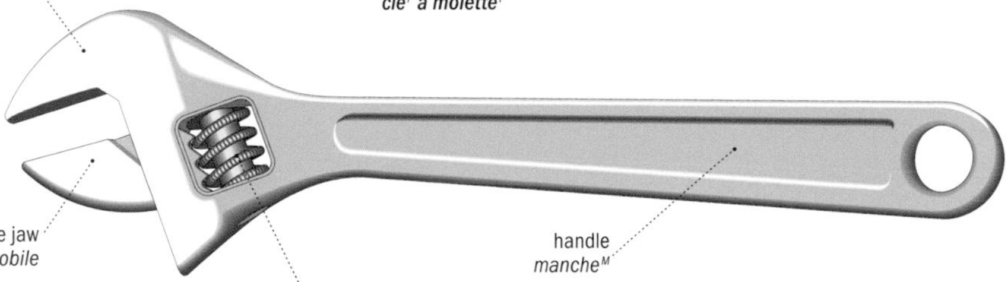

fixed jaw
mâchoire[F] fixe

movable jaw
mâchoire[F] mobile

thumbscrew
molette[F]

handle
manche[M]

ratchet box end wrench
clé[F] polygonale à cliquet[M]

flare nut wrench
clé[F] polygonale à têtes[F] fendues

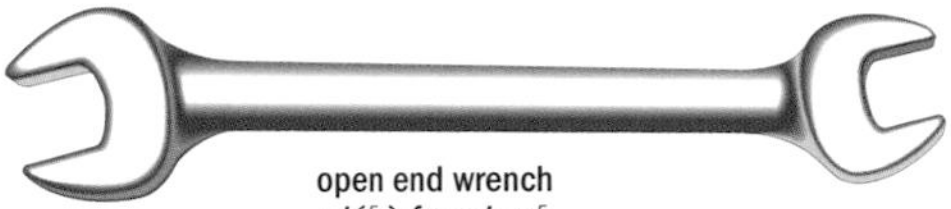

open end wrench
clé[F] à fourches[F]

box end wrench
clé[F] polygonale

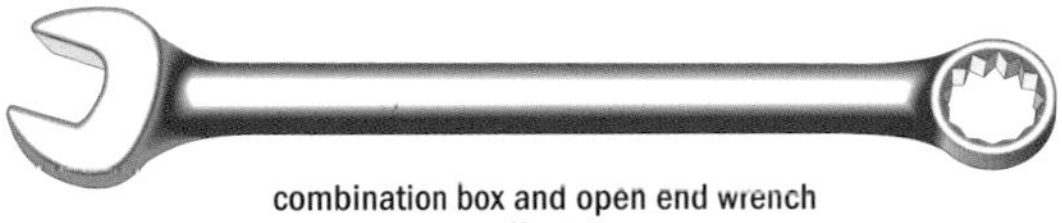

combination box and open end wrench
clé[F] mixte

ratchet socket wrench
clé[F] à douille[F] à cliquet[M]

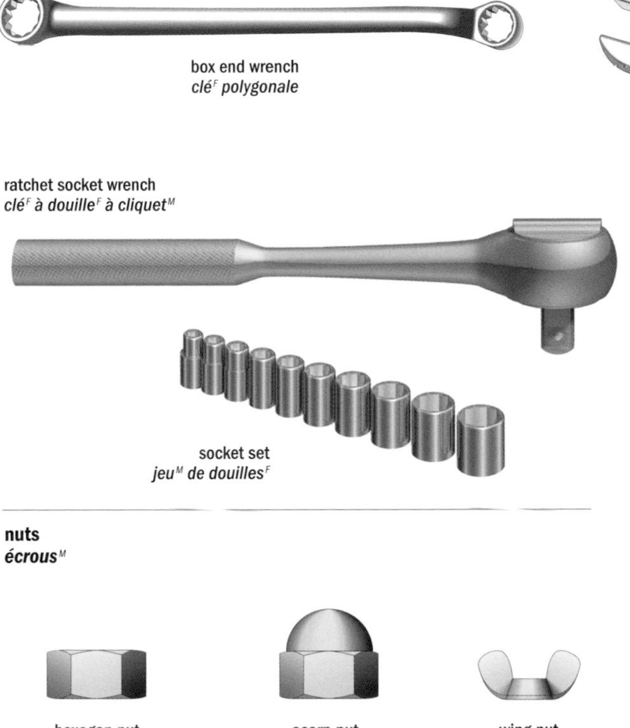
socket set
jeu[M] de douilles[F]
nuts
écrous[M]
hexagon nut
écrou[M] hexagonal
acorn nut
écrou[M] borgne
wing nut
écrou[M] à oreilles[F]

bolts
boulons[M]

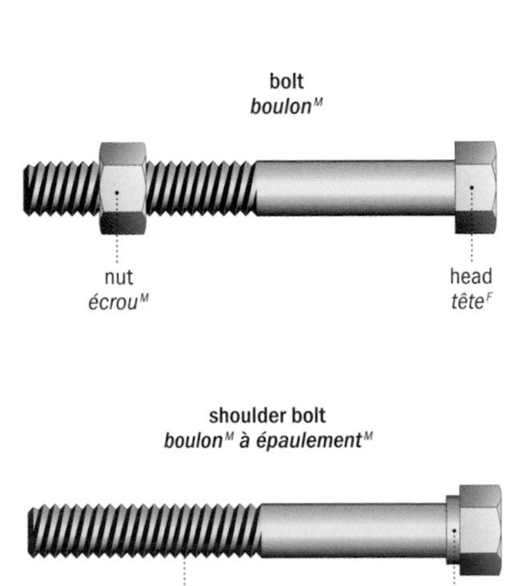
bolt
boulon[M]
nut
écrou[M]
head
tête[F]
shoulder bolt
boulon[M] à épaulement[M]
threaded rod
tige[F] filetée
shoulder
épaulement[M]

carpentry: gripping and tightening tools

C-clamp
***serre-joint**[M]*

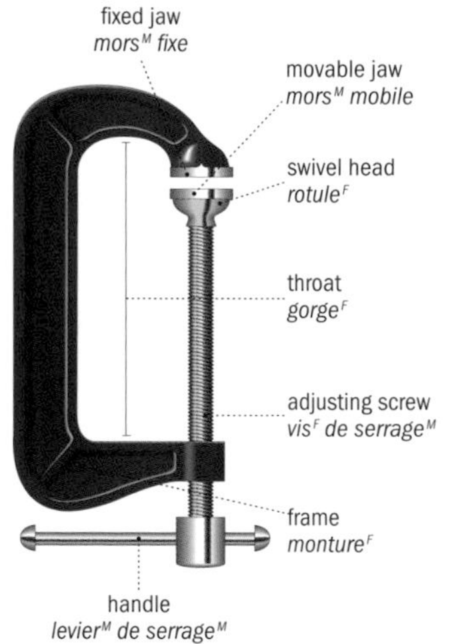
fixed jaw
mors[M] fixe
movable jaw
mors[M] mobile
swivel head
rotule[F]
throat
gorge[F]
adjusting screw
vis[F] de serrage[M]
frame
monture[F]
handle
levier[M] de serrage[M]

vise
***étau**[M]*

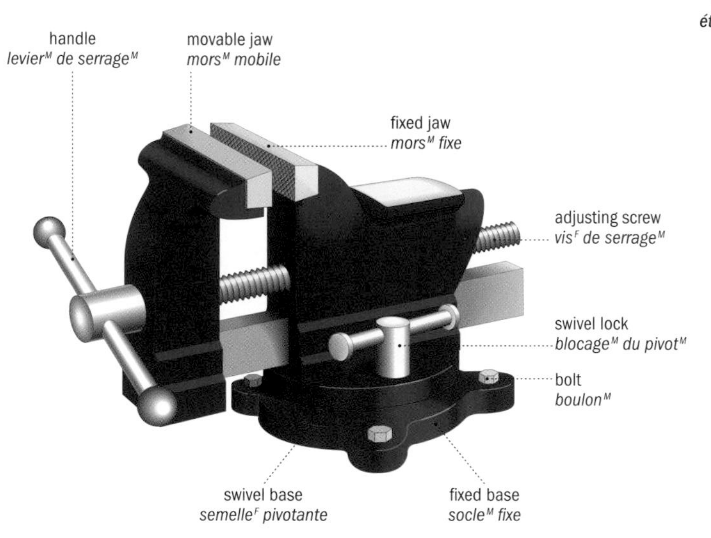
handle
levier[M] de serrage[M]
movable jaw
mors[M] mobile
fixed jaw
mors[M] fixe
adjusting screw
vis[F] de serrage[M]
swivel lock
blocage[M] du pivot[M]
bolt
boulon[M]
swivel base
semelle[F] pivotante
fixed base
socle[M] fixe

pipe clamp
***serre-joint**[M] **à tuyau**[M]*

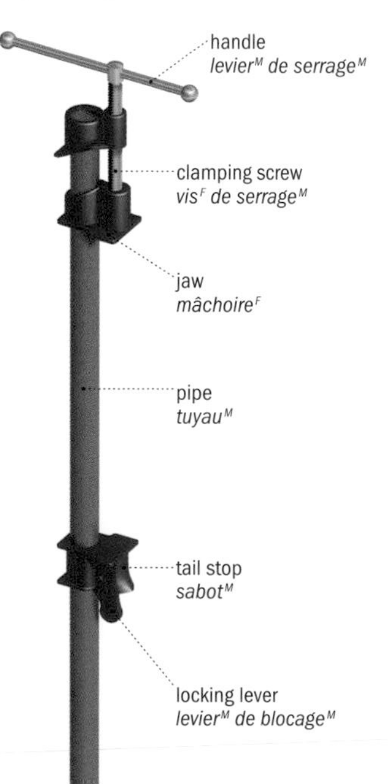
handle
levier[M] de serrage[M]
clamping screw
vis[F] de serrage[M]
jaw
mâchoire[F]
pipe
tuyau[M]
tail stop
sabot[M]
locking lever
levier[M] de blocage[M]

work bench and vise
***établi**[M] **étau**[M]*

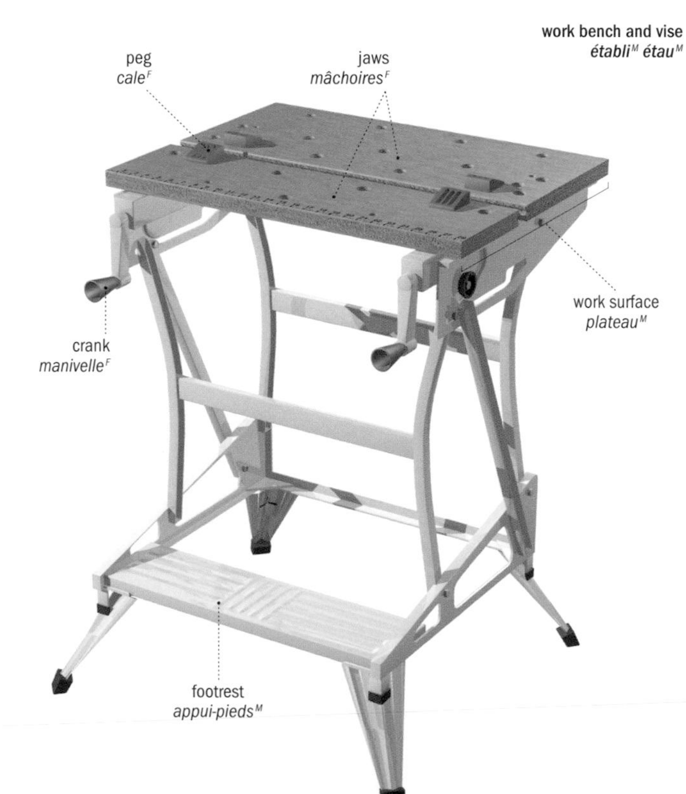
peg
cale[F]
jaws
mâchoires[F]
work surface
plateau[M]
crank
manivelle[F]
footrest
appui-pieds[M]

carpentry: measuring and marking tools

menuiserie[F] : instruments[M] de traçage[M] et de mesure[F]

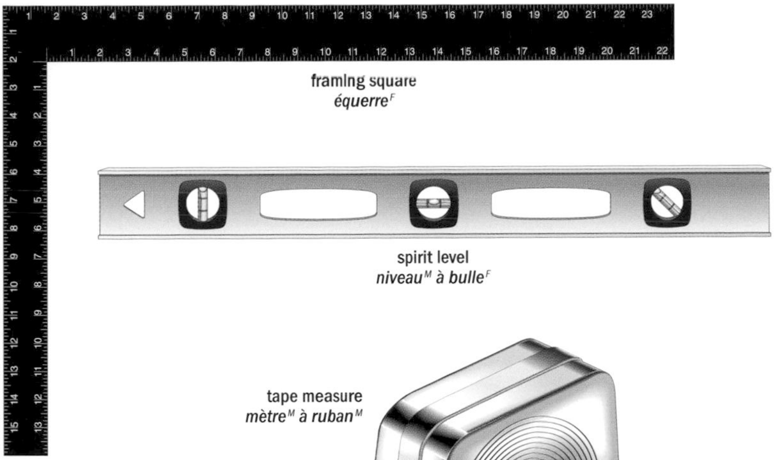

framing square
équerre[F]

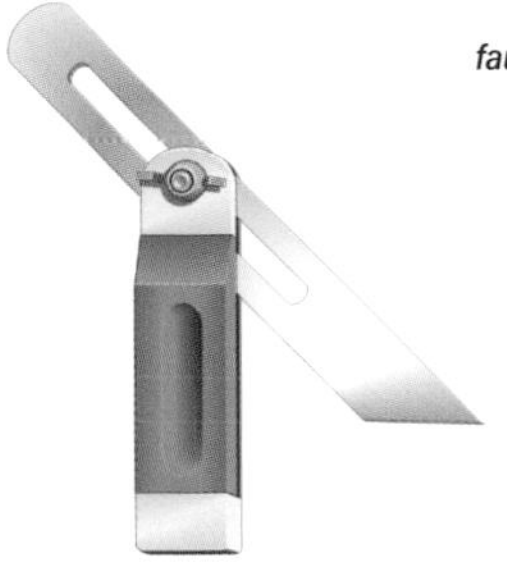

bevel square
fausse-équerre[F]

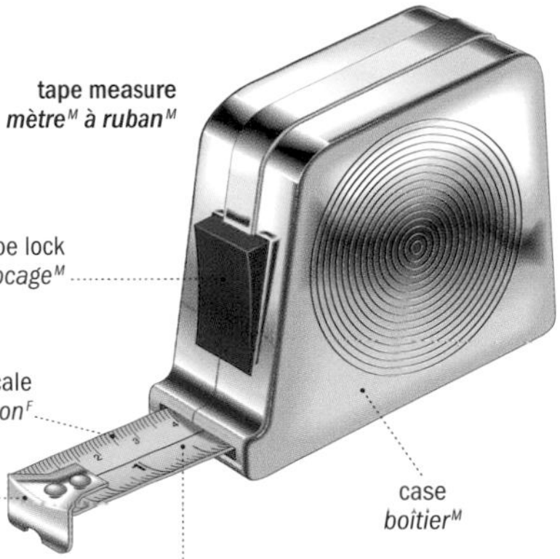

spirit level
niveau[M] à bulle[F]

tape measure
mètre[M] à ruban[M]

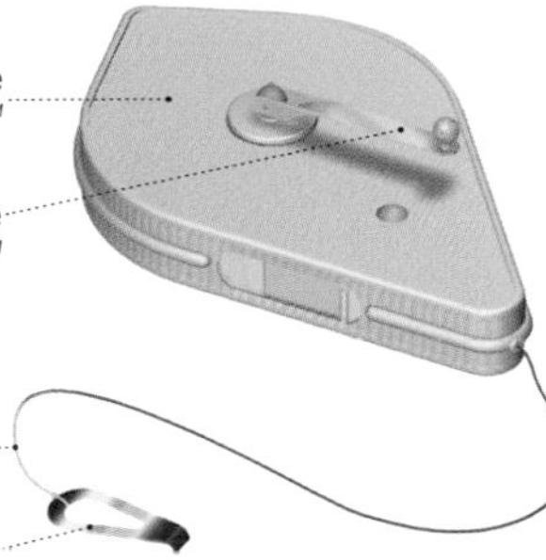

tape lock
bouton[M] de blocage[M]

scale
graduation[F]

hook
crochet[M]

tape
ruban[M]

case
boîtier[M]

chalk line
cordeau[M] à tracer

case
boîtier[M]

crank handle
manivelle[F] d'enroulement[M]

line
cordeau[M]

hook
crochet[M]

carpentry: miscellaneous material

menuiserie[F] : matériel[M] divers

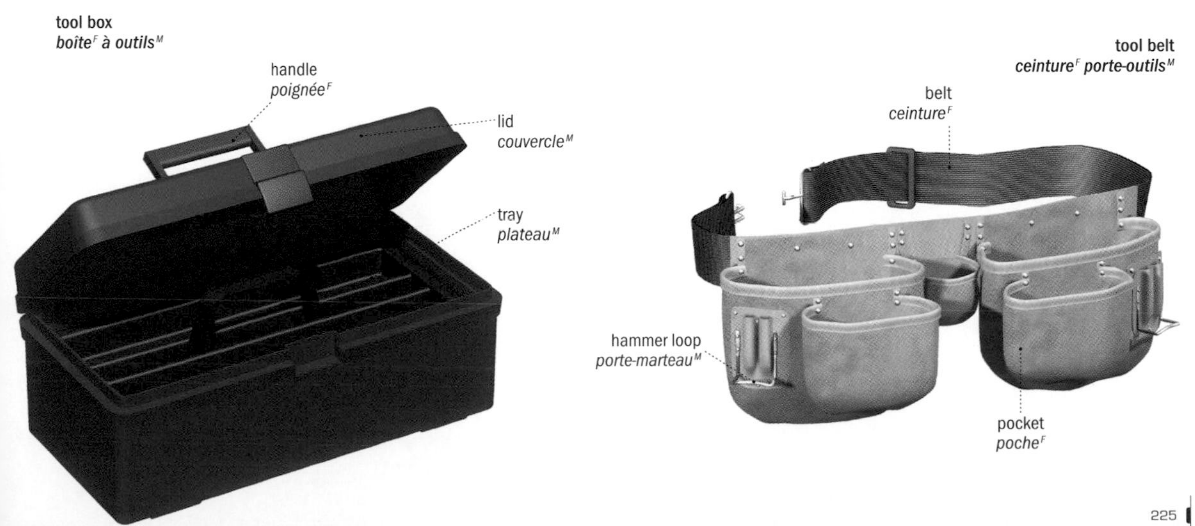
tool box
boîte[F] à outils[M]
handle
poignée[F]
lid
couvercle[M]
tray
plateau[M]
tool belt
ceinture[F] porte-outils[M]
belt
ceinture[F]
hammer loop
porte-marteau[M]
pocket
poche[F]

carpentry: sawing tools

menuiserie[F] : outils[M] pour scier

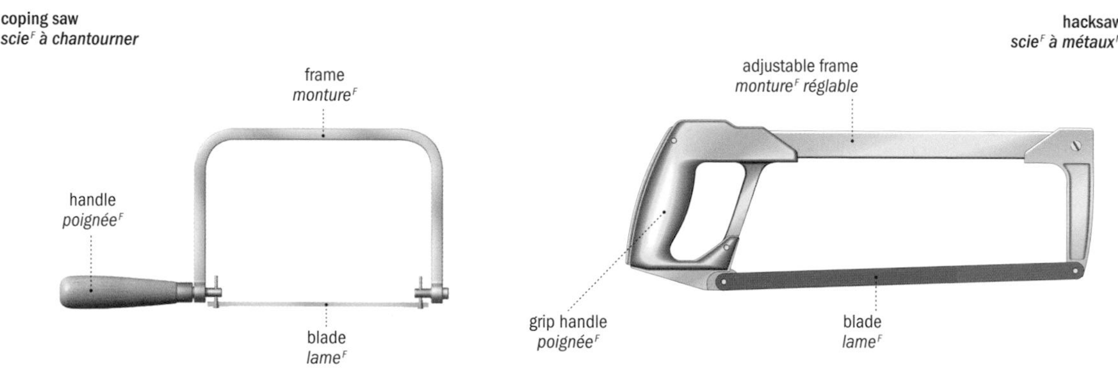
coping saw
scie[F] à chantourner
frame
monture[F]
handle
poignée[F]
blade
lame[F]
hacksaw
scie[F] à métaux[M]
adjustable frame
monture[F] réglable
grip handle
poignée[F]
blade
lame[F]

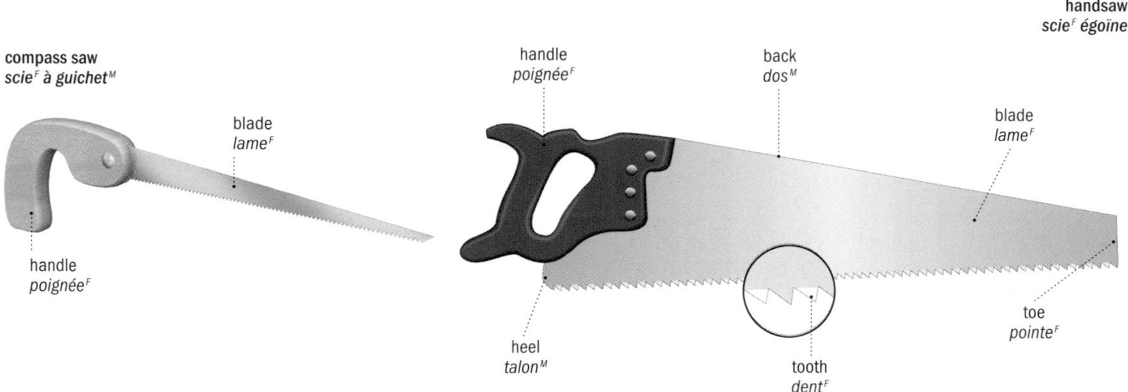
compass saw
scie[F] à guichet[M]
blade
lame[F]
handle
poignée[F]
handsaw
scie[F] égoïne
handle
poignée[F]
back
dos[M]
blade
lame[F]
toe
pointe[F]
heel
talon[M]
tooth
dent[F]

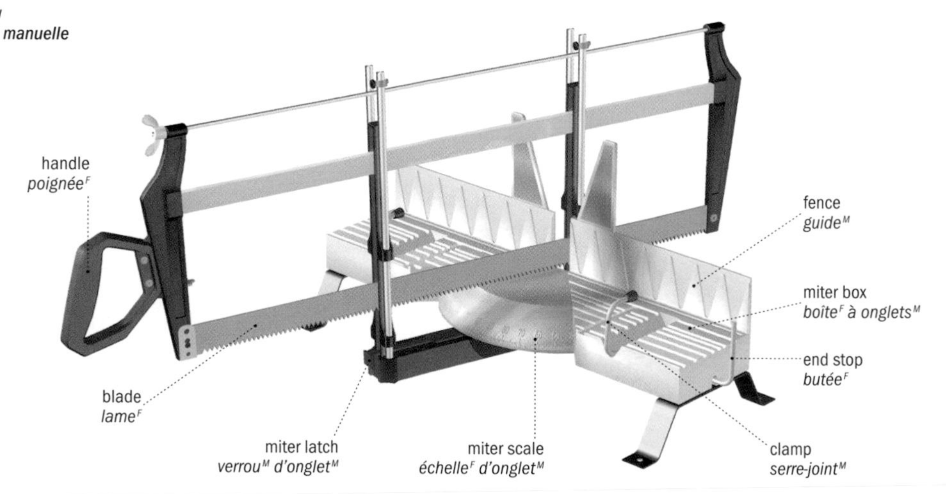
hand miter saw
scie[F] à onglet[M] manuelle
handle
poignée[F]
fence
guide[M]
miter box
boîte[F] à onglets[M]
end stop
butée[F]
blade
lame[F]
miter latch
verrou[M] d'onglet[M]
miter scale
échelle[F] d'onglet[M]
clamp
serre-joint[M]

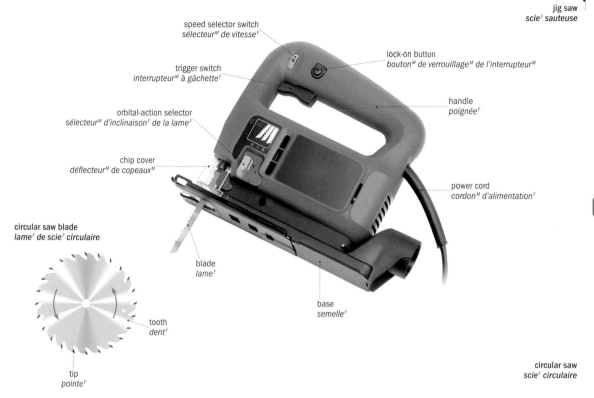

jig saw
scie[F] sauteuse

speed selector switch
sélecteur[M] de vitesse[F]

lock-on button
bouton[M] de verrouillage[M] de l'interrupteur[M]

trigger switch
interrupteur[M] à gâchette[F]

handle
poignée[F]

orbital-action selector
sélecteur[M] d'inclinaison[F] de la lame[F]

chip cover
déflecteur[M] de copeaux[M]

power cord
cordon[M] d'alimentation[F]

blade
lame[F]

base
semelle[F]

circular saw blade
lame[F] de scie[F] circulaire

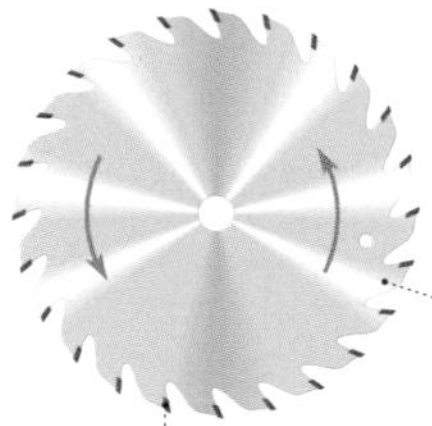

tooth
dent[F]

tip
pointe[F]

circular saw
scie[F] circulaire

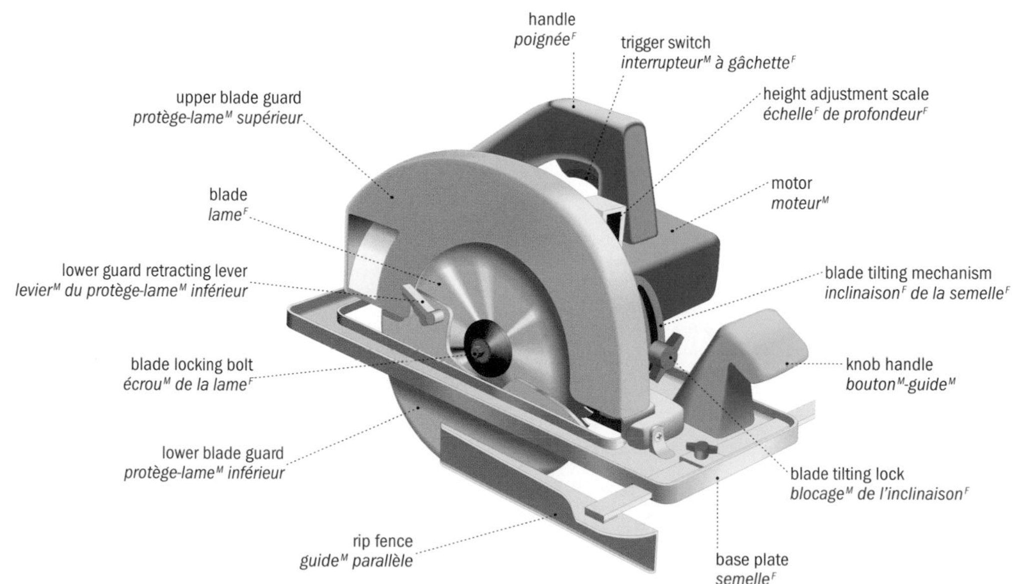
handle
poignée[F]
trigger switch
interrupteur[M] à gâchette[F]
upper blade guard
protège-lame[M] supérieur
height adjustment scale
échelle[F] de profondeur[F]
motor
moteur[M]
blade
lame[F]
lower guard retracting lever
levier[M] du protège-lame[M] inférieur
blade tilting mechanism
inclinaison[F] de la semelle[F]
knob handle
bouton[M]-guide[M]
blade locking bolt
écrou[M] de la lame[F]
lower blade guard
protège-lame[M] inférieur
blade tilting lock
blocage[M] de l'inclinaison[F]
rip fence
guide[M] parallèle
base plate
semelle[F]

carpentry: drilling tools

menuiserie[F] : outils[M] pour percer

cordless drill
perceuse[F]-visseuse[F] sans fil[M]

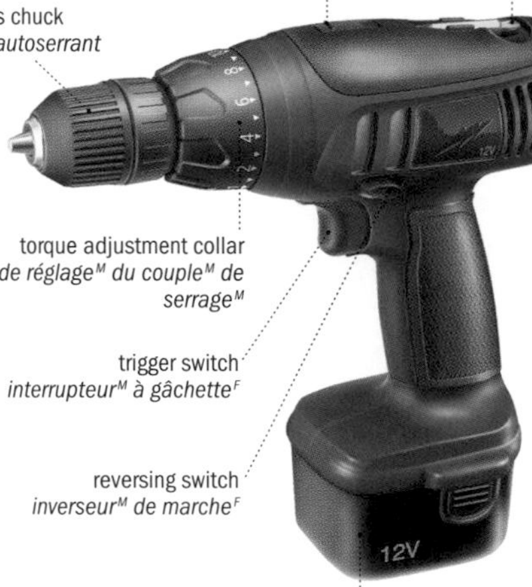

speed selector switch
sélecteur[M] de vitesse[F] de rotation[F]

screwdriver bit
embout[M] de vissage[M]

keyless chuck
mandrin[M] autoserrant

torque adjustment collar
bague[F] de réglage[M] du couple[M] de serrage[M]

trigger switch
interrupteur[M] à gâchette[F]

reversing switch
inverseur[M] de marche[F]

battery pack
batterie[F]

battery pack
batterie[F]

charger
chargeur[M]

chuck key
clé[F] de mandrin[M]

electric drill
perceuse[F] électrique

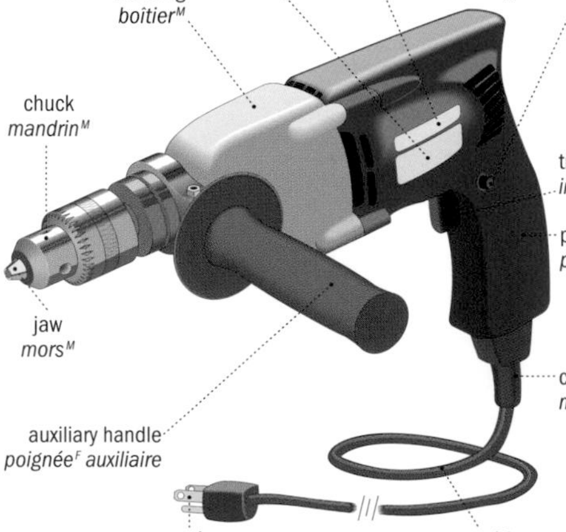

nameplate
plaque[F] signalétique

warning plate
plaque[F] d'instructions[F]

switch lock
blocage[M] de l'interrupteur[M]

housing
boîtier[M]

chuck
mandrin[M]

trigger switch
interrupteur[M] à gâchette[F]

pistol grip handle
poignée[F]-pistolet[M]

jaw
mors[M]

cable sleeve
manchon[M] de câble[M]

auxiliary handle
poignée[F] auxiliaire

plug
fiche[F]

cable
câble[M]

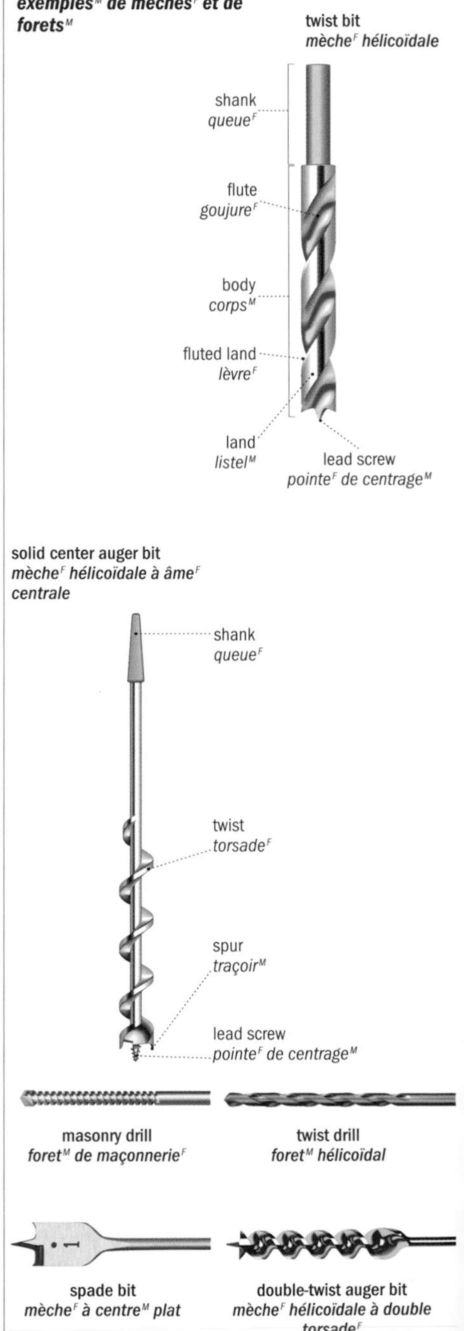
examples of bits and drills
exemples[M] de mèches[F] et de forets[M]
twist bit
mèche[F] hélicoïdale
shank
queue[F]
flute
goujure[F]
body
corps[M]
fluted land
lèvre[F]
land
listel[M]
lead screw
pointe[F] de centrage[M]
solid center auger bit
mèche[F] hélicoïdale à âme[F] centrale
shank
queue[F]
twist
torsade[F]
spur
traçoir[M]
lead screw
pointe[F] de centrage[M]
masonry drill
foret[M] de maçonnerie[F]
twist drill
foret[M] hélicoïdal
spade bit
mèche[F] à centre[M] plat
double-twist auger bit
mèche[F] hélicoïdale à double torsade[F]

carpentry: shaping tools

menuiserie[F] : outils[M] pour façonner

plane
rabot[M]

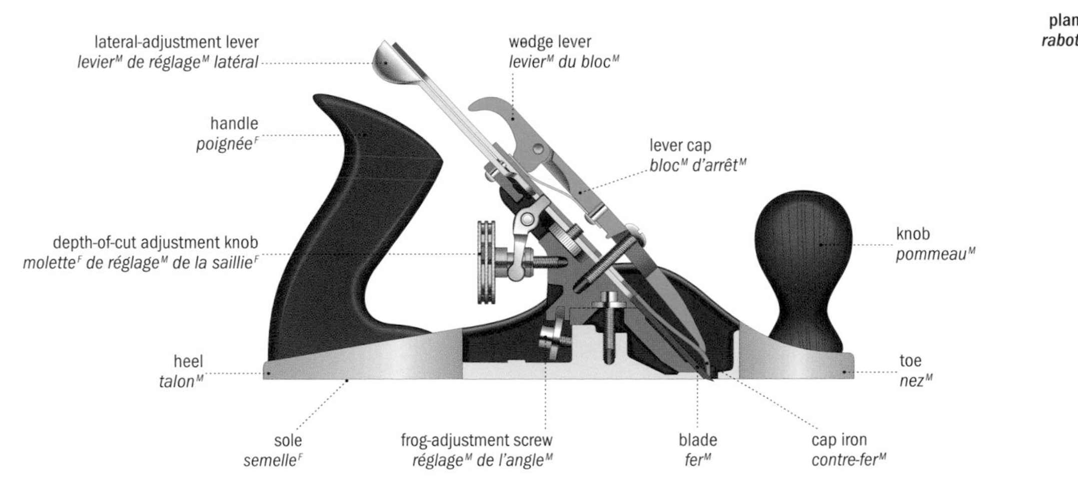
lateral-adjustment lever
levier[M] de réglage[M] latéral
wedge lever
levier[M] du bloc[M]
handle
poignée[F]
lever cap
bloc[M] d'arrêt[M]
depth-of-cut adjustment knob
molette[F] de réglage[M] de la saillie[F]
knob
pommeau[M]
heel
talon[M]
toe
nez[M]
sole
semelle[F]
frog-adjustment screw
réglage[M] de l'angle[M]
blade
fer[M]
cap iron
contre-fer[M]

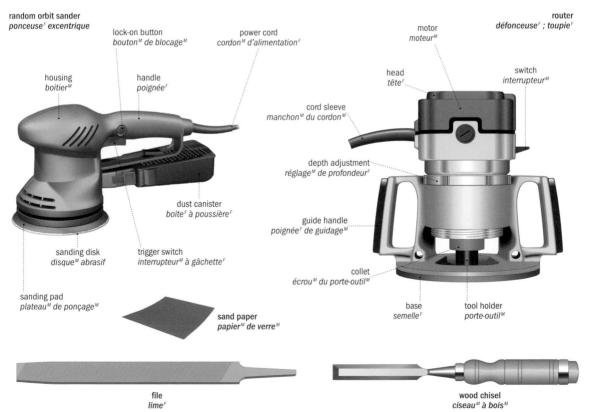

random orbit sander
ponceuse[F] excentrique

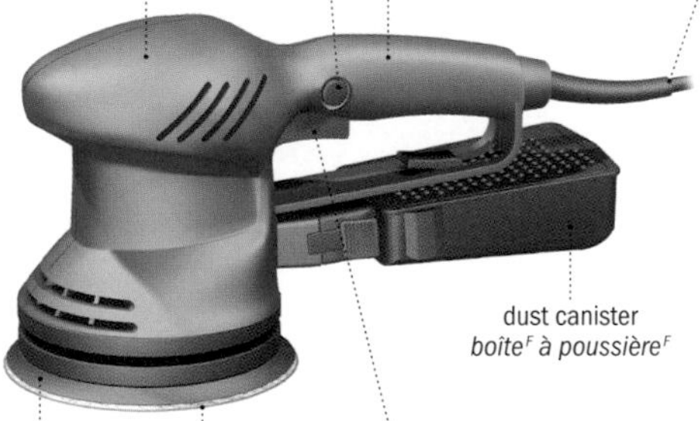

lock-on button
bouton[M] de blocage[M]

power cord
cordon[M] d'alimentation[F]

housing
boîtier[M]

handle
poignée[F]

dust canister
boîte[F] à poussière[F]

sanding disk
disque[M] abrasif

trigger switch
interrupteur[M] à gâchette[F]

sanding pad
plateau[M] de ponçage[M]

sand paper
papier[M] de verre[M]

router
défonceuse[F] ; toupie[F]

motor
moteur[M]

head
tête[F]

switch
interrupteur[M]

cord sleeve
manchon[M] du cordon[M]

depth adjustment
réglage[M] de profondeur[F]

guide handle
poignée[F] de guidage[M]

collet
écrou[M] du porte-outil[M]

base
semelle[F]

tool holder
porte-outil[M]

file
lime[F]

wood chisel
ciseau[M] à bois[M]

pleasure garden

jardin^M d'agrément^M

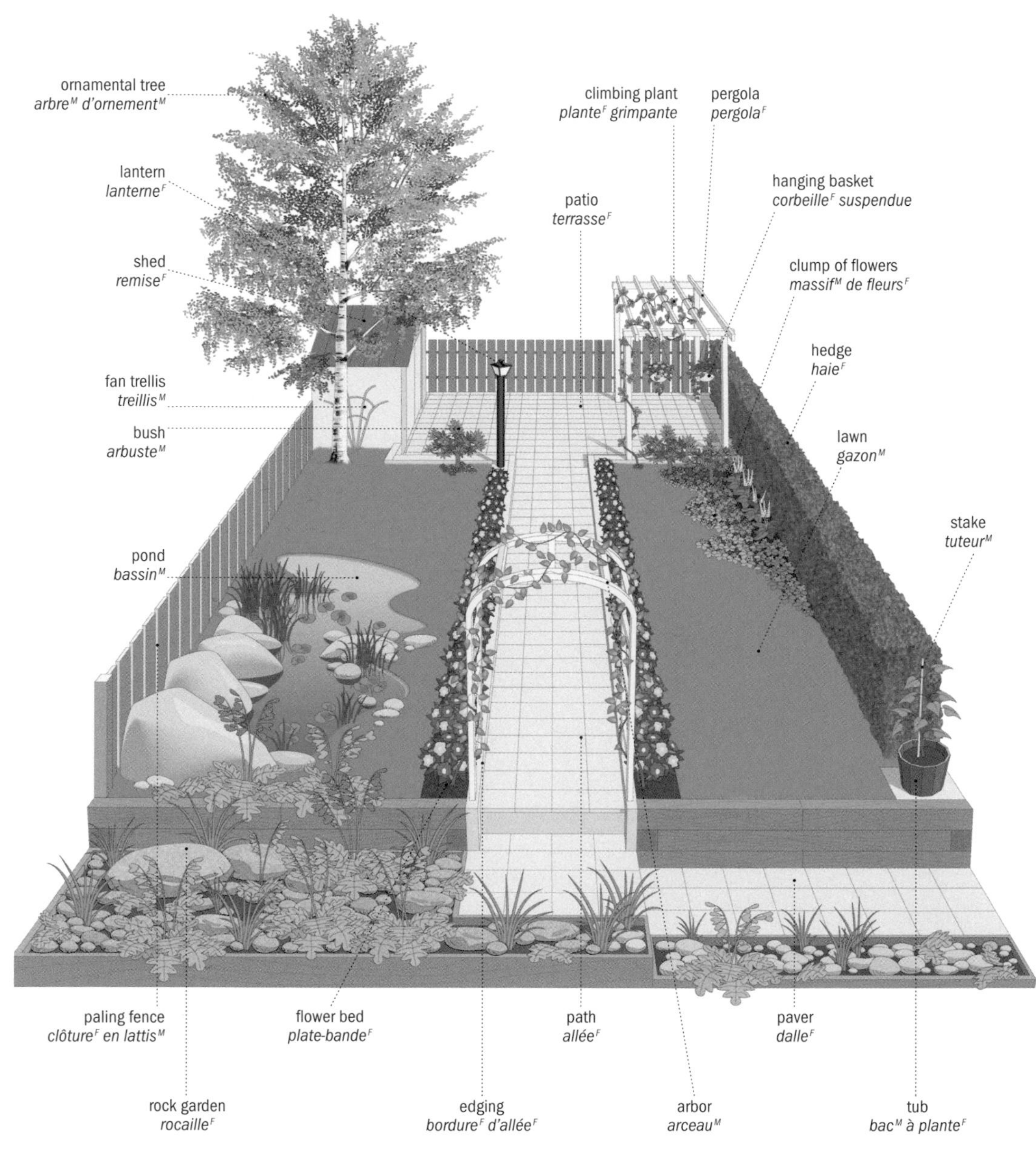
ornamental tree
arbre^M d'ornement^M
lantern
lanterne^F
shed
remise^F
fan trellis
treillis^M
bush
arbuste^M
pond
bassin^M
climbing plant
plante^F grimpante
pergola
pergola^F
patio
terrasse^F
hanging basket
corbeille^F suspendue
clump of flowers
massif^M de fleurs^F
hedge
haie^F
lawn
gazon^M
stake
tuteur^M
paling fence
clôture^F en lattis^M
flower bed
plate-bande^F
path
allée^F
paver
dalle^F
rock garden
rocaille^F
edging
bordure^F d'allée^F
arbor
arceau^M
tub
bac^M à plante^F

miscellaneous equipment

équipement[M] divers

compost bin
bac[M] à compost[M]
wheelbarrow
brouette[F]
tray
caisse[F]
handle
brancard[M]
leg
pied[M]
wheel
roue[F]

seeding and planting tools

outils[M] pour semer et planter

garden line
cordeau[M]

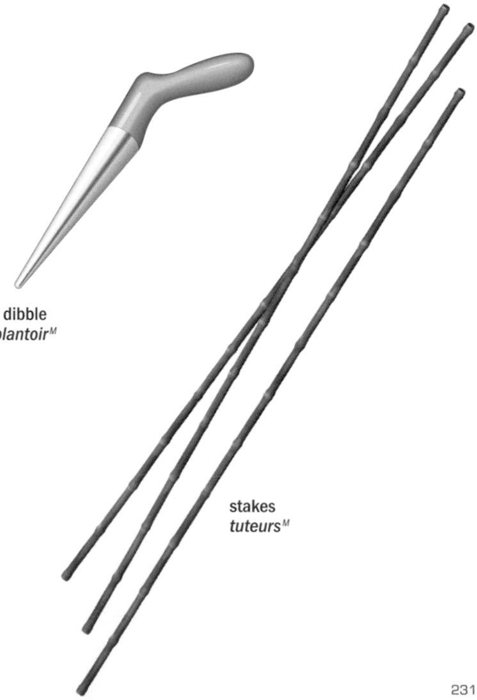

dibble
plantoir[M]

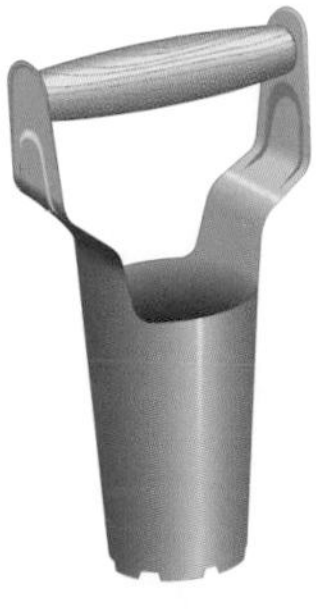

bulb dibble
plantoir[M] à bulbes[M]

seeder
semoir[M] à main[F]

stakes
tuteurs[M]

hand tools

jeu^M de petits outils^M

small hand cultivator
griffe^F à fleurs^F
trowel
transplantoir^M
weeder
tire-racine^M

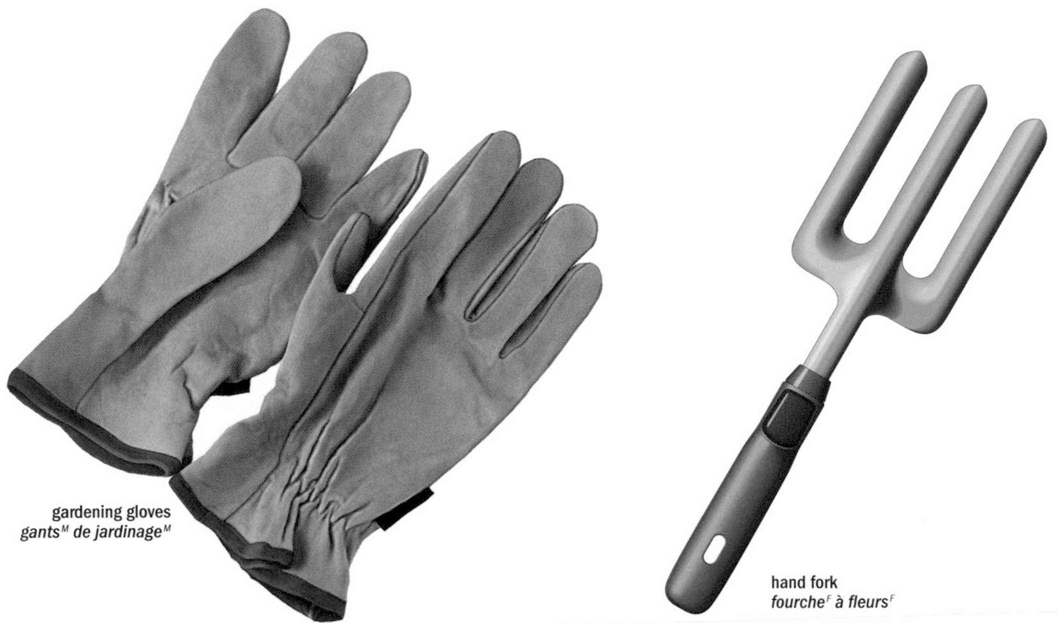
gardening gloves
gants^M de jardinage^M
hand fork
fourche^F à fleurs^F

tools for loosening the earth

outils^M pour remuer la terre^F

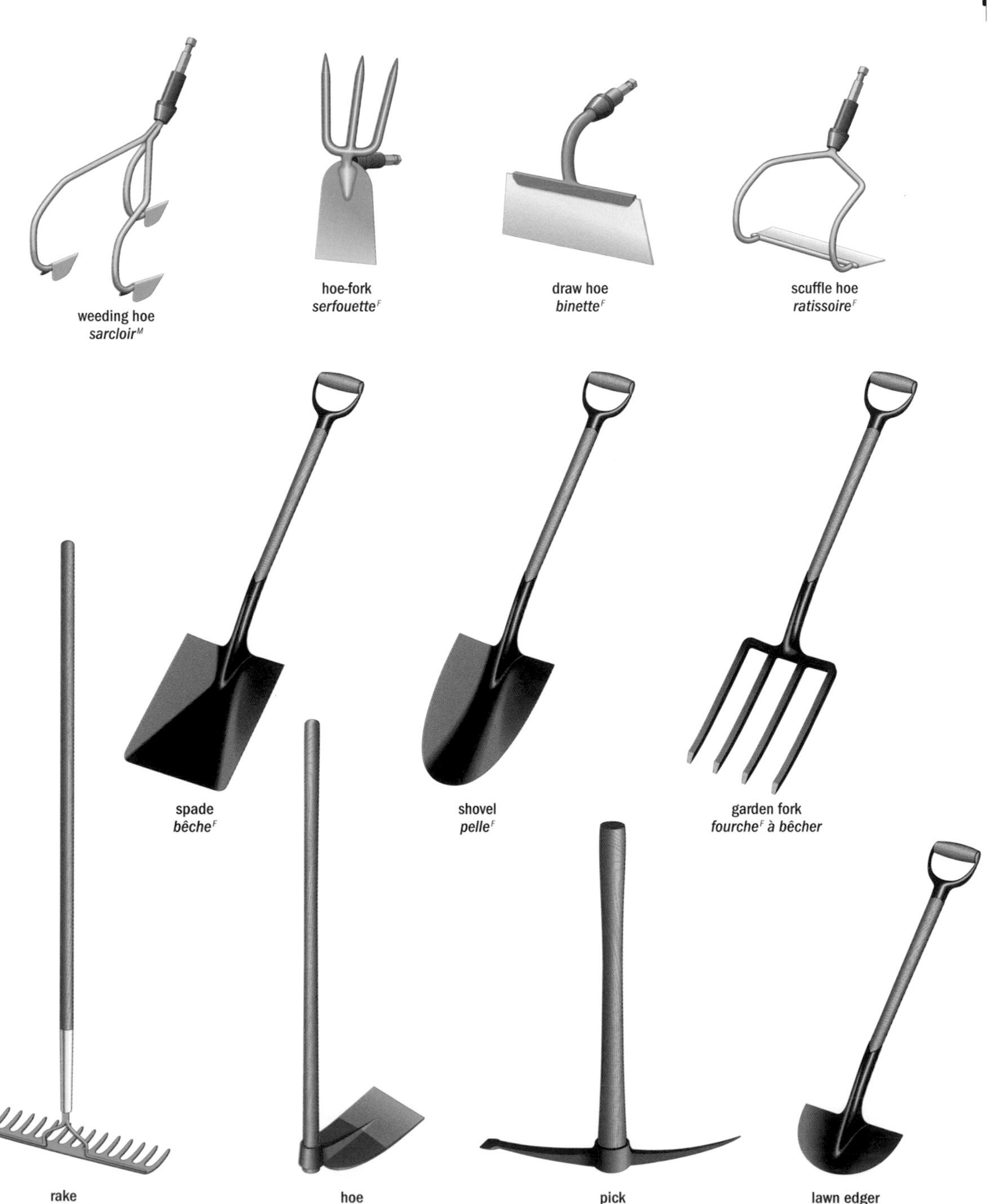
weeding hoe
sarcloir^M
hoe-fork
serfouette^F
draw hoe
binette^F
scuffle hoe
ratissoire^F
spade
bêche^F
shovel
pelle^F
garden fork
fourche^F *à bêcher*
rake
râteau^M
hoe
houe^F
pick
pioche^F
lawn edger
coupe-bordures^M

pruning and cutting tools

outils^M pour couper

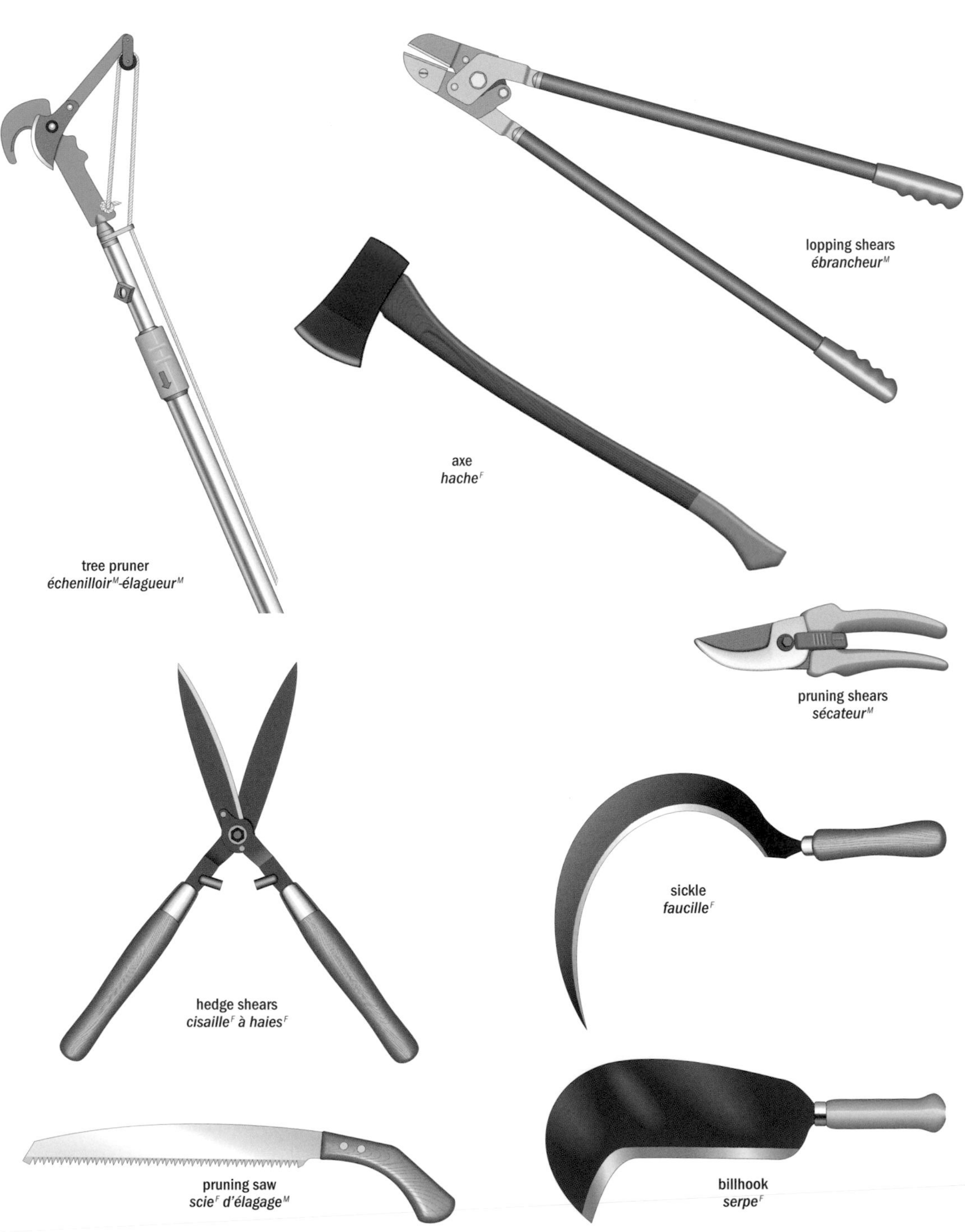
lopping shears
ébrancheur^M
axe
hache^F
tree pruner
échenilloir^M-élagueur^M
pruning shears
sécateur^M
sickle
faucille^F
hedge shears
cisaille^F à haies^F
pruning saw
scie^F d'élagage^M
billhook
serpe^F

hedge trimmer
*taille-haies*M

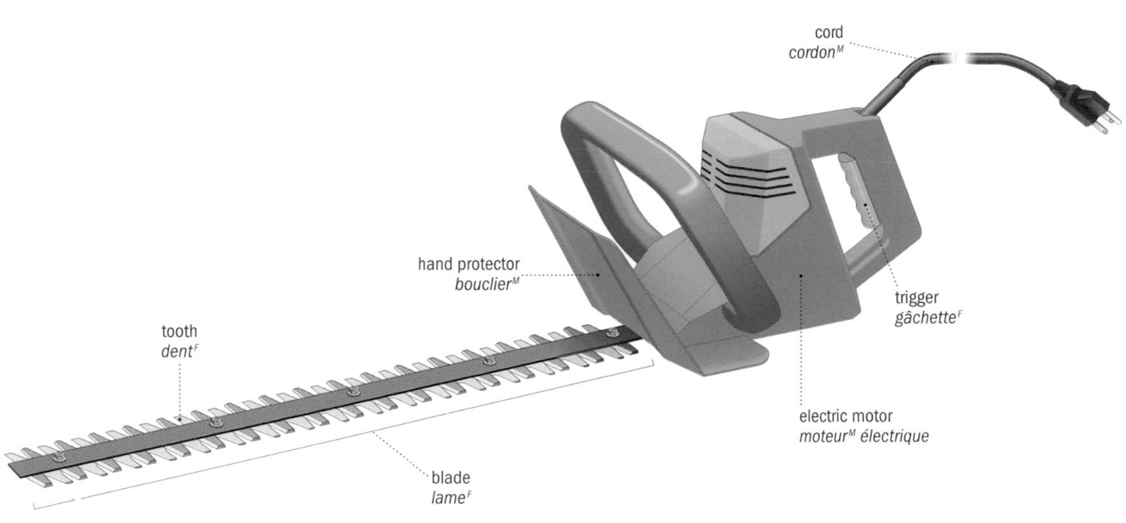
cord
cordonM
hand protector
bouclierM
trigger
gâchetteF
tooth
dentF
electric motor
moteurM électrique
blade
lameF

chainsaw
*tronçonneuse*F

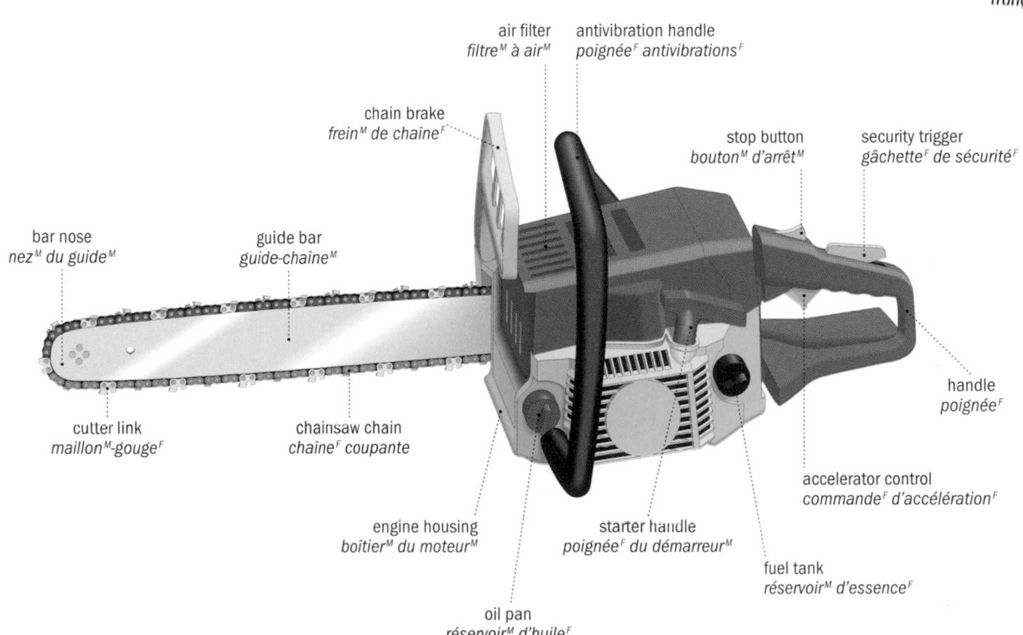
air filter
filtreM à airM
antivibration handle
poignéeF antivibrationsF
chain brake
freinM de chaîneF
stop button
boutonM d'arrêtM
security trigger
gâchetteF de sécuritéF
bar nose
nezM du guideM
guide bar
guide-chaîneM
handle
poignéeF
cutter link
maillonM-gougeF
chainsaw chain
chaîneF coupante
accelerator control
commandeF d'accélérationF
engine housing
boîtierM du moteurM
starter handle
poignéeF du démarreurM
fuel tank
réservoirM d'essenceF
oil pan
réservoirM d'huileF

watering tools

outils[M] pour arroser

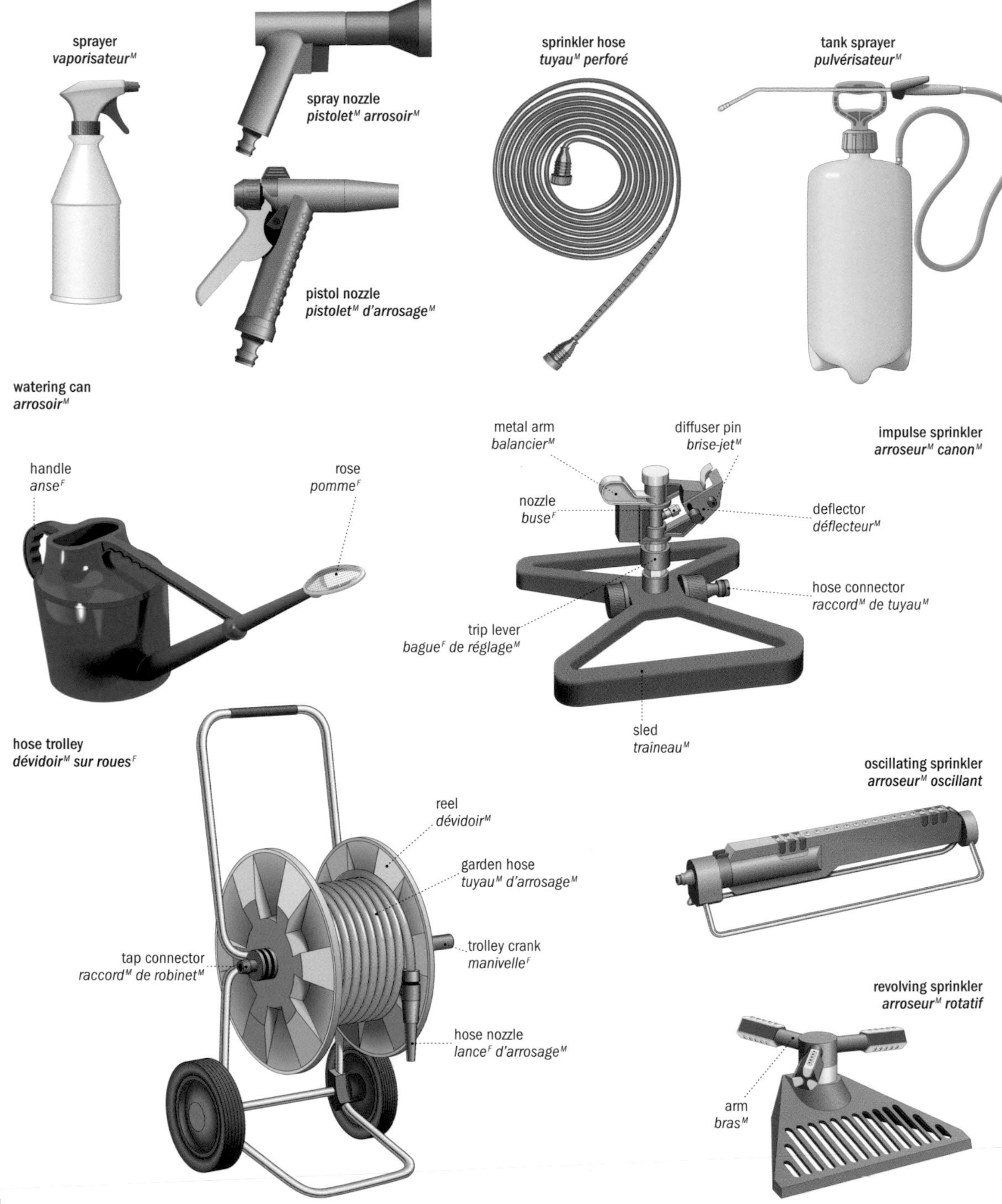
sprayer
vaporisateur[M]
spray nozzle
pistolet[M] arrosoir[M]
pistol nozzle
pistolet[M] d'arrosage[M]
sprinkler hose
tuyau[M] perforé
tank sprayer
pulvérisateur[M]
watering can
arrosoir[M]
handle
anse[F]
rose
pomme[F]
metal arm
balancier[M]
diffuser pin
brise-jet[M]
impulse sprinkler
arroseur[M] canon[M]
nozzle
buse[F]
deflector
déflecteur[M]
hose connector
raccord[M] de tuyau[M]
trip lever
bague[F] de réglage[M]
sled
traîneau[M]
hose trolley
dévidoir[M] sur roues[F]
reel
dévidoir[M]
garden hose
tuyau[M] d'arrosage[M]
trolley crank
manivelle[F]
tap connector
raccord[M] de robinet[M]
hose nozzle
lance[F] d'arrosage[M]
oscillating sprinkler
arroseur[M] oscillant
revolving sprinkler
arroseur[M] rotatif
arm
bras[M]

lawn care

soins[M] de la pelouse[F]

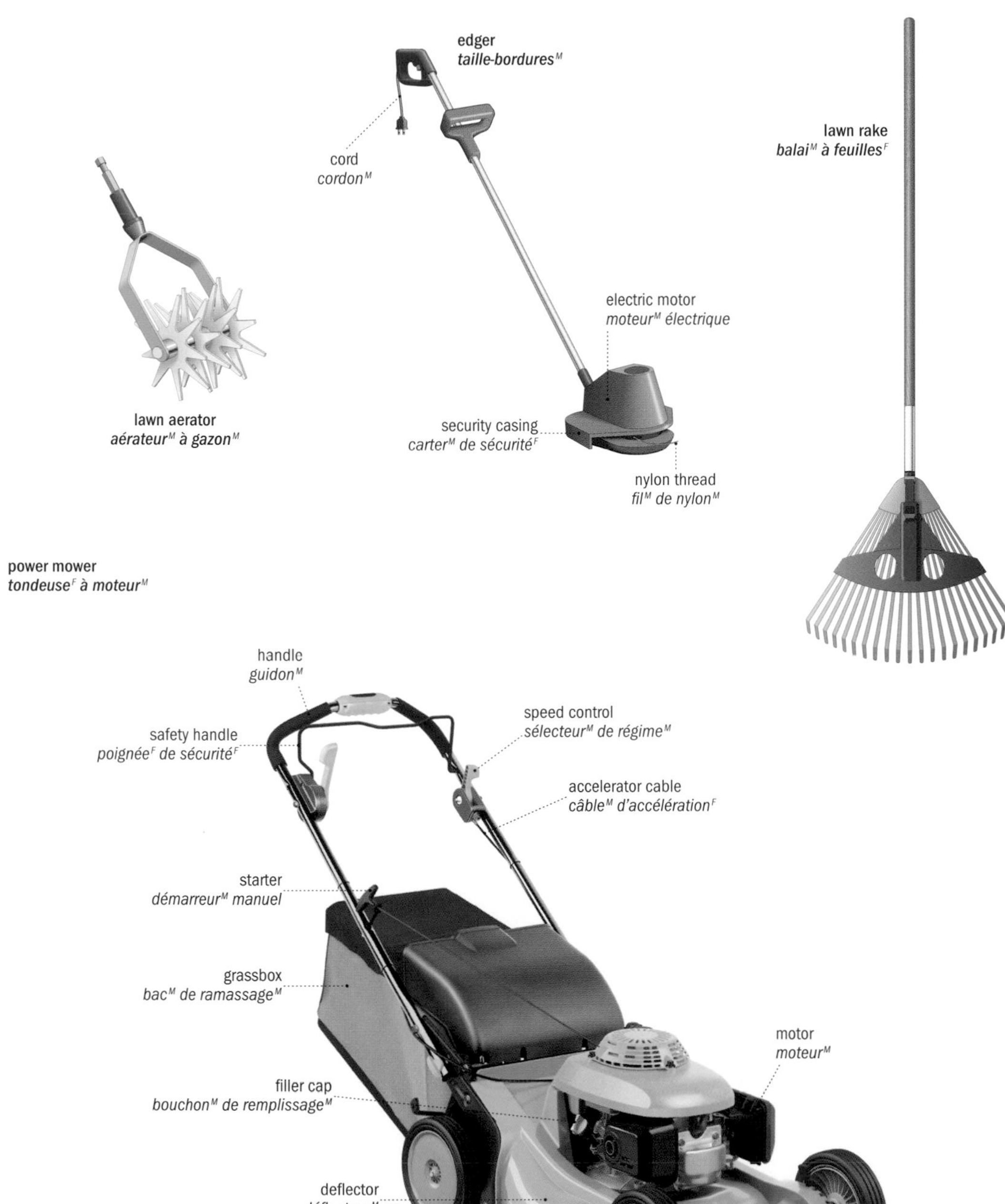
edger
taille-bordures[M]
cord
cordon[M]
lawn rake
balai[M] à feuilles[F]
electric motor
moteur[M] électrique
lawn aerator
aérateur[M] à gazon[M]
security casing
carter[M] de sécurité[F]
nylon thread
fil[M] de nylon[M]
power mower
tondeuse[F] à moteur[M]
handle
guidon[M]
safety handle
poignée[F] de sécurité[F]
speed control
sélecteur[M] de régime[M]
accelerator cable
câble[M] d'accélération[F]
starter
démarreur[M] manuel
grassbox
bac[M] de ramassage[M]
motor
moteur[M]
filler cap
bouchon[M] de remplissage[M]
deflector
déflecteur[M]
casing
carter[M]

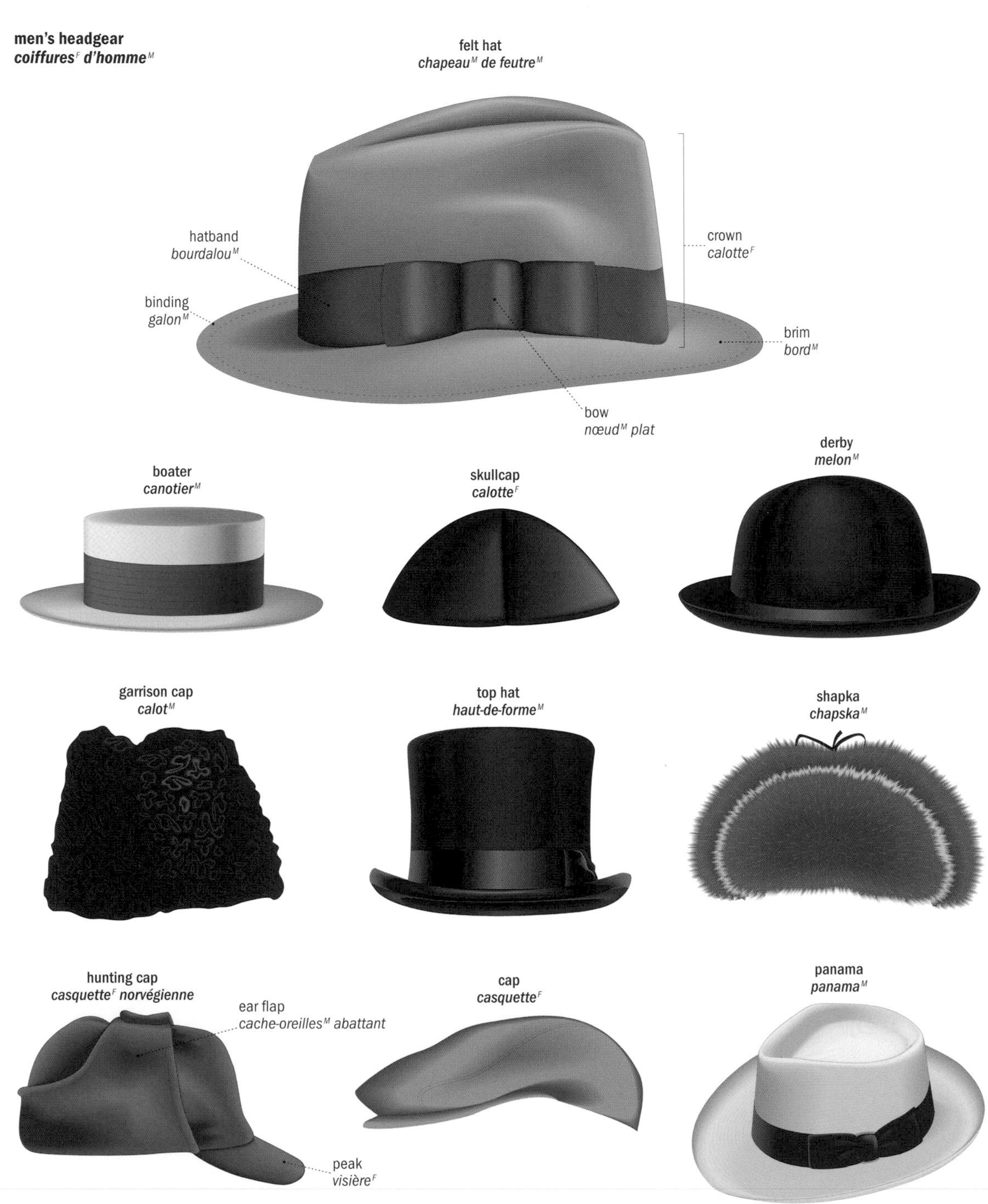
men's headgear
coiffures[F] d'homme[M]
felt hat
chapeau[M] de feutre[M]
hatband
bourdalou[M]
binding
galon[M]
crown
calotte[F]
brim
bord[M]
bow
nœud[M] plat
boater
canotier[M]
skullcap
calotte[F]
derby
melon[M]
garrison cap
calot[M]
top hat
haut-de-forme[M]
shapka
chapska[M]
hunting cap
casquette[F] norvégienne
ear flap
cache-oreilles[M] abattant
peak
visière[F]
cap
casquette[F]
panama
panama[M]

women's headgear
coiffures[F] de femme[F]

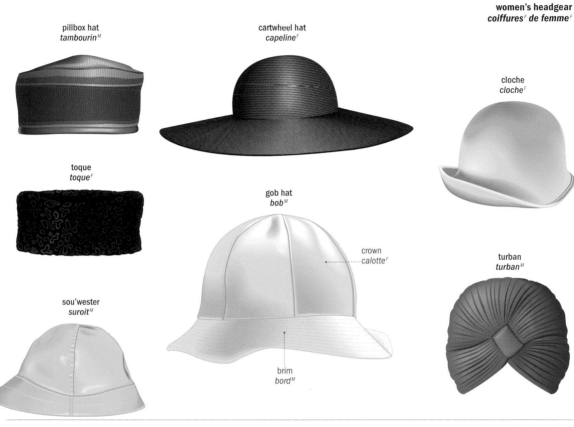

pillbox hat
tambourin[M]

cartwheel hat
capeline[F]

cloche
cloche[F]

toque
toque[F]

gob hat
bob[M]

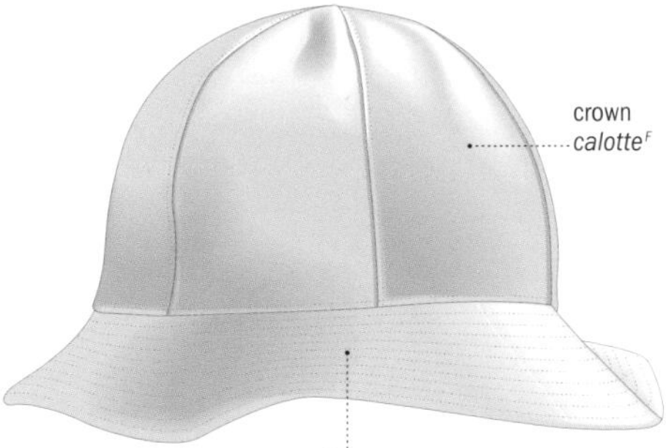

crown
calotte[F]

brim
bord[M]

turban
turban[M]

sou'wester
suroît[M]

unisex headgear
coiffures[F] unisexes

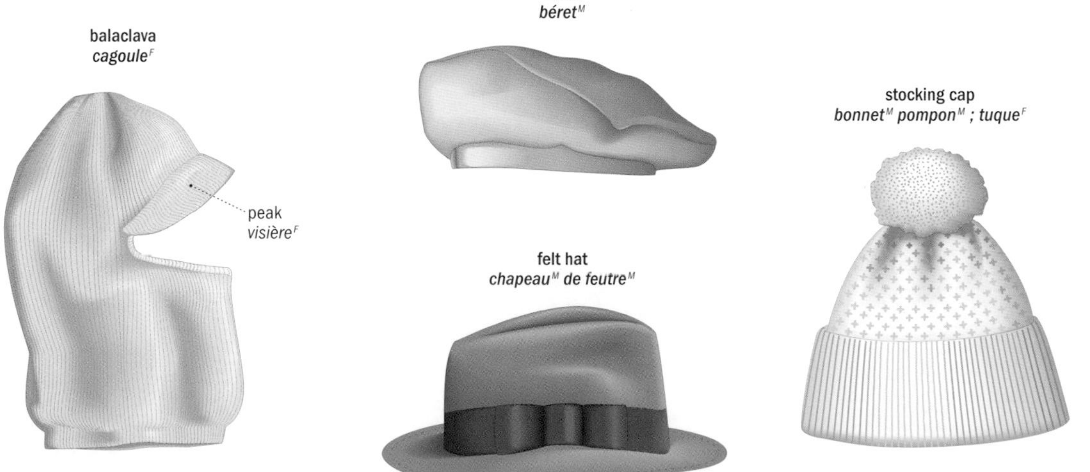
beret
béret[M]
balaclava
cagoule[F]
peak
visière[F]
stocking cap
bonnet[M] pompon[M] ; tuque[F]
felt hat
chapeau[M] de feutre[M]

shoes

chaussures[F]

men's shoes
chaussures[F] d'homme[M]

parts of a shoe
parties[F] d'une chaussure[F]
lining
doublure[F]
shoelace
lacet[M]
cuff
revers[M]
tongue
languette[F]
vamp
claque[F]
heel grip
glissoir[M]
stitch
surpiqûre[F]
quarter
quartier[M]
punch hole
perforation[F]
outside counter
talonnette[F] de dessus[M]
heel
talon[M]
top lift
bonbout[M]
waist
cambrure[F]
nose of the quarter
aile[F] de quartier[M]
tag
ferret[M]
eyelet tab
garant[M]
outsole
semelle[F] d'usure[F]
perforated toe cap
bout[M] fleuri
eyelet
œillet[M]
welt
trépointe[F]
heavy duty boot
brodequin[M] de travail[M]
chukka
chukka[M]
rubber
claque[F]
bootee
bottillon[M]
oxford shoe
richelieu[M]
blucher oxford
derby[M]

women's shoes
chaussures[F] de femme[F]

ballerina slipper
ballerine[F]

sandal
sandale[F]

sling back shoe
escarpin[M]-sandale[F]

pump
escarpin[M]

one-bar shoe
Charles IX[M]

T-strap shoe
salomé[M]

casual shoe
trotteur[M]

thigh-boot
cuissarde[F]

boot
botte[F]

ankle boot
bottine[F]

unisex shoes
chaussures[F] unisexes

mule
mule[F]

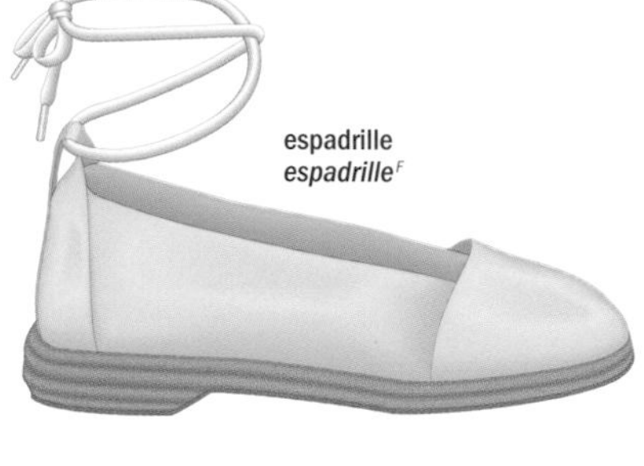

espadrille
espadrille[F]

tennis shoe
tennis[M]

loafer
loafer[M] ; flâneur[M]

sandal
nu-pied[M]

moccasin
mocassin[M]

thong
tong[M]

clog
socque[M]

sandal
sandalette[F]

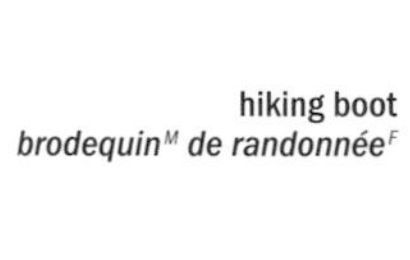

hiking boot
brodequin[M] de randonnée[F]

men's gloves
gants[M] d'homme[M]

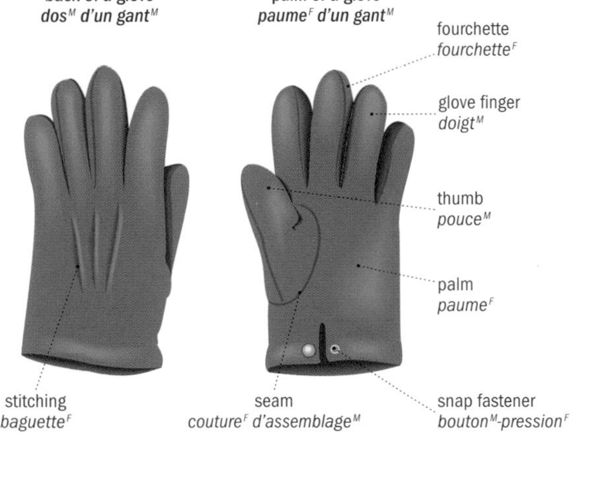

fourchette
fourchette[F]
glove finger
doigt[M]
thumb
pouce[M]
palm
paume[F]
stitching
baguette[F]
seam
couture[F] d'assemblage[M]
snap fastener
bouton[M]-pression[F]

back of a glove
dos[M] d'un gant[M]

palm of a glove
paume[F] d'un gant[M]

opening
fenêtre[F]

perforation
perforation[F]

driving glove
gant[M] de conduite[F]

mitten
moufle[F] ; mitaine[F]

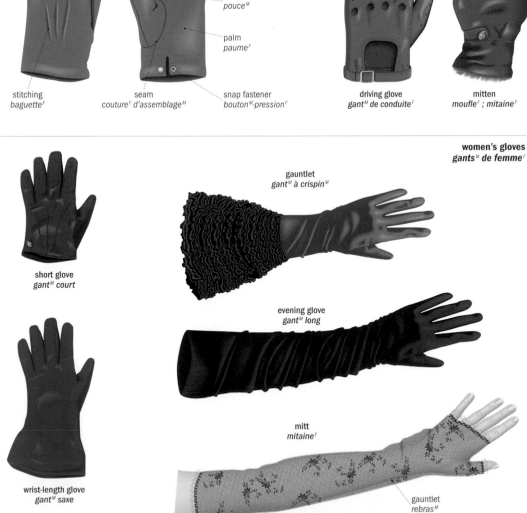

women's gloves
gants[M] de femme[F]

short glove
gant[M] court

wrist-length glove
gant[M] saxe

gauntlet
gant[M] à crispin[M]

evening glove
gant[M] long

mitt
mitaine[F]

gauntlet
rebras[M]

jackets
veston[M] et veste[F]

double-breasted jacket
veston[M] croisé
collar
col[M]
peaked lapel
revers[M] à cran[M] aigu
lining
doublure[F]
breast welt pocket
pochette[F]
sleeve
manche[F]
flap
rabat[M]
outside ticket pocket
poche[F]-ticket[M]
patch pocket
poche[F] plaquée
side back vent
fente[F] latérale
vest
gilet[M]
V-neck
encolure[F] en V
lining
doublure[F]
welt
patte[F]
front
devant[M]
seam
découpe[F]
welt pocket
poche[F] gilet[M]
adjustable waist tab
tirant[M] de réglage[M]
single-breasted jacket
veste[F] droite
lapel
revers[M]
notch
cran[M]
front
devant[M]
lining
doublure[F]
pocket handkerchief
pochette[F]
flap pocket
poche[F] tiroir[M]
back
dos[M]
sleeve
manche[F]
center back vent
fente[F] médiane

shirt
chemise[F]

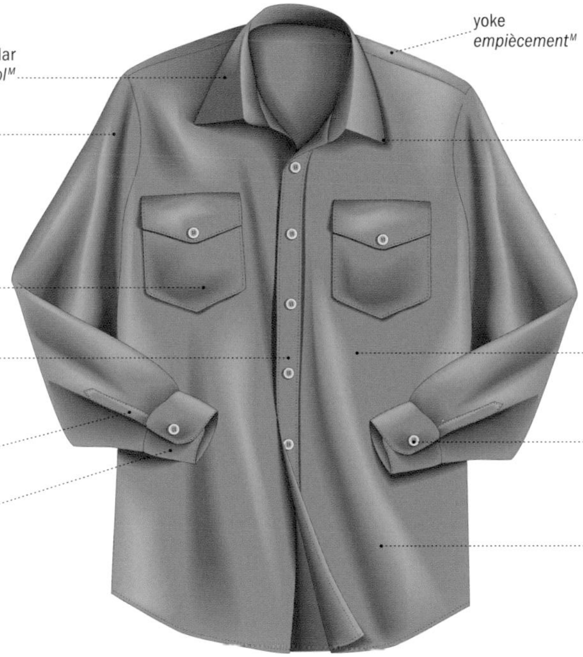

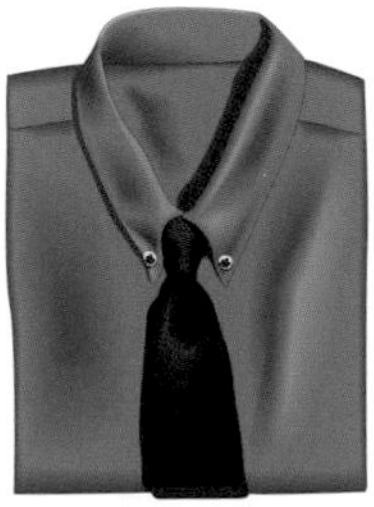

yoke
empiècement[M]

collar
col[M]

set-in sleeve
manche[F] montée

collar point
pointe[F] de col[M]

breast pocket
poche[F] poitrine[F]

front
devant[M]

buttoned placket
patte[F] de boutonnage[M]

button
bouton[M]

pointed tab end
patte[F] capucin[M]

cuff
poignet[M]

shirttail
pan[M]

collar stay
baleine[F] de col[M]

buttondown collar
col[M] pointes[F] boutonnées

ascot tie
ascot[F]

bow tie
nœud[M] papillon[M]

spread collar
col[M] italien

necktie
cravate[F]

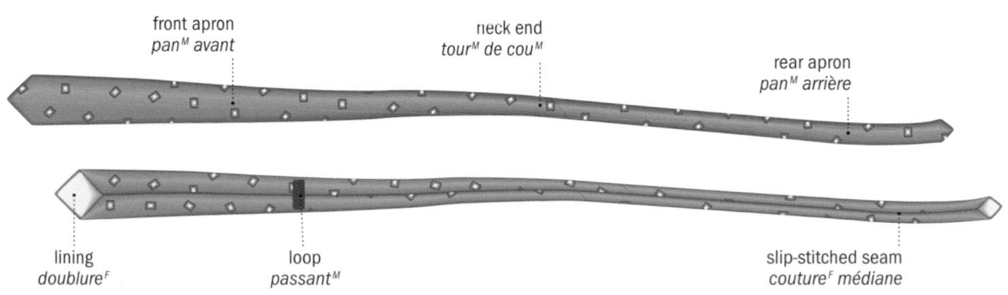
front apron
pan[M] avant
neck end
tour[M] de cou[M]
rear apron
pan[M] arrière
lining
doublure[F]
loop
passant[M]
slip-stitched seam
couture[F] médiane

pants
pantalon[M]

waistband extension
patte[F] boutonnée

knife pleat
pli[M] plat

fly
braguette[F]

belt loop
passant[M]

front top pocket
poche[F] cavalière

waistband
ceinture[F] montée

crease
pli[M]

cuff
revers[M]

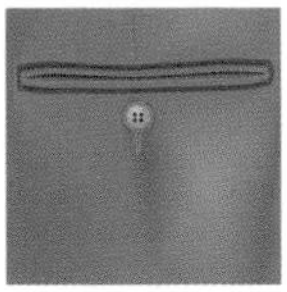

back pocket
poche[F]-revolver[M]

suspender clip
pince[F]

suspenders
bretelles[F]

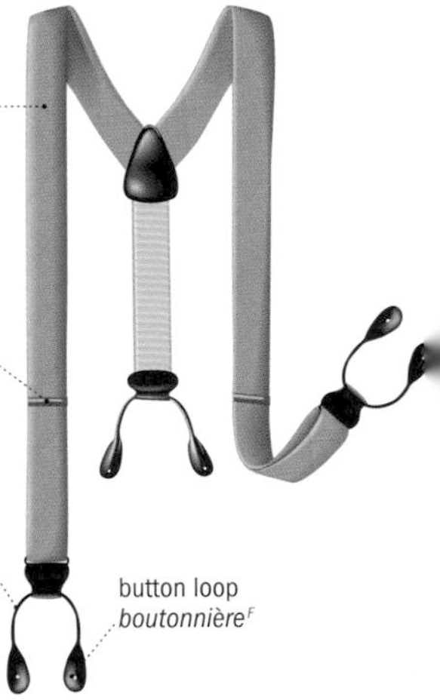

elastic webbing
bande[F] élastique

adjustment slide
coulisse[F]

leather end
patte[F]

button loop
boutonnière[F]

belt
ceinture[F]

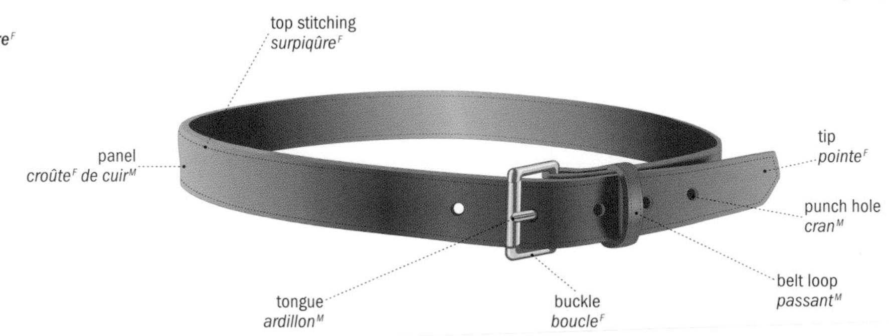
top stitching
surpiqûre[F]
panel
croûte[F] de cuir[M]
tip
pointe[F]
punch hole
cran[M]
belt loop
passant[M]
tongue
ardillon[M]
buckle
boucle[F]

underwear
sous-vêtements[M]

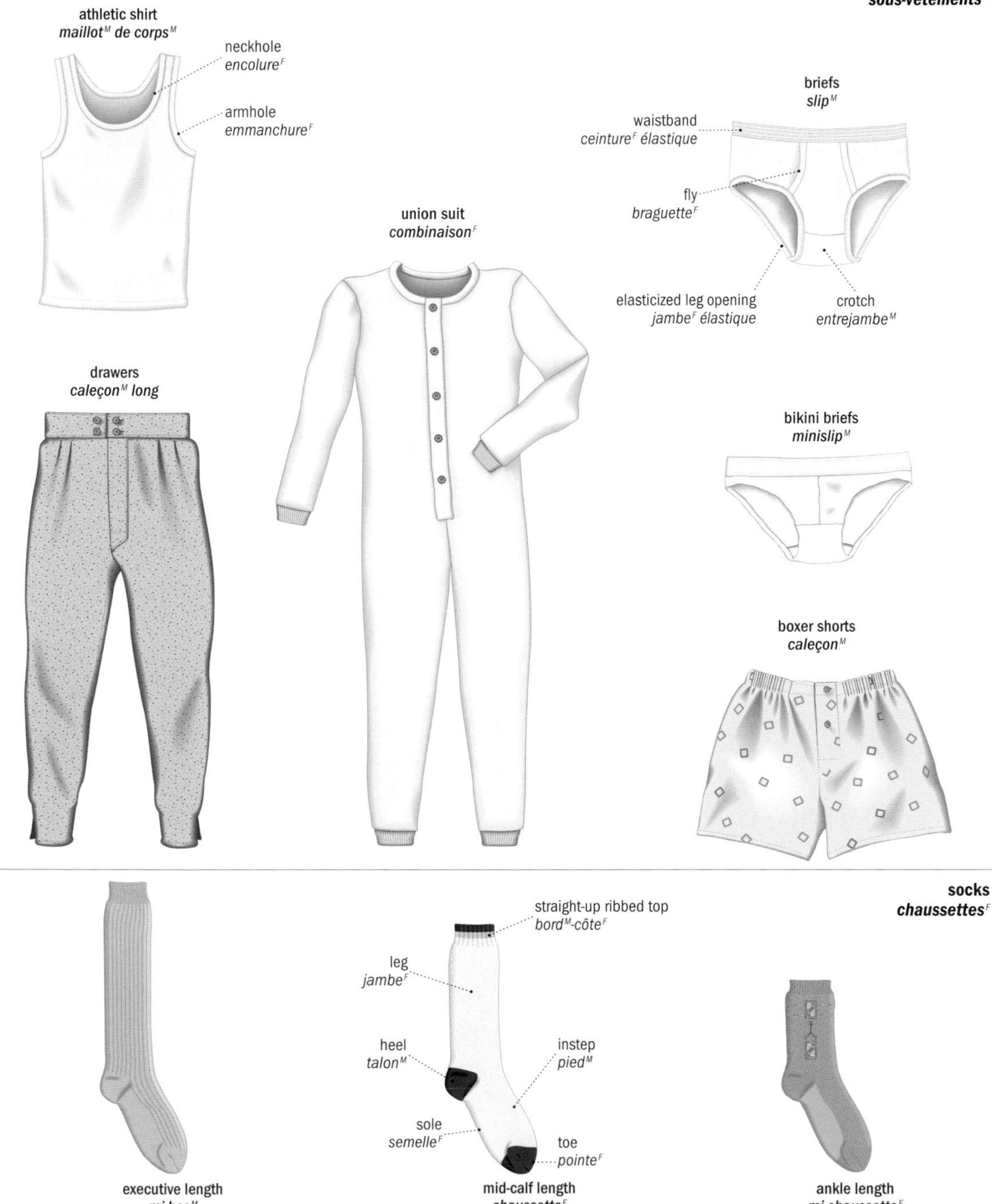
athletic shirt
maillot[M] de corps[M]
neckhole
encolure[F]
armhole
emmanchure[F]
briefs
slip[M]
waistband
ceinture[F] élastique
fly
braguette[F]
union suit
combinaison[F]
elasticized leg opening
jambe[F] élastique
crotch
entrejambe[M]
drawers
caleçon[M] long
bikini briefs
minislip[M]
boxer shorts
caleçon[M]
socks
chaussettes[F]
straight-up ribbed top
bord[M]-côte[F]
leg
jambe[F]
heel
talon[M]
instep
pied[M]
sole
semelle[F]
toe
pointe[F]
executive length
mi-bas[M]
mid-calf length
chaussette[F]
ankle length
mi-chaussette[F]

coats
manteaux[M] et blousons[M]

raincoat
imperméable[M]
collar
col[M]
raglan sleeve
manche[F] raglan
notched lapel
revers[M] cranté
tab
patte[F]
broad-welt side pocket
poche[F] raglan
buttonhole
boutonnière[F]
side panel
pan[M]
overcoat
pardessus[M]
notched lapel
revers[M] cranté
breast pocket
poche[F] poitrine[F]
breast dart
pince[F] de taille[F]
flap pocket
poche[F] à rabat[M]
trench coat
trench[M]
two-way collar
col[M] transformable
gun flap
bavolet[M]
double-breasted buttoning
double boutonnage[M]
belt
ceinture[F]
belt loop
passant[M]
frame
boucle[F] de ceinture[F]
epaulet
patte[F] d'épaule[F]
raglan sleeve
manche[F] raglan
sleeve strap loop
passant[M]
sleeve strap
patte[F] de serrage[M]
broad-welt side pocket
poche[F] raglan
three-quarter coat
paletot[M]

parka
***parka*[F] *; parka*[M]**

snap-fastening tab
patte[F] *à boutons*[M]*-pression*[F]

zipper
fermeture[F] *à glissière*[F]

sheepskin jacket
***canadienne*[F]**

duffle coat
***duffle-coat*[M] *; canadienne*[F]**

hood
capuchon[M]

yoke
empiècement[M]

frog
brandebourg[M]

patch pocket
poche[F] *plaquée*

toggle fastening
bûchette[F]

jacket
blouson*[M] *court

windbreaker
blouson*[M] *long

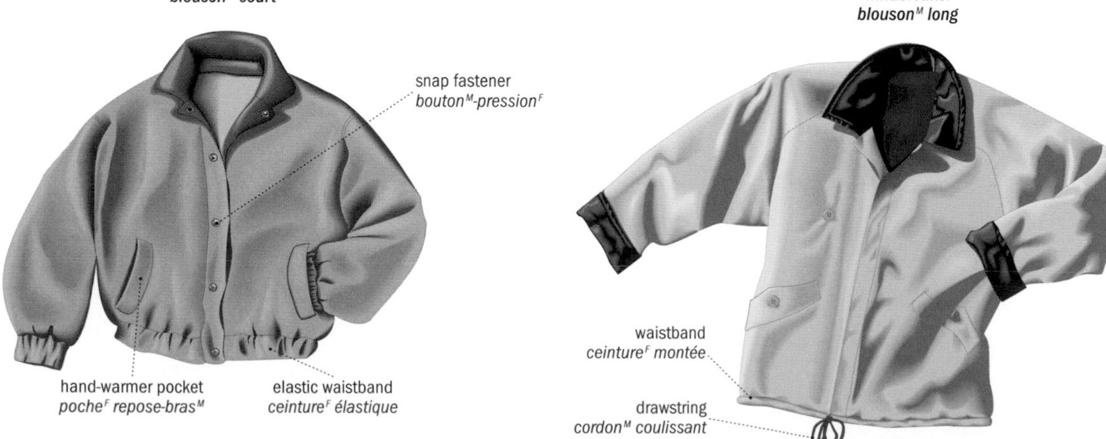
snap fastener
bouton[M]-pression[F]
hand-warmer pocket
poche[F] repose-bras[M]
elastic waistband
ceinture[F] élastique
waistband
ceinture[F] montée
drawstring
cordon[M] coulissant

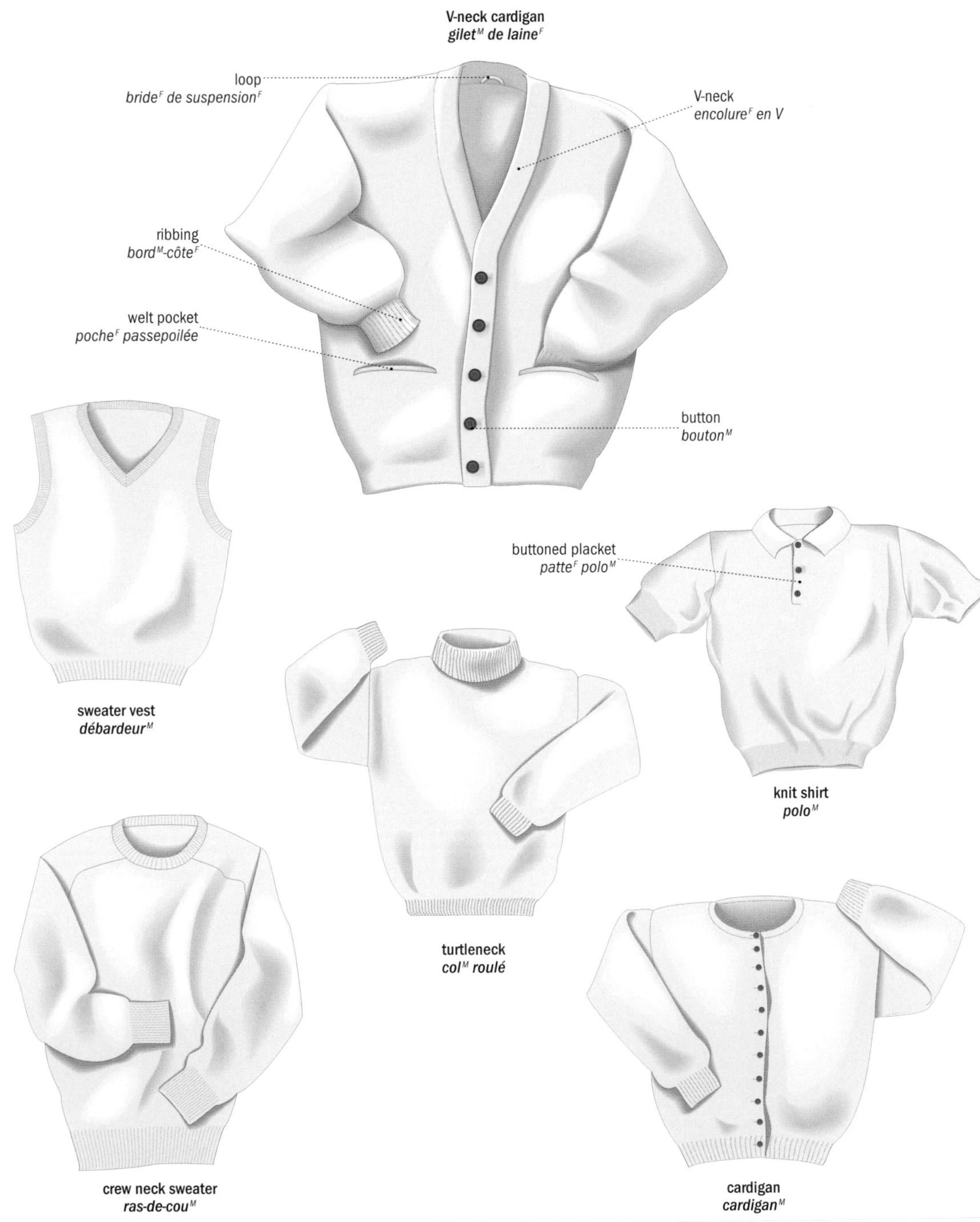

V-neck cardigan
gilet[M] de laine[F]
loop
bride[F] de suspension[F]
V-neck
encolure[F] en V
ribbing
bord[M]-côte[F]
welt pocket
poche[F] passepoilée
button
bouton[M]
buttoned placket
patte[F] polo[M]
sweater vest
débardeur[M]
knit shirt
polo[M]
turtleneck
col[M] roulé
crew neck sweater
ras-de-cou[M]
cardigan
cardigan[M]

coats
manteaux[M]

suit
tailleur[M]
jacket
veste[F]
skirt
jupe[F]
raglan
raglan[M]
raglan sleeve
manche[F] raglan
fly front closing
boutonnage[M] sous patte[F]
broad welt side pocket
poche[F] raglan

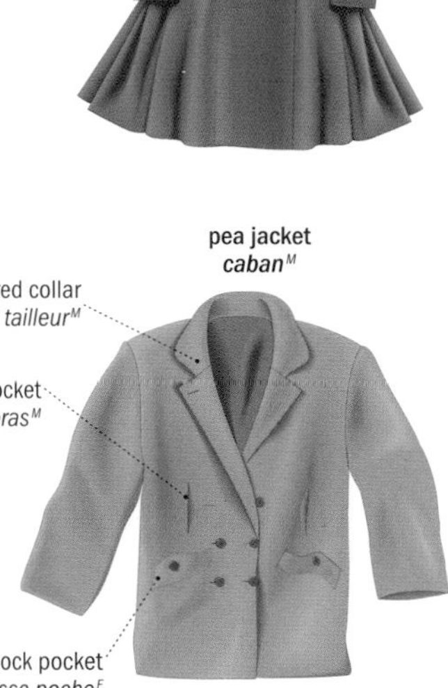
top coat
redingote[F]
pea jacket
caban[M]
tailored collar
col[M] tailleur[M]
hand-warmer pocket
poche[F] repose-bras[M]
mock pocket
fausse poche[F]

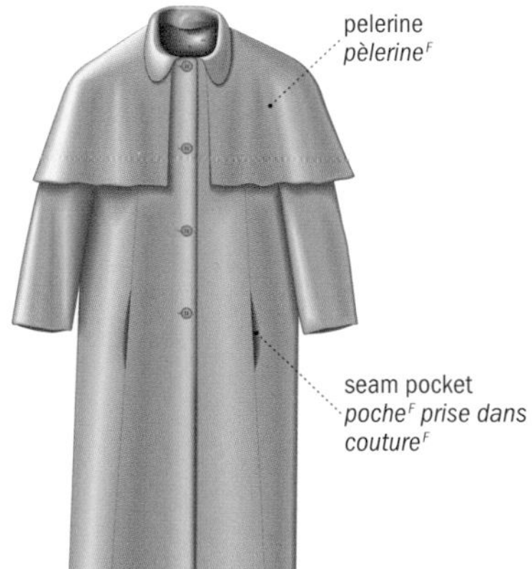
pelerine
pèlerine[F]
pelerine
pèlerine[F]
seam pocket
poche[F] prise dans une couture[F]

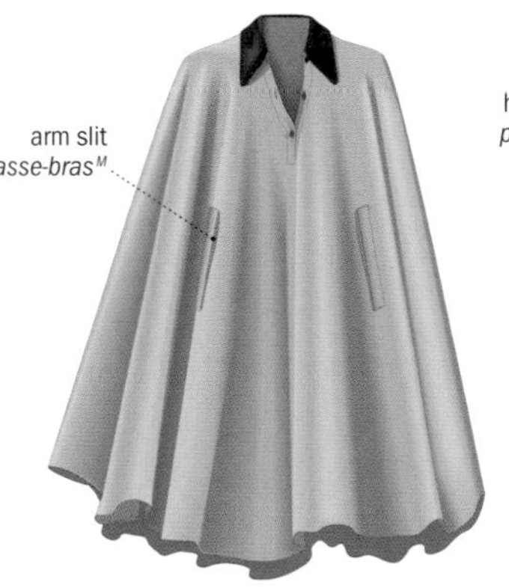
cape
cape[F]
arm slit
passe-bras[M]

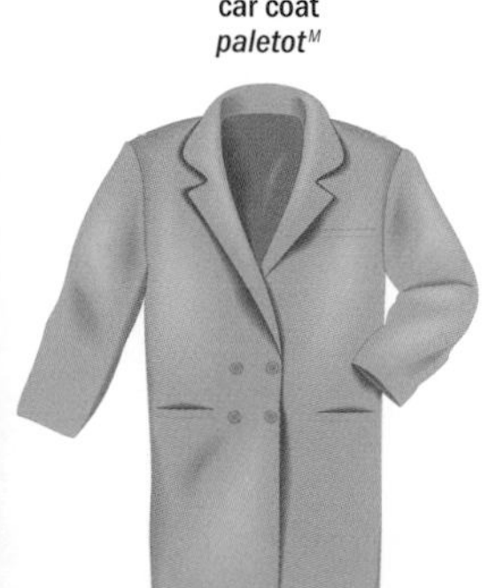
car coat
paletot[M]

jacket
veste[F]

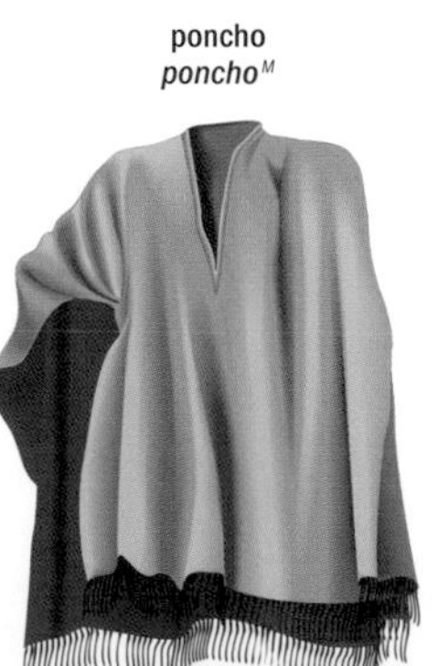
poncho
poncho[M]

overcoat
manteau[M]

examples of dresses
exemples[M] de robes[F]

sheath dress
robe[F] fourreau[M]

princess-seamed dress
robe[F] princesse[F]

coat dress
robe[F]-manteau[M]

polo dress
robe[F]-polo[M]

housedress
robe[F] d'intérieur[M]

shirtwaist dress
robe[F] chemisier[M]

drop-waist dress
robe[F] taille[F] basse

trapeze dress
robe[F] trapèze[M]

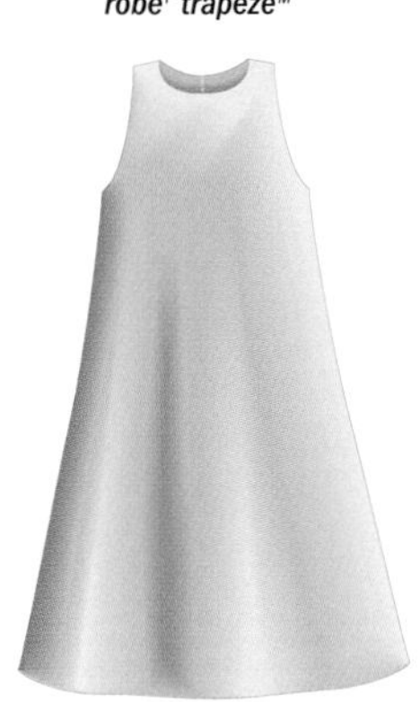

sundress
robe[F] bain[M]-de-soleil[M]

wraparound dress
robe[F] enveloppe[F]

tunic dress
robe[F] tunique[F]

jumper
chasuble[F]

examples of skirts
exemples[M] de jupes[F]

gored skirt
jupe[F] à lés[M]

kilt
kilt[M]

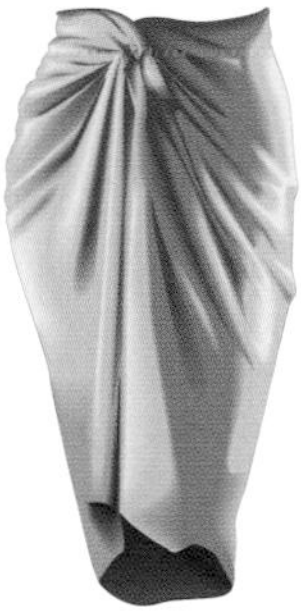

sarong
paréo[M]

wraparound skirt
jupe[F] portefeuille[M]

sheath skirt
jupe[F] fourreau[M]

ruffled skirt
jupe[F] à volants[M] étagés

straight skirt
jupe[F] droite

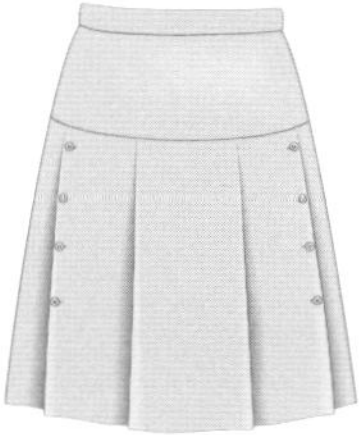

yoked skirt
jupe[F] à empiècement[M]

gathered skirt
jupe[F] froncée

culottes
jupe[F]-culotte[F]

examples of pleats
exemples[M] de plis[M]

inverted pleat
pli[M] creux

kick pleat
pli[M] d'aisance[F]

accordion pleat
plissé[M] accordéon[M]

top-stitched pleat
pli[M] surpiqué

knife pleat
pli[M] plat

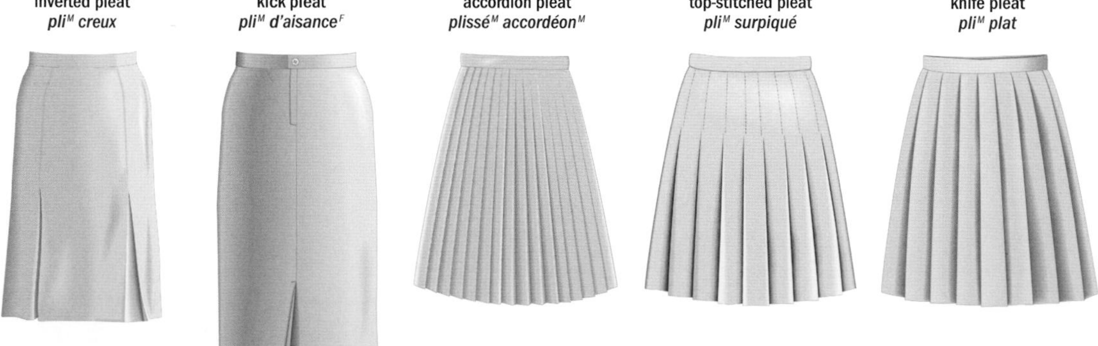

examples of pants
exemples[M] de pantalons[M]

shorts
short[M]

Bermuda shorts
bermuda[M]

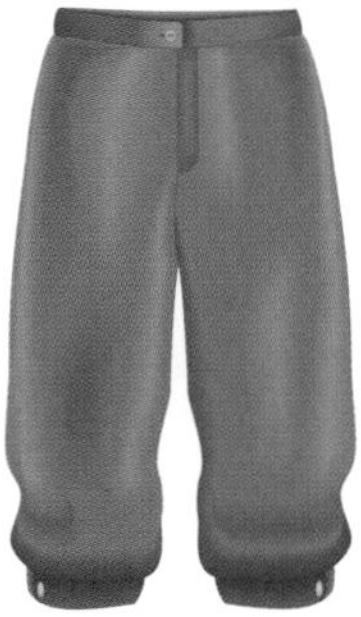

knickers
knicker[M]

pedal pushers
corsaire[M]

jeans
jean[M]

ski pants
fuseau[M]

footstrap
sous-pied[M]

jumpsuit
combinaison[F]-pantalon[M]

overalls
salopette[F]

bell bottoms
pantalon[M] pattes[F] d'éléphant[M]

jackets, vest and sweaters
vestes[F] et pulls[M]

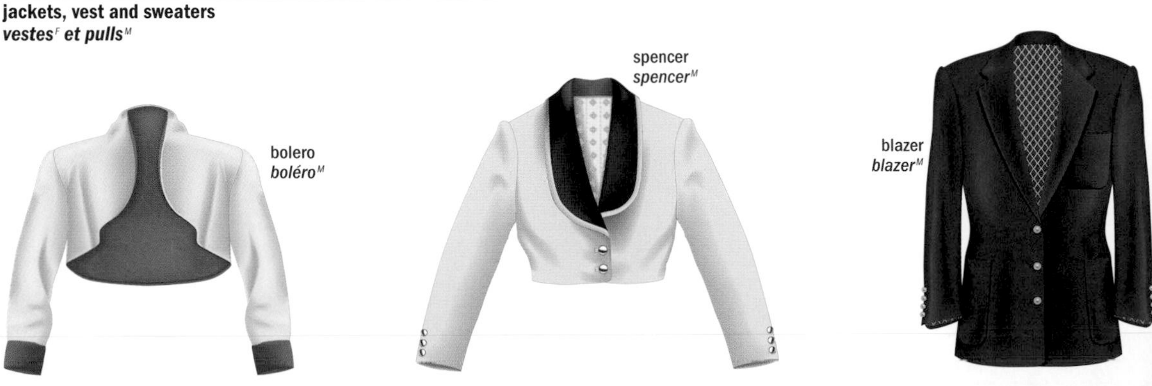
bolero
boléro[M]
spencer
spencer[M]
blazer
blazer[M]

safari jacket
saharienne[F]
gusset pocket
poche[F] *soufflet*[M]
vest
gilet[M]
twin-set
tandem[M]
crew neck sweater
ras-de-cou[M]
cardigan
cardigan[M]

examples of shirts
***exemples*[M] *de corsages*[M]**

body suit
***corsage*[M]*-culotte*[F]**

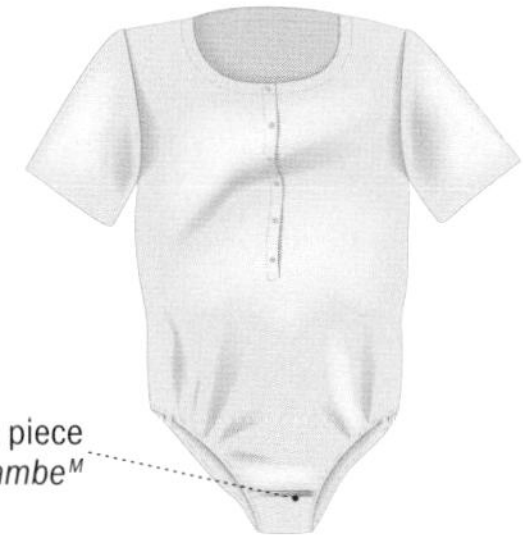

crotch piece
patte[F] *d'entrejambe*[M]

middy
***marinière*[F]**

yoke
empiècement[M]

gather
fronce[F]

shirttail
pan[M]

oversized shirt
***liquette*[F]**

classic blouse
chemisier*[M] *classique

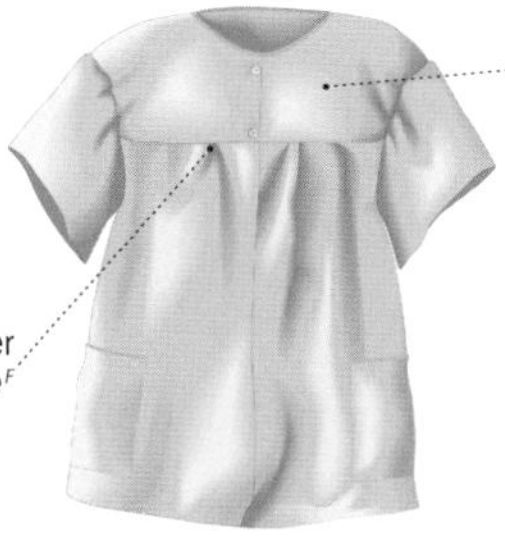

smock
***tablier*[M]*-blouse*[F]**

tunic
***tunique*[F]**

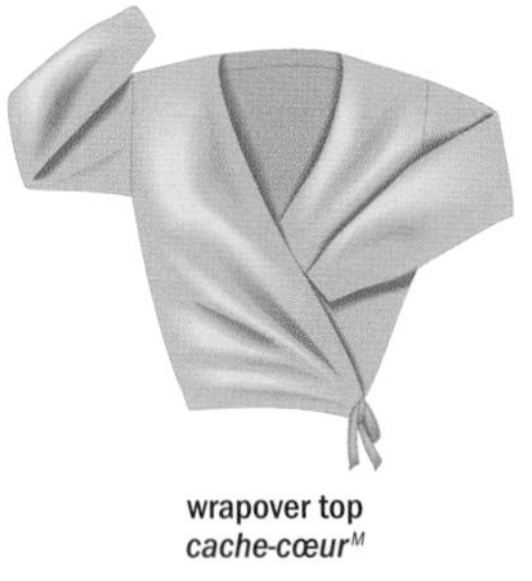

wrapover top
***cache-cœur*[M]**

polo shirt
***polo*[M]**

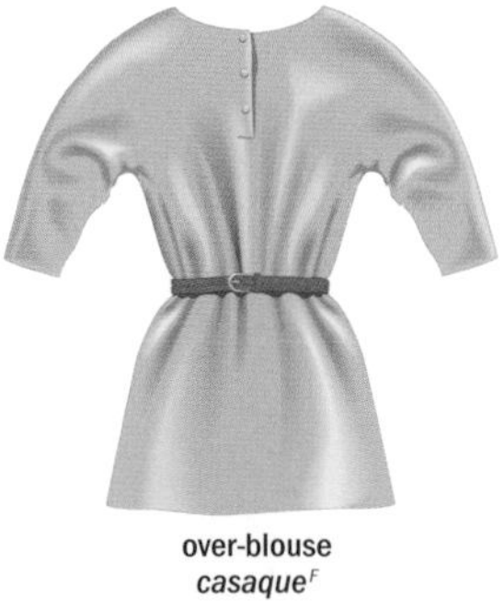

over-blouse
***casaque*[F]**

nightwear
vêtements[M] de nuit[F]

kimono
kimono[M]
nightgown
chemise[F] de nuit[F]
baby doll
nuisette[F]
pajamas
pyjama[M]
negligee
déshabillé[M]
bathrobe
peignoir[M]

hose
***bas*[M]**

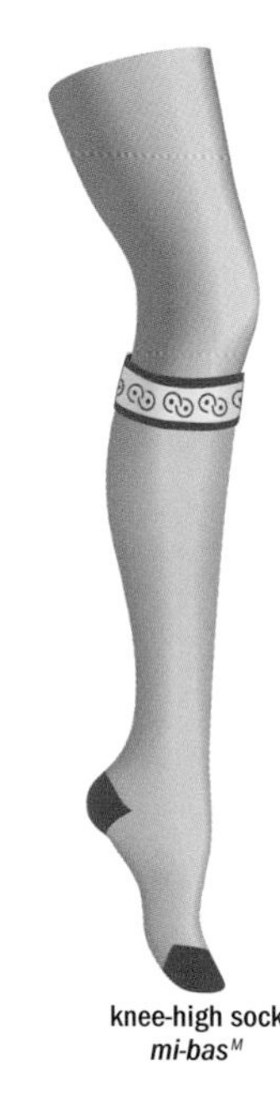

knee-high sock
mi-bas[M]

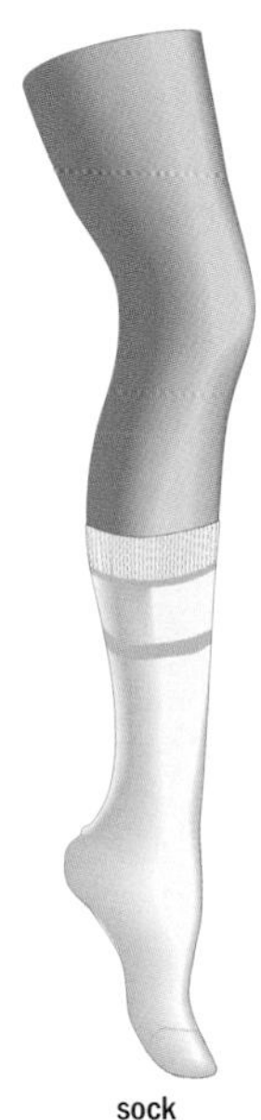

sock
chaussette[F]

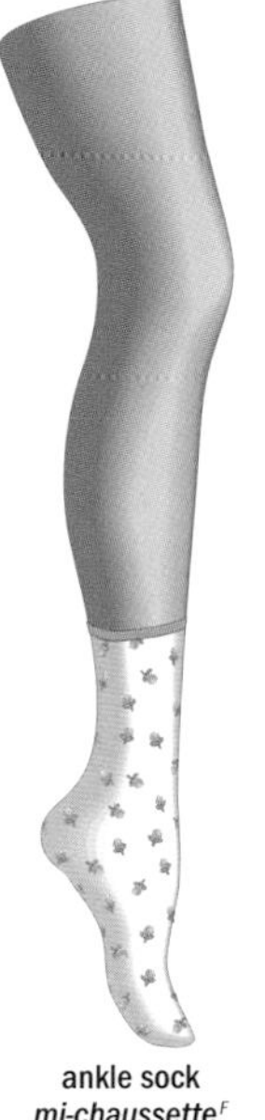

ankle sock
mi-chaussette[F]

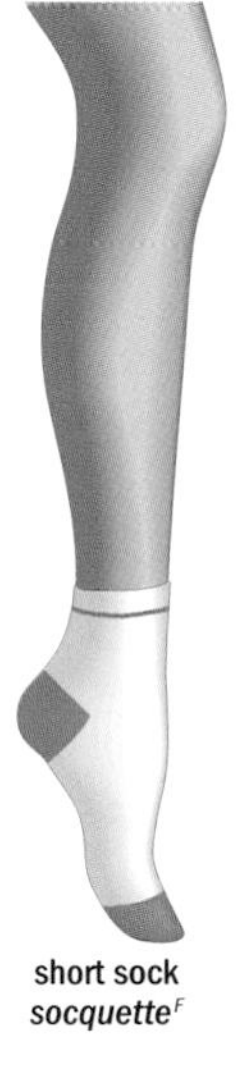

short sock
socquette[F]

panty hose
collant[M]

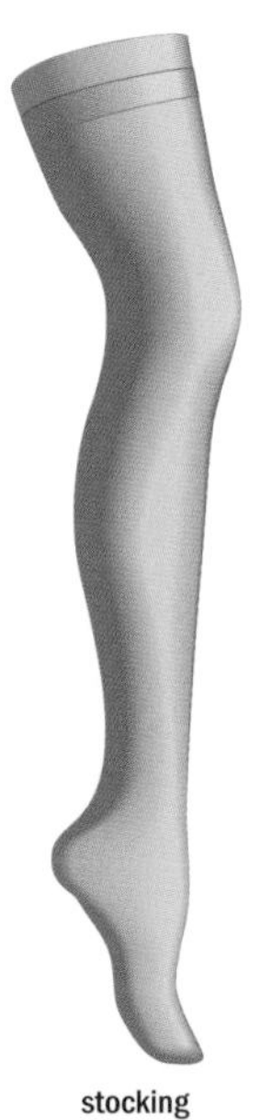

stocking
bas[M]

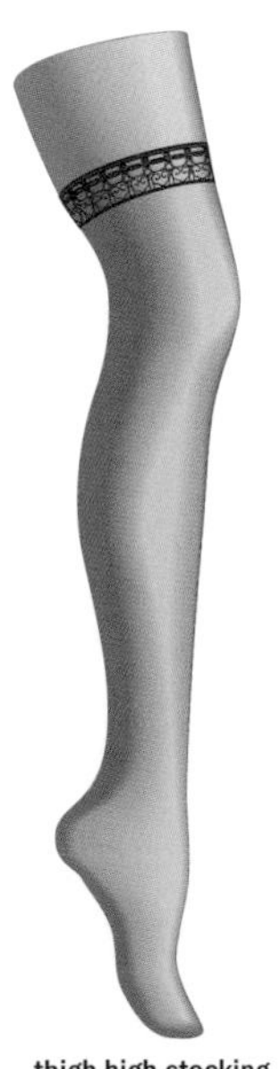

thigh-high stocking
bas[M]*-cuissarde*[F]

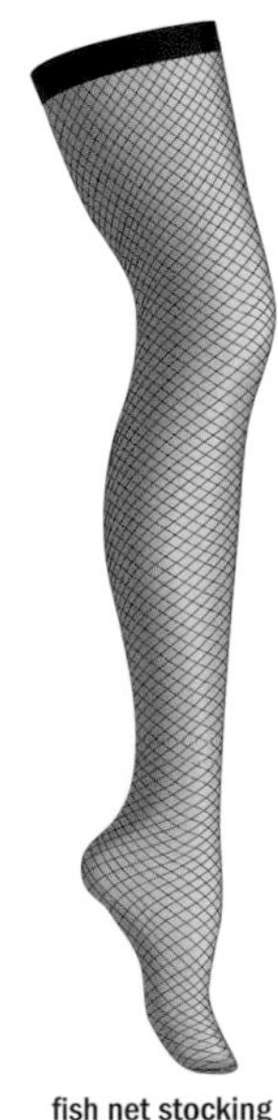

fish net stocking
bas[M] *résille*[F]

underwear
sous-vêtements [M]

corselette
combiné [M]

camisole
caraco [M] *; camisole* [F]

teddy
teddy [M] *; combinaison* [F]*-culotte* [F]

body suit
body [M] *; combiné-slip* [M]

panty corselette
combiné [M]*-culotte* [F]

half-slip
jupon [M]

princess seams
découpe [F] princesse [F]

foundation slip
fond [M] *de robe* [F]

slip
combinaison [F]*-jupon* [M]

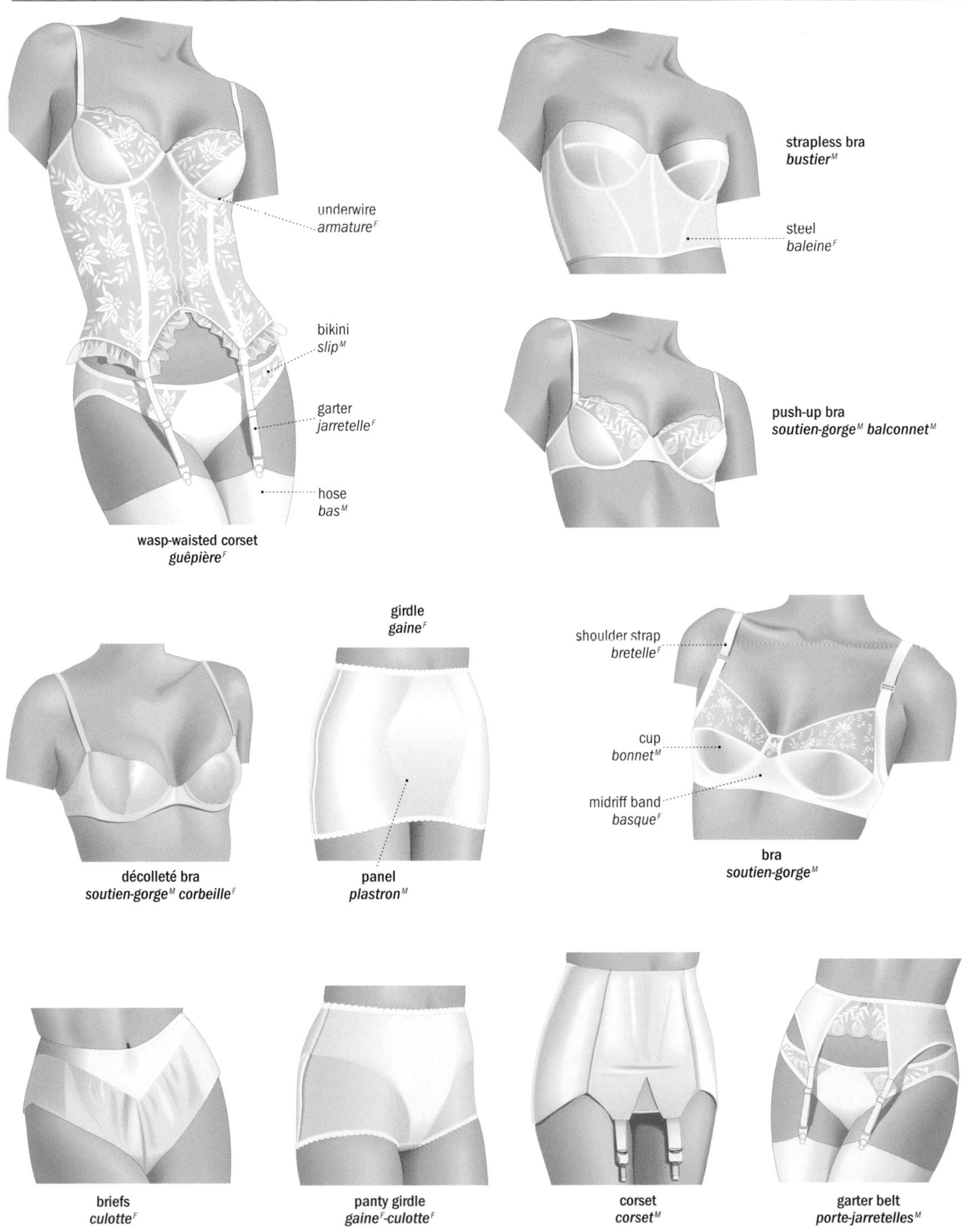
underwire
armature^F
bikini
slip^M
garter
jarretelle^F
hose
bas^M
wasp-waisted corset
guêpière^F
strapless bra
bustier^M
steel
baleine^F
push-up bra
soutien-gorge^M balconnet^M
girdle
gaine^F
shoulder strap
bretelle^F
cup
bonnet^M
midriff band
basque^F
décolleté bra
soutien-gorge^M corbeille^F
panel
plastron^M
bra
soutien-gorge^M
briefs
culotte^F
panty girdle
gaine^F-culotte^F
corset
corset^M
garter belt
porte-jarretelles^M

newborn children's clothing

vêtements[M] de nouveau-né[M]

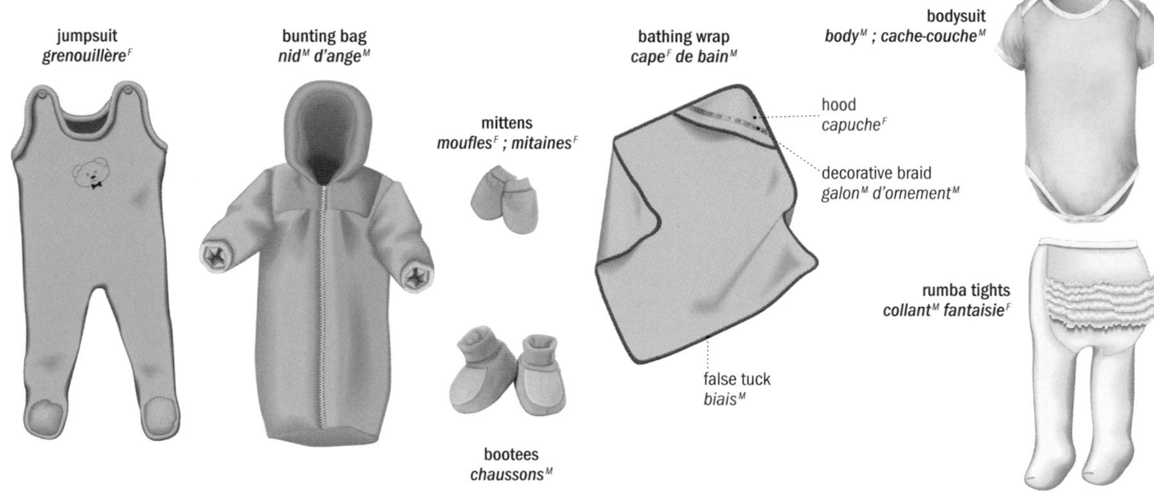
jumpsuit
grenouillère[F]
bunting bag
nid[M] d'ange[M]
mittens
moufles[F] ; mitaines[F]
bootees
chaussons[M]
bathing wrap
cape[F] de bain[M]
hood
capuche[F]
decorative braid
galon[M] d'ornement[M]
false tuck
biais[M]
bodysuit
body[M] ; cache-couche[M]
rumba tights
collant[M] fantaisie[F]

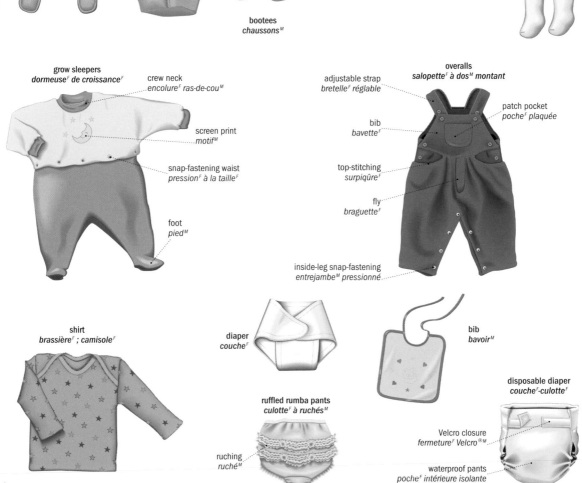

grow sleepers
dormeuse[F] de croissance[F]

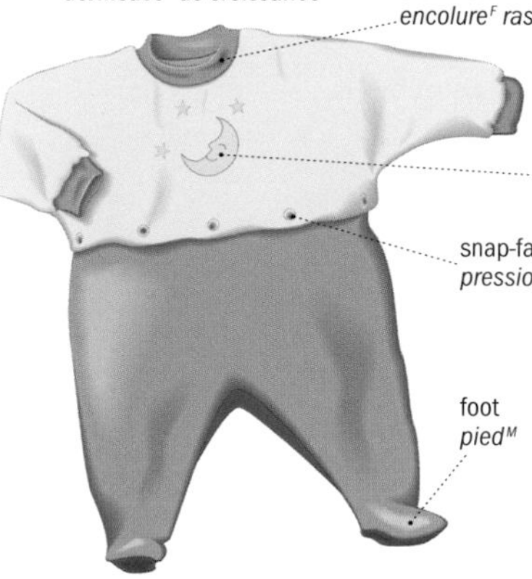

crew neck
encolure[F] ras-de-cou[M]

screen print
motif[M]

snap-fastening waist
pression[F] à la taille[F]

foot
pied[M]

overalls
salopette[F] à dos[M] montant

adjustable strap
bretelle[F] réglable

patch pocket
poche[F] plaquée

bib
bavette[F]

top-stitching
surpiqûre[F]

fly
braguette[F]

inside-leg snap-fastening
entrejambe[M] pressionné

shirt
brassière[F] ; camisole[F]

diaper
couche[F]

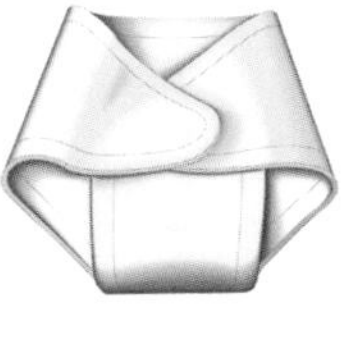

bib
bavoir[M]

ruffled rumba pants
culotte[F] à ruchés[M]

ruching
ruché[M]

disposable diaper
couche[F]-culotte[F]

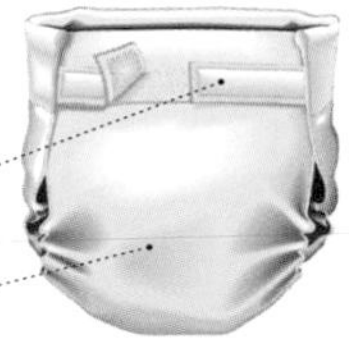

Velcro closure
fermeture[F] Velcro®[M]

waterproof pants
poche[F] intérieure isolante

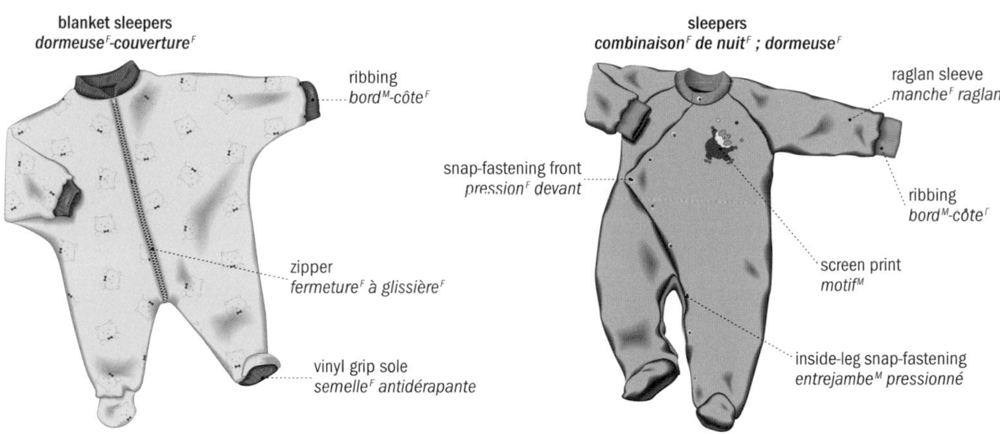
blanket sleepers
dormeuse[F]-couverture[F]
ribbing
bord[M]-côte[F]
zipper
fermeture[F] à glissière[F]
vinyl grip sole
semelle[F] antidérapante
sleepers
combinaison[F] de nuit[F] ; dormeuse[F]
raglan sleeve
manche[F] raglan
snap-fastening front
pression[F] devant
ribbing
bord[M]-côte[F]
screen print
motif[M]
inside-leg snap-fastening
entrejambe[M] pressionné

children's clothing

vêtements[M] d'enfant[M]

overalls
salopette[F] à bretelles[F] croisées

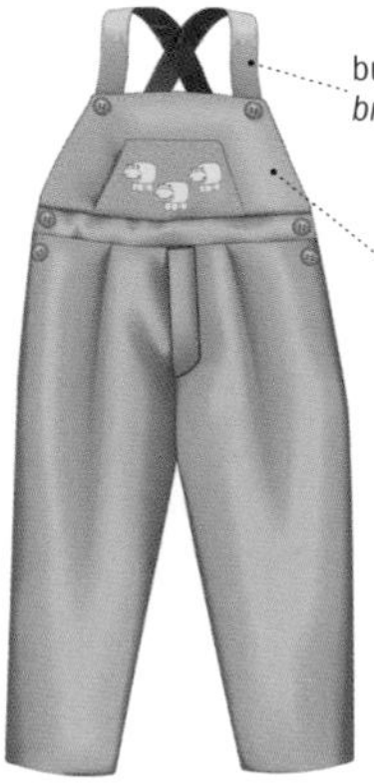

button strap
bretelle[F] boutonnée

bib
bavette[F]

snowsuit
habit[M] de neige[F]

hood
capuchon[M]

overalls
salopette[F]

pajamas
polojama[M]

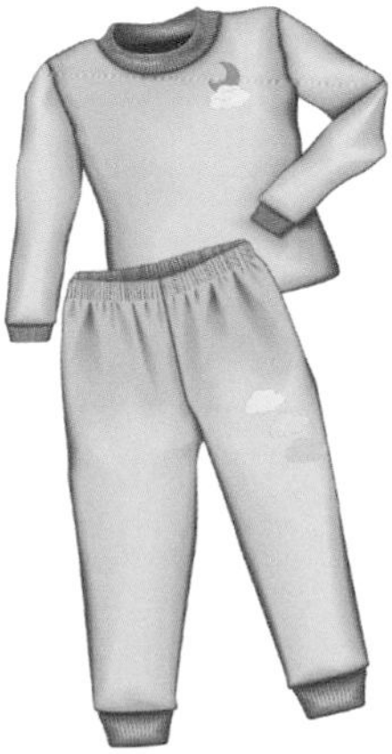

T-shirt dress
robe[F] tee-shirt[M]

rompers
barboteuse[F]

training set
tenue[F] d'exercice[M]

tank top
débardeur[M]

shorts
short[M]

jumpsuit
combinaison[F]

sportswear

tenue[F] d'exercice[M]

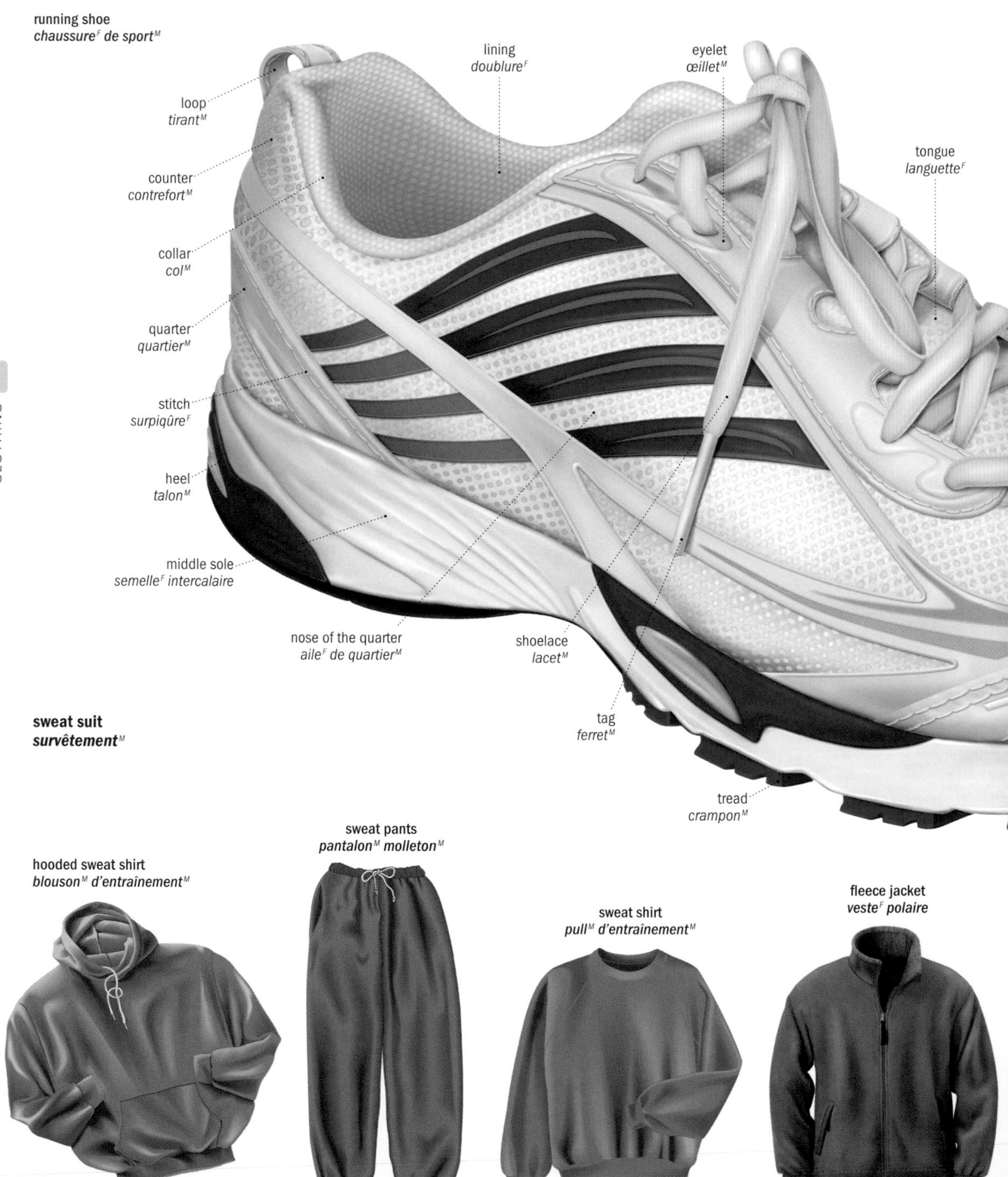
running shoe
chaussure[F] de sport[M]
loop
tirant[M]
counter
contrefort[M]
collar
col[M]
quarter
quartier[M]
stitch
surpiqûre[F]
heel
talon[M]
middle sole
semelle[F] intercalaire
nose of the quarter
aile[F] de quartier[M]
shoelace
lacet[M]
lining
doublure[F]
eyelet
œillet[M]
tongue
languette[F]
tag
ferret[M]
tread
crampon[M]
sweat suit
survêtement[M]
hooded sweat shirt
blouson[M] d'entraînement[M]
sweat pants
pantalon[M] molleton[M]
sweat shirt
pull[M] d'entraînement[M]
fleece jacket
veste[F] polaire

swimming trunks
slip[M] de bain[M]

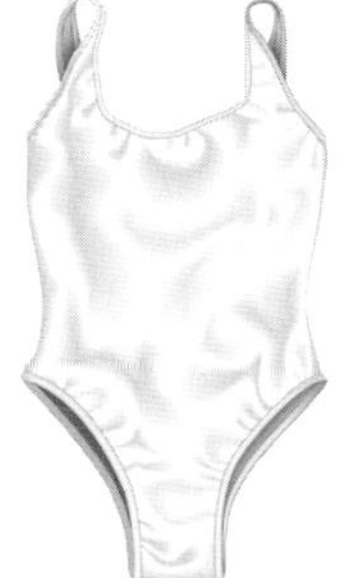

swimsuit
maillot[M] de bain[M]

exercise wear
vêtements[M] d'exercice[M]

footless tights
collant[M] sans pieds[M]

leotard
justaucorps[M]

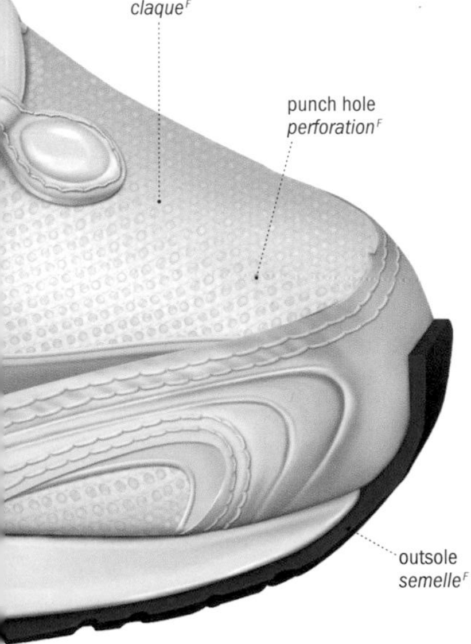
vamp
claque[F]
punch hole
perforation[F]
outsole
semelle[F] d'usure[F]

tank top
débardeur[M]

T-shirt
T-shirt[M]

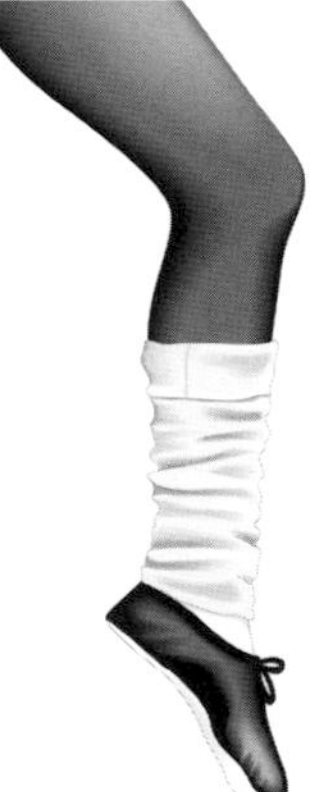

leg-warmer
jambière[F]

pants
pantalon[M]

anorak
anorak[M]

boxer shorts
short[M] boxeur[M]

shorts
cuissard[M]

jewelry

bijouterie^F

earrings
boucles^F d'oreille^F

clip earrings
boucles^F d'oreille^F à pince^F

screw earring
boucles^F d'oreille^F à vis^F

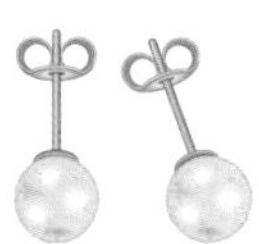

pierced earrings
boucles^F d'oreille^F à tige^F

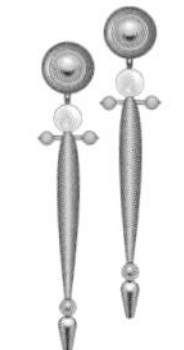

drop earrings
pendants^M d'oreille^F

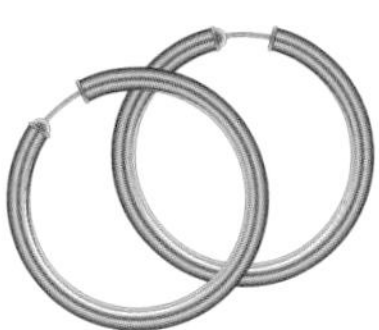

hoop earrings
anneaux^M

necklaces
colliers^M

matinee-length necklace
collier^M de perles^F, longueur^F matinée^F

velvet-band choker
collier^M-de-chien^M

pendant
pendentif^M

rope necklace
sautoir^M

opera-length necklace
sautoir^M, longueur^F opéra^M

bib necklace
collier^M de soirée^F

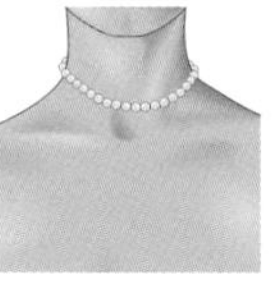

choker
ras-de-cou^M

locket
médaillon^M

bracelets
bracelets^M

identification bracelet
gourmette^F d'identité^F

bangle
bracelet^M tubulaire

charm bracelet
gourmette^F

rings
bagues^F

band ring
jonc^M

signet ring
chevalière^F

solitaire ring
bague^F solitaire^M

engagement ring
bague^F de fiançailles^F

wedding ring
alliance^F

nail care

manucure[F]

manicure set
trousse[F] de manucure[F]

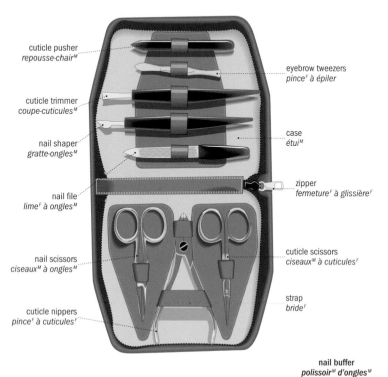

cuticle pusher
repousse-chair[M]

eyebrow tweezers
pince[F] à épiler

cuticle trimmer
coupe-cuticules[M]

nail shaper
gratte-ongles[M]

case
étui[M]

nail file
lime[F] à ongles[M]

zipper
fermeture[F] à glissière[F]

nail scissors
ciseaux[M] à ongles[M]

cuticle scissors
ciseaux[M] à cuticules[F]

cuticle nippers
pince[F] à cuticules[F]

strap
bride[F]

nail enamel
vernis[M] à ongles[M]

safety scissors
ciseaux[M] de sûreté[F]

nail buffer
polissoir[M] d'ongles[M]

chamois leather
peau[F] de chamois[M]

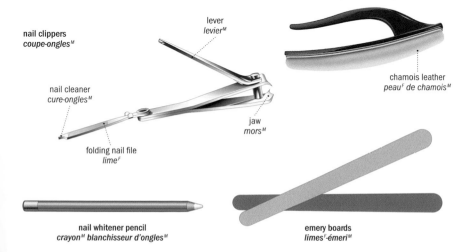

nail clippers
coupe-ongles[M]

lever
levier[M]

nail cleaner
cure-ongles[M]

jaw
mors[M]

folding nail file
lime[F]

nail whitener pencil
crayon[M] blanchisseur d'ongles[M]

emery boards
limes[F]-émeri[M]

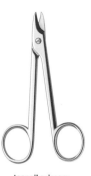

toenail scissors
ciseaux[M] de pédicure[F]

makeup

maquillage[M]

facial makeup
maquillage[M]

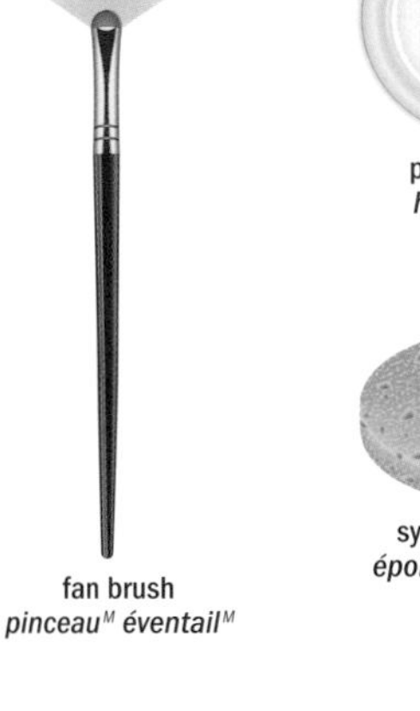

fan brush
pinceau[M] éventail[M]

powder puff
houppette[F]

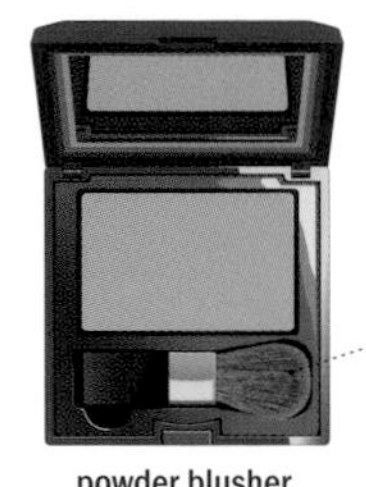
blusher brush
pinceau[M] pour fard[M] à joues[F]

powder blusher
fard[M] à joues[F] en poudre[F]

compact
poudrier[M]

pressed powder
poudre[F] pressée

synthetic sponge
éponge[F] synthétique

loose powder
poudre[F] libre

loose powder brush
pinceau[M] pour poudre[F] libre

liquid foundation
fond[M] de teint[M] liquide

eye makeup
maquillage[M] des yeux[M]

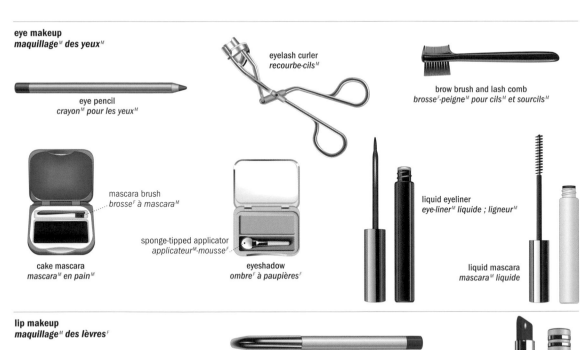

eye pencil
crayon[M] pour les yeux[M]

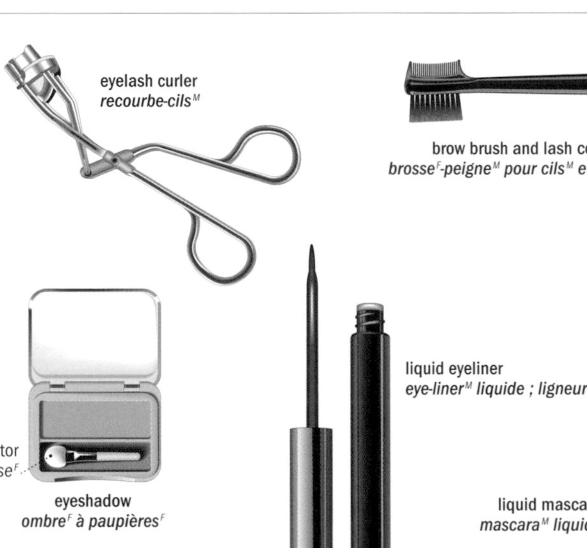

eyelash curler
recourbe-cils[M]

brow brush and lash comb
brosse[F]-peigne[M] pour cils[M] et sourcils[M]

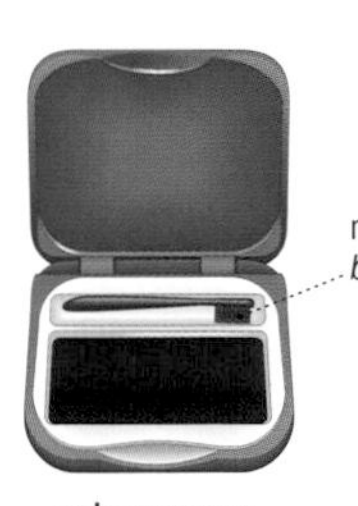
mascara brush
brosse[F] à mascara[M]

cake mascara
mascara[M] en pain[M]

sponge-tipped applicator
applicateur[M]-mousse[F]

eyeshadow
ombre[F] à paupières[F]

liquid eyeliner
eye-liner[M] liquide ; ligneur[M]

liquid mascara
mascara[M] liquide

lip makeup
maquillage[M] des lèvres[F]

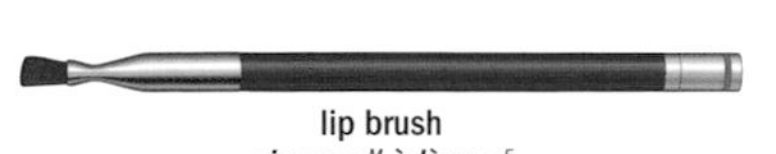

lip brush
pinceau[M] à lèvres[F]

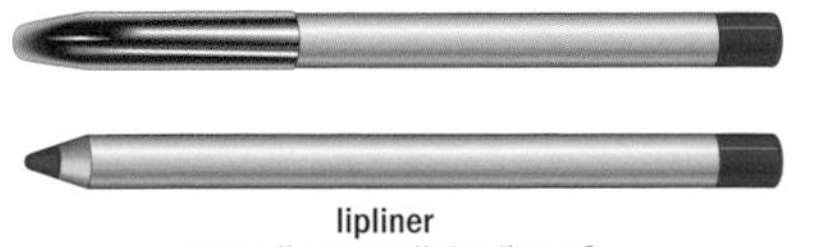

lipliner
crayon[M] contour[M] des lèvres[F]

lipstick
rouge[M] à lèvres[F]

body care

soins[M] du corps[M]

stopper
bouchon[M]
bottle
flacon[M]

toilet soap
savon[M] de toilette[F]

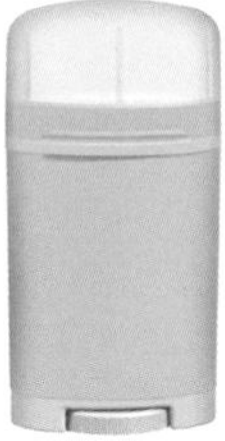

eau de parfum
eau[F] de parfum[M]

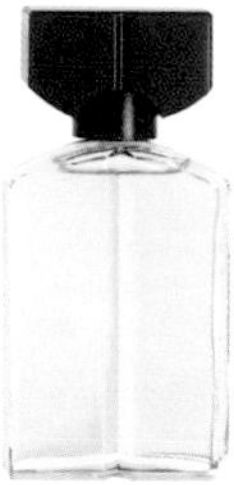

hair conditioner
revitalisant[M] capillaire

shampoo
shampooing[M]

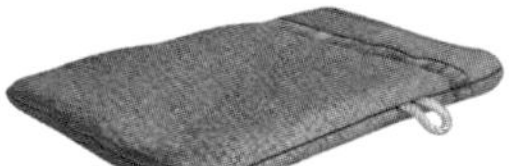

haircolor
colorant[M] capillaire

deodorant
déodorant[M]

eau de toilette
eau[F] de toilette[F]

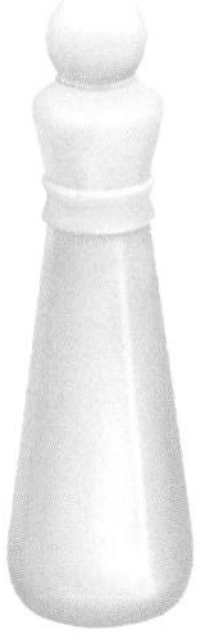

bubble bath
bain[M] moussant

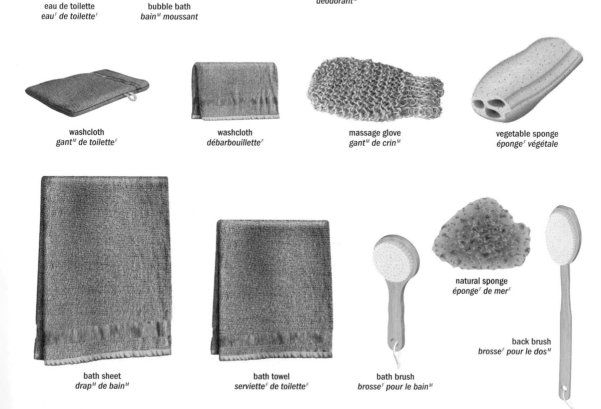

washcloth
gant[M] de toilette[F]

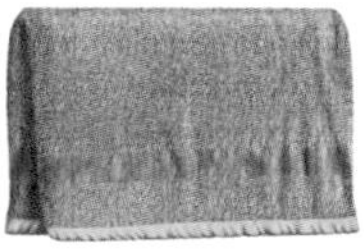

washcloth
débarbouillette[F]

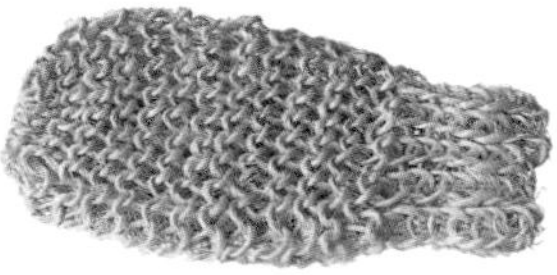

massage glove
gant[M] de crin[M]

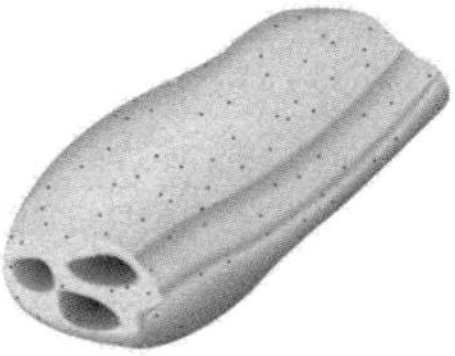

vegetable sponge
éponge[F] végétale

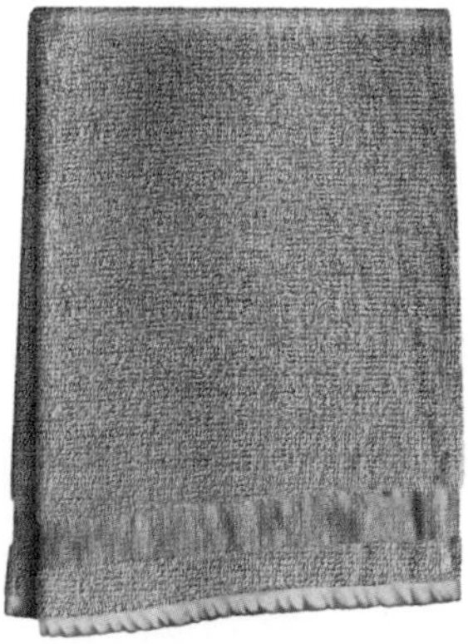

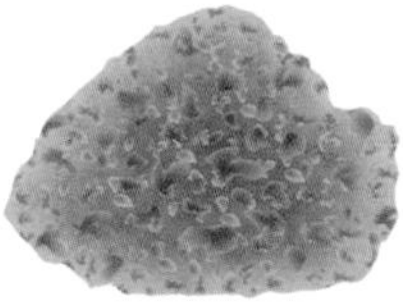

natural sponge
éponge[F] de mer[F]

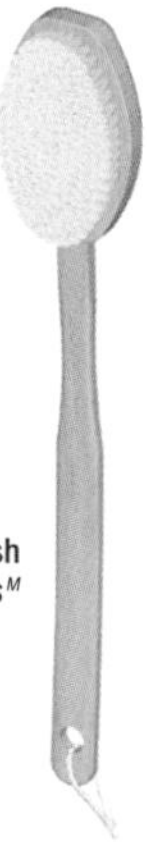

back brush
brosse[F] pour le dos[M]

bath sheet
drap[M] de bain[M]

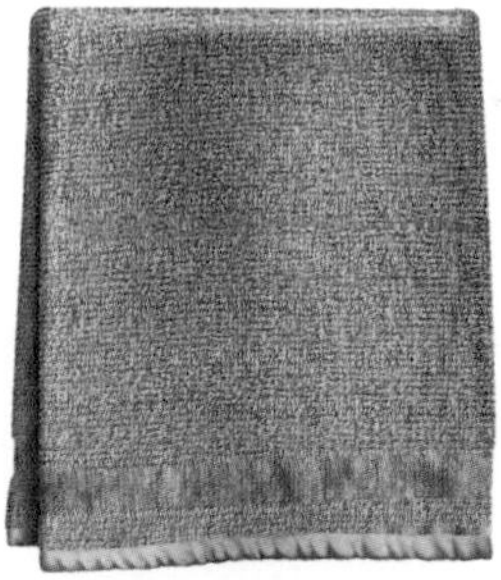

bath towel
serviette[F] de toilette[F]

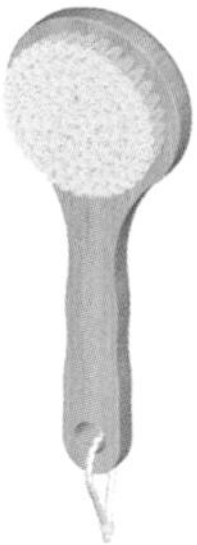

bath brush
brosse[F] pour le bain[M]

hairdressing

coiffure[F]

hairbrushes
brosses[F] à cheveux[M]

flat-back brush
brosse[F] pneumatique

round brush
brosse[F] ronde

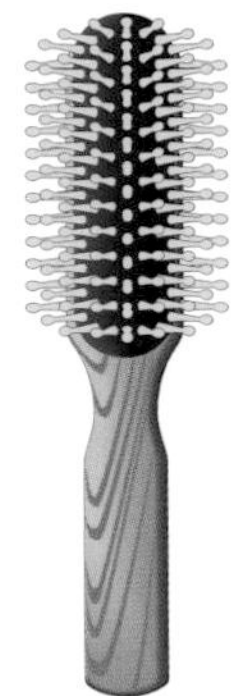
quill brush
brosse[F] anglaise

vent brush
brosse[F]-araignée[F]

combs
peignes[M]

Afro pick
peigne[M] afro

teaser comb
peigne[M] à crêper

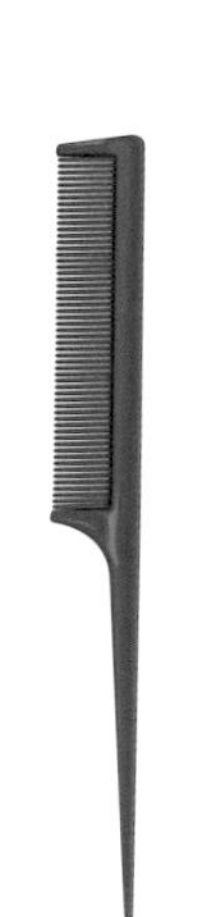
tail comb
peigne[M] à tige[F]

barber comb
peigne[M] de coiffeur[M]

pitchfork comb
combiné[M] 2 dans 1

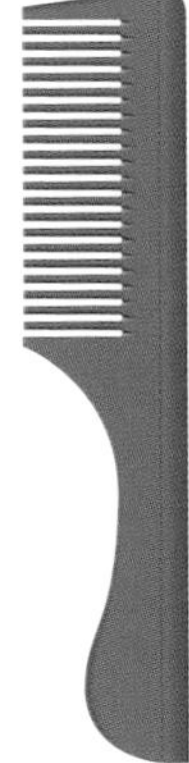
rake comb
démêloir[M]

hair roller
bigoudi[M]

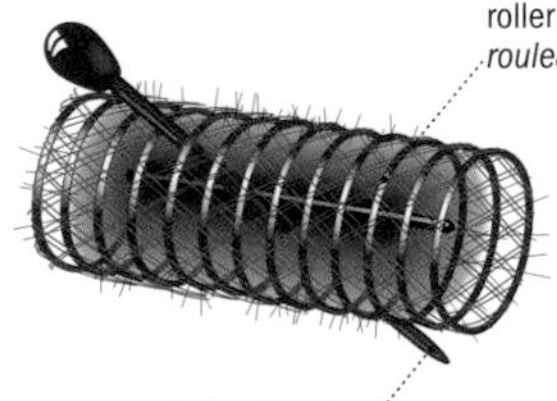
roller
rouleau[M]
hair roller pin
épingle[F] à bigoudi[M]

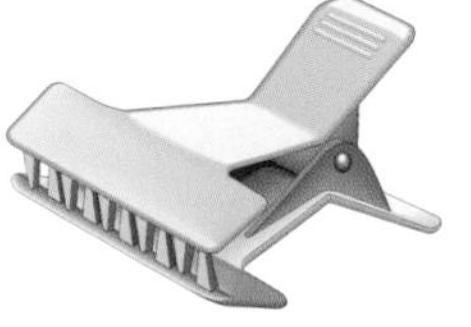
wave clip
pince[F] à boucles[F] de cheveux[M]

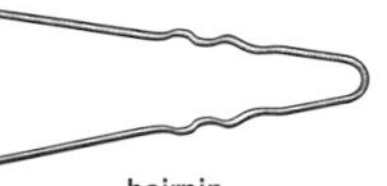
hairpin
épingle[F] à cheveux[M]

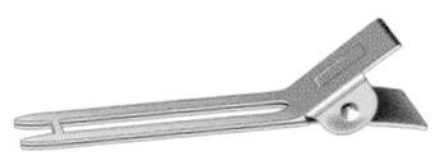
hair clip
pince[F] de mise[F] en plis[M]

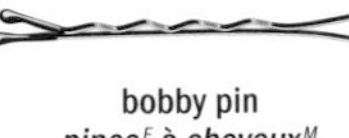
bobby pin
pince[F] à cheveux[M]

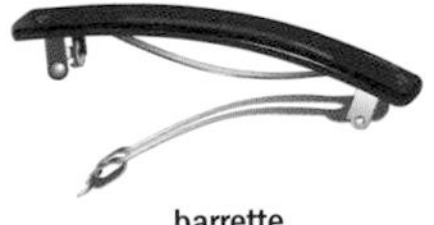
barrette
barrette[F]

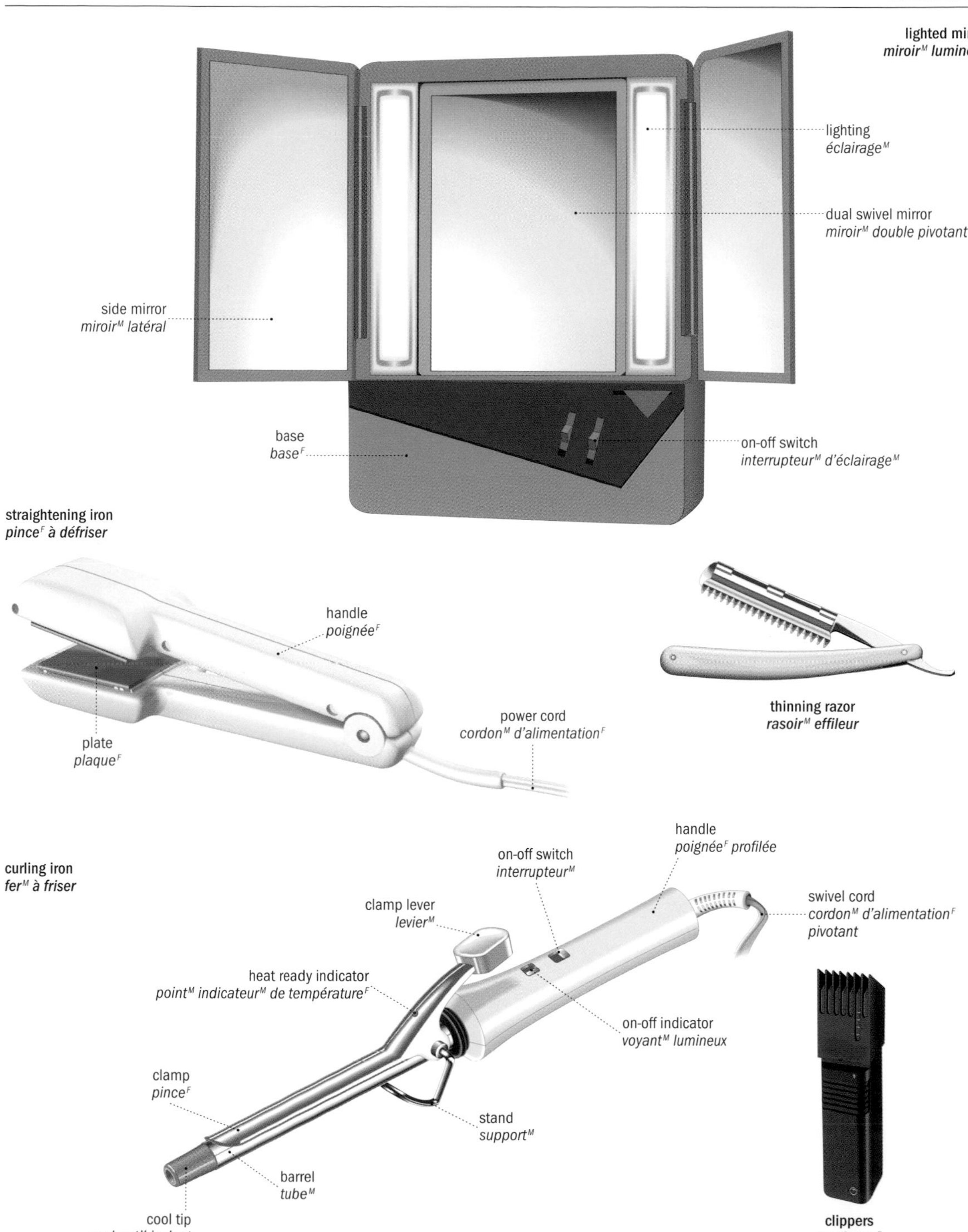
lighted mirror
miroir[M] lumineux
lighting
éclairage[M]
dual swivel mirror
miroir[M] double pivotant
side mirror
miroir[M] latéral
base
base[F]
on-off switch
interrupteur[M] d'éclairage[M]
straightening iron
pince[F] à défriser
handle
poignée[F]
plate
plaque[F]
power cord
cordon[M] d'alimentation[F]
thinning razor
rasoir[M] effileur
curling iron
fer[M] à friser
handle
poignée[F] profilée
on-off switch
interrupteur[M]
clamp lever
levier[M]
swivel cord
cordon[M] d'alimentation[F] pivotant
heat ready indicator
point[M] indicateur[M] de température[F]
on-off indicator
voyant[M] lumineux
clamp
pince[F]
stand
support[M]
barrel
tube[M]
cool tip
embout[M] isolant
clippers
tondeuse[F]

hairdressing

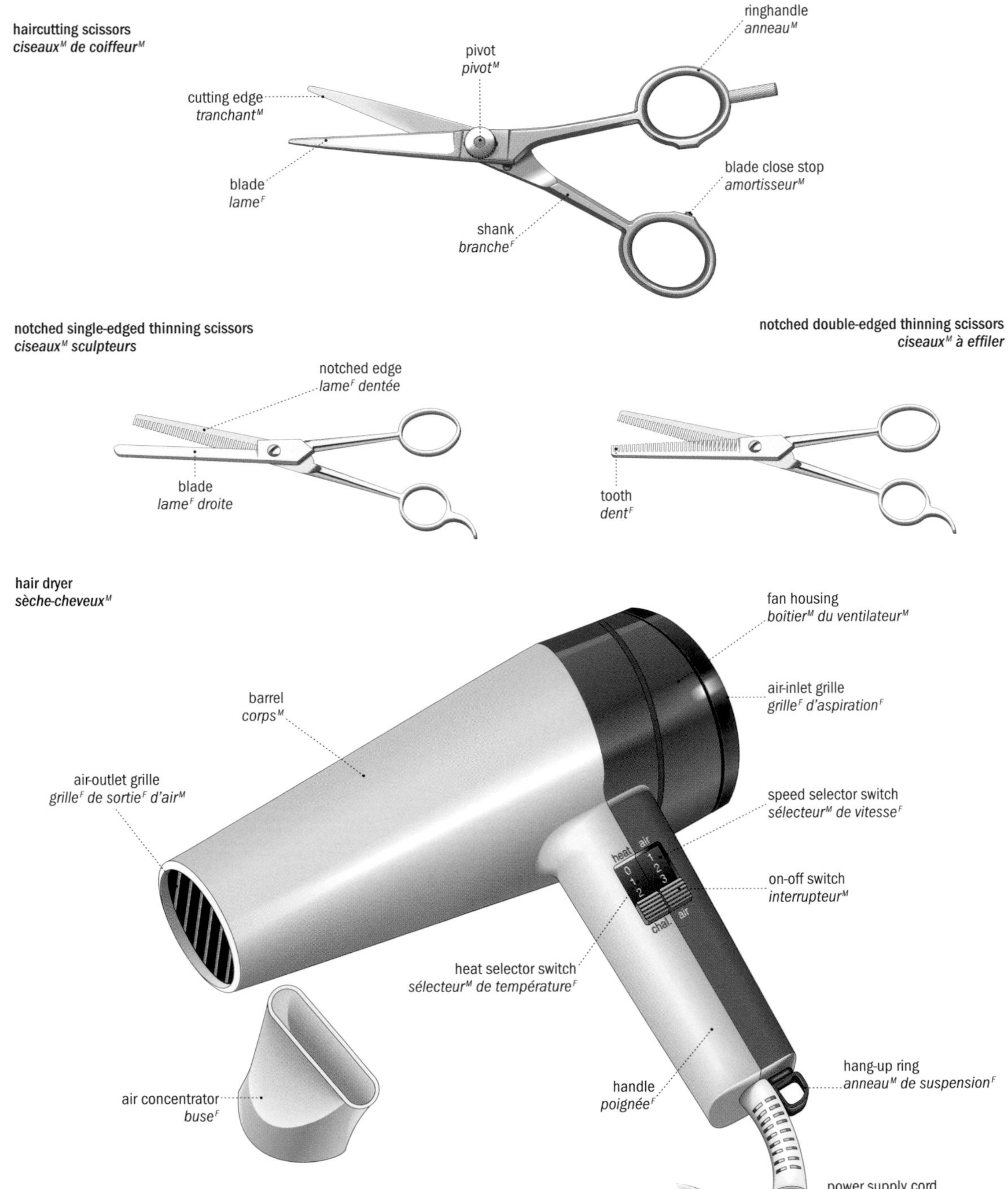
haircutting scissors
ciseaux^M de coiffeur^M
ringhandle
anneau^M
pivot
pivot^M
cutting edge
tranchant^M
blade close stop
amortisseur^M
blade
lame^F
shank
branche^F
notched single-edged thinning scissors
ciseaux^M sculpteurs
notched double-edged thinning scissors
ciseaux^M à effiler
notched edge
lame^F dentée
blade
lame^F droite
tooth
dent^F
hair dryer
sèche-cheveux^M
fan housing
boîtier^M du ventilateur^M
air-inlet grille
grille^F d'aspiration^F
barrel
corps^M
air-outlet grille
grille^F de sortie^F d'air^M
speed selector switch
sélecteur^M de vitesse^F
heat
air
0
1
2
1
2
3
chal.
air
on-off switch
interrupteur^M
heat selector switch
sélecteur^M de température^F
hang-up ring
anneau^M de suspension^F
handle
poignée^F
air concentrator
buse^F
power supply cord
cordon^M d'alimentation^F

shaving

rasage[M]

shaving foam
mousse[F] à raser

power cord
cordon[M] d'alimentation[F]

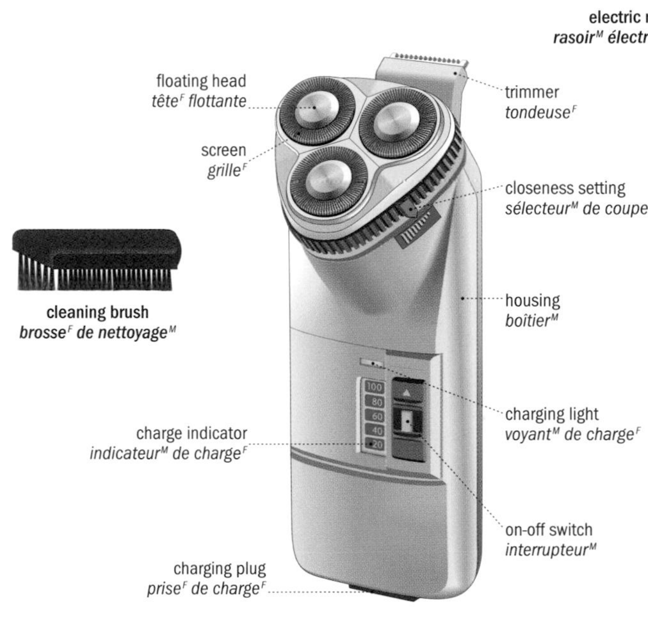
electric razor
rasoir[M] électrique
floating head
tête[F] flottante
screen
grille[F]
trimmer
tondeuse[F]
closeness setting
sélecteur[M] de coupe[F]
housing
boîtier[M]
charging light
voyant[M] de charge[F]
charge indicator
indicateur[M] de charge[F]
on-off switch
interrupteur[M]
charging plug
prise[F] de charge[F]

cleaning brush
brosse[F] de nettoyage[M]

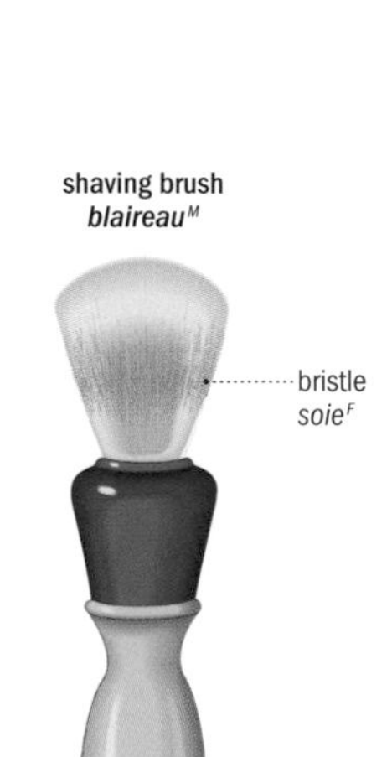
bristle
soie[F]

shaving brush
blaireau[M]

plug adapter
adaptateur[M] de fiche[F]

aftershave
après-rasage[M]

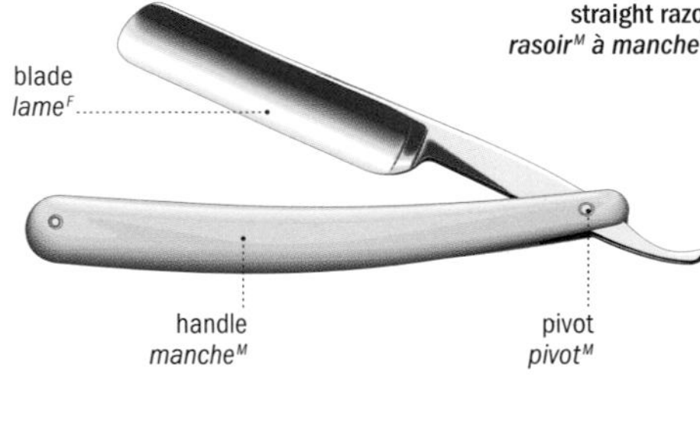
blade
lame[F]
handle
manche[M]
pivot
pivot[M]

straight razor
rasoir[M] à manche[M]

shaving mug
bol[M] à raser

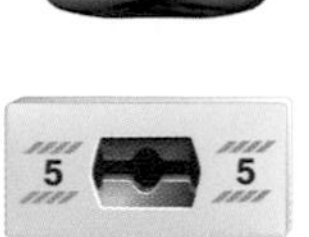

blade injector
distributeur[M] de lames[F]

double-edged blade
lame[F] à double tranchant[M]

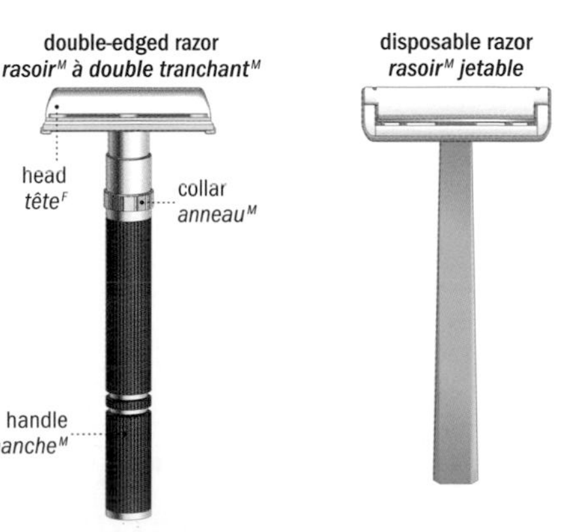
head
tête[F]
collar
anneau[M]
handle
manche[M]

double-edged razor
rasoir[M] à double tranchant[M]

disposable razor
rasoir[M] jetable

dental care

hygiène[F] dentaire

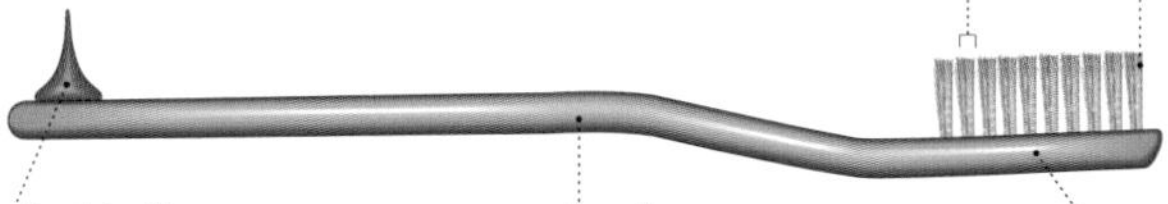

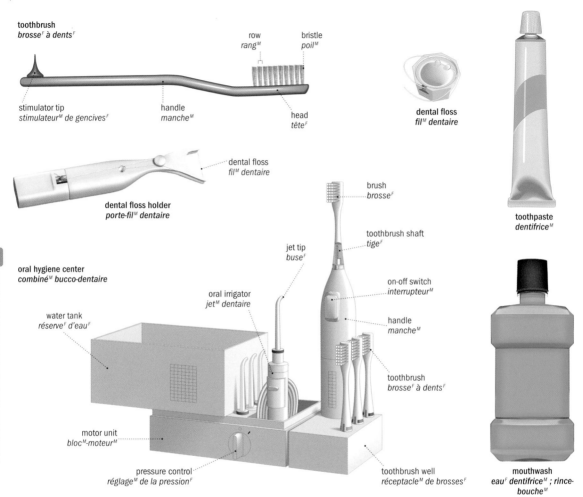

toothbrush
brosse[F] à dents[F]

row
rang[M]

bristle
poil[M]

stimulator tip
stimulateur[M] de gencives[F]

handle
manche[M]

head
tête[F]

dental floss
fil[M] dentaire

dental floss
fil[M] dentaire

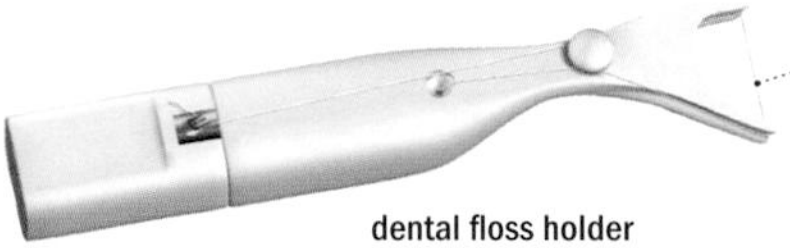

dental floss holder
porte-fil[M] dentaire

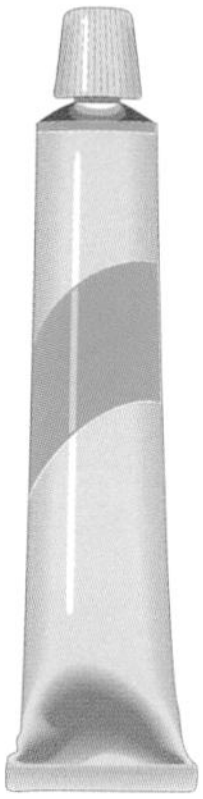

toothpaste
dentifrice[M]

oral hygiene center
combiné[M] bucco-dentaire

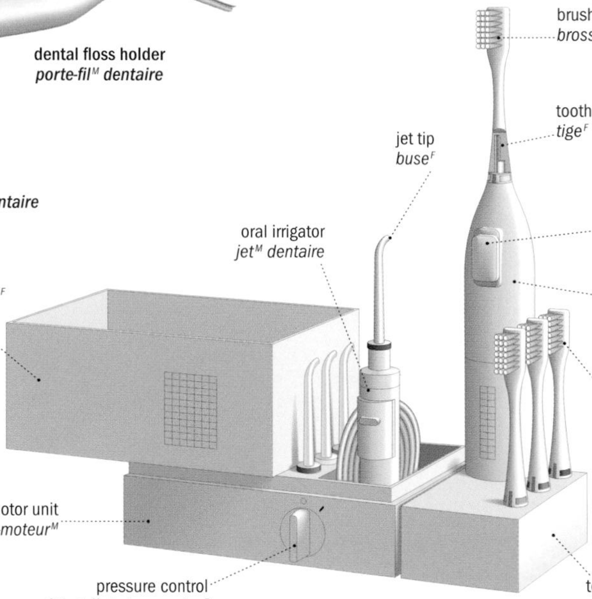

brush
brosse[F]

toothbrush shaft
tige[F]

jet tip
buse[F]

on-off switch
interrupteur[M]

oral irrigator
jet[M] dentaire

water tank
réserve[F] d'eau[F]

handle
manche[M]

toothbrush
brosse[F] à dents[F]

motor unit
bloc[M]-moteur[M]

pressure control
réglage[M] de la pression[F]

toothbrush well
réceptacle[M] de brosses[F]

mouthwash
eau[F] dentifrice[M] ; rince-bouche[M]

contact lenses

lentilles[F] de contact[M]

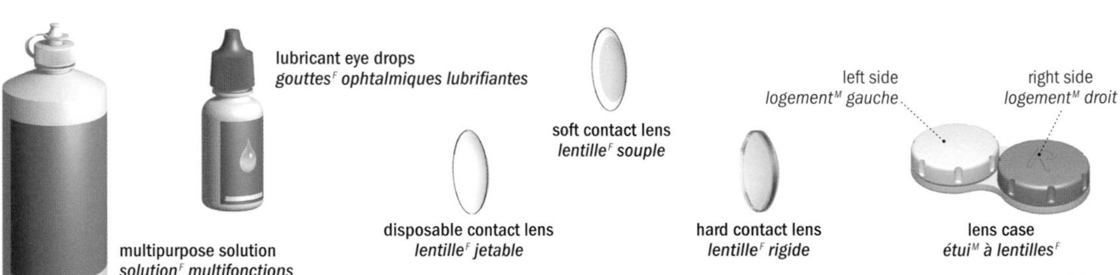

lubricant eye drops
gouttes[F] ophtalmiques lubrifiantes
soft contact lens
lentille[F] souple
left side
logement[M] gauche
right side
logement[M] droit
multipurpose solution
solution[F] multifonctions
disposable contact lens
lentille[F] jetable
hard contact lens
lentille[F] rigide
lens case
étui[M] à lentilles[F]

eyeglasses

lunettes^F

eyeglasses parts
parties^F des lunettes^F

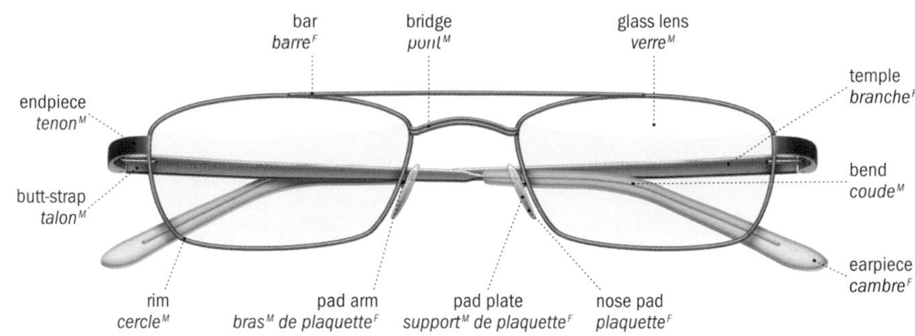
bar
barre^F
bridge
pont^M
glass lens
verre^M
temple
branche^F
endpiece
tenon^M
bend
coude^M
butt-strap
talon^M
earpiece
cambre^F
rim
cercle^M
pad arm
bras^M de plaquette^F
pad plate
support^M de plaquette^F
nose pad
plaquette^F

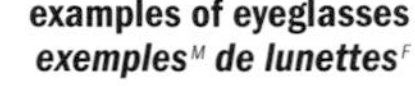

examples of eyeglasses
exemples^M de lunettes^F

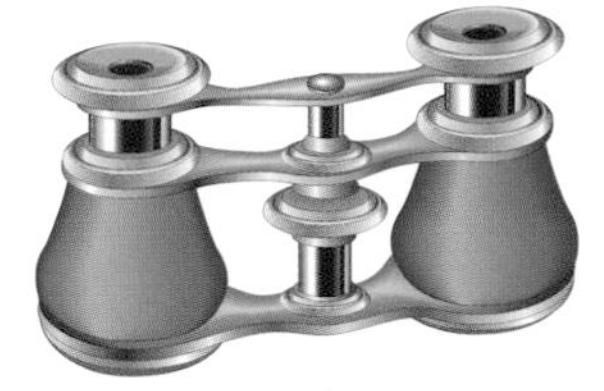

opera glasses
lorgnette^F

sunglasses
lunettes^F de soleil^M

half-glasses
demi-lune^F

umbrellas and stick

parapluies^M et canne^F

umbrellas
parapluies^M

umbrella stand
porte-parapluies^M

walking stick
canne^F

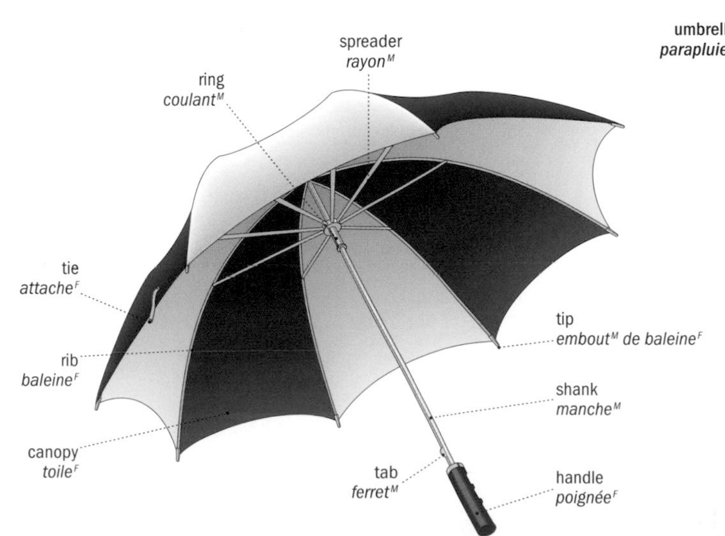
spreader
rayon^M
ring
coulant^M
tie
attache^F
tip
embout^M de baleine^F
rib
baleine^F
shank
manche^M
canopy
toile^F
tab
ferret^M
handle
poignée^F

PERSONAL ADORNMENT AND ARTICLES

leather goods

articles^M de maroquinerie^F

attaché case
mallette^F porte-documents^M

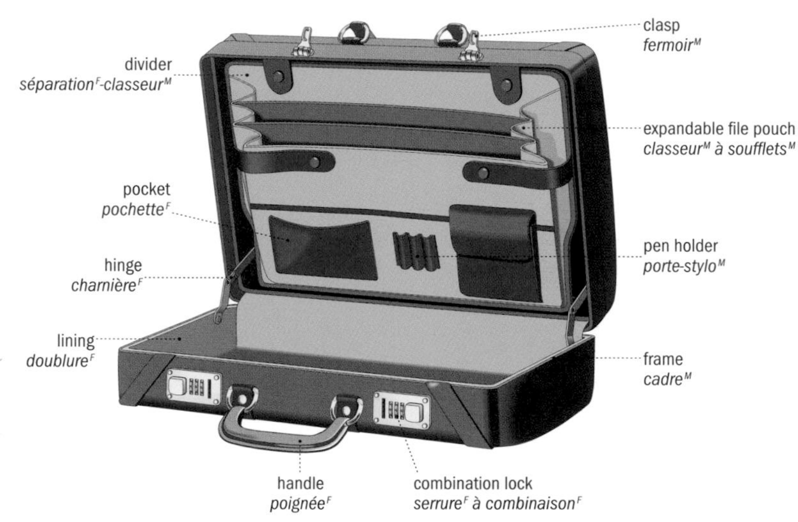

divider
séparation^F-classeur^M
clasp
fermoir^M
expandable file pouch
classeur^M à soufflets^M
pocket
pochette^F
hinge
charnière^F
pen holder
porte-stylo^M
lining
doublure^F
frame
cadre^M
handle
poignée^F
combination lock
serrure^F à combinaison^F

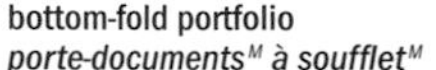

bottom-fold portfolio
porte-documents^M à soufflet^M

briefcase
serviette^F

retractable handle
poignée^F rentrante
exterior pocket
poche^F extérieure
tab
patte^F
key lock
serrure^F à clé^F
gusset
soufflet^M

checkbook/secretary clutch
portefeuille^M chéquier^M

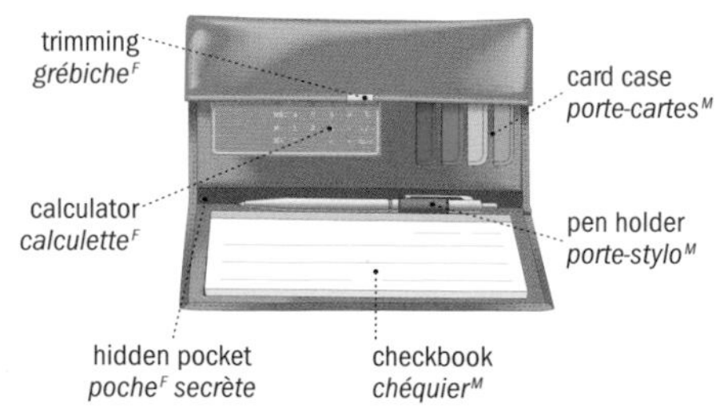

trimming
grébiche^F
card case
porte-cartes^M
calculator
calculette^F
pen holder
porte-stylo^M
hidden pocket
poche^F secrète
checkbook
chéquier^M

card case
porte-cartes^M

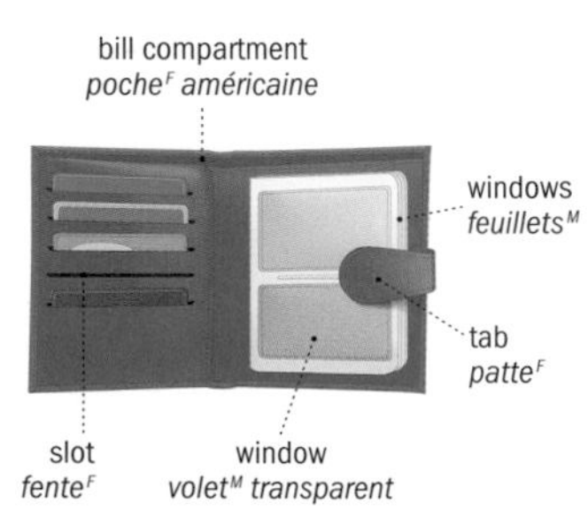

bill compartment
poche^F américaine
windows
feuillets^M
tab
patte^F
slot
fente^F
window
volet^M transparent

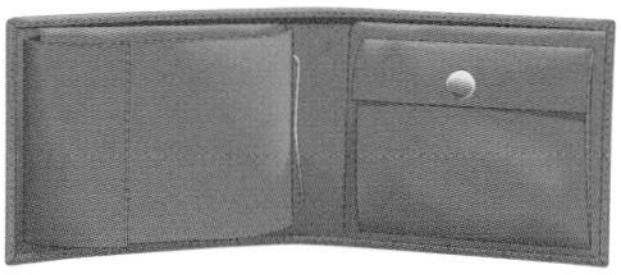

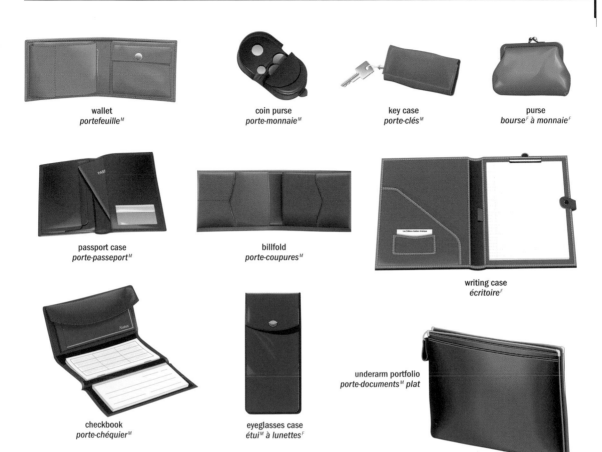

wallet
portefeuille[M]

coin purse
porte-monnaie[M]

key case
porte-clés[M]

purse
bourse[F] *à monnaie*[F]

passport case
porte-passeport[M]

billfold
porte-coupures[M]

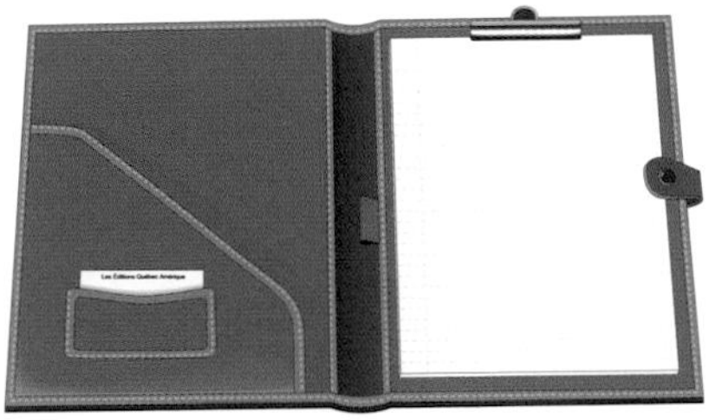

writing case
écritoire[F]

checkbook
porte-chéquier[M]

eyeglasses case
étui[M] *à lunettes*[F]

underarm portfolio
porte-documents[M] *plat*

handbags

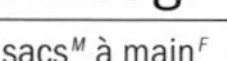

sacs[M] à main[F]

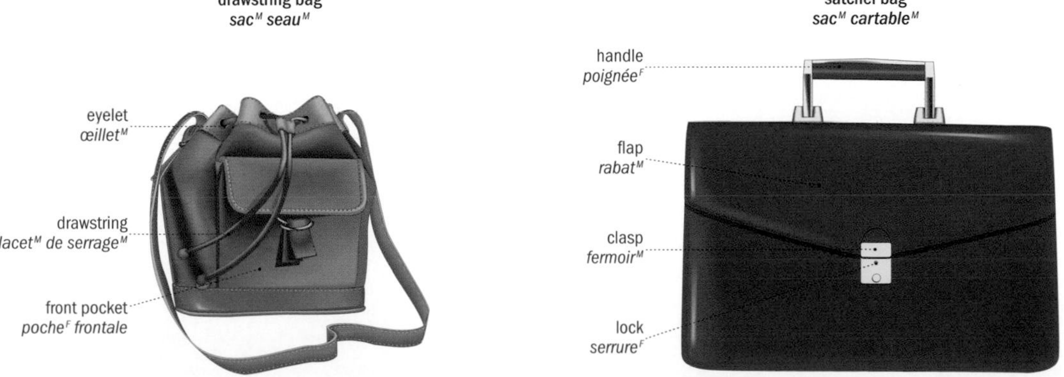
drawstring bag
sac[M] seau[M]
eyelet
œillet[M]
drawstring
lacet[M] de serrage[M]
front pocket
poche[F] frontale
satchel bag
sac[M] cartable[M]
handle
poignée[F]
flap
rabat[M]
clasp
fermoir[M]
lock
serrure[F]

handbags

box bag
sac[M] boîte[F]

drawstring bag
balluchon[M]

shoulder bag
sac[M] à bandoulière[F]

buckle
boucle[F]

shoulder strap
bandoulière[F]

muff
manchon[M]

hobo bag
sac[M] besace[F]

accordion bag
sac[M] accordéon[M]

gusset
soufflet[M]

tote bag
sac[M] fourre-tout[M]

men's bag
pochette[F] d'homme[M]

sea bag
sac[M] marin[M]

duffel bag
sac[M] polochon[M]

carrier bag
sac[M] à provisions[F]

shopping bag
cabas[M]

luggage

bagages[M]

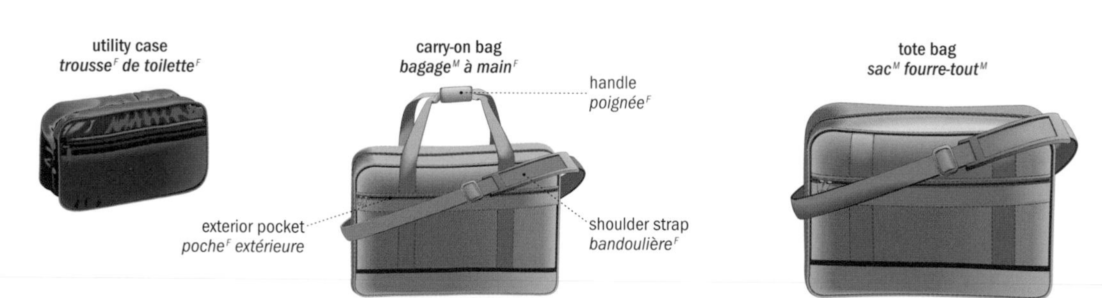
utility case
trousse[F] de toilette[F]
carry-on bag
bagage[M] à main[F]
handle
poignée[F]
exterior pocket
poche[F] extérieure
shoulder strap
bandoulière[F]
tote bag
sac[M] fourre-tout[M]

luggage

garment bag
housse^F à vêtements^M
zipper
fermeture^F à glissière^F
luggage carrier
porte-bagages^M
frame
armature^F
luggage elastic
sangle^F élastique
stand
béquille^F
backpack
sac^M à dos^M
retractable handle
poignée^F escamotable
upright suitcase
valise^F verticale
Pullman case
valise^F pullman^M
handle
poignée^F
identification tag
porte-adresse^M
frame
cadre^M
pull strap
dragonne^F
trim
garniture^F
wheel
roulette^F
weekender
valise^F fin^F de semaine^F
interior pocket
poche^F intérieure
curtain
panneau^M de séparation^F
garment strap
sangle^F serre-vêtements^M
lock
serrure^F
shell
coque^F
hasp
moraillon^M
trunk
malle^F
tray
plateau^M
latch
crampon^M de fermeture^F
cornerpiece
cantonnière^F
fittings
ferrure^F
handle
poignée^F

pyramid

pyramide^F

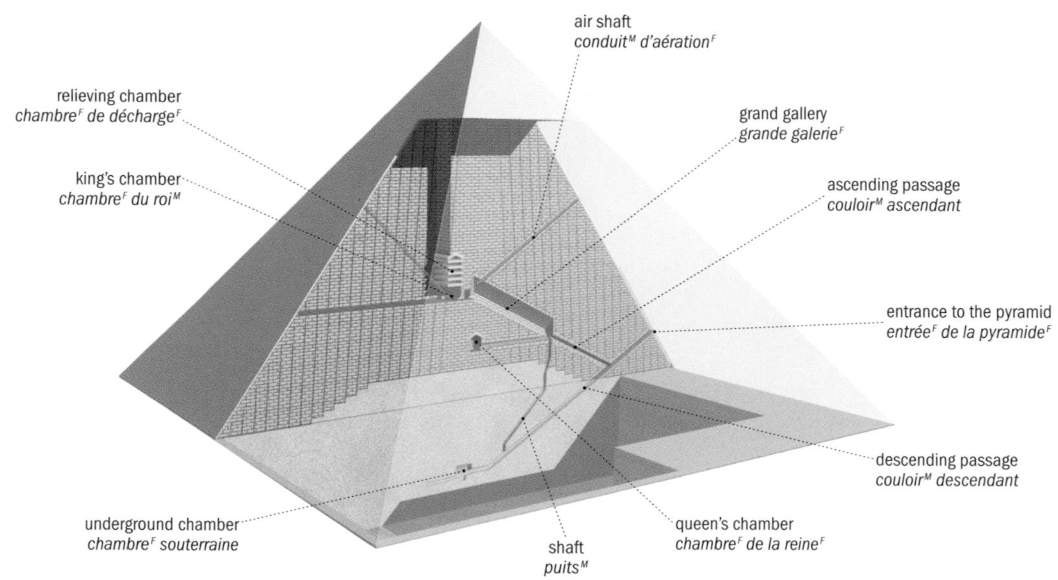
air shaft
conduit^M d'aération^F
relieving chamber
chambre^F de décharge^F
grand gallery
grande galerie^F
king's chamber
chambre^F du roi^M
ascending passage
couloir^M ascendant
entrance to the pyramid
entrée^F de la pyramide^F
descending passage
couloir^M descendant
underground chamber
chambre^F souterraine
queen's chamber
chambre^F de la reine^F
shaft
puits^M

Greek theater

théâtre^M grec

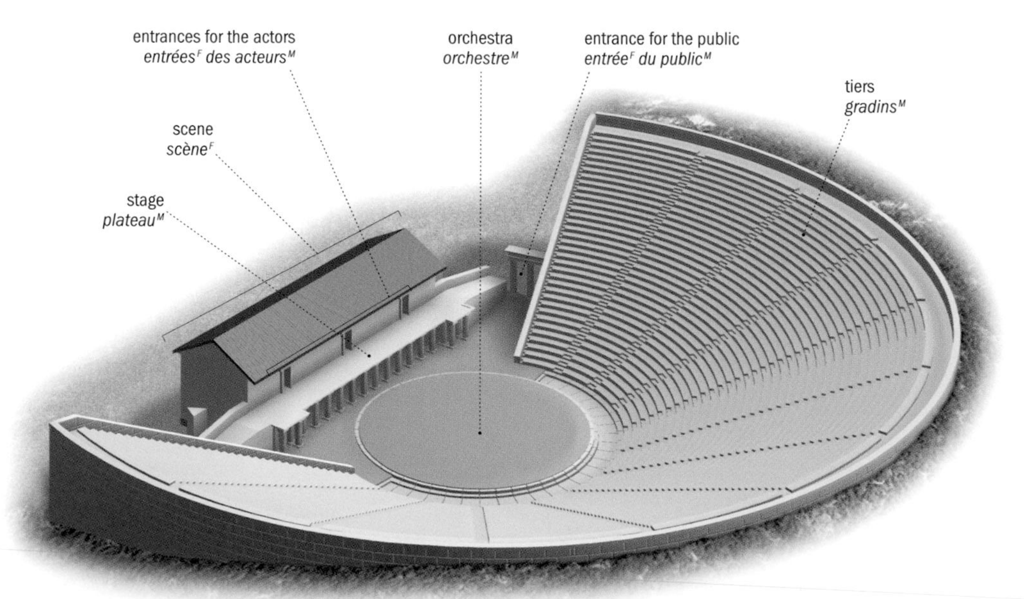
entrances for the actors
entrées^F des acteurs^M
orchestra
orchestre^M
entrance for the public
entrée^F du public^M
tiers
gradins^M
scene
scène^F
stage
plateau^M

Greek temple

temple^M grec

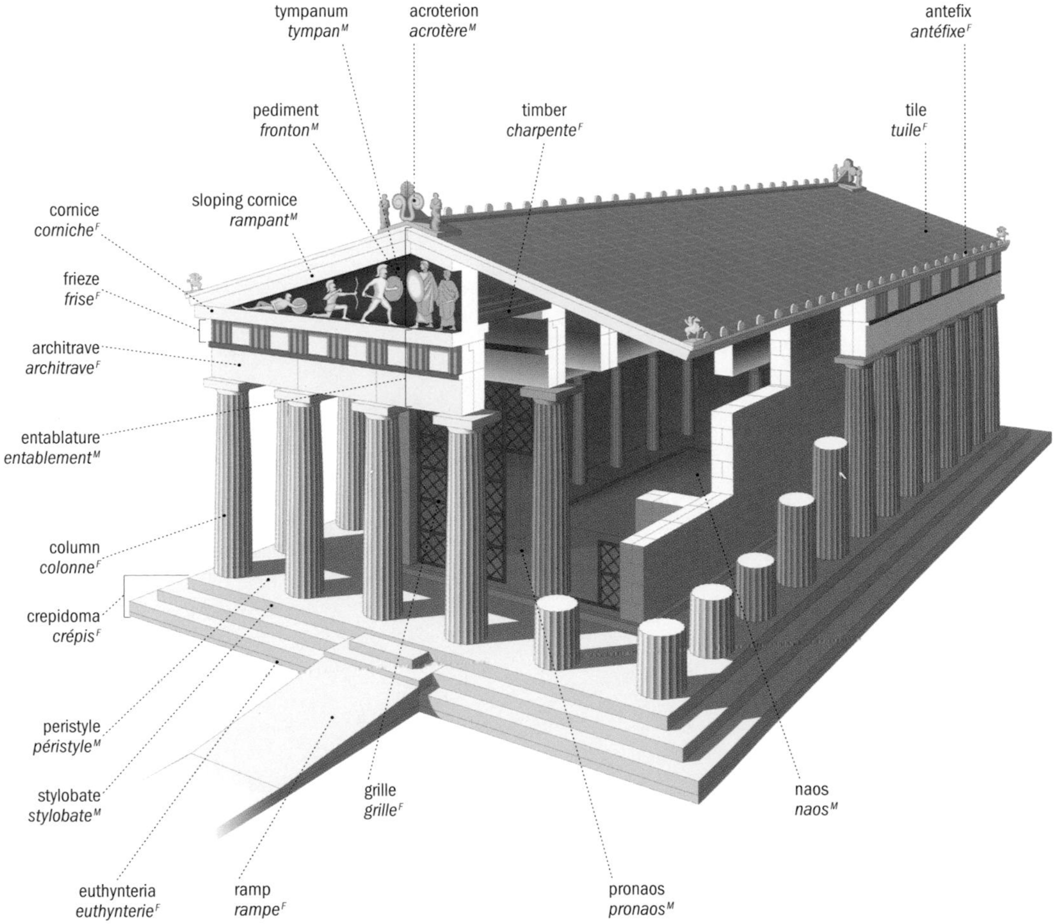

tympanum
tympan^M

acroterion
acrotère^M

antefix
antéfixe^F

pediment
fronton^M

timber
charpente^F

tile
tuile^F

cornice
corniche^F

sloping cornice
rampant^M

frieze
frise^F

architrave
architrave^F

entablature
entablement^M

column
colonne^F

crepidoma
crépis^F

peristyle
péristyle^M

stylobate
stylobate^M

grille
grille^F

naos
naos^M

euthynteria
euthynterie^F

ramp
rampe^F

pronaos
pronaos^M

plan
plan^M

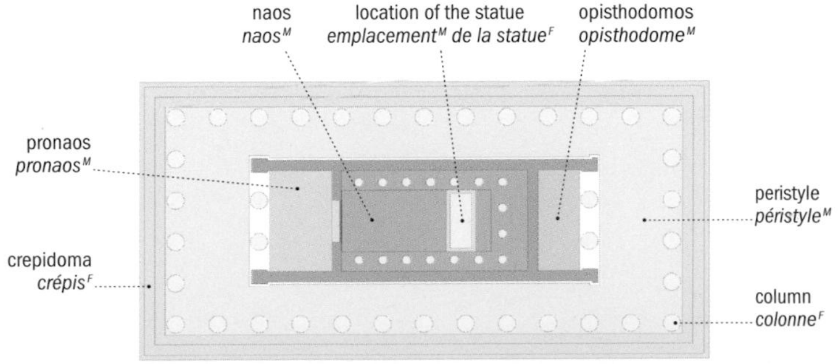

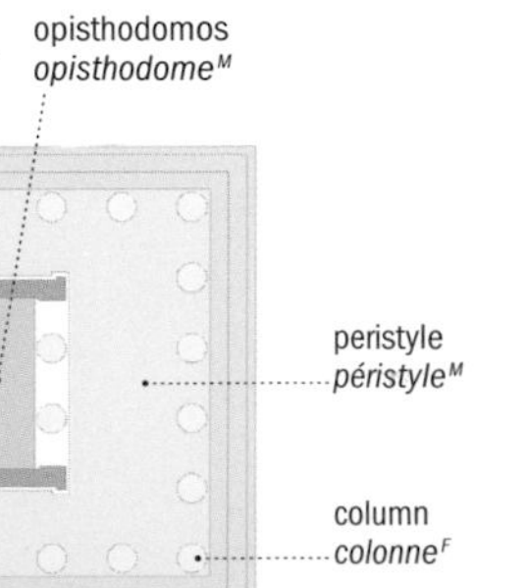
naos
naos^M
location of the statue
emplacement^M de la statue^F
opisthodomos
opisthodome^M
pronaos
pronaos^M
peristyle
péristyle^M
crepidoma
crépis^F
column
colonne^F

Roman house

maison^F romaine

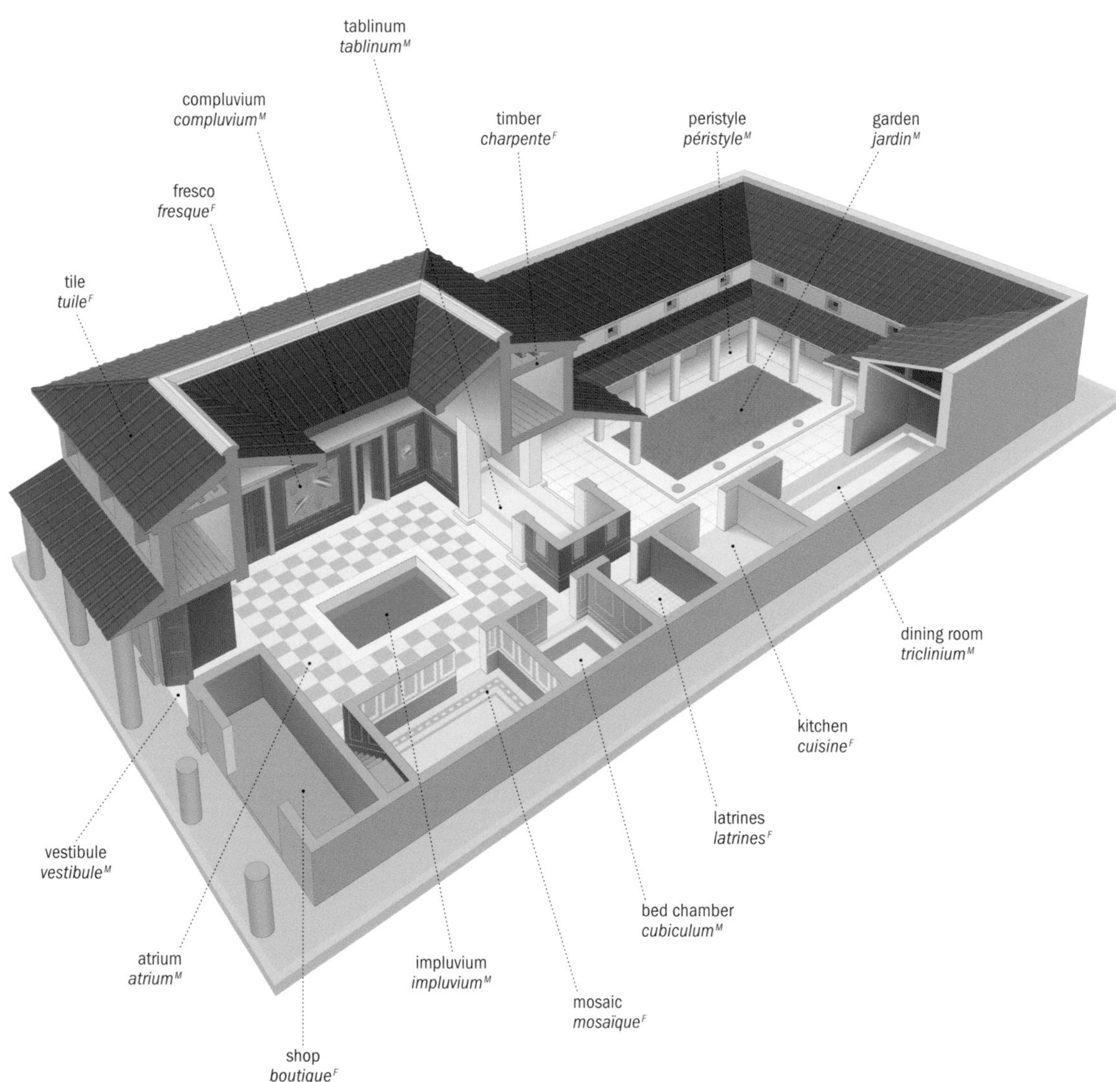
tablinum
tablinum^M
compluvium
compluvium^M
timber
charpente^F
peristyle
péristyle^M
garden
jardin^M
fresco
fresque^F
tile
tuile^F
dining room
triclinium^M
kitchen
cuisine^F
latrines
latrines^F
vestibule
vestibule^M
bed chamber
cubiculum^M
atrium
atrium^M
impluvium
impluvium^M
mosaic
mosaïque^F
shop
boutique^F

Roman amphitheater

amphithéâtre[M] romain

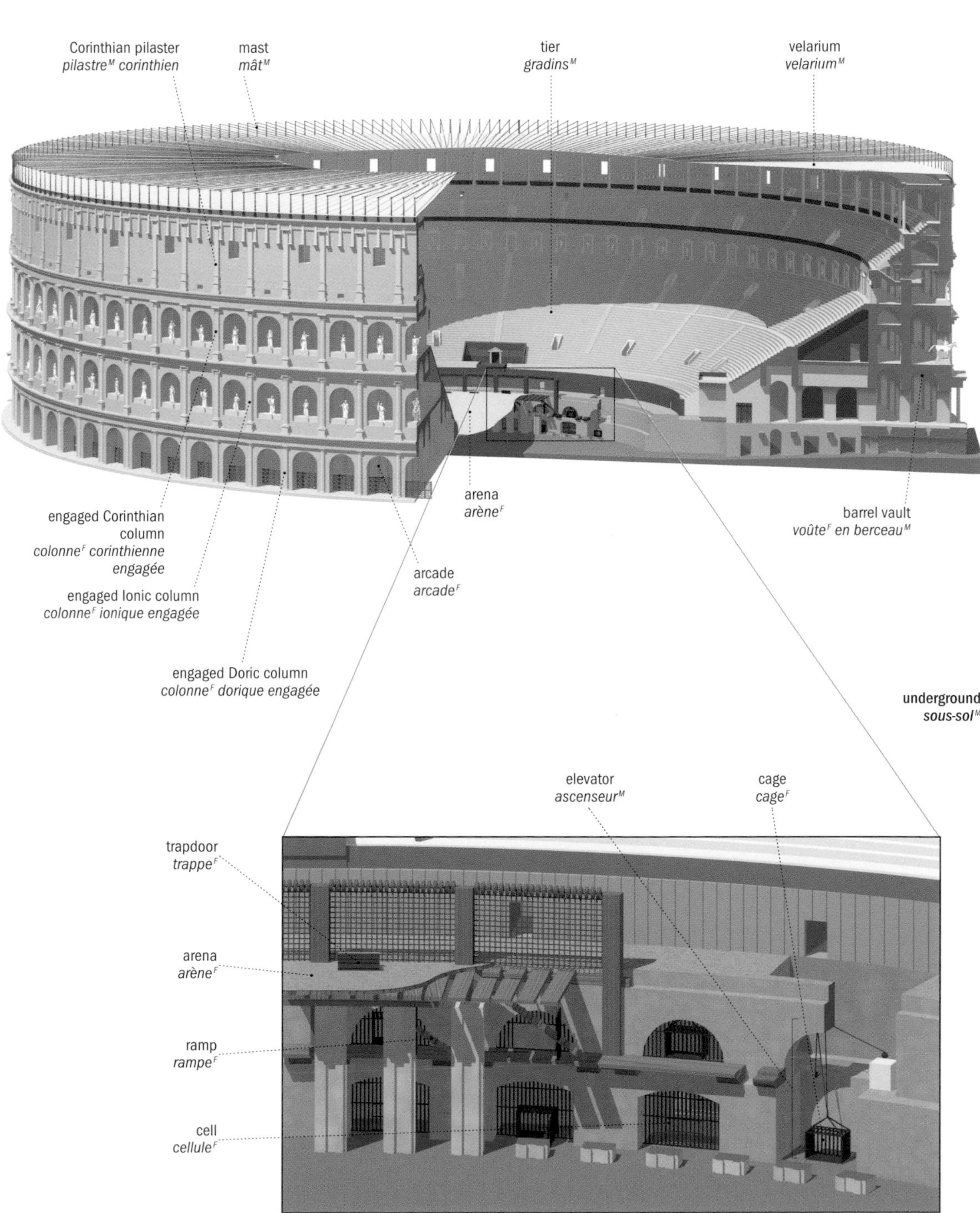
Corinthian pilaster
pilastre[M] corinthien
mast
mât[M]
tier
gradins[M]
velarium
velarium[M]
engaged Corinthian column
colonne[F] corinthienne engagée
engaged Ionic column
colonne[F] ionique engagée
engaged Doric column
colonne[F] dorique engagée
arena
arène[F]
arcade
arcade[F]
barrel vault
voûte[F] en berceau[M]
underground
sous-sol[M]
elevator
ascenseur[M]
cage
cage[F]
trapdoor
trappe[F]
arena
arène[F]
ramp
rampe[F]
cell
cellule[F]

castle

château[M] fort

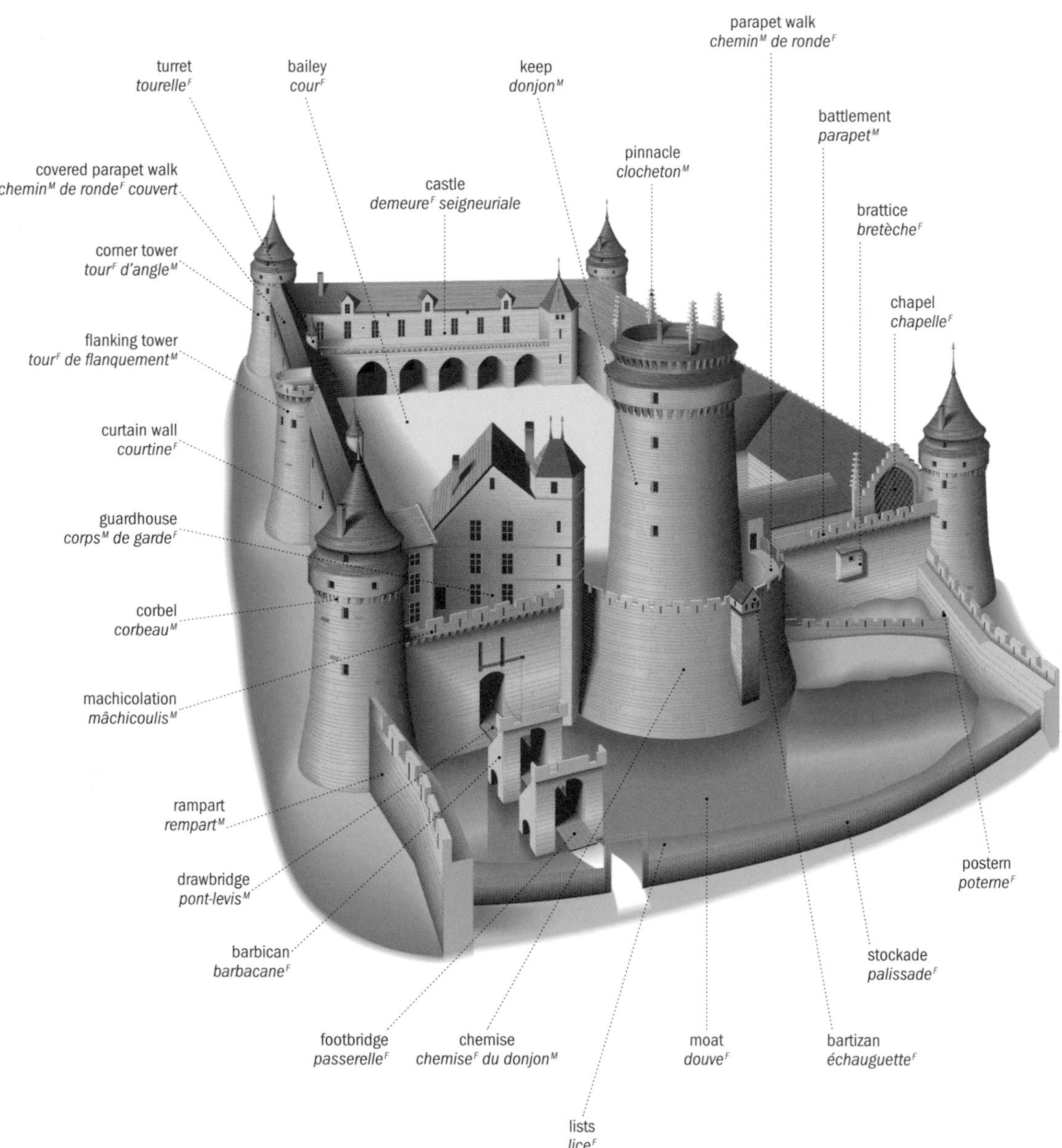
parapet walk
chemin[M] de ronde[F]
turret
tourelle[F]
bailey
cour[F]
keep
donjon[M]
battlement
parapet[M]
pinnacle
clocheton[M]
covered parapet walk
chemin[M] de ronde[F] couvert
castle
demeure[F] seigneuriale
brattice
bretèche[F]
corner tower
tour[F] d'angle[M]
chapel
chapelle[F]
flanking tower
tour[F] de flanquement[M]
curtain wall
courtine[F]
guardhouse
corps[M] de garde[F]
corbel
corbeau[M]
machicolation
mâchicoulis[M]
rampart
rempart[M]
postern
poterne[F]
drawbridge
pont-levis[M]
barbican
barbacane[F]
stockade
palissade[F]
footbridge
passerelle[F]
chemise
chemise[F] du donjon[M]
moat
douve[F]
bartizan
échauguette[F]
lists
lice[F]

pagoda

pagode^F

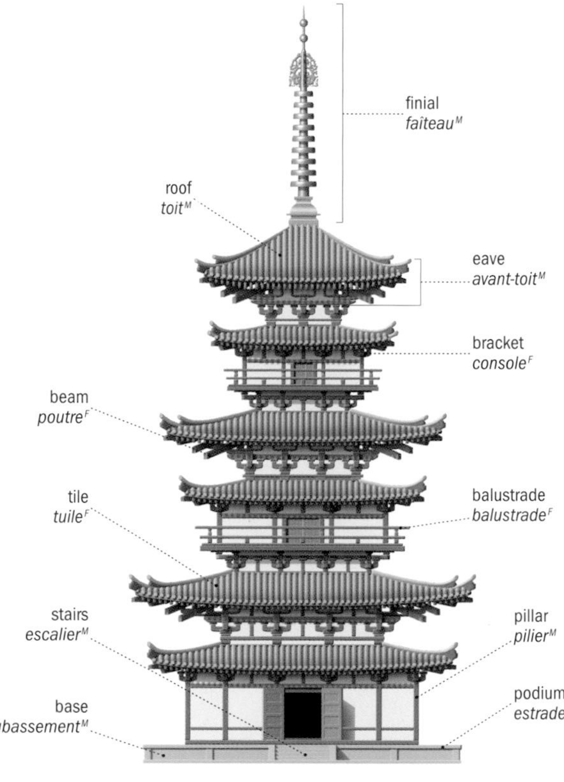
finial
faîteau^M
roof
toit^M
eave
avant-toit^M
bracket
console^F
beam
poutre^F
tile
tuile^F
balustrade
balustrade^F
stairs
escalier^M
pillar
pilier^M
base
soubassement^M
podium
estrade^F

Aztec temple

temple^M aztèque

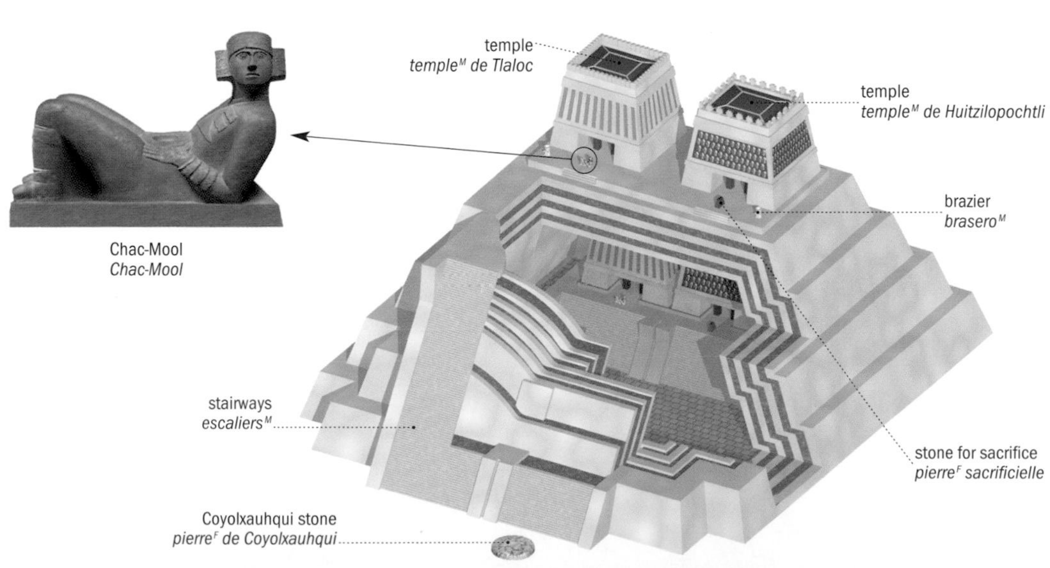
temple
temple^M de Tlaloc
temple
temple^M de Huitzilopochtli
Chac-Mool
Chac-Mool
brazier
brasero^M
stairways
escaliers^M
stone for sacrifice
pierre^F sacrificielle
Coyolxauhqui stone
pierre^F de Coyolxauhqui

cathedral

cathédrale^F

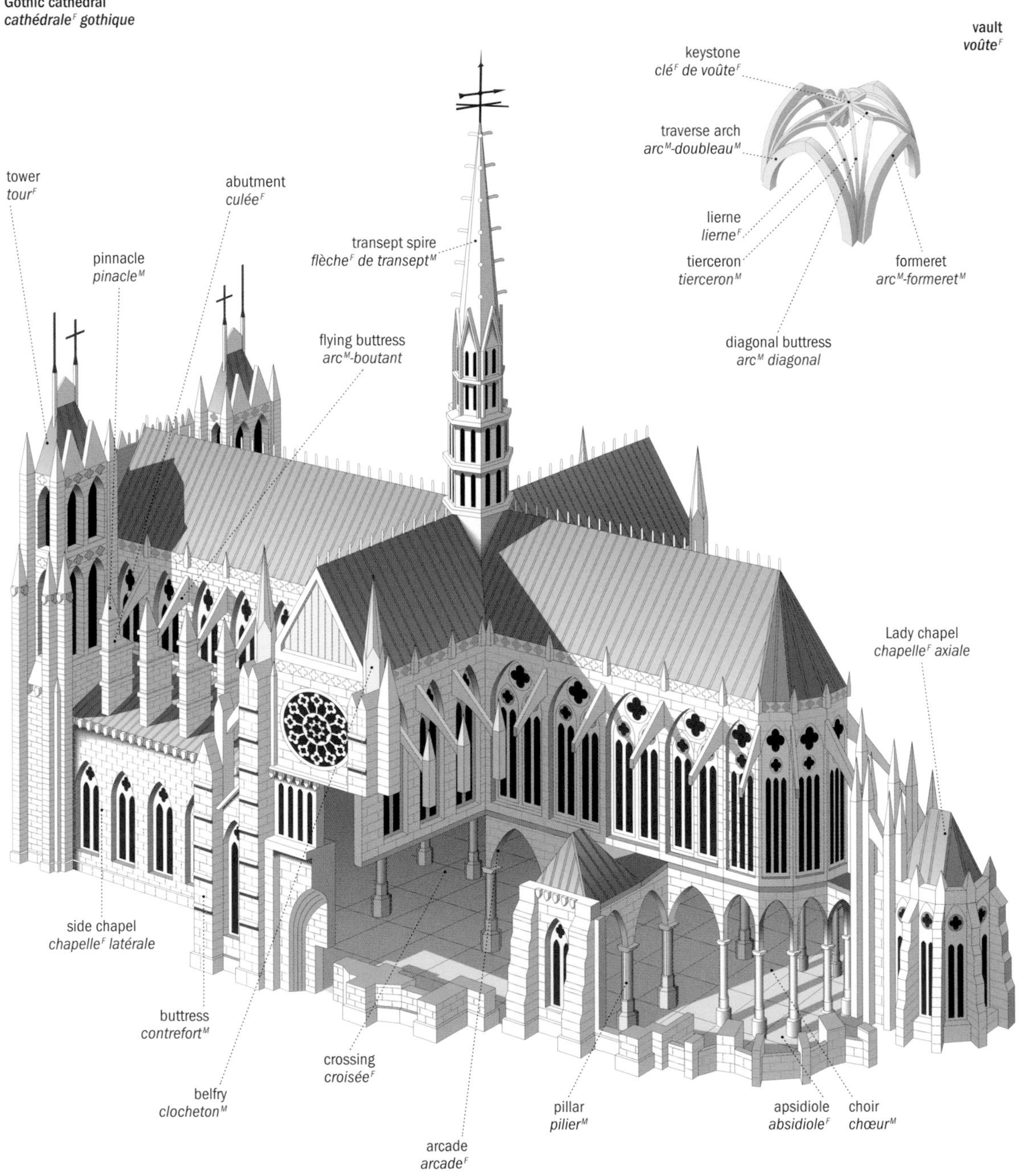

Gothic cathedral
cathédrale^F gothique
vault
voûte^F
keystone
clé^F de voûte^F
traverse arch
arc^M-doubleau^M
lierne
lierne^F
tierceron
tierceron^M
formeret
arc^M-formeret^M
diagonal buttress
arc^M diagonal
tower
tour^F
abutment
culée^F
pinnacle
pinacle^M
transept spire
flèche^F de transept^M
flying buttress
arc^M-boutant
Lady chapel
chapelle^F axiale
side chapel
chapelle^F latérale
buttress
contrefort^M
crossing
croisée^F
belfry
clocheton^M
arcade
arcade^F
pillar
pilier^M
apsidiole
absidiole^F
choir
chœur^M

façade
façade[F]

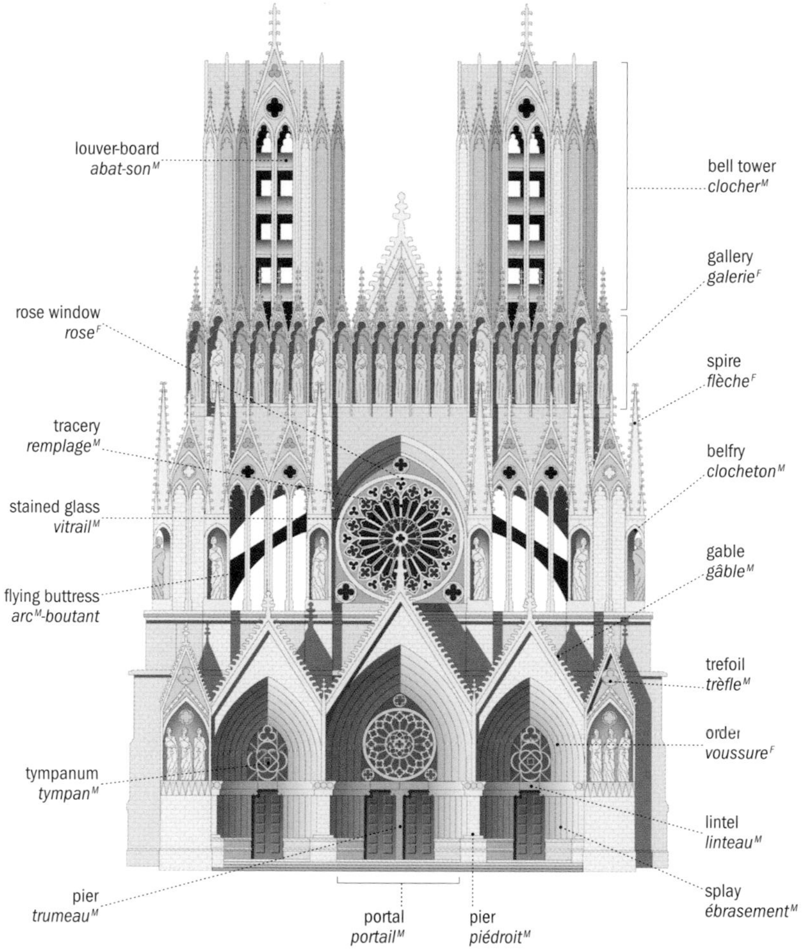

louver-board
abat-son[M]

bell tower
clocher[M]

gallery
galerie[F]

rose window
rose[F]

spire
flèche[F]

tracery
remplage[M]

belfry
clocheton[M]

stained glass
vitrail[M]

gable
gâble[M]

flying buttress
arc[M]*-boutant*

trefoil
trèfle[M]

order
voussure[F]

tympanum
tympan[M]

lintel
linteau[M]

splay
ébrasement[M]

pier
trumeau[M]

portal
portail[M]

pier
piédroit[M]

plan
plan[M]

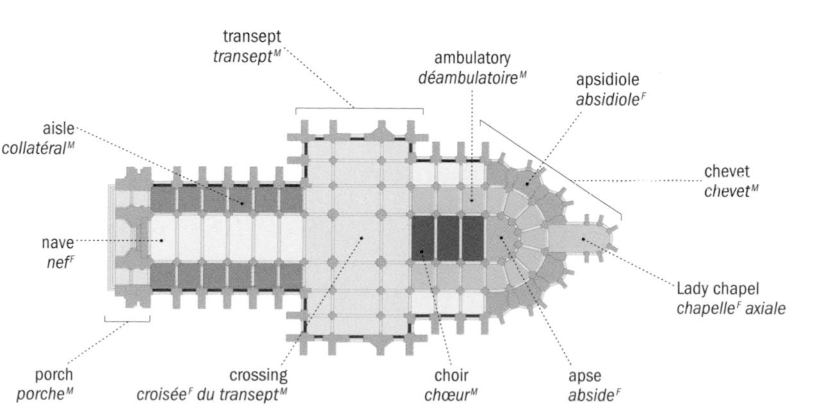
transept
transept[M]
ambulatory
déambulatoire[M]
apsidiole
absidiole[F]
aisle
collatéral[M]
chevet
chevet[M]
nave
nef[F]
Lady chapel
chapelle[F] axiale
porch
porche[M]
crossing
croisée[F] du transept[M]
choir
chœur[M]
apse
abside[F]

elements of architecture

éléments[M] d'architecture[F]

examples of doors
exemples[M] de portes[F]

manual revolving door
porte[F] à tambour[M] manuelle

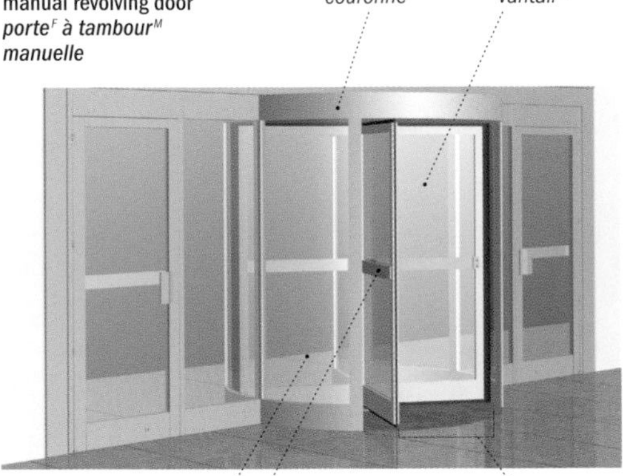
canopy
couronne[F]
wing
vantail[M]
enclosure
sas[M]
push bar
barre[F] de poussée[F]
compartment
compartiment[M]

automatic sliding door
porte[F] coulissante automatique

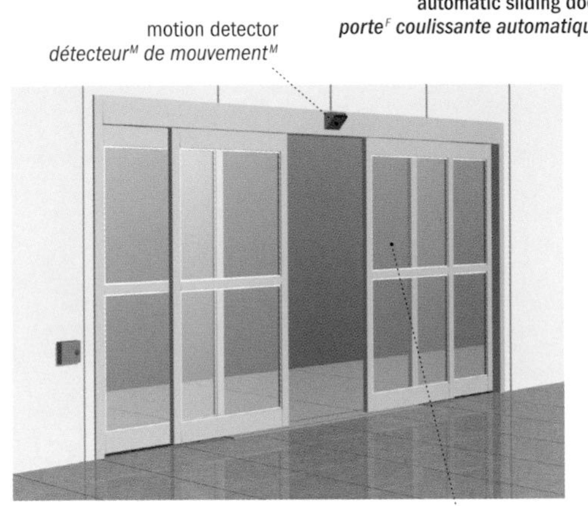
motion detector
détecteur[M] de mouvement[M]
wing
vantail[M]

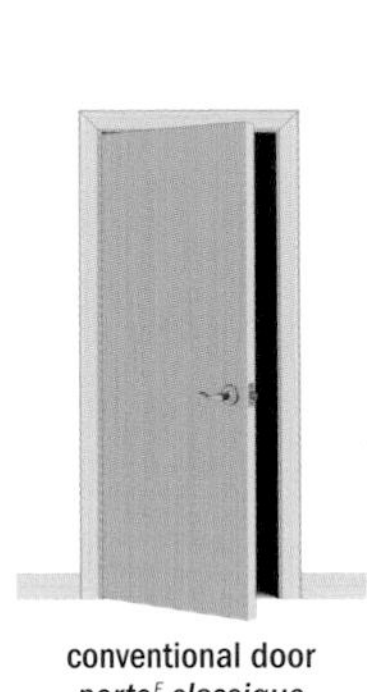

conventional door
porte[F] classique

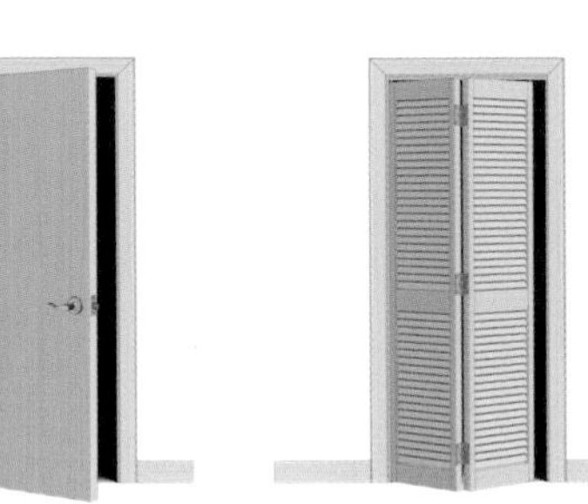

folding door
porte[F] pliante

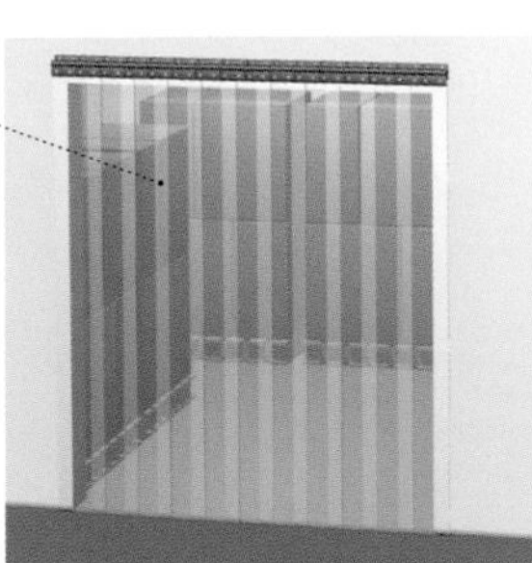
strip
lanière[F]

strip door
porte[F] à lanières[F]

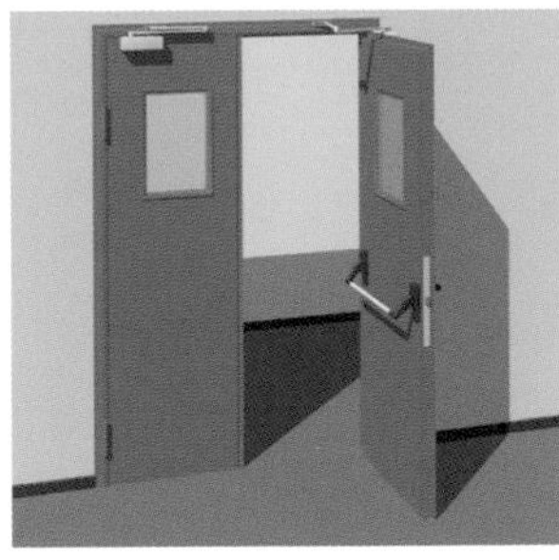

fire door
porte[F] coupe-feu

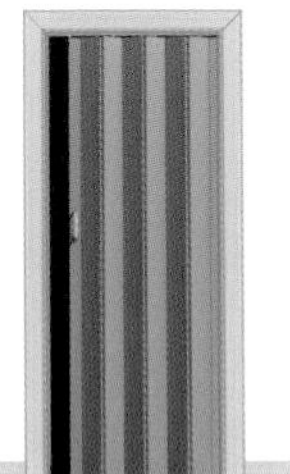

sliding folding door
porte[F] accordéon[M]

sliding door
porte[F] coulissante

sectional garage door
porte[F] de garage[M] sectionnelle

up and over garage door
porte[F] de garage[M] basculante

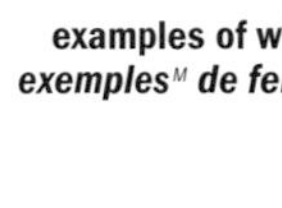

examples of windows
exemples[M] de fenêtres[F]

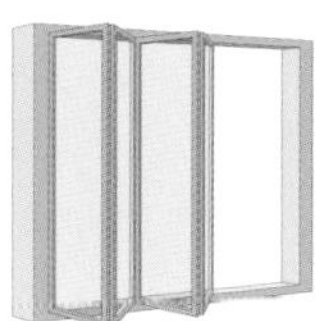

sliding folding window
fenêtre[F] en accordéon[M]

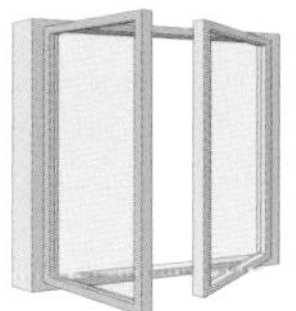

French window
fenêtre[F] à la française[F]

casement window
fenêtre[F] à l'anglaise[F]

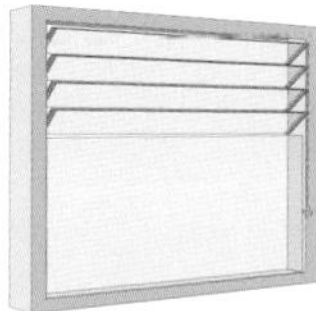

louvered window
fenêtre[F] à jalousies[F]

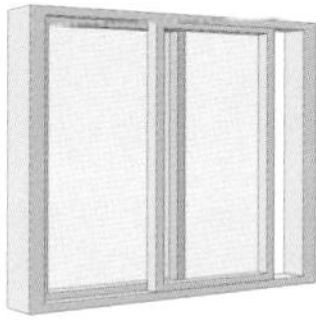

sliding window
fenêtre[F] coulissante

sash window
fenêtre[F] à guillotine[F]

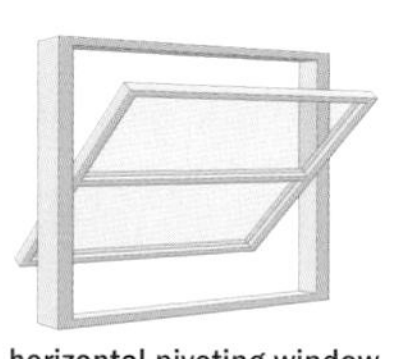

horizontal pivoting window
fenêtre[F] basculante

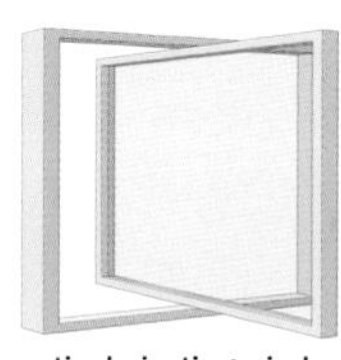

vertical pivoting window
fenêtre[F] pivotante

elevator

ascenseur[M]

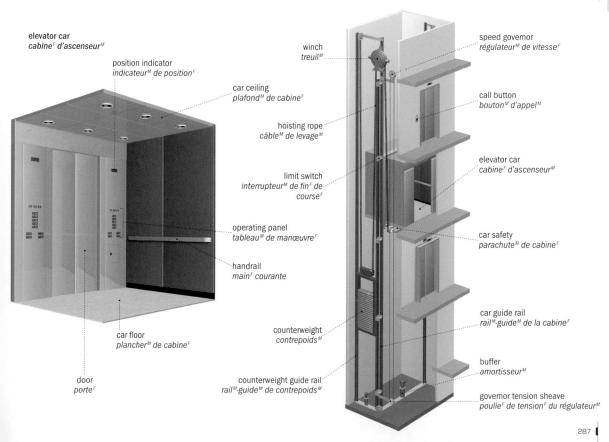

elevator car
cabine[F] d'ascenseur[M]

position indicator
indicateur[M] de position[F]

car ceiling
plafond[M] de cabine[F]

operating panel
tableau[M] de manœuvre[F]

handrail
main[F] courante

car floor
plancher[M] de cabine[F]

door
porte[F]

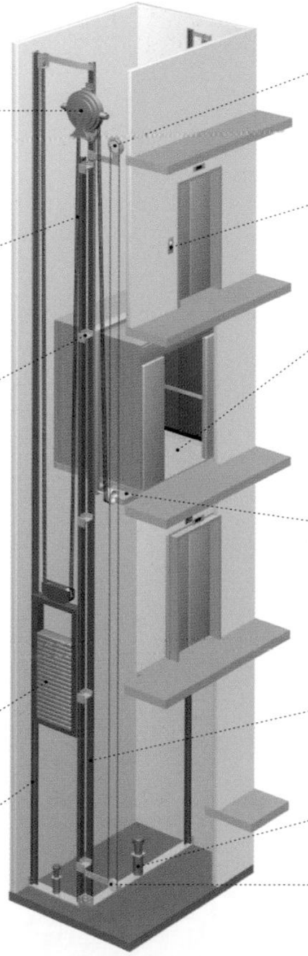

winch
treuil[M]

hoisting rope
câble[M] de levage[M]

limit switch
interrupteur[M] de fin[F] de course[F]

counterweight
contrepoids[M]

counterweight guide rail
rail[M]-guide[M] de contrepoids[M]

speed governor
régulateur[M] de vitesse[F]

call button
bouton[M] d'appel[M]

elevator car
cabine[F] d'ascenseur[M]

car safety
parachute[M] de cabine[F]

car guide rail
rail[M]-guide[M] de la cabine[F]

buffer
amortisseur[M]

governor tension sheave
poulie[F] de tension[F] du régulateur[M]

traditional houses

maisons^F traditionnelles

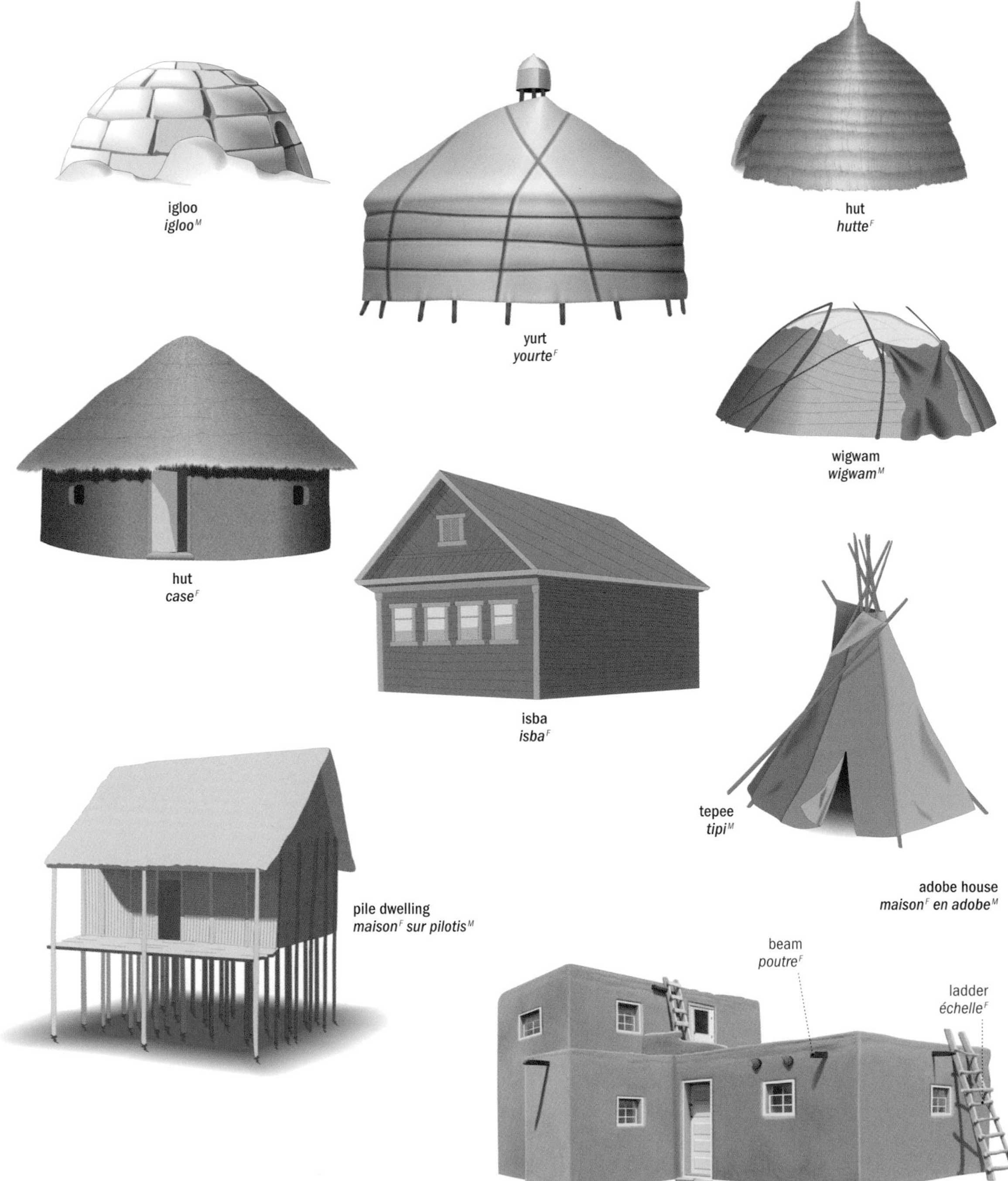
igloo
igloo^M
yurt
yourte^F
hut
hutte^F
wigwam
wigwam^M
hut
case^F
isba
isba^F
tepee
tipi^M
pile dwelling
maison^F sur pilotis^M
adobe house
maison^F en adobe^M
beam
poutre^F
ladder
échelle^F

city houses

maisons[F] de ville[F]

two-storey house
maison[F] à étage[M]

one-storey house
maison[F] de plain-pied[M]

semidetached house
maison[F] jumelée

town houses
maisons[F] en rangée[F]

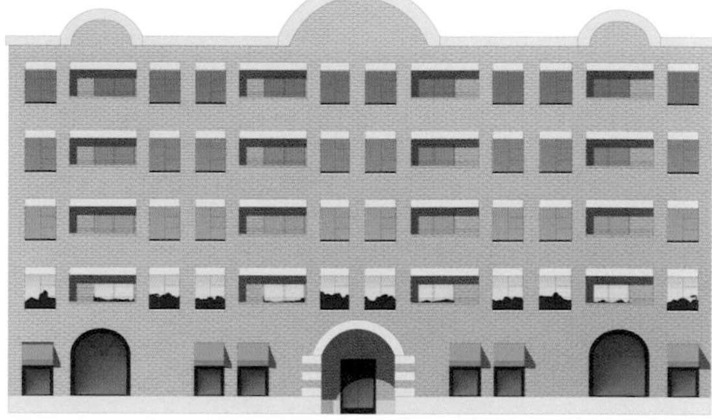

condominiums
appartements[M] en copropriété[F]

high-rise apartment building
tour[F] d'habitation[F]

sound stage

plateau^M de tournage^M

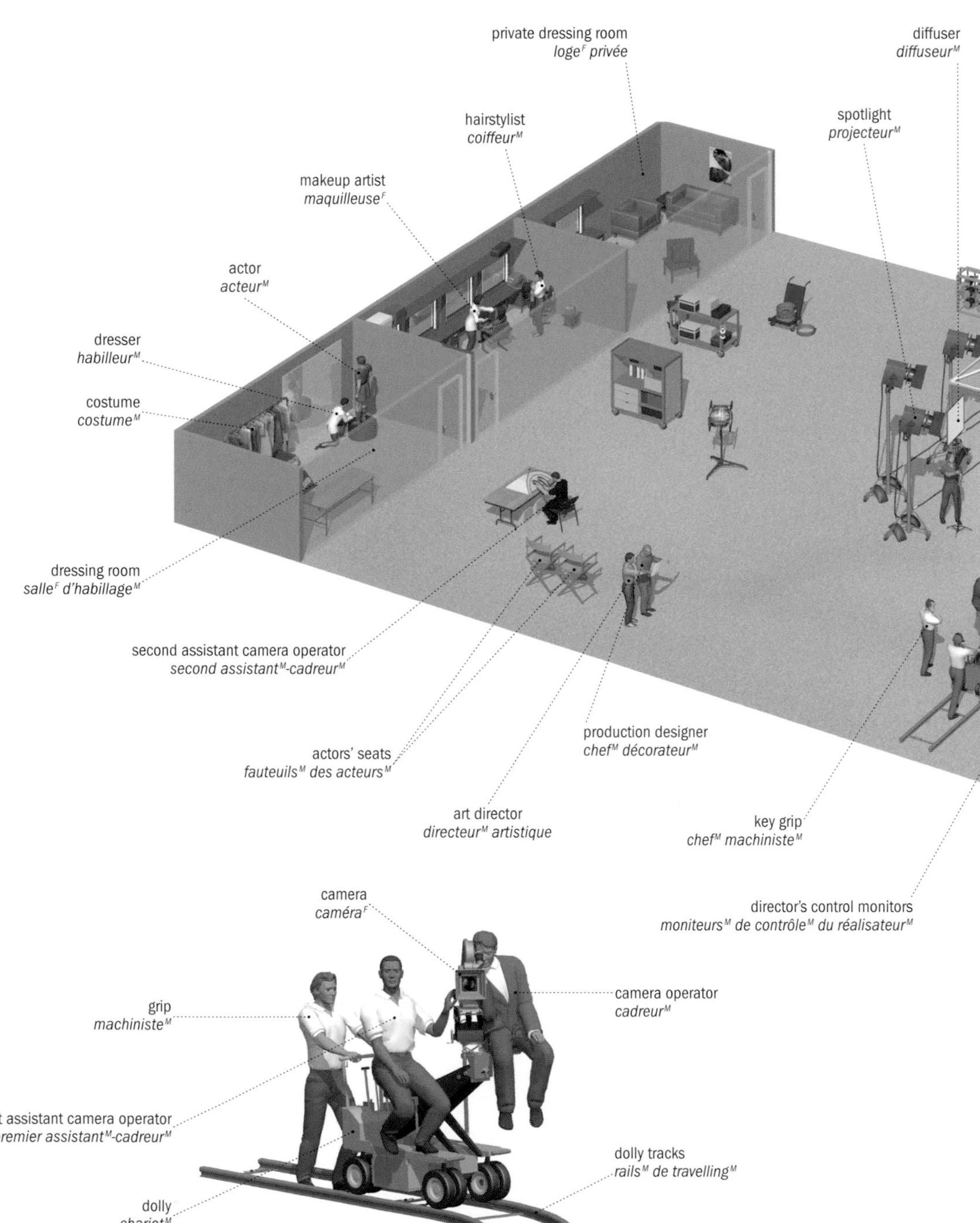
private dressing room
loge^F privée
diffuser
diffuseur^M
hairstylist
coiffeur^M
spotlight
projecteur^M
makeup artist
maquilleuse^F
actor
acteur^M
dresser
habilleur^M
costume
costume^M
dressing room
salle^F d'habillage^M
second assistant camera operator
second assistant^M-cadreur^M
actors' seats
fauteuils^M des acteurs^M
production designer
chef^M décorateur^M
art director
directeur^M artistique
key grip
chef^M machiniste^M
director's control monitors
moniteurs^M de contrôle^M du réalisateur^M
camera
caméra^F
camera operator
cadreur^M
grip
machiniste^M
first assistant camera operator
premier assistant^M-cadreur^M
dolly tracks
rails^M de travelling^M
dolly
chariot^M

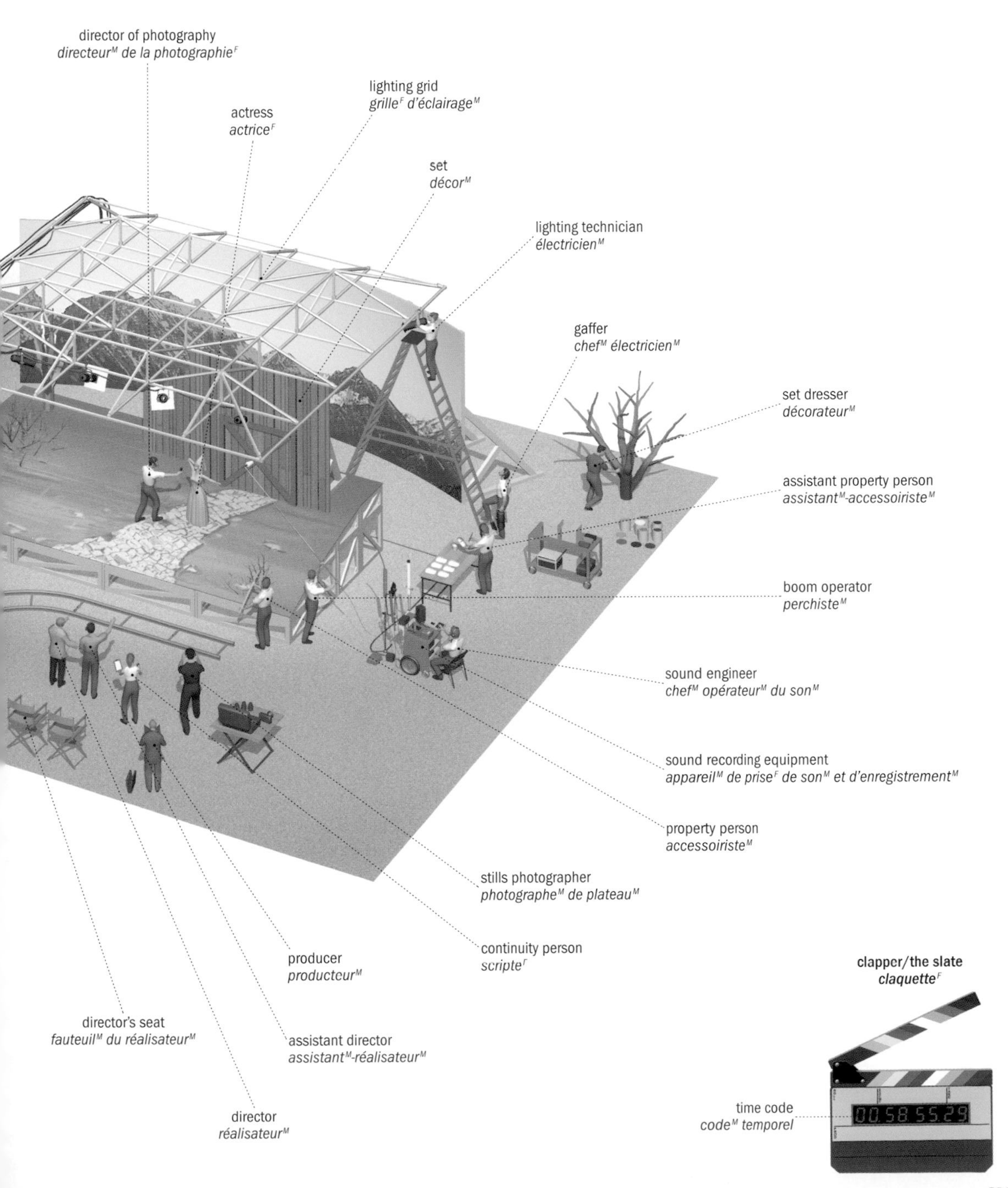
director of photography
directeur^M de la photographie^F
lighting grid
grille^F d'éclairage^M
actress
actrice^F
set
décor^M
lighting technician
électricien^M
gaffer
chef^M électricien^M
set dresser
décorateur^M
assistant property person
assistant^M-accessoiriste^M
boom operator
perchiste^M
sound engineer
chef^M opérateur^M du son^M
sound recording equipment
appareil^M de prise^F de son^M et d'enregistrement^M
property person
accessoiriste^M
stills photographer
photographe^M de plateau^M
continuity person
scripte^F
producer
producteur^M
director's seat
fauteuil^M du réalisateur^M
assistant director
assistant^M-réalisateur^M
director
réalisateur^M
clapper/the slate
claquette^F
time code
code^M temporel
00.58.55.29

theater

salle[F] de spectacle[M]

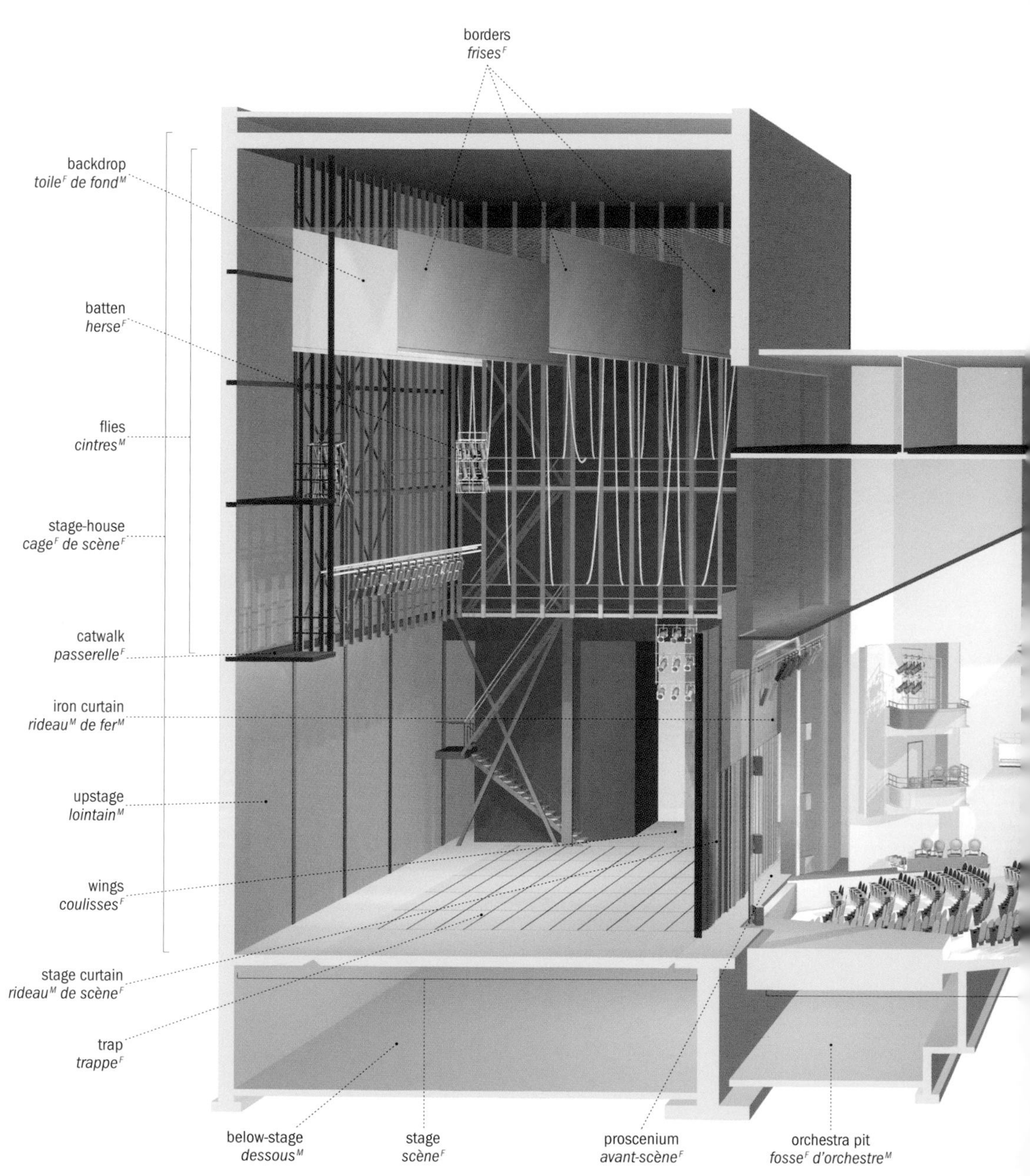
borders
frises[F]
backdrop
toile[F] de fond[M]
batten
herse[F]
flies
cintres[M]
stage-house
cage[F] de scène[F]
catwalk
passerelle[F]
iron curtain
rideau[M] de fer[M]
upstage
lointain[M]
wings
coulisses[F]
stage curtain
rideau[M] de scène[F]
trap
trappe[F]
below-stage
dessous[M]
stage
scène[F]
proscenium
avant-scène[F]
orchestra pit
fosse[F] d'orchestre[M]

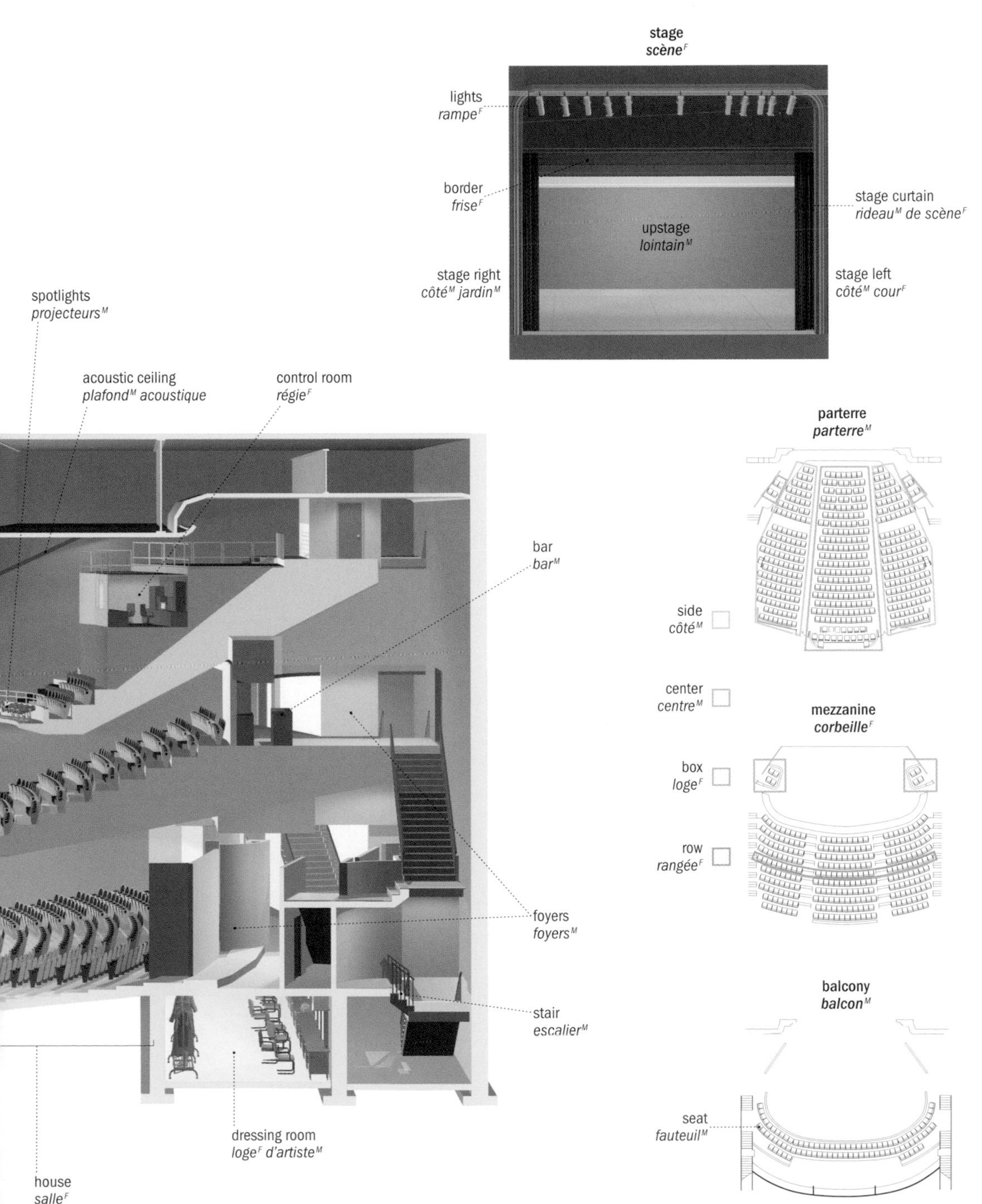
stage
***scène**^F*
lights
rampe^F
border
frise^F
stage curtain
rideau^M de scène^F
upstage
lointain^M
stage right
côté^M jardin^M
stage left
côté^M cour^F
spotlights
projecteurs^M
acoustic ceiling
plafond^M acoustique
control room
régie^F
parterre
***parterre**^M*
bar
bar^M
side
côté^M
center
centre^M
mezzanine
***corbeille**^F*
box
loge^F
row
rangée^F
foyers
foyers^M
balcony
***balcon**^M*
stair
escalier^M
dressing room
loge^F d'artiste^M
seat
fauteuil^M
house
salle^F

movie theater

cinéma[M]

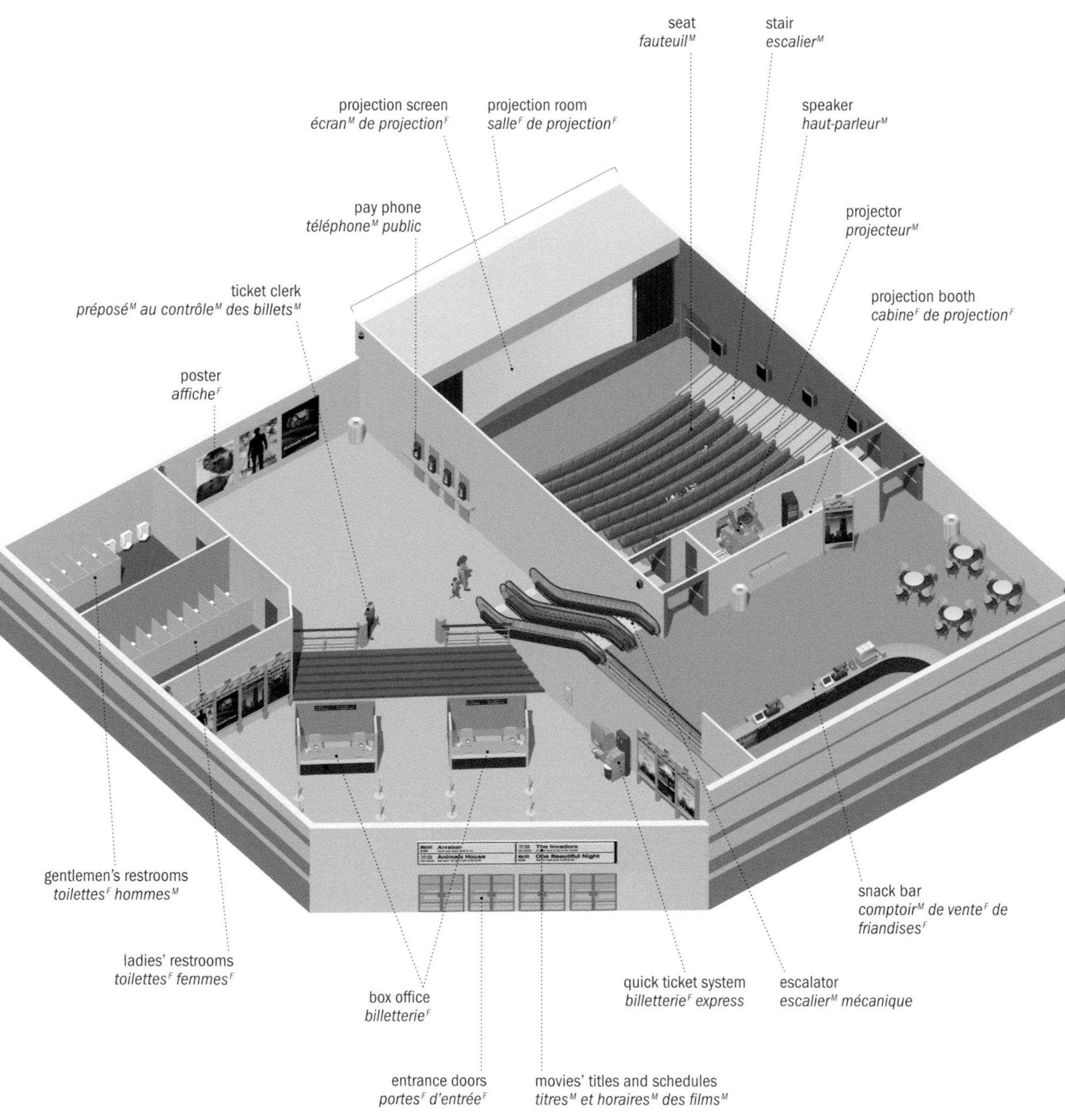
seat
fauteuil[M]
stair
escalier[M]
projection screen
écran[M] de projection[F]
projection room
salle[F] de projection[F]
speaker
haut-parleur[M]
pay phone
téléphone[M] public
projector
projecteur[M]
ticket clerk
préposé[M] au contrôle[M] des billets[M]
projection booth
cabine[F] de projection[F]
poster
affiche[F]
gentlemen's restrooms
toilettes[F] hommes[M]
snack bar
comptoir[M] de vente[F] de friandises[F]
ladies' restrooms
toilettes[F] femmes[F]
box office
billetterie[F]
quick ticket system
billetterie[F] express
escalator
escalier[M] mécanique
entrance doors
portes[F] d'entrée[F]
movies' titles and schedules
titres[M] et horaires[M] des films[M]

symphony orchestra

orchestre[M] symphonique

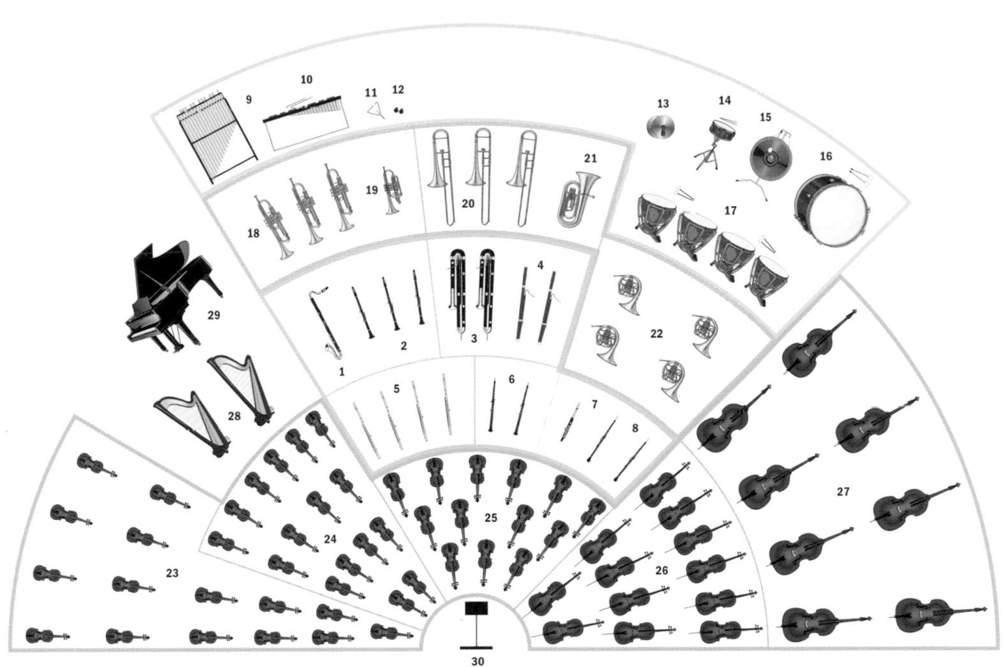
10
11
12
9
13
14
15
16
21
19
18
20
17
4
29
2
3
22
1
6
5
7
28
8
27
25
24
23
26
30

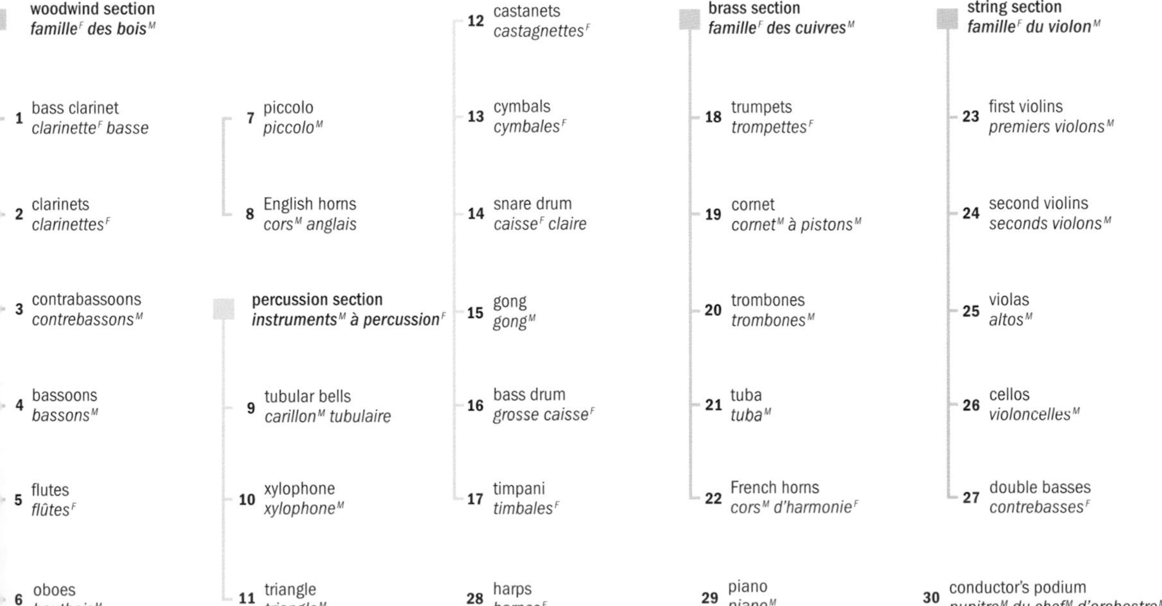

woodwind section
famille[F] des bois[M]

1 bass clarinet
clarinette[F] basse

2 clarinets
clarinettes[F]

3 contrabassoons
contrebassons[M]

4 bassoons
bassons[M]

5 flutes
flûtes[F]

6 oboes
hautbois[M]

7 piccolo
piccolo[M]

8 English horns
cors[M] anglais

percussion section
instruments[M] à percussion[F]

9 tubular bells
carillon[M] tubulaire

10 xylophone
xylophone[M]

11 triangle
triangle[M]

12 castanets
castagnettes[F]

13 cymbals
cymbales[F]

14 snare drum
caisse[F] claire

15 gong
gong[M]

16 bass drum
grosse caisse[F]

17 timpani
timbales[F]

28 harps
harpes[F]

brass section
famille[F] des cuivres[M]

18 trumpets
trompettes[F]

19 cornet
cornet[M] à pistons[M]

20 trombones
trombones[M]

21 tuba
tuba[M]

22 French horns
cors[M] d'harmonie[F]

29 piano
piano[M]

string section
famille[F] du violon[M]

23 first violins
premiers violons[M]

24 second violins
seconds violons[M]

25 violas
altos[M]

26 cellos
violoncelles[M]

27 double basses
contrebasses[F]

30 conductor's podium
pupitre[M] du chef[M] d'orchestre[M]

traditional musical instruments

instruments^M traditionnels

accordion
accordéon^M
bellows strap
fermeture^F du soufflet^M
treble register
registre^M des aigus^M
treble keyboard
clavier^M chant^M
key
touche^F
grille
grille^F
bellows
soufflet^M
button
bouton^M
bass keyboard
clavier^M accompagnement^M
bass register
registre^M des basses^F
harmonica
harmonica^M
bagpipes
cornemuse^F
drone pipe
bourdon^M
blow pipe
tuyau^M d'insufflation^F
stock
monture^F
windbag
sac^M
chanter
chalumeau^M
zither
cithare^F
soundboard
caisse^F de résonance^F
fingerboard
touche^F
open strings
cordes^F d'accompagnement^M
melody strings
cordes^F de mélodie^F
banjo
banjo^M
circular body
caisse^F circulaire

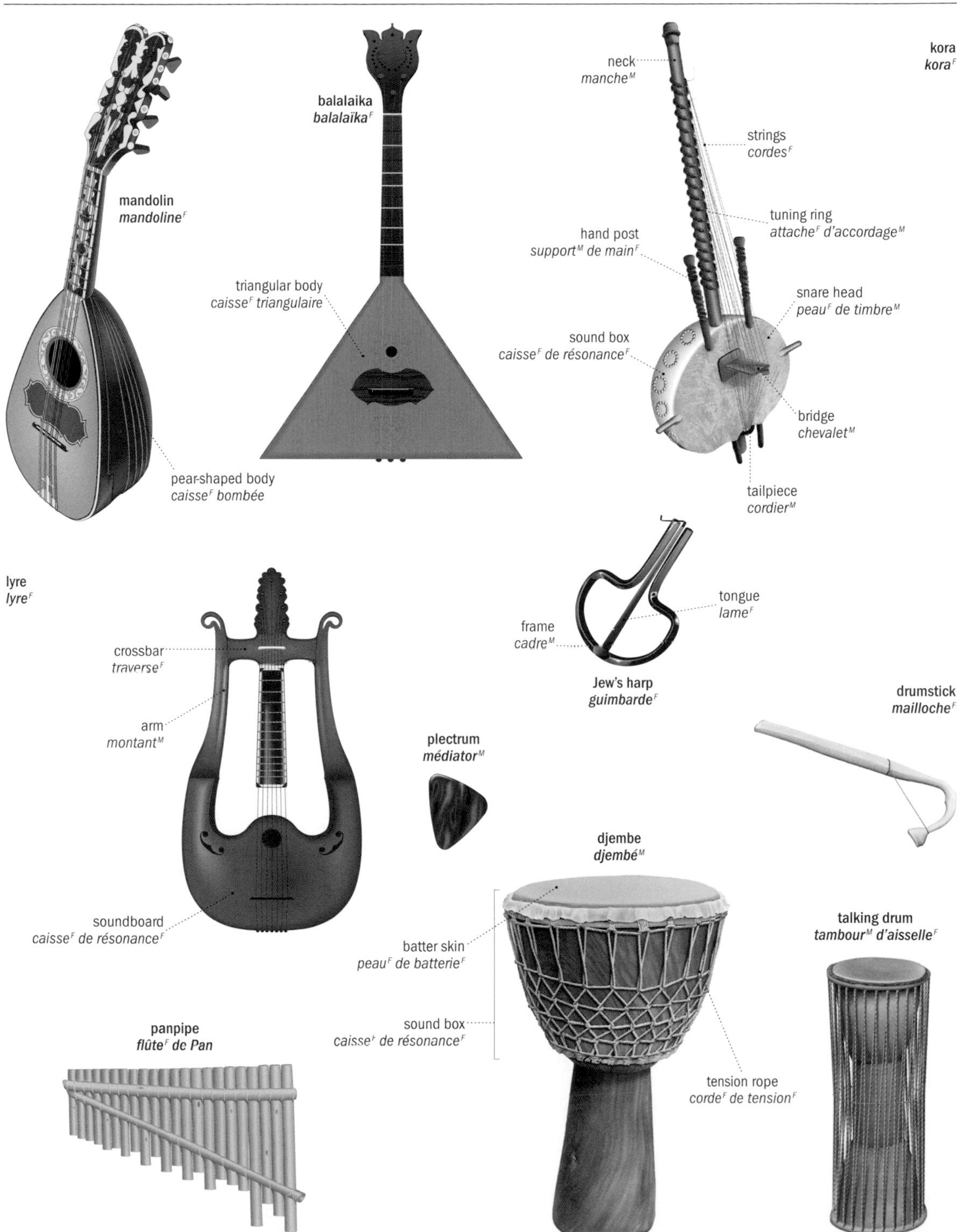
mandolin
mandoline F
pear-shaped body
caisse F bombée
balalaika
balalaïka F
triangular body
caisse F triangulaire
kora
kora F
neck
manche M
strings
cordes F
tuning ring
attache F d'accordage M
hand post
support M de main F
snare head
peau F de timbre M
sound box
caisse F de résonance F
bridge
chevalet M
tailpiece
cordier M
lyre
lyre F
crossbar
traverse F
arm
montant M
soundboard
caisse F de résonance F
plectrum
médiator M
Jew's harp
guimbarde F
tongue
lame F
frame
cadre M
drumstick
mailloche F
djembe
djembé M
batter skin
peau F de batterie F
sound box
caisse F de résonance F
tension rope
corde F de tension F
talking drum
tambour M d'aisselle F
panpipe
flûte F de Pan

musical notation

notation^F musicale

staff
portée^F

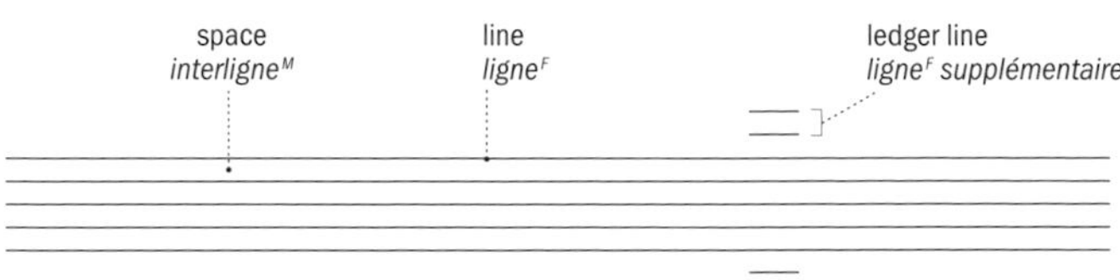

space
interligne^M
line
ligne^F
ledger line
ligne^F supplémentaire

clefs
clés^F

treble clef
clé^F de sol^M
bass clef
clé^F de fa^M
C clef
clé^F d'ut^M

time signatures
mesures^F

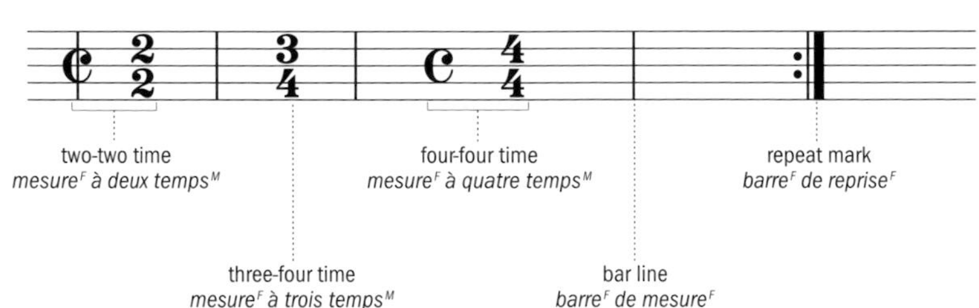

two-two time
mesure^F à deux temps^M
four-four time
mesure^F à quatre temps^M
repeat mark
barre^F de reprise^F
three-four time
mesure^F à trois temps^M
bar line
barre^F de mesure^F

intervals
intervalles^M

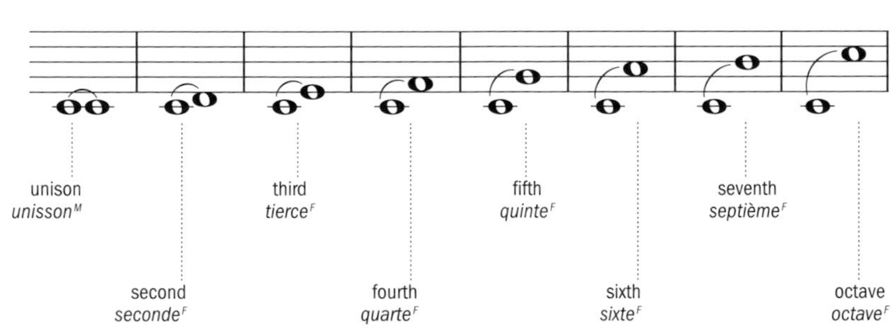

unison
unisson^M
third
tierce^F
fifth
quinte^F
seventh
septième^F
second
seconde^F
fourth
quarte^F
sixth
sixte^F
octave
octave^F

scale
gamme^F

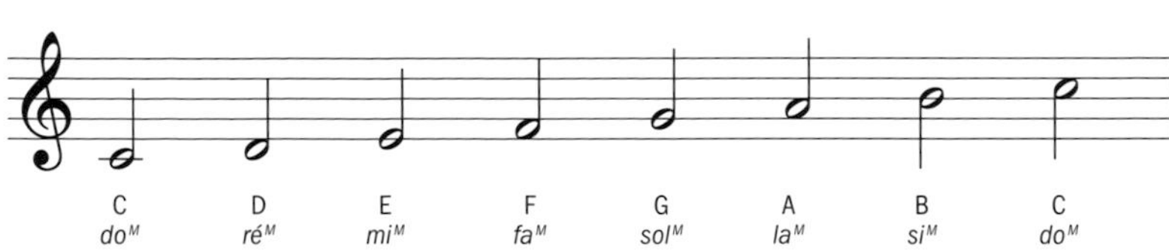

C
do^M
D
ré^M
E
mi^M
F
fa^M
G
sol^M
A
la^M
B
si^M
C
do^M

rest symbols
valeur^F des silences^M

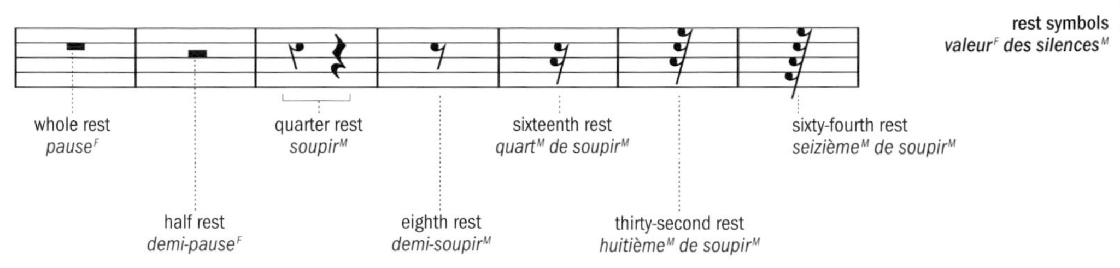
whole rest
pause^F
half rest
demi-pause^F
quarter rest
soupir^M
eighth rest
demi-soupir^M
sixteenth rest
quart^M de soupir^M
thirty-second rest
huitième^M de soupir^M
sixty-fourth rest
seizième^M de soupir^M

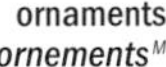

ornaments
ornements^M

appoggiatura
appoggiature^F
trill
trille^M
tr
turn
gruppetto^M
mordent
mordant^M

note symbols
valeur^F des notes^F

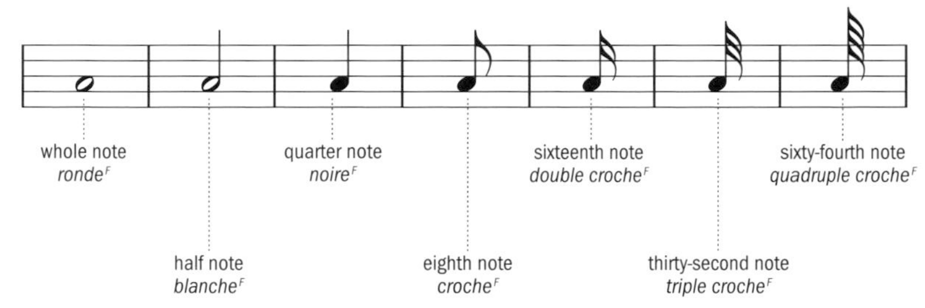
whole note
ronde^F
half note
blanche^F
quarter note
noire^F
eighth note
croche^F
sixteenth note
double croche^F
thirty-second note
triple croche^F
sixty-fourth note
quadruple croche^F

accidentals
altérations^F

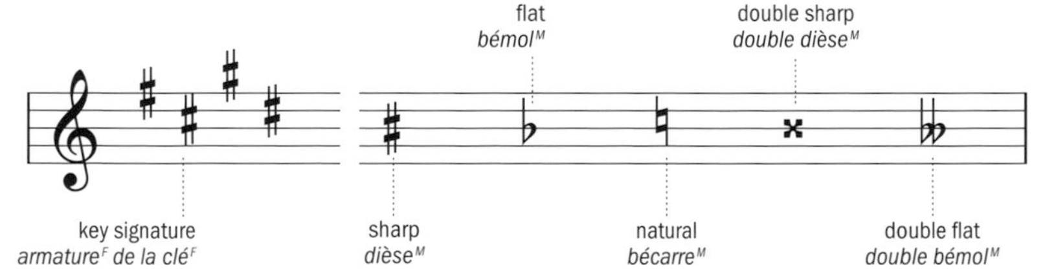
flat
bémol^M
double sharp
double dièse^M
key signature
armature^F de la clé^F
sharp
dièse^M
natural
bécarre^M
double flat
double bémol^M

other signs
autres signes^M

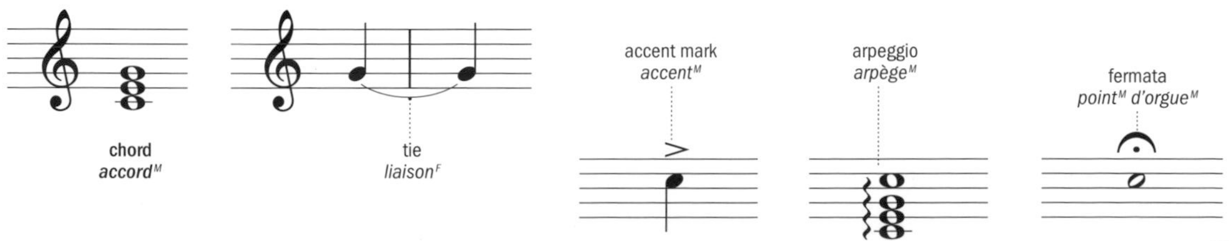
chord
accord^M
tie
liaison^F
accent mark
accent^M
arpeggio
arpège^M
fermata
point^M d'orgue^M

examples of instrumental groups

exemples^M de groupes^M instrumentaux

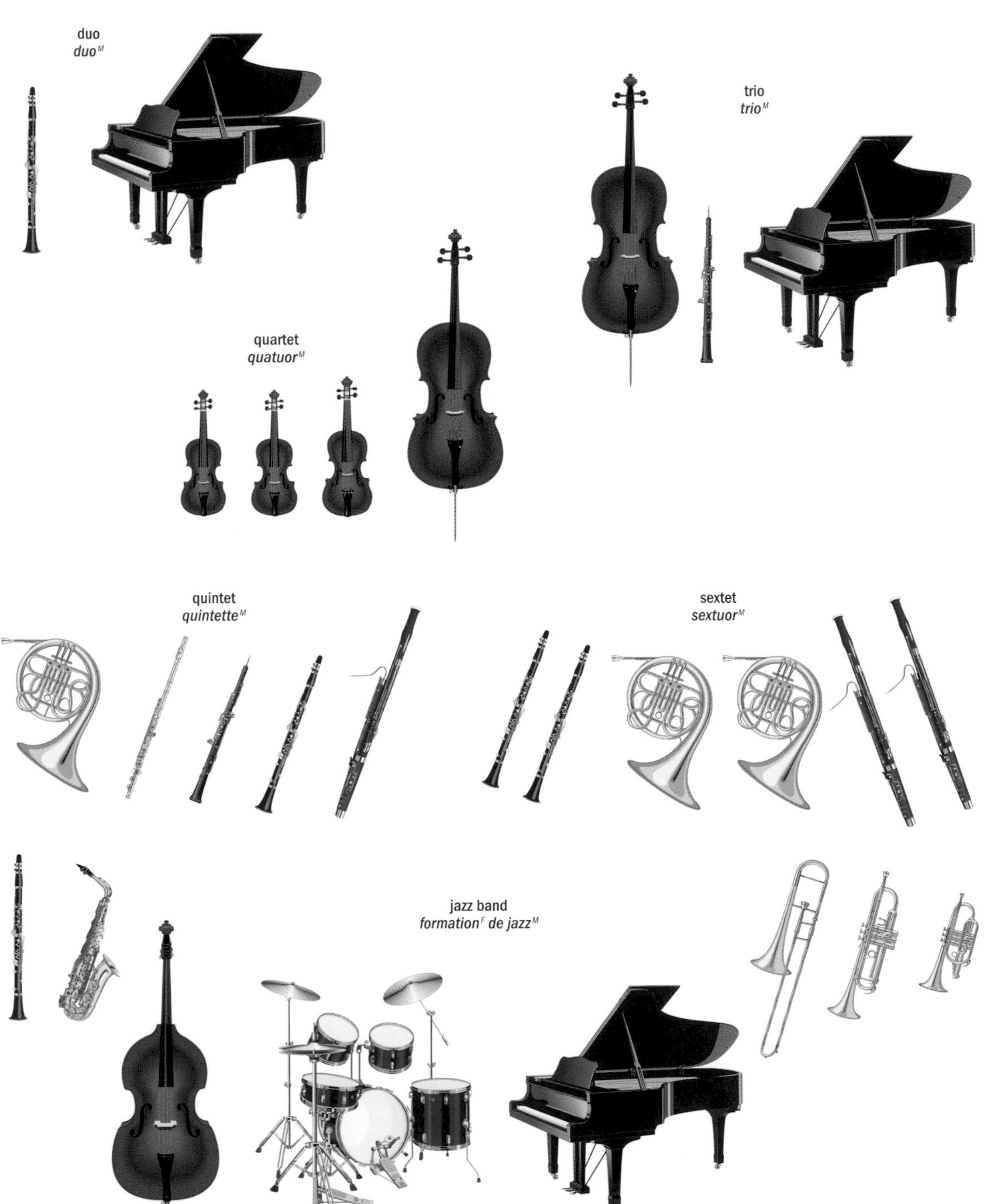
duo
duo^M
trio
trio^M
quartet
quatuor^M
quintet
quintette^M
sextet
sextuor^M
jazz band
formation^F *de jazz*^M

stringed instruments

instruments[M] à cordes[F]

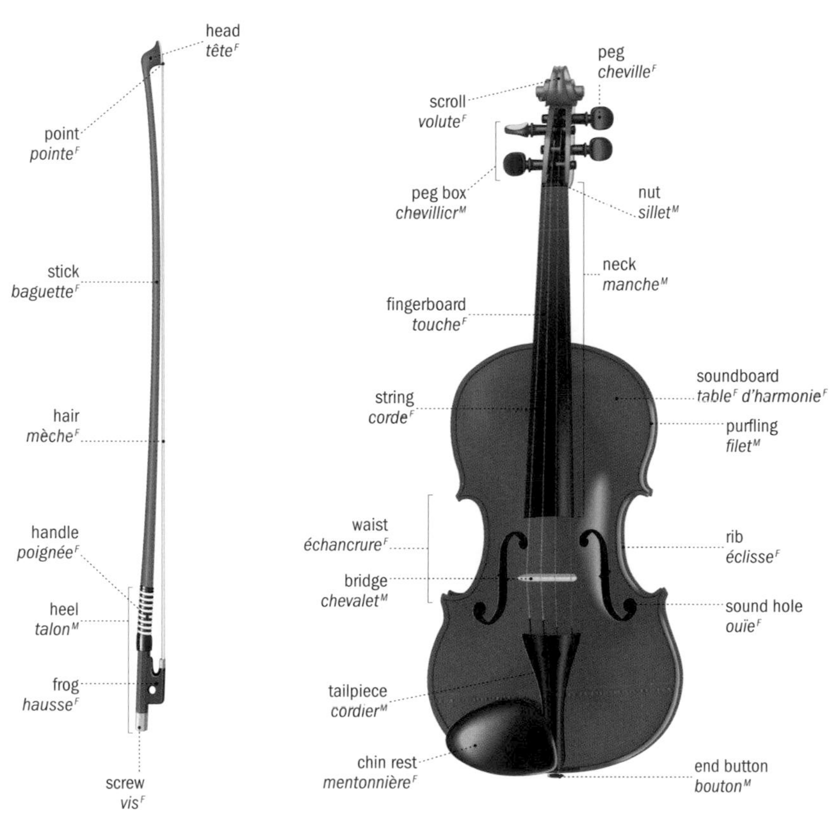
bow
archet[M]
head
tête[F]
point
pointe[F]
stick
baguette[F]
hair
mèche[F]
handle
poignée[F]
heel
talon[M]
frog
hausse[F]
screw
vis[F]
violin
violon[M]
peg
cheville[F]
scroll
volute[F]
peg box
chevillier[M]
nut
sillet[M]
neck
manche[M]
fingerboard
touche[F]
soundboard
table[F] d'harmonie[F]
string
corde[F]
purfling
filet[M]
waist
échancrure[F]
rib
éclisse[F]
bridge
chevalet[M]
sound hole
ouïe[F]
tailpiece
cordier[M]
chin rest
mentonnière[F]
end button
bouton[M]

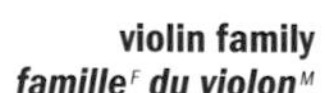
violin family
famille[F] du violon[M]

double bass
contrebasse[F]
cello
violoncelle[M]
viola
alto[M]
violin
violon[M]

stringed instruments

harp
harpe^F

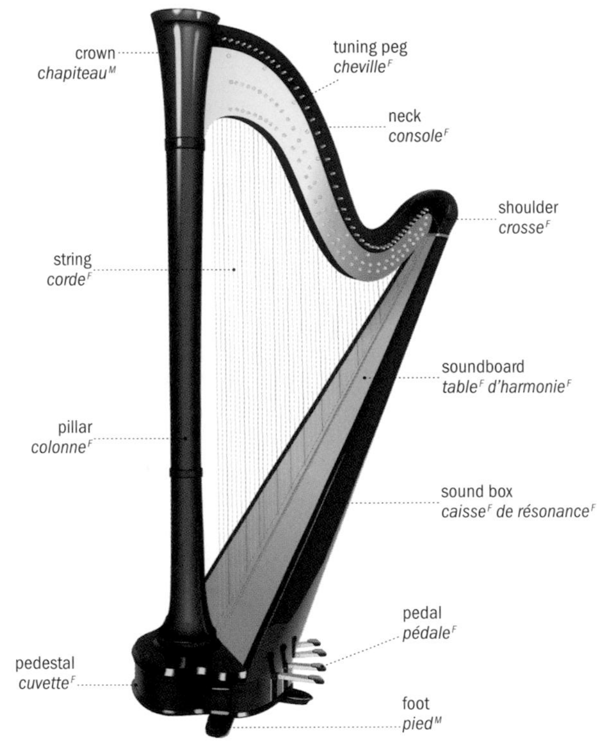
crown
chapiteau^M
tuning peg
cheville^F
neck
console^F
shoulder
crosse^F
string
corde^F
soundboard
table^F d'harmonie^F
pillar
colonne^F
sound box
caisse^F de résonance^F
pedal
pédale^F
pedestal
cuvette^F
foot
pied^M

acoustic guitar
guitare^F acoustique

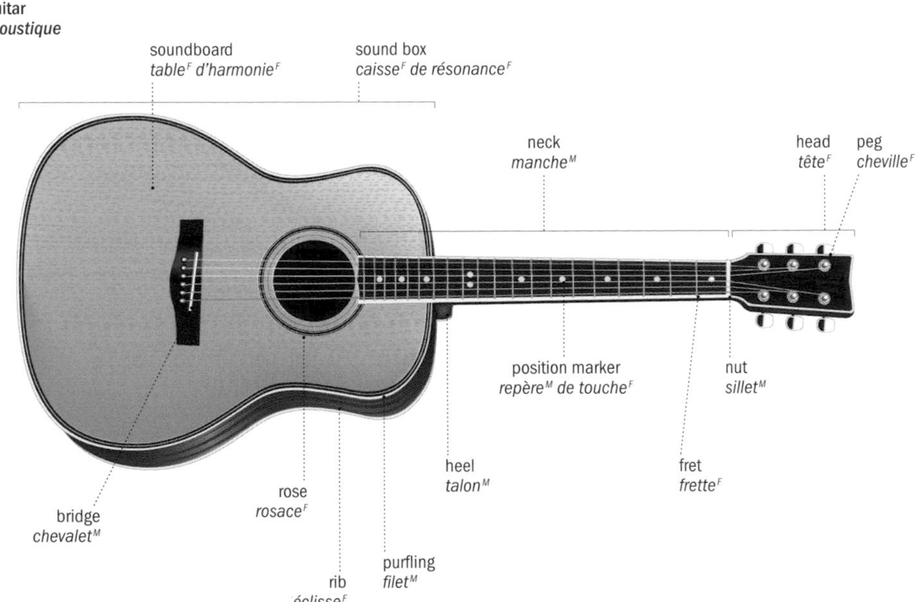
soundboard
table^F d'harmonie^F
sound box
caisse^F de résonance^F
neck
manche^M
head
tête^F
peg
cheville^F
position marker
repère^M de touche^F
nut
sillet^M
heel
talon^M
fret
frette^F
rose
rosace^F
bridge
chevalet^M
purfling
filet^M
rib
éclisse^F

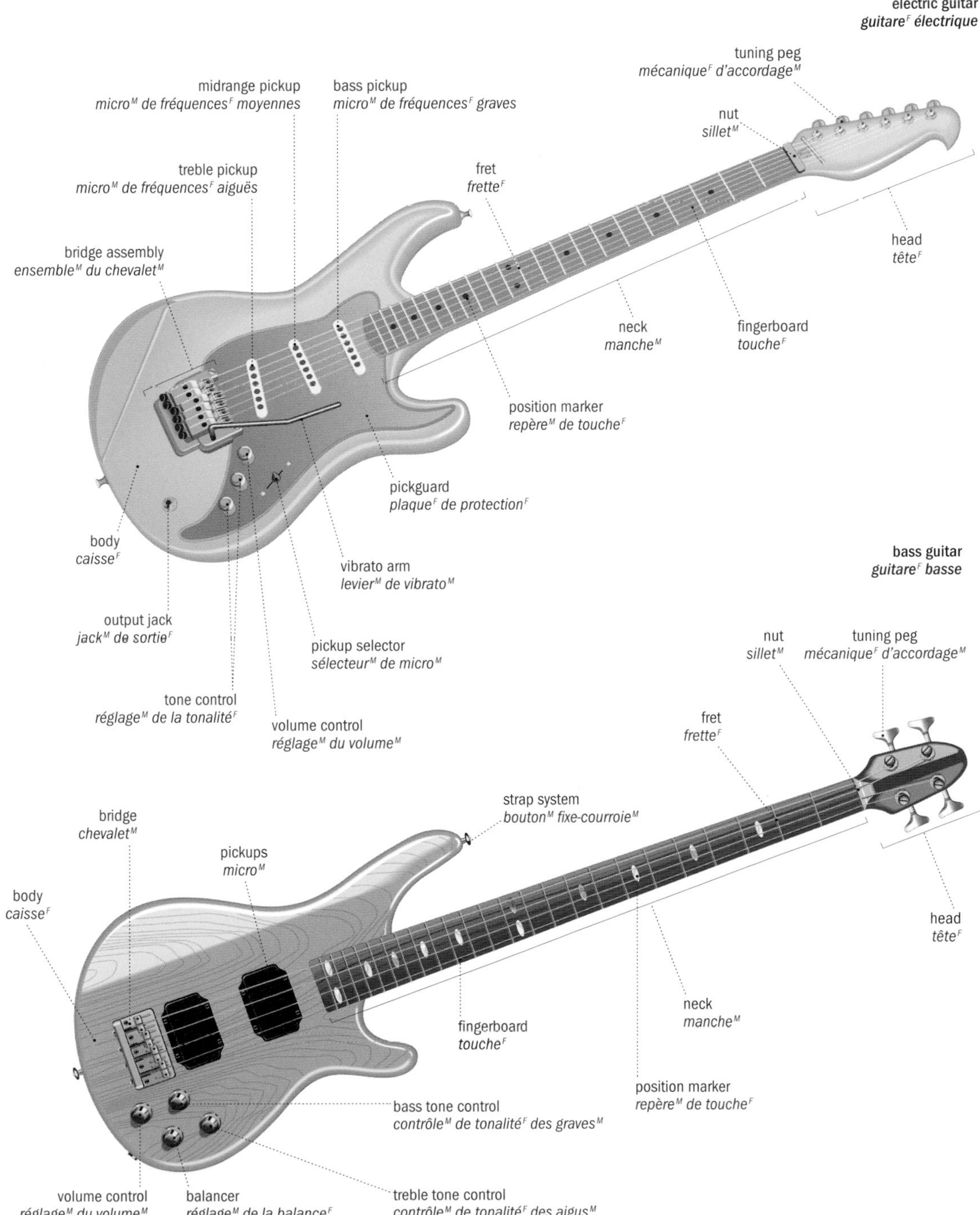
electric guitar
guitare^F électrique
tuning peg
mécanique^F d'accordage^M
midrange pickup
micro^M de fréquences^F moyennes
bass pickup
micro^M de fréquences^F graves
nut
sillet^M
treble pickup
micro^M de fréquences^F aiguës
fret
frette^F
bridge assembly
ensemble^M du chevalet^M
head
tête^F
neck
manche^M
fingerboard
touche^F
position marker
repère^M de touche^F
pickguard
plaque^F de protection^F
body
caisse^F
vibrato arm
levier^M de vibrato^M
output jack
jack^M de sortie^F
pickup selector
sélecteur^M de micro^M
tone control
réglage^M de la tonalité^F
volume control
réglage^M du volume^M
bass guitar
guitare^F basse
nut
sillet^M
tuning peg
mécanique^F d'accordage^M
fret
frette^F
strap system
bouton^M fixe-courroie^M
bridge
chevalet^M
pickups
micro^M
body
caisse^F
head
tête^F
neck
manche^M
fingerboard
touche^F
position marker
repère^M de touche^F
bass tone control
contrôle^M de tonalité^F des graves^M
volume control
réglage^M du volume^M
balancer
réglage^M de la balance^F
treble tone control
contrôle^M de tonalité^F des aigus^M

keyboard instruments

instruments^M à clavier^M

upright piano
piano^M droit

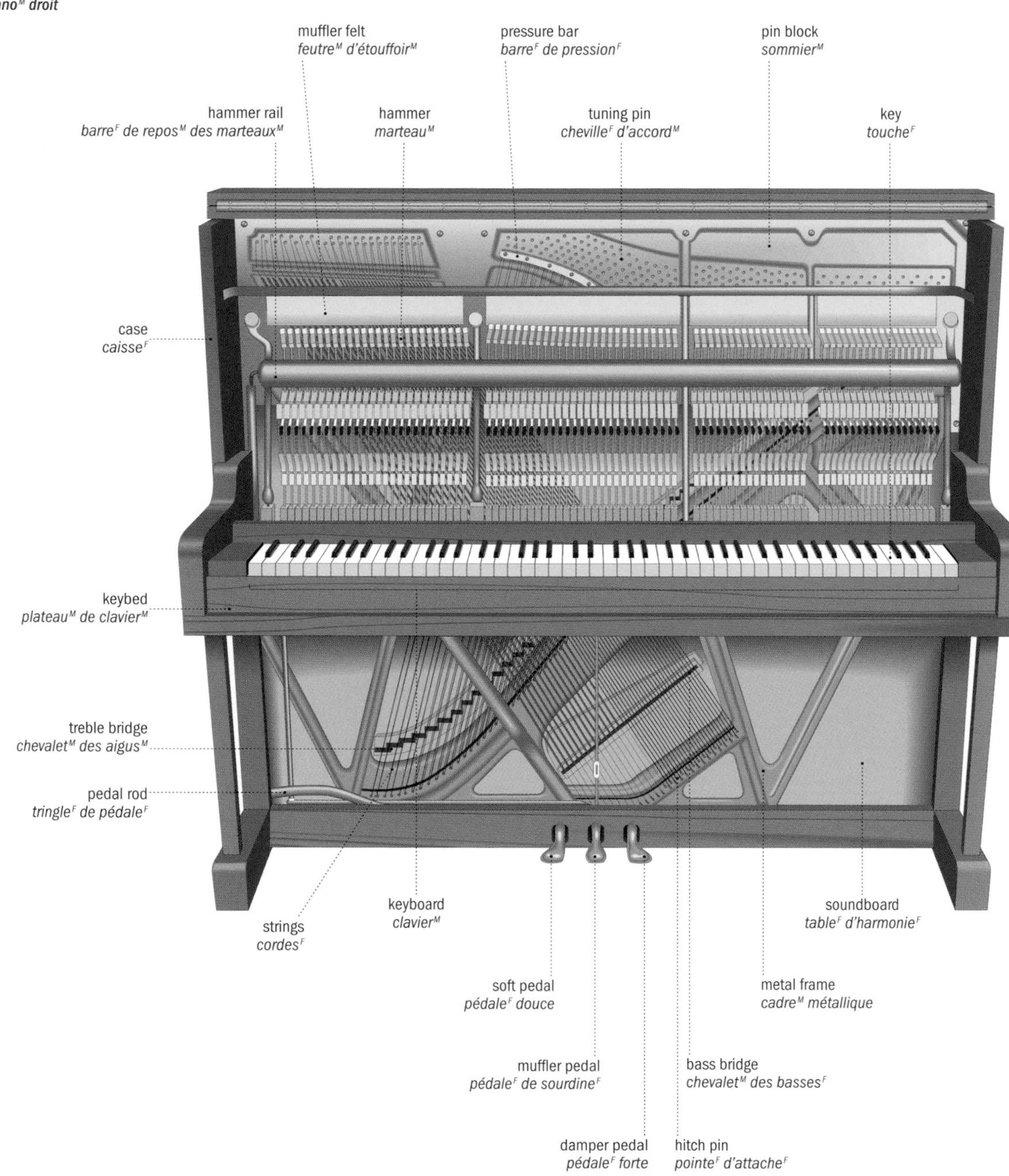
muffler felt
feutre^M d'étouffoir^M
pressure bar
barre^F de pression^F
pin block
sommier^M
hammer rail
barre^F de repos^M des marteaux^M
hammer
marteau^M
tuning pin
cheville^F d'accord^M
key
touche^F
case
caisse^F
keybed
plateau^M de clavier^M
treble bridge
chevalet^M des aigus^M
pedal rod
tringle^F de pédale^F
strings
cordes^F
keyboard
clavier^M
soundboard
table^F d'harmonie^F
soft pedal
pédale^F douce
metal frame
cadre^M métallique
muffler pedal
pédale^F de sourdine^F
bass bridge
chevalet^M des basses^F
damper pedal
pédale^F forte
hitch pin
pointe^F d'attache^F

organ
orgue[M]

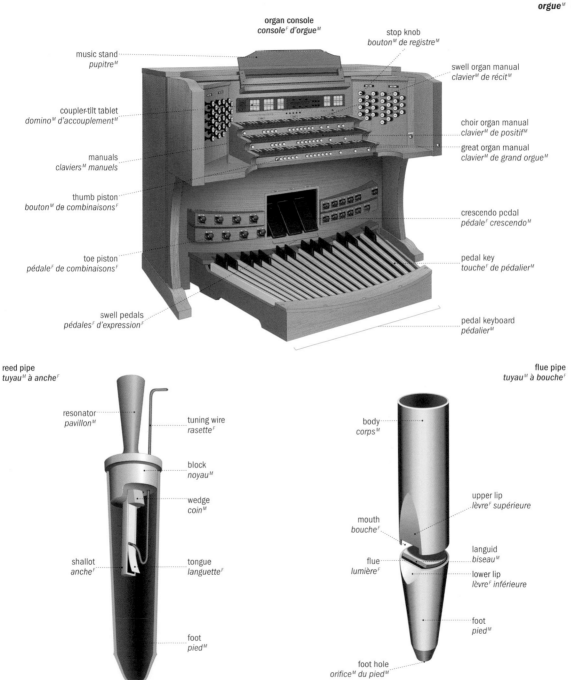

organ console
console[F] d'orgue[M]

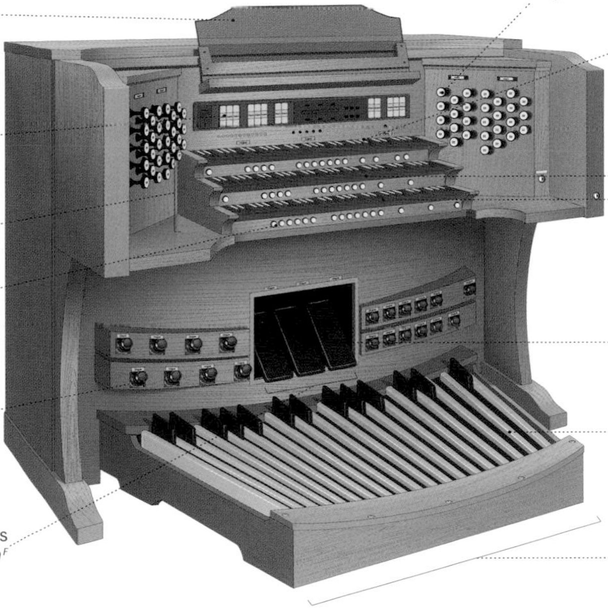

music stand
pupitre[M]

stop knob
bouton[M] de registre[M]

swell organ manual
clavier[M] de récit[M]

coupler-tilt tablet
domino[M] d'accouplement[M]

choir organ manual
clavier[M] de positif[M]

great organ manual
clavier[M] de grand orgue[M]

manuals
claviers[M] manuels

thumb piston
bouton[M] de combinaisons[F]

crescendo pedal
pédale[F] crescendo[M]

toe piston
pédale[F] de combinaisons[F]

pedal key
touche[F] de pédalier[M]

swell pedals
pédales[F] d'expression[F]

pedal keyboard
pédalier[M]

reed pipe
tuyau[M] à anche[F]

flue pipe
tuyau[M] à bouche[F]

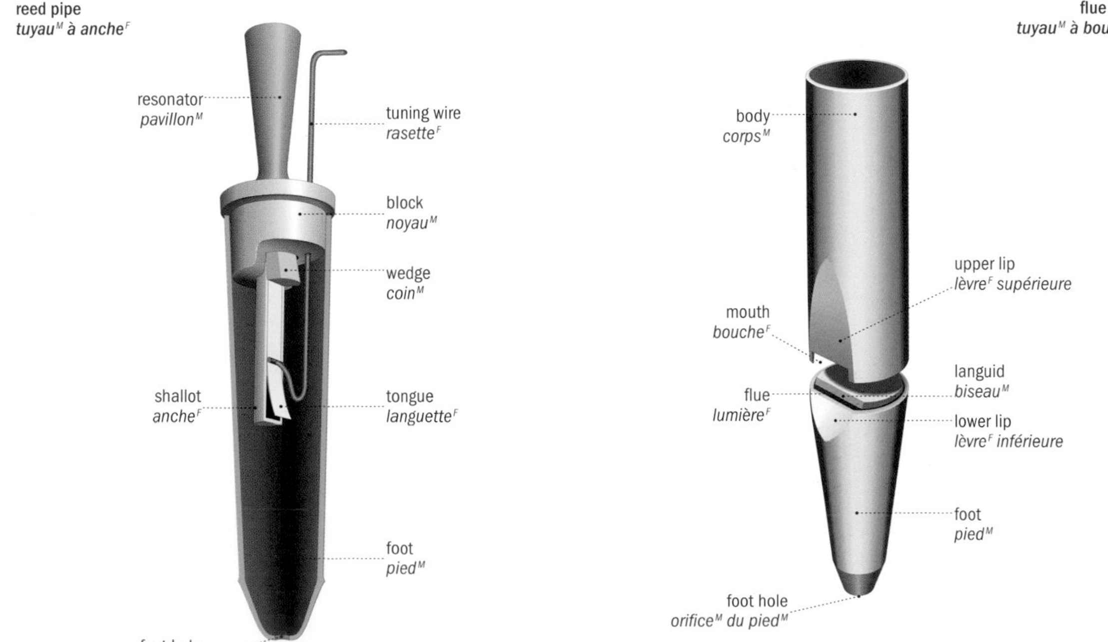
resonator
pavillon[M]
tuning wire
rasette[F]
block
noyau[M]
wedge
coin[M]
shallot
anche[F]
tongue
languette[F]
foot
pied[M]
foot hole
orifice[M] du pied[M]
body
corps[M]
upper lip
lèvre[F] supérieure
mouth
bouche[F]
languid
biseau[M]
flue
lumière[F]
lower lip
lèvre[F] inférieure
foot
pied[M]
foot hole
orifice[M] du pied[M]

wind instruments

instruments^M à vent^M

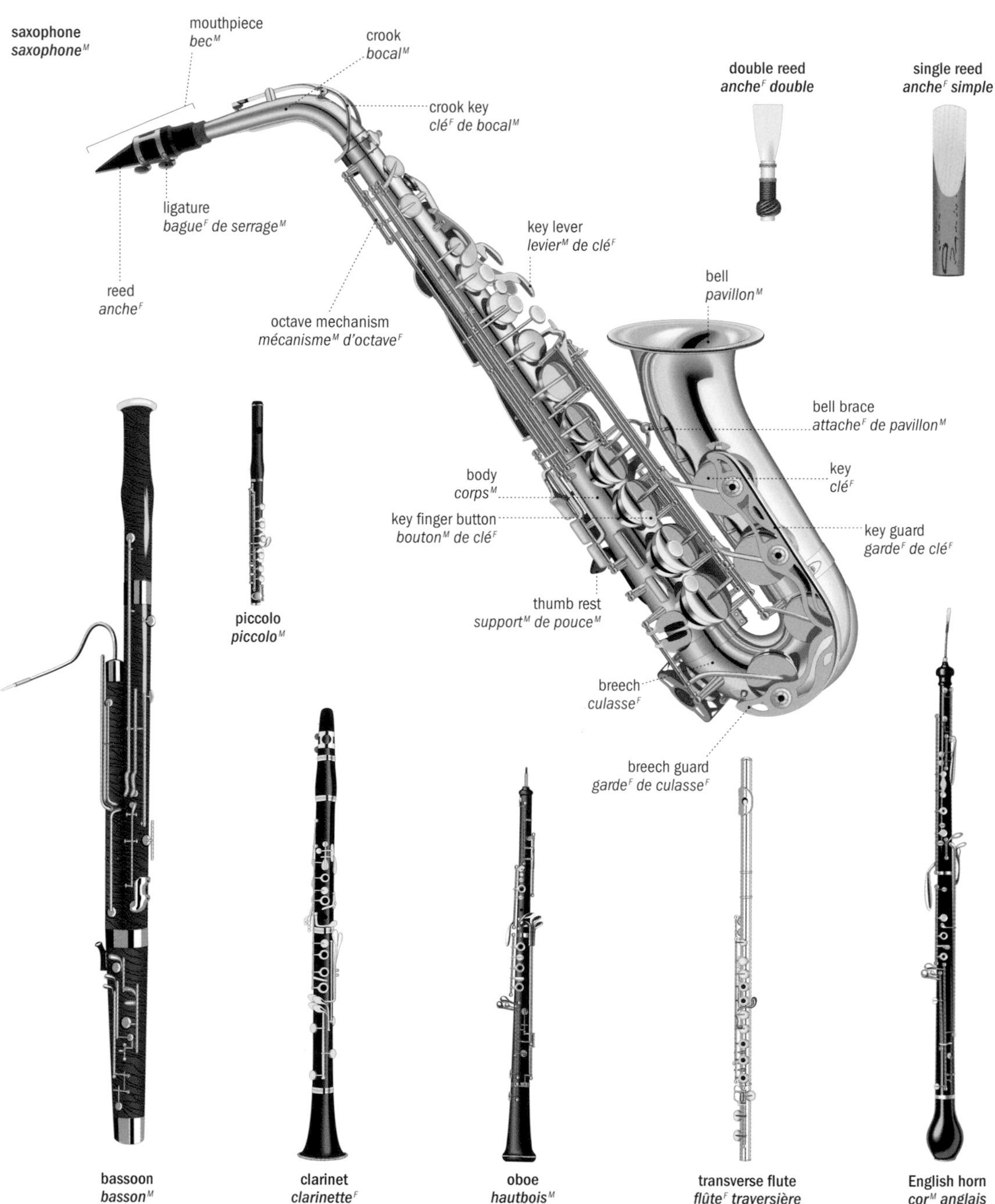
saxophone
saxophone^M
mouthpiece
bec^M
crook
bocal^M
crook key
clé^F de bocal^M
ligature
bague^F de serrage^M
reed
anche^F
octave mechanism
mécanisme^M d'octave^F
key lever
levier^M de clé^F
bell
pavillon^M
bell brace
attache^F de pavillon^M
key
clé^F
body
corps^M
key finger button
bouton^M de clé^F
key guard
garde^F de clé^F
thumb rest
support^M de pouce^M
breech
culasse^F
breech guard
garde^F de culasse^F
double reed
anche^F double
single reed
anche^F simple
piccolo
piccolo^M
bassoon
basson^M
clarinet
clarinette^F
oboe
hautbois^M
transverse flute
flûte^F traversière
English horn
cor^M anglais

trumpet
trompette[F]
key
bouton[M] *de piston*[M]
little finger hook
crochet[M] *de petit doigt*[M]
bell
pavillon[M]
mouthpipe
branche[F] *d'embouchure*[F]
ring
bague[F]
mouthpiece receiver
boisseau[M] *d'embouchure*[F]
mouthpiece
embouchure[F]
tuning slide
coulisse[F] *d'accord*[M]
first valve slide
coulisse[F] *du premier piston*[M]
spit valve
soupape[F] *d'évacuation*[F]
third valve slide
coulisse[F] *du troisième piston*[M]
thumb hook
crochet[M] *de pouce*[M]
valve
piston[M]
valve casing
corps[M] *de piston*[M]
second valve slide
coulisse[F] *du deuxième piston*[M]
mute
sourdine[F]
French horn
cor[M] ***d'harmonie***[F]
cornet
cornet[M] ***à pistons***[M]
bugle
clairon[M]
saxhorn
saxhorn[M]
tuba
tuba[M]
trombone
trombone[M]

percussion instruments

instruments[M] à percussion[F]

drums
batterie[F]

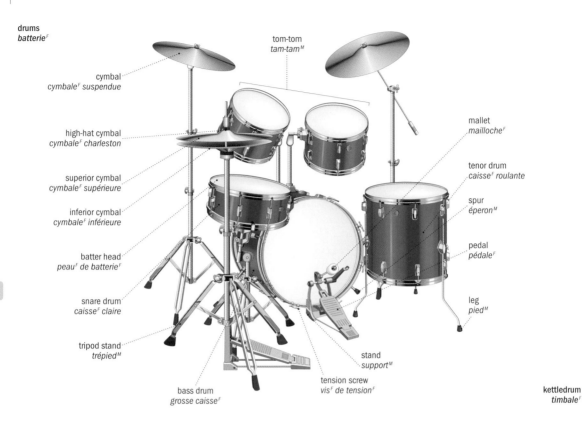

tom-tom
tam-tam[M]

cymbal
cymbale[F] suspendue

high-hat cymbal
cymbale[F] charleston

superior cymbal
cymbale[F] supérieure

inferior cymbal
cymbale[F] inférieure

batter head
peau[F] de batterie[F]

snare drum
caisse[F] claire

tripod stand
trépied[M]

bass drum
grosse caisse[F]

tension screw
vis[F] de tension[F]

stand
support[M]

mallet
mailloche[F]

tenor drum
caisse[F] roulante

spur
éperon[M]

pedal
pédale[F]

leg
pied[M]

kettledrum
timbale[F]

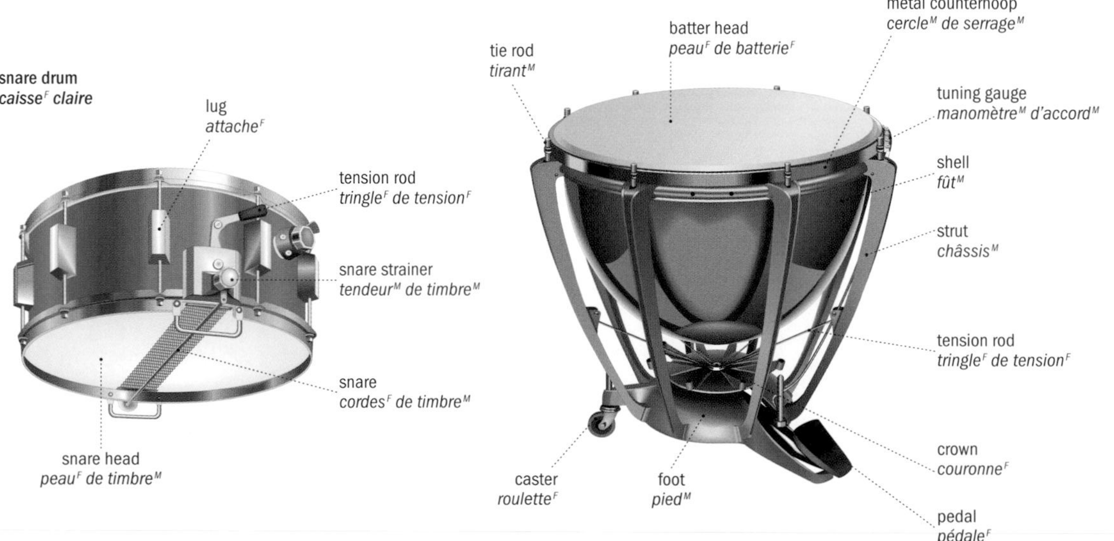
snare drum
caisse[F] claire
lug
attache[F]
tension rod
tringle[F] de tension[F]
snare strainer
tendeur[M] de timbre[M]
snare
cordes[F] de timbre[M]
snare head
peau[F] de timbre[M]
tie rod
tirant[M]
batter head
peau[F] de batterie[F]
metal counterhoop
cercle[M] de serrage[M]
tuning gauge
manomètre[M] d'accord[M]
shell
fût[M]
strut
châssis[M]
tension rod
tringle[F] de tension[F]
crown
couronne[F]
pedal
pédale[F]
caster
roulette[F]
foot
pied[M]

sleigh bells
grelots^M
set of bells
clochettes^F
sistrum
sistre^M
castanets
castagnettes^F
cymbals
cymbales^F
tambourine
tambour^M de basque^M
head
peau^F
jingle
cymbalette^F
triangle
triangle^M
metal rod
battant^M
bongos
bongo^M
wire brush
balai^M métallique
gong
gong^M
drum sticks
baguettes^F
xylophone
xylophone^M
resonator
tube^M de résonance^F
frame
châssis^M
bar
lame^F
tubular bells
carillon^M tubulaire
mallets
mailloches^F

electronic instruments

instruments[M] électroniques

sequencer
séquenceur[M]

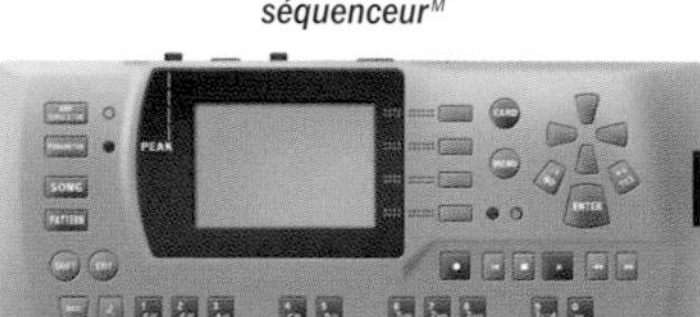

sampler
échantillonneur[M]

headphone jack
prise[F] casque[M]

function display
affichage[M] des fonctions[F]

disk drive
lecteur[M] de disquette[F]

expander
expandeur[M]

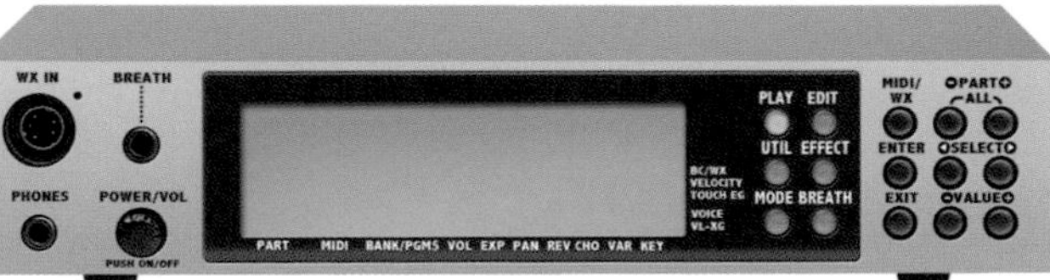
WX IN
BREATH
PHONES
POWER/VOL
PUSH ON/OFF
PLAY EDIT
UTIL EFFECT
MODE BREATH
BC/WX
VELOCITY
TOUCH EG
VOICE
VL-XG
PART MIDI BANK/PGMS VOL EXP PAN REV CHO VAR KEY
MIDI/WX
PART
ALL
ENTER
SELECT
EXIT
VALUE

synthesizer
synthétiseur[M]

system buttons
fonctions[F] système[M]

function display
affichage[M] des fonctions[F]

program selector
sélecteur[M] de programme[M]

voice edit buttons
programmation[F] des voix[F]

volume control
contrôle[M] du volume[M]

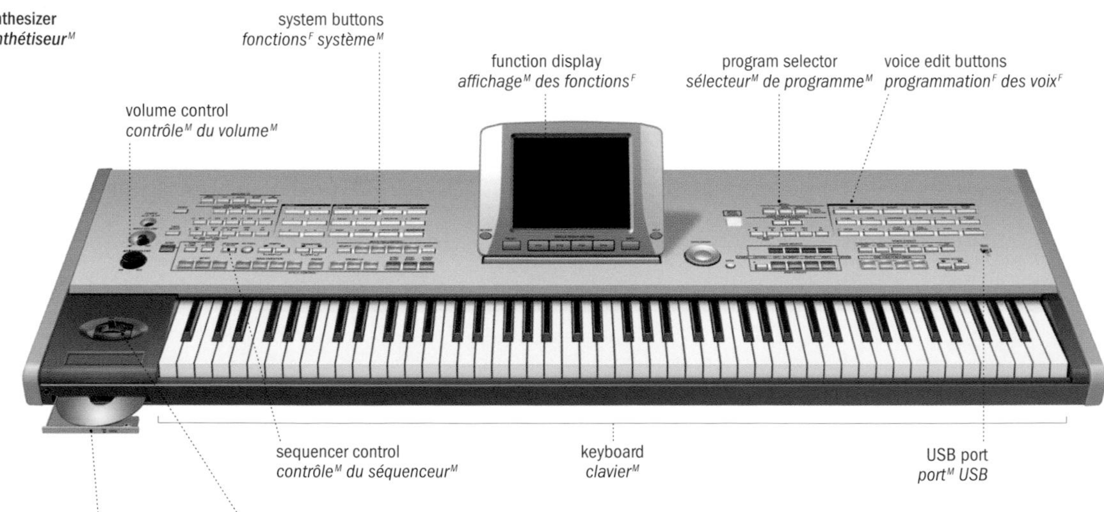

sequencer control
contrôle[M] du séquenceur[M]

keyboard
clavier[M]

USB port
port[M] USB

CD/DVD-ROM drive
lecteur[M] de CD/DVD-ROM[M]

pitch and modulation switch
modulation[F] de la hauteur[F] et du timbre[M] du son[M]

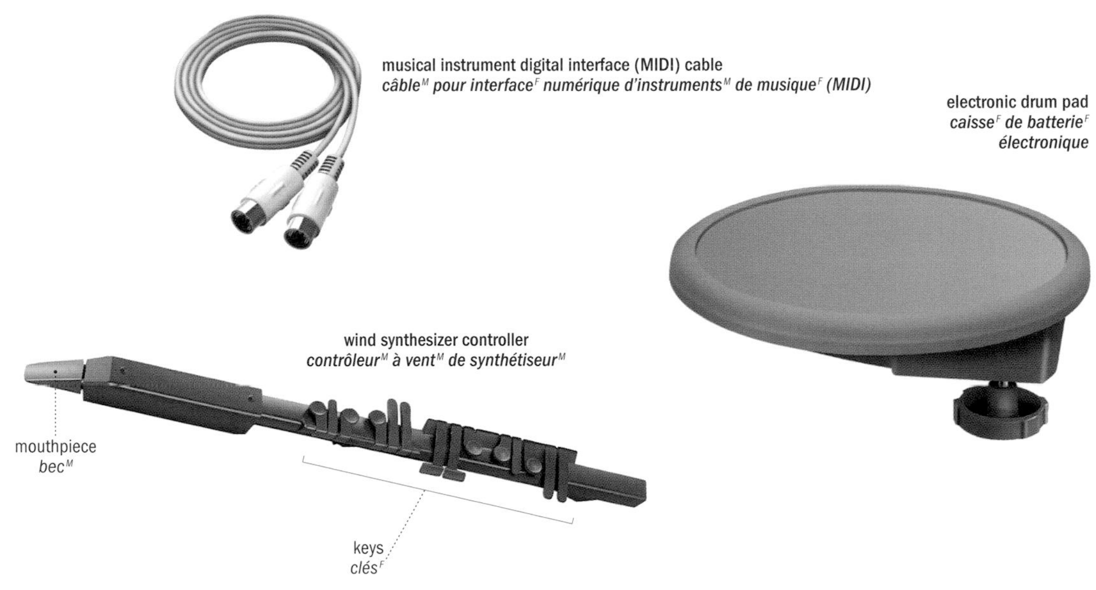

musical instrument digital interface (MIDI) cable
câble[M] pour interface[F] numérique d'instruments[M] de musique[F] (MIDI)
electronic drum pad
caisse[F] de batterie[F] électronique
wind synthesizer controller
contrôleur[M] à vent[M] de synthétiseur[M]
mouthpiece
bec[M]
keys
clés[F]

electronic piano
piano[M] électronique

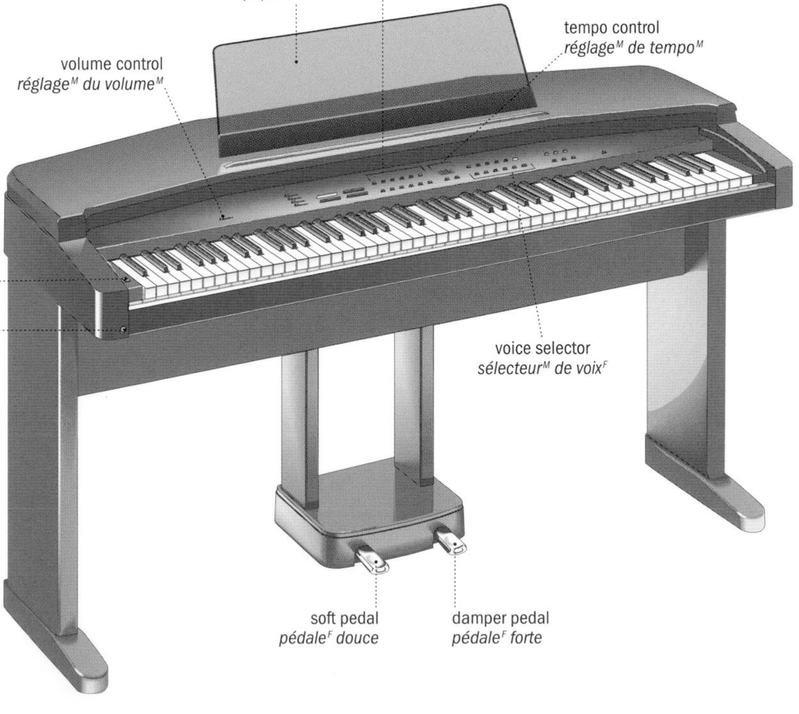

rhythm selector
sélecteur[M] de rythme[M]

music stand
pupitre[M]

tempo control
réglage[M] de tempo[M]

volume control
réglage[M] du volume[M]

power switch
interrupteur[M] d'alimentation[F]

headphone jack
prise[F] casque[M]

voice selector
sélecteur[M] de voix[F]

soft pedal
pédale[F] douce

damper pedal
pédale[F] forte

writing instruments

instruments^M d'écriture^F

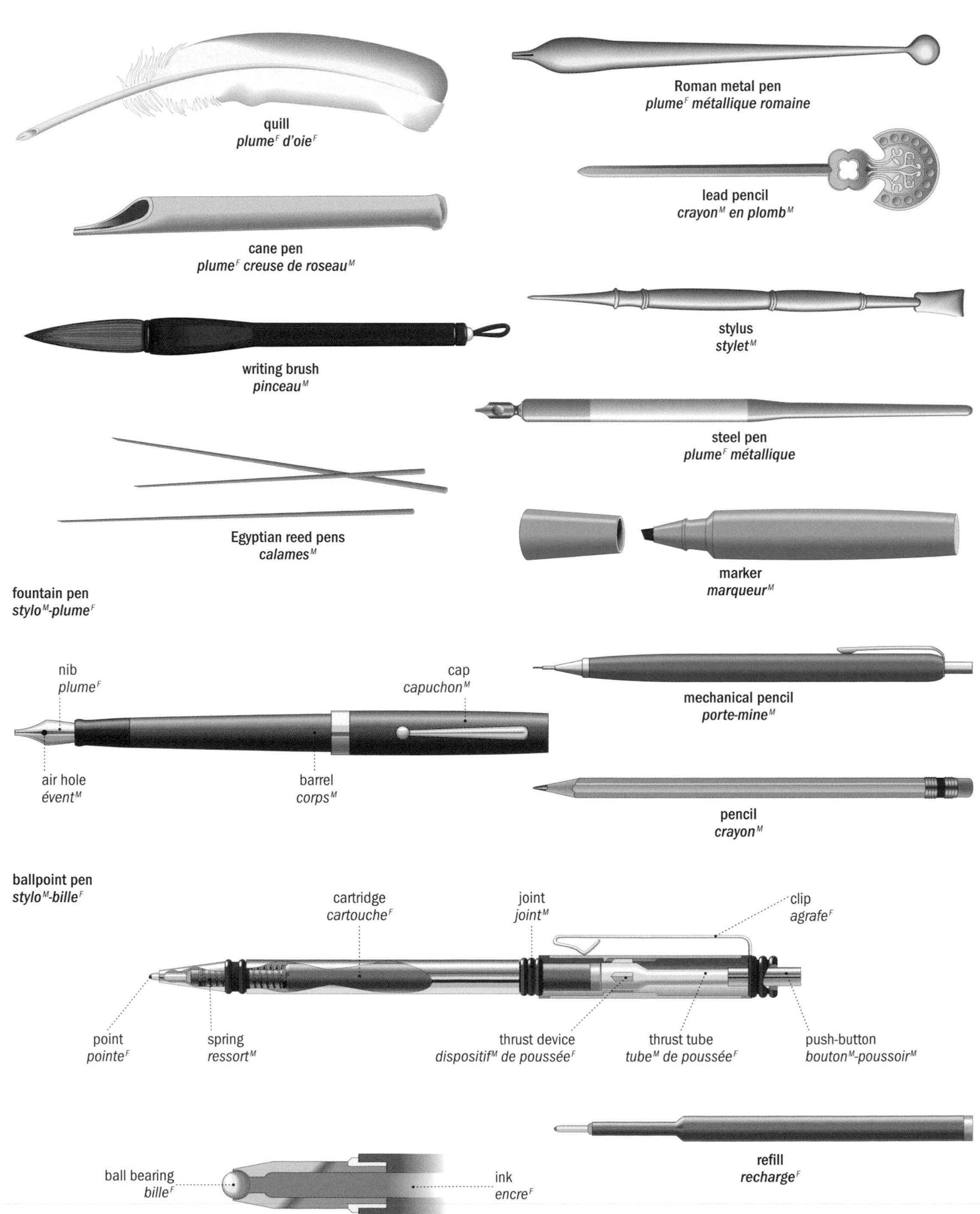
quill
plume^F d'oie^F
Roman metal pen
plume^F métallique romaine
lead pencil
crayon^M en plomb^M
cane pen
plume^F creuse de roseau^M
stylus
stylet^M
writing brush
pinceau^M
steel pen
plume^F métallique
Egyptian reed pens
calames^M
marker
marqueur^M
fountain pen
stylo^M-plume^F
nib
plume^F
cap
capuchon^M
air hole
évent^M
barrel
corps^M
mechanical pencil
porte-mine^M
pencil
crayon^M
ballpoint pen
stylo^M-bille^F
cartridge
cartouche^F
joint
joint^M
clip
agrafe^F
point
pointe^F
spring
ressort^M
thrust device
dispositif^M de poussée^F
thrust tube
tube^M de poussée^F
push-button
bouton^M-poussoir^M
refill
recharge^F
ball bearing
bille^F
ink
encre^F

newspaper

journal[M]

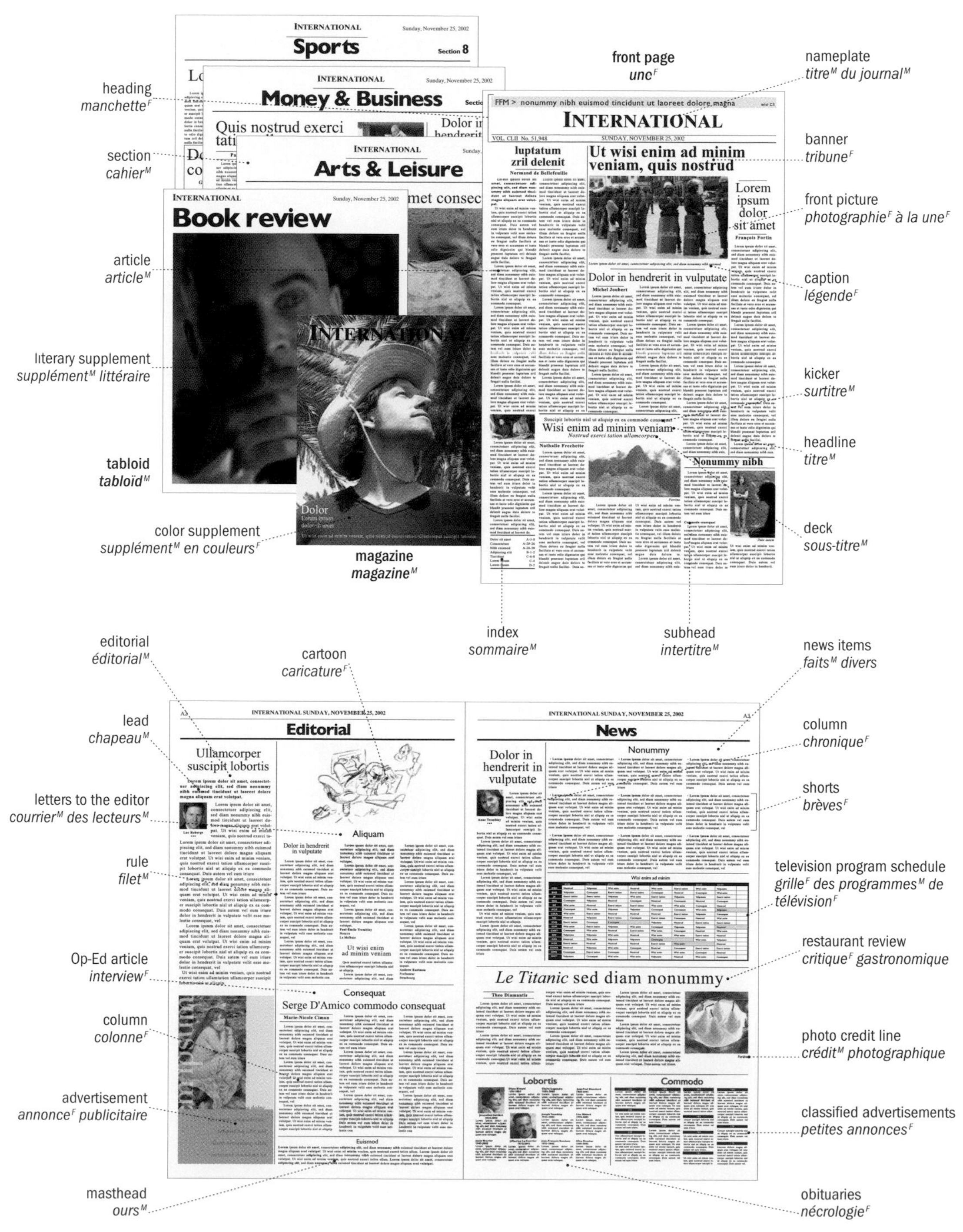

front page
une[F]
nameplate
titre[M] *du journal*[M]
heading
manchette[F]
banner
tribune[F]
section
cahier[M]
front picture
photographie[F] *à la une*[F]
article
article[M]
caption
légende[F]
literary supplement
supplément[M] *littéraire*
kicker
surtitre[M]
tabloid
tabloïd[M]
headline
titre[M]
color supplement
supplément[M] *en couleurs*[F]
magazine
magazine[M]
deck
sous-titre[M]
index
sommaire[M]
subhead
intertitre[M]
editorial
éditorial[M]
cartoon
caricature[F]
news items
faits[M] *divers*
lead
chapeau[M]
column
chronique[F]
letters to the editor
courrier[M] *des lecteurs*[M]
shorts
brèves[F]
rule
filet[M]
television program schedule
grille[F] *des programmes*[M] *de télévision*[F]
Op-Ed article
interview[F]
restaurant review
critique[F] *gastronomique*
column
colonne[F]
photo credit line
crédit[M] *photographique*
advertisement
annonce[F] *publicitaire*
classified advertisements
petites annonces[F]
masthead
ours[M]
obituaries
nécrologie[F]

photography

photographie^F

single-lens reflex (SLR) camera: front view
appareil^M à visée^F reflex mono-objectif^M : vue avant

exposure adjustment knob
correction^F d'exposition^F
accessory shoe
griffe^F porte-accessoires^M
hot-shoe contact
contact^M électrique
drive mode
mode^M d'acquisition^F
control panel
écran^M de contrôle^M
exposure mode
mode^M d'exposition^F
command control dial
sélecteur^M de fonctions^F
multiple exposure mode
surimpression^F
on-off switch
commutateur^M marche^F/arrêt^M
sensitivity
sensibilité^F
shutter release button
déclencheur^M
remote control terminal
prise^F de télécommande^F
self-timer indicator
témoin^M du retardateur^M
focus mode selector
mode^M de mise^F au point^M
camera body
boîtier^M
lens release button
déverrouillage^M de l'objectif^M
objective lens
objectif^M
depth-of-field preview button
vérification^F de la profondeur^F de champ^M

lenses
objectifs^M

telephoto lens
téléobjectif^M

zoom lens
objectif^M zoom^M

wide-angle lens
objectif^M grand-angulaire

macro lens
objectif^M macro

lens accessories
accessoires^M de l'objectif^M

lens cap
capuchon^M d'objectif^M
lens hood
parasoleil^M

polarizing filter
filtre^M de polarisation^F

digital reflex camera: camera back
appareil[M] à visée[F] reflex numérique : dos[M]

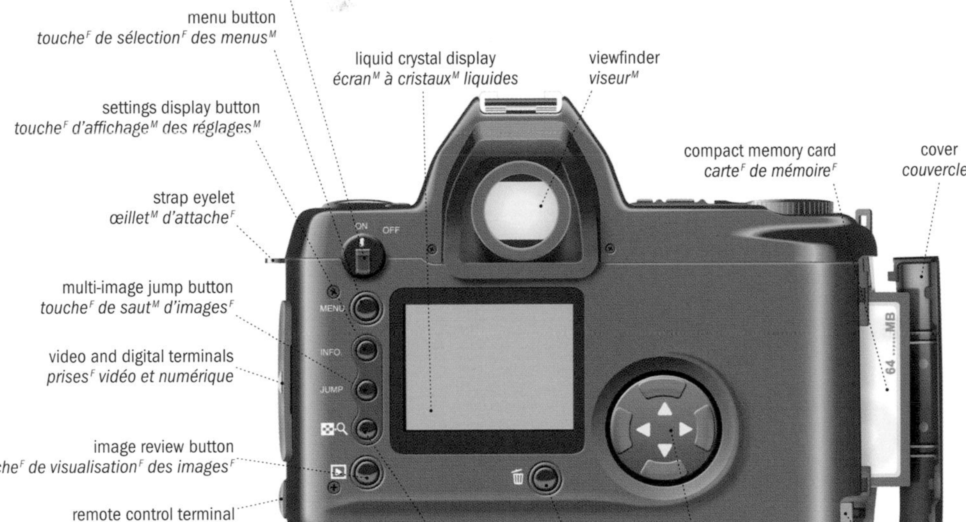
power switch
commutateur[M] d'alimentation[F]
menu button
touche[F] de sélection[F] des menus[M]
liquid crystal display
écran[M] à cristaux[M] liquides
viewfinder
viseur[M]
settings display button
touche[F] d'affichage[M] des réglages[M]
compact memory card
carte[F] de mémoire[F]
cover
couvercle[M]
strap eyelet
œillet[M] d'attache[F]
ON
OFF
multi-image jump button
touche[F] de saut[M] d'images[F]
MENU
INFO.
JUMP
64 MB
video and digital terminals
prises[F] vidéo et numérique
image review button
touche[F] de visualisation[F] des images[F]
remote control terminal
prise[F] de télécommande[F]
index/enlarge button
touche[F] d'index[M]/agrandissement[M]
erase button
touche[F] d'effacement[M]
four-way selector
sélecteur[M] quadridirectionnel
eject button
bouton[M] d'éjection[F]

still cameras
appareils[M] photographiques

Polaroid® camera
Polaroid®[M]

medium-format SLR (6 x 6)
appareil[M] reflex 6 X 6 mono-objectif[M]

ultracompact camera
appareil[M] ultracompact

compact camera
appareil[M] compact

disposable camera
appareil[M] jetable

view camera
chambre[F] photographique

broadcast satellite communication

télédiffusion[F] par satellite[M]

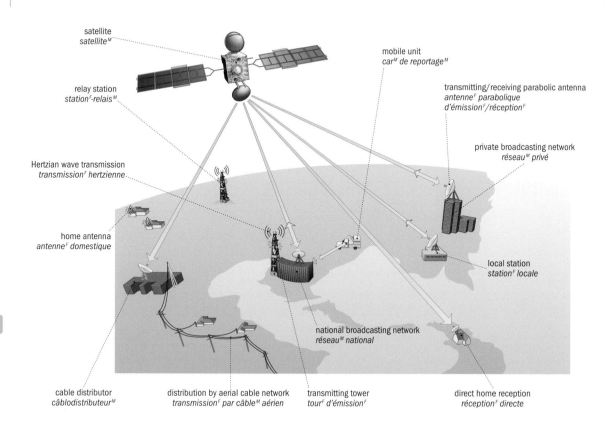

satellite
satellite[M]

mobile unit
car[M] de reportage[M]

relay station
station[F]-relais[M]

transmitting/receiving parabolic antenna
antenne[F] parabolique d'émission[F]/réception[F]

private broadcasting network
réseau[M] privé

Hertzian wave transmission
transmission[F] hertzienne

home antenna
antenne[F] domestique

local station
station[F] locale

national broadcasting network
réseau[M] national

cable distributor
câblodistributeur[M]

distribution by aerial cable network
transmission[F] par câble[M] aérien

transmitting tower
tour[F] d'émission[F]

direct home reception
réception[F] directe

telecommunication satellites

satellites[M] de télécommunications[F]

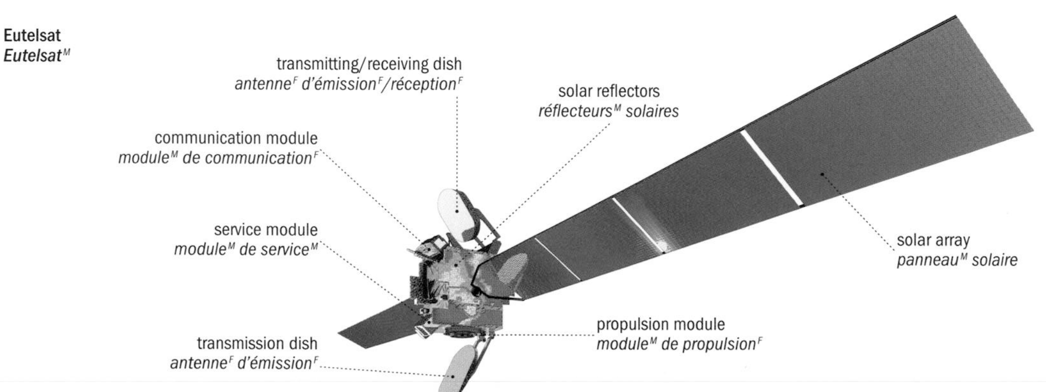

Eutelsat
Eutelsat[M]
transmitting/receiving dish
antenne[F] d'émission[F]/réception[F]
solar reflectors
réflecteurs[M] solaires
communication module
module[M] de communication[F]
service module
module[M] de service[M]
solar array
panneau[M] solaire
propulsion module
module[M] de propulsion[F]
transmission dish
antenne[F] d'émission[F]

telecommunications by satellite

télécommunications[F] par satellite[M]

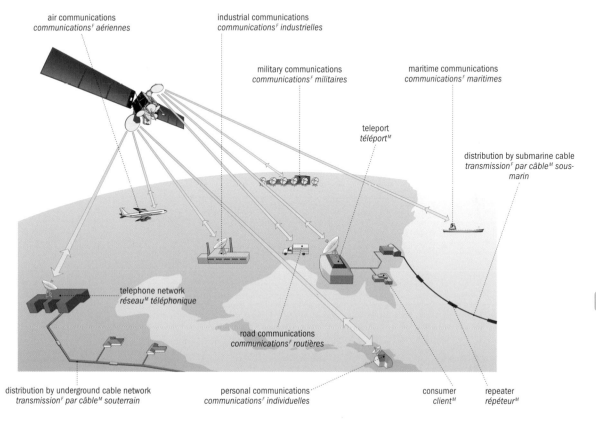

air communications
communications[F] aériennes

industrial communications
communications[F] industrielles

military communications
communications[F] militaires

maritime communications
communications[F] maritimes

teleport
téléport[M]

distribution by submarine cable
transmission[F] par câble[M] sous-marin

telephone network
réseau[M] téléphonique

road communications
communications[F] routières

distribution by underground cable network
transmission[F] par câble[M] souterrain

personal communications
communications[F] individuelles

consumer
client[M]

repeater
répéteur[M]

telecommunication satellites

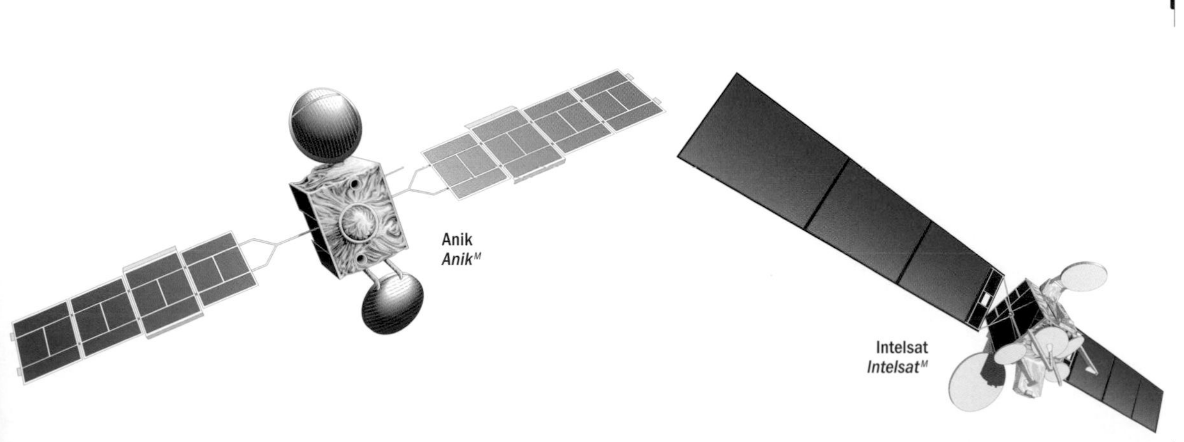
Anik
Anik[M]
Intelsat
Intelsat[M]

television

télévision[F]

liquid crystal display (LCD) television
téléviseur[M] à cristaux[M] liquides

plasma television
téléviseur[M] à plasma[M]

cathode ray tube (CRT) television
téléviseur[M] à écran[M] cathodique

cabinet
coffret[M]
screen
écran[M]
power button
interrupteur[M] d'alimentation[F]
tuning controls
boutons[M] de réglage[M]
remote control sensor
capteur[M] de télécommande[F]

picture tube
tube[M]-image[F]

electron gun
canon[M] à électrons[M]

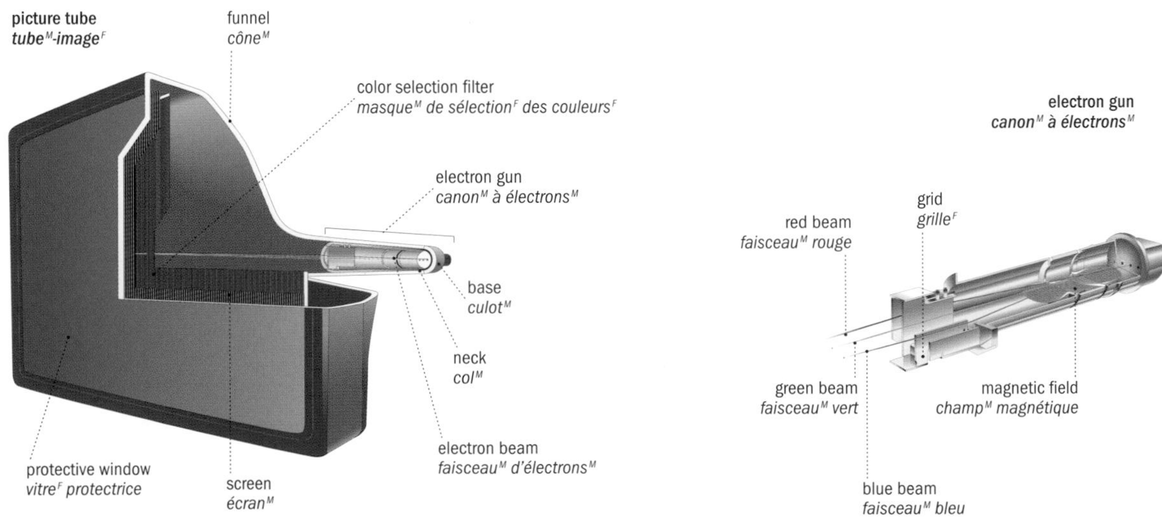
funnel
cône[M]
color selection filter
masque[M] de sélection[F] des couleurs[F]
electron gun
canon[M] à électrons[M]
base
culot[M]
neck
col[M]
electron beam
faisceau[M] d'électrons[M]
protective window
vitre[F] protectrice
screen
écran[M]
red beam
faisceau[M] rouge
grid
grille[F]
green beam
faisceau[M] vert
magnetic field
champ[M] magnétique
blue beam
faisceau[M] bleu

remote control
***télécommande*[F]**

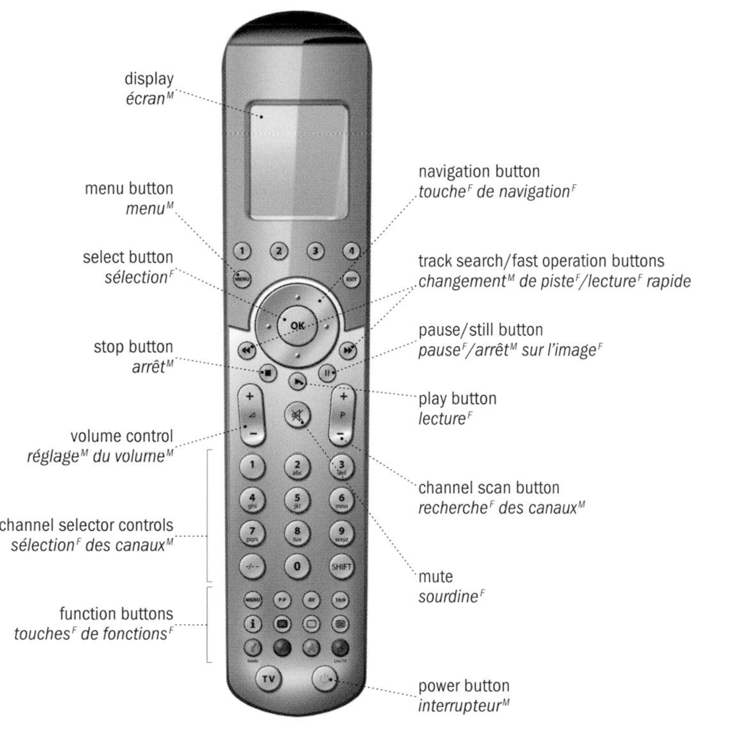
display
écran[M]
menu button
menu[M]
select button
sélection[F]
stop button
arrêt[M]
volume control
réglage[M] *du volume*[M]
channel selector controls
sélection[F] *des canaux*[M]
function buttons
touches[F] *de fonctions*[F]
navigation button
touche[F] *de navigation*[F]
track search/fast operation buttons
changement[M] *de piste*[F]*/lecture*[F] *rapide*
pause/still button
pause[F]*/arrêt*[M] *sur l'image*[F]
play button
lecture[F]
channel scan button
recherche[F] *des canaux*[M]
mute
sourdine[F]
power button
interrupteur[M]

DVD recorder
enregistreur*[M] *de DVD*[M] *vidéo

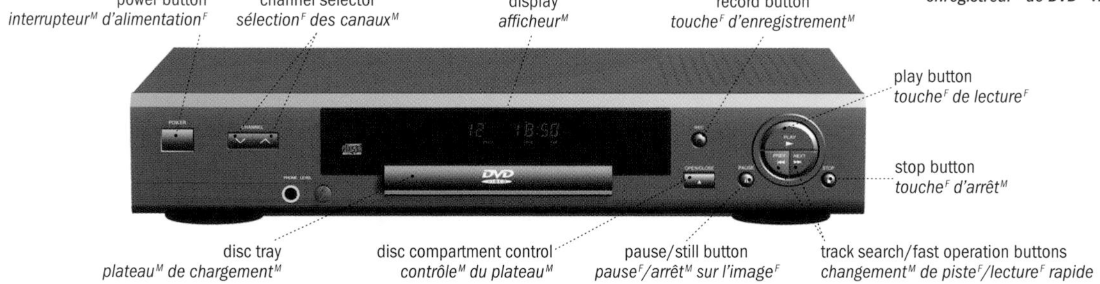
power button
interrupteur[M] *d'alimentation*[F]
channel selector
sélection[F] *des canaux*[M]
display
afficheur[M]
record button
touche[F] *d'enregistrement*[M]
play button
touche[F] *de lecture*[F]
stop button
touche[F] *d'arrêt*[M]
disc tray
plateau[M] *de chargement*[M]
disc compartment control
contrôle[M] *du plateau*[M]
pause/still button
pause[F]*/arrêt*[M] *sur l'image*[F]
track search/fast operation buttons
changement[M] *de piste*[F]*/lecture*[F] *rapide*

recording media
***supports*[M] *d'enregistrement*[M]**

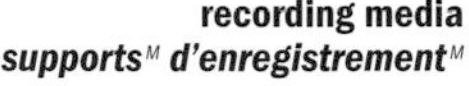

videocassette
cassette*[F] *vidéo

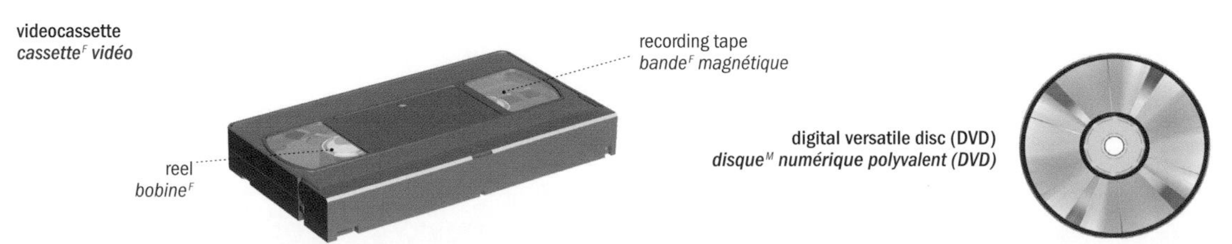
recording tape
bande[F] *magnétique*
reel
bobine[F]

digital versatile disc (DVD)
disque*[M] *numérique polyvalent (DVD)

COMMUNICATIONS AND OFFICE AUTOMATION

mini-DV camcorder: front view
caméscopeM mini-DV : vueF avant

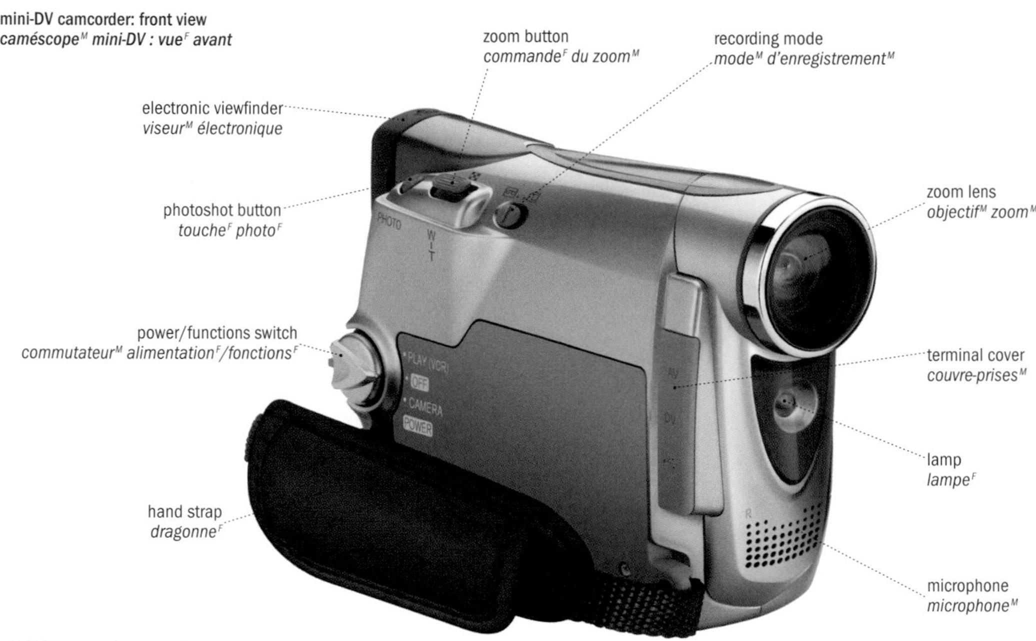
zoom button
commandeF du zoomM
recording mode
modeM d'enregistrementM
electronic viewfinder
viseurM électronique
photoshot button
toucheF photoF
zoom lens
objectifM zoomM
power/functions switch
commutateurM alimentationF/fonctionsF
terminal cover
couvre-prisesM
lamp
lampeF
hand strap
dragonneF
microphone
microphoneM

mini-DV camcorder: rear view
caméscopeM mini-DV : vueF arrière

videotape operation controls
commandesF de la bandeF vidéo
focus button
toucheF de miseF au pointM
nightshot button
toucheF de priseF de vuesF nocturne
eyepiece
oculaireM
liquid crystal display
écranM à cristauxM liquides
recording start/stop button
toucheF d'enregistrementM
rechargeable battery pack
pileF rechargeable
card slot
logementM de la carteF mémoireF
menu button
toucheF de menuM
speaker
haut-parleurM
backlighting button
toucheF de rétroéclairageM
widescreen/data code button
toucheF écranM large/codeM de donnéesF

television

dish antenna
antenne[F] parabolique

receiver
terminal[M] numérique

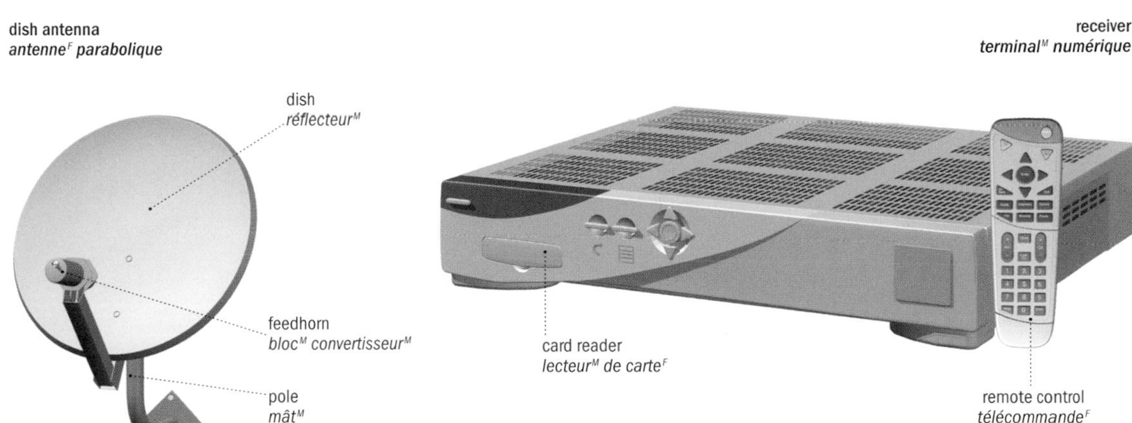
dish
réflecteur[M]
feedhorn
bloc[M] convertisseur[M]
pole
mât[M]
card reader
lecteur[M] de carte[F]
remote control
télécommande[F]

home theater
cinéma[M] maison[F]

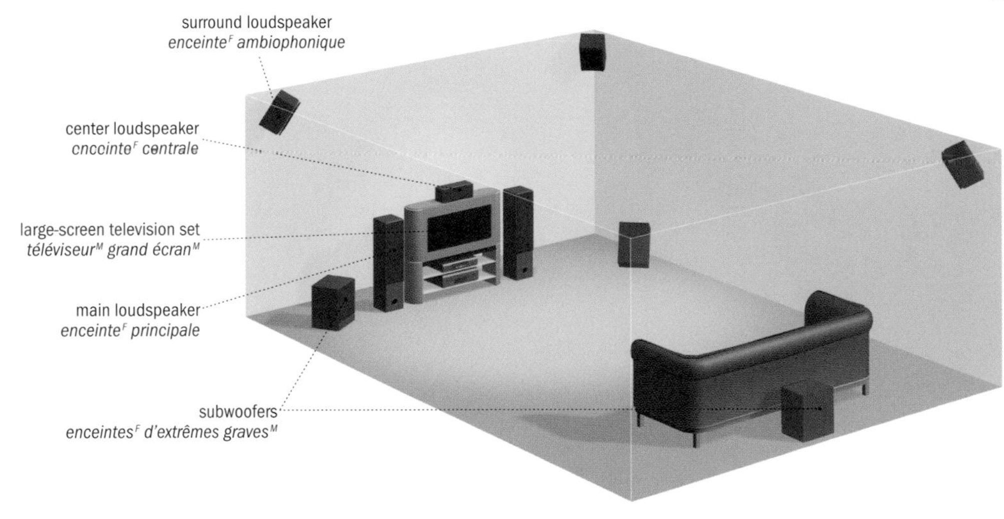
surround loudspeaker
enceinte[F] ambiophonique
center loudspeaker
cnceinte[F] centrale
large-screen television set
téléviseur[M] grand écran[M]
main loudspeaker
enceinte[F] principale
subwoofers
enceintes[F] d'extrêmes graves[M]

videocassette recorder (VCR)
magnétoscope[M]

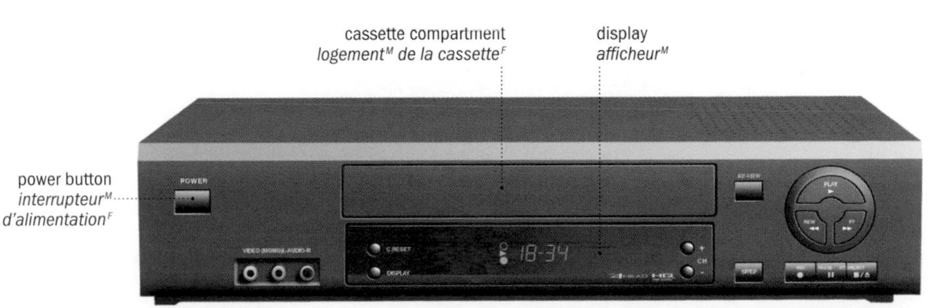
cassette compartment
logement[M] de la cassette[F]
display
afficheur[M]
power button
interrupteur[M] d'alimentation[F]
POWER
PLAY
18-34

sound reproducing system

chaîne[F] stéréo

ampli-tuner: front view
ampli[M]-syntoniseur[M] : vue[F] avant

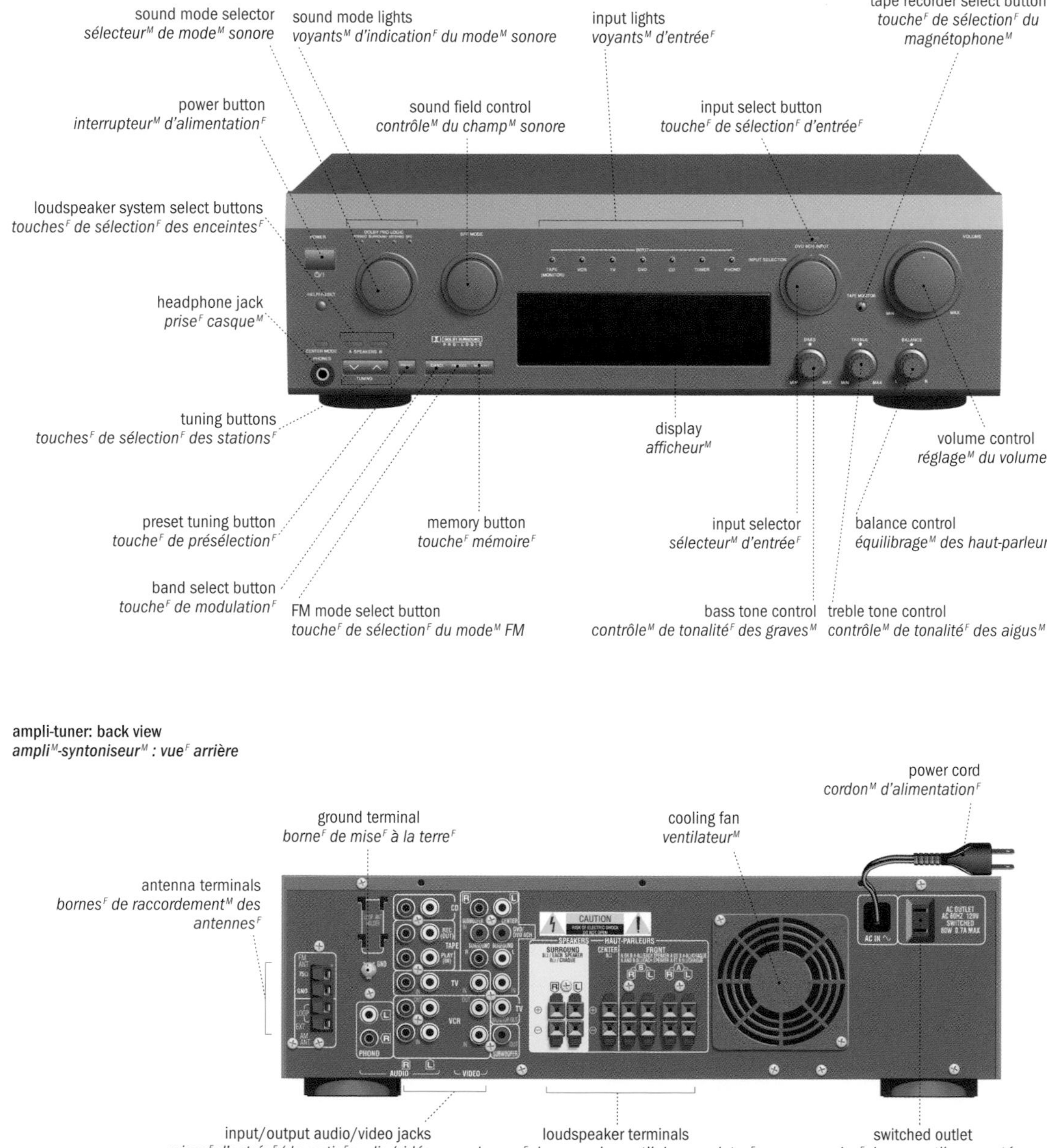
sound mode selector
sélecteur[M] de mode[M] sonore
sound mode lights
voyants[M] d'indication[F] du mode[M] sonore
input lights
voyants[M] d'entrée[F]
tape recorder select button
touche[F] de sélection[F] du magnétophone[M]
power button
interrupteur[M] d'alimentation[F]
sound field control
contrôle[M] du champ[M] sonore
input select button
touche[F] de sélection[F] d'entrée[F]
loudspeaker system select buttons
touches[F] de sélection[F] des enceintes[F]
headphone jack
prise[F] casque[M]
tuning buttons
touches[F] de sélection[F] des stations[F]
display
afficheur[M]
volume control
réglage[M] du volume[M]
preset tuning button
touche[F] de présélection[F]
memory button
touche[F] mémoire[F]
input selector
sélecteur[M] d'entrée[F]
balance control
équilibrage[M] des haut-parleurs[M]
band select button
touche[F] de modulation[F]
FM mode select button
touche[F] de sélection[F] du mode[M] FM
bass tone control
contrôle[M] de tonalité[F] des graves[M]
treble tone control
contrôle[M] de tonalité[F] des aigus[M]
ampli-tuner: back view
ampli[M]-syntoniseur[M] : vue[F] arrière
power cord
cordon[M] d'alimentation[F]
ground terminal
borne[F] de mise[F] à la terre[F]
cooling fan
ventilateur[M]
antenna terminals
bornes[F] de raccordement[M] des antennes[F]
CAUTION
input/output audio/video jacks
prises[F] d'entrée[F]/de sortie[F] audio/vidéo
loudspeaker terminals
bornes[F] de raccordement[M] des enceintes[F]
switched outlet
prise[F] de courant[M] commutée

COMMUNICATIONS AND OFFICE AUTOMATION

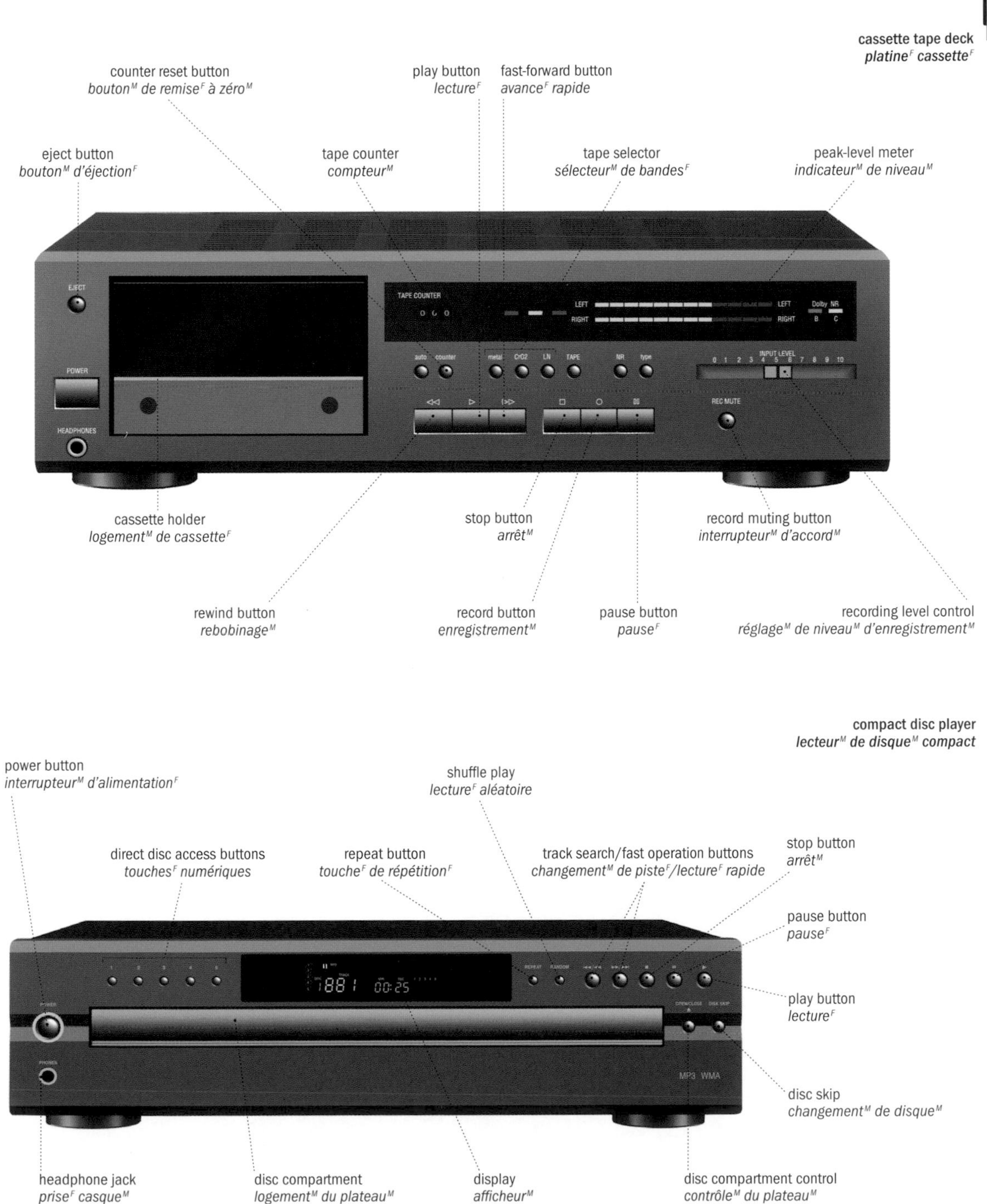
cassette tape deck
platine[F] cassette[F]
counter reset button
bouton[M] de remise[F] à zéro[M]
play button
lecture[F]
fast-forward button
avance[F] rapide
eject button
bouton[M] d'éjection[F]
tape counter
compteur[M]
tape selector
sélecteur[M] de bandes[F]
peak-level meter
indicateur[M] de niveau[M]
EJECT
TAPE COUNTER
LEFT
RIGHT
Dolby NR
B C
POWER
auto counter
metal CrO2 LN TAPE
NR type
INPUT LEVEL
0 1 2 3 4 5 6 7 8 9 10
REC MUTE
HEADPHONES
cassette holder
logement[M] de cassette[F]
stop button
arrêt[M]
record muting button
interrupteur[M] d'accord[M]
rewind button
rebobinage[M]
record button
enregistrement[M]
pause button
pause[F]
recording level control
réglage[M] de niveau[M] d'enregistrement[M]
compact disc player
lecteur[M] de disque[M] compact
power button
interrupteur[M] d'alimentation[F]
shuffle play
lecture[F] aléatoire
direct disc access buttons
touches[F] numériques
repeat button
touche[F] de répétition[F]
track search/fast operation buttons
changement[M] de piste[F]/lecture[F] rapide
stop button
arrêt[M]
pause button
pause[F]
REPEAT RANDOM
1 2 3 4 5
00:25
play button
lecture[F]
MP3 WMA
disc skip
changement[M] de disque[M]
headphone jack
prise[F] casque[M]
disc compartment
logement[M] du plateau[M]
display
afficheur[M]
disc compartment control
contrôle[M] du plateau[M]

COMMUNICATIONS AND OFFICE AUTOMATION

sound reproducing system

headphones
casque[M] d'écoute[F]

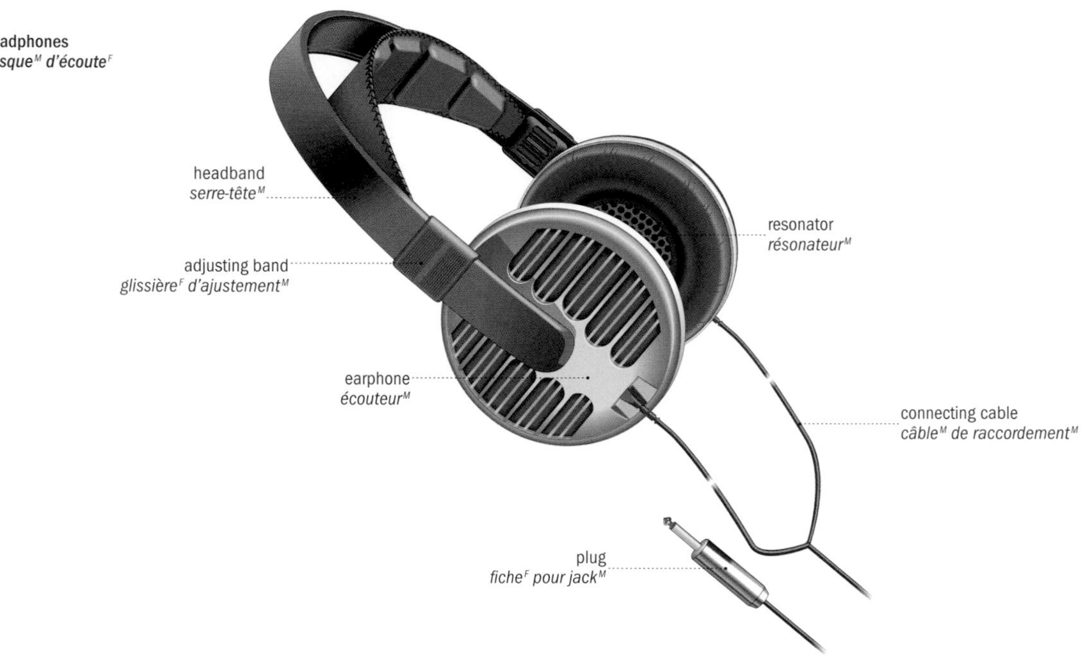
headband
serre-tête[M]
adjusting band
glissière[F] d'ajustement[M]
earphone
écouteur[M]
resonator
résonateur[M]
connecting cable
câble[M] de raccordement[M]
plug
fiche[F] pour jack[M]

loudspeakers
enceinte[F] acoustique

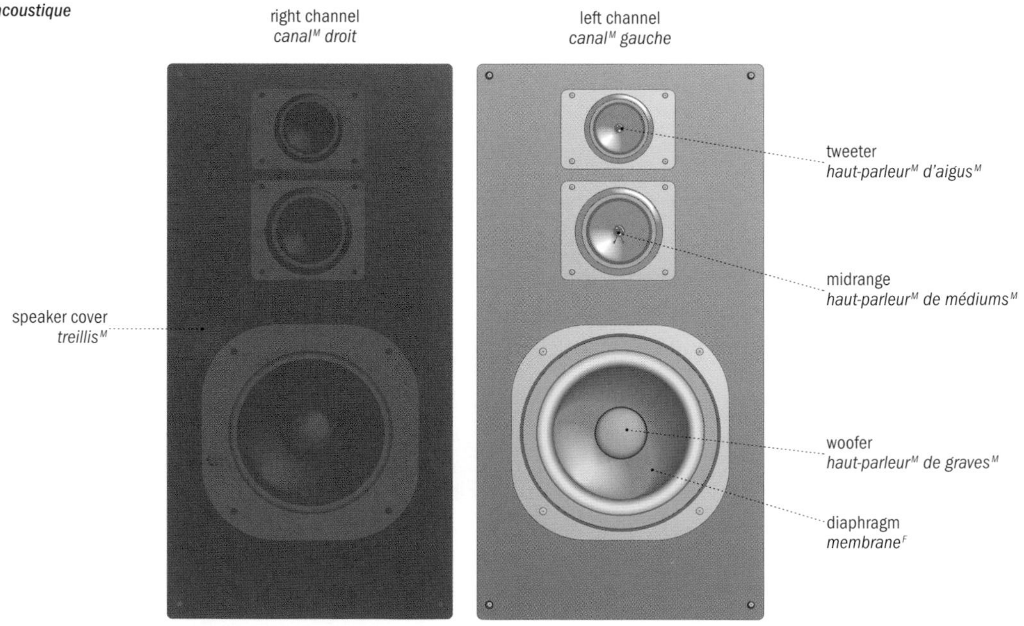

right channel
canal[M] droit

left channel
canal[M] gauche

speaker cover
treillis[M]

tweeter
haut-parleur[M] d'aigus[M]

midrange
haut-parleur[M] de médiums[M]

woofer
haut-parleur[M] de graves[M]

diaphragm
membrane[F]

mini stereo sound system

minichaîne[F] stéréo

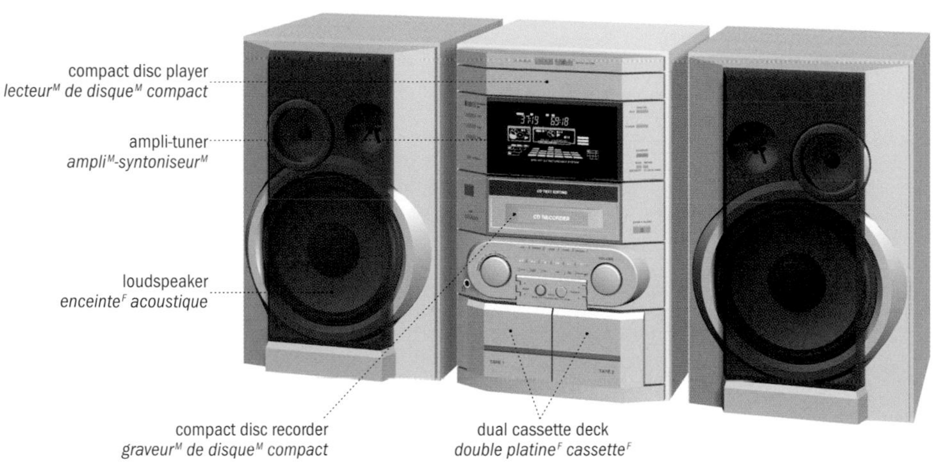
compact disc player
lecteur[M] de disque[M] compact
ampli-tuner
ampli[M]-syntoniseur[M]
loudspeaker
enceinte[F] acoustique
compact disc recorder
graveur[M] de disque[M] compact
dual cassette deck
double platine[F] cassette[F]

portable sound systems

appareils[M] de son[M] portatifs

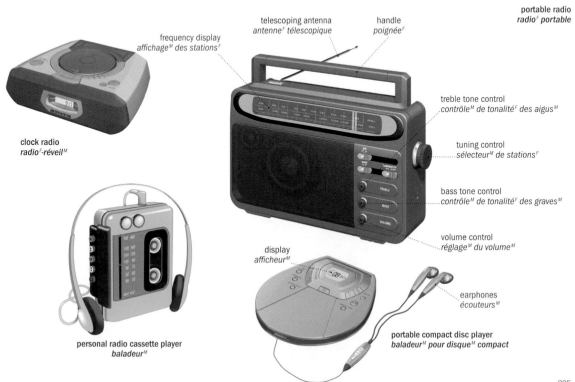

portable radio
radio[F] portable

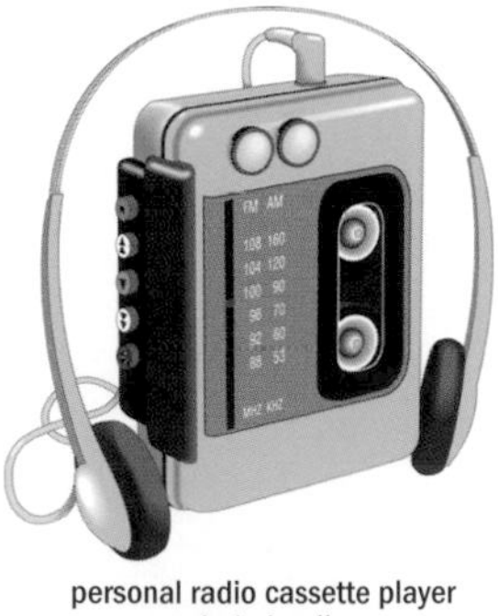

telescoping antenna
antenne[F] télescopique

handle
poignée[F]

frequency display
affichage[M] des stations[F]

treble tone control
contrôle[M] de tonalité[F] des aigus[M]

tuning control
sélecteur[M] de stations[F]

bass tone control
contrôle[M] de tonalité[F] des graves[M]

volume control
réglage[M] du volume[M]

clock radio
radio[F]-réveil[M]

display
afficheur[M]

earphones
écouteurs[M]

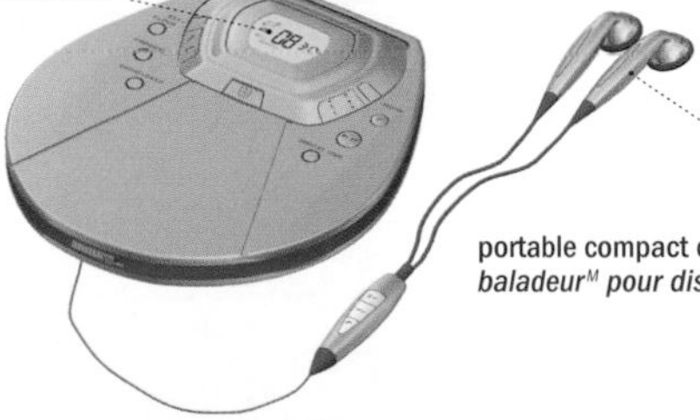

portable compact disc player
baladeur[M] pour disque[M] compact

personal radio cassette player
baladeur[M]

portable digital audio player
baladeur[M] numérique

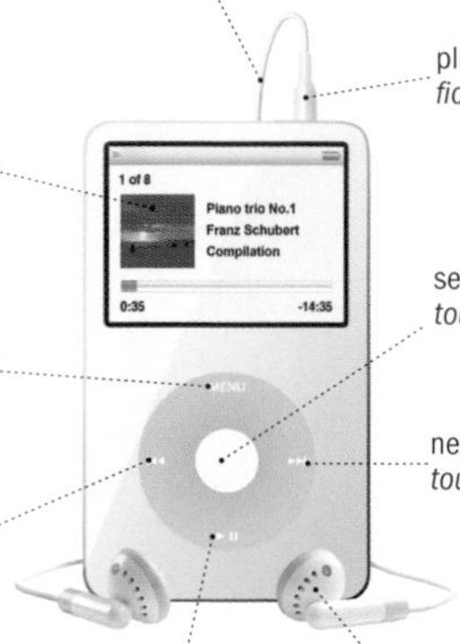

cable
cordon[M]

plug
fiche[F]

display
écran[M]

select button
touche[F] de sélection[F]

menu button
touche[F] menu[M]

next/fast-forward button
touche[F] suivant/avance[F] rapide

previous/rewind button
touche[F] précédent/retour[M] rapide

play/pause button
touche[F] lecture[F]/pause[F]

earphones
écouteurs[M]

satellite radio receiver
récepteur[M] de radio[F] par satellite[M]

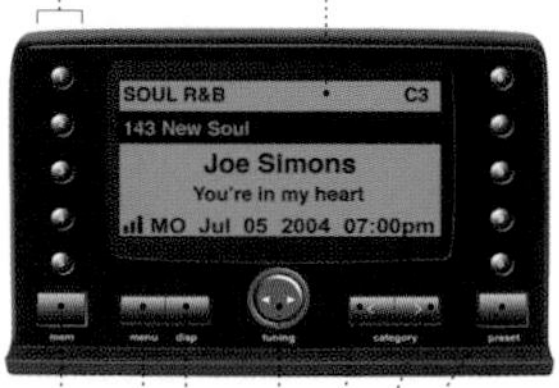

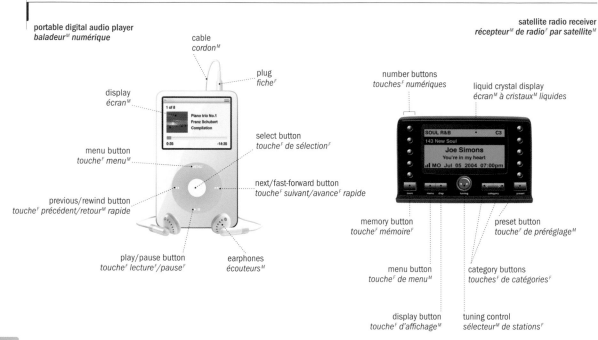

number buttons
touches[F] numériques

liquid crystal display
écran[M] à cristaux[M] liquides

memory button
touche[F] mémoire[F]

preset button
touche[F] de préréglage[M]

menu button
touche[F] de menu[M]

category buttons
touches[F] de catégories[F]

display button
touche[F] d'affichage[M]

tuning control
sélecteur[M] de stations[F]

portable CD/radio/cassette recorder
radiocassette[F] laser[M]

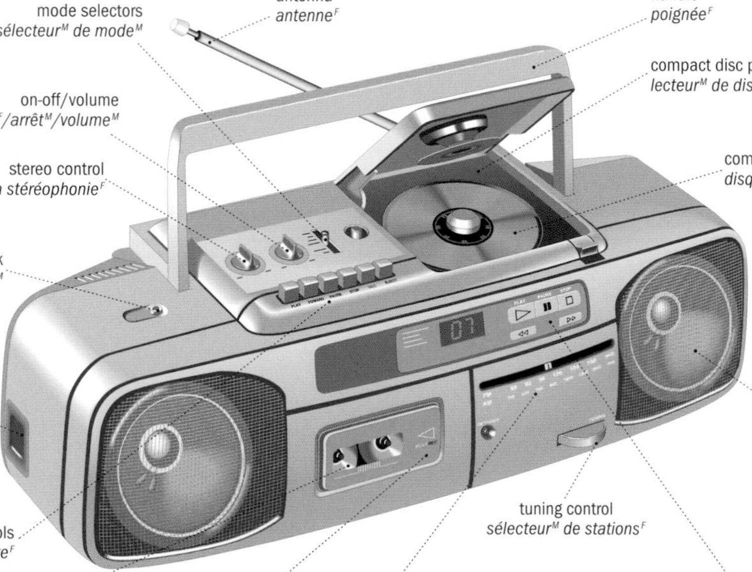

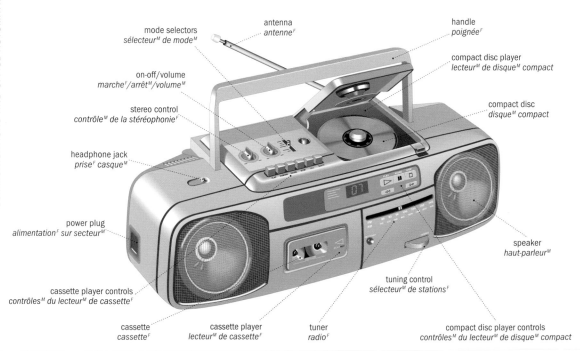

mode selectors
sélecteur[M] de mode[M]

antenna
antenne[F]

handle
poignée[F]

compact disc player
lecteur[M] de disque[M] compact

on-off/volume
marche[F]/arrêt[M]/volume[M]

compact disc
disque[M] compact

stereo control
contrôle[M] de la stéréophonie[F]

headphone jack
prise[F] casque[M]

power plug
alimentation[F] sur secteur[M]

speaker
haut-parleur[M]

tuning control
sélecteur[M] de stations[F]

cassette player controls
contrôles[M] du lecteur[M] de cassette[F]

cassette
cassette[F]

cassette player
lecteur[M] de cassette[F]

tuner
radio[F]

compact disc player controls
contrôles[M] du lecteur[M] de disque[M] compact

communication by telephone

communication[F] par téléphone[M]

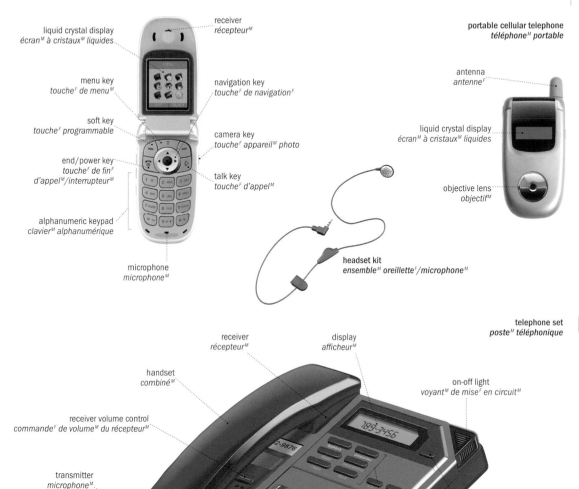

liquid crystal display
écran[M] à cristaux[M] liquides

receiver
récepteur[M]

menu key
touche[F] de menu[M]

navigation key
touche[F] de navigation[F]

soft key
touche[F] programmable

camera key
touche[F] appareil[M] photo

end/power key
touche[F] de fin[F] d'appel[M]/interrupteur[M]

talk key
touche[F] d'appel[M]

alphanumeric keypad
clavier[M] alphanumérique

microphone
microphone[M]

portable cellular telephone
téléphone[M] portable

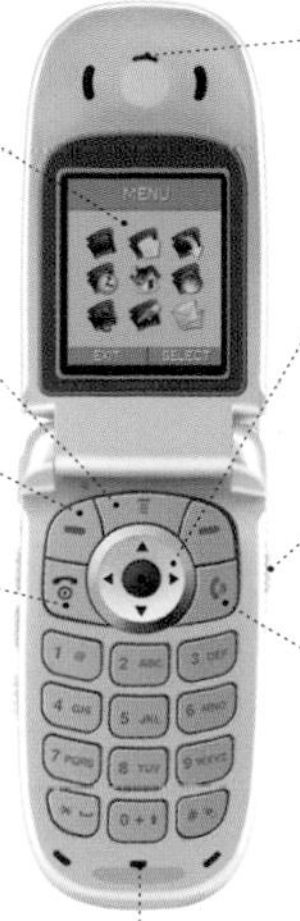

antenna
antenne[F]

liquid crystal display
écran[M] à cristaux[M] liquides

objective lens
objectif[M]

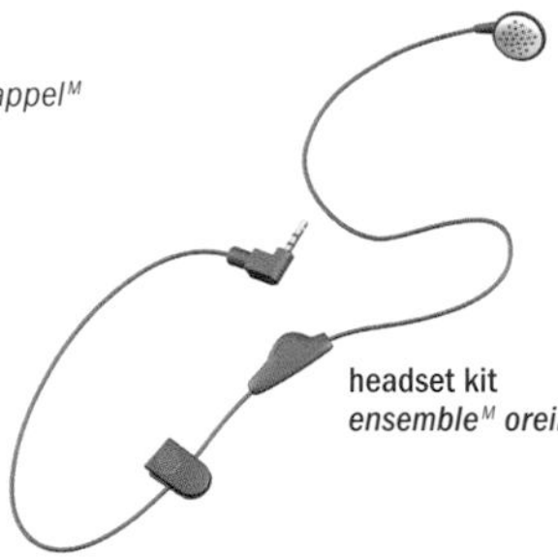

headset kit
ensemble[M] oreillette[F]/microphone[M]

telephone set
poste[M] téléphonique

receiver
récepteur[M]
display
afficheur[M]
handset
combiné[M]
on-off light
voyant[M] de mise[F] en circuit[M]
receiver volume control
commande[F] de volume[M] du récepteur[M]
transmitter
microphone[M]
display setting
réglage[M] de l'afficheur[M]
ringing volume control
commande[F] de volume[M] de la sonnerie[F]
handset cord
cordon[M] de combiné[M]
memory button
commande[F] mémoire[F]
function selectors
sélecteurs[M] de fonctions[F]
push buttons
clavier[M]
telephone index
répertoire[M] téléphonique
automatic dialer index
index[M] de composition[F] automatique

digital answering machine
répondeur[M] numérique

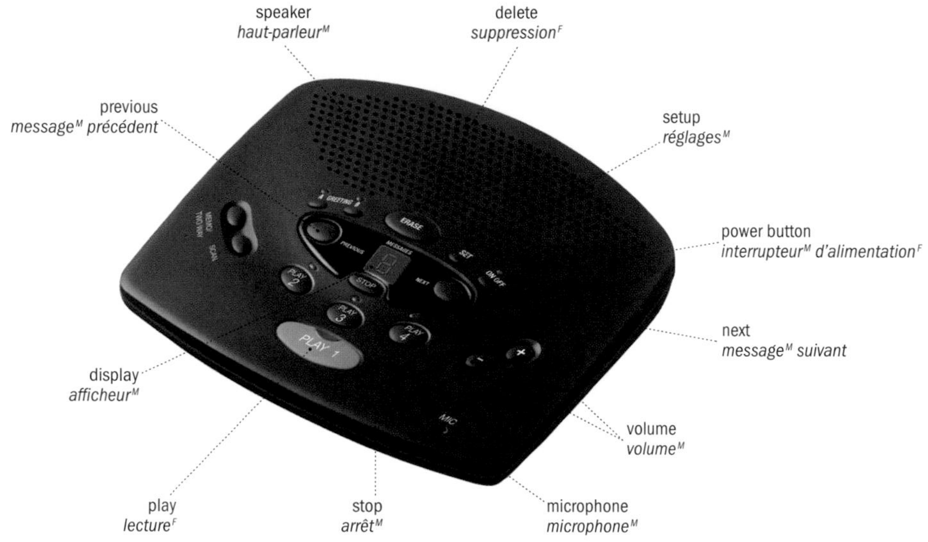
speaker
haut-parleur[M]
delete
suppression[F]
previous
message[M] précédent
setup
réglages[M]
power button
interrupteur[M] d'alimentation[F]
next
message[M] suivant
display
afficheur[M]
volume
volume[M]
play
lecture[F]
stop
arrêt[M]
microphone
microphone[M]

facsimile (fax) machine
télécopieur[M]

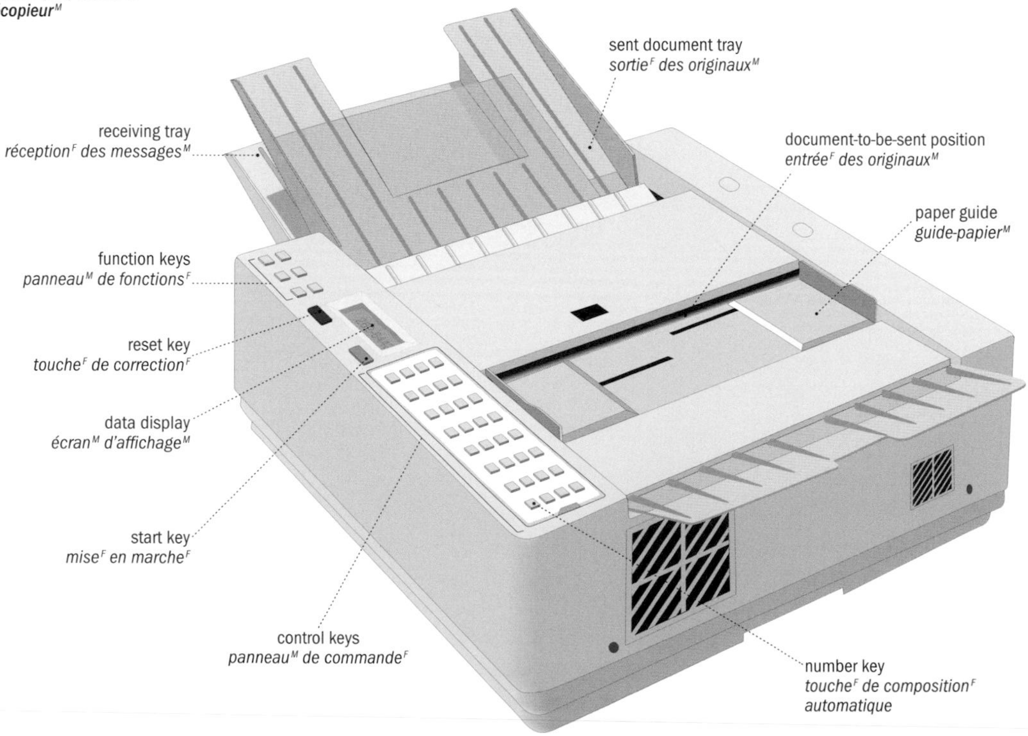

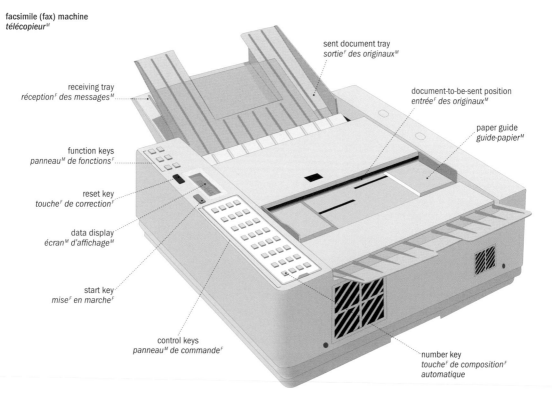

sent document tray
sortie[F] des originaux[M]

receiving tray
réception[F] des messages[M]

document-to-be-sent position
entrée[F] des originaux[M]

paper guide
guide-papier[M]

function keys
panneau[M] de fonctions[F]

reset key
touche[F] de correction[F]

data display
écran[M] d'affichage[M]

start key
mise[F] en marche[F]

control keys
panneau[M] de commande[F]

number key
touche[F] de composition[F] automatique

personal computer

micro-ordinateur[M]

video monitor
écran[M]

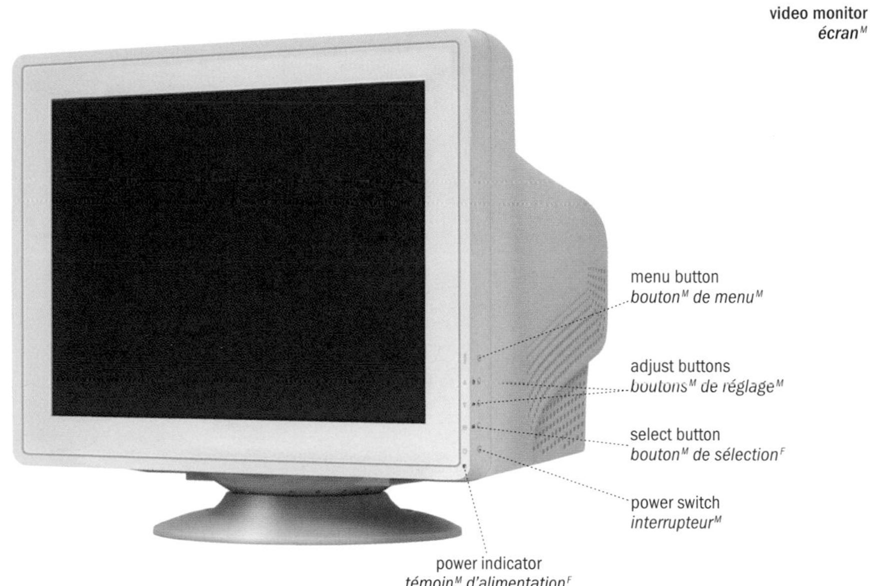
menu button
bouton[M] de menu[M]
adjust buttons
boutons[M] de réglage[M]
select button
bouton[M] de sélection[F]
power switch
interrupteur[M]
power indicator
témoin[M] d'alimentation[F]

tower case: back view
boîtier[M] tour[F] : vue[F] arrière

tower case: front view
boîtier[M] tour[F] : vue[F] avant

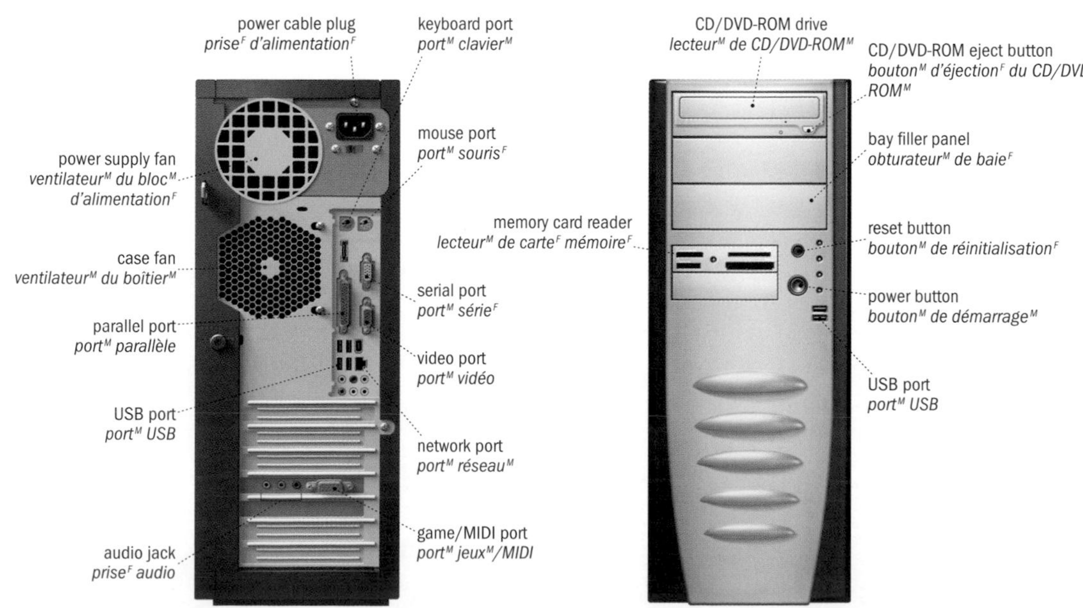
power cable plug
prise[F] d'alimentation[F]
keyboard port
port[M] clavier[M]
power supply fan
ventilateur[M] du bloc[M] d'alimentation[F]
mouse port
port[M] souris[F]
case fan
ventilateur[M] du boîtier[M]
serial port
port[M] série[F]
parallel port
port[M] parallèle
video port
port[M] vidéo
USB port
port[M] USB
network port
port[M] réseau[M]
game/MIDI port
port[M] jeux[M]/MIDI
audio jack
prise[F] audio
CD/DVD-ROM drive
lecteur[M] de CD/DVD-ROM[M]
CD/DVD-ROM eject button
bouton[M] d'éjection[F] du CD/DVD-ROM[M]
bay filler panel
obturateur[M] de baie[F]
memory card reader
lecteur[M] de carte[F] mémoire[F]
reset button
bouton[M] de réinitialisation[F]
power button
bouton[M] de démarrage[M]
USB port
port[M] USB

input devices

périphériques[M] d'entrée[F]

keyboard and pictograms
clavier[M] et pictogrammes[M]

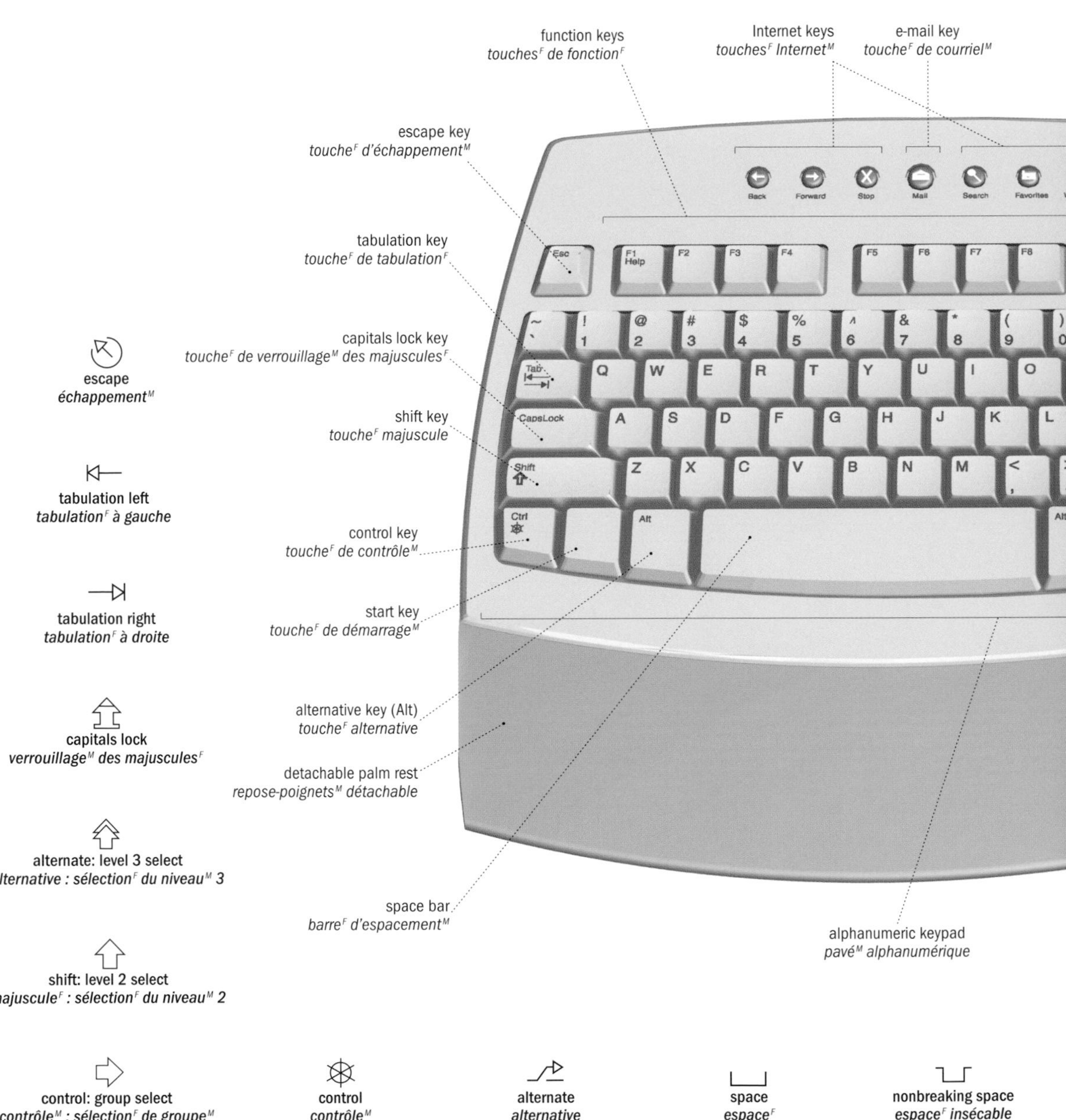
function keys
touches[F] de fonction[F]
Internet keys
touches[F] Internet[M]
e-mail key
touche[F] de courriel[M]
escape key
touche[F] d'échappement[M]
tabulation key
touche[F] de tabulation[F]
capitals lock key
touche[F] de verrouillage[M] des majuscules[F]
shift key
touche[F] majuscule
control key
touche[F] de contrôle[M]
start key
touche[F] de démarrage[M]
alternative key (Alt)
touche[F] alternative
detachable palm rest
repose-poignets[M] détachable
space bar
barre[F] d'espacement[M]
alphanumeric keypad
pavé[M] alphanumérique
Back
Forward
Stop
Mail
Search
Favorites
Esc
F1 Help
F2
F3
F4
F5
F6
F7
F8
Tab
CapsLock
Shift
Ctrl
Alt
escape
échappement[M]
tabulation left
tabulation[F] à gauche
tabulation right
tabulation[F] à droite
capitals lock
verrouillage[M] des majuscules[F]
alternate: level 3 select
alternative : sélection[F] du niveau[M] 3
shift: level 2 select
majuscule[F] : sélection[F] du niveau[M] 2
control: group select
contrôle[M] : sélection[F] de groupe[M]
control
contrôle[M]
alternate
alternative
space
espace[F]
nonbreaking space
espace[F] insécable

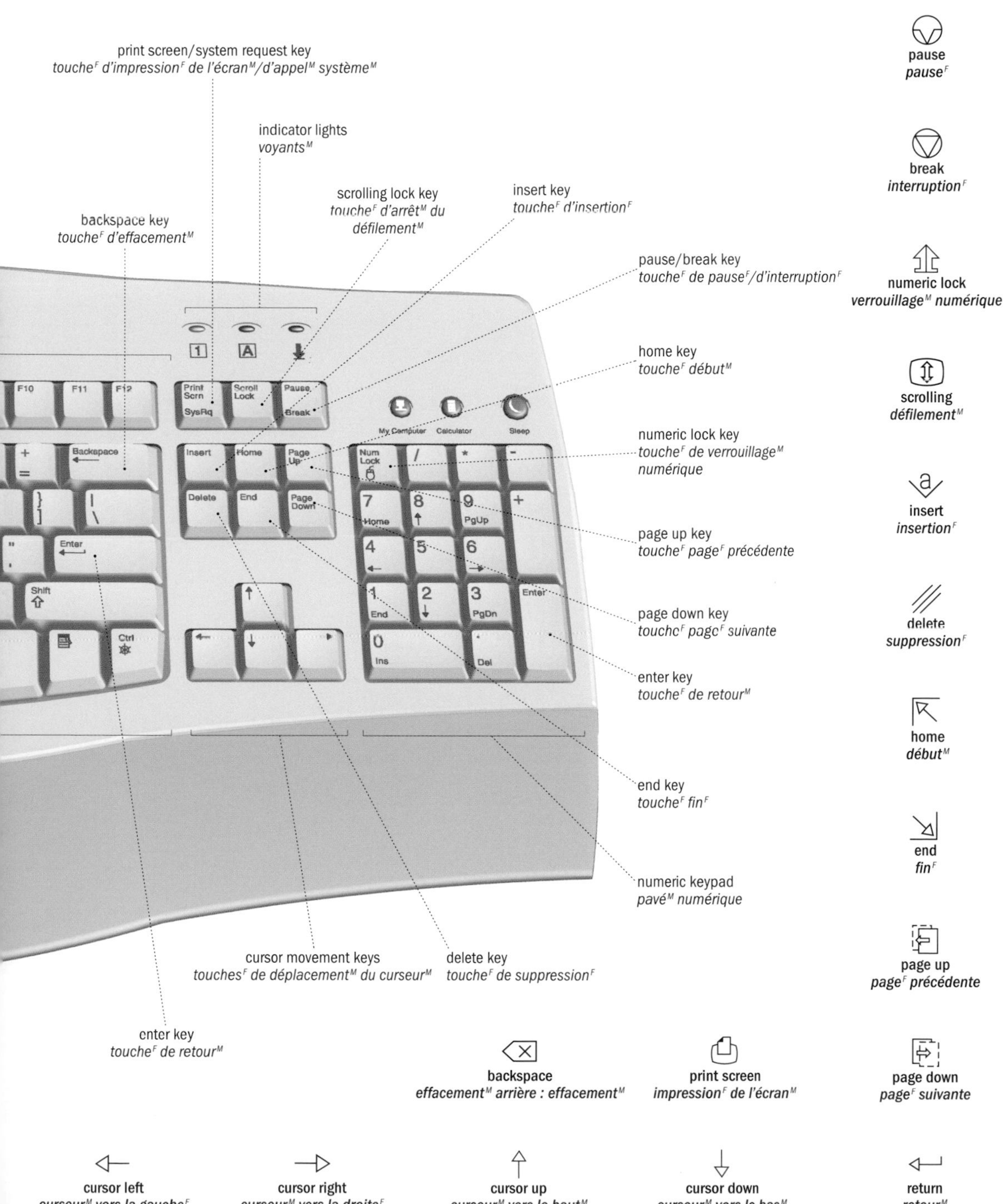
print screen/system request key
toucheF d'impressionF de l'écranM/d'appelM systèmeM
indicator lights
voyantsM
scrolling lock key
toucheF d'arrêtM du défilementM
insert key
toucheF d'insertionF
backspace key
toucheF d'effacementM
pause/break key
toucheF de pauseF/d'interruptionF
home key
toucheF débutM
numeric lock key
toucheF de verrouillageM numérique
page up key
toucheF pageF précédente
page down key
toucheF pageF suivante
enter key
toucheF de retourM
end key
toucheF finF
numeric keypad
pavéM numérique
cursor movement keys
touchesF de déplacementM du curseurM
delete key
toucheF de suppressionF
enter key
toucheF de retourM
F10
F11
F12
Print Scrn SysRq
Scroll Lock
Pause Break
My Computer
Calculator
Sleep
Backspace
Insert
Home
Page Up
Delete
End
Page Down
Num Lock
Enter
Shift
Ctrl
Home
PgUp
End
PgDn
Ins
Del

pause
*pause*F

break
*interruption*F

numeric lock
*verrouillage*M *numérique*

scrolling
*défilement*M

insert
*insertion*F

delete
*suppression*F

home
*début*M

end
*fin*F

page up
*page*F *précédente*

backspace
*effacement*M *arrière : effacement*M

print screen
*impression*F *de l'écran*M

page down
*page*F *suivante*

cursor left
*curseur*M *vers la gauche*F

cursor right
*curseur*M *vers la droite*F

cursor up
*curseur*M *vers le haut*M

cursor down
*curseur*M *vers le bas*M

return
*retour*M

input devices

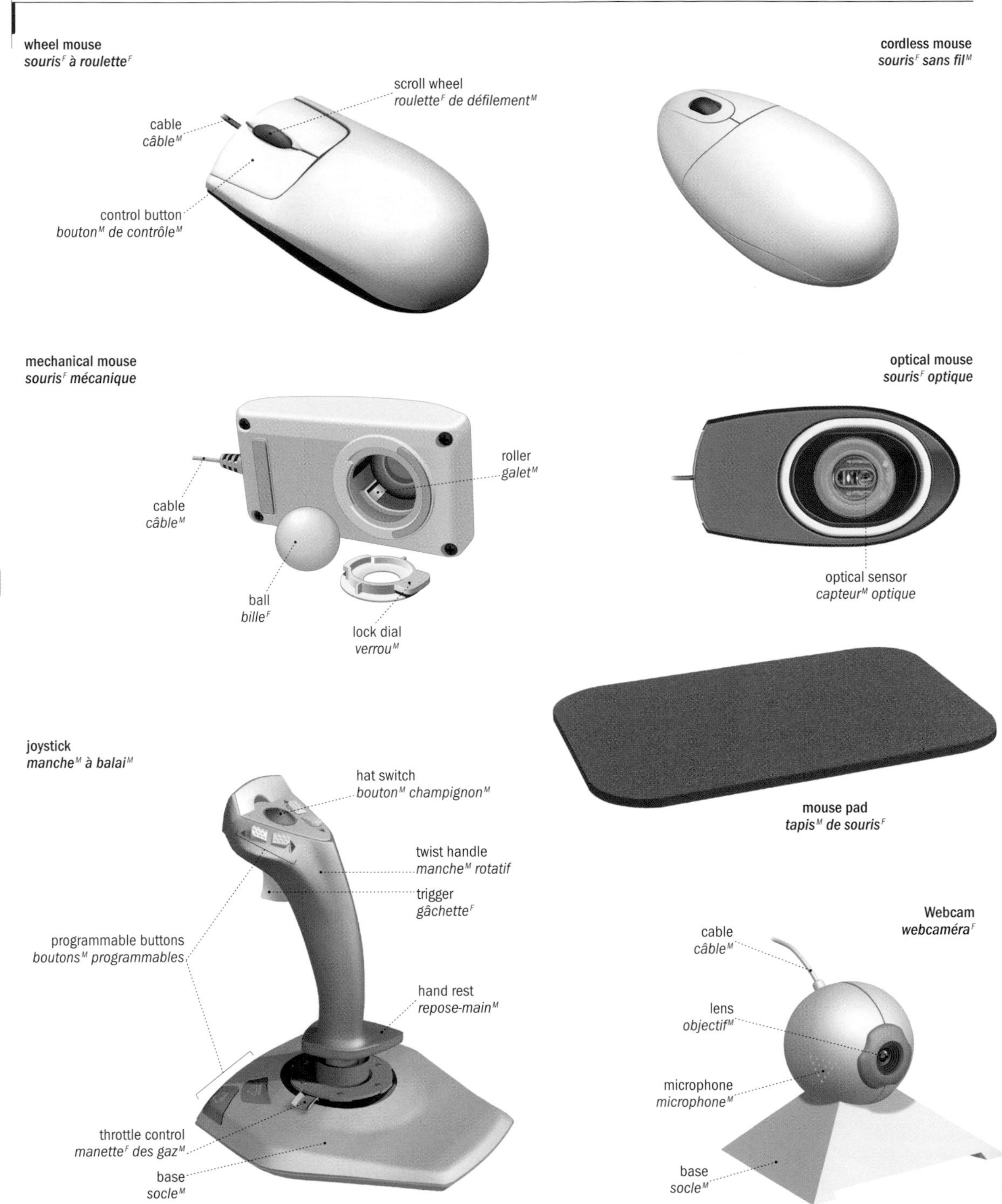
wheel mouse
souris^F à roulette^F
scroll wheel
roulette^F de défilement^M
cable
câble^M
control button
bouton^M de contrôle^M
cordless mouse
souris^F sans fil^M
mechanical mouse
souris^F mécanique
roller
galet^M
cable
câble^M
ball
bille^F
lock dial
verrou^M
optical mouse
souris^F optique
optical sensor
capteur^M optique
mouse pad
tapis^M de souris^F
joystick
manche^M à balai^M
hat switch
bouton^M champignon^M
twist handle
manche^M rotatif
trigger
gâchette^F
programmable buttons
boutons^M programmables
hand rest
repose-main^M
throttle control
manette^F des gaz^M
base
socle^M
Webcam
webcaméra^F
cable
câble^M
lens
objectif^M
microphone
microphone^M
base
socle^M

output devices

périphériques[M] de sortie[F]

inkjet printer
imprimante[F] à jet[M] d'encre[F]

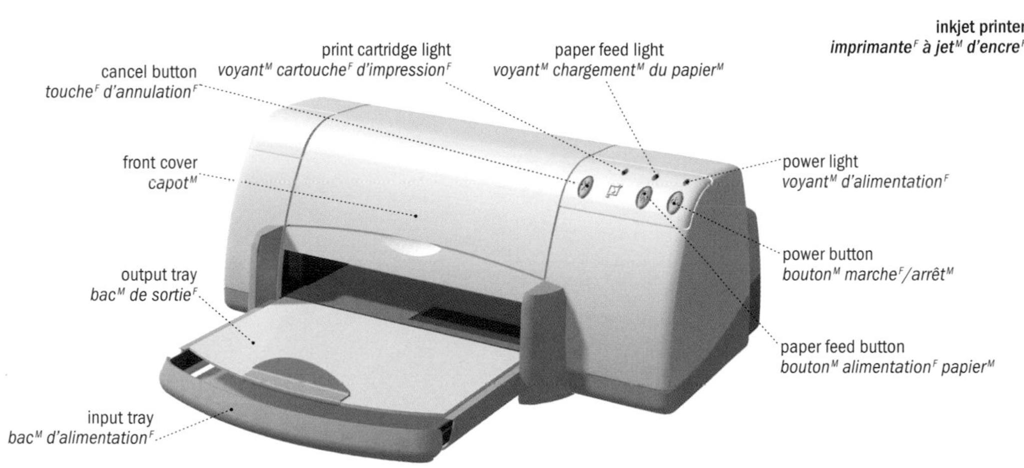
print cartridge light
voyant[M] cartouche[F] d'impression[F]
paper feed light
voyant[M] chargement[M] du papier[M]
cancel button
touche[F] d'annulation[F]
front cover
capot[M]
power light
voyant[M] d'alimentation[F]
power button
bouton[M] marche[F]/arrêt[M]
output tray
bac[M] de sortie[F]
paper feed button
bouton[M] alimentation[F] papier[M]
input tray
bac[M] d'alimentation[F]

data storage devices

périphériques[M] de stockage[M]

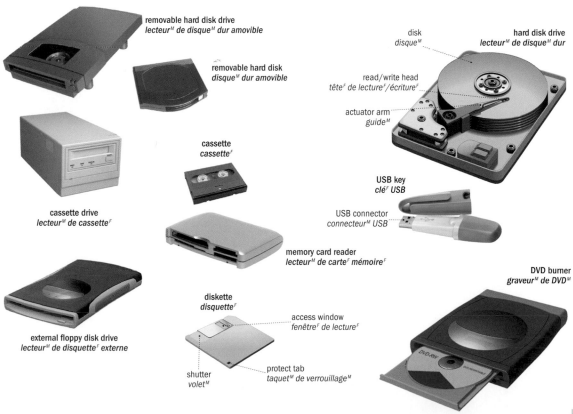

removable hard disk drive
lecteur[M] de disque[M] dur amovible

removable hard disk
disque[M] dur amovible

hard disk drive
lecteur[M] de disque[M] dur

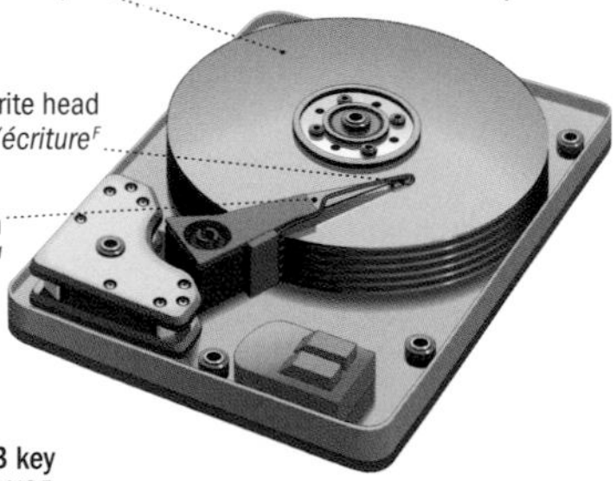

disk
disque[M]

read/write head
tête[F] de lecture[F]/écriture[F]

actuator arm
guide[M]

cassette
cassette[F]

cassette drive
lecteur[M] de cassette[F]

USB key
clé[F] USB

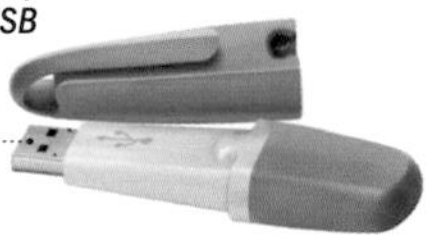

USB connector
connecteur[M] USB

memory card reader
lecteur[M] de carte[F] mémoire[F]

DVD burner
graveur[M] de DVD[M]

diskette
disquette[F]

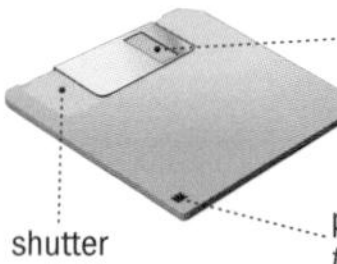

access window
fenêtre[F] de lecture[F]

external floppy disk drive
lecteur[M] de disquette[F] externe

protect tab
taquet[M] de verrouillage[M]

shutter
volet[M]

Internet

Internet[M]

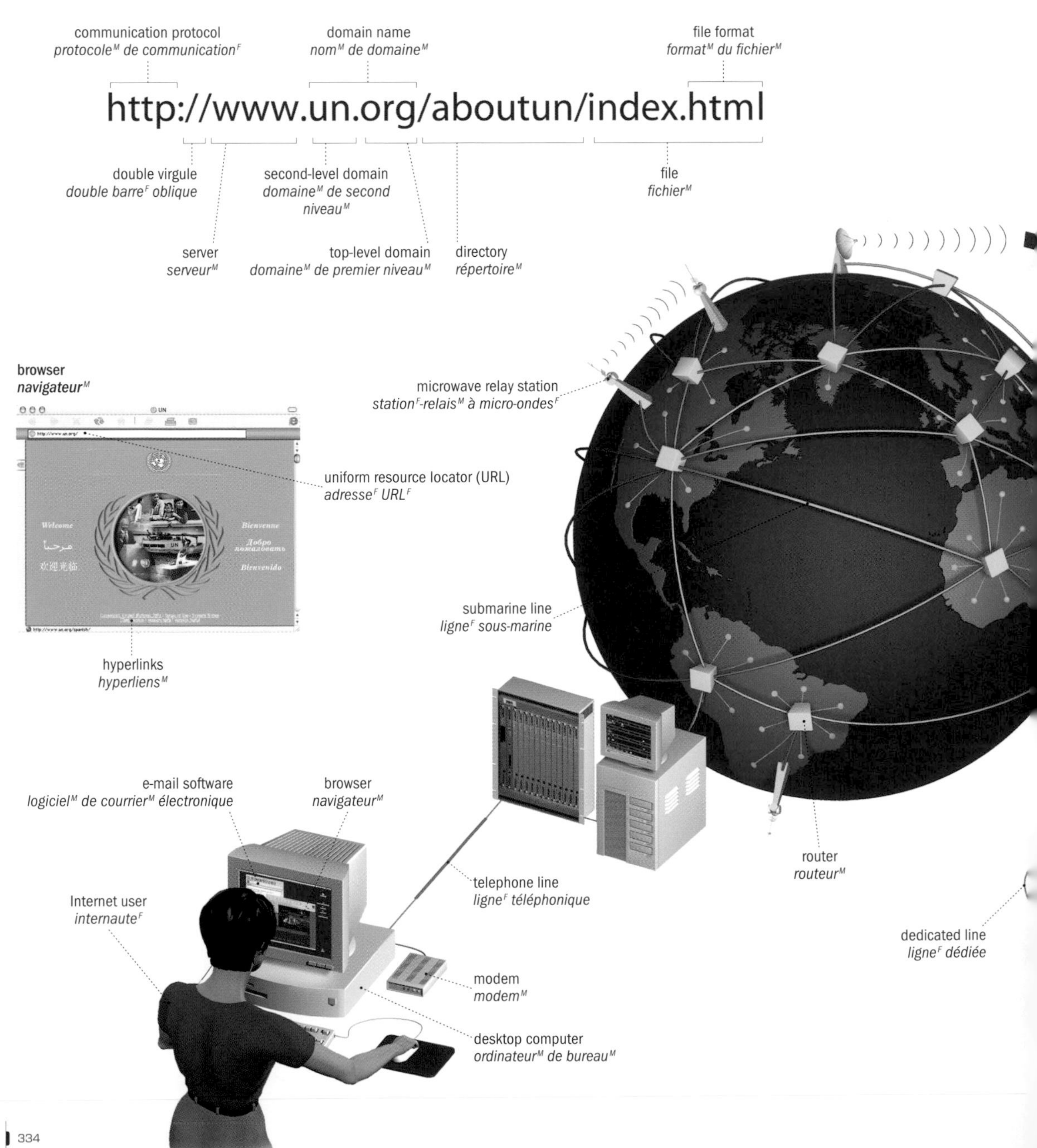
uniform resource locator (URL)
adresse[F] URL[F] (localisateur[M] universel de ressources[F])
communication protocol
protocole[M] de communication[F]
domain name
nom[M] de domaine[M]
file format
format[M] du fichier[M]
http://www.un.org/aboutun/index.html
double virgule
double barre[F] oblique
second-level domain
domaine[M] de second niveau[M]
file
fichier[M]
server
serveur[M]
top-level domain
domaine[M] de premier niveau[M]
directory
répertoire[M]
browser
navigateur[M]
UN
Welcome
مرحبا
欢迎光临
Bienvenue
Добро пожаловать
Bienvenido
uniform resource locator (URL)
adresse[F] URL[F]
hyperlinks
hyperliens[M]
microwave relay station
station[F]-relais[M] à micro-ondes[F]
submarine line
ligne[F] sous-marine
e-mail software
logiciel[M] de courrier[M] électronique
browser
navigateur[M]
Internet user
internaute[F]
telephone line
ligne[F] téléphonique
router
routeur[M]
dedicated line
ligne[F] dédiée
modem
modem[M]
desktop computer
ordinateur[M] de bureau[M]

Internet uses

utilisations[F] d'Internet[M]

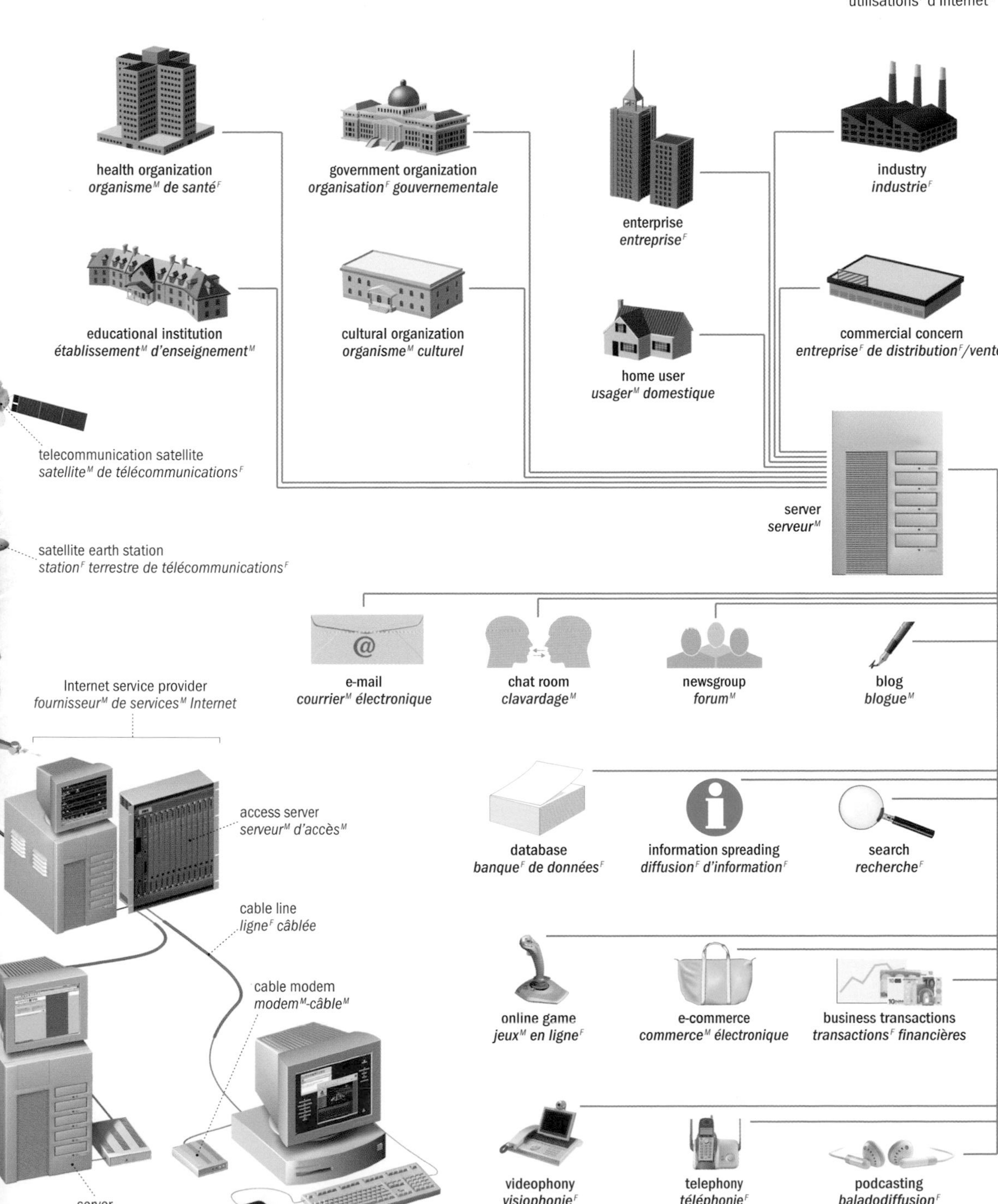

health organization
organisme[M] de santé[F]
government organization
organisation[F] gouvernementale
enterprise
entreprise[F]
industry
industrie[F]
educational institution
établissement[M] d'enseignement[M]
cultural organization
organisme[M] culturel
home user
usager[M] domestique
commercial concern
entreprise[F] de distribution[F]/vente[F]
telecommunication satellite
satellite[M] de télécommunications[F]
server
serveur[M]
satellite earth station
station[F] terrestre de télécommunications[F]
Internet service provider
fournisseur[M] de services[M] Internet
e-mail
courrier[M] électronique
chat room
clavardage[M]
newsgroup
forum[M]
blog
blogue[M]
access server
serveur[M] d'accès[M]
database
banque[F] de données[F]
information spreading
diffusion[F] d'information[F]
search
recherche[F]
cable line
ligne[F] câblée
cable modem
modem[M]-câble[M]
online game
jeux[M] en ligne[F]
e-commerce
commerce[M] électronique
business transactions
transactions[F] financières
videophony
visiophonie[F]
telephony
téléphonie[F]
podcasting
baladodiffusion[F]
server
serveur[M]

laptop computer

ordinateur[M] portable

laptop computer: front view
ordinateur[M] portable : vue[F] avant

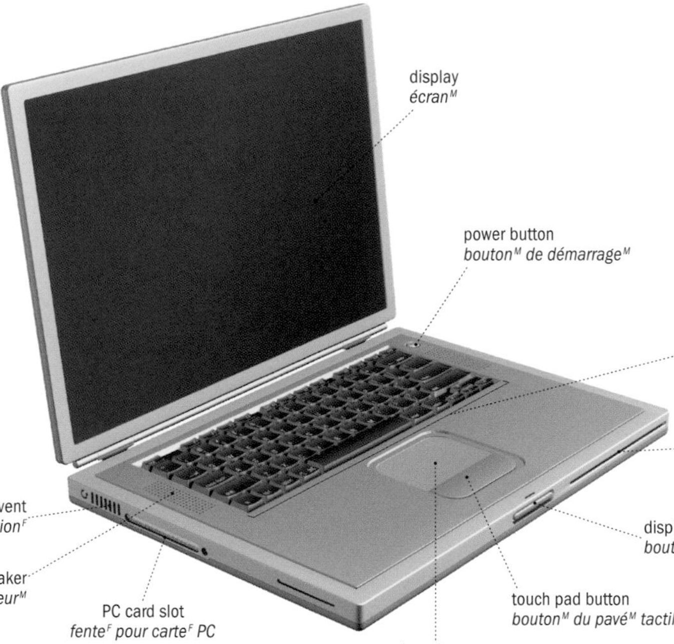

display
écran[M]

power button
bouton[M] de démarrage[M]

keyboard
clavier[M]

CD/DVD-ROM drive
lecteur[M] de CD/DVD-ROM[M]

cooling vent
fentes[F] d'aération[F]

display release button
bouton[M] de déverrouillage[M] de l'écran[M]

speaker
haut-parleur[M]

PC card slot
fente[F] pour carte[F] PC

touch pad button
bouton[M] du pavé[M] tactile

touch pad
pavé[M] tactile

laptop computer: rear view
ordinateur[M] portable : vue[F] arrière

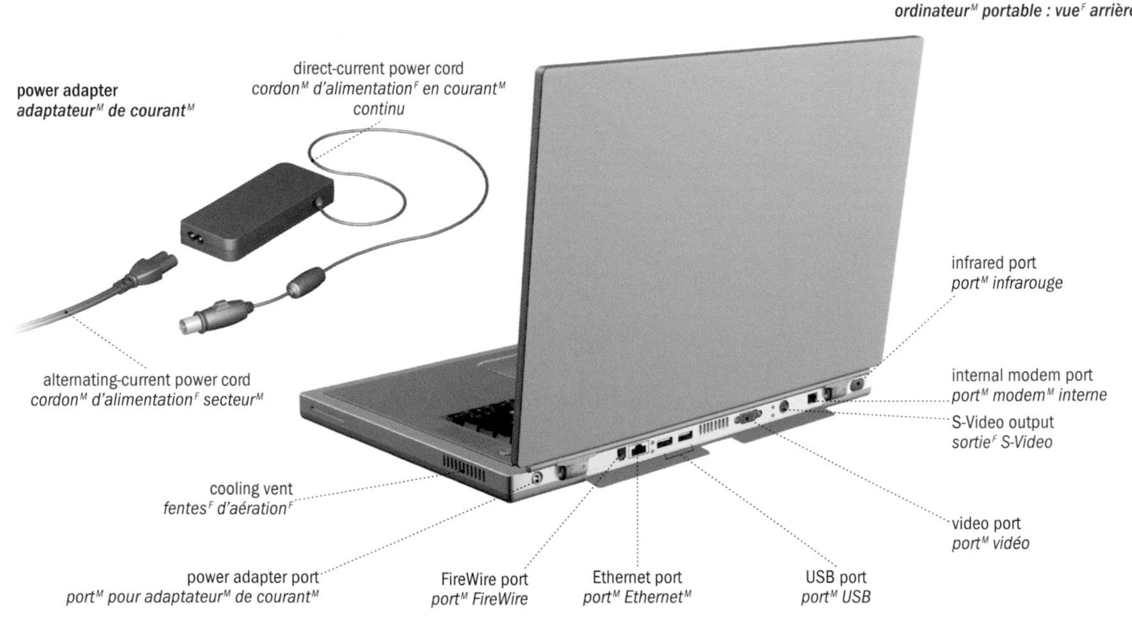
power adapter
adaptateur[M] de courant[M]
direct-current power cord
cordon[M] d'alimentation[F] en courant[M] continu
infrared port
port[M] infrarouge
alternating-current power cord
cordon[M] d'alimentation[F] secteur[M]
internal modem port
port[M] modem[M] interne
S-Video output
sortie[F] S-Video
cooling vent
fentes[F] d'aération[F]
video port
port[M] vidéo
power adapter port
port[M] pour adaptateur[M] de courant[M]
FireWire port
port[M] FireWire
Ethernet port
port[M] Ethernet[M]
USB port
port[M] USB

handheld computer/personal digital assistant (PDA)

ordinateur[M] de poche[F]

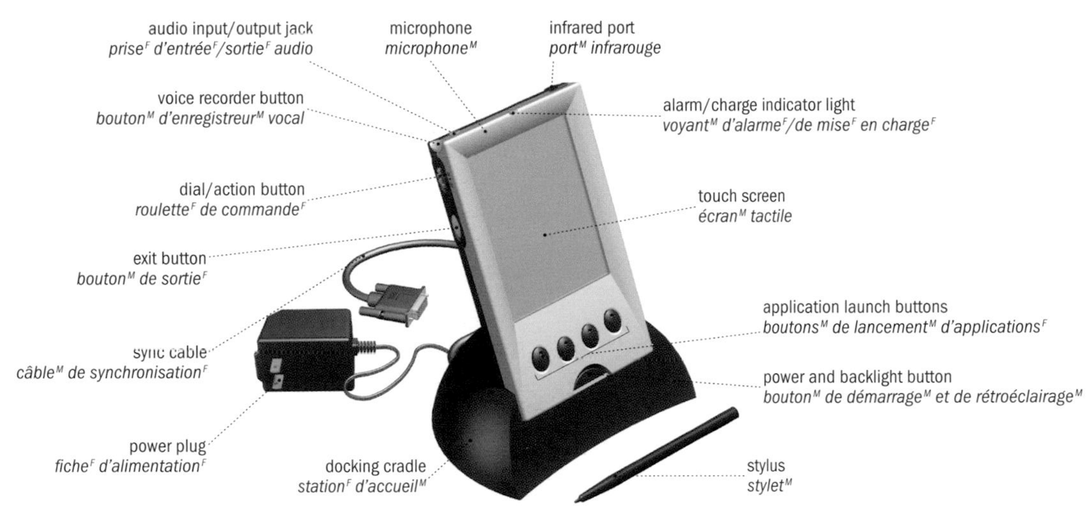
audio input/output jack
prise[F] d'entrée[F]/sortie[F] audio
microphone
microphone[M]
infrared port
port[M] infrarouge
voice recorder button
bouton[M] d'enregistreur[M] vocal
alarm/charge indicator light
voyant[M] d'alarme[F]/de mise[F] en charge[F]
dial/action button
roulette[F] de commande[F]
touch screen
écran[M] tactile
exit button
bouton[M] de sortie[F]
application launch buttons
boutons[M] de lancement[M] d'applications[F]
sync cable
câble[M] de synchronisation[F]
power and backlight button
bouton[M] de démarrage[M] et de rétroéclairage[M]
power plug
fiche[F] d'alimentation[F]
docking cradle
station[F] d'accueil[M]
stylus
stylet[M]

stationery

articles[M] de bureau[M]

scientific calculator
calculatrice[F] scientifique

printing calculator
calculatrice[F] à imprimante[F]

pocket calculator
calculette[F]

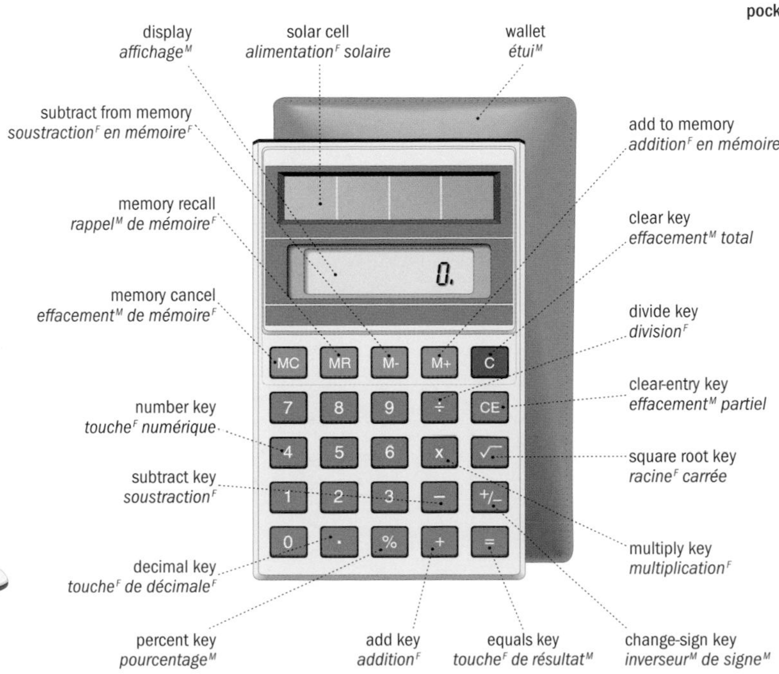

display
affichage[M]

solar cell
alimentation[F] solaire

wallet
étui[M]

subtract from memory
soustraction[F] en mémoire[F]

add to memory
addition[F] en mémoire[F]

memory recall
rappel[M] de mémoire[F]

clear key
effacement[M] total

memory cancel
effacement[M] de mémoire[F]

divide key
division[F]

clear-entry key
effacement[M] partiel

number key
touche[F] numérique

square root key
racine[F] carrée

subtract key
soustraction[F]

multiply key
multiplication[F]

decimal key
touche[F] de décimale[F]

percent key
pourcentage[M]

add key
addition[F]

equals key
touche[F] de résultat[M]

change-sign key
inverseur[M] de signe[M]

MC MR M- M+ C
7 8 9 ÷ CE
4 5 6 x √
1 2 3 – +/–
0 . % + =

stationery

for time management
pour l'emploi[M] du temps[M]

tear-off calendar
calendrier[M]-mémorandum[M]

calendar pad
bloc[M]-éphéméride[F]

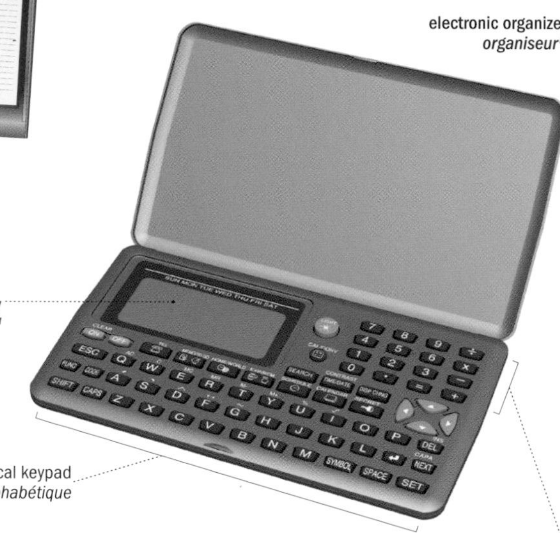
display
écran[M]
alphabetical keypad
pavé[M] alphabétique
numeric keypad
pavé[M] numérique

electronic organizer
organiseur[M]

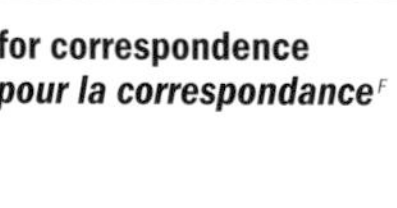

appointment book
agenda[M]

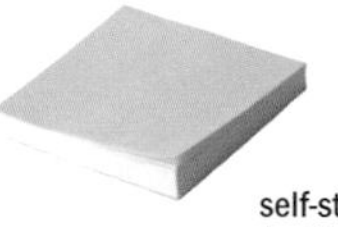

self-stick note
feuillet[M] adhésif

memo pad
bloc[M]-notes[F]

for correspondence
pour la correspondance[F]

stamp pad
tampon[M] encreur

rubber stamp
timbre[M] caoutchouc[M]

numbering machine
numéroteur[M]

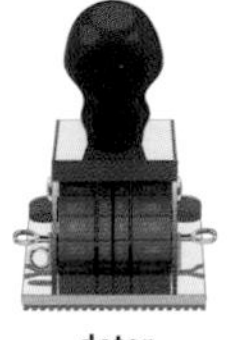

dater
timbre[M] dateur

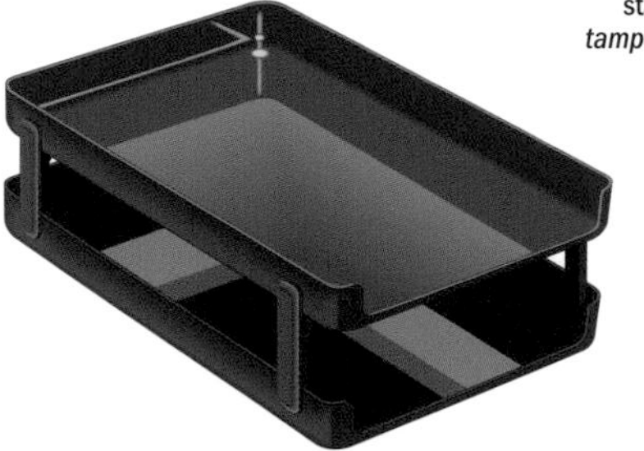

desk tray
boîte[F] à courrier[M]

rotary file
fichier[M] rotatif

telephone index
répertoire[M] téléphonique

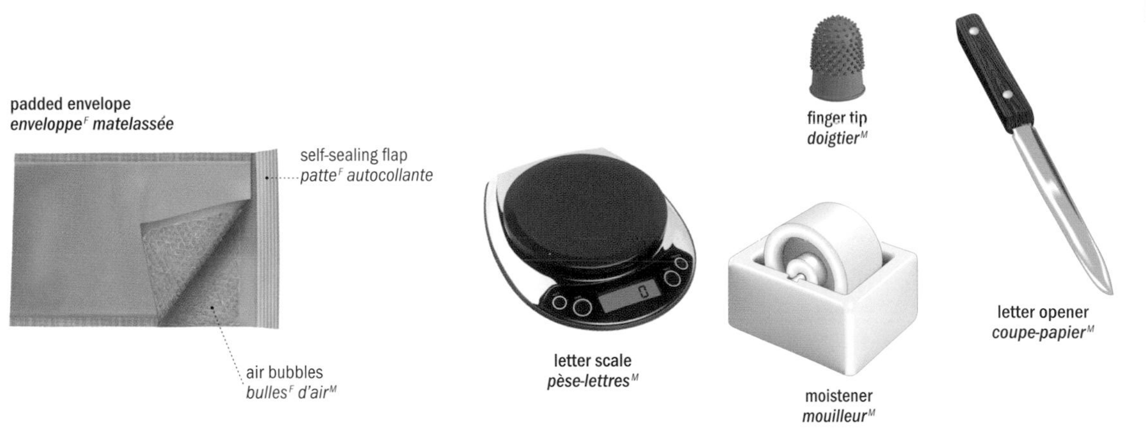
padded envelope
enveloppe^F matelassée
self-sealing flap
patte^F autocollante
air bubbles
bulles^F d'air^M
letter scale
pèse-lettres^M
finger tip
doigtier^M
moistener
mouilleur^M
letter opener
coupe-papier^M

for filing
pour le classement^M

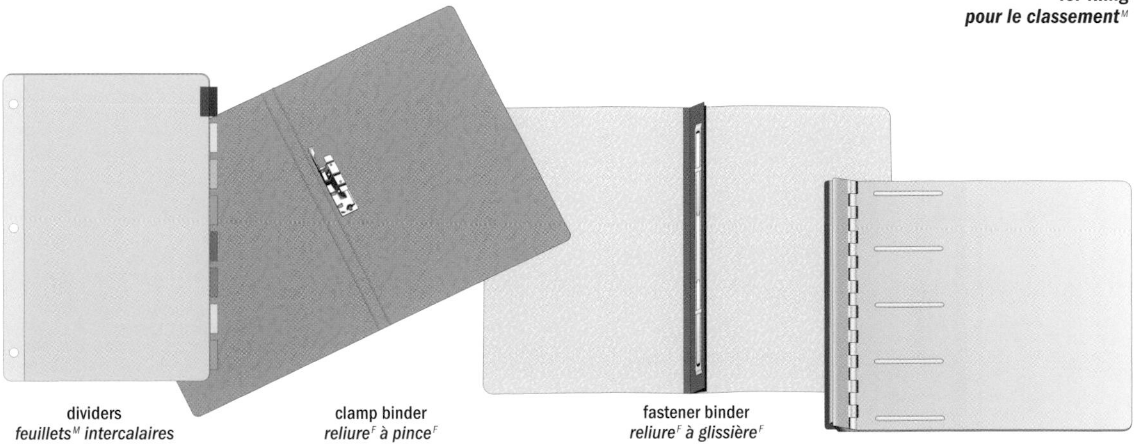

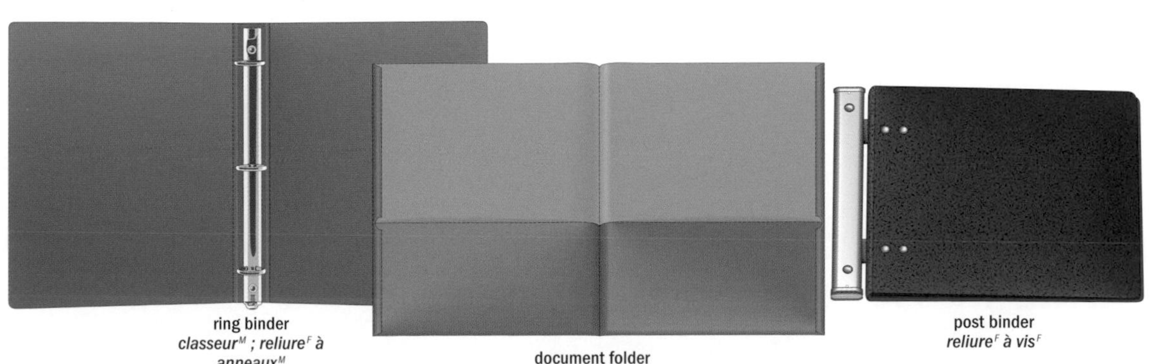
dividers
feuillets^M intercalaires
clamp binder
reliure^F à pince^F
fastener binder
reliure^F à glissière^F
spring binder
reliure^F à ressort^M
ring binder
classeur^M ; reliure^F à anneaux^M
document folder
pochette^F d'information^F
post binder
reliure^F à vis^F

stationery

self-adhesive labels
étiquettes[F] autocollantes
tab
onglet[M]
window tab
onglet[M] à fenêtre[F]
folder
chemise[F]
file guides
guides[M] de classement[M]
hanging file
dossier[M] suspendu
spiral notebook
reliure[F] spirale[F]
clipboard
planchette[F] à pince[F]
archboard
planchette[F] à arches[F]
filing box
boîte[F]-classeur[M]
label maker
pince[F] à étiqueter
paper punch
perforatrice[F]
comb binding
reliure[F] à anneaux[M] plastiques
expanding file
pochette[F] de classement[M]

stationery

miscellaneous articles
articles[M] divers

paper clips
trombones[M]

thumb tacks
punaises[F]

paper fasteners
attaches[F] parisiennes

pencil sharpener
taille-crayon[M]

eraser
gomme[F]

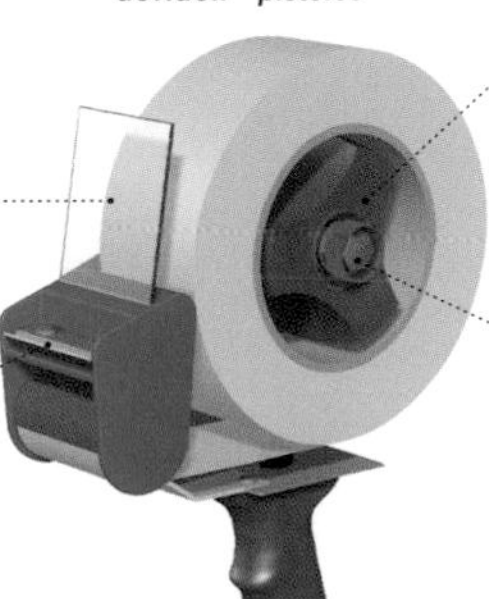
hub
moyeu[M]
tape guide
guide-bande[M]
tension-adjusting screw
vis[F] de réglage[M] de tension[F]
cutting blade
lame[F]
handle
poignée[F]

packing tape dispenser
dévidoir[M] pistolet[M]

bill-file
pique-notes[M]

staple remover
dégrafeuse[F]

glue stick
bâtonnet[M] de colle[F]

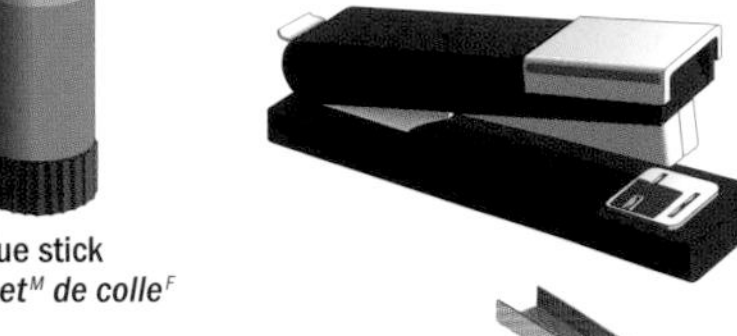

stapler
agrafeuse[F]

staples
agrafes[F]

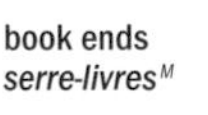

tape dispenser
dévidoir[M] de ruban[M] adhésif

book ends
serre-livres[M]

magnet
aimant[M]

paper clip holder
distributeur[M] de trombones[M]

pencil sharpener
taille-crayon[M]

posting surface
surface[F] d'affichage[M]

bulletin board
tableau[M] d'affichage[M] ; babillard[M]

cutting head
tête[F] de coupe[F]
waste basket
corbeille[F] à papier[M]

paper shredder
destructeur[M] de documents[M] ; déchiqueteuse[F]

waste basket
corbeille[F] à papier[M]

COMMUNICATIONS AND OFFICE AUTOMATION

road system

système[M] routier

cross section of a road
coupe[F] d'une route[F]

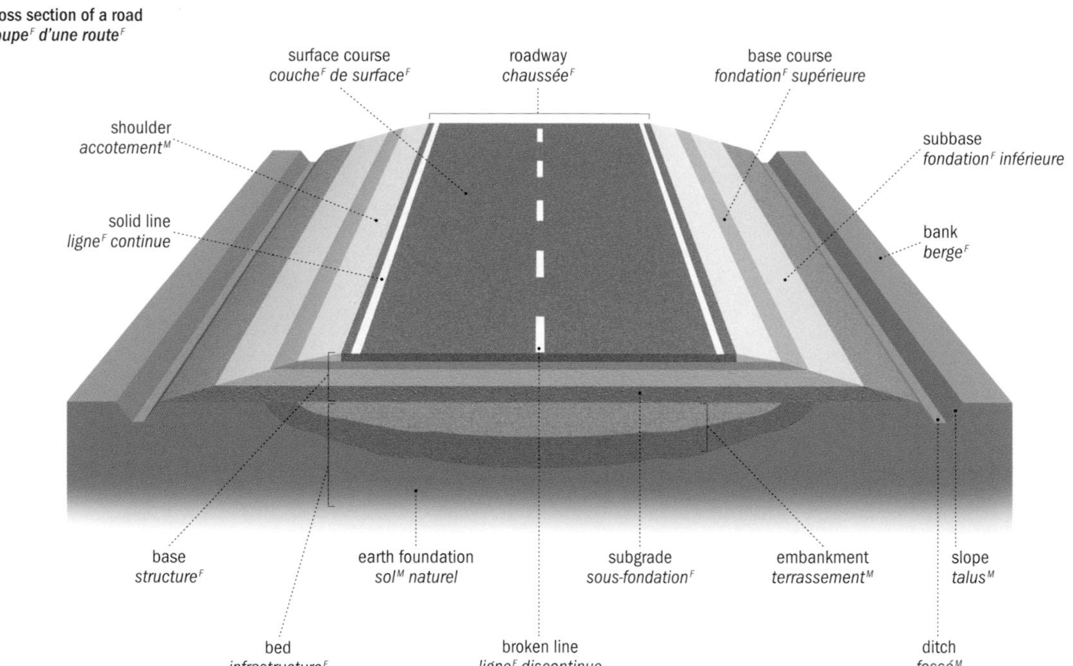
surface course
couche[F] de surface[F]
roadway
chaussée[F]
base course
fondation[F] supérieure
shoulder
accotement[M]
subbase
fondation[F] inférieure
solid line
ligne[F] continue
bank
berge[F]
base
structure[F]
earth foundation
sol[M] naturel
subgrade
sous-fondation[F]
embankment
terrassement[M]
slope
talus[M]
bed
infrastructure[F]
broken line
ligne[F] discontinue
ditch
fossé[M]

examples of interchanges
exemples[M] d'échangeurs[M]

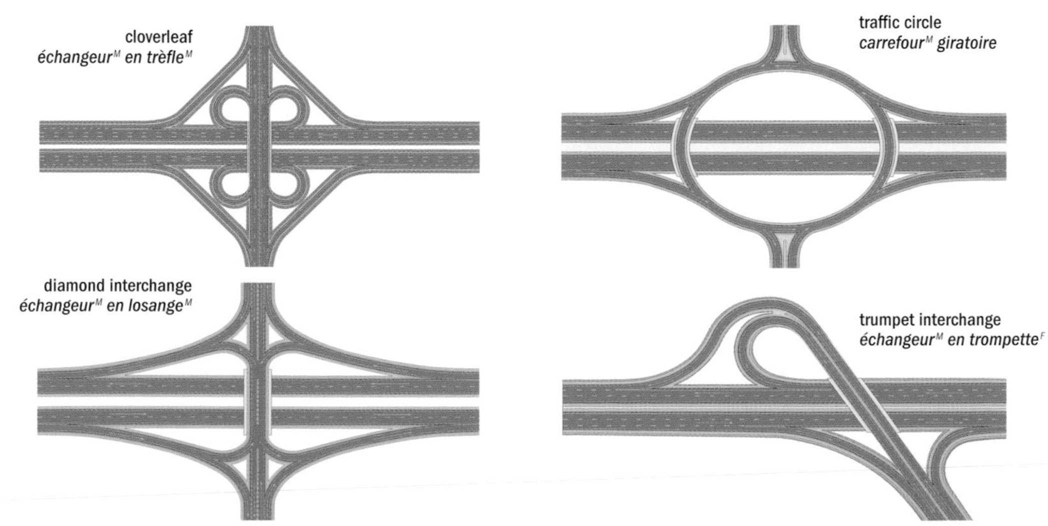
cloverleaf
échangeur[M] en trèfle[M]
traffic circle
carrefour[M] giratoire
diamond interchange
échangeur[M] en losange[M]
trumpet interchange
échangeur[M] en trompette[F]

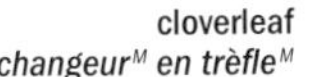

cloverleaf
échangeur^{M} en trèfle^{M}

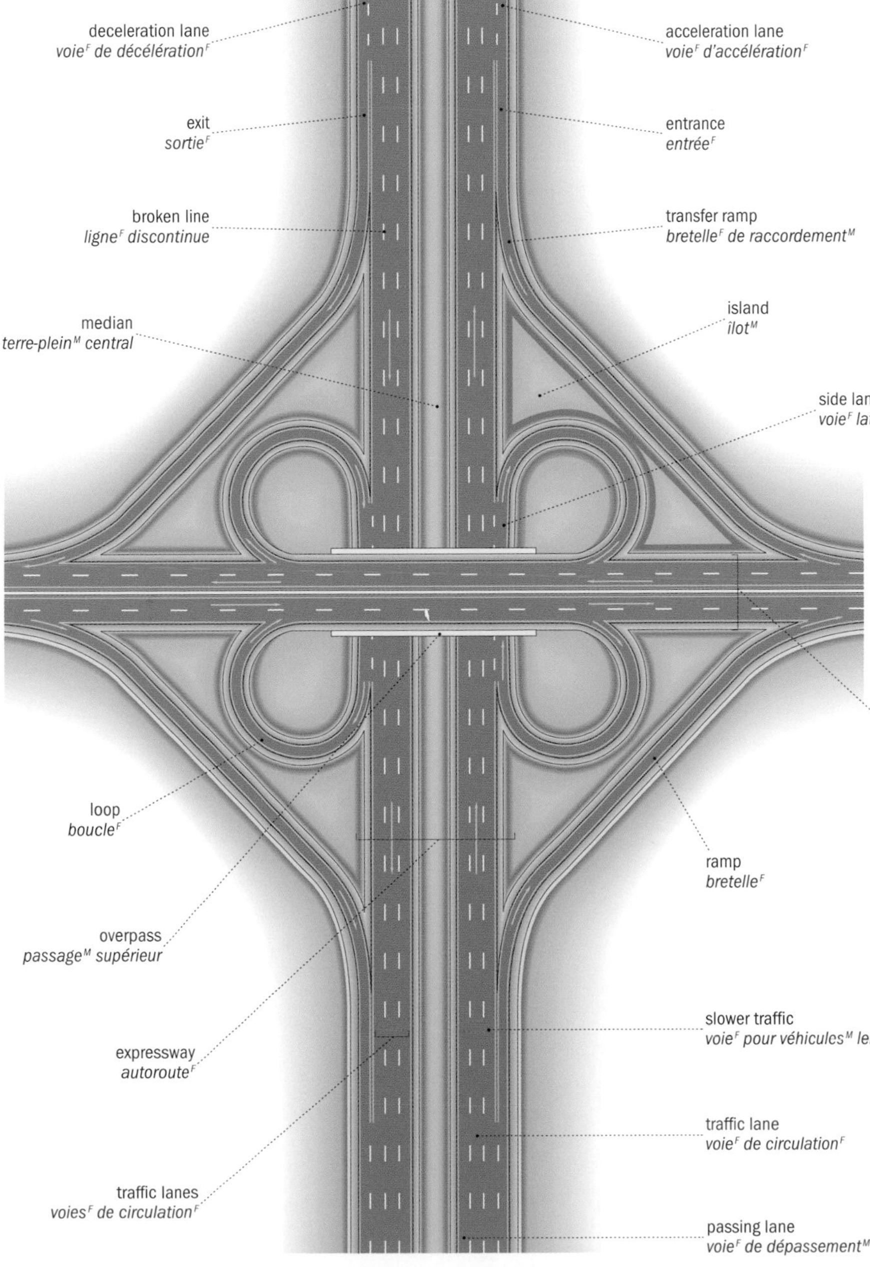

deceleration lane
voie^{F} de décélération^{F}

exit
sortie^{F}

broken line
ligne^{F} discontinue

median
terre-plein^{M} central

loop
boucle^{F}

overpass
passage^{M} supérieur

expressway
autoroute^{F}

traffic lanes
voies^{F} de circulation^{F}

acceleration lane
voie^{F} d'accélération^{F}

entrance
entrée^{F}

transfer ramp
bretelle^{F} de raccordement^{M}

island
îlot^{M}

side lane
voie^{F} latérale

highway
route^{F}

ramp
bretelle^{F}

slower traffic
voie^{F} pour véhicules^{M} lents

traffic lane
voie^{F} de circulation^{F}

passing lane
voie^{F} de dépassement^{M}

fixed bridges

ponts^M fixes

beam bridge
pont^M à poutre^F

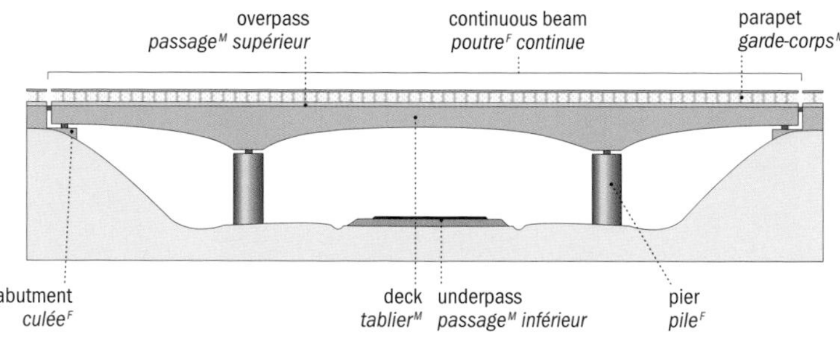
overpass
passage^M supérieur
continuous beam
poutre^F continue
parapet
garde-corps^M
abutment
culée^F
deck
tablier^M
underpass
passage^M inférieur
pier
pile^F

suspension bridge
pont^M suspendu à câble^M porteur

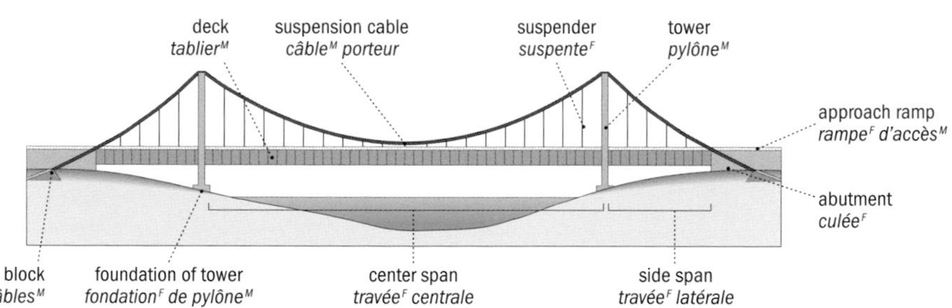
deck
tablier^M
suspension cable
câble^M porteur
suspender
suspente^F
tower
pylône^M
approach ramp
rampe^F d'accès^M
abutment
culée^F
anchorage block
massif^M d'ancrage^M des câbles^M
foundation of tower
fondation^F de pylône^M
center span
travée^F centrale
side span
travée^F latérale

cantilever bridge
pont^M cantilever

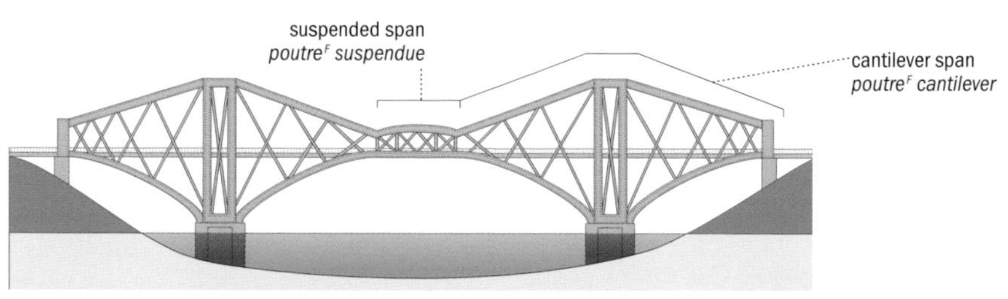
suspended span
poutre^F suspendue
cantilever span
poutre^F cantilever

movable bridges

ponts^M mobiles

swing bridge
pont^M tournant

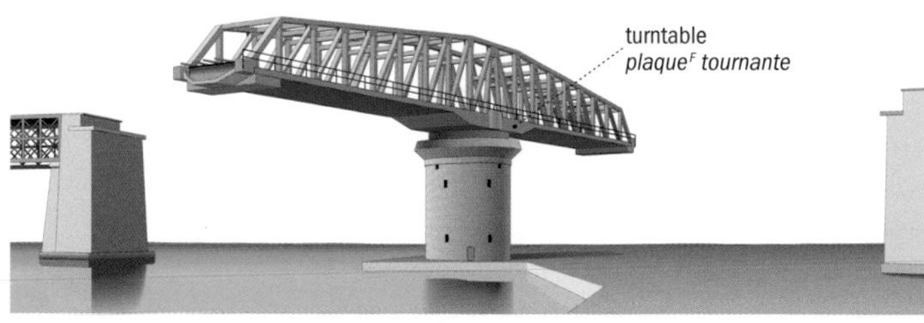
turntable
plaque^F tournante

movable bridges

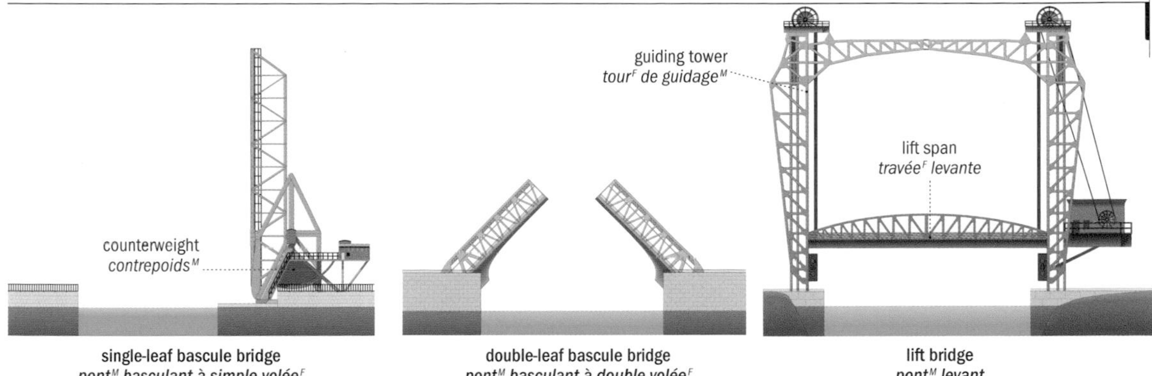
counterweight
contrepoids[M]
guiding tower
tour[F] *de guidage*[M]
lift span
travée[F] *levante*

single-leaf bascule bridge
***pont*[M] *basculant à simple volée*[F]**

double-leaf bascule bridge
***pont*[M] *basculant à double volée*[F]**

lift bridge
pont*[M] *levant

road tunnel

tunnel[M] routier

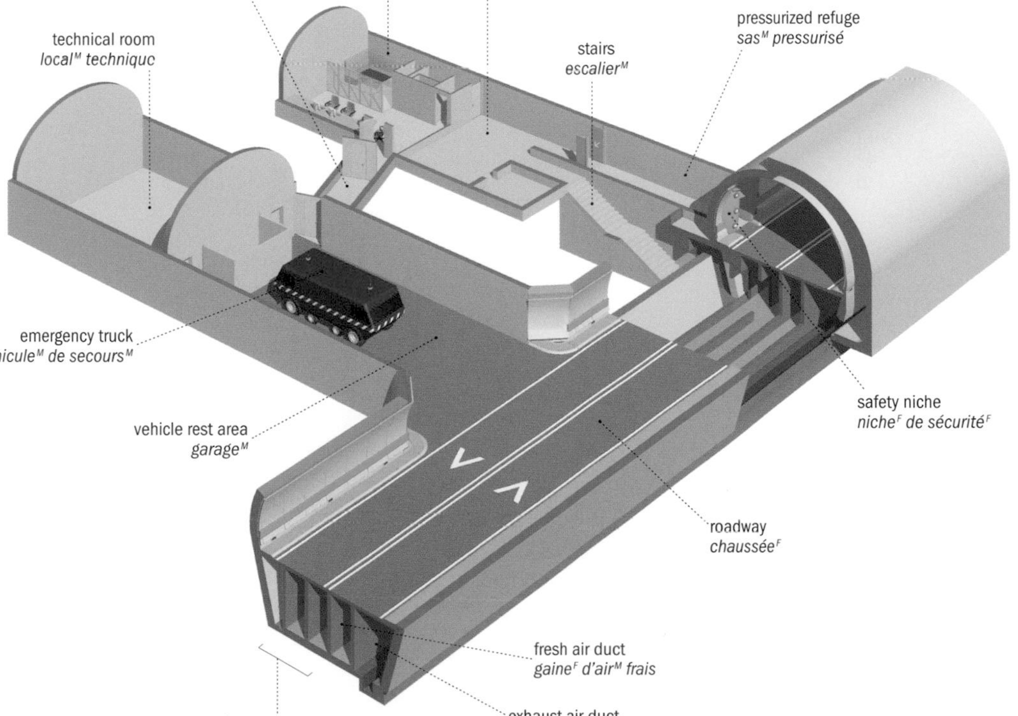

connecting gallery
galerie[F] *de liaison*[F]

emergency station
poste[M] *de secours*[M]

shelter
abri[M]

technical room
local[M] *techniquc*

pressurized refuge
sas[M] *pressurisé*

stairs
escalier[M]

emergency truck
véhicule[M] *de secours*[M]

safety niche
niche[F] *de sécurité*[F]

vehicle rest area
garage[M]

roadway
chaussée[F]

fresh air duct
gaine[F] *d'air*[M] *frais*

exhaust air duct
gaine[F] *d'air*[M] *vicié*

evacuation route
chemin[M] *d'évacuation*[F]

service station

station^F-service^M

gasoline pump
distributeur^M d'essence^F

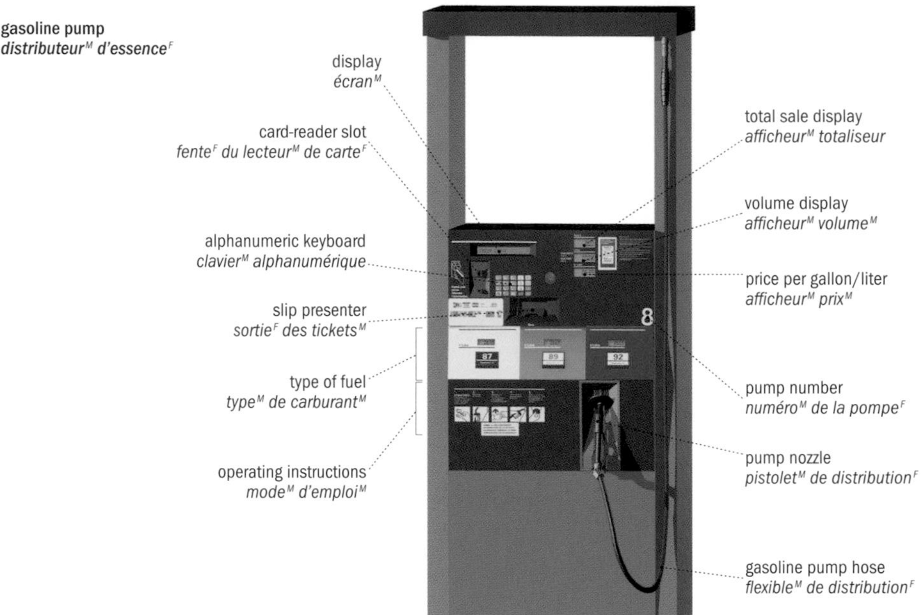
display
écran^M
card-reader slot
fente^F du lecteur^M de carte^F
alphanumeric keyboard
clavier^M alphanumérique
slip presenter
sortie^F des tickets^M
type of fuel
type^M de carburant^M
operating instructions
mode^M d'emploi^M
total sale display
afficheur^M totaliseur
volume display
afficheur^M volume^M
price per gallon/liter
afficheur^M prix^M
pump number
numéro^M de la pompe^F
pump nozzle
pistolet^M de distribution^F
gasoline pump hose
flexible^M de distribution^F
8
87
89
92

service station
station^F-service^M

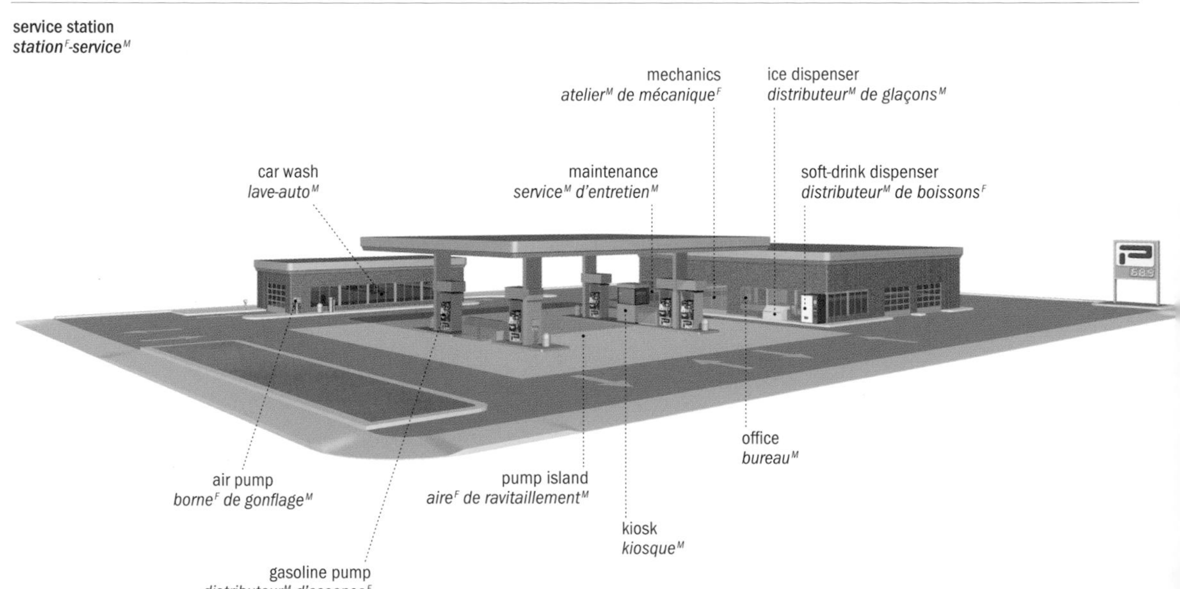
mechanics
atelier^M de mécanique^F
ice dispenser
distributeur^M de glaçons^M
car wash
lave-auto^M
maintenance
service^M d'entretien^M
soft-drink dispenser
distributeur^M de boissons^F
office
bureau^M
air pump
borne^F de gonflage^M
pump island
aire^F de ravitaillement^M
kiosk
kiosque^M
gasoline pump
distributeur^M d'essence^F

automobile

automobile[F]

sports car
voiture[F] sport[M]

examples of bodies
exemples[M] de carrosseries[F]

micro compact car
voiture[F] micro-compacte

hatchback
trois-portes[F]

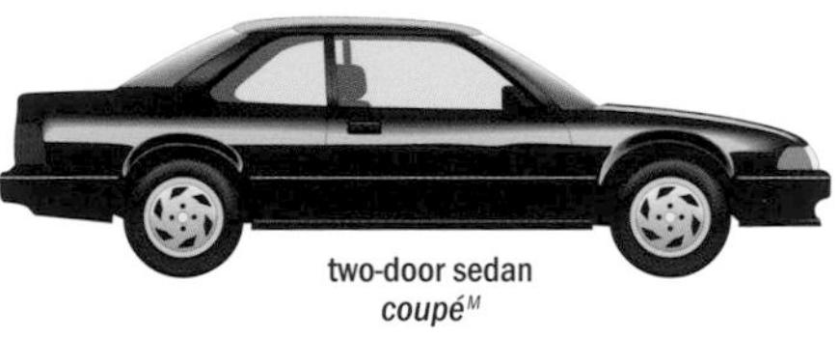

two-door sedan
coupé[M]

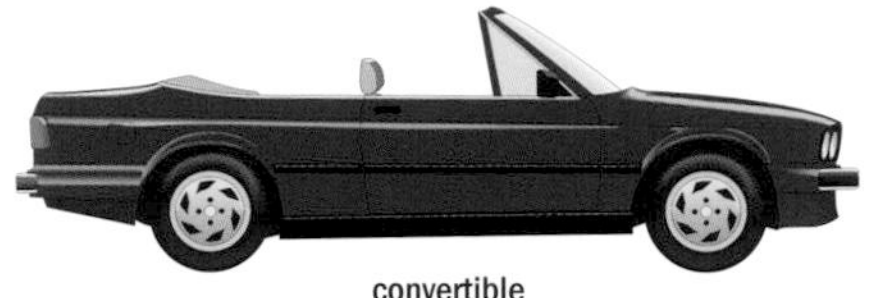

convertible
cabriolet[M] ; décapotable[F]

four-door sedan
berline[F]

station wagon
break[M] ; familiale[F]

minivan
fourgonnette[F]

sport-utility vehicle
véhicule[M] tout-terrain[M]

pickup truck
camionnette[F]

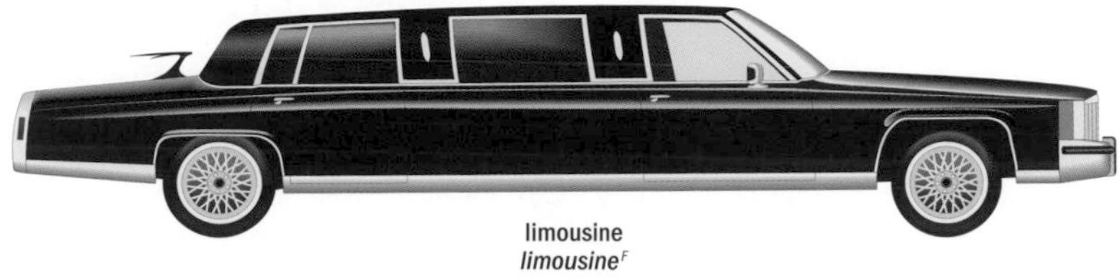

limousine
limousine[F]

automobile

body
*carrosserie*F

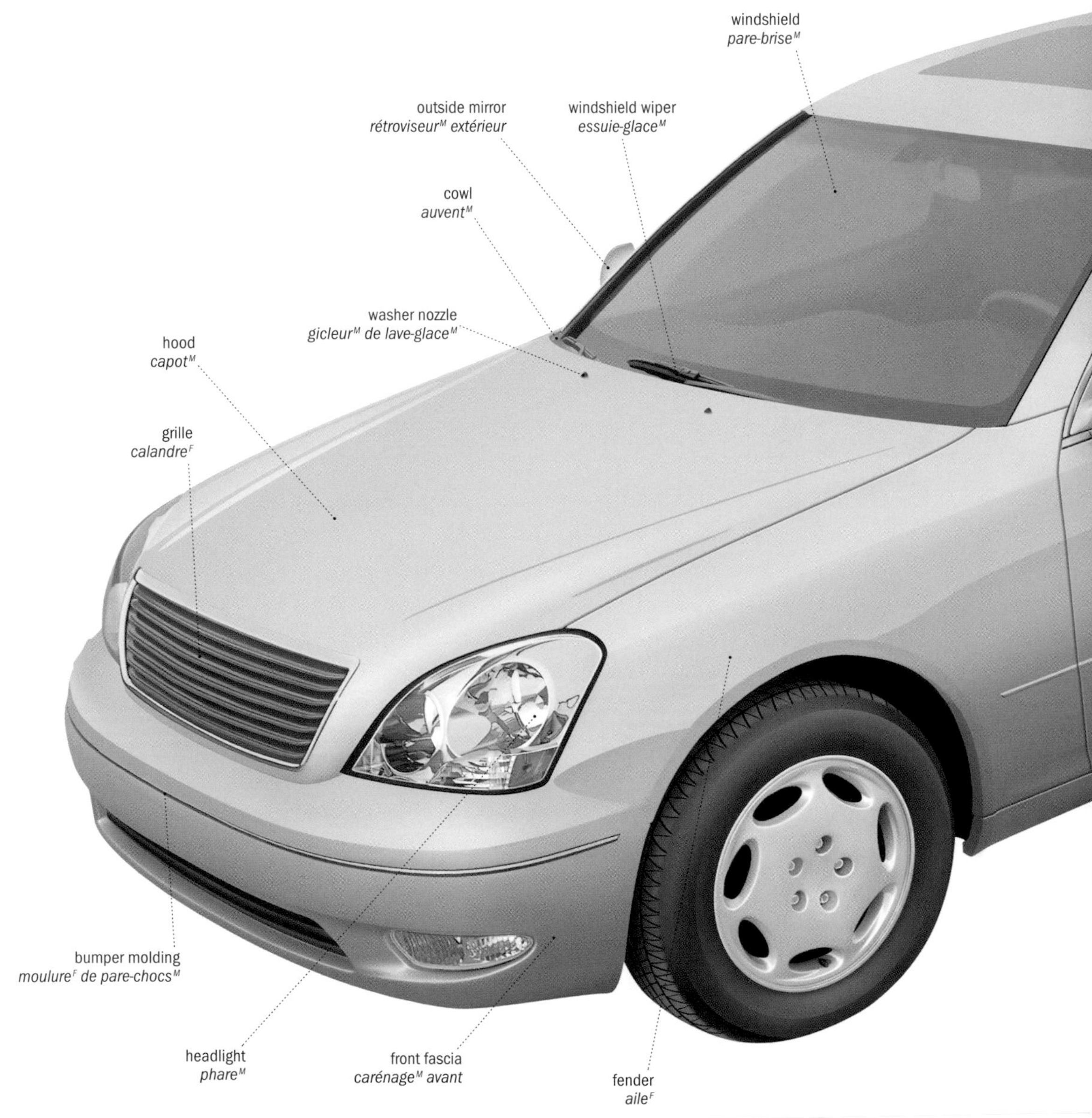
windshield
pare-briseM
outside mirror
rétroviseurM extérieur
windshield wiper
essuie-glaceM
cowl
auventM
washer nozzle
gicleurM de lave-glaceM
hood
capotM
grille
calandreF
bumper molding
moulureF de pare-chocsM
headlight
phareM
front fascia
carénageM avant
fender
aileF

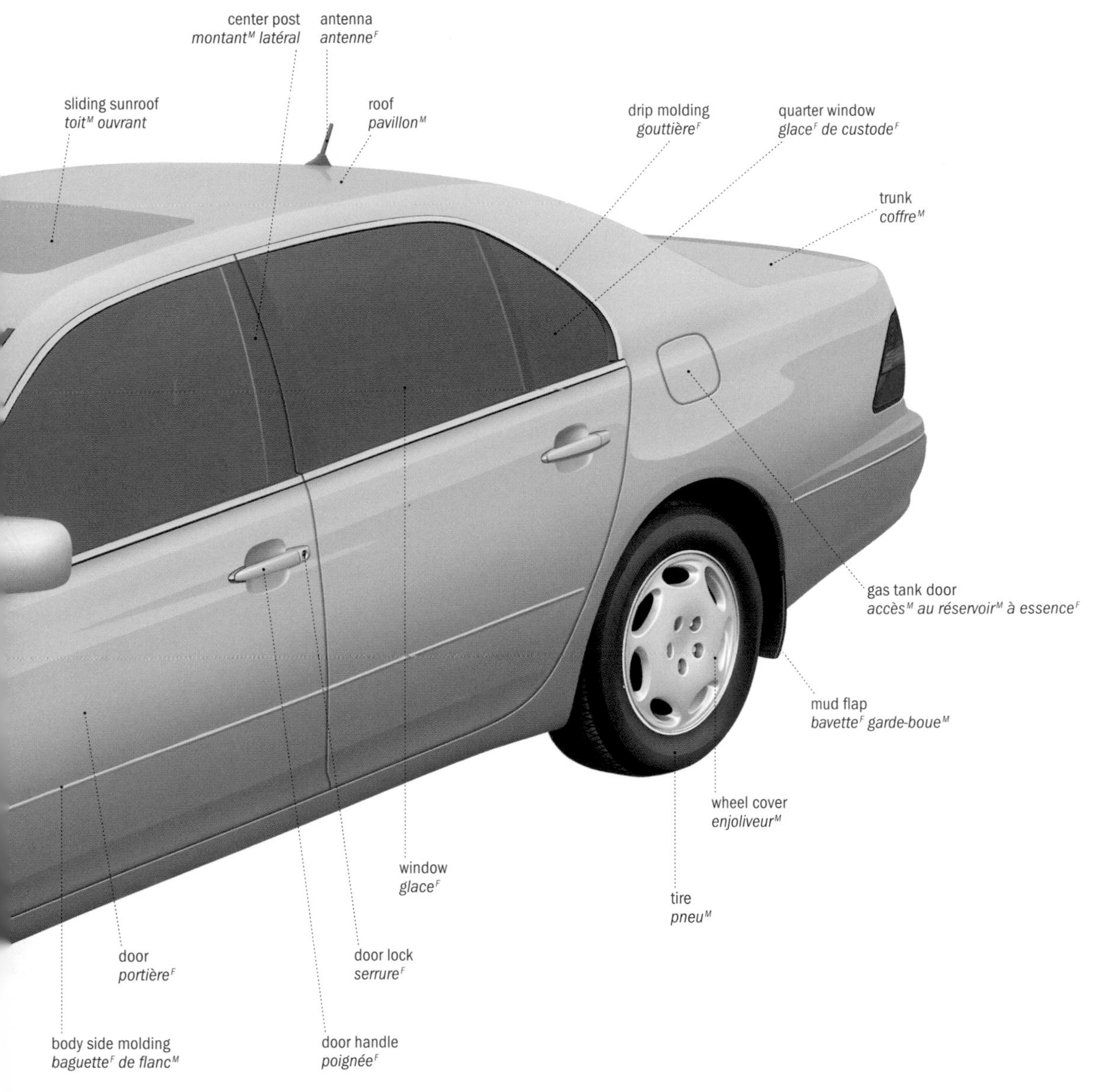
center post
montant[M] latéral
antenna
antenne[F]
sliding sunroof
toit[M] ouvrant
roof
pavillon[M]
drip molding
gouttière[F]
quarter window
glace[F] de custode[F]
trunk
coffre[M]
gas tank door
accès[M] au réservoir[M] à essence[F]
mud flap
bavette[F] garde-boue[M]
wheel cover
enjoliveur[M]
window
glace[F]
tire
pneu[M]
door
portière[F]
door lock
serrure[F]
body side molding
baguette[F] de flanc[M]
door handle
poignée[F]

automobile systems: main parts
principaux organes*[M] *des systèmes*[M] *automobiles

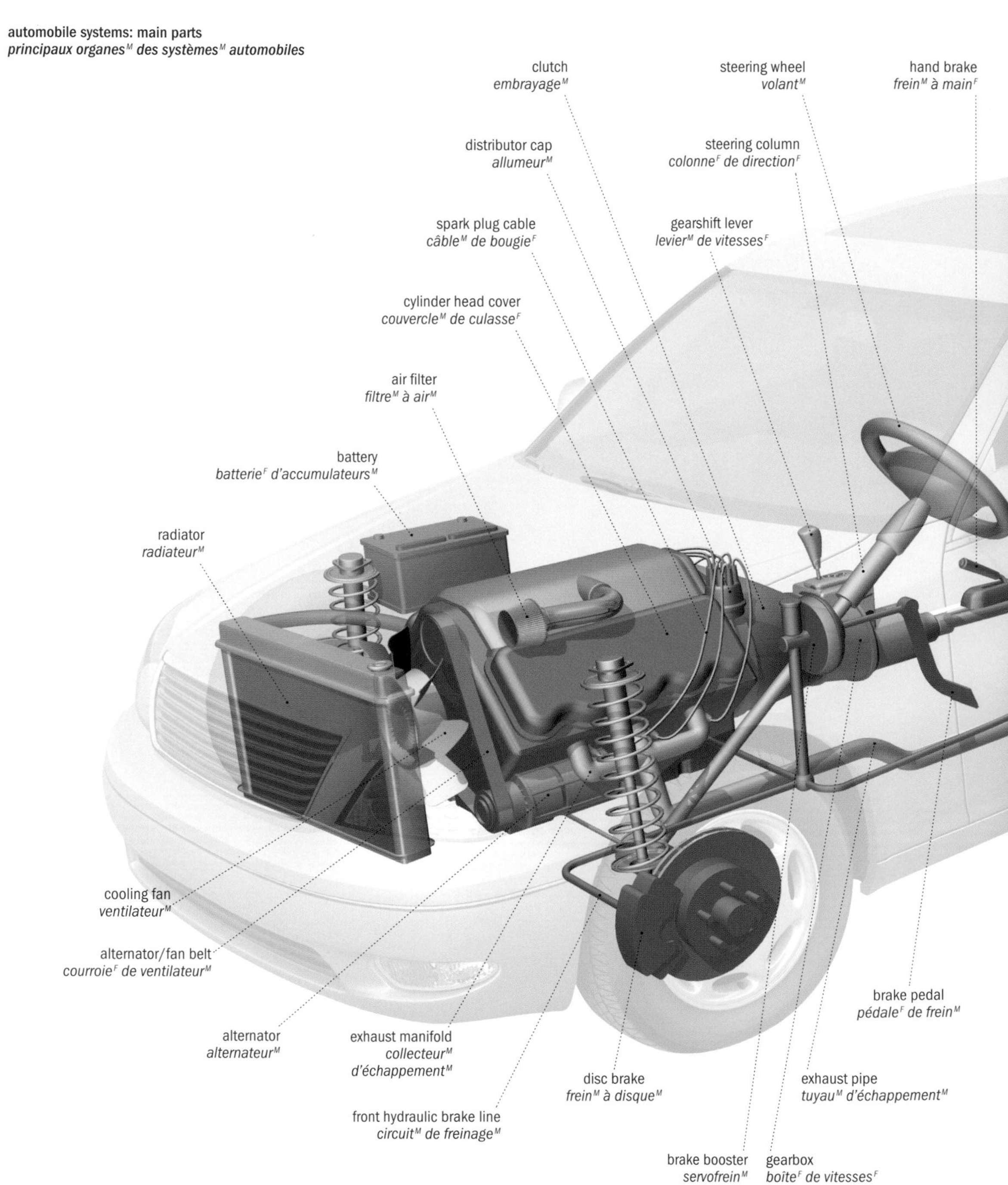
clutch
embrayage[M]
steering wheel
volant[M]
hand brake
frein[M] *à main*[F]
distributor cap
allumeur[M]
steering column
colonne[F] *de direction*[F]
spark plug cable
câble[M] *de bougie*[F]
gearshift lever
levier[M] *de vitesses*[F]
cylinder head cover
couvercle[M] *de culasse*[F]
air filter
filtre[M] *à air*[M]
battery
batterie[F] *d'accumulateurs*[M]
radiator
radiateur[M]
cooling fan
ventilateur[M]
alternator/fan belt
courroie[F] *de ventilateur*[M]
alternator
alternateur[M]
exhaust manifold
collecteur[M] *d'échappement*[M]
front hydraulic brake line
circuit[M] *de freinage*[M]
disc brake
frein[M] *à disque*[M]
brake pedal
pédale[F] *de frein*[M]
exhaust pipe
tuyau[M] *d'échappement*[M]
brake booster
servofrein[M]
gearbox
boîte[F] *de vitesses*[F]

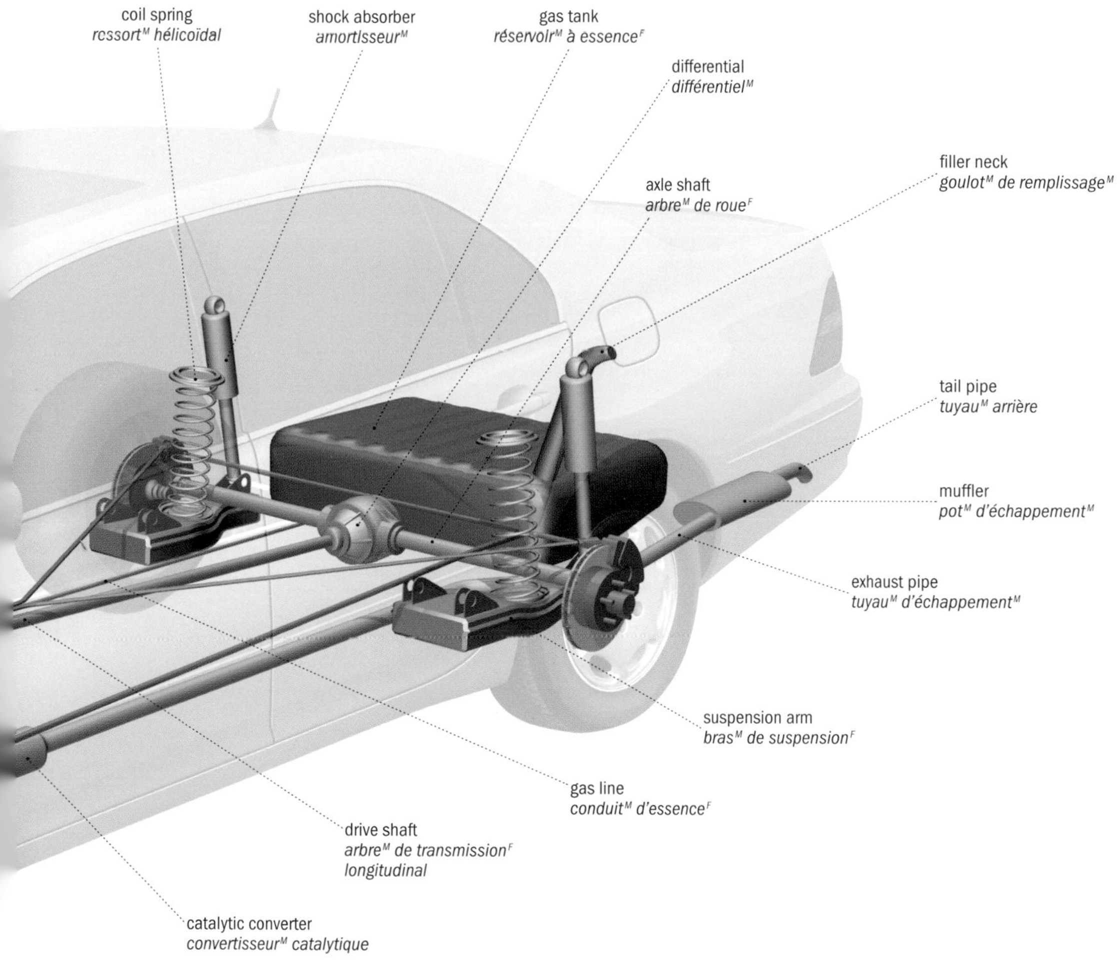

coil spring
ressort[M] hélicoïdal

shock absorber
amortisseur[M]

gas tank
réservoir[M] à essence[F]

differential
différentiel[M]

filler neck
goulot[M] de remplissage[M]

axle shaft
arbre[M] de roue[F]

tail pipe
tuyau[M] arrière

muffler
pot[M] d'échappement[M]

exhaust pipe
tuyau[M] d'échappement[M]

suspension arm
bras[M] de suspension[F]

gas line
conduit[M] d'essence[F]

drive shaft
arbre[M] de transmission[F] longitudinal

catalytic converter
convertisseur[M] catalytique

automobile systems
systèmes[M] automobiles

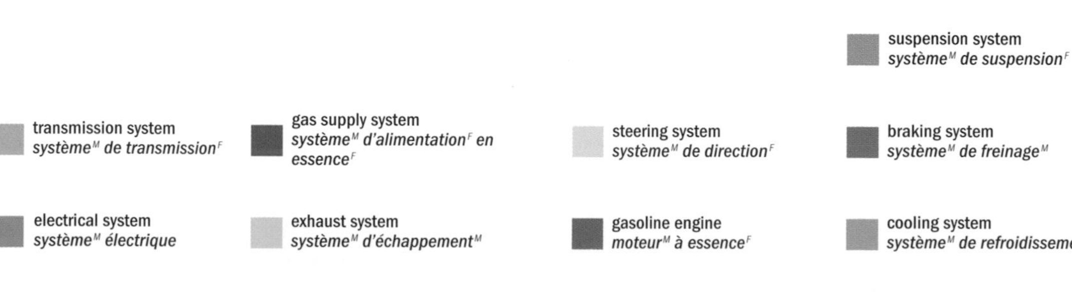
suspension system
système[M] de suspension[F]
transmission system
système[M] de transmission[F]
gas supply system
système[M] d'alimentation[F] en essence[F]
steering system
système[M] de direction[F]
braking system
système[M] de freinage[M]
electrical system
système[M] électrique
exhaust system
système[M] d'échappement[M]
gasoline engine
moteur[M] à essence[F]
cooling system
système[M] de refroidissement[M]

automobile

headlights
feux**[M] **avant

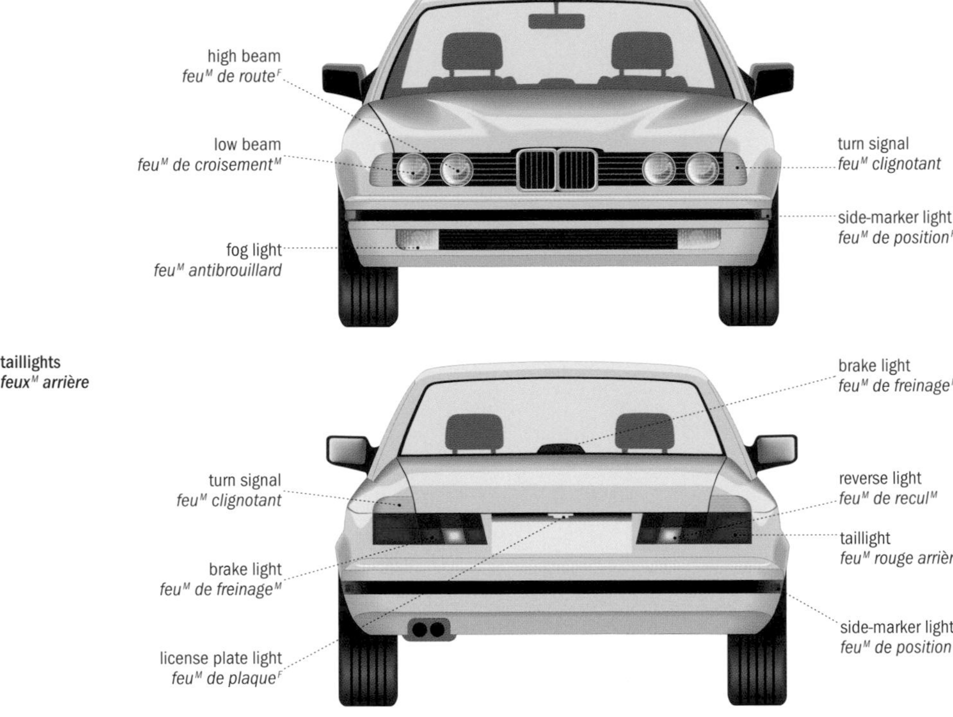
high beam
feu[M] de route[F]
low beam
feu[M] de croisement[M]
fog light
feu[M] antibrouillard
turn signal
feu[M] clignotant
side-marker light
feu[M] de position[F]

taillights
feux**[M] **arrière

turn signal
feu[M] clignotant
brake light
feu[M] de freinage[M]
license plate light
feu[M] de plaque[F]
brake light
feu[M] de freinage[M]
reverse light
feu[M] de recul[M]
taillight
feu[M] rouge arrière
side-marker light
feu[M] de position[F]

door
***portière**[F]*

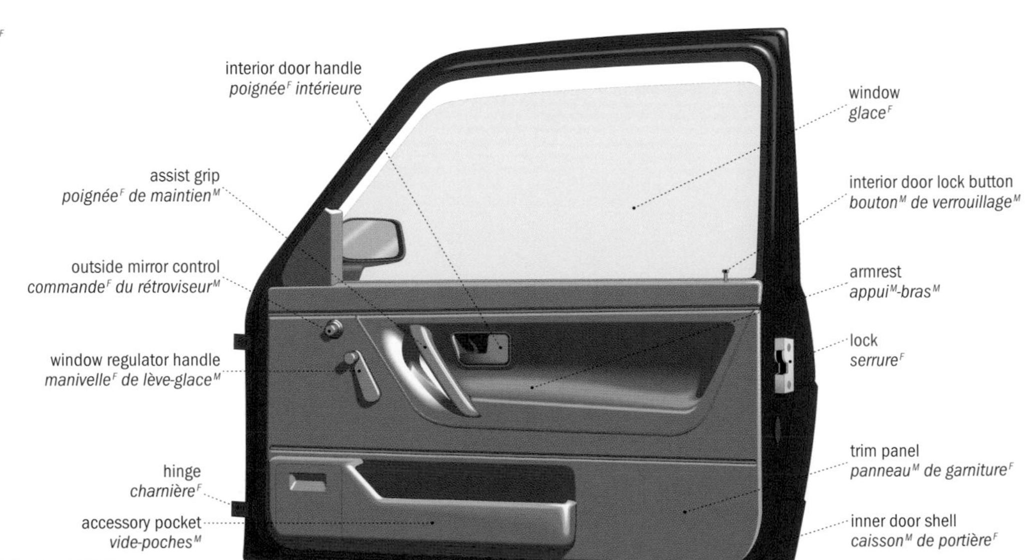
interior door handle
poignée[F] intérieure
assist grip
poignée[F] de maintien[M]
outside mirror control
commande[F] du rétroviseur[M]
window regulator handle
manivelle[F] de lève-glace[M]
hinge
charnière[F]
accessory pocket
vide-poches[M]
window
glace[F]
interior door lock button
bouton[M] de verrouillage[M]
armrest
appui[M]-bras[M]
lock
serrure[F]
trim panel
panneau[M] de garniture[F]
inner door shell
caisson[M] de portière[F]

bucket seat: front view
siège[M]-baquet[M] : vue[F] de face[F]

bucket seat: side view
siège[M]-baquet[M] : vue[F] de profil[M]

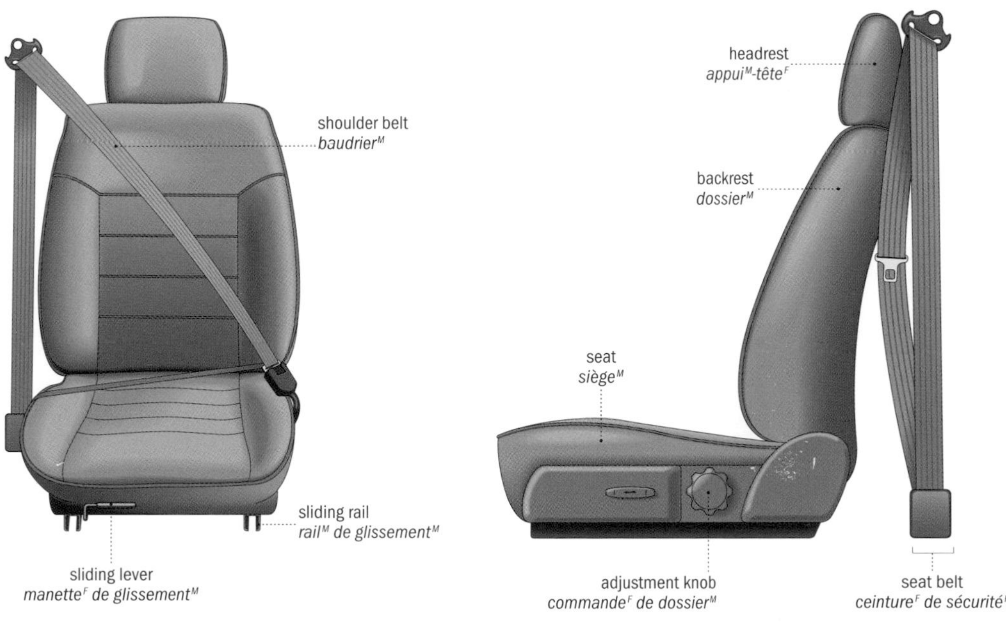
shoulder belt
baudrier[M]
sliding rail
rail[M] de glissement[M]
sliding lever
manette[F] de glissement[M]
headrest
appui[M]-tête[F]
backrest
dossier[M]
seat
siège[M]
adjustment knob
commande[F] de dossier[M]
seat belt
ceinture[F] de sécurité[F]

rear seat
banquette[F] arrière

armrest
appui[M]-bras[M]
webbing
sangle[F]
buckle
boucle[F]
bench seat
banquette[F]

dashboard
tableau[M] de bord[M]

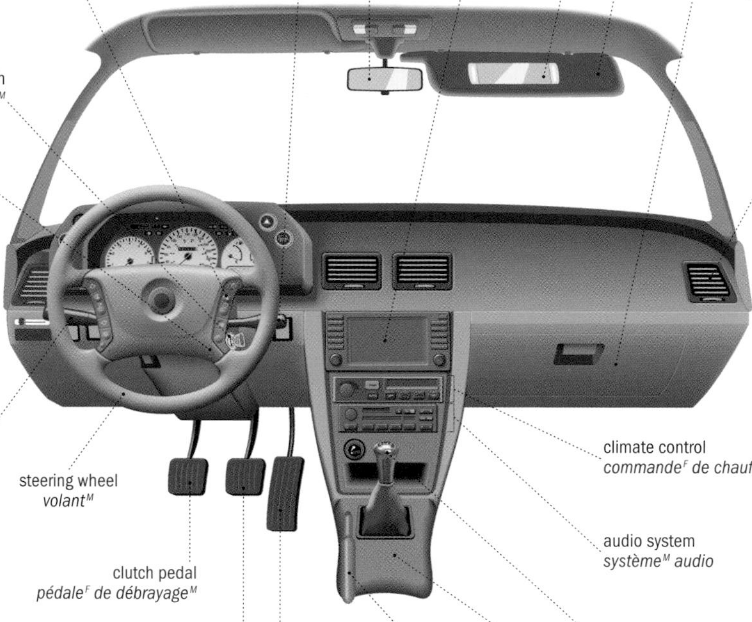

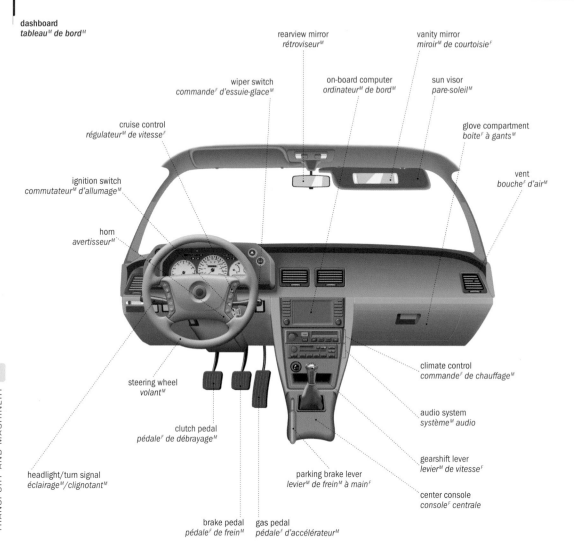

rearview mirror
rétroviseur[M]

vanity mirror
miroir[M] de courtoisie[F]

wiper switch
commande[F] d'essuie-glace[M]

on-board computer
ordinateur[M] de bord[M]

sun visor
pare-soleil[M]

cruise control
régulateur[M] de vitesse[F]

glove compartment
boîte[F] à gants[M]

ignition switch
commutateur[M] d'allumage[M]

vent
bouche[F] d'air[M]

horn
avertisseur[M]

climate control
commande[F] de chauffage[M]

steering wheel
volant[M]

audio system
système[M] audio

clutch pedal
pédale[F] de débrayage[M]

gearshift lever
levier[M] de vitesse[F]

headlight/turn signal
éclairage[M]/clignotant[M]

parking brake lever
levier[M] de frein[M] à main[F]

center console
console[F] centrale

brake pedal
pédale[F] de frein[M]

gas pedal
pédale[F] d'accélérateur[M]

air bag restraint system
système[M] de retenue[F] à sacs[M] gonflables

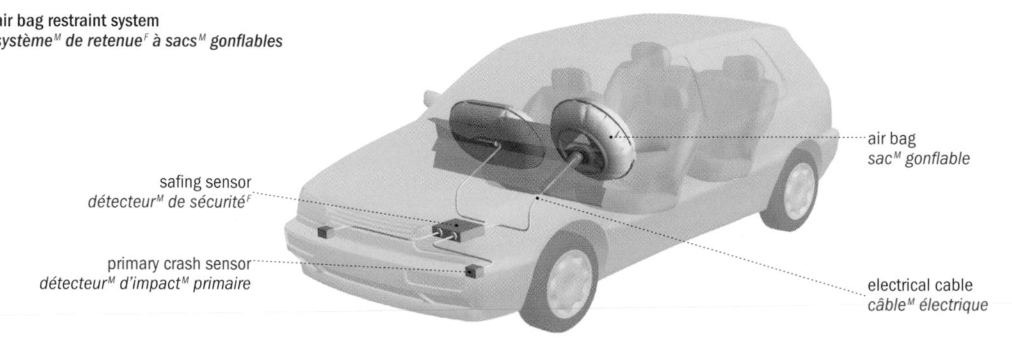
air bag
sac[M] gonflable
safing sensor
détecteur[M] de sécurité[F]
primary crash sensor
détecteur[M] d'impact[M] primaire
electrical cable
câble[M] électrique

instrument panel
instruments[M] de bord[M]

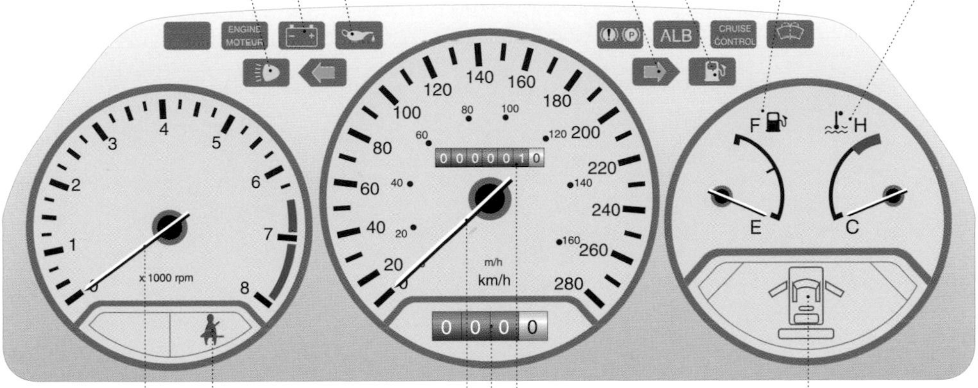

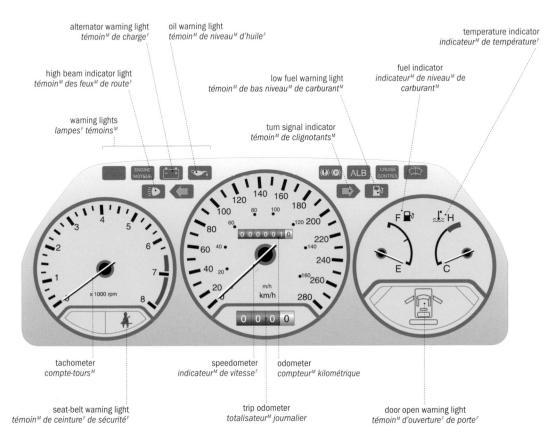

alternator warning light
témoin[M] de charge[F]

oil warning light
témoin[M] de niveau[M] d'huile[F]

temperature indicator
indicateur[M] de température[F]

high beam indicator light
témoin[M] des feux[M] de route[F]

low fuel warning light
témoin[M] de bas niveau[M] de carburant[M]

fuel indicator
indicateur[M] de niveau[M] de carburant[M]

warning lights
lampes[F] témoins[M]

turn signal indicator
témoin[M] de clignotants[M]

ENGINE MOTEUR

ALB

CRUISE CONTROL

x 1000 rpm

m/h

km/h

tachometer
compte-tours[M]

speedometer
indicateur[M] de vitesse[F]

odometer
compteur[M] kilométrique

seat-belt warning light
témoin[M] de ceinture[F] de sécurité[F]

trip odometer
totalisateur[M] journalier

door open warning light
témoin[M] d'ouverture[F] de porte[F]

windshield wiper
essuie-glace[M]

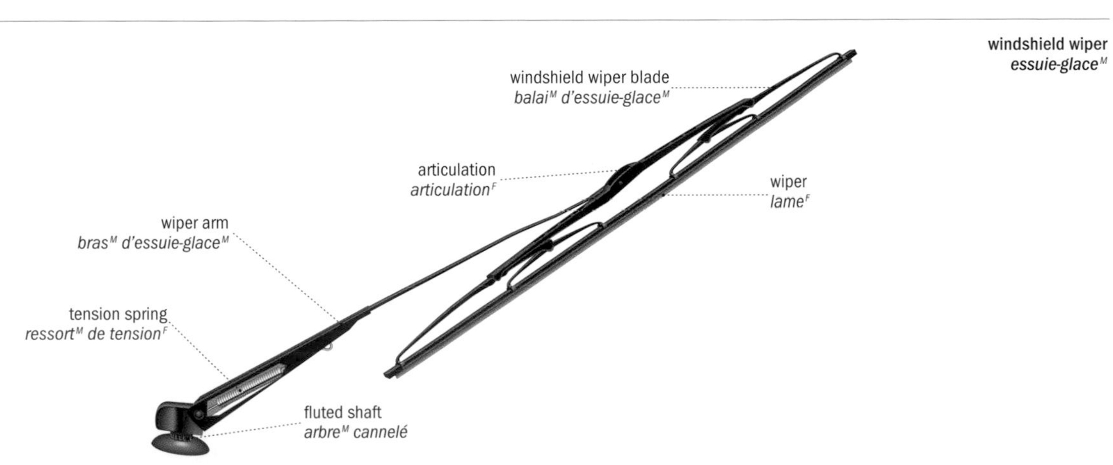
windshield wiper blade
balai[M] d'essuie-glace[M]
articulation
articulation[F]
wiper
lame[F]
wiper arm
bras[M] d'essuie-glace[M]
tension spring
ressort[M] de tension[F]
fluted shaft
arbre[M] cannelé

accessories
accessoires[M]

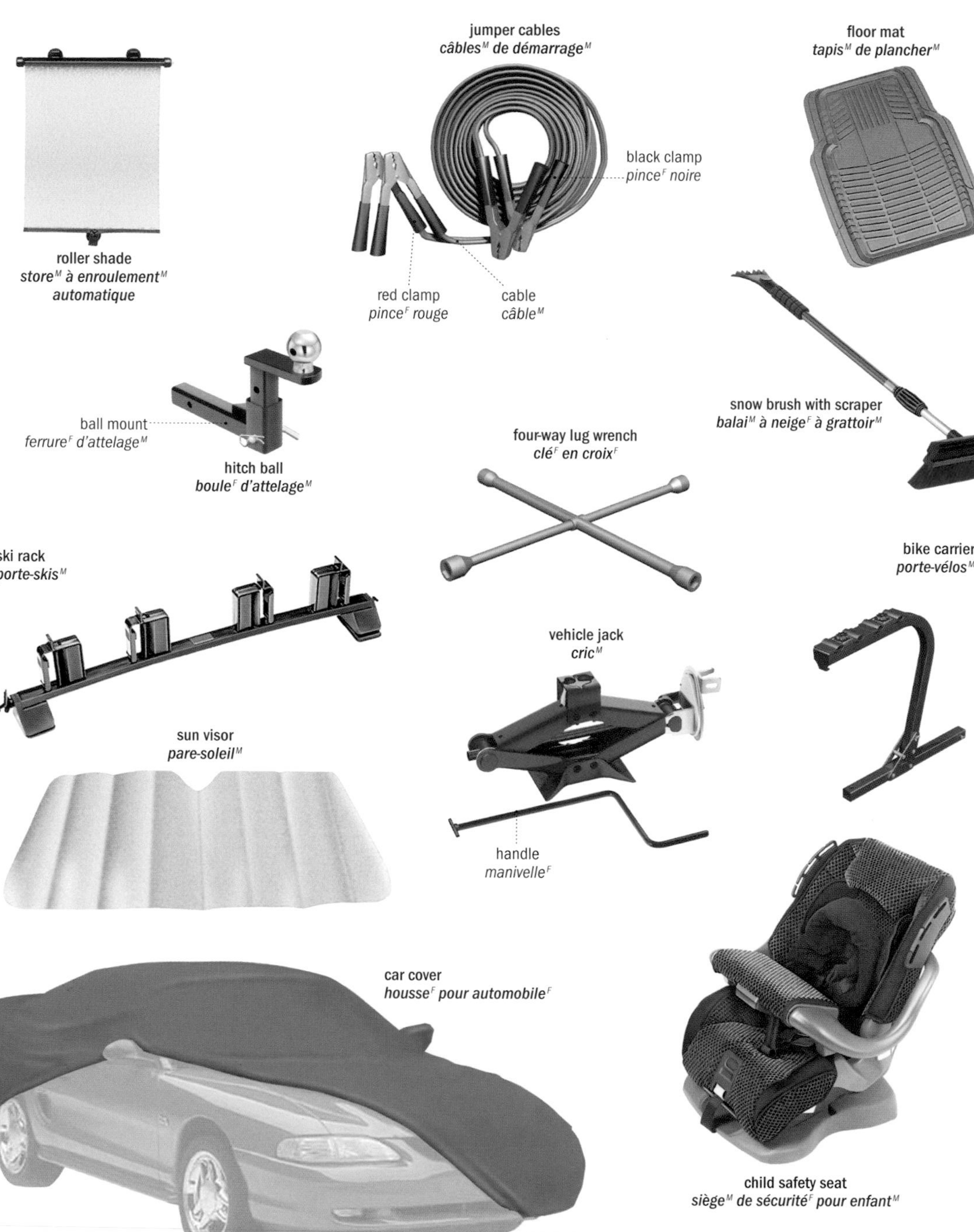
roller shade
store[M] à enroulement[M] automatique
jumper cables
câbles[M] de démarrage[M]
black clamp
pince[F] noire
red clamp
pince[F] rouge
cable
câble[M]
floor mat
tapis[M] de plancher[M]
ball mount
ferrure[F] d'attelage[M]
hitch ball
boule[F] d'attelage[M]
snow brush with scraper
balai[M] à neige[F] à grattoir[M]
four-way lug wrench
clé[F] en croix[F]
ski rack
porte-skis[M]
bike carrier
porte-vélos[M]
vehicle jack
cric[M]
sun visor
pare-soleil[M]
handle
manivelle[F]
car cover
housse[F] pour automobile[F]
child safety seat
siège[M] de sécurité[F] pour enfant[M]

brakes
freins[M]

disc brake
frein[M] à disque[M]

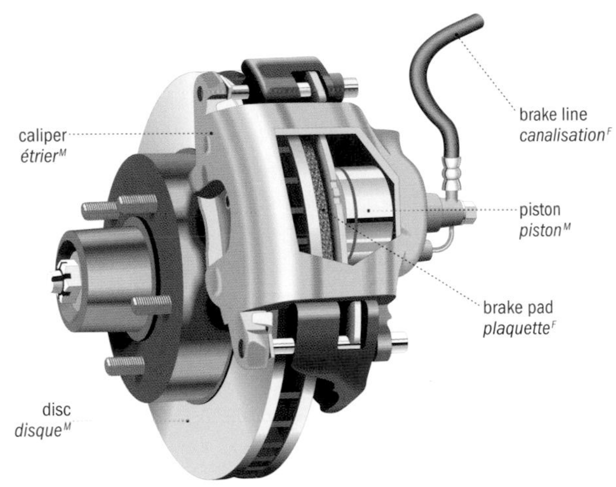
caliper
étrier[M]
brake line
canalisation[F]
piston
piston[M]
brake pad
plaquette[F]
disc
disque[M]

drum brake
frein[M] à tambour[M]

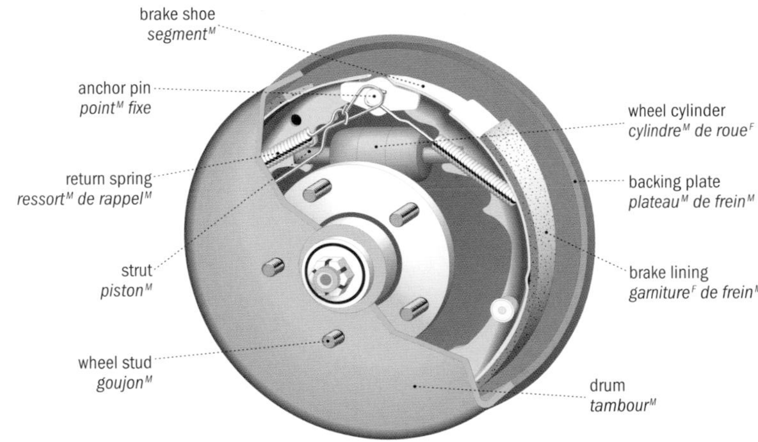
brake shoe
segment[M]
anchor pin
point[M] fixe
wheel cylinder
cylindre[M] de roue[F]
return spring
ressort[M] de rappel[M]
backing plate
plateau[M] de frein[M]
strut
piston[M]
brake lining
garniture[F] de frein[M]
wheel stud
goujon[M]
drum
tambour[M]

antilock braking system (ABS)
système[M] de freinage[M] antiblocage

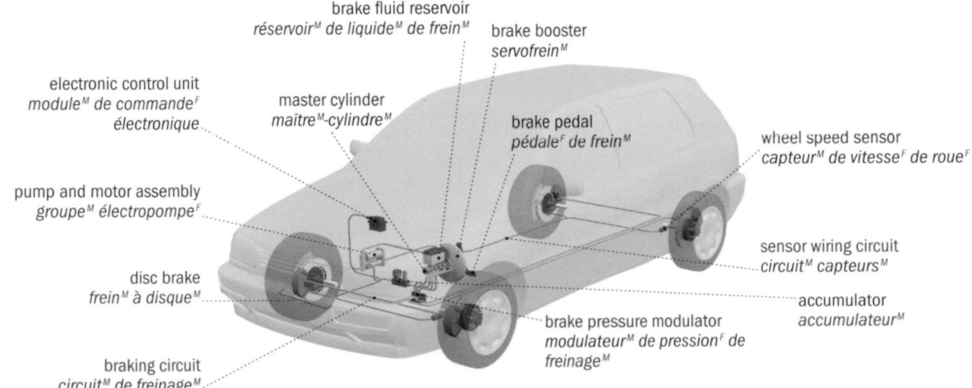
brake fluid reservoir
réservoir[M] de liquide[M] de frein[M]
brake booster
servofrein[M]
electronic control unit
module[M] de commande[F] électronique
master cylinder
maitre[M]-cylindre[M]
brake pedal
pédale[F] de frein[M]
wheel speed sensor
capteur[M] de vitesse[F] de roue[F]
pump and motor assembly
groupe[M] électropompe[F]
sensor wiring circuit
circuit[M] capteurs[M]
disc brake
frein[M] à disque[M]
accumulator
accumulateur[M]
brake pressure modulator
modulateur[M] de pression[F] de freinage[M]
braking circuit
circuit[M] de freinage[M]

TRANSPORT AND MACHINERY

tire

pneu[M]

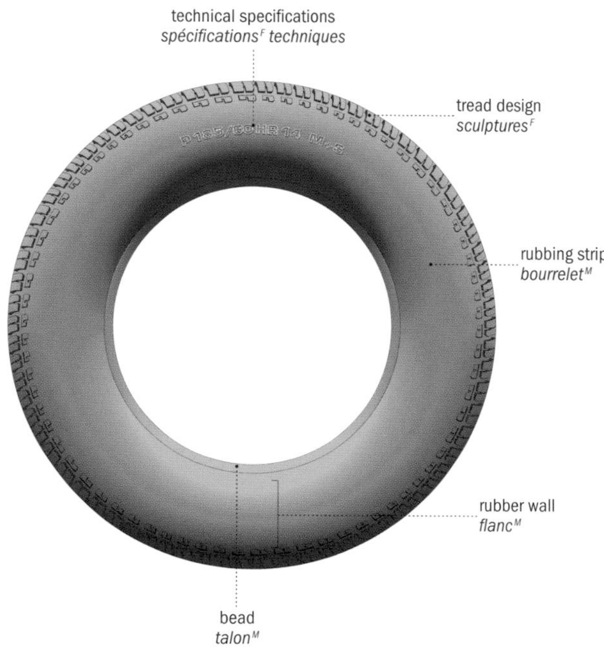
technical specifications
spécifications[F] techniques
tread design
sculptures[F]
rubbing strip
bourrelet[M]
rubber wall
flanc[M]
bead
talon[M]

examples of tires
exemples[M] de pneus[M]

performance tire
pneu[M] de performance[F]

all-season tire
pneu[M] toutes saisons[F]

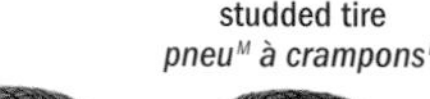

studded tire
pneu[M] à crampons[M]

winter tire
pneu[M] d'hiver[M]

touring tire
pneu[M] autoroutier

radiator

radiateur[M]

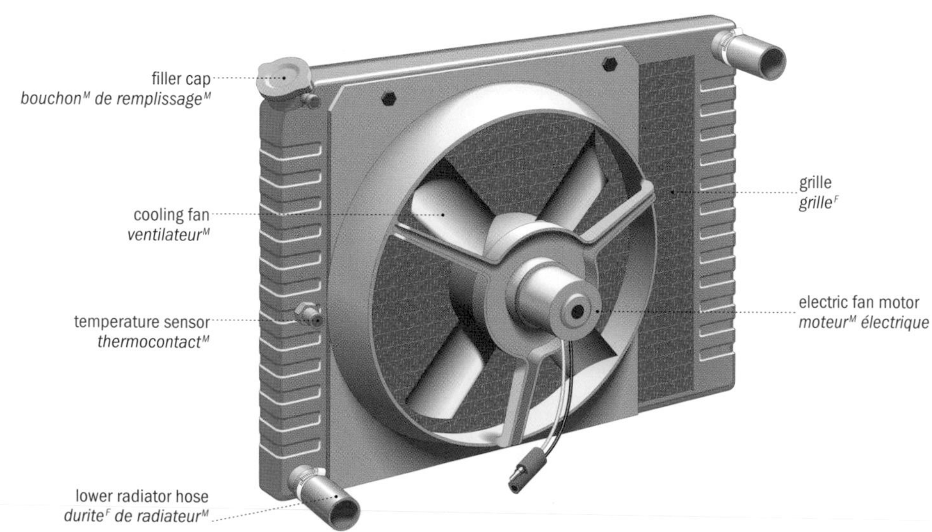
filler cap
bouchon[M] de remplissage[M]
cooling fan
ventilateur[M]
temperature sensor
thermocontact[M]
lower radiator hose
durite[F] de radiateur[M]
grille
grille[F]
electric fan motor
moteur[M] électrique

spark plug

bougie^F d'allumage^M

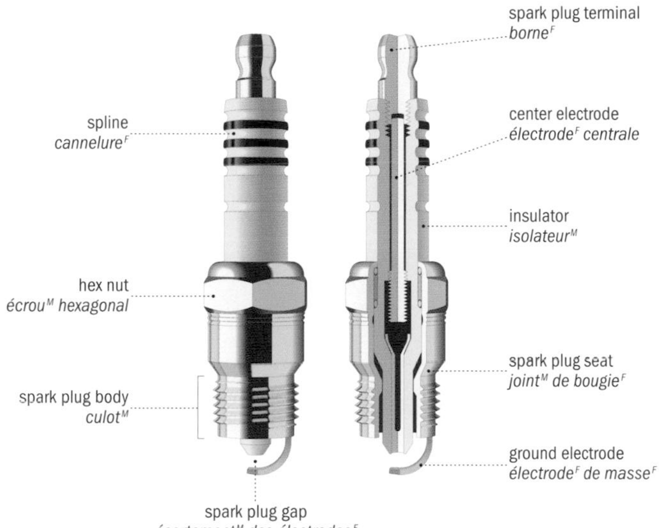
spark plug terminal
borne^F
spline
cannelure^F
center electrode
électrode^F centrale
insulator
isolateur^M
hex nut
écrou^M hexagonal
spark plug seat
joint^M de bougie^F
spark plug body
culot^M
ground electrode
électrode^F de masse^F
spark plug gap
écartement^M des électrodes^F

battery

batterie^F d'accumulateurs^M

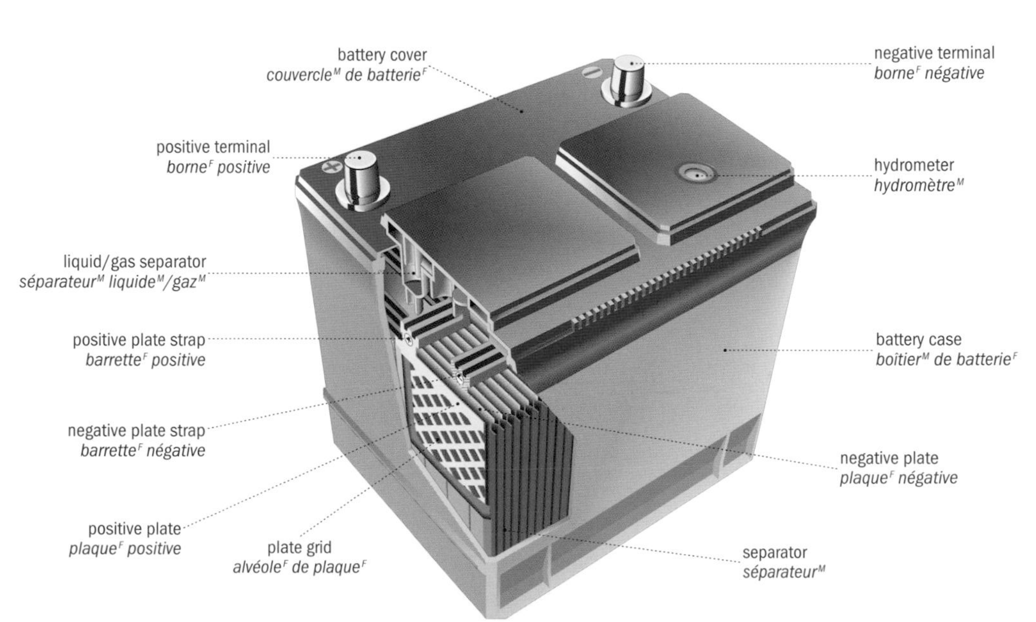
battery cover
couvercle^M de batterie^F
negative terminal
borne^F négative
positive terminal
borne^F positive
hydrometer
hydromètre^M
liquid/gas separator
séparateur^M liquide^M/gaz^M
positive plate strap
barrette^F positive
battery case
boîtier^M de batterie^F
negative plate strap
barrette^F négative
negative plate
plaque^F négative
positive plate
plaque^F positive
plate grid
alvéole^F de plaque^F
separator
séparateur^M

gasoline engine

moteur[M] à essence[F]

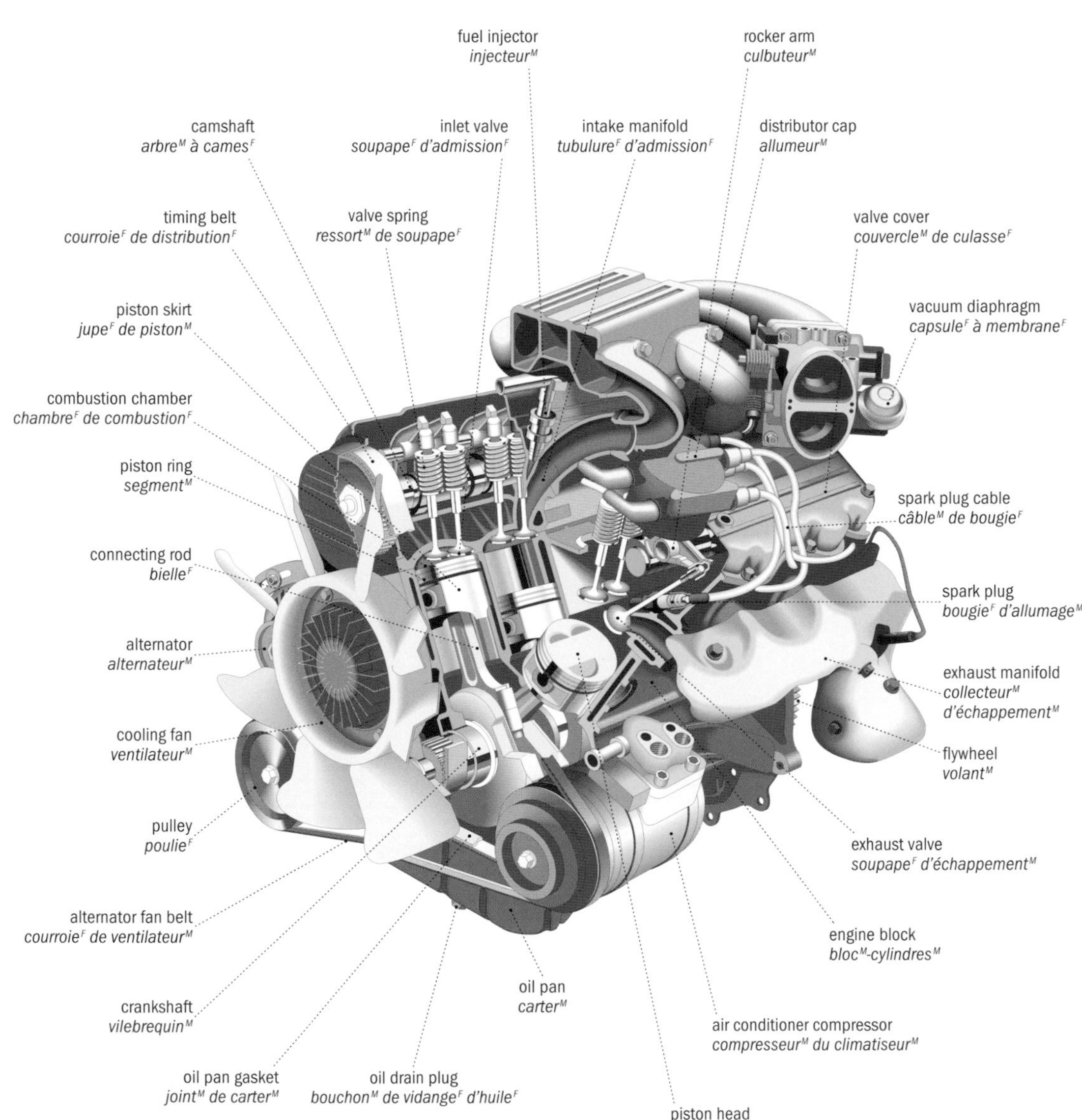
fuel injector
injecteur[M]
rocker arm
culbuteur[M]
camshaft
arbre[M] à cames[F]
inlet valve
soupape[F] d'admission[F]
intake manifold
tubulure[F] d'admission[F]
distributor cap
allumeur[M]
timing belt
courroie[F] de distribution[F]
valve spring
ressort[M] de soupape[F]
valve cover
couvercle[M] de culasse[F]
piston skirt
jupe[F] de piston[M]
vacuum diaphragm
capsule[F] à membrane[F]
combustion chamber
chambre[F] de combustion[F]
piston ring
segment[M]
spark plug cable
câble[M] de bougie[F]
connecting rod
bielle[F]
spark plug
bougie[F] d'allumage[M]
alternator
alternateur[M]
exhaust manifold
collecteur[M]
d'échappement[M]
cooling fan
ventilateur[M]
flywheel
volant[M]
pulley
poulie[F]
exhaust valve
soupape[F] d'échappement[M]
alternator fan belt
courroie[F] de ventilateur[M]
engine block
bloc[M]-cylindres[M]
oil pan
carter[M]
crankshaft
vilebrequin[M]
air conditioner compressor
compresseur[M] du climatiseur[M]
oil pan gasket
joint[M] de carter[M]
oil drain plug
bouchon[M] de vidange[F] d'huile[F]
piston head
piston[M]

TRANSPORT AND MACHINERY

camping trailers

caravane[F]

trailer
caravane[F] tractée

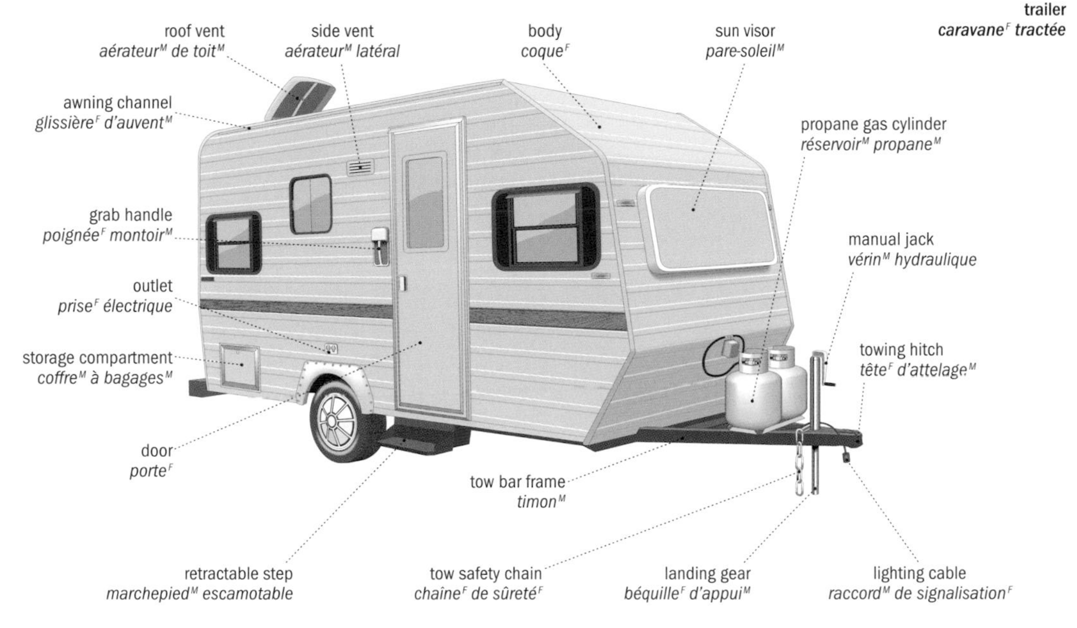
roof vent
aérateur[M] de toit[M]
side vent
aérateur[M] latéral
body
coque[F]
sun visor
pare-soleil[M]
awning channel
glissière[F] d'auvent[M]
propane gas cylinder
réservoir[M] propane[M]
grab handle
poignée[F] montoir[M]
manual jack
vérin[M] hydraulique
outlet
prise[F] électrique
towing hitch
tête[F] d'attelage[M]
storage compartment
coffre[M] à bagages[M]
door
porte[F]
tow bar frame
timon[M]
retractable step
marchepied[M] escamotable
tow safety chain
chaîne[F] de sûreté[F]
landing gear
béquille[F] d'appui[M]
lighting cable
raccord[M] de signalisation[F]

tent trailer
tente[F]-caravane[F]

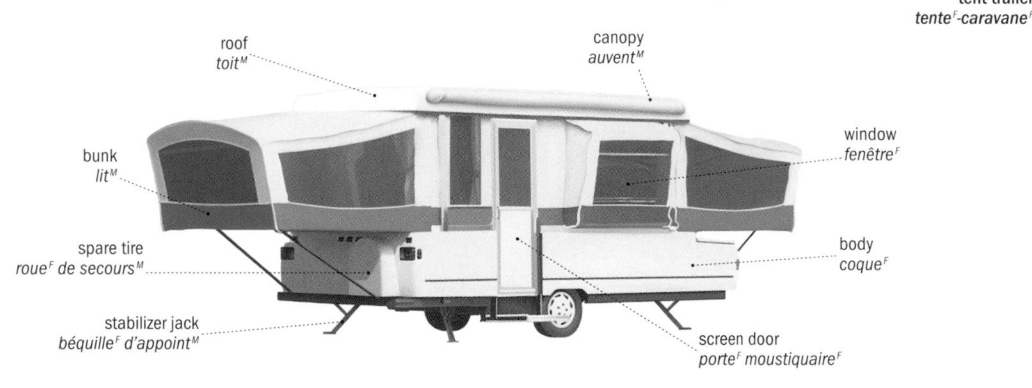
roof
toit[M]
canopy
auvent[M]
window
fenêtre[F]
bunk
lit[M]
body
coque[F]
spare tire
roue[F] de secours[M]
stabilizer jack
béquille[F] d'appoint[M]
screen door
porte[F] moustiquaire[F]

motor home
auto[F]-caravane[F]

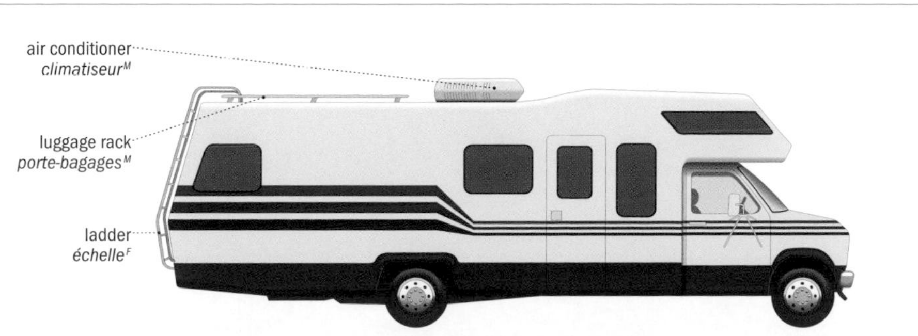
air conditioner
climatiseur[M]
luggage rack
porte-bagages[M]
ladder
échelle[F]

buses

autobus^M

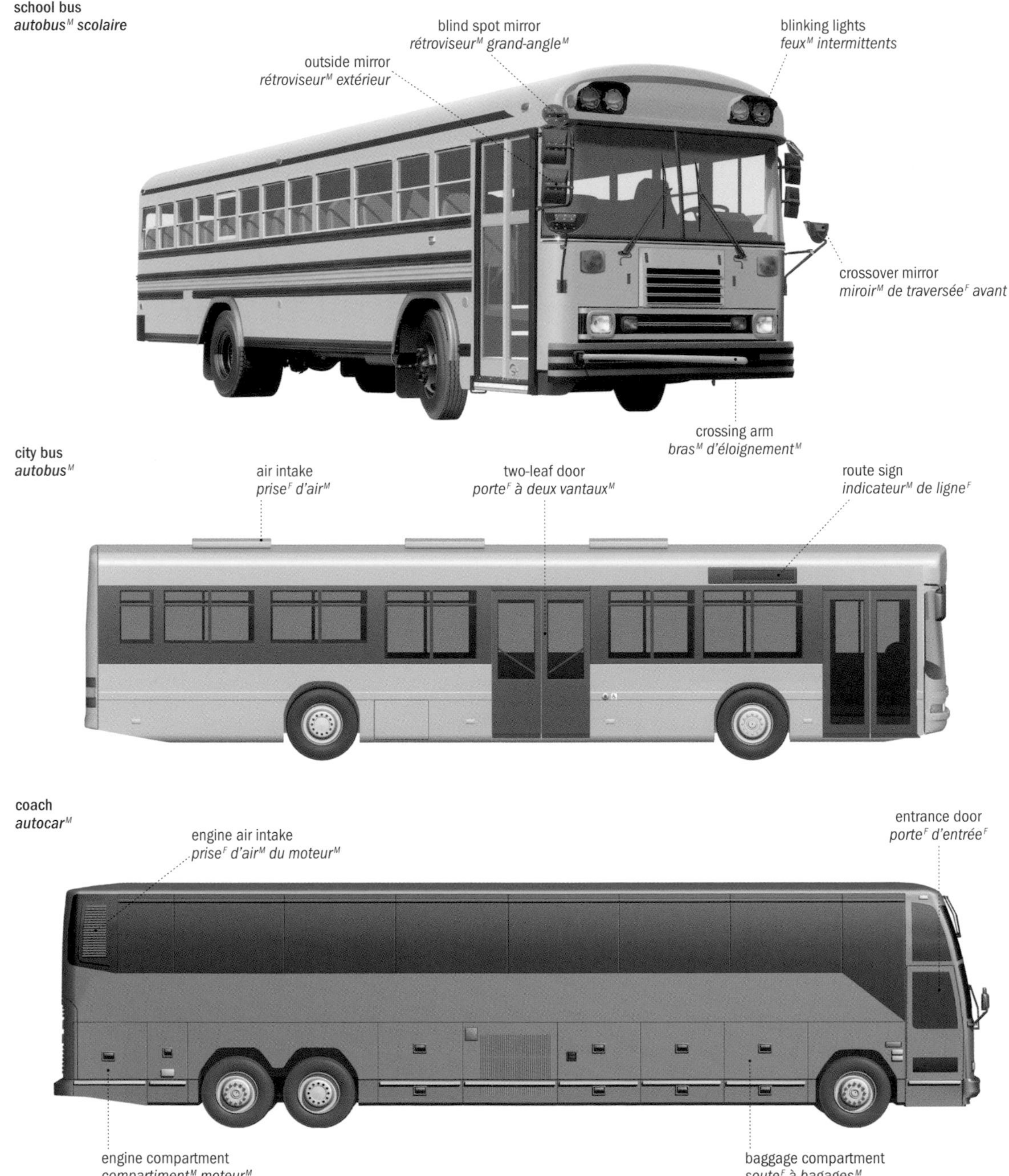
school bus
autobus^M scolaire
blind spot mirror
rétroviseur^M grand-angle^M
blinking lights
feux^M intermittents
outside mirror
rétroviseur^M extérieur
crossover mirror
miroir^M de traversée^F avant
crossing arm
bras^M d'éloignement^M
city bus
autobus^M
air intake
prise^F d'air^M
two-leaf door
porte^F à deux vantaux^M
route sign
indicateur^M de ligne^F
coach
autocar^M
engine air intake
prise^F d'air^M du moteur^M
entrance door
porte^F d'entrée^F
engine compartment
compartiment^M moteur^M
baggage compartment
soute^F à bagages^M

double-decker bus
***autobus*[M] *à impériale*[F]**

upper deck
impériale[F]
route sign
indicateur[M] *de ligne*[F]

minibus
***minibus*[M]**

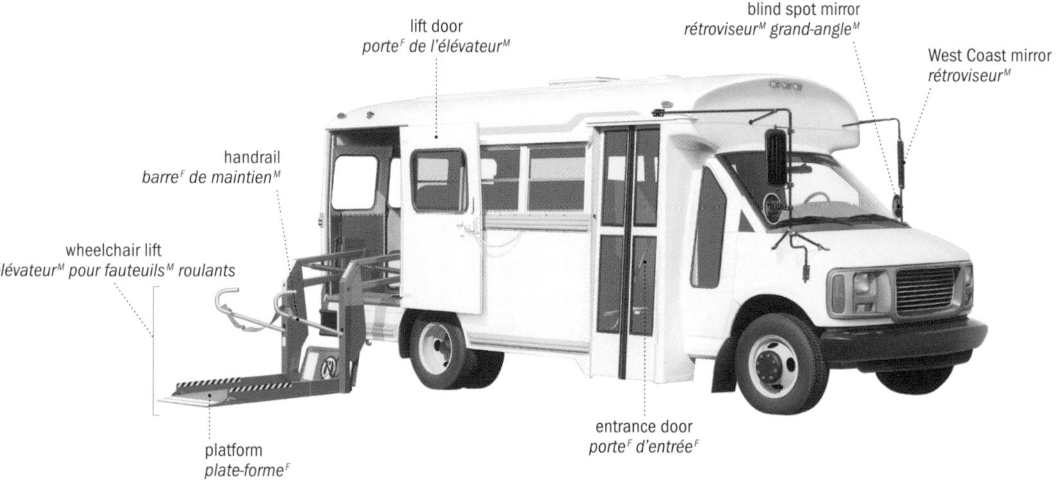
lift door
porte[F] *de l'élévateur*[M]
blind spot mirror
rétroviseur[M] *grand-angle*[M]
West Coast mirror
rétroviseur[M]
handrail
barre[F] *de maintien*[M]
wheelchair lift
élévateur[M] *pour fauteuils*[M] *roulants*
platform
plate-forme[F]
entrance door
porte[F] *d'entrée*[F]

articulated bus
autobus*[M] *articulé

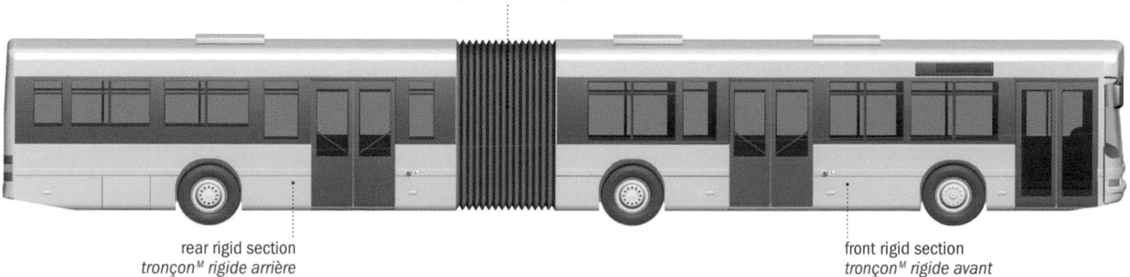
articulated joint
section[F] *articulée*
rear rigid section
tronçon[M] *rigide arrière*
front rigid section
tronçon[M] *rigide avant*

trucking

camionnage[M]

truck tractor
tracteur[M] routier

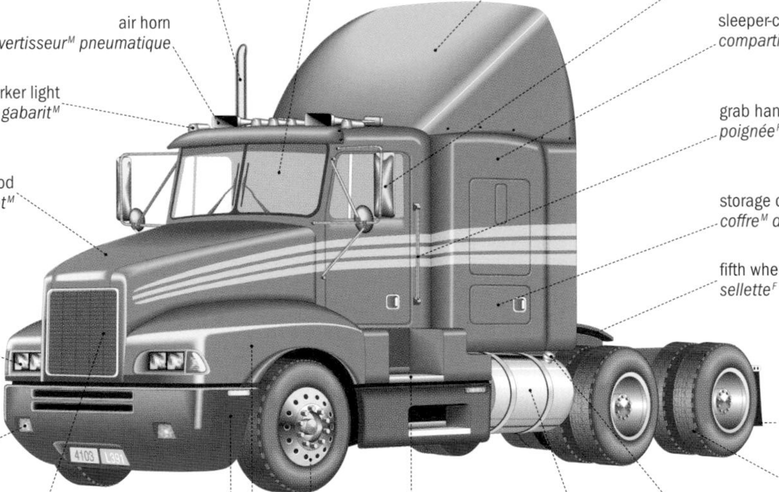

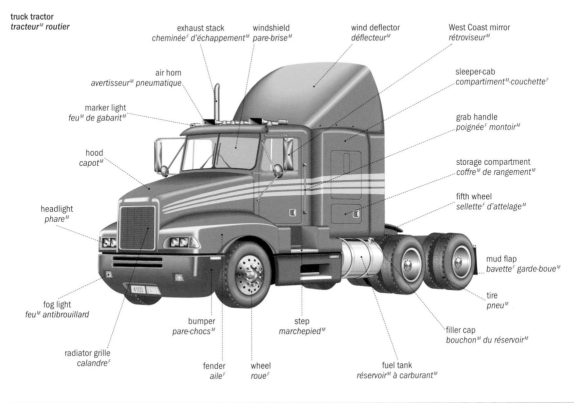

exhaust stack
cheminée[F] d'échappement[M]

windshield
pare-brise[M]

wind deflector
déflecteur[M]

West Coast mirror
rétroviseur[M]

air horn
avertisseur[M] pneumatique

sleeper-cab
compartiment[M]-couchette[F]

marker light
feu[M] de gabarit[M]

grab handle
poignée[F] montoir[M]

hood
capot[M]

storage compartment
coffre[M] de rangement[M]

headlight
phare[M]

fifth wheel
sellette[F] d'attelage[M]

mud flap
bavette[F] garde-boue[M]

tire
pneu[M]

fog light
feu[M] antibrouillard

bumper
pare-chocs[M]

step
marchepied[M]

filler cap
bouchon[M] du réservoir[M]

radiator grille
calandre[F]

fender
aile[F]

wheel
roue[F]

fuel tank
réservoir[M] à carburant[M]

examples of trucks
exemples[M] de camions[M]

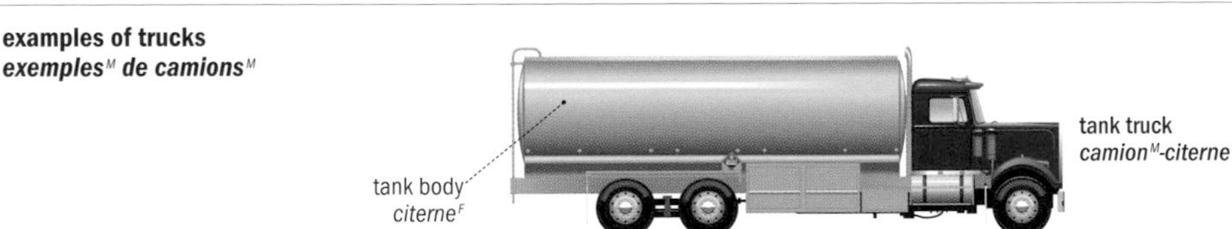
tank body
citerne[F]

tank truck
camion[M]-citerne[F]

tow truck
dépanneuse[F]

garbage collection truck
benne[F] à ordures[F] ; camion[M] à ordures[F]

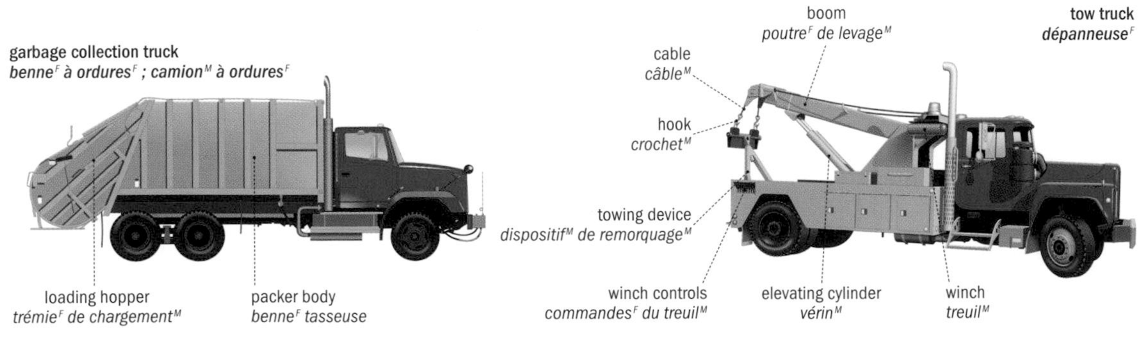
boom
poutre[F] de levage[M]
cable
câble[M]
hook
crochet[M]
towing device
dispositif[M] de remorquage[M]
loading hopper
trémie[F] de chargement[M]
packer body
benne[F] tasseuse
winch controls
commandes[F] du treuil[M]
elevating cylinder
vérin[M]
winch
treuil[M]

refrigerated semitrailer
semi-remorque[F] frigorifique

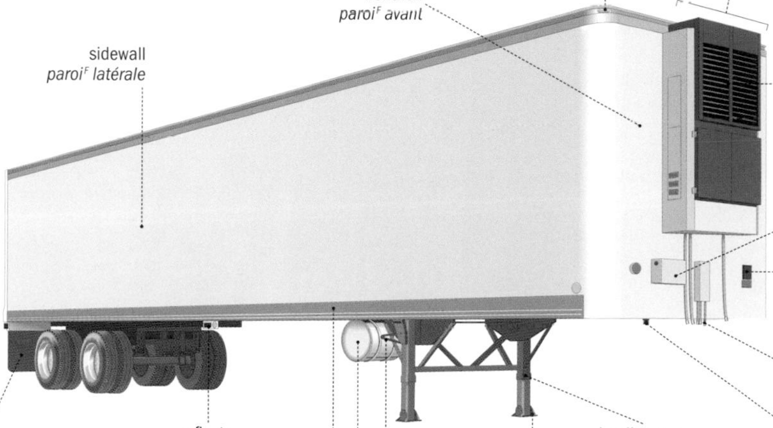

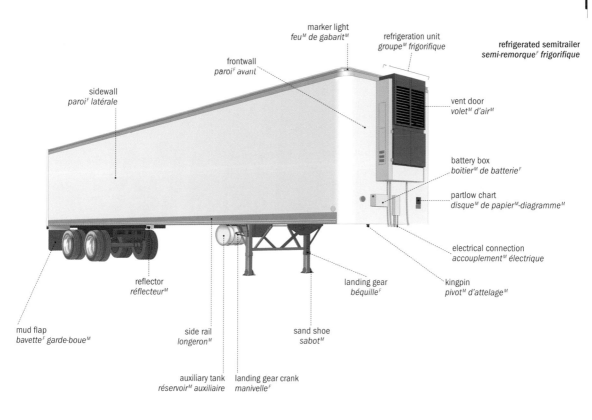

marker light
feu[M] de gabarit[M]

refrigeration unit
groupe[M] frigorifique

frontwall
paroi[F] avant

sidewall
paroi[F] latérale

vent door
volet[M] d'air[M]

battery box
boîtier[M] de batterie[F]

partlow chart
disque[M] de papier[M]-diagramme[M]

electrical connection
accouplement[M] électrique

kingpin
pivot[M] d'attelage[M]

landing gear
béquille[F]

reflector
réflecteur[M]

mud flap
bavette[F] garde-boue[M]

side rail
longeron[M]

sand shoe
sabot[M]

auxiliary tank
réservoir[M] auxiliaire

landing gear crank
manivelle[F]

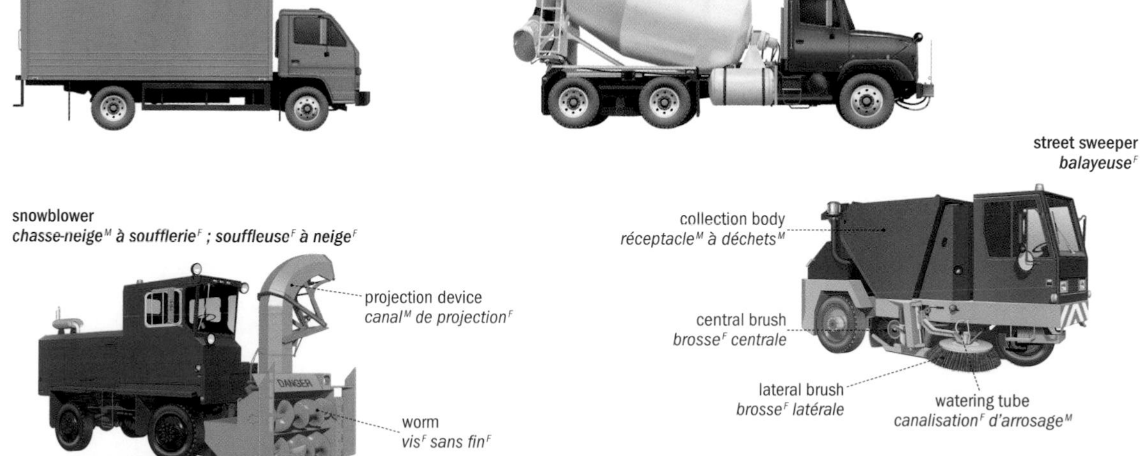
van straight truck
camion[M] porteur[M] fourgon[M]
concrete mixer truck
camion[M]-toupie[F] ; camion[M]-bétonnière[F]
street sweeper
balayeuse[F]
collection body
réceptacle[M] à déchets[M]
central brush
brosse[F] centrale
lateral brush
brosse[F] latérale
watering tube
canalisation[F] d'arrosage[M]
snowblower
chasse-neige[M] à soufflerie[F] ; souffleuse[F] à neige[F]
projection device
canal[M] de projection[F]
worm
vis[F] sans fin[F]
DANGER

motorcycle

moto^F

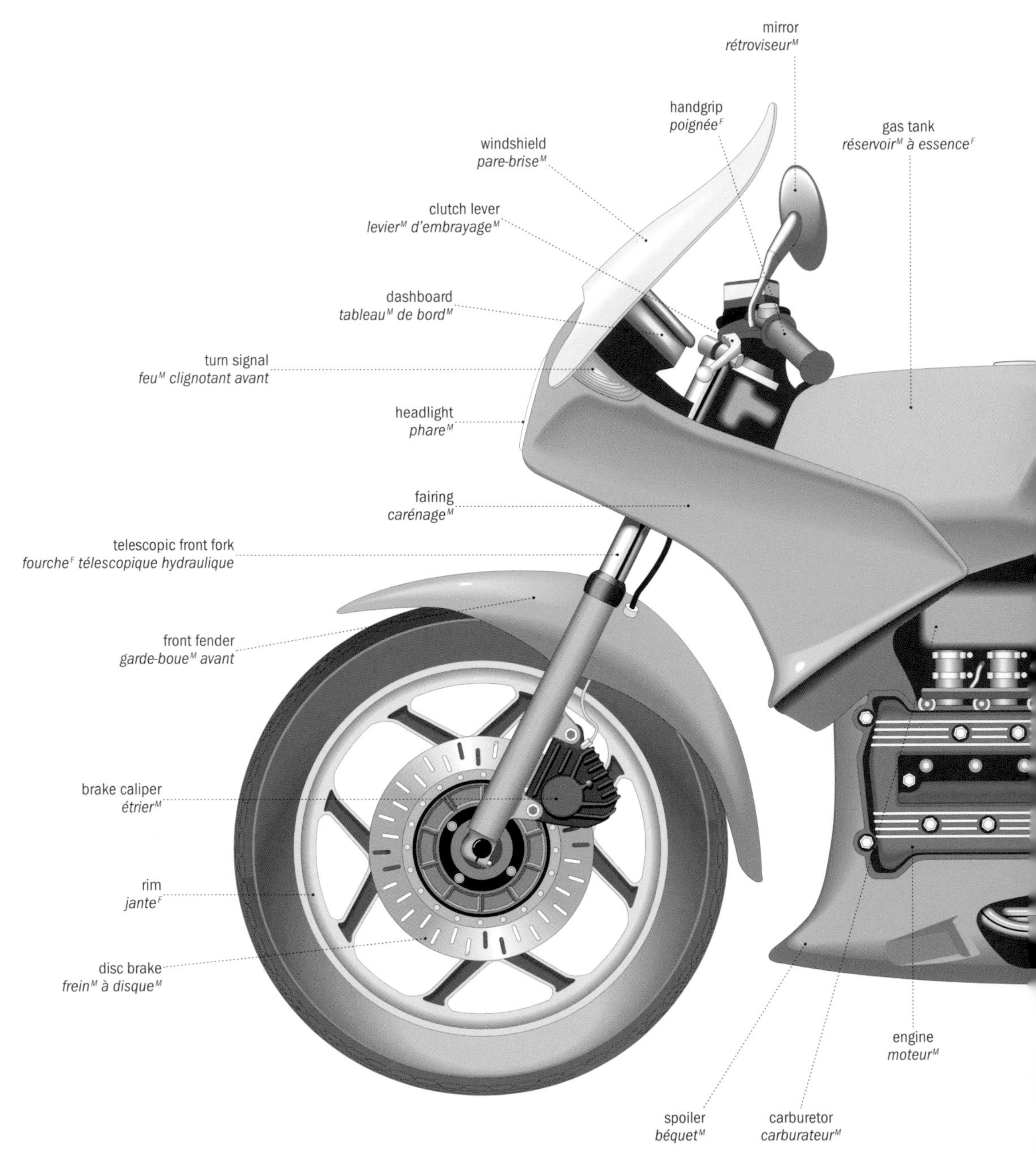
mirror
rétroviseur^M
handgrip
poignée^F
gas tank
réservoir^M à essence^F
windshield
pare-brise^M
clutch lever
levier^M d'embrayage^M
dashboard
tableau^M de bord^M
turn signal
feu^M clignotant avant
headlight
phare^M
fairing
carénage^M
telescopic front fork
fourche^F télescopique hydraulique
front fender
garde-boue^M avant
brake caliper
étrier^M
rim
jante^F
disc brake
frein^M à disque^M
engine
moteur^M
spoiler
béquet^M
carburetor
carburateur^M

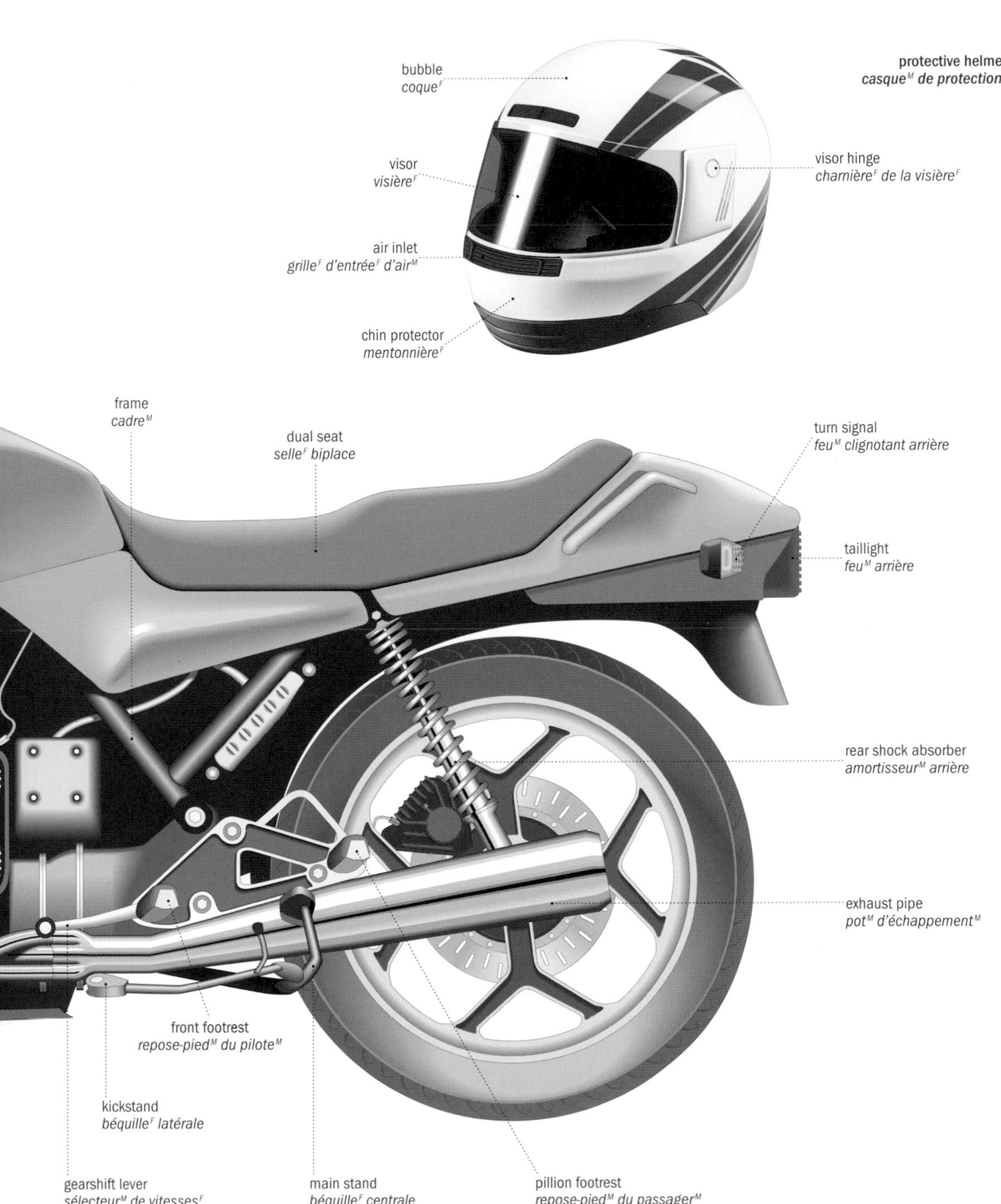
protective helmet
***casque*[M] *de protection*[F]**
bubble
coque[F]
visor
visière[F]
air inlet
grille[F] *d'entrée*[F] *d'air*[M]
chin protector
mentonnière[F]
visor hinge
charnière[F] *de la visière*[F]
frame
cadre[M]
dual seat
selle[F] *biplace*
turn signal
feu[M] *clignotant arrière*
taillight
feu[M] *arrière*
rear shock absorber
amortisseur[M] *arrière*
exhaust pipe
pot[M] *d'échappement*[M]
front footrest
repose-pied[M] *du pilote*[M]
kickstand
béquille[F] *latérale*
gearshift lever
sélecteur[M] *de vitesses*[F]
main stand
béquille[F] *centrale*
pillion footrest
repose-pied[M] *du passager*[M]

motorcycle

motorcycle dashboard
tableau[M] de bord[M]

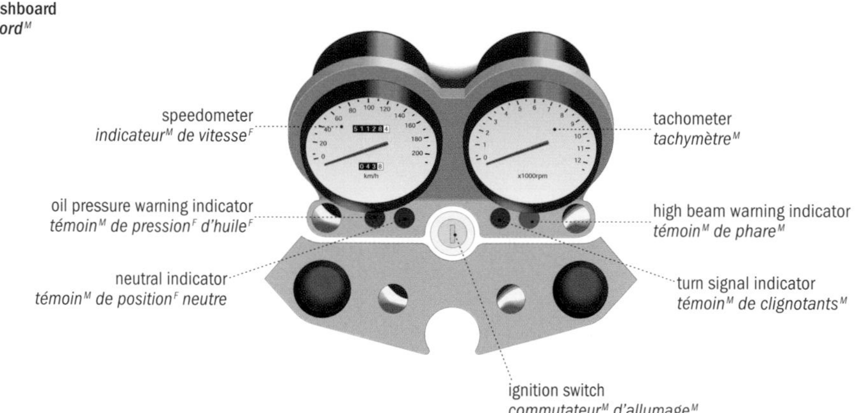
speedometer
indicateur[M] de vitesse[F]
tachometer
tachymètre[M]
oil pressure warning indicator
témoin[M] de pression[F] d'huile[F]
high beam warning indicator
témoin[M] de phare[M]
neutral indicator
témoin[M] de position[F] neutre
turn signal indicator
témoin[M] de clignotants[M]
ignition switch
commutateur[M] d'allumage[M]

motorcycle: view from above
moto[F] : vue[F] en plongée[F]

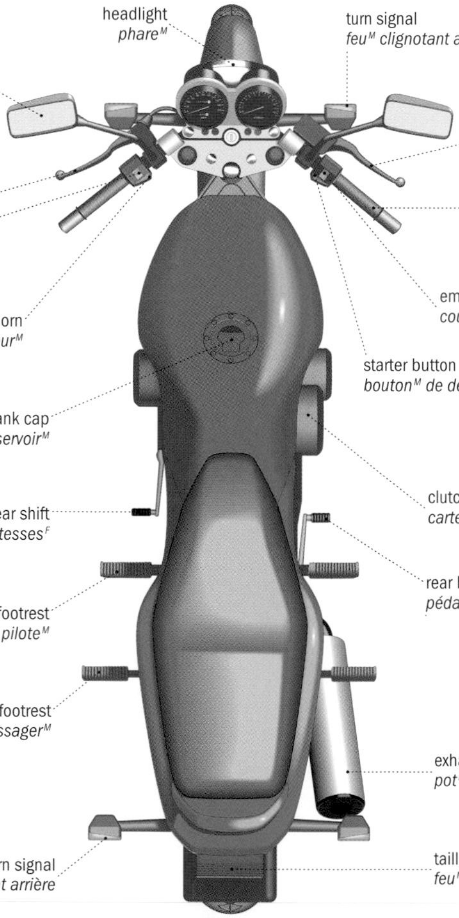

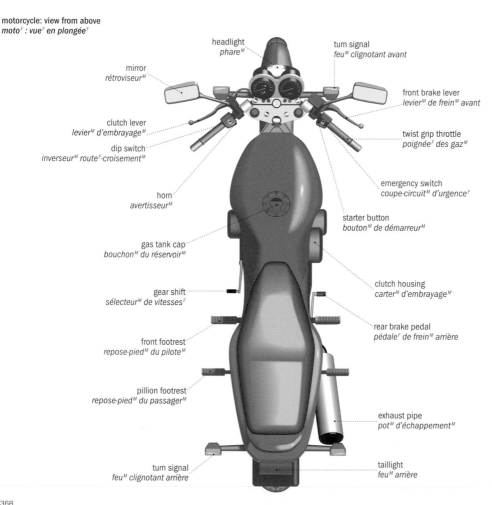

headlight
phare[M]

turn signal
feu[M] clignotant avant

mirror
rétroviseur[M]

front brake lever
levier[M] de frein[M] avant

clutch lever
levier[M] d'embrayage[M]

twist grip throttle
poignée[F] des gaz[M]

dip switch
inverseur[M] route[F]-croisement[M]

emergency switch
coupe-circuit[M] d'urgence[F]

horn
avertisseur[M]

starter button
bouton[M] de démarreur[M]

gas tank cap
bouchon[M] du réservoir[M]

clutch housing
carter[M] d'embrayage[M]

gear shift
sélecteur[M] de vitesses[F]

rear brake pedal
pédale[F] de frein[M] arrière

front footrest
repose-pied[M] du pilote[M]

pillion footrest
repose-pied[M] du passager[M]

exhaust pipe
pot[M] d'échappement[M]

turn signal
feu[M] clignotant arrière

taillight
feu[M] arrière

TRANSPORT AND MACHINERY

motor scooter
scooter[M]

seat
selle[F]

mirror
rétroviseur[M]

luggage rack
porte-bagages[M]

apron
tablier[M]

floorboard
plancher[M]

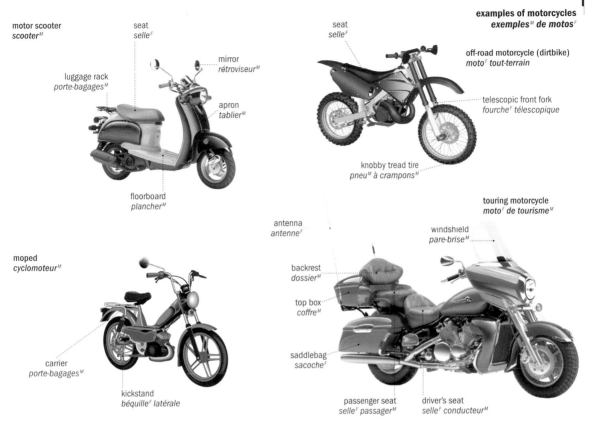

examples of motorcycles
exemples[M] de motos[F]

seat
selle[F]

off-road motorcycle (dirtbike)
moto[F] tout-terrain

telescopic front fork
fourche[F] télescopique

knobby tread tire
pneu[M] à crampons[M]

touring motorcycle
moto[F] de tourisme[M]

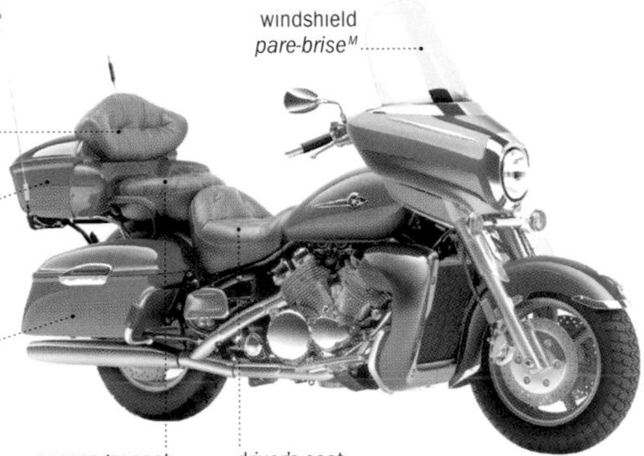

antenna
antenne[F]

windshield
pare-brise[M]

backrest
dossier[M]

top box
coffre[M]

saddlebag
sacoche[F]

passenger seat
selle[F] passager[M]

driver's seat
selle[F] conducteur[M]

moped
cyclomoteur[M]

carrier
porte-bagages[M]

kickstand
béquille[F] latérale

4 X 4 all-terrain vehicle

quad[M]

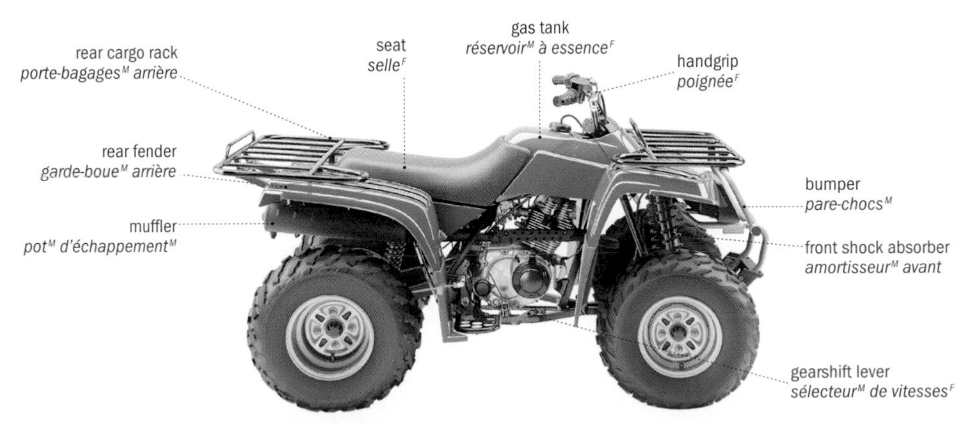
rear cargo rack
porte-bagages[M] arrière
seat
selle[F]
gas tank
réservoir[M] à essence[F]
handgrip
poignée[F]
rear fender
garde-boue[M] arrière
muffler
pot[M] d'échappement[M]
bumper
pare-chocs[M]
front shock absorber
amortisseur[M] avant
gearshift lever
sélecteur[M] de vitesses[F]

bicycle

bicyclette[F]

parts of a bicycle
parties[F] d'une bicyclette[F]

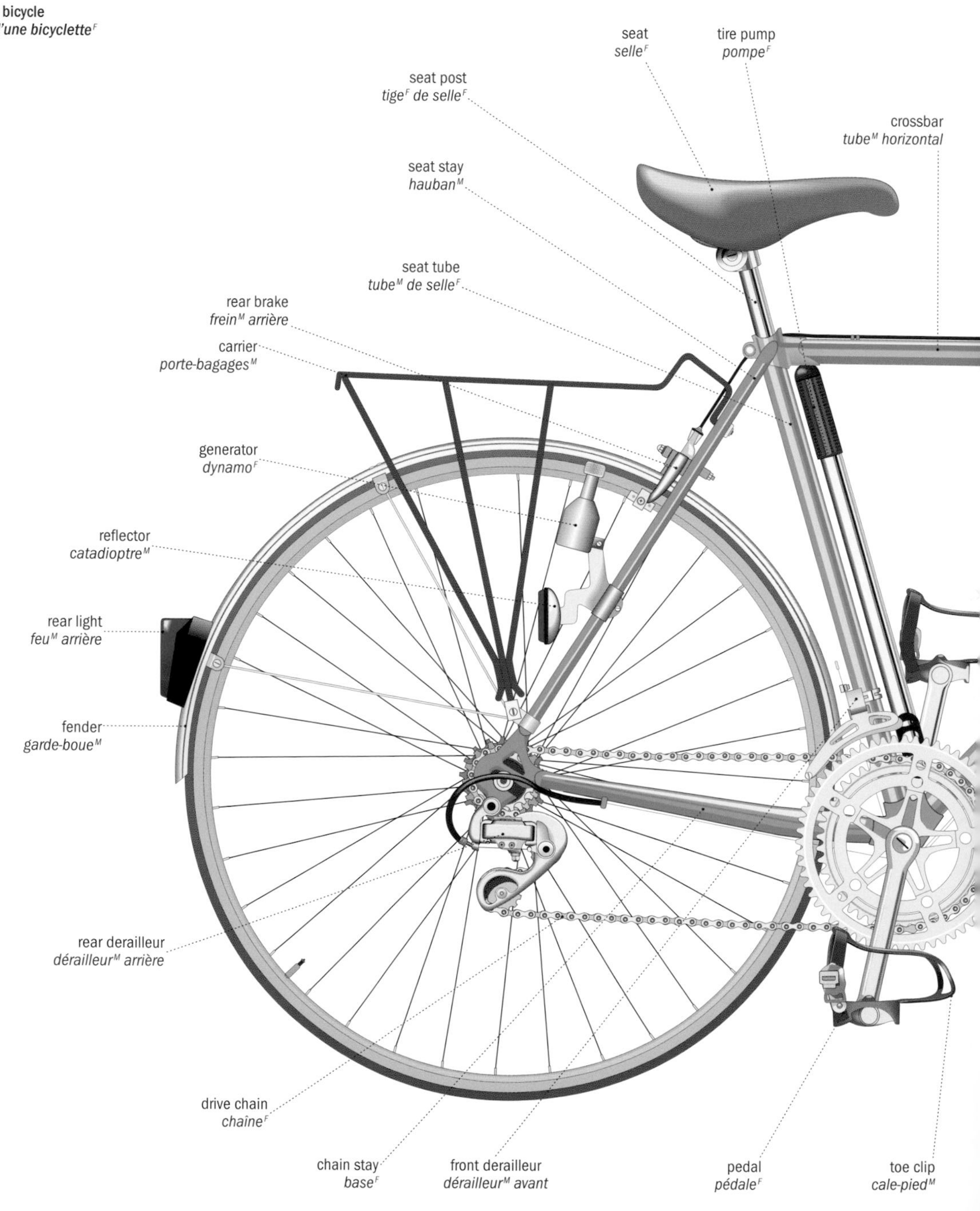
seat
selle[F]
tire pump
pompe[F]
seat post
tige[F] de selle[F]
crossbar
tube[M] horizontal
seat stay
hauban[M]
seat tube
tube[M] de selle[F]
rear brake
frein[M] arrière
carrier
porte-bagages[M]
generator
dynamo[F]
reflector
catadioptre[M]
rear light
feu[M] arrière
fender
garde-boue[M]
rear derailleur
dérailleur[M] arrière
drive chain
chaîne[F]
chain stay
base[F]
front derailleur
dérailleur[M] avant
pedal
pédale[F]
toe clip
cale-pied[M]

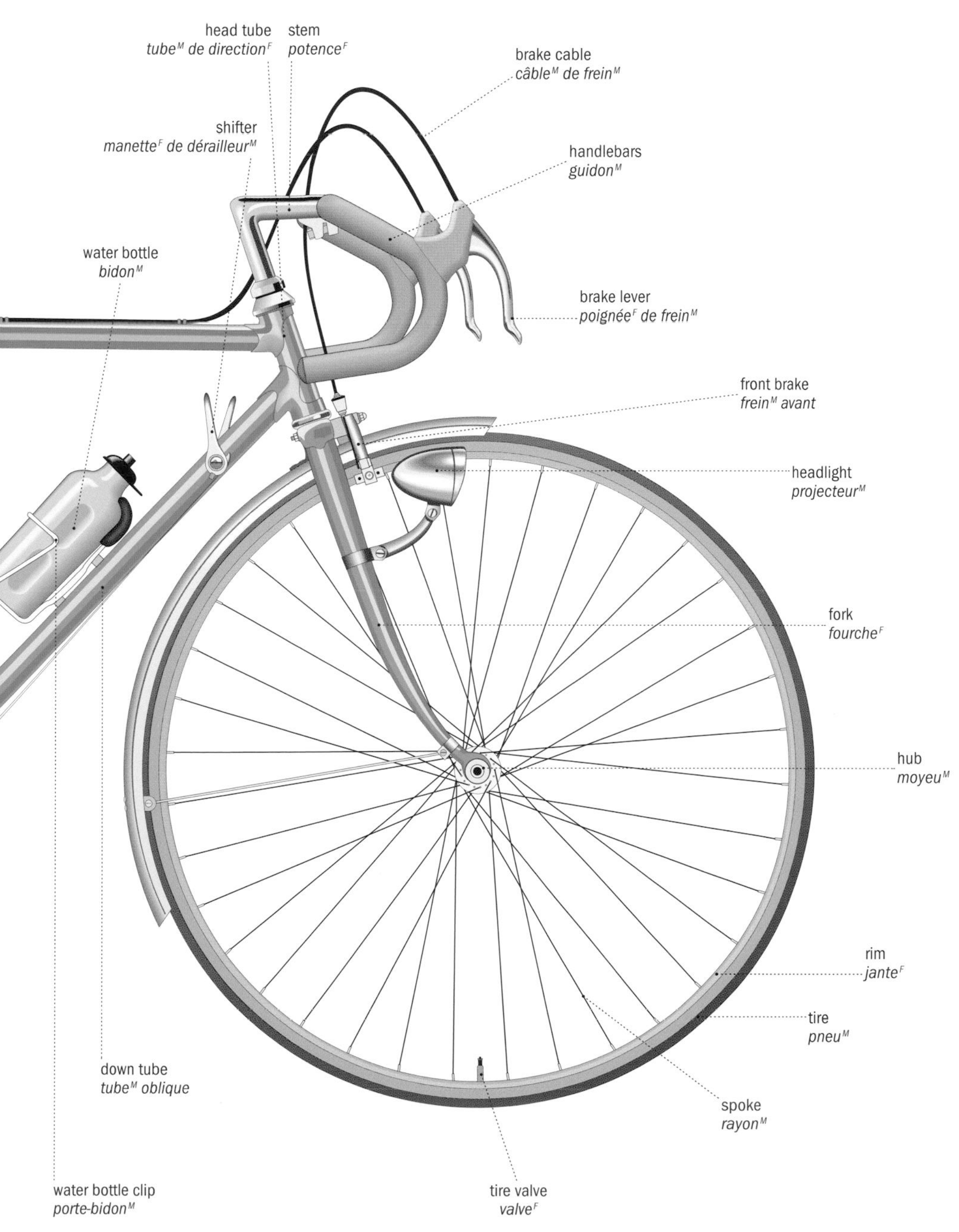
head tube
*tube*M *de direction*F
stem
*potence*F
brake cable
*câble*M *de frein*M
shifter
*manette*F *de dérailleur*M
handlebars
*guidon*M
water bottle
*bidon*M
brake lever
*poignée*F *de frein*M
front brake
*frein*M *avant*
headlight
*projecteur*M
fork
*fourche*F
hub
*moyeu*M
rim
*jante*F
tire
*pneu*M
down tube
*tube*M *oblique*
spoke
*rayon*M
water bottle clip
*porte-bidon*M
tire valve
*valve*F

bicycle

power train
mécanisme [M] ***de propulsion*** [F]

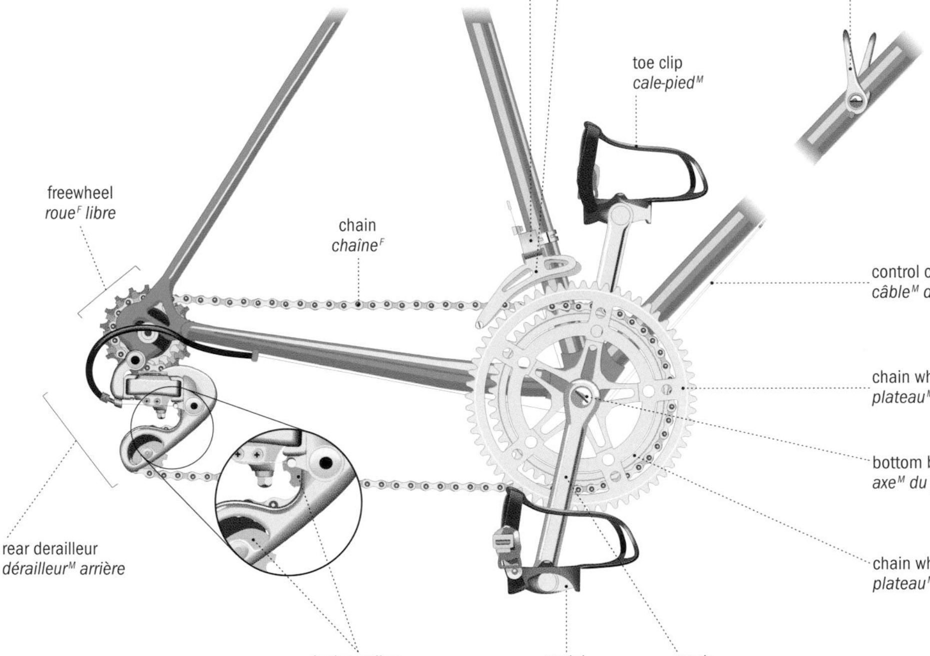

front derailleur
dérailleur [M] *avant*

chain guide
guide-chaine [M]

shifter
manette [F] *de dérailleur* [M]

toe clip
cale-pied [M]

freewheel
roue [F] *libre*

chain
chaîne [F]

control cable
câble [M] *de commande* [F]

chain wheel A
plateau [M] *A*

bottom bracket axle
axe [M] *du pédalier* [M]

rear derailleur
dérailleur [M] *arrière*

chain wheel B
plateau [M] *B*

jockey rollers
galets [M] *tendeurs*

pedal
pédale [F]

crank
manivelle [F]

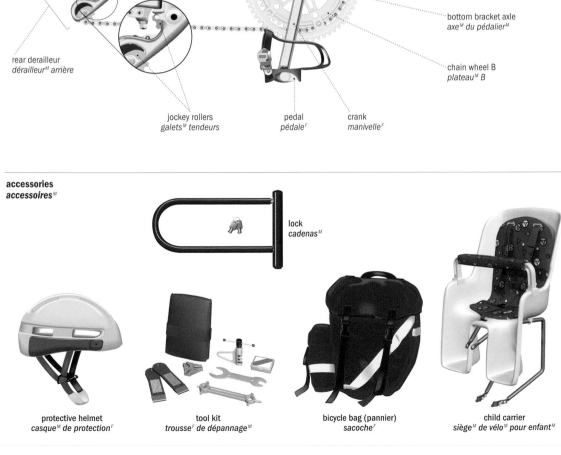

accessories
accessoires [M]

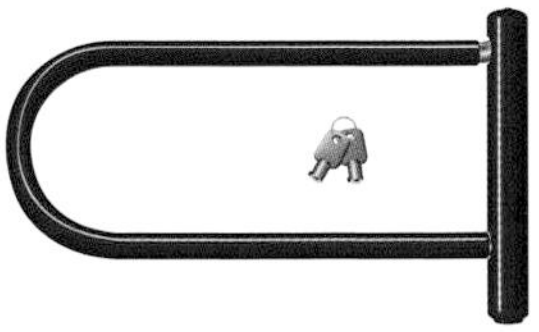

lock
cadenas [M]

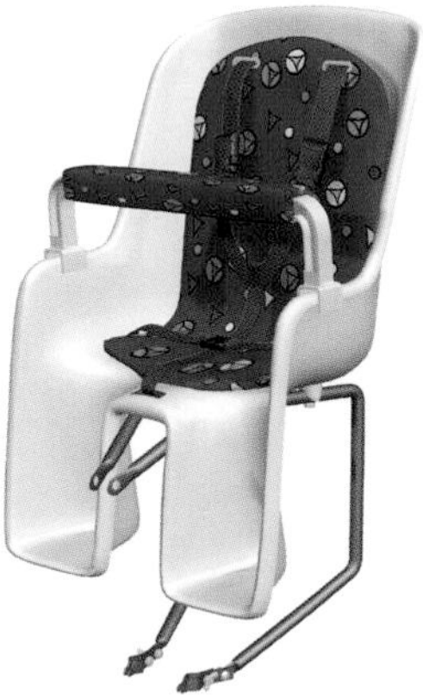

protective helmet
casque [M] ***de protection*** [F]

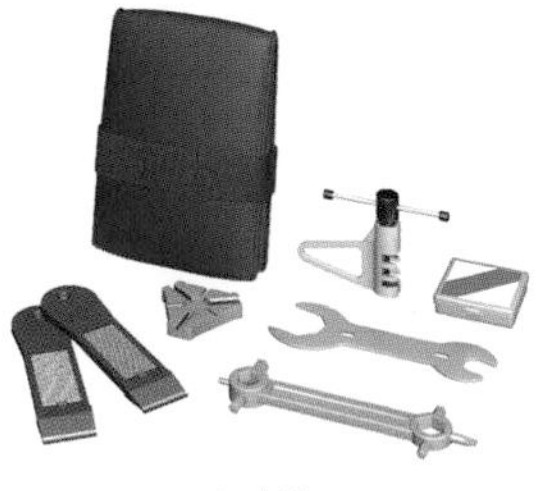

tool kit
trousse [F] ***de dépannage*** [M]

bicycle bag (pannier)
sacoche [F]

child carrier
siège [M] ***de vélo*** [M] ***pour enfant*** [M]

examples of bicycles
exemples^M de bicyclettes^F

child's tricycle
tricycle^M d'enfant^M
BMX bike
vélo^M cross^M
Dutch bicycle
bicyclette^F hollandaise
mountain bike
bicyclette^F tout-terrain
city bicycle
bicyclette^F de ville^F
road bicycle
bicyclette^F de course^F
touring bicycle
bicyclette^F de tourisme^M
tandem bicycle
tandem^M

passenger station

gare[F] de voyageurs[M]

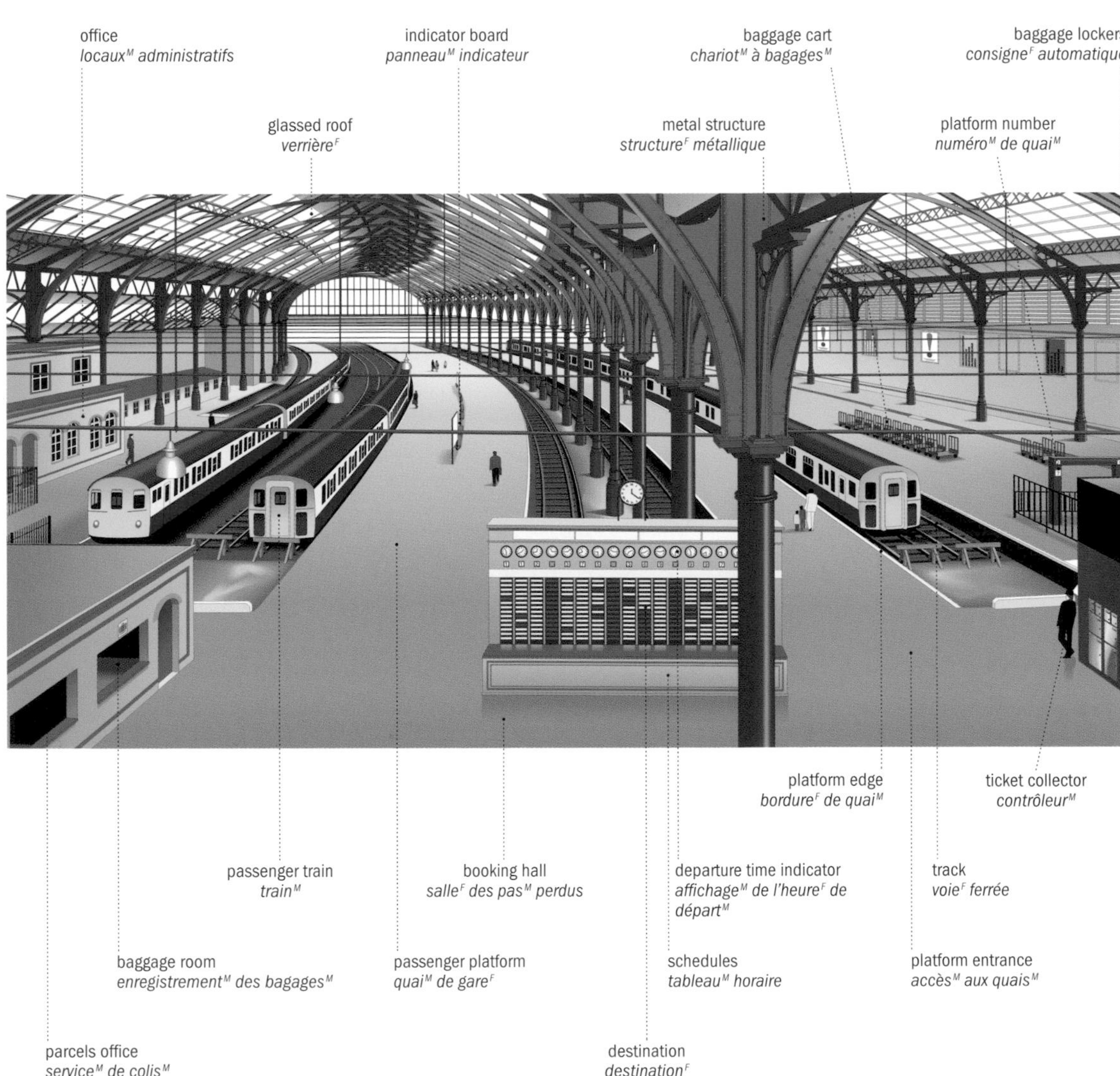
office
locaux[M] administratifs
indicator board
panneau[M] indicateur
baggage cart
chariot[M] à bagages[M]
baggage lockers
consigne[F] automatique
glassed roof
verrière[F]
metal structure
structure[F] métallique
platform number
numéro[M] de quai[M]
platform edge
bordure[F] de quai[M]
ticket collector
contrôleur[M]
passenger train
train[M]
booking hall
salle[F] des pas[M] perdus
departure time indicator
affichage[M] de l'heure[F] de départ[M]
track
voie[F] ferrée
baggage room
enregistrement[M] des bagages[M]
passenger platform
quai[M] de gare[F]
schedules
tableau[M] horaire
platform entrance
accès[M] aux quais[M]
parcels office
service[M] de colis[M]
destination
destination[F]

railroad station

gare[F]

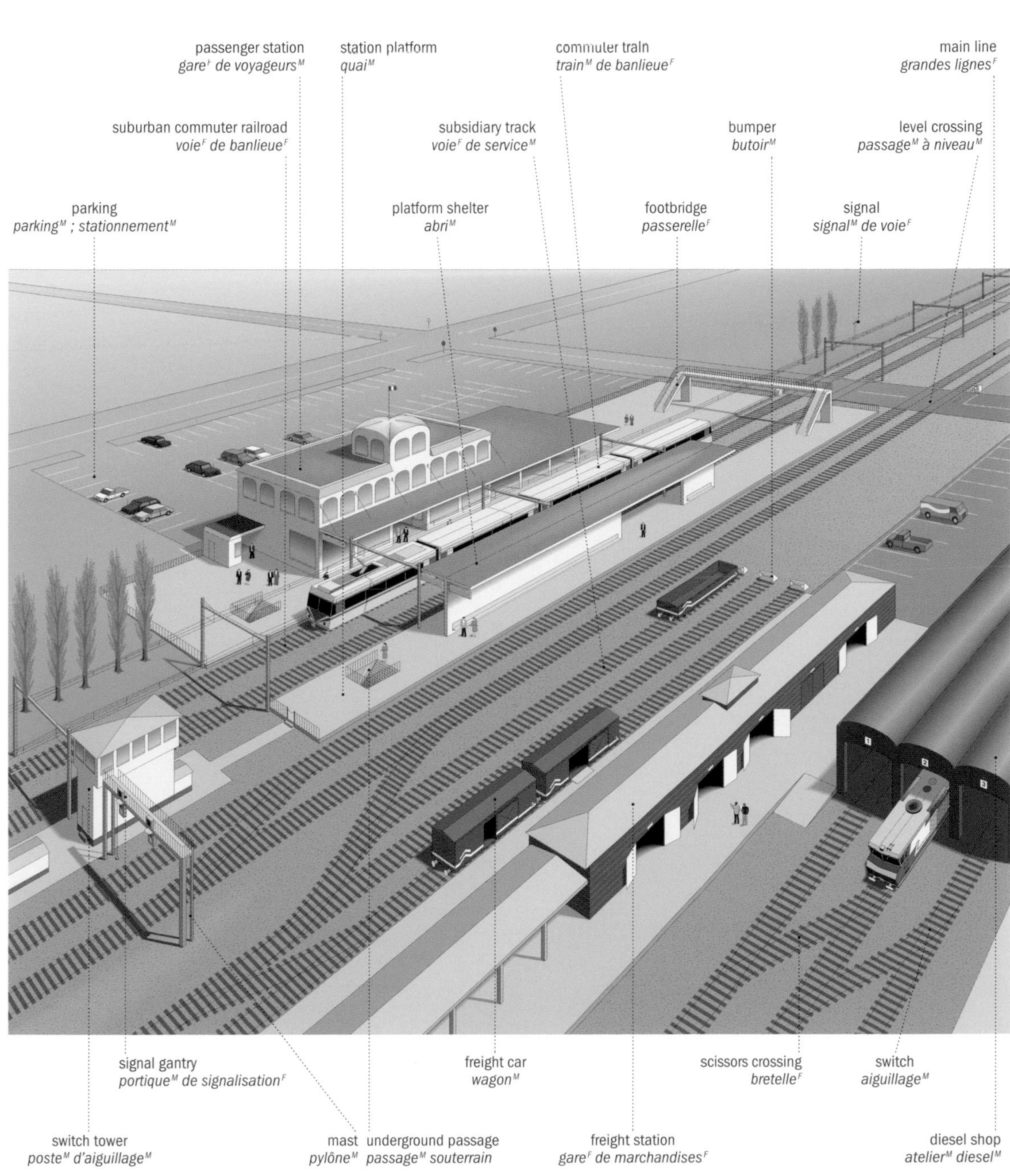
passenger station
gare[F] de voyageurs[M]
station platform
quai[M]
commuter train
train[M] de banlieue[F]
main line
grandes lignes[F]
suburban commuter railroad
voie[F] de banlieue[F]
subsidiary track
voie[F] de service[M]
bumper
butoir[M]
level crossing
passage[M] à niveau[M]
parking
parking[M] ; stationnement[M]
platform shelter
abri[M]
footbridge
passerelle[F]
signal
signal[M] de voie[F]
1
2
3
signal gantry
portique[M] de signalisation[F]
freight car
wagon[M]
scissors crossing
bretelle[F]
switch
aiguillage[M]
switch tower
poste[M] d'aiguillage[M]
mast
pylône[M]
underground passage
passage[M] souterrain
freight station
gare[F] de marchandises[F]
diesel shop
atelier[M] diesel[M]

high-speed train

train[M] à grande vitesse[F] (T.G.V.)

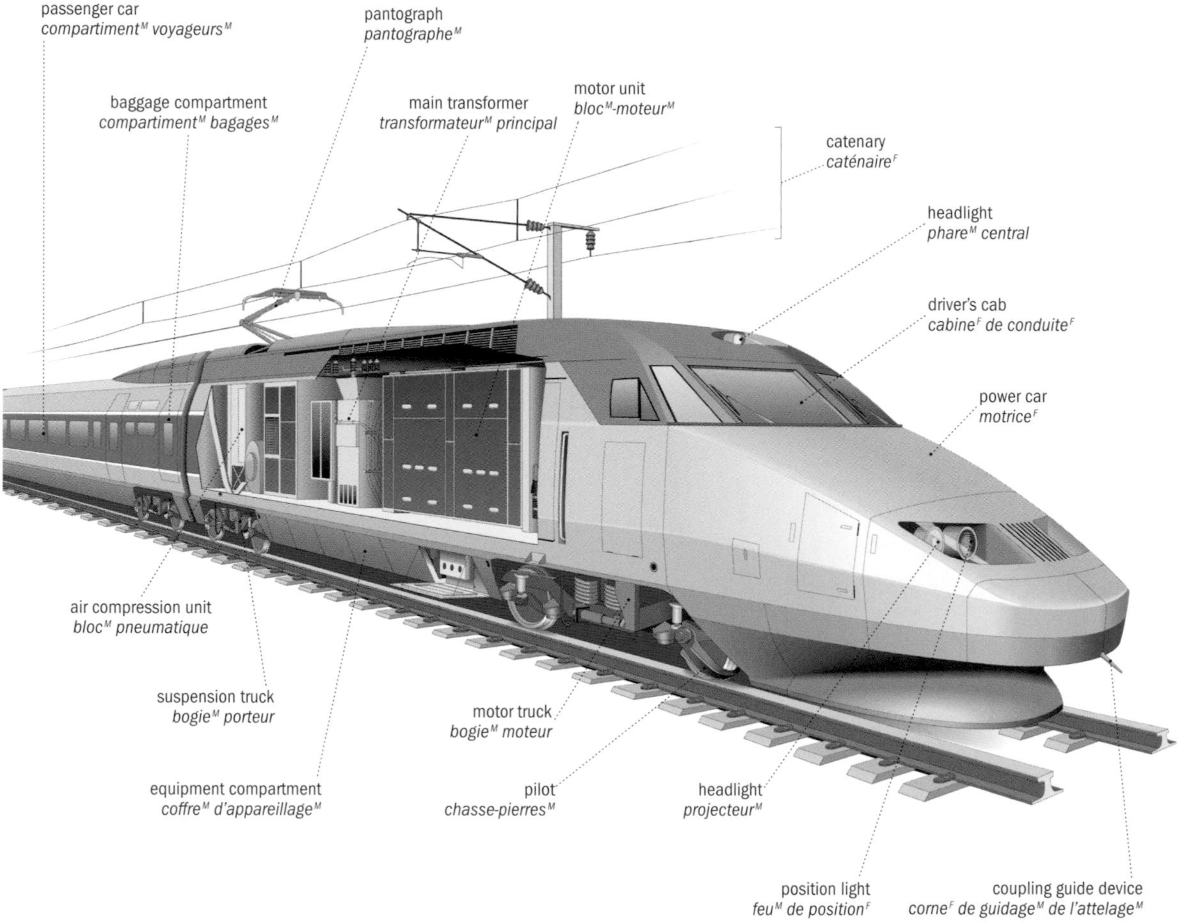

passenger car
compartiment[M] voyageurs[M]

pantograph
pantographe[M]

baggage compartment
compartiment[M] bagages[M]

main transformer
transformateur[M] principal

motor unit
bloc[M]-moteur[M]

catenary
caténaire[F]

headlight
phare[M] central

driver's cab
cabine[F] de conduite[F]

power car
motrice[F]

air compression unit
bloc[M] pneumatique

suspension truck
bogie[M] porteur

motor truck
bogie[M] moteur

equipment compartment
coffre[M] d'appareillage[M]

pilot
chasse-pierres[M]

headlight
projecteur[M]

position light
feu[M] de position[F]

coupling guide device
corne[F] de guidage[M] de l'attelage[M]

types of passenger cars

types[M] de voitures[F]

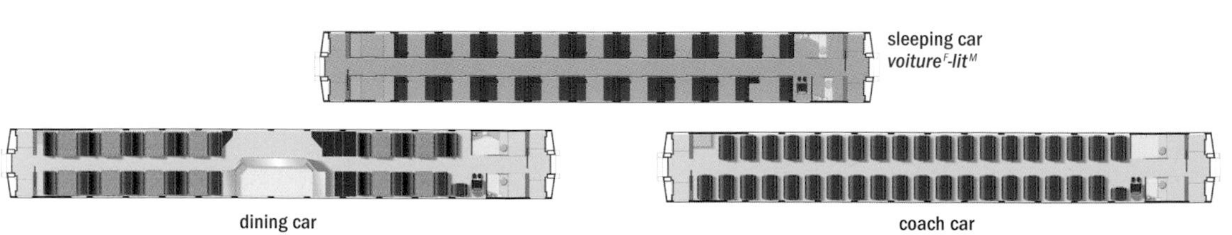
sleeping car
voiture[F]-lit[M]
dining car
voiture[F] restaurant[M]
coach car
voiture[F] classique

diesel-electric locomotive

locomotive^F diesel-électrique

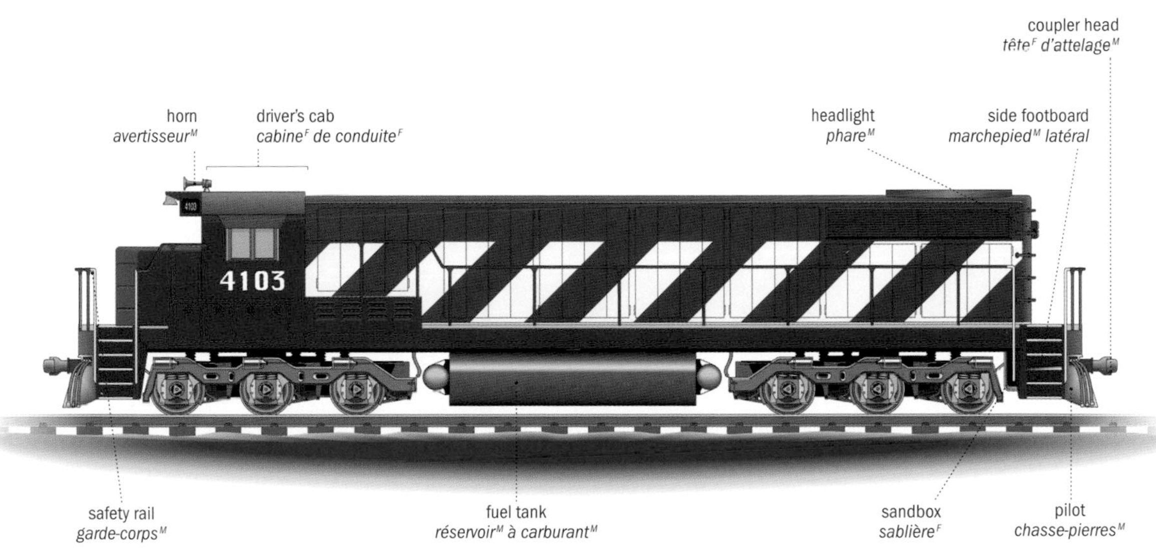
coupler head
tête^F d'attelage^M
horn
avertisseur^M
driver's cab
cabine^F de conduite^F
headlight
phare^M
side footboard
marchepied^M latéral
4103
safety rail
garde-corps^M
fuel tank
réservoir^M à carburant^M
sandbox
sablière^F
pilot
chasse-pierres^M

examples of freight cars

exemples^M de wagons^M

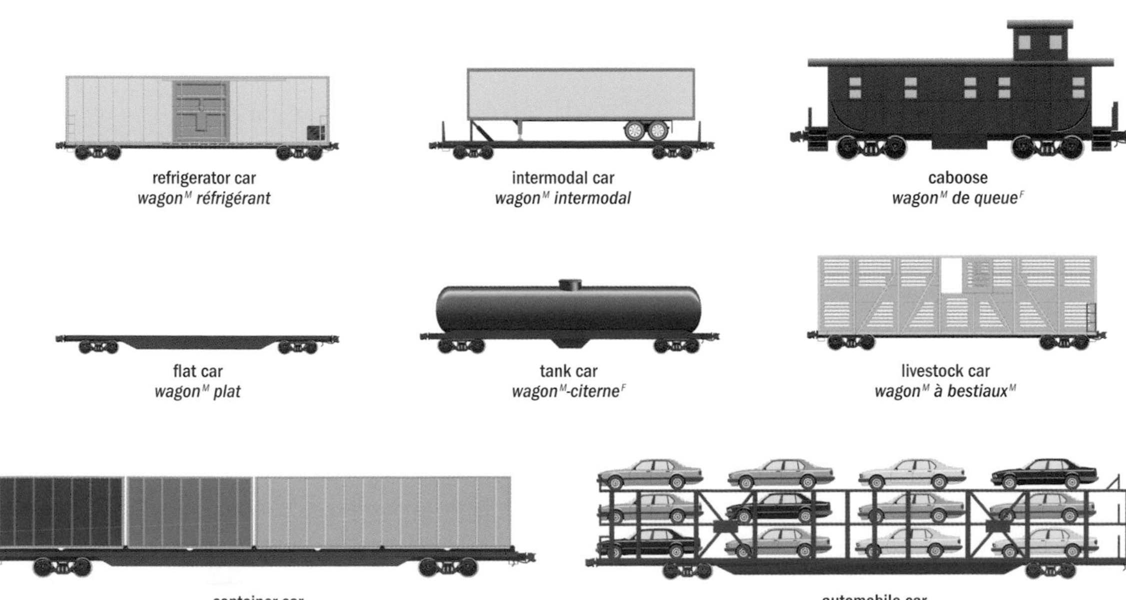
refrigerator car
wagon^M réfrigérant
intermodal car
wagon^M intermodal
caboose
wagon^M de queue^F
flat car
wagon^M plat
tank car
wagon^M-citerne^F
livestock car
wagon^M à bestiaux^M
container car
wagon^M porte-conteneurs^M
automobile car
wagon^M porte-automobiles^M

subway

chemin^M de fer^M métropolitain

subway station
station^F de métro^M

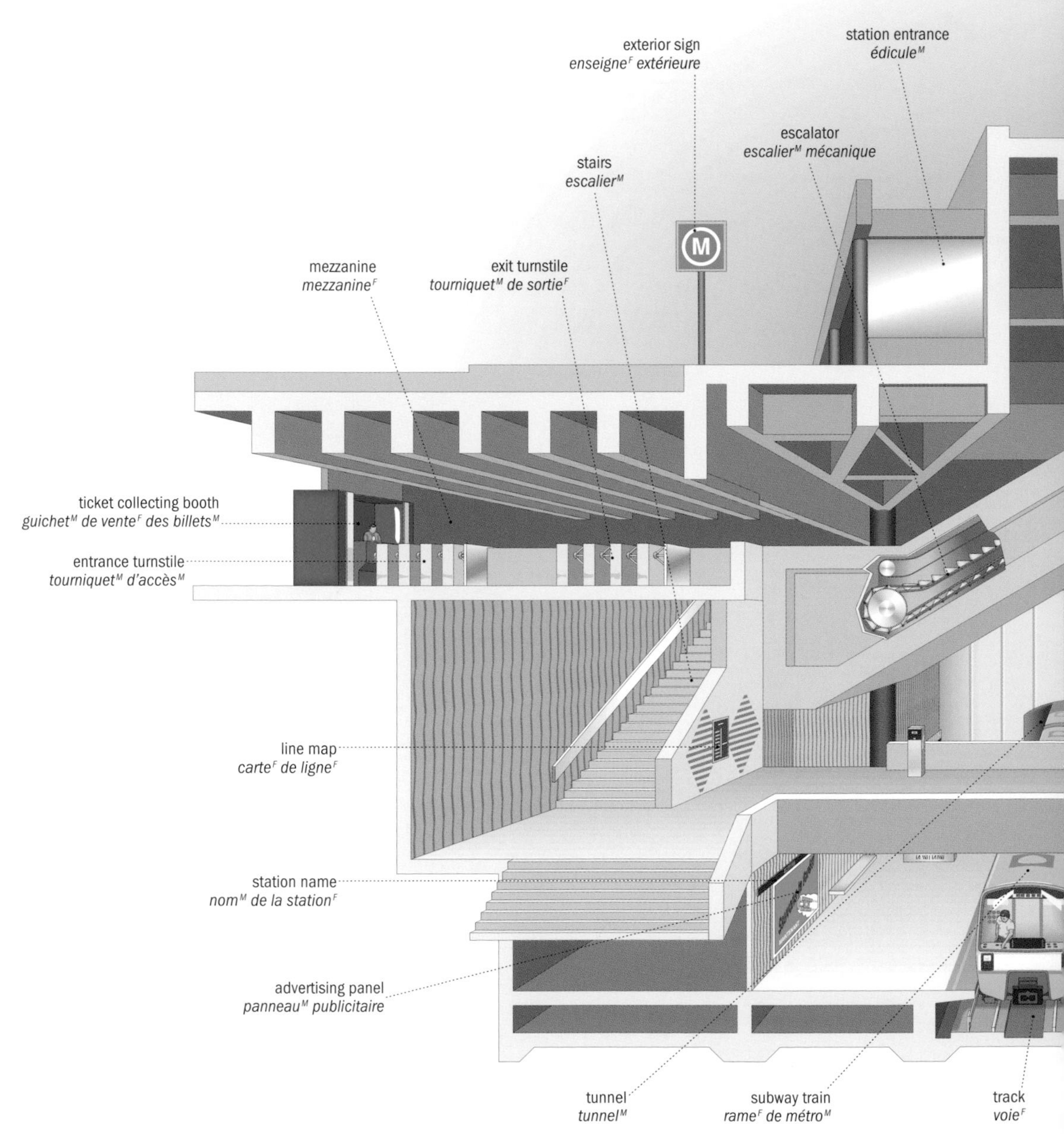

exterior sign
enseigne^F extérieure
station entrance
édicule^M
escalator
escalier^M mécanique
stairs
escalier^M
mezzanine
mezzanine^F
exit turnstile
tourniquet^M de sortie^F
ticket collecting booth
guichet^M de vente^F des billets^M
entrance turnstile
tourniquet^M d'accès^M
line map
carte^F de ligne^F
station name
nom^M de la station^F
advertising panel
panneau^M publicitaire
tunnel
tunnel^M
subway train
rame^F de métro^M
track
voie^F

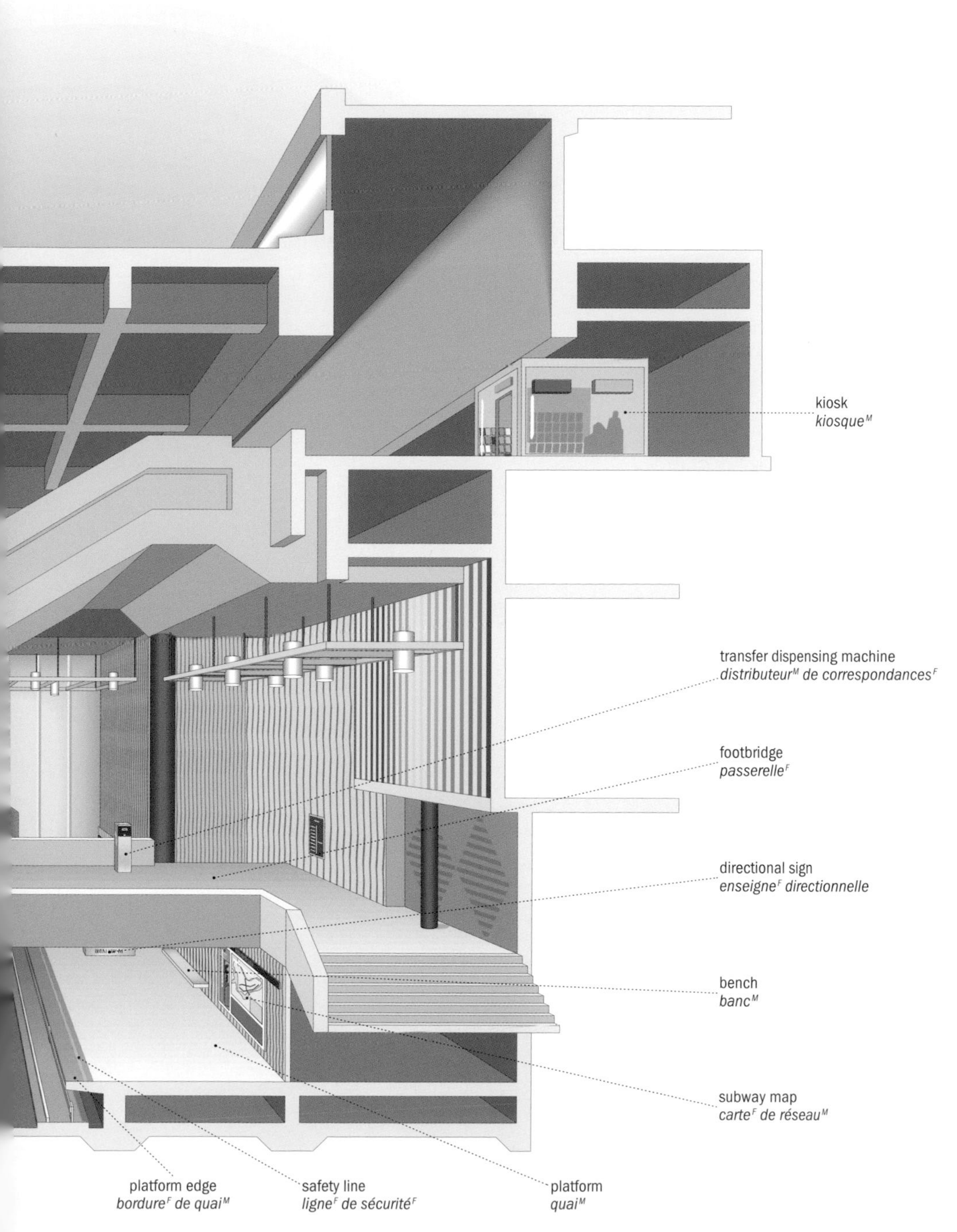
kiosk
*kiosque*M
transfer dispensing machine
*distributeur*M *de correspondances*F
footbridge
*passerelle*F
directional sign
*enseigne*F *directionnelle*
bench
*banc*M
subway map
*carte*F *de réseau*M
platform edge
*bordure*F *de quai*M
safety line
*ligne*F *de sécurité*F
platform
*quai*M

subway

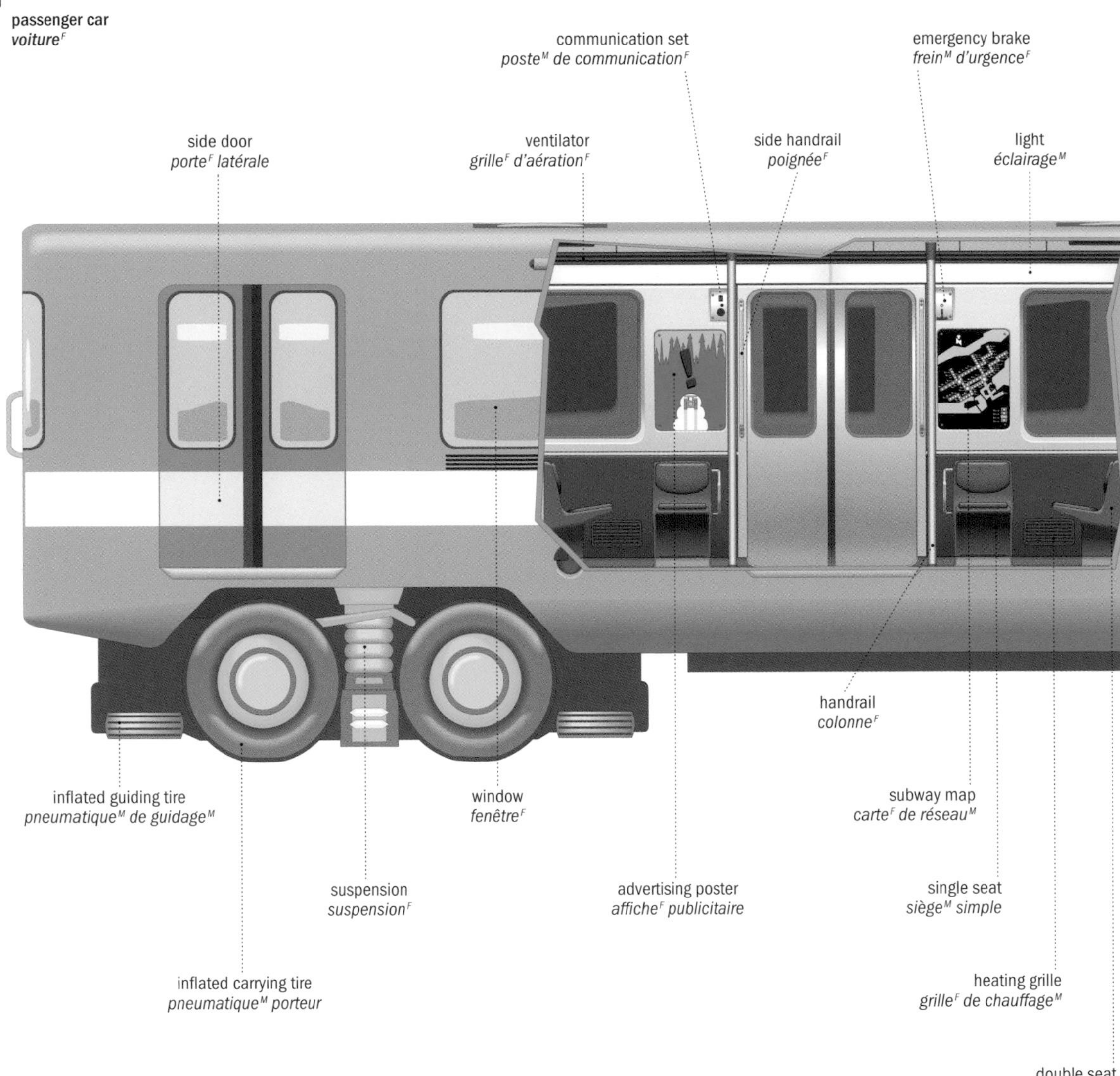
passenger car
voiture[F]
communication set
poste[M] de communication[F]
emergency brake
frein[M] d'urgence[F]
side door
porte[F] latérale
ventilator
grille[F] d'aération[F]
side handrail
poignée[F]
light
éclairage[M]
handrail
colonne[F]
inflated guiding tire
pneumatique[M] de guidage[M]
window
fenêtre[F]
subway map
carte[F] de réseau[M]
suspension
suspension[F]
advertising poster
affiche[F] publicitaire
single seat
siège[M] simple
inflated carrying tire
pneumatique[M] porteur
heating grille
grille[F] de chauffage[M]
double seat
siège[M] double

subway train
rame[F] de métro[M]

motor car
motrice[F]

trailer car
remorque[F]

motor car
motrice[F]

harbor

port^M maritime

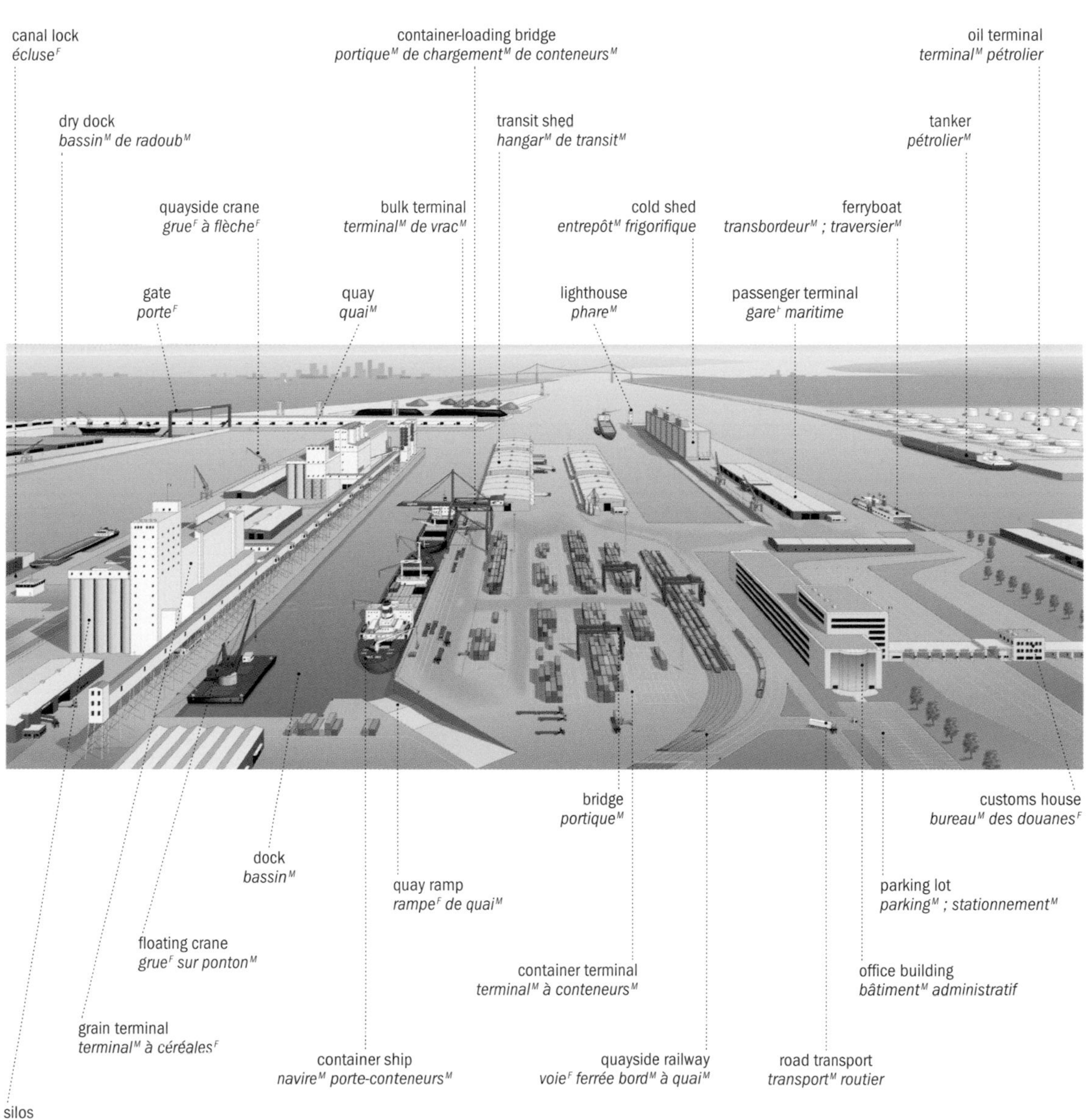
canal lock
écluse^F
container-loading bridge
portique^M de chargement^M de conteneurs^M
oil terminal
terminal^M pétrolier
dry dock
bassin^M de radoub^M
transit shed
hangar^M de transit^M
tanker
pétrolier^M
quayside crane
grue^F à flèche^F
bulk terminal
terminal^M de vrac^M
cold shed
entrepôt^M frigorifique
ferryboat
transbordeur^M ; traversier^M
gate
porte^F
quay
quai^M
lighthouse
phare^M
passenger terminal
gare^F maritime
bridge
portique^M
customs house
bureau^M des douanes^F
dock
bassin^M
quay ramp
rampe^F de quai^M
parking lot
parking^M ; stationnement^M
floating crane
grue^F sur ponton^M
container terminal
terminal^M à conteneurs^M
office building
bâtiment^M administratif
grain terminal
terminal^M à céréales^F
container ship
navire^M porte-conteneurs^M
quayside railway
voie^F ferrée bord^M à quai^M
road transport
transport^M routier
silos
silos^M

examples of boats and ships

exemples[M] de bateaux[M] et d'embarcations[F]

drill ship
navire[M] de forage[M]

derrick
tour[F] de forage[M]

bulk carrier
vraquier[M]

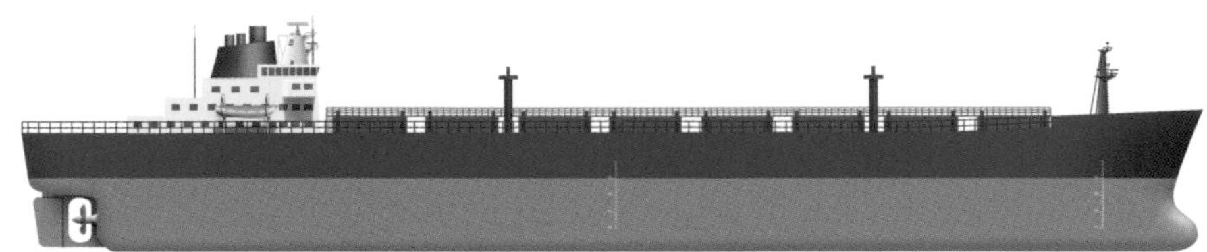

container ship
navire[M] porte-conteneurs[M]

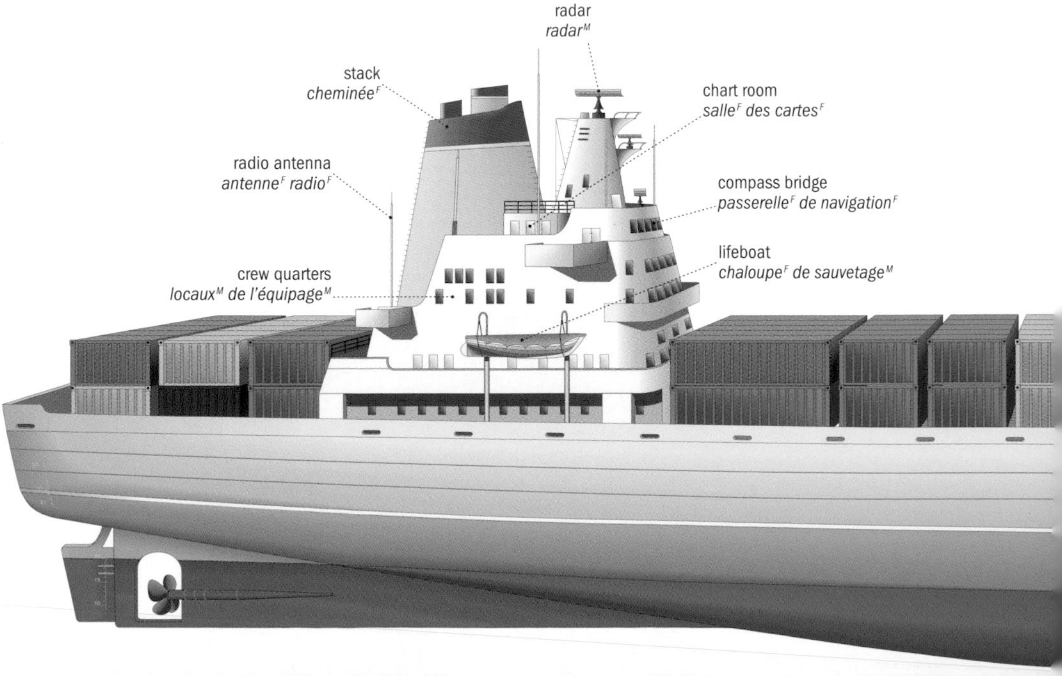

radar
radar[M]

stack
cheminée[F]

chart room
salle[F] des cartes[F]

radio antenna
antenne[F] radio[F]

compass bridge
passerelle[F] de navigation[F]

lifeboat
chaloupe[F] de sauvetage[M]

crew quarters
locaux[M] de l'équipage[M]

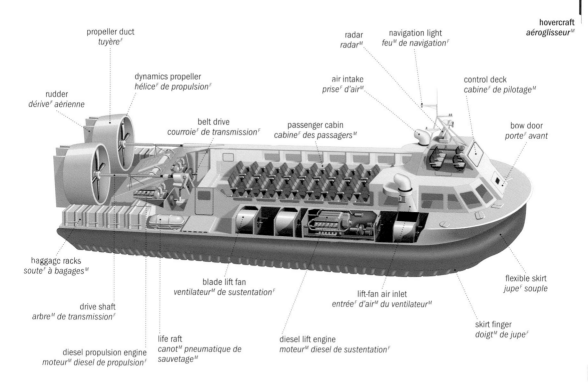

hovercraft
aéroglisseur[M]

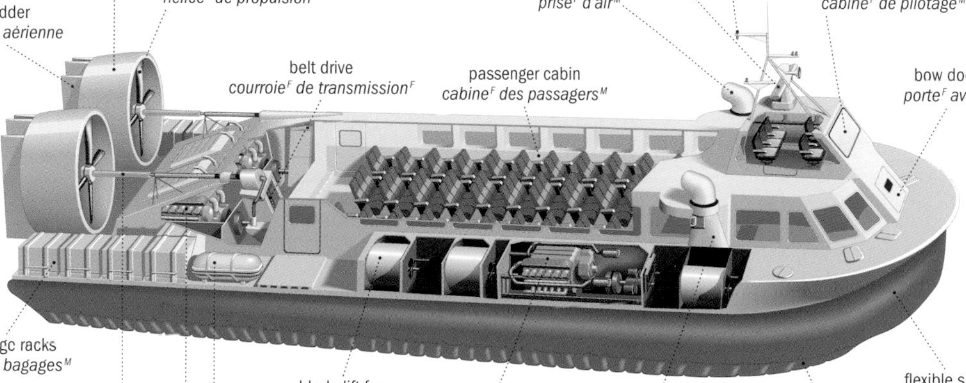

propeller duct
tuyère[F]

radar
radar[M]

navigation light
feu[M] de navigation[F]

dynamics propeller
hélice[F] de propulsion[F]

air intake
prise[F] d'air[M]

control deck
cabine[F] de pilotage[M]

rudder
dérive[F] aérienne

belt drive
courroie[F] de transmission[F]

passenger cabin
cabine[F] des passagers[M]

bow door
porte[F] avant

baggage racks
soute[F] à bagages[M]

flexible skirt
jupe[F] souple

blade lift fan
ventilateur[M] de sustentation[F]

lift-fan air inlet
entrée[F] d'air[M] du ventilateur[M]

drive shaft
arbre[M] de transmission[F]

skirt finger
doigt[M] de jupe[F]

life raft
canot[M] pneumatique de sauvetage[M]

diesel lift engine
moteur[M] diesel de sustentation[F]

diesel propulsion engine
moteur[M] diesel de propulsion[F]

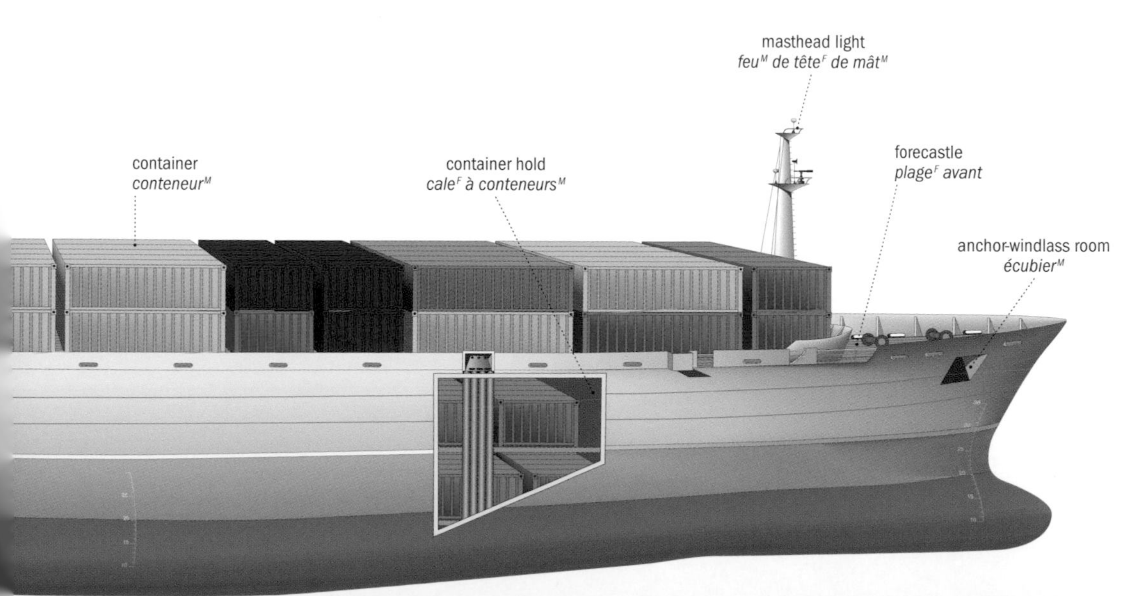
masthead light
feu[M] de tête[F] de mât[M]
container
conteneur[M]
container hold
cale[F] à conteneurs[M]
forecastle
plage[F] avant
anchor-windlass room
écubier[M]

examples of boats and ships

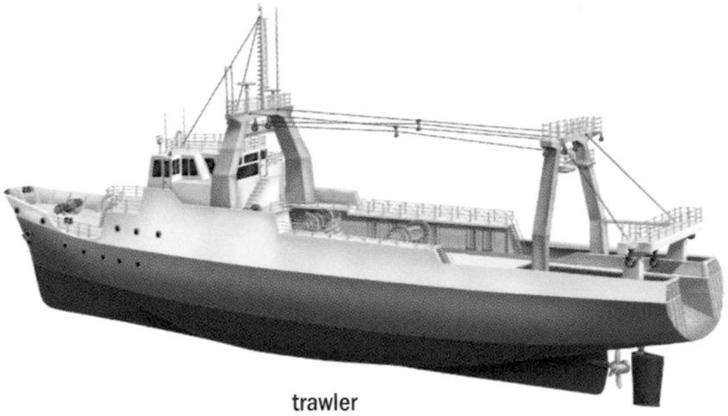

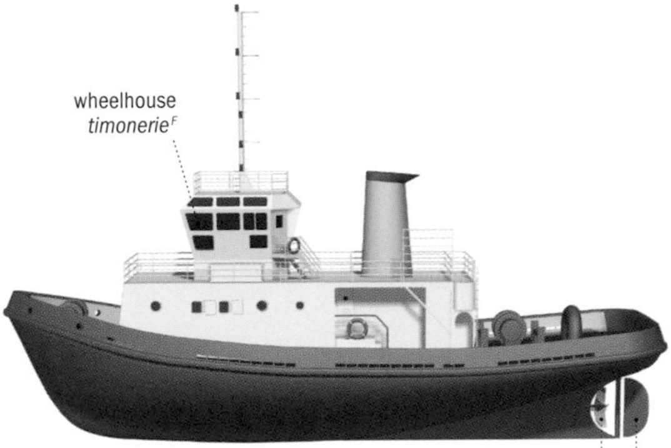

wheelhouse
timonerie[F]

trawler
chalutier[M]

tug
remorqueur[M]

propeller
hélice[F]

rudder blade
safran[M]

stem
étrave[F]

ice breaker
brise-glace[M]

rear propeller
hélice[F] arrière

stem propeller
hélice[F] d'étrave[F]

tanker
pétrolier[M]

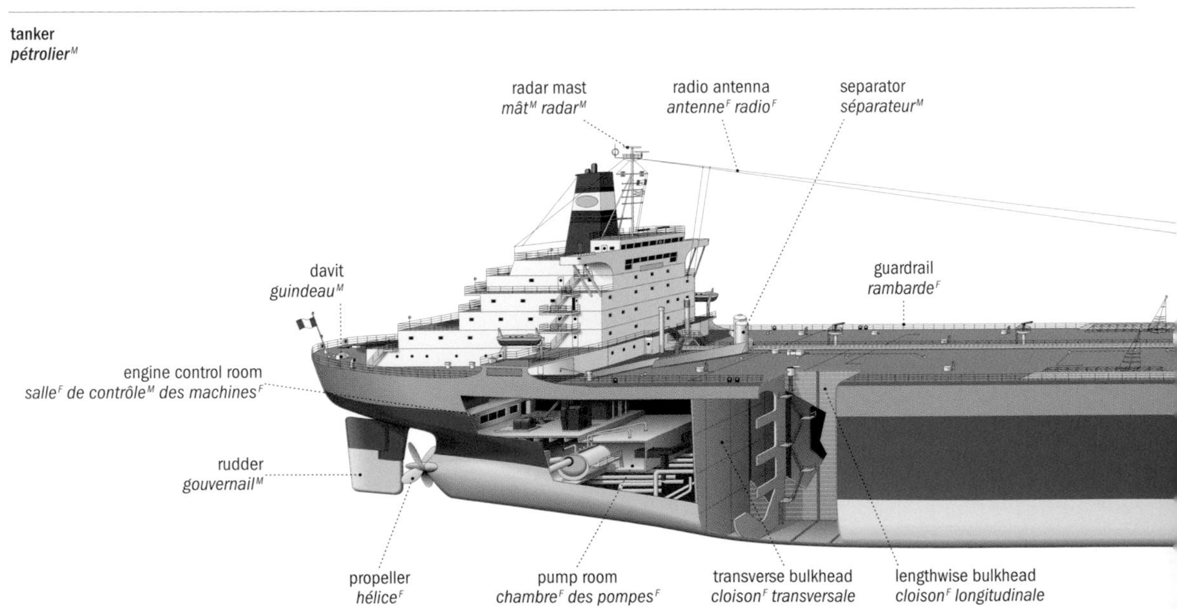
radar mast
mât[M] radar[M]
radio antenna
antenne[F] radio[F]
separator
séparateur[M]
davit
guindeau[M]
guardrail
rambarde[F]
engine control room
salle[F] de contrôle[M] des machines[F]
rudder
gouvernail[M]
propeller
hélice[F]
pump room
chambre[F] des pompes[F]
transverse bulkhead
cloison[F] transversale
lengthwise bulkhead
cloison[F] longitudinale

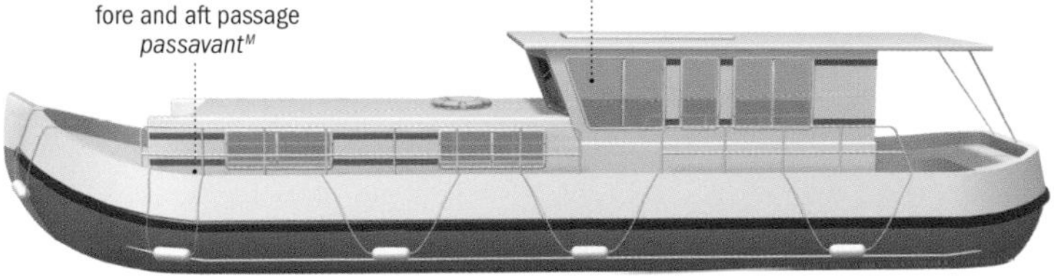

pilot house
cabine[F] de pilotage[M]

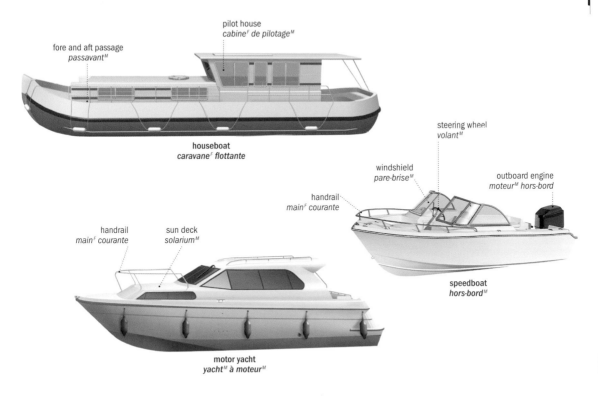

fore and aft passage
passavant[M]

houseboat
caravane[F] flottante

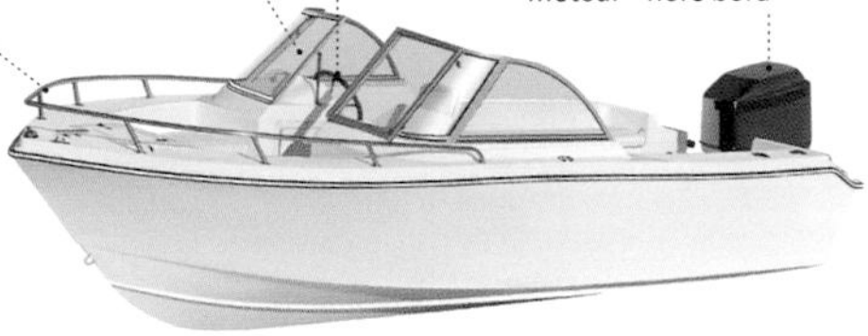

steering wheel
volant[M]

windshield
pare-brise[M]

outboard engine
moteur[M] hors-bord

handrail
main[F] courante

handrail
main[F] courante

sun deck
solarium[M]

speedboat
hors-bord[M]

motor yacht
yacht[M] à moteur[M]

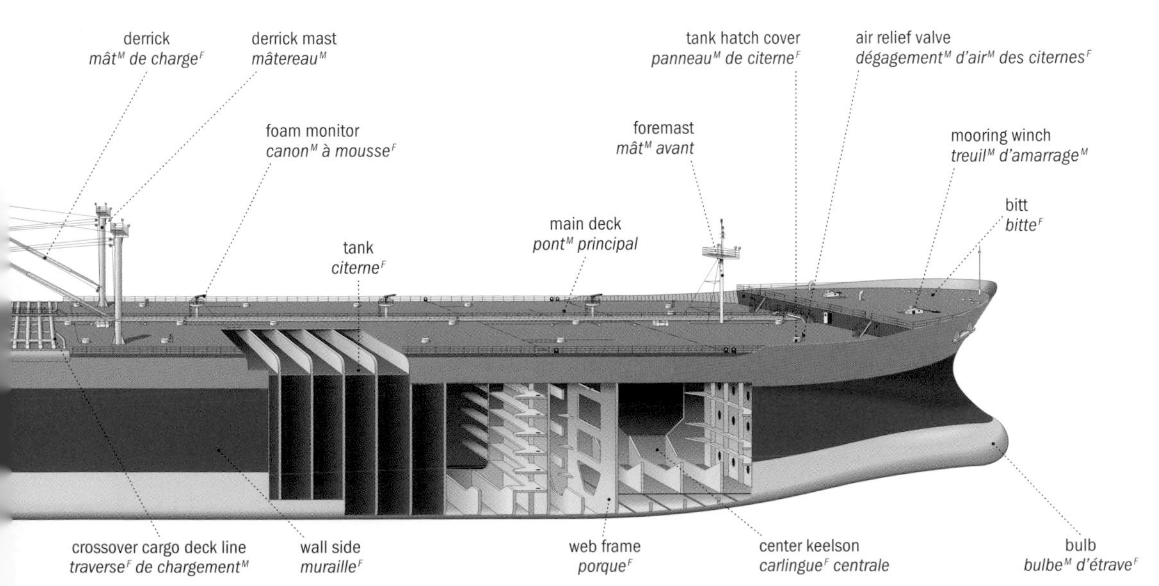
derrick
mât[M] de charge[F]
derrick mast
mâtereau[M]
foam monitor
canon[M] à mousse[F]
tank hatch cover
panneau[M] de citerne[F]
air relief valve
dégagement[M] d'air[M] des citernes[F]
foremast
mât[M] avant
mooring winch
treuil[M] d'amarrage[M]
bitt
bitte[F]
main deck
pont[M] principal
tank
citerne[F]
crossover cargo deck line
traverse[F] de chargement[M]
wall side
muraille[F]
web frame
porque[F]
center keelson
carlingue[F] centrale
bulb
bulbe[M] d'étrave[F]

examples of boats and ships

catamaran ferryboat
***transbordeur**[M]* ***; traversier**[M]*

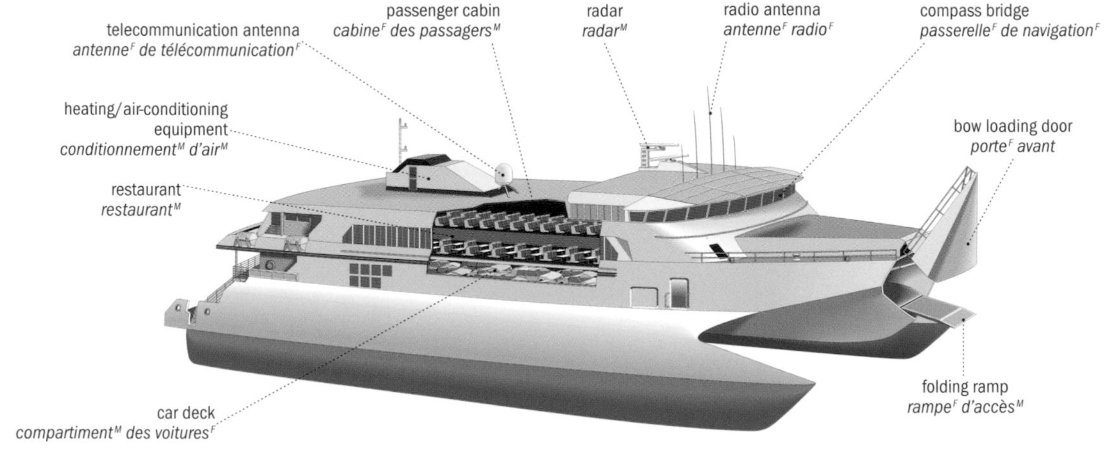
passenger cabin
cabine[F] des passagers[M]
radar
radar[M]
radio antenna
antenne[F] radio[F]
compass bridge
passerelle[F] de navigation[F]
telecommunication antenna
antenne[F] de télécommunication[F]
heating/air-conditioning equipment
conditionnement[M] d'air[M]
bow loading door
porte[F] avant
restaurant
restaurant[M]
folding ramp
rampe[F] d'accès[M]
car deck
compartiment[M] des voitures[F]

passenger liner
***paquebot**[M]*

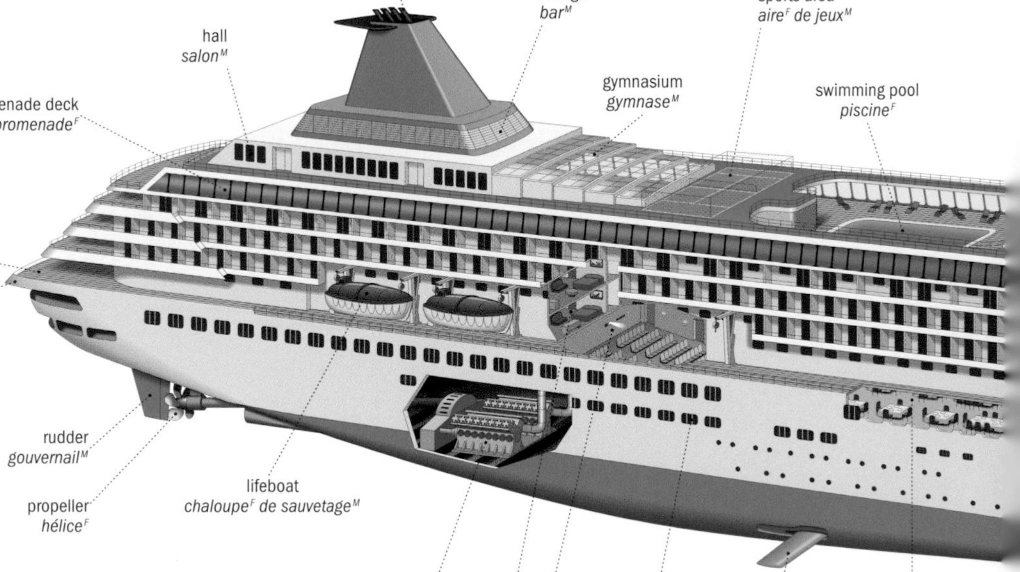

funnel
cheminée[F] antisuie

lounge
bar[M]

sports area
aire[F] de jeux[M]

hall
salon[M]

gymnasium
gymnase[M]

swimming pool
piscine[F]

promenade deck
pont[M]-promenade[F]

quarter-deck
plage[F] arrière

stern
poupe[F]

rudder
gouvernail[M]

lifeboat
chaloupe[F] de sauvetage[M]

propeller
hélice[F]

engine room
salle[F] des machines[F]

porthole
hublot[M]

dining room
salle[F] à manger

cabin
cabine[F]

movie theater
cinéma[M]

stabilizer fin
stabilisateur[M] de roulis[M]

hydrofoil boat
***hydroptère*[M]**

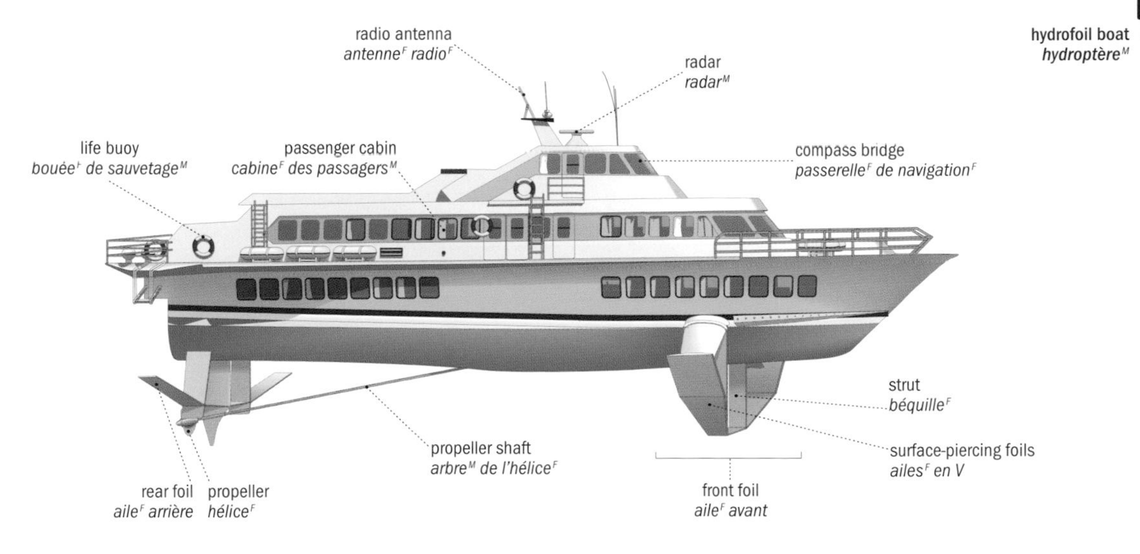
radio antenna
antenne[F] *radio*[F]
radar
radar[M]
life buoy
bouée[F] *de sauvetage*[M]
passenger cabin
cabine[F] *des passagers*[M]
compass bridge
passerelle[F] *de navigation*[F]
strut
béquille[F]
surface-piercing foils
ailes[F] *en V*
propeller shaft
arbre[M] *de l'hélice*[F]
rear foil
aile[F] *arrière*
propeller
hélice[F]
front foil
aile[F] *avant*

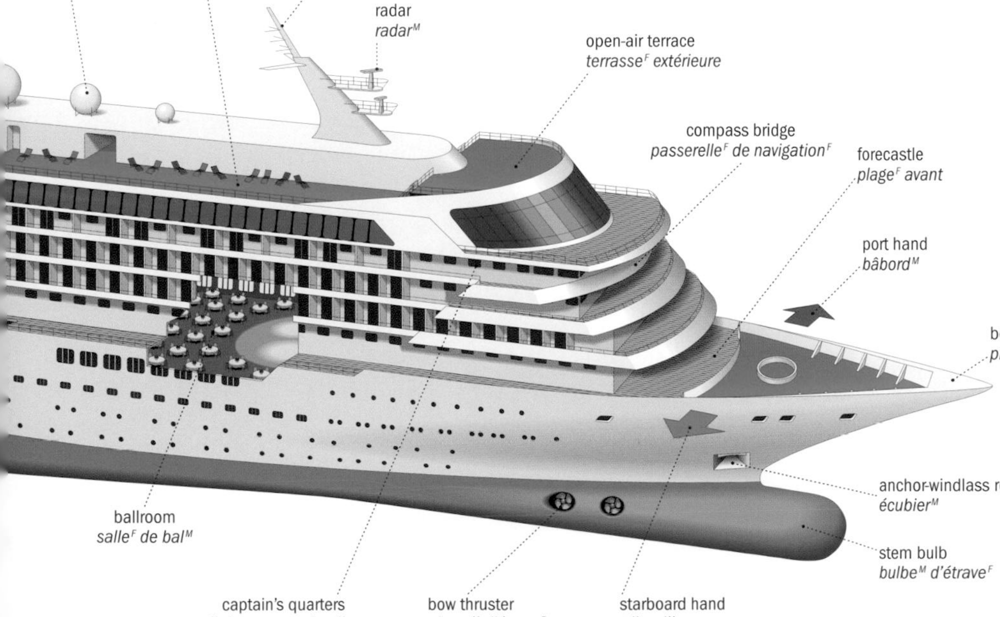

telecommunication antenna
antenne[F] *de télécommunication*[F]

radio antenna
antenne[F] *radio*[F]

sun deck
pont[M] *bain*[M] *de soleil*[M]

radar
radar[M]

open-air terrace
terrasse[F] *extérieure*

compass bridge
passerelle[F] *de navigation*[F]

forecastle
plage[F] *avant*

port hand
bâbord[M]

bow
proue[F]

anchor-windlass room
écubier[M]

ballroom
salle[F] *de bal*[M]

stem bulb
bulbe[M] *d'étrave*[F]

captain's quarters
appartement[M] *du commandant*[M]

bow thruster
propulseur[M] *d'étrave*[F]

starboard hand
tribord[M]

airport

aéroport[M]

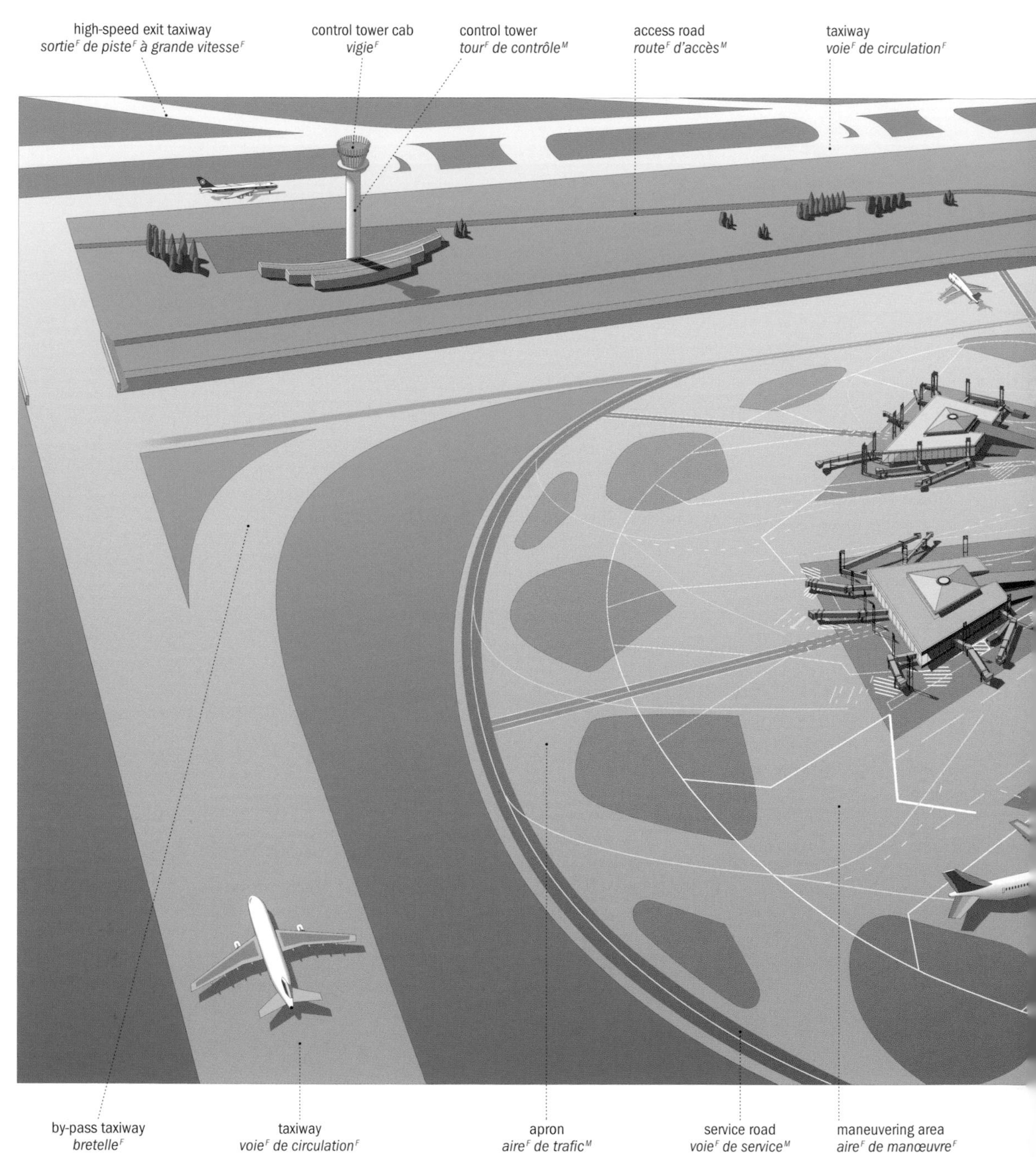
high-speed exit taxiway
sortie[F] de piste[F] à grande vitesse[F]
control tower cab
vigie[F]
control tower
tour[F] de contrôle[M]
access road
route[F] d'accès[M]
taxiway
voie[F] de circulation[F]
by-pass taxiway
bretelle[F]
taxiway
voie[F] de circulation[F]
apron
aire[F] de trafic[M]
service road
voie[F] de service[M]
maneuvering area
aire[F] de manœuvre[F]

passenger terminal
aérogare^F de passagers^M
maintenance hangar
hangar^M
parking area
aire^F de stationnement^M
telescopic corridor
passerelle^F télescopique
service area
aire^F de service^M
boarding walkway
quai^M d'embarquement^M
taxiway line
marques^F de circulation^F
radial passenger-loading area
aérogare^F satellite^M

airport

passenger terminal
aérogare[F]

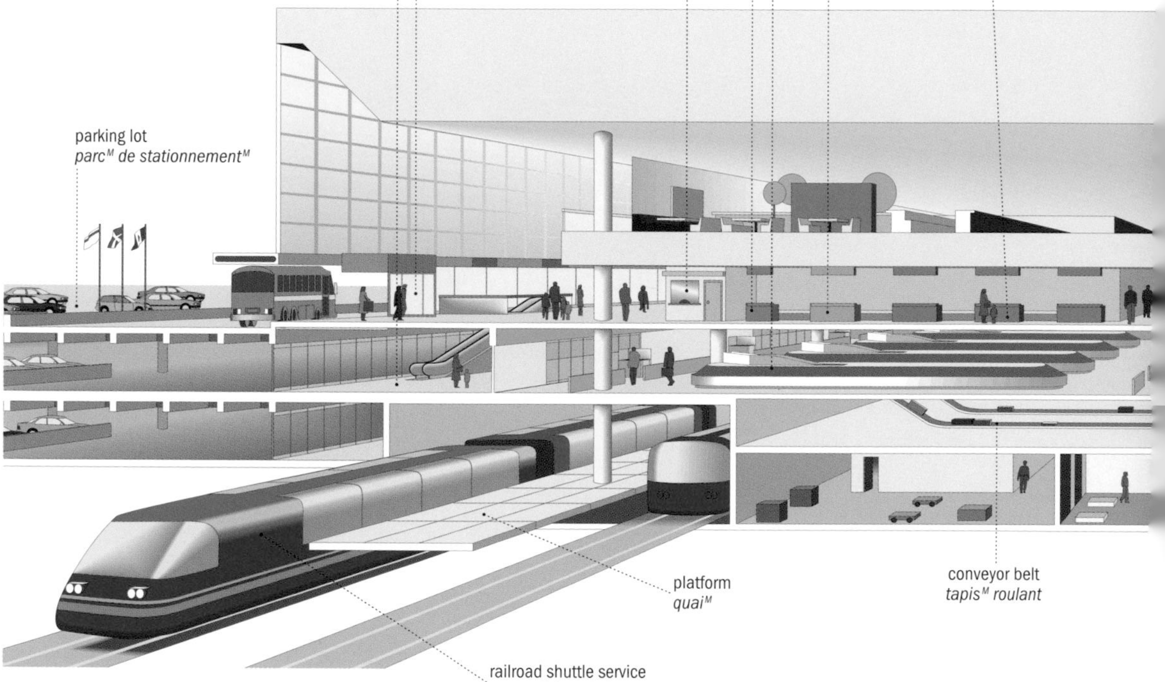

information counter
comptoir[M] *de renseignements*[M]

baggage claim area
zone[F] *de retrait*[M] *des bagages*[M]

hotel reservation desk
bureau[M] *de réservation*[F] *de chambres*[F] *d'hôtel*[M]

ticket counter
billetterie[F]

lobby
hall[M] *public*

automatically controlled door
porte[F] *automatique*

baggage check-in counter
comptoir[M] *d'enregistrement*[M]

parking lot
parc[M] *de stationnement*[M]

platform
quai[M]

conveyor belt
tapis[M] *roulant*

railroad shuttle service
navette[F] *ferroviaire*

runway
piste[F]

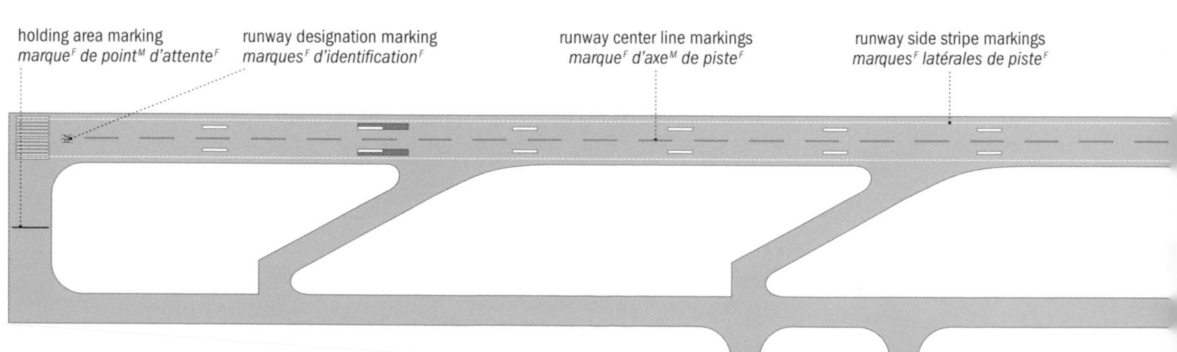
holding area marking
marque[F] de point[M] d'attente[F]
runway designation marking
marques[F] d'identification[F]
runway center line markings
marque[F] d'axe[M] de piste[F]
runway side stripe markings
marques[F] latérales de piste[F]

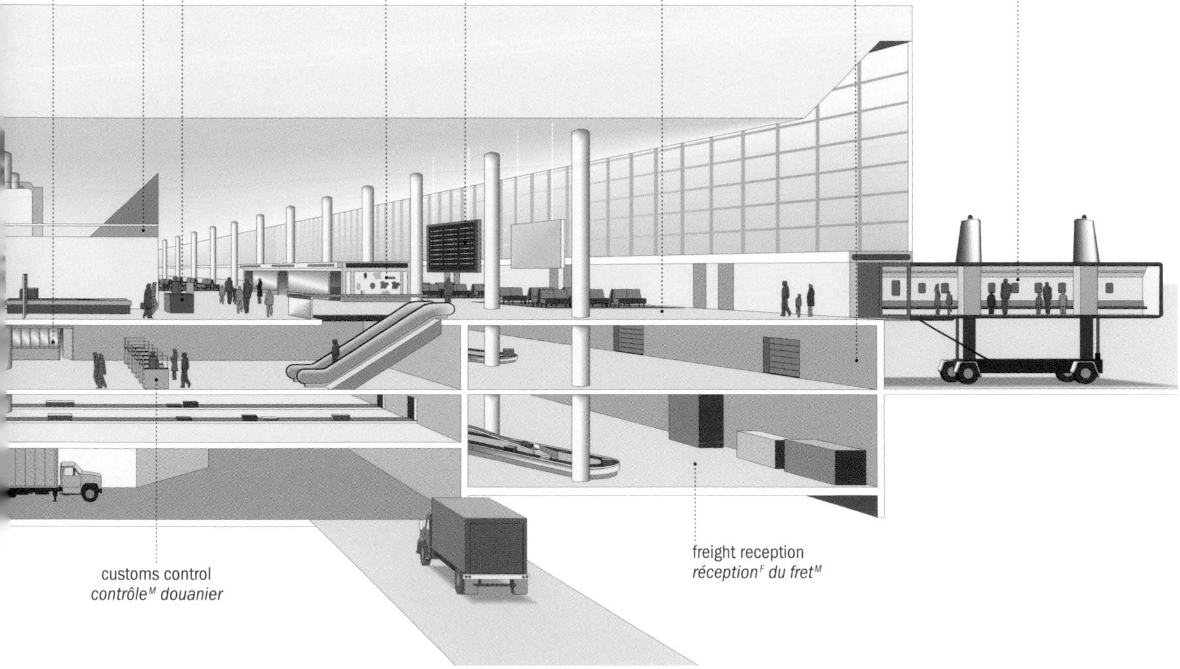

security check
contrôle[M] de sécurité[F]

duty-free shop
boutique[F] hors taxe[F]

observation deck
terrasse[F]

flight information board
tableau[M] d'affichage[M] des vols[M]

freight expedition
expédition[F] du fret[M]

passport control
contrôle[M] des passeports[M]

boarding room
salle[F] d'embarquement[M]

passenger transfer vehicle
transbordeur[M]

customs control
contrôle[M] douanier

freight reception
réception[F] du fret[M]

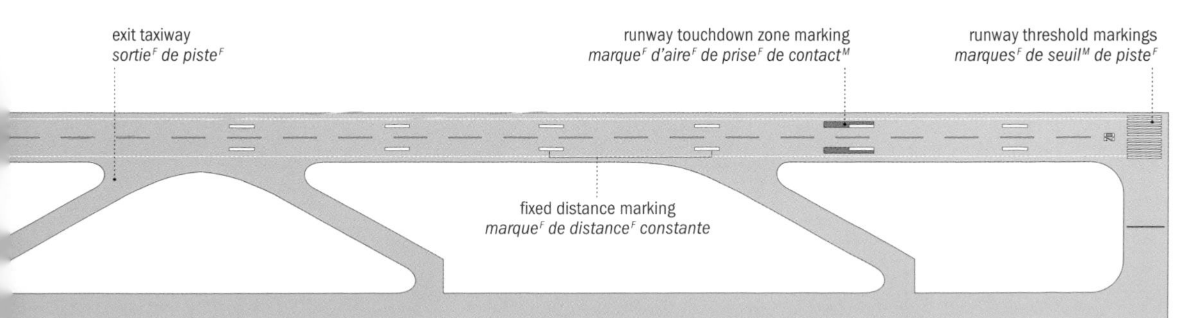
exit taxiway
sortie[F] de piste[F]
runway touchdown zone marking
marque[F] d'aire[F] de prise[F] de contact[M]
runway threshold markings
marques[F] de seuil[M] de piste[F]
fixed distance marking
marque[F] de distance[F] constante

long-range jet

avion[M] long-courrier[M]

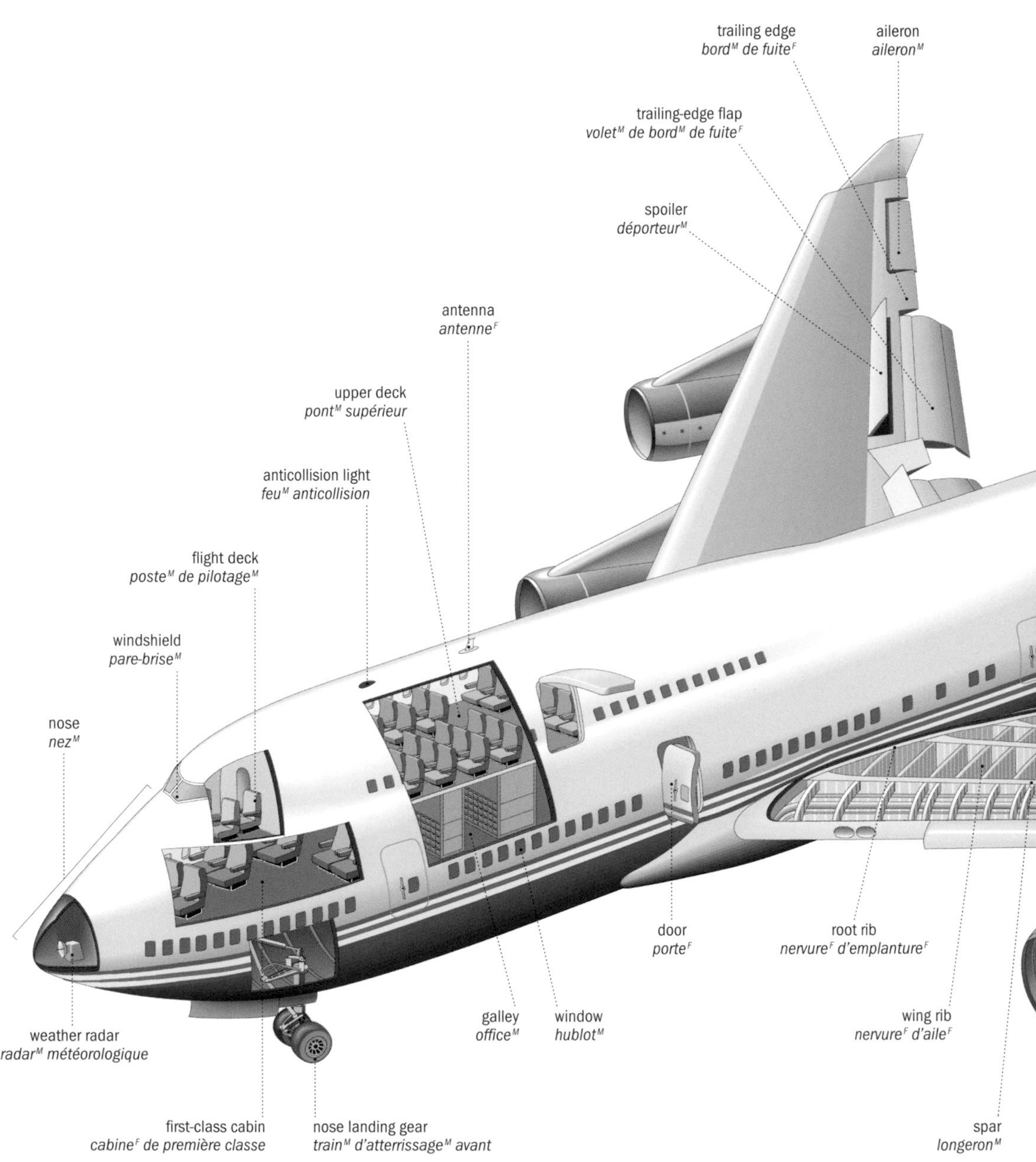
trailing edge
bord[M] de fuite[F]
aileron
aileron[M]
trailing-edge flap
volet[M] de bord[M] de fuite[F]
spoiler
déporteur[M]
antenna
antenne[F]
upper deck
pont[M] supérieur
anticollision light
feu[M] anticollision
flight deck
poste[M] de pilotage[M]
windshield
pare-brise[M]
nose
nez[M]
door
porte[F]
root rib
nervure[F] d'emplanture[F]
galley
office[M]
window
hublot[M]
wing rib
nervure[F] d'aile[F]
weather radar
radar[M] météorologique
first-class cabin
cabine[F] de première classe
nose landing gear
train[M] d'atterrissage[M] avant
spar
longeron[M]

long-range jet

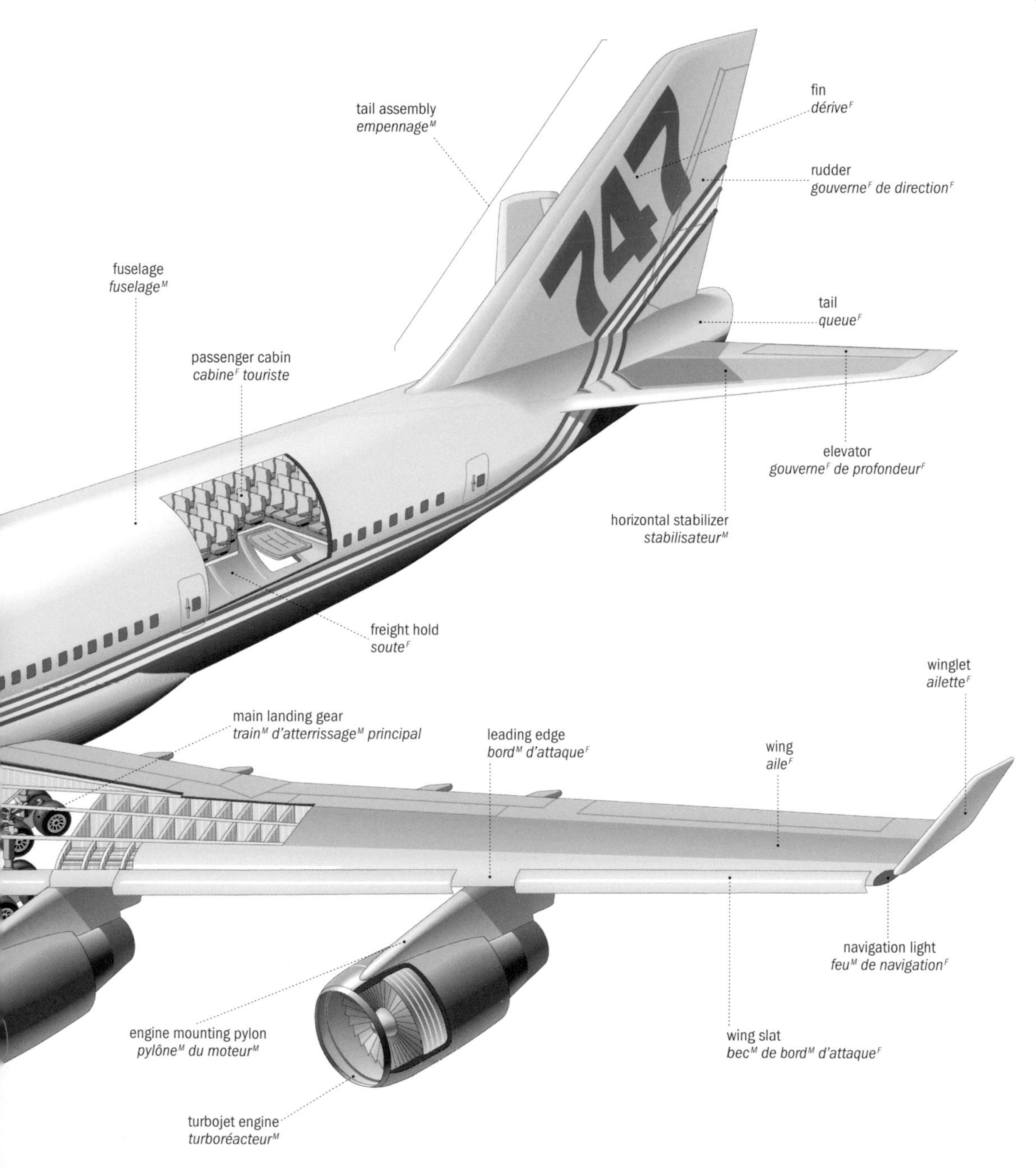
tail assembly
empennage^M
fin
dérive^F
rudder
gouverne^F de direction^F
747
fuselage
fuselage^M
tail
queue^F
passenger cabin
cabine^F touriste
elevator
gouverne^F de profondeur^F
horizontal stabilizer
stabilisateur^M
freight hold
soute^F
winglet
ailette^F
main landing gear
train^M d'atterrissage^M principal
leading edge
bord^M d'attaque^F
wing
aile^F
navigation light
feu^M de navigation^F
engine mounting pylon
pylône^M du moteur^M
wing slat
bec^M de bord^M d'attaque^F
turbojet engine
turboréacteur^M

examples of airplanes

exemples[M] d'avions[M]

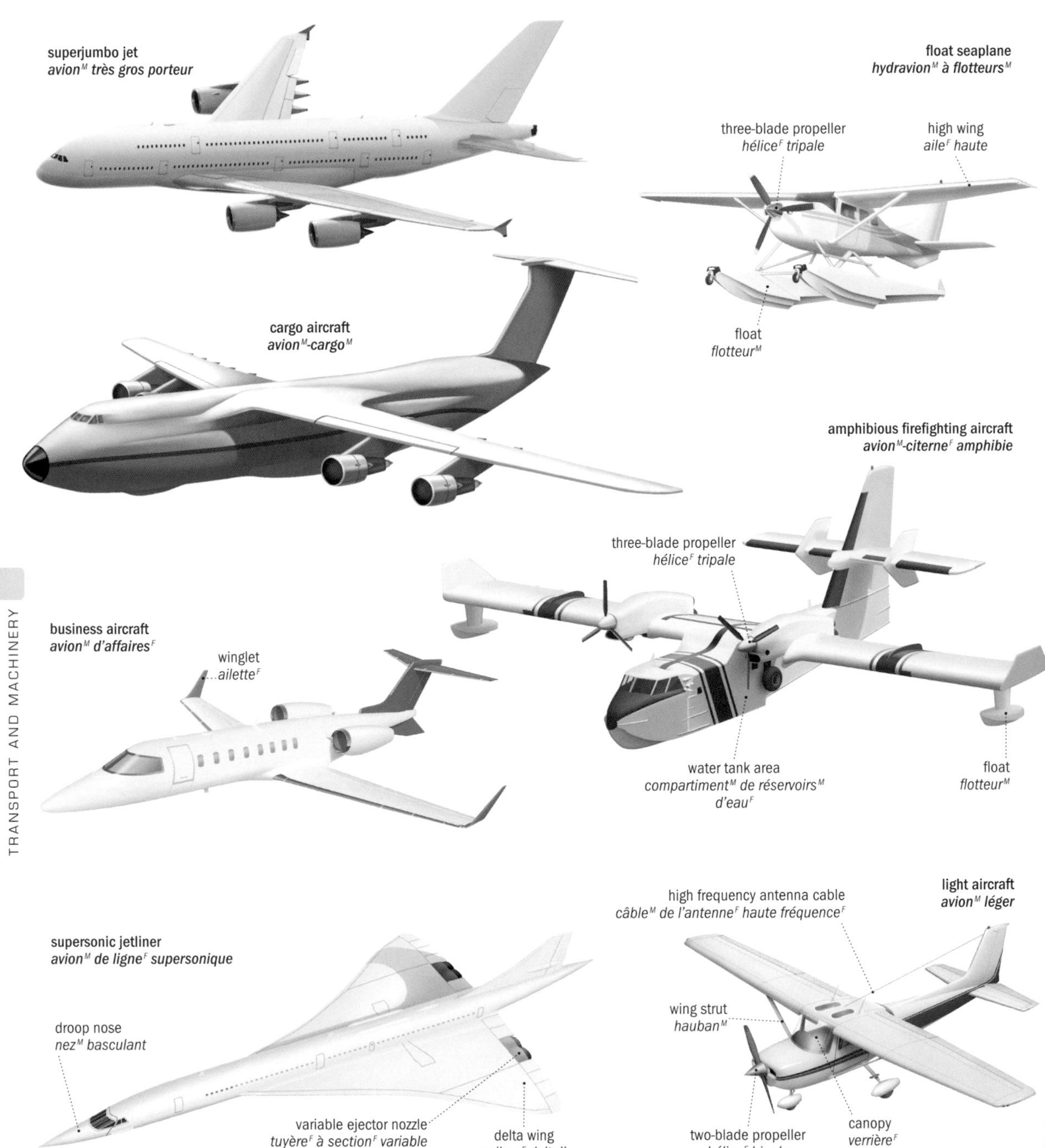
superjumbo jet
avion[M] très gros porteur
float seaplane
hydravion[M] à flotteurs[M]
three-blade propeller
hélice[F] tripale
high wing
aile[F] haute
float
flotteur[M]
cargo aircraft
avion[M]-cargo[M]
amphibious firefighting aircraft
avion[M]-citerne[F] amphibie
three-blade propeller
hélice[F] tripale
business aircraft
avion[M] d'affaires[F]
winglet
ailette[F]
water tank area
compartiment[M] de réservoirs[M] d'eau[F]
float
flotteur[M]
light aircraft
avion[M] léger
high frequency antenna cable
câble[M] de l'antenne[F] haute fréquence[F]
supersonic jetliner
avion[M] de ligne[F] supersonique
wing strut
hauban[M]
droop nose
nez[M] basculant
variable ejector nozzle
tuyère[F] à section[F] variable
delta wing
voilure[F] delta[M]
two-blade propeller
hélice[F] bipale
canopy
verrière[F]

movements of an airplane

mouvements[M] de l'avion[M]

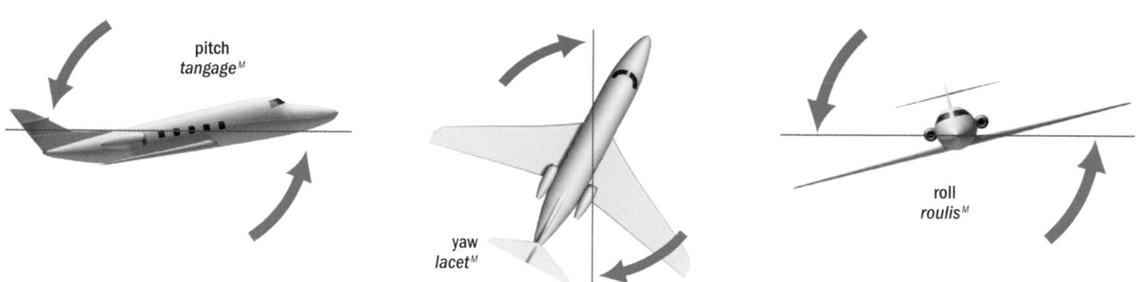
pitch
tangage[M]
yaw
lacet[M]
roll
roulis[M]

helicopter

hélicoptère[M]

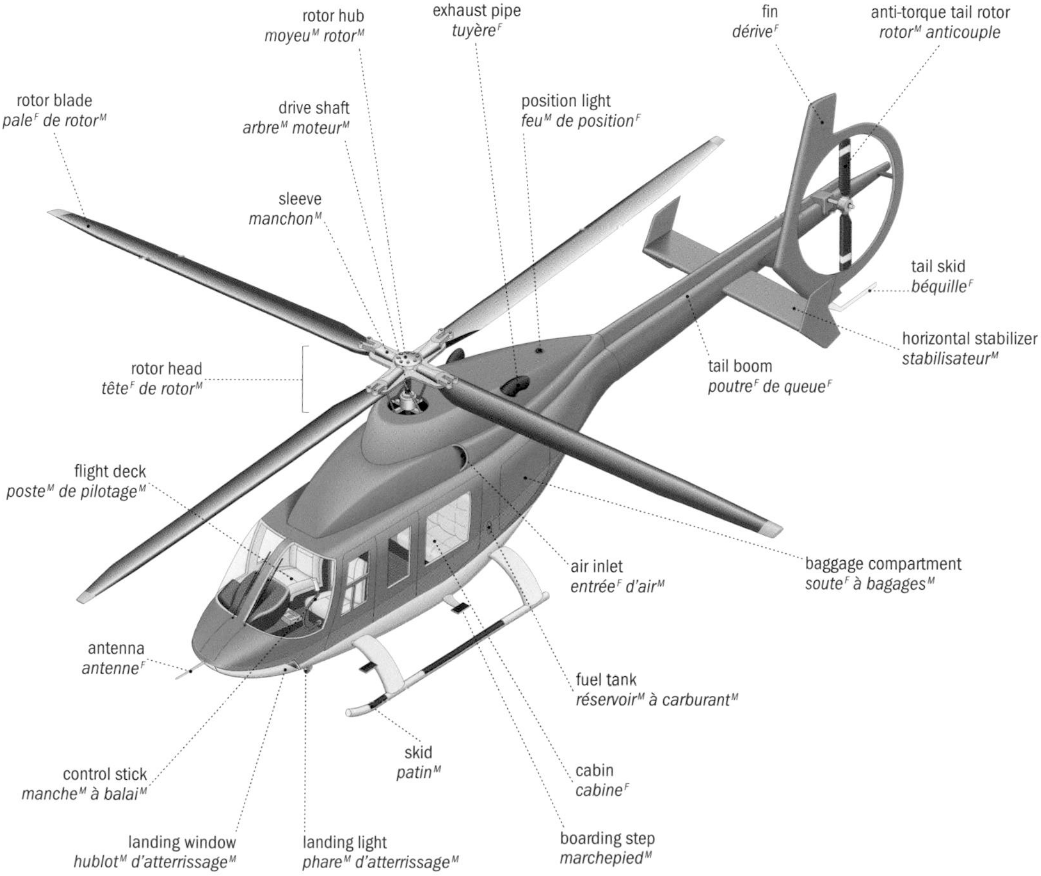

rotor hub
moyeu[M] rotor[M]

exhaust pipe
tuyère[F]

fin
dérive[F]

anti-torque tail rotor
rotor[M] anticouple

rotor blade
pale[F] de rotor[M]

drive shaft
arbre[M] moteur[M]

position light
feu[M] de position[F]

sleeve
manchon[M]

tail skid
béquille[F]

horizontal stabilizer
stabilisateur[M]

rotor head
tête[F] de rotor[M]

tail boom
poutre[F] de queue[F]

flight deck
poste[M] de pilotage[M]

air inlet
entrée[F] d'air[M]

baggage compartment
soute[F] à bagages[M]

antenna
antenne[F]

fuel tank
réservoir[M] à carburant[M]

skid
patin[M]

control stick
manche[M] à balai[M]

cabin
cabine[F]

landing window
hublot[M] d'atterrissage[M]

landing light
phare[M] d'atterrissage[M]

boarding step
marchepied[M]

material handling

manutention[F]

forklift truck
chariot[M] élévateur
mast
mât[M]
crosshead
tête[F] du vérin[M] de levage[M]
lifting chain
chaine[F] de levage[M]
hydraulic hoses
système[M] hydraulique
carriage
tablier[M]
fork arm
bras[M] de fourche[F]
fork
fourches[F]
overhead guard
toit[M] de protection[F]
mast-operating lever
levier[M] de manœuvre[F] du mât[M]
engine compartment
moteur[M]
frame
châssis[M]
hand truck
diable[M]
pallet truck
transpalette[F] manuelle
wing pallet
palette[F] à ailes[F]
top deckboard
plancher[M] supérieur
stringer
entretoise[F]
entry
entrée[F]
bottom deckboard
plancher[M] inférieur

cranes

grues^{F} et portique^{M}

tower crane
grue^{F} à tour^{F}

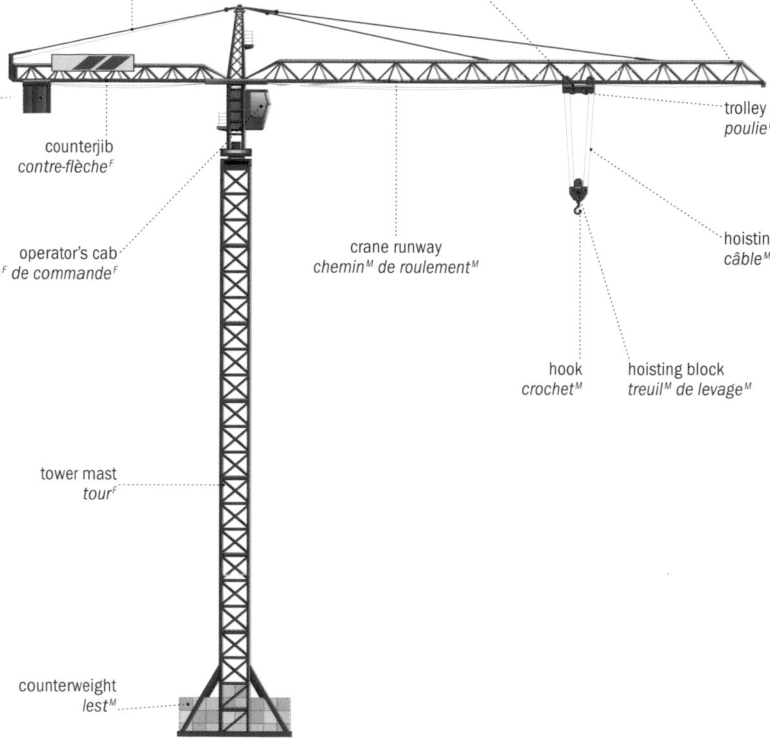

jib tie
lirant^{M}

trolley
chariot^{M}

jib
flèche^{F}

counterjib ballast
contrepoids^{M}

trolley pulley
poulie^{F} de chariot^{M}

counterjib
contre-flèche^{F}

operator's cab
cabine^{F} de commande^{F}

crane runway
chemin^{M} de roulement^{M}

hoisting rope
câble^{M} de levage^{M}

hook
crochet^{M}

hoisting block
treuil^{M} de levage^{M}

tower mast
tour^{F}

counterweight
lest^{M}

truck crane
grue^{F} sur porteur^{M}

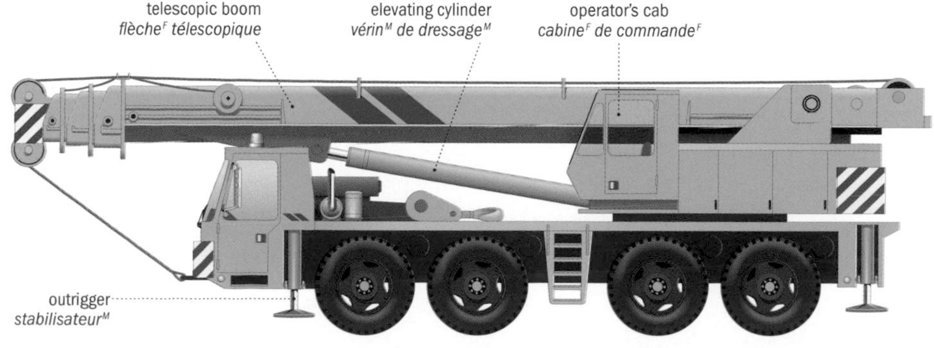
telescopic boom
flèche^{F} télescopique
elevating cylinder
vérin^{M} de dressage^{M}
operator's cab
cabine^{F} de commande^{F}
outrigger
stabilisateur^{M}

bulldozer

bouteur[M]

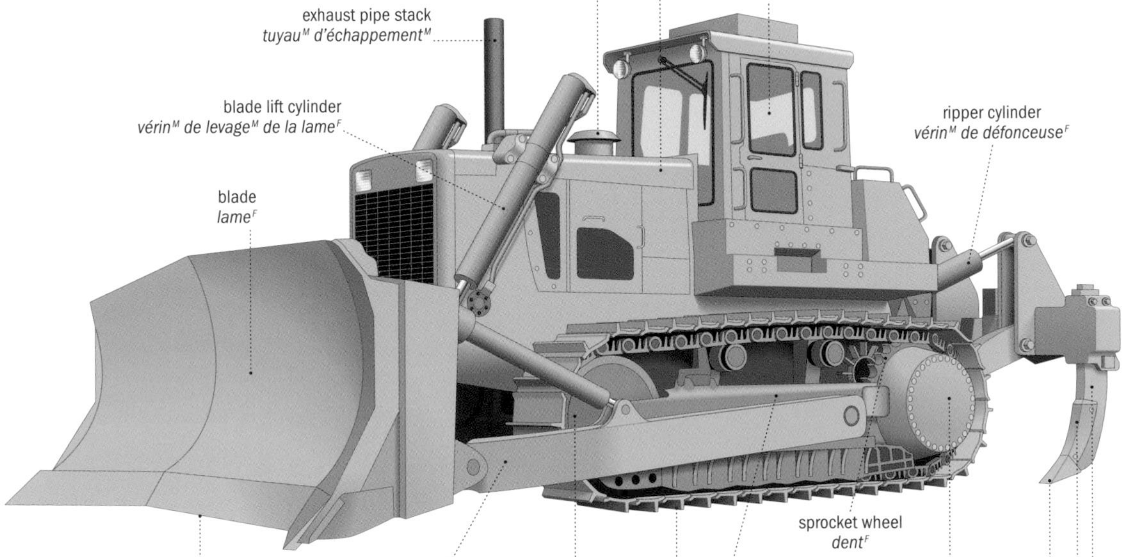

air pre-cleaner filter
filtre[M] à air[M]

diesel motor compartment
moteur[M] diesel

cab
cabine[F]

exhaust pipe stack
tuyau[M] d'échappement[M]

blade lift cylinder
vérin[M] de levage[M] de la lame[F]

ripper cylinder
vérin[M] de défonceuse[F]

blade
lame[F]

sprocket wheel
dent[F]

cutting edge
bord[M] tranchant

push frame
bras[M] du longeron[M]

track idler
roue[F] folle

final drive
barbotin[M]

track
chenille[F]

ripper tip tooth
pointe[F] de dent[F]

track roller frame
longeron[M] de chenille[F]

shank protector
sabot[M] de protection[F]

ripper shank
dent[F] de défonceuse[F]

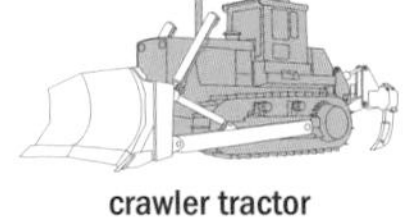

crawler tractor
tracteur[M] à chenilles[F]

blade
lame[F]

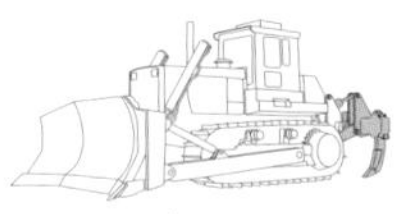

ripper
défonceuse[F]

wheel loader

chargeuse[F]-pelleteuse[F]

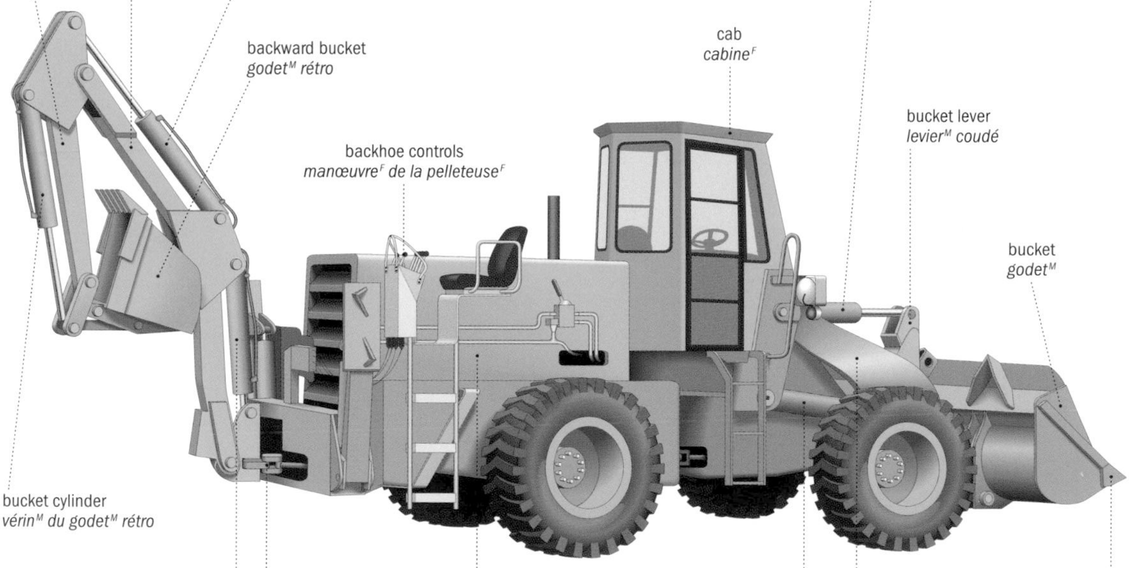

dipper arm
bras[M]

dipper-arm cylinder
vérin[M] du bras[M]

boom
flèche[F]

backward bucket
godet[M] rétro

backhoe controls
manœuvre[F] de la pelleteuse[F]

cab
cabine[F]

bucket cylinder
vérin[M] du godet[M]

bucket lever
levier[M] coudé

bucket
godet[M]

bucket cylinder
vérin[M] du godet[M] rétro

boom cylinder
vérin[M] de la flèche[F]

diesel engine compartment
moteur[M] diesel

lift arm
bras[M] de levage[M]

boom swing hinge pin
articulation[F] de la pelleteuse[F]

lift-arm cylinder
vérin[M] du bras[M] de levage[M]

cutting edge
dent[F] de godet[M]

front-end loader
chargeuse[F] frontale

wheel tractor
tracteur[M]

backhoe
pelleteuse[F]

scraper

décapeuse^F

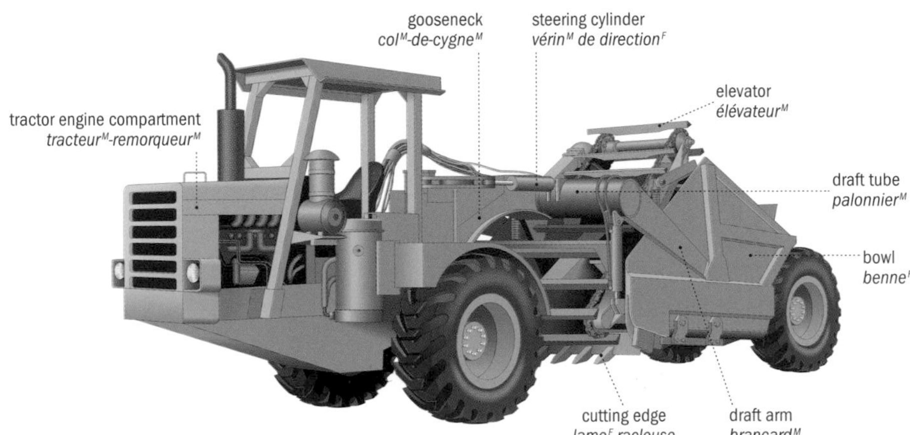
gooseneck
col^M-de-cygne^M
steering cylinder
vérin^M de direction^F
elevator
élévateur^M
tractor engine compartment
tracteur^M-remorqueur^M
draft tube
palonnier^M
bowl
benne^F
cutting edge
lame^F racleuse
draft arm
brancard^M

hydraulic shovel

pelle^F hydraulique

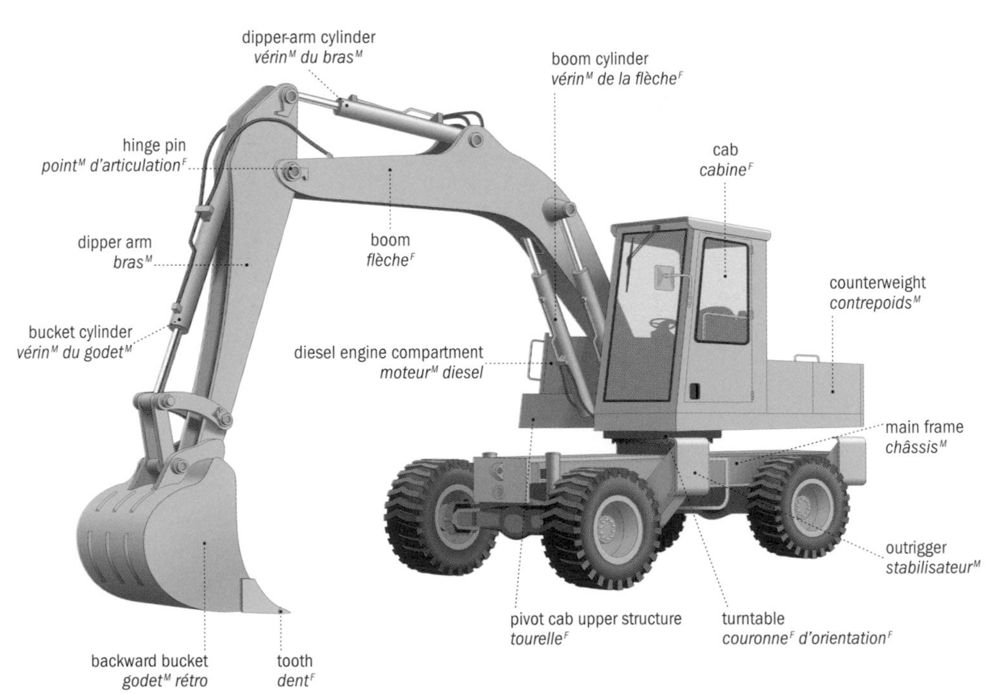
dipper-arm cylinder
vérin^M du bras^M
boom cylinder
vérin^M de la flèche^F
hinge pin
point^M d'articulation^F
cab
cabine^F
dipper arm
bras^M
boom
flèche^F
counterweight
contrepoids^M
bucket cylinder
vérin^M du godet^M
diesel engine compartment
moteur^M diesel
main frame
châssis^M
outrigger
stabilisateur^M
pivot cab upper structure
tourelle^F
turntable
couronne^F d'orientation^F
backward bucket
godet^M rétro
tooth
dent^F

grader

niveleuse^F

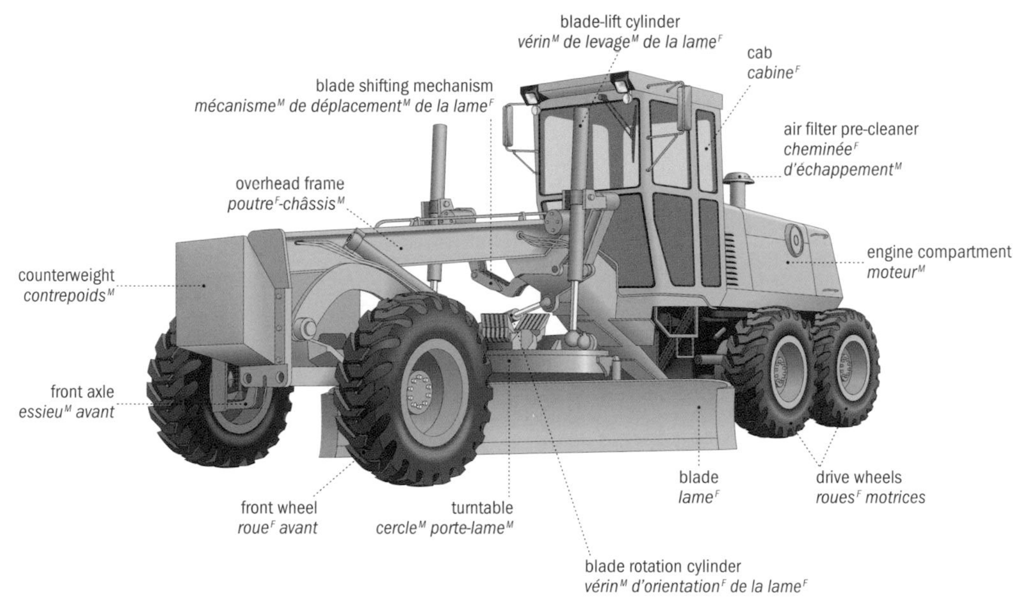
blade-lift cylinder
vérin^M de levage^M de la lame^F
cab
cabine^F
blade shifting mechanism
mécanisme^M de déplacement^M de la lame^F
air filter pre-cleaner
cheminée^F d'échappement^M
overhead frame
poutre^F-châssis^M
engine compartment
moteur^M
counterweight
contrepoids^M
front axle
essieu^M avant
blade
lame^F
drive wheels
roues^F motrices
front wheel
roue^F avant
turntable
cercle^M porte-lame^M
blade rotation cylinder
vérin^M d'orientation^F de la lame^F

dump truck

camion^M-benne^F

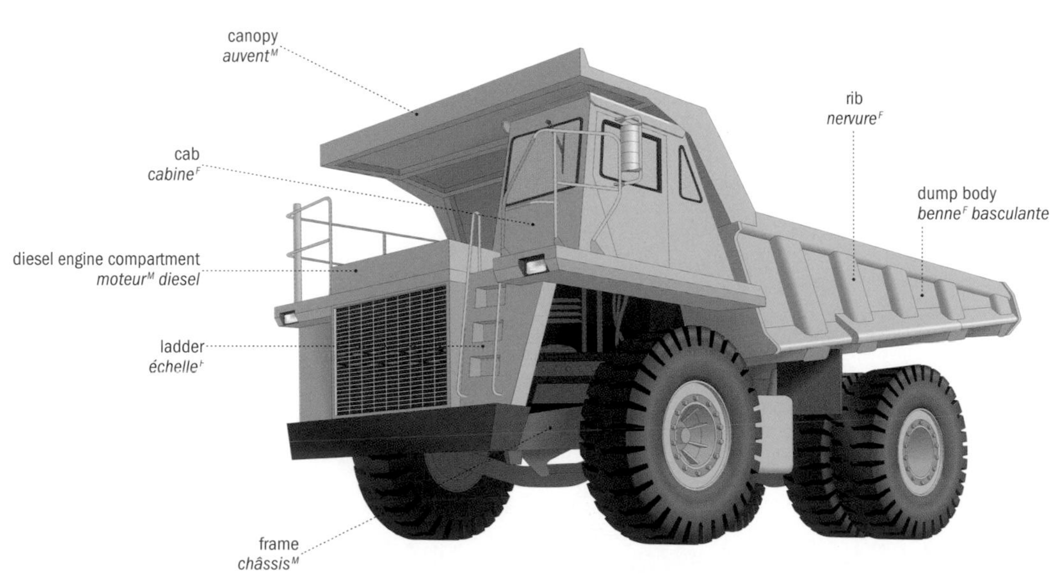
canopy
auvent^M
rib
nervure^F
cab
cabine^F
dump body
benne^F basculante
diesel engine compartment
moteur^M diesel
ladder
échelle^F
frame
châssis^M

production of electricity from geothermal energy

production[F] d'électricité[F] par énergie[F] géothermique

turbine
turbine[F]

generator
alternateur[M]

condenser
condenseur[M]

steam
vapeur[F]

separator
séparateur[M]

high-tension electricity transmission tower
transport[M] de l'électricité[F] à haute tension[F]

transformer (voltage increase)
élévation[F] de la tension[F]

water-steam mix
mélange[M] eau[F]-vapeur[F]

cooling tower
tour[F] de refroidissement[M]

upper confining bed
toit[M] imperméable

water
eau[F]

geothermal field
champ[M] géothermique

lower confining bed
substratum[M] imperméable

production well
puits[M] de production[F]

confined aquifer
aquifère[M] captif

injection well
puits[M] d'injection[F]

magma chamber
réservoir[M] magmatique

thermal energy

énergie[F] thermique

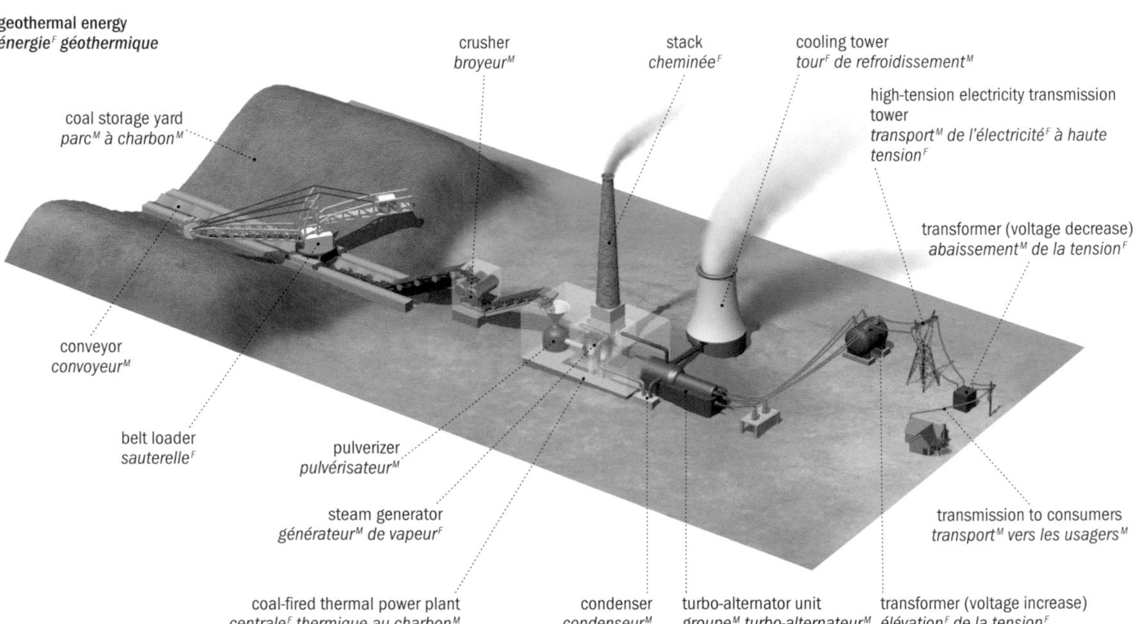
geothermal energy
énergie[F] géothermique
crusher
broyeur[M]
stack
cheminée[F]
cooling tower
tour[F] de refroidissement[M]
coal storage yard
parc[M] à charbon[M]
high-tension electricity transmission tower
transport[M] de l'électricité[F] à haute tension[F]
transformer (voltage decrease)
abaissement[M] de la tension[F]
conveyor
convoyeur[M]
belt loader
sauterelle[F]
pulverizer
pulvérisateur[M]
steam generator
générateur[M] de vapeur[F]
transmission to consumers
transport[M] vers les usagers[M]
coal-fired thermal power plant
centrale[F] thermique au charbon[M]
condenser
condenseur[M]
turbo-alternator unit
groupe[M] turbo-alternateur[M]
transformer (voltage increase)
élévation[F] de la tension[F]

oil

pétrole[M]

surface prospecting
prospection[F] terrestre

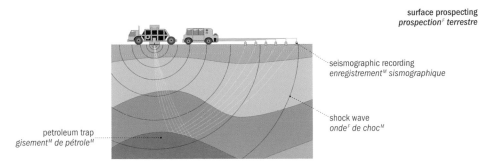

seismographic recording
enregistrement[M] sismographique

shock wave
onde[F] de choc[M]

petroleum trap
gisement[M] de pétrole[M]

drilling rig
appareil[M] de forage[M]

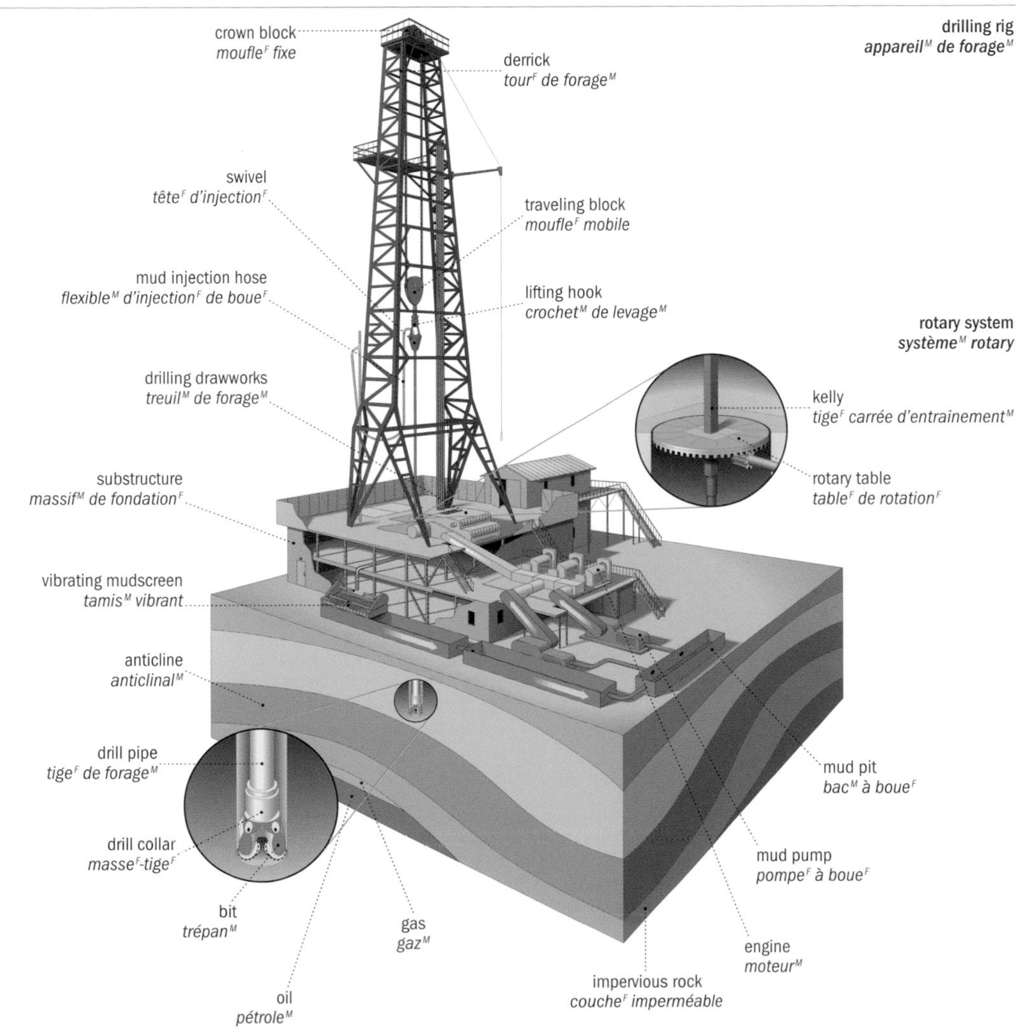
crown block
moufle[F] fixe
derrick
tour[F] de forage[M]
swivel
tête[F] d'injection[F]
traveling block
moufle[F] mobile
mud injection hose
flexible[M] d'injection[F] de boue[F]
lifting hook
crochet[M] de levage[M]
rotary system
système[M] rotary
drilling drawworks
treuil[M] de forage[M]
kelly
tige[F] carrée d'entraînement[M]
substructure
massif[M] de fondation[F]
rotary table
table[F] de rotation[F]
vibrating mudscreen
tamis[M] vibrant
anticline
anticlinal[M]
drill pipe
tige[F] de forage[M]
mud pit
bac[M] à boue[F]
drill collar
masse[F]-tige[F]
mud pump
pompe[F] à boue[F]
bit
trépan[M]
gas
gaz[M]
engine
moteur[M]
impervious rock
couche[F] imperméable
oil
pétrole[M]

floating-roof tank
réservoir^M à toit^M flottant

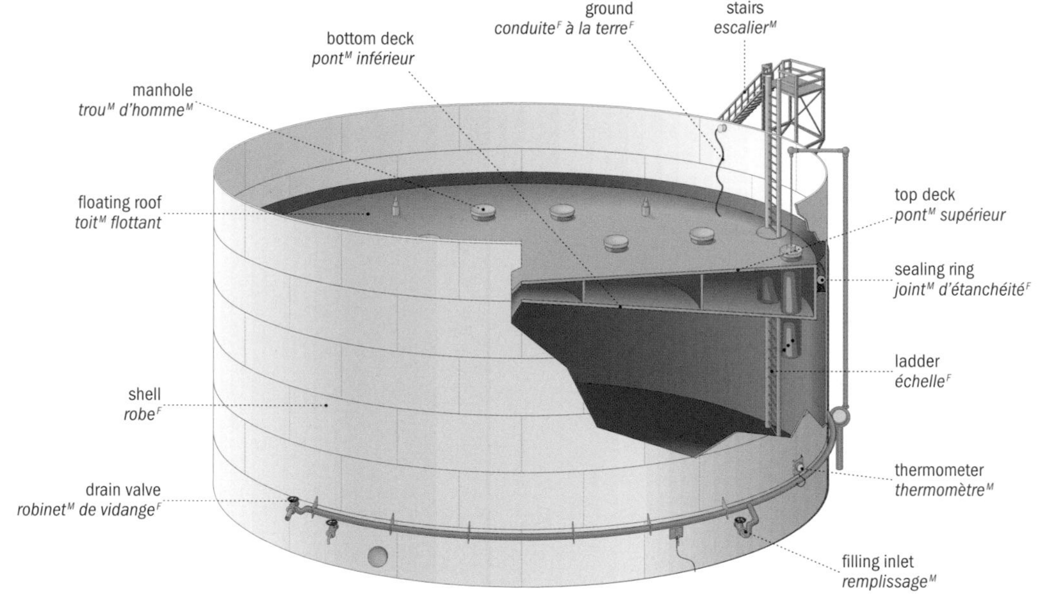
ground
conduite^F à la terre^F
stairs
escalier^M
bottom deck
pont^M inférieur
manhole
trou^M d'homme^M
floating roof
toit^M flottant
top deck
pont^M supérieur
sealing ring
joint^M d'étanchéité^F
ladder
échelle^F
shell
robe^F
thermometer
thermomètre^M
drain valve
robinet^M de vidange^F
filling inlet
remplissage^M

crude-oil pipeline
réseau^M d'oléoducs^M

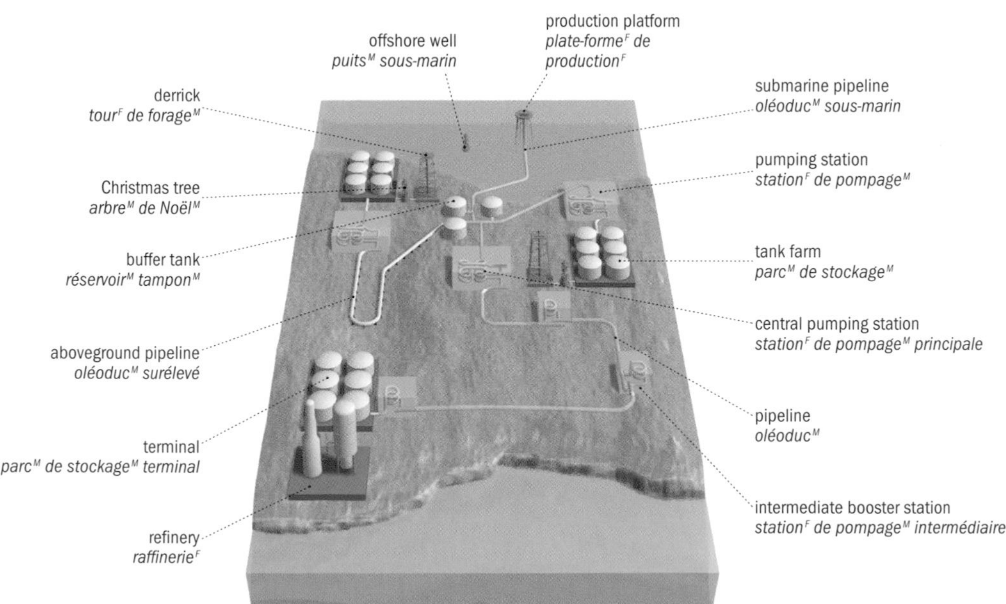
production platform
plate-forme^F de
production^F
offshore well
puits^M sous-marin
derrick
tour^F de forage^M
submarine pipeline
oléoduc^M sous-marin
pumping station
station^F de pompage^M
Christmas tree
arbre^M de Noël^M
buffer tank
réservoir^M tampon^M
tank farm
parc^M de stockage^M
central pumping station
station^F de pompage^M principale
aboveground pipeline
oléoduc^M surélevé
pipeline
oléoduc^M
terminal
parc^M de stockage^M terminal
intermediate booster station
station^F de pompage^M intermédiaire
refinery
raffinerie^F

refinery products
produits[M] de la raffinerie[F]

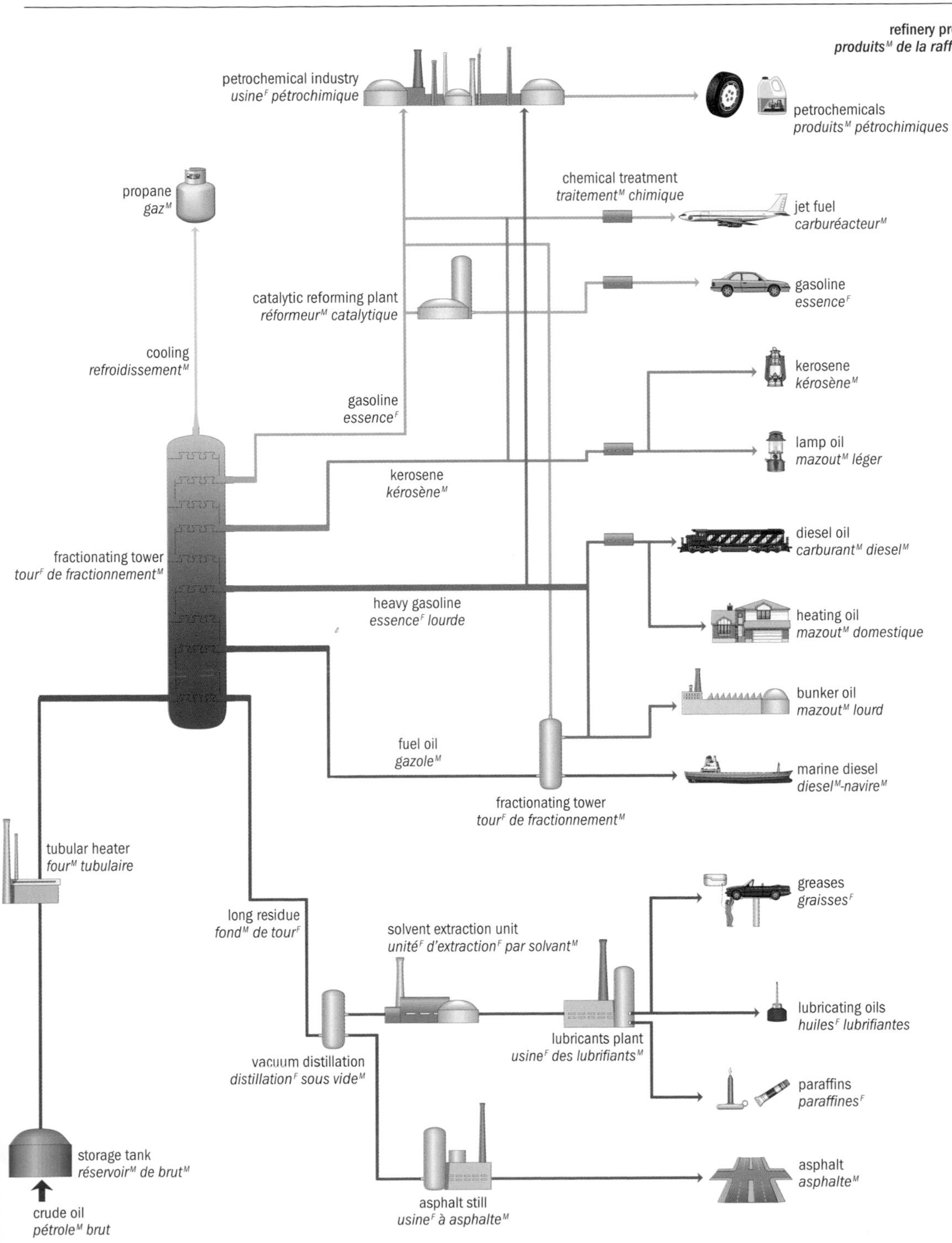
petrochemical industry
usine[F] pétrochimique
petrochemicals
produits[M] pétrochimiques
propane
gaz[M]
chemical treatment
traitement[M] chimique
jet fuel
carburéacteur[M]
catalytic reforming plant
réformeur[M] catalytique
gasoline
essence[F]
cooling
refroidissement[M]
kerosene
kérosène[M]
gasoline
essence[F]
lamp oil
mazout[M] léger
kerosene
kérosène[M]
diesel oil
carburant[M] diesel[M]
fractionating tower
tour[F] de fractionnement[M]
heavy gasoline
essence[F] lourde
heating oil
mazout[M] domestique
bunker oil
mazout[M] lourd
fuel oil
gazole[M]
marine diesel
diesel[M]-navire[M]
fractionating tower
tour[F] de fractionnement[M]
tubular heater
four[M] tubulaire
greases
graisses[F]
long residue
fond[M] de tour[F]
solvent extraction unit
unité[F] d'extraction[F] par solvant[M]
lubricating oils
huiles[F] lubrifiantes
lubricants plant
usine[F] des lubrifiants[M]
vacuum distillation
distillation[F] sous vide[M]
paraffins
paraffines[F]
storage tank
réservoir[M] de brut[M]
asphalt
asphalte[M]
crude oil
pétrole[M] brut
asphalt still
usine[F] à asphalte[M]

hydroelectric complex

complexe[M] hydroélectrique

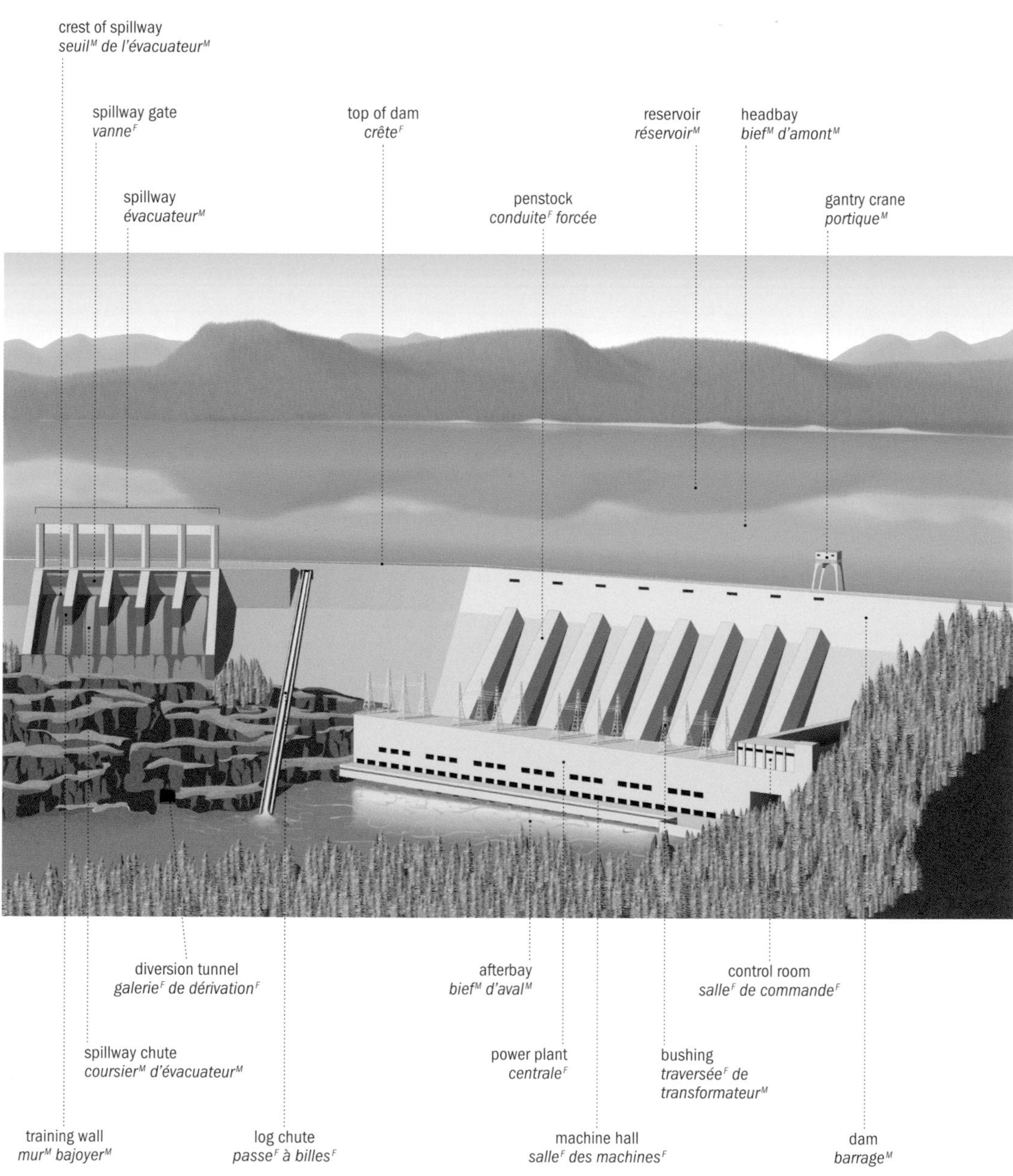
crest of spillway
seuil[M] de l'évacuateur[M]
spillway gate
vanne[F]
spillway
évacuateur[M]
top of dam
crête[F]
penstock
conduite[F] forcée
reservoir
réservoir[M]
headbay
bief[M] d'amont[M]
gantry crane
portique[M]
diversion tunnel
galerie[F] de dérivation[F]
afterbay
bief[M] d'aval[M]
control room
salle[F] de commande[F]
spillway chute
coursier[M] d'évacuateur[M]
power plant
centrale[F]
bushing
traversée[F] de transformateur[M]
training wall
mur[M] bajoyer[M]
log chute
passe[F] à billes[F]
machine hall
salle[F] des machines[F]
dam
barrage[M]

cross section of a hydroelectric power plant
coupe*[F] *d'une centrale*[F] *hydroélectrique

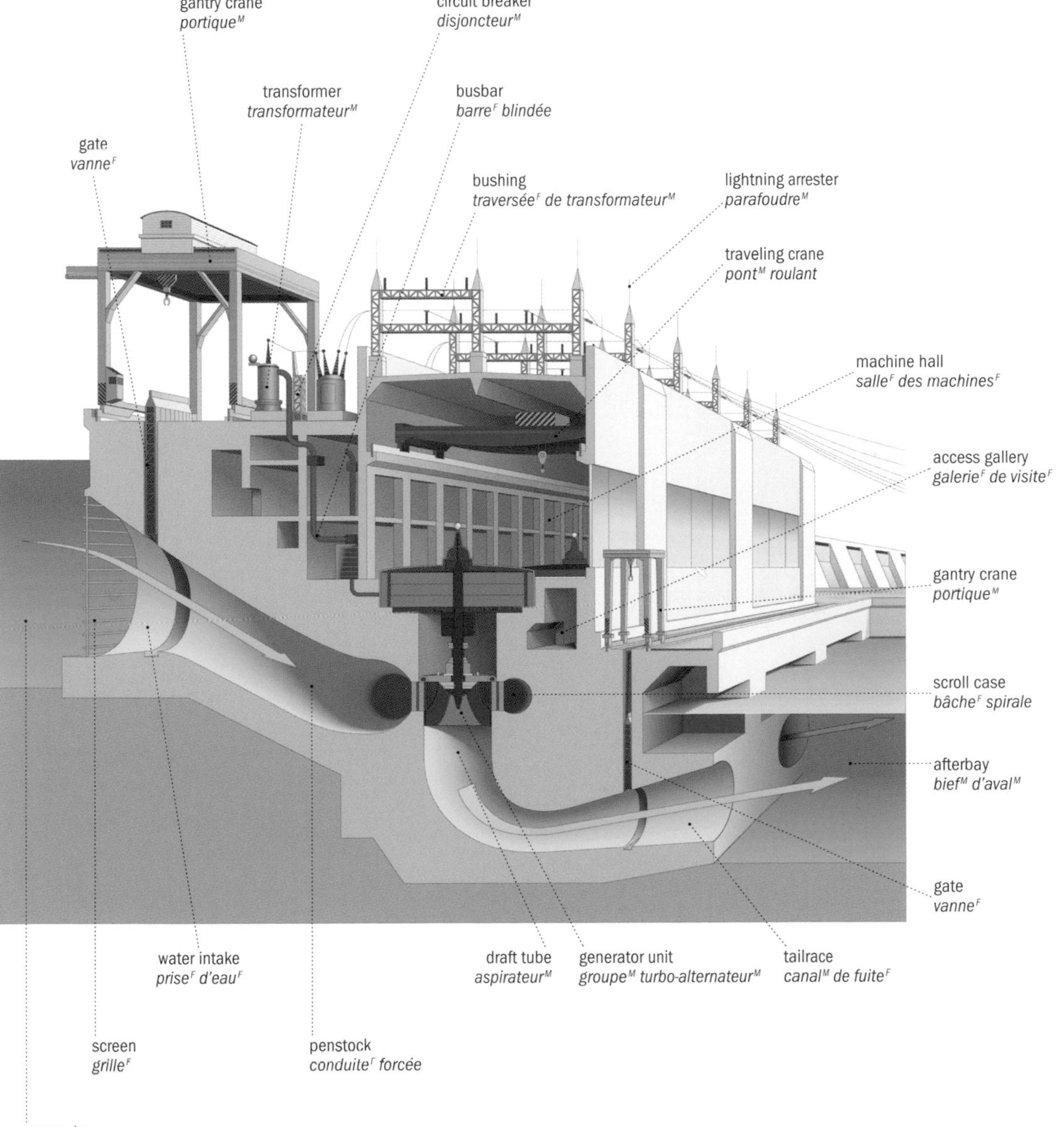
gantry crane
portique[M]
circuit breaker
disjoncteur[M]
transformer
transformateur[M]
busbar
barre[F] blindée
gate
vanne[F]
bushing
traversée[F] de transformateur[M]
lightning arrester
parafoudre[M]
traveling crane
pont[M] roulant
machine hall
salle[F] des machines[F]
access gallery
galerie[F] de visite[F]
gantry crane
portique[M]
scroll case
bâche[F] spirale
afterbay
bief[M] d'aval[M]
gate
vanne[F]
water intake
prise[F] d'eau[F]
draft tube
aspirateur[M]
generator unit
groupe[M] turbo-alternateur[M]
tailrace
canal[M] de fuite[F]
screen
grille[F]
penstock
conduite[F] forcée
reservoir
réservoir[M]

production of electricity from nuclear energy

production[F] d'électricité[F] par énergie[F] nucléaire

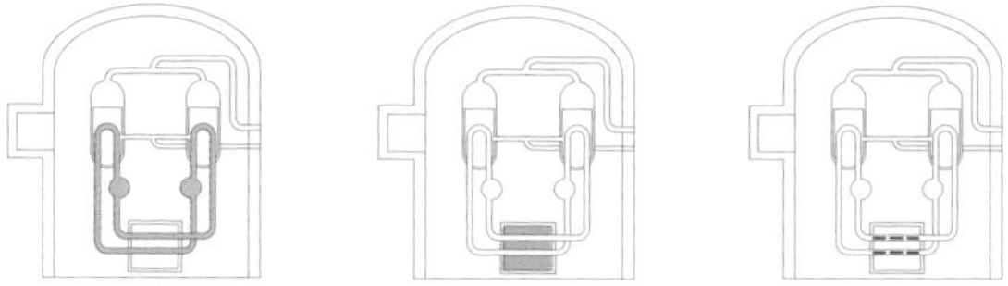

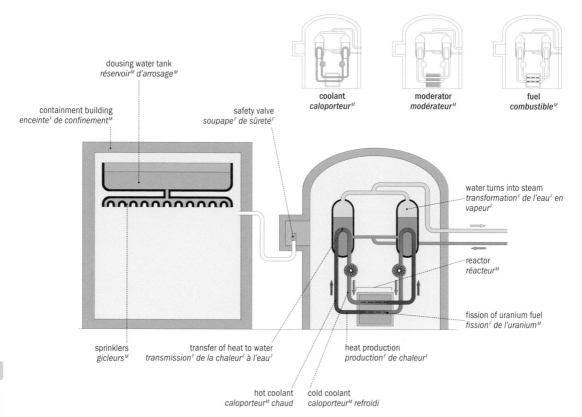

coolant
caloporteur[M]

moderator
modérateur[M]

fuel
combustible[M]

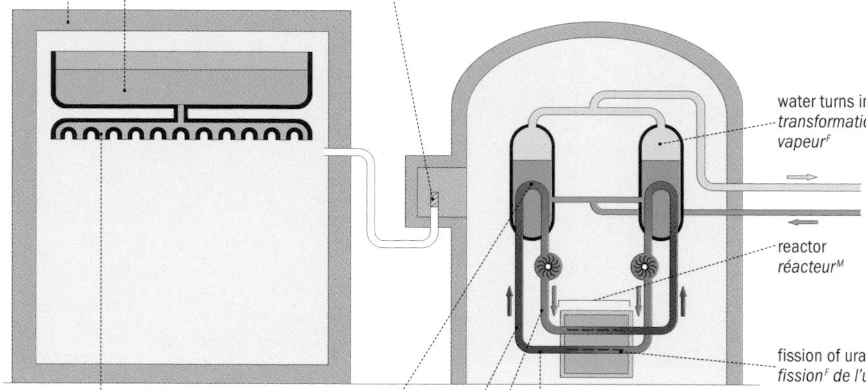

dousing water tank
réservoir[M] d'arrosage[M]

containment building
enceinte[F] de confinement[M]

safety valve
soupape[F] de sûreté[F]

water turns into steam
transformation[F] de l'eau[F] en vapeur[F]

reactor
réacteur[M]

fission of uranium fuel
fission[F] de l'uranium[M]

sprinklers
gicleurs[M]

transfer of heat to water
transmission[F] de la chaleur[F] à l'eau[F]

heat production
production[F] de chaleur[F]

hot coolant
caloporteur[M] chaud

cold coolant
caloporteur[M] refroidi

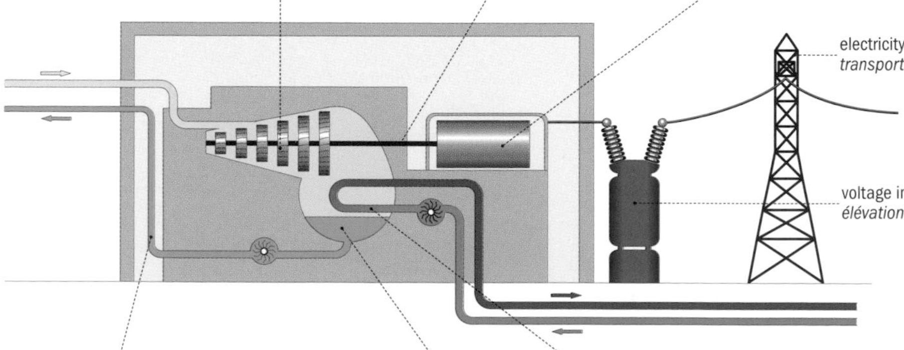

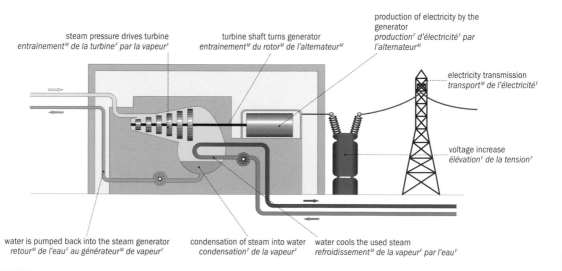

steam pressure drives turbine
entraînement[M] de la turbine[F] par la vapeur[F]

turbine shaft turns generator
entraînement[M] du rotor[M] de l'alternateur[M]

production of electricity by the generator
production[F] d'électricité[F] par l'alternateur[M]

electricity transmission
transport[M] de l'électricité[F]

voltage increase
élévation[F] de la tension[F]

water is pumped back into the steam generator
retour[M] de l'eau[F] au générateur[M] de vapeur[F]

condensation of steam into water
condensation[F] de la vapeur[F]

water cools the used steam
refroidissement[M] de la vapeur[F] par l'eau[F]

fuel bundle

grappe^F de combustible^M

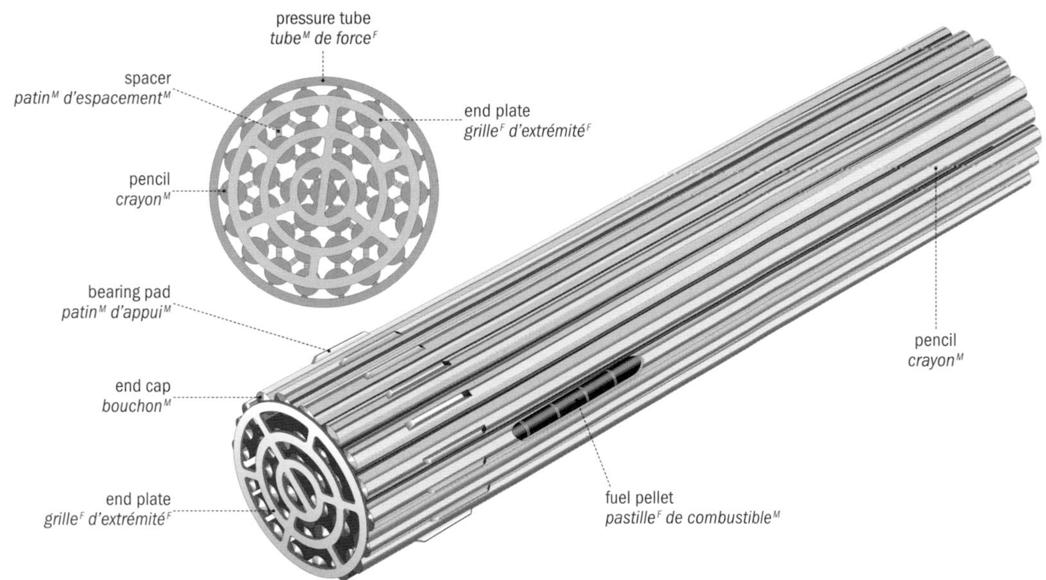
pressure tube
tube^M de force^F
spacer
patin^M d'espacement^M
end plate
grille^F d'extrémité^F
pencil
crayon^M
bearing pad
patin^M d'appui^M
pencil
crayon^M
end cap
bouchon^M
end plate
grille^F d'extrémité^F
fuel pellet
pastille^F de combustible^M

nuclear reactor

réacteur^M nucléaire

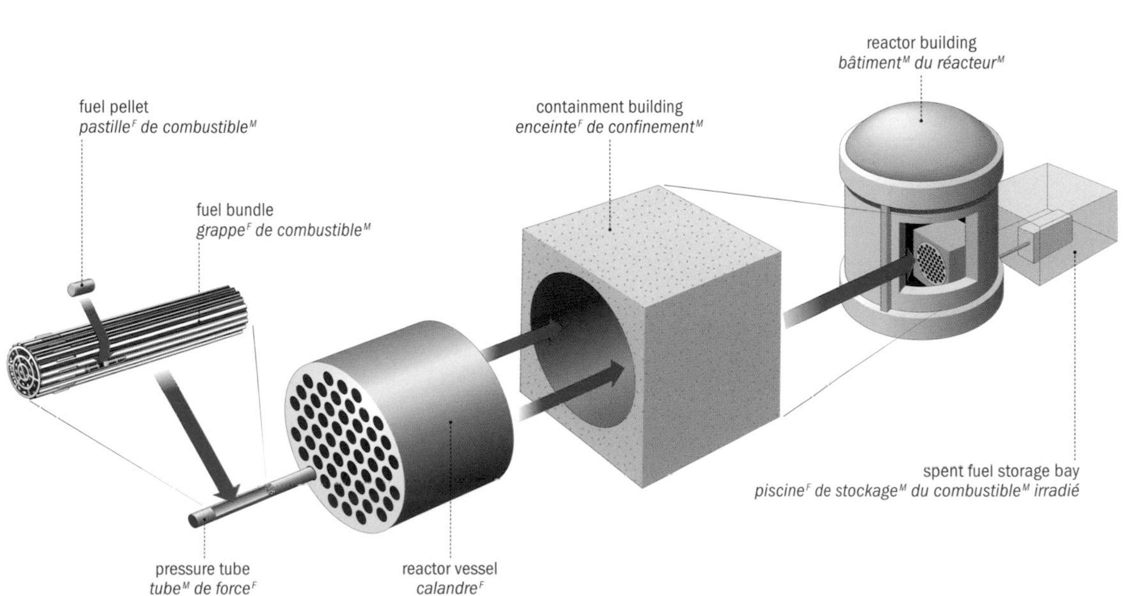
reactor building
bâtiment^M du réacteur^M
fuel pellet
pastille^F de combustible^M
containment building
enceinte^F de confinement^M
fuel bundle
grappe^F de combustible^M
spent fuel storage bay
piscine^F de stockage^M du combustible^M irradié
pressure tube
tube^M de force^F
reactor vessel
calandre^F

solar cell

photopile[F]

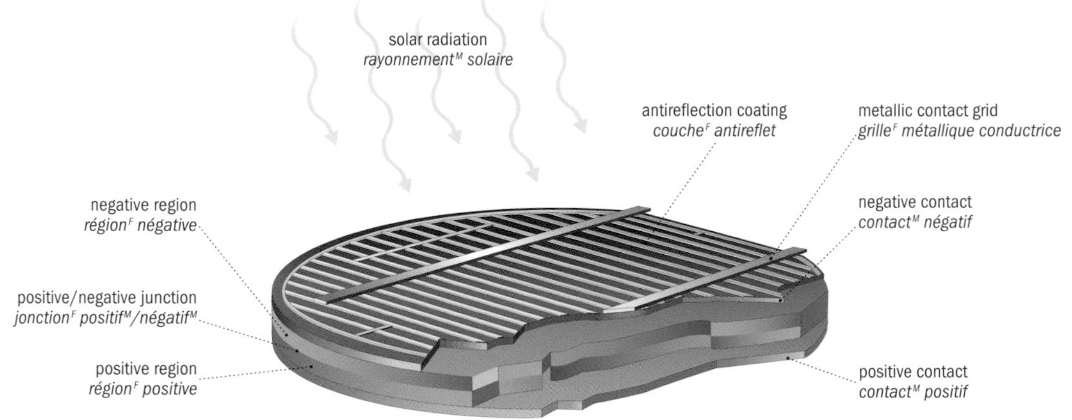
solar radiation
rayonnement[M] solaire
antireflection coating
couche[F] antireflet
metallic contact grid
grille[F] métallique conductrice
negative region
région[F] négative
negative contact
contact[M] négatif
positive/negative junction
jonction[F] positif[M]/négatif[M]
positive region
région[F] positive
positive contact
contact[M] positif

flat-plate solar collector

capteur[M] solaire plan

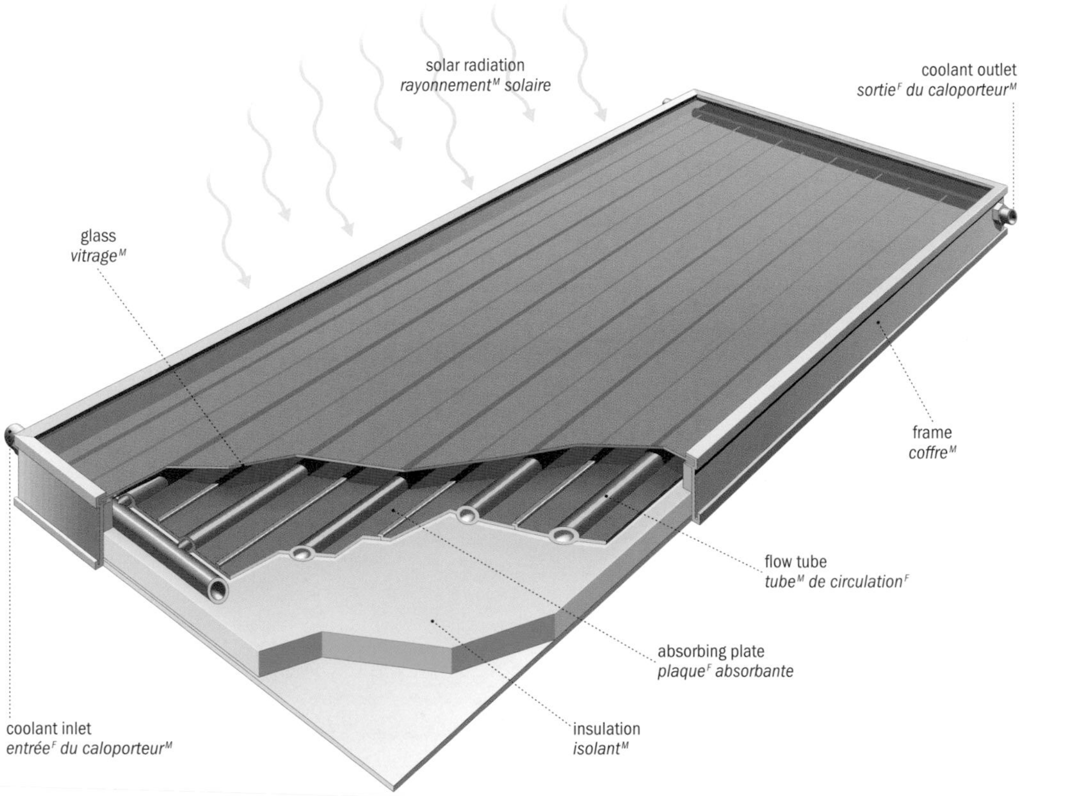

solar radiation
rayonnement[M] solaire

coolant outlet
sortie[F] du caloporteur[M]

glass
vitrage[M]

frame
coffre[M]

flow tube
tube[M] de circulation[F]

absorbing plate
plaque[F] absorbante

coolant inlet
entrée[F] du caloporteur[M]

insulation
isolant[M]

ENERGY

solar-cell system

circuit[M] de photopiles[F]

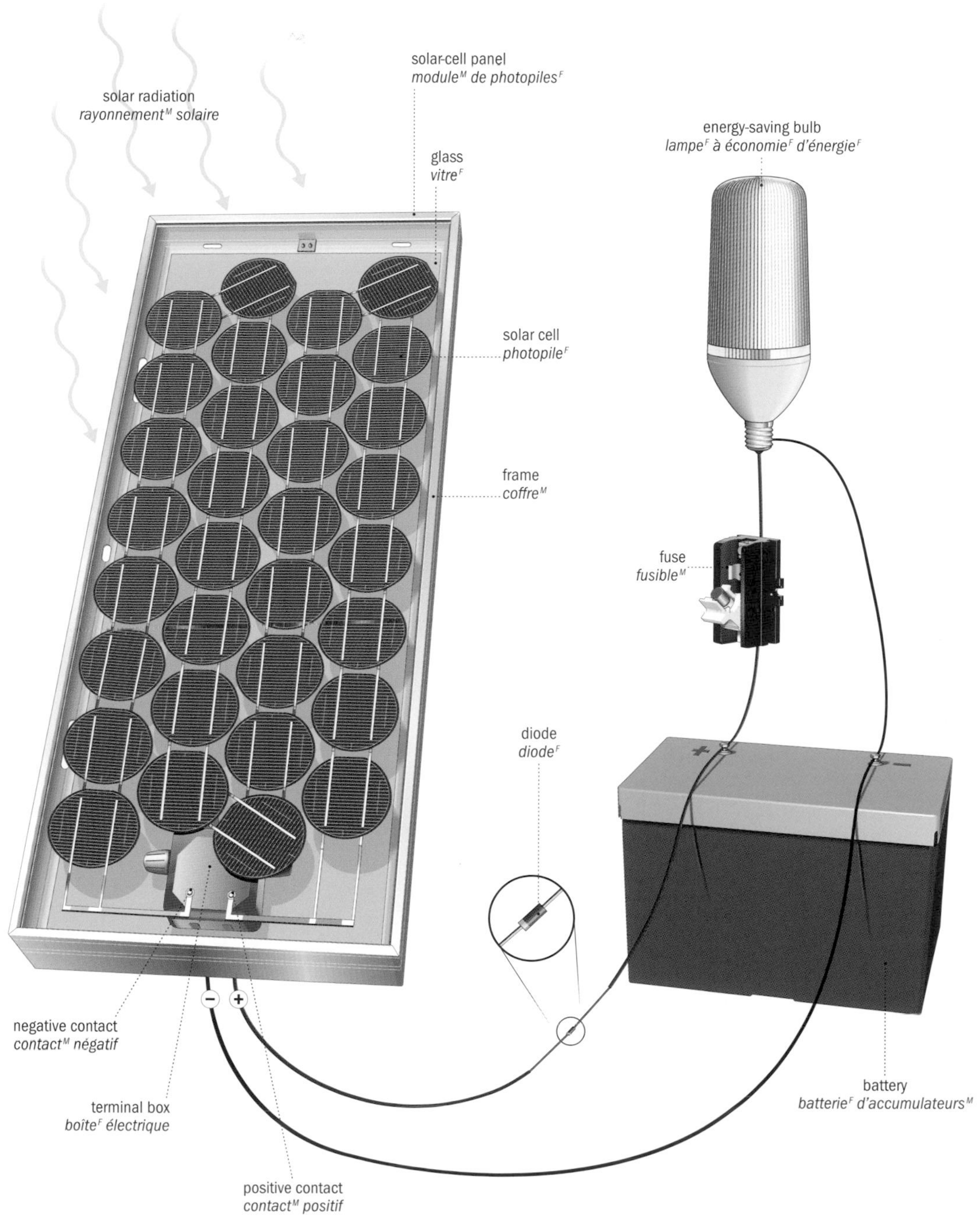
solar radiation
rayonnement[M] solaire
solar-cell panel
module[M] de photopiles[F]
glass
vitre[F]
energy-saving bulb
lampe[F] à économie[F] d'énergie[F]
solar cell
photopile[F]
frame
coffre[M]
fuse
fusible[M]
diode
diode[F]
negative contact
contact[M] négatif
terminal box
boîte[F] électrique
positive contact
contact[M] positif
battery
batterie[F] d'accumulateurs[M]

windmill

moulin^M à vent^M

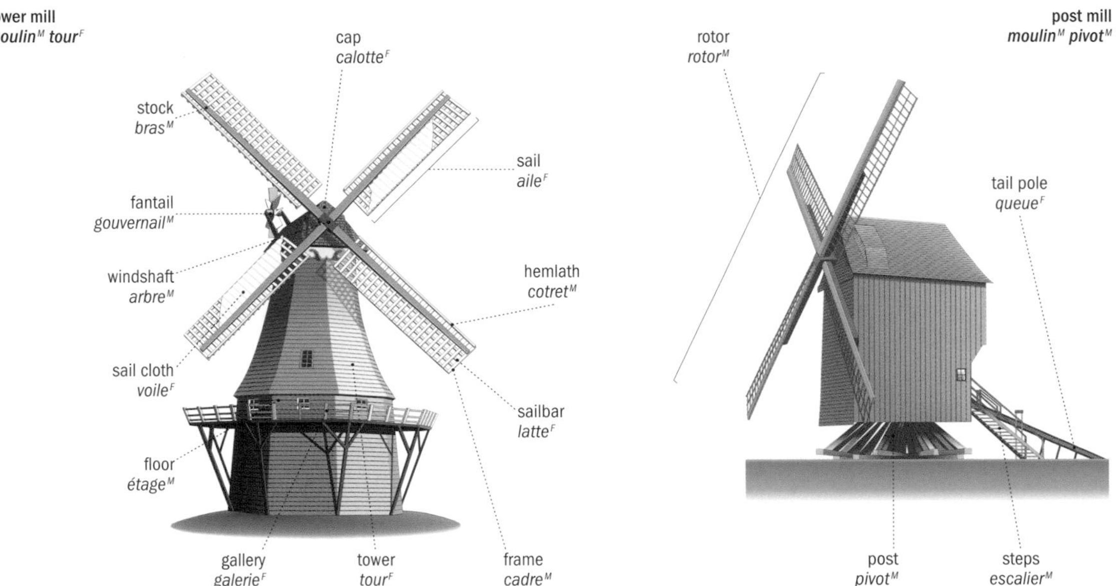
tower mill
moulin^M tour^F
cap
calotte^F
stock
bras^M
sail
aile^F
fantail
gouvernail^M
windshaft
arbre^M
hemlath
cotret^M
sail cloth
voile^F
sailbar
latte^F
floor
étage^M
gallery
galerie^F
tower
tour^F
frame
cadre^M
rotor
rotor^M
post mill
moulin^M pivot^M
tail pole
queue^F
post
pivot^M
steps
escalier^M

wind turbines and electricity production

éoliennes^F et production^F d'électricité^F

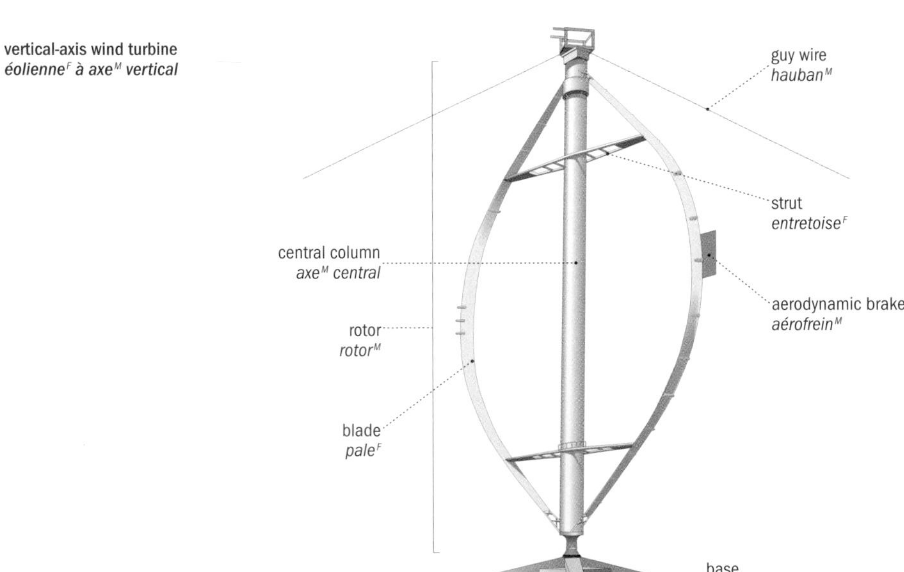
vertical-axis wind turbine
éolienne^F à axe^M vertical
guy wire
hauban^M
strut
entretoise^F
central column
axe^M central
aerodynamic brake
aérofrein^M
rotor
rotor^M
blade
pale^F
base
socle^M

ENERGY

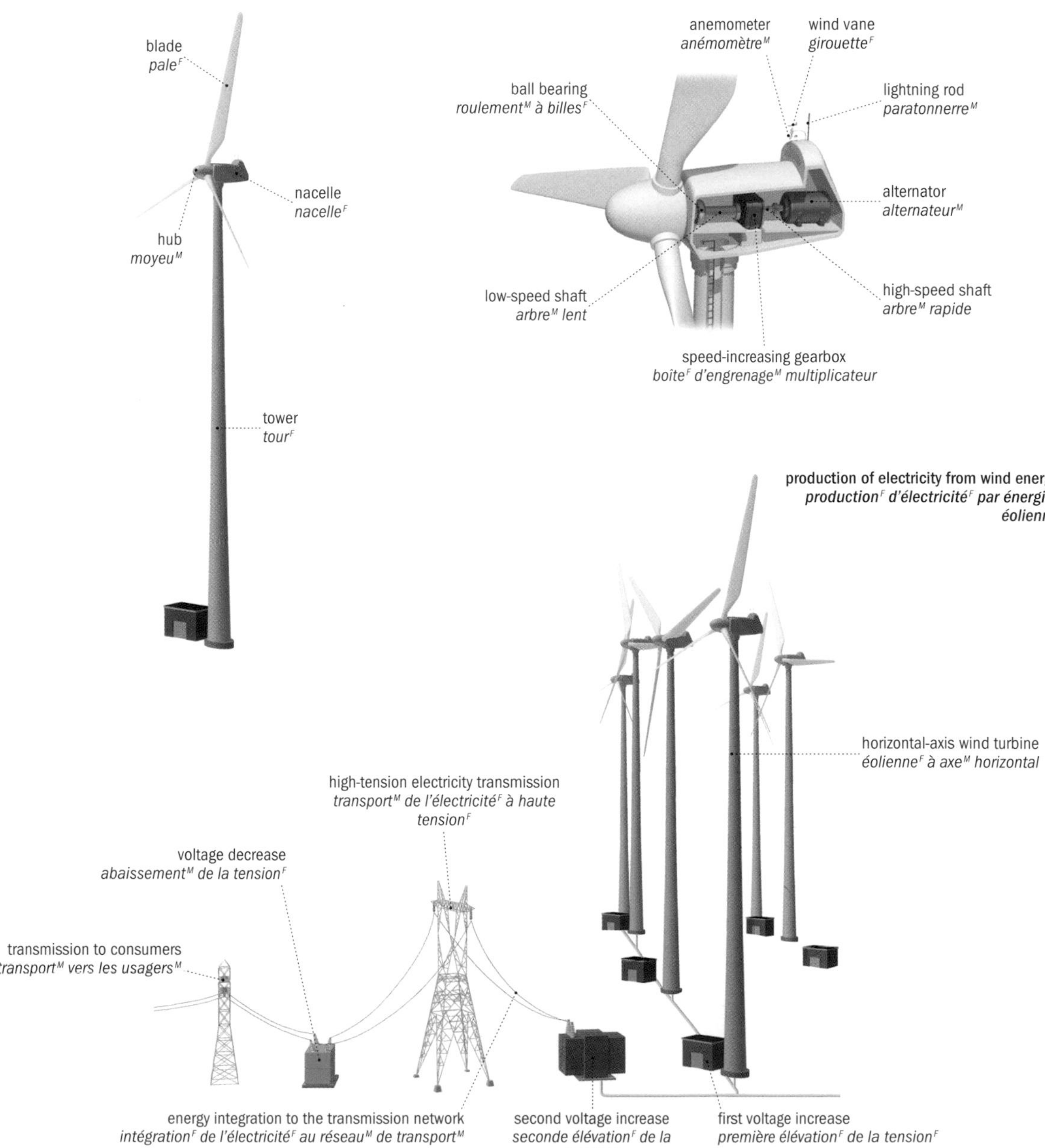
horizontal-axis wind turbine
éolienneF à axeM horizontal
blade
paleF
nacelle
nacelleF
hub
moyeuM
tower
tourF
nacelle cross-section
coupeF de la nacelleF
anemometer
anémomètreM
wind vane
girouetteF
ball bearing
roulementM à billesF
lightning rod
paratonnerreM
alternator
alternateurM
low-speed shaft
arbreM lent
high-speed shaft
arbreM rapide
speed-increasing gearbox
boiteF d'engrenageM multiplicateur
production of electricity from wind energy
productionF d'électricitéF par énergieF éolienne
horizontal-axis wind turbine
éolienneF à axeM horizontal
high-tension electricity transmission
transportM de l'électricitéF à haute tensionF
voltage decrease
abaissementM de la tensionF
transmission to consumers
transportM vers les usagersM
energy integration to the transmission network
intégrationF de l'électricitéF au réseauM de transportM
second voltage increase
seconde élévationF de la tensionF
first voltage increase
première élévationF de la tensionF

matter

matière[F]

atom
atome[M]

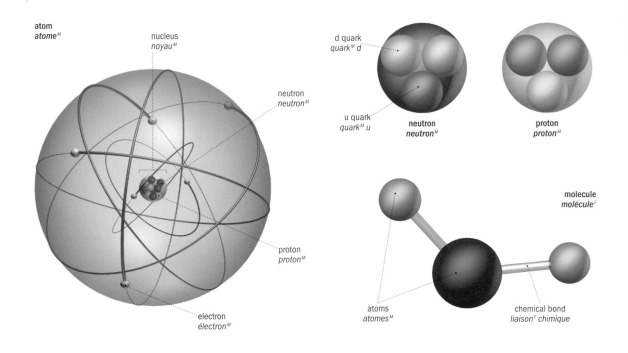

nucleus
noyau[M]

neutron
neutron[M]

proton
proton[M]

electron
électron[M]

d quark
quark[M] *d*

u quark
quark[M] *u*

neutron
neutron[M]

proton
proton[M]

molecule
molécule[F]

atoms
atomes[M]

chemical bond
liaison[F] *chimique*

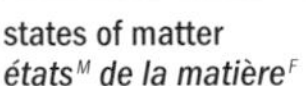

states of matter
états[M] ***de la matière***[F]

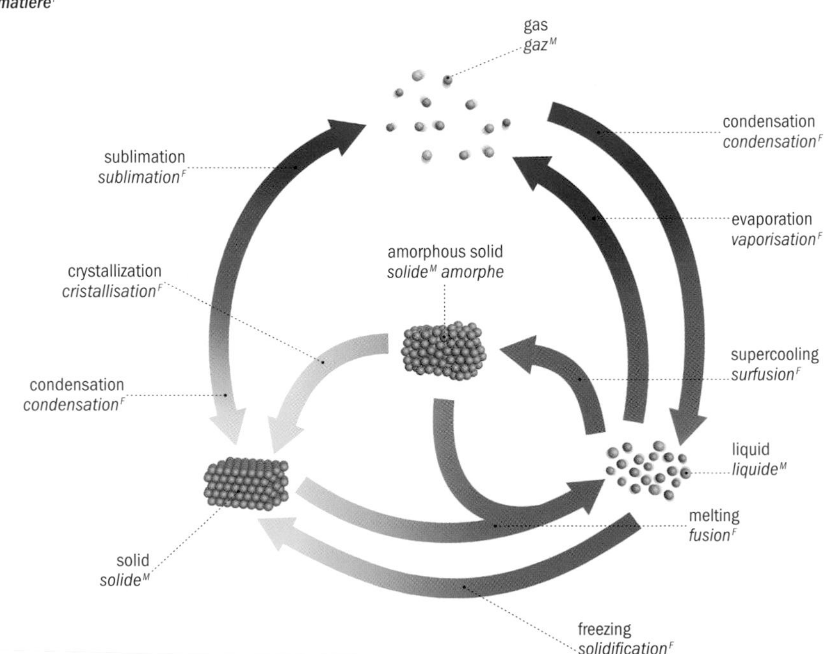
gas
gazM
condensation
condensationF
sublimation
sublimationF
evaporation
vaporisationF
amorphous solid
solideM amorphe
crystallization
cristallisationF
supercooling
surfusionF
condensation
condensationF
liquid
liquideM
melting
fusionF
solid
solideM
freezing
solidificationF

SCIENCE

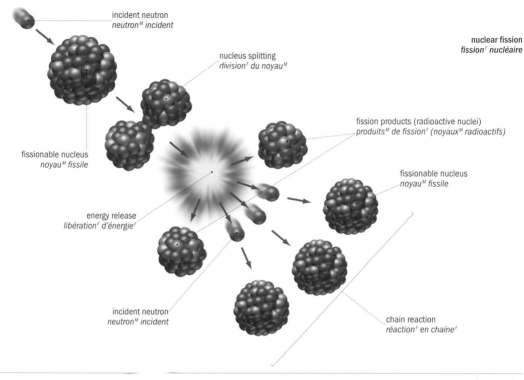

nuclear fission
fission[F] nucléaire

incident neutron
neutron[M] incident

nucleus splitting
division[F] du noyau[M]

fission products (radioactive nuclei)
produits[M] de fission[F] (noyaux[M] radioactifs)

fissionable nucleus
noyau[M] fissile

fissionable nucleus
noyau[M] fissile

energy release
libération[F] d'énergie[F]

incident neutron
neutron[M] incident

chain reaction
réaction[F] en chaîne[F]

heat transfer
transfert[M] de la chaleur[F]

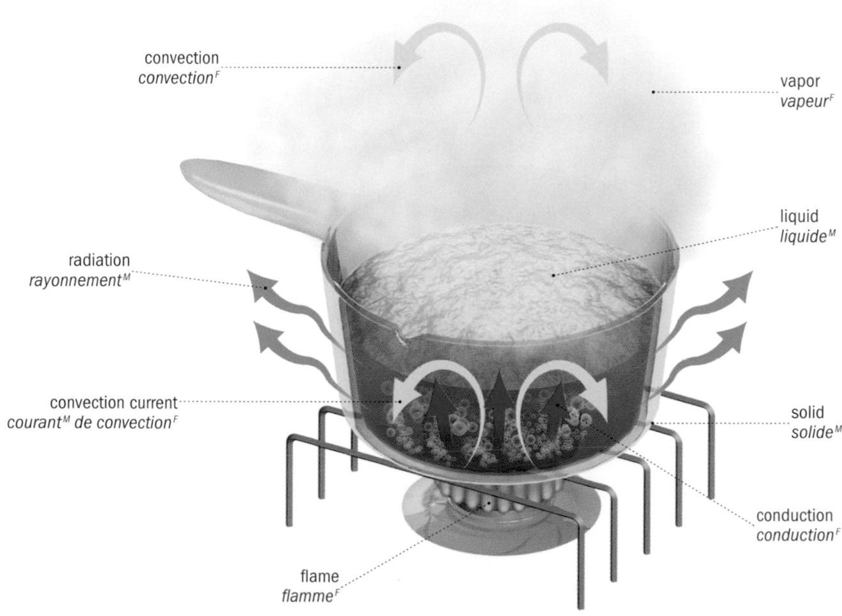
convection
convection[F]
vapor
vapeur[F]
liquid
liquide[M]
radiation
rayonnement[M]
convection current
courant[M] de convection[F]
solid
solide[M]
conduction
conduction[F]
flame
flamme[F]

magnetism

magnétisme^{M}

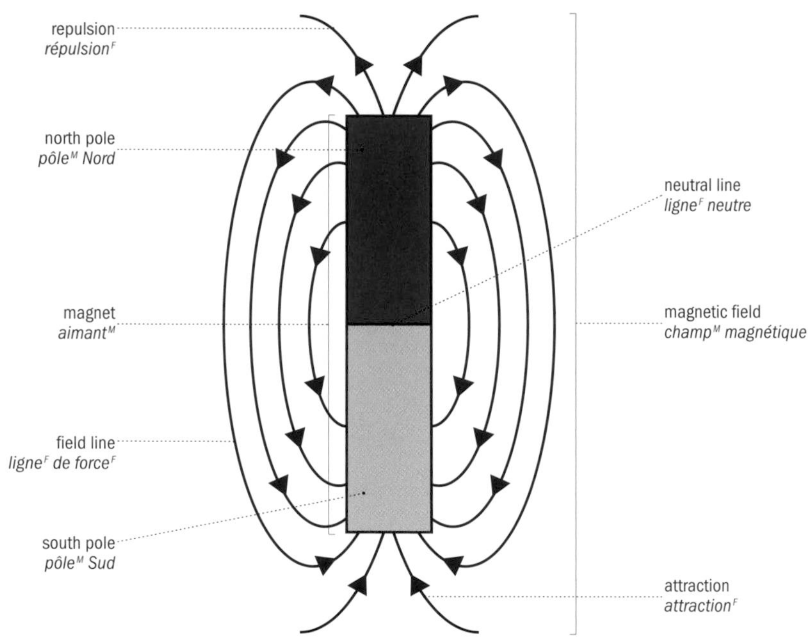
repulsion
répulsion^{F}
north pole
pôle^{M} Nord
magnet
aimant^{M}
field line
ligne^{F} de force^{F}
south pole
pôle^{M} Sud
neutral line
ligne^{F} neutre
magnetic field
champ^{M} magnétique
attraction
attraction^{F}

parallel electrical circuit

circuit^{M} électrique en parallèle^{F}

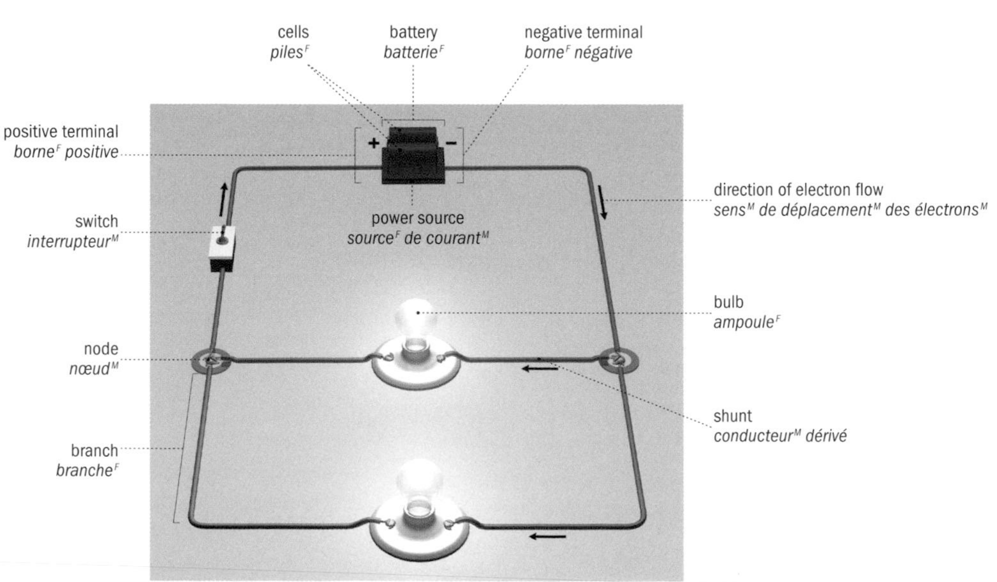
cells
piles^{F}
battery
batterie^{F}
negative terminal
borne^{F} négative
positive terminal
borne^{F} positive
+
–
switch
interrupteur^{M}
power source
source^{F} de courant^{M}
direction of electron flow
sens^{M} de déplacement^{M} des électrons^{M}
bulb
ampoule^{F}
node
nœud^{M}
shunt
conducteur^{M} dérivé
branch
branche^{F}

dry cells

piles[F] sèches

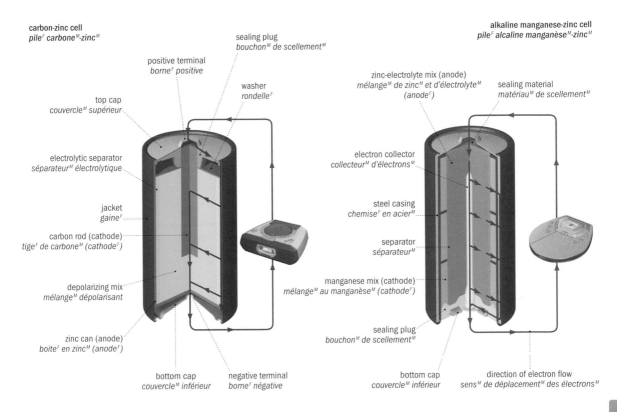

carbon-zinc cell
pile[F] carbone[M]-zinc[M]

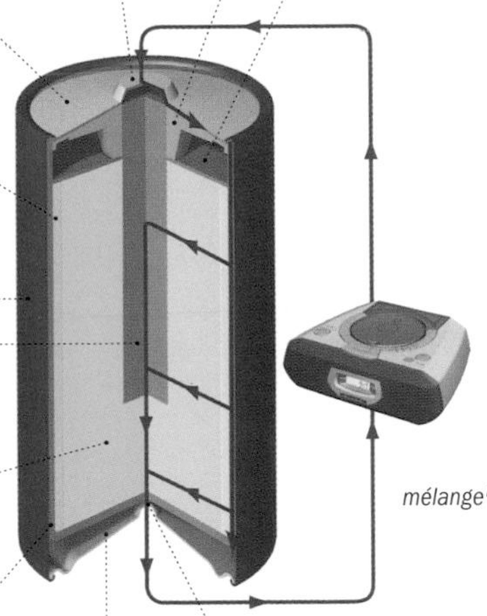

sealing plug
bouchon[M] de scellement[M]

positive terminal
borne[F] positive

washer
rondelle[F]

top cap
couvercle[M] supérieur

electrolytic separator
séparateur[M] électrolytique

jacket
gaine[F]

carbon rod (cathode)
tige[F] de carbone[M] (cathode[F])

depolarizing mix
mélange[M] dépolarisant

zinc can (anode)
boîte[F] en zinc[M] (anode[F])

bottom cap
couvercle[M] inférieur

negative terminal
borne[F] négative

alkaline manganese-zinc cell
pile[F] alcaline manganèse[M]-zinc[M]

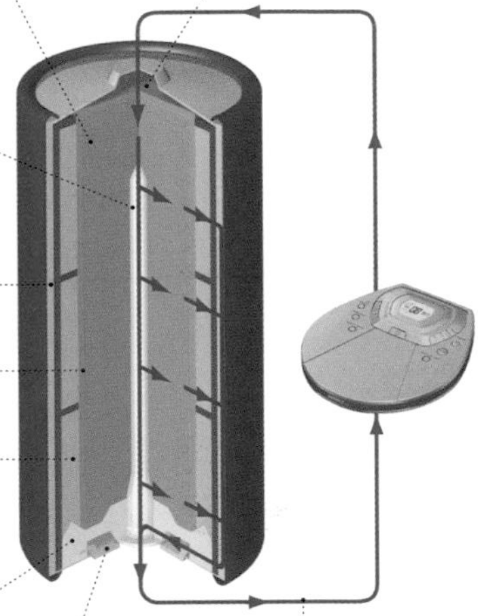

zinc-electrolyte mix (anode)
mélange[M] de zinc[M] et d'électrolyte[M] (anode[F])

sealing material
matériau[M] de scellement[M]

electron collector
collecteur[M] d'électrons[M]

steel casing
chemise[F] en acier[M]

separator
séparateur[M]

manganese mix (cathode)
mélange[M] au manganèse[M] (cathode[F])

sealing plug
bouchon[M] de scellement[M]

bottom cap
couvercle[M] inférieur

direction of electron flow
sens[M] de déplacement[M] des électrons[M]

electronics

électronique[F]

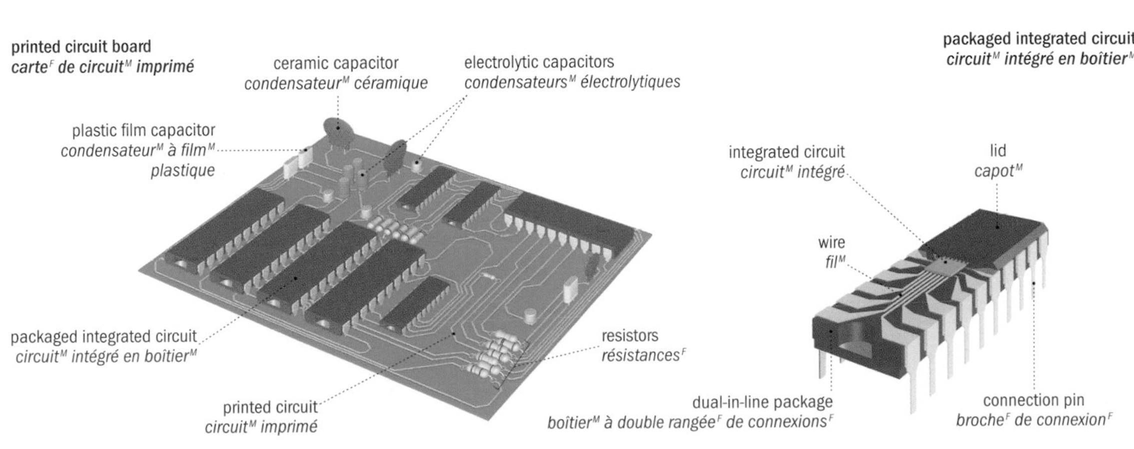
printed circuit board
carte[F] de circuit[M] imprimé
ceramic capacitor
condensateur[M] céramique
electrolytic capacitors
condensateurs[M] électrolytiques
plastic film capacitor
condensateur[M] à film[M] plastique
packaged integrated circuit
circuit[M] intégré en boîtier[M]
printed circuit
circuit[M] imprimé
resistors
résistances[F]
packaged integrated circuit
circuit[M] intégré en boîtier[M]
integrated circuit
circuit[M] intégré
lid
capot[M]
wire
fil[M]
dual-in-line package
boîtier[M] à double rangée[F] de connexions[F]
connection pin
broche[F] de connexion[F]

electromagnetic spectrum

spectre^M électromagnétique

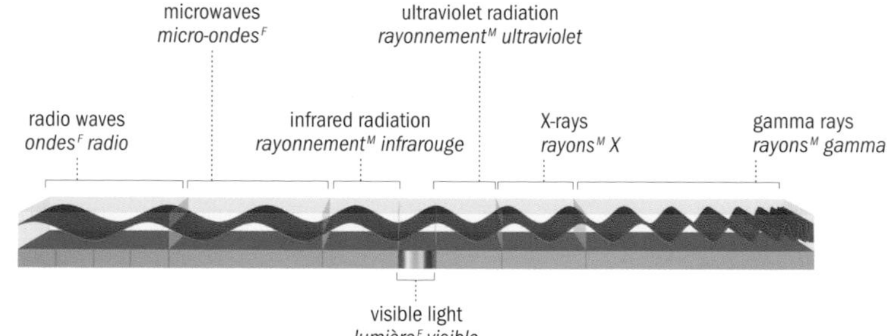
microwaves
micro-ondes^F
ultraviolet radiation
rayonnement^M ultraviolet
radio waves
ondes^F radio
infrared radiation
rayonnement^M infrarouge
X-rays
rayons^M X
gamma rays
rayons^M gamma
visible light
lumière^F visible

wave

onde^F

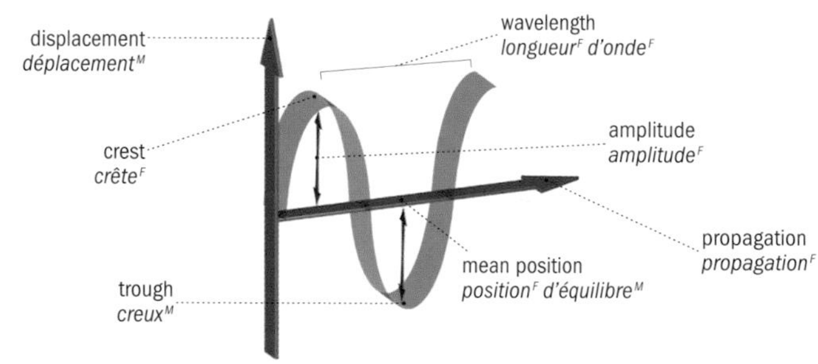
displacement
déplacement^M
wavelength
longueur^F d'onde^F
crest
crête^F
amplitude
amplitude^F
propagation
propagation^F
mean position
position^F d'équilibre^M
trough
creux^M

color synthesis

synthèse^F des couleurs^F

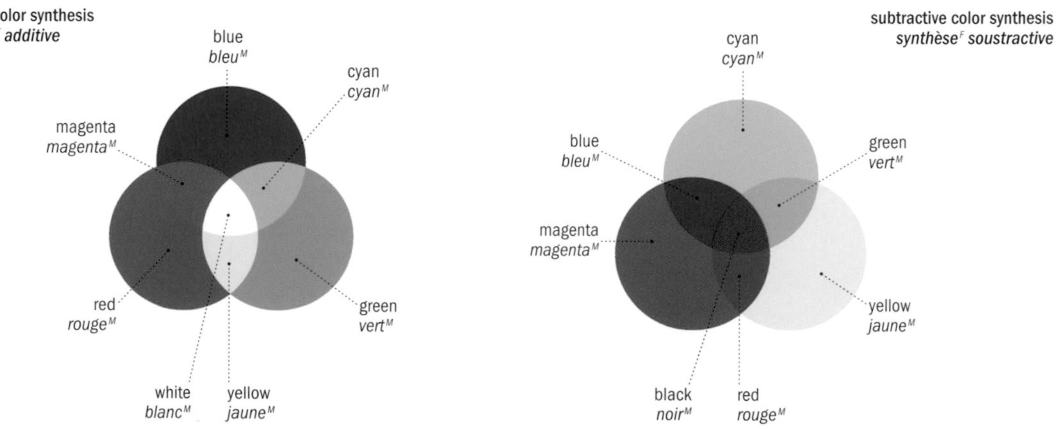
additive color synthesis
synthèse^F additive
blue
bleu^M
cyan
cyan^M
magenta
magenta^M
red
rouge^M
green
vert^M
white
blanc^M
yellow
jaune^M
subtractive color synthesis
synthèse^F soustractive
cyan
cyan^M
blue
bleu^M
green
vert^M
magenta
magenta^M
yellow
jaune^M
black
noir^M
red
rouge^M

vision

vision[F]

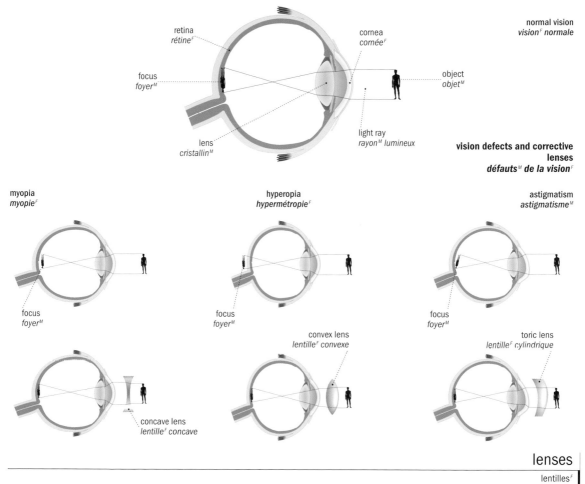

normal vision
vision[F] normale

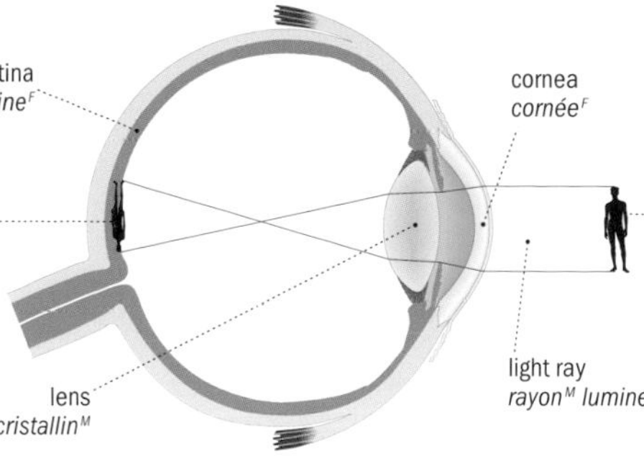

retina
rétine[F]

cornea
cornée[F]

focus
foyer[M]

object
objet[M]

light ray
rayon[M] lumineux

lens
cristallin[M]

vision defects and corrective lenses
défauts[M] de la vision[F]

myopia
myopie[F]

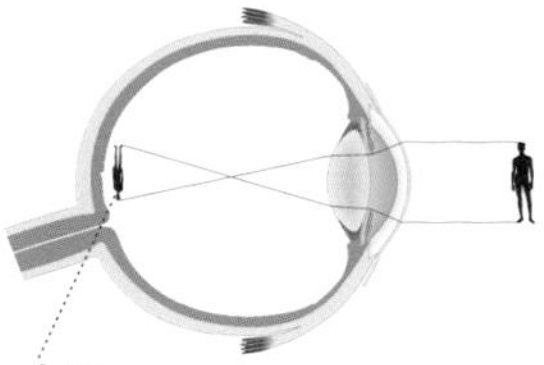

focus
foyer[M]

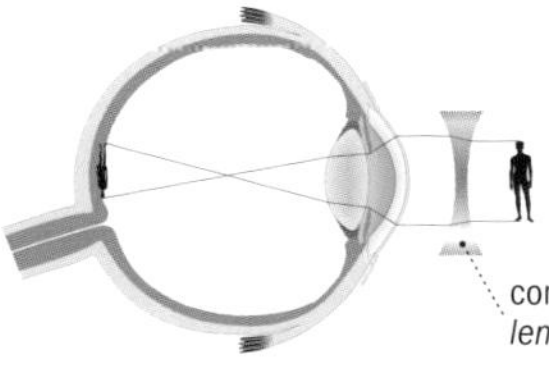

concave lens
lentille[F] concave

hyperopia
hypermétropie[F]

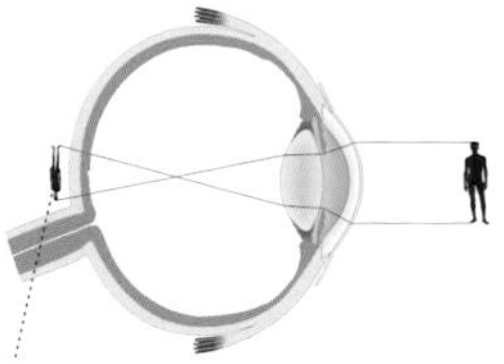

focus
foyer[M]

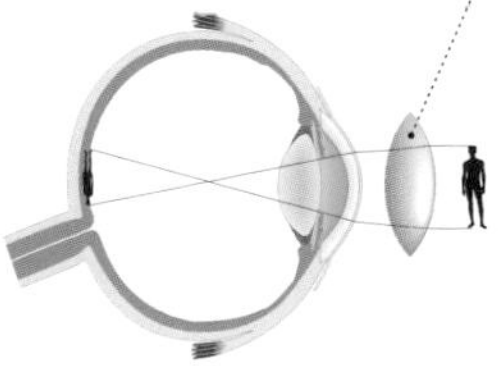

convex lens
lentille[F] convexe

astigmatism
astigmatisme[M]

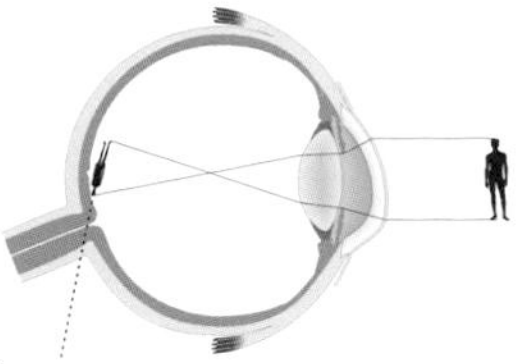

focus
foyer[M]

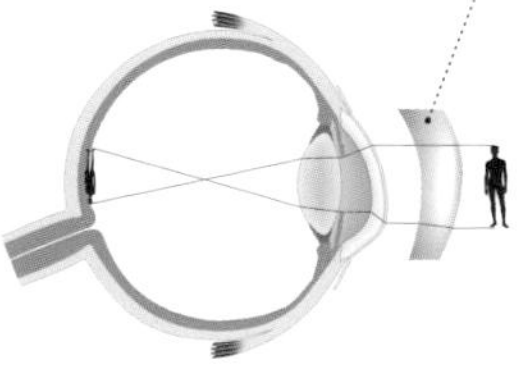

toric lens
lentille[F] cylindrique

lenses

lentilles[F]

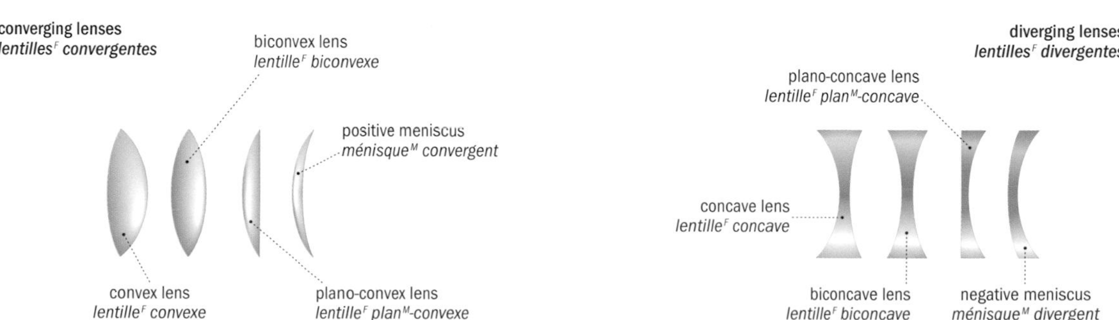

converging lenses
lentilles[F] convergentes
biconvex lens
lentille[F] biconvexe
positive meniscus
ménisque[M] convergent
convex lens
lentille[F] convexe
plano-convex lens
lentille[F] plan[M]-convexe
diverging lenses
lentilles[F] divergentes
plano-concave lens
lentille[F] plan[M]-concave
concave lens
lentille[F] concave
biconcave lens
lentille[F] biconcave
negative meniscus
ménisque[M] divergent

pulsed ruby laser

laser[M] à rubis[M] pulsé

reflecting cylinder
cylindre[M] réflecteur

photon
photon[M]

cooling cylinder
manchon[M] refroidisseur

fully reflecting mirror
miroir[M] à réflexion[F] totale

laser beam
faisceau[M] laser[M]

partially reflecting mirror
miroir[M] à réflexion[F] partielle

flash tube
tube[M] à éclairs[M]

ruby cylinder
cylindre[M] de rubis[M]

prism binoculars

jumelles[F] à prismes[M]

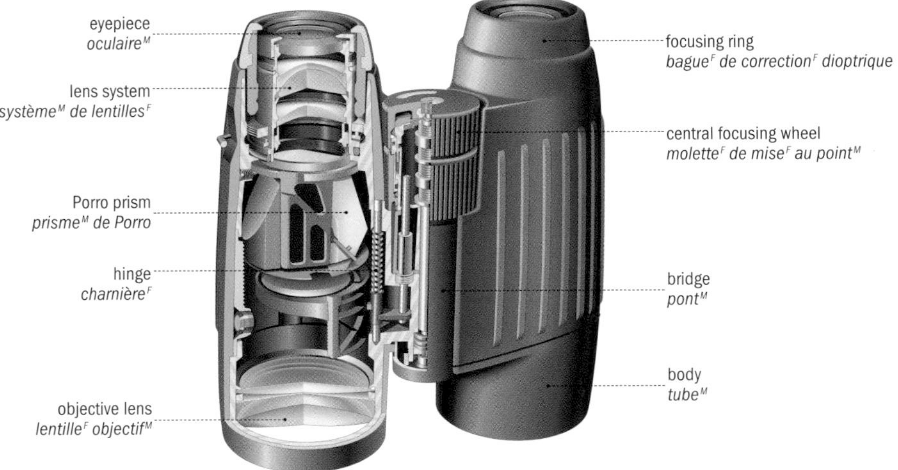
eyepiece
oculaire[M]
lens system
système[M] de lentilles[F]
Porro prism
prisme[M] de Porro
hinge
charnière[F]
objective lens
lentille[F] objectif[M]
focusing ring
bague[F] de correction[F] dioptrique
central focusing wheel
molette[F] de mise[F] au point[M]
bridge
pont[M]
body
tube[M]

telescopic sight

lunette[F] de visée[F]

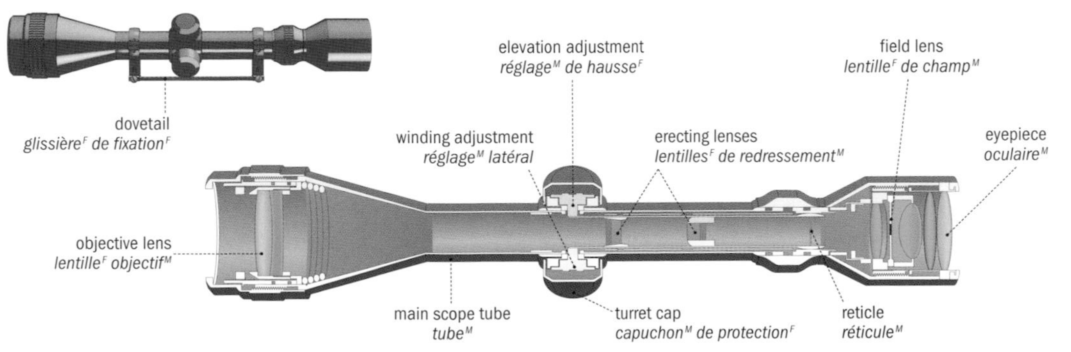
dovetail
glissière[F] de fixation[F]
elevation adjustment
réglage[M] de hausse[F]
field lens
lentille[F] de champ[M]
winding adjustment
réglage[M] latéral
erecting lenses
lentilles[F] de redressement[M]
eyepiece
oculaire[M]
objective lens
lentille[F] objectif[M]
main scope tube
tube[M]
turret cap
capuchon[M] de protection[F]
reticle
réticule[M]

magnifying glass and microscopes

loupe[F] et microscopes[M]

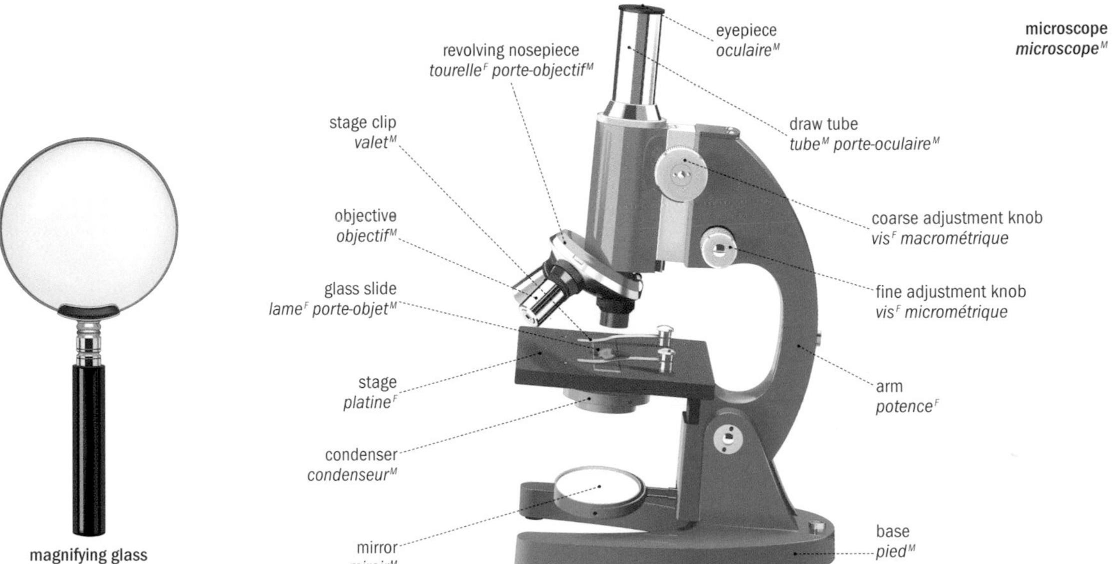
microscope
microscope[M]
eyepiece
oculaire[M]
revolving nosepiece
tourelle[F] porte-objectif[M]
draw tube
tube[M] porte-oculaire[M]
stage clip
valet[M]
coarse adjustment knob
vis[F] macrométrique
objective
objectif[M]
fine adjustment knob
vis[F] micrométrique
glass slide
lame[F] porte-objet[M]
stage
platine[F]
arm
potence[F]
condenser
condenseur[M]
base
pied[M]
mirror
miroir[M]
magnifying glass
loupe[F]

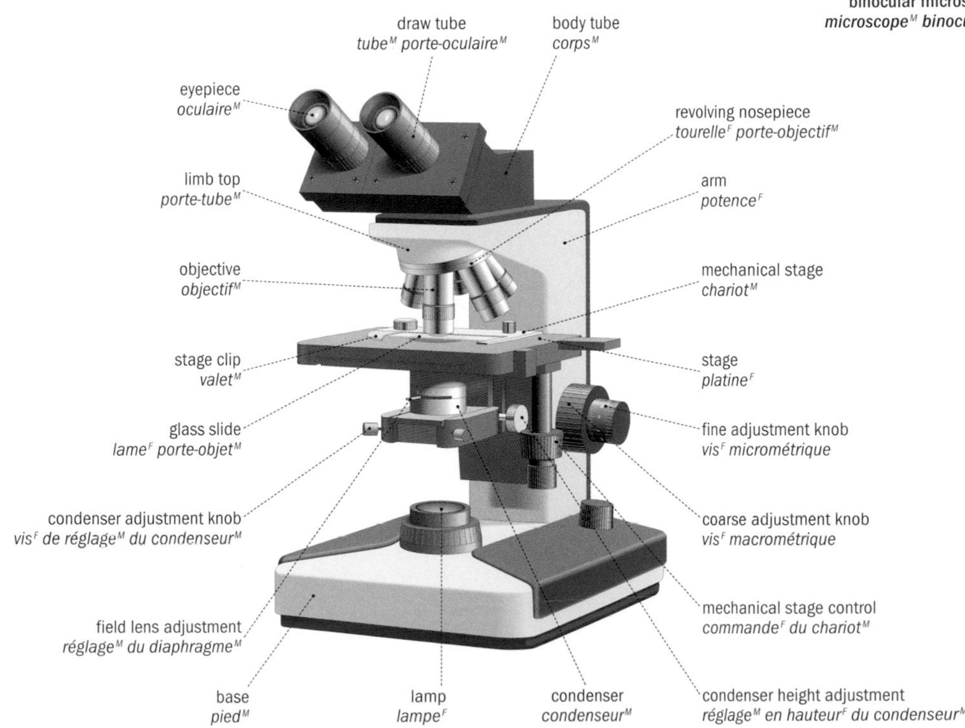
binocular microscope
microscope[M] binoculaire
draw tube
tube[M] porte-oculaire[M]
body tube
corps[M]
eyepiece
oculaire[M]
revolving nosepiece
tourelle[F] porte-objectif[M]
limb top
porte-tube[M]
arm
potence[F]
objective
objectif[M]
mechanical stage
chariot[M]
stage clip
valet[M]
stage
platine[F]
glass slide
lame[F] porte-objet[M]
fine adjustment knob
vis[F] micrométrique
condenser adjustment knob
vis[F] de réglage[M] du condenseur[M]
coarse adjustment knob
vis[F] macrométrique
field lens adjustment
réglage[M] du diaphragme[M]
mechanical stage control
commande[F] du chariot[M]
base
pied[M]
lamp
lampe[F]
condenser
condenseur[M]
condenser height adjustment
réglage[M] en hauteur[F] du condenseur[M]

SCIENCE

measurement of weight

mesure[F] de la masse[F]

beam balance
balance[F] à fléau[M]

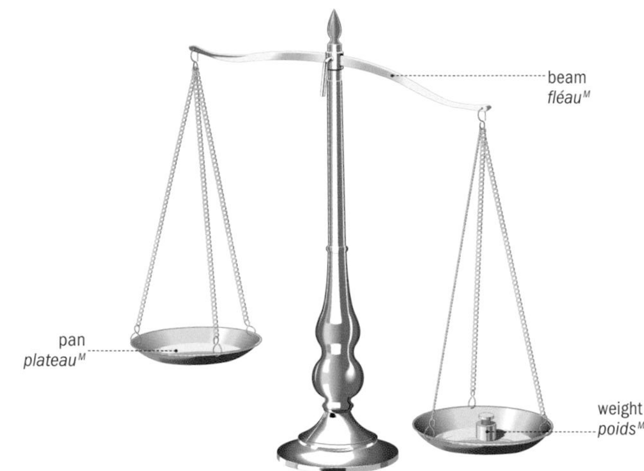
beam
fléau[M]
pan
plateau[M]
weight
poids[M]

steelyard
balance[F] romaine

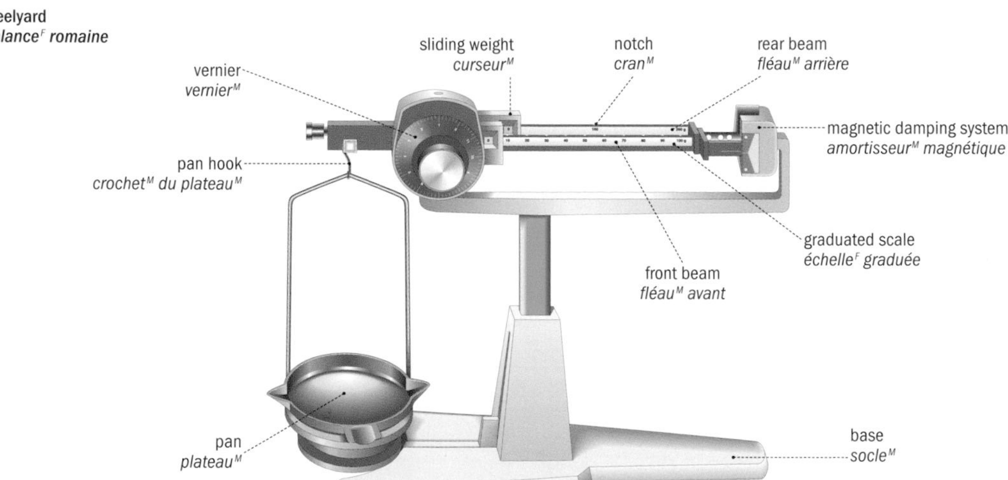
sliding weight
curseur[M]
notch
cran[M]
rear beam
fléau[M] arrière
vernier
vernier[M]
magnetic damping system
amortisseur[M] magnétique
pan hook
crochet[M] du plateau[M]
graduated scale
échelle[F] graduée
front beam
fléau[M] avant
pan
plateau[M]
base
socle[M]

Roberval's balance
balance[F] de Roberval

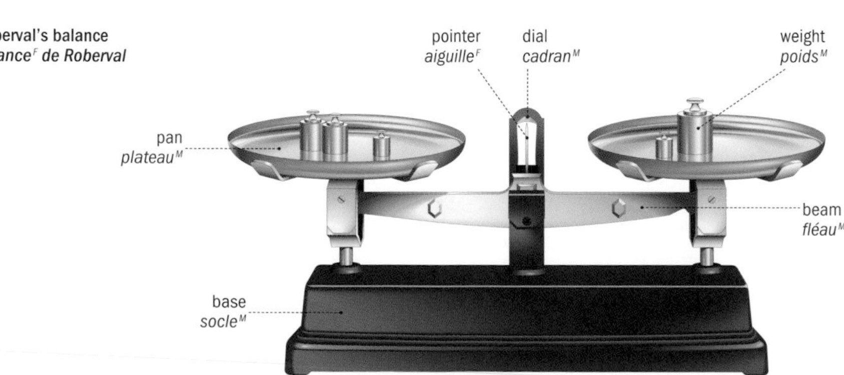
pointer
aiguille[F]
dial
cadran[M]
weight
poids[M]
pan
plateau[M]
beam
fléau[M]
base
socle[M]

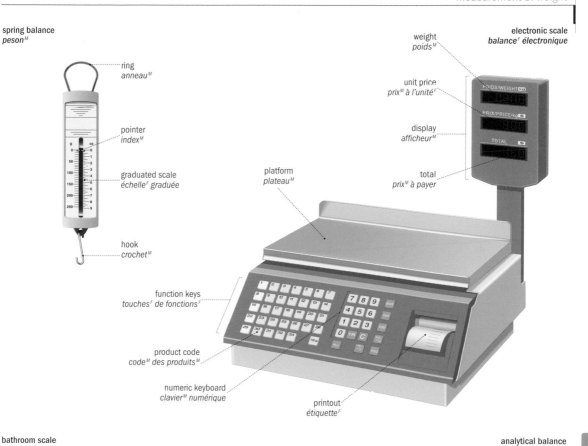

spring balance
peson[M]

ring
anneau[M]

pointer
index[M]

graduated scale
échelle[F] *graduée*

hook
crochet[M]

electronic scale
balance*[F] *électronique

weight
poids[M]

unit price
prix[M] *à l'unité*[F]

display
afficheur[M]

total
prix[M] *à payer*

platform
plateau[M]

function keys
touches[F] *de fonctions*[F]

product code
code[M] *des produits*[M]

numeric keyboard
clavier[M] *numérique*

printout
étiquette[F]

bathroom scale
pèse-personne[M]

analytical balance
***balance*[F] *de précision*[F]**

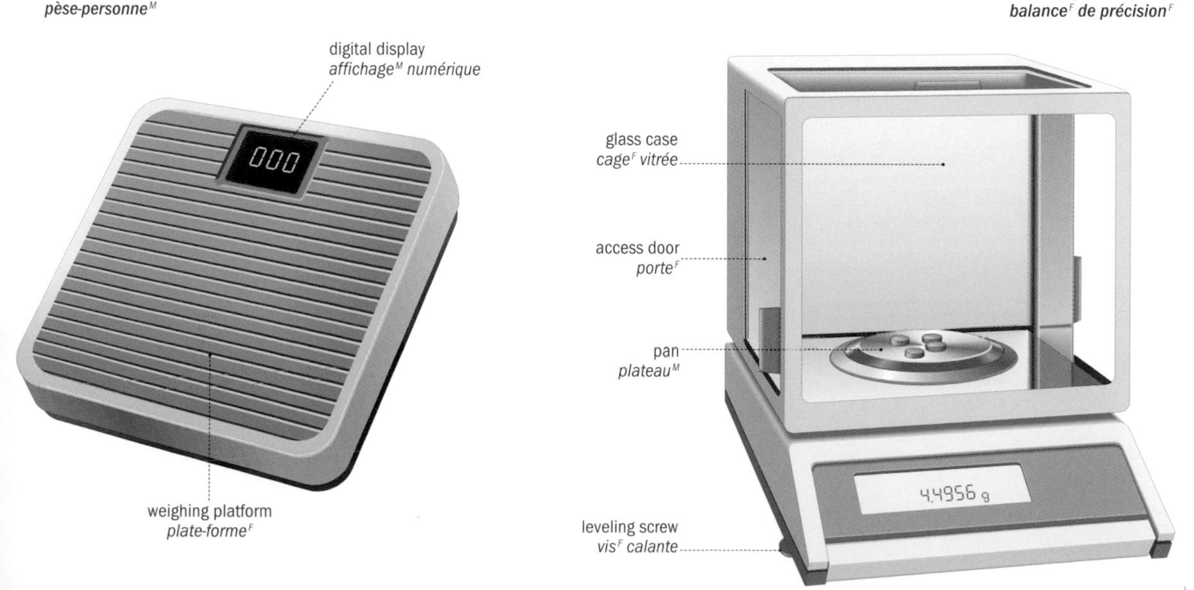
digital display
affichage[M] numérique
000
weighing platform
plate-forme[F]
glass case
cage[F] vitrée
access door
porte[F]
pan
plateau[M]
4.4956 g
leveling screw
vis[F] calante

measurement of temperature

mesure[F] de la température[F]

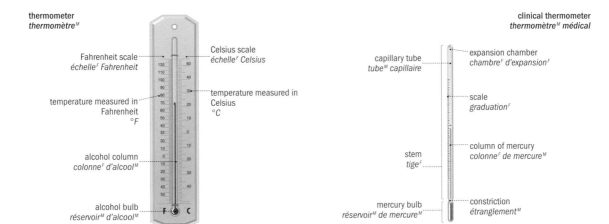

thermometer
***thermomètre*[M]**

Fahrenheit scale
échelle[F] Fahrenheit

Celsius scale
échelle[F] Celsius

temperature measured in Fahrenheit
°F

temperature measured in Celsius
°C

alcohol column
colonne[F] d'alcool[M]

alcohol bulb
réservoir[M] d'alcool[M]

clinical thermometer
thermomètre*[M] *médical

capillary tube
tube[M] capillaire

expansion chamber
chambre[F] d'expansion[F]

scale
graduation[F]

column of mercury
colonne[F] de mercure[M]

stem
tige[F]

mercury bulb
réservoir[M] de mercure[M]

constriction
étranglement[M]

measurement of time

mesure[F] du temps[M]

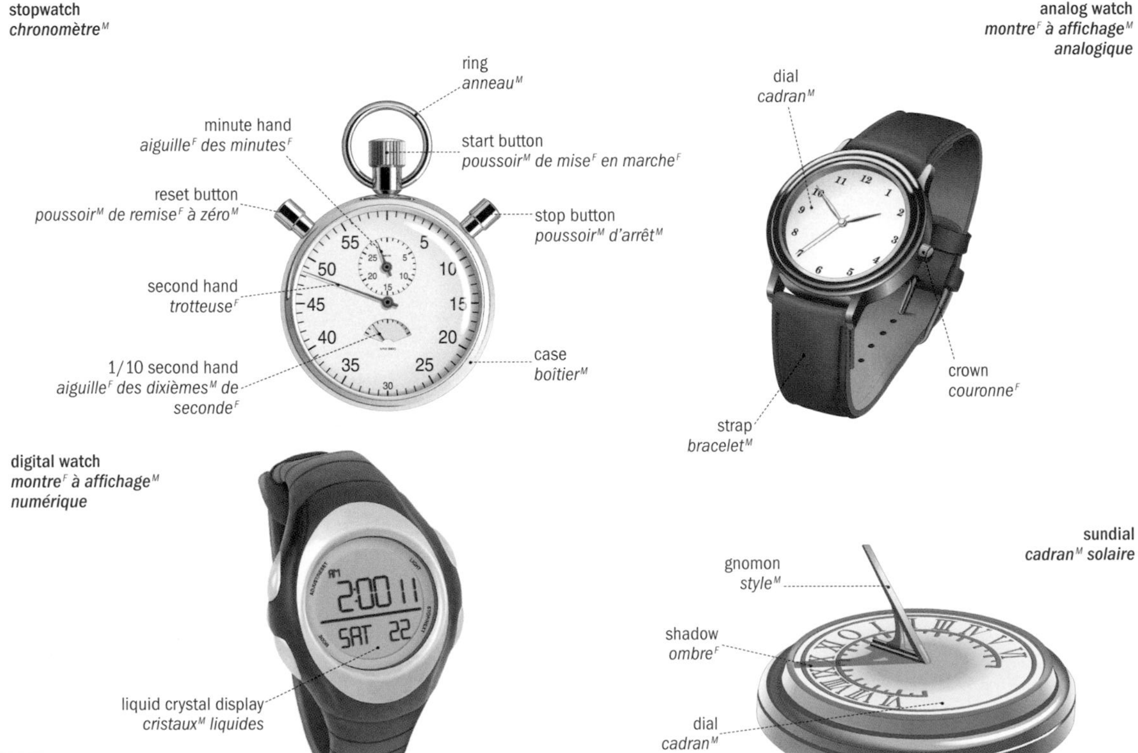
stopwatch
chronomètre[M]
ring
anneau[M]
minute hand
aiguille[F] des minutes[F]
start button
poussoir[M] de mise[F] en marche[F]
reset button
poussoir[M] de remise[F] à zéro[M]
stop button
poussoir[M] d'arrêt[M]
second hand
trotteuse[F]
1/10 second hand
aiguille[F] des dixièmes[M] de seconde[F]
case
boîtier[M]
analog watch
montre[F] à affichage[M] analogique
dial
cadran[M]
crown
couronne[F]
strap
bracelet[M]
digital watch
montre[F] à affichage[M] numérique
liquid crystal display
cristaux[M] liquides
sundial
cadran[M] solaire
gnomon
style[M]
shadow
ombre[F]
dial
cadran[M]

SCIENCE

measurement of length

mesure[F] de la longueur[F]

ruler
règle[F] graduée

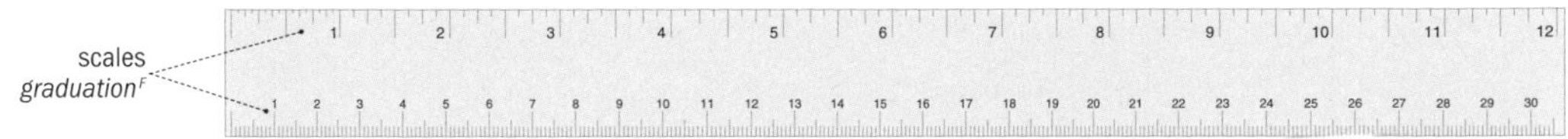
scales
graduation[F]

measurement of thickness

mesure[F] de l'épaisseur[F]

vernier caliper
pied[M] à coulisse[F] à vernier[M]

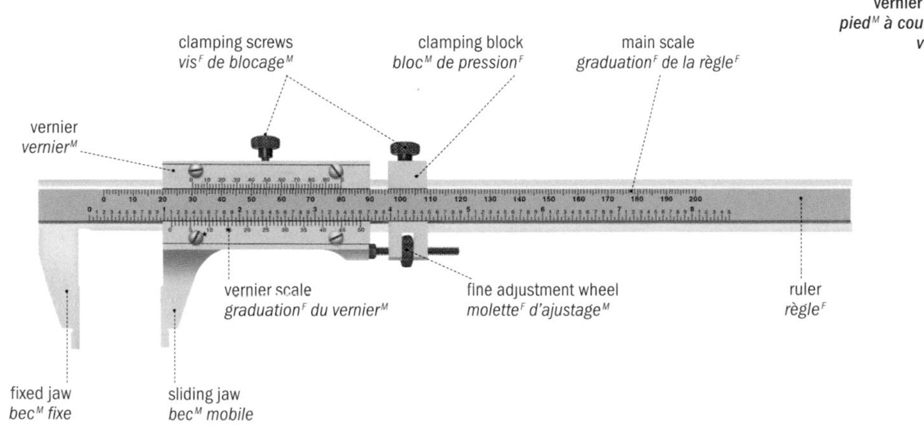
clamping screws
vis[F] de blocage[M]
clamping block
bloc[M] de pression[F]
main scale
graduation[F] de la règle[F]
vernier
vernier[M]
vernier scale
graduation[F] du vernier[M]
fine adjustment wheel
molette[F] d'ajustage[M]
ruler
règle[F]
fixed jaw
bec[M] fixe
sliding jaw
bec[M] mobile

micrometer caliper
micromètre[M] palmer[M]

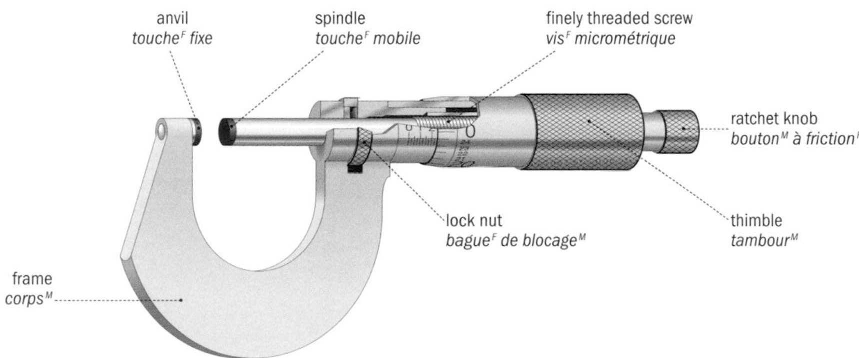
anvil
touche[F] fixe
spindle
touche[F] mobile
finely threaded screw
vis[F] micrométrique
ratchet knob
bouton[M] à friction[F]
lock nut
bague[F] de blocage[M]
thimble
tambour[M]
frame
corps[M]

international system of units

systèmeᴹ international d'unitésᶠ

unit of frequency
mesureᶠ de la fréquenceᶠ

Hz

hertz
hertzᴹ

unit of electric potential difference
mesureᶠ de la différenceᶠ de potentielᴹ électrique

V

volt
voltᴹ

unit of electric charge
mesureᶠ de la chargeᶠ électrique

C

coulomb
coulombᴹ

unit of energy
mesureᶠ de l'énergieᶠ

J

joule
jouleᴹ

unit of power
mesureᶠ de la puissanceᶠ

W

watt
wattᴹ

unit of force
mesureᶠ de la forceᶠ

N

newton
newtonᴹ

unit of electric resistance
mesureᶠ de la résistanceᶠ électrique

Ω

ohm
ohmᴹ

unit of electric current
mesureᶠ du courantᴹ électrique

A

ampere
ampèreᴹ

unit of length
mesureᶠ de la longueurᶠ

m

meter
mètreᴹ

unit of mass
mesureᶠ de la masseᶠ

kg

kilogram
kilogrammeᴹ

unit of temperature
mesureᶠ de la températureᶠ

°C

degree Celsius
degréᴹ Celsius

unit of thermodynamic temperature
mesureᶠ de la températureᶠ thermodynamique

K

kelvin
kelvinᴹ

unit of amount of substance
mesureᶠ de la quantitéᶠ de matièreᶠ

mol

mole
moleᶠ

unit of radioactivity
mesureᶠ de la radioactivitéᶠ

Bq

becquerel
becquerelᴹ

unit of pressure
mesureᶠ de la pressionᶠ

Pa

pascal
pascalᴹ

unit of luminous intensity
mesureᶠ de l'intensitéᶠ lumineuse

cd

candela
candelaᶠ

SCIENCE

biology

biologieᶠ

male
mâleᴹ

female
femelleᶠ

blood factor RH positive
facteurᴹ rhésus positif

Rh-

blood factor RH negative
facteurᴹ rhésus négatif

death
mortᶠ

*

birth
naissanceᶠ

mathematics

mathématiques[F]

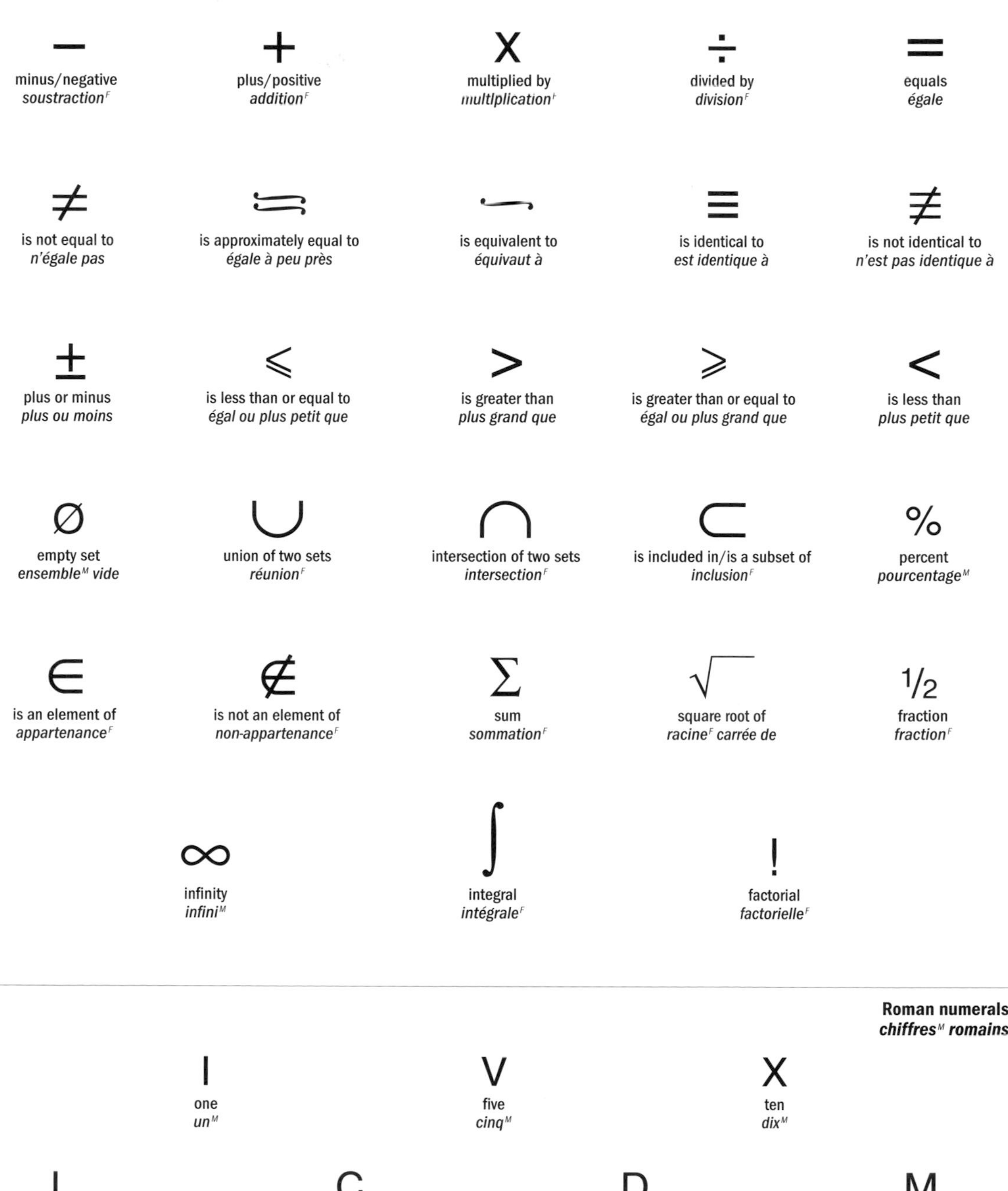
minus/negative
soustraction[F]
plus/positive
addition[F]
multiplied by
multiplication[F]
divided by
division[F]
equals
égale
is not equal to
n'égale pas
is approximately equal to
égale à peu près
is equivalent to
équivaut à
is identical to
est identique à
is not identical to
n'est pas identique à
plus or minus
plus ou moins
is less than or equal to
égal ou plus petit que
is greater than
plus grand que
is greater than or equal to
égal ou plus grand que
is less than
plus petit que
empty set
ensemble[M] vide
union of two sets
réunion[F]
intersection of two sets
intersection[F]
is included in/is a subset of
inclusion[F]
percent
pourcentage[M]
is an element of
appartenance[F]
is not an element of
non-appartenance[F]
sum
sommation[F]
square root of
racine[F] carrée de
1/2
fraction
fraction[F]
infinity
infini[M]
integral
intégrale[F]
factorial
factorielle[F]
Roman numerals
chiffres[M] romains
I
one
un[M]
V
five
cinq[M]
X
ten
dix[M]
L
C
D
M

fifty
cinquante[M]

one hundred
cent[M]

five hundred
cinq cents[M]

one thousand
mille[M]

geometry

géométrie^F

○

degree
degré^M

′

minute
minute^F

″

second
seconde^F

π

pi
pi^M

⊥

perpendicular
perpendiculaire^F

∥

is parallel to
parallèle

∦

is not parallel to
non parallèle

∟

right angle
angle^M ***droit***

obtuse angle
angle^M ***obtus***

∠

acute angle
angle^M ***aigu***

geometrical shapes

formes^F géométriques

examples of angles
exemples^M ***d'angles***^M

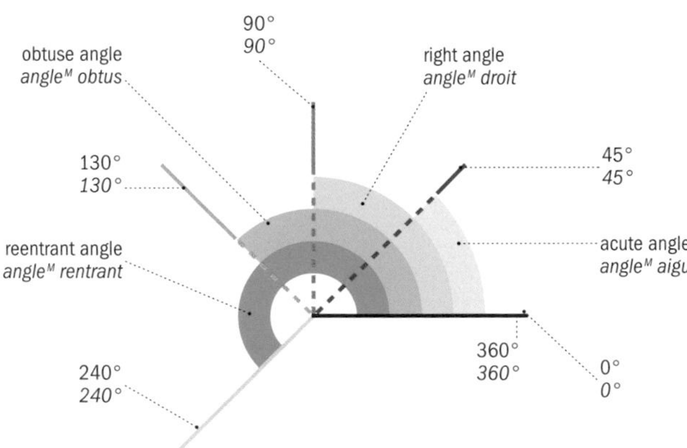
90°
90°
obtuse angle
angle^M obtus
right angle
angle^M droit
130°
130°
45°
45°
reentrant angle
angle^M rentrant
acute angle
angle^M aigu
360°
360°
240°
240°
0°
0°

plane surfaces
surfaces^F

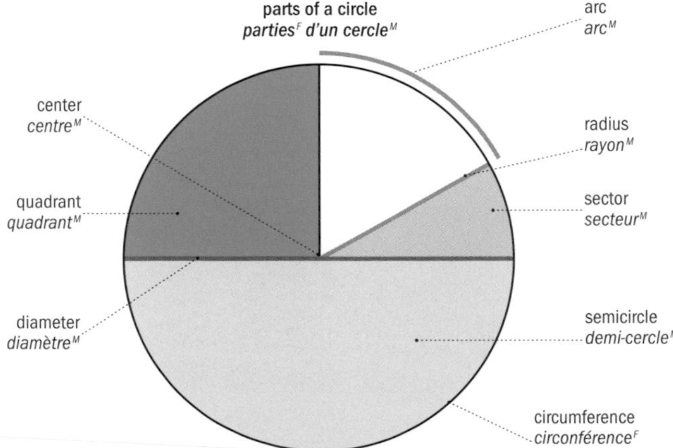
parts of a circle
parties^F d'un cercle^M
arc
arc^M
center
centre^M
radius
rayon^M
quadrant
quadrant^M
sector
secteur^M
diameter
diamètre^M
semicircle
demi-cercle^M
circumference
circonférence^F

polygons
polygones[M]

triangle
triangle[M]

square
carré[M]

rectangle
rectangle[M]

rhombus
losange[M]

trapezoid
trapèze[M]

parallelogram
parallélogramme[M]

quadrilateral
quadrilatère[M]

regular pentagon
pentagone[M] *régulier*

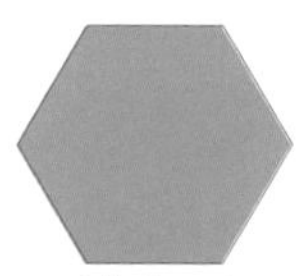

regular hexagon
hexagone[M] *régulier*

regular heptagon
heptagone[M] *régulier*

regular octagon
octogone[M] *régulier*

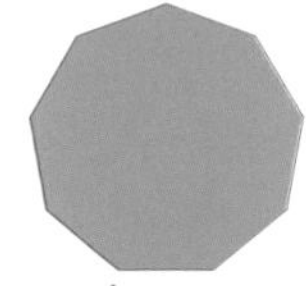

regular nonagon
ennéagone[M] *régulier*

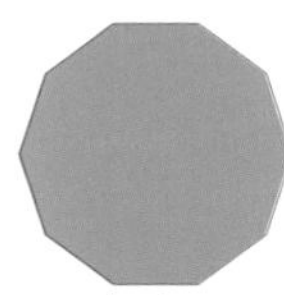

regular decagon
décagone[M] *régulier*

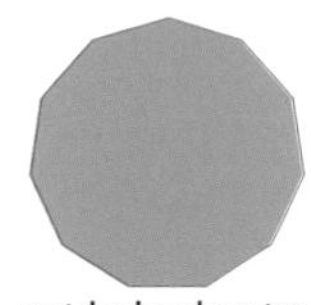

regular hendecagon
hendécagone[M] *régulier*

regular dodecagon
dodécagone[M] *régulier*

solids
volumes[M]

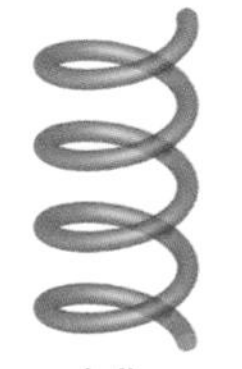

helix
hélice[F]

torus
tore[M]

hemisphere
hémisphère[M]

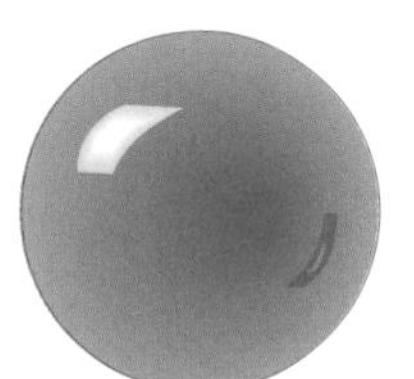

sphere
sphère[F]

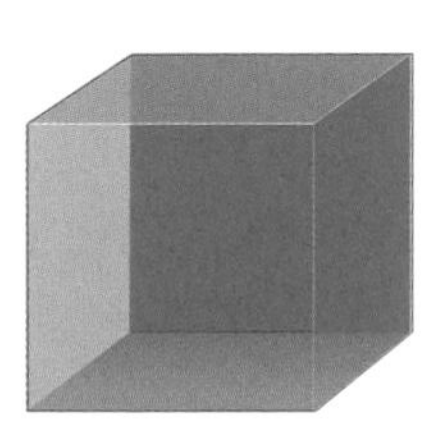

cube
cube[M]

cone
cône[M]

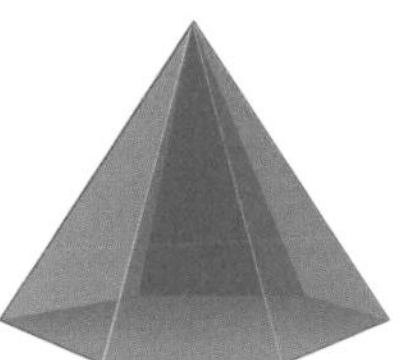

pyramid
pyramide[F]

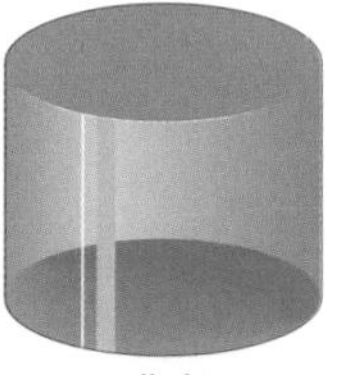

cylinder
cylindre[M]

parallelepiped
parallélépipède[M]

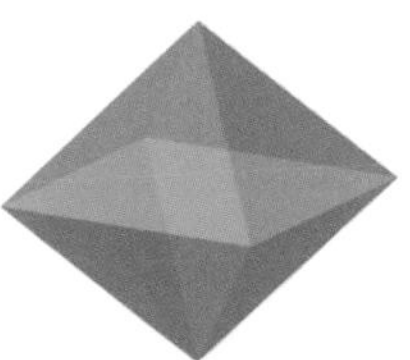

regular octahedron
octaèdre[M] *régulier*

agglomeration

agglomération[F]

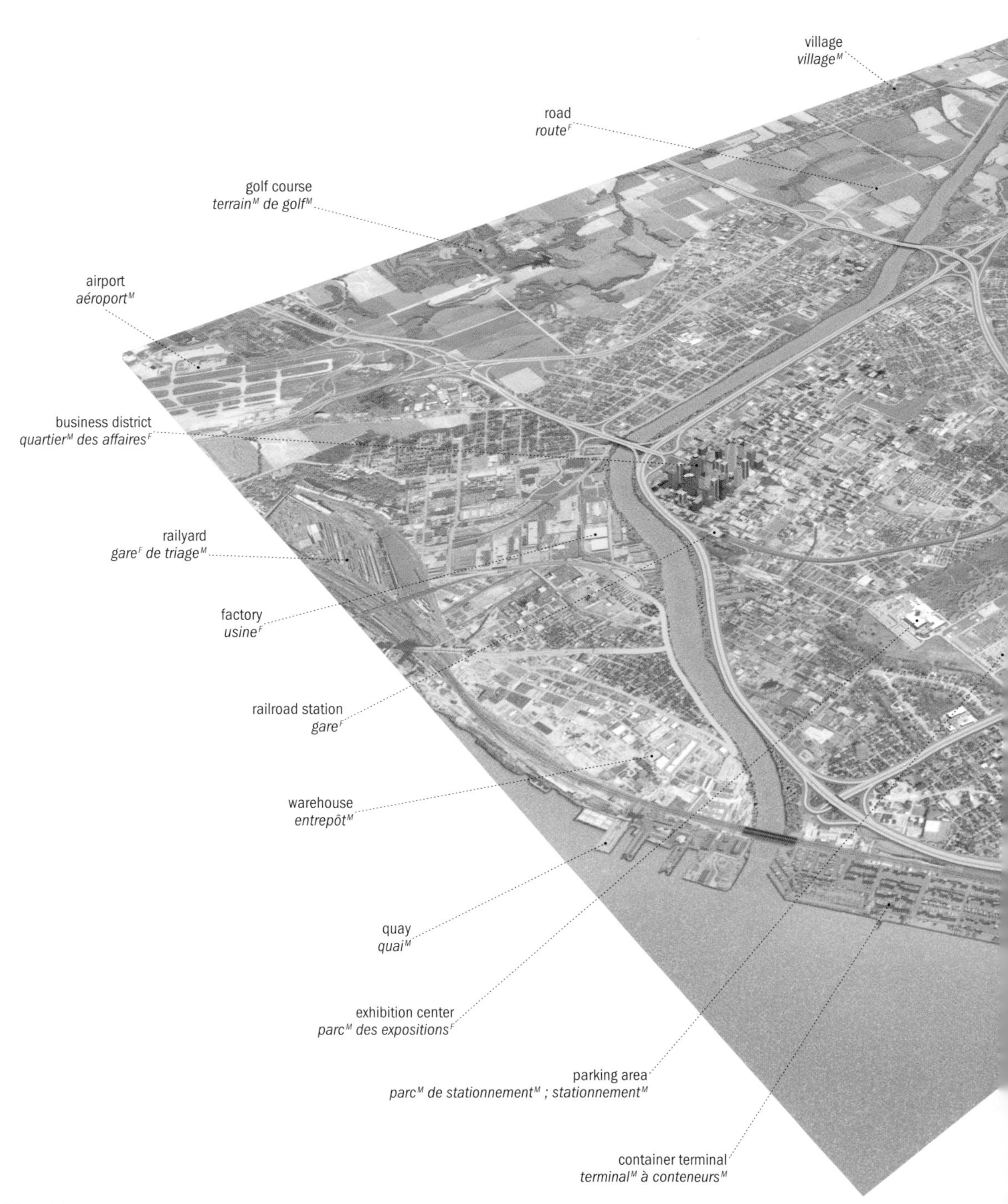
village
village[M]
road
route[F]
golf course
terrain[M] de golf[M]
airport
aéroport[M]
business district
quartier[M] des affaires[F]
railyard
gare[F] de triage[M]
factory
usine[F]
railroad station
gare[F]
warehouse
entrepôt[M]
quay
quai[M]
exhibition center
parc[M] des expositions[F]
parking area
parc[M] de stationnement[M] ; stationnement[M]
container terminal
terminal[M] à conteneurs[M]

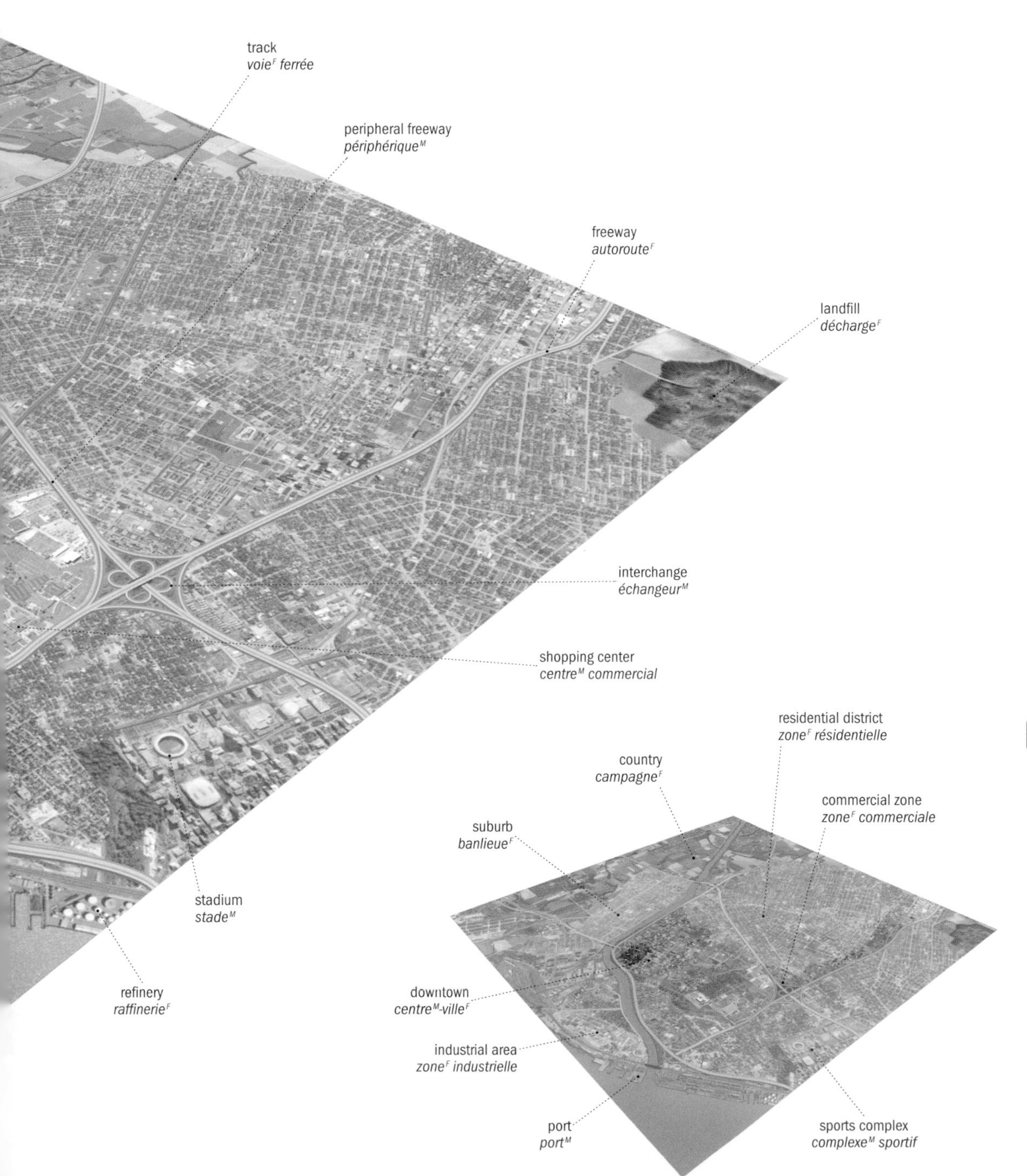
track
voie[F] ferrée
peripheral freeway
périphérique[M]
freeway
autoroute[F]
landfill
décharge[F]
interchange
échangeur[M]
shopping center
centre[M] commercial
stadium
stade[M]
refinery
raffinerie[F]
residential district
zone[F] résidentielle
country
campagne[F]
commercial zone
zone[F] commerciale
suburb
banlieue[F]
downtown
centre[M]-ville[F]
industrial area
zone[F] industrielle
port
port[M]
sports complex
complexe[M] sportif

downtown

centre[M]-ville[F]

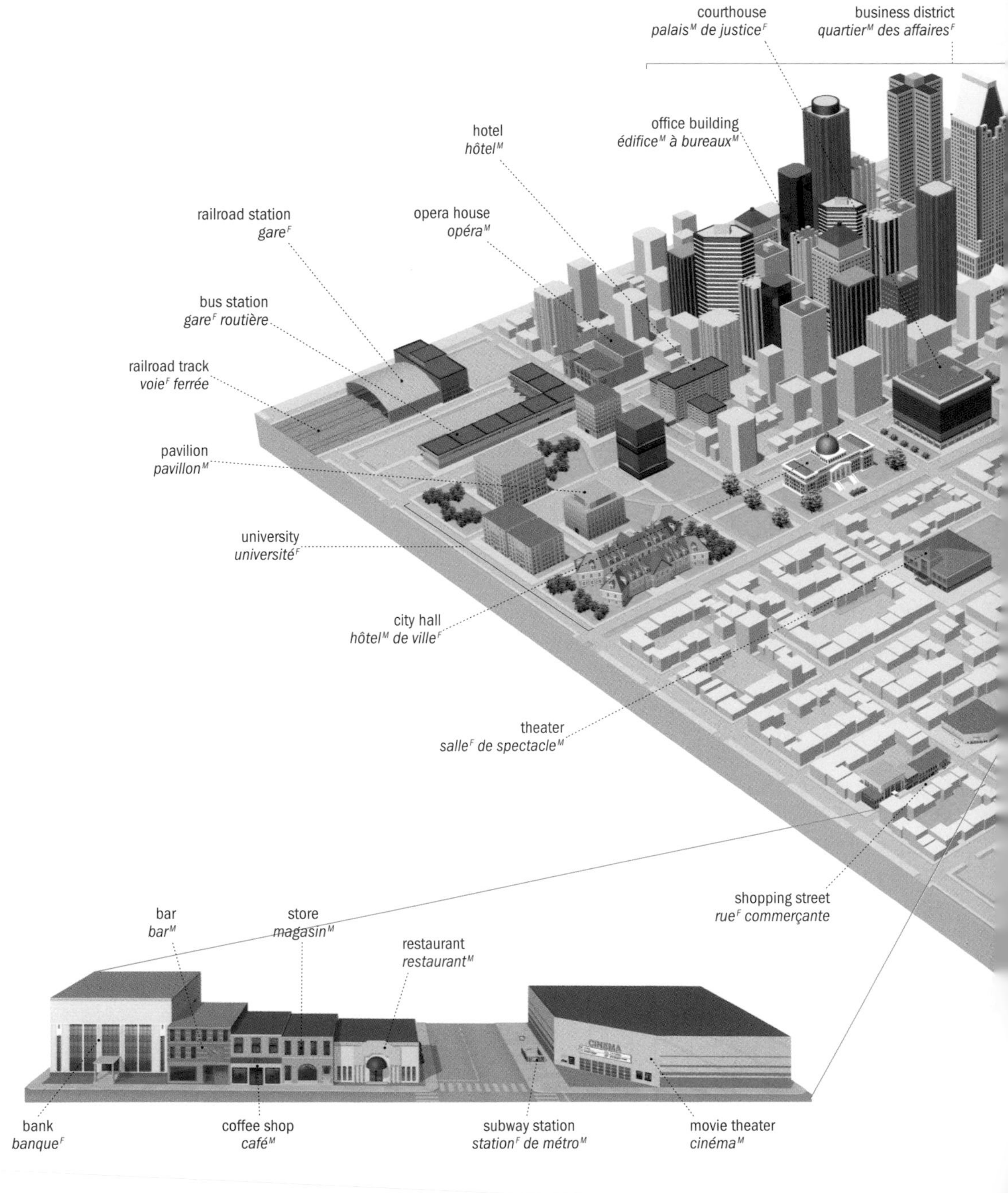
courthouse
palais[M] de justice[F]
business district
quartier[M] des affaires[F]
hotel
hôtel[M]
office building
édifice[M] à bureaux[M]
railroad station
gare[F]
opera house
opéra[M]
bus station
gare[F] routière
railroad track
voie[F] ferrée
pavilion
pavillon[M]
university
université[F]
city hall
hôtel[M] de ville[F]
theater
salle[F] de spectacle[M]
shopping street
rue[F] commerçante
bar
bar[M]
store
magasin[M]
restaurant
restaurant[M]
CINEMA
bank
banque[F]
coffee shop
café[M]
subway station
station[F] de métro[M]
movie theater
cinéma[M]

SOCIETY

downtown

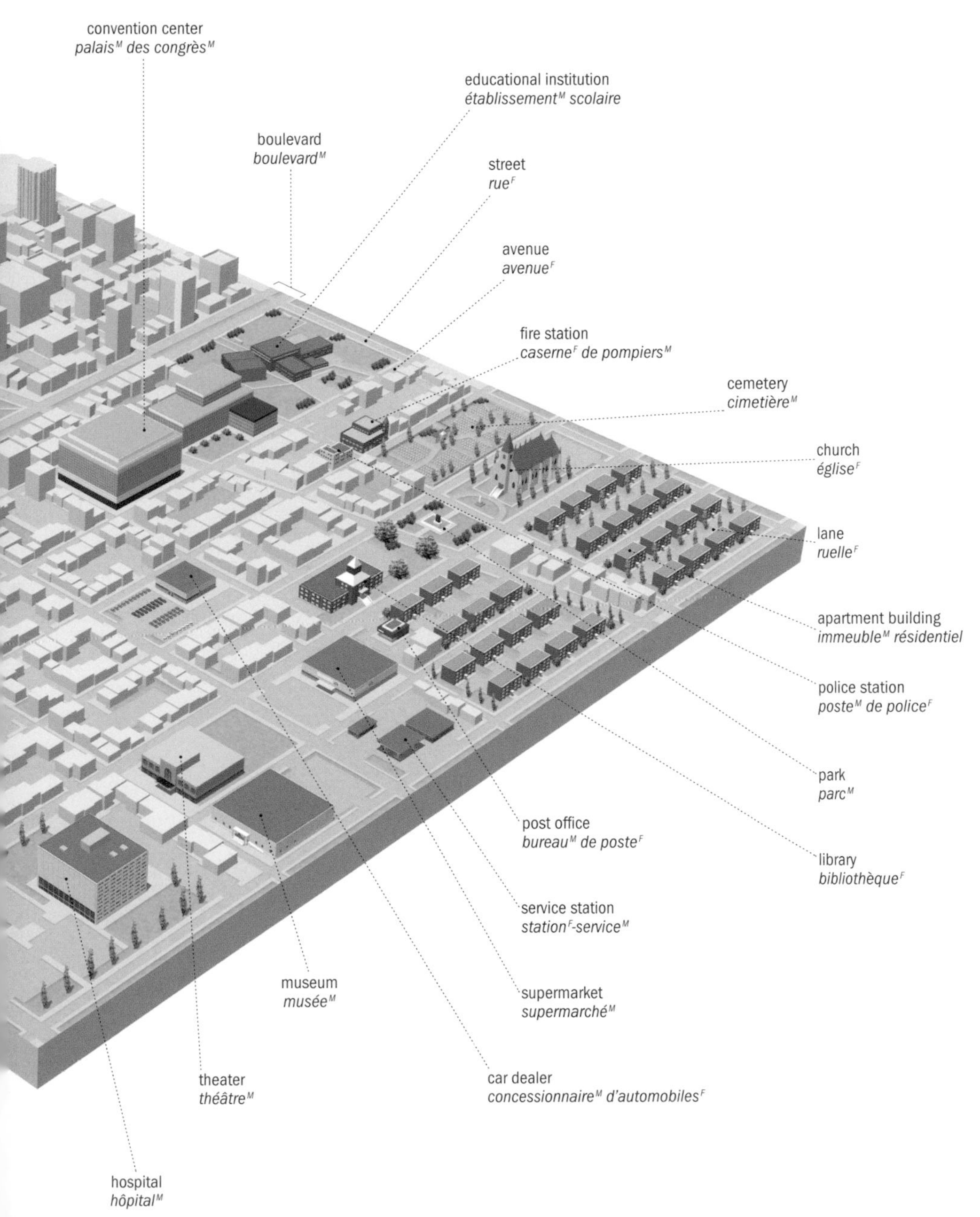

convention center
palais[M] des congrès[M]
educational institution
établissement[M] scolaire
boulevard
boulevard[M]
street
rue[F]
avenue
avenue[F]
fire station
caserne[F] de pompiers[M]
cemetery
cimetière[M]
church
église[F]
lane
ruelle[F]
apartment building
immeuble[M] résidentiel
police station
poste[M] de police[F]
park
parc[M]
post office
bureau[M] de poste[F]
library
bibliothèque[F]
service station
station[F]-service[M]
museum
musée[M]
supermarket
supermarché[M]
theater
théâtre[M]
car dealer
concessionnaire[M] d'automobiles[F]
hospital
hôpital[M]

SOCIETY

cross section of a street

coupe[F] d'une rue[F]

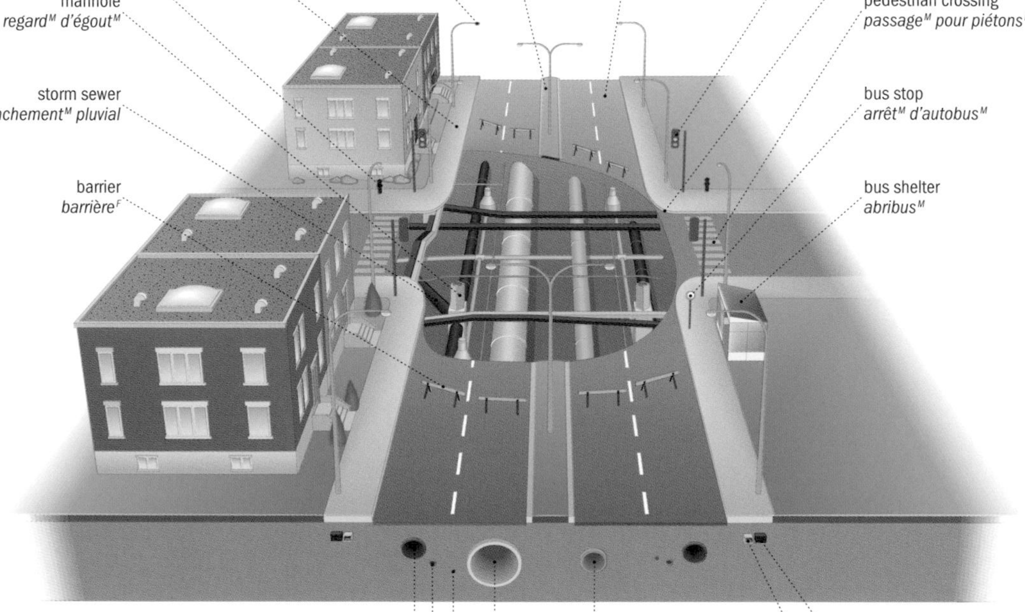

sidewalk
trottoir[M]

street light
réverbère[M]

median strip
terre-plein[M]

roadway
chaussée[F]

traffic lights
feu[M] de circulation[F]

fire hydrant
borne[F] d'incendie[M]

curb
bordure[F] de trottoir[M]

manhole
regard[M] d'égout[M]

pedestrian crossing
passage[M] pour piétons[M]

storm sewer
branchement[M] pluvial

bus stop
arrêt[M] d'autobus[M]

barrier
barrière[F]

bus shelter
abribus[M]

sewer
égout[M]

service main
conduite[F] d'eau[F] potable

electricity cable
câble[M] électrique

main sewer
égout[M] collecteur

telephone cable
câble[M] téléphonique

gas main
conduite[F] de gaz[M]

service main
conduite[F] d'eau[F] potable

traffic lights
feu[M] de circulation[F]

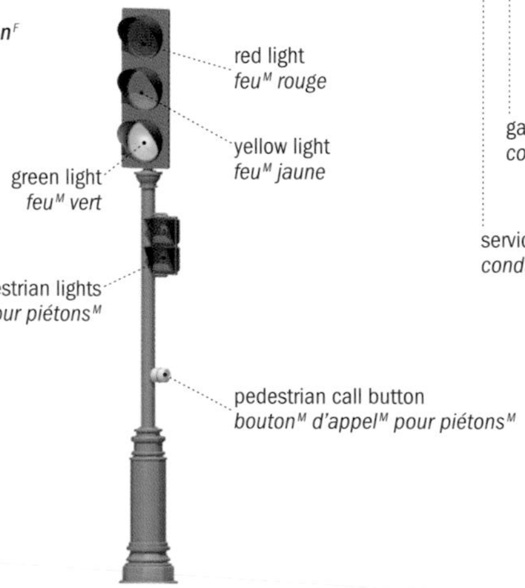

red light
feu[M] rouge

yellow light
feu[M] jaune

green light
feu[M] vert

pedestrian lights
feu[M] pour piétons[M]

pedestrian call button
bouton[M] d'appel[M] pour piétons[M]

office building

édifice[M] à bureaux[M]

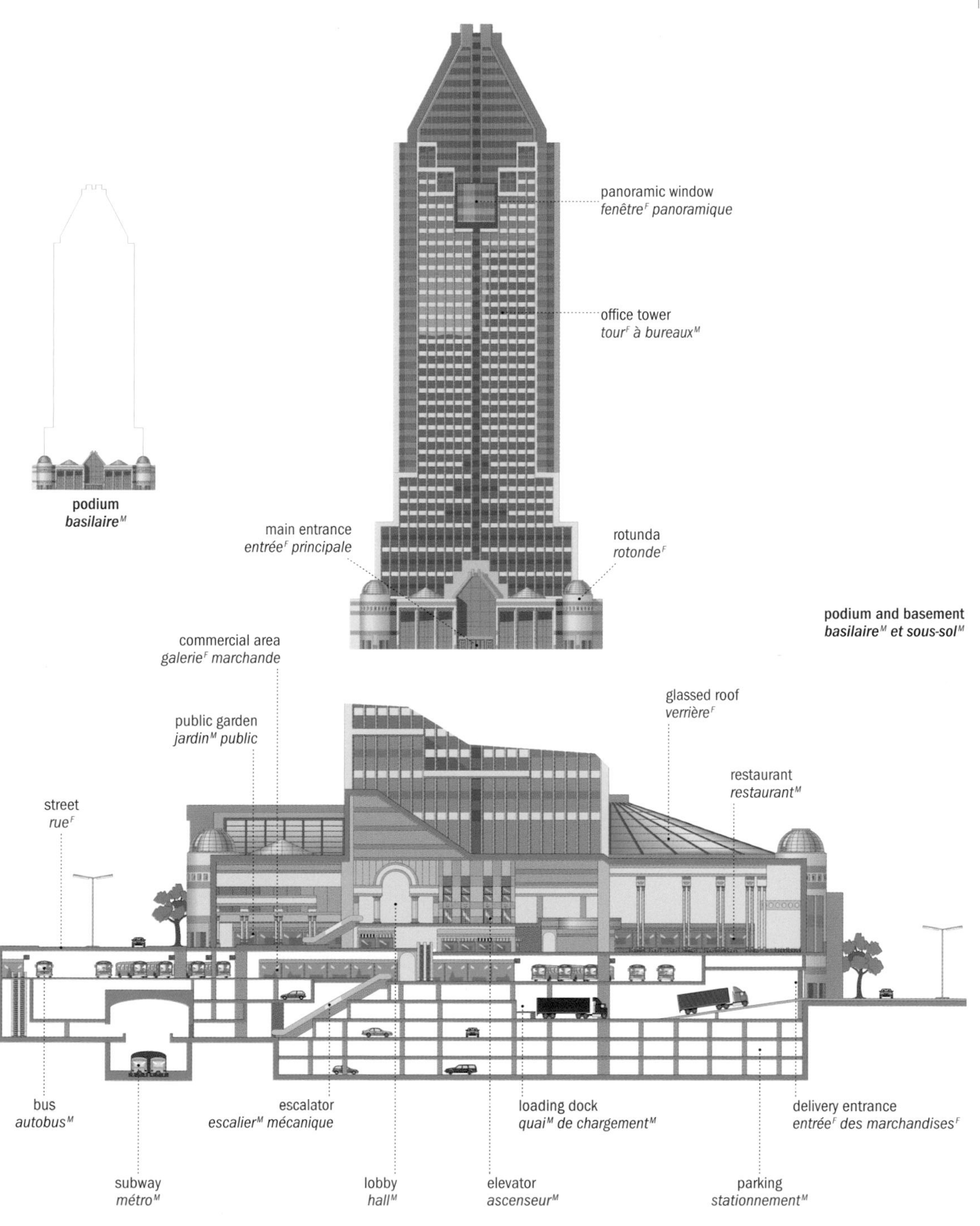

panoramic window
fenêtre[F] panoramique
office tower
tour[F] à bureaux[M]
podium
basilaire[M]
main entrance
entrée[F] principale
rotunda
rotonde[F]
podium and basement
basilaire[M] et sous-sol[M]
commercial area
galerie[F] marchande
glassed roof
verrière[F]
public garden
jardin[M] public
restaurant
restaurant[M]
street
rue[F]
bus
autobus[M]
escalator
escalier[M] mécanique
loading dock
quai[M] de chargement[M]
delivery entrance
entrée[F] des marchandises[F]
subway
métro[M]
lobby
hall[M]
elevator
ascenseur[M]
parking
stationnement[M]

shopping center

centre[M] commercial

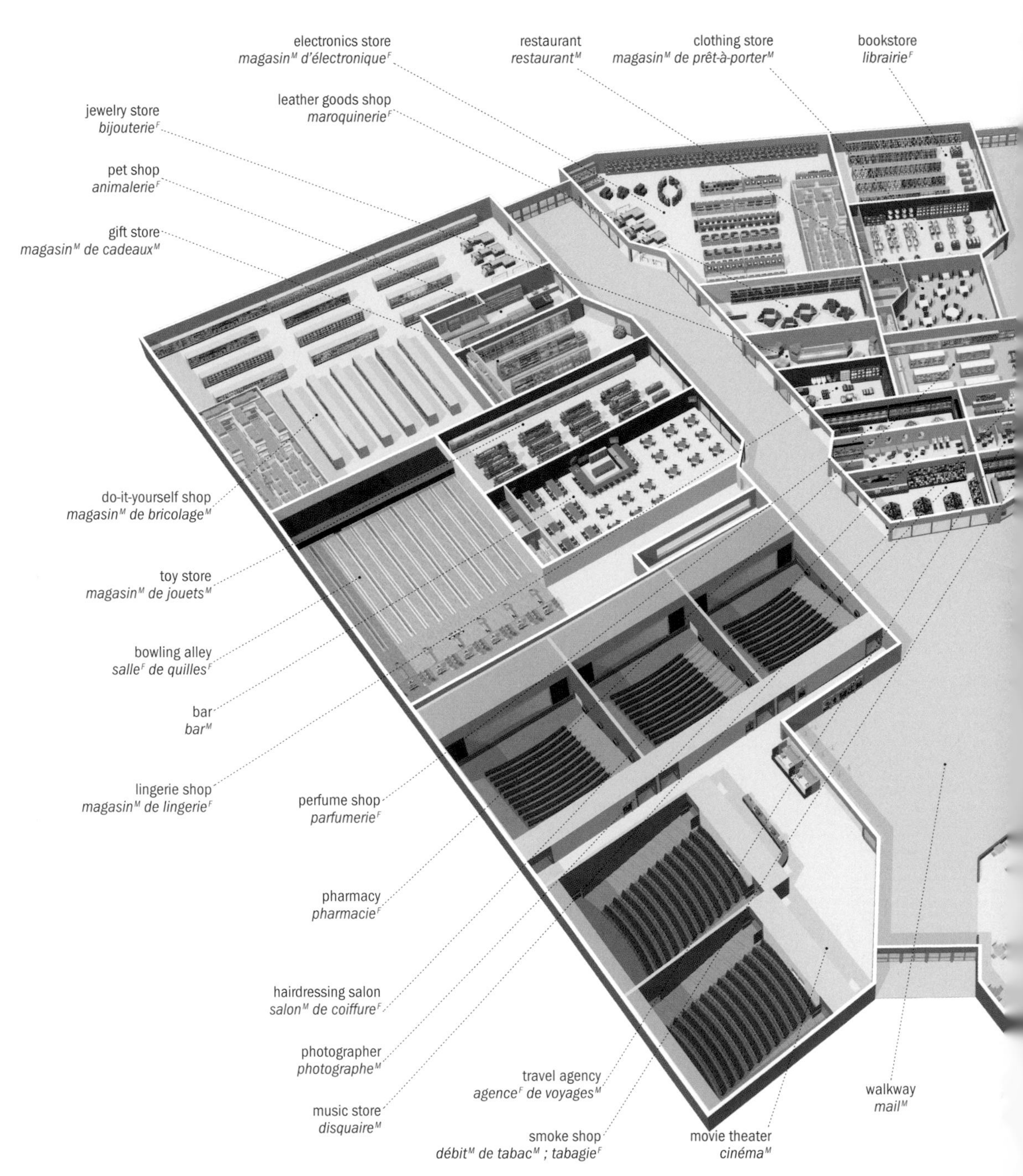
electronics store
magasin[M] d'électronique[F]
restaurant
restaurant[M]
clothing store
magasin[M] de prêt-à-porter[M]
bookstore
librairie[F]
jewelry store
bijouterie[F]
leather goods shop
maroquinerie[F]
pet shop
animalerie[F]
gift store
magasin[M] de cadeaux[M]
do-it-yourself shop
magasin[M] de bricolage[M]
toy store
magasin[M] de jouets[M]
bowling alley
salle[F] de quilles[F]
bar
bar[M]
lingerie shop
magasin[M] de lingerie[F]
perfume shop
parfumerie[F]
pharmacy
pharmacie[F]
hairdressing salon
salon[M] de coiffure[F]
photographer
photographe[M]
music store
disquaire[M]
travel agency
agence[F] de voyages[M]
smoke shop
débit[M] de tabac[M] ; tabagie[F]
movie theater
cinéma[M]
walkway
mail[M]

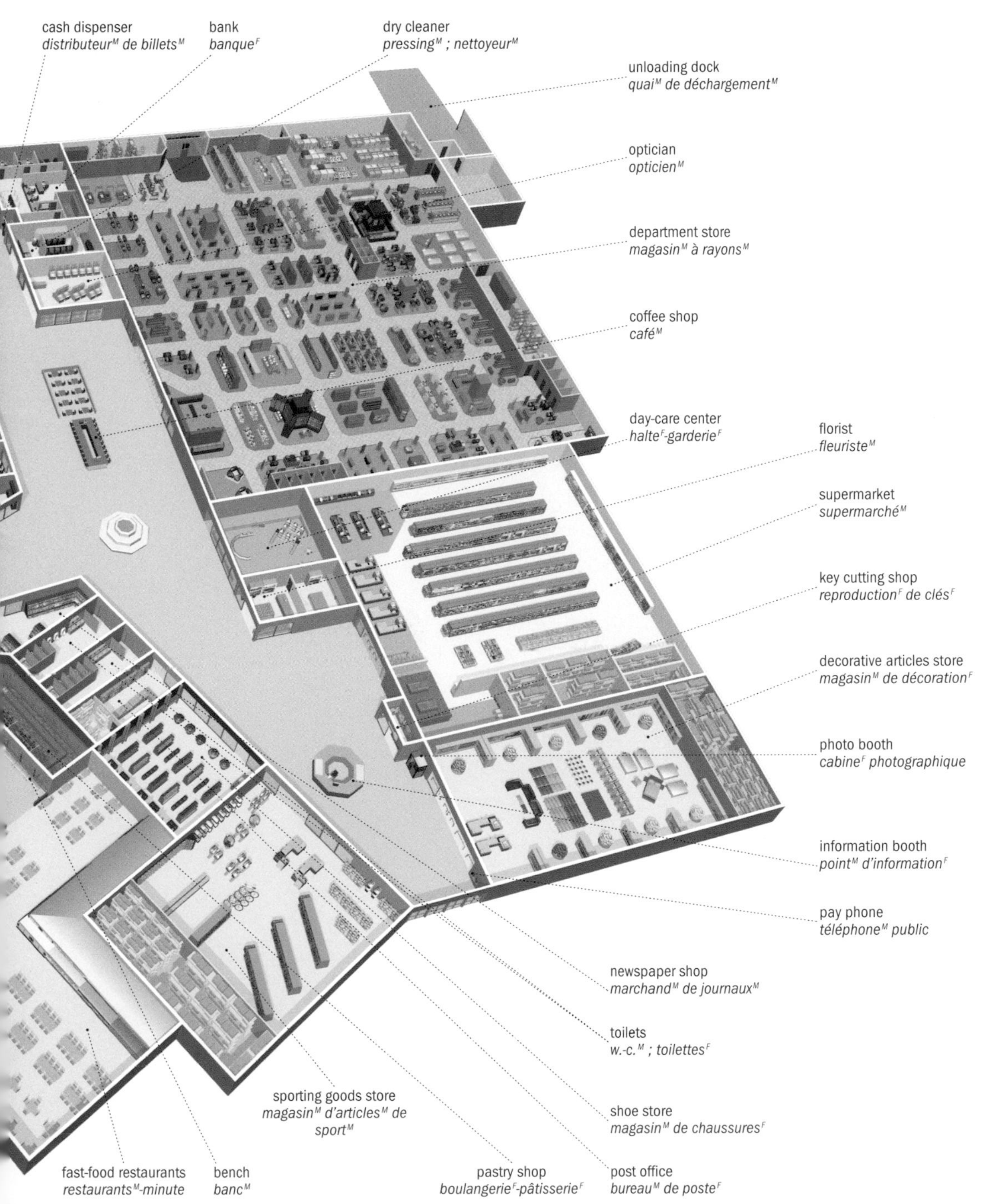
cash dispenser
distributeur[M] de billets[M]
bank
banque[F]
dry cleaner
pressing[M] ; nettoyeur[M]
unloading dock
quai[M] de déchargement[M]
optician
opticien[M]
department store
magasin[M] à rayons[M]
coffee shop
café[M]
day-care center
halte[F]-garderie[F]
florist
fleuriste[M]
supermarket
supermarché[M]
key cutting shop
reproduction[F] de clés[F]
decorative articles store
magasin[M] de décoration[F]
photo booth
cabine[F] photographique
information booth
point[M] d'information[F]
pay phone
téléphone[M] public
newspaper shop
marchand[M] de journaux[M]
toilets
w.-c.[M] ; toilettes[F]
sporting goods store
magasin[M] d'articles[M] de sport[M]
shoe store
magasin[M] de chaussures[F]
fast-food restaurants
restaurants[M]-minute
bench
banc[M]
pastry shop
boulangerie[F]-pâtisserie[F]
post office
bureau[M] de poste[F]

restaurant

restaurant[M]

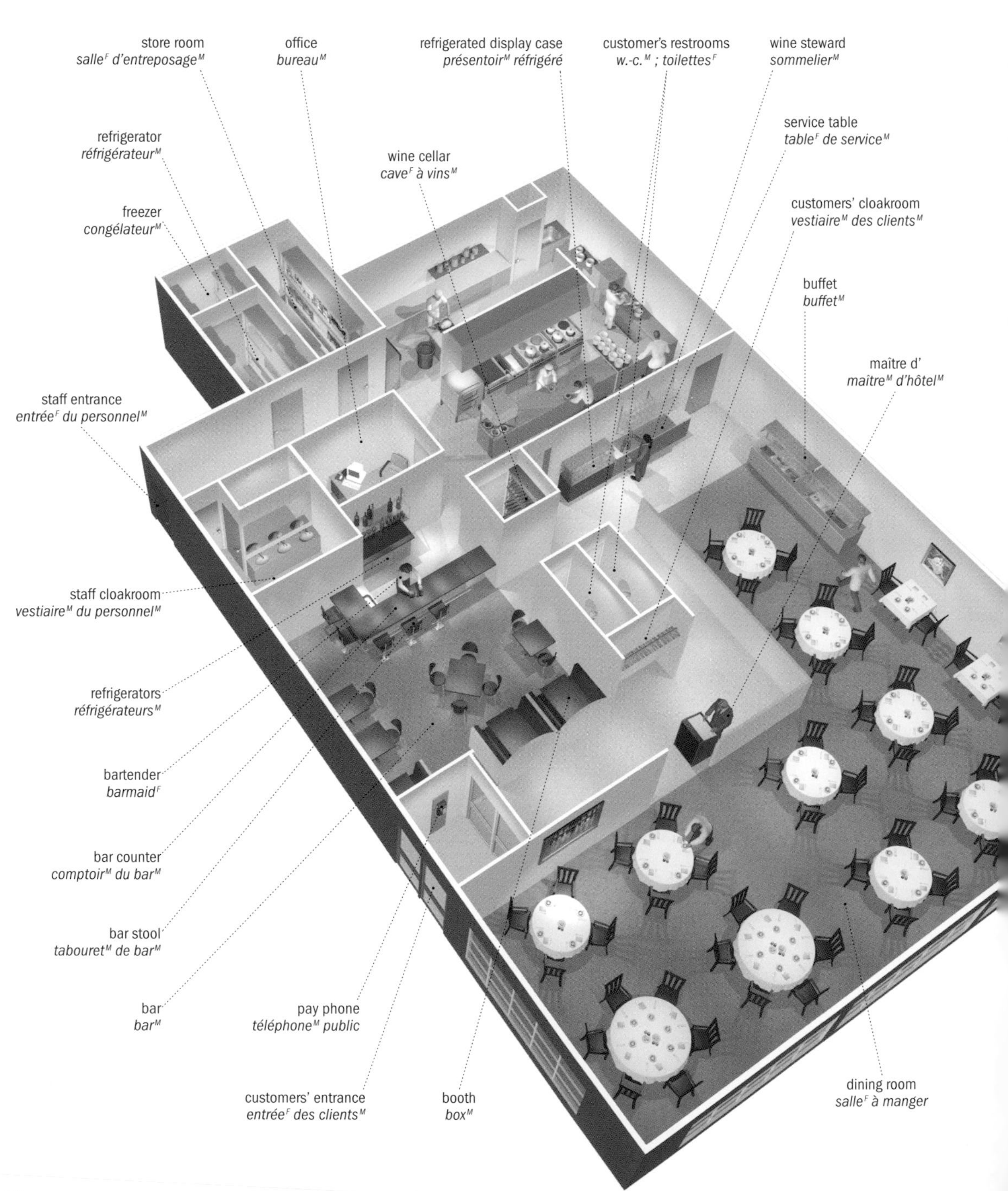
store room
salle[F] d'entreposage[M]
office
bureau[M]
refrigerated display case
présentoir[M] réfrigéré
customer's restrooms
w.-c.[M] ; toilettes[F]
wine steward
sommelier[M]
refrigerator
réfrigérateur[M]
service table
table[F] de service[M]
wine cellar
cave[F] à vins[M]
freezer
congélateur[M]
customers' cloakroom
vestiaire[M] des clients[M]
buffet
buffet[M]
maître d'
maître[M] d'hôtel[M]
staff entrance
entrée[F] du personnel[M]
staff cloakroom
vestiaire[M] du personnel[M]
refrigerators
réfrigérateurs[M]
bartender
barmaid[F]
bar counter
comptoir[M] du bar[M]
bar stool
tabouret[M] de bar[M]
bar
bar[M]
pay phone
téléphone[M] public
customers' entrance
entrée[F] des clients[M]
booth
box[M]
dining room
salle[F] à manger

SOCIETY

hotel

hôtel[M]

reception level
niveau[M] de la réception[F]

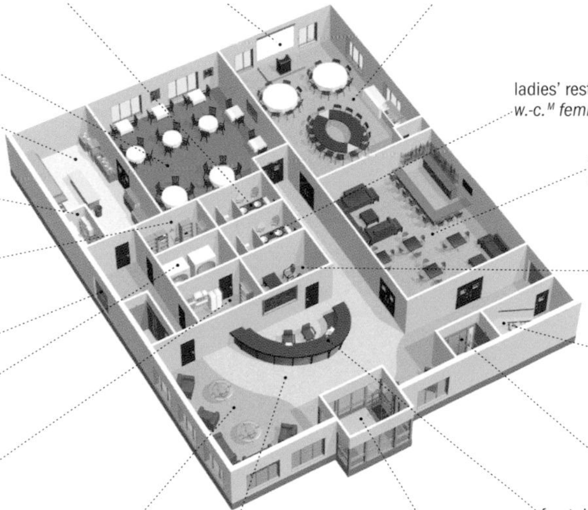

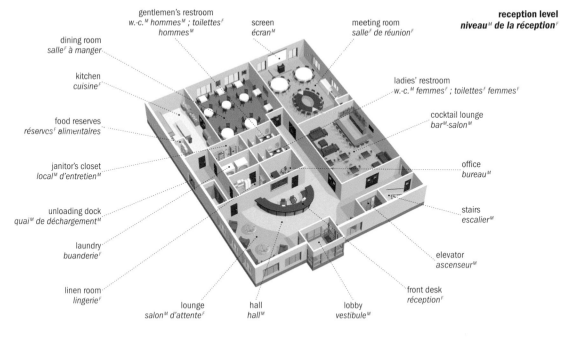

gentlemen's restroom
w.-c.[M] hommes[M] ; toilettes[F] hommes[M]
screen
écran[M]
meeting room
salle[F] de réunion[F]
dining room
salle[F] à manger
kitchen
cuisine[F]
ladies' restroom
w.-c.[M] femmes[F] ; toilettes[F] femmes[F]
cocktail lounge
bar[M]-salon[M]
food reserves
réserves[F] alimentaires
janitor's closet
local[M] d'entretien[M]
office
bureau[M]
unloading dock
quai[M] de déchargement[M]
stairs
escalier[M]
laundry
buanderie[F]
elevator
ascenseur[M]
linen room
lingerie[F]
front desk
réception[F]
lounge
salon[M] d'attente[F]
hall
hall[M]
lobby
vestibule[M]

hotel rooms
chambres[F] d'hôtel[M]

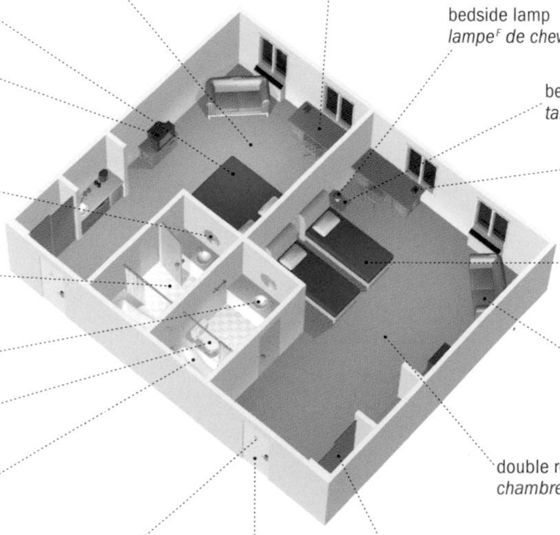

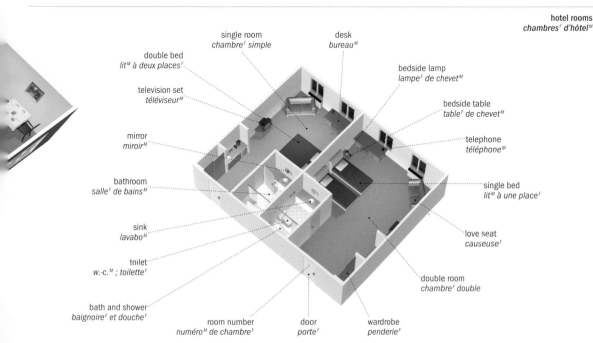

single room
chambre[F] simple
desk
bureau[M]
double bed
lit[M] à deux places[F]
bedside lamp
lampe[F] de chevet[M]
television set
téléviseur[M]
bedside table
table[F] de chevet[M]
mirror
miroir[M]
telephone
téléphone[M]
bathroom
salle[F] de bains[M]
single bed
lit[M] à une place[F]
sink
lavabo[M]
love seat
causeuse[F]
toilet
w.-c.[M] ; toilette[F]
double room
chambre[F] double
bath and shower
baignoire[F] et douche[F]
room number
numéro[M] de chambre[F]
door
porte[F]
wardrobe
penderie[F]

SOCIETY

court

tribunal[M]

jurors' room
salle[F] des jurés[M]

judges' bench
banc[M] des juges[M]

clerks' desk
table[F] des greffiers[M]

restroom
w.-c.[M] ; toilettes[F]

prosecution counsels' bench
banc[M] des avocats[M] de l'accusation[F] ; banc[M] des avocats[M] de la poursuite[F]

judges' office
cabinet[M] des juges[M]

courtroom
prétoire[M]

jury box
banc[M] du jury[M]

clerks' office
bureau[M] des greffiers[M]

witness stand
barre[F] des témoins[M]

audience
assistance[F]

cells
cellules[F]

security vestibule
couloir[M] de sécurité[F]

counsels' assistants
assistants[M] des avocats[M]

defense counsels' bench
banc[M] des avocats[M] de la défense[F]

prisoner's dock
banc[M] des accusés[M]

interview rooms
salles[F] d'entrevue[F]

lobby
vestibule[M]

examples of currency abbreviations

exemples[M] d'unités[F] monétaires

dollar
dollar[M]

cent
cent[M]

rupee
roupie[F]

euro
euro[M]

new shekel
nouveau shekel[M]

peso
peso[M]

yen
yen[M]

pound
livre[F]

SOCIETY

money and modes of payment

monnaie^{F} et modes^{M} de paiement^{M}

coin: obverse
pièce^{F} : avers^{M}

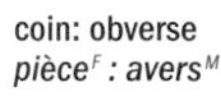

date
millésime^{M}

edge
tranche^{F}

banknote: front
billet^{M} de banque^{F} : recto^{M}

initials of the issuing bank
initiales^{F} de la banque^{F} émettrice

security thread
fil^{M} de sécurité^{F}

hologram foil strip
bande^{F} métallisée holographique

official signature
signature^{F} officielle

watermark
filigrane^{M}

color shifting ink
encre^{F} à couleur^{F} changeante

portrait
effigie^{F}

serial number
numéro^{M} de série^{F}

coin: reverse
pièce^{F} : revers^{M}

outer ring
couronne^{F}

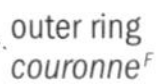

denomination
valeur^{F}

banknote: back
billet^{M} de banque^{F} : verso^{M}

flag of the European Union
drapeau^{M} de l'Union^{F} européenne

serial number
numéro^{M} de série^{F}

motto
devise^{F}

denomination
valeur^{F}

name of the currency
nom^{M} de la monnaie^{F}

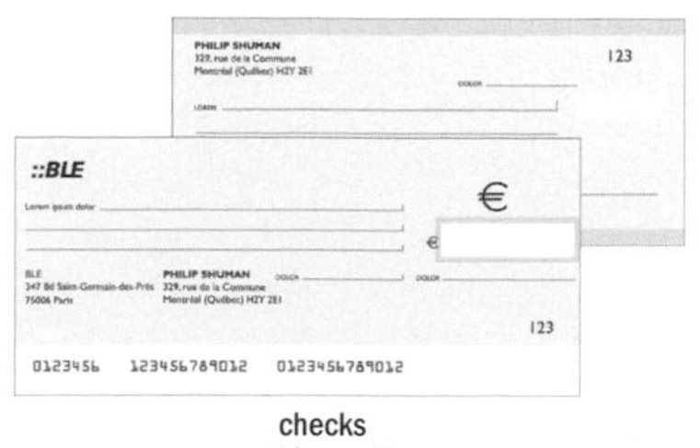

checks
chèques^{M}

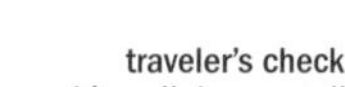

traveler's check
chèque^{M} de voyage^{M}

credit card
carte^{F} de crédit^{M}

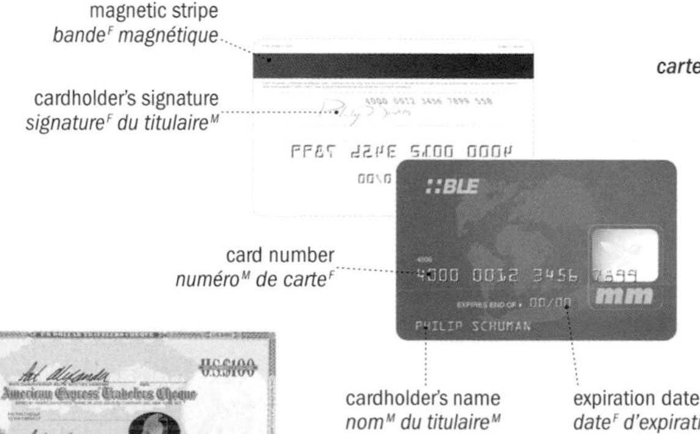

magnetic stripe
bande^{F} magnétique

cardholder's signature
signature^{F} du titulaire^{M}

card number
numéro^{M} de carte^{F}

cardholder's name
nom^{M} du titulaire^{M}

expiration date
date^{F} d'expiration^{F}

bank

banque[F]

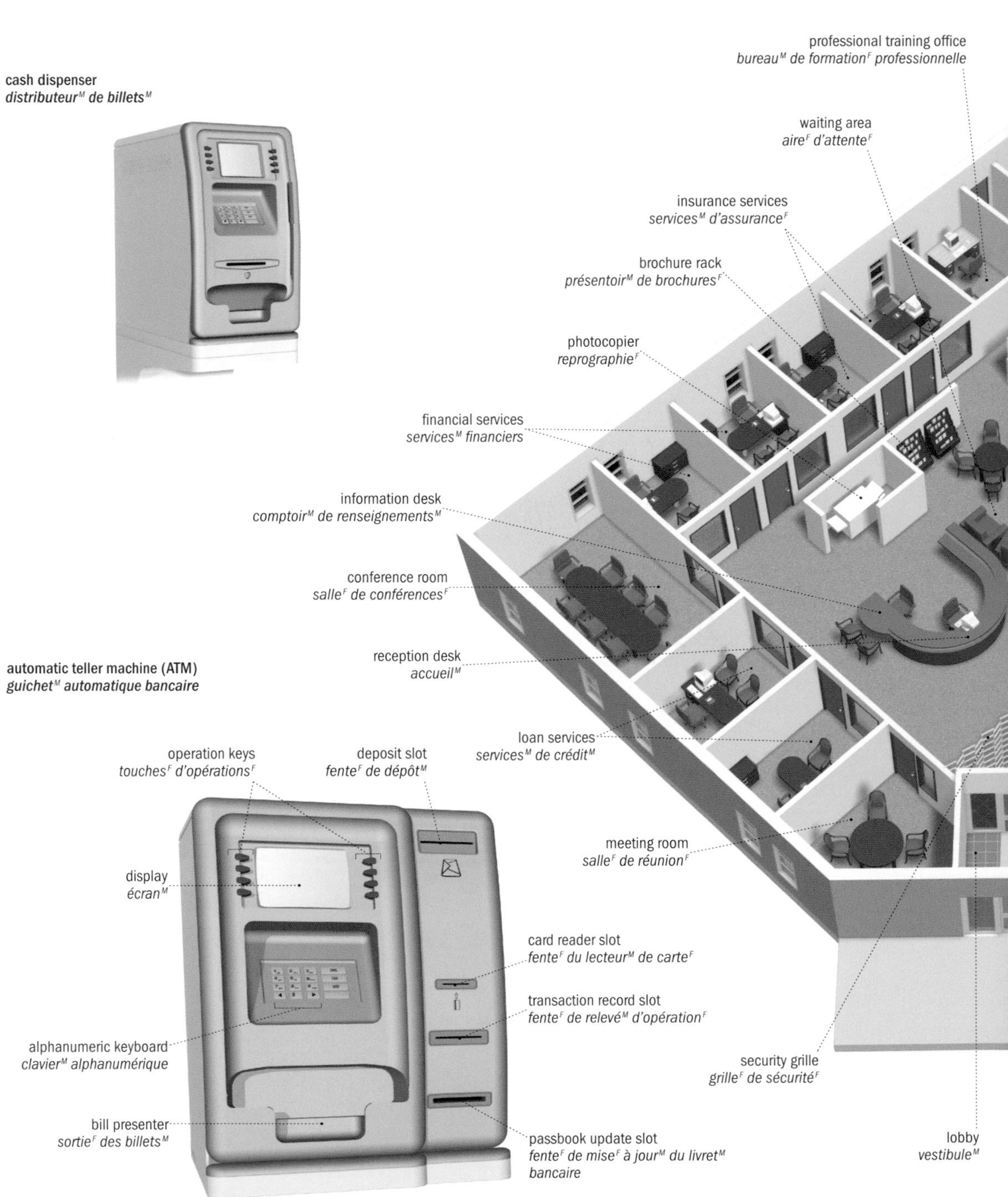

cash dispenser
distributeur[M] de billets[M]
professional training office
bureau[M] de formation[F] professionnelle
waiting area
aire[F] d'attente[F]
insurance services
services[M] d'assurance[F]
brochure rack
présentoir[M] de brochures[F]
photocopier
reprographie[F]
financial services
services[M] financiers
information desk
comptoir[M] de renseignements[M]
conference room
salle[F] de conférences[F]
reception desk
accueil[M]
automatic teller machine (ATM)
guichet[M] automatique bancaire
loan services
services[M] de crédit[M]
operation keys
touches[F] d'opérations[F]
deposit slot
fente[F] de dépôt[M]
display
écran[M]
meeting room
salle[F] de réunion[F]
card reader slot
fente[F] du lecteur[M] de carte[F]
transaction record slot
fente[F] de relevé[M] d'opération[F]
alphanumeric keyboard
clavier[M] alphanumérique
security grille
grille[F] de sécurité[F]
bill presenter
sortie[F] des billets[M]
passbook update slot
fente[F] de mise[F] à jour[M] du livret[M] bancaire
lobby
vestibule[M]

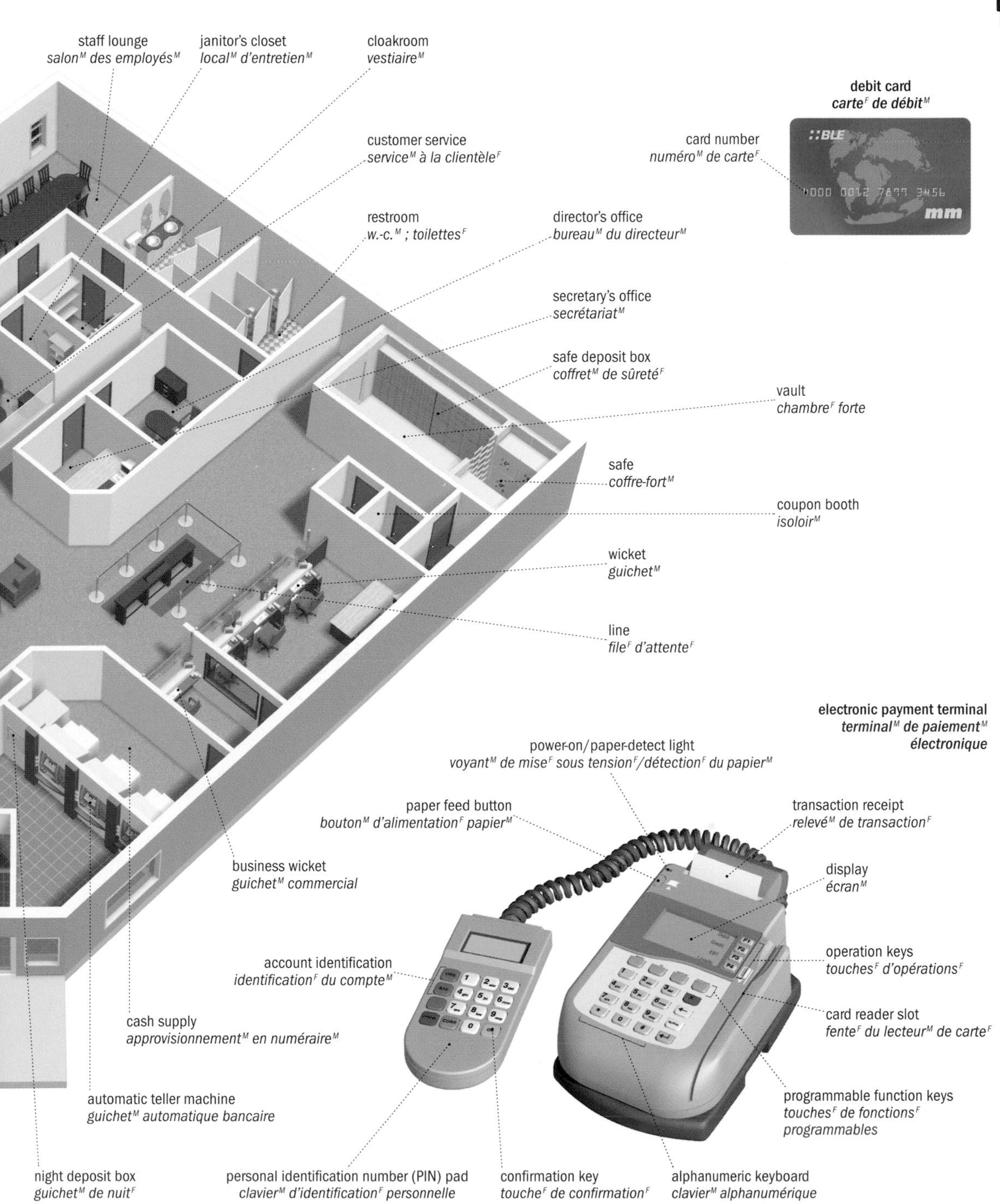
staff lounge
salon^M des employés^M
janitor's closet
local^M d'entretien^M
cloakroom
vestiaire^M
customer service
service^M à la clientèle^F
restroom
w.-c.^M ; toilettes^F
director's office
bureau^M du directeur^M
secretary's office
secrétariat^M
safe deposit box
coffret^M de sûreté^F
vault
chambre^F forte
safe
coffre-fort^M
coupon booth
isoloir^M
wicket
guichet^M
line
file^F d'attente^F
business wicket
guichet^M commercial
cash supply
approvisionnement^M en numéraire^M
automatic teller machine
guichet^M automatique bancaire
night deposit box
guichet^M de nuit^F
debit card
carte^F de débit^M
card number
numéro^M de carte^F
electronic payment terminal
terminal^M de paiement^M électronique
power-on/paper-detect light
voyant^M de mise^F sous tension^F/détection^F du papier^M
paper feed button
bouton^M d'alimentation^F papier^M
transaction receipt
relevé^M de transaction^F
display
écran^M
account identification
identification^F du compte^M
operation keys
touches^F d'opérations^F
card reader slot
fente^F du lecteur^M de carte^F
programmable function keys
touches^F de fonctions^F programmables
personal identification number (PIN) pad
clavier^M d'identification^F personnelle
confirmation key
touche^F de confirmation^F
alphanumeric keyboard
clavier^M alphanumérique

school

écoleF

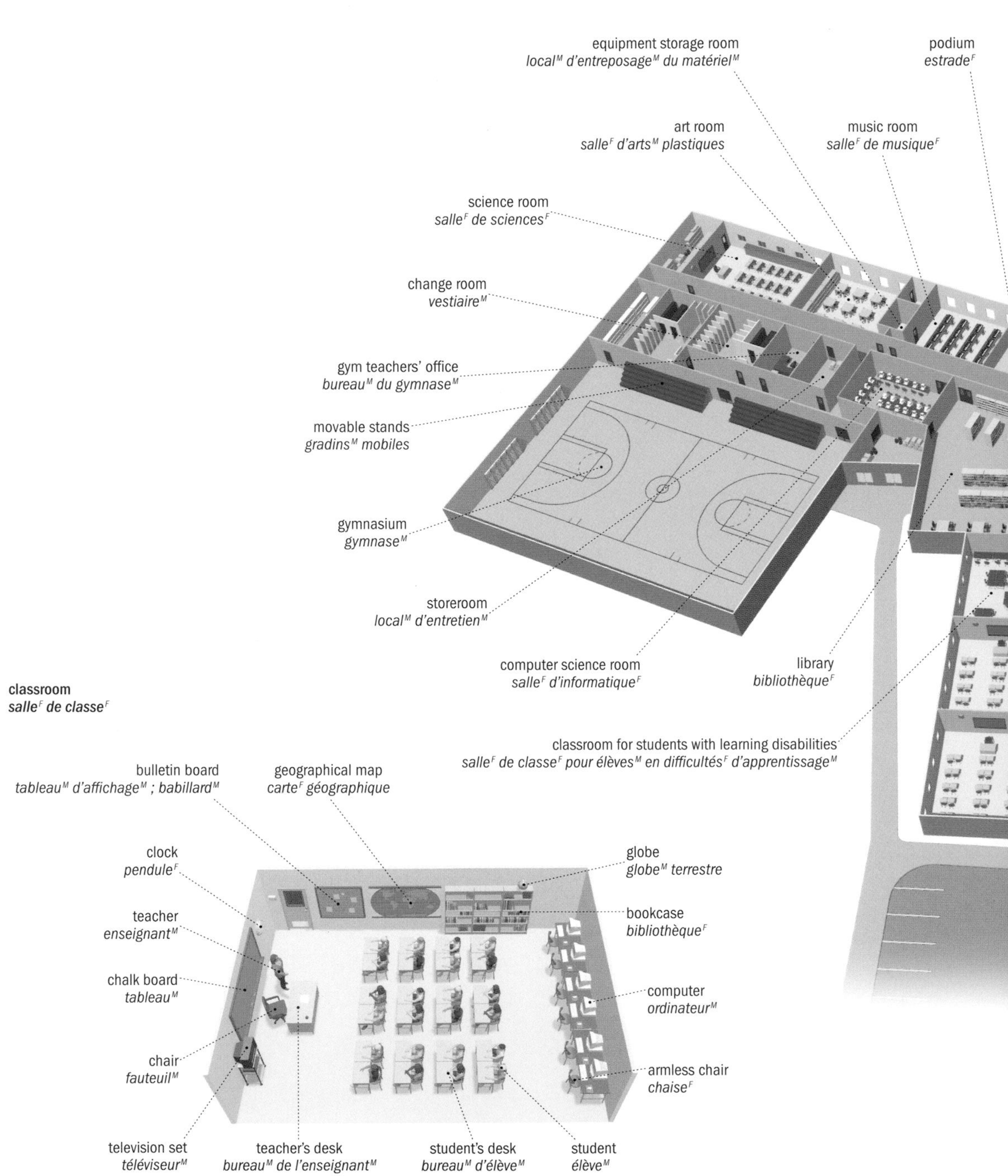
equipment storage room
localM d'entreposageM du matérielM
podium
estradeF
art room
salleF d'artsM plastiques
music room
salleF de musiqueF
science room
salleF de sciencesF
change room
vestiaireM
gym teachers' office
bureauM du gymnaseM
movable stands
gradinsM mobiles
gymnasium
gymnaseM
storeroom
localM d'entretienM
computer science room
salleF d'informatiqueF
library
bibliothèqueF
classroom for students with learning disabilities
salleF de classeF pour élèvesM en difficultésF d'apprentissageM
classroom
salleF de classeF
bulletin board
tableauM d'affichageM ; babillardM
geographical map
carteF géographique
clock
penduleF
globe
globeM terrestre
teacher
enseignantM
bookcase
bibliothèqueF
chalk board
tableauM
computer
ordinateurM
chair
fauteuilM
armless chair
chaiseF
television set
téléviseurM
teacher's desk
bureauM de l'enseignantM
student's desk
bureauM d'élèveM
student
élèveM

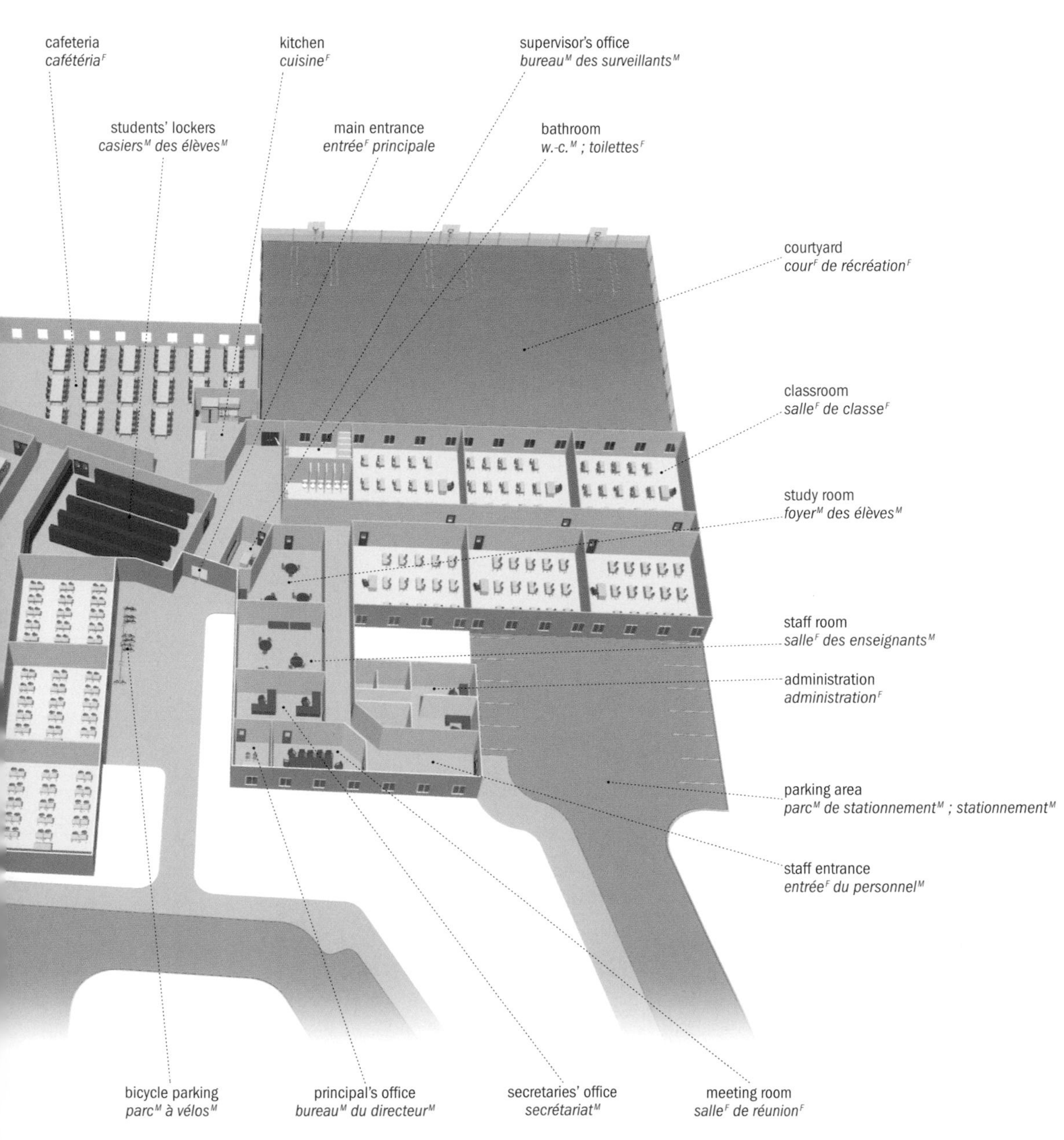
cafeteria
*cafétéria*F
kitchen
*cuisine*F
supervisor's office
*bureau*M *des surveillants*M
students' lockers
*casiers*M *des élèves*M
main entrance
*entrée*F *principale*
bathroom
*w.-c.*M ; *toilettes*F
courtyard
*cour*F *de récréation*F
classroom
*salle*F *de classe*F
study room
*foyer*M *des élèves*M
staff room
*salle*F *des enseignants*M
administration
*administration*F
parking area
*parc*M *de stationnement*M ; *stationnement*M
staff entrance
*entrée*F *du personnel*M
bicycle parking
*parc*M *à vélos*M
principal's office
*bureau*M *du directeur*M
secretaries' office
*secrétariat*M
meeting room
*salle*F *de réunion*F

Catholic church

église[F]

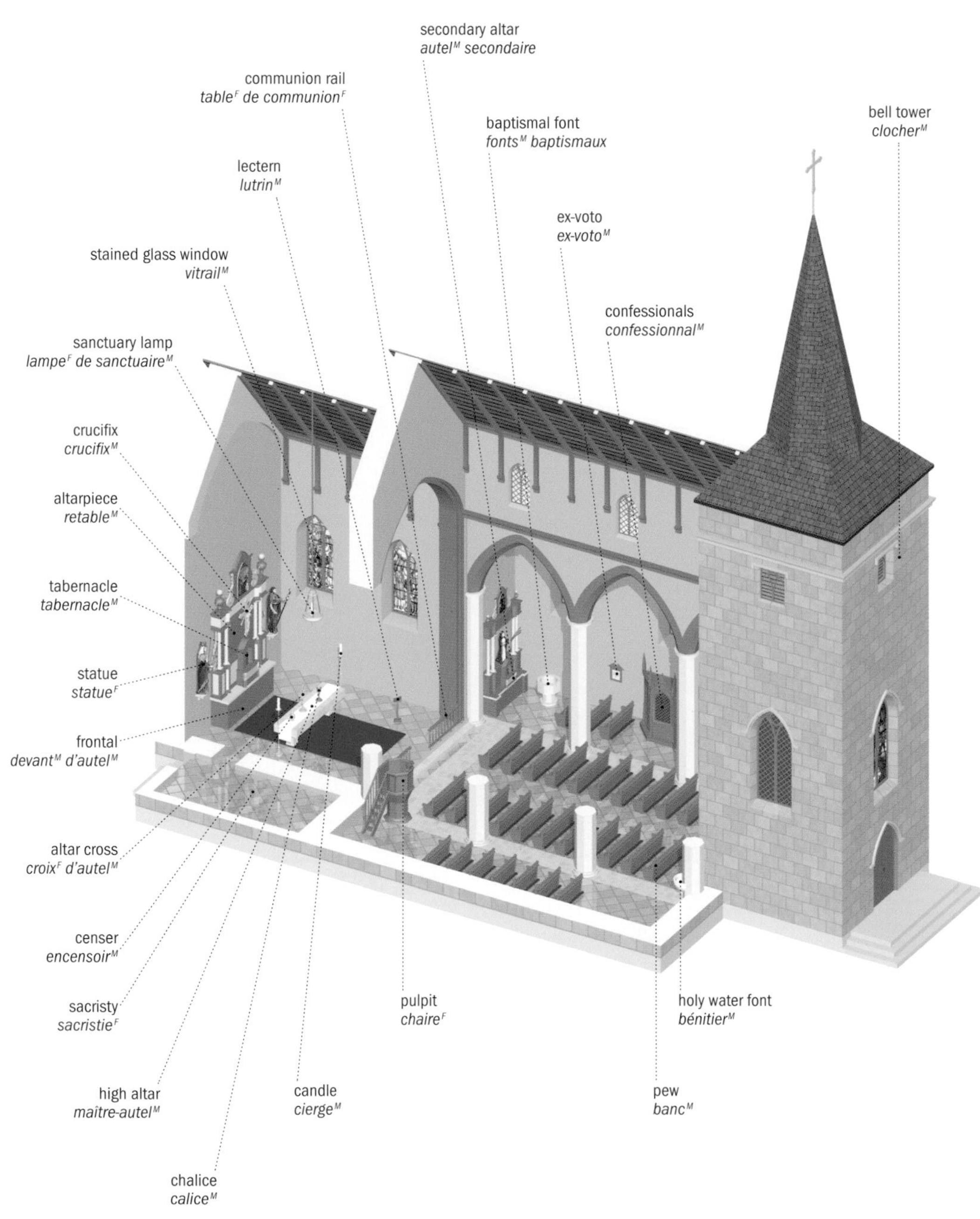
secondary altar
autel[M] secondaire
communion rail
table[F] de communion[F]
baptismal font
fonts[M] baptismaux
bell tower
clocher[M]
lectern
lutrin[M]
ex-voto
ex-voto[M]
stained glass window
vitrail[M]
confessionals
confessionnal[M]
sanctuary lamp
lampe[F] de sanctuaire[M]
crucifix
crucifix[M]
altarpiece
retable[M]
tabernacle
tabernacle[M]
statue
statue[F]
frontal
devant[M] d'autel[M]
altar cross
croix[F] d'autel[M]
censer
encensoir[M]
sacristy
sacristie[F]
pulpit
chaire[F]
holy water font
bénitier[M]
high altar
maître-autel[M]
candle
cierge[M]
pew
banc[M]
chalice
calice[M]

synagogue

synagogue[F]

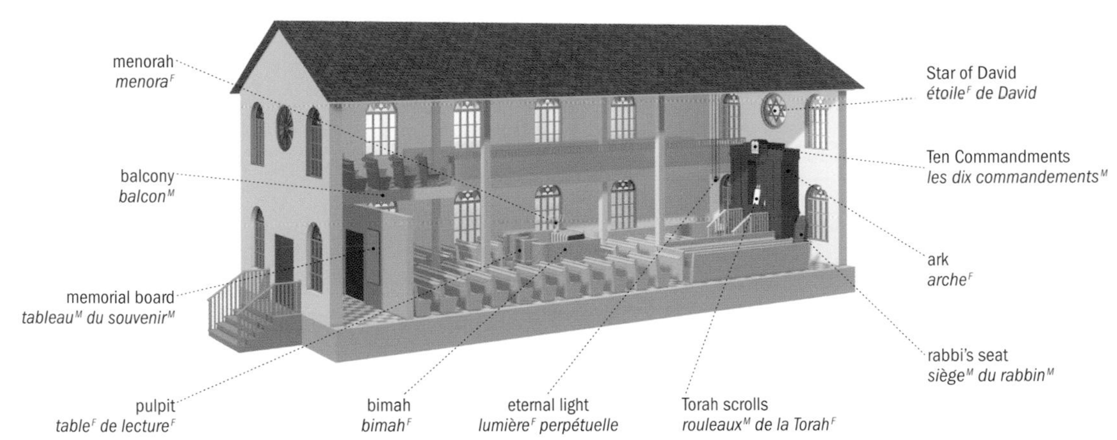
menorah
menora[F]
balcony
balcon[M]
memorial board
tableau[M] du souvenir[M]
pulpit
table[F] de lecture[F]
bimah
bimah[F]
eternal light
lumière[F] perpétuelle
Torah scrolls
rouleaux[M] de la Torah[F]
Star of David
étoile[F] de David
Ten Commandments
les dix commandements[M]
ark
arche[F]
rabbi's seat
siège[M] du rabbin[M]

mosque

mosquée[F]

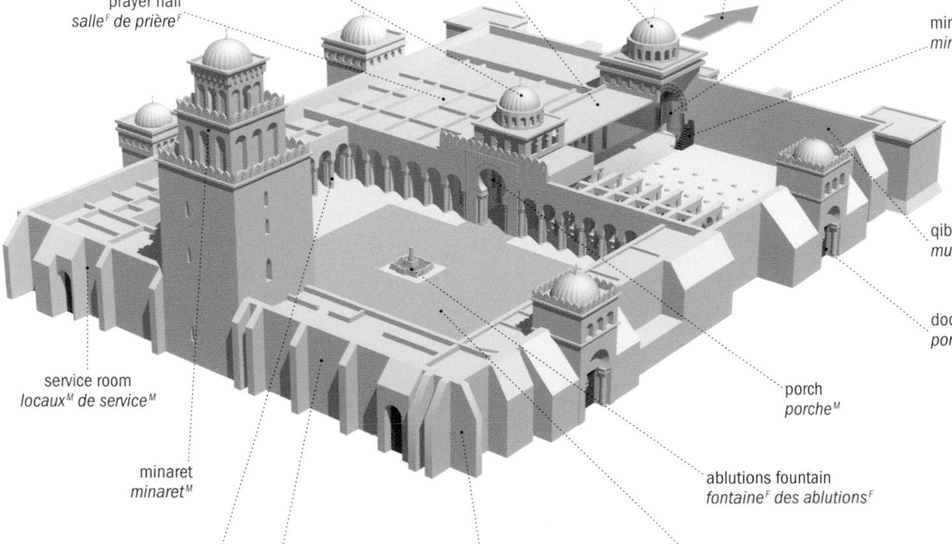

porch dome
coupole[F] du porche[M]

central nave
nef[F] centrale

mihrab dome
coupole[F] du mihrab[M]

direction of Mecca
direction[F] de La Mecque[F]

mihrab
mihrab[M]

prayer hall
salle[F] de prière[F]

minbar
minbar[M]

qibla wall
mur[M] de la qibla[F]

door
porte[F]

service room
locaux[M] de service[M]

porch
porche[M]

minaret
minaret[M]

ablutions fountain
fontaine[F] des ablutions[F]

shady arcades
portique[M]

reception hall
salle[F] de réception[F]

fortified wall
mur[M] fortifié

courtyard
cour[F]

flags

drapeaux[M]

Americas
***Amériques*[F]**

1 

Canada
Canada[M]

2 

United States of America
États-Unis[M] *d'Amérique*[F]

3 

Mexico
Mexique[M]

4 

Honduras
Honduras[M]

5 

Guatemala
Guatemala[M]

6 

Belize
Belize[M]

7 

El Salvador
El Salvador[M]

8 

Nicaragua
Nicaragua[M]

9 

Costa Rica
Costa Rica[M]

10 

Panama
Panama[M]

11 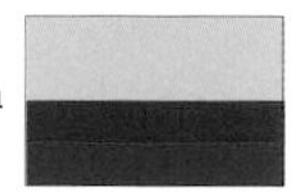

Colombia
Colombie[F]

12 

Venezuela
Venezuela[M]

13 

Guyana
Guyana[F]

14 

Suriname
Suriname[M]

15 

Ecuador
Équateur[M]

16 

Peru
Pérou[M]

17 

Brazil
Brésil[M]

18 

Bolivia
Bolivie[F]

19 

Paraguay
Paraguay[M]

20 

Chile
Chili[M]

21 

Argentina
Argentine[F]

22 

Uruguay
Uruguay[M]

Caribbean Islands
***Antilles*[F]**

23 

The Bahamas
Bahamas[F]

24 

Cuba
Cuba[F]

25 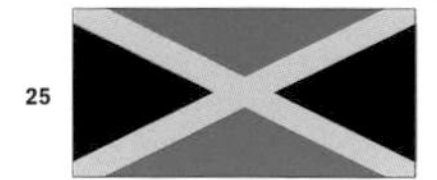

Jamaica
Jamaïque[F]

26 

Haiti
Haïti[M]

SOCIETY

27

Saint Kitts and Nevis
Saint-Kitts-et-Nevis[M]

28

Antigua and Barbuda
Antigua-et-Barbuda[F]

29

Dominica
Dominique[F]

30

Saint Lucia
Sainte-Lucie[F]

31 

Saint Vincent and the Grenadines
Saint-Vincent[M]*-et-les Grenadines*[F]

32 

Dominican Republic
République[F] *dominicaine*

33 

Barbados
Barbade[F]

34 

Grenada
Grenade[F]

35 

Trinidad and Tobago
Trinité-et-Tobago[F]

Europe
Europe[F]

36 

Andorra
Andorre[F]

37 

Portugal
Portugal[M]

38 

Spain
Espagne[F]

39 

United Kingdom
Royaume-Uni[M] *de Grande-Bretagne*[F] *et d'Irlande*[F] *du Nord*[M]

40 

France
France[F]

41 

Ireland
Irlande[F]

42 

Belgium
Belgique[F]

43 

Luxembourg
Luxembourg[M]

44 

Netherlands
Pays-Bas[M]

flags

45 
Germany
Allemagne[F]

46 
Liechtenstein
Liechtenstein[M]

47 
Switzerland
Suisse[F]

48 
Austria
Autriche[F]

49 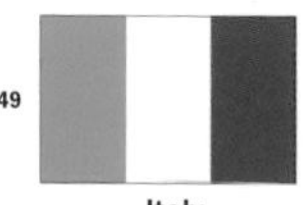
Italy
Italie[F]

50 
San Marino
Saint-Marin[M]

51 
Bulgaria
Bulgarie[F]

52 
Monaco
Monaco[M]

53 
Malta
Malte[F]

54 
Cyprus
Chypre[F]

55 
Greece
Grèce[F]

56 
Albania
Albanie[F]

57 
The Former Yugoslav Republic of Macedonia
Ex-République[F] *yougoslave de Macédoine*[F]

58 
Holy See (Vatican City)
État[M] *de la cité*[F] *du Vatican*[M]

59 
Serbia
Serbie[F]

60 
Montenegro
Monténégro[M]

61 
Bosnia and Herzegovina
Bosnie-Herzégovine[F]

62 
Croatia
Croatie[F]

63 
Slovenia
Slovénie[F]

64 
Hungary
Hongrie[F]

65 
Romania
Roumanie[F]

66 
Slovakia
Slovaquie[F]

67 
Czech Republic
République[F] *tchèque*

68 
Poland
Pologne[F]

69 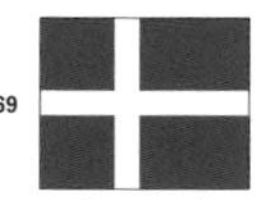
Denmark
Danemark[M]

70 
Iceland
Islande[F]

71 
Norway
Norvège[F]

72 
Lithuania
Lituanie[F]

73 
Sweden
Suède[F]

74 
Finland
Finlande[F]

75 
Estonia
Estonie[F]

76 
Latvia
Lettonie[F]

77 
Belarus
Bélarus[M]

78 
Ukraine
Ukraine[F]

79 
Moldova
République[F] *de Moldova*[F]

80 
Russia
Fédération[F] *de Russie*[F]

Africa
Afrique[F]

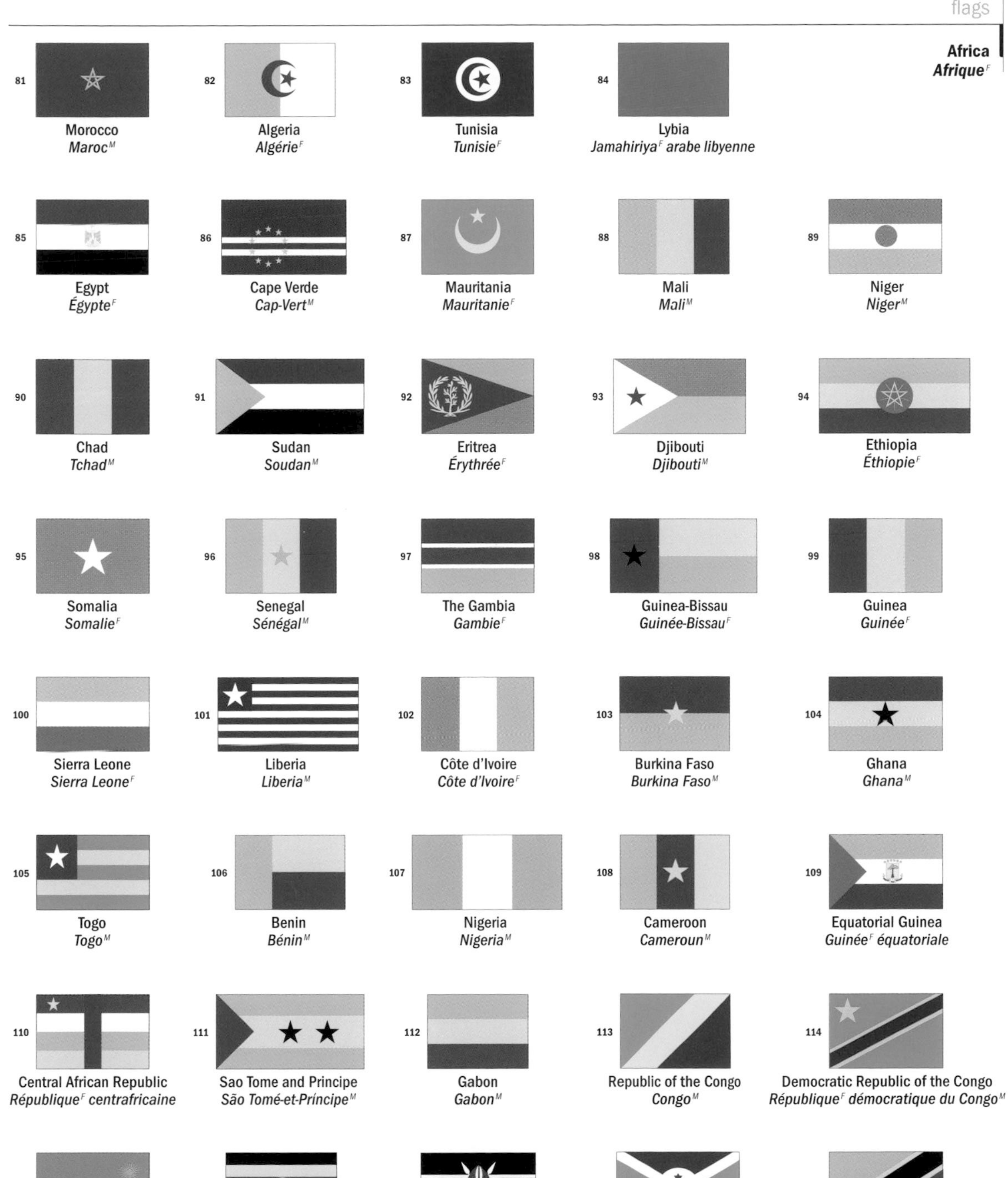

81 Morocco — *Maroc[M]*

82 Algeria — *Algérie[F]*

83 Tunisia — *Tunisie[F]*

84 Lybia — *Jamahiriya[F] arabe libyenne*

85 Egypt — *Égypte[F]*

86 Cape Verde — *Cap-Vert[M]*

87 Mauritania — *Mauritanie[F]*

88 Mali — *Mali[M]*

89 Niger — *Niger[M]*

90 Chad — *Tchad[M]*

91 Sudan — *Soudan[M]*

92 Eritrea — *Érythrée[F]*

93 Djibouti — *Djibouti[M]*

94 Ethiopia — *Éthiopie[F]*

95 Somalia — *Somalie[F]*

96 Senegal — *Sénégal[M]*

97 The Gambia — *Gambie[F]*

98 Guinea-Bissau — *Guinée-Bissau[F]*

99 Guinea — *Guinée[F]*

100 Sierra Leone — *Sierra Leone[F]*

101 Liberia — *Liberia[M]*

102 Côte d'Ivoire — *Côte d'Ivoire[F]*

103 Burkina Faso — *Burkina Faso[M]*

104 Ghana — *Ghana[M]*

105 Togo — *Togo[M]*

106 Benin — *Bénin[M]*

107 Nigeria — *Nigeria[M]*

108 Cameroon — *Cameroun[M]*

109 Equatorial Guinea — *Guinée[F] équatoriale*

110 Central African Republic — *République[F] centrafricaine*

111 Sao Tome and Principe — *São Tomé-et-Príncipe[M]*

112 Gabon — *Gabon[M]*

113 Republic of the Congo — *Congo[M]*

114 Democratic Republic of the Congo — *République[F] démocratique du Congo[M]*

115 Rwanda — *Rwanda[M]*

116 Uganda — *Ouganda[M]*

117 Kenya — *Kenya[M]*

118 Burundi — *Burundi[M]*

119 Tanzania — *République[F]-Unie de Tanzanie[F]*

flags

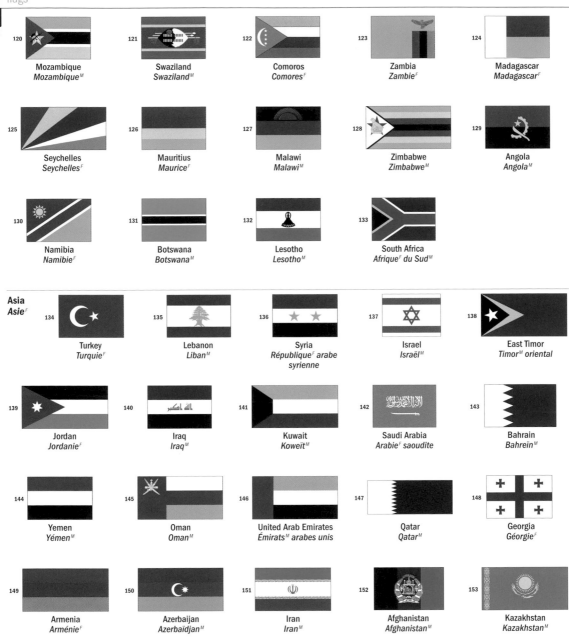

120 Mozambique *Mozambique*[M]

121 Swaziland *Swaziland*[M]

122 Comoros *Comores*[F]

123 Zambia *Zambie*[F]

124 Madagascar *Madagascar*[F]

125 Seychelles *Seychelles*[F]

126 Mauritius *Maurice*[F]

127 Malawi *Malawi*[M]

128 Zimbabwe *Zimbabwe*[M]

129 Angola *Angola*[M]

130 Namibia *Namibie*[F]

131 Botswana *Botswana*[M]

132 Lesotho *Lesotho*[M]

133 South Africa *Afrique*[F] *du Sud*[M]

Asia
Asie[F]

134 Turkey *Turquie*[F]

135 Lebanon *Liban*[M]

136 Syria *République*[F] *arabe syrienne*

137 Israel *Israël*[M]

138 East Timor *Timor*[M] *oriental*

139 Jordan *Jordanie*[F]

140 Iraq *Iraq*[M]

141 Kuwait *Koweït*[M]

142 Saudi Arabia *Arabie*[F] *saoudite*

143 Bahrain *Bahreïn*[M]

144 Yemen *Yémen*[M]

145 Oman *Oman*[M]

146 United Arab Emirates *Émirats*[M] *arabes unis*

147 Qatar *Qatar*[M]

148 Georgia *Géorgie*[F]

149 Armenia *Arménie*[F]

150 Azerbaijan *Azerbaïdjan*[M]

151 Iran *Iran*[M]

152 Afghanistan *Afghanistan*[M]

153 Kazakhstan *Kazakhstan*[M]

154 Turkmenistan *Turkménistan*[M]

155 Uzbekistan *Ouzbékistan*[M]

156 Kyrgyzstan *Kirghizistan*[M]

157 Tajikistan *Tadjikistan*[M]

158 Pakistan *Pakistan*[M]

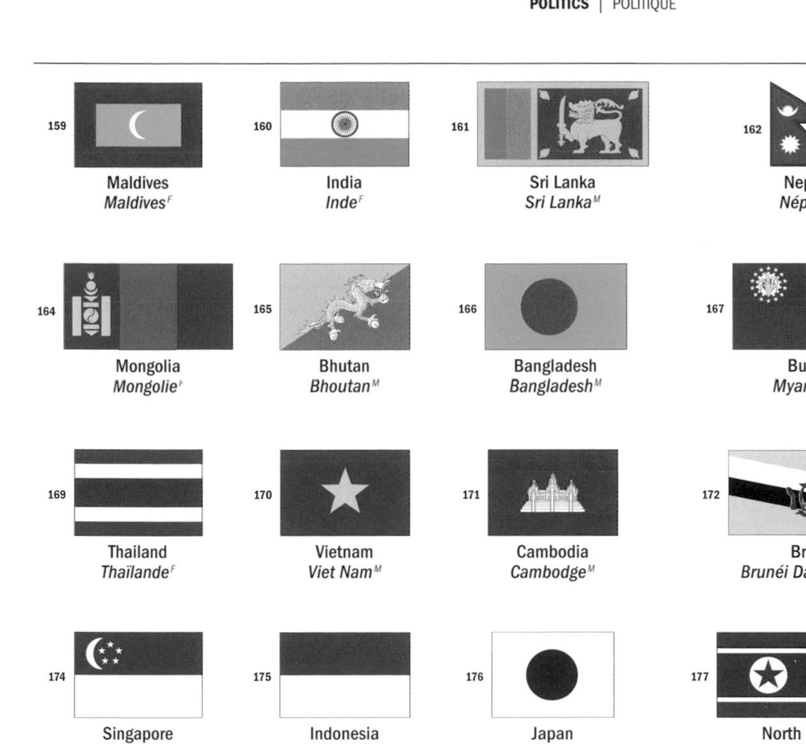

159 Maldives *Maldives[F]*

160 India *Inde[F]*

161 Sri Lanka *Sri Lanka[M]*

162 Nepal *Népal[M]*

163  China *Chine[F]*

164 Mongolia *Mongolie[F]*

165 Bhutan *Bhoutan[M]*

166 Bangladesh *Bangladesh[M]*

167  Burma *Myanmar[M]*

168  Laos *République[F] démocratique populaire lao*

169 Thailand *Thaïlande[F]*

170 Vietnam *Viet Nam[M]*

171 Cambodia *Cambodge[M]*

172  Brunei *Brunéi Darussalam[M]*

173  Malaysia *Malaisie[F]*

174 Singapore *Singapour[F]*

175 Indonesia *Indonésie[F]*

176 Japan *Japon[M]*

177 North Korea *République[F] populaire démocratique de Corée[F]*

178  South Korea *République[F] de Corée[F]*

Oceania and Polynesia
Océanie[F] et Polynésie[F]

179  Philippines *Philippines[F]*

180  Palau *Palaos[M]*

181  Federated States of Micronesia *Micronésie[F]*

182  Marshall Islands *Îles[F] Marshall*

183  Nauru *Nauru[F]*

184  Kiribati *Kiribati[F]*

185  Tuvalu *Tuvalu[M]*

186  Samoa *Samoa[F]*

187  Tonga *Tonga[F]*

188  Vanuatu *Vanuatu[M]*

189  Fiji *Fidji[F]*

190  Solomon Islands *Îles[F] Salomon*

191  Papua New Guinea *Papouasie-Nouvelle-Guinée[F]*

192  Australia *Australie[F]*

193  New Zealand *Nouvelle-Zélande[F]*

fire prevention

prévention^F des incendies^M

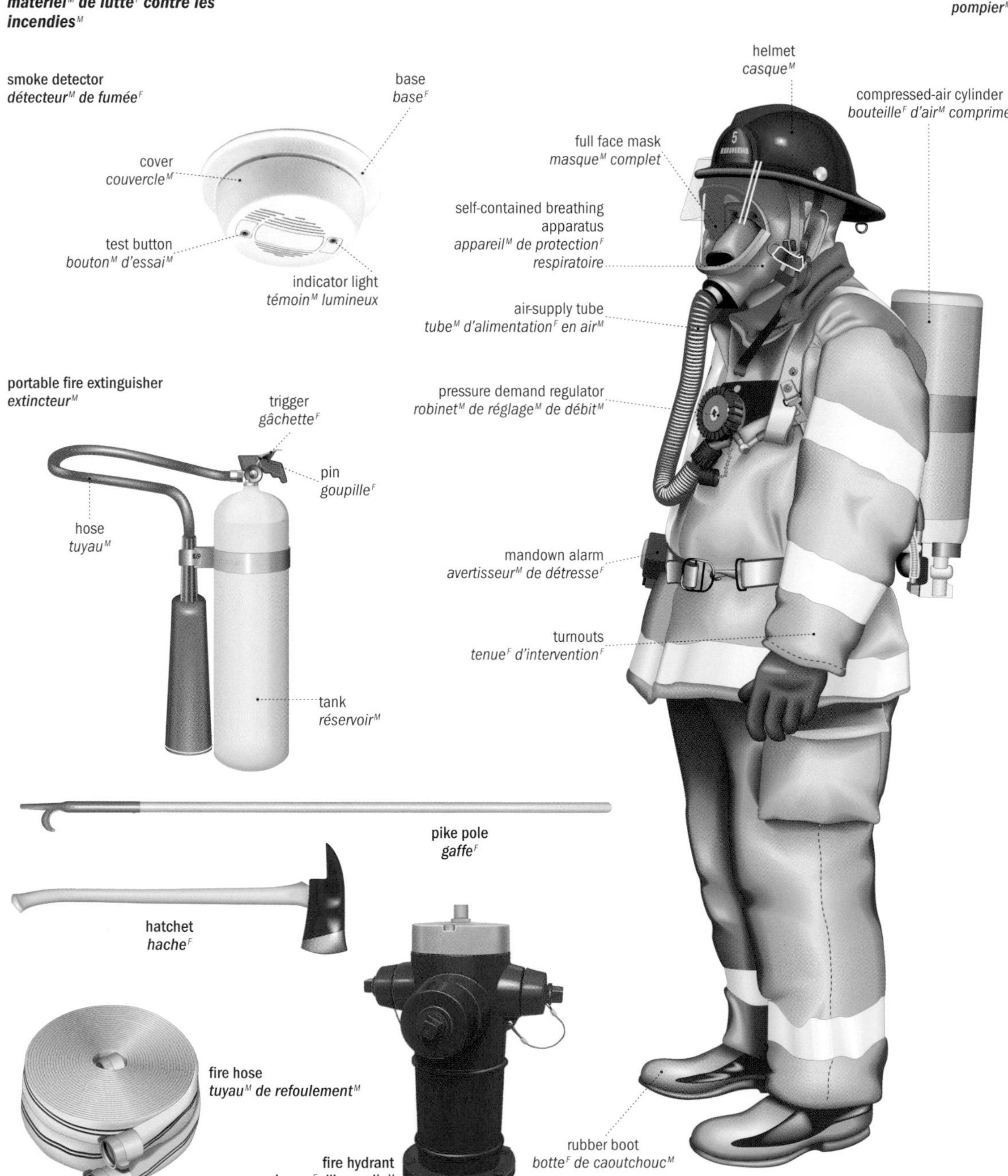
fire-fighting materials
matériel^M de lutte^F contre les incendies^M
smoke detector
détecteur^M de fumée^F
base
base^F
cover
couvercle^M
test button
bouton^M d'essai^M
indicator light
témoin^M lumineux
portable fire extinguisher
extincteur^M
trigger
gâchette^F
pin
goupille^F
hose
tuyau^M
tank
réservoir^M
pike pole
gaffe^F
hatchet
hache^F
fire hose
tuyau^M de refoulement^M
fire hydrant
borne^F d'incendie^M
firefighter
pompier^M
helmet
casque^M
compressed-air cylinder
bouteille^F d'air^M comprimé
full face mask
masque^M complet
self-contained breathing apparatus
appareil^M de protection^F respiratoire
air-supply tube
tube^M d'alimentation^F en air^M
pressure demand regulator
robinet^M de réglage^M de débit^M
mandown alarm
avertisseur^M de détresse^F
turnouts
tenue^F d'intervention^F
rubber boot
botte^F de caoutchouc^M

fire trucks
camions[M] d'incendie[M]

pumper
fourgon[M]-pompe[F]

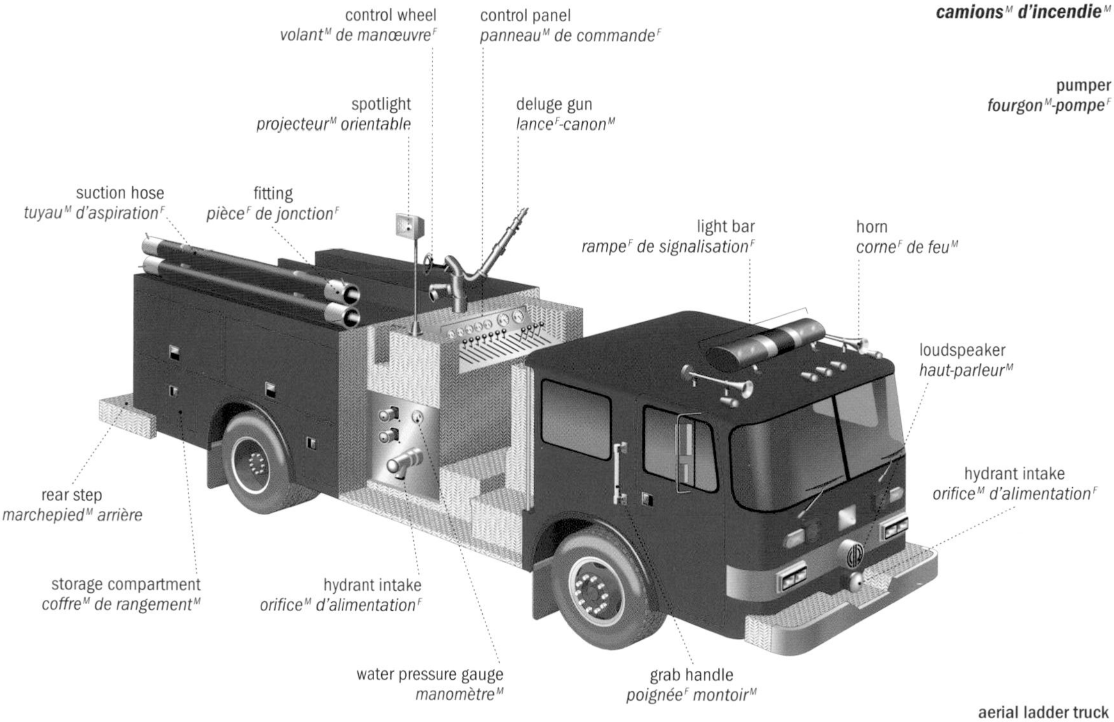

control wheel
volant[M] de manœuvre[F]

control panel
panneau[M] de commande[F]

spotlight
projecteur[M] orientable

deluge gun
lance[F]-canon[M]

suction hose
tuyau[M] d'aspiration[F]

fitting
pièce[F] de jonction[F]

light bar
rampe[F] de signalisation[F]

horn
corne[F] de feu[M]

loudspeaker
haut-parleur[M]

hydrant intake
orifice[M] d'alimentation[F]

rear step
marchepied[M] arrière

storage compartment
coffre[M] de rangement[M]

hydrant intake
orifice[M] d'alimentation[F]

water pressure gauge
manomètre[M]

grab handle
poignée[F] montoir[M]

aerial ladder truck
grande échelle[F]

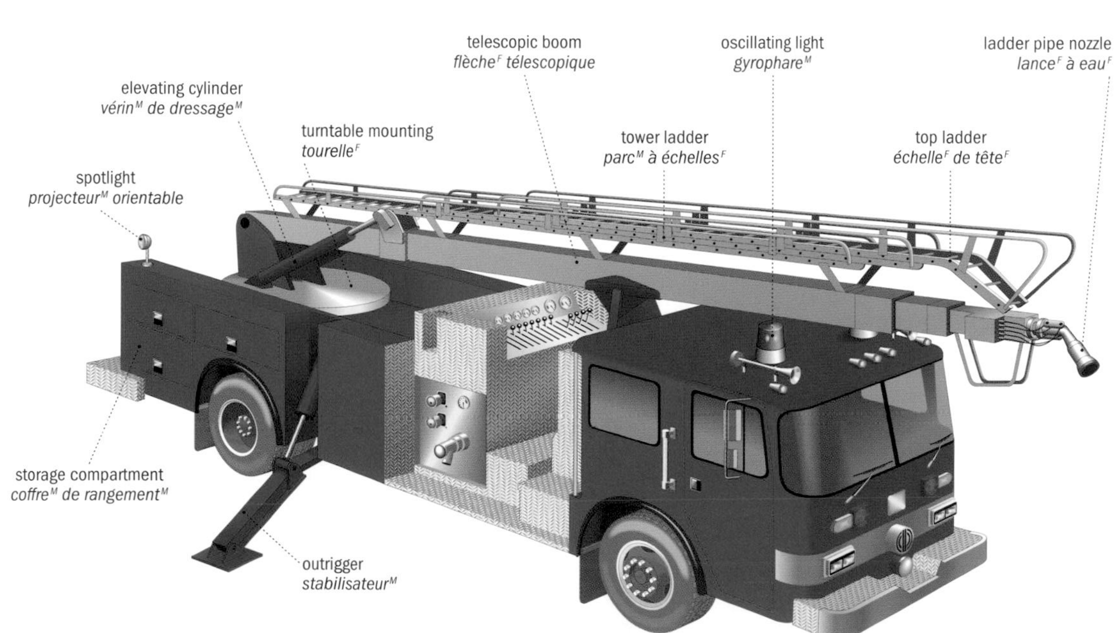
telescopic boom
flèche[F] télescopique
oscillating light
gyrophare[M]
ladder pipe nozzle
lance[F] à eau[F]
elevating cylinder
vérin[M] de dressage[M]
turntable mounting
tourelle[F]
tower ladder
parc[M] à échelles[F]
top ladder
échelle[F] de tête[F]
spotlight
projecteur[M] orientable
storage compartment
coffre[M] de rangement[M]
outrigger
stabilisateur[M]

SOCIETY

ear protection

protection[F] de l'ouïe[F]

safety earmuffs
serre-tête[M] antibruit

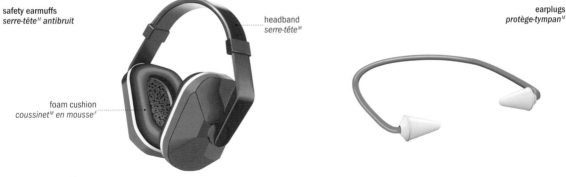

headband
serre-tête[M]

foam cushion
coussinet[M] en mousse[F]

earplugs
protège-tympan[M]

eye protection

protection[F] des yeux[M]

safety glasses
lunettes[F] de sécurité[F]

safety goggles
lunettes[F] de protection[F]

head protection

protection[F] de la tête[F]

hard hat
casque[M] de sécurité[F]

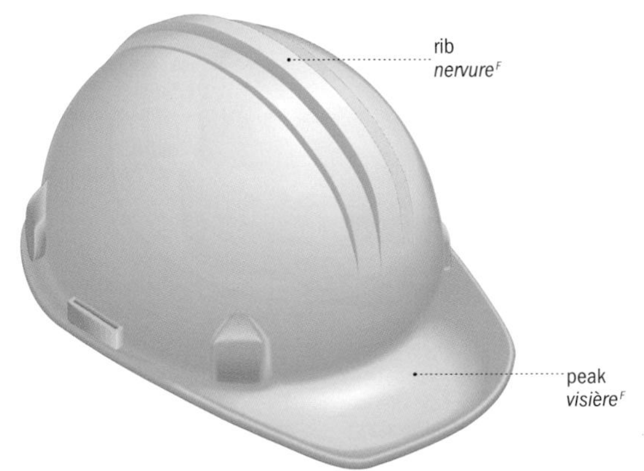
rib
nervure[F]
peak
visière[F]

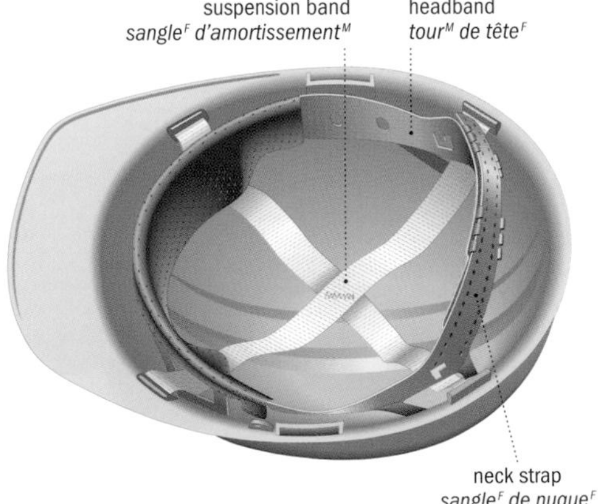
suspension band
sangle[F] d'amortissement[M]
headband
tour[M] de tête[F]
neck strap
sangle[F] de nuque[F]

respiratory system protection

protection^{F} des voies^{F} respiratoires

respirator
masque^{M} respiratoire

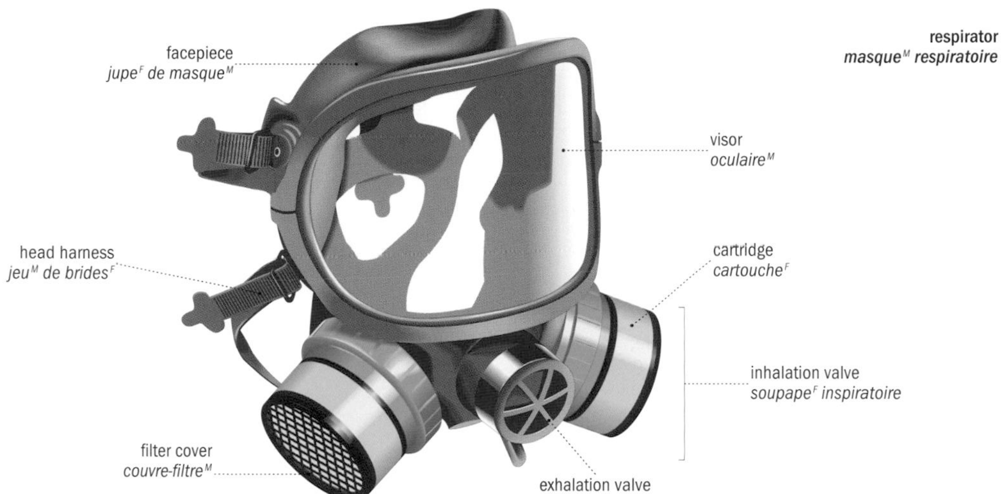
facepiece
jupe^{F} de masque^{M}
visor
oculaire^{M}
head harness
jeu^{M} de brides^{F}
cartridge
cartouche^{F}
inhalation valve
soupape^{F} inspiratoire
filter cover
couvre-filtre^{M}
exhalation valve
soupape^{F} expiratoire

operating mask
masque^{M} de chirurgie^{F}

half-mask respirator
masque^{M} bucco-nasal

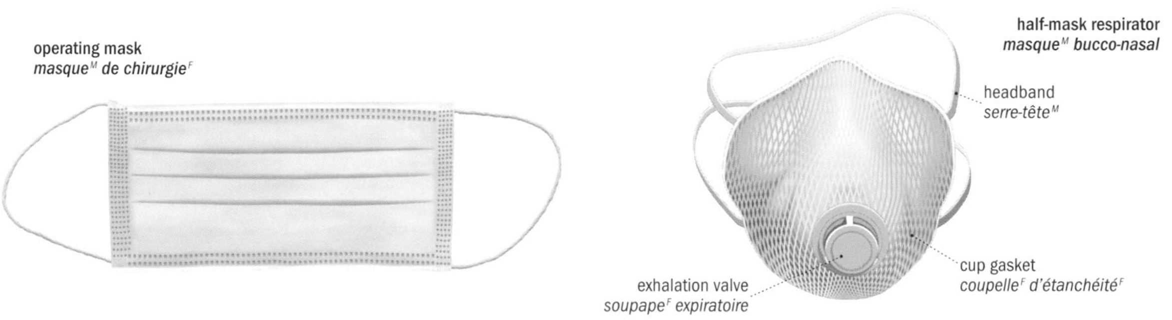
headband
serre-tête^{M}
cup gasket
coupelle^{F} d'étanchéité^{F}
exhalation valve
soupape^{F} expiratoire

foot protection

protection^{F} des pieds^{M}

safety boot
brodequin^{M} de sécurité^{F}

toe guard
protège-orteils^{M}

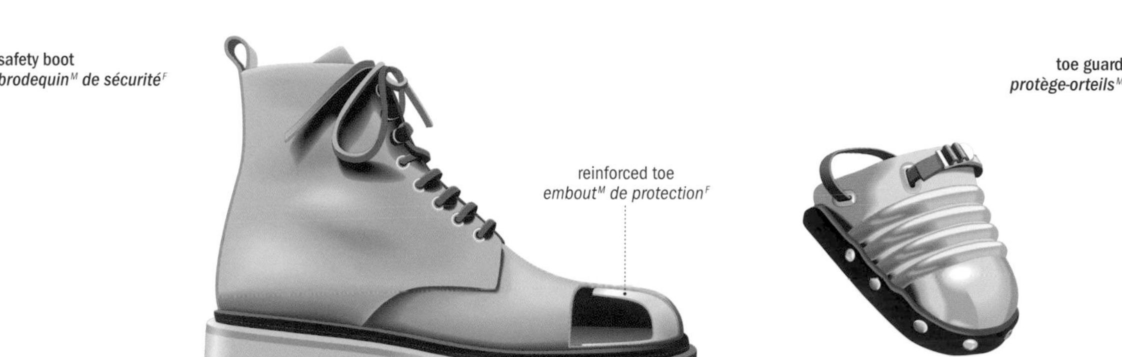
reinforced toe
embout^{M} de protection^{F}

first aid equipment

matériel[M] de secours[M]

stethoscope
stéthoscope[M]

Y-tube
tube[M] en Y[M]

sound receiver
récepteur[M] de son[M]

branch clip
lame[F]-ressort[M]

earpiece
embout[M] auriculaire

flexible tube
tube[M] flexible

branch
branche[F]

syringe
seringue[F]

bevel
biseau[M]

needle
aiguille[F]

needle hub
pavillon[M]

Luer-Lock tip
embout[M] Luer Lock

hollow barrel
corps[M] de pompe[F]

tip protector
protecteur[M] d'embout[M]

rubber bulb
bouchon[M]

finger flange
anneau[M] de retenue[F]

scale
graduation[F]

thumb rest
poussoir[M]

plunger
piston[M]

latex glove
gant[M] en latex[M]

syringe for irrigation
seringue[F] pour lavage[M] de cavités[F]

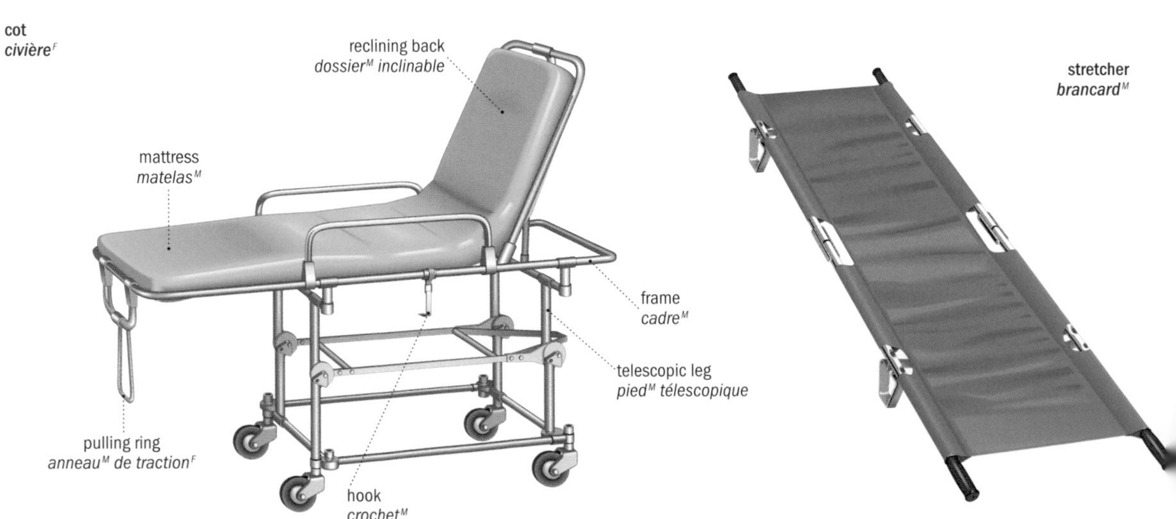
cot
civière[F]
reclining back
dossier[M] inclinable
mattress
matelas[M]
frame
cadre[M]
telescopic leg
pied[M] télescopique
pulling ring
anneau[M] de traction[F]
hook
crochet[M]
stretcher
brancard[M]

first aid kit

trousse^F de secours^M

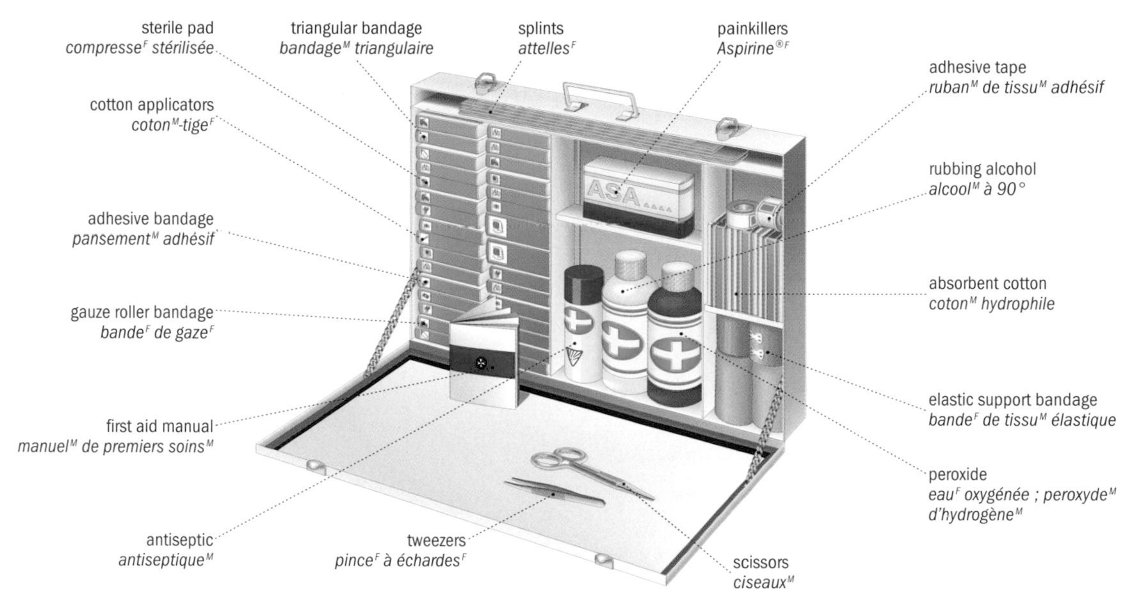
sterile pad
compresse^F stérilisée
triangular bandage
bandage^M triangulaire
splints
attelles^F
painkillers
Aspirine®^F
adhesive tape
ruban^M de tissu^M adhésif
cotton applicators
coton^M-tige^F
rubbing alcohol
alcool^M à 90°
adhesive bandage
pansement^M adhésif
absorbent cotton
coton^M hydrophile
gauze roller bandage
bande^F de gaze^F
elastic support bandage
bande^F de tissu^M élastique
first aid manual
manuel^M de premiers soins^M
peroxide
eau^F oxygénée ; peroxyde^M d'hydrogène^M
antiseptic
antiseptique^M
tweezers
pince^F à échardes^F
scissors
ciseaux^M

clinical thermometers

thermomètres^M médicaux

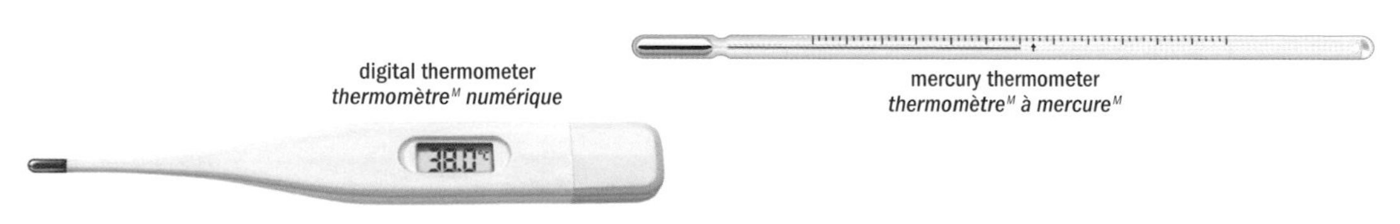
digital thermometer
thermomètre^M numérique
mercury thermometer
thermomètre^M à mercure^M

blood pressure monitor

tensiomètre^M

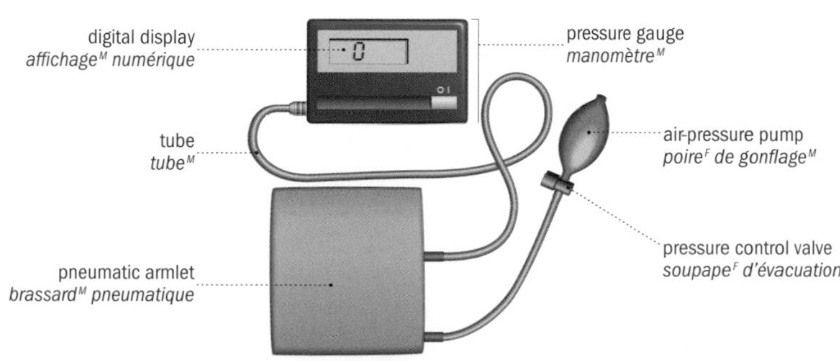
digital display
affichage^M numérique
pressure gauge
manomètre^M
tube
tube^M
air-pressure pump
poire^F de gonflage^M
pressure control valve
soupape^F d'évacuation^F
pneumatic armlet
brassard^M pneumatique

SOCIETY

hospital

hôpital[M]

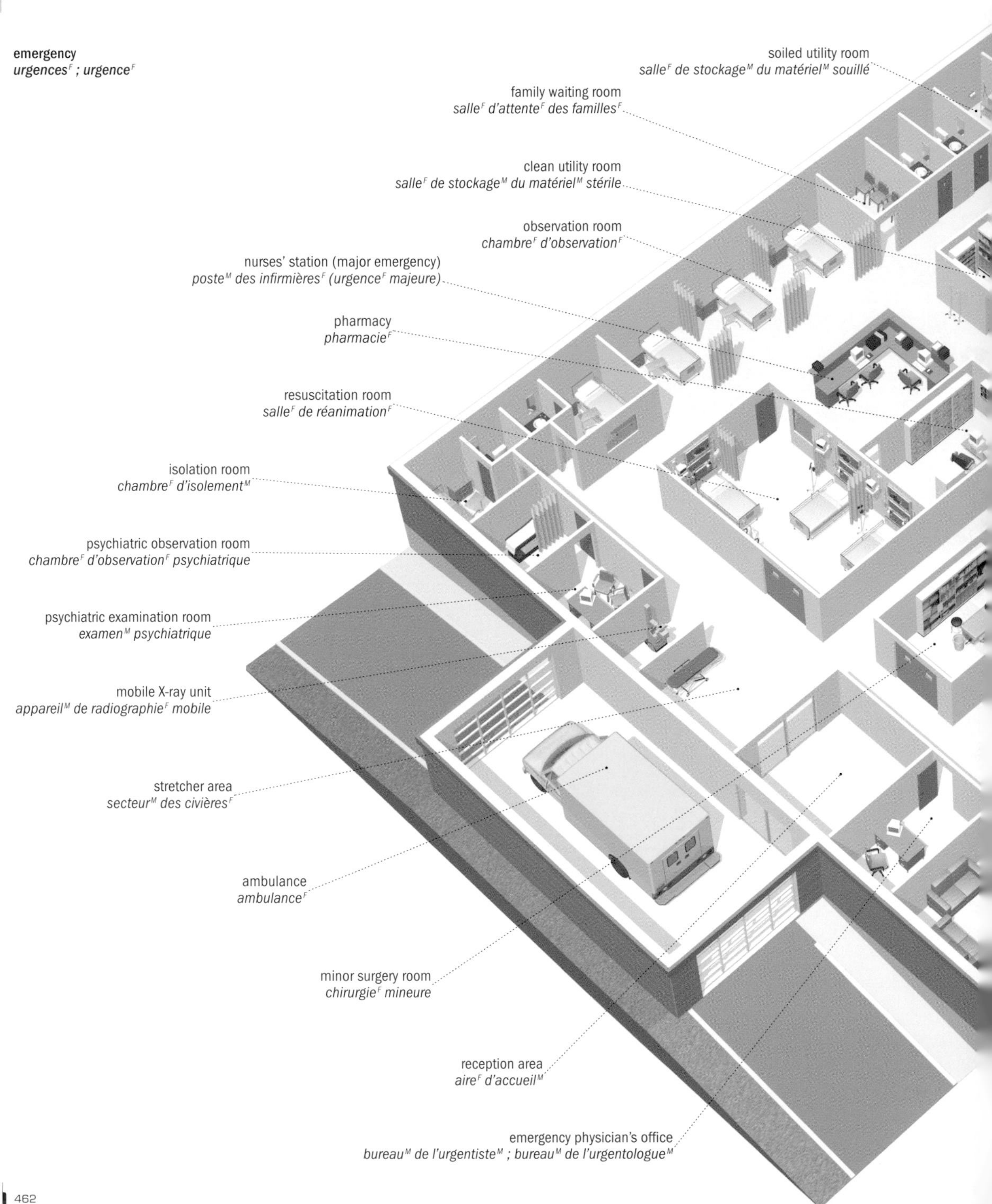
emergency
urgences[F] ; urgence[F]
soiled utility room
salle[F] de stockage[M] du matériel[M] souillé
family waiting room
salle[F] d'attente[F] des familles[F]
clean utility room
salle[F] de stockage[M] du matériel[M] stérile
observation room
chambre[F] d'observation[F]
nurses' station (major emergency)
poste[M] des infirmières[F] (urgence[F] majeure)
pharmacy
pharmacie[F]
resuscitation room
salle[F] de réanimation[F]
isolation room
chambre[F] d'isolement[M]
psychiatric observation room
chambre[F] d'observation[F] psychiatrique
psychiatric examination room
examen[M] psychiatrique
mobile X-ray unit
appareil[M] de radiographie[F] mobile
stretcher area
secteur[M] des civières[F]
ambulance
ambulance[F]
minor surgery room
chirurgie[F] mineure
reception area
aire[F] d'accueil[M]
emergency physician's office
bureau[M] de l'urgentiste[M] ; bureau[M] de l'urgentologue[M]

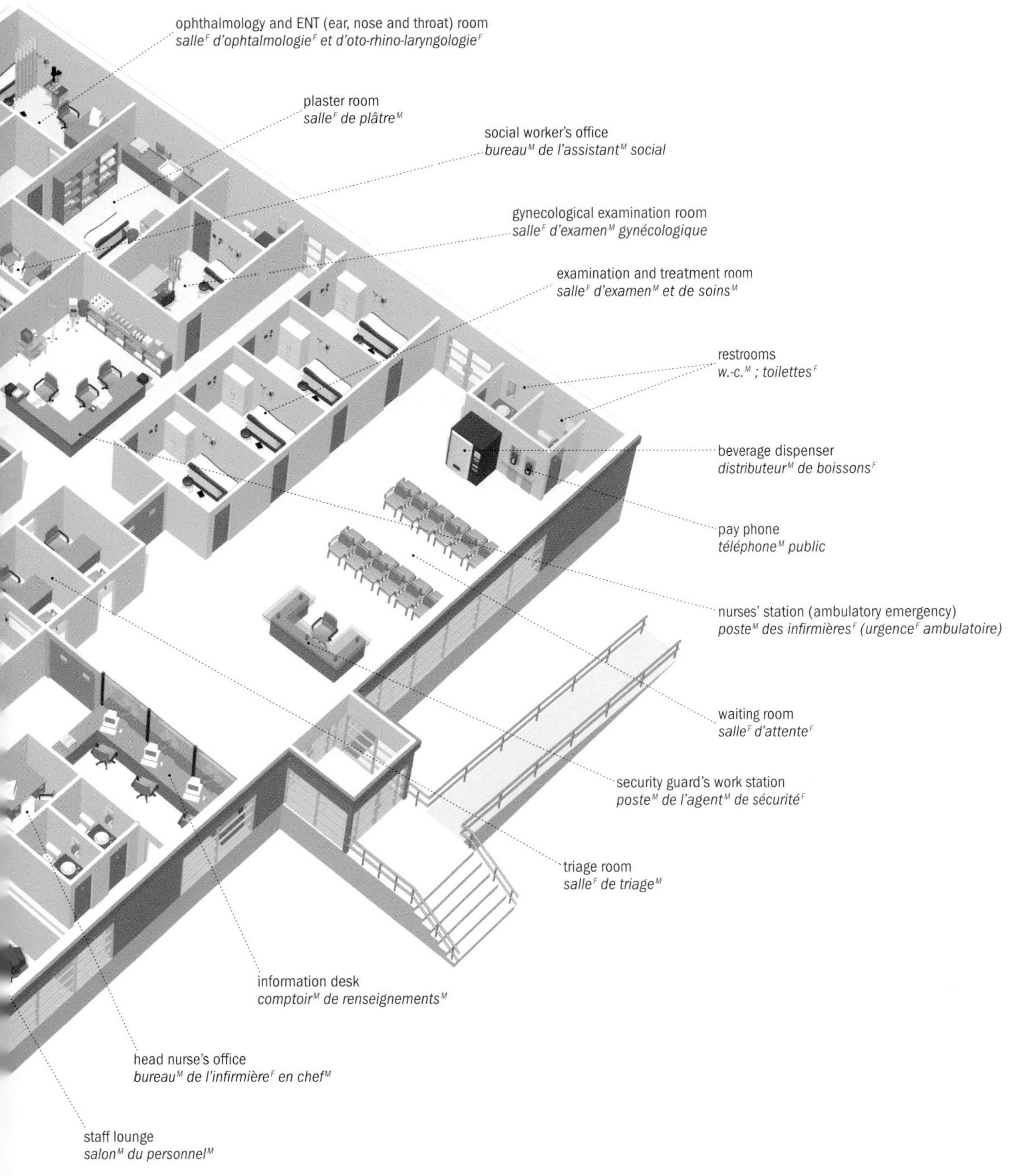
ophthalmology and ENT (ear, nose and throat) room
salle^F d'ophtalmologie^F et d'oto-rhino-laryngologie^F
plaster room
salle^F de plâtre^M
social worker's office
bureau^M de l'assistant^M social
gynecological examination room
salle^F d'examen^M gynécologique
examination and treatment room
salle^F d'examen^M et de soins^M
restrooms
w.-c.^M ; toilettes^F
beverage dispenser
distributeur^M de boissons^F
pay phone
téléphone^M public
nurses' station (ambulatory emergency)
poste^M des infirmières^F (urgence^F ambulatoire)
waiting room
salle^F d'attente^F
security guard's work station
poste^M de l'agent^M de sécurité^F
triage room
salle^F de triage^M
information desk
comptoir^M de renseignements^M
head nurse's office
bureau^M de l'infirmière^F en chef^M
staff lounge
salon^M du personnel^M

hospital

patient room
chambre[F] d'hôpital[M]

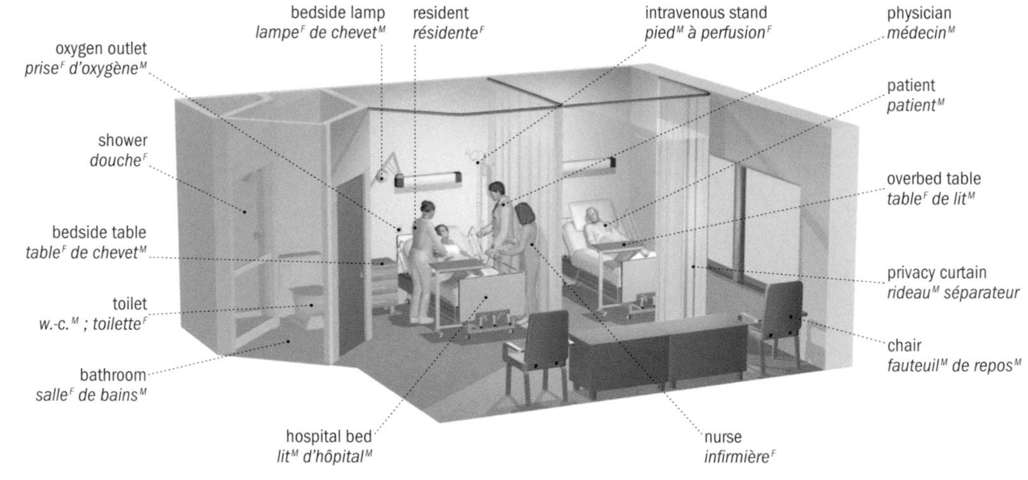
bedside lamp
lampe[F] de chevet[M]
resident
résidente[F]
intravenous stand
pied[M] à perfusion[F]
physician
médecin[M]
oxygen outlet
prise[F] d'oxygène[M]
patient
patient[M]
shower
douche[F]
overbed table
table[F] de lit[M]
bedside table
table[F] de chevet[M]
privacy curtain
rideau[M] séparateur
toilet
w.-c.[M] ; toilette[F]
chair
fauteuil[M] de repos[M]
bathroom
salle[F] de bains[M]
hospital bed
lit[M] d'hôpital[M]
nurse
infirmière[F]

operating suite
bloc[M] opératoire

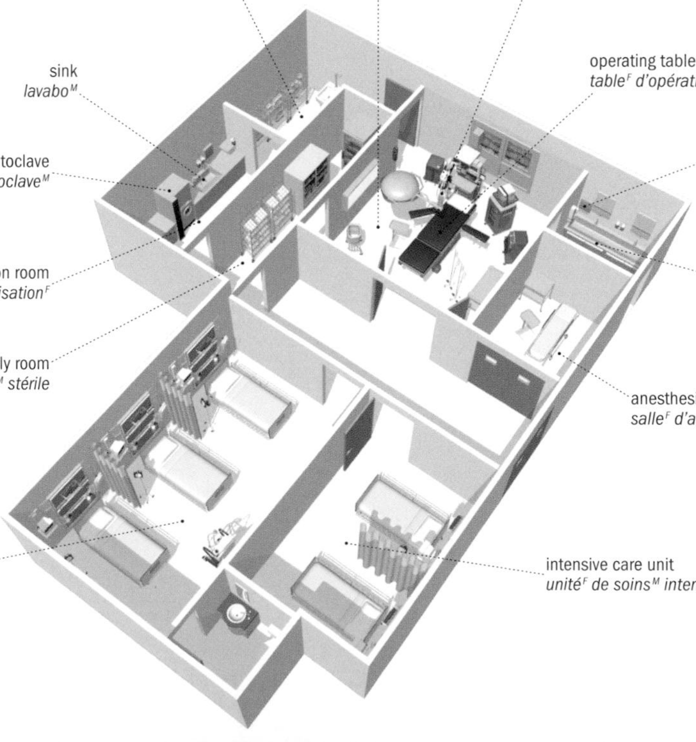

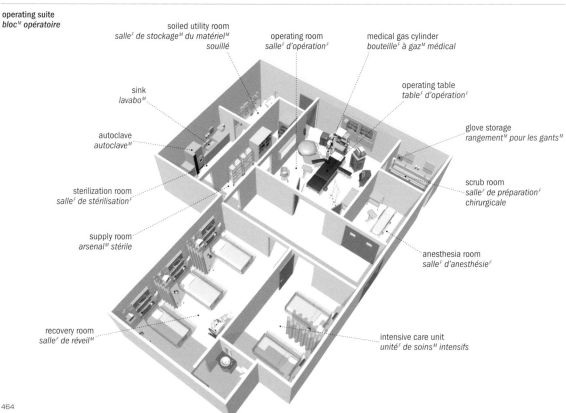

soiled utility room
salle[F] de stockage[M] du matériel[M] souillé

operating room
salle[F] d'opération[F]

medical gas cylinder
bouteille[F] à gaz[M] médical

sink
lavabo[M]

operating table
table[F] d'opération[F]

glove storage
rangement[M] pour les gants[M]

autoclave
autoclave[M]

sterilization room
salle[F] de stérilisation[F]

scrub room
salle[F] de préparation[F] chirurgicale

supply room
arsenal[M] stérile

anesthesia room
salle[F] d'anesthésie[F]

recovery room
salle[F] de réveil[M]

intensive care unit
unité[F] de soins[M] intensifs

ambulatory care unit
unité[F] de soins[M] ambulatoires

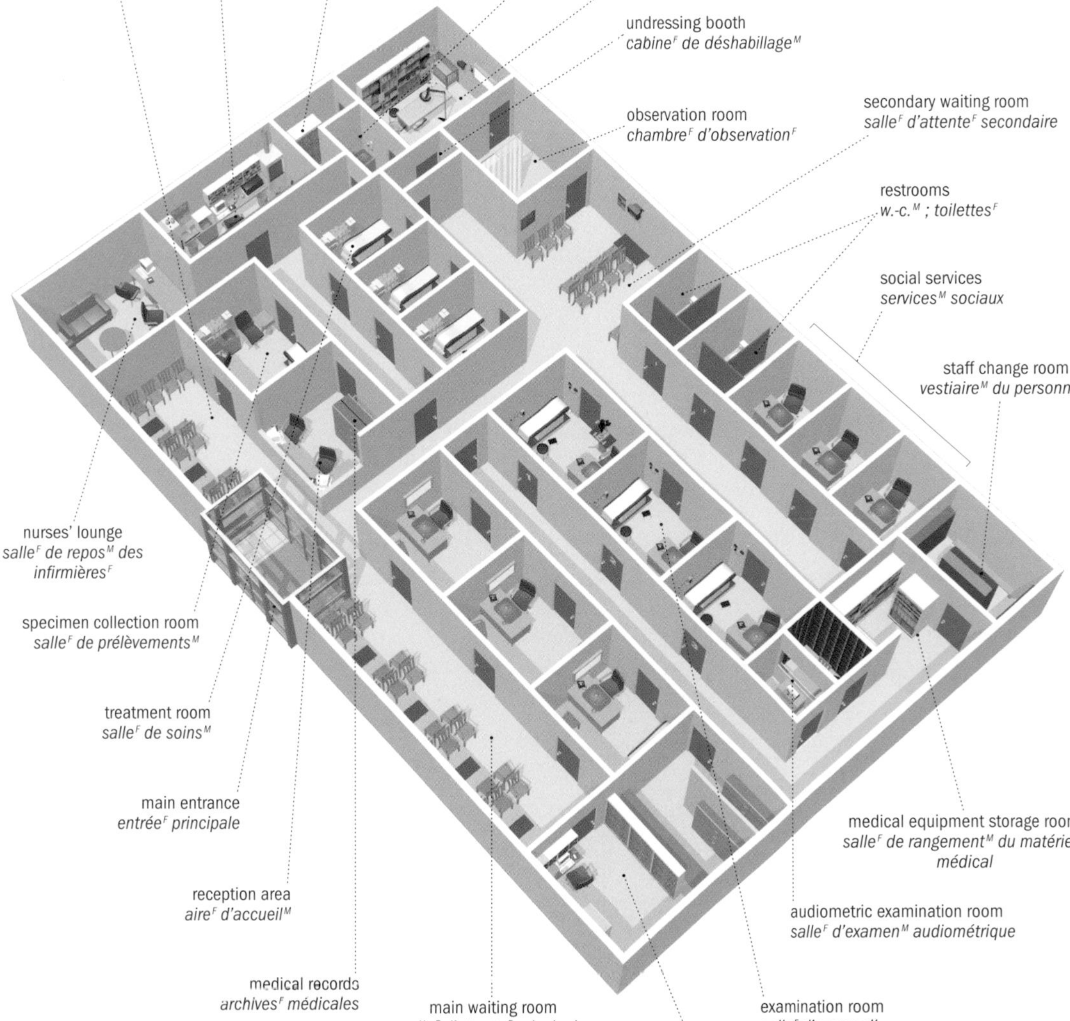

specimen collection center waiting room
salle[F] d'attente[F] du centre[M] de prélèvements[M]
surgeon's sink
lavabo[M] du chirurgien[M]
pathology laboratory
laboratoire[M] de pathologie[F]
sterilization room
salle[F] de stérilisation[F]
operating room
salle[F] d'opération[F]
undressing booth
cabine[F] de déshabillage[M]
observation room
chambre[F] d'observation[F]
secondary waiting room
salle[F] d'attente[F] secondaire
restrooms
w.-c.[M] ; toilettes[F]
social services
services[M] sociaux
staff change room
vestiaire[M] du personnel[M]
nurses' lounge
salle[F] de repos[M] des infirmières[F]
specimen collection room
salle[F] de prélèvements[M]
treatment room
salle[F] de soins[M]
main entrance
entrée[F] principale
reception area
aire[F] d'accueil[M]
medical records
archives[F] médicales
main waiting room
salle[F] d'attente[F] principale
pharmacy
pharmacie[F]
examination room
salle[F] d'examen[M]
audiometric examination room
salle[F] d'examen[M] audiométrique
medical equipment storage room
salle[F] de rangement[M] du matériel[M] médical

walking aids

aides^F à la marche^F

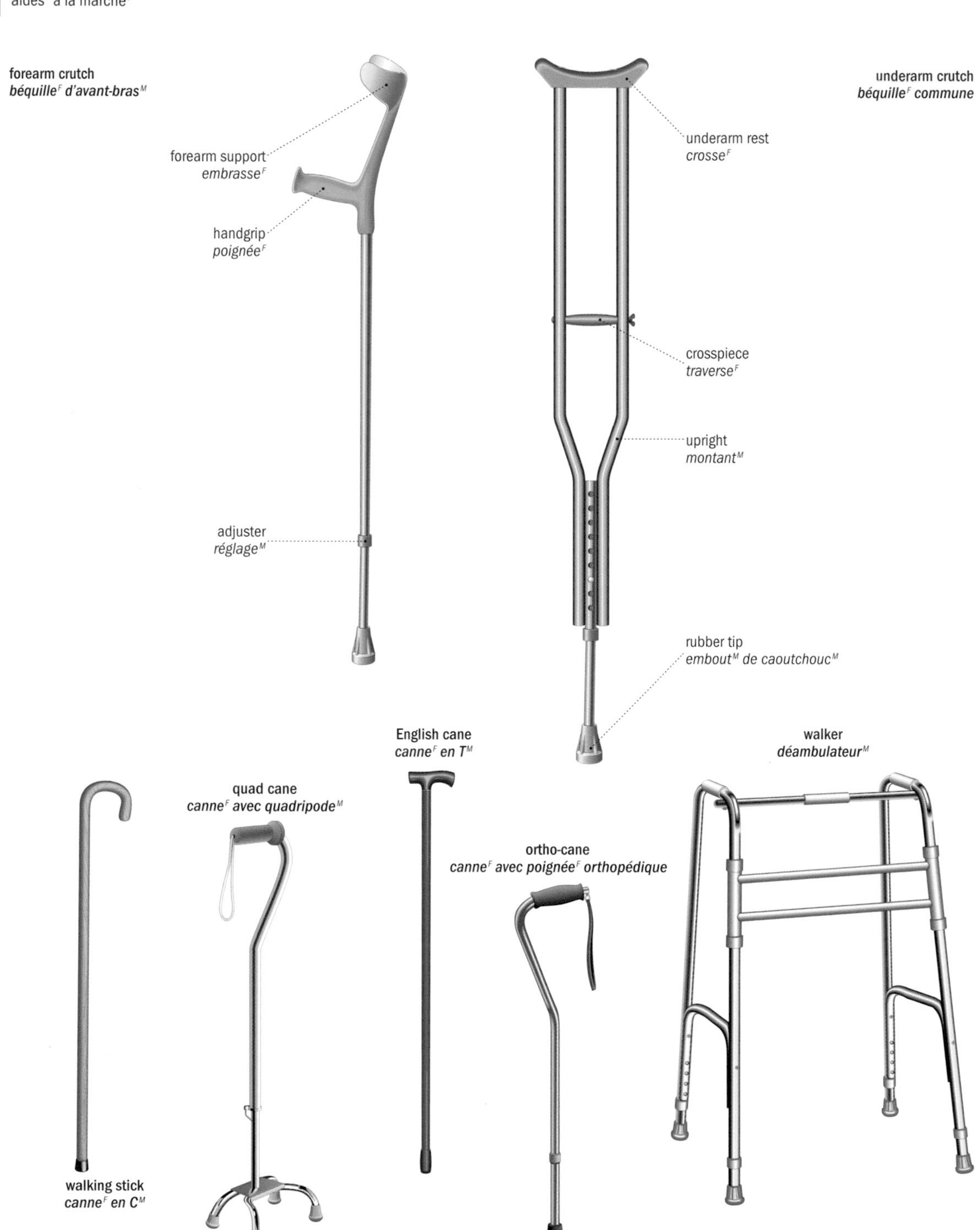
forearm crutch
béquille^F d'avant-bras^M
underarm crutch
béquille^F commune
forearm support
embrasse^F
handgrip
poignée^F
underarm rest
crosse^F
crosspiece
traverse^F
upright
montant^M
adjuster
réglage^M
rubber tip
embout^M de caoutchouc^M
English cane
canne^F en T^M
walker
déambulateur^M
quad cane
canne^F avec quadripode^M
ortho-cane
canne^F avec poignée^F orthopédique
walking stick
canne^F en C^M

wheelchair

fauteuil[M] roulant

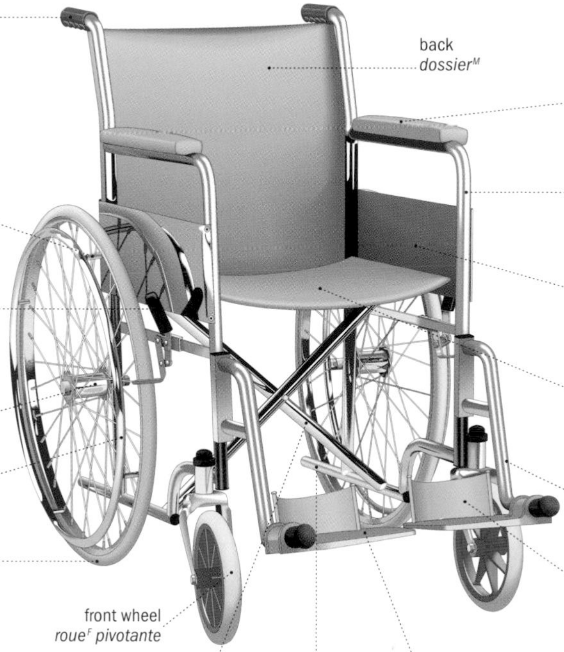

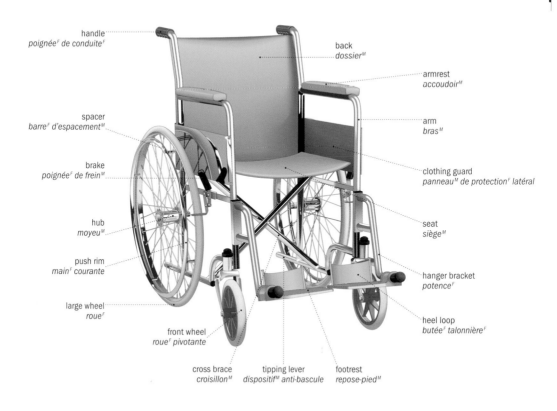

handle
poignée[F] de conduite[F]

back
dossier[M]

armrest
accoudoir[M]

spacer
barre[F] d'espacement[M]

arm
bras[M]

brake
poignée[F] de frein[M]

clothing guard
panneau[M] de protection[F] latéral

hub
moyeu[M]

seat
siège[M]

push rim
main[F] courante

hanger bracket
potence[F]

large wheel
roue[F]

heel loop
butée[F] talonnière[F]

front wheel
roue[F] pivotante

cross brace
croisillon[M]

tipping lever
dispositif[M] anti-bascule

footrest
repose-pied[M]

forms of medications

formes[F] pharmaceutiques des médicaments[M]

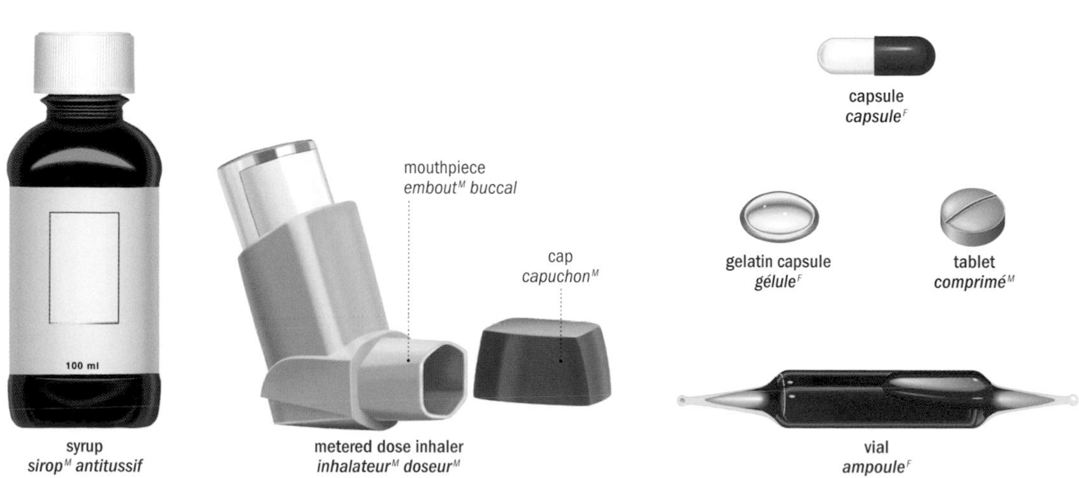
capsule
capsule[F]
100 ml
mouthpiece
embout[M] buccal
cap
capuchon[M]
gelatin capsule
gélule[F]
tablet
comprimé[M]
syrup
sirop[M] antitussif
metered dose inhaler
inhalateur[M] doseur[M]
vial
ampoule[F]

dice and dominoes

dés[M] et dominos[M]

ordinary die
dé[M] régulier

poker die
dé[M] à poker[M]

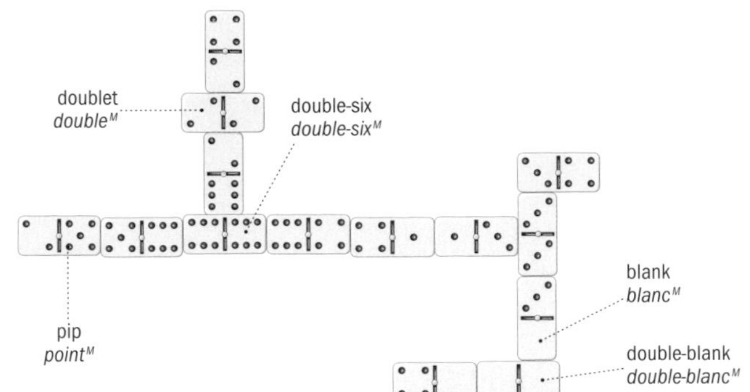
dominoes
dominos[M]
doublet
double[M]
double-six
double-six[M]
blank
blanc[M]
pip
point[M]
double-blank
double-blanc[M]

cards

cartes[F]

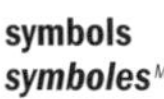

symbols
symboles[M]

heart
cœur[M]

diamond
carreau[M]

club
trèfle[M]

spade
pique[M]

joker
Joker[M]

ace
As[M]

king
Roi[M]

queen
Dame[F]

jack
Valet[M]

standard poker hands
combinaisons[F] au poker[M]

high card
carte[F] isolée

one pair
paire[F]

two pairs
double paire[F]

three-of-a-kind
brelan[M]

straight
séquence[F]

flush
couleur[F]

full house
main[F] pleine

four-of-a-kind
carré[M]

straight flush
quinte[F]

royal flush
quinte[F] royale

board games
jeux[M] de plateau[M]

backgammon
jacquet[M]

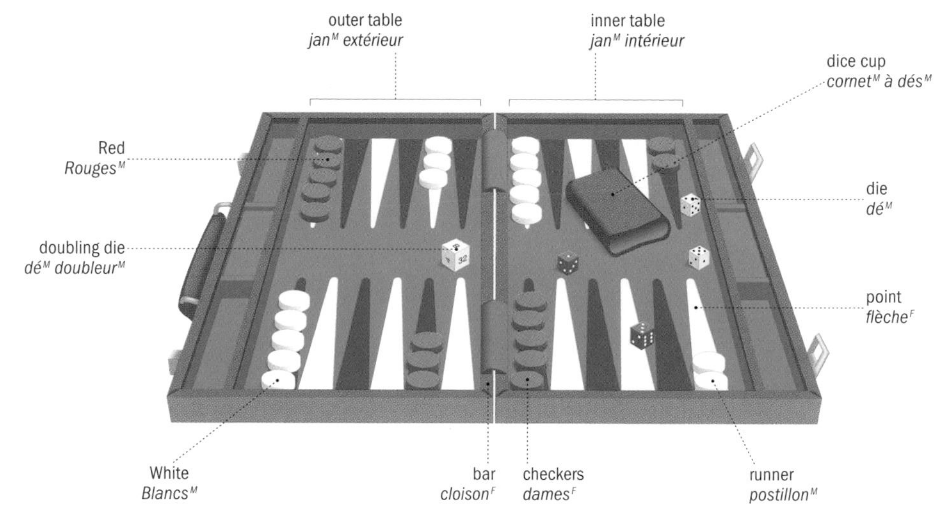
outer table
jan[M] extérieur
inner table
jan[M] intérieur
dice cup
cornet[M] à dés[M]
Red
Rouges[M]
die
dé[M]
doubling die
dé[M] doubleur[M]
point
flèche[F]
White
Blancs[M]
bar
cloison[F]
checkers
dames[F]
runner
postillon[M]

snakes and ladders
serpents[M] et échelles[F]

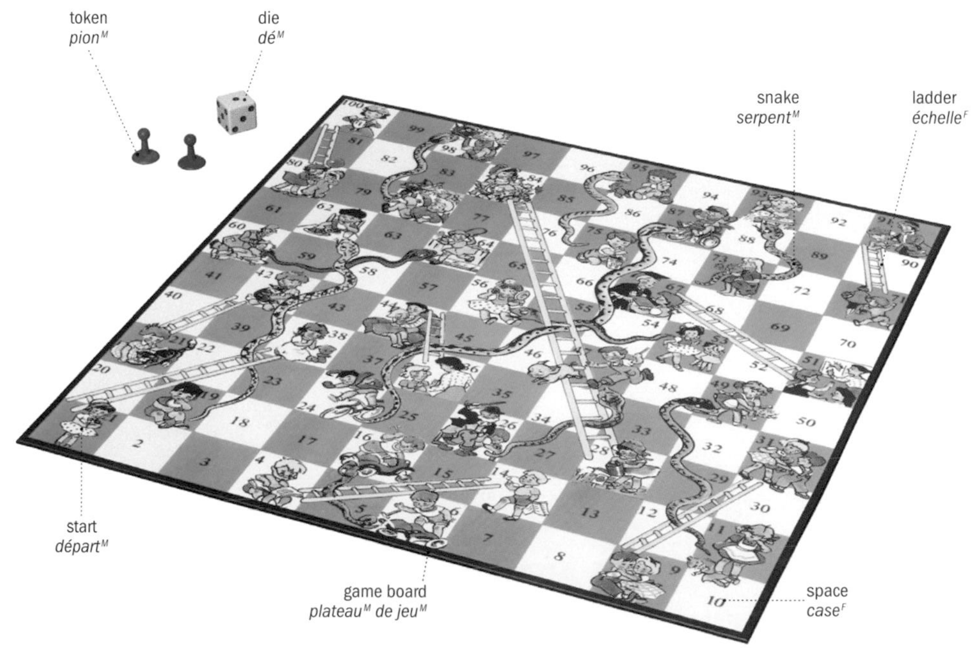
token
pion[M]
die
dé[M]
snake
serpent[M]
ladder
échelle[F]
start
départ[M]
game board
plateau[M] de jeu[M]
space
case[F]

board games

chess
échecs[M]

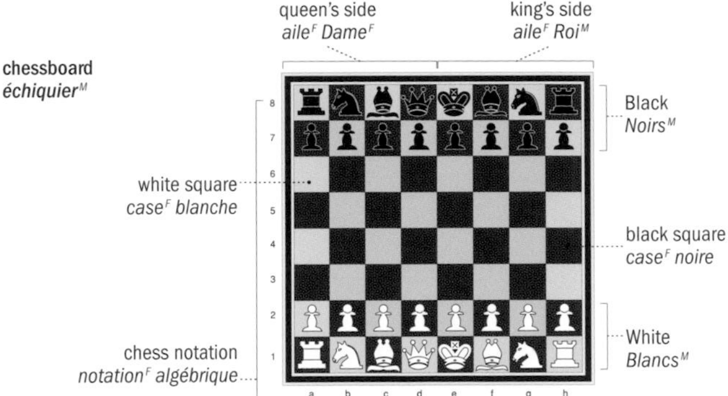
queen's side
aile[F] Dame[F]
king's side
aile[F] Roi[M]
chessboard
échiquier[M]
Black
Noirs[M]
white square
case[F] blanche
black square
case[F] noire
White
Blancs[M]
chess notation
notation[F] algébrique
8
7
6
5
4
3
2
1
a b c d e f g h

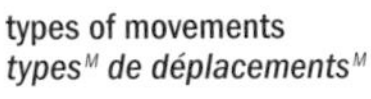
types of movements
types[M] de déplacements[M]

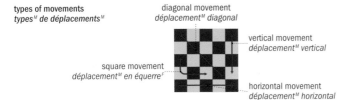

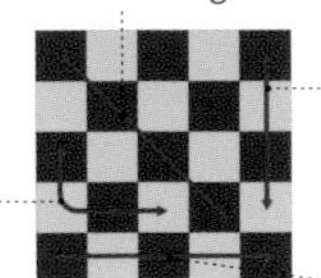
diagonal movement
déplacement[M] diagonal
vertical movement
déplacement[M] vertical
square movement
déplacement[M] en équerre[F]
horizontal movement
déplacement[M] horizontal

chess pieces
pièces[F]

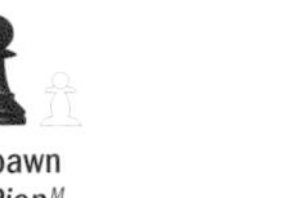
pawn
Pion[M]

rook
Tour[F]

bishop
Fou[M]

knight
Cavalier[M]

king
Roi[M]

queen
Dame[F]

go
go[M]

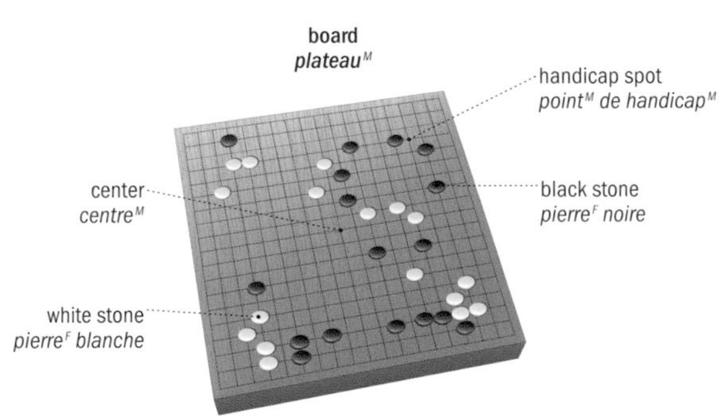
board
plateau[M]
handicap spot
point[M] de handicap[M]
center
centre[M]
black stone
pierre[F] noire
white stone
pierre[F] blanche

major motions
principaux mouvements[M]

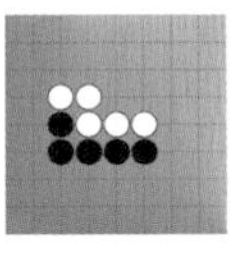
connection
connexion[F]

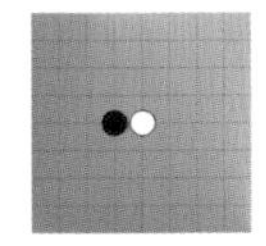
contact
contact[M]

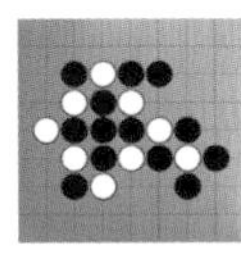
capture
capture[F]

checkers
jeu[M] de dames[F]

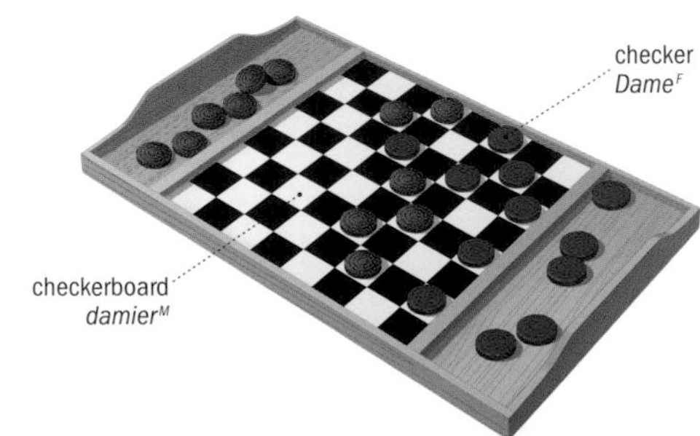
checker
Dame[F]
checkerboard
damier[M]

SPORTS AND GAMES

video entertainment system

systÃ¨me[M] de jeux[M] vidÃ©o

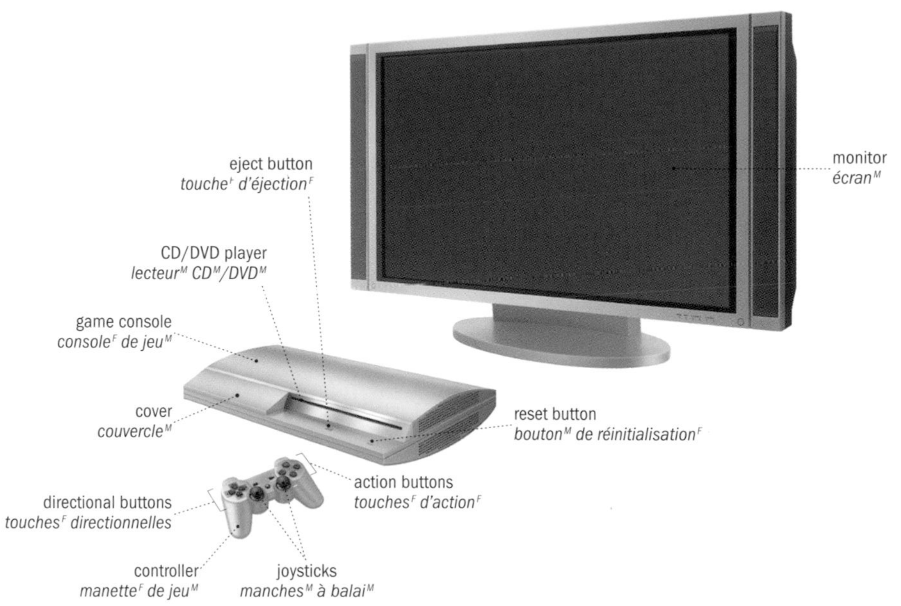
eject button
touche[F] d'Ã©jection[F]
CD/DVD player
lecteur[M] CD[M]/DVD[M]
game console
console[F] de jeu[M]
cover
couvercle[M]
directional buttons
touches[F] directionnelles
controller
manette[F] de jeu[M]
joysticks
manches[M] Ã balai[M]
action buttons
touches[F] d'action[F]
reset button
bouton[M] de rÃ©initialisation[F]
monitor
Ã©cran[M]

darts

jeu[M] de flÃ©chettes[F]

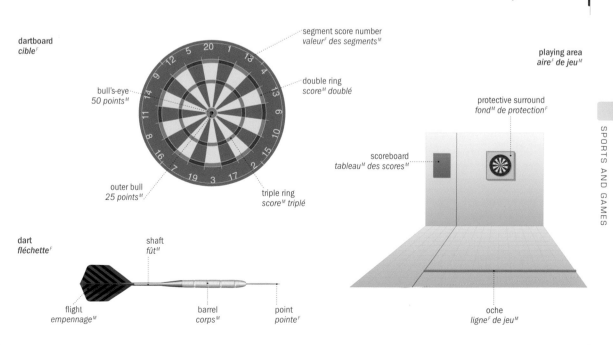

dartboard
cible[F]

segment score number
valeur[F] des segments[M]

double ring
score[M] doublÃ©

bull's-eye
50 points[M]

outer bull
25 points[M]

triple ring
score[M] triplÃ©

playing area
aire[F] de jeu[M]

protective surround
fond[M] de protection[F]

scoreboard
tableau[M] des scores[M]

oche
ligne[F] de jeu[M]

dart
flÃ©chette[F]

shaft
fÃ»t[M]

flight
empennage[M]

barrel
corps[M]

point
pointe[F]

arena

stade^M

long jump and triple jump
saut^M en longueur^F et triple saut^M

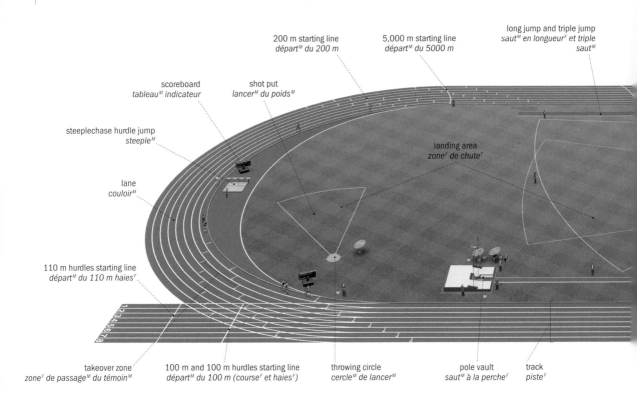

200 m starting line
départ^M du 200 m

5,000 m starting line
départ^M du 5000 m

scoreboard
tableau^M indicateur

shot put
lancer^M du poids^M

steeplechase hurdle jump
steeple^M

landing area
zone^F de chute^F

lane
couloir^M

110 m hurdles starting line
départ^M du 110 m haies^F

takeover zone
zone^F de passage^M du témoin^M

100 m and 100 m hurdles starting line
départ^M du 100 m (course^F et haies^F)

throwing circle
cercle^M de lancer^M

pole vault
saut^M à la perche^F

track
piste^F

equipment
***équipement**^M*

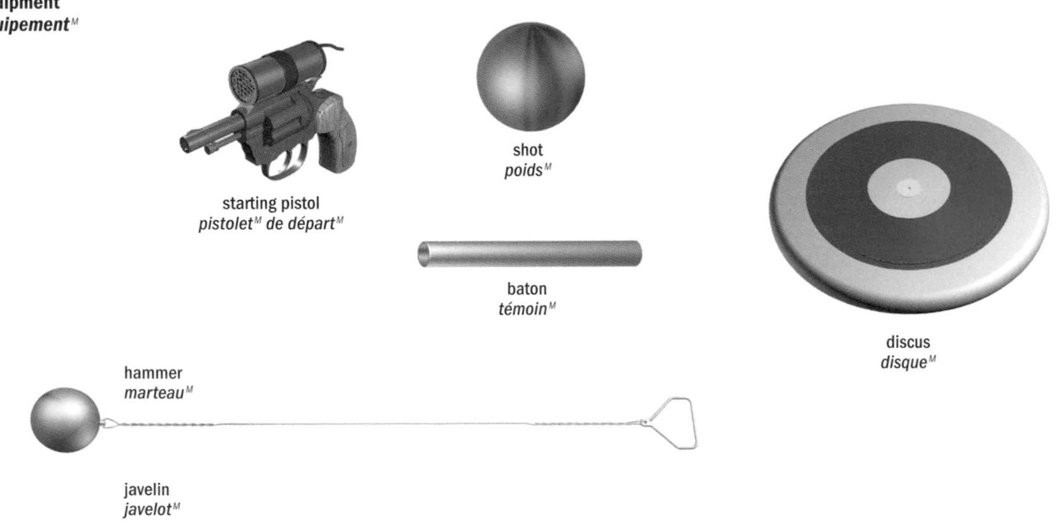
starting pistol
pistolet^M de départ^M
shot
poids^M
baton
témoin^M
discus
disque^M
hammer
marteau^M
javelin
javelot^M

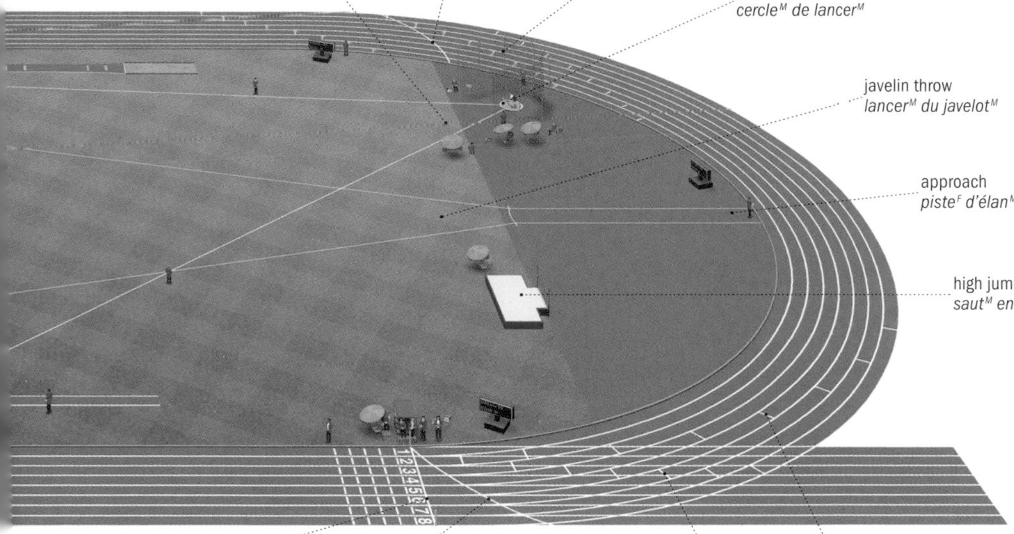

discus and hammer throw
lancer[M] disque[M] et marteau[M]

1,500 m starting line
départ[M] du 1500 m

safety cage
cage[F]

throwing circle
cercle[M] de lancer[M]

javelin throw
lancer[M] du javelot[M]

approach
piste[F] d'élan[M]

high jump
saut[M] en hauteur[F]

finish line
ligne[F] d'arrivée[F]

10,000 m and 4 x 400 m relay starting line
départ[M] du 10 000 m et du relais[M] 4 x 400 m

800 m starting line
départ[M] du 800 m

400 m, 400 m hurdles, 4 x 100 m relay starting line
départ[M] des 400 m (course[F], haies[F], relais[M])

athlete: starting block
athlète[F] : bloc[M] de départ[M]

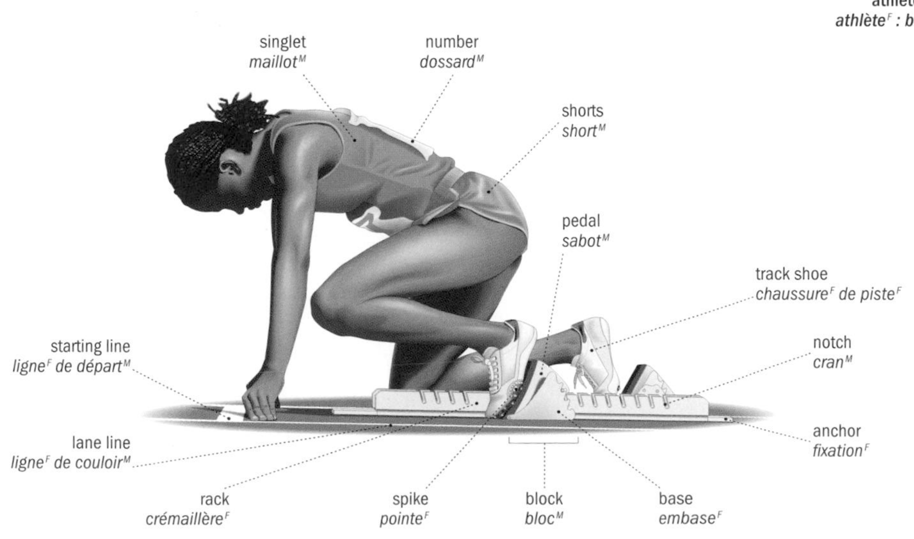
singlet
maillot[M]
number
dossard[M]
shorts
short[M]
pedal
sabot[M]
track shoe
chaussure[F] de piste[F]
notch
cran[M]
starting line
ligne[F] de départ[M]
anchor
fixation[F]
lane line
ligne[F] de couloir[M]
rack
crémaillère[F]
spike
pointe[F]
block
bloc[M]
base
embase[F]

baseball

baseball[M]

player positions
position[F] des joueurs[M]

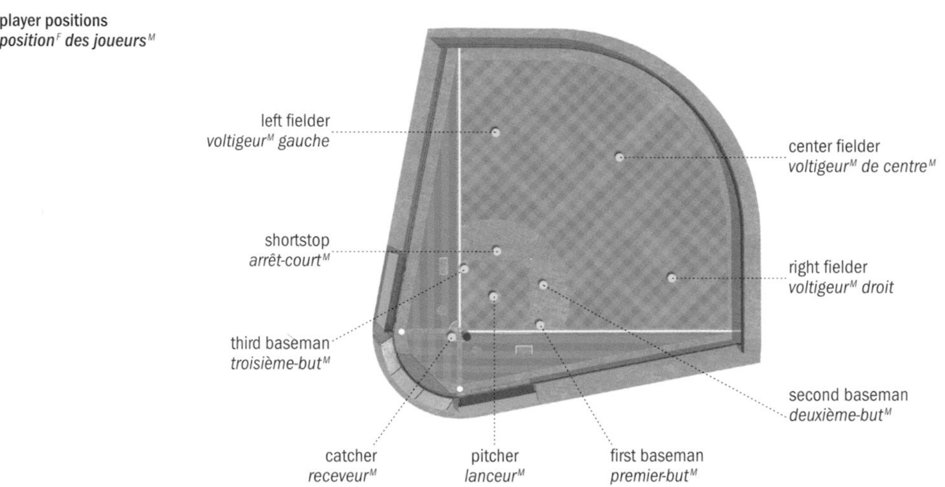
left fielder
voltigeur[M] gauche
center fielder
voltigeur[M] de centre[M]
shortstop
arrêt-court[M]
right fielder
voltigeur[M] droit
third baseman
troisième-but[M]
second baseman
deuxième-but[M]
catcher
receveur[M]
pitcher
lanceur[M]
first baseman
premier-but[M]

field
terrain[M]

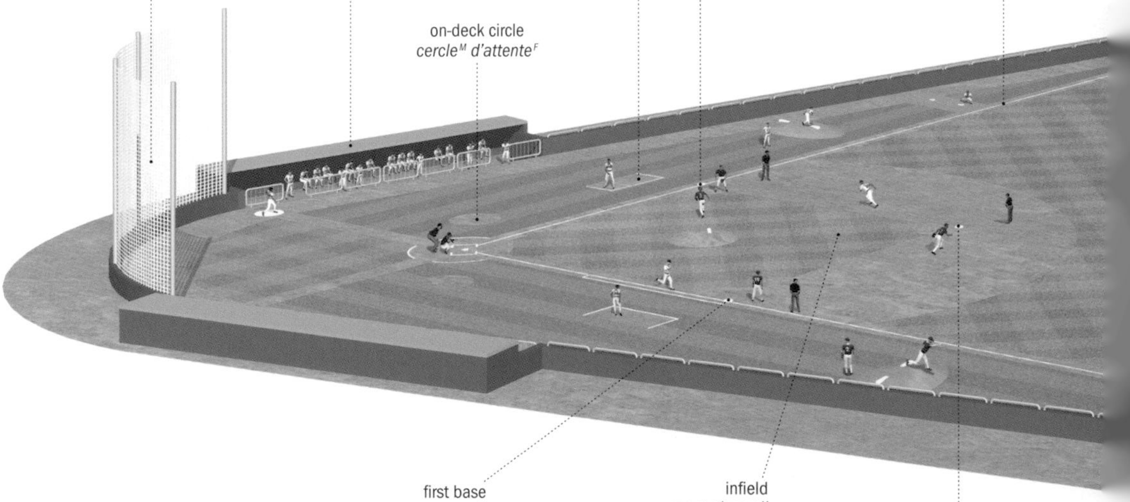

third base
troisième but[M]
coach's box
rectangle[M] des instructeurs[M]
foul line
ligne[F] de jeu[M]
dugout
abri[M] des joueurs[M]
backstop
écran[M] de protection[F]
on-deck circle
cercle[M] d'attente[F]
first base
premier but[M]
infield
avant-champ[M]
second base
deuxième but[M]

SPORTS AND GAMES

pitch
lancer^{M}

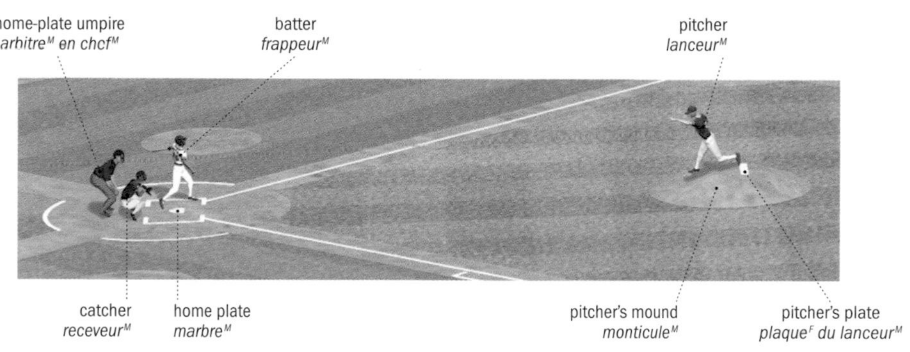
home-plate umpire
arbitre^{M} en chef^{M}
batter
frappeur^{M}
pitcher
lanceur^{M}
catcher
receveur^{M}
home plate
marbre^{M}
pitcher's mound
monticule^{M}
pitcher's plate
plaque^{F} du lanceur^{M}

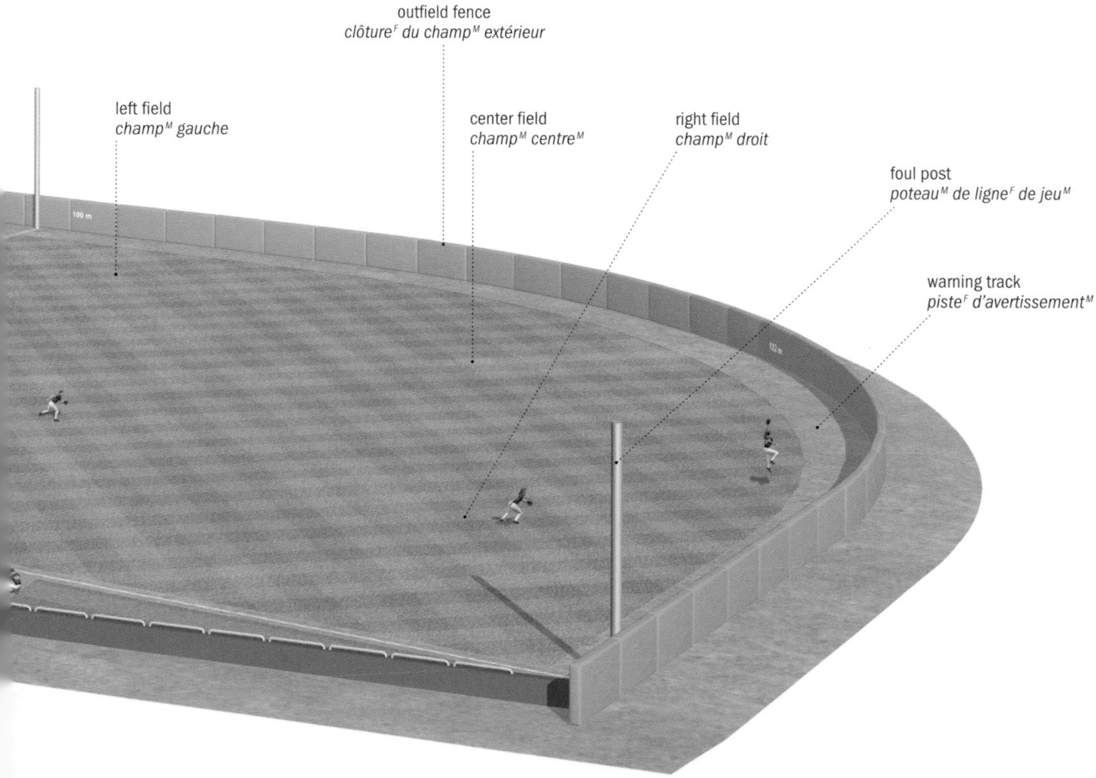

outfield fence
clôture^{F} du champ^{M} extérieur

left field
champ^{M} gauche

center field
champ^{M} centre^{M}

right field
champ^{M} droit

foul post
poteau^{M} de ligne^{F} de jeu^{M}

warning track
piste^{F} d'avertissement^{M}

SPORTS AND GAMES

baseball

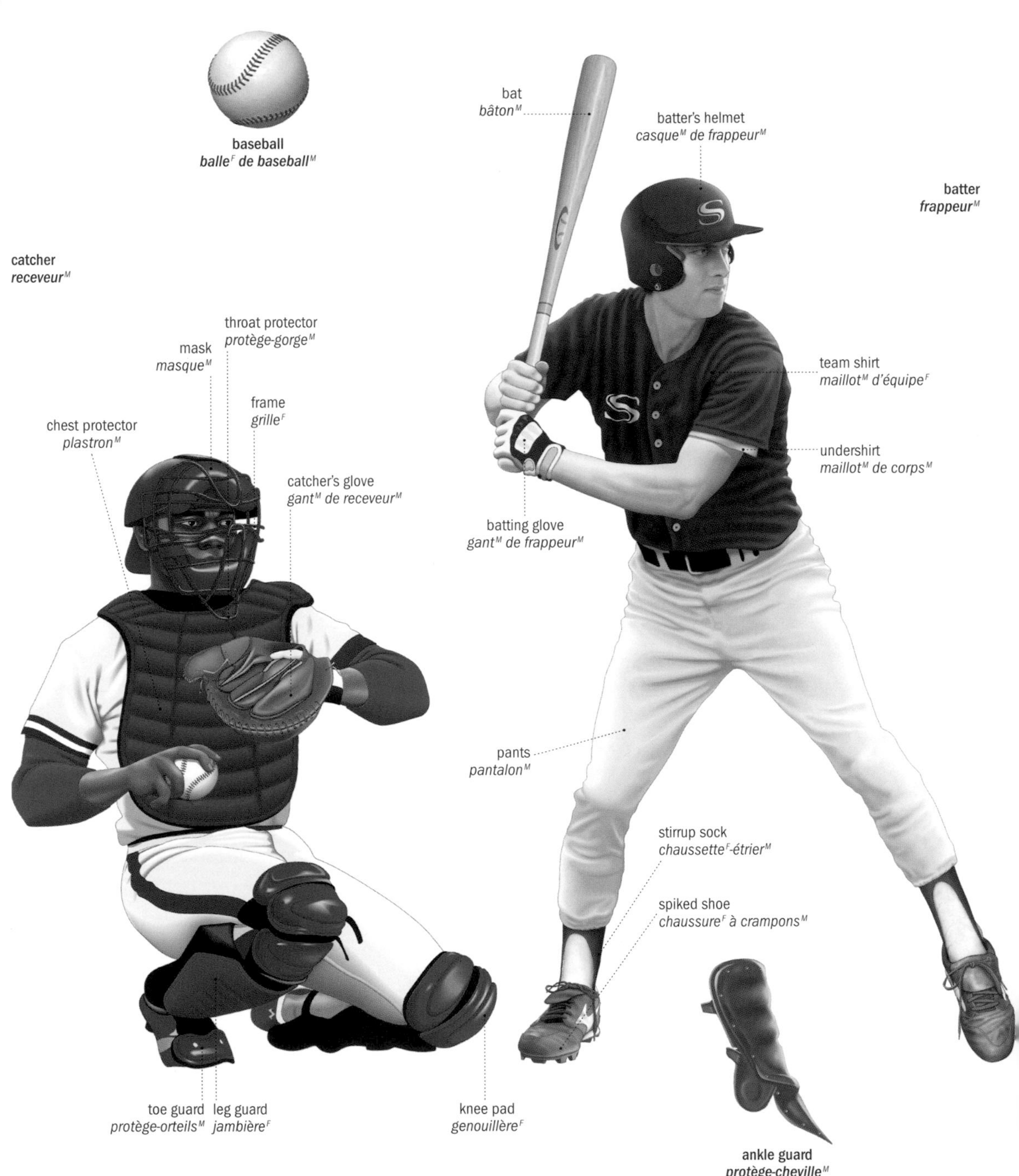
baseball
balle^F de baseball^M
bat
bâton^M
batter's helmet
casque^M de frappeur^M
batter
frappeur^M
catcher
receveur^M
throat protector
protège-gorge^M
mask
masque^M
frame
grille^F
chest protector
plastron^M
catcher's glove
gant^M de receveur^M
team shirt
maillot^M d'équipe^F
undershirt
maillot^M de corps^M
batting glove
gant^M de frappeur^M
pants
pantalon^M
stirrup sock
chaussette^F-étrier^M
spiked shoe
chaussure^F à crampons^M
toe guard
protège-orteils^M
leg guard
jambière^F
knee pad
genouillère^F
ankle guard
protège-cheville^M

baseball

bat
bâton[M]

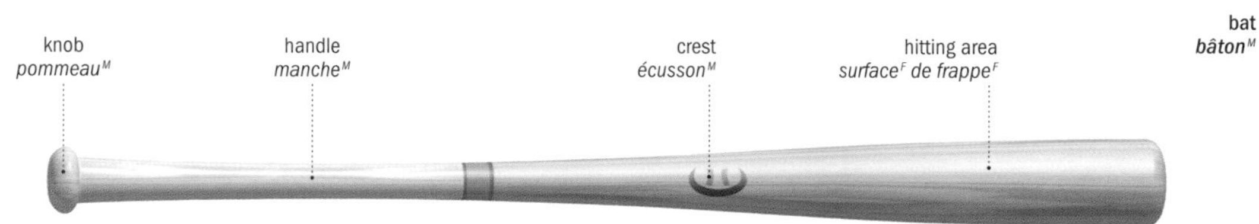
knob
pommeau[M]
handle
manche[M]
crest
écusson[M]
hitting area
surface[F] de frappe[F]

cross section of a baseball
coupe[F] de la balle[F]

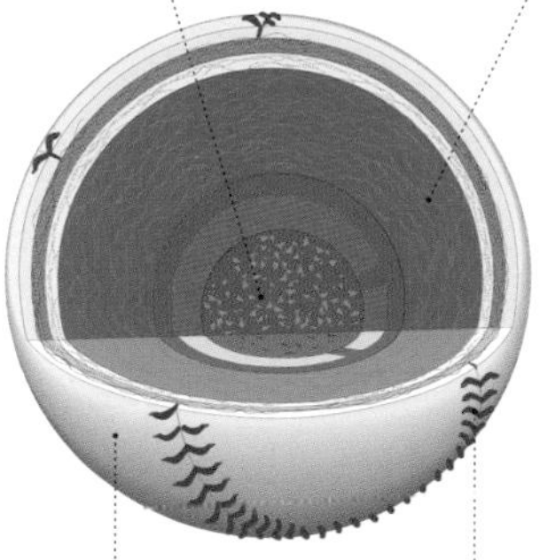

cork ball
balle[F] de liège[M]

yarn
balle[F] de fil[M]

cover
enveloppe[F]

stitches
couture[F]

fielder's glove
gant[M]

web
panier[M]

strap
patte[F]

thumb
pouce[M]

finger
doigt[M]

palm
paume[F]

heel
talon[M]

lace
lacet[M]

softball

softball[M]

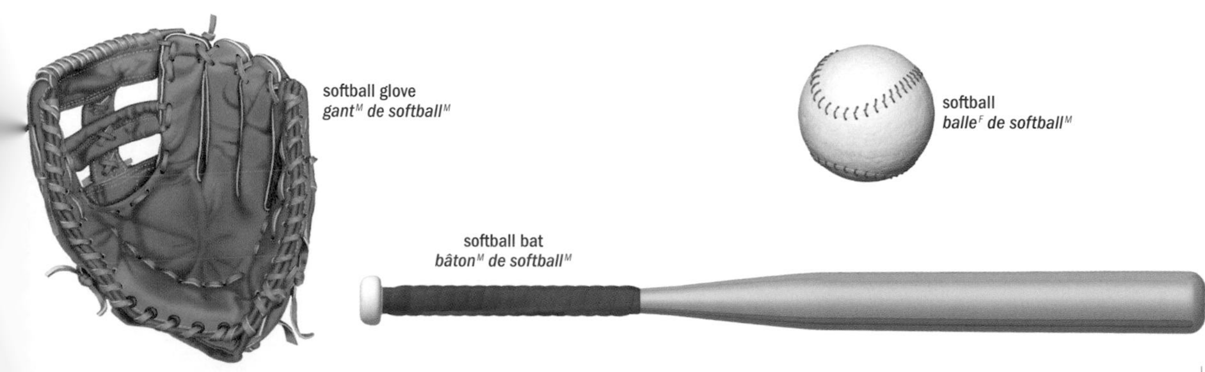

softball glove
gant[M] de softball[M]

softball
balle[F] de softball[M]

softball bat
bâton[M] de softball[M]

cricket

cricket^{M}

cricket player: batsman
joueur^{M} de cricket^{M} : batteur^{M}

helmet
casque^{M}

bat
batte^{F}

face mask
masque^{M}

glove
gant^{M}

pad
jambière^{F}

cricket shoe
chaussure^{F}

stud
crampon^{M}

cricket ball
balle^{F} de cricket^{M}

leather skin
enveloppe^{F}

seam
couture^{F}

bat
batte^{F}

handle
manche^{M}

willow
plat^{M}

front view
vue^{F} de face^{F}

side view
vue^{F} de profil^{M}

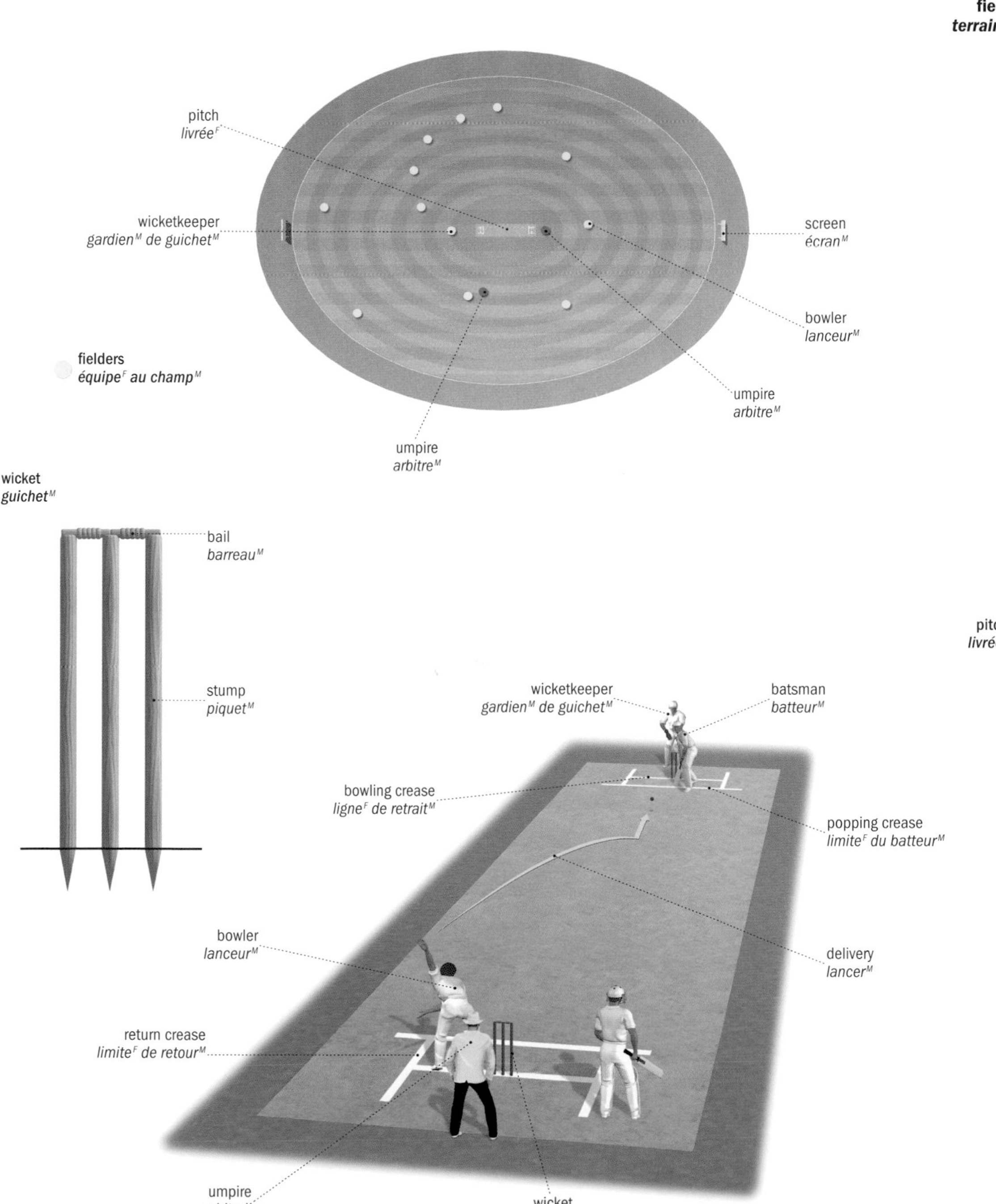
field
terrain M
pitch
livrée F
wicketkeeper
gardien M *de guichet* M
screen
écran M
bowler
lanceur M
fielders
équipe F *au champ* M
umpire
arbitre M
umpire
arbitre M
wicket
guichet M
bail
barreau M
stump
piquet M
pitch
livrée F
wicketkeeper
gardien M *de guichet* M
batsman
batteur M
bowling crease
ligne F *de retrait* M
popping crease
limite F *du batteur* M
bowler
lanceur M
delivery
lancer M
return crease
limite F *de retour* M
umpire
arbitre M
wicket
guichet M

soccer

football[M]

soccer player
footballeur[M]

team shirt
maillot[M] d'équipe[F]

shorts
short[M]

shin guard
protège-tibia[M]

sock
chaussette[F]

soccer ball
ballon[M] de football[M]

goalkeeper's gloves
gants[M] de gardien[M] de but[M]

interchangeable studs
crampons[M] interchangeables

soccer shoe
chaussure[F] de football[M]

playing field
terrain[M]

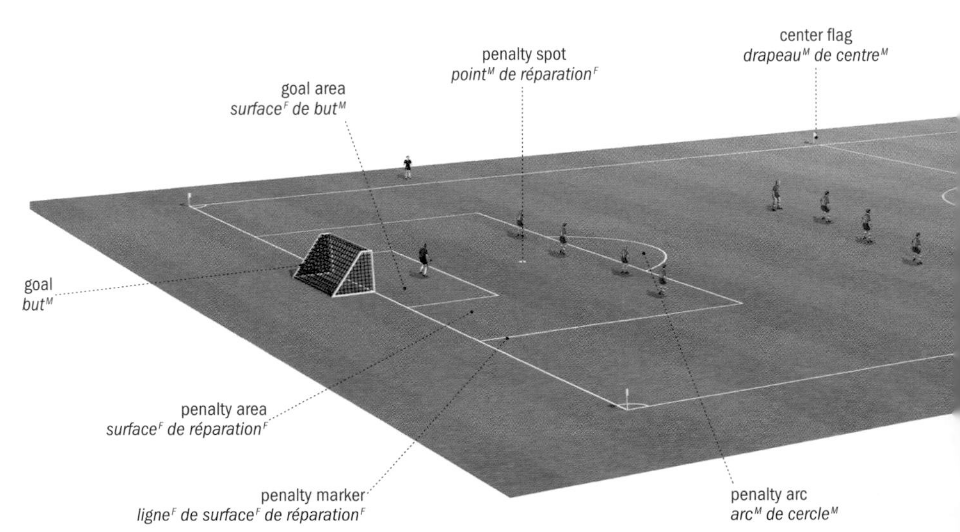
center flag
drapeau[M] de centre[M]
penalty spot
point[M] de réparation[F]
goal area
surface[F] de but[M]
goal
but[M]
penalty area
surface[F] de réparation[F]
penalty marker
ligne[F] de surface[F] de réparation[F]
penalty arc
arc[M] de cercle[M]

player positions
***position*[F] *des joueurs*[M]**

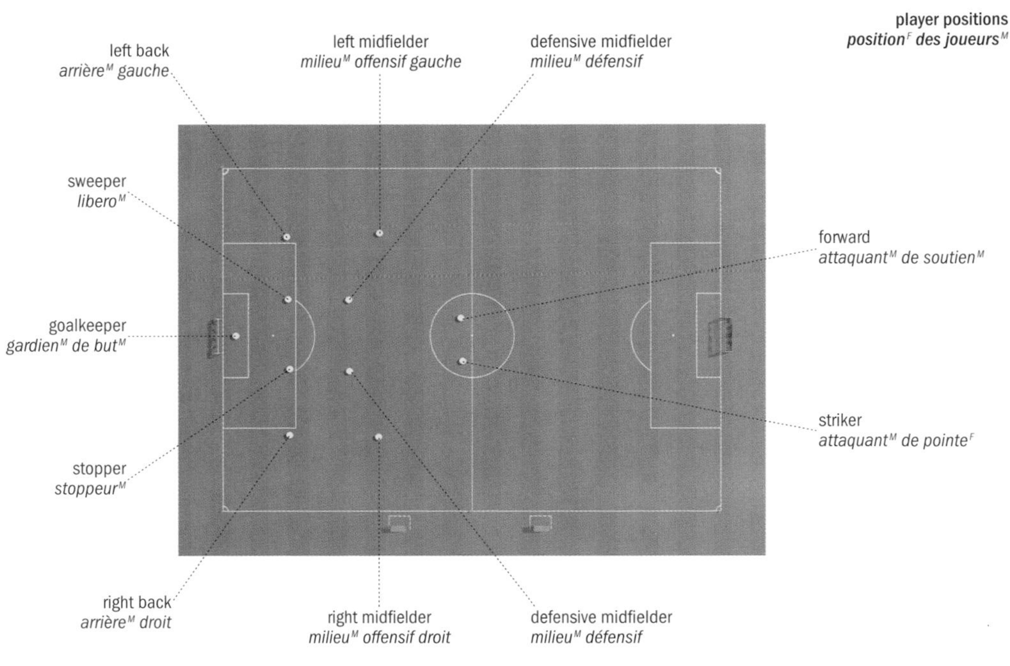
left back
arrière[M] *gauche*
left midfielder
milieu[M] *offensif gauche*
defensive midfielder
milieu[M] *défensif*
sweeper
libero[M]
forward
attaquant[M] *de soutien*[M]
goalkeeper
gardien[M] *de but*[M]
striker
attaquant[M] *de pointe*[F]
stopper
stoppeur[M]
right back
arrière[M] *droit*
right midfielder
milieu[M] *offensif droit*
defensive midfielder
milieu[M] *défensif*

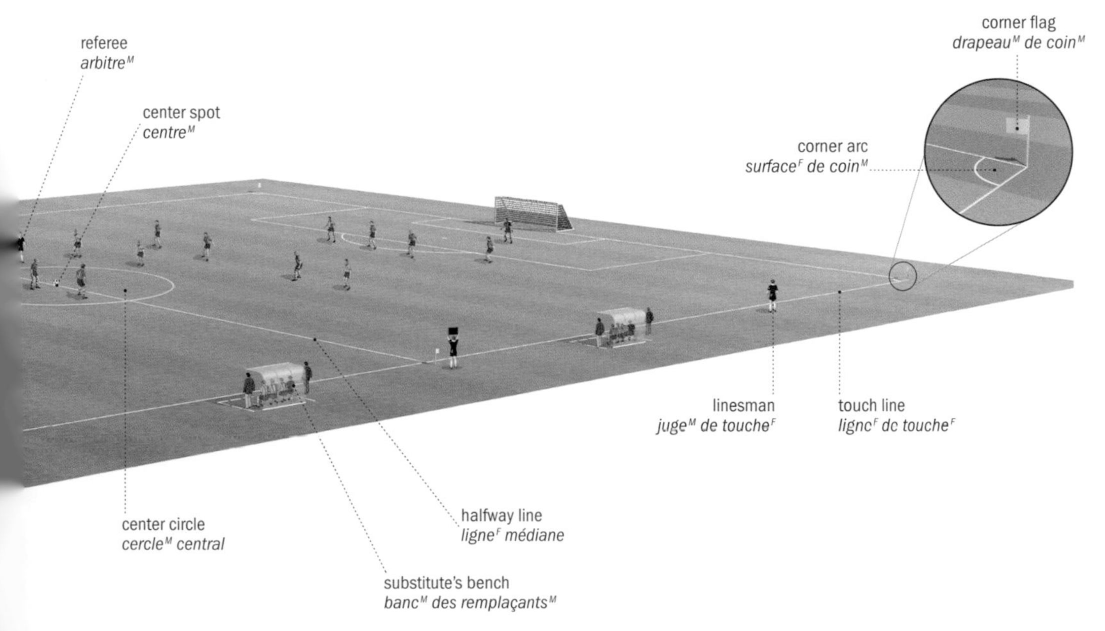
referee
arbitre[M]
center spot
centre[M]
corner flag
drapeau[M] *de coin*[M]
corner arc
surface[F] *de coin*[M]
linesman
juge[M] *de touche*[F]
touch line
ligne[F] *de touche*[F]
center circle
cercle[M] *central*
halfway line
ligne[F] *médiane*
substitute's bench
banc[M] *des remplaçants*[M]

rugby

rugby^M

players' positions
position^F des joueurs^M

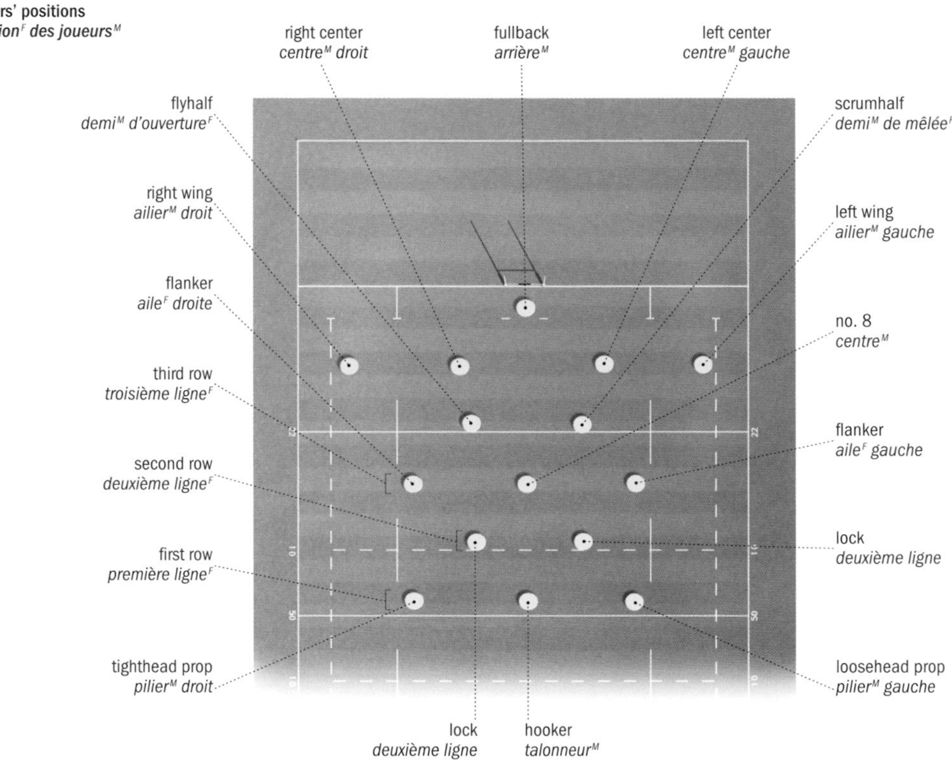
right center
centre^M droit
fullback
arrière^M
left center
centre^M gauche
flyhalf
demi^M d'ouverture^F
scrumhalf
demi^M de mêlée^F
right wing
ailier^M droit
left wing
ailier^M gauche
flanker
aile^F droite
no. 8
centre^M
third row
troisième ligne^F
flanker
aile^F gauche
second row
deuxième ligne^F
lock
deuxième ligne
first row
première ligne^F
tighthead prop
pilier^M droit
loosehead prop
pilier^M gauche
lock
deuxième ligne
hooker
talonneur^M

field
terrain^M

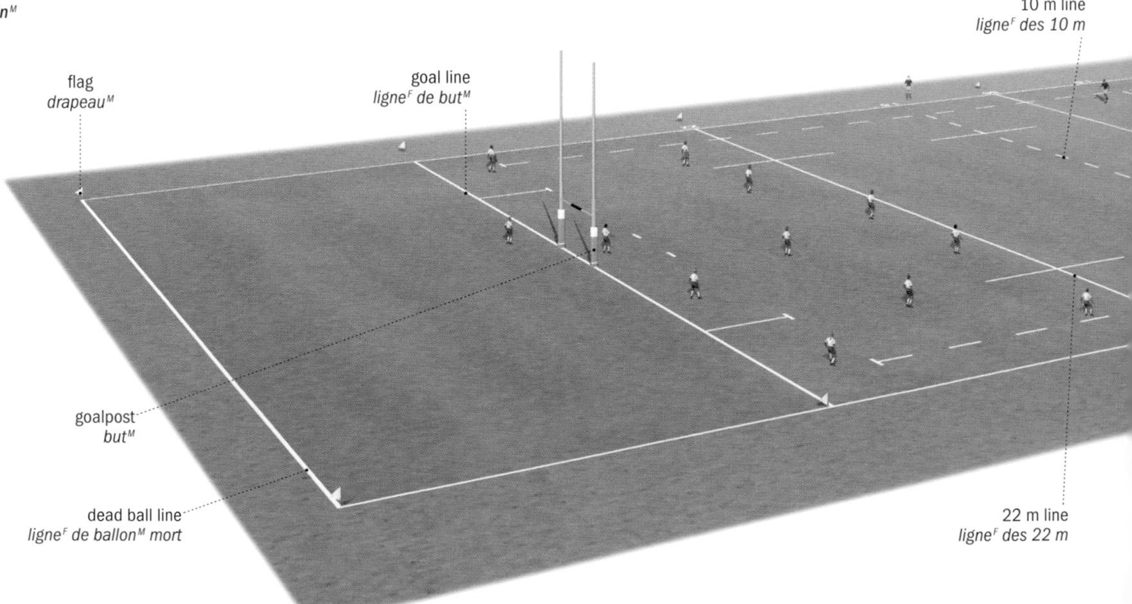
10 m line
ligne^F des 10 m
flag
drapeau^M
goal line
ligne^F de but^M
goalpost
but^M
dead ball line
ligne^F de ballon^M mort
22 m line
ligne^F des 22 m

SPORTS AND GAMES

rugby

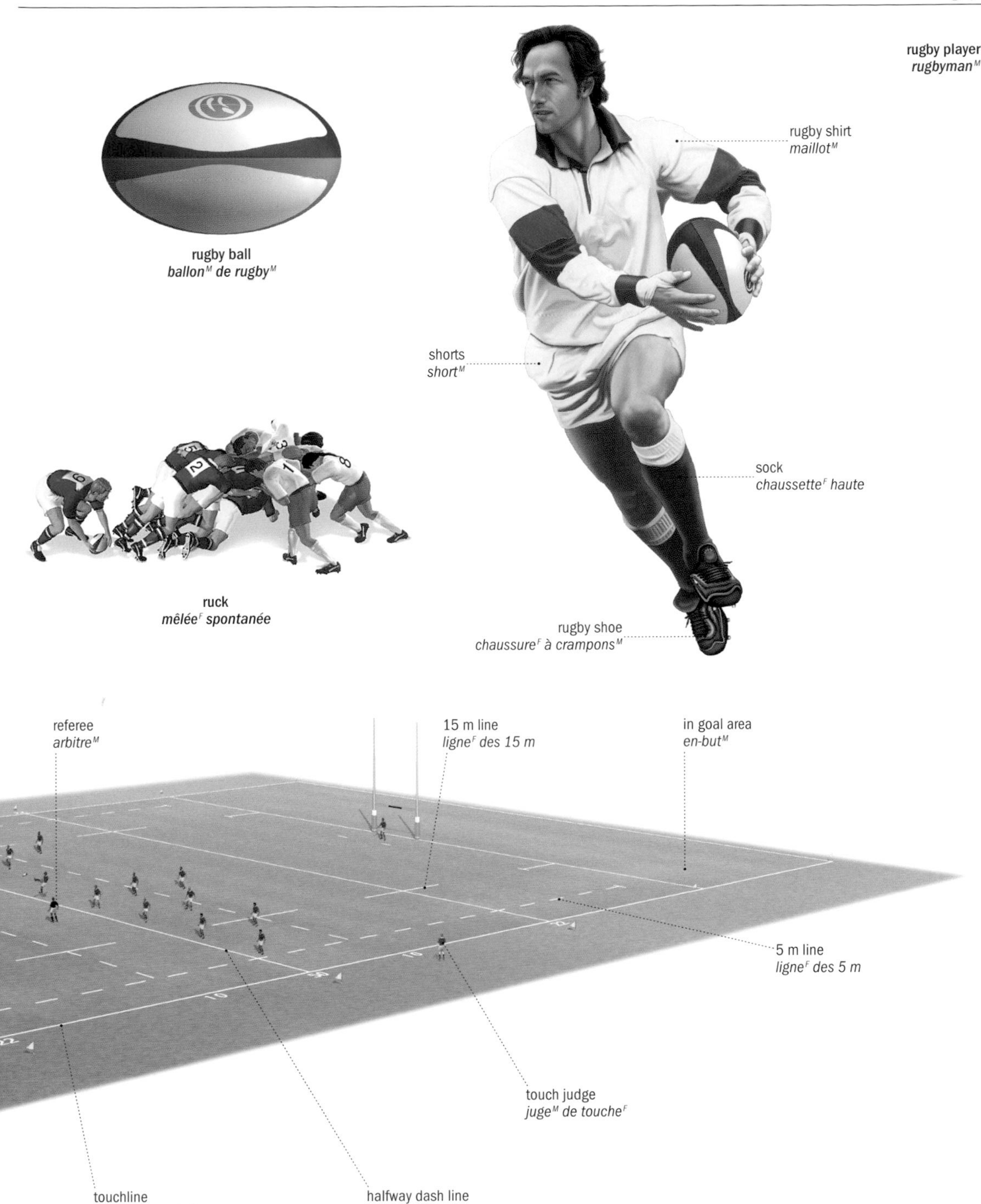
rugby player
*rugbyman*M
rugby shirt
*maillot*M
shorts
*short*M
sock
*chaussette*F *haute*
rugby shoe
*chaussure*F *à crampons*M
rugby ball
*ballon*M *de rugby*M
ruck
*mêlée*F *spontanée*
referee
*arbitre*M
15 m line
*ligne*F *des 15 m*
in goal area
*en-but*M
5 m line
*ligne*F *des 5 m*
touch judge
*juge*M *de touche*F
touchline
*ligne*F *de touche*F
halfway dash line
*ligne*F *médiane*

American football

football[M] américain

scrimmage: defense
mêlée[F] : défense[F]

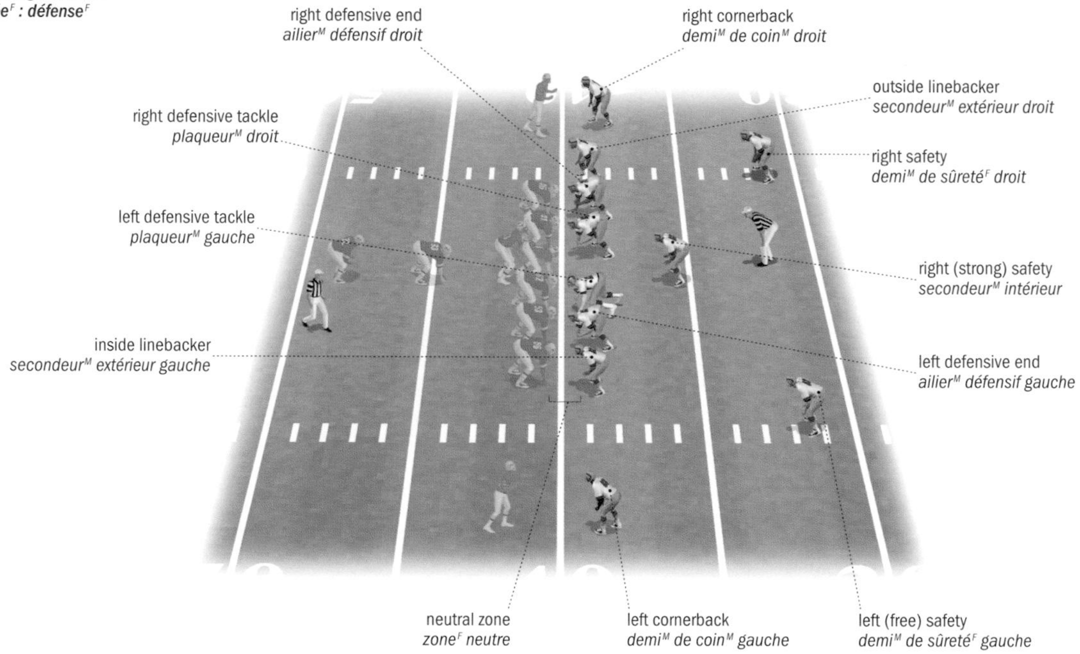

right defensive end
ailier[M] défensif droit

right cornerback
demi[M] de coin[M] droit

outside linebacker
secondeur[M] extérieur droit

right defensive tackle
plaqueur[M] droit

right safety
demi[M] de sûreté[F] droit

left defensive tackle
plaqueur[M] gauche

right (strong) safety
secondeur[M] intérieur

inside linebacker
secondeur[M] extérieur gauche

left defensive end
ailier[M] défensif gauche

neutral zone
zone[F] neutre

left cornerback
demi[M] de coin[M] gauche

left (free) safety
demi[M] de sûreté[F] gauche

playing field for American football
terrain[M] de football[M] américain

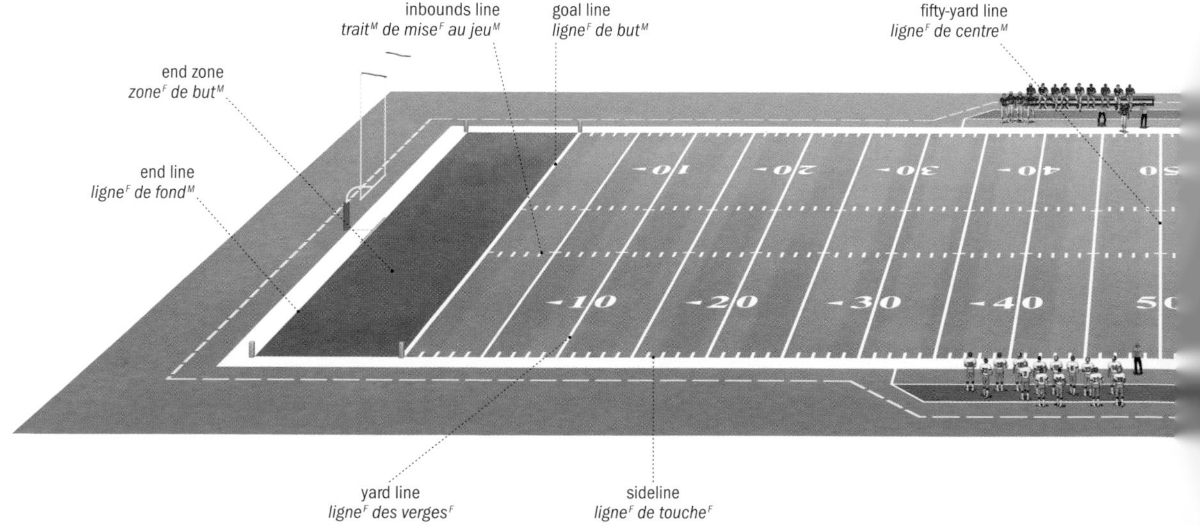
inbounds line
trait[M] de mise[F] au jeu[M]
goal line
ligne[F] de but[M]
fifty-yard line
ligne[F] de centre[M]
end zone
zone[F] de but[M]
end line
ligne[F] de fond[M]
yard line
ligne[F] des verges[F]
sideline
ligne[F] de touche[F]

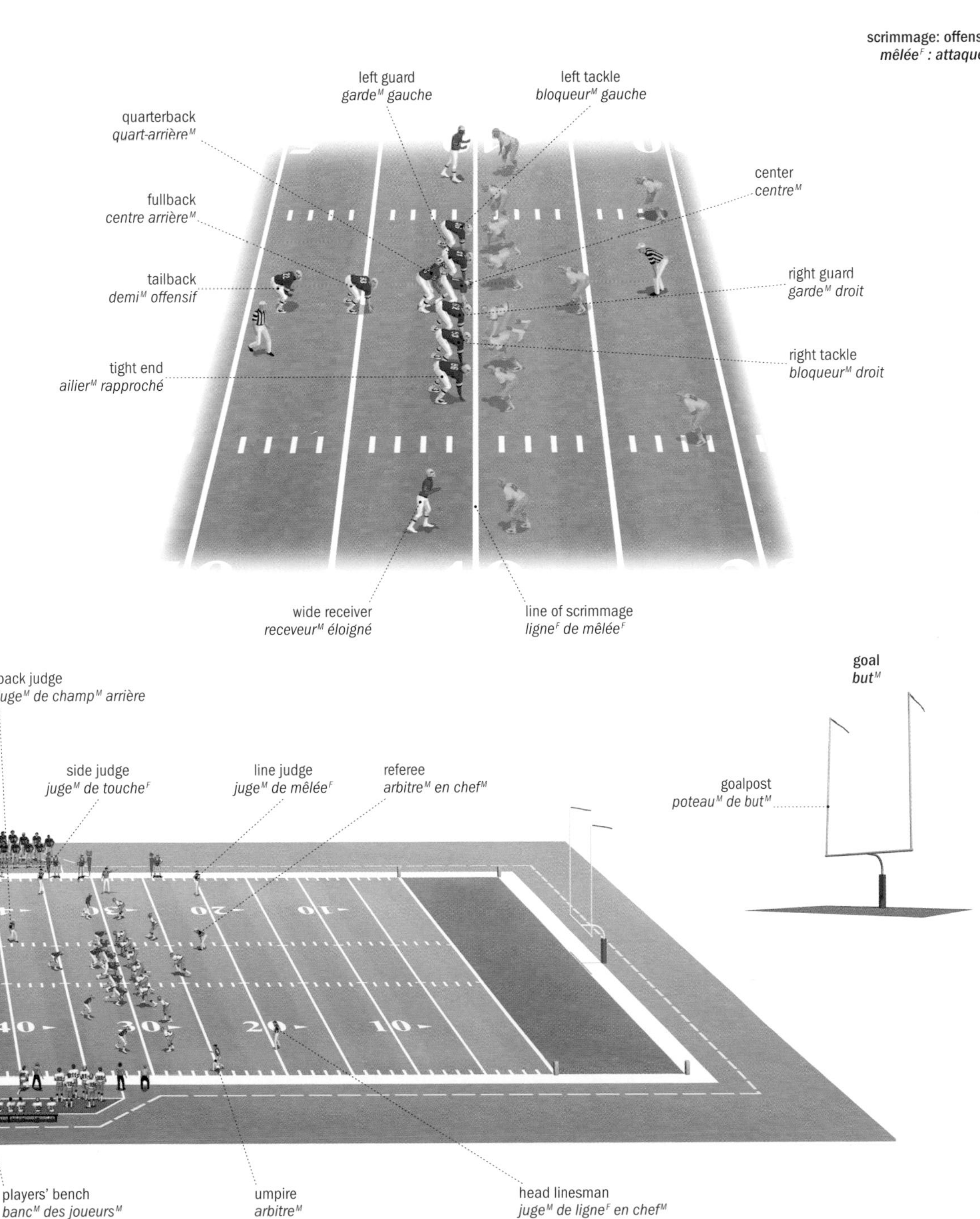
scrimmage: offense
mêlée^F : attaque^F
left guard
garde^M gauche
left tackle
bloqueur^M gauche
quarterback
quart-arrière^M
center
centre^M
fullback
centre arrière^M
tailback
demi^M offensif
right guard
garde^M droit
right tackle
bloqueur^M droit
tight end
ailier^M rapproché
wide receiver
receveur^M éloigné
line of scrimmage
ligne^F de mêlée^F
goal
but^M
back judge
juge^M de champ^M arrière
side judge
juge^M de touche^F
line judge
juge^M de mêlée^F
referee
arbitre^M en chef^M
goalpost
poteau^M de but^M
players' bench
banc^M des joueurs^M
umpire
arbitre^M
head linesman
juge^M de ligne^F en chef^M

American football

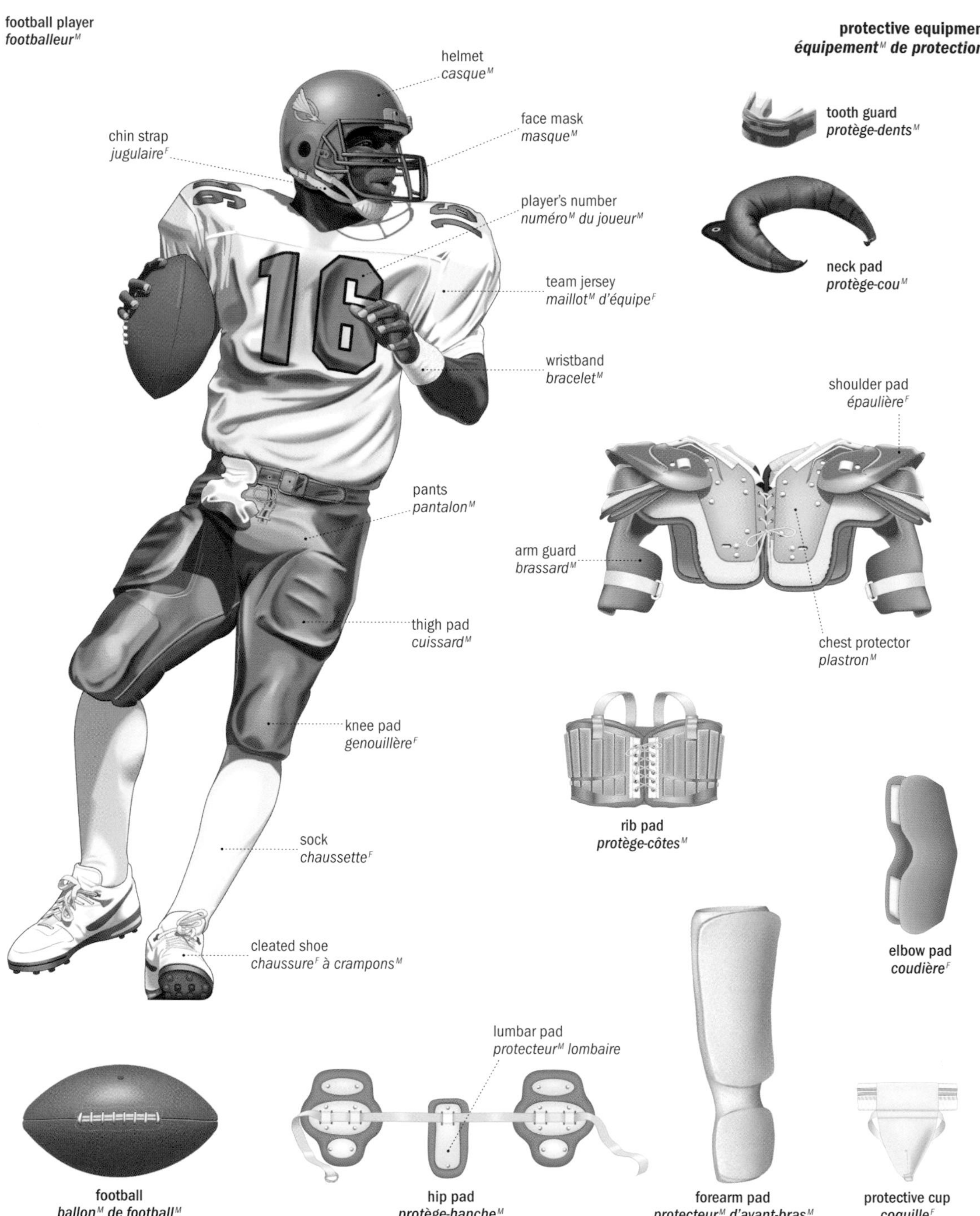
football player
footballeur
helmet
casque
chin strap
jugulaire
face mask
masque
player's number
numéro du joueur
team jersey
maillot d'équipe
wristband
bracelet
pants
pantalon
thigh pad
cuissard
knee pad
genouillère
sock
chaussette
cleated shoe
chaussure à crampons
football
ballon de football
protective equipment
équipement de protection
tooth guard
protège-dents
neck pad
protège-cou
shoulder pad
épaulière
arm guard
brassard
chest protector
plastron
rib pad
protège-côtes
elbow pad
coudière
lumbar pad
protecteur lombaire
hip pad
protège-hanche
forearm pad
protecteur d'avant-bras
protective cup
coquille

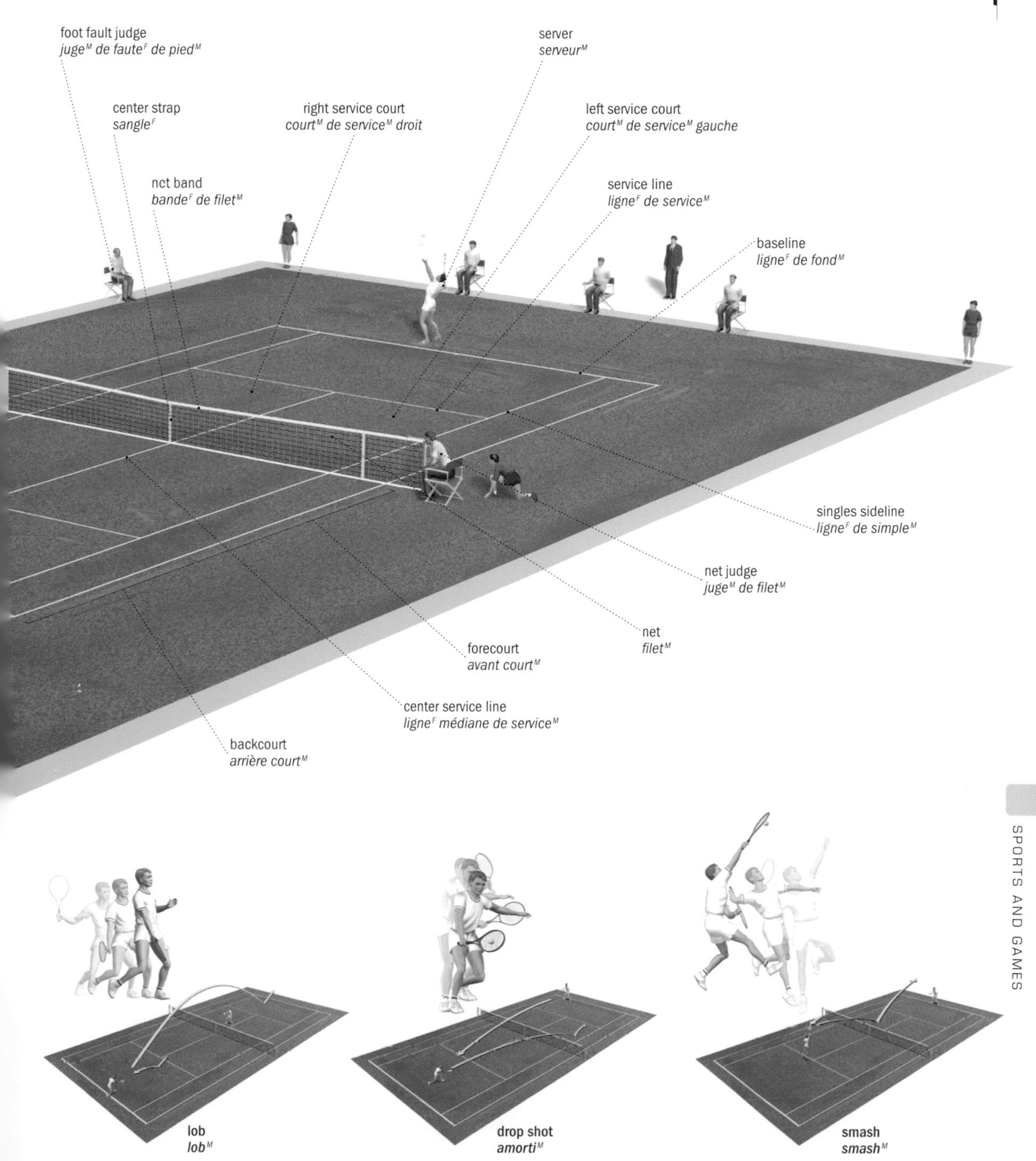
foot fault judge
juge[M] de faute[F] de pied[M]
server
serveur[M]
center strap
sangle[F]
right service court
court[M] de service[M] droit
left service court
court[M] de service[M] gauche
nct band
bande[F] de filet[M]
service line
ligne[F] de service[M]
baseline
ligne[F] de fond[M]
singles sideline
ligne[F] de simple[M]
net judge
juge[M] de filet[M]
net
filet[M]
forecourt
avant court[M]
center service line
ligne[F] médiane de service[M]
backcourt
arrière court[M]
lob
lob[M]
drop shot
amorti[M]
smash
smash[M]

tennis

tennis racket
raquette[F] de tennis[M]

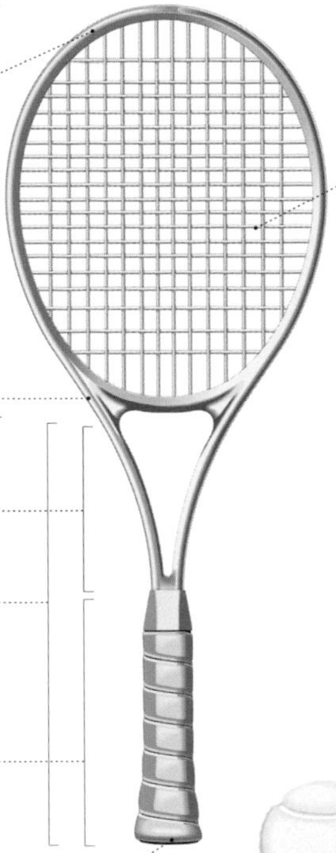

frame
cadre[M]

head
tête[F]

shoulder
épaule[F]

throat
cœur[M]

shaft
manche[M]

handle
poignée[F]

butt
talon[M]

stringing
tamis[M]

tennis ball
balle[F] de tennis[M]

tennis player
joueuse[F] de tennis[M]

polo shirt
polo[M]

tennis skirt
jupette[F]

wristband
serre-poignet[M]

sock
chaussette[F]

tennis shoe
chaussure[F] de tennis[M]

scoreboard
tableau[M] d'affichage[M]

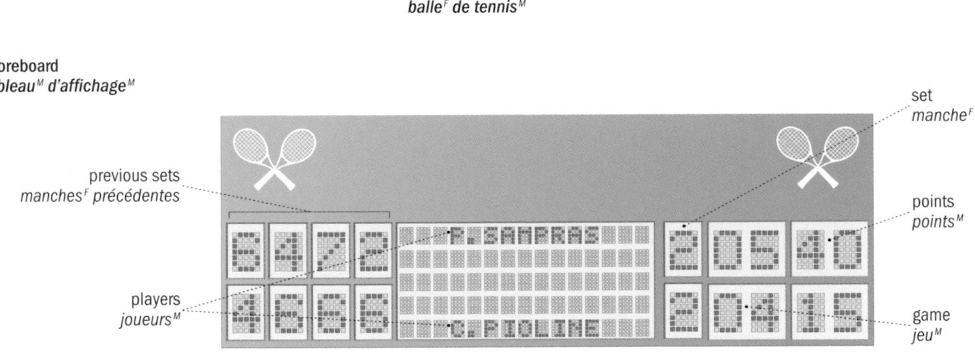
set
manche[F]
previous sets
manches[F] précédentes
points
points[M]
players
joueurs[M]
game
jeu[M]
6 4 7 2
P.SAMPRAS
2 0 5 40
4 6 6 6
C.PIOLINE
2 0 4 15

playing surfaces
surfaces[F] de jeu[M]

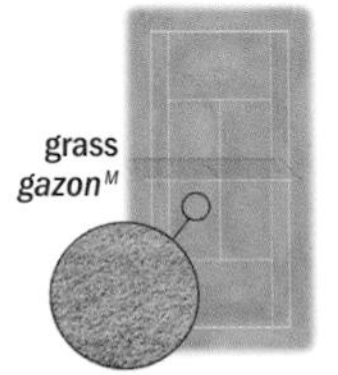

grass
gazon[M]

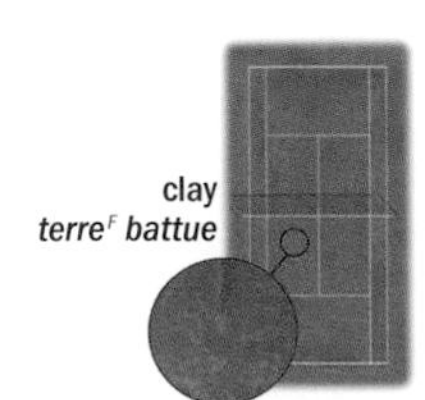

clay
terre[F] battue

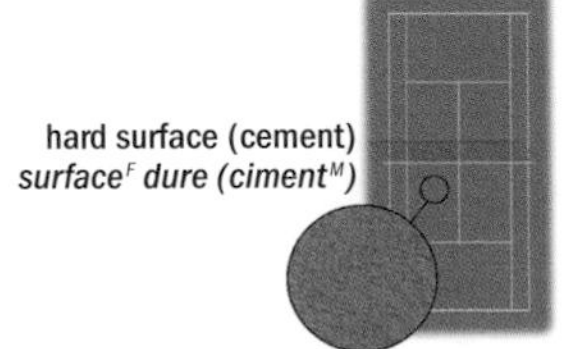

hard surface (cement)
surface[F] dure (ciment[M])

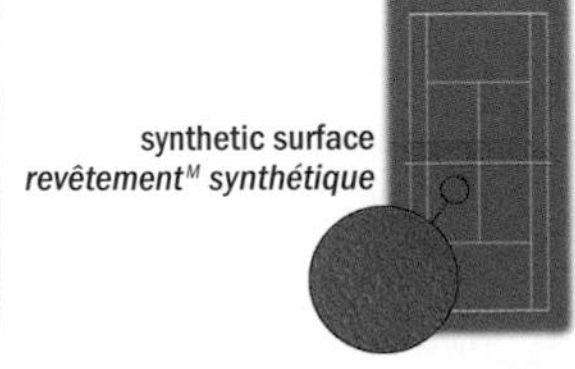

synthetic surface
revêtement[M] synthétique

table tennis

tennis[M] de table[F]

table
table[F]

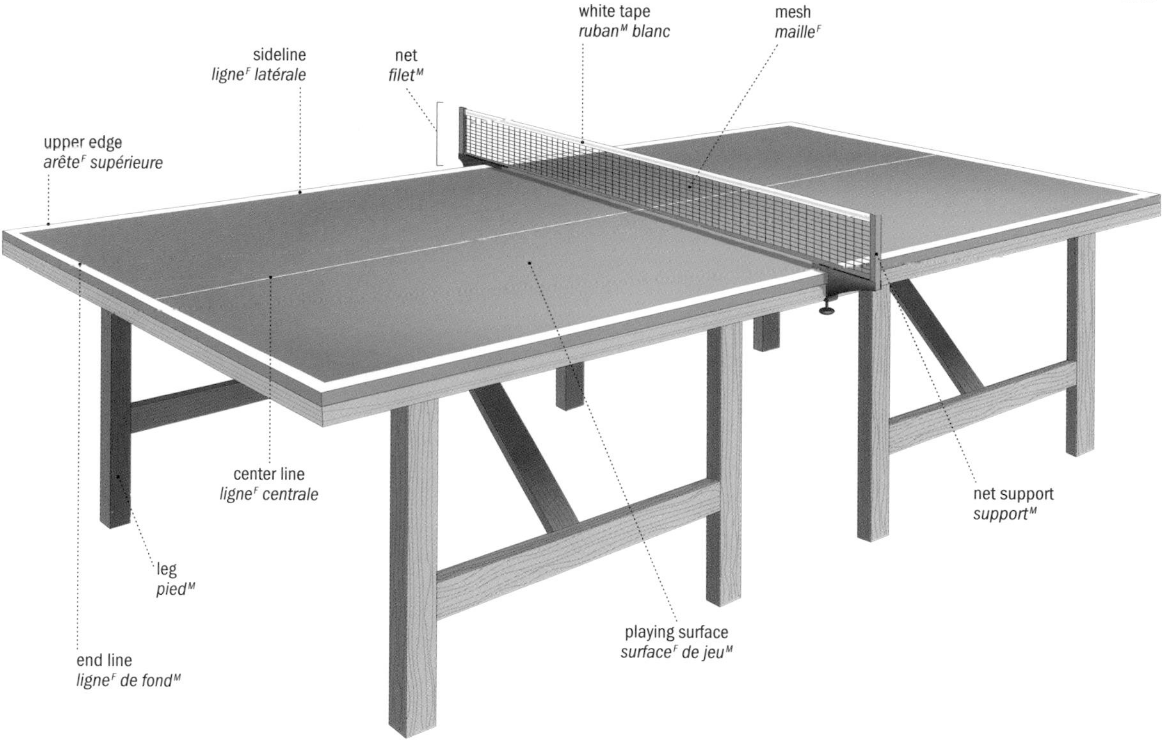

white tape
ruban[M] blanc

mesh
maille[F]

sideline
ligne[F] latérale

net
filet[M]

upper edge
arête[F] supérieure

center line
ligne[F] centrale

net support
support[M]

leg
pied[M]

playing surface
surface[F] de jeu[M]

end line
ligne[F] de fond[M]

table tennis paddle
raquette[F] de tennis[M] de table[F]

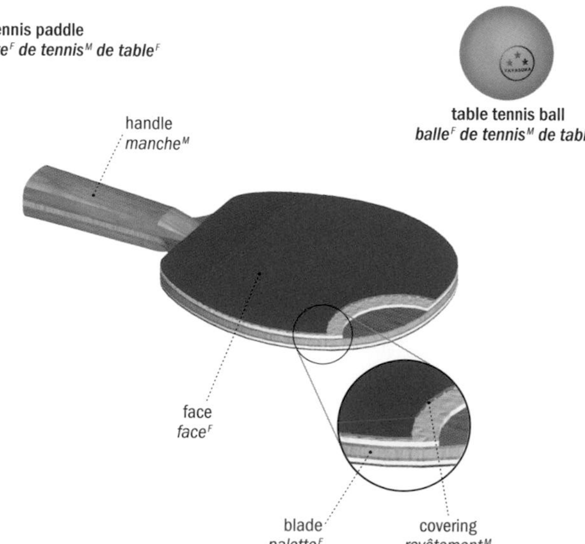
handle
manche[M]
face
face[F]
blade
palette[F]
covering
revêtement[M]

table tennis ball
balle[F] de tennis[M] de table[F]

types of grips
types[M] de prises[F]

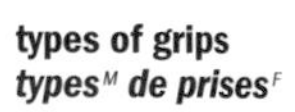

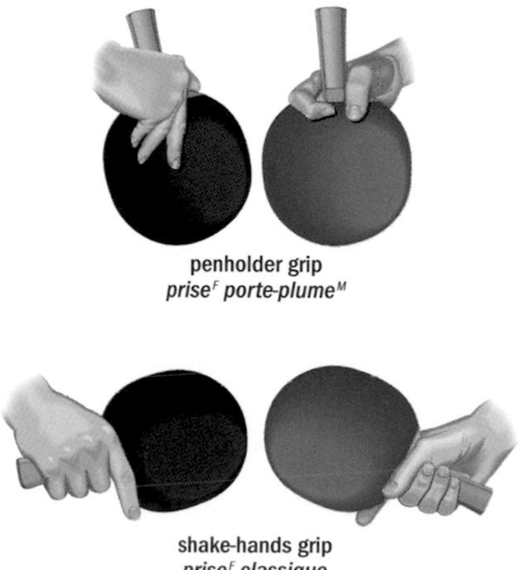

penholder grip
prise[F] porte-plume[M]

shake-hands grip
prise[F] classique

SPORTS AND GAMES

badminton

badminton[M]

court
terrain[M]

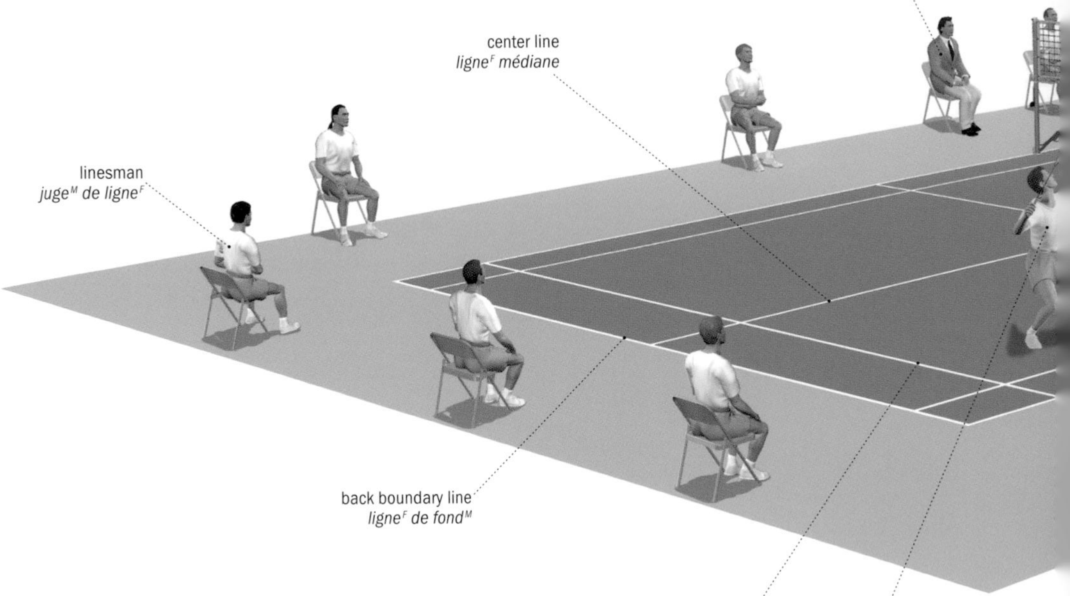

service judge
juge[M] de service[M]

center line
ligne[F] médiane

linesman
juge[M] de ligne[F]

back boundary line
ligne[F] de fond[M]

long service line
ligne[F] de service[M] long

server
serveur[M]

badminton racket
raquette[F] de badminton[M]

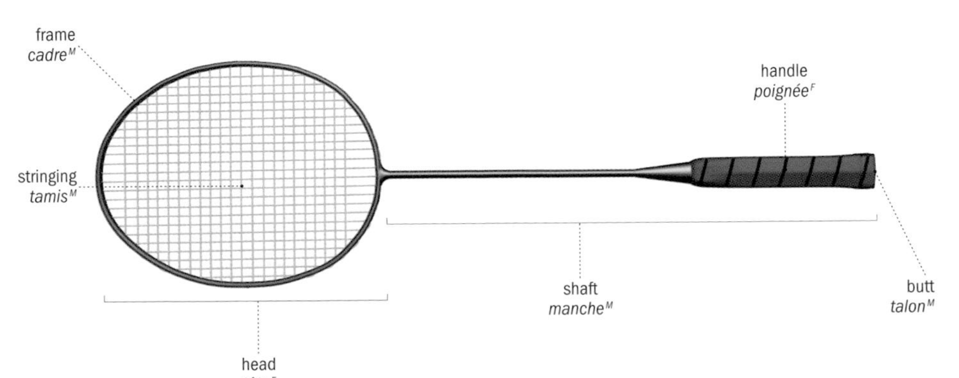
frame
cadre[M]
handle
poignée[F]
stringing
tamis[M]
shaft
manche[M]
butt
talon[M]
head
tête[F]

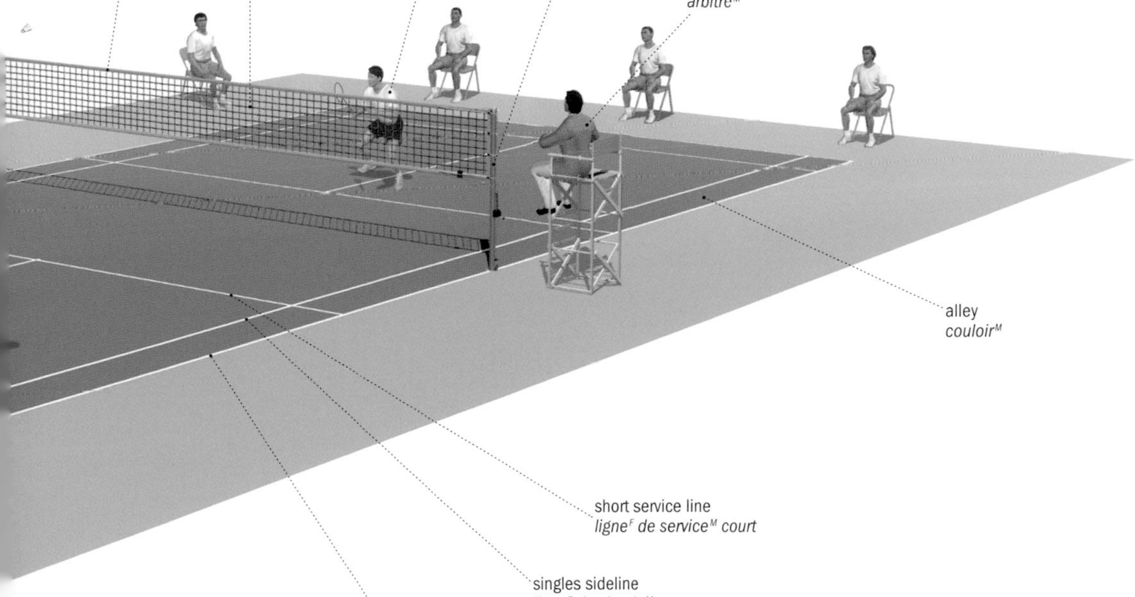

white tape
ruban[M] blanc

receiver
receveur[M]

net
filet[M]

post
poteau[M]

umpire
arbitre[M]

alley
couloir[M]

short service line
ligne[F] de service[M] court

singles sideline
ligne[F] de simple[M]

doubles sideline
ligne[F] de double[M]

service zones
zones[F] de service[M]

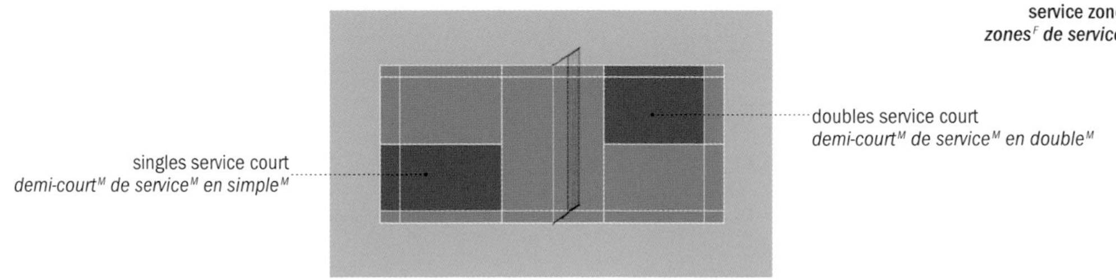
doubles service court
demi-court[M] de service[M] en double[M]
singles service court
demi-court[M] de service[M] en simple[M]

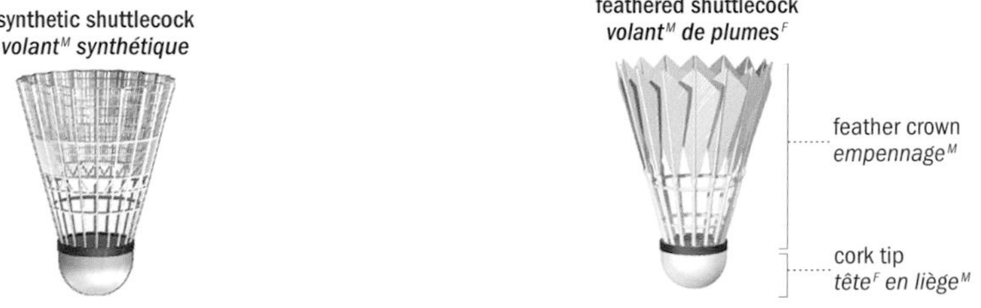
synthetic shuttlecock
volant[M] synthétique
feathered shuttlecock
volant[M] de plumes[F]
feather crown
empennage[M]
cork tip
tête[F] en liège[M]

gymnastics

gymnastique^F

event platform
podium^M des épreuves^F

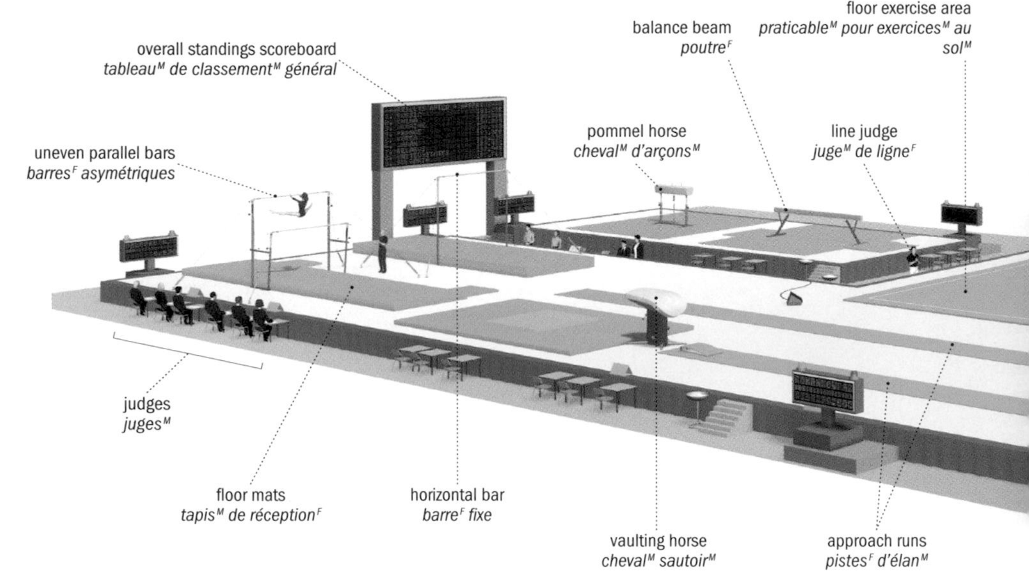

overall standings scoreboard
tableau^M de classement^M général
balance beam
poutre^F
floor exercise area
praticable^M pour exercices^M au sol^M
uneven parallel bars
barres^F asymétriques
pommel horse
cheval^M d'arçons^M
line judge
juge^M de ligne^F
judges
juges^M
floor mats
tapis^M de réception^F
horizontal bar
barre^F fixe
vaulting horse
cheval^M sautoir^M
approach runs
pistes^F d'élan^M

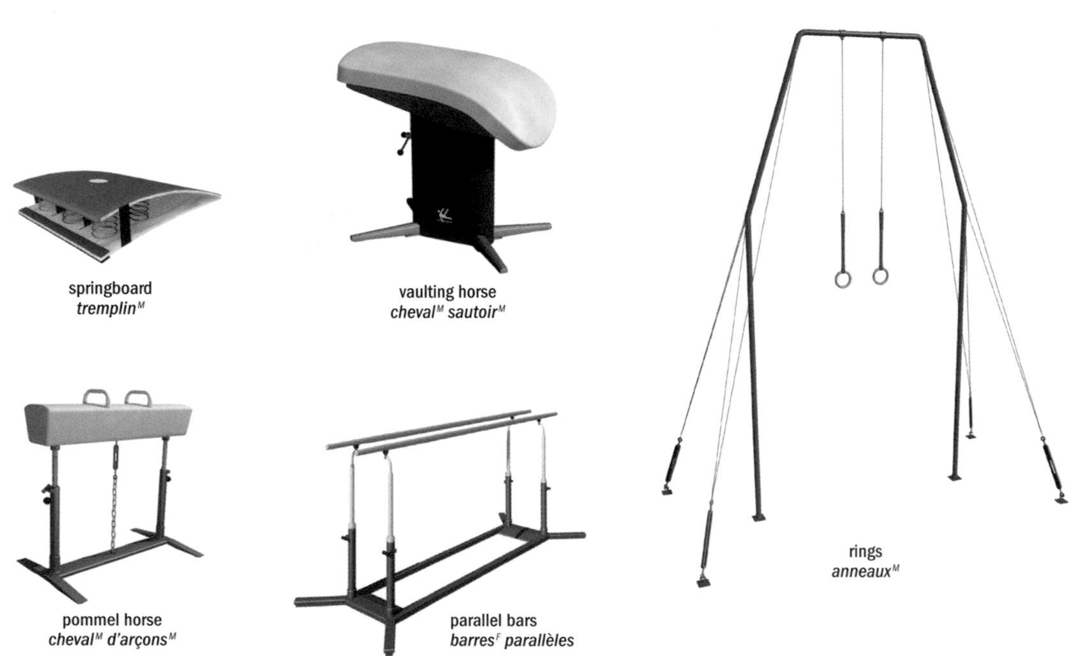

springboard
tremplin^M
vaulting horse
cheval^M sautoir^M
rings
anneaux^M
pommel horse
cheval^M d'arçons^M
parallel bars
barres^F parallèles

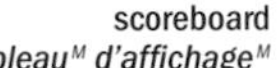

scoreboard
tableau[M] d'affichage[M]

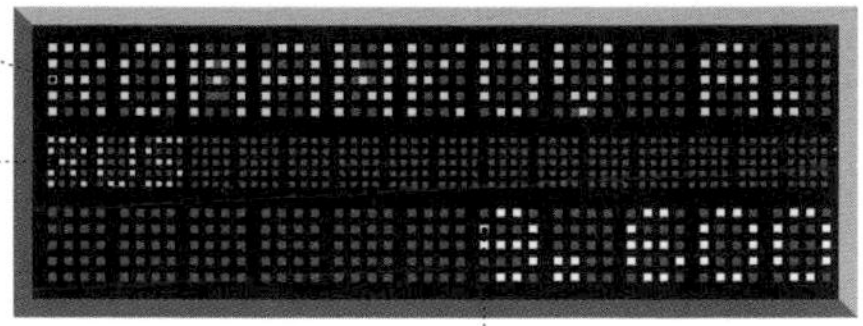

gymnast's name
nom[M] du gymnaste[M]

nationality
nationalité[F]

score
note[F]

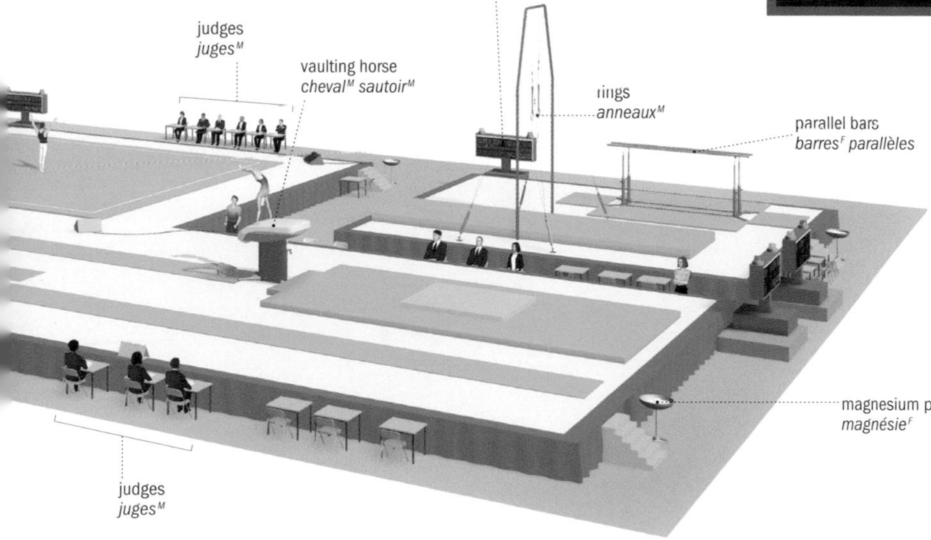

current event scoreboard
pointage[M] de l'épreuve[F] en cours[M]

judges
juges[M]

vaulting horse
cheval[M] sautoir[M]

rings
anneaux[M]

parallel bars
barres[F] parallèles

magnesium powder
magnésie[F]

judges
juges[M]

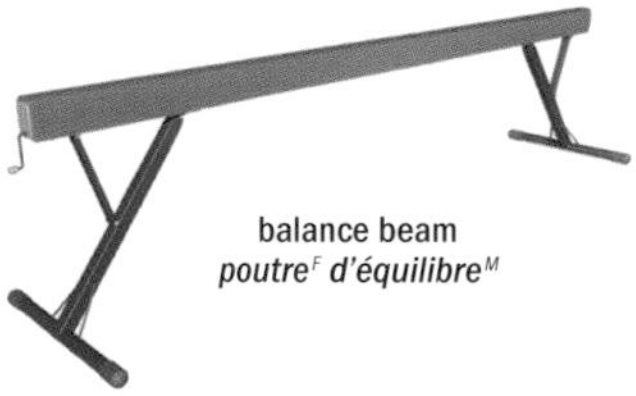

balance beam
poutre[F] d'équilibre[M]

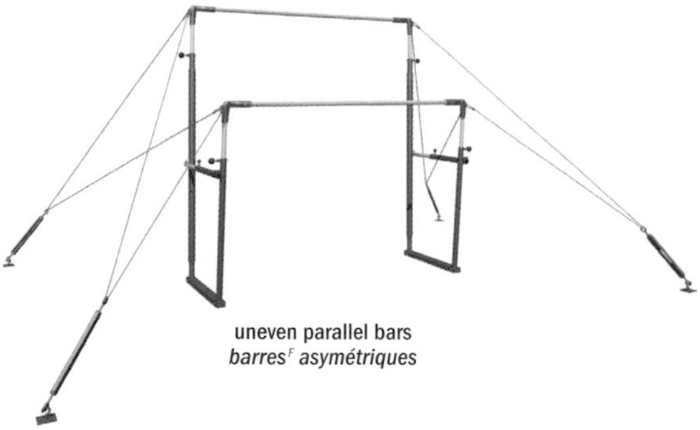

uneven parallel bars
barres[F] asymétriques

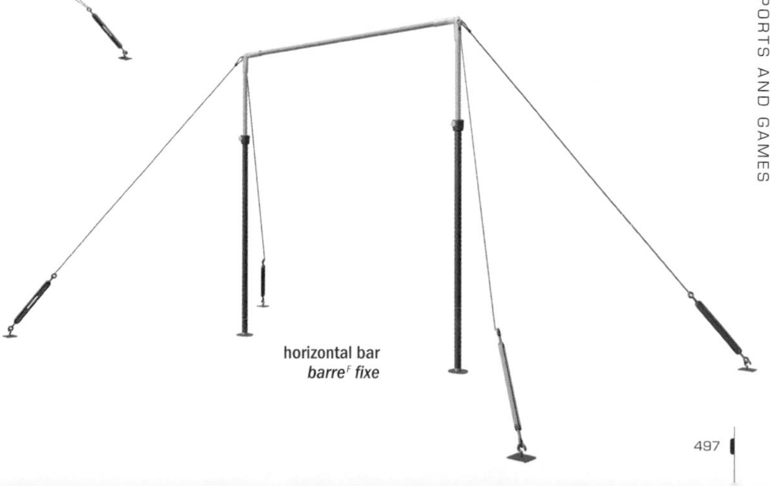

horizontal bar
barre[F] fixe

boxing

boxe[F]

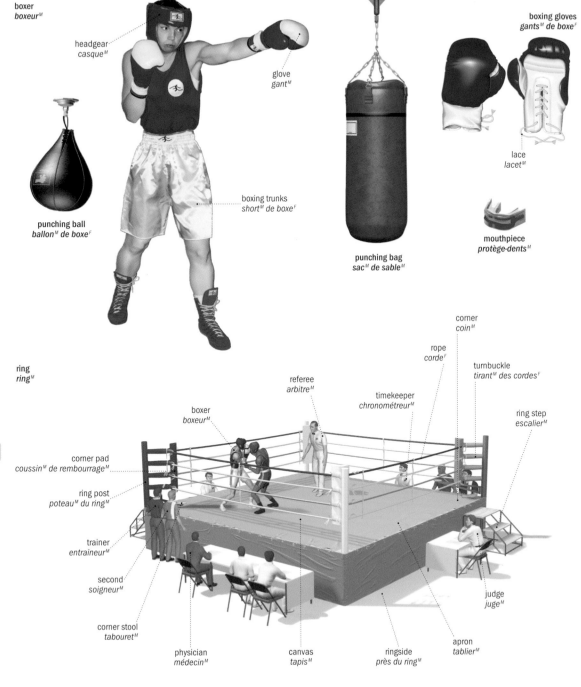

boxer
boxeur[M]

headgear
casque[M]

glove
gant[M]

boxing trunks
short[M] de boxe[F]

punching ball
ballon[M] de boxe[F]

punching bag
sac[M] de sable[M]

boxing gloves
gants[M] de boxe[F]

lace
lacet[M]

mouthpiece
protège-dents[M]

ring
ring[M]

corner
coin[M]

rope
corde[F]

turnbuckle
tirant[M] des cordes[F]

referee
arbitre[M]

timekeeper
chronométreur[M]

boxer
boxeur[M]

ring step
escalier[M]

corner pad
coussin[M] de rembourrage[M]

ring post
poteau[M] du ring[M]

trainer
entraîneur[M]

second
soigneur[M]

judge
juge[M]

corner stool
tabouret[M]

physician
médecin[M]

canvas
tapis[M]

ringside
près du ring[M]

apron
tablier[M]

judo
judo[M]

mat
tapis[M]
scorers and timekeepers
marqueurs[M] et chronométreurs[M]
medical team
équipe[F] médicale
contestant
combattant[M]
safety area
surface[F] de sécurité[F]
danger area
zone[F] de danger[M]
scoreboard
tableau[M] d'affichage[M]
contest area
surface[F] de combat[M]
referee
arbitre[M]
judge
juge[M]
examples of holds and throws
exemples[M] de prises[F]
judogi
judogi[M]
jacket
veste[F]
holding
immobilisation[F]
stomach throw
projection[F] en cercle[M]
sweeping hip throw
hanche[F] ailée
major outer reaping throw
grand fauchage[M] extérieur
major inner reaping throw
grand fauchage[M] intérieur
naked strangle
étranglement[M]
trousers
pantalon[M]
belt
ceinture[F]
arm lock
clé[F] de bras[M]
one-arm shoulder throw
projection[F] d'épaule[F] par un côté[M]

weightlifting

haltérophilie[F]

barbell
haltère[M] long

wristband
poignet[M] de force[F]

weightlifting belt
ceinture[F] d'haltérophilie[F]

sleeveless jersey
maillot[M] de corps[M]

trunks
culotte[F]

knee wrap
genouillère[F]

strap
lanière[F]

weightlifting shoe
chaussure[F] d'haltérophilie[F]

clean and jerk
épaulé[M]-jeté[M]

snatch
arraché[M]

fitness equipment

appareils[M] de conditionnement[M] physique

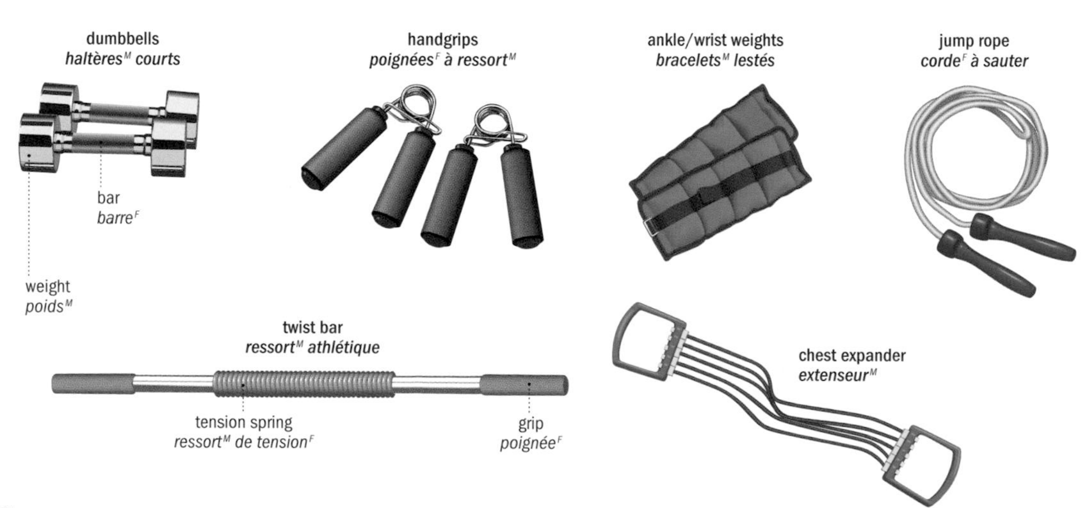
dumbbells
haltères[M] courts
bar
barre[F]
weight
poids[M]
handgrips
poignées[F] à ressort[M]
ankle/wrist weights
bracelets[M] lestés
jump rope
corde[F] à sauter
twist bar
ressort[M] athlétique
tension spring
ressort[M] de tension[F]
grip
poignée[F]
chest expander
extenseur[M]

fitness equipment

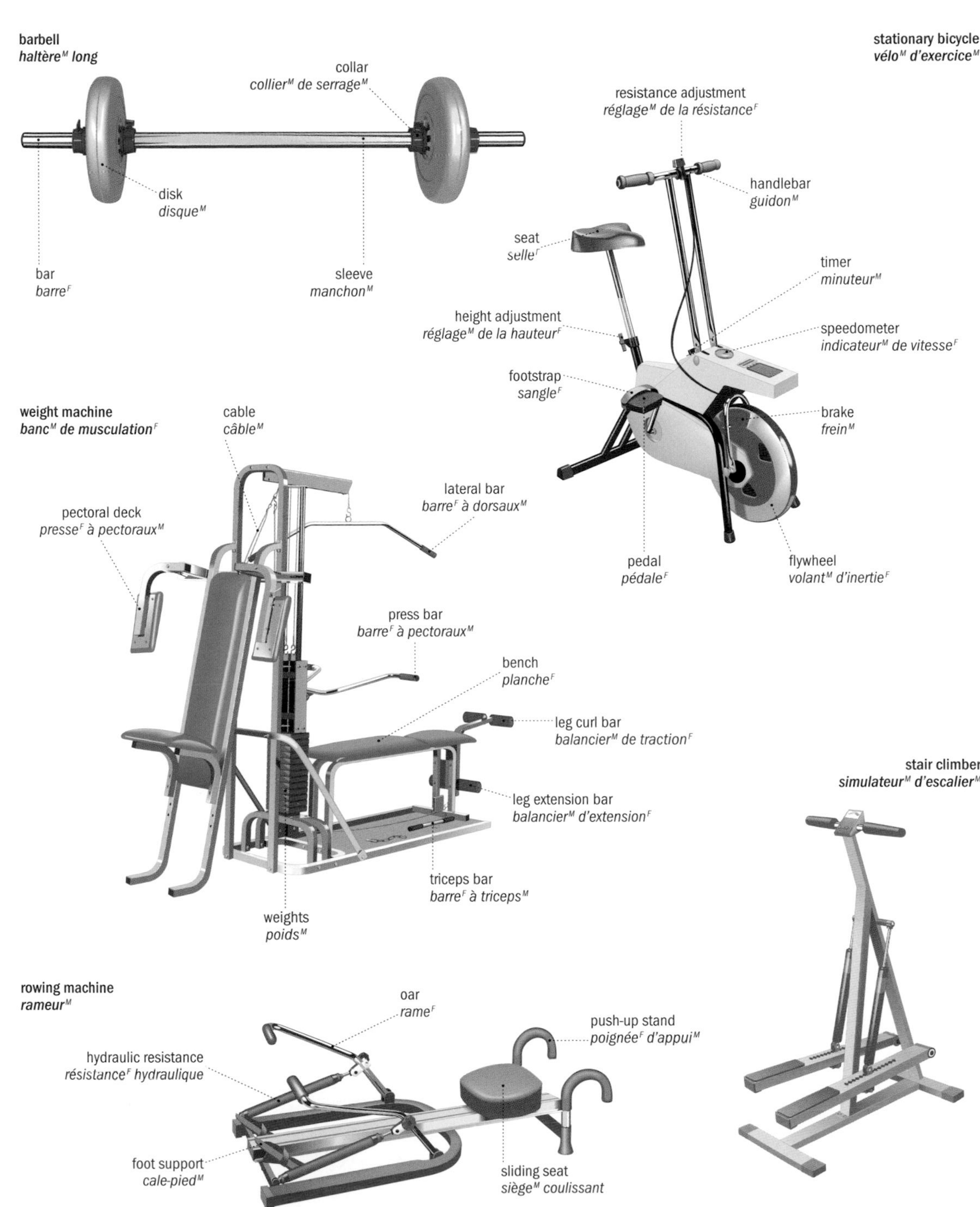
barbell
haltère[M] long
collar
collier[M] de serrage[M]
disk
disque[M]
bar
barre[F]
sleeve
manchon[M]
stationary bicycle
vélo[M] d'exercice[M]
resistance adjustment
réglage[M] de la résistance[F]
handlebar
guidon[M]
seat
selle[F]
timer
minuteur[M]
height adjustment
réglage[M] de la hauteur[F]
speedometer
indicateur[M] de vitesse[F]
footstrap
sangle[F]
brake
frein[M]
pedal
pédale[F]
flywheel
volant[M] d'inertie[F]
weight machine
banc[M] de musculation[F]
cable
câble[M]
pectoral deck
presse[F] à pectoraux[M]
lateral bar
barre[F] à dorsaux[M]
press bar
barre[F] à pectoraux[M]
bench
planche[F]
leg curl bar
balancier[M] de traction[F]
leg extension bar
balancier[M] d'extension[F]
triceps bar
barre[F] à triceps[M]
weights
poids[M]
stair climber
simulateur[M] d'escalier[M]
rowing machine
rameur[M]
oar
rame[F]
push-up stand
poignée[F] d'appui[M]
hydraulic resistance
résistance[F] hydraulique
foot support
cale-pied[M]
sliding seat
siège[M] coulissant

billiards

billard[M]

carom billiards
billard[M] français

pool
billard[M] pool

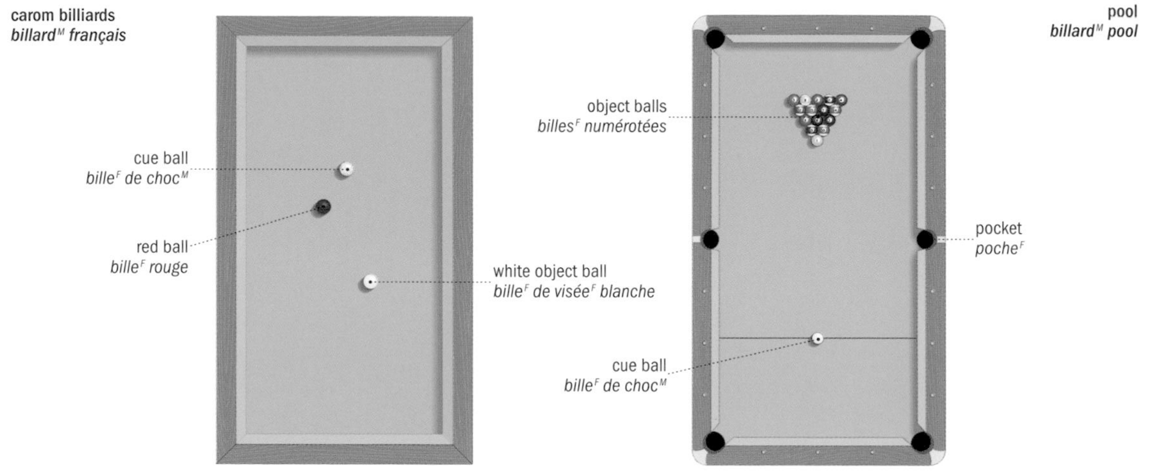

cue ball
bille[F] de choc[M]
red ball
bille[F] rouge
white object ball
bille[F] de visée[F] blanche
object balls
billes[F] numérotées
pocket
poche[F]
cue ball
bille[F] de choc[M]

table
table[F]

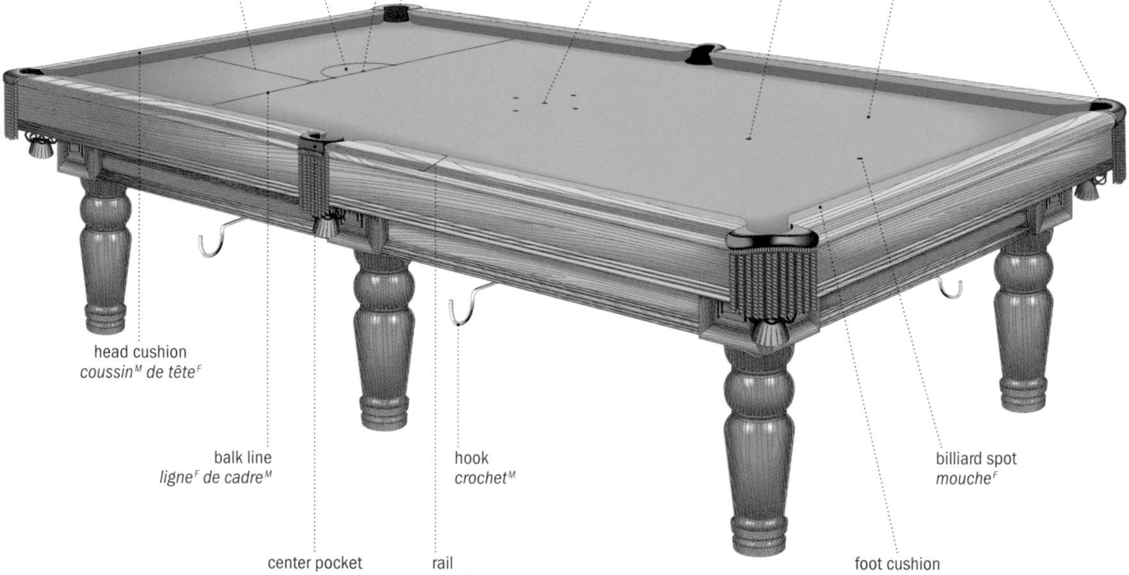

D
D[M]

balk line spot
mouche[F] de ligne[F] de cadre[M]

pyramid spot
mouche[F] supérieure

baize
tapis[M]

balk area
cadre[M]

bottom pocket
poche[F] inférieure

center spot
mouche[F] centrale

top pocket
poche[F] supérieure

head cushion
coussin[M] de tête[F]

balk line
ligne[F] de cadre[M]

hook
crochet[M]

billiard spot
mouche[F]

center pocket
poche[F] centrale

rail
bande[F]

foot cushion
coussin[M] arrière

billiards

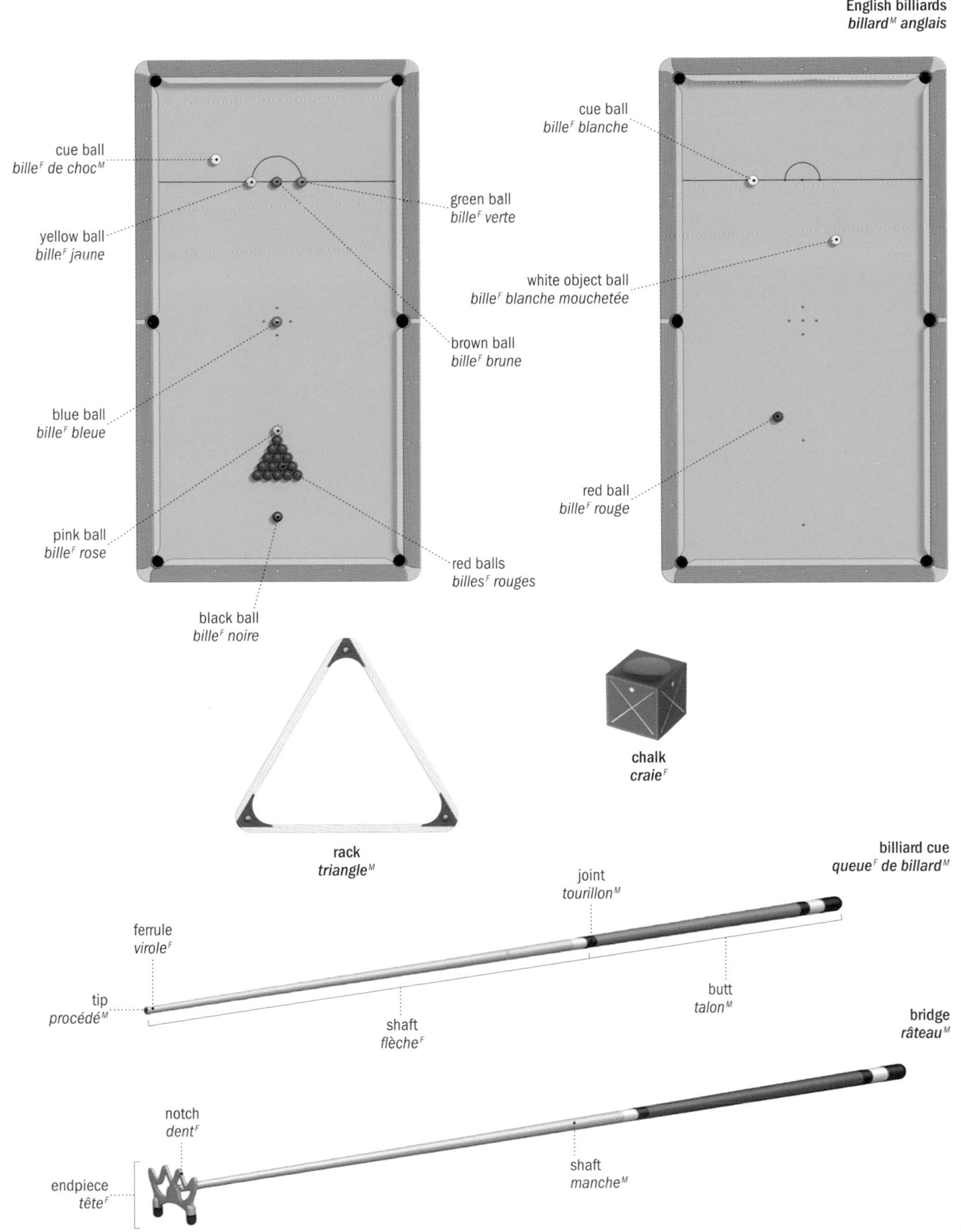
snooker
snooker^M
cue ball
bille^F de choc^M
yellow ball
bille^F jaune
green ball
bille^F verte
brown ball
bille^F brune
blue ball
bille^F bleue
pink ball
bille^F rose
red balls
billes^F rouges
black ball
bille^F noire
English billiards
billard^M anglais
cue ball
bille^F blanche
white object ball
bille^F blanche mouchetée
red ball
bille^F rouge
rack
triangle^M
chalk
craie^F
billiard cue
queue^F de billard^M
joint
tourillon^M
ferrule
virole^F
tip
procédé^M
shaft
flèche^F
butt
talon^M
bridge
râteau^M
notch
dent^F
endpiece
tête^F
shaft
manche^M

golf

golf^M

course
parcours^M

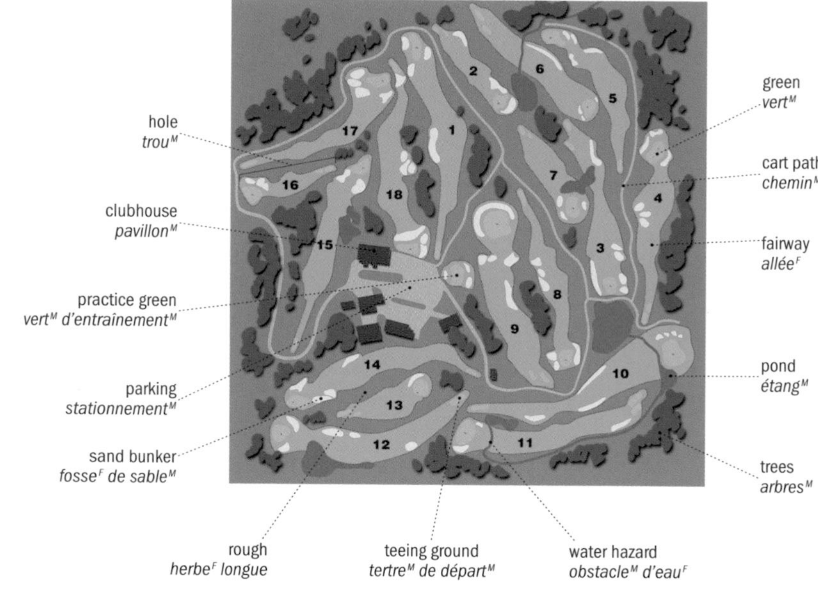

green
vert^M
cart path
chemin^M
fairway
allée^F
pond
étang^M
trees
arbres^M
water hazard
obstacle^M d'eau^F
teeing ground
tertre^M de départ^M
rough
herbe^F longue
sand bunker
fosse^F de sable^M
parking
stationnement^M
practice green
vert^M d'entrainement^M
clubhouse
pavillon^M
hole
trou^M
1
2
3
4
5
6
7
8
9
10
11
12
13
14
15
16
17
18

par 5 hole
trou^M de normale^F 5

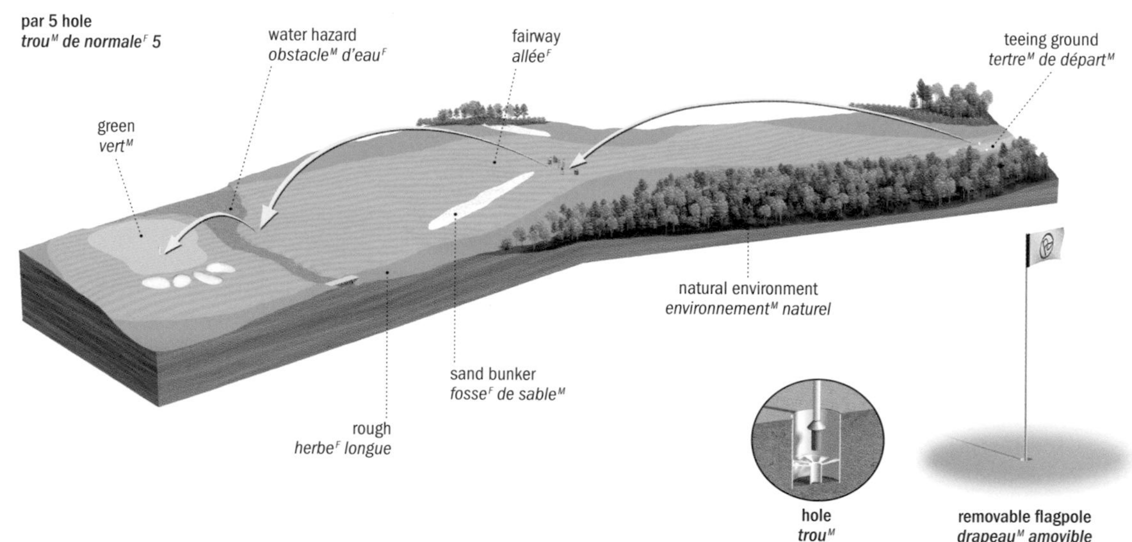

water hazard
obstacle^M d'eau^F
fairway
allée^F
teeing ground
tertre^M de départ^M
green
vert^M
natural environment
environnement^M naturel
sand bunker
fosse^F de sable^M
rough
herbe^F longue

hole
trou^M

removable flagpole
drapeau^M amovible

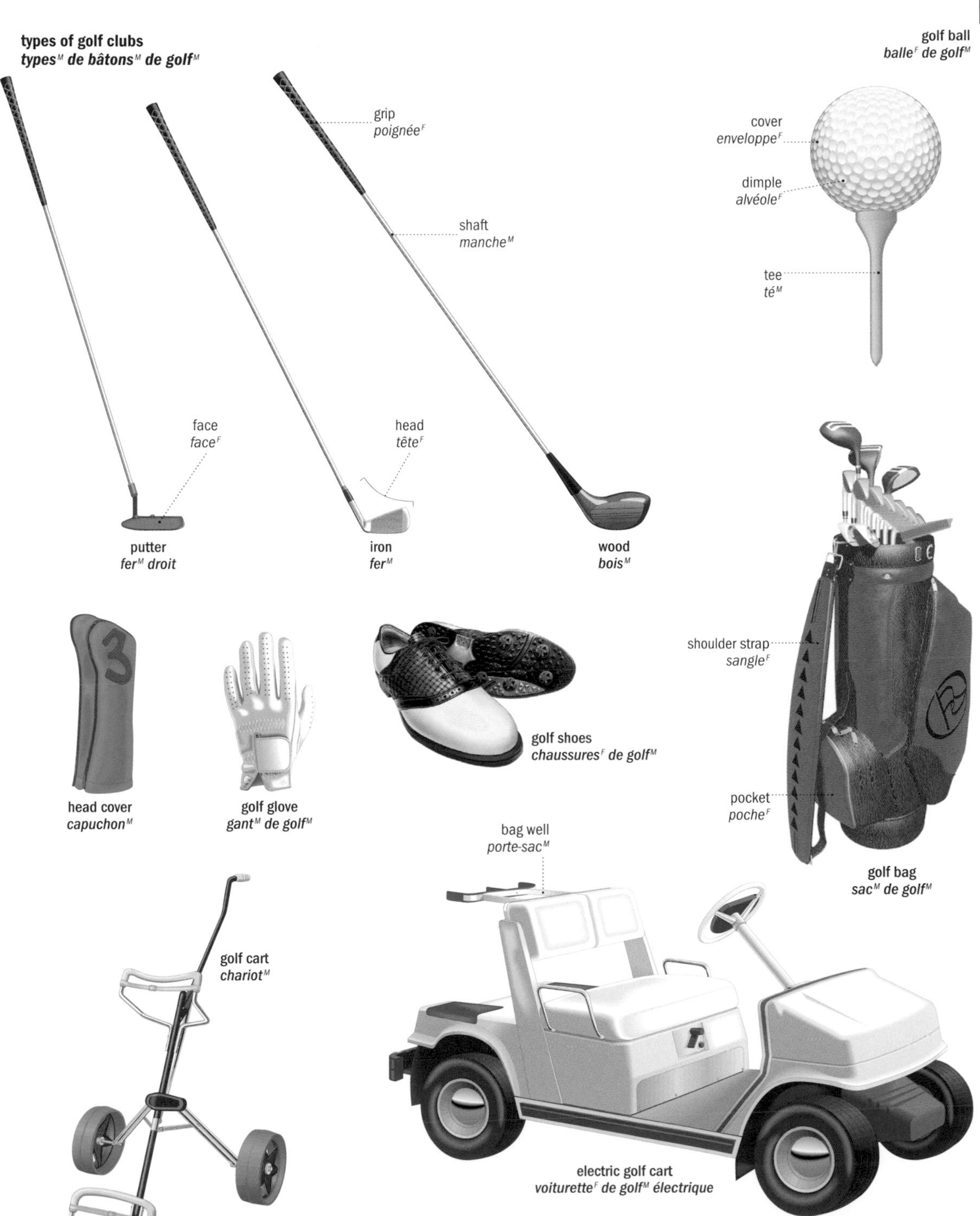
types of golf clubs
types de bâtons de golf
grip
poignée
shaft
manche
face
face
head
tête
putter
fer droit
iron
fer
wood
bois
golf ball
balle de golf
cover
enveloppe
dimple
alvéole
tee
té
head cover
capuchon
golf glove
gant de golf
golf shoes
chaussures de golf
shoulder strap
sangle
pocket
poche
golf bag
sac de golf
bag well
porte-sac
golf cart
chariot
electric golf cart
voiturette de golf électrique

ice hockey

hockey[M] sur glace[F]

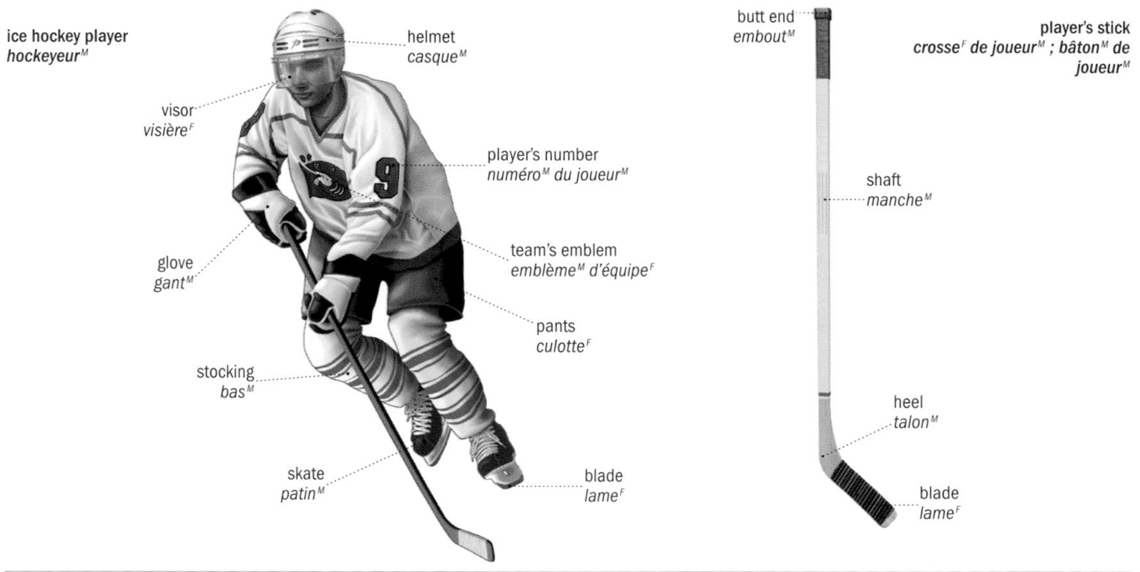
ice hockey player
hockeyeur[M]
helmet
casque[M]
visor
visière[F]
player's number
numéro[M] du joueur[M]
team's emblem
emblème[M] d'équipe[F]
glove
gant[M]
pants
culotte[F]
stocking
bas[M]
skate
patin[M]
blade
lame[F]
butt end
embout[M]
player's stick
crosse[F] de joueur[M] ; bâton[M] de joueur[M]
shaft
manche[M]
heel
talon[M]
blade
lame[F]

rink
patinoire[F]

face-off spot
point[M] de mise[F] au jeu[M]

right defense
défenseur[M] droit

left defense
défenseur[M] gauche

goal line
ligne[F] de but[M]

glass protector
vitre[F] de protection[F]

players' bench
banc[M] des joueurs[M]

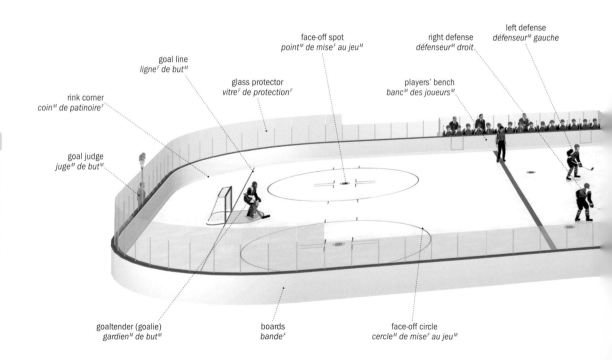

rink corner
coin[M] de patinoire[F]

goal judge
juge[M] de but[M]

goaltender (goalie)
gardien[M] de but[M]

boards
bande[F]

face-off circle
cercle[M] de mise[F] au jeu[M]

snowboarding

surf[M] des neiges[F]

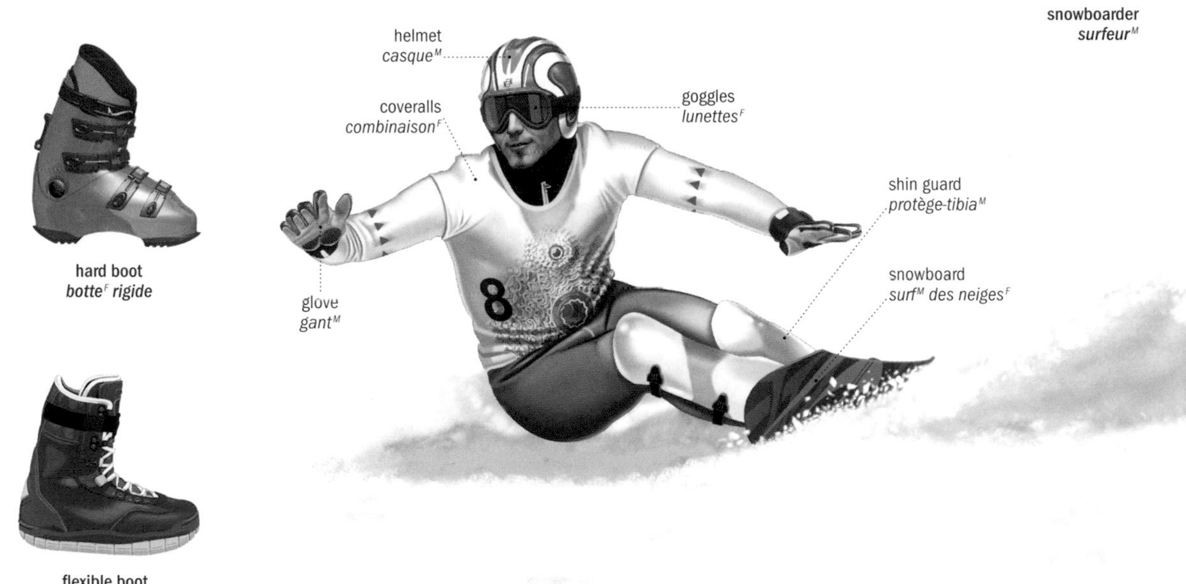
snowboarder
surfeur[M]
helmet
casque[M]
coveralls
combinaison[F]
goggles
lunettes[F]
shin guard
protège-tibia[M]
snowboard
surf[M] des neiges[F]
glove
gant[M]
hard boot
botte[F] rigide
flexible boot
botte[F] souple

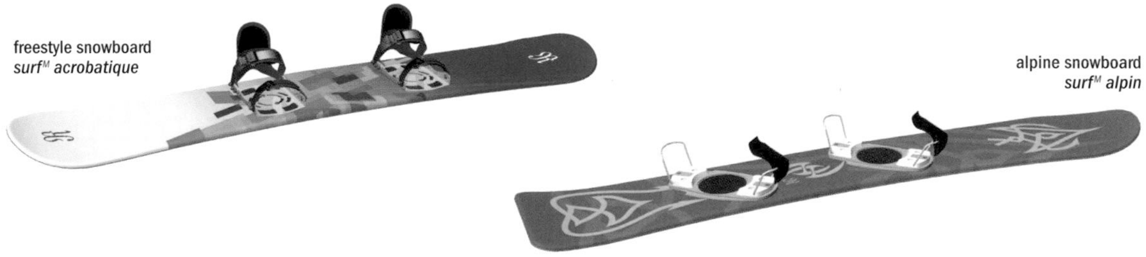
freestyle snowboard
surf[M] acrobatique
alpine snowboard
surf[M] alpin

ski jumping

saut[M] à ski[M]

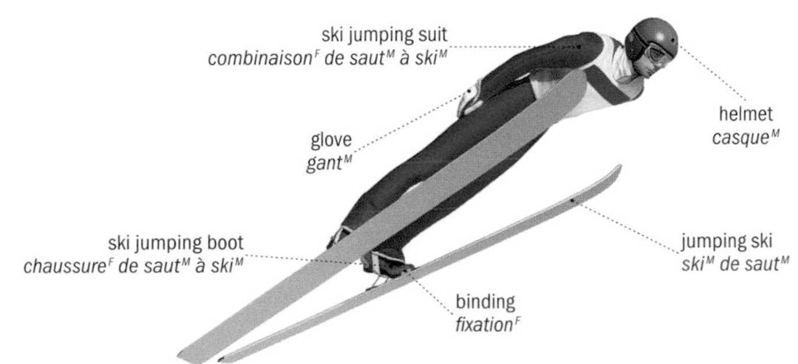
ski jumper
sauteur[M]
ski jumping suit
combinaison[F] de saut[M] à ski[M]
helmet
casque[M]
glove
gant[M]
ski jumping boot
chaussure[F] de saut[M] à ski[M]
jumping ski
ski[M] de saut[M]
binding
fixation[F]

cross-country skiing

ski[M] de fond[M]

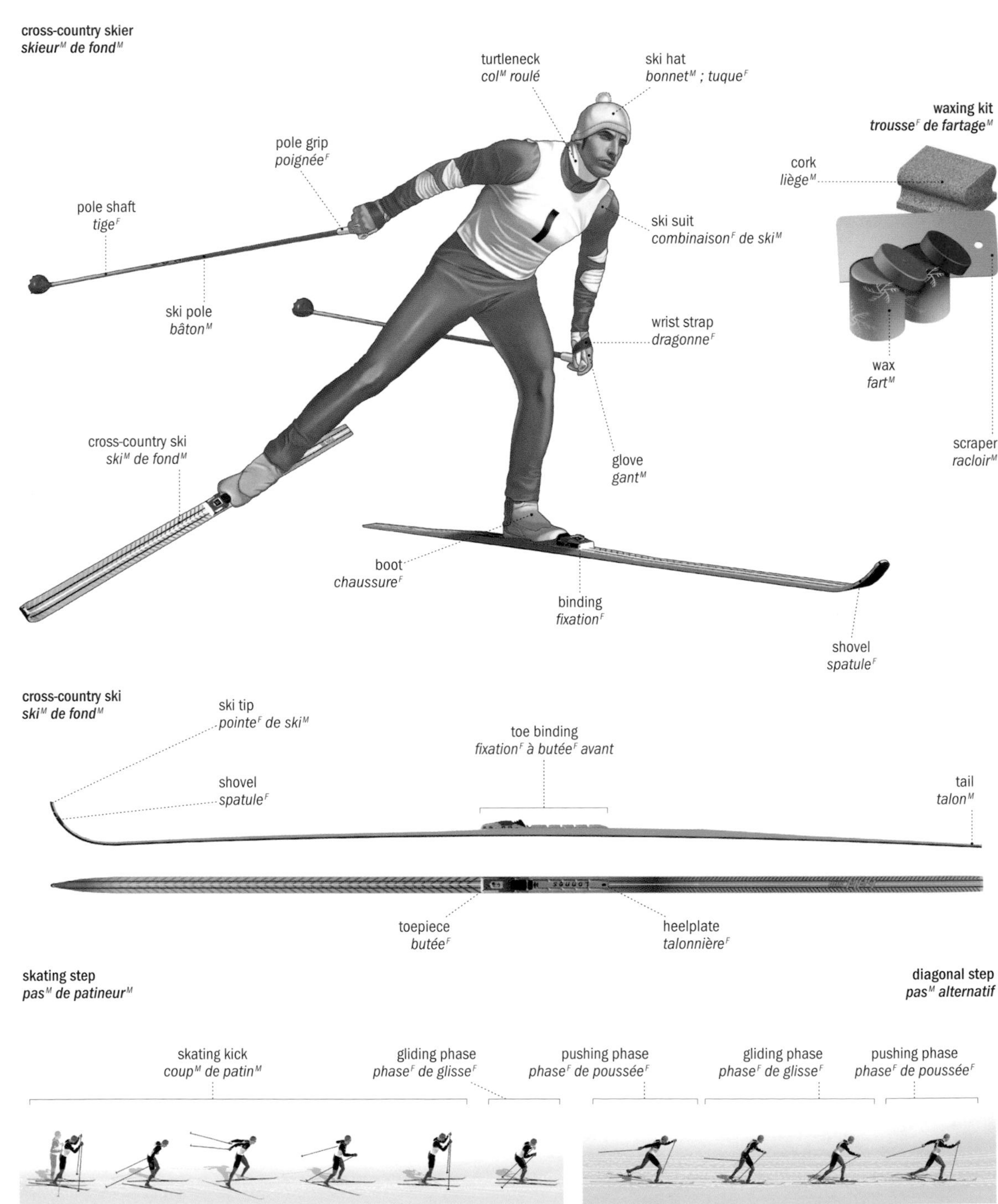
cross-country skier
skieur[M] de fond[M]
turtleneck
col[M] roulé
ski hat
bonnet[M] ; tuque[F]
waxing kit
trousse[F] de fartage[M]
pole grip
poignée[F]
cork
liège[M]
pole shaft
tige[F]
ski suit
combinaison[F] de ski[M]
ski pole
bâton[M]
wrist strap
dragonne[F]
wax
fart[M]
cross-country ski
ski[M] de fond[M]
glove
gant[M]
scraper
racloir[M]
boot
chaussure[F]
binding
fixation[F]
shovel
spatule[F]
cross-country ski
ski[M] de fond[M]
ski tip
pointe[F] de ski[M]
toe binding
fixation[F] à butée[F] avant
shovel
spatule[F]
tail
talon[M]
toepiece
butée[F]
heelplate
talonnière[F]
skating step
pas[M] de patineur[M]
diagonal step
pas[M] alternatif
skating kick
coup[M] de patin[M]
gliding phase
phase[F] de glisse[F]
pushing phase
phase[F] de poussée[F]
gliding phase
phase[F] de glisse[F]
pushing phase
phase[F] de poussée[F]

curling

curling[M]

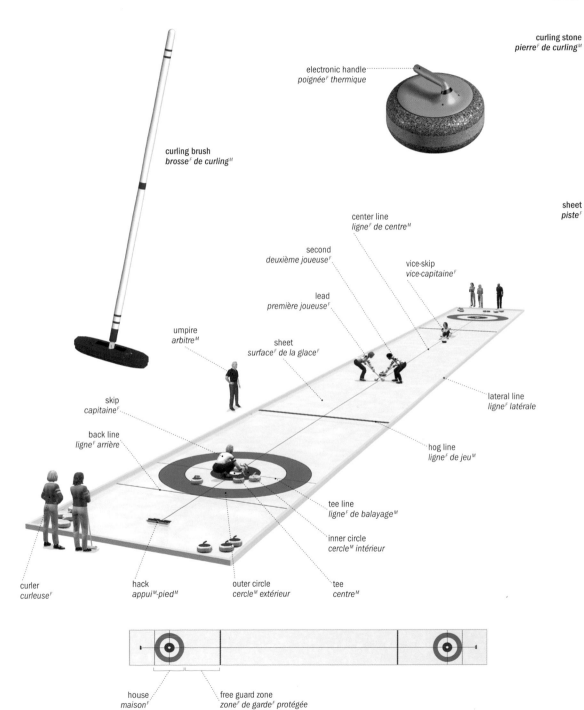

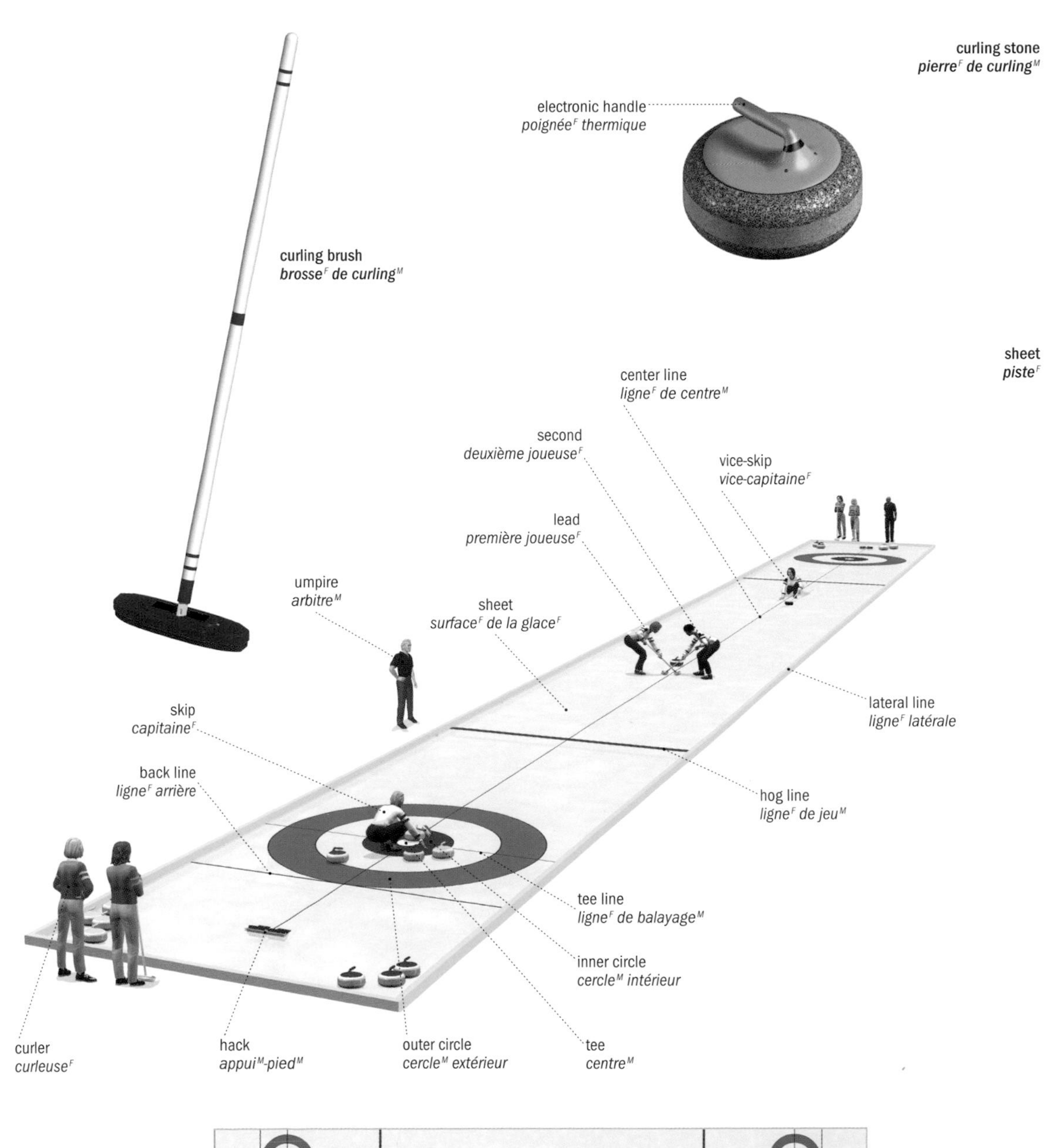
curling stone
pierre[F] de curling[M]
electronic handle
poignée[F] thermique
curling brush
brosse[F] de curling[M]
sheet
piste[F]
center line
ligne[F] de centre[M]
second
deuxième joueuse[F]
vice-skip
vice-capitaine[F]
lead
première joueuse[F]
umpire
arbitre[M]
sheet
surface[F] de la glace[F]
lateral line
ligne[F] latérale
skip
capitaine[F]
back line
ligne[F] arrière
hog line
ligne[F] de jeu[M]
tee line
ligne[F] de balayage[M]
inner circle
cercle[M] intérieur
curler
curleuse[F]
hack
appui[M]-pied[M]
outer circle
cercle[M] extérieur
tee
centre[M]
house
maison[F]
free guard zone
zone[F] de garde[F] protégée

swimming

natation[F]

starting block
plot[M] de départ[M]

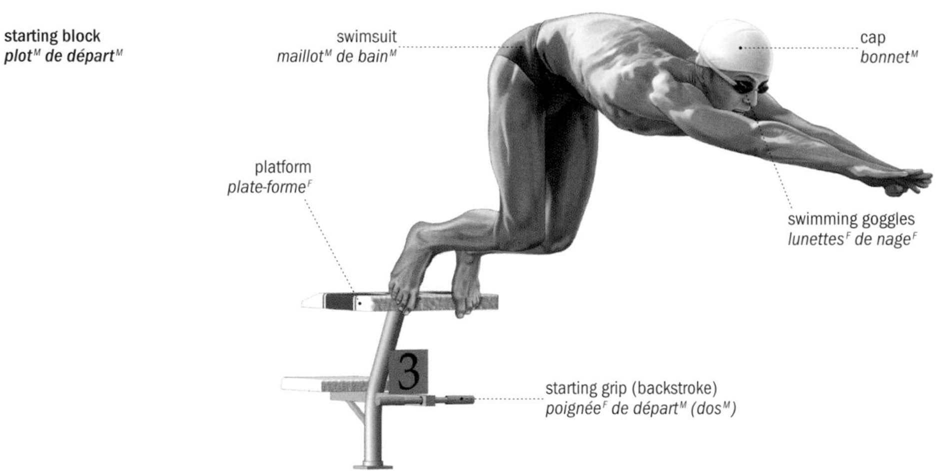
swimsuit
maillot[M] de bain[M]
cap
bonnet[M]
platform
plate-forme[F]
swimming goggles
lunettes[F] de nage[F]
3
starting grip (backstroke)
poignée[F] de départ[M] (dos[M])

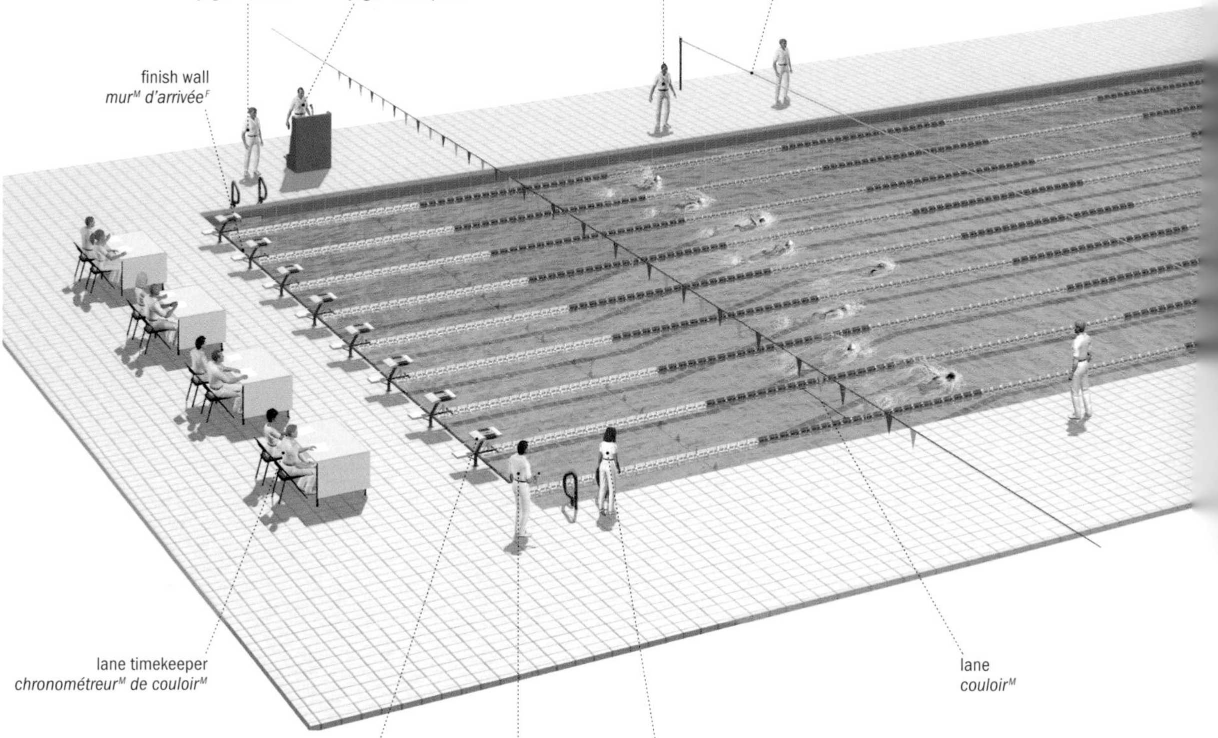

referee
juge[M] arbitre[M]

starter
juge[M] de départ[M]

stroke judge
juge[M] de nage[F]

false start rope
corde[F] de faux départ[M]

finish wall
mur[M] d'arrivée[F]

lane timekeeper
chronométreur[M] de couloir[M]

lane
couloir[M]

starting block
plot[M] de départ[M]

chief timekeeper
chronométreur[M] en chef[M]

placing judge
juge[M] de classement[M]

types of strokes
types^M de nages^F

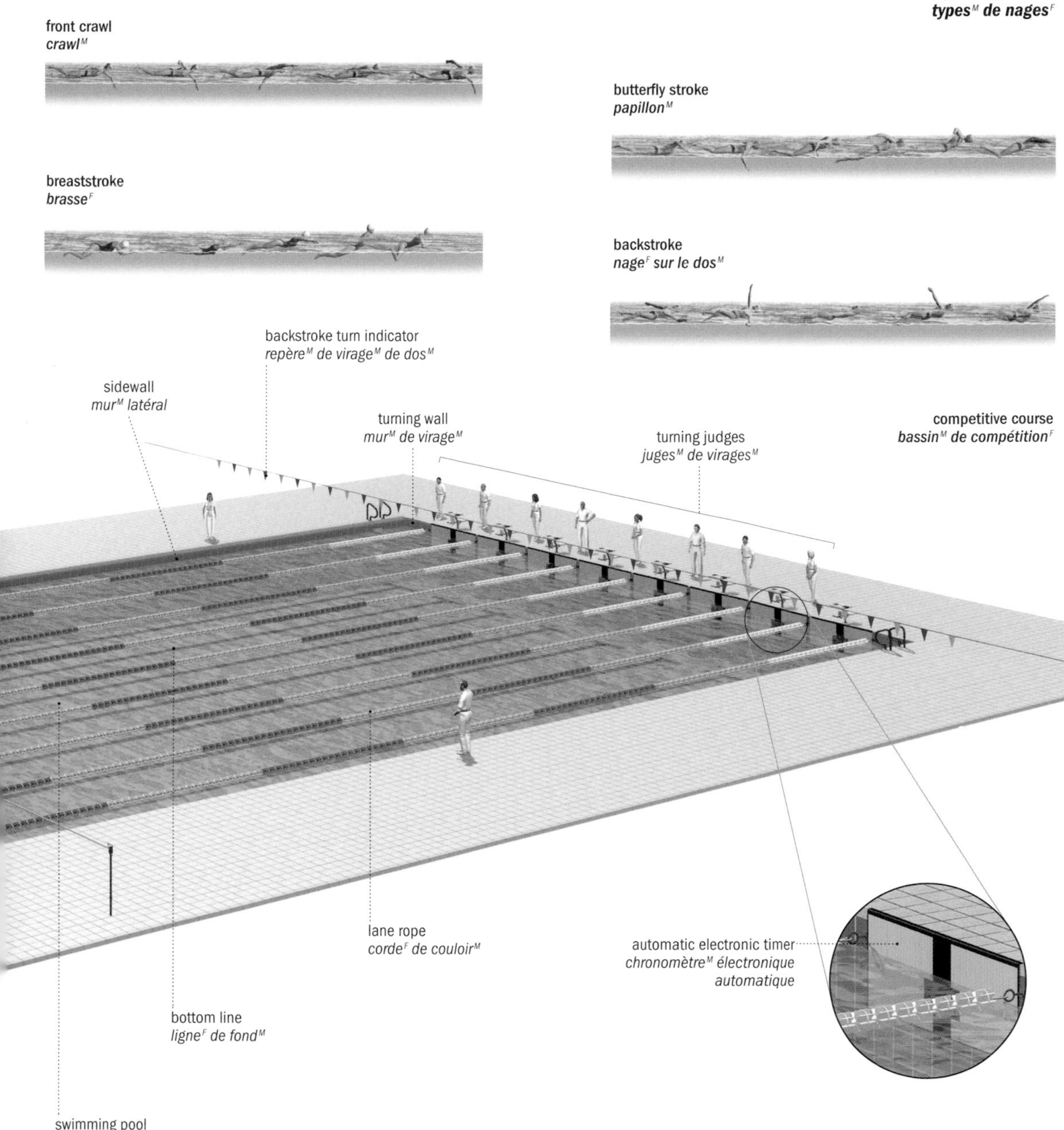
front crawl
crawl^M
butterfly stroke
papillon^M
breaststroke
brasse^F
backstroke
nage^F sur le dos^M
backstroke turn indicator
repère^M de virage^M de dos^M
sidewall
mur^M latéral
turning wall
mur^M de virage^M
turning judges
juges^M de virages^M
competitive course
bassin^M de compétition^F
lane rope
corde^F de couloir^M
automatic electronic timer
chronomètre^M électronique automatique
bottom line
ligne^F de fond^M
swimming pool
bassin^M

diving

plongeon[M]

starting positions
positions[F] de départ[M]
reverse
renversé
inward
retourné
backward
arrière
forward
avant
armstand
en équilibre[M]
flights
vols[M]
tuck position
position[F] groupée
straight position
position[F] droite
pike position
position[F] carpée

diving installations
plongeoir[M]

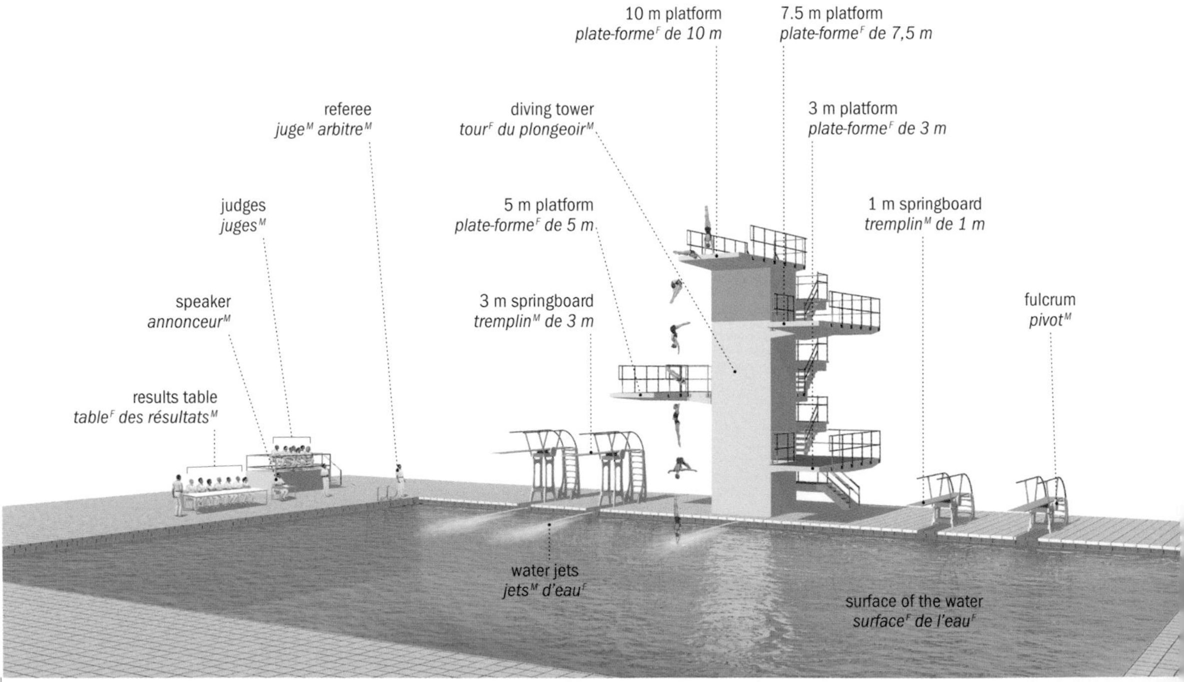

10 m platform
plate-forme[F] de 10 m
7.5 m platform
plate-forme[F] de 7,5 m
referee
juge[M] arbitre[M]
diving tower
tour[F] du plongeoir[M]
3 m platform
plate-forme[F] de 3 m
judges
juges[M]
5 m platform
plate-forme[F] de 5 m
1 m springboard
tremplin[M] de 1 m
speaker
annonceur[M]
3 m springboard
tremplin[M] de 3 m
fulcrum
pivot[M]
results table
table[F] des résultats[M]
water jets
jets[M] d'eau[F]
surface of the water
surface[F] de l'eau[F]

SPORTS AND GAMES

sailboard

planche[F] à voile[F]

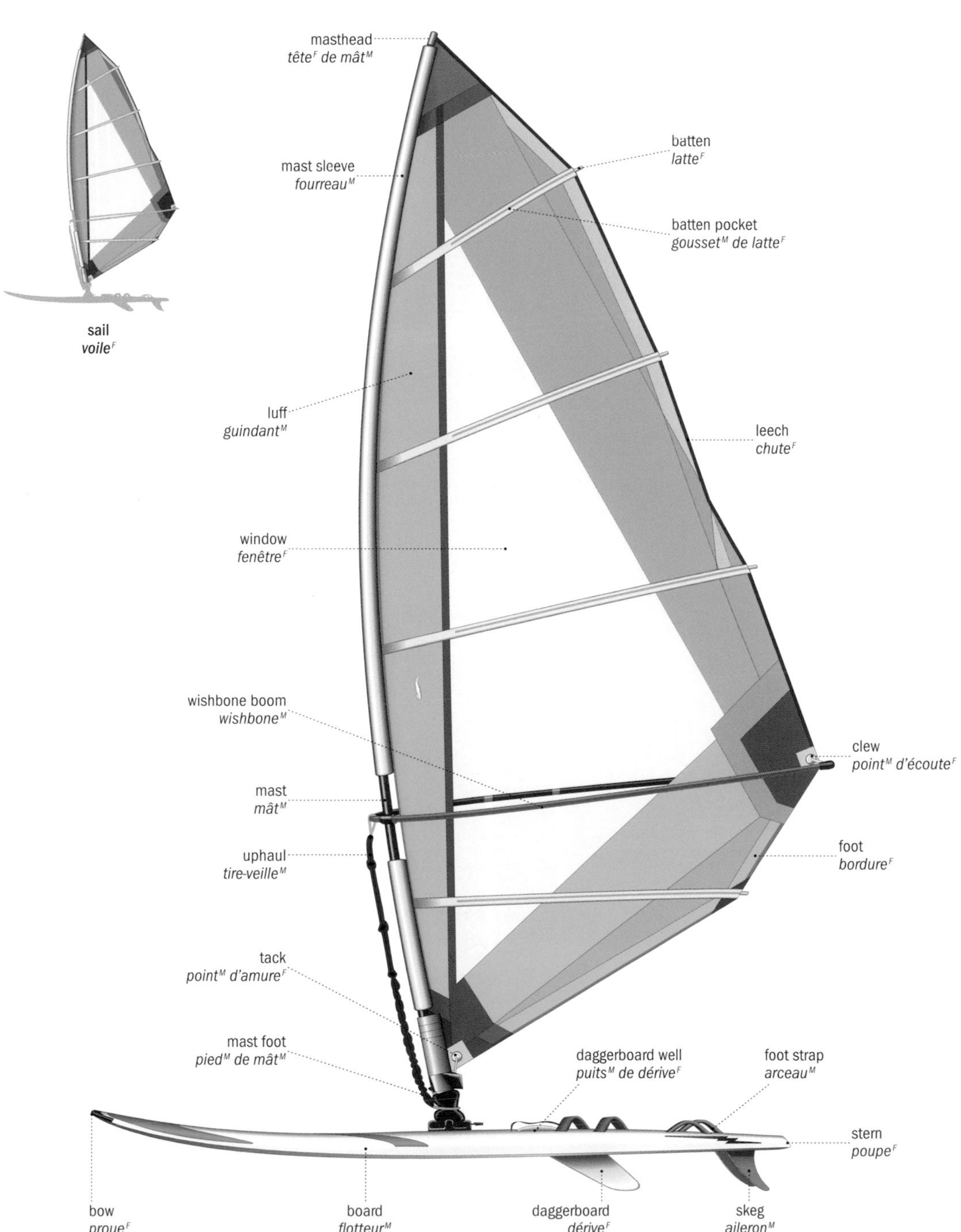
sail
voile[F]
masthead
tête[F] de mât[M]
mast sleeve
fourreau[M]
batten
latte[F]
batten pocket
gousset[M] de latte[F]
luff
guindant[M]
leech
chute[F]
window
fenêtre[F]
wishbone boom
wishbone[M]
clew
point[M] d'écoute[F]
mast
mât[M]
uphaul
tire-veille[M]
foot
bordure[F]
tack
point[M] d'amure[F]
mast foot
pied[M] de mât[M]
daggerboard well
puits[M] de dérive[F]
foot strap
arceau[M]
stern
poupe[F]
bow
proue[F]
board
flotteur[M]
daggerboard
dérive[F]
skeg
aileron[M]

sailing

voile^F

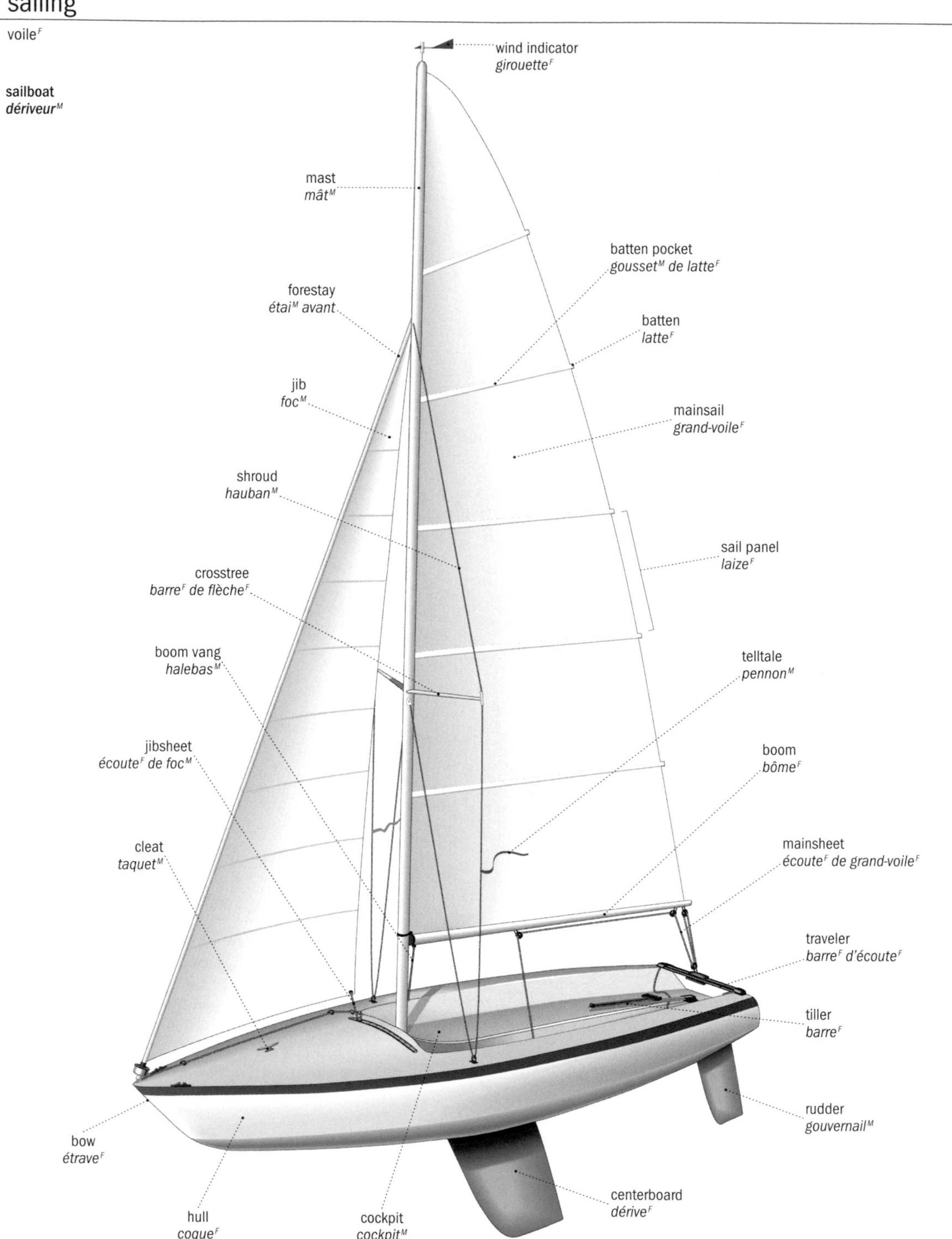

sailboat
dériveur^M
wind indicator
girouette^F
mast
mât^M
batten pocket
gousset^M de latte^F
forestay
étai^M avant
batten
latte^F
jib
foc^M
mainsail
grand-voile^F
shroud
hauban^M
sail panel
laize^F
crosstree
barre^F de flèche^F
boom vang
halebas^M
telltale
pennon^M
jibsheet
écoute^F de foc^M
boom
bôme^F
cleat
taquet^M
mainsheet
écoute^F de grand-voile^F
traveler
barre^F d'écoute^F
tiller
barre^F
rudder
gouvernail^M
bow
étrave^F
centerboard
dérive^F
hull
coque^F
cockpit
cockpit^M

multihulls
***multicoques*[M]**

monohulls
***monocoques*[M]**

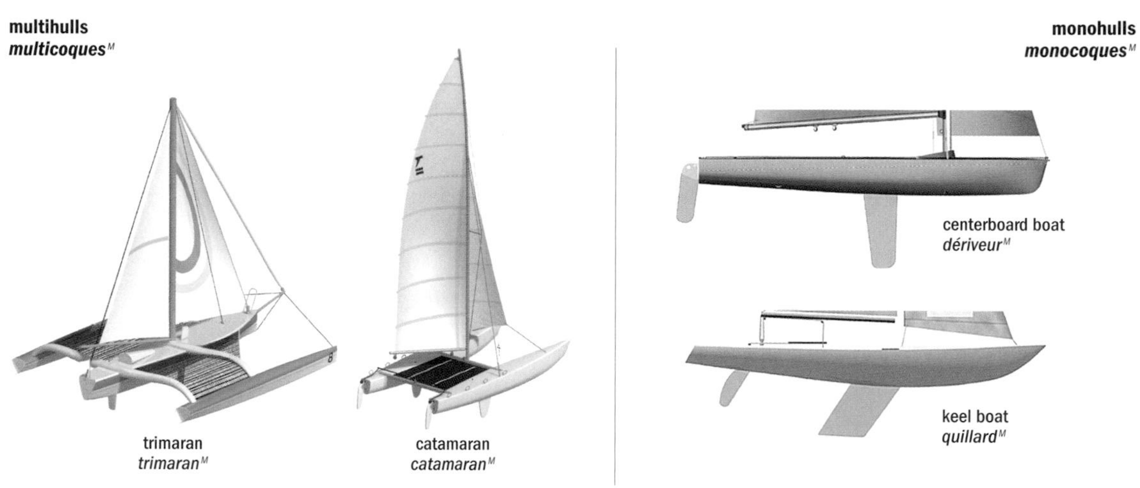
trimaran
trimaran[M]
catamaran
catamaran[M]
centerboard boat
dériveur[M]
keel boat
quillard[M]

upperworks
***accastillage*[M]**

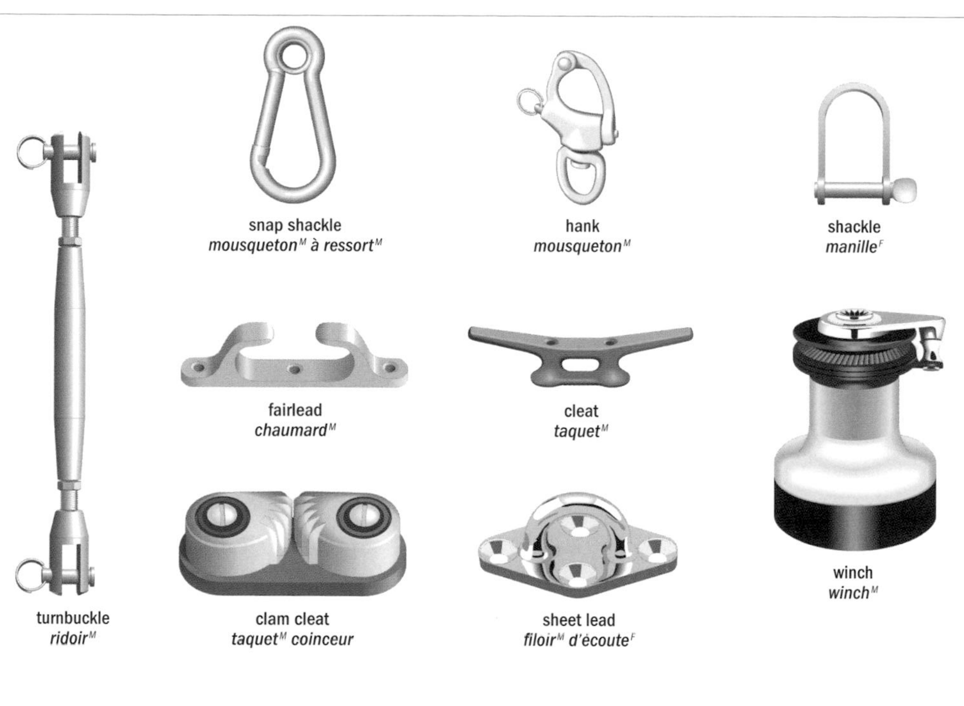
snap shackle
mousqueton[M] *à ressort*[M]
hank
mousqueton[M]
shackle
manille[F]
turnbuckle
ridoir[M]
fairlead
chaumard[M]
cleat
taquet[M]
winch
winch[M]
clam cleat
taquet[M] *coinceur*
sheet lead
filoir[M] *d'écoute*[F]

traveler
***barre*[F] *d'écoute*[F]**

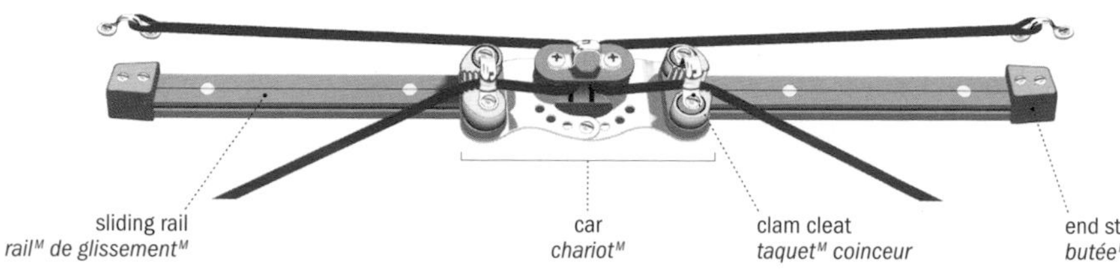
sliding rail
rail[M] *de glissement*[M]
car
chariot[M]
clam cleat
taquet[M] *coinceur*
end stop
butée[F]

road racing

cyclisme[M] sur route[F]

road-racing bicycle and cyclist
vélo[M] de course[F] et cycliste[M]

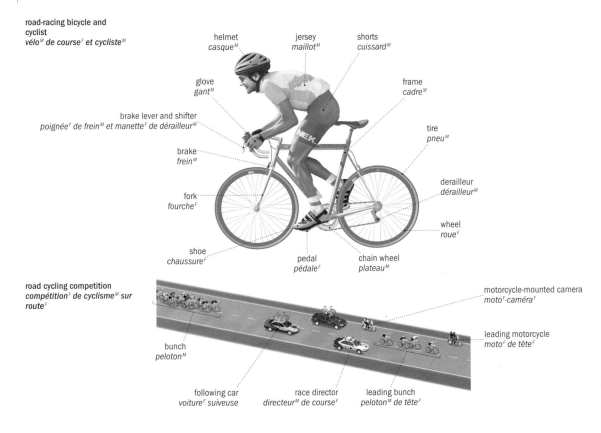

helmet
casque[M]
jersey
maillot[M]
shorts
cuissard[M]
glove
gant[M]
frame
cadre[M]
brake lever and shifter
poignée[F] de frein[M] et manette[F] de dérailleur[M]
tire
pneu[M]
brake
frein[M]
derailleur
dérailleur[M]
fork
fourche[F]
wheel
roue[F]
shoe
chaussure[F]
pedal
pédale[F]
chain wheel
plateau[M]

road cycling competition
compétition[F] de cyclisme[M] sur route[F]

motorcycle-mounted camera
moto[F]-caméra[F]
leading motorcycle
moto[F] de tête[F]
bunch
peloton[M]
following car
voiture[F] suiveuse
race director
directeur[M] de course[F]
leading bunch
peloton[M] de tête[F]

mountain biking

vélo[M] de montagne[F]

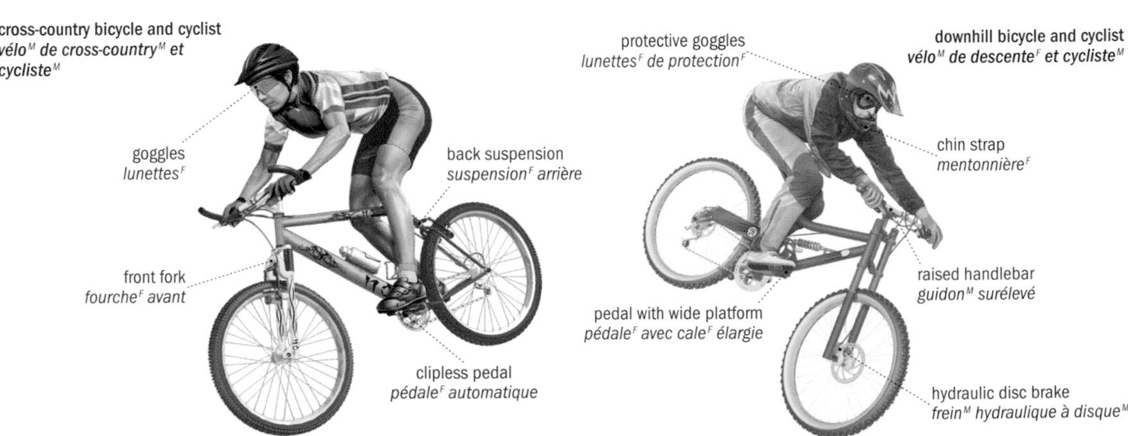
cross-country bicycle and cyclist
vélo[M] de cross-country[M] et cycliste[M]
goggles
lunettes[F]
back suspension
suspension[F] arrière
front fork
fourche[F] avant
clipless pedal
pédale[F] automatique
protective goggles
lunettes[F] de protection[F]
downhill bicycle and cyclist
vélo[M] de descente[F] et cycliste[M]
chin strap
mentonnière[F]
raised handlebar
guidon[M] surélevé
pedal with wide platform
pédale[F] avec cale[F] élargie
hydraulic disc brake
frein[M] hydraulique à disque[M]

personal watercraft

scooter[M] de mer[F] ; *motomarine*[F]

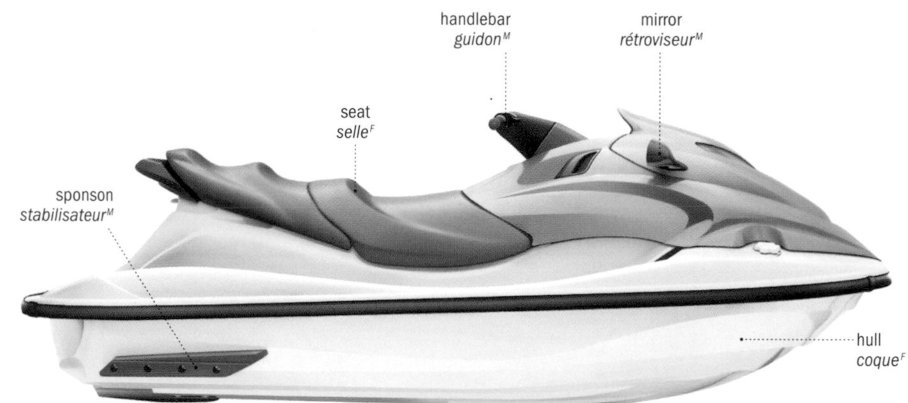
handlebar
guidon[M]
mirror
rétroviseur[M]
seat
selle[F]
sponson
stabilisateur[M]
hull
coque[F]

snowmobile

motoneige[F]

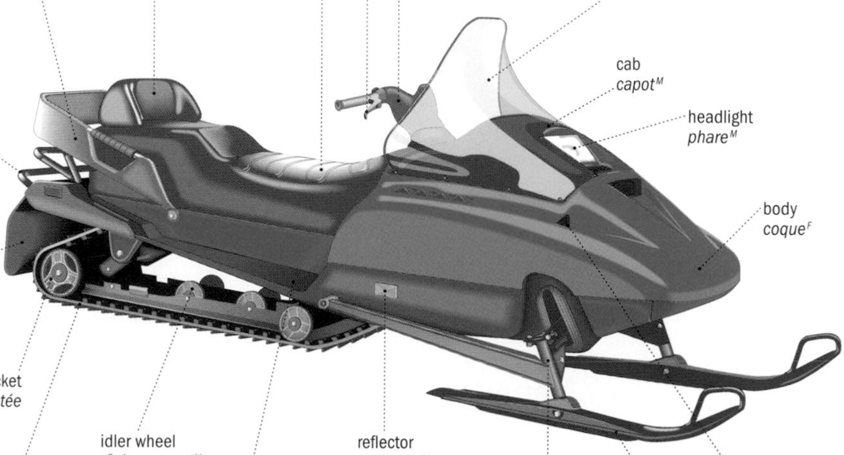

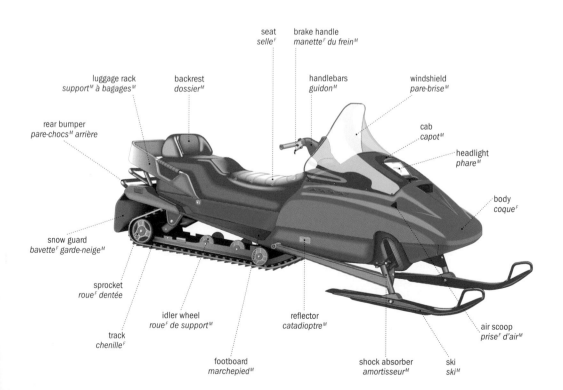

seat
selle[F]

brake handle
manette[F] *du frein*[M]

luggage rack
support[M] *à bagages*[M]

backrest
dossier[M]

handlebars
guidon[M]

windshield
pare-brise[M]

rear bumper
pare-chocs[M] *arrière*

cab
capot[M]

headlight
phare[M]

body
coque[F]

snow guard
bavette[F] *garde-neige*[M]

sprocket
roue[F] *dentée*

idler wheel
roue[F] *de support*[M]

reflector
catadioptre[M]

air scoop
prise[F] *d'air*[M]

track
chenille[F]

footboard
marchepied[M]

shock absorber
amortisseur[M]

ski
ski[M]

car racing

course[F] automobile

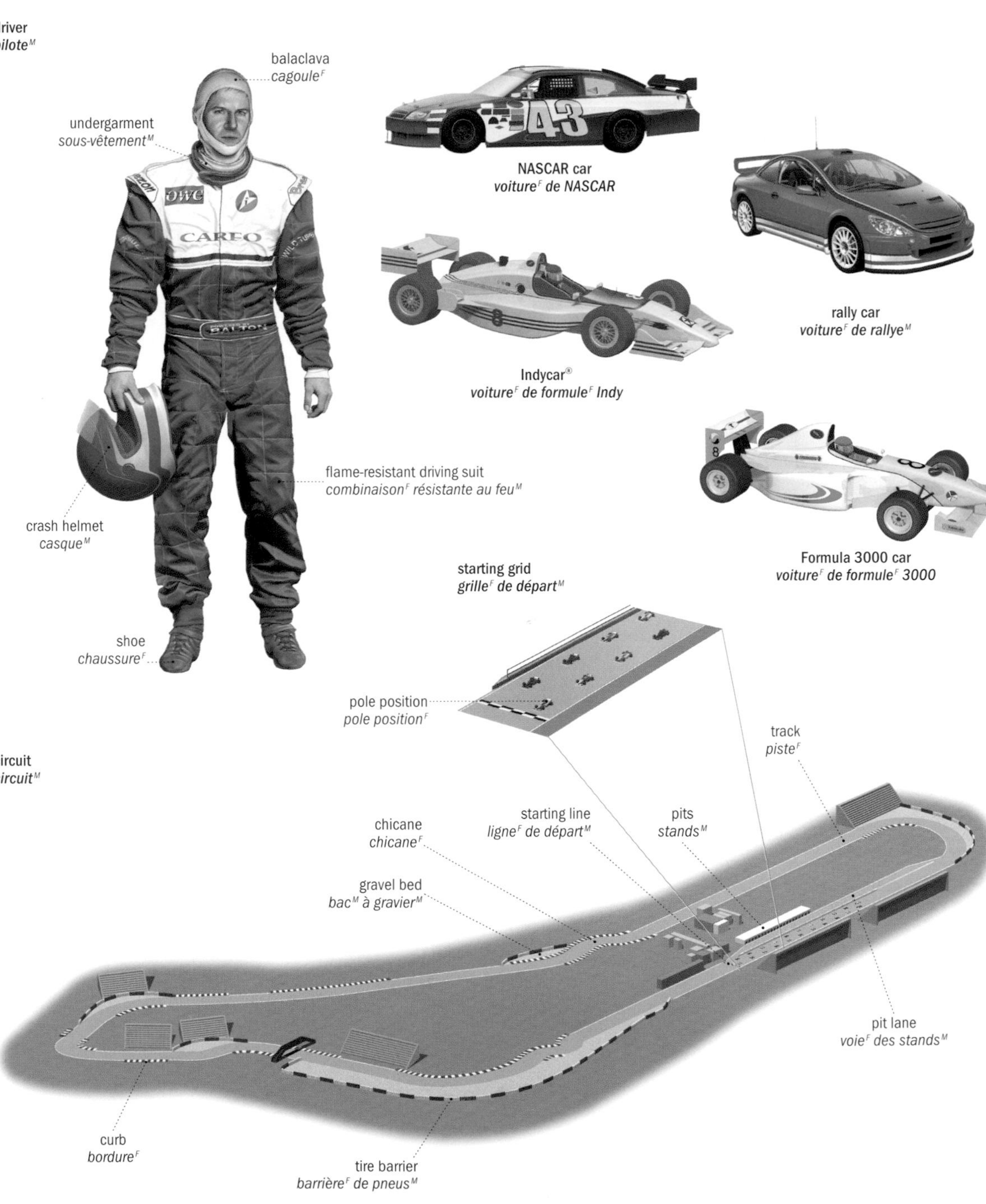
driver
pilote[M]
balaclava
cagoule[F]
undergarment
sous-vêtement[M]
flame-resistant driving suit
combinaison[F] résistante au feu[M]
crash helmet
casque[M]
shoe
chaussure[F]
NASCAR car
voiture[F] de NASCAR
rally car
voiture[F] de rallye[M]
Indycar®
voiture[F] de formule[F] Indy
Formula 3000 car
voiture[F] de formule[F] 3000
starting grid
grille[F] de départ[M]
pole position
pole position[F]
circuit
circuit[M]
track
piste[F]
chicane
chicane[F]
starting line
ligne[F] de départ[M]
pits
stands[M]
gravel bed
bac[M] à gravier[M]
pit lane
voie[F] des stands[M]
curb
bordure[F]
tire barrier
barrière[F] de pneus[M]

car racing

Formula 1® car
voiture[F] de Formule[F] 1

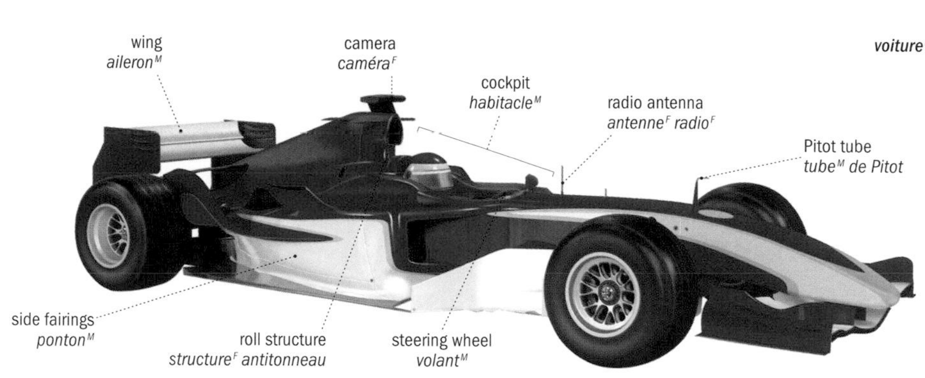
wing
aileron[M]
camera
caméra[F]
cockpit
habitacle[M]
radio antenna
antenne[F] radio[F]
Pitot tube
tube[M] de Pitot
side fairings
ponton[M]
roll structure
structure[F] antitonneau
steering wheel
volant[M]

motorcycling

motocyclisme[M]

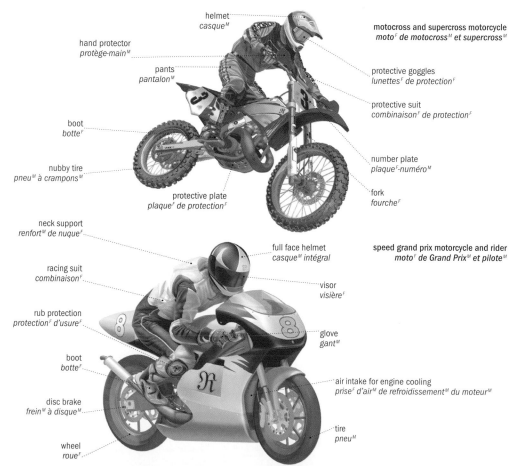

motocross and supercross motorcycle
moto[F] de motocross[M] et supercross[M]

helmet
casque[M]

hand protector
protège-main[M]

pants
pantalon[M]

boot
botte[F]

nubby tire
pneu[M] à crampons[M]

protective plate
plaque[F] de protection[F]

protective goggles
lunettes[F] de protection[F]

protective suit
combinaison[F] de protection[F]

number plate
plaque[F]-numéro[M]

fork
fourche[F]

speed grand prix motorcycle and rider
moto[F] de Grand Prix[M] et pilote[M]

neck support
renfort[M] de nuque[F]

racing suit
combinaison[F]

rub protection
protection[F] d'usure[F]

boot
botte[F]

disc brake
frein[M] à disque[M]

wheel
roue[F]

full face helmet
casque[M] intégral

visor
visière[F]

glove
gant[M]

air intake for engine cooling
prise[F] d'air[M] de refroidissement[M] du moteur[M]

tire
pneu[M]

skateboarding

planche^{F} à roulettes^{F}

skateboard
planche^{F} à roulettes^{F}

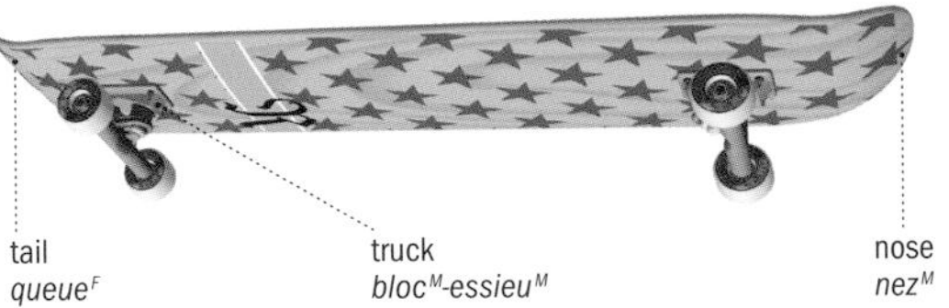
tail
queue^{F}
truck
bloc^{M}-essieu^{M}
nose
nez^{M}

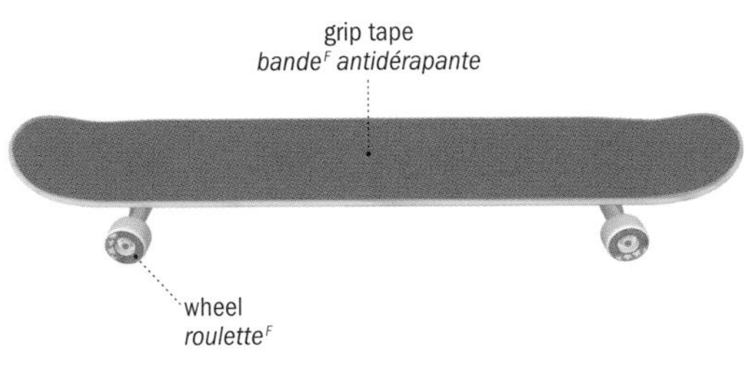
grip tape
bande^{F} antidérapante
wheel
roulette^{F}

skateboarder
planchiste^{M}

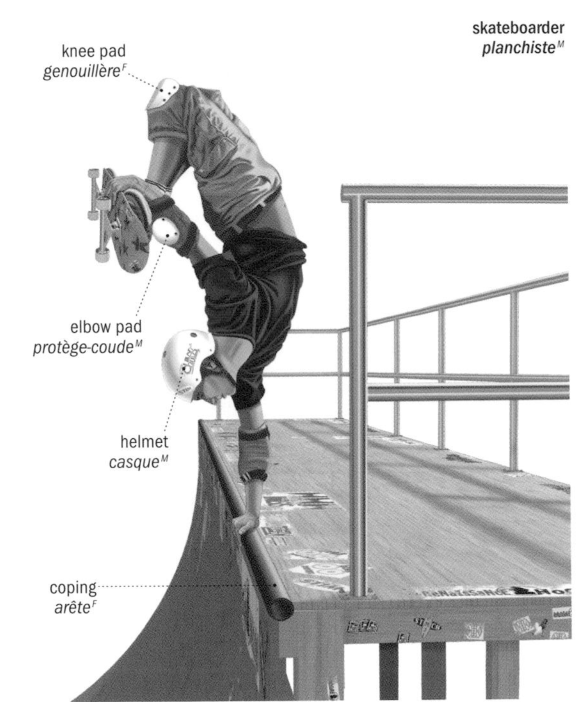
knee pad
genouillère^{F}
elbow pad
protège-coude^{M}
helmet
casque^{M}
coping
arête^{F}

ramp
rampe^{F}

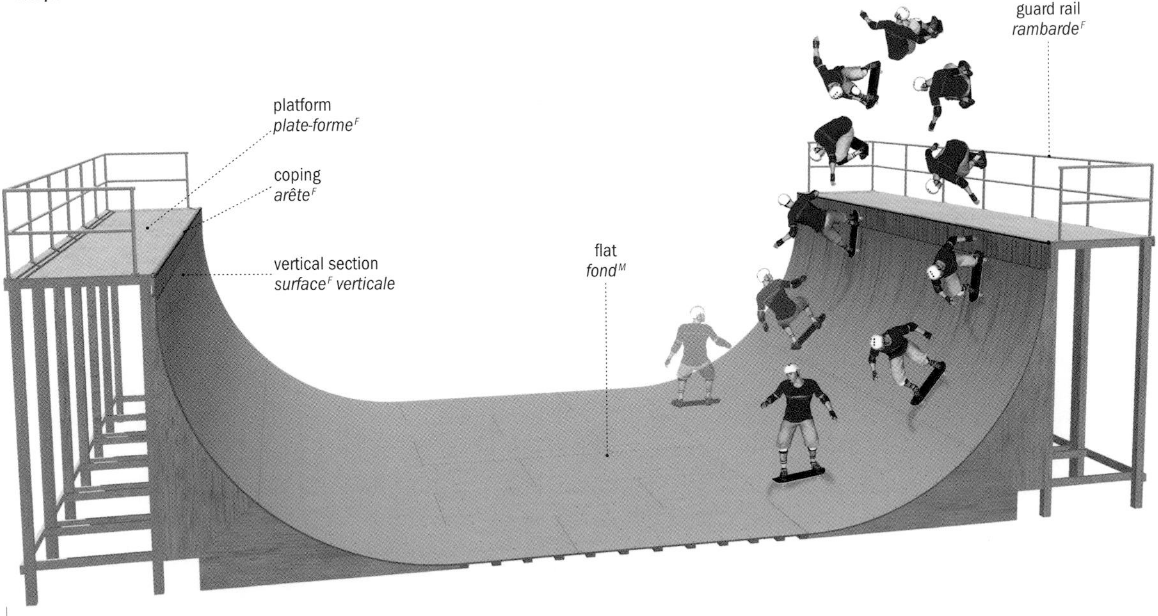

guard rail
rambarde^{F}

platform
plate-forme^{F}

coping
arête^{F}

vertical section
surface^{F} verticale

flat
fond^{M}

SPORTS AND GAMES

in-line skating

patin[M] à roues[F] alignées

acrobatic skate
patin[M] acrobatique
inner boot
chausson[M] intérieur
upper shell
coque[F] supérieure
frame
platine[F]
wheel
roue[F]
skater
patineuse[F]
helmet
casque[M]
elbow pad
coudière[F]
knee pad
genouillère[F]
wrist guard
protège-poignet[M]
in-line speed skate
patin[M] de vitesse[F]
in-line skate
patin[M] à roues[F] alignées
inner boot
chausson[M] intérieur
upper shell
coque[F] supérieure
in-line hockey skate
patin[M] de hockey[M]
ROLLER
adjusting buckle
boucle[F] de réglage[M]
boot
chaussure[F]
axle
essieu[M]
heel stop
frein[M] de talon[M]
wheel
roue[F]
truck
bloc[M]-essieu[M]

camping

camping[M]

examples of tents
exemples[M] de tentes[F]

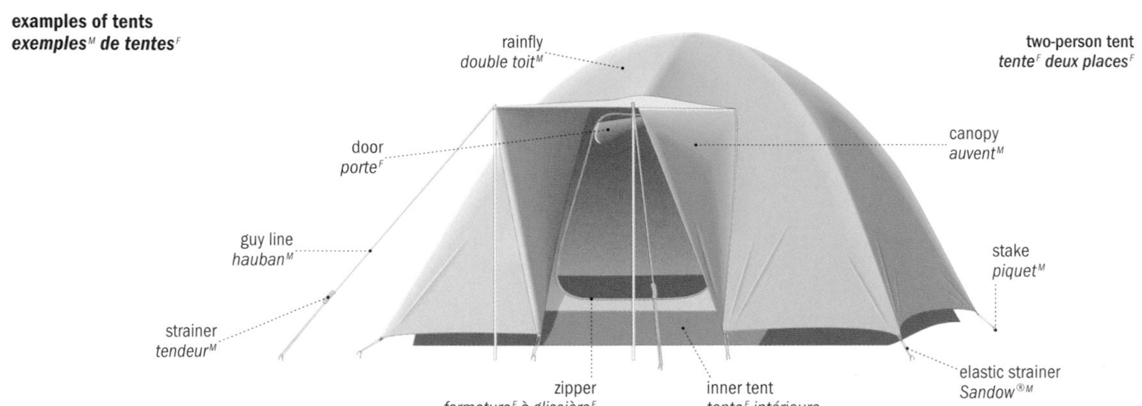

rainfly
double toit[M]
two-person tent
tente[F] deux places[F]
door
porte[F]
canopy
auvent[M]
guy line
hauban[M]
stake
piquet[M]
strainer
tendeur[M]
elastic strainer
Sandow®[M]
zipper
fermeture[F] à glissière[F]
inner tent
tente[F] intérieure

family tent
tente[F] familiale

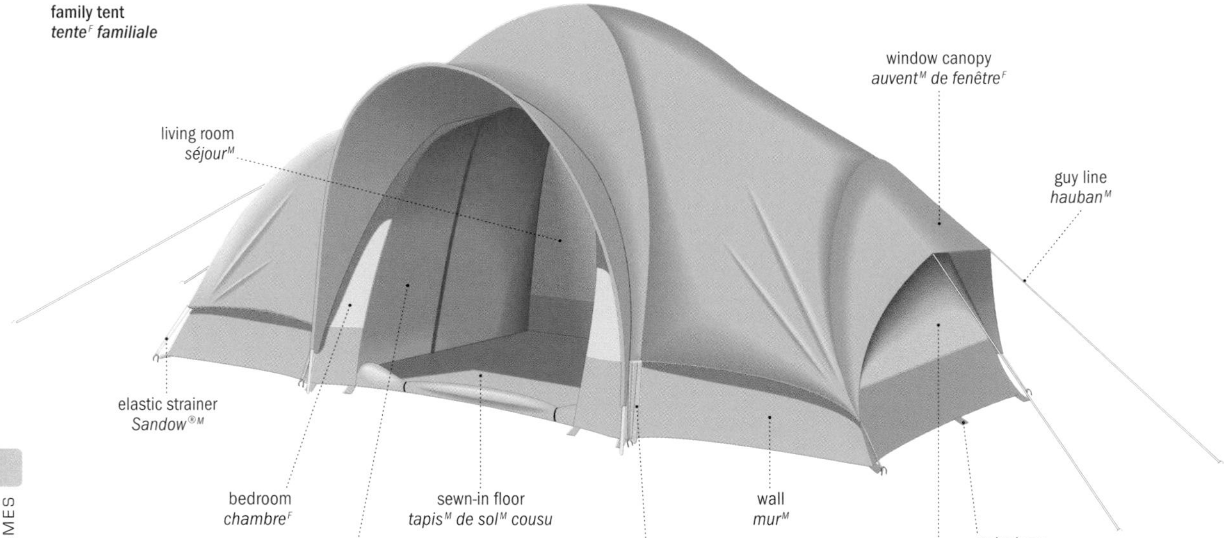

window canopy
auvent[M] de fenêtre[F]
living room
séjour[M]
guy line
hauban[M]
elastic strainer
Sandow®[M]
bedroom
chambre[F]
sewn-in floor
tapis[M] de sol[M] cousu
wall
mur[M]
stake loop
boucle[F] de piquet[M]
canvas divider
cloison[F]
frame
armature[F]
screen window
fenêtre[F] moustiquaire[F]

wagon tent
tente[F] grange[F]

wall tent
tente[F] rectangulaire

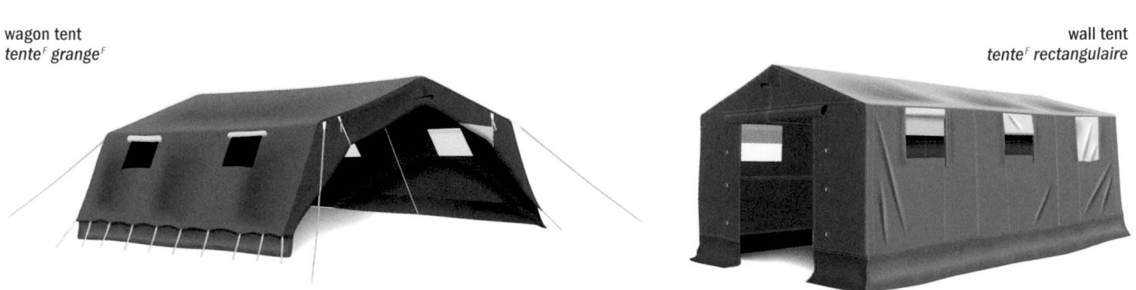

pup tent
tente[F] canadienne

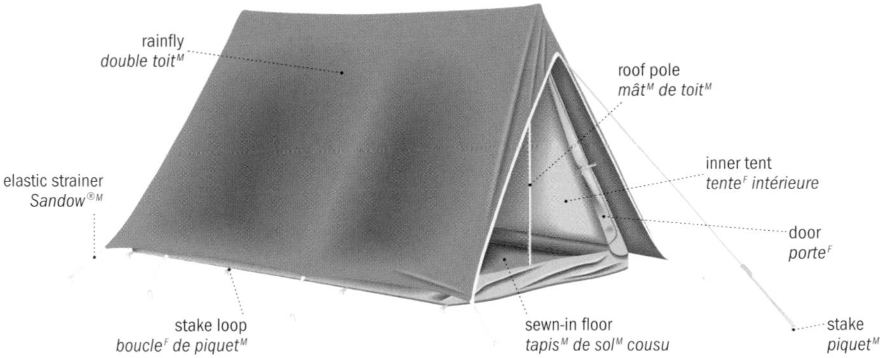

rainfly
double toit[M]

roof pole
mât[M] de toit[M]

elastic strainer
Sandow[®][M]

inner tent
tente[F] intérieure

door
porte[F]

stake loop
boucle[F] de piquet[M]

sewn-in floor
tapis[M] de sol[M] cousu

stake
piquet[M]

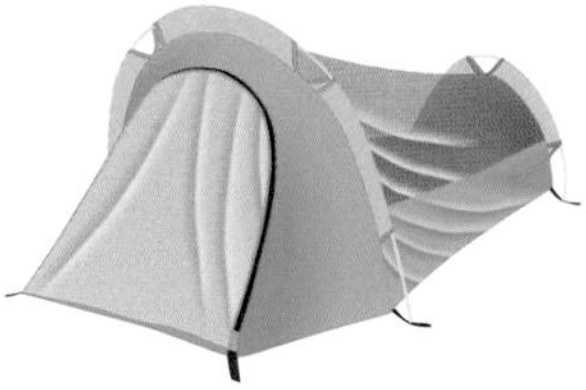

one-person tent
tente[F] individuelle

dome tent
tente[F] dôme[M]

pop-up tent
tente[F] igloo[M]

propane or butane accessories
accessoires[M] au propane[M] ou au butane[M]

lantern
lanterne[F]

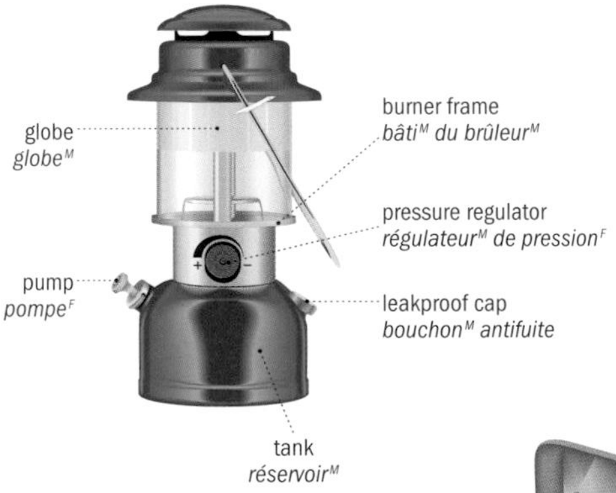

globe
globe[M]

burner frame
bâti[M] du brûleur[M]

pressure regulator
régulateur[M] de pression[F]

pump
pompe[F]

leakproof cap
bouchon[M] antifuite

tank
réservoir[M]

heater
chaufferette[F]

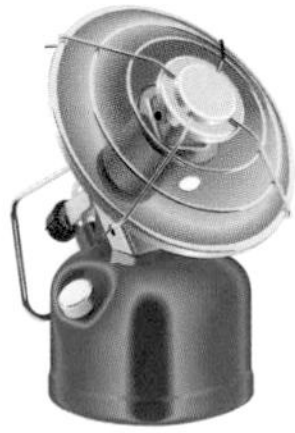

double-burner camp stove
réchaud[M] à deux feux[M]

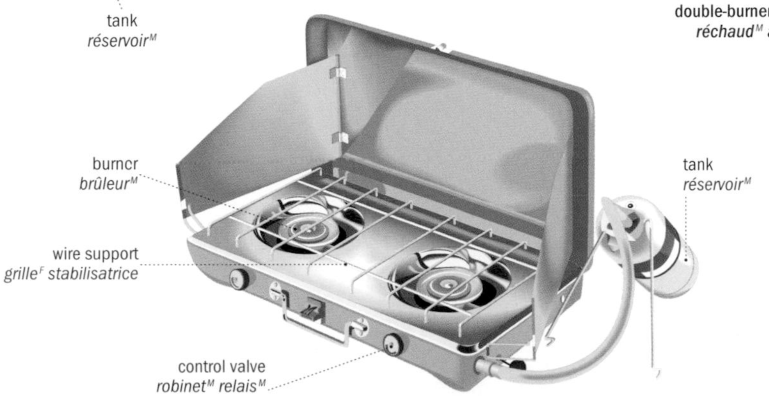

burner
brûleur[M]

tank
réservoir[M]

wire support
grille[F] stabilisatrice

single-burner camp stove
réchaud[M] à un feu[M]

control valve
robinet[M] relais[M]

camping

examples of sleeping bags
exemples[M] de sacs[M] de couchage[M]

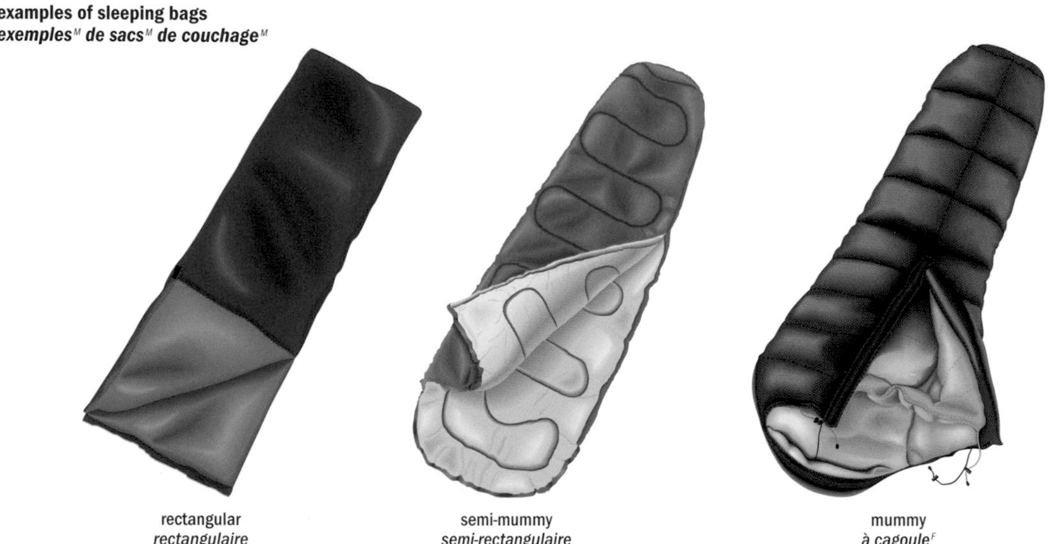

rectangular
rectangulaire

semi-mummy
semi-rectangulaire

mummy
à cagoule[F]

bed and mattress
lit[M] et matelas[M]

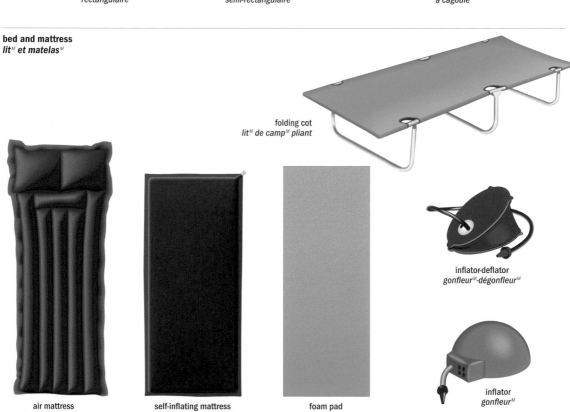

folding cot
lit[M] de camp[M] pliant

air mattress
matelas[M] pneumatique

self-inflating mattress
matelas[M] autogonflant

foam pad
matelas[M] mousse[F]

inflator-deflator
gonfleur[M]-dégonfleur[M]

inflator
gonfleur[M]

cutlery set
***ustensiles*[M] *de campeur*[M]**

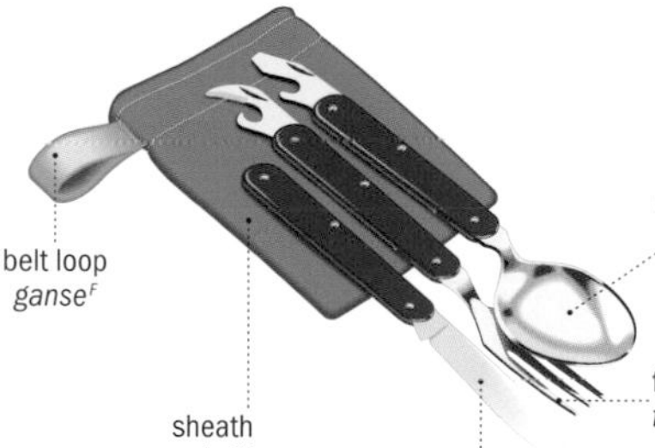

spoon
cuiller[F]

belt loop
ganse[F]

fork
fourchette[F]

sheath
étui[M]

knife
couteau[M]

cooking set
***popote*[F]**

plate
assiette[F] *plate*

saucepan
faitout[M]

handle
queue[F]

frying pan
poêle[F] *à frire*

coffee pot
cafetière[F]

cup
tasse[F]

camping equipment
***matériel*[M] *de camping*[M]**

Swiss Army knife
couteau[M] *suisse*

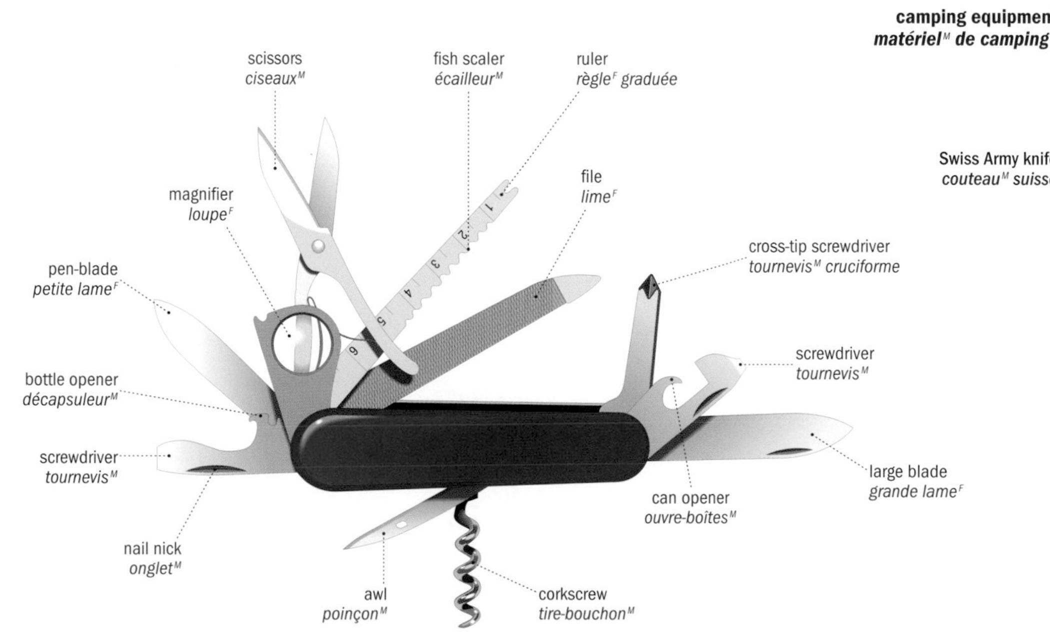
scissors
ciseaux[M]
fish scaler
écailleur[M]
ruler
règle[F] graduée
magnifier
loupe[F]
file
lime[F]
pen-blade
petite lame[F]
cross-tip screwdriver
tournevis[M] cruciforme
screwdriver
tournevis[M]
bottle opener
décapsuleur[M]
screwdriver
tournevis[M]
large blade
grande lame[F]
can opener
ouvre-boîtes[M]
nail nick
onglet[M]
awl
poinçon[M]
corkscrew
tire-bouchon[M]

camping

backpack
sac[M] à dos[M]
top flap
rabat[M]
shoulder strap
bretelle[F]
tightening buckle
boucle[F] de réglage[M]
side compression strap
sangle[F] de compression[F]
front compression strap
sangle[F] de fermeture[F]
strap loop
passe-sangle[M]
hip belt
ceinture[F]
folding shovel
pelle[F]-pioche[F] pliante
vacuum bottle
bouteille[F] isolante
bottle
bouteille[F]
stopper
bouchon[M]
cup
tasse[F]
hurricane lamp
lampe[F]-tempête[F]
canteen
gourde[F]
cooler
glacière[F]
water carrier
cruche[F]

bow saw
scie[F] de camping[M]

knife
couteau[M]

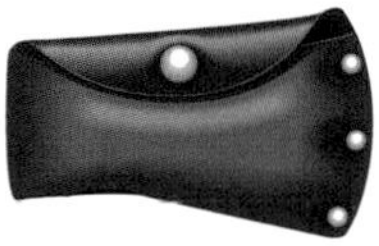

leather sheath
étui[M] de cuir[M]

sheath
gaine[F]

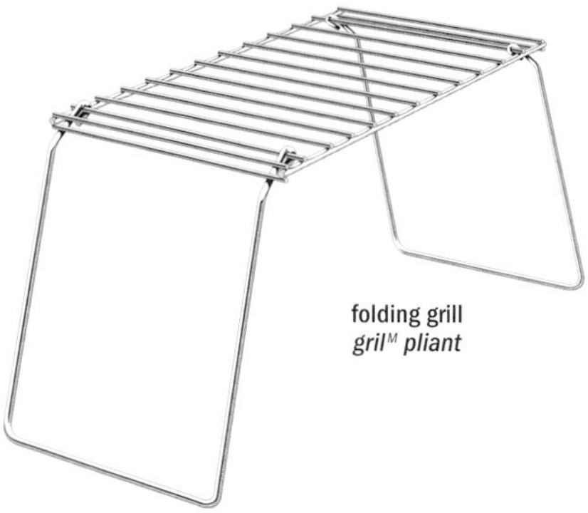

folding grill
gril[M] pliant

hatchet
hachette[F]

magnetic compass
boussole[F] magnétique

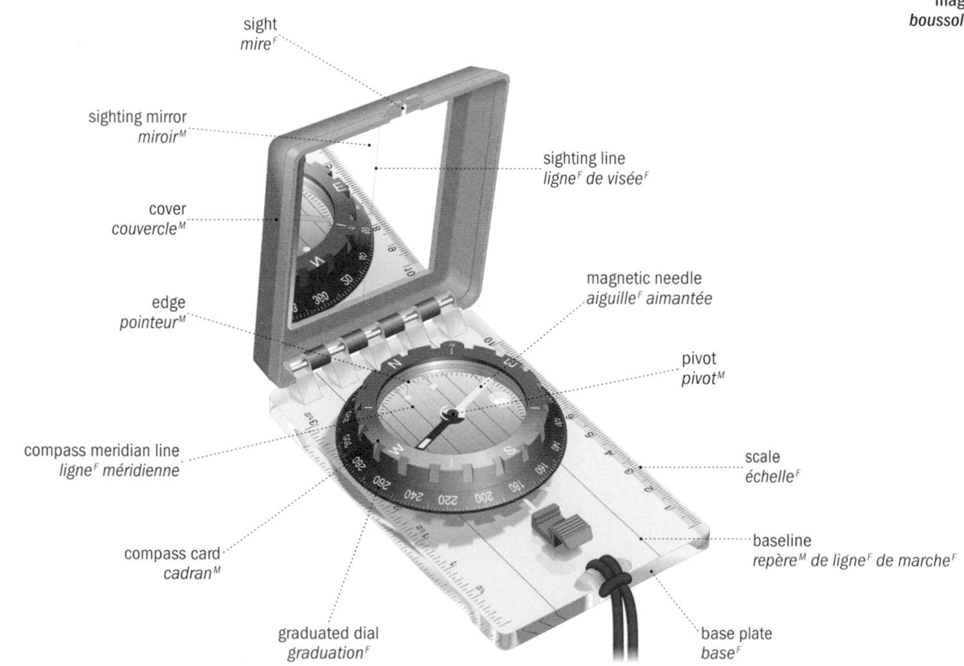
sight
mire[F]
sighting mirror
miroir[M]
sighting line
ligne[F] de visée[F]
cover
couvercle[M]
magnetic needle
aiguille[F] aimantée
edge
pointeur[M]
pivot
pivot[M]
compass meridian line
ligne[F] méridienne
scale
échelle[F]
baseline
repère[M] de ligne[F] de marche[F]
compass card
cadran[M]
graduated dial
graduation[F]
base plate
base[F]

hunting

chasse[F]

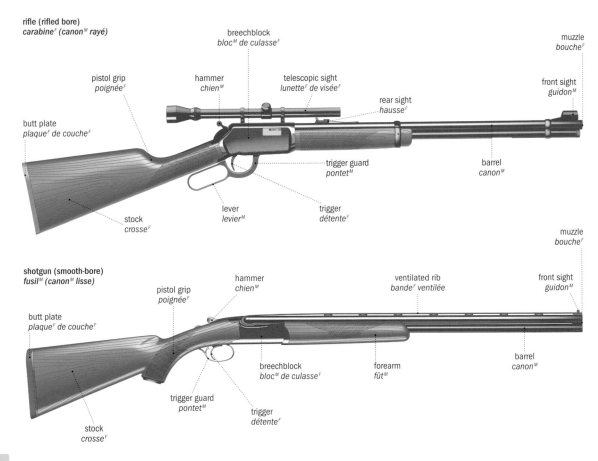

rifle (rifled bore)
carabine[F] (canon[M] rayé)

breechblock
bloc[M] de culasse[F]

muzzle
bouche[F]

pistol grip
poignée[F]

hammer
chien[M]

telescopic sight
lunette[F] de visée[F]

front sight
guidon[M]

rear sight
hausse[F]

butt plate
plaque[F] de couche[F]

trigger guard
pontet[M]

barrel
canon[M]

lever
levier[M]

trigger
détente[F]

stock
crosse[F]

shotgun (smooth-bore)
fusil[M] (canon[M] lisse)

muzzle
bouche[F]

hammer
chien[M]

ventilated rib
bande[F] ventilée

front sight
guidon[M]

pistol grip
poignée[F]

butt plate
plaque[F] de couche[F]

breechblock
bloc[M] de culasse[F]

forearm
fût[M]

barrel
canon[M]

trigger guard
pontet[M]

trigger
détente[F]

stock
crosse[F]

cartridge (shotgun)
cartouche[F] (fusil[M])

cartridge (rifle)
cartouche[F] (carabine[F])

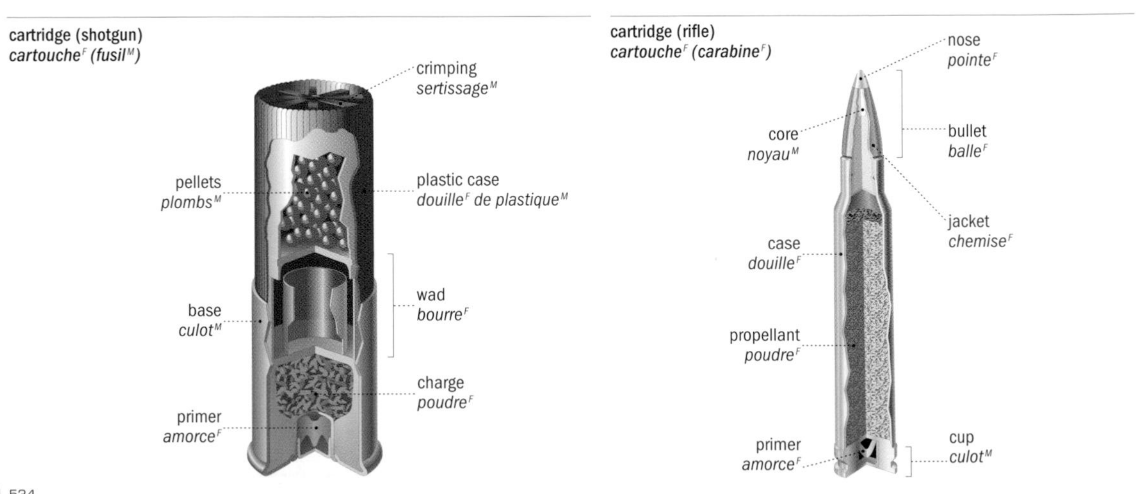
crimping
sertissage[M]
pellets
plombs[M]
plastic case
douille[F] de plastique[M]
base
culot[M]
wad
bourre[F]
charge
poudre[F]
primer
amorce[F]
nose
pointe[F]
core
noyau[M]
bullet
balle[F]
jacket
chemise[F]
case
douille[F]
propellant
poudre[F]
primer
amorce[F]
cup
culot[M]

SPORTS AND GAMES

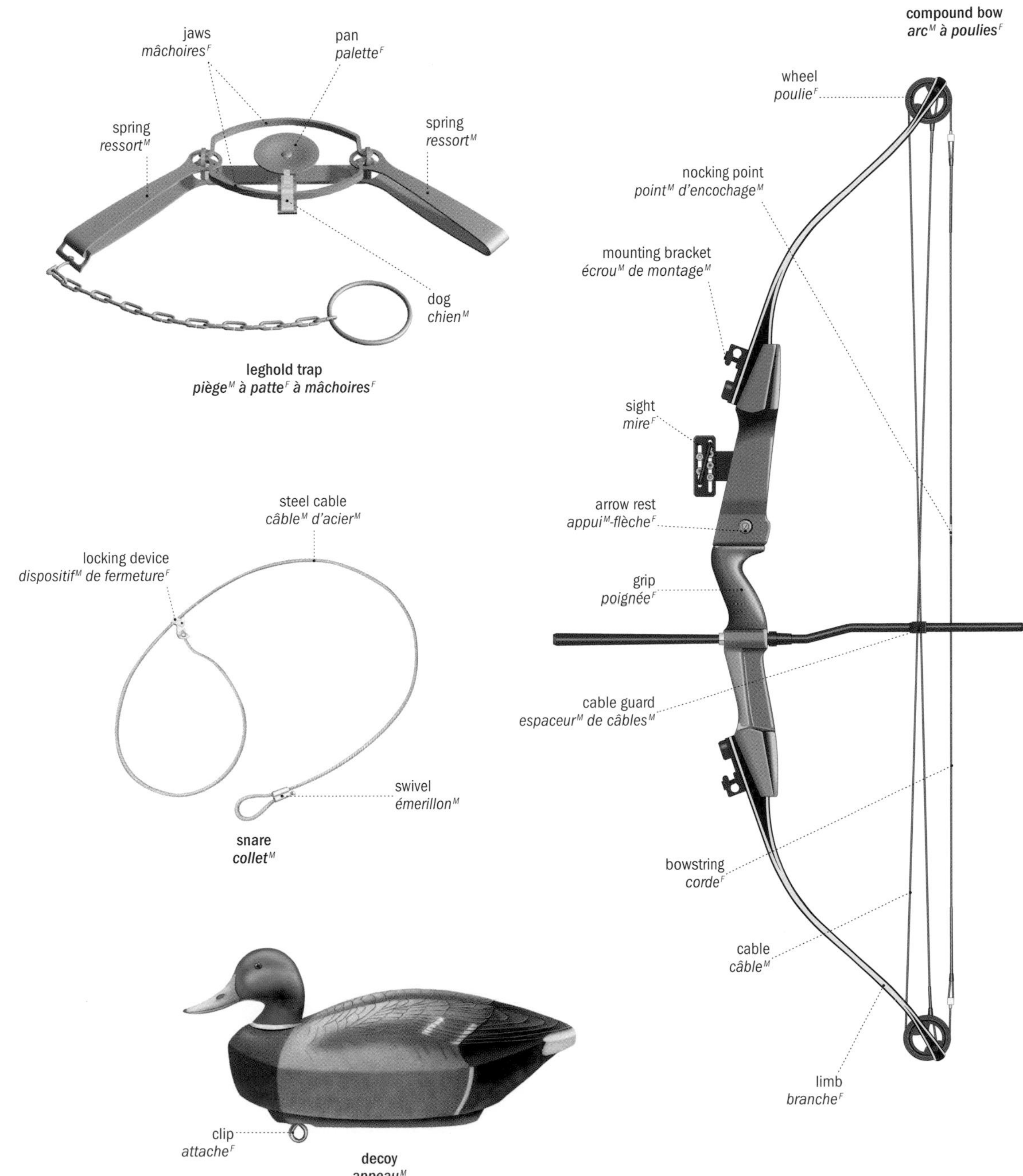
jaws
*mâchoires*F
pan
*palette*F
spring
*ressort*M
spring
*ressort*M
dog
*chien*M
steel cable
*câble*M *d'acier*M
locking device
*dispositif*M *de fermeture*F
swivel
*émerillon*M
clip
*attache*F
compound bow
*arc*M *à poulies*F
wheel
*poulie*F
nocking point
*point*M *d'encochage*M
mounting bracket
*écrou*M *de montage*M
sight
*mire*F
arrow rest
*appui*M*-flèche*F
grip
*poignée*F
cable guard
*espaceur*M *de câbles*M
bowstring
*corde*F
cable
*câble*M
limb
*branche*F

leghold trap
***piège*M *à patte*F *à mâchoires*F**

snare
***collet*M**

decoy
***appeau*M**

fishing

pêche[F]

flyfishing
pêche[F] à la mouche[F]

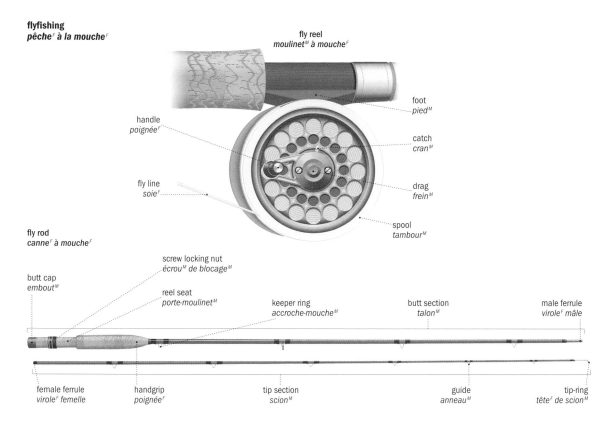

fly reel
moulinet[M] à mouche[F]

foot
pied[M]

handle
poignée[F]

catch
cran[M]

fly line
soie[F]

drag
frein[M]

spool
tambour[M]

fly rod
canne[F] à mouche[F]

screw locking nut
écrou[M] de blocage[M]

butt cap
embout[M]

reel seat
porte-moulinet[M]

keeper ring
accroche-mouche[M]

butt section
talon[M]

male ferrule
virole[F] mâle

female ferrule
virole[F] femelle

handgrip
poignée[F]

tip section
scion[M]

guide
anneau[M]

tip-ring
tête[F] de scion[M]

artificial fly
mouche[F] artificielle

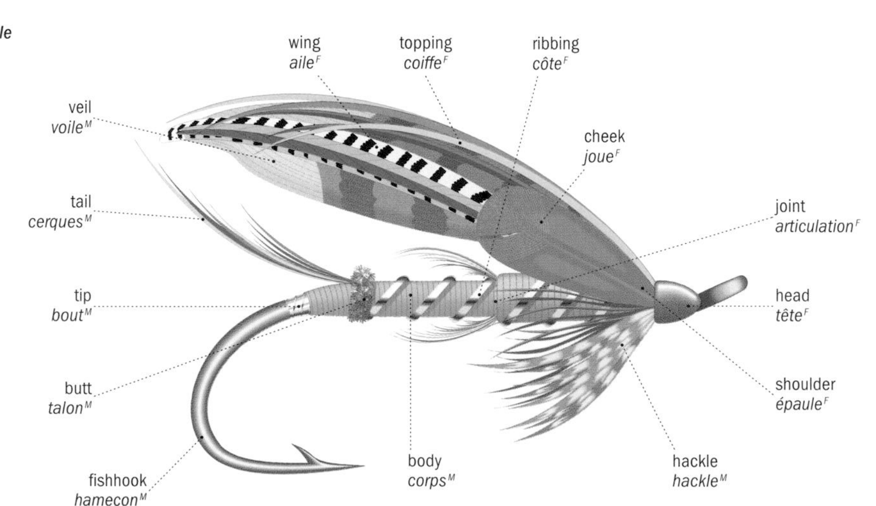
wing
aile[F]
topping
coiffe[F]
ribbing
côte[F]
veil
voile[M]
cheek
joue[F]
tail
cerques[M]
joint
articulation[F]
tip
bout[M]
head
tête[F]
butt
talon[M]
shoulder
épaule[F]
fishhook
hameçon[M]
body
corps[M]
hackle
hackle[M]

casting
pêche[F] au lancer[M]

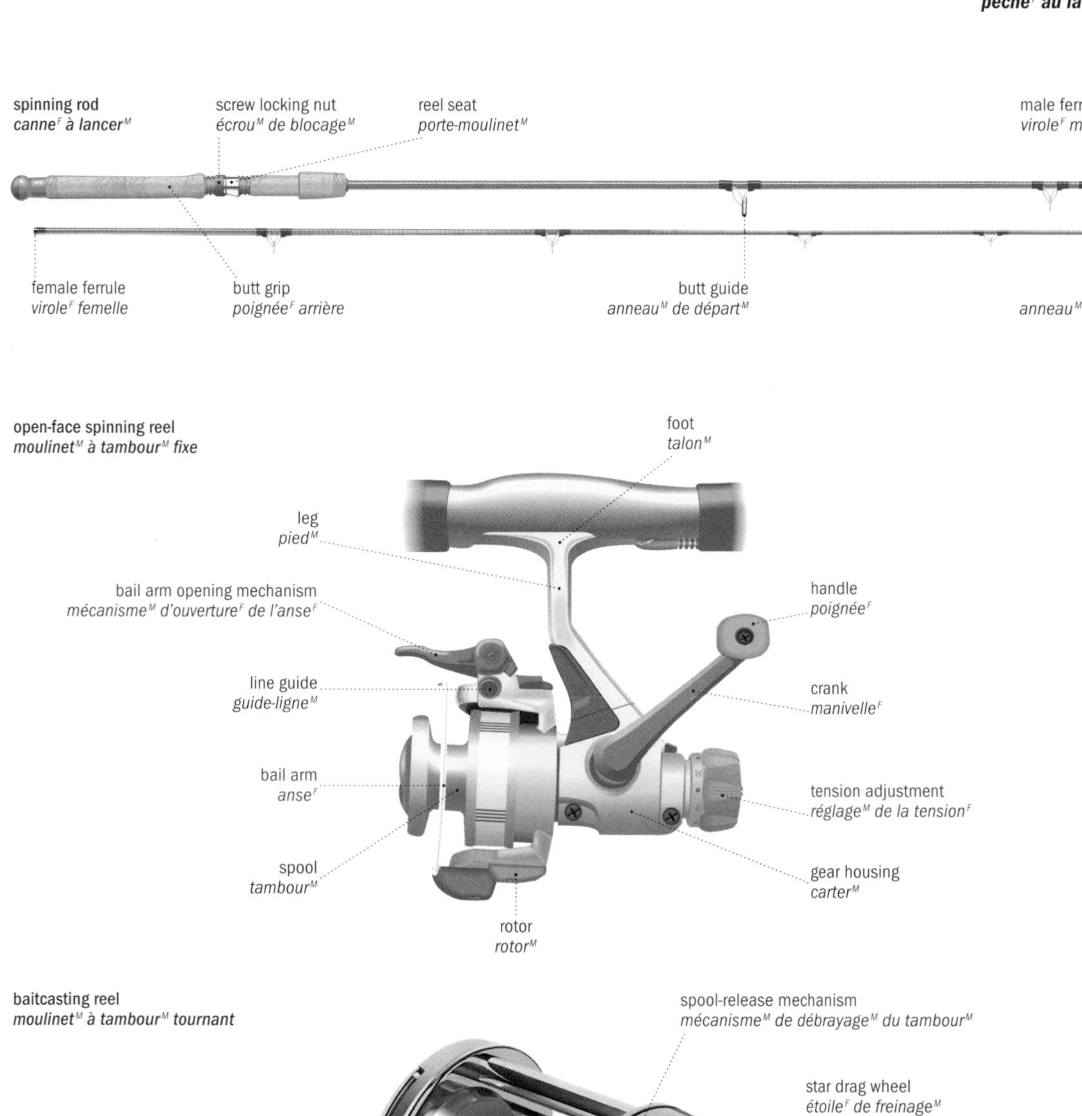
spinning rod
canne[F] à lancer[M]
screw locking nut
écrou[M] de blocage[M]
reel seat
porte-moulinet[M]
male ferrule
virole[F] mâle
female ferrule
virole[F] femelle
butt grip
poignée[F] arrière
butt guide
anneau[M] de départ[M]
tip-ring
anneau[M] de tête[F]
open-face spinning reel
moulinet[M] à tambour[M] fixe
foot
talon[M]
leg
pied[M]
bail arm opening mechanism
mécanisme[M] d'ouverture[F] de l'anse[F]
handle
poignée[F]
line guide
guide-ligne[M]
crank
manivelle[F]
bail arm
anse[F]
tension adjustment
réglage[M] de la tension[F]
spool
tambour[M]
gear housing
carter[M]
rotor
rotor[M]

baitcasting reel
moulinet[M] à tambour[M] tournant

spool-release mechanism
mécanisme[M] de débrayage[M] du tambour[M]

star drag wheel
étoile[F] de freinage[M]

spool
tambour[M]

spool axle
axe[M] de tambour[M]

crank
manivelle[F]

stand
pied[M]

fishing

fishhook
hameçon[M]

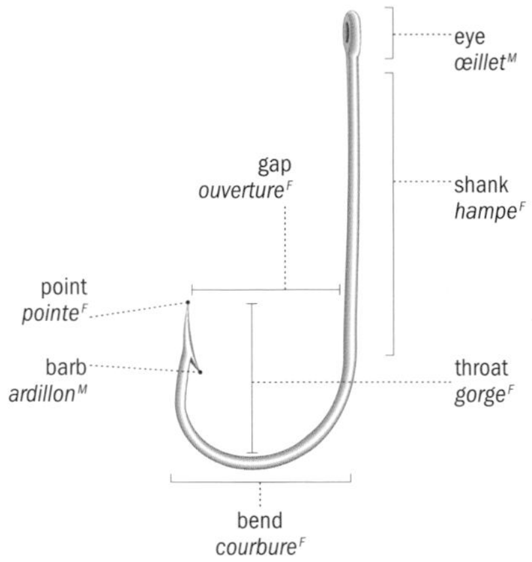

eye
œillet[M]

gap
ouverture[F]

shank
hampe[F]

point
pointe[F]

barb
ardillon[M]

throat
gorge[F]

bend
courbure[F]

float tackle
bas[M] de ligne[F]

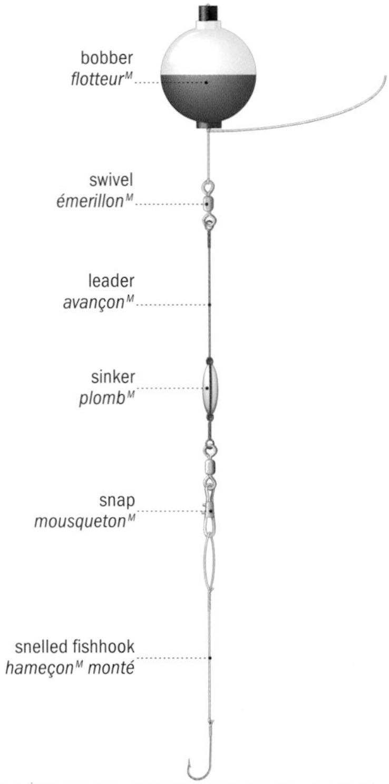

bobber
flotteur[M]

swivel
émerillon[M]

leader
avançon[M]

sinker
plomb[M]

snap
mousqueton[M]

snelled fishhook
hameçon[M] monté

spinner
cuiller[F]

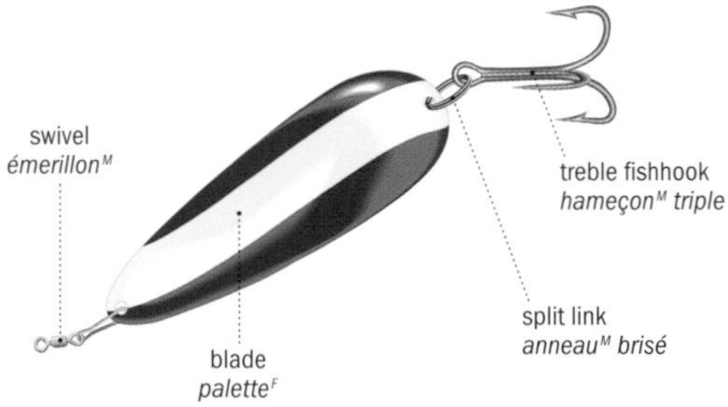

swivel
émerillon[M]

treble fishhook
hameçon[M] triple

split link
anneau[M] brisé

blade
palette[F]

clothing and accessories
vêtements[M] et accessoires[M]

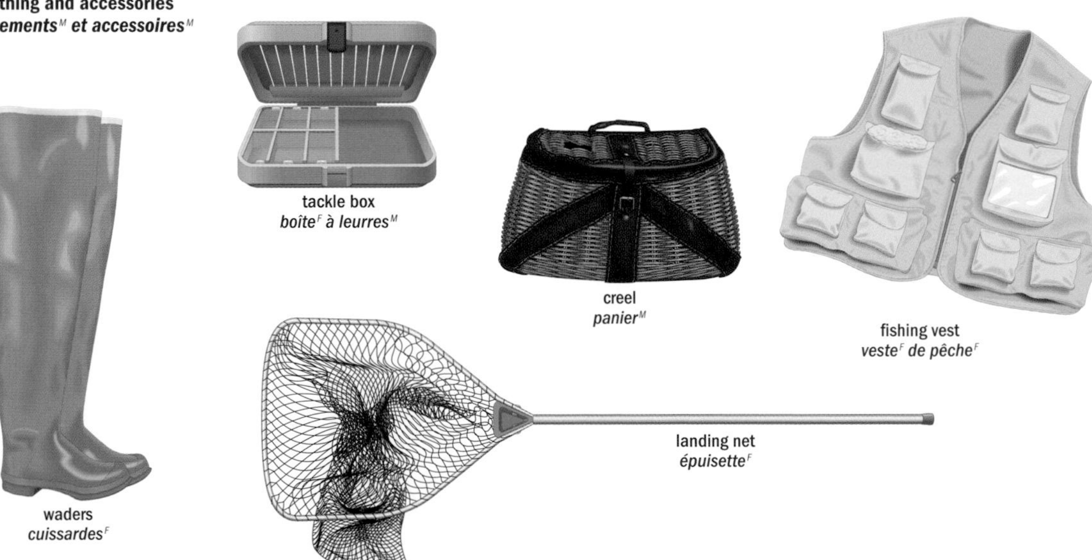
tackle box
boîte[F] à leurres[M]
creel
panier[M]
fishing vest
veste[F] de pêche[F]
landing net
épuisette[F]
waders
cuissardes[F]

English Index

ENGLISH INDEX

B

C

D

E

F

G

H

I

J

K

L

ENGLISH INDEX

M

N

O

P

Q

R

S

T

U

V

W

X

Y

Z

Index français

B

C

INDEX FRANÇAIS

D

E

F

G

INDEX FRANÇAIS

M

N

O

P

Q

R

T